The Political History of Modern Iran

The Political History of Modern Iran

Revolution, Reaction and Transformation, 1905 to the Present

Ali Rahnema

I.B. TAURIS
LONDON • NEW YORK • OXFORD • NEW DELHI • SYDNEY

I.B. TAURIS
Bloomsbury Publishing Plc
50 Bedford Square, London, WC1B 3DP, UK
1385 Broadway, New York, NY 10018, USA
29 Earlsfort Terrace, Dublin 2, Ireland

BLOOMSBURY, I.B. TAURIS and the I.B. Tauris logo are trademarks of Bloomsbury Publishing Plc

First published in Great Britain 2023

Copyright © Ali Rahnema, 2023

Ali Rahnema has asserted his right under the Copyright, Designs and Patents Act, 1988, to be identified as Author of this work.

For legal purposes the Acknowledgements on p. xix constitute an extension of this copyright page.

Cover design by www.paulsmithdesign.com

All rights reserved. No part of this publication may be reproduced or transmitted in any form or by any means, electronic or mechanical, including photocopying, recording, or any information storage or retrieval system, without prior permission in writing from the publishers.

Bloomsbury Publishing Plc does not have any control over, or responsibility for, any third-party websites referred to or in this book. All internet addresses given in this book were correct at the time of going to press. The author and publisher regret any inconvenience caused if addresses have changed or sites have ceased to exist, but can accept no responsibility for any such changes.

A catalogue record for this book is available from the British Library.

A catalog record for this book is available from the Library of Congress.

ISBN: HB: 978-0-7556-4398-1
       PB: 978-0-7556-4399-8
       ePDF: 978-0-7556-4400-1
       eBook: 978-0-7556-4401-8

Typeset by RefineCatch Limited, Bungay, Suffolk

To find out more about our authors and books visit www.bloomsbury.com and sign up for our newsletters.

Contents

List of Figures xv
Acknowledgements xix
Timeline xxi

INTRODUCTION 1
    Chat with Students Studying Modern Iranian History 1
    Cautions about Reading this Textbook 4
    The Approach of this Textbook 4
    Persia and Western Europe in the Nineteenth Century: Worlds Apart 6
    Persia in the Cave of Ephesus 8
    Plagues and Famines 12
    Persia at the Dawn of Twentieth Century 13

1 THE QUEST FOR A CONSTITUTIONAL MONARCHY UNDER THE QAJARS, 1905–11 15
    Qajar Shahs, Wars and Mismanagements 15
        The Babi Movement 17
        Nasereddin Shah and Amir Kabir 18
        Nasereddin Shah: 'From Concession to Concession' 19
        Intellectual Murmurs of Anti-Despotism and Constitutionalism 22
        Mozaffareddin Shah 26
    The Approaching Revolution 27
    The Constitutionalists Organize 28
        The First Flare-Ups 30
    Royal Decree Granting a Consultative Parliament 31
    Mohammad-Ali Shah's Rule 33
        The Constitutionalist Front 34
        The Despotic Front 36
    The 1st Majles, 7 October 1906–23 June 1908 38
        The Assassination of the Prime Minister 40
        First Assault on Parliament: The Failed Coup 42
        Attempt on the Shah's Life 43
        Second Coup: The Parliament is Shelled and Closed 43

Two Responses to Despotism 45
　The Religious Split in Response to Despotism 46
　Azarbayjan's Military Response to Despotism 47
　The Russian Occupation 49
　Two Significant Events Forgotten in the Midst of Civil War 50
　Constitutionalists Back in Power 51
　The 2nd Majles, 15 November 1909–25 December 1911 53
Seventeen Months of Interminable Crises: July 1910–December 1911 55
　Party Rivalries Intensify 55
　Political Assassinations 56
　Disarming the *Mojahedin* 56
　The Conservative Backlash and Mohammad-Ali Shah's Attempted Return 57
The Shuster Affair and the End of Iran's Independence 59
　Russia Defeats Constitutionalism and Annexes Its Zone of Influence 60

2　A STATE MADE DYSFUNCTIONAL, 1912–21 67

Facing Foreign Invasion 67
　Iran between Partial and Full Invasion, 1912–1914 68
　Iran's Initial Response to the First World War 69
　Iran's Chemistry with the Belligerent Powers 71
Fifteen Months of Strict Neutrality, 1 August 1914–14 November 1915 73
　The 3rd Majles 73
　Iranian Governments, the Majles and the Belligerent Powers 74
　The Rauf Bey Affair and the Fall of Ayn al-dowleh 77
Two Governments and a Shah 79
　The Pro-German Resistance Movement: The National Defence Committee 80
Governments in Tehran during the Last Two Years of the War 81
　Allied-Friendly Governments 82
　The Punishment Committee 83
　Iranian Governments Digesting the Russian Revolutions 85
British Forces in Iran 87
　The South Persian Rifles 87
　The British Dunsterforce 88
Mirza Kuchek Khan Jangali's Challenge 89
Famine, Influenza and Cholera 92
The Post-War British Design for Iran 94
　The Paris Peace Conference 95
　The 1919 Anglo-Persian Agreement 96
The Background to the 1921 Coup 99

Khiyabani's Movement: From Reform to Cautious Rebellion 100
The 1919 Treaty is Not Acceptable to Iranians 103
The Bolsheviks in Anzali and Its Consequences 104
Seeking Alternatives 106
What to do with the Cossacks 106
The Iron Committee 108
The Perfectly Coordinated Coup 110
Britain Protecting Its Interests in Iran 112

3 REZA SHAH: NATION-BUILDING, REPRESSION, EUROPEANIZATION AND MODERNIZATION, 1921–41 117

Prelude to Reza Khan's Rise 117
Europeanized Intellectuals Root for Dictatorship 117
From Theory to Practice 120
Uncomfortable Collaboration of Two Aspiring Dictators 120
Eliminating the Competition 122
Mirza Kuchek Khan and Gilan 122
Col. Pesyan's rebellion in Khorasan 123
Maj. Lahuti's coup in Tabriz 125
Reza Khan's Ascent to Power 126
From Minister of War to Prime Minister 128
Reza Khan, Prime Minister 131
The Republican Attempt 133
Reza Khan Regains Confidence 136
First Round of Political Serial Killings 137
Taming Semi-Autonomous Tribes 139
Last Stretch to the Throne 142
Reza Shah Pahlavi's Reign 143
Economic and Financial Development 145
Oil and Agriculture: Enclave Sectors 147
Infrastructure, Roads, Railroad and Urban Development 149
Judicial and Administrative Reform 152
Socio-cultural Europeanization 152
Dressing Iranians 153
Domestic Politics 157
Short honeymoon of party politics 158
The Despot 159
A New Opposition 162
The Crown Prince 163
Foreign Policy 163

4 MOHAMMAD-REZA SHAH: FOREIGN INVASION, OIL NATIONALIZATION AND THE COUP, 1941–53 169

Iran under Foreign Occupation 169
    The Persian Corridor: A Complicated Relationship 171
    The Tehran Conference: A Patronizing Pat on the Back 172
    The Economic Nightmare of the Occupation 173
        Inflation 173
        Food crisis 174
        Transportation crisis 175
    Pro-Axis Iranians 176
    Political Consequences of the Invasion 177
        Parties and labour unions 177
            Smaller parties 178
            The dominant parties 180
The Shah Overshadowed by Qavam 183
    The Failed Soviet Push for Oil Concessions and Its Consequences 185
    The Uprising of Khorasan Officers 187
    The Autonomous Movement of Azarbayjan 188
    Qavam Seduces and Deceives Stalin? 193
    Qavam Co-opts the Tudeh Party to Appease the Soviets 195
From Qavam's Fall to Mosaddeq's Rise 198
    Enter Iran's New Shii Game Changers 199
    Attempted Regicide and Its Consequence 205
The Oil Issue 207
    Battle over the 16th Majles 208
    Oil Nationalization 210
Mosaddeq's 28 Months in Office 213
    Mosaddeq's International Saga 215
    Britain's Economic Embargo 217
    Mosaddeq and Domestic Policies: The Kashani–Mosaddeq Alliance 218
    Mosaddeq and Domestic Policies: The Kashani–Zahedi Alliance 224
    The Coups 226

5 FROM POST-COUP TO POST-UPRISING, AUGUST 1953–JUNE 1963 233

Iran after the Coup 233
    Political Consequences of the Coup 235
    A Hot December in Tehran 237
    Zahedi's Brief and Grief 238

The Demise of the Tudeh Party 240
　　Exit Zahedi 242
Ala's Caretaker Government 243
　　The Devotees of Islam's Last Assassination Attempt and the Eclipse of
　　Kashani 244
　　The Shah's Expanding Purview, Western Anxieties and the Birth of
　　SAVAK 245
Eqbal in Office 248
　　Contrived Parties and Party Politics 249
　　Plots Destabilizing the Shah's Newly Found Confidence 250
Two Elections, Sharif Emami's Brief Premiership and a Cursed 20th
Majles 253
Amini's Premiership 257
　　The Anti-Corruption Campaign 258
　　The Mosaddeqist Opposition, the Shah and the US 259
　　Arsanjani and Land Reform 262
Alam, the White Revolution and the Eclipse of Mosaddeqists 264
　　A Tale of Two Congresses 265
　　Opposition to the White Revolution 269
Ayatollah Khomeyni, the New Contender for Power 271
　　The 5 June or 15 Khordad Uprising 272
　　The Alarming Political Aftermath of the 5 June Uprising 275
　　The Shah Looks to a Bright Future 276

6　THE SHAH'S PUSH TOWARDS THE GATES OF THE GREAT CIVILIZATION, 1964–77 281

The Architects of the New Iran and Their Enemies 281
　　Bullets Aimed at the Prime Minister 284
　　The Big Wheel Keeps on Turning 285
　　Bullets for the Shah 286
　　Domestic Politics 288
Landmarks of Transitioning to Despotism 289
　　Intuiting the Shah's Desires as State Policy 290
　　A Bonapartian Coronation 291
　　Iran's 2,500 Years of Monarchy: Just a Celebration? 293
　　The Shah, Nixon and Kissinger: Money Brings Political Romance 295
　　Arms Build-Up and the Regional Gendarme 297
　　The One-Party System 300
The Roaring Years: Economic and Cultural Transformations 303
　　Growing Prosperity and Crippling Convulsions 304
　　Economics is a Pain! 306

You Can't Tell a Market Economy What to Do 307
The Tangible Results of the Economic Boom 308
 The automobile industry 309
 Home appliances, food industries and department stores 309
The Queen's Soft Cultural Revolution 311
 Organization for the Intellectual Development of Children and Young Adults 312
 The Shiraz Arts Festival and the Theatre Workshop 314
 The Swinging and Sizzling Tehran of the 1970s 318
  Intellectual cafés and popular cabarets 318
  Movies and the television 319
  A new genre of hangouts 322

7 THE REVOLUTIONARY TRANSITION FROM MONARCHY TO REPUBLIC, MARCH 1977–MARCH 1979 327

The Rise of Subversive Forces 328
 The People's Fadai (Self-Sacrificing) Guerrillas: A Revolutionary Marxist Movement 328
 The People's Mojahedin (Holy Warriors): A Revolutionary Islamic Organization 332
 Ali Shariati, the Ideologue of a Revolutionary Islam 336
 CISNU, The Student Movement Abroad 340
Dismantling the Monarchy, Step by Step 343
 Carter in the White House 343
 Open Letters and Ten Nights of Poetry Reading 344
 Khomeyni Prods the Sleepy Religious Forces to Wake Up 345
 Mostafa Khomeyni's Death 346
 Khomeyni Regains his Voice 347
The Regime Retaliates, Retreats and Strikes Back 348
 Violent Street Demonstrations 349
 Khomeyni: Natural Leader of the Anti-Shah Movement 351
 The Shah Changes Tactics, Confusing his Supporters 351
 Change of Prime Ministers 352
 Two Days of Massive and Peaceful Demonstrations 353
 Black Friday and Its Consequences 354
 Strikes 355
 The Saint under the Apple Tree: Khomeyni at Neauphle-le-Château 356
The Shah Vacillates and Khomeyni Rams through the Revolution 359
 Shapur Bakhtiyar's Civilian Government 361
 The Guadeloupe Consensus 362

Planning the Shah's Departure 363
A Monarchy without the Monarch 364
Khomeyni Returns 365
Bazargan's Provisional Government 366
The 11 February 1979 Collapse 368
A Referendum on an Islamic Republic 370

8 KHOMEYNI'S ISLAMIC REPUBLIC, 1979–89 375
Mehdi Bazargan's Nine-Month Government: A Knife without a Blade 377
  New Revolutionary Institutions: Outside Bazargan's Reach 379
    The Islamic Revolution Committees 379
    The Revolutionary Islamic Courts 380
    Islamic Revolutionary Guard Corps 381
    The Foundation of the Oppressed/Disinherited 382
    Imam's Assistance/Relief Committee 383
    The Construction Jihad 384
  Pushing Out the Uncommitted, Making Room for Doctrinaires 385
  Ethnic Opposition, Self-Determination, and Clashes 386
    Kurdistan 386
    Turkman Sahra 388
    Khuzestan 389
  Three New Islamic Parties 390
    The Islamic Republic Party 390
    Muslim People of Iran's Republic Party 392
    The Mojahedin of the Islamic Revolution 394
    MIR and Forqan 395
  Iran's New Constitution: A Lost Opportunity 397
    The Assembly of Experts and the Rule of the Guardian Jurist 399
    Imposing Islamic homogeneity 400
  American Embassy Falls 403
    The Den of spies 404
The Rise and Fall of Bani-Sadr: The Paris Discourse is Gone for Good 407
  A Cultural Revolution 409
  The Failed US Rescue Operation 411
  Bani-Sadr's Initial Skirmishes with the IRP 412
  Imposing the Islamic Attire 413
  The Failed Nojeh Coup 414
  Iraq Attacks 415
  The End of Bani-Sadr and All Opposition Groups 417
    Bani-Sadr stands up to Khomeyni 418
    Bani-Sadr's alliance with the Mojahedin 420

The final blow by Khomeyni and his followers 420
Eight months of brisk and screaming turnovers, June 1981–
February 1982 422
Eight-Year Presidency of Seyyed Ali Khamenei 424
Crushing All Domestic Foes 425
    The Majority Fadais 426
    The Tudeh Party 427
    The unfortunate fate of Qotbzadeh and Shariatmadari 428
    Settling scores with Bazargan and the Hojatiyyeh Society 430
The Islamic Republic Party Implodes 431
The End of MIR 434
From a Defensive to an Offensive War 435
Khomeyni's Last Two Years: Haughtiness, Desperation and Anger 439
    The Absolute Rule of the Guardian Jurist: A New Landmark in Iranian Despotism 440
    Religion against Religion: Mohammaden vs American Islam 441
    Ending the War: Khomeyni Drinks the Poisoned Chalice 442
    The Mojahedin Attack: 'Operation Eternal Light' 443
    Prison Massacres 445
    The *Satanic Verses* 446
    The Montazeri Affair: Rise and Fall of Khomeyni's Heir 447

9 PRESIDENT RAFSANJANI, THE CRUSADER OF CONSTRUCTION, 1989–97 455

Transitioning to Post-Khomeyni Iran 455
The Rafsanjani–Khamenei Duo 458
Domestic politics, July 1989–July 1997 459
    The Duo Purging the Left Faction of the Imam's Line 462
    The Leader's Nightmare of a Western Cultural Onslaught 466
Rafsanjani's Economic Reform: Hopes and Challenges 468
    Privatization, Subsidies and Exchange Rate Unification 472
    Privatization and Militarization of the Economy 473
Rafsanjani's Political Conundrums 474
    Khamenei Challenges Rafsanjani 475
    Karbaschi, the Modernist and Entrepreneurial Mayor of Tehran 477
    The 5th Majles: The Right Splits into Traditional and Modern 479
    Assassinating the Opposition Abroad and Its Consequences 482
    Repression at Home 484
        Silencing Iranian Writers' Association 485
    The Challenge of Islamic Intellectuals 486

10 KHATAMI'S PRESIDENCY: A DEMOCRATIC OPPORTUNITY DEFLECTED AND FOREGONE, 1997–2005   491

Khatami's Sweeping Victory   493
   Khatami, His Cabinet and Initial Waves   494
   Khatami's Islam is Different from Khamenei's   497
Stifling Reform   498
   Attack on Karbaschi   499
   Gagging Nuri and Kadivar   500
State-Sponsored Terror   503
   The Execution of Darush Foruhar and Parvaneh Eskandari   504
   Hunting Writers and Intellectuals   505
The Rise of Iran's New Civil Society Press   507
   Assaulting Universities for Defending the Free Press   508
Laying Siege to the Reform Movement   512
   The Hajjariyan Affair   513
   Silencing the Independent Press   515
The Revolt of the Maverick 6th Majles   516
   The Judiciary Muzzles the Executive and the Legislative   518
Khatami's Re-election   520
   The Sad Fate of Reform: Acquiescence and Confrontation   522
Khatami's Foreign Policy   526
Khatami's Economic Legacy   529

11 THE AHMADINEJAD PRESIDENCY, 2005–13   535

Khamenei's Search for an Appropriate President   535
   Ahmadinejad, the Populist Miracle-Maker   537
   The Making of a President   539
   Ahmadinejad's Islamic Government: The Leader's Dream Come True   541
   A Bombastic and Sanctimonious President   543
Ahmadinejad's Atypical and Folksy Politics   546
   Iran's Nuclear Policy   546
   Holocaust Denying and Wiping Out the Zionist State   547
   International Sanctions   548
   Ahmadinejad's Economic Policies   549
   The Politics of Voluntaristic Economic Decisions   553
   Economic Performance during Ahmadinejad's Presidency   554
   The IRGC: Beneficiary of Ahmadinejad's Presidency   555
Society Pushes Back against Ahmadinejad   559
   Workers' Movement   559
   Teachers' Movement   560

Women's Movement 560
Scare Tactics against Intellectuals 561
Elections to the 8th Majles: The Ruling Elite Squabble as the People Abstain 562
The June 2009 Presidential Elections: The People Confront the Leader 564
　The Televised Debates, the Youth and Musavi's Green Wave 566
　Unexpected Election Results 568
　Where is My Vote: The Green Movement is Born 569
　Repression Works 572
Ahmadinejad's Turn to Fall Out with Khamenei 575
　The Rahim-Mashai Affair and its Consequences 575
　Ahmadinejad: Sudden Defender of Pre-Islamic Persia 577
　Frost Sets in between the Leader and His President 578
　The Moslehi Affair 579
　Ahmadinejad Besieged 580

12 ROWHANI: SMILES, HOPE AND MODERATION DASHED, 2013–21 585

Rowhani, the Surprise Victor of the 2013 Presidential Elections 586
Rowhani's First Term 2013–17: Somewhat Euphoric 590
　The Zarif-Soleymani Duo 590
　Rowhani's Illusions 592
　The Pashai Affair: Widening and Deepening Cultural Cleavages 595
　Social Movements and Demands 597
　The Domestic Balance of Forces 598
　Rowhani's Foreign and Nuclear Policy, 2013–17 599
　The Surprise Elections to the 10th Majles and the Fifth Assembly of Experts 602
Rowhani's Very Bumpy Second Term in Office 605
　The Enqelab Street Girl 606
　The Curse of Endemic Corruption 607
　Revolting Against Corruption 607
　Repressing Workers, Teachers, Environmentalists and Sufis 609
　Trump Pulls the Plug 610
The Second Social Calamity 611
　Rowhani's Nightmarish Final Months 614
In Closing 618

Notes 623
Bibliography 655
Index 667

Figures

1.1	The Great Game	17
1.2	Mirza Malkam Khan	20
1.3	Mirza Fathali Akhundzadeh	24
1.4	Iran: Spheres of Influence, 1900	27
1.5	Mozaffaredin Shah	28
1.6	Seyyed Abdollah Behbahani	29
1.7	The leaders of the Fadai detachments, Baqer Khan and Sattar Khan	48
2.1	Ahmad Shah	70
2.2	Mostowfi al-mamalek	75
2.3	Soleyman Mirza Eskandari	76
2.4	Hasan Vosuq al-dowleh	83
2.5	Stamp printed in Iran shows Sheykh Mohammad Khiyabani	101
2.6	Persian Cossack Brigade	107
2.7	Seyyed Ziaeddin Tabatabai	109
2.8	Reza Khan	109
3.1	Mohammad Tadayyon	128
3.2	Sheykh Khazal	139
3.3	Abdolhoseyn Teymurtash	157
4.1	Mr Churchill is greeted by the Shah of Persia, 1943	173
4.2	Ahmad Qavam	195
4.3	Jafar Pishevari	196
4.4	Abdolhoseyn Hajir	203
4.5	Gen. Ali Razmara	211
4.6	Mosaddeq with Allahyar Saleh (left of photo)	216
4.7	Premier Mosaddeq and the Shah, shortly after the premier's return from the USA	217
4.8	Mosaddeq with Hoseyn Fatemi (to his right) and Hoseyn Makki (third to his left)	222
5.1	Gen. Teymur Bakhtiyar	241
5.2	Manuchehr Eqbal	248
5.3	Gen. Mohammadvali Qarani	250
5.4	Jafar Sharif-Emami	254
5.5	Ali Amini	258

5.6	Assadollah Alam	265
5.7	The shah handing out land deeds. Hasan Arsanjani (right of photo) with Amini and Alam present	268
6.1	Hasan-Ali Mansur	282
6.2	Amir-Abbas Hoveyda	285
6.3	Coronation of the shah of Iran in 1967	292
6.4	Jamshid Amuzegar	303
6.5	Shiraz Arts Festival	314
7.1	Mahmud Taleqani gifts a Quran to Gholamreza Takhti	333
7.2	Ali Shariati	336
7.3	Gen. Nematollah Nasiri	340
7.4	Black Friday on Jaleh Square	354
7.5	Gen. Golamreza Azhari	360
7.6	The shah and the queen, Farah Diba, leaving Iran, with Shapur Bakhtyar (right of photo)	364
8.1	Ayatollah Khomeyni and Mehdi Bazargan	377
8.2	Mahmud Taleqani, Sadeq Qotbzadeh and Ebrahim Yazdi	382
8.3	Mohammad-Sadeq Givi-Khalkhali, Hoseyn-Ali Montazeri, Mohammad-Taqi Falsafi and Mostafa Chamran	388
8.4	Ayatollah Kazem Shariatmadari	393
8.5	Ayatollah Morteza Motahhari	396
8.6	Iranian demonstrator burning the American flag in the US Embassy	405
8.7	Poster with the Iranian leaders Mohammad Mosaddeq, Ayatollah Ruhollah Khomeyni, Ahmad Khomeyni and Abolhasan Bani-Sadr	406
8.8	Iran–Iraq War	416
8.9	Basiji Forces	436
8.10	Ayatollah Hoseyn-Ali Montazeri	448
9.1	Rafsanjani with newly elected Supreme Leader Ali Khamenei, 1989	457
9.2	Ali-Akbar Nateq-Nuri	465
9.3	Gholamhoseyn Karbaschi	478
10.1	Abdollah Nuri	495
10.2	Darush Foruhar and Parvaneh Eskandari	505
10.3	NOPO Special Forces	509
10.4	Mohammad-Reza Mahdavi-Kani at Friday Prayer, with nuclear negotiator, Ali Larijani, former foreign minister, Kamal Kharrazi, and commander of the IRGC, Yahya Rahim-Safavi	511
10.5	Saeed Hajjariyan	516
10.6	Judiciary Chief Sadeq Larijani sits next to former Judiciary Chief Ayatollah Hashemi-Shahrudi	520
10.7	President Mohammad Khatami	528

11.1	Mahmud Ahmadinejad's election poster with Mohammad-Ali Rajai (to the right)	537
11.2	The Bushehr Nuclear Power Plant	542
11.3	Mehdi Karrubi	565
11.4	Supporters of Mir-Hoseyn Musavi	566
11.5	Where is my vote?	569
11.6	Iranians run from the riot police, June 2009	571
12.1	Supporters of Iranian President Hasan Rowhani	586
12.2	Gen. Qasem Soleymani	591
12.3	Supreme Leader Ayatollah Ali Khamenei, Secretary of Drug Control and Police Chief Esmail Ahmadi Moqqadam, Army Commander Ataollah Salehi, Armed Forces Joint Chief of Staff Hasan Firuzabadi, Head of Revolutionary Guards Mohammad-Ali Jafari and Iran's defence minister, Mostafa-Mohammad Najjar	595
12.4	John Kerry and Javad Zarif	603
12.5	Assembly of Experts	604
12.6	Supreme Leader Ayatollah Ali Khamenei (on screen) speaking during an online meeting with members of the Iranian Parliament in Tehran, 27 May 2021	617

Acknowledgements

Every book has a story behind it. The temptation for this one was twofold. First, in spring 2018, I taught a course called 'Modern Iran: Political and Social Investigation' at the American University of Paris. This was the first time I was teaching a course on Iran. I enjoyed it immensely and my students in ME 3091C/PO 5002 seemed also to appreciate it. It seemed like a perfect double coincidence of joy and bliss. Once the course was over, the idea of writing a textbook on the modern history of Iran was implanted somewhere in my subconscious. But it was sublimated as I was involved with other projects. Then, in May 2020, out of the blue, Sophie Rudland of I.B. Tauris (Bloomsbury) wrote me asking if I would be interested in writing a textbook on Modern Iranian History. To me, her proposal was a beckoning. The kind assessment of the six anonymous reviewers of my proposal for the textbook gave me heart and reason to pursue this project. I am most indebted to the two anonymous readers of the final text and their observations and recommendations. The rest is history.

This book is dedicated to all of my students over the past thirty-five years. It also celebrates and salutes over a century of the idealistic and realistic efforts of the Iranian people and particularly its youth, chivalrously fighting against mighty odds, for a humane, democratic and inclusive society, free from fear, injustice, arbitrariness, despotism and poverty.

But whatever is worthwhile in this book reflects the efforts of those who taught me. I need to acknowledge them and express my gratitude to their teaching that marked me, made my eyes twinkle, my mind to investigate and think critically from primary to graduate school. They were the main reason I became a teacher. Thank you Khanoume Parvin (Dodangeh) at Miss Mary/Bahare No Primary School, Yahya Dehghanpur throughout my life, Khanoume (Aku) Alizadeh at Iranzamin High School, Joseph Ha and Nosratollah Rassekh at Lewis and Clark College, Arpad Von Lazar at the Fletcher School of Law and Diplomacy, Arthur MacEwan at Harvard University and Yves Goussault at the Institute for the Study of Economic and Social Development (IEDES), l'Université Paris 1 Panthéon-Sorbonne.

Finally, I am most grateful to Leyla Ebtehadj for her sharp eyes, good humour and compelling recommendations throughout this whole project, tirelessly editing and improving this text. The photos in this text are the fruits of her labour. Another angel, who does not wish to be named, heeded my call for help at a luncheon and subsequently spent a considerable amount of time improving it. Thank you M. H. Throughout this project, I benefitted from the guidance of two dear and life-long colleagues, Shahram Ghanbari and Ali Gheissari. Without Sediqeh Rahimi, who provided me with the much-needed newspapers and books, this work would have been more wanting. I am also grateful to Siavush Randjbar-Daemi for providing me with crucial documents.

Timeline

The Quest for a Constitutional Monarchy under the Qajars, 1905–11

17 June 1797	Having reunified the land, Aqa Mohammad Khan, founder of the Qajar dynasty, was assassinated.
5 September 1848	Nasereddin Shah Qajar, aged 17, ascended the throne and ruled for forty-eight years.
10 January 1852	Mirza Taqi Khan Farahani (Amir Kabir), Nasereddin Shah's modernizing chief minister was murdered on the king's orders after three years of service.
4 March 1857	After Persia's defeat in the Anglo-Persian War of 1856–7, the Peace Treaty of Paris was signed.
July 1872	Nasereddin Shah granted a concession to the British banker, Baron Julius de Reuter, for the effective control over the economy.
March 1890	Nasereddin Shah granted a 50-year monopoly for the production, sale and export of Iranian tobacco to Maj. Jerald Talbot, an Englishman.
1 May 1896	Nasereddin Shah was assassinated by Mirza Reza Kermani, a follower of Seyyed Jamaleddin Asadabadi.
1 May 1896	Crown Prince Mozaffareddin Shah, age 43, became king.
28 May 1901	Mozaffareddin Shah signed an oil concession with William Knox D'Arcy, a successful British entrepreneur.
12 December 1905	The governor of Tehran ordered the bastinadoing of two reputable sugar merchants alleged to have raised the price of sugar.
10 January 1906	Mozaffareddin Shah issued a royal decree granting a house of justice (*edalatkhaneh*).
5 August 1906	Mozaffareddin Shah issued a royal decree granting a national consultative parliament (*Majles showraye melli*).
7 October 1906	The first Constituent Assembly met in the presence of Mozaffareddin Shah and the diplomatic corps.

1 January 1907	Three key documents – the constitutional edict, the electoral law and the Constitution itself – were endorsed by Mozaffareddin Shah.
2 January 1907	Mozaffareddin Shah passed away.
19 January 1907	The 38-year-old pro-Russian, Mohammad-Ali Shah, was coronated.
31 August 1907	Britain and Russia signed a secret treaty, the Anglo-Russian Convention, in St. Petersburg, dividing Iran into two zones of influence.
8 October 1907	Mohammad-Ali Shah signed the Supplement to the Constitution, clarifying the ambiguities in the original Constitution.
8 February 1908	Two handmade bombs were thrown at the shah's motorcade.
26 May 1908	Oil gushed into the air at Masjed Soleyman. This was the first important oil find in the Middle East.
23 June 1908	Mohammad-Ali Shah ordered the bombing of the Majles (Parliament) and the arrest of constitutionalists.
24 June 1908	Mohammad-Ali Shah dissolved Parliament which had been in session for twenty months.
July 1908–March 1909	Civil war in Tabriz and mobilization of the constitutionalists in the provinces.
April 1909	Anglo-Persian Oil Company (APOC) was incorporated.
13 July 1909	Several thousand constitutionalists entered Tehran and faced no serious resistance.
16 July 1909	The constitutionalists removed Mohammad-Ali Shah Qajar and appointed Ahmad Shah, his 11-year-old son, as the new king.
15 November 1909	The 2nd Majles was inaugurated in the presence of Ahmad Shah.
8 August 1910	The constitutionalist heroes of Tabriz, Baqer Khan and Sattar Khan, were disarmed in Tehran.
January/February 1911	The deposed shah, Mohammad-Ali Shah and his two brothers, Shoao al-salṭanah and Salar al-dowleh, plotted in Vienna to return to power.
21 May 1911	Salar al-dowleh conquered Sanandaj in the name of his deposed brother.
25 December 1911	To forestall the Russian invasion of Iran, Eprem Khan, the staunch defender of constitutionalism, ordered the deputies to evacuate the Majles before padlocking it.
1 January 1912	The Russian flag was hoisted over government buildings in Tabriz.

A State Made Dysfunctional, 1912–21

10 March 1912	The former shah, Mohammad-Ali Qajar, retreated to Russia after a year-long attempt to regain his throne.
1912–14	The government is unable to impose its authority on the brigandage and banditry in the central provinces and preserve peace, while the Russians occupied the north.
21 July 1914	At the age of 15, Ahmad Shah was coronated king.
1 August 1914	Germany declared war on Russia and within a week the First World War began.
September 1914	Mirza Kuchek Khan and his guerrilla forces began harassing Russian forces in Gilan. His movement came to be known as the Jangalis (Men of the Woods).
1 November 1914	Ahmad Shah issued a royal edict, declaring Iran's neutrality.
4 January 1915	Ottoman troops occupied Urumiyeh in Azarbayjan, and some three weeks later, they clashed with Russian troops in Tabriz and Urumiyeh.
22 May 1915	British forces repulsed Ottoman forces, threatening oil installations in the south, and secured the resumption of oil flow.
5 December 1914	Almost three years after the 2nd Majles was forcefully interrupted, the 3rd Majles began work.
February/March 1915	Turkish forces led by Hoseyn Rauf Bey (Orbey) entered Iran from the west.
8 April 1915	500 troops in the British Indian Army landed at Bushehr and 300 more disembarked close by.
6 June 1915	The minister of interior, informed the deputies that if they refused to take sides against the Ottomans, the Russian Army would march on the capital.
8 August 1915	British troops occupied Bushehr in the south.
14 November 1915	Parliament disbanded, and the uncompromising politicians, deputies and clergy opposed to the Allied invasion migrated from Tehran to Qom and formed the openly pro-German National Defence Committee.
February 1916	The National Defence Committee was disbanded, and the Provisional National Government was formed at the behest of the Germans.
March 1916	Sir Percy Sykes arrived at Bandar Abbas to lead the South Persian Rifles (SPR), a military force composed of Persians and led by the British to oppose the Germans in Iran.

15 April 1917	The Provisional National Government departed from Iran, disbanded and dispersed.
July 1917	The Kerensky government announced the withdrawal of Russian forces from Iran.
August 1917	The British-led South Persian Rifles numbered some 5,500.
16 January 1918	Leon Trotsky, the new Bolshevik foreign minister, announced that the Anglo-Russian Convention of 1907 was null and void and hoped for the rapid withdrawal of British and Ottoman forces from Iran.
27 January 1918	Fresh British forces were dispatched to Iran from Iraq under the command of Maj. Gen. L. C. Dunsterville, an Indian Army officer.
February 1918	The Jangali movement was on the ascent. It had created a quasi-liberated zone in Iran.
14 August 1918	The six-month hostilities between Dunsterville and Mirza Kuchek Khan ceased, and a truce was negotiated between them, which was abrogated unilaterally by the British in March 1919.
11 November 1918	First World War officially ended.
23 January– 14 February 1919	At the behest of Britain, the Iranian delegation, headed by the minister of foreign affairs, was refused representation to the Paris Peace Conference.
9 August 1919	The Anglo-Persian Agreement which had been concealed from the Iranians and the international community was made public.
4 April 1920	Mohammad Khiyabani led a movement against the central government in Tabriz, renamed Azarbayjan as Azadestan, the land of the free, and promised a democratic and free government within the laws of the land.
18 May 1920	Confrontation between the Bolshevik and British fleets in the Caspian Sea culminated in the Red Army's occupation of Anzali.
3 June 1920	Kuchek Khan entered Rasht, announced the abolition of the monarchy and its replacement with a republic.
12 September 1920	The headquarters of Khiyabani's Azarbayjan Democratic Party were attacked and the next day, Khiyabani was shot dead by the Cossack forces of the central government in his pursuit.
22 December 1920	The British War Office announced that it intended to begin withdrawing its forces from Iran by 1 April 1921.

21 January 1921	Curzon encouraged Herman Norman, the British minister in Persia, to use all his influence to bring a strong government to power.
21 February 1921	Seyyed Ziaeddin Tabatabai and Lt Col. Reza Khan, commander of the Cossack Brigade, entered Tehran at the head of some 3,000 Cossacks and carried out an almost bloodless coup.
26 February 1921	The Iranian government, headed by Seyyed Zia signed the Russo-Persian Treaty of Friendship, putting to rest anxieties about an imminent Bolshevik invasion.

Reza Shah: Nation-Building, Repression, Europeanization and Modernization, 1921–41

24 May 1921	Seyyed Zia was removed from the office of prime minister.
22 June 1921	Inauguration of the 4th Majles.
29 July 1921	Col. Mohammad-Taqi Pesyan rebelled against the central government in Khorasan.
31 October 1921	Pesyan fell in battle.
2 February 1922	Maj. Abolqasem Lahuti rebelled against the central government in Tabriz and his rebellion was put down after nine days.
24 February 1922–26 October 1923	Iran went through six prime ministers.
30 November 1922	American Arthur Millspaugh began work as Iran's administrator-general of finance.
27 October 1923	Ahmad Shah appointed Reza Khan prime minister.
24 January 1924	Some two months after Ahmad Shah left the country, Reza Khan began his campaign to change the monarchy to a republic.
20 March 1924	Faced with staunch opposition, especially by the clergy, Reza Khan abandoned the idea of a republic.
20 July 1924	American vice consul in Tehran, Maj. Robert Imbrie, was attacked, wounded and finally killed in the hospital by a mob.
7 December 1924	Khazal bin Jabir al-Kabi, the powerful British-supported ruler of the oil-rich Khuzestan Province, surrendered to Reza Khan.

12 February 1925	The Majles addressed Reza Khan as 'commander-in-chief', the shah's official title, and gave him full powers within the law.
4 June 1925	A law was passed requiring civil registry of identity documents, including birth and death certificates.
31 October 1925	A special session of the Majles voted in favour of deposing the Qajar dynasty and provisionally named Reza Khan Pahlavi as the ruler of Iran.
12 December 1925	The Constituent Assembly voted to alter the Constitution and conferred the monarchy permanently on Reza Shah Pahlavi and his offspring.
27 December 1928	The Majles passed the 'uniform dress code', making the 'Pahlavi hat' obligatory for all Iranian men, except for clergy and seminary school students.
1 May 1929	Abadan oil refinery workers demonstrated and demanded higher wages and shorter hours.
29 April 1933	Reza Shah signed a new contract with the Anglo-Persian Oil Company.
3 October 1933	Reza Shah's trusted and powerful minister of court, Abdolhoseyn Teymurtash, was killed in prison.
11 July 1934	Reza Shah ended his 30-day trip to Turkey, where he met Mustafa Kemal Ataturk.
21 March 1935	Reza Shah ordered that the country's name as used in foreign-language correspondence be changed from Persia to Iran.
8 January 1936	The government officially imposed forced unveiling.
May 1936	After five years of study at Le Rosey, Switzerland, Mohammad-Reza Pahlavi, the crown prince returned to Iran at age 16.
11 September 1937	Reza Shah inaugurated the 11th Majles.
3 September 1939	Iran officially declared its neutrality after the outbreak of the Second World War.
20 August 1941	The British authorized Operation Countenance, the invasion plan of Iran.
25 August 1941	British and Soviet forces invaded Iran.
28 August 1941	Reza Shah ordered his troops to lay down their arms.
16 September 1941	Reza Shah was forced to abdicate by the British and the crown prince, Mohammad-Reza, became shah.

Mohammad-Reza Shah: Foreign Invasion, Oil Nationalization and the Coup, 1941–53

26 January 1942	The Tripartite Anglo-Soviet-Persian Treaty of Alliance, imposed by the belligerent forces, was ratified by the 13th Majles.
10 March 1942	The US declared Iran eligible for Lend Lease, opening the door to its presence in Iran.
Summer of 1942	Food riots broke out in the provinces.
7 January 1943	Britain took over the Port of Khorramshahr.
End of February 1943	Malnutrition in Tehran turned to famine and the daily death rate trebled.
February–March 1943	Typhus epidemic broke out in Tehran, Mashhad, Kerman and Zahedan.
February 1943–April 1944	European and US oil companies requested oil concessions in the south.
16 August 1943	The British began rounding up Iranian dignitaries and politicians for their alleged cooperation with the Germans.
9 September 1943	Iran officially joined the Allies and declared war on the Axis.
28 November 1943	US President Franklin Roosevelt, British Prime Minister Winston Churchill and Chairman of the Council of People's Commissars Joseph Stalin met in Tehran, at what was known as the Tehran Conference.
13–16 September 1944	A Soviet oil mission led by the Vice Commissar of Foreign Affairs Sergei Kavtaradze met with the shah and demanded an oil concession in the five northern provinces of Iran.
8 October 1944	The Iranian prime minister, Mohammad Saed, informed Kavtaradze that all oil concession negotiations, including the ones with the American oil companies were suspended until the end of the war.
21 June 1945	Stalin issued a top-secret decree, ordering exploration and prospecting for oil and gas in Azarbayjan.
6 July 1945	The Political Bureau of the Central Committee of the Soviet Communist Party ordered Mir-Jafar Baqerov to organize secessionist movements in Iran's Azarbayjan and other northern provinces.

14 July 1945	The specifics for 'creating the Azerbaijani Democratic Party' were outlined by the Soviet authorities after consultation with Jafar Pishehvari and Abdolsamad Kambakhsh in Baku.
15 August 1945	A group of pro-Tudeh officers rebelled in Khorasan.
25 August 1945	Jafar Pishehvari, a veteran communist, entered Tabriz.
3 September 1945	Establishment of the Azarbayjan Democratic Party (*Ferqehe democratic Azarbayjan*).
End of November 1945	A de facto dual-power system prevailed in Iran, and with the inauguration of Azarbayjan's Parliament on 12 December, this duality became official.
26 January 1946	Iran demanded that the Security Council investigate the dispute between Iran and the Soviet Union over Azarbayjan.
28 January 1946	Ahmad Qavam replaced Prime Minister Hakimi.
4 April 1946	Qavam-Sadchikov Agreement.
6 May 1946	The Soviets withdrew their forces from Iran.
1 August 1946	Qavam gave ministerial positions to three prominent members of the Tudeh Party but ousted them on 19 October 1946.
13 December 1946	The Soviet-initiated secessionist Azarbayjan movement folded. The Iranian Army entered Tabriz. Pishehvari fled to Baku and government forces entered Azarbayjan.
15 December 1946	The eleven-month Soviet-initiated Kurdish Republic of Mahabad, led by Qazi Mohammad, surrendered to the central government.
22 October 1947	The Majles annulled the Qavam-Sadchikov Agreement.
January 1948	Seyyeds Abolqasem Kashani and Mojtaba (Mirlowhi) Navab-Safavi issued fiery communiqués and organized a series of high-profile demonstrations and marches in Tehran.
4 February 1949	The shah escaped an assassination attempt at Tehran University.
17 July 1949	The Supplemental Agreement on oil was signed by Neville Gass, the director of AIOC, and Abbasqoli Golshayan, the Iranian minister of finance and was sent to the Majles for quick ratification.
23 October 1949	Establishment of the National Front (*Jebhehye Melli*) under the leadership of Mosaddeq.
4 November 1949	Abdolhoseyn Hajir, the powerful minister of court, was assassinated by a member of Navab-Safavi's Devotees of Islam.

26 June 1950	Gen. Haj Ali Razmara was appointed prime minister by the shah.
7 March 1951	Razmara was assassinated by Khalil Tahmasebi, a member of Navab-Safavi's Devotees of Islam.
20 March 1951	The shah signed the Oil Nationalization Law.
29 April 1951	Mohammad Mosaddeq became prime minister.
30 April 1951	The nine-point oil nationalization law was ratified by the Majles.
5 May–27 September 1951	Britain planned different military operations, from invasion of Iran's southern oil fields under the code name 'Operation Buccaneer' in late June to deployment of airborne troops to take over Abadan and the oil refinery in July.
7 October 1951	Mosaddeq flew to New York to defend Iran against a complaint lodged by Britain at the UN Security Council.
27 December 1951	Beginning of elections to the 17th Majles.
7 January 1952	Mosaddeq named *Time* magazine's Man of the Year for 1951.
28 May 1952	Mosaddeq attended the hearing of the International Court at The Hague regarding the UK complaint to the UN Security Council.
16 July 1952	Mosaddeq resigned and the shah accepted his resignation, appointing Qavam to replace him on 17 July.
18–21 July 1952	Crowds took to the streets demanding Mosaddeq's return.
21 July 1952	Qavam resigned and on the next day, the Majles voted in favour of Mosaddeq.
22 July 1952	The International Court of Justice ruled that it had no jurisdiction to deal with or rule over the dispute.
22 October 1952	Iran severed diplomatic ties with Britain.
28 February 1953	The anti-Mosaddeq forces formed around the Kashani–Zahedi–Behbahani axis caused unrest in Tehran to overthrow the prime minister but failed.
4 April 1953	Allen Dulles, director of the American Central Intelligence Agency (CIA), authorized a budget of $1 million to be used 'in any way that would bring about the fall of Mosaddeq'.
26 April 1953	Discovery of the body of assassinated Lt Gen. Mahmud Afshartus, Mosaddeq's chief of police.
25 June 1953	The plan to overthrow Mosaddeq was given official approval in Washington.
15 August 1953	The first coup began by officers and soldiers of the Iranian Army loyal to the shah failed.

16 August 1953	The shah fled the country and arrived in Baghdad.
19 August 1953	The second coup unfolded as planned and succeeded to overthrow Mosaddeq.

From Post-Coup to Post-Uprising, August 1953–June 1963

19 August 1953	Gen. Fazlollah Zahedi, the coup commander, became prime minister.
8 October 1953	The Mosaddeqist National Resistance Movement organized its first major demonstration.
1 December 1953	Tehran and London resumed diplomatic relations.
7 December 1953	Soldiers opened fire on students at Tehran University's Faculty of Engineering, killing three students.
21 December 1953	Mosaddeq's trial ended, and he was condemned to three years in prison.
5 August 1954	A new oil agreement was made between Ali Amini and the new head of the Consortium, Howard Page.
6 April 1955	The shah demanded Zahedi's resignation and appointed Hoseyn Ala as prime minister.
22 October 1955	The Iranian Parliament voted in favour of Iran joining the Baghdad Pact.
4 August 1956	Mosaddeq was 'released' from prison and placed under house arrest, 100 kilometres west of Tehran.
14 March 1957	The bill concerning the creation of the State Organization for Intelligence and Security (SAVAK) passed in the Majles.
3 April 1957	Manuchehr Eqbal became prime minister and Ala slipped back into his old position of court minister.
27 February 1958	The Qarani Affair.
3 October 1958	The first television network in Iran, Iran Television (ITV), owned by Habibollah Sabet, began transmitting.
23 December 1959	The American Armed Forces Radio and Television Services (AFRTS) started broadcasting its first television programme.
27 August 1960	The shah effectively annulled the election to the 20th Majles due to widespread rigging.
29 August 1960	The shah replaced Eqbal with Jafar Sharif-Emami as prime minister.

4 January 1961	A new round of elections for the 20th Majles began and the Majles was convened on 21 February 1961.
2 May 1961	A strike by Tehran's Teachers' Association led to the death of a teacher in front of the Majles.
5 May 1961	After eight months in office, the shah replaced Sharif Emami with Ali Amini.
9 May 1961	The shah dissolved the Majles, which remained closed for 27 months, reopening on 6 October 1963.
18 May 1961	Tehran witnessed an unprecedented National Front gathering at Jalaliyeh, officially permitted by the Amini Government.
21 January 1962	Tehran University was attacked by the military, mostly parachutists. Their bloody operation lasted for some two hours.
2 March 1962	Land reform began in Maragheh (Azarbayjan).
17 July 1962	The shah accepted Amini's resignation and two days later Asadollah Alam became prime minister.
25 December 1962	The National Front Congress opened in Tehran.
9 January 1963	Hasan Arsanjani organized the First Congress of Rural Cooperatives in Tehran at which the shah presented the 'six-point principles' of the White Revolution.
26 January 1963	The 'six-point principles' of the White Revolution was ratified in a national referendum.
5 June 1963	The pro-Khomeyni uprising.
27 August 1963	The Congress of Free Men and Women opened in Tehran to set the stage for the 21st Majles elections.
15 December 1963	Hasan-Ali Mansur, Amir-Abbas Hoveyda and Ataollah Khosravani founded the New Iran Party.
7 March 1964	Alam resigned and the shah appointed Hasan-Ali Mansur as prime minister.

The Shah's Push towards the Gates of the Great Civilization, 1964–77

13 October 1964	The Majles ratified the 'Status of Forces Agreement', exempting US military personnel from being held accountable for crimes committed in Iran.
4, November 1964	Khomeyni was arrested, placed on a plan and banished to Turkey and then Iraq.

21 January 1965	Mansur was shot twice in front of the Majles and died five days later.
27 January 1965	The shah appointed Amir-Abbas Hoveyda as prime minister.
10 April 1965	The shah escaped an assassination attempt on his life at the Marble Palace.
6 September 1965	The People's Mojahedin (Holy Warriors), a clandestine revolutionary Islamic group is found to launch an armed struggle.
15 September 1965	The shah is conferred the title 'Aryamehr'.
March 1966	The Jazani Group, a semi-clandestine Marxist-Leninist group is formed with the objective of fomenting radical political change.
11–21 September	The first Shiraz Art Festival.
26 October 1967	The shah coronated himself and Queen Farah.
25 October of 1968	Ali Shariati gave his first lecture at Hoseyniyeh Ershad.
8 February 1971	A guerrilla force later known as the People's Fadai Guerrillas, or the People's Self-Sacrificing Guerrillas, attacked and disarmed the Siyahkal Gendarmerie Station in Mazandaran.
1 March 1971	The British ended their presence in the Persian Gulf.
12–16 October 1971	The Persepolis celebrations of Iran's 2,500 years of monarchy.
30 November 1971	The Iranian Army occupied the three tiny islands of Greater Tonb, Lesser Tonb and Abu Musa in the Persian Gulf.
30 May 1972	President Nixon accompanied by Henry Kissinger arrived in Tehran. They gave the shah a carte blanche to purchase any number and type of conventional weapons available in the US arsenal.
August 1972	The shah rushed to the help of Sultan Qabus of Oman in his war against the Dhofar Marxist-Leninist rebels.
17 November 1972	Hoseyniyeh Ershad was sealed off by a cordon of police and Shariati went into hiding before being arrested on 29 September 1973.
2 March 1975	The shah imposed a one-party system and told Iranians to join the new Rastakhiz or Resurgence Party (later the National Resurgence Party of Iran).
11 December 1975	Sultan Qabus claimed victory over the rebellion.
March–November 1976	Amnesty International and the International Commission of Jurists published three damaging reports on Iran's human rights abuses.
20 January 1977	Inauguration of James Carter as US president.

The Revolutionary Transition from Monarchy to Republic, March 1977–March 1979

18/19 June 1977	Ali Shariati died in Southampton, UK.
7 August 1977	The shah replaced Hoveyda with Jamshid Amuzegar as prime minister.
19 August 1977	The government released some 650 political prisoners.
10 October 1977	The Goethe Institute in Tehran hosted ten days of poetry reading and speeches organized by the dissident Iranian Writers' Association.
23 October 1977	Mostafa Khomeyni, Ayatollah Khomeyni's elder son who had accompanied his father into exile, passed away in Najaf.
24 November 1977	Some 2,000 people attending a gathering of the National Front were attacked by busloads of agents, disguised as workers.
7 January 1978	*Ettelaat*, one of the country's leading newspapers, published a calumnious opinion piece against Khomeyni.
9 January 1978	Anti-shah and pro-Khomeyni rallies broke out in Qom and spread to Tehran, Tabriz, Mashhad, Esfahan and Ahvaz.
19 August 1978	Violence reached a new hysterical pitch when the Rex Movie Theatre in Abadan was set on fire by Khomeyni's supporters, causing the death of 377.
27 August 1978	The shah replaced Amuzegar with Jafar Sharif-Emami as prime minister.
5 September 1978	A wave of strikes swept factories, oil installations and workplaces.
8 September 1978	Troops fired on a crowd that had gathered at Jaleh Square in Tehran, killing about 400 people. The carnage came to be known as 'Black Friday'.
6 October 1978	Under pressure from the Iranian government, Khomeyni was forced to leave Iraq and went to France, settling at Neauphle-le-Château in the Yvelines.
6 November 1978	The shah appointed Gen. Gholamreza Azhari to form a military government and ordered the arrest of six former ministers and the former chief of SAVAK.
30 December 1978	The shah replaced Azhari with Shapur Bakhtiyar, an old Mosaddeqist and member of the National Front.

4 January 1979	The leaders of the US, UK, France and Germany gathered on the French Caribbean island of Guadeloupe, and one of the main items on their agenda was the Iranian crisis.
5 January 1979	US Gen. Robert Huyser, deputy commander of the Supreme Allied Command in Europe, arrived in Iran.
12 January 1979	Khomeyni announced the formation of the 'Council of the Islamic Revolution'.
16 January 1979	The shah and queen left Iran for Cairo.
1 February 1979	Khomeyni returned to Iran.
4 February 1979	Khomeyni introduced Mehdi Bazargan as the first provisional prime minister of the Iranian Revolution.
11 February 1979	The Iranian Army declared its 'neutrality', marking the victory of the people's revolution.
12 February 1979	The Kurdish Democratic Party of Iran (KDPI) occupied the police stations and gendarmerie outposts in Mahabad and emptied out the armouries.
15 February 1979	Heads began to roll as summary trials behind closed doors condemned generals Nematollah Nasiri, Reza Naji, Mehdi Rahimi and Manuchehr Khosrowdad to death for 'corruption on earth'.
18 February 1979	Five of Khomeyni's trusted clerics announced the formation of the Islamic Republic Party (IRP).
28 February 1979	Khomeyni ordered the expropriation of the assets belonging to the shah, the royal family and those associated with them.
28 February 1979	Khomeyni issued an edict creating the Islamic Revolutionary Guard Corps (IRGC).
18 March 1979	In Sanandaj, the capital of Kurdistan, the army headquarters, the gendarmerie outpost and Sanandaj's radio and television were overrun by anti-government forces and the town's main garrison was under siege.
31 March 1979	Of the total number of participants in the national referendum, 98 per cent voted for the Islamic Republic as their new system of government.

Khomeyni's Islamic Republic, 1979–89

1 May 1979	Ayatollah Morteza Motahhari was the first of many assassinated by the radical Muslim Forqan Group.

19 August 1979	The Assembly of Experts convened to review the draft of the new Constitution.
21 August 1979	The Office of Tehran's Prosecutor of the Islamic Revolutionary Courts and the minister of guidance ordered the closure of 41 dailies and weeklies.
22 October 1979	The shah flew from Mexico to the US and was rushed to New York Hospital.
4 November 1979	A group of students which came to be known as Student Followers of the Imam's Line, entered the grounds of the US Embassy and took 63 embassy staff as hostages.
3 December 1979	The new Constitution, including Rule of the Guardian Jurist, was approved by a referendum.
25 January 1980	Abolhasan Bani-Sadr won the first presidential election.
7 April 1980	The US government broke off all diplomatic ties with Iran and imposed full sanctions.
15 April 1980	The Student Followers of the Imam's Line occupied Tabriz University and launched the Cultural Revolution in Iranian universities.
24 April 1980	US launched the disastrous Operation Eagle Claw to free the American hostages.
5 July 1980	The Revolutionary Council announced that it was mandatory that women wear the veil.
12 July 1980	The Iranian press reported on a failed coup attempt (*Nojeh*) to overthrow the Islamic Republic.
22 September 1980	Iraq launched a full-scale land and air attack against Iran.
12 May 1981	Khomeyni announced that the People's Mojahedin needed to lay down their arms, embrace the Islamic Republic, stop threatening the state with armed uprising and recant from their past positions.
8 June 1981	Pro-Bani-Sadr and pro-Mojahedin forces clashed daily with pro-Khomeyni *Hezbollahi*s.
18 June 1981	The People's Mojahedin declared a defensive war on the Islamic Republic.
21 June 1981	Majles removed Bani-Sadr from office.
28 June 1981	The People's Mojahedin blew up the headquarters of the IRP, killing 75, including Ayatollah Beheshti.
29 July 1981	Masoud Rajavi, the leader of the Mojahedin, and Bani-Sadr, Iran's first president escaped from Iran.
2 October 1981	Ali Khamenei gained 94 per cent of the votes and became Iran's president.

24 May 1982	The Iranian Army and the IRGC, retook possession of Khorramshahr, forcing Iraqi forces to retreat.
13 July 1982	Iranian forces entered Iraqi territory.
16 July 1985	The Assembly of Experts met and secretly designated Hoseyn-Ali Montazeri as heir to Khomeyni.
17 September 1985	Khomeyni permitted the IRGC to expand its branches and constitute its own navy and air forces.
9 October 1986	Montazeri began openly questioning the excesses of the Islamic Republic.
9 February 1986	Iran captured the Faw Peninsula, 20 kilometres south-east of Basra.
1 June 1987	Rafsanjani and Khamenei requested that Khomeyni dissolve the Islamic Republic Party.
6 February 1988	Khomeyni issued an edict that an 'Expediency Discernment Council' be established to resolve the differences and conflicts between the Guardian Council and the Majles.
17 April 1988	Iran lost the Faw Peninsula and was forced to retreat.
3 July 1988	The USS *Vincennes*, launched two surface-to-air missiles at Iran Air commercial Flight 655, travelling from Bandar Abbas to Dubai, killing 290 onboard.
18 July 1988	Iran agreed to comply with Resolution 598, calling for a ceasefire with Iraq and a withdrawal of troops to international borders.
25 July 1988	The Mojahedin's National Liberation of Iran Army entered Iran from Iraq, hoping to overthrow the regime. They were routed within three days.
31 July 1988	Khomeyni ordered the execution of imprisoned Mojahedin who remained steadfast in their political beliefs.
31 July 1988	Montazeri warned that Khomeyni's decision would be construed as vindictiveness, and that violence and execution would not yield any results.
July–September 1988	Some 2,800 to 12,000 imprisoned members of the political opposition were executed.
14 February 1989	Khomeyni issued a fatwa against the author Salman Rushdie, condemning him to death.
26 March 1989	Khomeyni stripped Montazeri of his title of Deputy of the Leader.
24 April 1989	Khomeyni ordered the reappraisal and revision of the Constitution.
3 June 1989	Khomeyni passed away.

The Rafsanjani's Presidency, 1989–97

4 June 1989	The Assembly of Experts voted Hojatoleslam Ali Khamenei as Iran's new Leader replacing Khomeyni.
28 July 1989	Hashemi-Rafsanjani became Iran's new president.
19 August 1989	Rafsanjani encouraged the IRGC to become involved in the war reconstruction effort.
4 January 1990	Gholamhoseyn Karbaschi became the mayor of Tehran.
Mid-July 1990	The Assembly of Experts of the Leadership empowered the Guardian Council to ascertain the eligibility of applicants of the Assembly Experts. This set a dangerous precedence.
3 May 1991	Roland Dumas, the French foreign minister, visited Tehran, followed by Hans-Dietrich Genscher, the West German foreign minister.
22 May 1991	The Guardian Council announced that it had the right to supervise the Majles elections, including the rejection and approval of applicants' credentials.
November 1991	The influential monthly *Kiyan*, reflecting the views of modernist Islamic intellectuals appeared on the newsstands.
28 May 1992	The 4th Majles election resulted in the overwhelming victory of the conservative Right faction of the regime over its Left faction.
18 July 1992	Rafsanjani finally accepted the resignation of Mohammad Khatami, his minister of culture and Islamic guidance.
17 September 1992	Sadeq Sharafkandi, the leader of the Kurdish Democratic Party of Iran, along with two of his associates, were assassinated in Berlin.
11 June 1993	Rafsanjani won a second presidential term.
18 January 1996	The pro-Rafsanjani and moderate political group called the 'Executives of Construction' were born.
5 August 1996	Clinton signed the Iran–Libya Sanctions Act (ILSA).
6 August 1996	The Ministry of Intelligence plot to murder 21 members of Iranian Writers' Association failed.
11 April 1997	The German judiciary ruled that the Iranian political leadership had ordered the assassination of Kurdish political leaders in September 1992.
11 April 1997	European governments began recalling their ambassadors from Tehran.

Khatami in Power, 1997–2005

23 May 1997	Mohammad Khatami became Iran's president.
November 1997	The last EU ambassadors returned to Tehran.
7 January 1998	Khatami raised the issue of two Islams, one 'progressive' and the other 'reactionary', and announced that his Islam sought 'dialogue, understanding and peace with all nations'.
5 February 1998	An intellectually seductive newspaper called *Jameeh* (Society) appeared on the newsstands. It represented the Khatami-era professional, independent and inquisitive press.
17 February 1998	The US wrestling team received a warm welcome in Tehran.
7 June 1998	Karbaschi, mayor of Tehran, was put on trial and sentenced to five years in prison and twenty years suspension from all government services.
24 July 1998	The newspaper *Jameeh* (Society) published its last issue, but was followed by a string of new and bold newspapers.
August 1998	US President Bill Clinton sent a secret letter to President Khatami, attempting to establish contact with him through the Swiss ambassador in Tehran.
22 November 1998	Darush Foruhar and Parvaneh Eskandari, old members of the National Front and political dissidents were assassinated at their home by members of the Ministry of Intelligence.
3 December 1998	Marked the beginning of a series of assassinations carried out by the Ministry of Intelligence against dissident poets, writers, translators and intellectuals.
March 1999	The US removed its sanction against sales of spare aeroplane parts, food and medicine to Iran.
20 June 1999	Saeed Emami, the mysterious mastermind of the serial political killings, committed suicide in prison.
8 July 1999	Demonstrations broke out against the closure of the newspaper *Salam* in the universities and spread.
20 July 1999	24 high-ranking commanders of the IRGC denounced the demonstrations and warned Khatami that their patience was at an end, and if he did not reconsider, they would no longer wait.
30 October 1999	Abdollah Nuri, Khatami's former minister of interior was put on trial and charged with 'libeling and insulting the

	system's authorities and institutions', and 'propagating ideas against religious principles/standards and insulting religious sanctities'.
23 November 1999	Nuri was sentenced to five years in prison, given a five-year ban from press activities and fined.
18 February 2000	Khatami's reformist faction won a resounding victory in the elections to the 6th Majles.
12 March 2000	Saeed Hajjariyan, a prominent reformist ideologue and member of the Tehran City Council, survived an assassination attempt commanded a member of the IRGC.
17 March 2000	Madeleine Albright apologized to Iran for US involvement in the 1953 coup and for her support for Saddam Hussein during the Iran–Iraq War.
23 April 2000	The judiciary ordered twelve flagship reformist newspapers and weeklies be shut down, including Hajjariyan's *This Morning*.
19 June 2000	The unconstitutional closure of the press and the unnecessary arrest of individuals were denounced by 151 reformist deputies of the 6th Majles.
8 June 2001	Iranians elected Khatami as president for a second term.
29 January 2002	US President George W. Bush referred to Iran as a member of the 'axis of evil'.
21 May 2002	135 deputies of the 6th Majles wrote to Khamenei and warned that 'the country was at a fork in the road, either dictatorship and despotism' or a return to the Constitution and submission to democratic rules.
23 February 2003	The conservative Principlists (*usulgarayan*), in alliance with the Islamic Coalition of Mourning Groups, routed the reformist candidates in elections to the Second City and Rural Councils.
3 May 2003	Mahmud Ahmadinejad became Tehran's mayor.
December 2003	Khatami signed the Additional Protocol to the Nuclear Non-Proliferation Treaty (NPT).
11 January 2004	Some 140 reformist deputies of the 6th Majles took sanctuary in Parliament, protesting the widespread purge of reformist candidates for the 7th Majles by the Guardian Council.
1 February 2004	Some 125 deputies of the 6th Majles resigned in protest.
20 February 2004	The elections to the 7th Majles gave the candidates of Khamenei's conservative coalition a sweeping victory.

14 November 2004	Khatami temporarily suspended all uranium enrichment activities for the duration of negotiations with the International Atomic Energy Agency (IAEA).
24 June 2005	In a highly contested election, Mahmud Ahmadinejad became Iran's president.
3 August 2005	Khatami left the Presidential Palace.

The Ahmadinejad Presidency, 2005–13

17 September 2005	In his first address to the Security Council, Ahmadinejad asserted Iran's right to develop peaceful nuclear energy and prayed for the return of the Twelfth Shii Imam.
24 September 2005	The IAEA referred the purview of Iran's nuclear activities to the UN Security Council.
10 November 2005	The government ratified the by-laws of 'Quick Impact and Return Projects'.
22 December 2005	The Bus Workers' Syndicate went on strike, protesting work conditions.
29 January 2006	The government ratified the executive by-law of 'Justice Shares'.
11 April 2006	Ahmadinejad announced that Iran had completed the nuclear fuel cycle and joined the nuclear countries.
12 June 2006	Fifty-four women's rights activists were arrested during a rally.
2 July 2006	The Leader charged the government to implement Article 44 of Iran's Constitution and sell 80 per cent of all state-owned enterprises.
31 July 2006	The UN Security Council adopted Resolution 1696, the first of some five resolutions against Iran's nuclear activities.
August 2006	Women's rights activists launched a campaign called the 'One Million Signatures for the Repeal of Discriminatory Laws'.
12 December 2006	Ahmadinejad told members of the international conference *Reviewing the Holocaust: Global Vision* in Tehran that, 'Just as the Soviet Union was wiped out (*mahv*) ... so will the Zionist regime.'
14 March 2007	Police attacked and broke up a demonstration of teachers in front of the Majles protesting their wages and benefits.

Mid-April 2007	Some 60 per cent of schools in Tehran were experiencing work stoppages.
9 July 2007	Ahmadinejad dissolved the Management and Plan Organization (MPO).
14 March 2008	Only 51 per cent of the eligible voters in the country and 30 per cent of Tehranis voted during the 8th Majles elections.
10 March 2009	To everyone's surprise, Mir-Hoseyn Musavi announced his candidacy for the June presidential elections.
18 April 2009	Right before the presidential elections, Ahmadinejad distributed the profits of the 'justice shares' to some 9 million shareholders.
3 June 2009	The highly controversial presidential debate between Musavi and Ahmadinejad led to a resurgence of Musavi's popularity.
13 June 2009	The official results of the 12 June presidential election declared Ahmadinejad as the winner with 64.7 per cent of the votes.
13 June 2009	Khamenei confirmed the election results while Musavi and Karrubi contested them and called for their annulment.
15 June 2009	According to different sources, between 1 and 3 million supporters of Musavi and Karrubi participated in a spectacular show of force in Tehran, chanting, 'Where is my vote?'
19 June 2009	Khamenei rejected annulling the elections and ordered the people not to come out on the streets and warned that protesters would be responsible for bloodletting and violence.
17 July 2009	Ahmadinejad appointed Esfandiyar Rahim-Mashaei as his First Deputy.
18 July 2009	Khamenei issued a decree commanding Ahmadinejad to revoke Rahim-Mashaei's appointment. The president complied after a week.
1 August 2009	Some 100 reformist politicians, journalists and activists arrested after the June elections were put on a collective trial and accused of plotting against national security, disturbing public order and attempting a velvet revolution.
27–28 December 2009	The Green Movement rattled the regime for the last time as angry protesters clashed with security forces in Tehran and the provinces, leaving 11 dead in Tehran.

17 April 2011	Ahmadinejad removed Heydar Moslehi from his post as the minister of intelligence.
18 April 2011	Khamenei ordered Moslehi back to his office.
19 April 2011	Ahmadinejad provoked an unprecedented national crisis by refusing to carry out his state responsibilities. The president stayed at home for eleven days.
2 May 2011	One day after Ahmadinejad returned to his office, the security forces arrested his cultural adviser and the prayer leader of the President's Office, along with several individuals associated with Rahim-Mashaei's circle.
March 2012	The Council of the European Union disconnected Iran from the global SWIFT system, preventing it from cross-border financial transactions.
24 September 2012	Ahmadinejad arrived in New York on his last official trip, accompanied by an entourage of 140.

Rowhani: Smiles, Hope and Moderation Dashed, 2013–21

22 May 2013	The Guardian Council rejected the credentials of Ali-Akbar Hashemi-Rafsanjani and Mahmud Ahmadinejad, to stand for presidential elections. Both had been president for two terms.
14 June 2013	Hasan Rowhani was elected president.
24 September 2013	Rowhani was in New York attending the UN General Assembly and speaking to US President Barack Obama on the phone.
14 July 2015	Iran and the P5+1, the five permanent members of the Security Council plus Germany, reached a comprehensive nuclear deal, the Joint Comprehensive Plan of Action (JCPOA).
11 October 2015	The Majles approved JCPOA.
2 January 2016	A 'spontaneous' crowd of some 700 zealots chanting, 'Death to the Al Saud!' attacked, ransacked and firebombed the Saudi Embassy in Tehran.
3 January 2016	Saudi Arabia broke off diplomatic relations with Iran.

24 January 2016	Rowhani headed a 90-man team of economic and financial experts to Italy and France and signed a €50 million cooperation agreement with them.
19 December 2016	Rowhani signed the 'Charter on Citizen's Rights', committing his government to uphold the rights and freedoms of individuals, women and minorities.
7 January 2017	Workers at Haft Tapeh sugar-cane factory went on strike, and were followed by a string of strikes of various industries.
8 January 2017	The 82-year-old healthy and fit Hashemi-Rafsanjani was announced dead under suspicious circumstances.
19 May 2017	Rowhani won the presidential elections.
27 December 2017	An unassuming woman stood on an elevated electricity box in Tehran's very busy Enqelab Street, exposed her uncovered long black hair and waved a white headscarf on a stick. She was arrested.
28 December 2017	Demonstrations turned into riots in Mashhad and spread throughout Iran, lasting ten days, leaving some 25–50 dead.
24 and 25 January 2018	The Intelligence Organization of the Islamic Revolutionary Guard Corps (IOIRGC) arrested nine members of an environmental group called the Persian Wildlife Heritage Foundation. They were accused of acting as a front for the CIA and Israeli intelligence service, Mossad.
8 May 2018	President Donald Trump withdrew the US from the JCPOA and reimposed sanctions on Iran.
1 July 2018	Disturbances erupted in Ahvaz, Khorramshahr and Mahshahr as riot police attacked and tried to disperse crowds protesting the shortage of potable water and the saltiness of available water resources.
September 2018	Foreign firms that had entered the Iranian market after the nuclear deal began pulling out under the threat of US retaliation.
15 November 2019	The government announced the tripling of the price of a litre of non-rationed gasoline.
15 November 2019	Violent protests engulfed the country and the protester's main target of rage was Khamenei.
17 November 2019	Khamenei told a handful of top political, security and military officials that the Islamic Republic was in danger and they had to do whatever it took to end it.

25 November 2019	The government staged a pro-Khamenei counter-demonstration. The participants condemned the Leader's enemies and chanted, 'Death to America!' and 'Death to Israel!'
3 January 2020	President Trump ordered a drone attack on Baghdad, killing seven people, including Gen. Qasem Soleymani, the head of Iran's Qods Force, and Abu Mahdi al-Muhandis, the leader of Iraq's *Hezbollah*.
8 January 2020	The IRGC launched 'Operation Martyr Soleymani', firing 12 ballistic missiles at American forces stationed at Ayn al-Assad Airbase in Iraq.
8 January 2020	102 minutes after the end of the Iranian missile attack on the US base, a Ukrainian commercial plane which had taken off from Tehran's Imam Khomeini International Airport crashed 6 minutes after taking off, killing all 176 on board.
11 January 2020	The Commander of IRGC's Aerospace Force admitted that the Ukrainian plane had been mistaken for an incoming cruise missile and was shot down accidentally by the IRGC.
18 February 2020	Iran announced its first cases of Covid-19 and the country partially shut down for about two months.
24 May 2020	The Guardian Council rejected the credentials of Ali Larijani, who had been the speaker of the Majles for twelve years, Ahmadinejad, the two-term president, and Eshaq Jahangiri, Rowhani's vice president for eight years.
18 June 2021	The thirteenth presidential election of the Islamic Republic brought 49 per cent of eligible voters to the booths and resulted in the election of Ebrahim Raisi, the Leader's preferred candidate.
3 August 2021	Rowhani left the Presidential Office.

Introduction

Chapter Outline

Chat with Students Studying Modern Iranian History	1
Cautions about Reading this Textbook	4
The Approach of this Textbook	4
Persia and Western Europe in the Nineteenth Century: Worlds Apart	6
Persia in the Cave of Ephesus	8
Plagues and Famines	12
Persia at the Dawn of Twentieth Century	13

Chat with Students Studying Modern Iranian History

The textbook before you begins with a background to the Iranian Constitutional Revolution around the turn of the twentieth century and concludes twenty-one years into the twenty-first century. As such, it attempts to make sense of more than one hundred years. It is primarily a study in history – if we agree that thirty years must pass before we consider a topic historical – but it will also cover current events.

Iranians, like people of all those countries lacking solid institutions, political democracy and peaceful means of transferring power, enviously look at countries possessing these features and ask the same daunting question. Generation after generation, for over a hundred years, Iranians have wondered, 'why are we in the situation we are in, not benefitting from what they have?' and 'what did they do which we did not?'

A simple answer is that external and internal factors hindered Iranians from enjoying the life of their happier humankind. Features and characteristics indigenous and endogenous to Iran and Iranians, played a role, be it their long and mixed cultural and historical heritage, religions, values, beliefs, practices, institutions, geography, economic development and political evolution. There were also extrinsic and outside influences such as foreign encroachments, colonialism and imperialism.

A purpose of this textbook is to address those closely intertwined determining factors by reviewing and analysing the historical evidence during this period. Narrating the Iranian side of the story, and examining the initiatives, movements and advances, as well as the impediments, resistance and setbacks will provide palpable elements to begin understanding why Iran has yet failed to join the ranks of the democratic countries of the world.

Our study will demonstrate that in view of Iran's state of underdevelopment, economic, social, political and cultural, at the turn of twentieth century, change became a forced process, not an evolutionary one. For a hundred years, political actors and leaders took Iranians by the ears and pulled them forward or backward, depending on their ideological convictions and vision.

This historical narrative demonstrates how in the absence of democratic institutions, and legal mechanisms of checks and balances, individuals become the main builders and shapers of history. The imposition of their power clashes with the popular will, throwing society into cycles of protest, opposition and resistance.

Historical interludes of synergy, trust and complicity between Iranians and their leaders have existed, but such moments of democratic interaction, participation and experience have been rare and short-lived. The weakness of democratic institutions, civil society organizations, labour unions, interest groups, the press and parties allowed Iranian leaders in power to maintain their power. The rule of long-term non-democracy effectively and systematically hampered the emergence of democratic institutions. Attempts at their natural development was usually resisted forcefully. Iranian modern history narrates the hegemony of arbitrary rulers over democratic institutions and existing national covenants.

Our study of one hundred years of Iranian history illustrates that the separation and independence of powers, except for short interludes, remained a window dressing and a formality. The first move by authoritarian Iranian rulers consolidating their powers has always been to make the executive, legislative, judiciary and the press, subservient and submissive to their personal wish.

In the absence of democratic mediums of protesting and objecting national policies and prevailing socio-economic and political conditions, Iranian history has been regularly subjected to instability and crises. This book will recount a hundred years of uncertainty, insecurity, repression, fear, political breakdown and chaos. Yet, between the pages of these tragic years, students will be learning about a country searching for solutions, blending theories and experimenting with liberating ideas. This textbook tells the story of a people's hopeful and audacious quest for freedom, security and prosperity under the rule of law. It recounts how they participated in, organized, mobilized and led opposition movements, revolts and revolutions without attaining their ends.

In their search for a just and democratic society Iranians have proven resilience, lived life with a grain of salt and drawn upon a mixed bag of their cultural legacy to enjoy life, take hardship with a grain of salt and never give up on the idea of change and improvement. Their centuries-long collective cultural and political experience has inculcated them with a *carpe diem* philosophy of life, with a fair share of determinism and subversive defiance. This unstable mix of characteristics has always taken their rulers by surprise. While unrepresentative rulers have made life insecure, fearful and unstable for their subjects, Iranians too have made life insecure, fearful and unstable for their rulers.

Students will witness how, in the absence of control over their lives, Iranians vacillate between the dysphoria of repression and economic hardship, the euphoria of political, cultural and social victories, and the humdrums of a routine but generally uncertain life. The national and individual mood of Iranians can fluctuate between gloom and self-deprecation to jubilation and self-glorification.

This textbook narrates the struggle between Iranians and their rulers, Iranians and foreign powers, and finally, the strife among Iranians concerning class, religion, ideology, personal power and control. The above multifrontal struggles, the political cleavages marking each historical period and the absence of open arenas for discussing conflicting sides have resulted in an accumulation of unresolved and entrenched positions. Undemocratic regimes are sensitive to independent historical accounts and transparency. They regard them as a security-related issue, which could become seditious. The absence of participatory and democratic channels to resolve conflicts, and the freedom to openly report on disagreements and their socio-political consequences, has made the reading and reporting of Iranian history binary and contentious.

Another marker of this one-hundred-year study is that periods of combined social peace, smooth transitions, socio-political harmony, sustained economic construction, completed transformations and public participation in national projects are almost non-existent.

Iran's failure to implement political development has convoluted outcomes. The setbacks and regressions carry within them seeds of progression, almost perversely dialectical. Acquired rights, be they political or social, have never been sure and certain in Iranian history. Yet, as anti-democratic regimes impose their own values on society and set their own arbitrary red lines, Iran's evolving civil society, in a constant battle, transgresses and transcends those red lines. In the process, it learns what it wants and does not want. The social, political and economic hardships and uncertainties imposed by non-participatory despotic systems has mentally, psychologically and intellectually educated and induced Iranians to move closer to the necessity of democratic governance.

Cautions about Reading this Textbook

Students should be cautious of the narrator's unintended double bias, one general and another specific to Iranian historiography. The first is rooted in the choices made in any historical narrative. What a textbook on history contains is informed by what the narrator has determined to be most telling and relevant. Irrespective of claims to academic impartiality, the selection of sources, events highlighted, explanations and arguments provided and conclusions drawn are at the cost of ignoring other sources, downplaying other events and choosing not to provide explanations other than the ones provided.

In his classic work, *What is History*, E. H. Carr reminds us that, 'The facts speak only when the historian calls on them: it is he who decides to which facts to give the floor, and in what order or context.' So, 'the historian is necessarily selective'.[1] This raises the tangential issue that any historical work claiming definitiveness is false.

The second bias concerns the historiography of a country like Iran. In a politically polarized, contentious, litigious and binary society, Iranian sources, primary and secondary, are partial, and 'objective' accounts of events and personalities are rare, as narrators are writing or speaking because of their political involvement and engagement. Even later, secondary 'objective' accounts are based on originally partisan accounts. There is seldom a significant historical event on which consensus exists over causal and explanatory factors, or their place and impact on the evolution of Iranian society and history. A key feature of Iranian historiography is its litigiousness, making 'neutral' accounts almost impossible.

This second bias, specific to Iranian historiography, exasperates the first, especially when confronted with controversial and conflictual issues. Weaving throughout a hundred-year history, all competing and often contradictory theories and explanations cannot be presented. There will be voices that will not be heard. The narrator admits to possible biases caused by his reading and understanding of archives, newspapers, parliamentary speeches, interviews, chronicles, books and reports on events, personalities and causal relations. This brings us to another tangential issue, more research, representing alternative views of Iranian history will help inquisitive minds develop a better understanding.

The Approach of this Textbook

Once the material is selected, an approach to telling the story must be adopted. How is the information and analysis projected on paper, chronologically or thematically? The chronological approach in history is concerned with the orderly and time sensitive sequential presentation of facts, events, development and personalities. It enables establishing foundation, logical causal relations and backward and forward connections to understand the unfolding of history. The thematic approach to history breaks with chronology and centres its investigation on grand themes and ideas across history and time. This textbook uses the chronological approach as its frame and backbone, yet it hopes to be more than a timeline. Within that structure, themes are woven into the text, where and when they are pertinent to the event in the chronology.

The textbook reads through historical chronology by zooming in and out of the historical process. The zoom-out process, or the bird's-eye-view method of chronicling history, looks at people, events and action from an elevated aerial view. It is a *tour d'horizon*, a general survey approach to history, providing contours and forms, reporting on the salient feature without necessarily getting into the why of occurrences, interactions and decisions.

The merit of the bird's-eye-view method is that it provides general information suited for a survey-style history course. It explains and informs when there is no previous knowledge. It can sometimes jump years and decades to provide the big picture. You keep to the essentials. It is like a Modern Iran for Beginners.

The bird's-eye-view method, however, does not allow for sharpness, distinction, contrasts, nuance and context. It seldom has time for analysis, comparison and socio-economic investigation, leaving big gaps in the chronological unfolding of events. It can easily gloss over historically significant chains of cause and consequences to present the overall picture, falling into disconnectedness and fragmentations.

The zoom-in or the stray-dog's-view method of reporting history, on the other hand, is a close-up view of events, resembling what the stray dog sees as it wonders through history. The close-range rendition of history is a disaggregated, item by item, person by person and brick-by-brick narrative. Parts and constituent elements are well developed and sharp. Images are clear and exact.

The stray-dog's-view method recounts the particulars of the historical puzzle but cannot see how it fits into the overall image. Unless you zoom out, broader connections, interrelations, associations, alliances, schisms, affiliations and cleavages carrying through history, are lost. The obvious way to provide width and depth in this account of Iran's modern history, is to use both methods, provide the broad scope to introduce and the detail of a zoom-in to entice.

The objective of providing a clear, exciting and engaging political economy history of Iran is best obtained when micro events and even digressions, providing soul and spirit, can be judiciously woven into the macro narrative. This is easier said than done, the students and teachers will be the judge of it. The different sets of questions at the end of each chapter are tools for students to measure their understanding of the subject matter and offers teachers options by which they can test the grasp of their students. Some of the chapters have words in bold and corresponding explanatory glossaries at the end.

To proceed with the history of Modern Iran, students need to heed four possible problems. First, the issue of loyalty to the macro narrative, which becomes further complicated when adopting a general policy of avoiding single-causation explanations. Recounting the history of a hundred years by simplifying the complexities of historical processes can lead to the trap of historical reductionism. When the call for conciseness infringes upon thorough and interlaced presentation of facts and explanations, students may have to bear with wordy presentations.

Second, to convey a sense of time, environment, mood and ambiance of the historical periods covered, relevant information has been injected. Trying to produce a time-machine effect, rather than a timeline effect, requires details to create context, backdrop and décor. These minutiae help provide a richer historical image. When such information enlivens the text, brevity is sacrificed for clarity and almost real-life accounts.

Third, a historical textbook on Iran needs to cover a few closely interrelated disciplines. It is an account of the political, both domestic and international, social, economic, cultural, intellectual, religious and military developments. Once again, the brief is vast, if one wishes to provide a balanced account of all of those fields. In this study, the political, economic, social, religious and military events and issues take precedence, even though not evenly treated, and the cultural and intellectual are conjured when they significantly impact historical unfolding and cause a historical inflection point.

Finally, a history textbook on Iran will inevitably be full of complicated names, sometimes double-barrelled first and second names. Such complicated names are foreign to non-Iranians and often difficult to remember. Transliteration from Persian/Farsi to English makes the job of distinction more difficult. For a non-Iranian, distinguishing and remembering the names of three key figures of post-revolution Iran, Khomeyni, Khamenei and Khatami, can become difficult. But just as students memorize irregular verbs to master their grammar and fans of literature keep track of complex Russian names to make sense of plots in classical novels, so too should students of Iranian history memorize complicated names. Also, whereas all dates in the text are converted to the Gregorian calendar, reference to Persian sources in the Notes and the Bibliography will cite the Islamic and sometimes the Imperial calendars. Those students familiar with Persian will find it more convenient when the dates of Persian sources are in the original.

Persia and Western Europe in the Nineteenth Century: Worlds Apart

To provide context and perspective to our historical journey, Persia, as Iran was called at the time, will be contrasted to Europe. The comparative survey is to set the backdrop. In the nineteenth century, Europe became a global power. It experienced groundbreaking transformations in industry, technology and medicine. Intellectually, it grappled with liberalism, conservatism, positivism, rationalism, nationalism, humanism, anarchism, socialism, communism and imperialism.

In 1869, John Stuart Mill argued that, 'The legal subordination of one sex to the other is wrong' and is a chief hindrance 'to human improvement'. In the late 1800s, Charles Darwin's theory of evolution permanently marked scientific thought, while by 1896, Sigmund Freud was already using the term 'psychoanalysis'. By 1848, Karl Marx had written his Communist Manifesto and Nietzsche had popularized the phrase, 'God is dead,' by 1885.

In general, Western and Northern Europe of the nineteenth century were well on the road to completing their democracy project. Franchise was extended to the working man, parliamentary democracy was operational, free elections were respected, free press, independent associations and labour unions were active. States were thinking of the collective through welfare legislation and free and compulsory education. In 1815, *The Times* of London had a circulation of 5,000, and by the 1850s, it reached 50,000. By 1870, the literacy rate in Britain for males was about 80 per cent and around 73 per cent for females.

Gustave Flaubert's *Madame Bovary* appeared in April 1857, shocked Parisian literary circles and sold out its first print of 6,750 copies in two months. Flaubert faced trial for offending public morality and religion when he refused to alter the sexual passages in his book. The book was considered as a threat to public safety, and he was arrested. The Sixth Chamber of the Correctional Court at the Palais de Justice concluded that the charges against him were insufficiently proven, and acquitted him. The French judiciary system under the Second Empire clearly exercised its independence, separated state and religion and did not sacrifice the freedom of expression at the altar of threat to morality and public peace.

European engineers were the architects of the economic advances which created great wealth with political consequences for the rest of the world. From 1853 to 1870, Baron Haussmann installed some 15,000 to 20,000 gaslights in Paris, allowing nightlife in the city. In 1881, the first central public electricity generator began work in Surrey, UK. By 1870, Britain was connected to India via telegraph. By 1899, Marconi was sending wireless signals across the English Channel.

The steam-engine century allowed for automated, mechanized and consequently affordable mass production. Textile, shoe, machine, armament, trains and ship factories were born. The number of weaving looms in Britain jumped from 2,400 in 1803 to 250,000 in 1857. The rapid development of railways and canals helped in obtaining raw materials and distributing final goods. The nineteenth century witnessed the construction of some 250,000 kilometres of railroads in Europe. In 1880, some 6,000 locomotives operated in France, transporting some 51,600 passengers while unified Germany possessed 9,400 locomotives and hauled some 43,000 passengers per year.

In the 1880s, Britain, followed by France and Germany, led Europe in the production of breech-loading repeating rifles, rendering muzzle-loaded muskets obsolete. Long-range and rapid-firing artillery, both on land and at sea, gave the Europeans a marked advantage in their military campaigns. Machine guns made their appearance in 1881, and the classic British 10-round magazine Lee–Enfield rifle was introduced in November 1895, increasing the range of hitting a target from around 100 metres to some 500 metres. In 1884, a private company in England, commissioned by the government to produce arms, was capable of building and arming a battleship.

Between 1810 and 1820, vaccination decreased death rates from smallpox in England, and by 1853 the government had made it mandatory. The advances in health and medicine increased life expectancy and labour performance. The French invented the stethoscope in 1817, and the discovery of X-rays came in 1895. In 1861, England and Wales had some 14,400 physicians and surgeons and some 1,500 dentists. Improved public hygiene and better nutrition reduced death rates. In 1879, Louis Pasteur was developing his vaccines against anthrax, rabies and cholera. In 1892, the first effective anti-cholera vaccine was developed at Pasteur Institute in Paris.

From around 1820, Britain, France and Sweden experienced annual gross domestic product (GDP) growth rates of some 0.9–1.3 per cent. Optimists have suggested England witnessed an almost doubling of real wage rates for blue-collar workers between 1819 and 1851. Economic growth in Europe outstripped population growth, allowing for improvements in the standard of living, which in turn generated leisure time. In 1878, the concept of a weekend from Saturday afternoon to Monday morning took hold in Northern England. This gave the blue-collar workers the opportunity to have 'a leisurely midday meal at home, which was often followed by a weekly bath in the neighborhood bathhouse, an important institution at a time when few homes had running water', 'reading the paper', attending 'park concerts, soccer games, rowing, and bicycling and, of course, drinking in the local pub'.[2]

In international relations, realpolitik or the politics of pursuing one's own national interests without any regards for ethical considerations and colonial expansion, went hand in hand. By the end of nineteenth century, the British Empire occupied the same place that the Persian Empire (500–400 BCE) had once occupied. Technological and economic advances of Western European countries in the nineteenth century allowed them to control much of Asia, and all of Africa except for Ethiopia and Liberia. Exercising influence through trade and commerce, transitioned to military outposts to protect trade and then outright colonialization. The age of imperialism had begun.

Persia in the Cave of Ephesus

Around 475 BCE, when the Persian Empire of the Achaemenids was at the height of its power, it included West Asia, parts of South-East Europe, the Caucasus, North Africa and north-western regions of the Indian sub-continent. Darius and Xerxes ruled over some 44 per cent of the world's population. This first superpower was a model of centralized management through a quasi-federative system of *satrapies*, tolerant of its multi-cultural subjects, with some 2,500 kilometres of highways connecting its vast territory, a flourishing intercontinental trade, a clearly established taxing system and standard currency, weights and measures. The ears and eyes of the emperor inspected and reported on all affairs of the subjects in far-flung corners of the empire.

Providing a fairly accurate statistical picture of Persia in the nineteenth century is impossible. The inexistence of basic data, such as population census and civil registration records of births and deaths, let alone literacy rates, makes precision a far-fetched fantasy. Whereas the first full official census in England and Wales dated back to March 1801, the first population and housing census conducted in Iran was in 1956. Civil registration of births, deaths and marriages began on 1 July 1837 in England and Wales, and on 25 December 1918 in Iran.

This yawning gap in vital statistics between Persia and Europe in the nineteenth century was symptomatic of the disparities between the two, and indicated the political interest of rulers in the welfare of their subjects/citizens, centralized authority of government, legal provisions, organizational capabilities, trained staff and finally funding. Disregarding the general sense of irresponsibility and aloofness of Qajar monarchs towards their subjects, the absence of a codified legal system, mass illiteracy, dispersal of rural and nomadic populations, absence of transportation and the lack of funding and staff, made data generation impossible. In the nineteenth century, the coffers of the state were empty and the ears and eyes of the shah had ceased to function as they once did at the time of the Achaemenids.

So, any statistical picture of nineteenth-century Iran is primarily a guesstimate or a conjecture. Reports on Iran's population around 1850 vary between 4 and 10 million. The more likely estimate is put between 9 and 10 million. There were periodically large declines in population due to starvation and cholera. Nevertheless, it has been suggested that 'the average annual net growth rate of the population seems to have been a little over 0.5 per cent'.[3] The northern, north-eastern and north-western regions of the country housed about half of Iran's population.

Literacy rate at the beginning of twentieth century is sometimes put at 5 per cent of a population of less than 12 million. Other estimates suggest a population of some 10 million in 1900.[4] Based on a 5 per cent literacy rate of an estimated 10 million population, would imply that Iran had some 500,000 literates by 1900. The figure of half a million literates represents the equivalent of the total population of Tehran (200,000), Tabriz (200,00) and Esfahan (100,000) in 1900.[5] This number seems inflated, and the literacy rate of less than 2 per cent or about 200,000 at around 1905 seems more realistic.[6] We are, indeed, fishing in very muddy waters.

It was not until February 1898, that after trying and failing for ten years in Azarbayjan, Roshdiyeh (Mirza Hasan Tabrizi) opened the first modern primary boys' school in Tehran. The next one was opened in Rasht in 1899 and in Bushehr in 1900. It was not until 1903 that Parvaresh, the first girls' school opened in Tehran, although it was shut down forcefully after four days. Its founder reopened the school under the name of Namus in 1907. By this time, the Dushizegan School for girls had started operation with three grades in the private house of its owner. The hidebound religious opposition to women's education made the task of opening girls' schools most difficult.

The first printing press opened in Tabriz in 1818/19 and in 1825 in Tehran. The first lithographic press in Tehran began operation around 1833. During this period, the Quran was reprinted four times, Saadi's famous poetry books, *Bustan* and *Golestan*, were re-preprinted five times in total, while Mohammad-Baqer Majlesi's religious works were reprinted fourteen times. Newspapers had not existed in Iran until the appearance of the monthly, *News* (*khabar*), on 1 May 1837. This two-page lithographic printed paper included news of Iran, Italy, Turkey and Britain, and appeared irregularly for some three years. The weekly *Current Events* (*vaqaye etefaqiyeh*), which appeared on 7 February 1851, was a government publication of some 600–700 copies. It reported on court news, government promotions, the shah's overseas trips and news of foreign countries.

Between the 1850s and 1880s, 'the settled population numbered apparently some 6.5 million people, of which at least 5.5 million lived in rural settlements, and the remainder, numbering about 800,000, lived in towns of 10,000 inhabitants and over'.[7] Some 60 per cent of the population were peasants, around 8 per cent were townsmen and the rest were nomads.[8] 'At least 80 to 85 per cent of the total economically active population was engaged in agricultural production. The remaining 15 to 20 per cent was employed in the handicraft and services sectors of the economy.'[9] Agricultural land belonged overwhelmingly to the shah, religious endowments or land given by the shah to nobles, governors, tribal leaders and whomever he pleased, which had subsequently become their property.

Preponderantly, peasants worked the land as sharecroppers, and their standard living condition in mid-1850s, even in the fertile northern regions, was one of destitution, poverty and indebtedness. The economic condition of peasants or most Iranians stagnated throughout the nineteenth century. There is no evidence of any technical or organizational changes, even marginal, in agricultural production or any increase in productivity. 'There is also overwhelming evidence pointing to a considerable deterioration of the irrigation systems, which in turn implies a greater rain-fed and less intensive agriculture.'[10]

Iran was experiencing neither industrialization nor urbanization. Manufacturing was artisanal and handcraft-based. Workshops were concentrated in Esfahan, Kashan, Yazd, Shiraz and Mashhad, producing silk and cotton goods, shawls, carpets and cutlery. In the 1850s, cheap British cotton imports were chasing out home-made products. By 1857, Iran was an importer of manufactured good, most significantly cotton, wool and silk manufactures and was an exporter of raw materials, raw silk, wheat, barely, sheep, dried fruits and tobacco. In the absence of government concern or protection for home production, the number of silk looms dropped to a tenth of their levels at the beginning of the 1800s.

In the early 1860s, the government tried to establish modern factories producing paper, candle, glass, gunpowder, linen and sugar. By 1864, these factories proved unprofitable and were abandoned. At the same time, Persia's raw-silk production plummeted from 20,000 in 1860 to almost 6,000 bales a year in 1869 due to the silkworm disease in Gilan. Thanks to foreign capitalists keeping 'tight control over the collection and distribution of graine (silkworm eggs)', the silk industry revived after 1889.[11]

From the 1870s, two economic activities significantly impacted the Iranian economy. Carpet-weaving gained a new impetuous due to European firms providing mainly urban cottage industries with the raw materials and purchasing their final products for exports. By the end of the nineteenth century, carpets became a major Iranian export item, employing many of those who had been made redundant by the cheap import of manufactured goods.

The other key activity which boomed around 1875 was opium production. In 1871, some 870 cases were exported and by 1886, the number of cases exported reached 8,000. In the absence of a banking system, moneylenders in the bazaars and well-established merchants served the function of credit institutions, lending money to the government.

Iran's Economic Situation at the Start of Twentieth Century

Barring the telegraph, there was no significant technical progress in the economic sense of the term in either industry or agriculture. One could even observe economic regress in the sense of traditional know-how . . . Likewise, there was no significant increase in the accumulation of financial capital and rise in the stock of physical capital. (H. Katouzian)[12]

By the late 1880s, Persia's transportation system and facilities, including roads, bridges, aqueducts and caravansaries were not properly maintained and no new infrastructural projects were undertaken. The absence of a viable transportation network had grave consequences. In 1887, a rail network of 8,700 metres was established between Tehran and Ray (*Shahabdolazim*). A year later, a private initiative by the prominent Iranian merchant Haj Amin al-zarb began to connect Mahmudabad to Amol in the north (17 km). Having laid some 24 kilometres of the rail and built a caravanserai and warehouses at the terminus, the line was inaugurated in March–

April 1890, 'but was defunct after four years'.[13] Almost all traffic, passengers and goods was conducted using mules, horses and camels. The government's indifference and negligence towards improving the livelihood of the people, added to the Russian and British rivalry, stunted growth and economic development.

Plagues and Famines

Primarily due to inadequate sanitation and hygiene, cholera epidemics were recurrent in Persia. The autumn plague of 1830 is reported to have killed some 30,000 people. The 1835 cholera epidemic in Tabriz killed some 1,000 in two days out of a population of some 100,000.[14] In July 1846, there was a new outbreak. The estimated mortality was 12,000 in Tehran, 7,000 in Tabriz, some 7,000 in Yazd and 2,000 in Urumiyeh, a city of 25,000.[15] Between 1846 and 1857, cholera broke out five times in Tabriz.

It was not until 1850 that a faculty of medicine with European professors was established at Iran's first polytechnical school, Dar al-fonun, teaching engineering, mathematics, medicine, pharmacology, mining, literature and military sciences. In 1853, cholera ravaged central Iran. In 1858, forty-two graduates of Dar al-fonun were sent to Paris for further studies, five of whom were medical students. Probably the first of its kind, the National Hospital was opened in Tehran in 1873. In 1882, the first American Mission Hospital opened in Urumiyeh, with 40 beds and an operating room.

'The year 1861 was the first of the great famine years which succeeded one another at irregular intervals.' Plentiful wheat in Azarbayjan and Kermanshah could not be transported to Tehran, facing famine, due to inadequate transportation networks. Bread riots broke out in March and May and by summer, once the roads became accessible, food shortages were relieved. The 1861 famine in Tehran was followed by a severe cholera outbreak.

In the summer of 1862, cholera broke out in Mashhad, with deaths numbering 'between 100 and 120 a day'.[16] In the absence of any quarantine protocols, the disease was brought to Tehran in August 1862 by people fleeing from Mashhad. It later reappeared in Esfahan in 1869, killing 2,000 people before it spread to Bushehr. 'The most destructive cholera epidemics, in terms of mortality, were those of 1892–3.'[17] Between 1,000 and 1,600 were killed in Tehran before it spread to Mashhad, Shahrud, Rasht, Shiraz, Khuzestan, Kermanshah and Hamedan.

Famine returned almost ten years later. The 1870–1 great famine has been dubbed as 'the most tragic event in the modern economic and social history of Persia'.[18] Paucity of rainfall, two consecutive years of drought, decline in the output of wheat, market manipulation and hoarding of grain by landowners, governors and clerical landowners caused an unprecedented famine. Bread riots broke out in Bushehr, Qom and many other cities in 1870. In 1871, the situation worsened, 'Those who could not afford bread, ate dogs, cats, rats, and other animals, even dung and grass.'[19] Cannibalism was reported in the famine-hit provinces and 'at Qum a man was executed for cannibalism'.[20]

In May 1871, the death toll due to starvation in Esfahan and Mashhad was reported at 500 a day. In Tehran, the winter of 1871 was very hard on the poor and the undernourished. 'Three hundred deaths a night are said to have occurred from cold and starvation.'[21] As dead bodies lay scattered in the roads, the sanitary conditions worsened, inviting cholera and typhoid outbreaks. The outcome was a population loss of some 20–25 per cent of the estimated 6–7 million.

Persia at the Dawn of Twentieth Century

The 1870–1 famine had important social consequences. It forced some of the nomads who had lost their livestock to settle and cause large-scale population dislocations from drought-stricken area to the more prosperous north. By November 1871, some 20,000 to 30,000 flooded Gilan Province of some 10,000 inhabitants.[22] From Gilan many crossed into Russia. By 1897, Iranian migration to Russia numbered 74,000 with 72 per cent of them residing in the Caucasus. Most of them led wretched lives as menial day labourers, human beasts of burden, longshoremen and mine workers.[23]

In the severely afflicted areas, the drought and famine further impoverished the vulnerable social classes and reduced the purchasing power of large segments of society. 'The decline in business threw more and more people out of work, and considerable numbers of people from the upper classes fell into poverty, warding off starvation only by selling their household belongings.'[24]

Persia at the dawn of the twentieth century was unable to harness natural adversities and calamities. The agricultural and nomadic economy stagnated, and the impoverished population was regularly threatened by famine and plagues. The great majority of the people were illiterate and unfamiliar with technological advances. They lived in isolation from one another, following their provincial traditions and practices. Their worldview and values were mainly shaped by their religions. Persian rulers were unconcerned with the well-being of their people and uninterested in developing modern institutions, along with legal and administrative structures.

The shahs ruled according to their whim and were not bound by any social covenant or constitution. They indulged in their own opulent and extravagant lives, and left their people to their own devices, except when they needed to fill the state coffers or they got into wars. The conscript army, an important institution and medium of socialization and provision of a common identity, did not exist in the 1800s. Persia did not have a regular standing army by modern standards, and at times of war, it relied mainly on irregulars and mostly on nomadic cavalrymen of at most 100,000. These men were irregularly paid, if at all, inclined to loot, very poorly armed and without distinct uniforms. Nineteenth-century Persia was politically, economically, technologically, educationally, scientifically and militarily well behind Western and Northern Europe.

1

The Quest for a Constitutional Monarchy under the Qajars, 1905–11

Chapter Outline

Qajar Shahs, Wars and Mismanagements	15
The Approaching Revolution	27
The Constitutionalists Organize	28
Royal Decree Granting a Consultative Parliament	31
Mohammad-Ali Shah's Rule	33
The 1st Majles, 7 October 1906–23 June 1908	38
Two Responses to Despotism	45
Seventeen Months of Interminable Crises, July 1910–December 1911	55
The Shuster Affair and the End of Iran's Independence	59
Glossary	63

Qajar Shahs, Wars and Mismanagements

The founder of the Qajar dynasty, Aqa Mohammad Khan, was of Turkic origin and had been castrated at a young age at the hands of his father's political opponents. In 1788/9, he chose Tehran as his new capital. Some five years later, in 1794, he subdued Lotfali Khan Zand of the reigning dynasty. Two years later, he invaded the Caucasus and laid waste to Tiflis. Aqa Mohammad Shah was known for his cruelty. During his campaigns, he would give the vanquished women and children as slaves to his soldiers, and either kill or blind the adult males.

Having reunified the land, he coronated himself in March 1796 and was assassinated the following year, on 17 June 1797. Aqa Mohammad Shah was succeeded first by his nephew, Fathali Shah (1797–1834), and later by Mohammad Shah (1834–48), Nasereddin Shah (1848–96), Mozaffareddin Shah (1896–1907), Mohammad-Ali Shah (1907–9) and Ahmad Shah (1909–25).

During Fathali Shah's rule, Iran's aspirations as a powerful regional power were dashed by consecutive defeats at the hands of Imperial Russia. Two Russo-Persian wars led to the treaties of Golestan (1813) and the British-negotiated Turkmanchay (1828). These two humiliating treaties had long-term adverse effects on the country. Iran was forced to secede its long-held Caucasian territories, pay war indemnities, desist from navigating in the Caspian Sea, accept commercial treaties as demanded by Russia and comply by extraterritorial rights (capitulation rights) for Russian subjects in Iran.

The outcome of the Russo-Persian wars demonstrated the weakness of the poorly armed and trained Iranian troops, its absence of war-readiness and utter disorganization. Some 35,000 troops alone were lost during the second Russo-Persian War (1826–8). These wars marked a long and drawn-out period of Russian political domination and intervention in Iran.

After the death of Fathali Shah in 1834, Mohammad Shah tried to regain Iran's lost authority after the Russo-Persian wars, and turned his attention to Herat (Afghanistan) which had become a base of subversion against his rule. Afghanistan was on the border of the British Empire in India and the British were committed to keeping a weakened Iran from becoming militarily involved in the region.

In 1837, Mohammad Shah laid an eight-month siege to Herat. John MacNeil, a prominent British diplomat, conveyed to the shah that Britain was considering military action should Iran take Herat. To further dissuade the shah, the British occupied Khark Island in June 1838 and McNeil renewed the threat of war in August 1838. Finally, under threat of invasion in the south, Iran's siege ended in August 1838 and the troops were withdrawn.

Both Russo-Persian wars and the failure of the siege of Herat demonstrated that as of the 1840s, Iran was too weak to stand up to the Russo-British pincer encroachments (Figure 1.1). Iran was being squeezed between the British protecting their colony in India, and the Russians with expansionist and anti-British objectives. Behind Iran's veneer of independence stood a debilitated and frail kingdom at the mercy of Russo-British manipulations and machinations. Under the unshakeable dominion of foreign powers, Qajar monarchs were obsessed with maintaining their reign. Incapable of ascertaining centralized authority, monarchs left regional administration to their generally self-serving relatives and appointees. They, in turn, terrorized the people in pursuit of their private gain.

The people were consequently subjected to the threefold wrongs of the foreigners, monarchs and their appointees. Growing hardships and injustice resulted in social

"SAVE ME FROM MY FRIENDS!"

Figure 1.1 The Great Game. *Source: Wikimedia Commons.*

discontent and dissent. At times of interminable calamity, the oppressed turn to alternative political and religious solutions, heralded by new messengers of hope and seek change through force and individuals gain importance and come to shape history.

The Babi Movement

The Babi messianic religious movement led by Seyyed Ali-Mohammad Shirazi, known as the Bab, threatened Mohammad Shah's rule and the domination of the **Shii** religious establishment. Mohammad-Ali Shirazi was self-taught in Islamic jurisprudence, Shii reports and interpretations, but lacked formal training to become an *alem* or religious scholar. At 20, he spent a year in Karbala studying with **Sheykh Kazem Rashti**. A few months after his return to Shiraz, he claimed to have had the first of a series of dreams and visitations by spirits.

In 1844, Mohammad-Ali Shirazi claimed that he had received verbal inspirations from the Twelfth or the Hidden Shii Imam. Shirazi, pronounced himself the medium of communication with the twelfth Imam, who had been in occultation since 941. He subsequently went to claim that he was the Bab (the Gate) to the Twelfth Imam. In 1848, at age 29, Bab announced that he was Imam Mahdi himself, who had returned.

He abrogated Islamic rules and laws, the ***sharia***, changed the direction of prayers from Mecca to Shiraz, where he had lived and established a new calendar starting at Nowruz 1848, with nineteen months and nineteen days in each month. He replaced the Quran with his Persian book, *Bayan* (expression/declaration).

Bab's claim in 1848 that he was the Mahdi, fulfilled the millenarian Shii claim that the Hidden Imam would return some thousand years after the first occultation (874 CE). According to Shii teachings, the Mahdi would reappear to lead a socio-political and religious revolution to end impiety and unjust rule. Bab's message that he was the Hidden Imam did fall on the receptive ears of Iranians who were fed up with their economic, social and political condition. By claiming that he incarnated the Hidden Imam, Bab was de facto declaring war on both the Qajar political rule and the Shii religious establishment. His appeal and the spread of his followers threatened the Qajar dynasty's temporal power and rendered the powerful Shii establishment redundant.

Nasereddin Shah and Amir Kabir

Upon the death of Mohammad Shah at age 40, his 17-year-old son Nasereddin ascended to the throne in September 1848. His rise to power was concurrent with clashes between Bab's followers and regional and state troops in Mazandaran (July 1848), Neyriz (May–June 1850) and Zanjan (May 1850–January 1851). Reports have it that a third of the population at Neyriz (between Shiraz and Sirjan) and a quarter of Zanjan's inhabitants had become Babis. Anxious about the growing challenge of the Babi movement to the status quo, the clergy accused Bab of being a heretic. He was imprisoned, and shortly after faced a firing squad on 8 July 1850. Even though Bab had died, Babis actively participated in the Constitutional Revolution. The Babi movement later morphed into the Bahai movement.

During Nasereddin Shah's 48-year reign (1848–96), little was done to improve the socio-economic and political plight of Iranians. The country was, however, jolted by a three-year interlude of progress, when Mirza Taqi Khan Farahani (Amir Kabir) was appointed chief minister in October 1848 and given responsibility for the army. Amir Kabir had travelled to Russia, the Caucasus and Erzurum and had been exposed to the **Tanzimat reforms** in the Ottoman Empire. He had acquired a comprehensive vision for the country's development. To pursue his reform agenda, Amir Kabir repressed with a heavy hand all threats to the central government. He ordered the execution of Bab and quelled provincial revolts, which had flared up during the end of Mohammad Shah's reign.

Simultaneously, Amir Kabir focused on increasing revenues and cutting costs. The long and costly wars of Nasereddin Shah's predecessors, their financial indiscipline and the growing balance of trade deficit had depleted the coffers of the state. Amir Kabir's financial reforms focused on increasing revenues and cutting costs. He began by collecting unpaid taxes in the provinces, increasing tariffs, reducing salaries of government employees and launching an anti-corruption campaign against dishonest civil servants and clerics.

To boost revenues, he rescinded the Russian monopoly of fishing in the Caspian Sea and channelled its lucrative revenue back into the government's Treasury. Amir Kabir promoted modern agriculture in cash crops such as cotton and sugar cane as well as mining. On the international stage, he curtailed foreign influences by denying privileges and concessions to the Russians and the British.

Amir Kabir understood the importance of creating infrastructure in a backward country. With the meagre resources at his disposal, he launched into urban development, building dams and constructing water canals. He commissioned Iran's first modern high school/university somewhat similar to an école polytechnique called *Dar al-fonun* (Abode of Skills). All along, Amir Kabir sought to limit the power of the clergy and the religious courts by empowering customary law courts.

Amir Kabir's modernizing influence was, however, short-lived. He was abruptly dismissed on 16 November 1851, exiled to Kashan and extrajudicially murdered on 10 January 1852. The rise and fall of Amir Kabir typified the exercise of power by a despotic ruler. Iran of the nineteenth century lacked a judiciary, let alone an independent judiciary.

The court intrigues and jealousies of the queen mother and Aqa Khan Nuri, who later replaced Amir Kabir, were said to be instrumental in Amir Kabir's fall. However, it was mostly the fears, near-sightedness and the lack of acumen of the 21-year-old Nasereddin Shah which prevented the country from pursuing a more promising developmental path.

Other than during the brief period when Amir Kabir attempted to change the course of Iran's development, Nasereddin Shah spent the remaining 44 years of his reign neglecting the welfare and development of the country and embarking on recklessly auctioning the country's resources to foreign interests to raise money for court expenses and his travels overseas. The irresponsibility and frivolousness of Nasereddin Shah exposed the country to greater foreign presence, humiliation and increasing domestic squalor, resentment and hostility.

Nasereddin Shah's defeat in the Anglo-Persian War of 1856–7, enabled the British to establish a military foothold in Bushehr (27 January 1857) and later occupy Mohammareh (Khorramshahr). Iranian forces folded before the well-trained and well-armed British and Indian soldiers. According to the 4 March 1857 Peace Treaty of Paris, Iran was to abandon all claims to Herat and withdraw from every part of Afghanistan and in return British troops would withdraw from all 'ports, places and islands belonging to Persia'. Britain also obtained a **most-favoured-nation status**. By 1857, Iran's military reverses exposed the country to British and Russian financial and political dictates, granting of one-sided and exploitive concessions and increase in imports. Iran was neither a colony nor an independent state.

Nasereddin Shah: 'From Concession to Concession'

On 14 April 1890, Dr Jean-Baptiste Feuvrier, Nasereddin Shah's French physician, lamented Iran's string of concessions to foreigners and predicted that, 'Persia will soon be entirely in the hands of foreigners.'[1] In July 1872, Nasereddin Shah granted a concession to the British banker, Baron Julius de Reuter, for the effective control over the economy, from building roads, dams, railways and factories to exploiting raw materials (except gold and silver) and controlling national customs. The architects of this project were the prime minister, Mirza Hoseyn Qazvini Sepahsalar (Moshir al-dowleh), and Mirza Malkam Khan, the Armenian Christian intellectual, journalist and diplomat, who had converted to Islam. Both were modernists and reformists intent on propelling Iran out of its backwardness. The two must have believed that only an Englishman could achieve such goals.

> **The Concession that Could Have Crushed Iran**
>
> Lord George Curzon, British viceroy of India (1899–1905) wrote, that when the details of the concession were published, it was found to contain the most complete and extraordinary surrender of the entire industrial resources of a kingdom into foreign hands that has probably ever been dreamed of, much less accomplished, in history. (G. Curzon)[2]

Irrespective of the concession's long-term implications for the independence of the country, there were also moral and ethical problems with it. First, the prime minister, Moshir al-dowleh and Malkam Khan (Figure 1.2), chief of the Persian Legation in London, were alleged to have received substantial bribes brokering the

Figure 1.2 Mirza Malkam Khan. *Source: Wikimedia Commons.*

agreement. Second, following the signature of the concession, the shah received a £200,000 credit at 5 per cent interest from Reuter. Of this loan, £50,000 was used to finance the first of the shah's three European tours in 1873.

This was only the first of a string of loans for the shah's extravagant personal leisure, which later exposed the country to the financial and political dual-control of Britain and Russia. The Qajar monarchs viewed the coffers of state as their private purse and felt no accountability to the people, whom they regarded as their servants. Their irresponsible governance drove the country into the arms of an old colonial strategy, granting loans for political advantage. The indebted country accumulated loans incurred by shahs, khedives and sultans, and, incapable of paying interests, let alone the principal, it borrowed more until one day, it would succumb to the dominion of the colonizer.

Upon his return from Europe in 1873, and under domestic and mainly Russian pressure, Nasereddin Shah rescinded the Reuter concession after only one year and dismissed his prime minister, Moshir al-dowleh. However, through the intercession of the British minister in Tehran, in 1889, Reuter was compensated by receiving an exclusive 60-year concession to establish the Imperial Bank of Persia, a privately owned British bank incorporated and publicly floated in London, with its board of directors in London.[3] The bank was mandated to operate throughout Iran, with the exclusive authority to issue bank notes, the usual remit of national central banks. The concession also stipulated that the bank should provide the government with loans, which it fulfilled in 1892. The Imperial Bank of Persia would become a powerful lever for British economic and political control of Iran.

Between the first and second Reuter concessions (1872–9), Nasereddin Shah went on to make three unfortunate political and financial decisions, ratcheting up Russo-British involvement in Iran. After his second trip to Europe (1878), and greatly impressed by the Russian Cossack troops, Nasereddin Shah invited the Russians to create and train a similar regiment in Iran. Russian officers began their task in April 1879. By 1900, the Russians commandeered a Cossack brigade of some 1,500 men. The presence of an Iranian-Russian Cossack brigade irked the British, who in turn increased their economic pressure on the shah.

The shah's third trip to Europe (1889), had been an eventful one. On 20 July 1889, while still in England, the shah granted a 75-year lottery concession in Iran to an unnamed person. The mastermind and real holder of the concession was Malkam Khan, who eventually sold it to a British syndicate for £40,000. However, faced with the clergy's objection that lottery constituted a form of gambling, the shah was forced to rescind it. The shah fell out with Malkam Khan over his financial improprieties in the lottery concession. Malkam Khan, who had devoutly served Nasereddin Shah from 1871 and benefitted from the Qajar court, went on to launch from London, on 20 February 1890, his famous anti-Qajar and pro-constitutionalist paper *Qanun* (The Law).

In March 1890, the shah granted a second unsuccessful concession: a 50-year monopoly for the production, sale and export of Iranian tobacco to Maj. Jerald Talbot, an Englishman, whom he had met during his third trip to Europe in 1889. It is alleged that the shah and his new prime minister, Mohammad-Hasan Khan Etemad al-saltaneh, had received handsome bribes from Talbot to facilitate the signing of the concession and the creation of the Imperial Tobacco Corporation of Persia with a capital of £650,000. Tobacco was a major and flourishing export item, and some 200,000 people were involved in its production and sale. The concession jeopardized the livelihood of local tobacco producers, merchants and consumers, while the arrival of foreign employees generated cultural tensions. As Dr Feuvrier observed, 'The Persians could not, without resistance, submit to being obliged to buy from the English the tobacco which they themselves grow and gather in.'[4]

The concession raised widespread nationalist and anti-colonial feelings even inside the court. Riots erupted in Shiraz, Tabriz, Esfahan, Tehran, Mashhad, Yazd and Kashan. The anti-tobacco concession movement reached its climax once Mirza Hasan Shirazi, the Shii religious dignitary in Samara, was prompted by **Seyyed Jamaleddin Asadabadi (Afghani)** to issue a **fatwa** in November/December 1891 against the consumption of tobacco. The movement against the tobacco concession manifested the growing frustration with the shah's arbitrary whims, and on 6 January 1892, under domestic pressure and faced with stern warnings from Russia, Nasereddin Shah revoked the concession. To pay a hefty £500,000 compensation, the Iranian government had to borrow the sum at 7 per cent interest rate from the British-owned Imperial Bank of Persia.

On 1 May 1896, Nasereddin Shah was assassinated by Mirza Reza Kermani, a follower of Seyyed Jamaleddin Asadabadi. Kermani had acted alone and out of personal desperation, vengeance and anger mingled with a sense of anti-despotism. He told his interrogators that his motive for the assassination was that previously, he had been unjustly chained and beaten at length by Tehran's chief of police, Mohammad-Ali Sardar-Afkham (Vakil al-dowleh). Before he was hanged on 12 August 1896, Kermani accused the shah of fifty years of incompetence and injustice.

Intellectual Murmurs of Anti-Despotism and Constitutionalism

Halfway into Nasereddin Shah's rule, Iranian intellectuals had begun writing about Iran's abysmal political, economic and social conditions. Some of the main forefathers of this new trend of critical and modernist thinking were Mirza Fathali Akhundzadeh (1812–78), Mirza Yusef Khan Mostashar al-dowleh (1823–95), Mohammad-Khan Majd-al-molk (1809–81), Abdolrahim Talebof (1834–1911), Mirza Malkam Khan (1833–1908) and Haji Zeinolabeddin Maraghehi (1839–1910).

> ### Chronicles of the Times
>
> O Iran, your land is devastated, your inhabitants are ignorant and uninformed about the civilized world, they are deprived of freedom and your king is a despot . . . under the influence of despotism and the fanaticism of your clergy, your capabilities have become rusty . . . your people under the yolk of injustice of poverty have left the country . . . and are suffering as servants and day-workers in Ottoman, Russian and Afghani lands. (Fathali Akundzadeh, 1863)
>
> What is the reason for the staggering prosperity of foreign lands? Why is our country incapable of reaching it? If we are human beings why do we opt for ruin and destruction, like the owl? Wherever you look in our land there is devastation, cemeteries, filth, mud, infection, and darkness. (Abdolrahim Talebof, 1890)
>
> The underlying cause of Iran's present chaos and turmoil and the discontinuity of rule in one dynasty, which turns every day like a ring on many fingers, is nothing but ignorance and lawlessness. The main cause of those ruinations is injustice . . . One should weep for the desperate state of this country. (Zeinolabeddin Maraghehi, 1903)

These men had either travelled or lived abroad for most or part of their lives. They were concerned with the tragic state of political, social and economic backwardness of their country. As social reformers and harbingers of new perspectives, they searched for the roots of their country's misfortune and desolation. Comparing Iran to Western countries, some depicted Iran as 'uncivilized', 'barbaric' and 'savage', a country in a deep slumber of ignorance.[5]

Akhundzadeh was an atheist and a materialist who considered political despotism and religious fanaticism as the twin causes of Iran's backwardness. He employed the Persianized transcription of despotism (*dispotizm*) to describe Naseredd.n Shah's political system and the monarch's conduct. His transcriber or copyist explained the term *dispot* (despot) as a shah with 'unlimited and monopolistic control over the life and property of his people and one who always acts according to his personal whim and will'. Akhundzadeh described the people under the despot's rule, as 'base and wretched slaves', 'completely devoid of freedoms and human rights'.[6] Adopting a constitution, Akhundzadeh believed, would end despotism and usher in an Islamic Protestantism which would transform the faith according to the needs and necessities of modern times.[7]

On 2 April 1871, Akhundzadeh wrote to a friend that 'to eradicate injustice and oppression/cruelty, it is necessary for the oppressor to cease oppressing or for the oppressed to cease tolerating oppression and annihilate the oppressor'. He concluded that the oppressed needed to 'wake up from their slumber and dethrone the oppressor'.[8] Four years later, Akhundzadeh wrote that the only way to uproot despotism is to tell the oppressor to 'get lost'.[9]

Akhundzadeh was the most revolutionary among this new wave of intellectuals (Figure 1.3). His fellow critics for the most part believed in trying to convince Nasereddin Shah to introduce reforms from above. One such intellectual was Mostashar al-dowleh, the shah's chargé d'affaires in Paris, who in 1870 had written a treatise called *Resalehe yek kalameh* (Treatise of One Word). Deeply influenced by the French Constitution, Mostashar al-dowleh believed that to overcome backwardness and embark on 'progress' and 'civilization', countries needed to organize life around a codified constitution. The rule of law, approved by the people, was the magical solution as it defined and established the rights and responsibilities of rulers in secular domains.

Mostashar al-dowleh ascertained that, 'None of God's creatures, be they kings or others, have the right to command/judge, in other words they are not rulers/masters, but duty bound and accountable.' For Mostashar al-dowleh, it was time for the

Figure 1.3 Mirza Fathali Akhundzadeh. *Source: Wikimedia Commons.*

country to have citizens and not subjects. He wrote, 'the Shah and the pauper' had to be bound by the letter of the law and neither could act according to arbitrary will.[10]

Another prominent thinker was Abdolrahim Talebof, whose work called *Ketabe Ahmad* (Ahmad's Book) and published in 1906 became a highly influential text in constitutionalist circles.[11] For Talebof, a country without laws clearly regulating social and political activities was an uncivilized state where welfare and felicity were absent, and terror reigned.[12] In an absolutist monarchy, Talebof argued, the shah relegated the management of the realm to ministers who were solely responsible to him, yet ultimately the life and property of all subjects were at his mercy. In such a state, laws did not exist, and if they did, their making and execution were combined in one body and rested entirely in the hands of the shah.

Talebof considered the absence of separation in government branches tantamount to despotism. Echoing Akhundzadeh and Mostashar al-dowleh, Talebof wrote that in an absolutist system, 'sometimes murderers were rewarded and sometimes the innocent was executed'. The Qajar Shahs, he wrote, occupied themselves with expansionist wars, horseback-riding, hunting and other pleasures of life.[13]

Talebof characterized Iran, Arabia, Afghanistan and China as primitive absolutist and lawless monarchies.[14] Without written laws or edicts, the realm was governed by individual whims. A popularly elected legislative body, on the other hand, defended the people's interests and limited the shah's purview. In the absence of such a representative body, the people were deprived of making laws, controlling their lives, participating in the governance process and the administration of their country.[15] Talebof warned that if a sultan refuses to invite the people to participate and assist in administrating the country, 'they will come without an invitation and then they will sing another tune'.[16]

In around 1903, Haji Zeinalabedin Maraghehi published *Ebrahim Beyg's Travel Writings*. Maraghehi believed that Iran's chaotic political predicament was rooted in ignorance, lawlessness and oppression.[17] For him, as for his enlightened co-thinkers, despotism and oppression could only be abolished with the introduction of constitutional law.[18]

Maraghehi emphasized the importance of a modern and independent judiciary system as an antidote to despotism. He envisaged a court where the public prosecutor stood on one side of the aisle trying to prove guilt and the defence attorney stood on the other side trying to acquit 'the thief, the murderer and the treacherous'. The final verdict on the case, Maraghehi proposed, should be delivered by the court's majority vote once 'evidence and witnesses' had been heard.[19] Maraghehi insisted that a country could only succeed when the constitution mediated between the people and the government.[20] He believed that the constitution, Parliament, the laws and procedures, all served as a bumper or shield protecting the citizens from the encroachment of absolutist monarchs.[21]

Mozaffareddin Shah

When the 43-year-old crown prince, Mozaffareddin, became shah in May 1896, expectations were high among his subjects that he would be different from his authoritarian father and be amenable towards long-awaited reforms. The shah's ill health and his blind trust in Mirza Ali-Asghar Atabak also known under the names Amin-Soltan/Atabak Azam (hereafter referred to as Atabak) were to prove considerable hurdles. Atabak was an expert at giving concessions to foreigners, throwing the shah into another web of foreign loans, mortgaging the country's wealth and seeking cures in Europe. Unwilling to cut back on the expenditures of the court, the gap between revenues and expenditures had to be made up by more foreign loans.

In 1900, the Russians extended a £2.4 million loan to Iran at the rate of 5 per cent and squeezed the British out of their privileged financial position in the country. The terms of the loan conferred implicitly exclusive rights to the Russians to lend money to Iran. The loan would enable the shah to go on his first visit to Europe in April 1900, a trip that lasted some seven months.

On 28 May 1901, Mozaffareddin Shah signed a historical oil concession with William Knox D'Arcy, a successful British entrepreneur and gold miner in Australia. The agreement was brokered by Antoine Ketabchi, the Iranian Armenian director of Persian customs. Atabak, the prime minister who had pro-Russian proclivities, supported the arrangement believing that it would come to naught. The Russians, however, objected to the concession, assessing it as a portal to British domination in Persia. At the time, however, no one imagined that this concession would become such a golden goose.

The concession gave D'Arcy a sixty-year exclusive right to oil exploration, drilling and exportation for the entire country, excluding only the five northern provinces of Azarbayjan, Gilan, Mazandaran, Astarabad and Khorasan, which were regarded as Russia's sphere of influence (Figure 1.4). In return, D'Arcy agreed to pay the Persian government £20,000 in cash, with another £20,000 worth of shares, as well as an annual royalty which was defined somewhat vaguely as equal to 16 per cent of 'annual net profits'.

On 12 April 1903, Mozaffareddin Shah embarked on his second visit to Europe, which included England. To finance the journey, the shah secured a Russian loan of approximately £1 million. Upon completion of his six-month journey, the shah and his entourage had almost entirely exhausted the loan.

For his third European trip on 6 June 1905, the Persian government was looking again for fresh funds and this time it was the Imperial Bank of Persia which extended the loan. Clearly the British and the Russians were outdoing one another in an effort to undermine each other's influence in Iran. Their turf war in Iran was costing them considerably in loan after loan. The need to find an acceptable diplomatic modus vivendi in Iran and avoid war would eventually lead the British and the Russians to move towards the 1907 Anglo-Russian Convention.

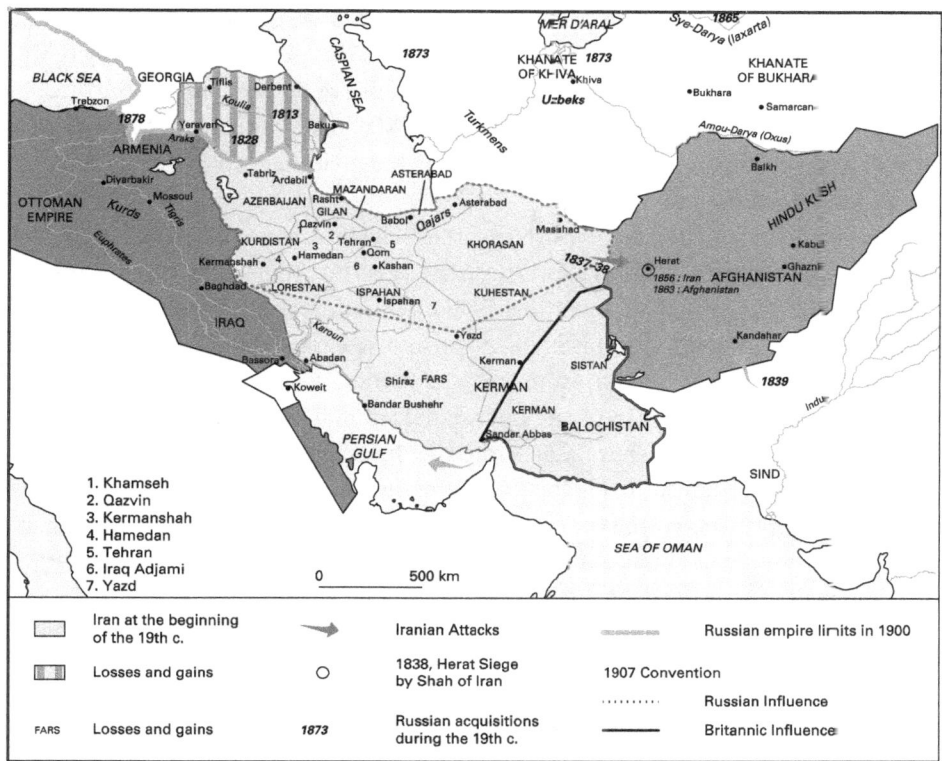

Figure 1.4 Iran: Spheres of Influence, 1900.

The Approaching Revolution

Iran's financial crisis and near bankruptcy produced riots against new tariffs in Tehran and Yazd (June 1903) and bread riots in Shiraz (August 1903). The shift from the production of staple crops to cash crops such as tobacco and opium for export, the paucity of rainfall in 1903, the shortage of bread, causing three years of semi-famine conditions, and the cholera epidemic of 1903–4, which led to the decline of 10–11 per cent of the population of Tehran and Esfahan, fanned discontent among the population.[22]

Iran's creditors relied on the country's custom revenues as the key source of repayment of their loans. This was the government's main collateral for obtaining loans. To make Iran's customs more effective and lucrative, the institution had been outsourced to Belgians. However, the more efficient the Belgians became in extracting revenues, the greater was the discontent among 'the **Bazaaris**, the artisans and certain groups of the religious classes and in particular the big merchants'.[23] While Iranian merchants were subjected to erratic price controls, insecure roads and precarity of life, their British and Russian counterparts benefitted from financial monopolies and security. Financial discrimination against Iranian merchants added insult to injury.

The 1904–5 Russo-Japanese War further disrupted trade between Iran and Russia, its major trading partner, and led to increases in the price of sugar, which was imported from Russia. In 1905, the price of wheat rose by 90 per cent and the price of sugar by 33 per cent in Tehran, Tabriz, Rasht and Mashhad.[24] Russia's defeat by Japan, an Asian power, further humiliated Iranians as they felt incapable of defending, let alone ridding themselves of Russia.

Between 1898 and 1904, Joseph Naus, the Belgian director of Persian customs tripled custom revenues, but his efforts translated also into higher prices of necessities and a general dislike for Naus and his Belgium employees. The growing power of Naus, who was appointed minister of posts and telegraphs and was the de facto minister of finance, was an affront to the sensitivities of Persians, in whose eyes he was responsible for the rise in prices and their economic hardship.

To prevent unrest, the government blamed the merchants. The government's heavy-handed policies to punish merchants for the price hikes backfired. In the provinces, clerics and people who voiced their grievances were shot or bastinadoed by the shah's governors. The stagnation and mismanagement of the country, compounded by the consequences of growing debts fuelled the demand for a constitution.

The Constitutionalists Organize

In October 1905, Mozaffareddin Shah returned home from his four-month European tour and found the country in crisis (Figure 1.5). While the shah procrastinated over the implementation of reforms and Ayn al-dowleh hoped to silence the opposition, the anti-despotic movement mobilized. This pro-constitutionalist movement had two modernist wings. Both were nationalist and egalitarian but one was secular and quasi-socialist, while the other was religious. Both chose to conduct their activities through societies or associations called *anjoman*s. Fearful of Ayn al-dowleh's repressive measures, these *anjoman*s were secret and clandestine.

Figure 1.5 Mozaffareddin Shah. *Source: Wikimedia Commons.*

Anjoman melli (National Society), sometimes referred to as the Central Society was founded in June 1904. Originally it had about sixty members and included the two notable constitutional preachers, Seyyed Jamaleddin Esfahani and Nasrollah Malek al-motekalemin. The outspoken anti-shah journalist Mohammad-Reza Mosavat-Shirazi, editor of the daily *Mosavat* (Equality), was also a member. This association had control over all others and possessed its own militia.

Another major *anjoman* was the Azarbayjan Association affiliated with the National Society. It operated in Tehran and had some 3,000 members. Despite its name, this society was a partisan of religious and ethnic unity in Iran and defended the rights of religious minorities.

On 7 February 1905, the influential Tehran cleric, Mohammad Tabatabai, recommended secret societies to combat injustice and despotism. In the past, Tabatabai had called on his followers to read newspapers out loud in coffee houses and other public places to awaken and educate the people. He, now called on like-minded people to discuss solutions to the country's problems and recommended reading Haji Zeinolabeddin Maraghehi's critical book which was banned in Iran.

According to Nazem al-eslam Kermani, the prominent chronicler of the Constitutional Revolution, he had been instructed by Tabatabai to invite friends to a secret society (*anjoman makhfi*). On 23 February 1905, they held the first of their many secret meetings. At these meetings, excerpts from Maraghehi's book were read out and discussed and members were encouraged to read the newspaper **Habl al-matin**, published in Calcutta.²⁵ Concerned participants unanimously emphasized the importance of laws as a solution to the predicaments of the country and the urgency of getting Seyyed Abdollah Behbahani, the other towering Tehran cleric, on board with Tabatabai and the constitutional drive (Figure 1.6). By 21 March 1905, members

Figure 1.6 Seyyed Abdollah Behbahani.

of the Secret Society were talking about the impossibility of reform without a revolution, awakening all who sought justice.

A radical nucleus within the *anjoman melli* later morphed into the revolutionary *ejtemaiyoun amiyoun* (Social Democrats), also known as the **mojaheds** or the crusaders/warriors. The Social Democrats were founded sometime between July and October 1905, with ties to the Russian Socialist Democratic Party. They had egalitarian, socialist, nationalist and constitutionalist ideals and aspired to the French revolutionary slogan of liberty, equality and fraternity.

By November 1905, a politico-religious alliance and accord was finally forged between Tabatabai and Behbahani in favour of a constitution and against Ayn al-dowleh while Sheykh Fazlollah Nuri, the other prominent Shii cleric of Tehran, remained steadfast to Ayn al-dowleh. When approached to join the constitutionalist front, in November, Nuri had told them that, 'the corrupt and outlaws need to be punished. We Iranians need the shah, Ayn al-dowleh, bastinadoing, and executioners ... all should be obedient to the shah and he who governs [Ayn al-dowleh].'[26]

The First Flare-Ups

As tensions rose over the sudden 60 per cent increase in sugar prices within a few days, on 12 December 1905, Ala al-dowleh, the governor of Tehran ordered the arrest and bastinadoing of two reputable sugar merchants alleged to have raised the price of sugar. The beating resulted in the immediate closure of the bazaar, the main market, and the commercial artery of the city. Crowds led by the two leading clerical figures Behbahani and Tabatabai, gathered at Masjede Shah to demand the removal of Ala al-dowleh and the establishment of a house of justice.

When Seyyed Jamaleddin Vaez-Esfahani, a fiery and popular preacher, began criticizing the injustices in the land, the conservative court cleric, Seyyed Abolqasem, Emam Jomeh (Friday Prayer Leader), the shah's son-in-law, accused him of slandering the shah and called him a Babi and an infidel. Seyyed Abolqasem ordered his followers, who were armed with sticks, to attack the crowd and disrupt the gathering.

On the next day, infuriated by the event, Tabatabai and Behbahani led a group of artisans, merchants, junior clerics and theology students to take sanctuary **bast** in the shrine of Shah Abdolazim in the south of Tehran. The number of protesters swelled to more than 2,000, demanding widespread reforms and Ayn al-dowleh's dismissal. In vain, Ayn al-dowleh tried to stem the tide by threatening and bribing its leadership.

The protest movement demanded the creation of a house of justice and tribunals in every province to address complaints against administrative excesses. This was a call for a national judicial system, based on Islamic laws. The protesters insisted on the dismissal of Naus and Ala al-dowleh, Tehran's governor, but dropped their demand for the removal of the prime minister, Ayn al-dowleh.

On 10 January 1906, Mozaffareddin Shah issued a royal decree granting a house of justice (*edalatkhaneh*). Even though Ala al-dowleh was dismissed, the shah retained Ayn al-dowleh and Naus. Both sides were able to save face, and the protesting clerical leaders left their one-month sanctuary on 12 January 1906. Amid the excitement of welcoming the protesters, for the first time the people chanted, 'Long live the Iranian nation (*zendeh bad mellate Iran*)!'[27] The concept of an Iranian nation composed of citizens was born.

By spring of 1906, secret societies in large Iranian cities were agitating for the rule of law and the ousting of despotism. Their *shabnameh* (night-letters) or tracts called for justice and the constitution. While Ayn al-dowleh dragged his feet hoping to delay the implementation of the House of Justice until the opposition was repressed or coopted, the movement intensified and its demand for a house of justice transitioned to demands for a parliament (Majles).

Frequent reports reached Tehran of self-serving and cruel provincial governors in Kerman, Khorasan and Shiraz driving people to destitution. In a letter, Mohammad Tabatabai complained to the shah about the brutality and injustices of governors in the provinces and told the shah that 'the solution to all corruptions and injustices was a parliament of justice, in which the guilds would resolve people's grievances, and the shah and the pauper would be equal in its eyes'. Tabatabai insisted that 'contrary to the claim that a parliament (Majles) is inconsistent with monarchy, an indestructible and upright monarchy is only possible with a parliament, without it, it would be meaningless and short-lived'.[28] Turning his wrath on Ayn al-dowleh and wishing to jolt the indecisive and weak shah, Tabatabai warned against the despotism of a single individual.

Prime Minister Ayn al-dowleh and his anti-constitutionalist partisans, lay and clerical, on the other hand, accused the constitutionalists (**mashruteh** *khahan*) of radicalism, anarchism, heresy and republicanism. Demonstrations, unrest and large gatherings at constitutionalist mosques were frequent, and confrontation was in the air. Fearing a public uprising, Ayn al-dowleh imposed a curfew, arrested constitutionalists, and filled the streets with government spies, Cossacks and soldiers. Meanwhile, the religious preachers, and especially Jamaleddin Vaez-Esfahani and Sheykh Mohammad Soltan al-motekallemin, a close associate of Abdollah Behbahani, rallied the people from the pulpit by denouncing 'autocracy and tyranny'.[29]

Royal Decree Granting a Consultative Parliament

In the summer of 1906, tension escalated as Seyyed Mohammad Tabatabai intensified his attacks from the pulpit on despotism, injustice and Ayn al-dowleh. He announced that the shah was innocent and alone and called for an end to arbitrary government. Ayn al-dowleh, who had failed to divide or buy off Tabatabai and Behbahani, responded by arresting clerics close to them. On 10 July 1906, as soldiers tried to arrest Sheykh Mohammad Soltan al-motekallemin, the crowd intervened. The soldiers opened fire, a seminary student was shot and a preacher was injured. This incident led to more clashes between soldiers and the people, the number of victims increased and the bazaar closed in protest, demanding Ayn al-dowleh's dismissal.

Meanwhile, the shah was becoming ever more convinced that the constitutionalist clerics were plotting against his monarchy. After 10 July, Tabatabai, Behbahani and their close followers feared for their lives. They decided to leave Tehran, and stayed in Qom on their way to Karbala and Najaf. More out of pragmatism than conviction, at this point Sheykh Fazlollah Nuri also joined the constitutionalist clergy.

The stand-off reached a new height when on 17 July 1906, nine merchants entered the British summer legation at Qolhak, in northern Tehran. Concerned with the safety of those who had remained behind in Tehran, Behbahani, who had been in touch with the British, organized the constitutionalists' safe stay (*bast*) at the British legation.

On 31 July 1906, Ayn al-dowleh resigned and the previous prime minister, Moshir al-dowleh, replaced him. The unrests did not abate. The shah requested the return of Tabatabai and Behbahani to Tehran, and they insisted on the urgency of a parliament. By 2 August 1906, prominent provincial clerics congregated at Qom in support of Tabatabai and Behbahani, while the crowd at the British Legation reached some 15,000. People from all walks of life, trades, guilds and even students filled the legation. The expenses, food and shelter in tents were provided by prominent Tehran merchants.

The demand for a constitution and a representative national assembly, a parliament which would limit the powers of the shah, evolved out of this *bast*. On 5 August 1906, Mozaffareddin Shah issued a royal decree granting a National Consultative Parliament (*Majles showraye melli*). By 14 August, having obtained satisfaction, the constitutionalists ended their four-week *bast* at the British Legation and began dismantling the more than 100 tents they had set up. The achievement was considered a 'National Victory'.[30]

The first Constituent Assembly met on 7 October 1906, and was composed of guild leaders, nobles, landowners, merchants and the clergy with the responsibility of drafting the Constitution. This historical occasion was inaugurated at Golestan Palace and in the presence of Mozaffareddin Shah and the diplomatic corps. Although by December 1906, rumours circulated that the crown prince, Mohammad-Ali, was opposed to a constitutional monarchy, all three documents – the constitutional edict, the electoral law and the Constitution itself – were endorsed by Mozaffareddin Shah on 1 January 1907. On the next day, Mozaffareddin Shah passed away at 6.00 am. The 38-year-old Mohammad-Ali Shah was coronated on 19 January 1907.

The Constitutional Law of 30 December 1906

The constitutional law of 1906 consisted of a short preamble and fifty-one articles, at least six of which corresponded, fully or in part, to articles in the Belgian constitution and at least five of which corresponded to provisions in the Bulgarian constitution of 1879, although none were *verbatim* translations.

Eligible voters
The 1st Constituent Assembly/Majles, composed of 156 deputies, was inaugurated on 7 October 1906. The deputies were elected only by: (1) Qajar princes, (2) nobles and notables, (3) clerics and seminary school students, (4) landed proprietors and farmers, (5) merchants and (6) members of guilds. Women, the illiterate, propertyless workers, peasants and petty tradesmen were barred from voting.

Parliament's brief
The Majles had legislative powers in conjunction with the Senate. It had the right to initiate legislation and approve international treaties and economic concessions and to control both the natural resources of the country and government finances. All treaties, concessions, contracts and loans between Persia and foreign nationals were subject to its approval. The Majles had the right to question ministers and could only request that the shah dismiss a minister who failed to provide satisfactory answers.

Mohammad-Ali Shah's Rule

Mohammad-Ali Shah had lived 26 years of his life as the crown prince in Tabriz, where he was tutored by a Russian in-house teacher, Serguy Markovitch Shapshal. The young prince was taught the Russian language and culture and subsequently became fond of Russia and the Russian court. Mohammad-Ali was not interested in any formal education. During his years in Tabriz, he was generally disliked because of his corruption, illegal land-grabbing, hoarding of wheat and barley, price-gouging and extortion. He pretended to be a devout Shii, who engaged in self-flagellation during the traditional mourning ceremonies of Ashura. When important decisions needed to be made, Mohammad-Ali relied on divinations (*estekhareh*).

While heir to the throne, Mohammad-Ali had opposed his father's decision to grant a parliament and a constitution. When he ascended to the throne, he played a cunning game: while publicly pledging allegiance to the Constitution, he actively plotted against it. Too weak to openly oppose the Constitution and Parliament, which had mobilized the people behind it, Mohammad-Ali Shah waited for the opportune moment to move against the constitutionalists.

Nevertheless, the new shah could not properly hide his dislike for Parliament. At his coronation, he invited all domestic and foreign dignitaries, but did not invite members of the Majles. Two weeks after his coronation, the shah was busy secretly gathering tribal forces from Azarbayjan to plot against Parliament. In April 1907, he appointed the widely unpopular Atabak as prime minister. *Habl al-matin*, the influential constitutionalist paper, characterized Atabak as the 'plunderer of the people', 'eradicator of security', 'devastator of justice', 'propagator of corruption' and 'protector of the lands of the infidels'.[31]

The Constitutionalist Front

The constitutionalists were a heterogeneous group gathered around the single objective of limiting the autocratic power of the monarchy and creating a modern independent state. They believed that a constitution, a representative legislature and the separation of powers would achieve this end. However, once the details of what those objectives meant to different adherents and how to operationalize them came to the fore, differences of opinion and dissent began. The Iranian Parliament from its inception witnessed the clash of ideas on the implementation of objectives, but it also became an arena where foreign powers invested in Iran, weighed in on issues, through their proxies.

> ### Who Were the Constitutionalists?
> The constitutional revolution was not a class-based movement and people from different walks of life participated in it to limit the Shah's power and obtain a constitution. (M. Etehadiyeh)[32]

The constitutionalists were roughly composed of four groups: the Tehran clergy led by Behbahani and Tabatabai; the Najaf clerical triumvirate of Akhund Molla Mohammad-Kazem Khorasani, Sheykh Abdollah Mazandarani and Mirza Hoseyn Khalili-Tehrani; segments of the enlightened notables and members of the Qajar family; and finally, merchants, guilds, journalists and commercial classes. The chief mobilizers and galvanizers were a mix of constitutionalist clerics, fiery preachers, liberals, social democrats, socialists, revolutionaries, secularists and **Azali Babis**. Members of this politicized core were also members of political *anjoman*s active in 1904–5 and the Freemasonry lodge of Réveil de l'Iran.

The some 140 *anjoman*s which operated in Tehran provided an ideal space for political activists to gather, exchange ideas and discuss the rapidly evolving political scene. These secret associations, whose aim had been to obtain a parliament, remained active after the ascent of Mohammad-Ali Shah to protect their political gains. Irrespective of their ideological differences, these powerful pre-party socio-political entities became a solid base of popular support for constitutionalism and the Majles. The shah viewed the *anjoman*s as a real threat and pushed the government to repress them.

Getting Mozaffareddin Shah to sign off on a parliament had been the initial battle, defending it against all its ill-wishers, domestic and foreign, was a much more difficult task. The deputies elected to the Parliament were inexperienced novices without any knowledge of parliamentary procedures or background in deliberations and manoeuvrings. It was not until the second Parliament that the notion of majority and minority party representation became officialized. In the first Parliament, the deputies were individual partisans of a vague notion of constitutionalism, who formed factions according to their respective interests. The task of confronting Mohammad-Ali Shah's assault against Parliament remained squarely on the decentralized, rather unruly, radicalized and sometimes armed associations (*anjoman*s).

Some of these associations were also the hub of Left-leaning, social democratic and radical constitutionalists journalists, who played a significant role in awakening and informing the people. Theses journalists were highly critical of the shah's despotism, and of a superstitious and reactionary Shiism. Influential constitutionalist editors – such as Jahangir Khan Shirazi and Soltan al-olama Khorasani, editors of *Suresrafil*, and Mohammad-Reza Mosavat-Shirazi, the editor of *Mosavat*, were all active members of *anjoman*s. Pro-constitutionalist papers such as Soltan al-olama Khorasani's *Ruh al-qodos* and Seyyed Jalaleddin Kashani's *Habl al-matin*, also played a key role in disseminating ideas such as, welfare, progress, freedom, parliamentarianism, the Constitution and nationalism.

Iranian members of the Freemasonry lodge *Le Réveil de L'Iran* (Iran's Awakening) played an important role in the Constitutional Revolution. *Le Réveil de L'Iran*, which was incorporated into the French Grand Orient in November 1907, had its first gathering in Tehran on 29 November 1906. The members of *Le Réveil de L'Iran* included radicals, moderates, clerical and military leaders, and even reactionaries in the constitutionalist movement.

Secret Societies and Freemasons

There is no doubt that the organization, concepts, and activities of the Iranian secret *anjoman*s, owed a great deal to, if not outright, European Masonic lodges. (M. Bayat)[33]

The question, however, remains whether Iranian constitutionalists learned their notions of anti-despotism, anti-religious fanaticism, nationalism and humanism from their Freemason lodges, or did they possess them and therefore joined the Freemasonries which upheld such ideals. In other words, was membership in *Le Réveil de L'Iran*, part of a mobilizing effort against despotism or did it provide actual schooling in the ways of European enlightenment or both?

The Despotic Front

Mohammad-Ali Shah was the leader of those with vested interests and exclusive rights in pre-constitutional Iran. The idea of common people rather than the nobles, notables and the elite becoming involved in government and especially controlling the finances of the state, irked the old establishment. The conservative, traditionalist and reactionary forces opposed Parliament as a legal and representative watchdog of the 'people' over the affairs of the state. They viewed the people as a rabble that needed to be put back in its resigned and obedient position.

The domestic anti-constitutionalist forces were composed of two groups. The first, with almost no popular support, was composed of the shah, courtiers, a good number of princes, governors and Qajar politicians, landowners and their functionaries, certain tribal leaders, and military notables whose privileges and arbitrary rule was curtailed by the Constitution.

In the 1st Majles, a small group of discontented pro-constitutionalist joined the anti-constitutionalists for power and financial gain. The most significant figure among this group was Mirza Javad Khan Saad al-dowleh. He, was a participant in drafting the Constitution, entered Parliament as a representative of the nobles and sided with the progressives on almost all controversial issues. In the summer of 1907, because of personal jealousies and perhaps careerism, he joined the anti-constitutionalists and gave up his seat.

The second group of anti-constitutionalists benefitted from popular support. The clergy enjoyed the support of believers. The conservative and anti-constitutionalist branch of the clergy, who had historically benefitted from their alliance with the court, traditionally opposed change, as a counter-religious force. This group was composed of the court cleric Seyyed Abolqasem Emam Jomeh, who had demonstrated his opposition to the idea of a constitution even before it was granted by Mozaffareddin Shah.

The most significant figure of this group was the prominent Sheykh Fazlollah Nuri, politically close to the much-disliked Prime Minister Ayn al-dowleh. Nevertheless, on 18 July 1906, he had reluctantly and belatedly joined the constitutionalists who had taken sanctuary in Qom. Before he fell out with them completely, Nuri pretended to cooperate with Behbahani and Tabatabai, even though he was loyal to Ayn al-dowleh and the shah.

Nuri feared that freedom and liberty would undermine the authority of the clergy and hammered at their disrupting influence on the faith. He viewed Parliament as a body mandated to implement Islamic laws (*sharia*) and not to legislate man-made laws. When the shah supported Nuri's cause and recommended a **mashrueh** or a constitution based on and bound by the *sharia*, the Majles refused the monarch's recommendation. The Parliament privileged a constitutional or a *mashruteh* system of governance. In June 1907, Nuri came out openly against the Constitution and labelled the Parliament as un-Islamic.

Mohammad-Ali Shah was the main beneficiary of Sheykh Fazlollah's anti-constitutional crusade. The shah benefitted from the prominence and religious arguments of anti-constitutionalist clerics, claiming that the law of the land had to be religious and that law-making by deputies was not for a Shii country. Sheykh Fazlollah Nuri labelled the constitutionalists Babis, heretics and infidels. Ultimately, he called for a vague system of *mashrutehe mashrueh*, in which divine laws would constitute the basis of legislature rather than man-made laws. In this system, the role of lawmakers became redundant and moot.

From outside the country, Russia was the major adversary of constitutionalism and a devout supporter of Mohammad-Ali Shah. After a humiliating defeat at the hands of the Japanese in 1905, followed by the 1905 revolution, the Tsarist government was fragile and vulnerable. Confronted with its own constitutionalist movement and its own Parliament (Duma) inaugurated on 27 April 1906, the Russians needed to restore their authority and position in Iran.

The anti-despotic demands of Iranian constitutionalist worried the Russians, especially the more radical brands with connections with revolutionary Social Democrats in the Caucasus. The constitutionalists threatened Russia's long-term political and financial investment in Iran. Both the Qajar and Tsarist regimes viewed their mode of despotic government as the sole guarantors of order and protectors of their respective religions.

Sharing Mohammad-Ali Shah's deep enmity towards constitutionalism, Parliament, a free press and the *anjoman*s was a Russian influential circle, which included the Russian ambassador, H. G. Hartwig, his close associate, Col. Vladimir Platonovich Liyakhov, who became Tehran's military governor in June 1908 and the Cossacks commanders serving under him, Perebinsov, Blazanov and Ushakov. The shah's old Russian teacher Sergei Shapshal, allegedly a Russian agent, was also an important figure in the anti-constitutionalist circle.

The 1st Majles, 7 October 1906–23 June 1908

Lacking a culture of orderly deliberation, discussion and negotiation, the first Parliament was plagued by inexperience, confusion and emotional haggling. Half of the deputies who represented the guilds were not politicized. They were often absent and did not play a significant role in the deliberations. The other half were politicized constitutionalists, composed of radicals and moderates. A handful of pro-despotic deputies were also present in this Majles. The radicals who had some semblance of organization in the Majles were known as the liberty-seekers (*azadi khahan*). They believed that power should be vested in Parliament. They also believed in individual rights and liberties, the freedom of expression, association and the press, equal rights before the law, secularism and free education. The radicals sought to minimize the political role of the monarch to that of a ceremonial ruler, and emphasized a strong legislature and executive, and control of government finances by the Majles.

The radicals were led by Seyyed Hasan Taqizadeh, the representative of the merchants of Tabriz, an eloquent speaker familiar with progressive Western ideas and an active member of several key parliamentary committees. The radicals associated with Iranian Social Democrats, founded sometime between July and October 1905, constituted the minority faction in Parliament, although their popular support among the *anjoman*s and the press gave them substantial political clout. Their relentless opposition to Mohammad-Ali Shah and his appointees endeared them to the public.

The moderates who constituted the majority were composed of reputable old politicians, established merchants and progressive clerics. The moderates were sceptical of radicalism and weary of direct confrontation with Mohammad-Ali Shah. The most influential anti-radical moderates were Seyyed Abdollah Behbahani, one of the two clerical pioneers of the constitutionalist movement, and a few affluent merchants such as Haji Amin al-zarb, Haji Mohammad-Taqi Bonakdar and Haji Mohammad-Esmail Aqa. Mohamamd-Ali Shah's appointment of Atabak as prime minister on 3 May 1907, had caused a rift among the two constitutionalist religious leaders. While Tabatabai opposed his appointment, Behbahani had supported it and stood by him. Atabak wooed the moderates and soon Behbahani and Haji Amin al-zarb rallied behind him. The prime minister sought to neutralize the opposition to the shah in the Majles.

The First Collision Course: Parliament and the Shah

From day one, the shah and the constitutionalists had very different understandings of the new constitutional order and who should be running the country. The shah felt as though nothing of substance had changed in the manner of governance, while the constitutionalists believed that the executive was responsible to the Majles. The shah viewed the demands of Parliament in limiting his political powers as excessive and anti-constitutional. Their fundamental disagreement on the purpose of a parliament and the role of the sovereign and their respective relation to the people made reconciliation between the shah and Parliament difficult. The shah saw Iranians as subjects and Parliament considered them as citizens.

The Second Collision Course: Reformist and Revolutionary Deputies

Within the constitutionalists, the radicals were convinced that the shah was bent on destroying Parliament, just as the tsar was obsessed with getting rid of the Duma. The radicals were eager to see a French or English parliamentary system in Iran and were weary of a Russian experience with constitutionalism. The moderates, on the other hand, were reformists who believed that the constitutional process could be best secured through some sort of reconciliation between the shah and Parliament for the sake of order and stability. The reformists' reconciliatory position towards the shah was viewed as treasonous to the cause of the people by the revolutionaries.

One of the most important tasks of the 1st Majles was to draft a 'Supplement to the Constitution', clarifying the ambiguities in the original Constitution. Work on this document began in mid-February 1907, and after great strife, was signed on 8 October 1907 by a reluctant Mohammad-Ali Shah, who renounced his absolutist powers. Sheykh Fazlollah Nuri sided with the shah and opposed the liberal and inclusive articles of the text. On 21 June 1907, Sheykh Fazlollah Nuri led his followers to the shrine of Shah Abdolazim and began his three-month sanctuary (*bast*), conducting his anti-constitutionalist activities through pamphlets and leaflets.

Nuri claimed that the Supplement to the Constitution, debated in the Majles, was in opposition to religious laws (*sharia*) on three accounts. First, the notion of equality of all Iranians before the law undermined the legal distinction between Muslims and non-Muslims. Second, the civil rights stipulated, such as the freedom of expression and of the press were contrary to the *sharia*. Third, man-made laws needed to be supervised and vetted by a group of *mujtahids* (religious experts) to ensure that they complied with the *sharia*. Nuri claimed that the Majles had fallen into the hands of heretics, materialists and Babis, in effect declaring a religious war on the constitutionalists. In a few other cities, such as Rasht and Tabriz, a number of clerics joined the anti-constitutional front, while in Parliament, Mohammad-Taqi Harati defended Nuri's position.

The Assassination of the Prime Minister

The radicals suspected that the shah was doing his utmost to take control of the Majles through manoeuvrings, promising favours and even bribing deputies, all the while aided by his prime minister, Atabak, and by Fazlollah Nuri. On 31 August 1907, a month before the signing of the Supplement to the Constitution by the shah, Atabak was assassinated in front of the Majles. The 22-year-old Abbas Aqa Tabrizi, a moneychanger from Tabriz, had fired the three fatal shots. Moments later, the assailant committed suicide. A note identifying him as a *fadai* (self-sacrificer) was found in his pocket. Abbas Aqa Tabrizi was a member of Heydar Amuoqlu's clandestine revolutionary organization, the armed chapter of the Social Democrats (*Ejtemaiyun Amiyun*).

The Anglo-Russian Convention

On 31 August 1907, the same day that Atabak was assassinated in Tehran, the British and Russians signed a secret treaty, the Anglo-Russian Convention, in St. Petersburg, dividing Iran into two zones of influence. Northern Iran, including Tehran and Esfahan, went to Russia and southern Iran, including Sistan and Baluchestan, went to the British. Neither power was to seek commercial or political concessions in the other country's zone of influence. Each country was given a free hand in its own zone of influence and both agreed on dividing the revenues from Iran's customs and fisheries to finance Iran's debts to the two countries. Both countries recognized Iran's strict independence and integrity. The sliver of land between the two zones, including Yazd and Shiraz, remained a neutral zone. The Anglo-Russian Convention was a colonial design against the sovereignty of Iran. Its contents were communicated to Parliament almost a month after it was signed.

Iran's Response to the Anglo-Russian Convention

From North to South, Persia is ours: we are neither minors needing a guardian, nor lunatics needing a keeper. (*Habl al-matin*)[34]

The assassination of the prime minister had weakened the anti-constitutionalists and the moderates in Parliament. It had also scared the shah and the despotic front, leading Nuri to end his three-month-long anti-constitutionalist sanctuary in September 1907. The assassination had been a stern warning by the radical constitutionalists. Yet, it also opened the door to claims by the despotic front that Iran was moving towards instability and chaos.

The Supplement to the Constitution

After seven months of conflict, the Supplement to the Constitution was ratified and signed on 8 October 1907 by Mohammad-Ali Shah. It stipulated that:

a. All Iranians were equal before the law. Their lives, property, honour and homes were protected, and they were entitled to due process if accused of a crime.
b. All Iranians had the right to privacy of communications and were entitled to the freedom of association and the press.
c. The powers of the realm emanated from the people.
d. The legislative, judiciary and executive branches of government constituted separate and independent powers.
e. The legislative power was shared by the shah, the Majles and the Senate, each with the right to initiate legislation.
f. The Majles could dismiss any minister or the entire government through a vote of no confidence.
g. A group of five religious experts (*mojtaheds*) would vet all legislation to assure that no proposals would be at variance with Islamic laws.
h. The monarchy was stipulated as a Divine Right entrusted to the shah by the people.

On 6 November, the radical constitutionalist paper *Ruh al-qodos* assessed Iran's political situation thus: 'The tyrant falleth aye by self-wrought ill. The Rook is lost, the Pawn advances still. Bishop and Knight, we to the task will bring. The Premier's slain – 'tis check-mate to the King.'[35] On 12 November, the shah, accompanied by several princes, went to the Majles and pledged allegiance to the Constitution and the safeguarding of Iran's independence. All the while and under the influence of his Russian advisers, the shah was preparing his forces for an attack on Parliament and the people knew it.

Two weeks after his oath of allegiance, the shah organized an army led by Amir Bahador and called on the Majles not to interfere with his plan to repress the *anjoman*s, which he called a bunch of bandits. The *anjoman*s in return attacked the shah, Amir Bahador, Shapshal and Sheykh Fazlollah Nuri at their gatherings and in their newspapers. They blamed the shah and the sheykh for the country's problems and asked for their dismissal.

First Assault on Parliament: The Failed Coup

On 15 December 1907, a mob of 600–700 thugs armed with clubs and machetes was mobilized from Tehran's poorer quarters to attack the Majles. They were led by Mohammad Khan Sani-Hazrat and Khosrow Khan Sardar-Etemad (Moqtader-nezam), agents of the religio-political despotic front. Once they were repulsed by the *anjoman* forces, the thugs retreated to Meydane Tupkhaneh, joining Amir Bahador's forces. There, the pro-despotic forces engaged in beating up the people.

In the afternoon, Prime Minister Naser al-molk, suspected of constitutionalist sympathies, had been summoned to the court and put in chains. After the intercession of the British Legation, the Oxford-educated Naser al-molk was allowed to leave the country for London the next day. After a day of hesitation and uncertainty during which deputies took refuge in Parliament and the bazaar shut down in protest, the constitutionalists counter-attacked.

On 16 December, the shah demanded the dissolution of Parliament and the expulsion of a few deputies, including Taqizadeh and the fiery preachers Jamaleddin Esfahani and Malek al-motekallemin. But by this time, the tides had turned. Some 3,000 members of the *anjoman*s, many of them armed, had surrounded Parliament. As the day progressed, the constitutionalist forces swelled up to about 6,500 as people from all walks of life joined in. Concurrently, telegrams from the provinces started to pour in, supporting the constitutionalists. Telegrams from Tabriz called for the dismissal of the shah and clashes occurred between constitutionalists and anti-constitutionalists in Tabriz and Esfahan.

Deeply concerned about his future, the shah backed off, agreed to the dismissal of some of his advisers, met with parliamentary leaders and once again went through the meaningless process of pledging his allegiance to the Constitution. The crisis was over in a few days with hardly any bloodshed. 'Peace had been made, but it felt to be a hollow truce.'[36] On 22 December 1907, through the new Prime Minister Nezam al-saltaneh, the shah sent a sealed message to Parliament. Written on the back of a Quran, Mohammad-Ali Shah once again pledged to protect the Constitution.

About a week later, the three Najaf religious dignitaries sent an unprecedented telegram to Behbahani and Tabatabai, in response to their complaints about Nuri. Nuri's Islamic arguments against Parliament compelled the Najaf **Sources of Imitation (*maraje taqlid*)** to take a religious position. Kazem Khorasani, Abdollah Mazandarani and Hoseyn Khalili-Tehrani, threw their weight behind the constitutionalist and sealed Nuri's fate. They announced that since Nuri had been an impediment to public peace and was a corruptor, his opinion, ruling and intervention in all matters were prohibited (*haram*).[37] The Najaf triumvirate took the bold step of excommunicating Nuri for his political positions.

Attempt on the Shah's Life

On the surface, it seemed as though the shah and Parliament were mending fences. Yet, the relation between the two remained tenuous. The Parliament had decided to punish the shah's men for murdering a prominent Zoroastrian merchant and an active constitutionalist. This infuriated the monarch. Then, on 8 February 1908, two handmade bombs were thrown at the shah's motorcade. The shah escaped the attack, but his servant and a number of bystanders were killed. On the next day, the shah ordered the bastinado of Tehran's governor, Azizollah Zafar al-saltaneh, for negligence.

On 10 February, an attempt was made on the life of Gholamhoseyn Ghaffari (*Saheb-ekhtiyar*), a Qajar notable and proponent of Mohammad-Ali Shah. He escaped the attack, but his gardener and servant were killed. Heydar Amuoghlu and his secret society were held responsible for the plot to assassinate Mohammad-Ali Shah. Heydar and three others were arrested and soon released under pressure from the secret societies and the radical deputies.

The shah now feared for his life and did not leave the palace. He felt powerless and angered by his inability to punish his assailants. He complained about the treatment he was receiving, the chaos in the country and the impunity of the radicals.

Second Coup: Parliament is Shelled and Closed

By June 1908, the shah and the constitutionalists were once again at cross-purposes. The shah demanded that newspapers and vocal preachers stop criticizing and denouncing him. The Majles, in turn, demanded the dismissal of six close collaborators of the shah, who were suspected of plotting against the Parliament, including Shapshal, the shah's Russian instructor and Amir Bahador.

On 2 June 1908, Russian Minister Hartwig and British Chargé d'Affaires Marlaine informed the Iranian minister of foreign affairs that they believed the *anjoman*s and the constitutionalists 'had transgressed all bounds and wish now to depose the Shah'. Both men threatened that this would not be tolerated and were it to happen, they would 'be compelled to interfere'.[38] Given the timing of this warning, it was clear that the two powers were establishing a pretext for what was to follow.

On 3 June 1908, Mohammad-Ali Shah left his palace for Baqe Shah, a residence just outside the city. He was accompanied by Shapshal, Liyakhov and his Cossacks.

There, the shah agreed to Liyakhov's suggestion to 'abolish the constitution, disperse the Majles, . . . and to return to the former absolute form of government'.[39]

On 5 June, the shah lured, arrested and exiled five pro-constitutionalists, among them, Qajar princes. When twelve deputies were sent to negotiate, the shah had them arrested. The Majles objected to these illegal arrests, and the *anjoman*s assembled in the Sepahsalar Mosque, near the Majles building. The shah responded by ordering their dispersal and the arrest of their leaders. The shah's forces took over all telegraph offices, cutting the provinces from Tehran before proclaiming martial law. Mohammad-Ali Shah appointed Liyakhov as military governor of Tehran and moved to disarm the militia belonging to the *anjoman*s. On 14 June 1908, Mohammad-Ali Shah demanded the expulsion from the capital of eight outspoken constitutionalist preachers and journalists, including Malek al-motakalemin, Seyyed Jamaleddin Esfahani, Mirza Jahangir Khan (*Suresrafil*) and Mohammad-Reza Shirazi (*Mosavat*).

The provinces were calling to depose the shah, and Tabriz, Esfahan and Kerman threatened to send troops to Tehran in support of the Constitution. On 19 June, some 10,000 members of various secret societies, accompanied by constitutionalist deputies and leaders, congregated at Sepahsalar Mosque. To avoid bloodshed by the shah's Cossacks, the constitutionalist deputies dispersed the huge crowd. The deputies worried that clashes would provide a pretext for the Russians and the British to intervene.

Boldened by the constitutionalists' conciliatory reaction, the shah closed all newspapers on 21 June 1908. On the next day, acting from a position of power, the shah sent word that he was ready for negotiations with the Majles while simultaneously announcing that the Majles was working against the Constitution. He threatened that anyone who disobeyed his directives would be harshly punished.

On 23 June 1908, at 6 am, 20 Cossacks tried to arrest the constitutional leaders but were repulsed from the Sepahsalar Mosque by constitutionalist riflemen. Some 1,000–2,000 Cossacks and soldiers set siege to the Parliament. Liyakhov, who had the full support of the Russian minister, Hartwig, arrived on the scene an hour later. Accompanied by his Russian officers, Liyakhov stationed his troops, brought in heavy artillery and aimed his guns at the Majles. He subsequently ordered his troops to fire on the Majles and the Sepahsalar Mosque adjacent to it.

The brunt of the fighting fell on some 100 riflemen of *Anjoman Azarbayjan* and some members of *Anjoman Mozaffari*, who defended the Majles. By noon, the Cossacks prevailed. The Parliament and mosque, symbols of Iran's religious and political pride, independence and identity had been laid to waste by Mohammad-Ali Shah.

Constitutionalists were arrested and their homes looted. Some 300 were killed, 500 were wounded and another 300 arrested. Even the houses of the shah's uncle and aunt were not spared. Some leading constitutionalists, including Taqizadeh and Ali-Akbar Dehkhoda found refuge in the British Legation, while others found sanctuary at the French and Ottoman embassies.

The shah took revenge on the outspoken press and preachers. Jahangir Khan Shirazi, Sheykh Ahmad Ruh al-qodos and Malek al-motakalemin were captured and murdered. Jamaleddin Esfahani managed to escape from Tehran but was subsequently murdered in Borujerd. Both Abdollah Behbahani and Mohammad Tabatabai, and their sons, who had been in the Majles during the attack, were arrested and subsequently exiled.

On 24 June 1908, Mohammad-Ali Shah dissolved Parliament and ended the 20-month constitutional experience. The historical period between the coup of 23 June 1908 and the fall of Mohammad-Ali Shah in July 1909 is known as the Short/Lesser Despotism (*Estebdad Saqir*). Mohammad-Ali Shah, propped up by a domestic despotic front and openly incited by the Russians, had staged a coup against Iran's nascent democratic movement. The 1907 Anglo-Russian Entente had also made Britain complicit in the coup, though it was not directly involved. Despotism had returned, the Constitution was rescinded and political freedoms were to remain suspended for a year and a half.

Lenin on the Counter-Revolution

There has been a counter-revolution in Persia – a peculiar combination of the dissolution of Russia's first Duma, and of the Russian insurrection at the close of 1905 . . . The exploits of the Cossacks in mass shootings, punitive expeditions, manhandling and pillage in Russia, are followed by their exploits in suppressing the revolution in Persia. (V. I. Lenin)[40]

Lenin on Europe and the Democratic Tide in Asia

Essentially, what we see now going on in the Balkans, Turkey and Persia is a counter-revolutionary coalition of the European powers *against* the mounting tide of democracy in Asia. (V. I. Lenin)[41]

Two Responses to Despotism

The June 1908 assault on constitutionalism was made possible by two intertwined forces, one religious and the other political. The response to despotism, therefore, had to be fought on both those fronts. The constitutionalist clergy had to refute the accusation that modern democracy was incompatible with Shiism. In this political confrontation, in the guise of religion, the two opposing spokesmen of Shiism had to determine whether parliamentarianism and constitutionalism were reconcilable with the faith. The deliberations and outcome of this sensitive and polarizing intra-faith struggle would leave its marks on the future generations. The political and military response to despotism was less conflictual for Iranians as the just/good and the unjust/bad sides were more delineated.

The Religious Split in Response to Despotism

Sheykh Fazlollah Nuri had played from the start a central role in articulating and propagating a religious justification for despotism. He posited that the notions of parliamentary legislation and representation were contrary to the *sharia*. He had emphasized that absolute monarchy was an extension of prophethood, and as such was a pillar of an Islamic system of governance. Nuri and his clerical followers believed that the preservation and protection of Islam was incumbent upon the ruler and the religious experts (*olama*).

According to Nuri, Islam prohibited man-made laws. It was a complete religion and when dealing with novel occurrences, unforeseen in primary religious sources, it was the responsibility of the *olama* to derive edicts from the religious sources. By pitting that which was religiously authorized (*mashrueh*) against man-made laws which constituted the Constitution (*mashruteh*), Nuri concluded that constitutionalism dethroned and dispossessed Islam and constitutionalists were apostates.

During the Short/Lesser Despotism, the centre of religious opposition to despotism shifted from Tehran to Najaf. Shortly after shelling the Majles, the Shii dignitaries of Najaf, Akhund Molla Kazem Khorasani and Sheykh Abdollah Mazandarani, wrote a sharp letter to Mohammad-Ali Shah counselling him not to oppose constitutional rule. Weeks later, as news of Tabriz's heroic resistance in July reached Najaf, Hoseyn Khalili-Tehrani joined the other two Shii Sources of Imitation (*maraje taqlid*), Khorasani and Mazandarani, to warn the shah that fighting in Tabriz and its blockade were tantamount to what Yazid had done to Imam Hoseyn.

In August 1908, the shah responded that, as the defender of the faith, he would not compromise with apostates. He claimed that all Iranians were against a constitutional system which opposed the faith and the foundations of Shiism. On 13 November 1908, a large gathering was organized at Baqe Shah to discuss the most suitable type of government. In the presence of the shah, princes, notables, merchants and clergy, Nuri proclaimed once again that a constitutional government was incompatible with the *sharia* and presented the shah with a petition to renounce it. The petition was signed by many clerics, including Nuri, Seyyed Abolqasem Emam Jomeh and Seyyed Javad Zahir al-eslam.

The anti-constitutional clergy claimed that Iran's Moslems opposed a consultative assembly as 'it would bring about the destruction of religion ... and of the Islamic law'.[42] The culmination point of the despotic front's dramatic show came on 19 November 1908. Invoking his absolute obedience to Islamic laws and the *olama*'s edict, Mohammad-Ali Shah announced that he had abandoned the idea of parliamentarism as it was contrary to Islam.

Faced with the shah's intransigence and the country's back-peddling to despotism, the key religious sources of authority in Najaf issued a fatwa. They called on the people to rid the country of the shah's despotic rule and announced that the restoration of constitutionalism was a religious obligation incumbent upon all Shii. The Najaf Sources of Imitation were increasingly worried about the threat of a Russian military intervention in Tabriz. Their order to wage holy war (*jihad*) against tyranny and despotism was certainly an important factor in favour of the constitutionalists.

Azarbayjan's Military Response to Despotism

Less than a week after the June shelling of the Majles, Iran had been in the grips of a civil war. While Tehran had acquiesced to despotism, Tabriz took up the mantle of combatting it and held out as the country's hub of anti-despotism. The Tabriz branch of the Social Democrats (*ejtemaiyoun amiyoun*), known for its radical anti-despotism and anti-clericalism, had effectively announced its independence from the shah and taken control of the political and judicial affairs of the province. The eleven-month fight in Tabriz, to keep the flag for independence and freedom flying can be divided into three periods.[43]

The first period, from July to August 1908, was marked by the bravery of Baqer Khan and Sattar Khan whose defence of two districts in Tabriz prevented the city from caving to the royalists (Figure 1.7). Both men were members of the Provincial Association of Azarbayjan's militia. Sattar Khan claimed that he was fighting against despotism under orders from the three Sources of Imitation in Najaf. The royalists, in turn, accused all constitutionalists of being Babis, heretics and enemies of Islam.

The Revolutionary Social Democrats of the Caucasus

The Social Democratic Moslem branch of Transcaucasia sent volunteers, arms, and funds to Tabriz. Heydar Amu oghli, who had fled to Baku on the eve of the coup, returned to Tabriz. Reportedly he was able to exert great influence upon the mojahedin and Sattar Khan himself. (M. Bayat)[44]

The Revolutionary Russo-Iranian Front against Their Despotic Regimes

An estimated 800 Transcaucasian mojahedin reportedly crossed the frontier to join Sattar Khan's forces in Tabriz; another 350 volunteers went to the province of Gilan. The sheer number, in addition to the great store of firearms smuggled into northern Iran by the Russian revolutionaries, alarmed the tsar's envoy in Tehran. (M. Bayat)[45]

The second period of the civil war in Tabriz started around August 1908. During this time, the constitutionalists repelled all the royalist and Cossack forces sent from Tehran, cleansed the city, consolidated their positions and pushed the assailants outside the city. By mid-October 1908, the constitutionalists were fully in control of Tabriz and the royalists were on the run. Liberated Tabriz was safe enough for constitutionalists, such as Taqizadeh and Mohammad-Reza Mosavat, who had fled the country after the coup, to return to Tabriz.

The third period, from February 1909, was marked by the government forces imposing a full blockade on the city, preventing all transportation and food from entering Tabriz. In March 1909, having suffered another defeat, the government forces began negotiations on lifting the siege which was causing considerable hardship.

Russian Designs: Lyakhov in Tehran, Znarsky in Tabriz

That Russia, with the knowledge of the powers, is fighting the Persian revolution with every means at her command, from intrigue to the sending of troops, is a fact. That her policy is to occupy Azerbaijan, is likewise beyond doubt. (V. I. Lenin)[46]

Figure 1.7 The leaders of the Fadai detachments, Baqer Khan and Sattar Khan.
Source: Via Getty Images.

The Russian Occupation

Russian troops numbering some 4,000, under Gen. Znarsky, crossed the frontier, violated the sovereignty of Iran and entered Tabriz on 30 April 1909. Their arrival was a blessing and a curse. They ended the blockade by government forces and allowed desperately needed food to enter the city. Mohammad-Ali Shah's siege of Tabriz had made the invading Russians seem like liberators. The city was now under Russian control. A few days earlier, Howard Baskerville had been killed in battle. The 25-year-old American Princeton graduate had taught at the Presbyterian Memorial School in Tabriz. He had formed and trained a group of militias called the 'salvation army' and had fought along with the constitutionalist militia.[47]

Before Tabriz fell to Russian troops, the heroism of its citizens and their international allies had become a shining beacon of resistance for the rest of Iran. The resistance in Tabriz had allowed for Social Democratic cells to flourish in Rasht. Members of these cells included Mirza Kuchek Khan, Abdolkarim Moez al-soltan, his brother Abdolhoseyn Moez al-soltan and the Armenian Eprem Khan. These constitutionalists formed alliances with the revolutionary Russian Social Democratic Party, the Armenian Social Democrat Henchackian Party, and the Armenian Revolutionary Federation or Dashnaks and received volunteers from these organizations. 'Funds, weapons, and expertise never ceased to flow from Transcaucasia to Gilan.'[48]

On 8 February 1909, Rasht was in the hands of constitutionalists. Less than a month later, some 300 Caucasian revolutionary volunteers were present in the city. Among them were Mensheviks, Bolsheviks, Anarchists, members of the Hemmat Organization, a Moslem-socialist revolutionary group based in Baku (1904/5), Dashnaks and Henchacks.[49]

From 1909, resistance to the despotic forces spread to Anzali, Mashhad, Esfahan, Shiraz and Lar. Once, in January 1909, the Bakhtiyari tribesmen under the leadership of Samsam al-saltaneh (Najafqoli Bakhtiyari), had taken over Esfahan and the town had fallen in the hands of the constitutionalists, other towns followed suit, one by one. This was the first time that the Bakhtiyaris, one of the most powerful and influential Iranian tribes had come to the support of constitutionalists.

In February, Rasht had flipped, followed by Hamedan, Shiraz, Bandar Abbas and Bushehr in March and Mashhad in April. In most of these towns, local assemblies had been established, and Mohammad-Shah had lost his grip on the country. From Rasht and Esfahan, the constitutionalist forces converged on Tehran. Defying warnings by the British and the Russians to abort their advance, the constitutionalist forces hastened towards Tehran.

On 13 July 1909, several thousand constitutionalists entered Tehran, met with 'no serious resistance' and established their headquarters at Baharestan 'the ruined seat of the former parliament'.⁵⁰ The liberating forces were led by Sardar Asad Bakhtiyari (Aliqoli Khan), Sepahdar Tonokaboni (Mohammadvali Khan) and Eprem Khan. Three days later, Mohammad-Ali Shah took refuge at the summer Russian Legation while Liyakhov surrendered to Sardar Asad Bakhtiyari, Samsam al-saltaneh's brother. The fact that the shah felt safer in the Russian legation rather than anywhere else in his own country told the sorry story of his rule.

Two Significant Events Forgotten in the Midst of Civil War

Before Ahmad Shah's ascension to the throne, and amidst the civil war, two events occurred with significant consequences. First, on 26 May 1908, oil gushed some 21 metres into the air at Masjed Soleyman. This was the first important oil find in the Middle East. D'Arcy's investments, explorations and drillings which had produced no serious results for seven years, suddenly became a most lucrative endeavour.

But D'Arcy had sold most of his shares by 1908 to the British Burmah Oil Company. Back in 1905, D'Arcy and Burmah Oil had agreed to create the Concessions Syndicate Ltd to finance their explorations in Iran. In April 1909, the Anglo-Persian Oil Company (APOC) was incorporated and replaced the Concessions Syndicate Ltd. Its shares were sold to 'the public in Glasgow and London (but not Tehran)' and 'bought up in half-an-hour by local investors'.⁵¹

In May 1909, under instructions from the British government and APOC, Maj. Percy Cox, the British consul-general at Bushehr, had approached Sheykh Khazal and reached an agreement with him. Khazal was to find a suitable site for an oil refinery in Abadan and would subsequently assist in the building of a pipeline. The British Foreign Office and APOC now worked in close collaboration and in July 1909, the 'Abadan Agreement' was signed between Sheykh Khazal, APOC and Percy Cox.

Sheykh Khazal was more than a tribal leader. He was the patron of Khuzestan's Arab tribes. He had always enjoyed close relations with the British and was inclined to secede from Iran to establish his own autonomous entity. While the Russians were maintaining Mohammad-Ali Shah's hopeless rule, the British were busy expanding their economic interests by negotiating with local powers.

The second key event was the ominous landing of 100 British Royal Navy soldiers at Bushehr on 10 April 1909. While northern troops under the command of Sepahdar and Eprem Khan were approaching Qazvin, the British moved to impose their authority on their zone of influence and repress the constitutionalist movement of Seyyed Morteza Ahrami-Tangestani, who had taken over Bushehr. The British gunboat was reportedly sent to protect foreigners and trade routes. The Iranian constitutionalists feared that the British had come to stay as part of the 1907 Anglo-Russian partition agreement.

Constitutionalists Back in Power

Immediately after the liberation of Tehran, some 500 constitutionalist notables, warriors and dignitaries formed a supreme assembly and appointed some 25 members to a high commission to govern temporarily. The High Commission's first executive order on the evening of 16 July 1909 was to remove Mohammad-Ali Shah Qajar and appoint Ahmad Shah, his 11-year-old son, as the new king. Mohammad-Ali Shah was given safe passage to Russia. Until Ahmad Shah reached the legal age of 18, Ali-Reza Azod al-molk, head of the Qajar tribe, was named regent.

The High Commission appointed the cabinet, the chief of police, governors of Esfahan, Azarbayjan and Zanjan, issued the order for elections to the second Majles and replaced Seyyed Abolqasem, the Emam Jomeh, with his constitutionalist brother, Seyyed Mohammad. Eprem Khan, an Armenian revolutionary, connected with the revolutionaries in the Caucasus, and one of Tehran's liberators became Tehran's chief of police. When Tonokaboni, the minister of war, objected to Eprem Khan's appointment because of his religion, Sardar Asad defended his nomination.

On 17 July, a revolutionary court composed of eight members, representing the key religious, military and political constitutionalist leaders was formed to try the supporters of despotism and Mohammad-Ali Shah's cohorts. It is said that six of the eight were Freemasons, including the presiding judge, Sheykh Ebrahim Zanjani, who was said to have 'joined the *Réveil de l'Iran* lodge', affiliated with the anti-clerical French Grand Orient Masonry Lodge.[52]

On 30 and 31 July 1909, the revolutionary court sentenced to death Mohammad Khan Sani-Hazrat, one of the leaders of the first attack on the Majles, and Ali-Naqi Mafakher al-molk, governor of Tehran and instrumental in the repression of constitutionalists, and carried out the sentence. Fifteen days after the constitutionalists had taken back Tehran (31 July 1909), Sheykh Fazlollah Nuri, whose role in the attacks on the Majles was clear, was put on trial and executed by hanging before a large crowd.

Sheykh Ebrahim Zanjani, the presiding judge, based his ruling on the 1907 fatwa of the three eminent Najaf jurists, who had pronounced Nuri a corruptor. But Zanjani had put his own spin on the use of the word corruptor by the Najaf jurists. He interpreted the word as 'Corruptor on Earth', which according to the Quran was punishable by death.

'From the interrogations of Sani Hazrat and Mafakher, it became evident that the Sheykh [Nuri] had been the mastermind of all' that had happened during the 15

December 1907 attack on the Majles.[53] By executing a notable and high-ranking *mojtahid*, the constitutionalists settled scores with political and religious despotism. The debate on religious despotism and its relation to political despotism found its echo in the seminal work of Allameh Naini, an enlightened student of Akhund Khorasani and Sheykh Mazandarani.

With the triumph of the constitutionalists, exiled politicians were invited to return to Tehran, the nascent free press resumed its activities, new newspapers appeared, the *anjoman*s regrouped and political parties quickly replaced and absorbed the secret societies. Politically, Iran was at last breathing an air of freedom and liberty, yet political, religious and personal cleavages of all kinds remained. Relations between the pro-Russian Sepahdar Tonokaboni, who assumed the posts of provisional prime minister and minister of war, and the pro-British Sardar Asad Bakhtiyari, who became minister of interior, had begun to sour as they jockeyed for hegemony. The secularists pushed the boundaries of the freedom of the press against the clerical establishment and sometimes religious beliefs.

A week after Nuri's hanging, Seyyed Hasan Habl al-matin, the younger brother of Jamaleddin and the new editor of *Habl al-matin*, was arrested, fined 250 Tomans and imprisoned. His newspaper was banned for 23 months for an article that was deemed anti-Arab and anti-clerical. As well as outmanoeuvring the Russo-British influence, the lingering issue for the constitutionalists was to find a way to reconcile political democratization and economic modernization with traditionalism and what the Shii establishment believed to be Islam.

Meanwhile, the old ruling oligarchy and influential families were finding their way back into positions of power. 'The political and economic power of the old ruling class remained intact.'[54] After the ousting of Mohammad-Ali Shah, the heterogeneous armed liberators of Tehran and defenders of the constitutional cause, *mojahedin*, began to disintegrate. Each armed group had their allegiance to their political or tribal leaders, who in turn had their respective agendas and wished to have the support of their armed men, without their interference.

Most significantly, the central government had serious problems imposing its authority in Tehran and the provinces. In Tehran, some 2,000 armed men of rival militias roamed around the city and sometimes extorted and pillaged. They were accused of 'bullying the populace, taking ransoms, and refusing to follow orders'.[55] The Bakhtiyari *mojahedin* were charged with lewdness: 'they spend day and night singing, playing music and whoring'.[56] Within a month after the establishment of constitutional rule, the central government faced rebellious bands of pro-despotic bandits in Zanjan, Rasht and Ardebil, which were eventually defeated.

In the north, some of these anti-governmental bands were supported by the Russians, who remained well entrenched in Tabriz. The Russian military presence in the north made a mockery of Iran's national sovereignty and independence. By 13

July 1909, 'there were about 4000 Russian troops at Tabriz, 1700 between Rasht and Qazwin, and some 600 more in other places in the North of Persia'.[57] Fearing the breakout of hostilities between Russian troops and the *mojahedin* in Tabriz and the subsequent increase of Russian troops, the government adopted a conciliatory approach. At the insistence of the Russian government, the national heroes, Sattar Khan and Baqer Khan, accompanied by their *mojahedin* left Tabriz and arrived in Tehran on 16 April 1910.

> **Russians in Iran**
>
> Some days ago, at Qazwin, several Russian soldiers, their stomachs surcharged with vodka, spread terror through the streets of the town, scandalizing the inhabitants and maltreating women and children, while a Russian officer, instead of striving to restrain his subordinates, wounded three passers-by, and insulted the police who had intervened. After this noble exploit the soldiers, filled with fury, set fire to a grocer's shop. E. G. Browne)[58]

The 2nd Majles, 15 November 1909–25 December 1911

On 15 November 1909, the 2nd Majles was inaugurated in the presence of Ahmad Shah. The new deputies were no longer representatives of guilds or professions and even though the number of deputies was to be 120, the Majles began work with 61 in attendance. The newly elected deputies were confronted with immense problems. The Treasury was empty, the country was heavily indebted to Britain and Russia and provincial administration was in chaos. Brigands operated freely in southern Iran, rendering the trade routes insecure and Russia continued to despatch soldiers to Iran. The Russians and British were making their presence felt more than ever in their respective zones of influence.

By mid-1910, the deputies were mainly divided into two parties with armed supporters on the outside. The Democrats, successors to the Social Democrats (*Ejtemaiyun amiyun*), were represented by about 20 to 27 deputies. They were mainly journalists, some notables, professionals and clerics familiar with Western ideas. Many of them came from the northern regions and included figures such as Seyyed Hasan Taqizadeh, Mohammad-Ali Tarbiyat, Mohammad-Reza Shirazi, Hoseynqoli Khan Navab and Soleyman Mirza Eskandari. Their supporters outside the Majles were led by Heydar Khan Amuoghlu and Mohammad-Ali Rasulzadeh, who had links with the Social Democrats in Baku. The Democrats had their own newspaper, *Iran no* (New Iran), and their own armed forces called the *garde fateh* (Victorious Guard), numbering some 300.

The Democrats had egalitarian and socialist ideals and believed in land reform and structural social and economic changes. They believed in equality of all, irrespective of religion, race and nationality before the law; freedom of expression, press and association; a strong and centralized state; special attention to women's education; free and obligatory education; and 'the complete separation of politics and religion'.[59] Their foreign policy was based on nationalism and a strong opposition to British and Russian involvement in Iran's politics and economy.

Seyyed Hasan Taqizadeh, the Westernized, secularist and influential deputy in the 1st Majles, had fled Tehran after the Majles was shelled. He returned to Tehran on 6 August 1909 amidst a warm and most popular welcome, while musical bands played in his honour. Until his forced departure on 16 July 1910, after the assassination of Abdollah Behbahani, Taqizadeh remained the undisputed leader of the Democrats and then passed on the baton to Soleyman Mirza Eskandari, the red Qajar prince.

The Social Moderate Party (*ejtemaiyoun etedaliyoun*) or the reformists had some 30 representatives. They included intellectuals, princes, bureaucrats, cabinet ministers, landed aristocrats, tribal leaders, merchants and the clergy. Seyyed Abdollah Behbahani and Mohammad Tabatabai supported the Social Moderates as did Sepahdar Tonokaboni. Some of the prominent deputies of the Social Moderates included Ali-Akbar Dehkhoda, Asadollah Khan Kordestani and Mirza Sadeq Khan Mostashar al-dowleh.

The Social Moderates believed in the principles of equality and justice. They considered themselves realists as distinct from idealists and promoted gradual change with an eye to the existing socio-political conditions and relations. The Social Moderates argued against 'rushed modernization' and revolutionary approaches to change as detrimental to society and promoted political moderation. They were in favour of some degree of political centralization but stood openly against economic centralization. They opposed monopolies, hoarding, lotteries and consumption of alcoholic beverages. In foreign affairs, the Social Moderates sought a rapprochement with other powers. Even though they were committed to the freedom of thought, speech, press and association, they limited it to the prescriptions of religious law.[60]

The Social Moderates had two newspapers, *Ruznamehye Majles* (Parliament's Daily) and *Vaqt* (Time). They had their own armed forces, called Mohy's Guards (*garde Mohy*), numbering some 500. This armed group was formed by Abdolhoseyn Khan Moez al-saltaneh, who received the title of Sardar Mohy because of his role in the liberation of Tehran and was appointed the undersecretary of the Ministry of War. The Social Moderates formed a majority coalition of some 40 members with two smaller parties while the Democrats formed the minority party.

As of February 1911, Iran was experimenting with a multi-party parliamentary system, with the Social Moderates and their allies sitting on the right of the aisle in Parliament and the Democrats on the left. Even though both sides of the isle were committed to reforms in the country, they engaged in lengthy discussions, often delaying decisions at a time when the country faced mounting financial and security problems both internal and external.

> **Iranians and the Trial and Error of Party Politics**
>
> The Persians, however, are a peculiar people, and being totally inexperienced in the technique of democratic forms of government, once the line of political cleavage was established, there quickly developed an intense and bitter rivalry and even personal animosity between the members of the Moderate party . . . and the Democratic party. (M. Shuster)[61]

Seventeen Months of Interminable Crises, July 1910–December 1911

From late May 1910, there was a heightened tension in the air. Sepahdar Tonokaboni, who was both prime minister and minister of interior, moved against the radical and highly critical newspapers. On 26 May 1910, *Irane no* (New Iran), a paper close to the Democrats was shut down and its editor put on trial. It had written an article arguing that *qisas*, or the Islamic Law of Talion was 'incompatible with modern political and philosophical principles'.[62] The debate over the brief of religion, religious laws and the separation of religion and politics permeated within secularist constitutionalists and the Democrats in Majles.

On 30 May 1910, Hasan Khan Amin al-molk, was assassinated at his home. He had been a confidant, informer and partisan of Mohammad-Ali Shah. After the constitutionalist victory, he had allied himself with Sepahdar Tonokaboni and 'became a leading figure in the struggle against the Democrat Party'.[63] The Social Moderates accused Heydar Amuoghlu and the Democrats of his assassination.

Party Rivalries Intensify

From early June, an anti-Democrat front composed of the Social Moderates, Behbahani, Haj Amin al-zarb, Sardar Mohy and Baqer Khan was formed. One of their main demands was the exile of Taqizadeh. They informed the Najaf triumvirate about Taqizadeh's radical policies, accused him of being a Republican and demanded his removal from the Majles. The Democrats viewed these agitations against them as an attempt on the part of Behbahani and the Social Moderates to undermine their power in the Parliament and outside.

The anti-Taqizadeh hysteria reached a new climax when the Najaf religious leaders, Kazem Khorasani and Abdollah Mazandarani, wrote to the Majles and ruled that Taqizadeh's 'outlook was opposed to the Islamicness of the country and the holy *sharia* laws'. In this undated letter written before 8 July 1910, and probably kept secret, the Najaf Sources of Imitation ordered Taqizadeh's dismissal from Parliament and his immediate exile from the country.[64]

Political Assassinations

On 16 July 1910, four masked men entered Abdollah Behbahani's house at night. Two went up to the roof, where he was sitting on his bed surrounded with six of his aides and relatives. The men shot Behbahani dead and escaped. On the next day, some 10,000 gathered around Behbahani's house, the Majles and the Bazaar closed, as Tehran went into shock. A tract dated 20 July 1910 opined that Taqizadeh was responsible for the savagery and promised that the culprits would be punished. Taqizadeh fled the country.

The Social Moderates attributed the assassination to the Democrats. They held Heydar Amuoghlu and Taqizadeh responsible for the assassination. The assassins did belong to Heydar Amuoghlu's militia. Amuoghlu was arrested, held for some forty days in prison and freed without trial. It is said that his connections with the Democrats and Eprem Khan were instrumental in his quick release. Amuoghlu was later ambushed but managed to escape again.

On 31 July 1910, the Social Moderates retaliated. Unable to find Taqizadeh, Ali-Mohammad Khan Tarbiyat and Seyyed Abdolrazzaq were shot and killed at Lalehzar / Mokhber al-dowleh Square. Tarbiyat was Taqizadeh's nephew, and he had been put in charge of creating a unified *mojahedin* force, the National Guard, for a short period in April 1909. Abdolrazzaq was a constitutionalist activist close to the radical wing of the Democrats. The four assailants were 'all commanders of Mohy's Guards'.[65] Sardar Mohy was close to Sepahdar Tonokaboni and the Moderates. The political assassinations and counter-assassinations created an atmosphere of lawlessness, terror and fear.

Disarming the *Mojahedin*

On 11 July 1910, the regent Ali-Reza Azod al-molk, appointed Hasan Mostofi al-mamalek as prime minister. Mostofi al-mamalek was close to the Democrats and his cabinet was committed to putting an end to the lawlessness caused by the armed activities of rival militias. After the July assassinations, the fragile political equilibrium was even more destabilized. On 3 August 1910, the Majles ratified a four-item law to disarm all non-military personnel and close all subversive publications and associations detrimental to public peace.

Eprem Khan, the chief of police, along with pro-Democrat militias of Sardar Asad and Heydar Amuoghlu moved to disarm the armed allies of the Moderates, Sattar Khan, Baqer Khan and Sardar Mohy, gathered at Park Atabak. On 8 August 1910, some 1,000 government forces under the command of Eprem Khan, armed with a few cannon and machine guns surrounded some 300 *mojahedin* of Sattar-Baqer-Mohy.

This was a bleak and bitter moment in the history of the constitutional movement. A seven-hour war broke out between old comrades-in-arms, *mojahedin*, costitutionalist heroes and anti-despotic commanders who had liberated Tehran. Baqer Khan surrendered and Sattar Khan was wounded. The casualties on both sides were between 20 and 25.

Public reaction to the campaign of disarmament was negative. 'Protesting the Park Atabak incident, Tehran's bazaar shut down for five days and people blamed the government.'[66] Humiliating Sattar Khan and Baqer Khan and neutralizing their *mojahedin* had deprived Tabriz of its potential defensive shield against Russian intransigence.

The Conservative Backlash and Mohammad-Ali Shah's Attempted Return

The 90-year-old regent, Azod al-molk, died on 22 September 1910 and the Majles replaced him with Naser al-molk. This appointment turned the tide against the Democrats. On his return to Iran from Europe, Naser al-molk appointed Sepahdar Tonokaboni as his prime minister. Tonokaboni was one of the biggest landowners of northern Iran, a pro-Russian, and an anti-Democrat politico-military figure. 'Sepahdar was chosen to be the new prime minister, with Anglo-Russian full support.'[67]

While introducing his government to the Majles on Saturday, 11 March 1911, Tonokaboni pointed out the killings and lawlessness in the capital, the chaos in the provinces and the abuse of freedoms by the press and asked for 'full powers'. The new government's first task was to 'eliminate corruption and terrorism' and subsequently to prevent the press from abusing its freedoms.[68] Tonokaboni, presented himself as the iron-fisted politician who was going to reinstate order and cleanse the country of extremist, terrorist elements.

Both Tonokaboni and Naser al-molk considered the Democrats as extremists and terrorists responsible for the country's misfortunes. On 29 March 1911, Heydar Amuoghlu and later Mohammad-Amin Rasulzadeh, the editor of the Democrat's paper *New Iran*, were forced into exile. Just as the Democrats had eliminated the *mojahedin* of Sattar-Baqer-Mohy and the Moderates, now it was the turn of the Moderates to dismantle the *mojahedin* of Heydar Amuoghlu and Yar-Mohammad Kermanshahi.

Since January/February 1911, the deposed Mohammad-Ali Shah and his two brothers, Shoao al-Salṭanah and Salar al-dowleh, had been plotting in Vienna to return to power. On 21 May 1911, Salar al-dowleh conquered Sanandaj in the name of his deposed brother and entered Kermanshah with some 2,000 troops on 28 July 1911. In the meantime, Mohammad-Ali Shah's well-armed troops had entered Torkaman Sahra. The path to the old despot's successful come-back was paved. Starting from 20 July, Mohammad-Ali Shah's troops invaded Gorgan, Babol and Shahrud in the north and were marching towards Tehran.

The Russians hoped that with the return of Mohammad-Ali Shah, they would be able to defeat the constitutionalist movement and regain their weakened hold on the country. Tonokaboni's close ties to the Russians were well known, 'given his debt to the Russian Bank and the location of his estates in the Russian Zone'.[69] Tonokaboni was accused of collaboration with the deposed Mohammad-Ali Shah. On 25 July 1911, the Majles dismissed him and appointed Samsam al-saltaneh prime minister.

To thwart a despotic come back, Samsam al-salteneh and Eprem Khan, Iran's chief of police, took matters into their own hands. They arrested a few well-known anti-constitutionalists, compelling some sixty influential pro-Russian politicians to take refuge in the Russian Legation. The remnants of the *mojahedin* reconvened and the estranged Sardar Mohy of the Moderates and Yar Mohammad Kermanshahi of the Democrats joined forces again against the return of despotism.

On 27 September, after a battle that lasted six full weeks, government troops declared victory over Mohammad-Ali Shah's army. With the defeat of Mohammad-Ali, Russia adopted an even more aggressive posture towards Iran. 'Their consulates in Tabriz, Rasht, Mashhad and Astarabad, unabashedly intervened in local affairs.'[70]

While the Russians pursed their own objectives, the British were discreetly but in tandem following theirs. In the provinces, tribal elements, most likely prodded by the British, had started taking control of Lorestan, Azarbayjan and Khorasan. They withheld taxes and effectively defied the weakened central government. The breakdown in security in the south had led to the further deployment of British forces. 'On October 27 the first detachment of Indian troops landed in Bushehr.'[71] The British excuse was that the Iranian government failed to secure the southern trade routes. The country was disintegrating under domestic problems and foreign intrigues.

The Shuster Affair and the End of Iran's Independence

To put the country's finances in order, the Majles hired the American Morgan Shuster as a financial expert. Shuster and his three assistants arrived in Iran on 12 May 1911. The immediate brief of the American team was to reorganize the finances of the country in which no previous record of receipts and expenditures existed, a national budget was wanting and the Treasury had a deficit of some $400,000. Shuster was also faced with the two different sets of Iranian debts to Russia and Britain. The Majles had appointed Shuster as treasurer-general.

> ### Shuster's View of Iran
> Imagine, if you will, a fast decaying government amid whose tottering ruins a heterogeneous collection of Belgian customs officers, Italian gendarmes, German artillery sergeants, French savants, doctors, professors and councilors of state, Austrian military instructors, English bank clerks, Turkish and Armenian courtiers, and last, but not least, a goodly sprinkling of Russian Cossack officers, tutors and drill instructors all go through their daily task of giving the Imperial Persian Government a strong shove toward bankruptcy, with a sly side push in the direction of their own particular political or personal interests. (M. Shuster)[72]

Shuster's proposed reforms would bring him into direct conflict with the old Qajar bureaucracy, the big landowners, the British and most importantly, the Russians. Deep vested interests and widespread corruption opposed his plans for a total reorganization of the finances, including a budget for each ministry. Troubles began when Shuster decided to create 'a special gendarmerie force' which would operate under his direct command. It was to 'assist and cooperate with the civilian officers of the Treasury in the collection of the different kinds of taxes throughout the Empire'.[73]

Shuster sped up his efforts in July by seeking the employment of Capt. C. E. Stokes, a British subject, to command and train what would be a 12,000-strong force, in charge of collecting the revenues due to the government throughout the land. Shuster's reforms were to the benefit of the whole country and threatened the Russian and British hold on their respective zones of influence.

On 19 August 1911, while war was raging between government troops and the former Shah's troops, Russia issued a threat: should the Persian government engage Capt. Stokes and his men, Russia 'would reserve to itself the right to take such measures as it might judge to be necessary for the safeguarding of its interests in the

North of Persia'.[74] The British sided with the belligerent Russian position and both made it clear that, despite the letter of the Anglo-Russian Convention, neither country cared to respect Iran's independence and integrity.

On 4 October 1911, the government ordered Shuster to confiscate the estates of insurgent princes Shoa al-saltaneh and Salar al-dowleh, who had tried to bring back the former shah. When Shuster's Treasury Gendarmes went to take over Shoa al-saltaneh's property in Mansuriyeh, Dowlatabad and Mansurabad, they clashed with Russian Cossacks who were protecting the property but succeeded in taking over the said property. On 2 November, embarrassed and humiliated by the tenacity of Shuster's forces, the Russians issued the first of a string of ultimatums, with the intention of occupying Iran. The Russian consul-general demanded the return of Shoa al-saltaneh's property and an apology for having 'insulted' Russian consular officers during the clashes over the property.

From this date onwards, the cycle of Shuster's resistance to the illegal and bullying acts of Russian interventionism endeared him to the people and the Majles. Both the Democrats and the Moderates in the Majles supported his reforms. Yet, his honesty and sense of Iranian nationalism also earned him the enmity of the Russians and the British, as well as that of local influential landowners and corrupt government officials. Shuster succeeded in extracting the just taxes that Ala al-dowleh, a member of the royal family, had first refused to pay. The Iranian government, however, began to fear that Shuster's relentless defence of Iranian rights against Russia and the Majles' refusal to heed Russian demands, would lead to a Russian invasion.

Russia Defeats Constitutionalism and Annexes Its Zone of Influence

On 18 November, Russia broke diplomatic relations over Iranian refusal to heed the first ultimatum. By November, there were some 4,000 Russian troops in Iran. The last Russian ultimatum, made on 29 November, had demanded Shuster's dismissal, guarantees that Iran would obtain the satisfaction of Russia and Britain before it hired foreign subjects, and indemnity for the expenses incurred by dispatching Russian troops. Russia had given the Iranian government forty-eight hours to comply or else it would invade Tehran. Russian belligerence had momentarily united all waring domestic parties and militias.

The Majles refused the ultimatum on 30 November, setting off widespread anti-Russian demonstrations. There was a spree of assassinations against anti-constitutionalist politicians, who were suspected of collusion with the former Shah. Meanwhile some 4,000 Russian troops were moved to Qazvin, only 150 kilometres north-west of Tehran. While Iran was resisting Russian annexation, troops of the despotic former Shah were making another bid in Kermanshah, Shahroud, Damqan and even Mashhad, all of them with the support of the Russians.

Faced with the imminent occupation of Tehran, the government of Samsam al-saltaneh, supported by Eprem Khan, decided to accept the terms of the Russian ultimatum, dissolve the Majles and give full powers to the government. During the last session of the 2nd Majles on Tuesday, 19 December 1911, it refused to empower the government to deal with the Russian ultimatum. Sheykh Mohammad Khiyabani, the constitutionalist radical, had passionately defended Shuster in the name of nationalism and Islam and equated him with reform and independence of Iran.[75]

In Praise of the 2nd Majles

The Medjlis was the only permanent check in the governmental fabric on the reactionary tendencies of numbers of the grandees and cabinet officials, as well as on corruption among many Persian officials of all ranks. (M. Shuster)[76]

The Second Coup against the Majles, 1911

The Medjlis stood for an honest and progressive administration of Persia's affairs. On the day that this body was destroyed, with the connivance of the foreign powers, the last hope of honest or representative government in Persia disappeared. (M. Shuster)[77]

On 25 December 1911, under orders from Naser al-Molk, Eprem Khan, the staunch defender of constitutionalism, ordered the deputies to evacuate the Majles before padlocking it. The government was trying to prevent further Russian advances. 'Meanwhile thousands of Russian troops, with Cossacks and artillery, were pouring into Northern Persia, from Tiflis and Julfa by land and from Baku across the Caspian to the Persian port of Enzeli, whence they took up their 220-mile march over the Elburz mountains towards Kasvin [Qazvin] and Teheran.'[78]

In Tabriz and Gilan, nationalist rebellions against the occupying Russian forces were forcefully repressed and the Russian Cossacks began an unprecedented massacre of civilians, women and children as well as political and military constitutionalists. 'On Christmas Day arrived sinister rumours of frightful bloodshed both at Tabriz and Resht, with open threats on the part of the Russian Government of field court martials and wholesale executions.'[79]

The life of the 2nd Majles, along with Iran's baby steps towards constitutional democracy and independence came to an end on 25 December 1911. On the first day of 1912, the Russian flag was hoisted over government buildings in Tabriz. After the Russian occupation of Iran, Parliament remained closed for three years and power was concentrated in the hands of the executive, with Naser al-molk at its apex. 'Iranian society entered a period known as "Naser al-molk's dictatorship."'[80]

Factual and Analytical Questions

1. Golestan and Torkamanchay treaties: When, what, why and consequences?
2. Reuter concession: When, what, why and consequences?
3. What were Nasereddin Shah's three disastrous political and financial decisions ratcheting up Russo-British involvement in Iran (1872–89)?
4. The shah who granted a national consultative parliament: Who, when and why?
5. Who were the leading constitutionalist clerics in Tehran and Najaf?
6. The Anglo-Russia Convention of 1907: Why, impact and consequences?
7. The Short/Lesser Despotism: When, what led to it, why and consequences?
8. Democrats and Moderates in the 2nd Majles: What did they stand for, what was their social base, how did they differ?
9. Who were the *mojahedin*? Homogeneous or heterogeneous? What led to disarming them and what were its consequences?
10. What was the role of the secret associations (*anjoman*s)?

Seminar Questions

1. What was the impact of the search for markets and scramble for colonies by Western powers on Iran (Persia) in the nineteenth century?
2. What were the causes and consequences of Iran's indebtedness during the reigns of Nasereddin and Mozaffareddin Shah?
3. What were the causes and objectives of the Constitutional Revolution?
4. What role did the clergy play in the Constitutional Revolution?
5. The *mojahedin*: the solution or the problem of the constitutionalist movement?

Discussion Questions

1. Threatened by the colonial aspirations of Britain and Russia, Persia was doomed to become a semi-colony?

2 The political and economic underdevelopment of Persia was primarily the consequence of political despotism and religious fanaticism.
3 Had Atabak not been assassinated and an attempt not made on Mohammad-Ali Shah's life, the shah would not have shelled the Majles.
4 Was Azarbayjan the protector of Iran's constitutionalism?
5 Morgan Shuster: Saviour or exterminator of Iran's independence?
6 Was Iran an occupied semi-colony by January 1912?

Glossary

Azali Babis Mirza Yahya Nuri (sobhe azal) was born in 1830. His followers considered him as the successor to Seyyed Mohammad-Ali Shirazi, known as the Bab. Yahya became the leader of Azali Babis, while his older brother Mirza Hoseyn-Ali Nuri, later became Bahaollah, the founder of the Bahai religion. Yahya did not have a clerical background but had visitations and theophanies.

bast A religiously sanctioned political tradition, where people with grievances seek protection in a mosque or a neutral space while they negotiate with the government, knowing that they are immune from assault and arrest. This is a non-violent form of protest with participants usually leaving their sanctuary once satisfaction is received.

Bazaari Bazaar is a permanent traditional and usually covered marketplace. The grand bazaar of Tehran and other urban centres in are the homes to various retail and wholesale shops and stands, grouped by specific crafts. This was the hub of commerce and the heart of cities. The bazaar represented money, power and religious piety. Bazaars were usually home to the principal mosques in a city. *Bazaari* is a catchall term referring to all of those social classes working in the bazaar, from the big merchants (*tojjar*) and the master craftsmen (*ostad/usta*) to the apprentices (*shagerd*) and footboys (*pado*). It could connote conservatism as well as political and religious consciousness. The bazaar represented a solid source of financial revenue for the state and as such constituted an important barometer of socio-political satisfaction with the state and government. When the bazaar protested, governments usually took heed. The bazaar had traditional ties with the clergy and political activists and played a crucial role in the constitutional movement, oil-nationalization movement and the 1979 fall of the Pahlavi dynasty.

fatwa This is an authoritative and legal ruling by a qualified religious jurist (*mojtahed*) fully knowledgeable in Islamic jurisprudence (*fiqh*). It is binding on believers. A fatwa is usually in response to a question and reflects the opinion of the jurist based on his research into the sources of Islamic jurisprudence.

Habl al-matin The Strong Cord, a most influential constitutionalist newspaper, started publication in Calcutta on 19 December 1893. Its editor was Seyyed Jalaleddin Moayyed al-Eslam Kashani. This was a liberal, reformist, anti-despotic, nationalist and anti-Russian newspaper. It had Pan-Islamist proclivities and its name was the Persian translation of *Al-Urwah al-Wuthqa*, published by Seyyed Jamaleddin Afghani and Mohammad Abduh in March 1884.

mashrueh A constitutional system based on religious laws or the *sharia* and dismissing man-made laws. Fazlollah Nuri was the principal proponent of this constitutional system and his supporters came to be known as champions of religious law or *mashrueh khahan*.

mashruteh A constitutional system, limiting or constraining the power of the monarch and based on a mixture of man-made and religious laws. In this system the legitimacy of laws was primarily, but not entirely rooted in the will of the people. The champions of this constitutional system came to be known as *mashruteh khahan*.

mojahedin Those who engage in struggle (*jehad*). The holy warriors, *mojahedin*, is a term with religious connotations. The Quran praises the *mojahedin*, or those who strive with their life in His cause, in Sura Al-Nisa, Aya 95. *Mojahedin*, in the context of the Constitutional Revolution generally referred to active supporters of the Constitution and specifically to its armed defenders.

most-favoured-nation status This is a reciprocal commercial agreement providing both sides with best trade conditions, such as low tariff rates and minimum trade barriers. Politically, it confirms an equal standing between the countries involved.

Seyyed Jamaleddin Asadabadi (Afghani) Born in 1838/9, was a pioneer of Islamic revivalism as a political tool against European imperialism. He is credited as the founder of the pan-Islamic movement. Afghani was a modernist and rationalist cleric. Politically he was a globe-trotting internationalist who believed in revolution when reform was no longer possible to overthrow despotism.

sharia Literally means the well-trodden path to water. *Sharia* is the path to reach proximity to God and refers to the totality of Islamic laws, while *fiqh* or Islamic jurisprudence is the human understanding of divine laws. To derive Islamic law, Islamic jurists rely on four sources: the Quran, the tradition of the prophet (*sunnat/hadith*), consensus (*ijma*) and analogy (*qiyas*) for the Sunnis and reason (*aql*) for the Shii.

Sheykh Kazem Rashti Born between 1784 and 1799, he had dreams and visions of Shii religious figures. He became a student and follower of Sheykh Ahmad Ehsai, the founder of the mystical Sheykhi school (Sheykhiyeh), which is considered as the origin of Babism and Bahaism. Rashti believed that the Twelfth Imam, who was in occultation, was in the world and he encouraged his followers to seek him out.

Shii Moslems follow the two main schools of belief, the Sunnis and Shiis. Each possess their own sub-schools. Both schools share the core fundaments of monotheism, the prophethood of Mohammad and the day of resurrection. The Shiis believe that the Prophet intended his successor to be Ali, from his household. They believe in the Twelve Imams, the offsprings of Ali, as successors to the Prophet and hold that the Twelfth Imam, is in occultation and will appear. They also believe in the justice of God.

Sources of Imitation (*maraje taqlid*) Plural for *marja taqlid* or Source of Imitation. For the Shii, the most qualified Islamic jurists, who have written their thesis on Islamic practices in the realms of worship, family, commercial and penal activities become religious leaders of their community. Believers follow the rulings of one such qualified jurist to remain on the rightful religious path and find proximity to God.

Tanzimat reforms Tanzimat in Turkish means 'reorganization'. These reforms promulgated in the Ottoman Empire in 1839–76, were to modernize and secularize the traditional and religious system. The reforms included legal, economic and political changes in tune with European commercial, criminal and civil laws. It guaranteed security of life, property and dignity to all, regardless of their religion. The reforms were crowned with the first Ottoman Parliament in 1876.

2

A State Made Dysfunctional, 1912–21

Chapter Outline

Facing Foreign Invasion	67
Fifteen Months of Strict Neutrality, 1 August 1914–14 November 1915	73
Two Governments and a Shah	79
Governments in Tehran during the Last Two Years of the War	81
British Forces in Iran	87
Mirza Kuchek Khan Jangali's Challenge	89
Famine, Influenza and Cholera	92
The Post-War British Design for Iran	94
The Background to the 1921 Coup	99
The Perfectly Coordinated Coup	110
Glossary	114

Facing Foreign Invasion

Besieged by Russia and Britain, Iranians developed a sense of peoplehood, nationhood and concern for the homeland. Russo-British complicity against Iranian democracy and independence caused incessant humiliations and reinforced Iran's nascent sense of nationalism. Iranians traced their national identity to their geographical location, their common history, religion and quest for a constitutional monarchy.

Iran's constitutionalist-nationalist experience had created its own heroes and leaders, as well as a newfound respect for their defence of Iran's national sovereignty, irrespective of social class, religion and ethnicity. Foreigners, such as Baskerville and

Shuster who strove for Iran's welfare, were viewed as national heroes while Iranian collaborators working for the benefit of foreigners were viewed as Iranian only in name.

Nationalism implied protecting the independence of the country from foreign aggression (national sovereignty) and safeguarding the rule of the people by the people from its internal opponents (popular sovereignty). Throughout the nineteenth century, Russia and Britain had advanced their national interests through Iranian politicians and leaders, sometimes transparently and sometimes opaquely. A salient feature of colonies and semi-colonies lies in binary political leadership. Politicians split between those who support popular and national sovereignty and those who privilege the interest of foreigners at the cost of their own national interests. Nationalist politicians are distrustful of foreign political and economic deals not favourable to the motherland and disdainful towards those who wish to silence or manipulate the will of the people by derailing the constitutional process.

Mutually beneficial political and economic deals have a give-and-take element in them. Only deals forcefully imposed by a crushingly strong party over a very weak party can be non-reciprocal and one-sided. The unequal balance of military and economic power between Iran and the Russo-British pair, facilitated the imposition of unfair treaties, with all gains accruing to the stronger parties. The only safeguard against such politico-economic foreign encroachments is the protest movement of the people targeting both the foreign intervening powers and their own collaborating governments.

A whole array of Iranian politicians and leaders did greater service to foreign powers than their own country and without consent of Parliament. They argued that the political and economic concessions they advanced were done in the spirit of guaranteeing Iran's national sovereignty. Thus appeared the Iranian notion of politicians being either servants and servitors (*khadem*) or traitors (*khaen*) to the people's cause.

Iran between Partial and Full Invasion, 1912–1914

The 1907 Anglo-Russian Convention almost sealed the fate of Iran's quest for independence and constitutionalism. Forces of reaction and enemies of constitutionalism had returned. Closing the second Majles and disrupting Iran's constitutional experience nearly ended the hope of national and popular sovereignty. With the Majles dissolved, power in Tehran was in the hands of Naser al-molk, the regent, who repressed Democrats and nationalists, sent them into exile and closed down their papers.

On 10 March 1912, the former shah, Mohammad-Ali Qajar, retreated to Russia after a year-long attempt to regain his throne. On 29 March 1911, the Russians took vengeance on the holy city of Mashhad. Claiming that the lives of their subjects were in danger, their guns opened fire on the Shrine of Imam Reza, killing and wounding innocent pilgrims and passers-by. The reprehensible brutality of Russians in Mashhad further intensified the Iranian dislike of the invading forces.

During May 1912, government forces engaged in a bitter struggle in Kermanshah with Salar al-dowleh, Mohammad-Ali's brother who claimed the throne. On 19 May 1912, Eprem Khan lost his life during a final and successful battle against Salar al-dowleh's army. The slain 40-year-old Armenian military commander and chief of national police who had valiantly served the constitutionalist cause was given a hero's burial in Tehran.

Meanwhile in the neutral zone, lawlessness prevailed. The famous warlord and brigand, Nayeb Hoseyn Kashi, and his sons raided and pillaged villages between Yazd and Kerman, taking women and children prisoners. On 11 September 1912, some 2,000 mounted Bakhtiyari troops sent by the central government from Esfahan to put an end to Nayeb Hoseyn Kashi's activities, failed in their mission. From the summer of 1913, the gendarmes were in continuous battle with provincial brigands and unruly tribes in Lorestan and Fars. The central government was unable to exert its authority even in the provinces unoccupied by foreign forces.

In dark hours, and under pressure, Iran extended more economic concessions to the two imperialist powers. On 6 February 1913, and in the absence of the Majles, Ala al-saltaneh's government gave Russia the right to build a railway from Julfa to Tabriz, and three days later, the British Syndicate was permitted to build a railway between Mohammareh (Khorramshahr) and Khoramabad in Lorestan. Ala al-saltaneh's government had come to power at the behest of the British and with Russian consent. His minister of interior, Abdolmajid Ayn al-dowleh, had been 'imposed on him by the Russians'.[1]

In the north, Russian troops caused havoc in the occupied territories of Tabriz, Rasht and Anzali. Russians had appointed their own Iranian operatives as governors and made headways into the neutral zone. In the south, insecurity reigned on the roads, with raids on commercial caravans. On 23 August 1913, the British complained strongly about attacks on unsafe southern routes, leading to the pillage of British and Indian merchants. At this time, Britain maintained control in its zone of influence primarily through the tribes financially and politically beholden to it. Sheykh Khazal, the Bakhtiyaris and the Qashqais each had their own separate agreements and understandings with the British. These understandings and alliances would go through considerable alteration before the war's end.

Iran's Initial Response to the First World War

On 21 July 1914, at the age of 15, and before having reached the legal age of 18, Ahmad Shah was coronated and assumed his royal responsibilities (Figure 2.1).[2] Eleven days later, on 1 August 1914, Germany declared war on Russia and within a

Figure 2.1 Ahmad Shah. *Source: Wikimedia Commons.*

week the First World War had begun. Even though Iranians referred to it as the 'European War', it immediately knocked on their door.

Iran's attempt to guard itself from being drawn into the war was doomed in advance. When war broke out in Europe, Azarbayjan was under Russian military occupation and the south was a British zone of influence. The presence of Allied Powers on its soil compromised Iran's hope for neutrality. On 30 September 1914, Asim Bey, the Ottoman ambassador to Iran, reminded Ala al-saltaneh, the Iranian foreign minister, that Russian military presence violated Iran's neutrality and constituted a threat to the Ottomans. Only if the Russians were to withdraw their forces, would the Ottomans respect Iran's neutrality. On 6 October 1914, Russia officially refused to evacuate its forces and Iran prepared for the worse.

As a last-ditch effort, on 1 November 1914, Ahmad Shah issued a royal edict declaring Iran's neutrality. Naively and helplessly, the shah assured the warring parties of Iran's 'friendly relations' with each, hoping that his promise would keep the belligerent parties off the Iranian soil. However, Iran did not possess the military power to enforce its policy of neutrality. Two weeks after the proclamation of Iran's neutrality, on 15 November, 10,000 Turkish soldiers entered Iran and pushed towards Russian fortifications in Khoy, north-east of Iran.

This first Ottoman encroachments was responded to by a note of 'protest' from the Iranian Foreign Ministry. This too was the first of many such notes, demonstrating the central government's military and political impotence. The First World War exposed Iran's military and political inferiority not only in respect to Europe, but also to the Muslim **Sublime Porte**.

On 4 January 1915, Ottoman troops occupied Urumiyeh, and some three weeks later, they clashed with Russian troops in Tabriz and Urumiyeh. The fate of Russo-Ottoman fighting in Iran swung like a pendulum from one side to the other until the Dilmaqan Battle of 15 April 1915, after which the united Russian and Armenian troops defeated and chased out the Ottoman troops from northern Iran.

On 26 January 1915, the Ottomans opened a new front in the south, threatening British oil installations. Aided by Iranian tribal forces, the Turks raided Ahvaz from Amara. Sheykh Khazal and the Bakhtiyaris, traditional allies of the British and protectors of the oil fields and pipelines, shirked their responsibility. They were inclined towards the advancing Turkish forces and even disrupted the oil flow. On 3 March 1915, British troops dispatched to Ahvaz to protect the oil installations were heavily defeated. In April 1915, the British Admiralty panicked about the safety of oil flow from Iran's southern fields. On 22 May, British forces advanced on the rivers of Karun and Karkheh, secured the resumption of oil flow and began reparations on the pipelines.

Iran's Chemistry with the Belligerent Powers

Russia and Britain had a political and military advantage in Iran. Aside from a military presence, each had their own respective network of functionaries, protégés and Iranian political collaborators reaching high up into the Iranian government. Both countries had also important financial strangleholds on the country through their respective banks. Geographically speaking, the Russians shared a border in the north and felt as though Iran was their backyard, while for the British, Iran was of great geopolitical interest as a crucial buffer shielding India from potential Russian designs. The 1907 Russo-British Convention was supposed to end the costly rivalry of the two countries in Iran.

The discovery of oil, the subsequent construction of a 220-kilometres pipeline from Masjed Soleyman to Abadan and the completion of the Abadan oil refinery in August 1912 made controlling Iran indispensable to Britain. Right before the outbreak of the war, the British Royal Admiralty at the behest of First Lord of the Admiralty Winston Churchill had switched from coal to oil. By June 1914, oilless Britain had secured its source of supply by acquiring 51 per cent of the private Anglo-Persian Oil Company. When the war broke out, Britain was heavily dependent on Iranian oil and therefore most concerned with the security of Iran's southern oilfields.

Despite their firm implantation on Iranian soil, the Allied Powers suffered from a major setback in establishing their dominion. Their presence and meddling were deeply resented by Iranians. What the Germans lacked in terms of a historical foothold and strong ties with Iranian politicians, notables and clergy, was made up by Iranian goodwill and trust towards them. The German model of development, industrialization, militarization and centralized administration appealed to Iranians. Germany's historically non-aggressive and non-exploitative foreign policy towards Iran, in addition to Kaiser Wilhelm II's proclaimed love for Islam, made him and his country a darling of the people. 'Whether the hatred towards Russia and Britain and the attraction for Germany made sense or not, it was prevalent.'[3]

Intellectuals, *bazaaris*, Democrats, Moderates, anti-colonialists and nationalists who had long loathed Russian and British presence in Iran saw Germany as a liberating force. For devout Iranian Muslims, the Kaiser, affectionately referred to as **haji** Wilhelm, was a Muslim king. The widescale and effective German propaganda machine played an important role in attracting nationalist Iranians to their cause. Just as T. E. Lawrence was to mobilize the Arabs to obtain their independence from the ruling Ottomans, foment revolt and open an anti-Ottoman front behind their lines, the Germans had their own anti-British plans in the Middle East.

German agents, fluent in Persian, Turkish and Arabic and familiar with the terrain and the people's culture and ways of life, were commissioned to draw Iran into the war on the German side and foster insurrection in Afghanistan and the British Raj. Wilhelm Wassmuss, Oskar von Niedermayer, Max Otto Schuenemann and Werner Otto von Hentig were German agents instructed to incite rebellion in Iran and Afghanistan against Britain. None of them became as famous and as effective as Wassmuss, 'the most successful German agent in Persia', who stirred up considerable amounts of trouble against the British.[4]

As soon as the war began, Radolf von Kardorff, the German chargé d'affaires, successfully attracted the nationalist Iranian press to the Central Powers. Von Kardorff sent emissaries to the provinces and the tribes to preach Germany's friendship towards Iran and attended Shii mourning ceremonies at the house of Iranian notables. On 11 November 1914, a fatwa was issued by Constantinople's Grand Mufti Urguplu Hayri, ordering Muslims to wage jihad against the Allied Powers, thus strengthening German hands in Muslim lands.

In early January 1915, at Hasan Taqizadeh's behest, young Iranian nationalists converged on Berlin from Cambridge, Paris and Istanbul. Taqizadeh had been invited by German officials and had travelled from the US to form a resistance movement against Russian and British presence in Iran. The group known as the Berlin Circle, financed by Germany, was composed of outstanding figures such as Hoseyn Kazemzadeh Iranshahr, Ebrahim Purdavud, Mirza Mohammad Khan Qazvini and Mohammad-Ali Jamalzadeh. On 24 January 1916, *Kaveh*, the mouthpiece of young Germanophile, anti-colonial and nationalist Iranians published its first issue. The responsibility of Iranians, Taqizadeh believed, was to mobilize their countrymen to throw in their lot with the Central Powers, assure Iran's independence and take vengeance on Iran's enemies, Russia and Britain.

As much as the Germans were popular with Iranians, the Turks were looked upon with suspicion. The old Sunni–Shii cleavage, animosity between Ottomans and

Persians and the growing influence of Pan-Turkism among Ottoman politicians, especially Enver Pasha, around 1911, raised serious concerns about Turkish irredentist designs. The initial Ottoman incursions in Iran and their mistreatment of the population had exasperated the initial misgivings and added to the popular antipathy towards the invading Turkish forces.

Fifteen Months of Strict Neutrality, 1 August 1914–14 November 1915

Iran's official handling of the war was a function of the military presence and threat of Russia and subsequently Britain. Throughout the war, the central government was reacting to successive crises over which it had no control. In the absence of a viable army and sound finances, central governments possessed no effective authority especially in the provinces, which were either under foreign occupation or in defiance of Tehran. The alarming turnover in governments and the inability of appointed prime ministers to form a government was rooted in their political and executive impotence in the face of invading powers. The durability of governments, at this time, was primarily a function of their degree of loyalty to Russia and Britain.

For some fifteen months, from 1 August 1914 to 14 November 1915, Iran adhered to a policy of 'strict neutrality', even though Iranian politicians had chosen their respective camps. During this period, the young shah acted as a constitutional and nationalist leader. The Iranian Parliament was in session and could counter and even ouster governments which were leaning towards the Allied Powers. Newspapers were playing an active role in domestic and international politics. Even though foreign armies were roaming in different parts of the country, none were threatening the capital. Under exceptionally constrained circumstances, Iranian politicians and deputies in general displayed a united front against the belligerent forces intent on forcing or cajoling Iran to enter the war on their side.

The 3rd Majles

Almost three years after the second Majles was forcefully interrupted, the 3rd Majles began work on 5 December 1914 with 68 deputies. Unlike the constraining regulations of the two previous elections, candidates did not face any financial or educational conditions for elections and therefore the composition of the Majles was more diverse. However, in comparison with the deputies to the 2nd Majles, the number of landowners and clerics had increased, while the number of merchants decreased and civil servants remained constant.

The Parliament was composed of four major political groups. Mirza Soleyman Eskandari headed the Democrat Party, and Mirza Mohammad-Sadeq Tabatabai led the Moderate Party (old Social Moderates). Two new factions came to play a decisive role in the Majles. The newly constituted Religious Group (*heyate elmiyyeh*), primarily composed of clerics and headed by Seyyed Hasan Modarres, and the Independents, with their swing vote, had no official leadership figure. Irrespective of their political stance and disagreements on domestic policies, the deputies were, by and large, nationalists and constitutionalists who opposed Russian and British presence on Iranian soil. The Majles became a powerful hub of patriotism and an impediment to Russian and British designs in Iran.

The relation between the shah and Parliament during the 3rd Majles displayed political maturity and a healthy transition to a constitutional monarchy. Every time prime ministers needed to be appointed, Ahmad Shah asked Parliament for its preference. Once the deputies decided on their choice, the shah appointed that person. This procedure defined the shah's role as a reigning and not a ruling monarch.

Even before its inauguration, Britain and, in particular, Russia had been hostile to the resumption of parliamentary activities. The Allied Powers in Iran were aware of their negative image among the population. They knew that even if they could come to terms with the executive, the people's representatives would resist compromising Iran's national interest. Russia and Britain, therefore, pressured the executive to close the Majles. The Germans, on their part, befriended the Democrat and the Moderate deputies in the Majles. The alliance between the Democrats and the Moderates in the Majles delighted the Germans and infuriated Russia and Britain.

For the next eleven months, both the shah and the 3rd Majles stood their ground as much as they could against Russian and British opposition by objecting to the violation of their neutrality and refusing imposed nominations. On 2 March 1915, during its 14th session, Haj Ez al-mamalek Ardalan, the deputy from Kermanshah, objected to the violation of Iran's neutrality and chastised the deputies for their silence and inaction to propose a solution. Although, committed to respecting Iran's neutrality, the deputies avoided attacking or even mentioning the name of the belligerent powers on Iranian soil during their public sessions. The deputies fought their real battles in closed private sessions for which there were no minutes.

Iranian Governments, the Majles and the Belligerent Powers

Soon after the First World War broke out on 18 August 1914, Hasan Mostowfi al-mamalek replaced Ala al-saltaneh as prime minister. Mostowfi al-mamalek was known for his political independence, patriotism and moral integrity. Russia considered him as pro-German and was displeased with his appointment. The British were unhappy with Mostowfi al-mamalek because he had not appointed Abdolhoseyn Farmanfarma and Hasan Vosug al-dowleh to his cabinet. In line with the position of the Majles, Mostowfi al-mamalek ascribed to a strict neutrality policy, and in November 1914, he requested that the press 'respect Iran's neutral status'. Under pressure from Russia and Britain to abandon his policy of strict neutrality, Moswtofi al-mamalek resigned (Figure 2.2).

On 11 March 1915, Hasan Moshir al-dowleh replaced Mostowfi al-mamalek. The University of Moscow-educated new prime minister was a constitutionalist, an opponent of the Anglo-Russian Convention of 1907, committed to Iran's neutrality and an upstanding Iranian politician respected by all. Upon his assumption of office, the British, Russians and French diplomatic representatives demanded that Moshir al-dowleh stop objecting to the presence of Russian troops in Iran and dismiss Mokhber al-saltaneh (Mehdiqoli Hedayat), the German-educated governor of Fars, as well as the Swedish commander of the gendarmerie in Fars. Moshir al-dowleh refused to comply and asked for a moratorium on repaying the interest of monies borrowed from Russia and Britain.

On 8 April, 500 troops in the British Indian Army landed at Bushehr and 300 more disembarked close by. Foreign troops were entering Iran from the north, west and south. After forty-four days in office, Moshir al-dowleh resigned because of escalating hostilities between Russian and Ottoman troops in the Kermanshah region, the crippling financial situation and constant Russian threats of marching on Tehran. Intrigues by Charles Marling, the new British chargé d'affaires, were instrumental in the fall of Moshir al-dowleh's government.

On 24 April 1915, the British and Russian envoys in Tehran tried to impose their handpicked prime minister. Javad Saad al-dowleh, the pro-Russian, who had become

Figure 2.2 Mostowfi al-mamalek. *Source: Wikimedia Commons.*

a staunch anti-constitutionalist, had long been groomed for this position. The two envoys met with Ahmad Shah and demanded, 'the resignation of Moshir al-dowleh, the appointment of Saad al-dowleh as prime minister, the closure of Majles, the banning of the press, the dismissal of Swedish officials in the gendarmerie, and the expulsion of the German and Ottoman diplomatic corps'.[5] A surprise nocturnal visit by the German and Ottoman envoys to the shah foiled the ploy. Mostowfi al-mamalek, the choice of the Majles, was no longer interested in the position. Fearful of an outright Allied Powers puppet prime minister, the deputies settled with Abdolmajid Ayn al-dowleh, a compromise candidate with an anti-constitutionalist past.

On Monday, 26 April 1915, Ayn al-dowleh came to the Majles as the new prime minister and introduced his cabinet five days later. Ayn al-dowleh had the support of Russia and Britain. Marling found the political situation convenient for advancing British interests and 'pressed the shah to include Farmanfarma and Mirza Hasan Khan, Vusug ud-Daula' in the cabinet.[6]

Around 11 May, Ayn al-dowleh requested full powers from the Majles. There was talk of using such powers first to close the press and then the Majles, handing over complete authority to the Russo-British-backed executive. In a show of support for constitutionalism and nationalism, the deputies opposed Ayn al-dowleh's bid for absolute power. The attempt at circumventing the Majles irked the deputies, especially the Democrats.

During the 38th session of the Majles, on 20 May 1915, Soleyman Mirza Eskandari, the leader of the Democrats and deputy chair of the Majles, observed that the success of any government policy and reform was incumbent upon ensuring Iran's neutrality in the war even though its neutrality was being consistently violated (Figure 2.3).

Figure 2.3 Soleyman Mirza Eskandari. *Source: Wikimedia Commons.*

On 6 June 1915, in a closed meeting, Abdolhoseyn Mirza Farmanfarma, the minister of interior, informed the deputies that the Russian Army in Qazvin was about to march on the capital. Russia had set a single condition for not attacking Tehran. It demanded that the Majles issue a public statement of 'hatred' towards the Ottoman government.[7] The deputies, committed to Iran's policy of strict neutrality, did not comply. The tug of war between the Russo-British forces and the Iranian Parliament continued.

The Rauf Bey Affair and the Fall of Ayn al-dowleh

Around February–March 1915, Turkish forces led by Hoseyn Rauf Bey (Orbey) entered Iran from the west, operating in the Khaneqeyn and Qasr Shirin areas. Under the command of Enver Pasha, the Ottoman minister of war, Rauf Bey, was dispatched to the area with 1,800 men and a few machine guns. He was to coordinate his activities in Iran with the German agents Wilhelm Wassmuss and Oskar von Niedermayer. The German operatives quickly parted ways with Rauf Bey over strategy and the realization that 'the Ottoman's intended to annex Azarbayjan'.[8]

In late March and early April, news came of clashes between the local population and tribes, particularly the Sanjabis, with Rauf Bey's invading Ottoman forces. The Sanjabis under Shir-Mohammad Khan Samsam al-mamalek were standing up to Rauf Bey's forces. On 6 April 1915, from his base in Khaneqeyn, Rauf Bey demanded the surrender and punishment of Samsam al-mamalek and threatened that if his demands were not met, he would march on Kermanshah.

The prospect of Ottomans as liberating forces quickly turned into a bitter nightmare as Turkish forces, acting as colonial invaders, looted Persian and Kurdish villages. Count Georg Kanitz, the German military attaché, reported on 'the wretched tragedy of plunder, arson, defilement of women and senseless bloodbaths' caused by Rauf Bey's forces.[9] Turkish brutality posed problems for Germany's design to win over Iranians against their old Russo-British oppressors.

> ### British Response to German Agitation
> In the face of Wassmuss' successful stirring up of anti-Entente activity in the region, in May 1915, the British found themselves forced to send in troops from India to occupy Bushire lest they would be driven from this strategic port by Wassmuss' local Tangestani allies led by their chief Ra'is Ali Delvari. (O. Bast)[10]

In early June 1915, Rauf Bey's forces in Kerend (some 100 km west of Kermanshah) were attacked by the Iranian Guran and Sanjabi tribes who, despite heavy casualties, freed their prisoners and forced the Turks to retreat. During the turbulent 6 July 1915 Majles session, the Rauf Bey Affair came to a head. The Democrat deputies censured Abdolhoseyn Farmanfarma, the minister of interior, for the people's plight in Kermanshah and his mishandling of the Rauf Bey Affair. The deputies in favour of Farmanfarma's dismissal criticized 'the tumult, killings, lootings and destructions' in Kermanshah.[11]

The Democrats were fond of neither Farmanfarma nor Ayn al-dowleh and considered both as pro-Russian and pro-British. The deputies sought the right opportunity to oust both of them and bring back the independent-minded Mostowfi al-mamalek's to power. During the 6 July 1915 meeting, Ayn al-dowleh, the prime minister, walked out of the Majles and informed the deputies that they should look for another prime minister. He resigned on 12 July, but that was not the end of the story.

Between Ayn al-dowleh's resignation and the second round of Mostowfi al-mamalek's premiership, Russia and Britain intervened again to close Parliament. On 24 July 1915, the British and Russian chargés d'affaires paid a visit to Ahmad Shah and demanded the closure of Parliament. The shah responded, 'I cannot comply, since I have sworn allegiance to the Constitution.'[12] The Russo-British diplomatic representatives threatened and reminded him of the dire consequences of his decision for his dynasty and the country. Despite a diplomatic shotgun at his head, the young shah stood his ground. After almost two months of negotiations and flexing of muscles, Ayn al-dowleh was finally replaced by Mostowfi al-mamalek on 4 August 1915.

Having failed to impose the Ayn al-dowleh government on Parliament, the Russo-British duo resorted to military action. On 5 August, 1,000 Russian soldiers moved from Qazvin to Tehran, only to return to Qazvin the next day. While Russian troops were threatening Tehran, 1,000 additional Russian soldiers arrived at Anzali on the Caspian coast. In July 1915, the British forces had come under attack in Bushehr by the Tangestani tribes, who were supported by the Germans. On 8 August 1915, the British landed troops at Bushehr, occupied the city, raised the Union Jack over all government buildings and overprinted Iranian postal stamps with: 'Bushire under British occupation.'

From September 1915, the domestic and international situation further deteriorated. The government's inability to pay its 7,000 gendarmes, bloody clashes around Bushehr between British occupying forces and Iranian tribes (8 August–16 October), growing insecurity in the provinces, talk of a secret treaty between Iran and Germany, the rising price of bread in Tehran and the ever-growing animosity of Russia towards Mostowfi al-mamalek's government did not bode well. The congregation of western tribes in the plains of Mahidasht in Kermanshah and their open challenge to the Russian and British invading forces, pushed the country towards a precipice. In late October, tensions rose as the Russians claimed that three wagonloads of bombs and explosives had been smuggled to Tehran for subversive purposes and threatened Iran with reprisals. This claim was part of a trumped-up charge that a coup was in progress against the Allied Powers in Tehran, thus providing an excuse to occupy the capital.

The growing interference of Russia and Britain in Iranian affairs, accompanied by increasing foreign occupation, stunted the country's embryonic political development. In major war-torn and occupied cities, the press was muzzled, the circulation of information was controlled and dissenting views were not tolerated. In late October 1915, less than a month before the nationalist forces emigrated to Qom, eighteen publications of different political leanings had appeared in Tehran. In the provinces, including Khorasan, Esfahan, Shiraz, Qazvin and Hamedan, nineteen weeklies or semi-weeklies were published. By 21 March 1916, 'Iranian publication were limited to four, diffused in Tehran: Thunder (*Raad*), New Age (*asre jadid*), Guidance (*Ershad*), and Information (*Ettelaat*).'[13]

Two Governments and a Shah

On 14 November 1915, the tide turned and Iran entered a new phase in its relations with Russia and Britain. Under the impending Russian invasion of Tehran, Parliament was disbanded and the uncompromising politicians, deputies and clergy opposed to the Allied invasion migrated from Tehran to Qom. This group, known as the *mohajerin* (Migrants), were accompanied by gendarmerie forces and the German chargé d'affaires, along with his retinue. The pro-German Migrants included ordinary people, merchants, notables, poets, journalists and intellectuals. Their aim was to establish a dual power without denouncing the shah. In effect, until the end of the war the shah had two spokesmen, the pro-Russo-British government in Tehran and the pro-German self-proclaimed government which was on the move. Neither side officially committed Iran to enter the war. From 14 November 1915 until 11 November 1918, even the 'inclined or biased neutrality' of Ayn al-dowleh's government was set aside.

Neutrality had become a meaningless concept as in the absence of the Majles, Russia and Britain dictated their wishes to the ever-revolving governments in Tehran. Under the threat of imminent occupation of Tehran by Russian troops in Qazvin, Ahmad Shah also intended to migrate accompanied by his government. In a private session, the shah informed the deputies of his decision, but the Russian and British diplomatic representatives eventually 'convinced' him not to leave Tehran. In return, they promised that Russian troops would not enter Tehran. Abdolhoseyn Farmanfarma played a decisive role in convincing the shah to stay in Tehran. Russian troops camping 150 kilometres from Tehran continued to act as a sword of Damocles, a constant reminder of where true power resided.

The Pro-German Resistance Movement: The National Defence Committee

The Migrants are said to have been anywhere between hundreds and thousands. Among them were forty-one Majles deputies, twenty were Democrats, eight Moderates, another eight Independents and five were from the Religious Group. The presence of Seyyed Hasan Modarres, the influential cleric who had defended Ayn al-dowleh during the Rauf Bey Affair, symbolized the new nationalist and anti-Russo-British United Front. The coalition of Democrats and Moderates that had come under great strain during Ayn al-dowleh's government was once again forged.

The National Defence Committee, openly pro-German, was founded in Qom on 15 November 1915, under the auspices of Democrat deputies. The German Max Otto Schuenenmann played a determining role in its formation. The establishment of an authoritative decision-making body opposing Russo-British hegemony energized the provincial political forces that were waiting for a national leadership to emerge. The National Defence Committee's motto was: 'Long live resistance, may Iran's freedom and democracy endure forever.'[14] The committee was the embryo of a revolutionary provincial government. Upon its creation, messages of support, emphasizing the importance of national sovereignty and the right to self-determination, poured in from Kordestan, Esfahan, Arak, Hamedan and Kermanshah. The National Defence Committee succeeded in whipping up an unprecedented sense of patriotism and nationalism. On 19 November, the British Consulate in Shiraz fell to the supporters of the Committee, and all British residents were sent to Wassmuss in Tangestan (Bushehr).

On 24 November 1915, a united front of all nationalist political tendencies, composed of four deputies each representing the four major Majles factions, took over the leadership of the National Defence Committee. This committee, aided by the Germans, began communicating and liaising with the provinces, collecting money, overseeing finances and procuring arms. The various diffuse and uncoordinated military forces fighting the Russian, British and local surrogate troops were now called the National Forces or the National Encampment.

Mostowfi al-mamalek's government in Tehran was no less patriotic than the National Defence Committee. Mostowfi al-mamalek invited the Migrants to return, arguing that he was incapable of serious decision-making about the country's future in the absence of the Majles. The National Defence Committee hoped to create a nationwide resistance movement against Russia and Britain, eventually expelling them with German support. It, therefore, dragged its feet and contended itself with encouraging news of the victorious National Forces. On the fronts, however, the military reality was different from what the National Defence Committee hoped.

Russia and Britain had well-armed troops in Iran and could regularly replenish them while the Germans had a few well-trained agents and were forced to depend on the efficiency of Ottoman troops in Iran.

In December 1915, the Russian troops routed the National Forces in Saveh and Qazvin, and advanced to 80 kilometres of Qom. A month after arriving in Qom, the Migrants were once again on the move, fleeing before the advancing Russian troops. On 19 December 1915, the National Defence Committee escaped to Kashan, and then to Esfahan. On 6 January 1916, under pressure from advancing Russian troops, they left Esfahan, travelling westwards in the bitter winter, and arrived in Kermanshah around the first week of February.

During their short stay in Kermanshah, the National Defence Committee was disbanded. At the behest of the Germans, a provisional national government, headed by Rezaqoli khan Nezam al-saltaneh, was formed. Nezam al-saltaneh, known for his patriotism and uprightness, had joined the resistance movement while he was the governor of Lorestan and Borujerd back in November 1915. A swath of land in western Iran and close to the Ottoman border, consisting of Kordestan, Hamedan, Malayer, Nahavand, Tuserkan and Borujerd, was under the nominal control of the Provisional National Government, which had begun appointing governors and even dispatching ambassadors to Istanbul and Berlin.

But gradually, a sense of despair set in among members of the resistance movement. The nationalists on the run felt as though German promises of arms and financial aid were empty words. The National Forces had only received some 1,000 old French Lebel rifles captured on the European front. On 12 April 1916, the Provisional National Government was forced to leave Qasr Shirin in Iran and cross over to Ottoman Iraq, where it remained in exile for six months.

On 2 July 1916, Ali-Ihsan Bey's troops defeated the Russian Army and occupied Kermanshah again. Under the protection of Ottoman troops, the Provisional National Government returned to Kermanshah for another nine months. Occupation of Baghdad on 11 March 1917 by British forces once again threatened the Provisional National Government in Kermanshah. On 15 April 1917, Ottoman forces withdrew from Kermanshah and the Provisional National Government departed from Iran, disbanded and dispersed. 'By March 1918, Mashad was under British control followed by Qazvin, Hamadan and Kermanshah in April'.[15]

Governments in Tehran during the Last Two Years of the War

During the last two years of the First World War, Ahmad Shah had remained the rallying symbol of both the Tehran and the Provisional National Government and had tried his best to show his allegiance to the Russo-British powers. The shah was effectively a hostage of the Allied Powers in Tehran. When anti-Allied provincial leaders enquired about the shah's position on British and Russian presence in Iran, Ahmad Shah took pains to respond that he was committed to firm and friendly political relations with the Allied Powers and did not intend to alienate them.

Allied-Friendly Governments

With the departure of Mostowfi al-mamalek, who tried to steer a neutralist course and who had kept contact with the National Defence Committee, the central government in Tehran came under various degrees of Allied control. On 25 December 1915, Ahmad Shah appointed Abdolhoseyn Farmanfarma as his prime minister, while the Russo-British forces 'obtained total control of Tehran'.[16] However, until the end of the war, it was not easy for the Allied Powers to exert a uniform degree of authority over the eight prime ministers who came to power within a period of thirty-five months. The rapid rate of turnover of Iranian governments was, in large part, due to the rivalry between the Russians and the British for greater sway over Iranian governments.

Farmanfarma, whose policies were based on cordial and close relations with both Russia and Britain, was ousted on 4 March 1916 at the instigation of the Russians who had fallen out with him. After their victory in Kermanshah, the Russians wanted a politician more amenable to their designs and Mohammadvali Khan Sepahsalar Tonokaboni replaced Farmanfarma.

Between 3 and 5 August 1916, an important agreement with significant consequences was signed between Prime Minister Sepahsalar Tonokaboni and the British minister, Charles Marling, and the Russian minister, M. de Etter. The negotiations leading to this agreement had begun under the Farmanfarma cabinet. This financial and military agreement further strengthened the Russo-British hold on Iran.

The 'Sepahsalar Agreement', which was signed under *force majeure*, allowed the Russians to increase their Cossack troops in the north to some 11,000, but more significantly, gave a free hand to the British to create a force of equal strength in the south. Even though these Russo-British troops were supposed to operate under the auspices of Iran's Ministry of War, this would remain only on paper. The agreement officialized Russian military control in the north and the British military hold in the centre and south. The 1907 'neutral zone' now shrank to Tehran. The 'Sepahsalar Agreement' also empowered Russia and Britain to oversee and direct Iran's financial affairs. The five-man Mixed Financial Commission, with only two Iranian representatives, was established to carry out this task.

The rapid advance of Turkish troops in Iran and the fall of Hamadan on 11 August 1916 rekindled hope among the nationalists. Ottoman victories destabilized the pro-

Allied government of Sepahsalar Tonokaboni, alarmed the Allied Powers and emboldened the Central Powers and their supporters. Ahmad Shah was displeased that the 'Sepahsalar Agreement' was conducted without his participation and consent.

On 14 August 1916, with the blessing of the Russian chargé d'affaires, the shah replaced Sepahsalar Tonokaboni with Hasan Vosuq al-dowleh. Pressure by the British prevented Vosuq al-dowleh from appointing ministers of his choice. His cabinet ended up being 'composed of mainly [George Percy] Churchill's friends.[17] George Churchill was the influential oriental secretary to the Persian Legation who read, wrote and spoke Persian fluently. He was widely knowledgeable about Iranian politicians and familiar with behind-the-scenes political dealings.

The Punishment Committee

The increasing meddling of Russia and Britain in Iranian politics fostered an atmosphere of resentment among Iranians. Frustrated with their own impotence to expel the Russo-British forces, Iranians turned their wrath towards those politicians widely rumoured to be the appointees, functionaries, facilitators and friends of Russia or Britain.

A few months after Vosuq al-dowleh took office in August 1916, three veterans of the constitutionalist movement, two of whom were former high-ranking officers in the Cossack Brigade, formed a clandestine terrorist organization called the Punishment Committee (Figure 2.4). Mirza Ebrahim Khan Monshizadeh, Asadollah Khan Abolfathzadeh and Mohammadnazar Khan Meshkat al-mamalek led the organization. Soon, they recruited Karim Davargar, a 35-year-old veteran just returning from the war fronts and known for his unsuccessful attempt to assassinate

Figure 2.4 Hasan Vosuq al-dowleh. *Source: Wikimedia Commons.*

Sheykh Fazlollah Nuri. The leadership trio provided Davatgar and his confederates with money and arms to carry out assassinations.

The Punishment Committee intended to secure Iran's welfare and progress by eliminating local spies 'occupying sensitive political positions because they were supported and assisted by foreigners'.[18] After the arrest of Monshizadeh, a leader of the Punishment Committee, he told his interrogators that 'a committee [such as this one] only takes shape in a country where governments engage in illegal and violent activities'. He added that 'it was the intolerable violence of Vosuq al-dowleh's government that generated a deep sense of vengeance in us'.[19]

The organization's assassination list included, among others, Sepahsalar Tonokaboni, Zel al-soltan, Kamran mirza, Abdolhoseyn Farmanfarma and Seyyed Ziaeddin Tabatabai (Seyyed Zia). To attain their objective of eliminating traitors, spies and servants of foreign governments, the Punishment Committee first assassinated Mirza Ebrahim Khan, the director of Tehran's granary, on 17 February 1917. Terrors in the name of saving the motherland lasted some five months, rocking the Vosuq al-dowleh government. It sowed terror among those compromised politicians who felt as though they would be the next victims. Fearing for his life, Seyyed Zia hired eight bodyguards, without whom he would not walk around Tehran.

The victims of the Punishment Committee included Matin al-saltaneh, the Oxford-educated editor of the pro-Allied newspaper *New Age* (*Asre jadid*) on 22 May, and the cleric, Mirza Mohsen Mojtahed, a close associate and supporter of Vosuq al-dowleh, on 7 June 1917. The Punishment Committee also ordered the assassination of Karim Davatgar, one of their own. Davatgar had demanded more money and threatened that he would expose the organization. On 4 May 1917, he, too, was assassinated. The Punishment Committee, whose numbers were no more than twenty, became bold enough to tell Ala al-saltaneh, the prime minister, whom he should assign as deputy minister of finance.[20]

The police were under the false assumption that the Punishment Committee was acting on behalf of Germany. On 23 July 1917, less than two months after Mohammad-Ali Ala al-saltaneh became prime minister, members of the Punishment Committee were arrested. It was not until 3 September 1918, or less than a month after Vosug al-dowleh became prime minister for a second time, that Monshizadeh and Abolfathzadeh, the leaders of the Punishment Committee, were liquidated in Semnan while under arrest. A few days before, two other members of the committee were hanged in Tehran chanting, 'Death to the traitors!' and 'Long live the Punishment Committee!'[21] Ehsanollah Khan Doostdar, a member of the Punishment Committee, was able to escape. He joined Mirza Kuchek Khan Jangali and later fell out with him.

> ### Russia and Iran
>
> Had Russia continued to absorb Northern Persia, by protecting rich landowners and merchants in Khorasan, by collecting the revenue due to the Persian Government from her 'subjects' in Azerbaijan, by buying villages in the province of Astrabad for nominal prices through an exercise of pressure and importing Russian subjects to work them, and in many other nefarious ways, the independence of the country would have been lost within a generation. The collapse of Russia gave Persia one more chance of working out her own salvation. (P. Sykes)[22]

Iranian Governments Digesting the Russian Revolutions

On 2 April 1917, eighty-eight former Majles deputies addressed an enthusiastic telegraph to the president of the Russian Duma. In their message, the Iranian parliamentarians supported the February Revolution in Russia and concluded with, 'Long live a liberal (freedom-loving) Russia.'[23] In July 1917, Kerensky the leader of the newly formed provisional government, ordered the Russian commander, Baratoff, to stop his advance through Persia and announced the withdrawal of Russian forces at the earliest possible moment.

Iranians enthusiastically welcomed Russia's shift towards constitutionalism, democracy and peaceful coexistence with its neighbours. Suddenly the spectre of Iran's oldest nemesis seemed to dissipate, dramatically altering the balance of power with the Allied Powers in Iran. As the Russian revolution unfolded, Iranians felt more relieved and less besieged.

On 29 May 1917, Vosuq al-dowleh resigned partially out of fear of the Punishment Committee and partially because of the change in power relations and the liberal political climate caused by the February Revolution. Ahmad Shah again appointed Mohammad-Ali Ala al-saltaneh as prime minister. Ala al-saltaneh had served as Persia's minister plenipotentiary in London for seven years and had been quite generous towards the British and the Russians by giving them concessions during his first term as prime minister. Even though he became prime minister with British approval and 'was personally friendly to Great Britain,'[24] Ala al-saltaneh's government proved to be less cooperative with the British than expected.

> **Russian Troops in Iran after the Order to Withdraw**
>
> Before the autumn [1917] the Russian troops in Persia were everywhere demoralized, and the position of the officers was pitiable, everything that they stood for having crumbled away. (P. Sykes)[25]

Against British recommendations, Ala al-saltaneh had prevented Percy Sykes from being officially presented to the shah as 'the Commander of the South Persian Rifles'. The prime minister pursued the idea of a unified Iranian military force for 'the whole country'.[26] On 9 October 1917, Ala al-saltaneh sent a key memo to Charles Marling, in which he refused to recognize the South Persian Rifles and proposed that: 'British Indian officers and troops should be withdrawn from Persia altogether; the South Persian Rifles should be handed over to the Governor General of Fars and fall under the direct control of the Persian Government until other officers arrived to organise the proposed uniform force.'[27] Ala al-saltaneh also asked for the abrogation of the 1907 Anglo-Russian Convention.

In the middle of Ala al-saltaneh's almost six-month term in office, George Churchill became impatient and disgruntled with the prime minister's non-compliant and even anti-British politics. Churchill quickly arranged to replace him with Abdolmajid Ayn al-dowleh, a long-time favourite and reliable friend of the Allied Powers. Even though Russia was losing its grip on Iranian politics, the British needed to demonstrate that their authority was intact.

The October Revolution had broken out before Ala al-saltaneh was replaced with Ayn al-dowleh on 19 November 1917. The Bolshevik Revolution caused further confusion and disarray among Russian troops in Iran who had already been ordered to retreat some four months earlier. The British came to lose a key military ally in the region and needed to fill in the vacuum created by the gradual departure of Russian troops.

For the British this was an opportunity as well as a threat. Ayn al-dowleh's government lasted some one and a half months before the shah appointed the nationalist, well-respected and popular Hasan Mostowfi al-mamalek, on 7 January 1918. Mostowfi al-mamalek was disliked by the Russians and not particularly liked by the British. From the fall of Vosuq al-dowleh's first government on 29 May 1917 until the formation of his second government on 7 August 1918, four prime ministers came and went. 'In part British hostility or indifference to any cabinet but one headed by Vusuq ud-Daula inhibited the formation of a stable government.'[28]

British Forces in Iran

The South Persian Rifles

The 'Sepahsalar Agreement' had given rise to a military force called the South Persian Rifles. This newly found force was under the command of the British Brig. Gen. Percy Sykes and composed of British, Indian and predominantly Iranian local tribesman. Sykes had arrived in Bandar Abbas in March 1916, and his force was to replace the gendarmerie under the command of Swedish officers suspected of pro-German tendencies.

The South Persian Rifles were mandated to exert military control over the British zone of influence in Iran, counter-German activities in the region, secure trade routes and the port facilities on the Persian Gulf, safeguard borders with British India as well as protect British oil interests in the south. According to the 'Sepahsalar Agreement', provincial officials loyal to the Tehran government were required to collaborate with Sykes in his endeavour to create this force.

> ### The South Persian Rifles (SPR)
> Thus, the British Government, through the agency of the South Persian Rifles meddled their way into southern Persia in 1916 and muddled out of it in 1921. (F. Safiri)[29]

Having secured Kerman, the South Persian Rifles entered Yazd on 14 August and joined Col. Bielomestonov's Russian troops in Esfahan on 11 September 1916. Having marched through central Iran, Sykes and his troops entered Shiraz exactly a month later and were greeted by Farmanfarma, the governor and Qavam al-Molk.[30] Despite initial resistance by the government in Tehran and some of the Iranian troops in Shiraz, by November 1916, some 3,000 gendarme forces were absorbed into the South Persian Rifles, leading to the formation of the British-commanded Fars Brigade. By August 1917, the South Persian Rifles numbered some 5,500.

In April 1918, the government of Mostowfi al-mamalek 'openly adopted an anti-South Persian Rifles line and was resisting British pressures to accept the force.'[31] In early May 1918, Sowlat al-dowleh led the Qashqais in a revolt against the British and other tribes of Fars joined in. Subsequently, British forces stationed in Bushehr were reinforced and numbered some 10,000 soldiers.

The clergy supported Sowlat al-dowleh's position and called on the people to rise and wage jihad against the British. Sykes and his 1,600 South Persian Rifles supported by Indian troops moved against Sowlat al-dowleh Qashqai's forces on 24 May 1918.

In the spring and summer of 1918, the South Persian Rifles survived numerous mutinies in their local ranks as Iranian soldiers deserted, refusing to fight against their own tribes. The British responded by court-marshalling and executing the deserting and mutinous forces.

> ## Lt. Col. Hugh Gough, British Consul at Shiraz in July 1918
>
> There exists 'A genuine desire on the part of large numbers of Persians to see their country free from all foreign interference. However much the Persian patriot may be derided, still it is a fact that patriotism does exist in Persia, and that such feelings animate some of our enemies.' (F. Safiri)[32]

During June and July, Shiraz became a besieged city. By October 1918, right before the end of the Great War, Sykes defeated Sowalat al-dowleh. A key factor in the British victory was that Qavam al-Molk 'was bought off at a very early stage'. In cooperation with Farmanfarma, Qavam al-Molk maintained some 2,000 to 3,000 soldiers, and 'lent some of these troops to the South Persian Rifles for operations in July against Saulat [Sowalat al-dowleh]'.[33] The South Persian Rifles disbanded in July 1921 after the February coup led by Seyyed Zia and Reza Khan.

The British Dunsterforce

Tides began to turn rapidly as of 16 January 1918. Leon Trotsky, the new Bolshevik foreign minister, sent a note to the Iranian chargé d'affaires at Petrograd that Russia considered the Anglo-Russian Convention of 1907 as null and void and hoped for the rapid withdrawal of British and Ottoman forces from Iran. The Brest-Litovsk Peace Treaty, signed between the Bolshevik government and the Central Powers on 3 March 1918, confirmed the evacuation of Russian and Turkish troops from Iran. This was a golden opportunity for Britain to replace Russia and extend its dominion over Iran.

Fresh forces were dispatched to Iran to ensure British military hegemony. On 27 January 1918, Maj. Gen. L. C. Dunsterville, an Indian Army officer, set out on an approximately 900-kilometre trek from Baghdad to Anzali on the Caspian Sea. Dunsterville and his party 'of twelve officers, two clerks and forty-one drivers' travelled in 41 Ford cars.[34] His special mission was to recruit and train locals to secure the northern provinces of Iran and the Russian littoral areas around the Caspian from the rebel forces of Mirza Kuchek Khan, replace the withdrawing Russian troops and hold off the Turks. Dunsterville's troops which gradually joined him were composed of some 400 Australian, Canadian, New Zealand and South African officers and non-commissioned officers. This special force, known as Dunsterforce, was accompanied by an armored car brigade, a lethal novelty at the time. At its peak, this force had some 1,000 officers and non-commissioned officers. To meet their financial needs, the Dunsterforce hauled large sums of Persian silver and British gold.

On 15 February 1918, Dunsterville and his party of some fifty arrived in Qazvin and were joined by an armoured car before heading to Anzali. Dunsterville's stay at Anzali was cut short by the joint revolutionary committee of Bolsheviks and Mirza Kuchek Khan, compelling him to move his forces back to Hamedan on 20 February 1918. In Hamedan, several **White Russian** officers joined Dunstreville's forces. But most significantly, Dunsterville succeeded in convincing Maj. Gen. Lazar Bicherakov and his Cossack troops to join forces with him in return for financial assistance to him and his men. Their first agreed upon mission was to attack Kuchek Khan's army and clear 'the road from Kasvin [Qazvin] to the Caspian'.[35]

On 11 June, Dunsterville's some 800 troops, accompanied by the White Russian Gen. Bicherakov's Cossack troops, two British armoured cars and two British airplanes, set out to battle with Mirza Kuchek Khan who held the strategic Manjil Bridge, 110 kilometres from Qazvin and halfway to Anzali. They met resistance from Kuchek Khan's forces, repulsed them and arrived in Anzali on 27 June 1918. Between 18 and 21 July, Kuchek Khan's forces known as the Jangalis ambushed Dunsterville's forces in Rasht and both sides incurred heavy losses. By this time, the Jangali forces were estimated to be between 2,500 and 5,000.[36] The role played by the Royal Air Force and the armoured cars were instrumental in bringing the Jangali forces to the negotiating table. On 14 August 1918, a ceasefire was negotiated between Dunsterville and Mirza Kuchek Khan.

In late August, once Dunsterville was in Baku, a new central command was formed of all British troops south of the Caspian called the North Persia Force (Norpeforce). On 31 August 1918, Brig. Gen. H. F. Bateman-Champain took charge of the North Persia Force and the Dunsterforce headquarters at Qazvin. On 22 September 1918, the War Office disbanded the Dunsterforce.

The formation and operations of the South Persian Rifles and the Dunsterforce demonstrated the extent of Britain's military involvement in neutral Iran. Within six months, Dunsterville's expeditionary force became the North Persia Force claiming around 5,000 soldiers. The South Persian Rifles secured the safety of the Anglo-Persian Oil Company's interests and the flow of oil. The North Persia Force was formed in reaction to the Bolshevik challenge in Iran and India.

Mirza Kuchek Khan Jangali's Challenge

Kuchek Khan (Yunes), born in Rasht (1880–1), was active in the Gilan constitutionalist movement and marched with Sardar Mohy on Tehran against Mohammad-Ali Shah in the summer of 1909. After the closure of the Majles in December 1911, Kuchek

Khan became a founding member of the Pan-Islamist, nationalist and anti-colonial Alliance of Islam Group (*Heyat Ettehad Eslam*). Once the First World War broke out, he founded the Alliance of Islam Group in Fuman and its surrounding forests, and gradually expanded his organization throughout Gilan and Mazandaran. Kuchek Khan believed in guerrilla warfare as the most suitable means of engaging the invading Russian army. 'Friends and foe saw in him an ardent patriot, an idealistic defender of justice, straightforward yet humble, without interest in personal gain and glory.'[37]

In September 1914, he began harassing Russian forces in Gilan. Kuchek Khan's guerrillas came to be known as the Jangalis (Men of the Woods). By May and August 1915, they were inflicting severe blows to the Russian Cossacks in the region. The hit-and-run operation of the Jangalis and the local support for them made their elimination impossible. Every engagement and successful attack by the Jangalis enhanced their popularity and authority.

> ### Dunsterville on Kuchek Khan
>
> The so-called Jangali movement was started by a well-known revolutionary of the name of Mirza Kuchik Khan, an honest, well-meaning idealist. His programme includes all the wearisome platitudes that ring the changes on the will-o'-the-wisp ideals of liberty, equality and fraternity. 'Persia for the Persians' and 'Away with the foreigners' are other obvious items . . . (L. C. Dunsterville)[38]

In November 1915, Kuchek Khan's men in Gilan fought under the banner of the National Forces, the loose military organization loyal to the National Defence Committee. Kuchek Khan's attacks on Russian troops and their local allies added to their fame in the region and gradually the whole country. Kuchek Khan gave a voice to the neglected and the downtrodden. 'Their victories even impacted the landlord–tenant relations. Landlords no longer foulmouthed the peasants since many of them carried weapons and fought alongside the Jangalis.'[39]

By the summer of 1917, even though Kuchek Khan's headquarters remained in Fuman, Rasht was governed with his consent. On 10 June 1917, following the February Revolution in Russia, the Jangalis published their semi-weekly newspaper, *Jangal* (Forest). The heading on its front page set in red was: 'This paper only defends the rights of Iranians and is the enlightener of Muslim thoughts.' In its first editorial, the paper defended democratic processes, the Constitution and called for free elections to the 4th Majles.[40]

The paper insisted that the Jangalis were law-abiding citizens, loyal to Ahmad Shah, thirsty for structural reforms and opposed to cession from Iran. It systematically opposed the 1907 Anglo-Russian Convention, all concessions given to Russia and Britain, presence of Russian forces in the north and the British South Persian Rifles. The Jangalis criticized and derided Iranian political collaborators of the Russians and the British. They assured the public that they had revolted and taken up arms to defend the motherland and would lay them down once the country was free of foreign intruders and domestic oppressors. Their repeated objective was the opening of the Majles, strengthening constitutionalism and the 'eradication of oppression and despotism'.[41]

Sykes on Kuchek Khan

Kuchik Khan was regarded as the hero of Persia. He had the support of his countrymen, of the Germans, and of the Turks (P. Sykes)[42]

From December 1917, *Jangal* became critical of Ayn al-dowleh's government and questioned the shah's intentions and motives in appointing him. The Jangalis considered the new government as the outcome of plans made by 'London's Royal Court' and labelled some ministers as corrupt, traitorous, and servants of foreigners.[43] *Jangal* accused a group of Iranian notables and politicians of corruption and acting on behalf of foreign interests.[44] It denounced the continual circulation of power among them, preventing Iran from breaking out of its miserable vicious circle.

After the 1917 October Revolution, *Jangal* warned that Iranians had had enough. It argued that given the situation in Russia and the spread of Bolshevik ideas, 'unheeded warnings today would result in more radical demands tomorrow'.[45] By February 1918, the Jangali movement was on the ascent. It had created a quasi-liberated zone in Iran, conducted an anti-corruption crusade in local government offices, and established a functioning justice system where Gilanis could petition for a court hearing in Fuman. Kuchek Khan had 'sympathizers in the Cabinet itself, Kasvin (Qazvin) was full of his agents, as well as Hamadan and all other large towns. He was acclaimed, as the saviour of Persia, who was going to turn the foreigners out and bring back the golden age.'[46]

From March 1918, the tone of *Jangal* towards Ahmad Shah became more radical. Even though the Jangali movement pronounced its loyalty to the shah, it warned against British designs in Iran and the activities of anglophile courtiers. On 7 August 1918, Hasan Vosuq al-dowleh was back in office as prime minister and set out to annihilate the Jangali movement.

On 27 March 1919, the British unilaterally abrogated the ceasefire agreement with the Jangali movement, issuing an ultimatum and demanding the surrender of the Jangalis. For its part, the Vosuq al-dowleh government succeeded in driving a wedge between Kuchek Khan and his close collaborators by appeasing some and promising others, who had become war-weary, safe conduct. The appointment of Sardar Moazam Khorasani (Abdolhoseyn Teymurtash) as governor of Gilan, on 27 March 1919, played a significant role in uprooting the Jangalis. Ahmad Kasmai and his followers were the first to break away from Kuchek Khan, followed by Dr Ebrahim Heshmat who surrendered his forces, having been assured of safe conduct. On 13 May 1919, Heshmat was hanged on Teymourtash's watch.

From spring of 1919, the dwindled, scattered and disorganized forces of Kuchek Khan were hunted down and on the run. Even though the governor and the Cossack commander in Gilan threatened anyone helping and sheltering Kuchek Khan and his forces with execution and the expropriation of their property, Kuchek Khan survived.

By September 1919, Kuchek Khan had regrouped. He was joined by Ehsanollah Khan Doostdar and Khalou Qorban and once again became a threat. Ehsanollah Khan had strong communist tendencies and considered his alliance with Kuchek Khan as one of political expediency. Kuchek Khan's experiences had radicalized him. He wrote, 'Present-day revolutions tempt us to proclaim a republic and free the toilers from the clutches of the leisure classes, as in all other countries. Furthermore, the courtiers resist administrating the country based on the constitutional law and democracy.'[47] Unable to subdue Kuchek Khan, Vosuq al-dowleh's government signed a truce with him on 14 January 1920.

Famine, Influenza and Cholera

With the outbreak of the First World War, a series of man-made and war-related calamities, in addition to natural adversities, led to a human catastrophe of great proportions. As foreign armies invaded Iran, traditional agricultural and pastoral economic life, the mainstay of Iranians, came to a halt. War exasperated the law of the survival of the fittest. The result was a staggering number of dead due to famine, starvation and disease. The death toll by 1919 is estimated at anywhere between 1 and 2 million, or 10 to 20 per cent of the population.[48]

In 1916 and 1917, the paucity of rain caused havoc with predominantly dry farming in Iran. The 1917 harvest was particularly a bad one. This was compounded by the disruption of normal agricultural activities caused by warring foreign forces, especially in Azarbayjan, Kermanshah, Hamedan, Gilan, Khorasan and Fars. The invading troops needed food provisions which were primarily requisitioned and at times purchased. 'In the north-east province of Khorasan, Russian troops blockaded all roads and prohibited any transfers of grain, except those destined for the Russian army.'[49] The sad state of roads and communication facilities in Iran had been aggravated by the war, and troop movements by the Russians, Ottomans and the

British further prevented transportation of grain to areas in dire need. The requisitioning of beasts of burden by the invading forces, further disrupted the pre-war distribution networks.

> ### Famine on the Way between Kerend and Kermanshah, April 1918
>
> The whole land had been skinned bare of supplies by Turk and Russian, and it was now in the throes of famine . . . They commandeered unscrupulously and without payment, and what they could not consume or carry off they destroyed. There was no seed wheat, and consequently no crops had been sown. Many tillers of the soil had fled for their lives; those who had remained were dying of hunger . . . It was desolation and ruin everywhere. (M. H. Donohoe)[50]

In 1918, famine was also due to 'the Turkish and Russian armies advancing and retreating in Western and North-western Persia', while 'the disbanded Russian troops, and the fleeing Assyrians all looted foodstuffs and stock, besides inflicting loss of life'.[51] In Azarbayjan, many fled the terror of Russian troops and died of hunger and the cold during their trek.

Pressure on grain supplies during the war period had domestic causes as well. The hoarding and speculation by local traders and landowners and the corruption of local and national officials, including Ahmad Shah, added to the price hike and unavailability of bread for those who could not afford the mounting prices. Sometimes, 'The wheat was there, but not the money to pay for it.'[52] Without a proper military force, the central government was unable to impose law and order. Its loss of authority resulted in banditry and looting by local armed groups and tribes.

> ### The Almost-Twenty Times Hike in the Price of Wheat
>
> The highest price I know of quoted for wheat has been 230 tomans, or about £70, for one kharwar = 800 lb., the normal price being 12 tomans or, say, 70 shillings. (L. C. Dunsterville)[53]

In Hamedan, 'among the population of 50,000 over 30 per cent were on the verge of starvation and for a very large percentage death was inevitable'.[54] On 6 May 1918, the British consul in Hamedan put the daily starvation deaths in the city at 200, while another source reported 160 cases of death daily during the first two weeks of May 1918. An eyewitness with the Dunsterforce observed, 'Hamadan was a city of horrors. The unburied victims of famine men, women and children were lying in the streets and in the fields adjoining British Headquarters.'[55] Hunger forced the enfeebled starving population of Hamadan to eat grass. 'A short course of this diet proved as fatal as the want of bread, for it invariably caused peritonitis and a lingering, agonizing death.'[56]

From mid-August 1918, the country was hit by the Spanish flu epidemic. War-torn and underdeveloped, Iran was neither medically nor organizationally prepared for the catastrophe. Casualties among the rural population were higher than the urban. The influenza seriously weakened the ill and the hungry, reducing their chances of survival.

The flu reached Tehran in late September 1918. A second and more virulent wave came in late September and ravaged Hamedan, Kermanshah, Shiraz and Kerman. 'Shiraz lost 10,000 out of its 50,000 inhabitants.'[57] A third wave of the flu afflicted Baluchestan in January 1919 but remained limited to this province. 'The flu came into an environment already beset by the calamities of war, famine, and disease.'[58]

The Killer Flu

In the province of Khorasan, for example, the city of Mashhad had two-thirds of its 100,000 citizens sick with the flu. The epidemic killed about 3,500 people in that area: a 5% mortality rate within city limits, and 7% in outlying villages.

One observer noted that villages around Yazd had lost up to 25% of their population to influenza, and villages in the Kerman district were reported to have had a 30%-40% casualty rate. (A. Afkhami)[59]

When the 1918 influenza hit Iran, malaria was already widespread in rural areas, exasperating the death rates. The rural population was overwhelmingly afflicted with malaria which had become endemic. The accumulated consequences of famine, malaria and the flu were catastrophic. 'With between 8.0% and 21.7% of its total population dead, Iran ranks as one of the countries most devastated by the 1918–19 pandemic.'[60]

The Post-War British Design for Iran

On 30 October 1918, Turkey requested an armistice, and within eight days all Central Powers began negotiations with the Allied Powers. On 11 November, the First World

War officially ended. In Iran, the pro-British Hasan Vosuq al-dowleh was in the fourth month of his second term as prime minister. The Bolsheviks had renounced the 1907 Anglo-Russian Convention and withdrawn their troops. Britain was the only country in Iran with a major military presence of some 20,000 troops in the north, centre and south. With Russia out of the picture, Britain remained unrivaled in Iran, a privileged position it sought to consolidate and render unassailable. To 'guarantee the exclusiveness of Britain's position' meant shutting out all other political powers from political, financial, and military interaction with Iran.[61]

The Paris Peace Conference

The Paris Peace Conference of 18 January 1919 provided a platform for Iran to obtain the international community's confirmation and promise that it was once and for all free from political, military, and financial intervention and control of all powers. From 21 November 1918, Iran sought the 'right of representation at the Peace Conference with the right to vote'.[62] Iran's representatives at the Conference demanded the 'abrogation of Treaties and Concessions prejudicial to [its] independence and integrity', and indemnities for damages caused by foreign belligerent armies during the war.[63] According the American minister in Iran, John Caldwell, Iran hoped to establish 'a strong independent state that will no longer be a pawn in the international game of the large imperial powers'.[64]

For the British, Iran's official representation at the Conference was unacceptable as it compromised Britain's exclusive hold on Iran and raised issues jeopardizing the monopolistic control it wished to exercise. Percy Cox, the British minister in Iran, believed that Iran was inept at governing itself. He maintained that unless Britain, its 'protector', secured 'a mandate' to reform the country, it would fall into chaos and Bolshevik hands.[65] Britain decided to prevent Iran from making its case before the Peace Conference, exclude other powers from involvement in Iran's fate and conclude an exclusive agreement with the Vosug al-dowleh government, which would place the country 'under some form of British protection'.

On 23 January 1919, the Iranian delegation, headed by the minister of foreign affairs, Moshaver al-mamalek, entered Paris. On 14 February 1919, he officially wrote to Monsieur Dutasta, the secretary-general of the Conference, requesting Iran's admission to the Conference. Robert Lansing, US secretary of state under US President Woodrow Wilson recalled that, 'At Paris I asked of Mr. **Balfour** three times that the Persians have an opportunity to be heard before the Council of Foreign Ministers because of their claims and boundaries and because their territory had been a battle ground. Mr. Balfour was rather abrupt in refusing to permit them to have a hearing.'[66]

Britain blocked Iran's representation at the Conference on the grounds that Iran was a neutral country and had not participated in the war. Britain successfully prevented Iran from presenting its case at the Paris Peace Conference as an independent country whose neutrality had been violated during the war. Having reminded Iran of its dependent and inferior status in the international community, the British negotiated a secret deal with the Vosuq al-dowleh government.

The 1919 Anglo-Persian Agreement

Britain hoped to secure a long-term solid footing in Iran through an agreement that provided Iran with a semblance of independence, while it contained the trappings of what could be later interpreted as a protectorate. Furthermore, Britain hoped to sell this project as highly advantageous to Iran and expected Iranians to naively embrace it. The British gambled on Iranian sheepishness, the erosion of Iranian nationalism and the ability to buy off opposition.

Reaching a satisfactory agreement with Iran as quickly as possible became a pressing issue. After the end of the War the British Treasury, under the guidance of **John Maynard Keynes**, tried to put the country's finances in order. Keynes considered Britain's 'level of expenditure, about £2,550,000 per month' in Iran, mainly on military missions, as too high and called for expenditure cuts.[67] The economic imperatives compelled the British to withdraw their military forces from Iran quickly. To George Curzon, the keen imperialist who had become the British foreign secretary in October 1919, the evacuation of British military forces would be a disaster.

On 9 August 1919, after some nine months of secret negotiations, the Anglo-Persian Agreement which had been concealed from Iranians and the international community was made public. Britain's main Iranian interlocutors during the negotiations had been Vosuq al-dowleh, the prime minister, Sarem al-dowleh, minister of finance, and Nosrat al-dowleh Firuz, minister of justice and the eldest son of Abdolhoseyn Farmanfarma. 'The British came to call these men 'the Triumvirate' and to put great faith in their judgement.'[68]

The text of the 1919 Agreement began with a 'categorical' reiteration on the part of the British government 'to respect absolutely the independence and integrity of Persia'. The British government granted a loan of £2 million to the Persian government at an annual rate of 7 per cent. The loan was to finance two major 'reforms'. First, 'The British Government will supply, at the cost of the Persian government, the services of whatever expert advisers may, after consultation between the two Governments, be considered necessary for the several departments of the Persian Administration.' Second, 'The British Government will supply, at the cost of the Persian government, such officers and such munition and equipment of modern type as may be adjudicated necessary by a joint commission of military experts, British and Persian . . . in respect of the formation of a uniform force . . .' The British government also announced that it was 'prepared to co-operate with the Persian Government for the encouragement of Anglo-Persian enterprise ... both by means of railway construction and other forms of transport ...'. Finally, the two governments agreed to appoint 'a joint Committee of experts for the examination and revision of the existing Customs Tariff ...'.⁶⁹

To Iranians suspicious of long-held British colonial designs, the 1919 Agreement reeked of foul play. Britain seemed to be cornering Iran to accept its monopoly and exclusive position in financial, military, administrative and industrial domains. The Agreement was an exclusivity treaty, designating Britain as the only country with a unique dominion over Iran. What was fair and equitable to the British was more explicit in one of the two letters attached to the 9 August 1919 Agreement. Britain assured the Persian government that it 'will not claim the cost of maintenance of British troops sent into Persia for the defence of her neutrality'. In return, Britain requested 'a similar assurance that the Persian Government will not claim indemnity for damage done by British troops in Persian territory'.⁷⁰

The irony was hyperbolic in that Iran would agree that British troops had invaded it to protect its neutrality. Vosuq al-dowleh claimed that the treaty was signed under exceptional circumstances and emergency conditions. In his eyes, it prevented the greater evil of domestic chaos, financial collapse and Bolshevik domination and was, therefore, the least of evils. Furthermore, given the military might of Britain, Vosuq al-dowleh reasoned that it would not have allowed any other country to come to Iran's help and he was, therefore, obliged to sign the treaty.

An American Political Scientist's Assessment of the 1919 Agreement

But whatever be the present intention of the British Government or the legal aspect of the question, it is useless to disguise the fact that in all human probability Persia will remain de facto under the virtual protection of Great Britain for an indefinite time to come. (A. Hershey)⁷¹

The French and the Treaty

Over and above its content and manner of presentation, what shocked French officials most about the Treaty was its premature implementation. [Charles] Bonin [the French minister in Tehran] describes this procedure as 'the invasion of British functionaries and officers implementing a treaty not yet ratified'. (M. Habibi).⁷²

> ### The US Secretary of State on the 1919 Treaty
>
> The Anglo-Persian agreement has caused a very unfavorable impression upon both the President and me and we are not disposed to ask our Minister at Teheran to assist the British Government or to ask him to preserve a friendly attitude toward this agreement . . . The secrecy employed and the silence observed seem contrary to the open and frank methods which ought to have prevailed and may well impair the bases of a peace inspired by friendliness. We cannot and will not do anything to encourage such secret negotiations or to assist in allaying the suspicion and dissatisfaction which we share as to an agreement negotiated in this manner. (L. Lansing)[73]

No sooner was the agreement made public that a widespread wave of opposition formed against it. Even though a few papers such as those of Seyyed Zia and Malek al-shoara Bahar defended the Agreement, the majority rallied against it. The Iranian sense of nationalism and patriotism was once again aroused. Demonstrations and meeting were organized, and the clergy condemned it from the pulpit.

'Thus, not only the modern nationalists, but the ulama and religious community, Democrats and popular constitutionalists (e.g. Mostwafi al-mamalek), the Gendarmerie and some of the Cossack officers were united in the belief that Iran had become a British protectorate.'[74] Under martial law, the government repressed the opposition. Within a month, Vosuq al-dowleh's reacted by arresting seventeen members of the opposition at Sheykh Abdolhasan Mosque in Tehran and banishing them to Qazvin. Four former ministers were arrested and exiled to Kashan.

Even Ahmad Shah, who had materially benefitted from British largess, publicly expressed his opposition to the Agreement during his visit to in Paris. Asked to support the Agreement, the shah announced that: 'a constitutional monarch was not permitted to opine on foreign policy issues without their ratification by the Majles'.[75] The treaty remained illegal as long as it was not ratified by the Majles. Preparations for and elections to the 4th Majles had been underway since May 1917. Suddenly, the inauguration of Parliament had become of great importance. Vosuq al-dowleh added to his own unpopularity by ensuring that all candidates were first and foremost in favour of the Treaty. He was aided in this objective by the British consular officers in the provinces.

Irrespective of its flaws and merits, the 1919 Treaty unveiled corruption at the highest political echelons in Iran and Great Britain. The moral and ethical scandal surrounding the Treaty became further proof of the injustice and perverse designs of the those who imposed it and the betrayal of those who signed it on behalf of Iran.

Forty-seven years after the scandal involving Iranian politicians and diplomats receiving money to facilitate the 1872 agreement with Baron Julius de Reuter, the

Iranian ruling class was again implicated in a similar affair. After considerable haggling over the just price of the bribe between the Triumvirate and the shah on the Iranian side and Curzon and Cox, on the British side, both parties reached a convenient private agreement. The money-grabbing shah who had been receiving a monthly 'subsidy' of 15,000 tomans from the British since 1916, was promised 'Britain's friendly support as long as he acted in accordance with the policy and advice of the British Government.' This implied supporting Vosuq al-dowleh's government, as was the term for the continued receipt of his original salary during Vosuq al-dowleh's first cabinet.

The Triumvirate was offered asylum 'if the occasion developed', and were paid a handsome sum of £131,000, instead of the £200,000 that they had adamantly asked for.[76] Half of this sum (200,000 tomans) was paid in cash to Sarem al-dowleh on 11 and 13 August 1919 and the other half (200,000 tomans) was placed in Vosuq al-dowleh's account in the British owned Shahi Bank. This sum was paid out of the £2 million British loan to Iran.

To obtain the 1919 Treaty, palms had been greased, and special promises had been made in secret, veiled from the eyes of respective legislatures, rendering the parties involved on both sides bribe-givers and bribe-takers, common criminals. The popular reaction to Vosuq al-dawleh, and the 1919 Agreement, was expressed by the famous Iranian poet of the time, Mirzadeh Eshqi, who wrote, 'O Vosuq al-dowleh, Iran was not your dad's property/holding.'

The Background to the 1921 Coup

Between the signature of the Anglo-Persian Agreement in August 1919 and the February 1921 coup, Iran lived through 18 tumultuous months. Germany had been the model country for Iranian nationalists and intellectuals in 1915. By 1919, it was the Bolshevik Revolution and communism that appealed to radical Iranians, who were disappointed with political developments at home. The repudiation of all Russian concessions and treaties, and the later annulment of debts owed to Tsarist Russia were unprecedented acts of goodwill and fraternity towards Iran. Here was a regime that did not seem greedily interested in taking advantage of Iran's financial misfortunes.

The rudiments of communism encapsulated in slogans promoted uprooting of poverty through equality, and the promise of bread, land, electricity and peace fell on receptive ears. The dismantling of old socio-economic relations and ridding the country of British colonialism appealed to progressive nationalists. The movements of Mirza Kuchek Khan and Mohammad Khiyabani, combining elements of nationalism, anti-colonialism, anti-despotism, progressive Shiism and socialism, were very much influenced by the Bolshevik movement and revolution.

Khiyabani's Movement: From Reform to Cautious Rebellion

Mohammad Khiyabani was born in 1880, some 70 kilometres from Tabriz. He went to seminary school and was 17 when he read Abdolrahim Talebof's influential work *Ketabe Ahmad* (Ahmad's Book). For some three to four years, he led the noon congregational prayers at Tabriz's Jame Mosque and the evening prayers at Karim Mosque. He took up arms in Azarbayjan during the constitutional movement, joined the *Mojahedin* and entered the Tabriz branch of the Democrat Party. He was elected to the 2nd Majles from Tabriz. In Parliament, he was a chief proponent of Morgan Shuster and an ardent opponent of Russia's ultimatum. Khiyabani knew French and Russian and was familiar with the works of 'Voltaire, Montesquieu, and Jean-Jacques Rousseau.'[77]

Following the February Revolution in Russia, Iran's northern provinces which had been under repressive Russian military domination could breathe again. In April 1917, Kiyabani revitalized the Azarbayjan Democratic Party (*Ferqehe Democratic Azarbayjan*), which had been dormant for five years. Soon the Democratic Party established branches throughout the province.

The weekly party publication, *Tajaddod* (Modernity), first appeared on 9 April 1917. It carried articles by Khiyabani and expressed the ideas and concerns of the Azarbayjan Democratic Party. In his article on 30 April 1917, Khiyabani insisted on the thorough application of the Constitution and pressed the central government of Vosuq al-dowleh to begin elections to the Majles. Khiyabani, like Mirza Kuchek Khan, was anxious to see Iran return to parliamentary democracy.

On 24 August 1917, the first 'Provincial Conference' of Azarbayjan, with 480 representatives from various cities, convened in Tabriz at the behest of Kiyabani (Figure 2.5). The mandate of this provincial parliament/council was to choose patriotic representatives who would supervise the proper implementation of the Constitution, oversee the honest conduct of government officials and help rebuild the country.

From August 1917 to August 1918, Khiyabani made recommendations and preached democracy, fairness, liberty, nationalism and honesty. He warned against dictatorship, called for democratic rule, respect for the Constitution and holding immediate elections to the 4th Majles. He pleaded with politicians in Tehran that delaying parliamentary elections reflected poorly on the shah and made people angry towards him. Khiyabani believed that central governments had to be composed of ethical, upright, patriotic, reformist, constitutionalist and well-trusted figures. He considered the types of Vosuq al-dowleh and Ayn al-dowleh as 'reactionary and despotic' politicians who were repressive and corrupt. In the same breath, Khiyabani insisted that 'Azarbayjan seeks the independence of Iran ... and has already declared

Figure 2.5 Stamp printed in Iran shows Sheykh Mohammad Khiyabani. *Source: Via Getty Images.*

itself an integral part of it.'[78] His numerous articles and speeches reveal no indications of separatism or pan-Turkism.

The second Vosuq al-dowleh government (8 August 1918–3 July 1920) radicalized Khiyabani. Two issues strengthened his pessimism towards the central government and pushed him to refuse its authority. The revelation of the Anglo-Persian 1919 treaty was a hard blow for Iranian nationalists, who felt betrayed. The public's adverse reaction to Vosuq al-dowleh overlapped with the elections to the 4th Majles. Preparations for this election had been underway since 5 May 1917, when the shah issued his royal edict for its commencement.

Khiyabani strongly believed that discussion, ratification or dismissal of the 1919 Treaty had to be left to the 4th Majles. As the very long parliamentary elections were coming to an end, there were widespread rumors and reports that Vosuq al-dowleh was engineering the process to ensure the success of deputies favourable to the treaty. On 10 November 1919, candidates of the Azarbayjan Democratic Party won a decisive victory in Tabriz.

On 3 April 1920, the police surrounded the headquarters of the Azarbayjan Democratic Party to arrest Mirza Baqer, a democrat. The people came to Mirza Baqer's help and clashes ensued between the police and pro-Democrats. Kiyabani's supporters occupied the police station and took control of the city. On 4 April, Khiyabani addressed a large crowd and declared that the people's revolt in Tabriz was against Vosuq al-dowleh's government which had signed the 'ruinous' 1919 Treaty. He announced that Azarbayjan would henceforth be called Azadestan (Land of the Free). Khiyabani wished to distinguish Iran's Azarbayjan from the anti-Bolshevik separatist Azarbayjan Democratic Republic, established on 26 May 1918 in Arran (Russia). By renaming Azarbayjan, Khiyabani sought to distance his movement from any pan-Turkist and irredentist claims of uniting the two Azarbayjans.

After the uprising, Khiyanabi's supporters armed themselves, and all military and police units in Tabriz paid allegiance to him. The Khiyabani movement aimed at 'ensuring freedom, irrespective of sex and religion', 'providing welfare and equality before the law' and upholding 'liberty, independence and equality'.[79] On April 22, Khiyabani, who addressed the people daily since the uprising, announced that 'the Tabriz uprising was for establishing a democratic and free government within the laws of the land'.[80] Soon, Khiyabani's anti-colonial, anti-despotic and socially conscious and responsible movement spread to other cities in Azarbayjan. Government offices were occupied in Zanjan, Ahar, Maragheh, Urumiyeh, Khoy and Ardebil.

In May 1920, Maj. Cecil John Edmonds, a British political officer with the North Persian Forces, met with Ahmad Kasravi, a member of an anti-Khiyabani minority faction within the Tabriz Democrats. Edmonds encouraged Kasravi and his friends to get rid of Khiyabani. After the plot was discovered, a number were arrested and Kasravi fled to Tehran. Edmonds had also met with Khiyabani during his visit to Tabriz, offered him a 60,000-toman cheque and requested that he stop criticizing Vosuq al-dowleh and cease emphasizing his friendly relations with the British.

Khiyabani on Modern Monarchies

Today kings have to either disappear or leave the running of the country to the majority. In today's world, despotism can no longer rule. (M. Khiyabani)[81]

When Moshir al-dowleh formed his government on 28 June 1920, Mokhber al-saltaneh Hedayat became his minister of finance. On 5 September 1920, Hedayat was dispatched to Tabriz as the new governor with full powers to put an end to Khiyabani's uprising. Hedayat had a dim view of Khiyabani and believed that he and a few of his supporters 'had intimidated the people through terror' and 'wished to secede from Iran'.[82] On 12 September 1920, the headquarters of the Azarbayjan Democratic Party was attacked.

At the time of the attack, Khiyabani had dispatched his military forces from Tabriz and Ardebil to Qarjehdagh/Qarehdagh and Ahar to put an end to Amir Ershad's brigandage in the area. The commander of his elite National Guard forces, Maj. Mir-Hoseyn Hashemi, had betrayed him and had ordered his troops out of Tabriz on the pretext of a nocturnal military manoeuvre on the night before the attack.

On 13 September, Khiyabani was shot dead by the Cossack forces in his pursuit. Mokhber al-saltaneh Hedayat claimed that Khiyabani had committed suicide. After three days of pillage, widespread arrests and bloodletting, the Khiyabani movement was vanquished. After the February 1921 coup, Reza Khan confided in Mokhber al-saltaneh Hedayat that, 'had you, not ended the sedition in Tabriz, our job would have been more difficult in Rasht [repressing the Kuchek Khan revolt]'.[83]

Khiyabani's five-month rule had mixed achievements. He had shut down opposition newspapers and arrested those who conspired against him, but not a single person was executed in the name of the revolution and a general amnesty had been granted on 23 June 1920. Numerous new schools for boys and girls, both at the primary and secondary level, were founded and the First of May was officially recognized as Labour Day, with a garden party to honour it.

The Democrats had promoted plays, music and concerts. They closed liquor stores and brothels, and outlawed gambling and the use of royally conferred/sold titles such as 'al-dowleh', 'al-saltaneh' or 'al-mamalek'. Khiyabani revived the memory of Howard Baskerville, the American hero of Iran's constitutional movement, and extolled him for 'sacrificing his life for the cause of Iran's freedom'.[84] The Democrats founded poor and elderly houses and centres for handicapped people and their Food Commission distributed cheap bread to the needy.

The 1919 Treaty is Not Acceptable to Iranians

In March 1920, ten months after the signature of the Anglo-Persian Treaty, Esmond Ovey reported to the British Cabinet that the situation in Iran was disappointing. To realize the objectives of the 1919 Treaty, he recommended a British-backed despotic executive system in Iran, with a dictatorial cabinet propped by British advisors, guiding Iranian ministers from behind the scenes. He proposed a dictatorial prime minister for a transitional period, who would improve the lot of Iranians, stabilize the financial situation and create a united army. Ovey recommended opening Parliament but warned against idealistic temptations and suggested an engineered election, where suitable candidates would fill the Majles. Ovey's recommendation would come true eight months later with the 21 February 1921 coup led by Seyyed Zia and Reza Khan.

The British first tried to weather the anti-Treaty storm by forcefully supporting Vosuq al-dowleh. In June 1920, they threatened to discontinue the monthly gratuity of 15,000 tomans, which they had been paying to Ahmad Shah, if he continued to undermine Vosuq al-dowleh. Soon, however, the British realized that Vosuq al-dowleh had become a liability and needed to be replaced by a more nationally acceptable figure. On 28 June 1920, Hasan Moshir al-dowleh, the nationalist, honest and constitutionalist who in the past had supported the 1919 Treaty, became prime minister.[85]

Moshir al-dowleh's premiership was a significant step towards the slow death of the Treaty. Moshir al-dowleh infuriated Curzon by delaying the implementation of the Treaty until the new Parliament would decide its fate. Furthermore, Moshir al-dowleh prevented the assortment of British advisers from taking up their 'advisory' positions in various ministries. Herman Norman, Britain's new minister in Iran, replacing Percy Cox, believed that Moshir al-dowleh's popular government needed to be supported by Britain and the Treaty to be approved by the Majles.

To support his policy, Norman sent Curzon reports written by Sydney Armitage-Smith, the British chief financial advisor to the Persian government, and Lt Col. Harold Dickson, the British chief military advisor. The two Englishmen wrote in support of the Moshir al-dowleh government and condemned Vosuq al-dowleh's policies and initiatives. Curzon's response was curt. He retorted that Norman should stop sending him such long and confusing reports. It enraged Curzon that his men in Tehran saw the 1919 Treaty and Vosuq al-dowleh as direct sources of Iran's recent wave of resentment towards the British.

From late October 1920, Curzon was frustrated with the dimming fate of the 1919 Treaty. He became even aggressive towards Norman and Gen. Edmund Ironside who pursued their own agenda and turned a deaf ear to Curzon's instructions. Ironside had taken command of the North Persia Force in Qazvin on 4 October. By 29 October 1920, disenchanted and enraged, Curzon washed his hands of Iranian politics and informed Norman that henceforth, he and Ironside would be responsible for securing British interests in Iran

The Bolsheviks in Anzali and Its Consequences

On 18 May 1920, confrontation between the Bolshevik and British fleets in the Caspian Region, culminated in the Red Army's attack on British headquarters in Anzali. The Red Army's campaign was against British-supported White Russians in the region, especially the anti-Bolshevik Russian Lt Gen. Anton Denikin. The White Russians fled the city, Anzali was occupied by the Red Army and the Bolsheviks seized the entire British flotilla. The British forces on the ground did not engage and retreated swiftly from Anzali and Rasht, leaving behind clothing, blankets, ammunition, food and most importantly petrol. The flight of British forces gave rise to the fear of an imminent Bolshevik takeover of the country.

Shortly after the Bolshevik landing in Anzali, 'a provisional revolutionary government' was established under the leadership of Kuchek Khan and backed by the Red Army. The Soviets, however, promised not to interfere in Iranian affairs. On 3 June 1920, Kuchek Khan entered Rasht and was welcomed as a hero. He announced the abolition of the monarchy and its replacement with a republic. From here on, the Jangalis became a socialist organization called 'Iran's Red Revolution Group'.[86] Kuchek Khan became the chief commissar and the commissar of war of the revolutionary committee governing Rasht.

From the outset, Kuchek Khan and the more radical elements of his coalition clashed. In the long debate over the fate of old government representatives, such as Issa Sadiq and Mohsen Sadr al-ashraaf, Kuchek Khan intervened to prevent their execution, demanded by the radicals. On 14 June 1920, the Cossack forces which had been resisting the authority of the new government were at last subdued and a declaration was issued in the name of 'The Soviet Republic of Iran' announcing the surrender of some 800 Cossacks. Once again, Kuchek Khan stepped in to prevent the execution of the Iranian Cossacks.

By June, tensions had heightened as hardened communist members of the Baku based Justice Party, arrived in Rasht after May 1920 to pursue a Sovietization programme. The communist newcomers clashed with Kuchek Khan, who opposed communist propaganda in Iran. The newly arrived members of the Justice Party published their communist literature in their publications, 'Red Iran', 'Red Revolution' and 'Communist'.

Ehsanollah Khan Doostdar pressed for closer cooperation between the Jangalis and the Soviets, but Kuchek Khan steered an independent course. Conflict between the two escalated when Kuchek Khan refused entrance to 700 communists who had come by boat from Baku. Avoiding a clash, Kuchek Khan left Rasht and went to Fuman. In a letter, Kuchek Khan informed Lenin that he would not go back to Rasht unless Soviet officials ceased their intervention in Iranian matters.

On 9 August 1920, Yakov Blumkin, the **Cheka** representative in Gilan, engineered a coup against Kuchek Khan. Kuchek Khan's supporters were rounded up by Bolshevik forces and he was labelled as a counter-revolutionary. Ehsanollah Khan Doostdar became the new chief commissar and Khalou Qorban the new commissar of war. The commissar of interior was Seyyed Jafar Javadzadeh Badkubehi (Seyyed Jafar Pishehvari).[87]

In his isolated hideout, Kuchek Khan rejected any cooperation with the new Revolutionary Committee in power and hammered at the notion that he would not compromise the independence of his country for any cause. He reminded his new Soviet foes that, 'We have lived honorably, have gone through the revolutionary stages honorably and we shall die honorably.'[88]

The Red opposition was weakened by inner divisions and feuds. In 1920, Rasht exchanged hands between government forces and the Reds led by Ehsanollah Khan, until it fell to government forces and the communists took flight. A year later, on 14 August 1921, old friends who had turned foes, had mended fences. With the help of Heydar Amuoghlu, they united to form a new Revolutionary Committee dedicated to restoring freedom, combatting the monarchy and counter-revolutionaries and improving the people's lot. Kuchek Khan again became the chief commissar and the commissar of finance.

Continued Bolshevik presence on Iranian soil and the revival of the Jangali movement rattled Ahmad Shah who feared for his life. The Soviet-backed Jangali movement also posed a threat to the British Empire. During summer and autumn of 1920, the central government lived in the fear of a sweeping Bolshevik attack on Tehran.

Seeking Alternatives

On 22 December 1920, the British War Office announced that it intended to begin withdrawing its forces from Iran by 1 April 1921. The First of April was 'that famous end to the financial year for all Service Departments' in Britain.[89] The British did not wish to incur any more expenses by keeping their forces in Iran after this date. Norman panicked and asked that Norpeforce not be withdrawn until the autumn of 1920, and that the South Persian Rifles remain in Iran for another full year.

He believed that without this extension, Iran would become defenceless before a Bolshevik onslaught and enter a period of chaos. The British, however, were fixed on their departure schedule and Norman had to pursue an alternative course. On 3 January 1921, Norman informed Curzon that the fall of Ahmad Shah would not be an unfortunate event but finding a replacement might be difficult. For once, Curzon agreed with Norman that all alternatives to Ahmad Shah would be better than him. Yet, both men worried about the disorder and disintegration that would ensue after his fall. By this time, out of fear of an imminent Bolshevik takeover, Ahmad Shah was himself ready to abdicate and desperately wanted to leave the country. He was only restrained by the British. The shah's desperate mood made the idea of finding an alternative for him more compelling.

Norman and Ironside were, therefore, looking for alternatives with certain credentials. Their successful candidate needed to be daring, iron-willed, authoritarian, up-and-coming, anti-communist and with a clean political slate on whom Britain could rely. Finding all those features in one person proved difficult, therefore the Norman-Ironside team opted for a civilian and an officer.

What to Do with the Cossacks

On 25 August 1920, Cossack forces, under the command of the White Russian Col. Vsevolod Staroselski, were defeated by the combined Jangali and Bolshevik forces around Anzali and forced to retreat. Rasht fell to the revolutionary forces on 28 August. On 23 September, supported by British aviation, the Cossacks re-entered Rasht but retreated again on 22 October, enabling the revolutionaries to retake Rasht. Russians fighting against Russians was taking its toll on the morale of Cossack troops. During these campaigns, Staroselski, commander of the Cossack forces in Iran, was leading his unpaid and disheartened troops (Figure 2.6).

Staroselski was appointed by Ahmad Shah to his position in 1917 and had the shah's full support. The Russian general was suspicious of British designs and believed

Figure 2.6 Persian Cossack Brigade. *Source: Brooklyn Museum.*

that talk of dissolving the Cossack division disheartened and weakened the resolve of his fighting men.

On 6 October 1920, the War Office informed Gen. Almeyr Haldane, the chief of staff of British forces in Iraq, that to deal with foreign and domestic threats, it intended to keep British troops in Iran until spring 1921. Haldane, in turn, informed Gen. Edmund Ironside of this decision. Ironside's mandate as the commander of the Norpeforce was to check the advance of the Bolsheviks, get rid of Staroselski, work towards a combined force under British command and organize the eventual withdraw of British forces.

Staroselski's retreat from Rasht in August 1920 provided Ironside and Norman with an excuse to remove him. Both men argued that it would be best to have a nominal Iranian commander of the Cossack forces with British officers managing the military operations. Ironside and Norman also accused Staroselski of incompetence, corruption and anti-British propaganda. Moshir al-dowleh agreed on dismissing Staroselski but rejected the idea of having British officers managing the military operations. Although Norman insisted on the employment of British officers, effectively giving the command of Cossack forces to Britain, Moshir al-dowleh refused to comply and resigned on 25 October 1920.

On 27 October, Norman's candidate, Fatollah Akbar (Sepahdar Rashti), a wealthy landowner from Gilan and an old constitutionalist, became prime minister. Before his appointment, he had promised Norman to carry out British demands. Three days after taking office, Akbar arranged for the immediate departure of Staroselski from Tehran. At this time, Staroselski's 3,500 Cossack force, which had retreated from Rasht, was at the British Aqa Baba Camp near Qazvin.

On 4 November, Iranian newspapers reported that close to 100 Russian officers were expelled and given fifteen days to leave the country. Upon Staroselski's ousting the affairs of the Cossack Brigade were handed over by Ironside to Lt Col. Henry Smyth, whose position and responsibility among the Cossacks was unofficial and even secret. When the Cossacks arrived in Qazvin, they had no winter clothing and many of them were struck by malaria. Smyth quickly whipped the Cossacks, who were in a pitiful state, into a viable and efficient fighting force.

Qasem Khan Vali (Sardar Homayun) had been dispatched from Tehran as the nominal commander of the Cossack Brigade. But Ironside and Smyth decided that Sardar Homayun was not cut out for the job, while they were both impressed with Reza Khan and his demeanour. They immediately made 'him commander of the Cossack Brigade at least temporarily'.[90]

The Iron Committee

In December 1920, Sardar Moazam Khorasani (Teymurtash) and Seyyed Zia contacted the prime minister, Akbar. Both men were pro-British figures and well known to the British Embassy in Iran. They had been in contact with Norman and were acting on behalf of the British. They urged the prime minister to accept the British proposal of forming a national army under British control and pressed for the gendarmerie and the police to be also placed under the command of British officers.

By 7 December, Norman, Seyyed Zia and Sardar Moazam Khorasani (Teymurtash) had been plotting a mini coup. In case certain ministers were to disagree with British control of the Iranian army, the plan was for Seyyed Zia and Teymurtash to take over their ministerial posts. Unimpressed by Seyyed Zia and Teymurtash, on 9 December 1920, Curzon warned Norman against becoming entangled in such ploys.

Seyyed Zia, the editor of the daily *Raad* (Thunder) had been openly a staunch supporter of Vosuq al-dawleh and the 1919 Treaty. He was well known in British circles and well connected with influential British diplomatic and military figures. Back in late November 1919, Vosuq al-dowleh chose Seyyed Zia, who had no previous foreign service experience, to head a diplomatic mission to Baku. It was on this trip that Seyyed Zia and Capt. Kazem Sayyah met with the British colonel, Henry Smyth. All three men would later collaborate in the February 1921 coup. Seyyed Zia later claimed that on his recommendation, by November 1920, Smyth had become the de facto director of the Cossack Brigade.

The Iron Committee

With the change in the political climate, and the surge in anti-elite propaganda in the Persian press, Sayyed Zia became a more viable choice to head the semi-clandestine Iron Committee, a quasi-revolutionary party financed by the British legation to foster popular anti-Bolshevik sentiments. (A. Amanat)[91]

Sometime around 1919, the secret Iron Committee began operating in Tehran under the leadership of Seyyed Zia (Figure 2.7). Members of this pro-British and anti-Communist organization considered themselves as patriots who were fed up with foreign interventions. Their number, both civilian and military, did not exceed twenty. Seyyed Zia had invited four members, Capt. Kazem Khan Sayyah, Maj. Masud Khan Keyhan, Adl al-molk Dadgar and Mansur al-saltaneh Adl, to a closed meeting to discuss the coup and the suitability of Reza Khan for participating in the coup.

It was Capt. Kazem Khan Sayyah who had recommended Reza Khan to Seyyed Zia. At the time, Capt. Sayyah and Maj. Keyhan were training the Cossacks at Qazvin under the dual command of Henry Smyth and Reza Khan. Maj. Keyhan was Smyth's second-in-command, while Capt. Sayyah was Gen. Ironside's official translator. Sayyah had a high opinion of Reza Khan for commanding the military aspect of the coup, because 'he was tall, ill-tempered, solemn and loved by his men'. While all members agreed on involving Reza Khan, Maj. Keyhan opposed the idea, arguing that, 'this Cossack officer is both illiterate and a coward. If he attains power, he will be become dangerous for both these reasons'.[92] The four in favour finally convinced Maj. Keyhan.

Seyyed Zia intended to form a strong centralized government that would end anarchy and turmoil, while 'working rationally with the British'. He envisioned himself

Figure 2.7 Seyyed Ziaeddin Tabatabai. *Source: Wikimedia Commons.*

Figure 2.8 Reza Khan. *Source: Wikimedia Commons.*

as a Mussolini-like prime minister, with dictatorial powers and reliant on a 'national military force'.[93] He needed, therefore, a partner with Reza Khan's characteristics to obtain and remain in power.

> **Ironside on the Coup**
>
> I fancy that everyone thinks that I engineered the *coup d'etat*. I suppose I did strictly speaking.[94]

On 21 January 1921, Curzon encouraged Norman to use all of his influence to bring a strong government to power. Before his departure from Qazvin on 16 February 1921, Ironside spoke to Reza Khan who had been promoted to Lt Col. and who now commanded the Cossack Brigade. Reza Khan pledged to keep the shah on his throne and not to conduct any offensive action against the withdrawing British forces. At a meeting, with Smyth present, Ironside informed Reza Khan 'that Britain would not oppose his seizing power if he would agree not to depose Ahmad Shah'.[95] To Ironside, Reza Khan seemed 'a strong and fearless man who had his country's good at heart'.[96]

The Perfectly Coordinated Coup

> **British Support for the Coup**
>
> The idea of a strong anti-Bolshevik government had the British Embassy's blessing. The Embassy . . . unanimously supported the Cossacks and misters [Walter Alexander] Smart . . . and [Godfrey] Havard, the Embassy counsellor, supported this idea. (Seyyed Zia)[97]

> **'Coordination'**
>
> Britons acted as intermediaries between Sayyid Zia and the Cossacks. Contemporary accounts named legation Oriental Secretary Walter Alexander Smart as 'privy to the whole proceeding.' In addition to Lt Cols Smyth and W. G. Grey (who both admitted involvement), legation staffer Victor Mallet and Captain C. J. Edmonds also may have been involved. (M. Zirinsky)[98]

> ### 'Greasing the Right Palms'
> I received the money ... the 25,000 tomans monthly allowance that the British paid for the salary of the Cossacks and gendarmes ... I paid all the postponed salaries of the Cossack soldiers and officers in addition to a bonus ... Payments to Reza Khan and Cossack officers were apart. (Seyyed Zia)[99]

> ### 'Gaining Iranian Compliance'
> Norman also served as midwife at the birth of Seyyid Zia's government. On 20 February 1921, having heard that the Cossacks were nearing Tehran, Norman, 'sent for General Westdahl, the Swedish chief of police, and impressed on him the importance, in case the Cossacks should enter the town, of seeing that his men confined themselves to their proper duty of maintaining public order and did not become involved in any fighting which might take place'. (M. Zirinsky)[100]

The night before the coup, Friday, 20 February 1921, the Cossacks congregated at Karvansaraye Sangi, near Karaj. Five key players swore on the Quran not to shed one another's blood, even if they became the worst of enemies. The coup plotters included Col. Reza Khan Mirpanj, Maj. Ahmad Agha Khan (Amir-Ahmadi), Maj. Masud Khan Keyhan, Capt. Kazem Khan Sayyah and Seyyed Zia.

On 21 February 1921, the duo, Seyyed Zia and Reza Khan, entered Tehran at the head of some 3,000 Cossacks of the Hamedan and Qazvin regiments. They carried out an almost bloodless coup, perfectly accomplished and met with no resistance. The coup was presented as an urgent move on the part of patriots or revolutionaries, as Norman called them, to save Tehran, the country and the crown from the Bolsheviks after the departure of British troops.

Seyyed Zia and Reza Khan kept Ahmad Shah on the throne, pledged their friendship to Britain and imposed martial law on Tehran, Qom, Qazvin, Semnan, Damqan and Kashan. Seyyed Zia set aside his turban and became prime minister, Col. Reza Khan became Sardar Sepah (chief of staff) and commander of the Cossack Brigade, Capt. Kazem Khan Sayyah was promoted to the rank of colonel and became Tehran's military governor and Maj. Masud Khan Keyhan was appointed minister of war. The Eton and Cambridge-educated British minister, Herman Norman gleefully reported that, 'Seyyid Zia-ed-din was appointed virtual dictator by the revolutionaries.'[101]

The ousted prime minister, Fatollah Akbar, sought sanctuary at the British Legation. On the morrow of the coup, some 80–100 politicians, clergy and activists of all shades, pro- and anti-British were arrested. In their eyes, it was not only Seyyed Zia, but also his British mentors who had thrown them in jail. Old politicians, notables, landowners and ministers, including Farmanfarma, Nosrat al-dowleh (his son), Ayn al-dowleh, Saad al-dowleh, Mohammadvali Tonokaboni (Sepahsalar Azam), Ahmad Qavam and Akbar-Mirza Sarem al-dowleh were arrested. 'Amongst these prisoners were some thirty of the richest and most influential people in Persia.'[102] From the opposite side of the aisle, Hasan Modarres, Hashem Ashtiyani, Mohammad Farrokhi-Yazdi and Ali Dashti were also rounded up. Contrary to past cabinets, only one of Seyyed Zia's ministers had any previous ministerial experience, the rest were all new faces, some of them quite unknown in political circles.

Britain Protecting Its Interests in Iran

The Seyyed Zia and Reza Khan team was friendly toward Britain and enjoyed its support after it came to power. Five days after the coup, on 26 February, the Iranian government signed the Russo-Persian Treaty of Friendship, putting to rest anxieties about an imminent Bolshevik invasion. The agreement renounced all previous agreements between the two countries, including Iranian concessions given to Russia in the past. It also prohibited the formation, presence or transit of any third forces in their respective territories, hostile to the signatories. All Soviet troops, including those stationed in Rasht and Azarbayjan, were evacuated by 23 June 1921.

By 1921, Britain had become completely dependent on Iranian oil. Losing its control over its oil interests in Iran would have been catastrophic for the British, both commercially and militarily. In January 1921, about a month before the Seyyed Zia and Reza Khan coup, the British Admiralty reported that Britain's petroleum needs, both for military and commercial ships, were being entirely supplied by Iran's southern oil fields. British imports stood at 350,000 tons annually and it was predicted to reach 500,000 tons.

The Anglo-Persian Oil Company supplied the petroleum needs of the British Admiralty at a discount rate. If Britain was to obtain her fuel from any other source than Iran it would have been obliged to pay six to seven times more. The British Admiralty warned that even with much higher prices, it was doubtful that Britain could secure its petroleum needs from anywhere else. Therefore, access to Iranian oil, honouring of old oil agreements and the maintenance of friendly commercial and political relations with a strong government in Iran was more important to Britain than hanging onto the dead letter of the 1919 Treaty.

Factual and Analytical Questions

1. Why was Iran's neutrality during the First World War not respected by the Central and Allied Powers? How realistic was Iran's 'strict neutrality policy'?
2. Explain the dual power in Iran between 14 November 1915 and 11 November 1918. What caused it?
3. When was the National Defence Committee created? What did it stand for? Why was it unsuccessful?
4. What was the 'Sepahsalar Agreement' of August 1916? What were its long-term consequences?
5. What was the mandate of the South Persian Rifles in Iran and how did it differ from the Dunsterforce?
6. What was Iran hoping to attain at the Paris Peace Conference? Was it successful?
7. What were the terms of the Anglo-Persian Agreement of 1919?
8. What were the political demands of Kuchek Khan and Khiyabani?
9. Why did the Red Army invade Anzali in May 1920?
10. How real was the threat of a Bolshevik invasion of Iran in the summer and autumn of 1920?
11. What was the Iron Committee? What role did it play in the February 1921 coup?
12. What role did the prospect of a British withdrawal of their military forces play in the February 1921 coup?

Seminar Questions

1. To what extent could economically and militarily underdeveloped countries such as Iran conclude non-zero-sum deals with colonial occupational powers?
2. 'The Tehran and the National Defence Committee were equally unpatriotic and unrepresentative of the people as they both relied on foreign powers for support.' Discuss.
3. 'The instability of Iranian governments during the First World War was the result of Russo-British meddling in Iranian politics in pursuit of their respective national interests.' Discuss.
4. 'How and why did Mirza Kuchek Khan and Sheykh Mohammad Khiyabani and their movements shift from constitutionalism and parliamentarianism to armed resistance?' Discuss.
5. Discuss the validity of Professor Hershey's statement on the 1919 Anglo-Persian Agreement that: 'whatever be the present intention of the British Government or the legal aspect of the question, it is useless to disguise the fact

that in all human probability Persia will remain de facto under the virtual protection of Great Britain for an indefinite time to come'.
6 'The February 1921 coup was the work of the British'. Discuss and provide the pros and cons arguments.
7 'The February 1921 coup was intended to secure British commercial and military oil need.'

Discussion Questions

1 Why were the Germans preferred to the Russian and British forces in Iran during the First World War? Why did Iranians never warm to the presence of their Ottoman Muslim brothers in Iran during the war?
2 'Pro-Allied prime ministers were not all stooges or lackeys.' Discuss this statement and support your arguments with cases.
3 'Were Mirza Kuchek Khan and Sheykh Mohammad Khiyabani patriots, or Iranians in the service of foreigners intent on seceding from Iran?'
4 What did Iran's exclusion from participation in the Paris Peace Conference demonstrate in terms of international power politics?
5 How did the Bolshevik Revolution influence Iran?
6 'The British had differing and even opposing views of how to proceed with the Anglo-Persian Agreement of 1919 and how to deal with the post-British withdrawal of their forces.' Discuss.
7 Assess and evaluate Khiyabani's five-month rule, according to its aims and objectives.
8 Was Staroselski's ousting by Norman and Ironside the prelude to the February 1921 coup?
9 Why did the February 1921 coup face no resistance?

Glossary

Balfour, Arthur British prime minister, 1902–5 and British foreign secretary, 1916–19, under Prime Minister Lloyd George. On 2 November 1917, in a letter to Lord Lionel Rothschild, the leader of the Anglo-Jewish community, Balfour extended British support for 'the establishment in Palestine of a national home for the Jewish people'. This became known as the Balfour Declaration and formed the basis for the creation of the State of Israel.

Cheka The commonly known abbreviation for the first Soviet secret police organization, the All-Russian Extraordinary Commission. Founded in December 1917, it was placed under the leadership of Felix Dzerzhinsky, who personally dispatched Blumkin to Gilan, and had offices across the Soviet Union.

Haji Haj or pilgrimage to Mecca, like prayers and fasting is one of the obligatory acts of worship (*ebadat*) for all Muslims. A person who has fulfilled this obligation and returned from the pilgrimage is called a Haji.

Keynes, John Maynard One of the most influential economists of the twentieth Century and the father of Keynesian economics. Keynes was appointed financial representative for the Treasury to the Paris Peace Conference at Versailles in 1919. At the Conference, he opposed the imposition of heavy war reparations on Germany and later wrote his authoritative criticism called the *Economic Consequences of the Peace*, published in 1919.

Sublime Porte Bab-e Ali or the Sublime Porte, is a figure of speech referring to the seat of the imperial government of the Ottoman Empire.

White Russian The term refers to those Russians who after the October Revolution of 1917, remained loyal to the Romanovs and fought against the new Bolshevik government during the civil war of 1917–20.

3

Reza Shah

Nation-Building, Repression, Europeanization and Modernization, 1921–41

Chapter Outline

Prelude to Reza Khan's Rise	117
Reza Khan, Prime Minister	131
Reza Shah Pahlavi's Reign	143
The Despot	159
Glossary	167

Prelude to Reza Khan's Rise

Europeanized Intellectuals Root for Dictatorship

In December 1920, a group of European-educated intellectuals founded the Young Iran Society. Its members produced the first post-war issue of *Kaveh*, published in Berlin. Hasan Taqizadeh, the veteran constitutionalist, identified the paper's objective as 'the dissemination of European civilization in Iran, a holy war against hideboundness/fanaticism, serving national identity and unity, and striving for the cleanliness and protection of Farsi language and literature…' Taqizadeh emphasized 'the unconditional embrace and propagation of European civilization' and Iran's 'absolute surrender' to the European way of life. This included, 'the universal adoption of rites, rituals, manners, science, industry, life and in general the conditions/state of Europe (*farangestan*), except the language'. Over-emphasizing a newly found absolute truth, Taqizadeh, wrote: 'In appearance/outwardly and substance/inwardly, physically, and spiritually, Iran must become Europeanized and that is all.'[1] This was not an invitation but a blatant command.

On 6 August 1921, some five months after the February coup, *Kaveh* was calling for political stability and continuity, a strong army, a reformed financial system, public education and the employment of numerous knowledgeable and efficient foreign advisors.[2] *Kaveh* had become a solid protagonist of law and order and a strong centralized government. Taqizadeh, the freedom-loving partisan of constitutionalism, was condemning 'the radical ideas of freedom-lovers', who fostered chaos.[3] The new trend among educated intellectuals was the disavowal of the constitutional experience as a futile exercise that had failed to obtain tangible economic results.

Many of those who contributed to *Kaveh*, went on to join the *Nameye Farangestan* (Letter of Europe), which first appeared in May 1924. In its first issue, *Letter of Europe* paid allegiance to *Kaveh* and wrote, 'We wish to Europeanize Iran. We wish to channel the flood of modern civilization towards Iran. We wish to retain the innate and advantageous moral character of Iran and follow the crucial axiom that Iran must become Europeanized physically and spiritually, in appearance/outwardly and in substance/inwardly.'[4]

The *Letter of Europe* had a sharp anti-religious slant and strongly favoured the separation of religion from politics. It believed that the public's deep-rooted religiosity was the cause of Iran's underdevelopment and prevented any legal and peaceful solution to the country's problems. It assessed Iran's 18-year constitutional experience as negative and an impediment to development. Instead of 'majority rule of the ignorant', Iran's European-educated intellectuals were calling for a Mussolini-type leader with 'new ideas', a 'man of action', 'serious' and 'learned'. *Letter of Europe* believed that a 'dictator' was needed to lead the revolution.

To obtain those freedoms enjoyed by Europeans, they promoted the rule of a 'learned dictator', an 'ideal dictator' who would 'make people taste true pleasures of life'. The price for attaining a European democratic system was to embrace a dictatorship. *Letter of Europe* proclaimed, 'If you see a person around yourselves with such characteristics, support him and bestow this position [ideal dictator] on him'. In May 1924, Reza Khan was the single military-politician showing autocratic tendencies and thirst for more power.[5]

The idea of a dictatorial figure Europeanizing Iran with an iron fist was gradually developing inside the country from around January 1923 or some sixteen months before *Letter of Europe* began publication in Berlin. The 34-year-old Ali-Akbar Davar, who had spent some ten years in Switzerland and studied law at Geneva University, returned to Iran immediately after the 1921 coup. Davar had collaborated with Seyyed Zia when the latter published his radical newspaper *Sharq* (East) in September

1909. On 28 January 1923, Davar published his influential pro-Reza Khan paper called *Marde Azad* (Free Man). Davar borrowed the name from his French political idol **George Clemenceau**, who had published a daily by this name (*L'Homme libre*) in 1913. Issa Sadiq, a close friend of Davar and a supporter of Reza Khan, became the paper's manager and a regular contributor.

Between January and October 1923, while Reza Khan was striving to become prime minister, Davar articulated an ideological defense for a constructive despot taking power. For Davar, the Constitutional Revolution and its achievements of 'freedom, equality and independence were empty words and poetry' incapable of solving poverty and economic underdevelopment.[6] Iranians, he argued, were poor, hungry, scruffy, bare-footed, dirty, lice-ridden, diseased and illiterate, living in squalor and filth.

Therefore, a European style of economic welfare was only possible by a forced Iranian industrial revolution. Iranians, Davar believed, would become humans *only* once poverty had been eradicated through industrialization, the development of mines and the construction of railways. He claimed that 'without roads, freedom and equality were useless to us'.[7]

Davar's arguments for the urgency of a despot taking the helm were fourfold. First, he posited that Iranians were 'undoubtedly' ignorant of how to conduct their lives in the modern world and were 'spontaneously' incompetent at attaining progress.[8] Second, left to their own devices, Davar believed that they would neither 'become humans' nor join the civilized world. 'Iranians,' he claimed, 'were Iran's enemies, not the provocations, interventions and transgressions of foreigners'.[9] Third, according to Davar, Iranians were 'incapable of comprehending reason and logic and even if they did, they would not follow it without coercion and force'.[10] Finally, Davar argued that 'despotic government has made the Iranian spirit so dependent on coercion and force that if you were to present him with a thousand arguments, he would not pay any attention to them, unless he was lashed, banished and imprisoned'.[11]

Davar's assessment of his countrymen was not very flattering. He viewed them as subhumans and beasts of burden who needed to be civilized by the 'force and violence' of a government using its 'fist' and 'sword'.[12] Davar had one single candidate in mind for this task. He invited Reza Khan to take control of the country, 'silence the demagogues', 'smash the teeth of opponents' and 'change all habits and customs' with 'the bayonet'.[13] Once Reza Khan became prime minister, Davar, the theoretician of his regime, addressed him as 'the messiah and the savior'.[14]

By 1921, the Constitutional Revolution had left Iranian intellectuals disappointed as it had failed to deliver the solution to the country's multiple problems. Both in Europe and in Iran, a new and educated stratum now came to look down upon the masses as uneducated, ignorant and incapable of change. Anxious to see rapid change and contemptuous of their own people, they sought a dictator, a redeemer, who would fix the people and the country. They wished for a strong central government, security, stability, national unity, secularization and Europeanization. Both the educated elite and British Gen. Ironside saw in Reza Khan the kind of man needed to impose security and civilize the nation: a strong military dictator with an iron fist.

> **Culture Wars**
>
> Many educated Iranians despaired of their country ever developing into a modern nation as long as the policies of a progressive elite could be sabotaged by the conservative majority, and thus began advocating for a strong state that could overcome societal resistance. The coup d'état of 1921 brought to power a leader who would build such a state: Reza Khan Pahlavi. (H. E. Chehabi)[15]

From Theory to Practice

After the February 1921 coup, a new generation of young, educated Iranians, different in class and educational background from the old aristocratic grandees, formed various political groups. This new blood was impatient with the pace of economic progress and disillusioned with the performance of the old political elite. This new breed of nationalists saw the country's salvation in forced and top-down modernization. They believed in sacrificing democracy and constitutionalism at the altar of rapid and coerced modernization, progress and Europeanization.

Acting as ideologues and stalwarts of Reza Khan's dictatorial nationalism, these political novices helped make him prime minister and subsequently shah. They advocated their cause through forming political parties, founding newspapers and campaigning in the forthcoming elections for the 4th (1921–3) and the 5th (1924–5) Majles.

Amongst the proponents of these views were Ali-Akbar Davar, Mohammad Tadayyon, Abdolhoseyn Teymurtash, Reza Tajaddod and Zeinolabeddin Rahnema. The political groups were numerous. *Tajaddod* (Renewal/Modernity) Party, formed in 1921, with a newspaper published three times a week under the same name; the Radical Party, formed around December 1922, with its newspaper, *Marde Azad* (Free Man), first published on 28 January 1923; or the Independent Democrat Party, founded around late 1921. With the help of Reza Khan, these parties were able to obtain a majority in the 5th Majles.

Uncomfortable Collaboration of Two Aspiring Dictators

The first public announcement signed by Reza, the head of the Cossack Brigade and the commander-in-chief, was intentionally intimidating and terrifying. On

22 February 1921, Tehran woke up to a communique called, 'I command', with nine short and forceful directives, pasted up onto walls and doors of the capital. It ordered the people to be 'quiet and submissive to military commands' and 'observe the curfew imposed from 8.00 pm by martial law'. It outlawed any assembly of greater than three and banned all publications until the formation of a new government. It ordered the closure of liquor shops, theatres, cinemas, gambling houses and photography shops. Reza threatened all those disobeying these orders with the 'harshest retributions' meted out by military courts.

> ## Seyyed Zia
>
> In those days, the curse of dictatorship as the antidote against communism was much in vogue. Seyyed Zia had been created to counter communism and in tune with fashionable world political trends of the day, he was a fascist. Yet he had failed to gather around him suitable companions for this purpose, or perhaps he did not have any . . . (Malak al-shoara Bahar)[16]

Reza Khan's stern words, becoming of a Cossack and conveying the image of a no-nonsense, pugnacious soldier, however, were written by Seyyed Zia. Within two days of the coup, Zia had arrested everyone who was anyone in Iranian politics, with a few exceptions, and got Ahmad Shah to endorse him as his prime minister, while Reza Khan would be Sardar Sepah, commander of the army and of the Cossack Division. Relying on Reza Khan's military clout, Seyyed Zia, the Iranian brain behind the coup, rode roughshod. He was mistaken to believe he could shape and control Reza, the uncouth Cossack commander and his junior coup partner.

On 27 February, Seyyed Zia unveiled the second stage of his revolutionary plans. He addressed his 'fellow countrymen' and placed all blame for the country's predicaments on the wealthy and property-owning notables and grandees, who in the past had taken turns in ruling the country. He accused the traditional political elite of corruption and wrong-doing and promised to bring them to justice. Seyyed Zia called for improving the living condition of peasants by distributing state and crownlands among them. He emphasized the primordial role of the army and promised to prioritize its needs. Finally, he announced the annulment of the by now defunct Anglo-Persian Agreement of 1919.

Seyyed Zia acted out his favourite role as a civilian dictator, while Reza carried out his duties as a military dictator. The two dictators could not coexist indefinitely. Soon, Zia fell out with Reza over his meddling in civilian issues and his increasing demands for military expenditures. Having alienated the old ruling classes, the wealthy and the opposition, whom he had imprisoned, as well as the shah and the court, the expenditures for which he had curtailed, Zia found himself isolated. Three months after becoming prime minister, the bombastic and lone wolf, obsessed with governing as a dictator, was ousted on 24 May 1921. He left the country immediately. Not many grieved his departure except for the British Legation in Tehran. In their assessment, 'the hopes which had been raised of introducing an honest Administration into the country disappeared'.[17]

Eliminating the Competition

With Seyyed Zia out of the political picture, Reza Khan who had become minister of war on 26 April 1921, pursued his plan of climbing to the summit of power.

Reza Khan's first order of priority was the difficult task of establishing safety and security through a land which had fallen to disorder after the First World War. In every corner, a tribal or regional leader had his own armed men, collected taxes and spent them as he saw fit and imposed his own law. Vast areas of the country were autonomous fiefdoms, outside the central government's effective jurisdiction and reach. To demonstrate his military might and establish his right to power, Reza Khan had to gradually subdue different kinds of military challenges to his military authority.

To achieve this, he relied on the expansion and empowerment of his crucial power base, the Cossacks. His politics became intertwined with the welfare and performance of his both repressive and liberating army. He promoted his trusted commanders, assured the regular payment of his soldiers, vigorously moved to integrate the gendarmerie and the police into and under the leadership of the Cossacks, and strove to improve their weapons and training. Reza's first objective was to create a strong and efficient national army.

Mirza Kuchek Khan and Gilan

On 26 February 1921, a Soviet–Persian treaty of friendship was concluded in Moscow, under which the Red Army was to gradually withdraw from Persian territory. On 31 May 1921, Ahmad Qavam replaced Seyyed Zia as prime minister, and on 14 June, Reza Khan showed off 5,000 of his well-disciplined men to Ahmad Shah during a parade. On 23 June, one day after the 4th Majles opened, Soviet forces were evacuated from Gilan, and the Baku-based communist party called Justice Party (*Hezbe Edalat*) issued a manifesto welcoming the opening of the Majles. Since the Bolshevik landing at Anzali in May 1920, Gilan had undergone major political transformations.

By late June 1921, Reza Khan amassed some 1,200 Cossacks to put an end to the Gilan insurrection. In the meantime, Kuchek Khan had begun negotiations with Qavam's government. On 2 July 1921, Kuchek Khan, the socialist and nationalist, fell out with the Soviet representatives over their meddling in Iranian affairs.

By August 1921, the Jangali movement in Mazandaran had begun to crumble. Amir-Asad Tonokaboni, a Jangali rebel whose 800-strong troops had an alliance with

Ehsanollah Khan, joined the government forces and was pardoned. The government forces attacked rebel positions, defeated them, killing some 300 and taking some 200 prisoners. Ehsanollah Khan and his 400 men took refuge in the Deylaman forests.

On 15 August 1921, Kuchek Khan issued a proclamation announcing a federal republican government, with himself as chief commissar and commissar of finance, Khalu Qorban as war commissar, and Heydar Amuoghlu as commissar of foreign affairs. This was an unsuccessful attempt at keeping an unstable coalition.

On 22 September, Kuchek Khan quarrelled with Khalu Qorban over the control of Gilan's finances and armaments. This led to hostilities on 2 and 3 October, during which the two sides fought each other for eighteen hours. Some 400 were killed and Kuchek Khan evacuated Rasht. Khalu Qorban switched sides and joined the government forces against Kuchek Khan.

In October 1921, Reza Khan joined his forces in Gilan, concluded an agreement with Khalu Qorban and entered Rasht triumphantly on 15 October. Amuoghlu was arrested and killed after Rasht was taken. Ehsanollah Khan left Anzali for Baku on 20 October 1921 and four days later, Anzali fell to government forces. Khalu Qorban, who had completely changed colours, obtained the rank of major, while his men were absorbed in the Cossack Brigade. He was later appointed provisional governor of Anzali.

Reza Khan stayed in Gilan to claim the ultimate trophy of bringing in Kuchek Khan dead or alive but returned to Tehran on 3 November 1921. Nevertheless, he made a name for himself as a victorious commander, who had put down one of Iran's longest rebellions. His popularity was on the rise and his position strengthened.

The government offered a prize of 10,000 tomans for Kuchek Khan's capture alive and 5,000 for his dead body. Hunted down by government forces sweeping the area, Kuchek Khan finally succumbed to the cold and died of frostbite on 6 December 1921. His decapitated head was brought to Tehran by Khalu Qorban. Kuchek Khan became a legendary figure of Iran's struggle for independence, justice, republicanism and anti-despotism.

Col. Pesyan's rebellion in Khorasan

Mohammad-Taqi Pesyan was a valiant soldier who had fought on the side of the Iranian Provisional Government and against Russia during the war and went to Berlin in 1916. He was educated and cultured. Pesyan knew French, English and German, and was a writer and a poet. He became a pilot in the German Air Force and later joined the infantry. In Berlin, 'he was in contact with Iranian radicals led by Hasan Taqizadeh and grouped around the periodical *Kaveh*, for which he occasionally wrote articles'.[18]

Pesyan returned to Iran in 1920 and in September of that year became commander of the gendarme forces in Khorasan. He quickly fell out with Ahmad Qavam, the governor, over regular payment of his troops. Pesyan regarded Qavam as an impediment to reorganizing and empowering the gendarmes and bringing security to Khorasan. He supported Seyyed Zia's seizure of power in February 1921, arrested Qavam on Zia's orders and dispatched him to Tehran, where he was jailed. On 3 April 1921, Seyyed Zia appointed Pesyan as military governor of Khorasan.

Pesyan declared martial law in Mashhad, replaced civilian governors of major towns with gendarme officers, began collecting unpaid taxes from big landlords and with the help of the Belgian financial administrator, tried to put Khorasan's finances in order. He then moved against the high officials of Imam Reza's very lucrative shrine and charged them with 'systematically embezzling Shrine revenues'.[19]

When Seyyed Zia was removed from office in late May 1921, the shah reinstated Pesyan as commander of the gendarmes but stripped him of his administrative post. In early June, Najd al-saltaneh was appointed as interim governor. Having been warned not to meddle in Khorasan's political affairs, Pesyan was convinced that this was the work of Ahmad Qavam, the newly appointed prime minister, whom he considered as self-serving and corrupt. Pesyan feared that the removal of Seyyed Zia by Reza Khan implied the return of the old corrupt politicians and the inefficient order.

Pesyan's Motive to Rebel

It was this counter-coup which Colonel Pasyan refused to accept and which led him to attempt to defend, from his base in Mashhad, the wider political project of which the Sayyid had been the chief exponent. (S. Cronin)[20]

Pesyan wrote to the shah, asking to be relieved of his military duties. The shah refused his request. Troubled by the turn of events and mistrustful of Qavam and the politics in Tehran, Pesyan began disobeying orders of the central government, while claiming his loyalty to the shah. On 29 July, Pesyan placed Najd al-saltaneh under house arrest and officially relieved him of his duties. Pesyan was rebelling against Qavam's government, imprisoning government officials and taking control of Khorasan.

Even though he was strict and disciplinarian, Pesyan was admired by the people and appreciated for his nationalism. His growing popularity, backed by the strength of some 6,000 gendarmes, along with his talk of ending injustice and despotism and his murmurs of 'the Republic of Khorasan', were alarming to the central government. Rumour of Pesyan marching on Tehran unnerved Reza Khan who was aware of the colonel's popularity and prestige. For those looking for an educated and Europeanized strongman, Pesyan was a serious alternative to Reza Khan. Already facing the threat of Kuchek Khan and the Gilan movement, Reza Khan did not have enough troops to spare for the Khorasan front.

On 27 August 1921, Qavam sent an urgent message to Amir Shokat al-molk Alam, the powerful governor of Qaenat and Sistan, instructing him to mobilize his forces and move against the rebellious Pesyan. Qavam referred to Pesyan as an offensive and mad rebel and instructed Alam to pardon Pesyan's gendarmes who had joined his forces and 'annihilate' the rest.[21] By September, the politically Left and radical National Committee of Khorasan, with Pesyan as its president, had taken control of Mashhad.

Around 30 September 1921, under orders from Qavam, Farajollah Khan, the governor of Shirvan, and the Kurdish militia forces of Sardar Moazez, the governor of Bojnurd, occupied Quchan in Khorasan. With his troops scattered across Khorasan to ward off possible attacks, Pesyan personally led some 24 gendarmes to confront the far numerically superior forces. On 3 October 1921, Pesyan fell in battle at the age of 29 and was decapitated. Even though his loyal associate, Maj. Esmail Khan, rebelled again in his name and took over Mashhad, his uprising was put down. The influential Iranian poets, Iraj Mirza and Aref Qazvini, eternalized Pesyan's memory as a nationalist hero and a lover of freedom and justice.

Maj. Lahuti's coup in Tabriz

On 22 January 1922, Hasan (Moshir al-dowleh) Pirnia replaced Ahmad Qavam as the third post-coup prime minister. The British Legation reported that at this time, 'Reza Khan remains virtually a military dictator.'[22] On 31 January 1922, news came that the gendarme detachment at Sharafkhaneh, 86 kilometres west of Tabriz (Azarbayjan), had mutinied and arrested Maj. Mahmud Khan Puladin, the commander of the gendarmes, his adjutant and the governor of Sharafkhaneh. On their way to Sufiyan and Tabriz, the rebel forces cut the telephone and telegraph lines and destroyed the railroad tracks.

On 2 February 1922, having forced the Cossacks defending the city to retreat and take shelter in their barracks, the 500–600 rebellious gendarmes took control of Tabriz. On the next day, the gendarme officers spoke of marching onto Tehran. The rebels were immediately joined by some 270 members of the Edalat Party (Justice Party) as well as members of Khiyabani's Democrat Party. The rebel forces occupied all government buildings including the police station and disarmed the Cossacks. Once Mehdiqoli (Mokhber ol-saltaneh) Hedayat, the governor of Tabriz surrendered and was given sanctuary, Tabriz was fully in rebel hands. The discipline and behaviour of the gendarmes was exemplary, and no cases of looting or lawlessness were reported after their victory.

The gendarmes were led by Maj. Abolqasem Lahuti, a 35-year-old poet, journalist, constitutionalist and a leftist political activist. Lahuti had been condemned to death once, allegedly for his political activities, when he served with the gendarmes and fled the country. He lived in Istanbul before returning to Tabriz and rejoining the gendarmes.

Lahuti and his men had organizational, economic and political grievances. They opposed Reza Khan's unification of the gendarmes with the Cossacks and believed that they would be subordinated to the Cossacks. The gendarmes, contrary to the Cossacks, had not been paid for three months and were living in poor conditions. Finally, they considered their 'coup' as a political vendetta against those who had shed the blood of Mohammad Khiyabani and were also concerned with the news of Reza Khan's 'legal infringements' and his 'dictatorial tendencies'.[23] For the British, however, 'This revolution had both Bolshevik and Kemalist elements in it'.[24]

> ### The Lahuti Coup
> The Lahuti coup is significant as it constitutes the last of a series of freedom-seeking rebellions which began in Tabriz in 1908 to restore a constitutionalist system. (K. Bayat)[25]

Reza Khan was absent from Tehran at the time of the Lahouti uprising, sending off Ahmad Shah to Europe. He immediately returned to Tehran and ordered the dispatch of 3,800 Cossacks to Tabriz. On 9 February 1922, the rebel forces were defeated by the superior forces of Habibollah Khan Sheybani. Lahouti took flight and accompanied with some 350 rebels crossed into Soviet territory. A short reign of terror ensued the entrance of government forces. 'Some of the gendarmes who had surrendered to government forces were shot on the spot.'[26] The government forces and the irregulars of Khalu Qorban began looting and pillaging on the afternoon of 9 February 1922. Finally, martial law was imposed on Tabriz to bring back order and some 60 people were arrested.

Reza Khan's Ascent to Power

Reza Khan never hid his disdain for sharing power. The soldier was anything but a democrat. On 15 August 1921, less than two months after the 4th Majles had been inaugurated, Reza, the minister of war, told M. Saunders, the British military attaché in Iran, that he intended to close the Majles 'immediately [if] he finds that it is of no real assistance to him'.[27] In time, Reza came to learn how to subdue the Majles and use it for his own political benefit. But before grappling with the Majles, he needed more domestic military success. To make his bid for prime minister, Reza had to show that he was indispensable for the security of the country.

The success and glory of the army were Reza's ticket to higher echelons of power. Reza needed to unite and strengthen the army to tame insubordinate provincial forces, who remained independent of and unanswerable to central governments. His military and political plans required channeling unavailable money to the army. His appropriation of funds meant forceful intervention in civilian affairs, causing discontent among the legally minded, the opposition press, Majles deputies and politicians anxious about his growing arbitrary power.

By the end of August 1922, Reza Khan could boast about stopping Kuchek Khan's rebellion in Mazandaran and Gilan, suppressing the Pesyan uprisings in Khorasan and defeating the Lahuti rebellion in Tabriz. He also neutralized Simitqu (Simko) or Esmail Aqa Shikak, the powerful chief of the Lur Shikak tribe, who had for long controlled a good part of Azarbayjan and Urumiyeh in particular. Simitqu who represented Kurdish nationalist sentiments and had long revolted against the central government, was defeated on 12 August 1922 by government forces and retreated to Ottoman territory.

Reza Khan's success in consolidating the power of the central government made him feel more entitled to demand additional powers. In a report dated 11 December 1921, Saunders wrote that Reza Khan 'is now more a military dictator than ever, controls the Cabinet, has the greatest contempt for the Medjliss and is feared by the Shah'.[28]

The financial situation was further aggravated towards the end of 1921. The government found itself unable to pay civil servants, teachers, the police and the army. The minister of war now felt entitled to appropriate the 'daily revenue from the Customs and Excise Departments'.[29] By January 1922, Reza Khan claimed a standing army of 23,000, and reorganized into five district commands. To counter-criticism of his interventions in civilian matters and his heavy-handed methods, Reza whipped up nationalist feelings by claiming that it was unnecessary for Iranians to be under the command of foreign officers.

Transferring Branches of the Minister of Finance to Ministry of War

When we arrived in Teheran, the Administration of Indirect Taxation, – comprising the important opium, tobacco, excise, and miscellaneous indirect taxes, – the Administration of Public Domains, the Alimentation Service, and the financial agency of Teheran, were administered directly and their net revenues received by the Ministry of War. In addition, that ministry received the surplus revenues of the Telegraphs Administration of the Ministry of Posts and Telegraphs. (A. Millspaugh)[30]

Incapable of resolving the financial situation, unable to secure a much-discussed US loan, unwilling to accept Britain's conditions for a loan, and under pressure from Reza Khan's increased meddling with state affairs, Qavam resigned on 26 January 1923. The US loan of 1.1 millions tomans from the Standard Oil Company materialized in May 1922 during Pirnia's Premiership. Reza Khan quickly appropriated 0.9 million tomans of this sum for the army.

Between 20 and 22 January 1922, when Qavam fell and Moshir al-dowleh Pirnia took office, Reza Khan placed a Cossack colonel, a loyal supporter, in charge of Tehran's granary. This position was previously under the purview of the Ministry of Finance. By the time Pirnia came to office, the sensitive position of controlling bread in Tehran had slipped into Reza Khan's hands.

From Minister of War to Prime Minister

Between 24 February 1921 and 26 October 1923 (4th Majles), Iran went through six prime ministers. Support for the prime ministers, who were appointed by the shah, vacillated. Group loyalties and alliances in the Majles shifted as deputies from the Reformists (Modarres), the Socialists (Eskandari) and the pro-Reza Khan parties led by Tadayyon, jockeyed for power (Figure 3.1). Between Zia and Reza Khan, three prime ministers (Qavam, Pirnia and Mostowfi al-mamalek) came and went. Each remained in power between three and eight months.

With his growing military prestige and popularity Reza Khan grew tired of hearing that the February 1921 coup had been a British affair. It was time for him to re-write history and ascertain his unrivalled authority. On 22 February 1922, the anniversary of the coup, Reza Khan publicly announced that he alone had been responsible for conceiving and executing the coup. He claimed that he 'had not been in any way inspired from any other quarter'. The minister of war interfered in civilian matters again, threatening that, 'If I see anything further in the papers about the causes of the coup d'état, that paper will be suppressed, and its editor will be liable to severe punishment.'[31]

Figure 3.1 Mohammad Tadayyon. *Source: Wikimedia Commons*.

Spreading his wings during the final days of Pirnia's premiership, Reza Khan extended his financial and administrative dominion and acted as a veritable prime minister only interested in the Ministry of War. He took over more revenue-generating departments such as opium and the lucrative crown and state lands. The government was unable to stand up to his excesses, although the Majles placed pressure by demanding that Reza Khan replace the military governors that he had appointed in the provinces with civilian ones.

In May 1922, a few hard-nosed newspapers, especially Mohammad Dehqan's *Haqiqat* (The Truth), published anti-British articles attributing the February coup to Herman Norman, the British minister in Tehran, and accusing the British of instigating unrest among Iranian tribes. *Haqiqat* also published a scathing attack on Reza Khan maintaining that he considered the troops as 'his private servants', oppressed the people and illegally interfered in the appointment of the premier.[32]

Reza Khan reacted harshly to *Haqiqat*'s criticisms and demanded its closure. If Prime Minister Pirnia failed to close the paper, Reza Khan threatened he would make sure that the prime minister would never again be admitted to the court.

Fed up with the Reza Khan's incessant interferences, Pirnia refused to close *Haqiqat* and preferred to resign. *Haqiqat* was a widely read pro-communist paper, labelled as 'the Organ of Iran's Communist Party'.[33] It was also closely affiliated with the newly found communist labour union, General Union of Central Workers, which claimed widespread membership among Iran's industrial workforce. After Pirnia's resignation, with Seyyed Hasan Modarres's solid support, Qavam became prime minister for a second time on 4 June 1922. A few weeks later, *Haqiqat* was shut down.

The news of Simitqu's defeat and fall of the impregnable Chahriq fortress on 12 August 1922, neutralized the bad publicity Reza Khan was getting for physically abusing, intimidating and arresting journalists and citizens as well as for muzzling the press. Reza Khan felt elated that the Majles, government and the shah congratulated him on his defeat of the Kurdish rebel.

But on 5 October 1922, Reza Khan came under renewed pressure from the Majles. The deputy from Tabriz criticized the continuation of martial law in the provinces and warned about dangers threatening the Constitution and the independence of the country. Modarres tried to defend Reza Khan in his own nuanced way. He referred to the power of the Majles, saying that it could censure Reza Khan and dismiss him, then added that the minister of war had costs and benefits and his benefits outstripped his costs. Meanwhile, the Iranian press gave wide coverage to Majles' dissatisfaction with Reza Khan.

The minister of war, however, took offense to Modarres' insinuation that the Majles could dismiss him. He sulked and resigned on 7 October 1922. During the next three days, Reza Khan orchestrated insecurity and lawlessness in Tehran. Suddenly innocent people were murdered without any motives, thefts were reported throughout the city and military personal, clad in civilian clothes, clashed with citizens. In the provinces, military commanders went so far as to order the closure of commerce and government services, demanding the return of Reza Khan.

On 10 October, as if he had won a national plebiscite, Reza Khan returned to office. Accepting the good counsel of Farajollah Bahrami, his teacher, advisor and ghostwriter, Reza Khan made his peace with the Majles. The following week, he promised to repeal martial law and desist from interfering with revenues from excise or indirect taxes and the crown lands.

On 30 November 1922, the Michigan-born and Johns Hopkins-educated Arthur Millspaugh began work as Iran's administrator-general of finance. Millspaugh and his team of nine American financial and fiscal experts were charged with putting Iran's dismal finances in order. Entrusting Millspaugh with Iran's finances reflected the faith Iranians had in Americans as disinterested and honest brokers. In December 1922, after ten months of full control over all revenue sources, including crown lands and indirect taxes, the minister of war handed over the finances of the country to Millspaugh.

Reza Khan and Millspaugh

Since Millspaugh could do little without force to back up the tax collectors, there was a natural alliance between him and Reza Khan. (G. E. Baldwin)[34]

When Qavam assumed office for a second time in June 1922, he had the support of Modarres and the Reformists in the Majles, which constituted the majority. The Socialists, led by Soleyman Mirza Eskandari constituted the minority faction. But gradually, the pro-Reza-Khan Independent Democrat Party, and the nucleus of the Modernity/Revival Party led by Tadayyon, sided with the Socialists, strengthening the opposition against Qavam.

On 11 January 1923, Tadayyon criticized Qavam's government for the mistreatment of prisoners at police stations. He objected to the closure of three newspapers and the arrest of an editor and asked Qavam to be accountable for these shortcomings. During the same session, Eskandari repeated Tadayyon's grievances, lamented the unaccountability of Qavam and accused him of having received a $150,000 bribe for an oil concession. Qavam rejected all the charges, but Eskandari accused him of being a liar and said, 'This unworthy man says nonsense, he is dishonest, a traitor and a thief'.[35]

A week after this incident in the Majles, Reza Khan told Saunders that Qavam's cabinet was useless, describing its members as 'interested purely in personal gain'. At the same meeting, Reza Khan announced 'his intention of turning them out of office'.[36] Nine days later, on 27 January 1923, under pressure from pro-Reza Khan factions, Qavam resigned.

With the support of the Socialists in the Majles, Hasan Mostowfi al-mamalek became prime minister on 15 February 1923, but less than two months later, Davar's pro-Reza Khan paper, *Free Man*, accused the new prime minister of being indecisive, and incompetent. From mid-April, supporters of Reza Khan openly agitated for the fall of Mostowfi al-mamalek, calling for Reza Khan to replace him. By early June, *Free Man* was openly calling the prime minister a shameless rascal in the hands of Soviet foreign policy. Despite its incessant invectives, Davar's paper remained unmolested.

During June 1923, Modarres and his Reformist faction in Majles tilted towards Reza Khan and threw their weight behind bringing down Mostowfi al-mamalek. Reza Khan had learnt how to use the division between Modarres the reformist, and Eskandari the socialist, pitting one constitutionalist against the other to achieve his own anti-constitutionalist ends. On 12 June 1923, the 4th Majles decided to censure the prime minister. Mostowfi al-mamalek, an honest and upright politician, defended his policies and declared that he would rather resign than strike a deal with his new opposition in the Majles. As Mostowfi al-mamalek and his cabinet left the Majles in protest, Reza Khan stayed behind. The minister of war clearly indicated that he felt no obligation to display loyalty.

On 14 June 1923, Hasan Pirnia became prime minister once again. The 4th Majles held its last session on 21 June 1923. By August, Reza-Khan's supporters had called on him to become prime minister. On 28 August, Davar's *Free Man* wrote, 'Sardar Sepah, why don't you take the reins of government and become prime minister ... You hold the power in your hands, why not use it to save the country, fearlessly and without hesitation?'[37]

By October 1923, Reza Khan had paved the way for his own premiership. To eliminate all future rivalry with Qavam, the minister of war ordered his arrest along with fifteen others. On 8 October, Qavam was accused of having plotted to assassinate Reza Khan, while he was prime minister. Ahmad Shah had to intercede on Qavam's behalf and saved him from execution.

On 11 October, Reza Khan displayed his military might and supervised the military manoeuvres of 1,200 soldiers at Karaj. He intentionally got Tehran's population worried by spreading rumours of an impending coup. He then sent word to Pirnia, the prime minister, not to attend the cabinet meetings or else. On 23 October 1923, Pirnia resigned. In the absence of the Majles, Ahmad Shah, who was rushed to leave Iran, appointed Reza Khan as prime minister on 27 October

Reza Khan, Prime Minister

In the newly formed cabinet, Reza Khan was both prime minister and minister of war. What came as surprises were Soleyman Eskandari as minister of education, Amanollah (Ezz al-mamalek) Ardalan as minister of public works and Qasem

Suresrafil as the acting minister of interior. All three were members of the Socialist Group. Clearly, Reza Khan wished to show that while he stood above everyday politics, he could be friendly with Iran's northern Bolshevik neighbours.

> ### Iran's American Administrator-General of Finance's View of Reza Khan
> There seems little question that Reza Khan Pahlevi possessed not merely the devotion of his army but also the confidence of the people. He was the natural rallying-point of nationalism; he was the logical leader and therefore marked to bear the symbol of leadership; he was the best hope of the country. (A. Millspaugh)[38]

As prime minister, Reza Khan issued a proclamation to explain why he needed to carry out his military operations, put an end to the internal chaos and bring peace and security in the provinces before he could accept the responsibility of taking his 'second step'. His second step would be to satisfy 'national aspirations' and reach 'progress and transformation.' Reza Khan emphasized his preference for 'action' rather than 'words' and informed his countrymen that 'his political programme consisted of protecting the rights of the country/state, and the application/execution of the law'.[39]

On 1 November 1922, the Turkish Grand National Assembly abolished the Sultanate. Almost a year later, on 3 November 1923, Ahmad Shah left Tehran for Europe. While Mehmet VI had felt obliged to leave Constantinople after the Parliament's verdict, Ahmad Shah was taking flight, leaving the political scene to a prime minister he dreaded. Fearing for his life, Ahmad Shah was effectively abdicating before Reza Khan put into motion the wheels that would eventually dethrone him. Ahmad Shah's hurried departure provided Reza Khan with a golden opportunity. The power of the new prime minister and minister of war was now, unrivalled.

By the time Reza Khan became prime minister, the effects of Millspaugh's financial restructuring were already coming to fruition. For the first time, all state revenues were centralized in the Treasury, very strict control was applied over expenditures and the monthly deficit of 0.9 million tomans was reduced to 0.2 million tomans. Millspaugh succeeded in collecting arrears and with the increased power of the central government to ensure tax collection, aimed at a domestic surplus for the financial year 1924–5. Millspaugh's balanced budget was approved by the 4th Majles before it was dissolved. Millspaugh presented a 24-million-toman budget to the Council of Ministers for 1924–5, out of which 10 million were allocated to the Ministry of War.

With the shah gone, the Majles was the only power that could confront and contain Reza Khan. But Reza Khan had become a master at manipulating the levers of power.

The 5th Majles was inaugurated on 12 February 1924. Reza Khan succeeded in sending to the 5th Majles deputies loyal to him, from the Modernity/Revival Party and the Independent Democratic Party. With the help of his military commanders, elections were engineered in the provinces, while Tehran's elected deputies were generally genuine. Reza Khan was elected as deputy from at least 12 constituencies, but not from Tehran. In the 5th Majles, the Modernity/Revival Party, Reza Khan's political tool, had a resounding majority. The Socialists and Reformists had been reduced to minority parties anxiously observing the game plan of the young Reza Khanists.

The Republican Attempt

From around 24 January 1924, some two months after Ahmad Shah left the country, the campaign for a regime change was launched. The local press, such as Ali Dashti's *Shafaq Sorkh* (Red Dawn) and Mirza Hasan Khan Saba's *Setareh Iran* (Iran's Star), attacked Ahmad Shah, while praising the prime minister and revelling in the idea of a republican Iran with Reza Khan as president. Reza Khan preferred to remain in the shadows, having his partisans launch the idea. He wished to appear like an impartial observer, studying the public's reactions to the idea of a republic and then proceeding accordingly.

Reza Khan had become a gifted politician. While promising to the petrified crown prince that he would not undermine the throne, he was actively preparing his demise. At this time, Reza Khan wished to be regarded as a modern revolutionary who would transform Iran politically and economically by becoming its first president. The objective was, however, to monopolize all power. As time showed, the form was not important.

> ### Why a Republic
> Today the Iranian people welcome with open arms Sardar Sepah, as President of the Republic. This is not because they want a republic . . . but because they would like to give unimpeded, absolute power to Sardar Sepah in pursuit of his endeavors. (*Iran's Star*)[40]

Since Reza Khan had already demonstrated his despotic leanings, many came to see his republicanism as a guise towards becoming a different kind of shah. The press became embroiled in the controversy and Reza Khan showed little tolerance for his critics. On 14 January 1924, Mohammad Farrokhi-Yazdi was exiled to Qom for his articles against Reza Khan. Farrokhi was a talented and outspoken socialist and patriot, poet and journalist, whose paper, *Toufan* (Storm), had been suppressed several times in the past.

On 13 February, Reza Khan met with Majles deputies and discussed with them the advisability of adopting a republican form of government given Ahmad Shah's lack of interest in the affairs of the state. In the meantime, newspapers such as *Nasime Shomal* (Northern Breeze), which questioned the appropriateness of a republican form of government, were closed, while papers supporting the idea of a republic and criticizing the shah were left unmolested.

> ## The Republican Fever
>
> On 16 February 1924, Saunders, the British Military Attaché reported that, 'Articles in favour of a republic and in abuse of the Shah are of daily occurrence, and no adequate steps are being taken to put a stop to this form of press propaganda.'[41]

On 1 March 1924, a republican rally attracted some 4,000 people, but successive meetings on 4 and 6 March were countered by pro-shah forces at which scuffles broke out and the police interfered. From 12 March 1924, Reza Khan ordered a 'spontaneous' popular movement in the provinces in support of the republican idea. The Ministry of War sent telegrams to all provincial military commanders ordering them to mobilize the press, parties, guilds, clergy and people from all walks of life in their districts against the Qajars and in favour of a republican regime.

People were directed to write articles in the local press, hold meetings and most importantly, flood the Majles with telegrams expressing these ideas. The people were told to put pressure on their deputies and demand the immediate dethroning of Ahmad Shah, the establishment of a republic and alteration of the Constitution. The Ministry of War insisted that these orders had to be carried without the people realizing that the army was behind it.

During the second week of March, concerts and plays were performed at Tehran's Grand Hotel to promote the idea of an Iranian Republic. The pro-Republican social, political and cultural propaganda activities were coordinated by a committee of 12, formed in late February, and with Reza Khan's full support. The orchestrated pressure from the urban and rural population, the broad telegram drive and the propaganda campaign in the press, were in preparation for the Majles session, when the republic would at last be put to vote and Reza Khan would become Iran's first president.

Still in Europe and worried about the mounting campaign against him, Ahmad Shah contacted the clergy to begin organizing his own an anti-republican movement. On 4 March 1924, the clergy in Qom informed their counterparts in Tehran that 'a republic was counter to the Islamic law, and if they gave their sanction to it, it would be the end of Islam'.[42]

An alliance took shape between clergy, merchants, common people, the deputies led by Modarres and even some army commanders – such as Lt Gen. Jan Mohammad Khan – to save the monarchy. Not all of these people were in favour of Ahmad Shah or against Reza Khan, but they feared a republic and viewed it as an idea concocted in London and anti-Islamic'.[43] Meanwhile, Mostowfi al-mamalek reported that the 'British Ambassador was not in favor of a republic as he did not approve of a concentration of powers in the hands of one group.'[44]

During the fourth parliamentary session, held on 16 March 1924, Modarres accused the army and the prime minister of election-rigging. Tadayyon challenged Modarres and demanded proof.

On 18 March 1924, the Majles was getting ready for the crucial vote. Both sides were testing the waters and verbal clashes between them heightened. Offended by the exchanges, Tadayyon, Reza Shah's key parliamentary proponent and the leader of the pro-republican faction, left the hearings in protest and called on members of the Modernity/Revival faction to follow him out.

With this abrupt end to the heated Majles session, Hoseyn Khan Bahrami, a Radical Party deputy from Zanjan and an ardent supporter of the republic, got into a heated argument with Modarres and slapped him in the face. Modarres's turban went flying off. Soon word got out that a respected anti-republican member of the clergy had been insulted by one of Reza Khan's republican supporters. This incident completely turned the tide against the republican movement. Bahrami's blow helped the continuity of the monarchial system. A republican Iran was delayed for another 55 years.

On Wednesday 19 March 1924, Tehran was feverish and restless. The republic which had seemed like a done deal was being seriously defied. Groups of young demonstrators roamed the city shouting, 'Death to Tadayyon', while others congregated outside the Majles, protesting against the republic.[45] By the time the motion to change the regime came to the Majles floor, the republicans were licking their wounds. On Thursday, 20 March 1924, a huge crowd of many thousands made their way to the Majles, chanting, 'We are followers of the Quran, we don't want a republic!' and 'Long live the king and death to Sardar Sepah.'[46]

On that same Thursday afternoon, the 7th session of the Majles was convened. The motions on the table were: '1- Change the constitutional monarchy to a republic; 2- Enable the deputies of the 5th Majles to change the constitution according to welfare/expediency of the country and the regime; 3- Once the vote was made public, the Majles would announce the regime change.'[47] The deliberations, however, were cut short as no decision was reached. The pro-republicans had lost their majority in Parliament and the anti-republicans succeeded in delaying discussions and a vote.

At around 4.30 pm on the same afternoon, Reza Khan entered the Majles with his close lieutenants and soldiers. He ordered his men to attack and disperse the large anti-republican crowd that had found its way in the Majles. In the melee and brawl inside the Majles, Reza Khan assaulted Sheykh Mehdi Soltan, an anti-republican speaker. The beating caused the crowd to insult and attack the prime minister. When the Majles president, Motamen al-molk, reproached Reza Khan for the action of his troops, Reza Khan apologized and added, 'now that the people are not in favor, I will abandon the idea of a republic'.[48] Forcing the republic seriously backfired and Reza Khan learned of the clergy's power and authority.

Between 30 March and 1 April 1924, Reza Khan changed tactics and carefully prepared the next stage of his march to power. His course of action demonstrated political astuteness. He issued a proclamation, announcing that having consulted with the religious dignitaries in Qom, he had decided to abandon the establishment of a republic and committed himself to defending Islam, securing its grandeur and assuring public respect for the clerical institution (*rowhaniyat*). Pragmatism prevailed, and Reza Khan made his peace with a temporary defeat and called for unity.

Reza Khan had to regain his lost authority, popularity and confidence. Playing the role of the offended and unappreciated diligent servant of the people, he offered his resignation as prime minister on 7 April 1924. Three days before, Ahmad Shah had dismissed him and asked the Majles to appoint Mostowfi al-mamalek in his place. Reza Khan's resignation was a theatrical coup to demonstrate that he was irreplaceable.

Immediately after Reza Khan's resignation, the powerful regional commanders of the western and eastern armies sent menacing telegrams threatening to march on Tehran in his support. Within two days, the Majles had given him an overwhelming vote of confidence and turned down Ahmad Shah's request for a new prime minister. Emboldened, Reza Khan asked the people for their oath of allegiance so that he may pursue what was good for them and the country. On 11 April 1924, Reza Khan met with the crown prince and made amends. Two days later, he presented his cabinet to the Majles, got his programme approved and embarked on the next stretch of his march to the summit.

Reza Khan Regains Confidence

After the destabilizing republican fiasco, Reza Khan sought to improve his image among the people and their deputies, neither of which he trusted. He learnt that for people to be content, they needed their bread and security, as well as respect for their religion, as interpreted by their religious leaders. Until the time when he could forcefully impose his will on the clergy, Reza Khan needed to gnaw at their power. The inability of the Modernity faction in Parliament to ram the republic through the Majles, taught him that he could not trust party politics as a reliable tool for an ascent to power.

Even though Reza Khan tried political flexibility and tolerance, he soon found it cumbersome and reverted to his old coercive ways. To renew his bid for ultimate power, he first presented himself as an ardent Muslim by participating in popular religious ceremonies. And once again, he relied on repressing quasi-independent tribal leaders and improving internal security relying upon his loyal army. Reza Khan's most important instrument for furthering his cause during this period was propaganda and his ability to engineer crises, from which he would emerge victorious. As of 10 April 1924, Reza Khan had his eyes on the prize. He told a group of his close supporters to lay low for two to three months and then, 'by means of newspaper or other propaganda, to work on public opinion to bring about the abdication of the shah and his substitution by a Shah from another family'.[49]

First Round of Political Serial Killings

To scare and send a warning to insubordinate tribal chiefs, Reza Khan ordered the arrest and imprisonment of Mortezaqoli Eqbal al-saltaneh Makui, considered as the most powerful tribal chief in Azarbayjan and the defiant governor of Maku. Upon his imprisonment, his personal jewellery and precious belongings were expropriated and handed over to Reza Khan.

Eqbal al-saltaneh was subsequently transferred from Tabriz to Tehran and was one of the first in a long series of 'sudden' deaths in prison. His death, on 10 May 1924, is said to have been ordered by Reza Khan. Col. Mohammad Dargahi, who was appointed chief of police in December 1923 by Reza Khan and served him loyally until December 1929, was said to be implicated in the political assassinations and the 'sudden' death of numerous political prisoners.

In June 1924, an anonymous leaflet circulated in the Majles, accusing Reza Khan of financial misconduct. He was alleged to have taken '5 of the 18 crores allotted annually to the army'.[50] This must have been some sort of army food ration. The officer of the Military Finance Department, who was believed to have been at the origin of the leaflet, went missing and was subsequently found dead. Reza Khan, who was facing some resistance in the army, could not stand for such sensitive leaks in the army.

Cracks in discipline had become manifest during the central government's May 1924 campaign against the Lorestan uprising. Over a 100 of the 2,000 reinforcements dispatched from Tehran had refused to go to the front, taking sanctuary in Shah Abdolazim and Qom. Among those who got to the front, many evaded the frontlines. Reza Khan's republican thrust had weakened his grip both on soldiers and country. By the end of June, voices were calling for his resignation, while demonstrations against him and popular demands for the return of Ahmad Shah to take over state affairs remained strong.

On 4 July 1924, Mirzadeh Eshqi (Mohammad-Reza Kordestani), a passionate, sharp-tongued socialist, a patriotic writer, poet and journalist who had long been at loggerheads with Reza Khan, was shot in his house and died a few hours later in hospital. The 30-year-old Eshqi had been a vocal opponent of the republic. The publication of his acerbic newspaper, *Qarne Bistom* (Twentieth Century) on 28 June 1924 had infuriated Reza Khan, who ordered its immediate closure.

Eshqi had mocked the republic, comparing it to Nasereddin Shah's despotic rule, when the opposition was repressed, battered and lashed. The word on the street was that Reza Khan had ordered Dargahai to assassinate Eshqi. Those newspapers, such as *Siyasat* (Politics), that wished to pursue the why, who and how of Eshqi's murder were suppressed and the editors of 12 opposition papers, fearing for their lives, took sanctuary in the Majles. Eshqi's murder caused considerable anguish and disquiet in society.

> ### Reza Khan's Reaction to the Assassination of Eshqi
> What is the importance of one murder, why don't you deplore the many killed in our wars?[51]

A few weeks earlier, Tehran fell into a state of supernatural religious frenzy. Word had gone round that in a public drinking place (*saqakhaneh*) on Sheykh Hadi Street, a Bahai who had been disrespectful to religious sanctities had suddenly gone blind. The 'divine retribution' was considered a miracle. On 7 and 8 July, Tehran celebrated the miracle, became embroiled in an anti-Bahai hysteria and people flocked to the new sacred site, expecting to be healed.

Two weeks after Eshqi's assassination, on Friday, 20 July 1924, the American vice consul in Tehran, Maj. Robert Imbrie, was attacked, wounded several times and finally killed in the hospital by a mob.[52] Imbrie had gone to visit the site and taken pictures of the place and the people seeking a miracle cure. The large crowds who gathered daily at the new pilgrimage spot had taken offense that he was photographing them. Someone on a motorbike accused Imbrie of intending to poison the water basin, rousing the people to attack him and his companion. The police present at the scene did not intervene. Imbrie had tried to get away, but his carriage was stopped and its passengers were once again attacked by a group of soldiers and the mob.

Once Imbrie was transported to the Police Hospital, another group including military personnel entered the hospital, attacked Imbrie and left him for dead. On the next day, Reza Khan imposed martial law to prevent the insecurity and unrest that reigned. Some 200–300, many of them clerics, were arrested and the opposition press was suppressed.

Within 19 weeks, a disliked reactionary tribal khan, a popular revolutionary poet and the American Consul were murdered. Public opinion believed that Reza Khan had engineered the murders to crush the continuing opposition to him and villainize the clergy and their devout fold by presenting them as fanatical and violent. Reza Khan, however, came out of the affair empowered. The minister of war proved that he could unleash chaos whenever it served his political agenda. As Reza Khan consolidated his reign of terror, no one dared pry into the murders. The judiciary and the police answerable only to him, turned a blind eye. The minority deputies in the Majles were paralyzed by death threats against them, while the majority were charmed by Reza Khan's modernity project.

Taming Semi-Autonomous Tribes

To consolidate the centralization process, Reza Khan had to end the semi-autonomous and quasi self-sovereign status of various tribal chiefs whose special deals with the British placed certain provinces under British protection. Furthermore, Reza Khan was intent on bringing the oil fields, pipelines and oil industry under the control and the military protection of the central government. This meant overpowering powerful tribal chiefs, such as Sheykh Khazal and the Bakhtiyaris, who provided the British with such military services and came under their protection (Figure 3.2).

In August 1923, the American financial advisors looking into the accounts of Bakhtiyari tribes identified 1.5 million tomans of arears and eventually settled for 0.5

Figure 3.2 Sheykh Khazal. *Source: Wikimedia Commons.*

tomans. The protection of oil fields and the pipelines had been provided by the Bakhtiyari tribes, under contract with the British. In January 1924, Prime Minister Reza Khan made it known that he wished to see Iranian regular troops take over such duties from the Bakhtiyaris as soon as possible.

In May 1924, the Lor tribes attacked government forces around Khorramabad, and incurred heavy casualties on them. The uprising was a reprisal against the treacherous killing of two Lor chiefs in March 1924. Reza Khan, who was facing political problems in Tehran, kept the uprising and his military reversals out of the news and poured reinforcements in the area.

Subduing Lorestan was an important step towards subjugating Sheykh Khazal in neighbouring Khuzestan. The government offered the Lors an amnesty, which they were reluctant to accept. During Reza Khan's visit in mid-September, the southern-Lor chiefs had refused to meet with him. But, by 30 November 1924, when Reza Khan moved his troops to the south to overcome Khazal, the road from Khorramabad to Dezful was open, indicating that the Lor chiefs had reached some sort of an arrangement with the central government enabling government troops to pass through peacefully.

Khazal bin Jabir al-Kabi was the chief of the Mehaisan tribal confederation and the Sheykh of Mohammareh (Khorramshahr) and its surrounding. For all intents and purposes, the oil-rich Khuzestan Province was under Khazal's rule. The discovery of oil in Masjed Soleyman (1908), the Anglo-Persian Oil Company's construction of a refinery at Abadan (1912) and the protection of the oil pipelines and storage tanks had made the security of Khuzestan indispensable for Britain.

In 1910, Britain had entered into an agreement with Khazal, confirming his autonomous authority from the central government in Iran and extending to him a quasi-protectorate status. With British support, Khazal considered himself the Emir of Arabestan (Khuzestan) and entertained the idea of carving out his autonomous Arab region from the rest of Iran. Khazal was also a prominent Freemason with his own lodge.

Sheykh Khazal Protected by the British and the APOC

His Majesty's Government will be prepared to afford to you [Sheikh Khaz'al] the support necessary for obtaining a satisfactory solution in the event of encroachment of the Persian Government on your jurisdiction and recognised right or your property in Persia. (C. Ghani).[53]

While he was under British protection, Khazal had failed to contribute anything to the central treasury from the taxes he had collected, and the port revenues accrued to him. On 4 November 1923, only nine days after Reza Khan became prime minister, Khazal was informed that he was expected to pay the arrears in taxes on state and crown lands. 'Now that Tehran was pressing him to settle his accounts, he approached the British authorities and wanted Britain to support his scheme for the partition of Iran, with himself as the ruler of Southern Persia.'[54]

Through the intermediary of the British minister, Percy Loraine, a tenuous and temporary understanding was reached between Khazal and the central government. Khazal even made a small contribution to the Treasury and paid for two Rolls-Royce armoured cars that the Ministry of War had purchased in England.

By mid-September 1924, Khazal was certain that Reza Khan was preparing an imminent attack. In a preemptive move, Khazal went on the offensive and called for Reza Khan's overthrow and the return of Ahmad Shah. 'Khazal was unaware that his support among British officialdom in Iran was dwindling.'[55] Khazal's anti-Reza Khan movement picked up some momentum in mid-October as leaders of the Lor, Qashqai, Mamasani, Boyer Ahmadi and some of the Bakhtiyari tribes entered into an alliance with him. By this time, both Khazal and Reza Khan were moving around their troops and preparing for battle.

On 7 November, Reza Khan went to Esfahan and from there to Shiraz to be closer to his troops and the theatre of war. On 13 November, Loraine rushed back to Iran from his honeymoon in London and met with Khazal in Ahvaz. On the following day, faced with Reza Khan's overwhelming troops and Britain's refusal to stand by him, Khazal sent a note of submission to Reza Khan, asking for forgiveness.

On 7 December 1924, Reza Khan received Khazal's surrender, granted him pardon, and established the central government's rule over Khuzestan. Four months later, while Loraine was absent from Tehran, Khazal was arrested on his boat (19 April 1925), abducted, and brought to Tehran. Even though Khazal had been elected to the First Constituent Assembly of 1925, which had conferred the crown on Reza Khan, he remained under surveillance in Tehran until 4 June 1936, when he was murdered at his own home. It is believed that Reza Khan had given the order to eliminate him.

Thanks to a change in British policy towards Khazal and British mediation, Reza Khan succeeded in subduing Khazal, probably his stiffest tribal adversary, without any major clashes. Reza Khan, 'the conqueror of Khuzestan', returned to Tehran triumphantly as a war hero. Khazal's Lor and Bakhtiyari allies, weakened and on the defensive, each reached a political accord with the central government. The power and hold of the insubordinate southern tribal chiefs had, thus, been broken.

Reza Khan used the alliance between Ahmad Shah and Khazal to discredit the shah among the people. With the help of the British, who had now put their eggs into Reza Khan's basket, the pretender to the throne could present himself as a nationalist who had unified the country and chased away British surrogates, allied with Ahmad Shah.

Last Stretch to the Throne

After obtaining Khazal's surrender and before returning to Tehran on 1 January 1925, Reza Khan went to the holy cities of Karbala and Najaf, the seats of Shii Sources of Imitation, to obtain the *olama*'s consent for a change in dynasty. On 8 February 1925, the prime minister met with a group of deputies and informed them that based on the documents in his possession, Ahmad Shah and the crown prince had been directly implicated in Khuzestan's unrests. He told them that he wished to put an end to the court's intrigues and was giving the Majles five days to come up with a solution. On 12 February, the Majles issued a statement addressing the prime minister as commander-in-chief, a title officially belonging to the shah, and giving him full powers within the law. The statement emphasized that Reza Khan could not be removed from power, except by the Majles.

On 22 February, commemorating the fourth anniversary of the coup, Reza Khan claimed to have 'destroyed all centres of corruption and destruction and uprooted social pains'. He concluded that 'a soldier needs to overcome all barriers'.[56] On 5 May 1925, the Majles voted to abolish all titles given in the past by Qajar kings. Reza Khan discarded his title, Sardar Sepah, which had been given to him by Ahmad Shah and adopted the surname Pahlavi. He was freeing himself from the last vestiges of the Qajars.

In September, Ahmad Shah made it known that he was returning to Iran. This announcement triggered a series of peculiar events. Tehran faced a bread shortage, bread prices skyrocketed and rumours circulated that Reza Khan was at the source of this penury. On 23 September, a few thousand, mostly women, congregated at the Majles, entered it by force and chased away the deputies. Even though Tehran was under martial law, the police did not intervene. The crowd demanded bread and the shah's return. When the riots intensified on the next day, mounted troops attacked and dispersed the people and calm was quickly restored.

The bread riots enabled Reza Khan to arrest some 800 opponents, mainly the shah's supporters, including numerous women. Among those arrested were the court's chief of protocol and several members of the crown prince's close associates. Reza Khan blamed the court for instigating the riots. The commotion was enough to scare the shah and prompt him to delay his return.

Two weeks after the bread riots, on 9 October, a flurry of telegrams addressed to the prime minister and the Majles deputies reached Tehran, demanding the non-admission of the shah back in the country and his removal from power. Military commanders in the provinces had orchestrated this nationwide inpour of petitions. Ahmad Shah's fear of returning had made him seem like an uncaring monarch and turned the mood in Tehran against him. Groups of people held small demonstration around the prime minister's home in the Hasanabad area, criticizing Ahmad Shah and demanding his dethronement.

The Majles met on the afternoon of 29 October 1925 to discuss the telegrams requesting a change in dynasty. The session was interrupted, and the deputies dispersed when gun shots were heard. Vaez Qazvini, a socialist said to be pro-Bolshevik and owner of the publication *Nasihat* (Advice), was erroneously assassinated in the Majles instead of Malek al-Shoara Bahar, a poet, journalist and deputy. Bahar, an initial supporter of Reza Khan, had fallen out with him and became an outspoken critic of his bullying tactics and autocratic bid for power. Bahar was also one of the leaders of the unsuccessful attempt in July 1924 to impeach Reza Khan. His would-be assassins had made a mistake but were successful in scaring and intimidating other insubordinate deputies and journalists.

On 31 October 1925, a special session of the Majles voted in favour of deposing the Qajar dynasty and provisionally named Reza Khan Pahlavi as the ruler of Iran until a constituent assembly could decide on the permanent form of government. In the Majles, only five deputies, Modarres, Taqizadeh, Mosaddeq, Ala and Yahya Dowlatabadi, spoke against Reza Khan's ascent to the throne. On 12 December 1925, the Constituent Assembly voted to alter the Constitution and conferred the monarchy permanently on Reza Pahlavi and his offspring. Four days later (16 December), Reza Shah Pahlavi sat on the royal Marble Throne and proclaimed his kingship.

Almost five years after the bloodless coup of 1921, Reza Khan had peacefully replaced the Qajar dynasty and founded the Pahlavi dynasty. During these years, Reza Khan had outmaneuvered all of his political opponents. He demonstrated a sharp political acumen, but the recipe for his success had rested in the loyalty and strength of his soldiers. Reza Shah's rise to power was not so different from all those warring soldiers who had established their dynasties in the past. The one difference was that Reza Khan's army had no worthy internal rival to force drawn-out bloodshed. Furthermore, very sensitive to his image abroad, instead of closing the Majles, he had mastered the art of engineering elections and manipulating the parliamentary system to his own advantage.

Reza Shah Pahlavi's Reign

There were not many tears shed for the deposed Ahmad Shah. Reza Shah Pahlavi ruled Iran as an uncontested and feared despot from 16 December 1925 to 16 September 1941. His almost 16-year rule transformed the country administratively, economically, culturally and socially. Reza Shah was a veritable state builder. He established central authority in a country where military weakness of past central governments, local tribal chiefs and brigands terrorized the provincial population. Reza Shah created a modern army and introduced military conscription. He completed unprecedented legal reforms, implemented registries, undertook fundamental infrastructural investments and laid grounds for modern industry and finance. He also created the national paraphernalia associated with state-building, giving Iranians a national identity.

If state-building is indivisible from respect for human rights, political freedoms, freedom of choice in clothing, accountability to the people and the alternation of executive power, then Reza Shah was not a state-builder. In his modern despotic state, he purposefully increased the risk of political and civil activities and the exercise of political rights and freedoms. Reza Shah's legacy includes material and social accomplishments along with failures in the realm of political freedoms, human rights and good government.

Iran's modernization from above reflected the vision of one man. Reza Shah, the uneducated Cossack had suddenly become the architect of a country, and his will became the command of his lieutenants and the builders of the country. Modernization, industrialization, centralization and unification appealed to Reza Shah as they possessed a soldierly facet of order, security, discipline and decorum. Reza Shah's modernization project and state-building followed a military-fashioned centralized and hierarchical chain of command leaving no room for meaningful consultation or democratic procedures in micro or macro domains and policies.

Opening Lines of Reza Shah's 1933 National Anthem

Long live our King of Kings, and may his glory make immortal our land. For Pahlavi improved Iran, A hundredfold from where it once used to stand.

Patriotism or nation-worshipping (*vatan parasti*) was equated with shah-worshipping (*shah parasti*) and both stood at the heart of Reza Shah's proposed new Iranian identity. The nation/Shah-worshipper was supposed to place the state/Shah above private and religious considerations. Reforms such as national conscription (1925), changing the calendar from lunar to solar (1925), a new dress code (1927), altering the national flag with the Pahlavi crown (1933), rial instead of qaran as the new currency (1929), a new national anthem (1933), the use of Iran instead of Persia by foreigners (1935) and the abolition of titles (May 1925 and June 1935) were all attempts at creating a unified modern national image worthy of being worshipped.

Unable to declare Iran a secular state, as Kemal Ataturk had done with Turkey, Reza Shah wished to dilute as much as possible the role of religion and the concomitant power of the clergy. By replacing Islam with Iran's pre-Islamic civilization, he hoped to forge a modernized national identity. His secularization drive echoed the agenda of his political supporters, the young Europeanized intellectuals.

Economic and Financial Development

The Millspaugh mission had laid the grounds for Reza Shah's financial and administrative modernization. For five years, Millspaugh and his team of American advisors worked hard to put Iran's finances in order and turn considerable budget deficits into surpluses. They organized the ledgers, enforced financial laws, centralized the tax and revenue system, collected arrears from notables and ran a tight budget. The simple fruit of their work was that the Iranian Treasury was no longer empty and teachers and soldiers got paid on time. Reza Khan had welcomed Millspaugh on his arrival, and the two worked in perfect harmony. In time relations between the two became complicated. 'Over the Shah's increasing demands for military funds,' the two fell out and Millspaugh left in 1927.[57]

> **Millspaugh's Departure**
>
> Reza Shah terminated Millspaugh's mission 'on grounds of Millspaugh's increasingly domineering conduct and his repeated noncompliance with the Shah's requests for increased military expenditure'. (M. Bonakdarian)[58]

In an economically backward country such as Iran, with mountainous and inaccessible regions, infrastructure was a first-order priority. Commerce, troop movements and travel needed roads, bridges, tunnels, railroads, ports and airports. Rural development required irrigation projects, modernization and mechanization of agriculture, reform of the feudal land-holding system and connecting isolated and scattered villages and cities. Cities needed urban planning, roads, schools, universities, hospitals, electricity, water supply systems and sewage.

Economic strategies adopted during Reza Shah's rule can be divided into two broad historical phases. First, during 1925–30, the government adopted a laissez-faire approach, encouraging private initiative, free trade and foreign investment. In May 1927, the important step towards realizing the old Iranian dream of monetary autonomy was taken and the law establishing the state-owned National Bank of Iran (Bank Melli) was ratified by the Majles. The Melli Bank, run by a German manager, began operation in September 1928, and by January 1931, some 70 German financial experts helped running it.

The years 1930 to 1941 marked the second and predominantly statist phase of Reza Shah's economic policies. This was partially due to Reza Shah's impatient drive to industrialize Iran. If private capital did not have the funds, then the government needed to become aggressively involved in raising the capital and investing it. The great economic depression in the West had slowed down private commerce and private capital formation.

Hence, the government took a leading role in industrialization, investment, employment and controlling international commerce through establishing trade monopolies on tea, sugar, textiles, cotton and motor vehicles. Consumers were obliged to purchase imported goods from government organizations. These measures were followed by a series of export monopolies, among them rice and carpets. In 1930 and 1931, a series of laws were passed, expanding the state's role in the economy, while providing protection for domestic industries.

During this protectionist economic period, the Melli Bank became the engine for mobilizing private savings for the government's industrial and infrastructural projects. The Melli Bank subsequently gave birth to two specialized state banks: the Agricultural and Industrial Bank in June 1933 and the Mortgage Bank in January 1939. The Agricultural and Industrial Bank was responsible for financing the establishment of processing industries such as textile, tobacco, sugar and tar. By 1940, the Melli Bank had played a central role in monetizing society and commercializing the economy through its 89 branches throughout Iran.

In March 1935, under the auspices of Abdolhoseyn Davar, minister of finance, and with the financial know-how of a Swiss expert, Iran opened its first state-run insurance company. This, too, became an arm of the government to collect and redirect capital. Davar was the first Iranian to take out an insurance policy against a house fire on 6 November 1936. Insurance premiums collected by the Iranian Insurance Company increased from 5 million rials in 1936 to 24 million rials in 1941.

In 1934, the Department of Industry took control of all government industrial undertakings, and in October of that year, private firms needed permission from this department to begin work. By the end of the 1930s, some 64 state industries had been set up, including cotton mills, knitting factories, sugar-beet refineries, cement and small chemical plants, tea-processing factories, a small copper refinery, fertilizer-mixing plants, food canneries, coal mines and brick, match, cigarette, paper, shoe and soap factories.[59] In 1920, Iran's industrial sector, aside from the oil industry, employed some 6,700 workers. 'By 1940 the numbers had grown to some 170,000, the bulk of this increase having taken place in the 1930s.'[60]

Reza Shah's Policy of Modernization

Not only established 'the groundwork for the appearance of a profoundly different middle class' but also the foundation of an urban proletariat. (E. Ehlers and W. Floor)[61]

Reza Shah's industrialization drive, however, ignored the internal logic and workings of modern capitalism. Factories were not always built with an eye to profits and efficiency or even generating employment, but for their demonstration effect of national grandeur. Most were ostentatious projects. The eight sugar refineries that began operation between 1932 and 1938, 'operated at a substantial loss, amounting to 50–70 million rials annually between 1938 and 1941'.[62]

Oil and Agriculture: Enclave Sectors

Throughout Reza Shah's rule, the highly lucrative oil sector remained an enclave economy, and its activities continued beyond government control. The Anglo-Persian Oil Company (APOC), changed its name in 1935 and became the Anglo-Iranian Oil Company (AIOC), a British-owned and British-controlled enterprise. It was a modern, capital intensive and technologically advanced industry with no meaningful backward or forward linkage with the rest of the Iranian economy. The Abadan refinery, built and operated by the British, was one of the biggest in the world, with some 10 million tons of oil going through it annually (1940). APOC had around 3,500 foreign and 20,000 Iranian employees.

Iranians always believed their country was being exploited by APOC. 'While oil production had increased by 23-fold between 1914 and 1929, the royalties to the Iranian government had increased by less than 5-fold.'[63] From 1928 to 1931, Abdolhoseyn Teymurtash, Reza Shah's powerful minister of court, conducted three rounds of negotiations with APOC to revise the terms of the old contract and increase Iran's revenues. These negotiations did not bear fruit. In June 1932, it was announced that based on the 1931 accounts of APOC, Iran's share of net profits would amount to £306,872. This was a dramatic fall in revenue compared to Iran's take in 1929 and 1931, 'of £1,437,000 and £1,288,312'.[64]

On 26 November 1932, Reza Shah asked for the APOC files and threw them in the fireplace in a fit of rage. On the next day, Hasan Taqizadeh, the new minister of finance, informed APOC's director in Tehran that the D'Arcy Concession was cancelled. Reza Shah announced that he would only sign an agreement that would safeguard Iran's vital interests. On 30 November 1932, the Majles approved the cancellation. The British government intervened on the part of APOC, sending an intimidating protest note, and carrying out naval war manoeuvres in the Persian Gulf. During January 1933, the British took their case before the League of Nations. The League advised that the parties renegotiate and hammer out a new agreement. Reza Shah signed a new agreement on 29 April 1933.

The new contract extended the original duration of the D'Arcy Concession. Whereas Iran could have legally terminated the D'Arcy Concession in 1961, it now committed itself until 1993. The renegotiated contract also enabled APOC to remain exempt from payment of duty on its exports of petroleum and imports of equipment. APOC 'gained the additional privilege of not having to surrender its foreign exchange to the Persian government', and exemption 'from liability to national and local taxes for a period of thirty years'. The company had 'succeeded in avoiding Persian demands for either representation upon the board or for a shareholding'.[65]

On the bright side, the new contract limited the concession area to 100,000 square miles (160,934 sq. km) to be chosen by the company, but within the bounds of its original concession area. The new contract calculated Iran's royalty based on tonnage (4 shilling/ton of petroleum) rather than the previous nebulous formula of 16 per cent of profits. The calculation of the profit figure by APOC remained a contentious issue and Iran was barred from inspecting the company's financial books. The new agreement entitled Iran to 'a sum equivalent to 20 per cent of the APOC's profits distributed to ordinary shareholders in excess of £671,250. A minimum aggregate payment of £750,000 was guaranteed and the company consented to price oil products for the Persian market at favourable rates.'[66]

To settle outstanding financial disagreements, Iran was to receive £1 million and APOC committed itself to accelerating 'the process of Persianization', which essentially remained an unkept promise. The new treaty was an improvement on the previous one, except for the 32-year extension. However, Iranian nationalists continued to view Britain as the bullying capitalist, always at Iran's throat.

Why Sign the New Agreement

Reza Shah's fears of British-instigated revolts by ethnic Arabs in oil-producing areas and possible military intervention compelled him to accept British negotiator's terms. (M. Elm)[67]

During Reza Shah's tenure, the standard of living, welfare and condition of life stagnated in rural areas. By 1940, the share of urban population was 22 per cent. Some 78 per cent of the population living in rural Iran did not benefit from Reza Shah's modernization and development efforts. The Iranian rural economy based mostly on dry-farming and primitive methods of agriculture stagnated. The Iranian countryside, except for the northern regions, was caught in an interminable poverty cycle, constantly exposed to malnutrition and disease.

The yawning rural–urban gap was also present between the upper and lower classes in Tehran. The relative glitter and comforts of Tehran's leisure class contrasted with the stagnation and poverty of the lower urban classes. The squalor of most rural areas and urban lower classes exemplified the trappings of two types of a dual society, both in appearance and in soul. Tehran of the rich and the poor was equally apart as Tehran and the rest of Iran.

Infrastructure, Roads, Railroad and Urban Development

> **Road-Building**
> Before 1921, nothing was done directly by the state to improve the condition of Iran's roads. (J. Bharier)[68]

In 1923, the Department of Roads and Bridges was created in the Ministry of Public Works and drew up a Nine-Year Road Plan. Iran had some 3,200 kilometres of almost entirely unpaved roads in 1925. By 1938, this figure had increased to 22,500 kilometres. In 1920, there were 'not more than ten' cars in Tehran. In 1924, Iran had some 1,000 vehicles, 'about half of which were in the oil company's concession area'.[69] By 1938, there were some 25,000 motor vehicles of various sorts in Iran. By 1940, some 100 municipal buses operated in Tehran alone. The increase in motor vehicles was concurrent with the opening of garages and service stations. By 1939, Iran had approximately 140 garages with a concentration in Tehran, Abadan, Tabriz and Kermanshah.

An important concern for Reza Shah was the urban transformation and modernization of cities, especially Tehran. According to the 1940 census, Iran had a population of 18,338,867. Tehran's population in 1940 was 540,087 as compared to 310,039 in 1932. Col. Karim Buzarjomehri was appointed acting mayor of Tehran in 1923 and subsequently served as mayor for ten years. He was an officer of the Cossack Brigade and was trusted by Reza Shah. With great caution and many caveats, Buzarjomehri's mark on Tehran can be compared to Baron Haussmann's on Paris. Both men were known for their arrogance and autocratic behaviour, and while Haussmann had attended the most prestigious Parisian high schools and had subsequently studied law, Buzarjomehri was said to be illiterate. Both had the support of their royal patrons and had grandiose ideas about their respective capitals.

Buzarjomehri began his modernization of Tehran in February–March 1925. Hoping to standardize and introduce some order in Tehran's housing projects, he announced that the construction of new houses had to be approved by Tehran's municipality. From 1927, works began on boulevards, roundabouts and widening streets and various parts and neighbourhoods of the city were connected. In 1930, the destruction of the eight-sided wall surrounding Tehran was begun and the moats around the city were filled up. Tehran's first psychiatric ward and fire station were also built during Buzarjomehri's office.

On 13 November 1933, the Majles passed a law on expanding and widening streets and squares in municipalities. 'Such towns as Hamadan, Kermanshah and Ahvaz were provided with avenues which radiated from a central circle. At the circle rose a statue of Reza Shah, usually of marble but sometimes of painted plaster which soon deteriorated.'[70] By 1939, most of Tehran's main streets were widened, and were first cobble-stoned and then asphalted. The approximately 30-kilometre road connecting Shemiran in the north of Tehran via Qolhak to Shah Abdolazim in the south of Tehran (the old Shemiran road), was completely asphalted as was Pahlavi Street, and planted with oriental plane trees (*chenar*) and wide water gutters were installed on either side. The delightful Pahlavi Street ran some 17 kilometres and connected Reza Shah's Saadabaad Palace in the north of Tehran to his Marble Palace in the city centre.

Government expenditure on buildings grew from 2 million rials in 1926 to 31.4 million rials in 1940. Most of this rapid increase in urbanization was concentrated in Tehran, while many governmental buildings were reconstructed in the provinces. New brick government buildings popped up in Tehran's city centre. By 1941, Tehran had buildings of six stories, while one-storey houses and shops, which Reza Shah disliked, gave way to an increasing number of Two-storey buildings. To provide Tehranis with green space, the government converted wastelands into parks, and by 1930, the capital had 'some 71,000 square meters in promenades and parks'.[71]

In Tehran, Urban Development and Renewal Aimed at Two Goals

On the one hand, it included clearing and reconstructing degraded areas, in particular in the central and northwestern parts of the old city. On the other, the 'construction of very impressive administrative buildings, together with several palaces in a quasi- European style'. (E. Ehlers and W. Floor)[72]

The impressive government buildings of the Tehran Railway Station, Museum of Ancient Iran, Tehran University, Melli Bank, police headquarters, Ministry of Justice and the Marble Palace are all products of the Reza Shah era. The architects of these impressive modern buildings were inspired by pre-Islamic Iranian, as well as modern European architecture and planning. They included the Polish Leshek Vladislav Dezidery Gorodetsky/Horodecki (Tehran Railway Station), the French André Godard (Museum of Ancient Iran and Tehran University), the German H. Heinrich (Bank Melli), the Armenian Iranian Gabriel Guevrekian (Police Headquarters and Ministry of Justice) and the Armenian Iranian Leon Tadousian (Marble Palace).

Eager to attract tourists and develop his birthplace Mazandaran, where he had financial interests, Reza Shah built a chain of modern, luxury hotels in Chalus, Amol, Ramsar and Babolsar. He also built Hotel Gachsar, on the road between Tehran and

Chalus, as well as, and two hotels, one in Abe Ali, some 65 kilometres from Tehran and the other at Dar Band, north of Tehran. These imposing hotels had all the amenities of modern European hotels and were completed with the help of German, British and Italian craftsmanship.

In tandem with urbanization, the Reza Shah era witnessed the spread of modern services and amenities. In the mid-1920s, electricity was available in APOC areas of operation, while the rest of the country was mainly in the dark with a few electricity-generating plants operating in the large cities. Significant annual addition to electricity generation began in 1933. In 1937, a new 8,000 horsepower generator was installed in Tehran and by 1939, 'practically every town in the country had electricity'.[73]

By 1939, the construction of Tehran's very modern grain silos was completed and inaugurated by the shah and the crown prince. At this time, Tehran possessed 21 telephone call boxes as well as public lavatories and urinals. The number of post offices grew from about 220 in 1915 to about 460 in 1931. From 1936, construction began on some 25 modern hospitals throughout the country. The 500-bed hospital in Tehran (later it had 1,000 beds) built by German architects and engineers, the 100-bed-capacity hospitals in Shiraz and Esfahan and the 32-bed hospital in Zanjan were among them. Improvements in services during the Reza Shah era, however, remained lopsided between rural and urban Iran and within the urban centres. In 1940, even Tehran remained deprived of piped water and a sewage system.

The Trans-Iranian Railway

Measured in terms of foreign exchange requirements, the length of roads which could have been built, other investments which were foregone or the recurrent costs to the state, the Trans-Iranian Railway must stand out as one of the classic examples of conspicuous investment in a developing country. (J. Bharier)[74]

One of Reza Shah's major infrastructural accomplishments was the construction of the Trans-Iranian Railway connecting Bandar Shah Harbour on the Caspian Sea to Bandar Shahpur Harbour on the Persian Gulf. The 1,394-kilometre-long project was built by the Germans, Americans, Danes and British. Work began in October 1927 and needed about 230 tunnels and 4,100 bridges to complete in August 1938. The massive project, opening a major artery through the inaccessible country, cost £30 million and what made it a major feat was that it was financed internally. 'In 1940 there was a bi-weekly service in both directions between Tehran and Bandar Shah and between Tehran and Karaj.'[75]

Judicial and Administrative Reform

Ali-Akbar Davar became minister of justice when Hasan Mostowfi reshuffled his cabinet on 12 February 1927. Davar served in that position for seven years. He immediately requested and obtained permission from the shah and Majles to dissolve the previous Justice Department, completely overhaul it and draw up a new legal code. Davar convened a team of legal experts, who prepared some 120 legal bills, all of which were approved by the Majles.

His fundamental reforms provided the country with new civil, commercial and criminal codes largely based on the Napoleonic codes. A significant outcome of these reforms was the abolition of old religious courts. Once the legal structure was created, Davar recruited a new body of judges to run the new courts throughout the country. When on 26 April 1927, Reza Shah opened the reformed Courts of Justice, he issued a royal decree abolishing Iran's **Capitulation** treaty with other countries.

On 10 April 1923, the law for recording deeds and properties was passed through the Majles. Before this date, documents were not officially registered by a government agency and their authenticity and legitimacy was only recognized by religious law devoid of state authorization. On 4 June 1925, a law was passed requiring civil registry of identity documents, including birth and death certificates. This was followed by laws enforcing land transactions and the registration of land records. To operationalize registry laws, state-approved and state-supervised offices for recording documents had to be established and staffed.

The Office of Official Documents, opened on 17 March 1932, was established on the model of French and Belgium notary offices. The management of these offices was left to the private sector, and the directors were usually former members of the clergy. The Ministry of Justice maintained a supervisory role with regards to these offices. The recording and certification of documents such as for marriage and divorce and the sale and purchase of property were authorized and legalized in these offices. These offices replaced the traditional religious offices which conducted such affairs.

Socio-cultural Europeanization

Modern education, in contrast to religious schooling and learning from the West, was a fundamental aspect of Reza Shah's vision for Iran. In 1911, Iran had 123 primary schools, 'two secondary schools and three higher colleges'.[76] By 1924, it had 638 primary schools and 86 high schools and 7 colleges, which were combined to form Tehran University on 30 May 1934. By 1940, the number of primary schools jumped to 2,331 and high schools to 321. Studying abroad became systematized in 1929, with the annual dispatch of 100 students. Between 1922 and 1938, some 848 students had been sent overseas to study.

On 6 September 1927, the Majles passed a law, making sports compulsory in schools. From 1934, the government became interested in modern sports for the youth as a means of promoting teamwork, discipline, individual betterment and leadership, as well as moral and physical development. Emphasis was placed on organizing sports events for both boys and girls and promoting scout activities. 'In the year 1936, Iran counted 1,694 Boy Scout and sports associations, the latter including old sports (*zurkhaneh*), soccer, tennis, volleyball, basketball, boxing, cycling, wrestling, boating, swimming, and different sports.'[77] In 1938, the government turned to the construction of swimming pools in Tehran and several provincial centres. The most famous of these swimming pools was at Manzariyeh, located in northern Tehran, where a regular summer camp was held annually for boy and girl scouts.

By 1940, Tehran had around 12 cinemas, screening mostly American and German films in their original language and with Persian captions, which most people could not read. In November 1933, the first Iranian speaking movie, *The Lor Girl* (*Dokhtar Lor*) made its debut at Tehran's Mayak (Didehban) movie theatre. The iconic Café Naderi, traditional hangout of Iranian literati and intellectuals, was opened in 1928, followed by Café Pars in 1934 on Lalehzar No Street.

Tehran's elite had two private and exclusive clubs, where women appeared without a veil. Tehran Club, mostly frequented by the British, and Iran Club, founded by Teymurtash, were the nocturnal entertainment jewels of the Iranian leisure class and the foreign diplomatic corp.

Dressing Iranians

Premodern Variety

Like all other premodern societies, premodern Iran was characterized by great sartorial variety, as different regions, tribes, religious groups, and social classes had their own specific clothes. (H. Chehabi)[78]

The Constitutional Revolution had created a socio-political opening giving vent to repressed claims and demands. Women's education, their social role and the extension of their rights came to the fore. The proponents of women's rights confronted those religious leaders who opposed their rights. Back in 1907, *Habl al-matin* had published an anonymous letter by a woman challenging Sheykh Fazlollah Nuri's claim that: 'Learning for women is against religion.'[79]

The women's drive for change fell on the receptive ears of Reza Shah and the young modernizers around him, who were invested in Europeanizing the appearance of Iranians. They looked most favourably on dressing men and women in the image of

Europeans. From 1919, women's publications in Tehran and the provinces increased, and with it a gradual murmur of unveiling.

Reza Shah's women's liberation movement became closely intertwined with secularization and the struggle against the religious establishment. Europeanization could not be detached from neutralizing the power of upholders of traditional Islam who saw a contradiction between women's individual freedoms and the teachings of the faith. Having defeated all claimants to power such as the Qajars, tribal leaders, local warlords, old politicians and revolutionary movements, the clergy remained the last bastion of resistance to Reza Shah's drive to despotism. To monopolize authority, Reza Shah approached secularization in a gradual, trial-and-error manner, in the same manner as he had moved against his other opponents.

> ### Reza Shah on the New Dress Code
> I would like us to look like them so they [Europeans] would not mock us.[80]

Changing or modernizing the appearance of Iranians began in August 1927, with the government's decision to impose a uniform headwear for men called the '**Pahlavi hat**'. It was first imposed on civil servants and then on school pupils. Sixteen months later, on 27 December 1928, the Majles passed the 'uniform dress code', making the 'Pahlavi hat' obligatory for all Iranian men, except for clergy and seminary school students. Turkey had already gone through the same process. To replace the fez, the Turkish Hat Law was passed on 25 November 1925.

The imposition of unveiling was slower and more intricate. It was officialized on 8 January 1936. Reza Shah knew that unveiling would bring on, the wrath of the clergy. He, therefore, had to make his move when he was in an unassailable political position. In October 1927, Reza Shah still wished to keep the clergy on his side, and in a speech to their representatives hammered at 'his passionate devotion to Islam'.[81]

But five months later, on 22 March 1928, a golden opportunity presented itself. Reza Shah rushed to Qom, entered the holy shrine of Hazrat Masumeh with his boots on and assaulted the renowned cleric, Sheykh Mohammad-Taqi Bafqi. The cleric's crime was that he had reproached the queen and shah's two daughters for wearing white **chadors** instead of black ones, and chiding one of them, for accidentally exposing part of her hair and body. From 1928, the police were informed that unveiled women were not prohibited from going out on the streets.

> ### Women and City
> In 1928 women were admitted to cafés and cinemas, and since that time they have taken full part in the social world. (P. Elwell-Sutton)[82]

Reza Shah's 30-day trip to Turkey, which ended on 11 July 1934, deeply marked him. He was highly impressed by what Ataturk had achieved in Turkey, especially in terms of women's rights, secularization and economic progress. Reza Shah's visit had convinced him to increase the tempo of his Europeanization and industrialization drive at home. Upon his return, Reza Shah turned his attention to women's attire.

In Ataturk's Turkey, no particular law had prohibited wearing the veil but the policy to stamp it out was begun by municipalities banning its use. The drive to suppress the veil in Turkey occurred after women received full universal suffrage on 5 December 1934. Reza Shah followed Ataturk's model of unveiling women, but not his revolutionary step of legalizing women's suffrage.

> ### The Herculean Task of Unveiling
> Unveiling and putting women on an equal status with men seemed more difficult than splitting Alborz Mountain . . . only the will of Reza Shah made this crucial reform possible. (I. Sadiq)[83]

On 13 May 1935, under the auspices of Reza Hekmat (Sardar Fakher), the minister of education, the Ladies' Centre opened its doors. The Centre's honorary president was Shams Pahlavi, Reza Shah's eldest daughter, and its purpose was to prepare public opinion among women and their families for banning the veil. This centre provided a state-sponsored anti-veil platform, under the cover of sports, lectures, adult literacy classes and plays both in Tehran and some 50 other cities. Its members were mainly school teachers and civil servants at the Ministry of Education.

Reza Shah's forceful imposition of the new dress code, on both men and women, led those more used to their traditional attire to resist and push back. The clergy assessed the rapid changes as an attack on the morality and chastity of their flock and rallied against it. To realize his secularization and Europeanization drive, as well as removing the last barrier to his absolute power, Reza Shah embarked on subduing and pacifying the clergy.

On 19 June 1935, Mohammad-Ali Foroughi's government decided on a new headgear for men. The proper full-rimmed chapeaux (bowler hat) replaced the Pahlavi Hat as men's obligatory headwear. When Mashhad's clergy opposed the move, the city plunged into turmoil. On 14 July 1935, Gen. Iraj Matbui, commander of the Western Corps, ordered his troops to attack a large crowd of thousands at Gowharshad Mosque, where Sheykh Mohammad-Taqi Bohlul had roused the people with his speeches against the government and its dress-code policies. The bloody repression of the unarmed people led to some 130 to 1,700 dead and about 300 wounded. Some 800, among them Mashhad's prominent religious figures, were arrested and many were exiled. The Gowharshad uprising was brutally quelled and Reza Shah overpowered the clergy.

Heads rolled after the Gowharshad uprising. Mohammadvali Asadi, the popular and honest custodian of Imam Reza's shrine, was arrested and executed. During the days leading to the attack on Gowharshad, Asadi had suggested coming to terms with the religious opposition and avoiding violence. Prime Minister Forughi, who had tried to intercede on behalf of Asadi, his in-law, lost his position some twenty days before Asadi's execution on 21 December 1935.

> ## The Tempo of Unveiling Women
>
> This 'varied greatly, according to the disposition of the local officials; on the whole, the most vigorous methods were used in the most fanatical districts, such as Tabriz, where the campaign was pushed through with the aid of much roughness and even cruelty on the part of the police'. (N. Butler)[84]

In July 1935, the government introduced co-education primary schooling until the fourth grade. More significantly, for the academic year 1935–6, girls were prohibited from wearing the veil at school.[85] During the same academic year, unveiled girls were admitted to the Teacher Training College and the faculties of literature and sciences.[86] With the appointment of Mahmud Jam as prime minister on 3 December 1935, 'the official procedure of banning the veil accelerated'.[87]

On Wednesday, 8 January 1936, the new building of the Teacher Training College was inaugurated by Reza Shah and the queen, accompanied by the princesses, Shams and Ashraf. Diplomas were handed out to the graduates and for the first time, female members of the royal family appeared without a veil at an official ceremony. All women in attendance, graduating students, wives of government officials and the girl scouts present were also unveiled. For Reza Shah, this special day signalled the official beginning of unveiling. He was promoting the new dress model for women by setting his own female family members as example. From February 1936, local authorities were ordered to impose the ban on the veil, and the promotion of gender mixing became an undeclared state policy.

Mehdiqoli Hedayat, the longest-serving prime minister under Reza Shah, spoke of two kinds of civilization, that of walking the boulevards and that of attending laboratories and libraries. He believed the civilization that prevailed during Reza Shah's rule was that of the boulevards demanded by the 'promiscuous and the degenerates'.[88]

Domestic Politics

Reza Shah appointed six men as prime ministers during his rule: Mohammad-Ali Forughi (19 December 1925), Hasan Mostowfi (7 June 1926–28 May 1927), Mehdiqoli Hedayat (31 May 1927–12 September 1933), Mohammad-Ali Forughi for a second time (17 September 1933–2 December 1935), Mahmud Jam (3 December 1935–26 October 1939), Ahmad Matin-Daftari (26 October 1939–24 June 1940), Ali Mansur (24 June 1940–27 August 1941) and finally, Mohammad-Ali Forughi for the third time (27 August 1941).

Prime ministers came and went at Reza Shah's will. One day they were told to form a government and on another to resign on the spot. During Reza Shah's rule, prime ministers and ministers simply reported the shah's will and command to various government units and enabled its proper execution. They had no rights and yet, were held fully responsible for the projects associated with their ministry. Usually, the cabinet met three times a week and on Saturdays and Wednesdays the shah presided.

> ### A British Diplomat's View of Iran in 1933
> In spite of its occidental veneer we are not dealing with a modern state, but with an oriental despotism. (V. A. L. Mallet)[89]

Figure 3.3 Abdolhoseyn Teymurtash. *Source: Wikimedia Commons.*

For seven years (16 December 1925–24 December 1932), Abdolhoseyn Teymurtash (Figure 3.3), the minister of court, acted as the plenipotentiary prime minister, the Grand Vizier and the powerful number two in the Pahlavi regime. During those years, prime ministers Forughi, Mostowfi and Hedayat were mere figureheads. The shah had told his cabinet that, 'Teymurtash's word is my word'.[90] Teymurtash would draw up and sign agreements, then present them to the cabinet for their approval. He would tell the cabinet that the shah 'has been informed and has approved'. This was the code word for ministers to sign whatever document was presented to them without reading it.

While in power, Teymurtash controlled Reza Shah's excesses. The two were complete opposites in class background, education, culture, social skills and public relations, yet both shared a love for power, Europeanization, secularization, jingoistic nationalism and heavy-handed tactics. As complementary as they were, Teymurtash, the worldly, multi-lingual, suave politician, became eventually too powerful for Reza Shah's taste. To everyone's surprise, Teymurtash, who had been instrumental in consolidating Reza Shah's power, was dismissed on 24 December 1932, put on trial, imprisoned and finally killed in prison on 3 October 1933. After Teymurtash, Reza Shah had no one to trust other than Davar. The tireless Davar, who had served Reza Shah and his country loyally, committed suicide in February 1937. The fear that Reza Shah would one day turn against him led him to desperation.

Short honeymoon of party politics

In Turkey, Ataturk had relied on his Republican People's Party to forge modernization and reform. The party's **Six Arrows** became the roadmap for Ataturk's reforms. Similarly, Reza Shah aimed at creating a stable and permanent majority party in Iran. In early July 1927, he prompted Teymurtash to found the *Hezbe Irane No* (New Iran Party). The party reflected Reza Shah's ideals of modernization, nationalism and 'opposition to all reactionary and subversive ideas', and was described by the British Legation in Iran as being 'on Fascist lines'.[91]

In September 1927, the New Iran Party came under attack by Tadayyon, the powerful minister of education, and Col. Mohammad Dargahi, the chief of police. This open opposition could not have been without Reza Shah's support, who suddenly forbade cabinet members 'to join political parties of any sort' and ordered them 'not to participate in the activities of the New Iran Party'.[92] Reza Shah was not familiar with party politics and apparently feared creating a strong organization which could overshadow him.

In October 1927, Reza Shah ordered the abolition of the religiously oriented *Hezbe Zedde Ajnabi* (Anti-Foreigners Party), which he had helped create. This mysterious organization was said to be organized by Col. Mohammad Dargahi, the chief of police, and Sheykh Mohammad Khalesizadeh, a long-time opponent of the republican movement.

By 15 October 1927, the New Iran Party ceased all public political activities. It had barely lasted 10 weeks. Towards the end of the dispute over the New Iran Party, which reflected Reza Shah's inner wrangling and possible machinations, the shah expressed his disdain with party politics. He told Mehdiqoli Hedayat's cabinet that, 'each country has its own regime, ours is a one-person regime'.[93] Teymurtash had to find a party system which would be suited to an absolute one-person regime.

Faced with Reza Shah's fear of an all-powerful single party, such as Ataturk's Republican People's Party, Teymurtash changed his strategy. He placed his emphasis on a new party, with a much more limited objective. The Progress Party's (*Hezbe Taraqi*) brief was to identify pro-government candidates, engineer their election to the Majles and assure their support of government bills in the Majles. This was not an ideological or policy-making party, but a facilitating tool of the executive based on patron–client relations.

Teymurtash's Progress Party held a large majority in the 6th, 7th and 8th Majles and worked effectively to push ahead Reza Shah's wishes. Deputies elected to the 7th Majles, opened on 6 October 1928, and the 8th Majles, on 16 December 1930, were for all intents and purposes appointees of the Court. Some 95 per cent of the deputies to the 7th Majles and 90 per cent of the members of the 8th Majles belonged to the Progress Party. Influential figures such as Mosaddeq and Modarres were prevented from being elected to the 7th Majles.

By the time the 11th Majles was opened by the shah on 11 September 1937, and the 12th Majles was inaugurated on 24 October 1939, the legislative had become a mere window dressing, which Reza Shah was happy to keep. The Majles had become so subdued that it did not even discuss issues, but just rubber-stamped whatever was brought to it. Reza Shah had obtained his political end, without creating a single powerful party.

The Despot

In February 1928, the French minister in Iran wrote about Reza Shah's mood change. He reported on the shah's excessive bouts of anger, violence, vulgar language, physical assault and restlessness. The British Legation's assessment of Reza Shah's mode of interaction with his people was telling. 'The army fears the Shah and the people fear both … His [the Shah's] unpopularity is as great as ever, but fear hold the discontented and allows the Shah and his government to put through reforms …'[94]

The shah's verbal and physical violence, his paranoia of plots against him and his vindictiveness worsened with time. His mood swings made his decisions even more arbitrary. One day he would dismiss a close associate or loyal officer on trumped-up charges, and on the next, he could either order their death or bring them back to power. In 1933, before the foreign community at a racecourse, Reza Shah kicked a subject in the stomach and then rewarded him with 100 tomans.

Reza Khan had already begun eliminating all opposition before he became shah. After wearing the crown, he went on to systematically jail, exile or execute his allies and his close military and civilian associates. In time, Reza Shah placed great reliance on his chiefs of police and their direct reports to him. Reza Shah's police state entered a new phase when he named Mohammad-Hoseyn Ayrom chief of police on 23 March 1931. Through Ayrom's eyes and ears, Reza Shah kept tabs on the activities of all military and civilian notables and politicians. Supersensitive to meetings between Iranians and members of foreign embassies, Reza Shah constantly suspected plots against him. In July 1933, Victor Mallet of the British Legation observed that, 'The fact remains that the Shah's earlier popularity has long since vanished and he is now almost universally loathed and detested.'[95]

> ## Killing the Opposition
> Like Mustafa Kemal's arranged murder of Turkish communist leaders, or fascist Italy's assassination of parliamentarian Giacomo Matteotti, Reza Khan's 'modernist' use of extra-judicial violence was quite effective in silencing the opponents of his dictatorship. (A. Matin-Asgari)[96]

Aside from the Bakhtiyari, Qashqai, Lor and Boyerahmadi, tribal leaders and the military officers who were executed each year on charges of treason and tumult, Reza Shah left behind a long trail of victims. The list of politicians, military officers and tribal chiefs executed or mysteriously killed includes: Col. Mahmud Pulladin, commander of the Royal Guards (February 1928); Shmuel Hayyim, a deputy in the 5th Majles, leader of the Jewish community and journalist (December 1931); Esmail Khan Sowlat al-dowleh, chief of the Qashqai tribe and member of 8th Majles (March 1933); Teymurtash, minister of court (October 1933); Sardar Asad Bakhtiyari (Sardar Asad), minister of war (March 1934); Sheykh Khazal (June 1936), Hasan Modarres, the influential cleric and deputy of Majles (December 1937); Nosrat al-dowleh Firuz, minister of finance (January 1938); Farrokhi-Yazdi, the revolutionary deputy of the 7th Majles and journalist (October 1939); and Arbab Keykhosrow, the Zoroastrian deputy from the 2nd to the 12th Majles, known for his honesty and uprightness, and father to Bahram Shahrokh, the anti-Shah Persian broadcaster of Berlin Radio (July 1940).

Some were lucky because they were imprisoned, exiled or banished but not put to death. A selected list of those who were allowed to run for their lives included: Hoseyn Dadgar, minister of interior, a deputy from the 6th to the 9th Majles (exiled May/June 1935); Farajollah Bahrami, Reza Shah's man of confidence, his teacher and head of the Royal Secretariat (arrested May 1935 and exiled); Ali Dashti, journalist (arrested May 1935 and banished); Zeinolabeddin Rahnema, journalist and deputy of the 5th and 6th Majles (arrested May 1935 and exiled); and Reza Tajaddod, deputy of 4th and 5th Majles, journalist and judge (arrested May 1935 and exiled).

> **Reporting on Repression in Iran of 1936**
>
> Arrests are so regular a feature of the Shah's system of government that they hardly need to be singled out any longer for special attention. (H. Seymour)[97]

Among those imprisoned more than once before being banished were Mohammad-Taqi Bahar, also known as Malek al-Shoara, who had been deputy of the 3rd to 6th Majles, and was a poet and journalist (November/December 1929 for the first time and again February/March 1933). There was another category of players who outsmarted Reza Shah. Ayrom, the dreaded chief of police, and Hasan Taqizadeh, Reza Shah's minister of finance and minister in France, both left Iran while still in power and preferred not to return home, fearing for their lives.

From 1935 Europeanization and industrialization in tandem with wanton domestic repression picked up speed. No one dared ask why journalists, deputies, politicians, poets and officers were being arrested and imprisoned. National unification had been gained and the roads were secured at the price of insecurity of citizens. Flattery and adulation of Reza Shah reached new heights in 1937. After a first statue of him was erected on Rah Ahan Square, a second statue was unveiled with great pomp on Baharestan Square on 12 September 1937. By 1941, and until his departure, Tehran saw five different statues of Reza Shah being erected, the last of which was unveiled on 6 May 1941.

> **A British Assessment of Reza Shah's Rule in 1940**
>
> The government's remedy for discontent is vigilant police, a controlled press and now a controlled wireless broadcasting system. (R. Bullard)[98]

The austere soldier had developed quite an appetite for land acquisition during his rule. He continued to accumulate wealth by forcefully dispossessing landowners either through outright confiscation or through coercing them to sell at nominal prices. Reza Sha's annual income from 'all his properties in 1932–33 was about one million tomans'.[99] By 1935, it was reported that Mazandaran and Gilan, two of Iran's most agriculturally prosperous provinces, 'are now largely owned by the Shah'.[100] In June 1940, he added large tracts of fertile land in Langaroud (Gilan Province) to his estates. In the summer of 1941, Reza Shah bought a large piece of land in Tehran for a tenth of the market price per square metre, to build a hotel. By the time he left the country in 1941, 'he owned about 10 per cent of the agricultural estates ...'[101]

A New Opposition

Even though Iranian society seemed to have succumbed to Reza Shah's reign of repression and despotism, new voices of opposition were emerging. On 1 May 1929, Abadan oil refinery workers demonstrated and demanded higher wages and shorter hours. The strike was led by Yusuf Eftekhari, dispatched 'from the Communist University of Toilers of the East (KUTIV) in Moscow'.[102] The arrest of some 45 demonstrators led to a series of strikes on 6 May involving some 9,000–10,000 refinery workers. After the arrest of some 200 and their banishment to Lorestan, the protest movement died out. 'The 1929 refinery strike signified the emergence of the organized working class in Iran and furnished a template for industrial militancy which was to reappear . . .'[103]

In May 1931, there was another communist-led strike among the textile workers in Isfahan. Fearing the spread of communism and labour actions, on 9 June 1931, the government of Mehdiqoli Hedayat, outlawed 'participation in any group or association 'whose aim and conduct is opposition to the Iranian constitutional monarchy, or contains communistic ideology'.[104]

Between 6 and 8 May 1937, Taqi Arani, Mohammad Bahrami, Ziaeddin Alamuti and Abbas Azari were arrested. These communist intellectuals neither belonged to the proletariat nor were they syndicalists. What came to be known as the communist Group of Fifty-Three was composed of different clusters of Left intellectuals and activists, who had no organizational ties with one another. Rokn al-din Mokhtari, Reza Shah's last chief of police (April 1936–September 1941), who had succeeded Ayrom, took credit for the arrests.

The Arani Group, closely associated with the Group of Fifty-Three, was primarily an intellectual group of university graduates and students founded by Arani, a German-educated science teacher who had worked with the *Letter of Europe* during his stay in Berlin. On 21 January 1934, Taqi Arani, Iraj Eskandari and Bozorg Alavi began publication of *Donya* (The World). All three had been attracted to Marxism during their stay in Europe. *Donya* was an intellectual review, propagating scientific socialism and dialectical materialism in the language of scientific articles, not discernable by the uninitiated.

Donya was 'Iran's first Marxist magazine' and 'gradually drew in many intellectuals, political activists and European-educated individuals who shared a commitment to social and political activism'.[105] Young, progressive and curious students and intellectuals gathered on Monday nights at Arani's house to discuss Left cultural, scientific and political issues. The Arani Group outlived, *Donya* which ceased publication after its twelfth issue in the summer of 1935.

Before going on trial between 2 and 15 November 1938, members of the group were mistreated and flogged in prison and were finally sentenced to three to ten years in prison. Taqi Arani, received the maximum ten-year prison term and allegedly died of typhus in prison on 4 February 1940.

In early November 1937, students at Tehran University Medical School went on strike, opposing the edict whereby 50 per cent of graduates, chosen by lot, had to serve in the Army Medical Service. The unusual strike continued for several days and ended with the arrest of its twelve leaders. Around the same time, rumours circulated of arrests in the army and among the cadets at the Officers' School. In November 1939, twelve officers and cadets were arrested and charged with plotting against national security and court-martialled. The group's leader, Mohsen Jahansuz, who had pro-German tendencies was executed in March 1940.

The Crown Prince

In May 1936, after five years of study at Le Rosey, Switzerland, Mohammad-Reza Pahlavi, the crown prince returned to Iran at the age of 16. He enrolled in the Military Academy and graduated in 1938 as second lieutenant. Mohammad-Reza accompanied his father on his numerous visits across Iran, participating in official inauguration of various projects, and attending annual military reviews and maneuvers. On 25 April 1939, he married Princess Fowziyeh Fuad, the sister of King Farouk of Egypt. The young prince made appearances at cultural and sports events and received foreign dignitaries, but remained in his father's long shadow.

On his 21st birthday (27 October 1939), the crown prince attended the finals of the Olympic Game trials at the newly inaugurated Amjadiyeh sports stadium. Attending sports events at Amjadiyeh on his birthday later became an annual routine. On April 23, 1940, he inaugurated the Tehran Broadcasting Station and in February 1941, the crown prince and Princess Ashraf Pahlavi attended incognito a masked ball at the elite and trendy Tehran Club.

In February 1941, some six months before the occupation of Iran by Britain and the Soviet Union, Reader Bullard, the British minister in Iran, expressed a low opinion of Mohammad-Reza, reporting that the 'Crown Prince commands no respect or affection' and 'is not credited with much strength of character'.[106]

Foreign Policy

Reza Shah had never fully trusted the British. He maintained cordial relations with the Soviets but courted the United States and Germany both commercially and diplomatically. From 1925, Iran was employing German financial advisors and in February 1929, both countries granted most-favoured-nation status to each other. Hjalmar Schacht, president of the German Central Bank and minister of economics, visited Tehran in November 1936, and met with the shah in Ramsar, cementing Iran–German commercial ties with an annual £3 million trade deal.

High-powered German firms became involved in industrializing Iran by establishing 'textile, glass, hardware factories, chemical and agricultural machinery plants, throughout the country'.[107] By June 1938, German firms and technicians were involved in mining, oil-prospecting and building the Tehran radio station.

The evolution of Iran's trade relations with Germany was a fair indicator of the political and economic bonding of these two countries from 1936. Between 1920 and 1924, only 2 per cent of Iran's imports had been coming from Germany. This figure gradually increased to 25 per cent between 1935 and 1939. Concomitantly, the share of Iran's exports to Germany during the same period grew from 0 to 32 per cent.

Economic coalescence was not isolated from political proximity. In March 1936, German Chancellor Adolf Hitler sent to Reza Shah a signed picture in a frame decorated with the eagle and swastika of the Third Reich. In 1937, Baldur von Schirach, the 30-year-old head of the Hitler Youth, visited Iran. Reza Shah insisted on distinguishing Iran from the rest of the Arab world, emphasizing that Iranians were Aryans and viewing this as a sense of kinship with Hitler's Germany. In March 1935, Reza Shah had already ordered that the country's name as used in foreign-language correspondence be changed from Persia to Iran. Economic ties in addition to ideological affinity became the Trojan Horse of German infiltration in Iran. By September 1939, some 1,500 Germans lived in Tehran.

Two days after the outbreak of Second World War (1 September 1939), Iran officially declared its neutrality. By mid-December 1939, the British Legation in Tehran was reporting that 'the major portion of Iranian current opinion is much in favor of Germany'.[108] From January 1941, the British minister in Iran warned the Iranian government of the growing number of Germans in Iran, some of whom it believed to be officers. At the time, German engineers were still working on industrial projects and Iran saw no reason to expel them.

On 9 July 1941, the foreign technicians employed in Iran's industry and commerce were estimated at 2,590 Englishmen, 690 Germans, 390 Russians, 310 Italians and 260 Greeks. Once the Soviet Union was attacked by Germany on 22 June 1941 and it joined the Allies, Britain and the Soviet Union found common interests in Iran and planned a joint Soviet–British attack on Iran.

By mid-July 1941, the new Soviet–British allies were pursuing two policies in Iran. While their ministers pressed the Iranian government to reduce the number of Germans in the country, considered as 'fifth columnists', they were studying the potential of the Trans-Iranian Railway network 'as a channel of supply to Russia'.[109] By mid-August, having agreed on their plan of attack, the British and Soviets requested the Iranian government to expel most Germans. For the belligerent powers, the excessive number of Germans in Iran was their agreed-upon excuse for invasion.

Operation Countenance, the British invasion plan of Iran, was authorized on 20 August 1941. The British needed Iranian oil and the Trans-Iranian Railway to help the Soviets. On 25 August 1941, Ali Mansur, the prime minister informed Bullard that: 'All Germans are going, good and bad.'[110] On the same day Operation Countenance began.

A neutral Iran was once again attacked and invaded. The British attacked from the south with their land, air and naval forces of some 20,000. The Soviets invaded from the north with land and air forces of approximately 40,000. Iran was to relive the nightmarish experience of the First World War. Tabriz, Ardebil, Rasht, Bandar Pahlavi, Ahvaz, Zanjan, Qazvin, Mashhad and even the outskirts of Tehran were bombed, leaving behind some 200 to 800 dead

Reza Shah's army, his pride and joy, collapsed within two days. On the third day, 28 August, the shah ordered his troops to lay down their arms. Reza Shah's army had grown from around 23,000 in 1922 to 105,000 in 1938 at the cost of approximately 40 per cent of the annual national budget. In action, other than a few like Admiral Gholamali Bayandor in the south and his brother Yadollah Bayandor in the north, the Iranian military proved to be a flop. Reza Shah had purchased his weapons, airplanes and ships from Czechoslovakia, Sweden, Britain, the US, Italy, Belgium and Germany, but weapon modernization was not enough to resist the invasion.

On 16 September 1941, Reza Shah was forced to abdicate, but there was debate on his replacement. The India Office was in favour of Soltan Hasan Qajar and the reinstalment of the Qajar dynasty. Bullard believed that his country could impose anyone it wished to replace Reza Shah, but he wrote, 'Acceptance of the Crown Prince offers I think, solution least disturbing to the country.'[111]

The British Kingmakers

His Majesty's Government, therefore, agreed that Mohamed Reza should be given a trial subject to good behaviour . . .[112]

The crown prince pledged allegiance to the Constitution on 17 September 1941, while foreign troops surrounded Tehran without entering the city. Reza Shah, accompanied by a handful of his immediate family, embarked on the steamship *Bandra* on 27 September in Bandar Abbas. He was sent into exile in Johannesburg. Reza Shah's departure did not sadden many. Had it not been for their resentment at having the country invaded, people would have probably rejoiced.

The British Legation in Tehran reported that there was no alternative to the crown prince. In a chillingly colonial manner, it posited that, 'The present Shah, if unsuitable, can be got rid of later.'[113] The British had once again become kingmakers in an Iran which had lost its sovereignty, cohesion and central authority.

Factual and Analytical Questions

1. Why were Iranian intellectuals disappointed with the constitutional experience and why did they turn towards dictatorship as the solution to economic progress?
2. When and why was Seyyed Zia Tabatabai ousted from power?
3. Assess the rise and fall of Kuchek Khan's Gilan movement.
4. Through the review of specific episodes, explain the power relationship between the clergy and Reza Khan between 1924 and 1928.
5. How did Reza Khan subdue the semi-autonomous tribes? Why was the tribal pacification campaign crucial to his bid for monarchy?
6. Between 1921 and 1925, what role did the army play both militarily and politically in Reza Shah's ascent to power?
7. How was the nationalism promoted by Reza Shah identical with Shah/state worshipping and to what end?
8. Assess the significance, impact and limitations of the Millspaugh Mission.
9. How did Reza Shah change the face of Tehran?
10. What were the most important aspects of Davar's legal reforms?
11. Were Reza Shah's reforms modelled on Ataturk's? Was he equally successful in their implementation?
12. Explain and assess the role of political repression during Reza Shah's rule.

Seminar Questions

1. Compare and contrast the ideas developed in *Kaveh* and *Letter of Europe* with those in *Free Man*.
2. How were the three revolts of Kuchek Khan, Pesyan and Lahouti alike, and how were they different from one another?
3. What prompted Reza Khan to establish a republic? Why was his republican quest unsuccessful?
4. 'Reza Shah succeeded as a military commander and state-builder but failed at political development.' Discuss the merits and short-comings of state-building without political democracy.
5. Describe and explain the statist and protectionist economic policies adopted by Reza Shah? Why?
6. 'Unveiling could be explained solely by Reza Shah's Europeanization and secularization drive.' Discuss with a view of the shah–clergy tug of war.
7. Was Reza Shah's foreign and economic policy biased towards Germany? How and why?

Discussion Questions

1. To what extent did the rise of fascism in Europe before the Second World War impact the non-democratic proclivities of Iranian intellectuals supporting Reza Khan?
2. Why does coercion and force rather than dialogue and consensus become instrumental in the ideology of Iranian modernists in the 1920s.
3. Were Kuchek Khan and Col. Pesyan treasonous, foreign-inspired secessionists or anti-despotic, constitutionalist nationalists?
4. 'Ahmad Shah was responsible for his own dethronement.' Discuss.
5. 'The fruits of Reza Shah's industrialization and modernization drive were mainly reaped by a small segment of the urban population.' Discuss with a view to Reza Shah's agricultural policies.
6. Why did Reza Shah change the way Iranians dressed?

Glossary

Capitulation Extra-territorial jurisdiction is granted when a sovereign state provides immunity from prosecution under its own laws to the citizens of a foreign state living in its territory. It limits and constrains the self-sovereignty of the country granting capitulation. A crime committed by a foreigner will be persecuted by the laws of the foreign country and the courts of the country that has extended capitulation will have no jurisdiction over the accused.

chador This is a loose outer garment worn by women, covering their hair and full body. It is open all the way in the front and must be held by one hand under the chin. This traditional cloak is worn by women when they leave their homes. In rural Iran and among the nomads, the head and body gear can take different forms.

Clemenceau, George French prime minister, 1906–9 and then 1917–20, was nicknamed Tiger. He was known for his strong leadership and popularity during the war, and his iron fist and repressive style of dealing with the opposition. He was an advocate of the separation of church and state since his youth when he had been an insurgent during the Paris Commune.

Pahlavi hat A special type of cap with a circular top and a visor, commonly known by its French name, *képi*. The Pahlavi hat could have been an imitation of the *képi* used in the French army, however, the German Brownshirts in the 1920s wore the same headgear.

Six Arrows Ataturk's socio-economic, political and cultural plans for a new Turkey. It consisted of: (1) republicanism, (2) nationalism, (3) populism, (4) statism, (5) secularism and (6) revolution.

4

Mohammad-Reza Shah Foreign Invasion, Oil Nationalization and the Coup, 1941–53

Chapter Outline

Iran under Foreign Occupation	169
The Shah Overshadowed by Qavam	183
From Qavam's Fall to Mosaddeq's Rise	198
The Oil Issue	207
Mosaddeq's 28 Months in Office	213
Glossary	230

Iran under Foreign Occupation

Following the invasion, the Iranian army came apart at the seams. Panic-stricken and leaderless, officers and soldiers in the provinces deserted in flocks. In the north, the Soviets disarmed the police and gendarmes and confiscated goods belonging to Iranian merchants, under the pretext that they were German goods and dispatched them to the Soviet Union. The Soviets requisitioned lorries and private motor vehicles and seized government buildings. With the breakdown in transportation, products such as sugar beet in Azarbayjan began to rot, reducing the output of sugar. Construction work on roads and railways came to a halt and workers were laid off. In the south, the British confiscated various government buildings in Ahvaz, Bandar

Shahpur and Hengam Island. With the disintegration of the army and the breakdown of central administration, law and order collapsed. Brigandage, raids, looting and robbery began in Lorestan, Kordestan, Fars and Khuzestan. By October 1941, the Kurdish tribes rebelled against the central government, seeking an independent government.

Iran was to remain under foreign occupation for almost five years. British and Soviet forces invaded the country on 25 August 1941, and Soviet troops departed on 6 May 1946. During this 56-month period, Iran experienced the coming and going of ten prime ministers: Mohammad-Ali Foruqi (27 August 1941–8 March 1942); Ali Soheyli (9 March 1942–30 July 1942); Ahmad Qavam (19 August 1942–13 February 1943); Ali Soheyli (17 February 1943–16 March 1944); Mohammad Saed (26 March 1944–9 November 1944); Mortezaqoli Bayat (21 November 1944–17 April 1945); Ebrahim Hakimi (10 May 1945–3 June 1945); Mohsen Sadr (6 June 1945–21 October 1945); Ebrahim Hakimi (31 October 1945–20 January 1946); and finally Ahmad Qavam (28 January 1946–1 December 1947). The average duration of each government was five and a half months, reflecting the country's political instability. Of the ten, three (Ali Soheyli, Ahmad Qavam and Ebrahim Hakimi) were called on to serve twice.

The British Prime Minister on 27 August 1941

Now that it seems that the Persian opposition is not very serious, I wish to know what are the plans for pushing on and joining hands with the Russians, and making sure we have the railway in working order in our hands. (Winston Churchill)[1]

On 6 September 1941, British Prime Minister Winston Churchill informed his foreign secretary that, 'Undoubtedly we must acquire complete military control of Persia during the war.'[2] This meant full control over all transportation and communication facilities in the country for war purposes as well as full press censorship.

Just as the British had decided on Reza Shah's replacement, they continued to play a significant role in changing and appointing prime ministers. During the first period of Soheyli's premiership, Adrian Holman, the British chargé d'affaires in Iran, wrote:

> Soon after he had taken office, it became clear that he was as incapable as his predecessor of obtaining swift decisions on matters of vital interest to us. The question of finding a better Prime Minister was taken up with the Foreign Office, but it was decided that for the moment no more suitable candidate was available, and he was, therefore allowed to stay.[3]

The Persian Corridor: A Complicated Relationship

The invasion forces, especially the British and later the Americans, wished to be appreciated and if possible, loved by the Iranians. The aggressors needed undeserved sympathy, while continuing their unwanted stay. The British, despite their heavy propaganda attempts, were hardly successful at winning the hearts of the common people. The Russians, with their long unsavoury history of expansionism in Iran and their enmity towards the Constitutional Revolution were in the same disadvantageous position as the British. The Soviet's appealing new ideology promising the moon to the workers and peasants, however, was successful in attracting the intellectuals and the budding Iranian working class.

The Tripartite Anglo-Soviet-Persian Treaty of Alliance, imposed by the belligerent forces and negotiated by Mohammad-Ali Foroughi's government, was finally ratified by the 13th Majles on 26 January 1942. The Majles was under pressure to vote in favour of the Treaty as Iran's considerable sterling balances in Britain were frozen until the Treaty was signed. The Treaty undermined Iran's neutrality whilst stipulating that Britain and the Soviet Union would 'respect the territorial integrity, sovereignty and political independence of Iran' and 'would withdraw their troops from Iran six months after the end of hostilities between the Allies and Germany through an armistice or the conclusion of peace'.

In fact, the Tripartite Treaty provided the invading forces unrestricted use and control of 'all means of communication throughout Persia, including railways, roads, rivers, aerodromes, ports, pipelines, and telephone, telegraph and wireless installations'. The operationalization of this key stipulation had major political and economic consequences on the country. Article 7 of the Treaty committed the Allied Powers to a vague notion of using 'their best endeavors to safeguard the economic existence of the Persian people against privations and difficulties arising as a result of the present war'.[4]

The Anglo-Soviet-Persian Treaty legitimized the invasion and upheld the sovereignty, control and supremacy of the belligerent parties over all Iranian affairs during their occupation. The function of the Iranian central government was consequently reduced to facilitating and feeding of the Persian Corridor, connecting the south of Iran to the Soviet border in the north. All other considerations were secondary. In October 1942, the British forced the Iranian government to declare Abadan a Special Military Zone where martial law was to be applied under an Iranian military governor 'accompanied' by a British military adviser.

Following Germany's attack on the Soviet Union in September 1941, the latter became a recipient of US **Lend Lease** on 7 November 1941. Four months later, on 10 March 1942, because of the Persian Corridor, the US declared Iran also eligible for

Lend Lease, opening the door to its presence in Iran. The US acted as an auxiliary of Great Britain in delivering supplies through the Persian Corridor to the USSR.

In September 1942, the US was assigned the full responsibility of moving supplies up the Persian Corridor. The American forces who had arrived without any prior knowledge of the Iranian authorities gradually took control of the supply and transit operations within the British Zone. On 7 January 1943, they took over the Port of Khorramshahr, and on 1 April 1943 they took command of the southern sector of the Iranian railway.

In time, the Americans, who first numbered a few hundred, became the most numerous operating in the Persian Corridor. By February 1944, they numbered 29,961 and employed 40,682 civilian Iranians on their Persian Corridor projects. The opening of the Black Sea route to the port of Odessa by the end of 1944 relieved pressure from the Persian Corridor. The Trans-Iranian Railway, however, continued to serve as the main channel for getting fuel to the Soviet Union from the Abadan refinery. The American army's stay in Iran lasted four years and a month. The US Military Iranian Mission reached the Persian Gulf in November 1941 and the last of what became the Persian Gulf Service Command, left Khorramshahr on 31 December 1945.

The Tehran Conference: A Patronizing Pat on the Back

A forced marriage had been imposed on Iran when on 9 September 1943, it officially joined the Allies and declared war on the Axis. So, it made sense for US President Franklin D. Roosevelt, British Prime Minister Winston Churchill and Chairman of the Council of People's Commissars Joseph Stalin to meet in Tehran (28 November 1943). On 1 December 1943, the three 'recognized' Iran's 'assistance' in the war effort and acknowledged that 'the war has caused special economic difficulties' for the country. To redress the problem, in very vague terms, they agreed 'to make available to the government of Iran such economic assistance as may be possible ...' Iran was promised that her claims would be heard and given full consideration after the war by members of the United Nations, and the three heads of states promised to respect and maintain 'the independence, sovereignty and territorial integrity of Iran'.[5]

This was a casual pat on Iran's back and a passing recognition of its economic and human plight during the occupation. On the surface, everything was rosy. The young Shah went to visit Roosevelt, who was staying at the Soviet Embassy, and received Churchill in the Library of the Soviet Embassy (Figure 4.1). Stalin, in turn, drove to the Marble Palace to pay his respects to the shah. After the Allied leaders departed, three streets in Tehran were named after each of them.

Figure 4.1 Mr. Churchill is greeted by the Shah of Persia, 1943. *Source: Via Alamy Images.*

The Economic Nightmare of the Occupation

Economically, Iran's international trade, monetary and fiscal policy as well as industrial and agricultural policy were dictated by the occupying forces. The Persian Corridor or the Bridge to Victory, created three interrelated economic crises, completely out of the Iranian government's control. The occupation triggered inflation, as well as a food and transportation crisis. These adversities hindered Iran's economic development for five years.

Inflation

The staggering rise in prices during the occupation amounted to hyper-inflation. During the first year following the invasion, the price of certain items increased as follows: potatoes 500 per cent, onions 600 per cent, charcoal 300 per cent, wood 300 per cent, rice 270 per cent and cheese 600 per cent. Arthur Millspaugh, the American financial advisor who had become a first-hand expert in the Iranian economy, described the post-occupation inflation as rooted in reduced imports due to 'military demands on shipping', aggravated by reduced domestic production resulting from the 'disorganization and disorder', caused by the invasion and Reza Shah's abdication. 'The loss of popular confidence in the national currency,' had, in turn, prompted producers and traders to hoard.

The decrease in supply and increase in demand, Millspaugh argued, was further fuelled by the Allied need for Iranian currency to pay for local goods and most significantly for labour. The Allies were purchasing the little goods available on the market. The money put into circulation by the Iranian government and spent by the

Allies, at its peak, reached the equivalent of $6 million a month. This sudden injection of liquidity in a market that could barely provide for its own population sent the price of goods skyrocketing.

For Millspaugh, 'speculation and profiteering' by those who had something to sell in a sellers' market also accounted for inflation.[6] As long as the war lasted, economic unpredictability reigned and black markets flourished, it benefitted well-connected Iranian businessmen and contractors to make their special deals with the Allies and make handsome profits by providing necessary war commodities. Wartime occupation further disrupted the import of spare parts for machines and factories, decreasing the incentive to invest in production, hence the serious decline in capital formation and the contraction in the economy during this period.

Food crisis

By late September 1941, Iranian cities were facing bread and sugar shortages due to delays in sending food supplies from Soviet-occupied territories. Tehran and the southern parts of the country were dependent on these supplies. From November 1941, bread, the main staple of most Iranians was scarce and its quality deteriorated, while tea and sugar became scarce everywhere except for the northern Soviet-occupied territories. Tehran also faced a shortage of rice and charcoal.

Within a month of the occupation, the price of bread increased by 66 per cent and local bread riots erupted throughout the country. These were forcefully repressed by the occupying forces. In Hamedan, British troops opened fire on protesters, whilst in Rasht, Soviet forces arrested some 100 protesters. Items such as sugar and cigarettes were rationed. The influx of some 26,000 Polish refugees from Russia, exasperated the food crises in Iran.

In August 1942, the food perspective seemed more optimistic. The northern regions, as well as Khuzestan, Kermanshah and Khorasan had a bumper crop. The Soviet policy of preventing foodstuff from leaving their northern zone of influence and breakdown in transportation due to the transit of goods to the Soviet Union, however, caused distribution problems. In September 1942, the Qavam government established the Ministry of Food to handle the food crisis. But by mid-October 1942, Tehran faced a new crisis as its wheat reserves were down to only a couple of days. The price of bread jumped, yet the Allied Powers refused to allow the movement of wheat from their surplus grain zones of occupation. The spectre of famine, as in the First World War, loomed.

In the fall of 1942, Iran was forced to sell 10,000 tons of potato to the British military authorities while the Russians were demanding Iran to provide their forces with '5,000 tons of wheat, 15,000 tons of barley and 30,000 tons of rice'.[7] It was not until November 1942, once food shortages had become dire, that the Ministry of Food followed the advice of J. K. Sheriden, the American adviser, and reduced the purchase of 26,000 eggs per day for the Polish refugees to 2,400 per day.

On 4 December 1942, a Food Agreement was signed by British, American and Iranian government officials. The Agreement assured that the Americans and the British would make up for Iran's deficiency of cereals until the 1943 harvest. But the British used their promise of food provision as a political lever to assure a more pro-British attitude on the part of Iranian governments. 'The American Minister at Tehran reported on December 9 [1942] that the British authorities in Iran had for some reason failed to bring to Tehran the 3500 tons of barley and 1500 tons of flour earmarked for Iran and held at Basra.'[8]

By February 1943, the food situation was further aggravated. In Tehran, the quality of bread was so poor that it was almost inedible and outside Tehran even the poor-quality bread could not be found. Bread riots broke out in Shiraz, Esfahan and Mashhad. By the end of February, malnutrition in Tehran was turning to famine and the daily death rate trebled. The shortage of kerosene, in oil-rich Iran, further aggravated the plight of the poor and generated deep anti-British sentiments. Even though by July 1943 the food situation had slightly improved, conditions were far from normal. In August, riots broke out in Kermanshah, Hamedan and Malayer over the price and quality of bread. The distribution of bread remained rationed through coupons.

The typhus epidemic of February 1943 in Tehran added to the people's suffering and made everyday life a continuing plight. By March 1943, typhus broke out in Mashhad, Kerman and Zahedan and the general epidemic continued throughout the winter of 1943. This calamity was followed by locust swarms in Sistan, Baluchestan, Northern Khorasan, Esfahan and the vicinities of Tehran.

Transportation crisis

A different kind of pressure was placed on the meagre Iranian economy as Lend Lease supplies started to reach Iran and had to be transported to Russia. 'By March 1942 a force of 67,000 native workmen and 14,000 donkeys were working on roads.'[9] In late December 1942, the Soviet Transportation Directorate demanded 1,000 Iranian civilian lorries for their war transit requirements. The scarcity of tires added to the depleting stock of lorries dispatched to meet the military demands of the Allies.

To expedite the transit of goods and war materials to Russia, the British and the Soviets took full control of the Trans-Iranian Railway each in their respective zones. By 1942, the railway extension from Ahvaz to Khorramshahr was completed by the British. Dock facilities at Bandar Shahpur were expanded, and railway terminals at Khorramshahr were constructed. Wharves were built to increase the port capacity of unloading cargo. During 'the busiest months of 1943 and 1944 the combined Anglo-American operations in the Persian Corridor used about 100,000 natives.'[10]

The construction of the 720-kilometre-road between Andimeshk and Qazvin was completed and asphalted in 1944, mainly by the Americans. While the transportation network expanded, its impact on the well-being of Iranians was adverse. The distribution of goods for the purpose of domestic consumption was not a priority and was limited to essential items such as wheat, oil and rice.

Pro-Axis Iranians

From April 1942, the British had begun identifying pro-Axis Iranian personalities, some of whom were arrested and exiled, while others were placed under close surveillance. In August, another round of Iranians, were arrested and interrogated for pro-Axis activities, raising the fury of the Iranian press. The Iranian government was forced to hand over its arrested citizens to British authorities for interrogation. Those suspected of pro-Axis activities were interned in British camps at Kermanshah and Ahvaz.

On 7 December 1942, Lt Gen. Fazlollah Zahedi, the commander of the Esfahan Division, was arrested by the British on charges of pro-Axis activities and banished to British Mandated Palestine, where he stayed for three years. On 12 August 1943, Franz Mayer, the key agent and organizer of the German fifth column in Iran, was arrested by the British in Tehran. Mayer had organized the pro-German clandestine *Hezbe Kabud* (Azure Party) under the leadership of Habibollah Nobakht.

The main object of the Azure Party was to form pro-German military cells for the purpose of 'sabotage, espionage, and insurgence in different parts of the country, with the help of and in collaboration with German agents'.[11] The Azure Party soon became popular among nationalist officers, who had been embarrassed by the army's pitiful performance during the occupation and wished to see the quick departure of the invading armies. The Azure Party was more anti-Allies and anti-occupation than pro-German, and its members 'established numerous and widespread cells within the armed forces'.[12]

After Mayer's arrest and the confiscation of his documents, the British rounded up 137 Iranians, including 70 workers of the Trans-Iranian Railway. Some 30 prominent Iranians were also arrested and sent to the British-controlled Arak (Sultanabad) prison on charges of collaboration with Mayer and affiliation with the Azure Party. The American minister in Iran, who had studied the Mayer documents, concluded that we 'see no good reason to doubt their authenticity although they do not appear conclusive as to the guilt of many persons named therein'.[13]

The arrests of the alleged German fifth column which started on 16 August 1943 and were concluded by the end of October 1943, included the former Prime Minister Ahmad Matin-Daftari, former Minister Mohammad Sajadi, Supreme Court Judge Ali Heyat, the deputy from Shiraz in the 13th Majles and the head of the Azure Party, Habibollah Nobakht, along with Jafar Sharif-Emami, Jahangir Tafazoli, Mohammad-Hoseyn Hesam-Vaziri and Mahmud Sharvin. The prominent Seyyed Abolqasem Kashani was also arrested for his membership in the Azure Party and his relations with Mayer. The military brass arrested included Generals Mohammad-Sadeq Kupal, Farajollah Aqevli and Abolhasan Purzand, and Colonels Nader Batmanqelich, Sadeq

Foruhar and Hoseyn Manuchehri, better known as Bahram Ariyana, who supervised the Azure Party cells in the army.

Political Consequences of the Invasion

Reza Shah's early experience with political parties and party politics had been unsuccessful. When he left the country in 1941, even though martial law was in place, the press censored and assemblies were outlawed, Iran experienced a political opening. Under foreign occupation, political parties mushroomed in an atmosphere of political pluralism and competition.

Iran was an invaded constitutional monarchy. The powers of the young Mohammad-Reza Shah were curtailed not only by the Constitution, but by the occupying forces' control of the legislative, judiciary and executive. Iran under occupation had a weakened and ceremonial master, the shah, and a strengthened and effective master, the Allies. The one power that constantly tested the patience of the invading forces was the Majles. The British and the Americans were inclined to close the Majles.

Bullard, the British minister in Iran, considered it as 'a collection of persons entirely unfitted by character and training for so delicate a task'.[14] In December 1942, the American minister in Iran, Louis Dreyfus, wrote, 'It has seemed clear to me for some time that the dissolution of the Majlis is necessary if there is to be continuity of government and anything substantial accomplished.'[15] And it might well have been dissolved had it not been for the rather unexpected opposition of the of the Russian ambassador who said the 'moment was inopportune'.[16]

A year later, during the late 1943 election to the 14th Majles, the British once again voiced their preference for either an indefinitely postponed Majles or a dissolved one. Before the invasion, Reza Shah had been the main threat to the government of the people. After the invasion, the occupying forces assumed this role. Even though the Majles was temporarily closed during Qavam's first government, it continued to function. During Qavam's second government there was also a 16-month interregnum between the end of the 14th Majles (12 March 1946) and the beginning of the 15th Majles (17 July 1947).

Parties and labour unions

Since 1932, Iran had been deprived of parties and party politics. Reza Shah's abdication enabled political parties and organizations to flourish, test their viability and often wither away. By 1944, Iran possessed some 60–100 parties and political organizations. Trade unions became active, attracting a growing number of adherents, and the press blossomed despite limitations and censures. Within five years of Reza Shah's departure, the Iranian press numbered 274 dailies, weeklies and monthlies.

By 1946, two powerful political parties dominated the political scene. The numerically and organizationally hegemonic *Hezbe Tudeh Iran* (Party of Iran's Masses), hereafter the Tudeh Party, represented the left and *Hezbe Eradeh Melli* (National Will Party) spoke for the right. In addition, there were a plethora of smaller and short-lived parties, some of which formed coalitions and morphed into other parties, while others just petered out after Majles elections.

Most of the parties that appeared after 1941, except for the Tudeh Party, were devoid of a solid social base and were reliant on the fortunes of their leaders. As the political success of their leaders surged, and chances of obtaining advantageous government or parliamentarian positions increased, membership bulged. However, once their leaders lost their political clout and allure, the party nosedived and disappeared.

Smaller parties

In December 1941, Ali Dashti founded *Hezbe Edalat* (the Justice Party). Dashti had been the editor of the progressive, modernist and critical newspaper *Shafaqe Sorkh* (Red Dawn), during the first part of Reza Shah's rule. He was imprisoned by Reza Shah and later became one of his supporters. Dashti was an influential deputy to the 13th Majles from Damavand. The Justice Party was a liberal pro-British and pro-court party, with its own newspaper, no ideological backbone and some 400 members. Among its most prominent members were Jamal Emami, Ebrahim Khajehnouri and Jamshid Alam. The party wielded considerable power in the 14th Majles and remained active until 1948. Later, some of its members such as Jamal Emami became opponents of the Mosaddeq government.

The *Mihan Parastan* (Party of the Patriots) made its debut on 6 January 1942. Financed by the court, it was openly anti-Tudeh and promoted national integrity, unity and a revival of Iran's past glory. It was founded by Ali Jalali, a law school graduate, and some of its members included Majid Yektai, Shojaeddin Shafa and Mohammad Pursartip. The party also had some provincial support in Lorestan. Abbas Masudi, the owner of the daily *Ettelaat*, ran as a candidate of this party and was elected from Tehran to the 14th Majles. Later, Jalali was recruited by the CIA and became instrumental in the coup against Mosaddeq, conducting propaganda, logistic and agitation operations right before the 19 August 1953 coup.

Hezbe Esteqlal (Independence Party), a small chameleon party which constantly changed colours was founded in 1941 by Abdolqadir Azad. *Hezbe Peykar* (Combat Party) was an independent socialist-leaning party founded by Khosrow Eqbal in 1942 and was composed of a group of his young and radical university and lawyer friends such as Jahangir Tafazoli, Jalal Shadman and Reza Azarakhshi. It was opposed to the Tudeh Party and Dashti's Justice Party. The Combat Party produced at least three newspapers, *Peykar* (Combat), *Daria* and *Irane ma* (Our Iran), in which some of Iran's future intellectual luminaries wrote. On 20 June 1944, during Mohammad

Saed's first government, the three parties Patriots, Combat and Independence, joined forces to create *Hezbe Mihan* (the Motherland Party), which attracted young nationalists such as Karim Sanjabi, Ali Shaygan, Abdolhoseyn Aliabadi and Mehdi Azar, who later became prominent figures in Mosaddeq's National Front.

The Motherland Party's social reformist platform promoted 'from each according to his/her ability and to each according to his/her work and the utility he/she accrues to society'.[17] The party was a nationalist and freedom-loving organization committed to cleansing the faith of religious superstition. It was dedicated to cooperation with the Allied Forces but vied to combat reactionary political organizations that relied on and cooperated with foreign powers.

By March 1945, the Motherland Party could mobilize some 500 people, mainly students, for its meetings, during which the speakers attacked Seyyed Zia, Ali Soheyli, Tadayyun and Reza Shah's old despotic rule. Their rallies ended with chants of, 'Long live Mosaddeq!' By October 1945, members of the Motherland Party and the Tudeh Party clashed in Tehran and the provinces. After about 16 months, the Motherland Party disintegrated and its members gravitated towards either the Tudeh Party or *Hezbe Iran* (the Iran Party), one of the main forces of the future (*Jebhehye Melli*) National Front.

On 5 May 1944, the Iran Party was born out of the Engineers Association, a group of European-educated engineers and university professors gathered around Gholamali Farivar, who represented the group in the 14th Majles from Tehran. The Iran Party appealed to the new, educated professional classes and university students. It attracted reformist engineers, lawyers and academics committed to modernity, social democracy, nationalism and freedom. The most eminent members of the Iran Party, who later became key players in Mosaddeq's National Front, were Allahyar Saleh, Ahmad Zirakzadeh, Kazem Hasibi, Jahangir Haqshenas and Mahmud Nariman. From 1945, *Jebheh* (the Front) became the party's newspaper.

On 22 September 1947, another political formation called *Ettehad* (Alliance) brought together three smaller parties. Of these, *Mardom* (People's Party), founded in December 1941 by Mohammad-Sadeq Tabatabai and Mortezaqoli Bayat, was the most important. Mohammad-Sadeq Tabatabai, a veteran of the constitutional movement, was the son of Ayatollah Mohammad Tabatabai, one of the two leaders of the constitutional movement. The People's Party believed in a parliamentary system, the rule of law and the independence of the judiciary. It considered itself a nationalist and social-democratic party. In the 14th Majles, Mohammad-Sadeq Tabatabai's party entered a coalition with Seyyed Ziaeddin Tabatabai's National Will Party, and Mohammad-Sadeq Tabatabai obtained the second-highest vote in Tehran.

Finally, a small socialist-leaning anti-fascist party created with British support called *Hamrahan* (Fellow Travellers/Confederates) was founded by Mostafa Fateh in October 1942. It was supposed to be the Iranian equivalent of the British Labour Party. In April 1943, the Fellow Travellers/Confederates published a socialist newspaper called *Emruz va Farda* (Today and Tomorrow). Under the anti-fascist union between Britain and the Soviet Union, many of those who closely collaborated with Fateh's party were also members of the Tudeh Party. There was even talk of the two parties joining forces during the election to the 14th Majles. This did not happen, but it was decided that the two parties would not run their candidates against one another. The Fellow Travellers/Confederates Party sent two deputies to the 14th Majles and fizzled out soon afterwards.

The dominant parties
Eradeh Melli (The National Will Party) was established by Seyyed Ziaeddin Tabatabai, upon his return from Palestine on 1 October 1943. Seyyed Zia was prompted to return by A. C. Trott, the oriental secretary at the British Legation in Tehran on behalf of the Foreign Office, and Bullard, the minister in Tehran.[18] Right before Seyyed Zia's return to Iran, Mozaffar Firuz, his close collaborator, launched the newspaper *Raad Emruz* (Today's Thunder) as the National Will Party's mouthpiece. In its first issue, *Today's Thunder* claimed that it strived for a 'new, free, and independent Iran'. Seyyed Zia was disliked by the Soviets, and vigorously supported by the British. His party was known for its pro-shah and anti-Tudeh political stance. The National Will Party had 30 deputies in the 14th Majles, and benefitted from the support of some 23 other deputies.

The Tudeh Party was founded on 29 September 1941. The public face and official leader of the party was the prominent social democrat and nationalist, Soleyman Eskandari. Most members of the Arani Group joined the Tudeh Party after their release. The Tudeh Party was the pro-Soviet communist party of Iran, although it shied away from calling itself publicly as such, and instead claimed to be a nationalist and reformist party committed to parliamentary democracy. The party considered itself the representative of the oppressed classes, namely workers, peasants, progressive intellectuals and craftsmen. It was a non-clandestine and legal party, opposed to dictatorship and colonialism. The Tudeh Party was born in the era of British–Soviet cooperation in a united anti-fascist front.

The first issue of the newspaper *Mardom* (People), associated with the Tudeh Party, appeared on 1 February 1942. The entire first page of the *People*'s second issue, 3 February 1942, was penned by Iraj Eskandari and dedicated to the Iranian communist hero, Taqi Arani. This paper became popular among intellectuals, radicals and communists as an anti-fascist paper. The anti-fascist front in Iran implied Soviet–British collaboration and brought together pro-British and pro-Soviet Iranian activists.

Mardom was originally established at the behest and with the full organizational and financial support of Mostafa Fateh, a close associate of Anne Lambton, the powerful and enigmatic British press attaché and political analyst. Lambton was thoroughly familiar with the Persian language and was the director of Victory House, the British Cultural Centre and the anti-fascist propaganda unit. The idea of *the People* as an anti-fascist publication, supporting the Tudeh Party's cause came from Lambton.

> ## Who Provided for the Communist-Leaning, Anti-Fascist *The People*?
>
> The money came from the British and the paper it was printed on came from the Soviets. (B. Khosravi)[19]

At the start of the anti-fascist front (1941–5), Tudeh Party members worked closely with Lambton, through Fateh, who was also a director at the Anglo-Persian Oil Company (APOC). APOC also contributed financially to *The People*. Ehsan Tabari and Bozorg Alavi, the towering theoretical and intellectual figures of the Tudeh Party were Anne Lambton's employees at Victory House. Fateh had been their sponsors. The ideologically unstable alliance between Fateh and Eskandari lasted some seven months, and Fateh left *The People* around October 1942. Once the British withdrew their support, *The People* relied solely on Soviets financial support. The Tudeh Party also had its own independent newspaper, *Siyasat* (Politics), which appeared on 22 February 1942 and *Rahbar* (Leader), which it produced in January 1943. Both were under the editorship of Iraj Eskandari.

After the departure of Reza Shah, the Tudeh Party's growing membership was staggering. Intellectuals, professionals, educated government employees, students and women, as well as growing numbers of politicized workers joined its ranks. As the military successes of the Axes Forces winded down, and organized pro-German supporters were rounded up, the Tudeh Party's progressive, democratic and egalitarian socio-political message attracted greater numbers of supporters.

The Tudeh Party promised the establishment of a democratic regime, which would uphold individual and political freedoms, while guaranteeing national sovereignty and independence. It was committed to social reform and opposed despotism, exploitation and colonialism. In May 1943, the Tudeh Party assured that it would not tolerate interference from any country, not even from Iran's northern neighbour, the USSR. The Tudeh Party's promises opened a new, and humanistic horizon for Iran's toilers, intellectuals and professionals.

In addition to Tehran, the Tudeh Party pursued its objectives through 'Provincial Committees' established in Azarbayjan, Gilan, Mazandaran, Khorasan and Esfahan. Whereas in October 1942, the Tudeh Party had some 4,000 members, its membership in 1944 swelled to some 49,000. The CIA placed the Tudeh Party's '1945 strength at 69,000', while Eskandari claimed 100,000 members for the same period. By 1946, membership in Iran was estimated at between 75,000 and 250,000, with 40,000 members only in Tehran.[20] The Tudeh Party claimed that in 1945, 70 per cent of its members were workers, 20 per cent intellectuals and 10 per cent peasants.

The Tudeh Party had established two important wings, one clandestine and military and the other public and trade unionist. From its inception officers with communist leanings had gravitated towards the Party headquarters. To avoid suspicions, they had been instructed to form 'friendly gatherings'.[21] By 1942, a significant number of these officers, including Col. Abdolreza Azar, Maj. Ali-Akbar Eskandani and Capt. Khosrow Ruzbeh were members of the Tudeh Party's military organization. In the spring of 1942, the officers elected their own Executive Committee and been assigned a liaison person with the Central Committee of the Tudeh Party.

The British View of the Tudeh Party

The Tudeh Party is the only seriously organized political party in Persia. (Military Attaché's Intelligence summary)[22]

In the spring of 1942, the Tudeh Party organized a nationwide labour union. The Central Council of Iran's Workers and Toilers (CCIWT) succeeded in mobilizing a considerable number of adherents under the leadership of Reza Rusta. Rusta was a communist and an experienced trade union organizer. In Tehran alone, the CCIWT had some 1,000 members. During the 14th Majles elections, the CCIWT played an important role in close cooperation with the Tudeh Party in securing votes for Tudeh candidates. The Central Council of Iran's Workers and Toilers morphed into the Central United Council of Iran's Workers and Toilers (CUCIWT) on 1 May 1944. In June 1944, the CUCIWT (*Showraye motahedeh markaziye kargaran va zahmatkeshan Iran*) had its own paper *Zafar* (Victory), and by 1945, it had over 100,000 members.

The 14th Majles became the battleground of some forty parties that had come to the fore since September 1941. Some 800 candidates competed for 136 seats. The elections to the 14th Majles generated considerable excitement in June 1943, even though the country was under occupation. The British used their influence in the South and the Soviets in the North to assure the election of deputies favourable to their interests, while the shah and the army supported their own designated candidates. Even though Tehran and most provinces were under military governorship, the army's grip over Iran was much weaker than it had been during Reza Shah's rule.

Elections to the 14th Majles were one of Iran's most open, pluralistic and competitive campaigns. The Tudeh Party presented 20–39 candidates, some of whom were not party members but political allies.[23] It held rallies and campaigned freely in Tehran and important provincial cities. Of the Tudeh Party-affiliated deputies, 10 were elected and the credentials of 1, Jafar Pishehvari, from Tabriz was rejected. The remaining 9 formed the **Tudeh Faction/Group in the 14th Majles**. Later, Rahmanqoli Khalatbari was excluded from the Tudeh Party, and the Tudeh Group dwindled down to 8. Out of the 8 Tudeh-affiliated deputies, 5 – Ardashes Avanesiyan, Iraj Eskandari, Reza Radmanesh, Abdolsamad Kambakhsh and Fereydun Keshavarz – were members of the Tudeh Party's 11-member Central Committee, elected during the First Congress of the Tudeh Party on 1 August 1944.

Faced with the opportunity of a relatively free election, the British military attaché lamented 'the venomous spite of so-called Nationalists and Communists' and reported that, 'Chaos has gone so far as that it is unlikely that it can be checked except by a firm hand, untroubled by constitutional or democratic principles.' He concluded that the elections were more likely to create 'disorder', than 'a better parliament'.[24] The deputies to the 14th Majles, which convened on 26 February 1944, were mostly authentic representatives of the people and almost half of them were new faces.

The Shah Overshadowed by Qavam

With his sudden ascent to the throne, the young shah was obliged to pay his respects to the Iranian Constitution and accept his role as a reigning monarch wielding minimum executive power. Yet, he remembered the absolute authority, power and status of his father and coveted it. While the allies occupied the country, the shah's margin of manoeuvre remained narrow. In an attempt to circumvent the government, he tried to enter into direct and private contact with the British minister. Embarrassingly, Bullard turned down the shah's offer and reminded him that he could not go behind the back of the Iranian government and Britain's Soviet allies. The shah was testing the waters and getting a sense of how he could create his own political niche.

The Shah's Personal Finances

Only months after the new Shah had come to power, the British government intercepted a telegram from a European bank to an American financial institution and learned that 'the Shah has one million (repeat one million) dollars in America and that he is now looking for safe investment for his money'. (A. Milani)[25]

The shah, like his father, very much identified with the army and took steps to regain his father's power base among the armed forces. While his father had won the respect of his officers in the field, the shah had to earn their trust and respect from scratch. The shah needed to establish personal networks with Iran's top military brass and have them report directly to him. The shah's first disagreement with Ahmad Qavam, who succeeded Soheyli on 19 August 1942, was over matters concerning the armed forces, police and Ministry of War.

The shah insisted on the chief of the general staff taking orders directly from him, thus circumventing the minister of war. Qavam, however, was intent on limiting the shah's power by keeping the army under government control. In September 1942, Qavam instructed the chief of police to report to the prime minister rather than the shah.

In November 1942, Qavam sought to further strengthen his position. He demanded full powers in the domains of food, security, transportation and price stabilization from the Majles. On 8 December 1942, 'several thousand persons, including women and children' demonstrated outside the Majles.[26] They protested bread shortages, looted shops on the main streets of Tehran, set fire to Qavam's house and clashed with the police. Calm was restored when, in a show of support for Qavam's government, a battalion of British troops arrived in Tehran from Qom on 9 December 1942. Rumours claimed that the shah had instigated this unrest.

But Qavam's shrewd political acumen turned the situation around. Tehran's military governor, Gen. Ahmad Amir-Ahmadi, used the pretext of the disturbances to close the Majles, impose a curfew, fully repress the press and make some 150 arrests, among them newspaper editors and schoolmasters. Even though the Majles was reopened on 20 December 1942, the sudden repressive measures in Tehran strengthened Qavam's hand and relieved him of the considerable pressure from the shah, the 13th Majles and the critical press. Qavam then appointed as minister of war Gen. Amir-Ahmadi, whom he had succeeded to co-opt. The shah was quickly learning that faced with seasoned politicians such as the 66-year-old Qavam, he would need to carefully prepare his next moves.

Qavam also moved against the opposition by restricting newspaper-publishing and having the government publish a Daily News Sheet. It was not until January 1943, that four newspapers were allowed to resume publication. Of the 40 newspapers that appeared before the crackdown, only 13 were allowed to continue publication by the end of January 1943.

Qavam had the respect and support of the British and the Soviets but was politically inclined towards the Americans. To benefit from foreign know-how, Qavam began hiring American advisors in various establishments such as the army, police, gendarmerie and the ministries of food, health and finance. On 12 November 1942, the Majles approved the return of Arthur Millspaugh at the head of a Financial Mission. Millspaugh entered Tehran on 29 January 1943 as administrator-general of the Finances and by February 1945, his mission had 47 employees.

By February 1943, living conditions worsened as the food crisis loomed once again. Bread was rationed, prices shot up and the very poor quality of bread mixed with barley made what was available hardly edible. By mid-February, Tehran was on the verge of starvation. In the eyes of the public, the British were the main culprits.

The shah's mistrust of Qavam and his desire to take effective control of the army, made cooperation between them ever more difficult. In early February 1943, Qavam clashed with the shah over the minister of interior's breach of protocol and his reporting to the shah rather than the prime minister. Farajollah Bahrami, the minister of interior, was the shah's nominee and Qavam forced him to resign. The shah wished for a subservient prime minister, which Qavam was not. In the end, Qavam resigned on 13 February and the Majles voted in favour of Ali Soheyli, while the shah supported Saed. Soheyli took up office on 17 February 1943.

Outraged by the anti-British articles in the press, the British minister in Iran forced Ali Soheyli to once again muzzle the press. By 26 April 1943, eleven newspapers were closed and the Tudeh Party was denied a permit to hold a May Day rally. Even though Soheyli yielded to the British, he proved to hold his ground against the shah.

In August 1943, the shah tried to force Ali Soheyli to yield control of the army. The decision on who should control the army was delegated to a joint government–Majles commission. To the shah's chagrin, the commission ruled that the minister of war was fully responsible for the army and the shah was only entitled, in certain cases, to approve proposals made by the minister of war.

The Failed Soviet Push for Oil Concessions and Its Consequences

Iran's weakened international political position emboldened companies and countries to push for oil concessions. The occupation of Iran presented an opportunity for the Allies to extract new and profitable economic agreements. In the autumn of 1943, the Dutch–British Royal Dutch Shell Company and the Standard Oil Company of New York requested oil concessions in the South. In early April 1944, the American Standard Vacuum Oil Company, which had already entered negotiation for an oil concession in February 1943, was joined by Sinclair Oil Company.

Prime Minister Mohammad Saed, who had replaced Soheyli on 26 March 1944, was in favour of extending an oil concession to American companies. Private talks of an oil concession in the North to Sinclair were leaked to the Iranian press and met with staunch Soviet opposition. The follow up discussions on oil concessions to the Dutch, British and American companies were subsequently aborted.

The successful Normandy landings on 6 June 1944 and the liberation of Paris on 25 August 1944 signalled imminent Allied victory, termination of hostilities and the division of the spoils of war. In September 1944, the Soviets sent an oil mission to Tehran led by the vice commissar of foreign affairs, Sergei Kavtaradze. The mission met with the prime minister and the shah on 13 and 16 September 1944.

The Soviets wanted an oil concession in the five northern provinces of Iran. Unsatisfied with Prime Minister Saed's response that the Cabinet and Majles would have to decide on the matter, Kavtaradze met with the shah to further push for immediate exploration rights. On 8 October 1944, Saed informed Kavtaradze that all oil concession negotiations, including the ones with the American oil companies were suspended until the end of the war. 'Kavtaradze replied that this decision could have unhappy consequences.'[27] The Tudeh Party staged demonstrations against Saed and attacked him in its newspapers.

On 21 October 1944, 'a considerable body of Russian soldiers in military trucks and conspicuously armed with tommy-guns paraded rapidly through certain sections of the city [Tehran] and notably before the Parliament building'.[28] The Tudeh Party and its affiliated labour union organized an anti-Saed demonstration on 27 October in Tehran, attracting a large crowd in front of Parliament.[29] The demonstration was orderly and the crowd chanted, 'Death to the prime minister!' The presence of armed Red Army troops, however, was revealing and ill-boding.

Three days later, the Tudeh Party, which had previously announced its opposition to interference of any country in Iran's affairs, including its northern neighbour, mobilized a demonstration in Tabriz, demanding that the Iranian government accept the Soviet oil concession. The Soviet army units took advantage of the situation and disarmed the local police and confined the Iranian army to their barracks. Similar anti-government Tudeh Party demonstrations were held in Ardebil, Rasht, Qazvin, Bandar Pahlavi, Mashhad and Esfahan.

On 8 November 1944, the Tudeh Party organized celebrations marking the 27th anniversary of the October Revolution. Forces of the military governor of Tehran pre-empted the gathering. They occupied the headquarters of the Central United Council of the Trade Union Workers and the Tudeh Party Club and arrested around 17 trade unionists. The ongoing demonstrations fuelled by Tudeh Party sympathizers weakened the Saed government. Under Soviet pressure and a barrage of Tudeh Party propaganda, as well as nationalist criticism, Saed resigned on 9 November 1944.

The Iranian government's decision to refuse granting an oil concession caused a political crisis between Iran and the Soviet Union. The Soviets were disappointed to discover that Mortezaqoli Bayat, the new prime minister, was as uncooperative as Saed. On 2 December 1944, the 14th Majles laid to rest all negotiations on oil concessions. Mohammad Mosaddeq introduced a bill, barring Iranian governments from signing oil concessions with foreign interests without the Majles' consent. Mosaddeq's historical bill was ratified by 80 votes to 7. It stipulated that anyone violating the provisions of the bill would face three to eight years of prison. A week after the Majles approved Mosaddeq's bill, an enraged Kavtaradze left Tehran.

On 30 April 1945, Hitler committed suicide and on 2 May 1945, German forces surrendered after the fall of Berlin. With the end of the war in Europe, the Tudeh Party and its trade union organization notched up their activities by adopting a more aggressive policy towards Iranian governments unfriendly to their cause. While fostering labour strife to obtain greater worker benefits, the Tudeh Party employed its highly organized members and sympathizers to pursue its own political ends, which included securing Soviet interests in Iran.

From mid-1944, the friendly anti-fascist cooperation of allies in Iran was abandoned and competition became increasing sharp and tense between the Soviet Union on the one hand and the US and Britain on the other hand. From 1945, the dress rehearsal for what came to be the cold war was played out in Iran.

On 30 May 1945, for the first time since 1929, oil workers in Kermanshah went on strike. When after a week some 350 workers refused to resume work, they were dismissed by AIOC. On 6 June 1945, the honest and soft-mannered Ebrahim Hakimi was replaced by the hardliner Mohsen Sadr, who would stand up to the rise of Tudeh-affiliated militancy.

Mosaddeq and some 30 independent deputies in the Majles, along with members of the Tudeh Faction opposed Sadr's appointment. Mosaddeq believed that Sadr's government did not represent the people, but the court. In the Majles, Mosaddeq hammered at the need for an immediate withdrawal of foreign troops from Iran. On 5 August, the Tudeh Party staged an orderly 5,000-strong march to the Majles. Intolerant of mounting criticism of his government, and increasing anti-government Tudeh Party agitation in the provinces, Sadr placed Tehran under martial law and prohibited all future demonstrations.

The Uprising of Khorasan Officers

Late during the night of 15 August 1945, a group of pro-Tudeh officers rebelled in Khorasan. This was a planned and thought-out uprising, coordinated with the Tudeh Officers' Organization in Tehran, but without the permission of the Tudeh Party. Under the leadership of Maj. Ali-Akbar Eskandani, 19 officers and 6 soldiers left the Mashhad garrison in two army trucks and a jeep. They took along, money, supplies, clothing, arms and military equipment.

The rebels travelled 500 kilometres to Gonbad Kavus, in the northern province of Gorgan. On their way they disarmed a military garrison and began distributing propaganda leaflets, inviting the people to join their revolutionary cause. The rebellious forces reached Gonbad Kavus on 18 August, where they met with the provincial representatives of the Tudeh Party and were informed of the Party's position of non-assistance. They subsequently moved further west and made camp in the wooded outskirts of Gorgan where they were joined by six more officers, including Col. Abdolreza Azar who had arrived from Tehran. Eskandani and Azar were among the first officers to join the Tudeh Party's clandestine Officers' Organization.

On Monday, 20 August, the 31-strong rebels made their way back to Gonbad Kavus to rest. Under the presumed protection of the Soviet garrison in the city, they believed they would be safe. On Monday afternoon, as the rebels moved out of the city, they were attacked by government forces as they drove past the local gendarmerie and police garrisons. Eskandani and 6 other officers were killed, 9 were arrested and the rest, including Col. Abdolreza Azar, eventually escaped to the Soviet Union with the help of the Tudeh Party.

Some 40 members of the Officers' Organization of the Tudeh Party who had been allegedly connected with the uprising were arrested in Tehran and the provinces. They were subsequently banished to Kerman. The connection between the communist officers in Tehran suspected of collusion with the officers in Khorasan remains undetermined. The Khorasan Officers' uprising was defeated in five days.

The Khorasan officers saw themselves as the vanguards of the anti-monarchic and people's revolution in Iran. Worried that after the war, reactionary forces would again impose their will on the country, they believed that 'peaceful parliamentary struggles were futile' and hoped to win the support of the Tudeh Party's leadership after staging the rebellion and creating a 'revolutionary base'.[30]

The pro-Tudeh rebellious officers were under the illusion that the Tudeh Party would eventually support their armed movement. The uprising demonstrated the schism between the revolutionary communism of officers committed to armed action and the reformist leadership of the Tudeh Party, which at times employed a revolutionary rhetoric. Little did the rebels know that the Tudeh Party and the Soviets, resented independent initiatives and actions not emanating from and closely controlled by the apex of the Tudeh Party or the Soviet authorities.

Pro-Tudeh activities in 1945 had to fit into the Soviet Union's broad national interests. Neither the Soviet Army in the region nor and the Tudeh authorities supported the uprising of the Khorasan officers. The Tudeh Party condemned the rebellion as a childish and angry act without a plan or proper decision-making.

Two days after the rebellion by the Khorasan officers had been crushed, martial law was announced in Tehran. The Tudeh headquarters in Shiraz were attacked and burnt down, and brawls broke out between the supporters of the Tudeh Party and Seyyed Zia's partisans in Shahi. On 14 September 1945, the military governor in Tehran forcefully broke up a Tudeh Party meeting at its headquarters, and subsequently occupied and closed the headquarters of the Tudeh Party and the Central United Council of the Trade Union Workers. Several Tudeh Party and Trade Union leaders were arrested, many, including Fereydun Keshavarz, a Tudeh Party deputy, were beaten up and at least nineteen newspapers, mostly Tudeh-affiliated, were closed.

The Autonomous Movement of Azarbayjan

From late October 1944, Azarbayjan witnessed a surge of regular and almost daily political and trade union activities in favour of Kavtaradze's demand for a Soviet oil concession. Iranian Azarbayjan, which the Soviets called Southern Azarbayjan, was gradually being prepared to secede from Iran and join Soviet Azarbayjan. On 10 April 1944, at the behest of the Soviets, 4,000 copies of the Azari language *Vatan*

Yolanda (For the Cause of the Homeland), was published and distributed in Tabriz. The paper's editor was Mirza Ebrahimov, a Soviet Azarbayjani who had been sent from Baku with his 27 staff members. In July 1944, Azarbayjan had formed its own Tudeh-affiliated labour union called the Provincial United Council of the Trade Union Workers and Toilers of Azerbayjan. This organization was headed by the communist Mohammad Biriya and openly supported by the Soviet Union.

In Azarbayjan, where the occupying Red Army supported pro-Soviet activities and intervened to disarm the local police, the central government's power was nominal. On 1 November 1944, Dadash Taqizadeh, the Tudeh Party leader in Maragheh, rebuked Saed's government and demanded that an oil concession be granted to the Soviet Union. Similar demonstrations by the Tudeh Party occurred in Azarbayjan's major cities, such as Rezaiyeh, Salmas, Ardebil and Tabriz.

Between December 1944 and February 1945, the idea of freeing Azarbayjan from the Persian (Fars) yoke was discussed in the Soviet high circles. The idea of separating Azarbayjan from Iran was staunchly pursued by Mir-Jafar Baqerov, the secretary-general of Soviet Azarbayjan's Communist Party, who was a partisan of the Azari national identity, irredentism and the Soviet way of life. Baqerov and Hasan Hasanov, the special Soviet envoy to Iran, became the instruments and administrators of forging an autonomous pro-Soviet Azarabyjan

It was clear that Soviet political and cultural interests in Azarbayjan were rooted in economic and oil interests. On 21 June 1945, Stalin issued a top secret decree, ordering the exploration and prospecting for oil and gas in Azarbayjan. Two and a half months later, explorations began in Gilan, Mazandaran, Gorgan and Azarbayjan.

On 6 July 1945, the Political Bureau of the Central Committee of the Soviet Communist Party ordered Baqerov to organize secessionist movements in Iran's Azarbayjan and other northern provinces. To finance the Azarbayjan secessionist movement, a budget of a million rubles, or the equivalent of 6,086,426 rials, was allocated to the Central Committee of the Azarbayjan Communist Party. On 14 July 1945, the specifics for 'creating the Azerbaijani Democratic Party' were outlined by the Soviet authorities, after consultation with Pishehvari and Kambakhsh in Baku.[31]

The Soviet Reaction to Iran's Refusal of Granting an oil Concession

The oil concession crisis of 1944 was a watershed for Soviet policy: the Soviet Union embarked on a policy of subversion in northern Iran only after that event. (E. Mark)[32]

From 23 August 1945, clashes erupted in the Soviet-controlled Northern areas involving Tudeh Party sympathizers and government forces. Tudeh activists began imposing their administrative control over the region as they forced changes of governors and commanding officers of the gendarmerie in various areas. When government troops were dispatched to Northern cities of Sari and Shahi, where Tudeh sympathizers clashed with Seyyed Zia's sympathizers, Soviet troops halted their advance and sent them back.

On 25 August 1945, Jafar Pishehvari, a veteran communist entered Tabriz. He was Baqerov's candidate for implementing Soviet plans in Azarbayjan. Pishehvari had been Gilan's commissar of interior in August 1920, after the Soviet-initiated coup against Kuchek Khan. He had been imprisoned with the Group of 53 but had never officially joined the Tudeh Party. The Tudeh Party had supported Pishehvari's candidacy during the 14th Majles elections.

From May 1943 to May 1945, Pishehvari edited a paper called *Ajir* (Siren), which appeared three times a week. *Siren* was a radical paper, staunchly anti-capitalist, anti-fascist, anti-colonial and pro-Soviet. It acted as the mouthpiece for Azarbayjan and posed itself as the protector of Azaris. *Siren* approved the granting of an oil concession to the Soviet Union in the North. It severely criticized Saed and Seyyed Zia and became increasingly anti-British and anti-US.

On 3 September 1945, *Ferqehe democratic Azarbayjan* (Azarbayjan Democratic Party) was born in Tabriz and its 12-point declaration was pasted in Azari on city walls. The declaration emphasized that Azari should be the official language of education and government correspondence and called for the liberation of Azarbayjan from the repressive Tehran government. It promised the eradication of unemployment, promotion of industrialization and land to landless peasants.

The Soviet Reaction to the Azarbayjan Democratic Party

The creation of the Azerbaijani Democratic Party in 1945 was met with enthusiasm by all progressive strata of Iran and the peoples inhabiting that country.[33]

Soviet-driven political developments sped up as the Azarbayjan Democratic Party (ADP) launched a bilingual Azari-Persian newspaper, *Azarbayjan*, on 5 September 1945, and both the Azarbayjan Tudeh Party and the Trade Union Workers and Toilers of Azerbayjan joined the ADP.

Despite the Tudeh Party's initial strong opposition to the creation of the Azarbayjan Democratic Party (ADP) and Pishehvari's leadership, disgruntled Tudeh Party members eventually bowed to the Soviet line and supported the ADP. The architects of the ADP ingeniously appropriated the name of Mohammad Khiyabani's independent and patriotic party.

> **Jafar Baqerov to Marshal Beria, Chief of Soviet Union's People's Commissariat for Internal Affairs (NKVD) on 21 October 1945**
>
> Twenty-one experienced NKVD and NKGB operatives of the Azerbaijan SSR have been selected who are capable of organizing work to liquidate people and organizations interfering with the development of the autonomy movement in Iranian Azerbaijan (gendarmes, policemen, officers of the Iranian Army, et al). All these comrades are to organize armed partisan detachments from the local population.[34]

From mid-November, under the command and patronage of some eighty Soviet security experts, groups of 300 to 400 were armed and trained in rural and urban areas of Azarbayjan, while missions of intimidation and assassination were conducted against landowners.

Ebrahim Hakimi replaced Mohsen Sadr as prime minister on 31 October 1945. Faced with the critical political and military developments in Azarbayjan, he informed the Soviet Embassy representatives in Tehran of the government's decision to dispatch the army to Azarbayjan. The Soviets denied any knowledge of the alarming situation in Azarbayjan and consigned the permission to dispatch troops to the Central Command of the Soviet Army in Iran. Tensions escalated when Iranian army units advancing towards Azarbayjan were stopped on more than one occasion in Karaj and Qazvin, making a mockery of Hakimi's address to the Majles that 'the government would not permit rebellion and would punish those responsible for creating trouble'.[35]

At the end of the Great Congress of the People of Azarbayjan, held on 23 November 1945, a letter signed by 150,000 attendants was addressed to the shah, the president of the Majles and the prime minister. The letter emphasized the Congress' commitment to the national integrity of Iran and made no mention of secession. It proposed a self-governed and self-determined Azarbayjan within Iran, with, nonetheless, Azari as its official language. In conclusion, the message to Tehran was that it did not seek violence but was ready to fight for its objectives. This was a shrewd subterfuge on the part of Soviet advisors to neutralize claims that the ADP was rebelling against the central government.

On the same day that the Great Congress of the People of Azarbayjan met, the US sent an urgent message to the Soviet government concerning the rebellion in Azarbayjan. The US urged the British and Soviet governments to issue 'instructions to their commanders, and that arrangements be made immediately for the complete withdrawal of all foreign troops from Iran by January 1, 1946'.[36] This was a soft warning to the Soviets to end their occupation, as agreed by all three allies in Tehran. Five days later,

Vyacheslav Molotov, the Soviet minister of foreign affairs, brushed off the US warning on the timing of troop withdrawal from Iran and denied any uprising in Azarbayjan.

With the inauguration of Azarbayjan's Parliament on 12 December, the de facto secession at the end of November 1945 became official. By this time, the armed ADP forces known as *Fadais* had disarmed and cleansed all government forces from the province. They entered Tabriz on 14 December 1945 and took control of the 1,000 government forces, who laid down their arms.

By mid-December 1945, the ADP was in full control of Azarbayjan. It had formed its own government led by Pishehvari composed of ten ministerial portfolios. As a sign of respect towards Iran's national and territorial integrity, the Pishehvari government did not include a minister of foreign affairs, even though it did have a Ministry of National Army (*qoshune melli*). Meanwhile, Soviet forces continued to violate Iranian national sovereignty by thwarting government troops from reaching Azarbayjan. Later, Soviet advisers from Baku assisted the ministers of Azarbayjan's National Government to efficiently run their respective ministries.

With ADP in control of Azarbayjan, Pishehvari, the prime minister, and Baqerov pushed for complete secession and the establishment of a Soviet Republic before the departure of Soviet forces from Iran. Some key members of the Tudeh Party's Central Committee, however, such as 'Ardeshir [Ardashes] Avanesiyan, Iraj Eskandari and Abdolsamad Kambakhsh were not in favour of Iranian Azarbayjan joining Soviet Azarbayjan.'[37] Concurrently, the Soviet Union was caught in a diplomatic tussle with its two war allies over Iran. If Stalin could obtain an oil concession in the north without antagonizing his old Western allies, he was willing to sacrifice the Azarbayjan Democrat Party.

At the 13 December 1945 Moscow meeting of the three foreign ministers, the US asserted that if the Azarbayjan problem was not resolved, the issue would be brought before the January meeting of the United Nations. Stalin told US Secretary of State James Byrnes that, the 'Soviet Union was not afraid of having the Iran question raised at UNO meeting and no one need blush if it should come up.'[38] Stalin complained also that the Hakimi government was hostile to the Soviet Union.

On 26 January 1946, in a letter to the president of the Security Council, Iran demanded that the Council investigate the dispute between the two countries over Azarbayjan. The Council recommended bilateral negotiations between Iran and the Soviet Union and left the door open to future discussions of the matter if issues were not resolved.

Soviet Arms for Azarbayjan

From October 1945 to January 1946, Azarbayjan received 110,516 German-made Mauser rifles, 350 machine-guns, 87 automatic rifles, 1,086 pistols, 3,000 mortar-shells, and 2,651,416 cartridges. (J. Hasanali)[39]

The US diplomatic activities through the UN agitated and embarrassed the Soviets. As news trickled in of Soviet reinforcements and tanks arriving in Azarbayjan and heading towards Kurdestan during early March 1945, the US became more anxious about a Soviet invasion and the spread of the crisis. The US and Britain pushed the Iranian government to take its case to the Security Council, despite Soviet threats against it, and maintained pressure on the Soviet Union to comply by the Tripartite Treaty.

As important as diplomatic pressure may have been, Stalin was impervious to such manoeuvrings. Yet, on 24 March 1946, in absolute secrecy, Stalin ordered the evacuation of Soviet troops from Iran by 30 April 1946. This sudden decision may well have been due to secret American threats delivered through non-conventional and untraceable channels. US President Harry S. Truman later referred to a US ultimatum to Stalin over troop withdrawals, but no record of such an ultimatum has been found in the US archives.

Qavam Seduces and Deceives Stalin?

On 28 January 1946, Ahmad Qavam replaced Prime Minister Hakimi. Qavam was a seasoned politician, and acceptable to both the Tudeh faction in the Majles and the Soviets. On 6 May 1946, some thirteen weeks after Qavam came into office, the Soviets withdrew their forces from Iran. Seven months later, on 13 December 1946, the Soviet-initiated secessionist Azarbayjan movement folded. Pishehvari fled to Baku and government forces entered Azarbayjan. Qavam was the charmer and wizard that had pulled off the impossible, completely overshadowing the shah and constantly a few steps head of the British, Americans and Soviets.

The Azarbayjan crisis, which brought the world close to a major US–Soviet confrontation, and threatened international peace, was defused rather unexpectedly. Whereas Stalin viewed Hakimi as hostile and refused to meet with him, he was most friendly towards Qavam. Four days after Qavam introduced his cabinet, he was on his way to Moscow to meet Stalin. They met on 21 February 1946 and discussed the Soviet troops' withdrawal from Iran and the Azarbayjan crisis. Nine days later, while Qavam was still in Moscow, the British withdrew their forces from Iran, and most significantly, the Soviets announced withdrawing their forces from Mashhad, Shahrud and Semnan, located in eastern Iran. Qavam was trying out his calculated policy of appeasement towards Moscow, without yielding on the fundamental interests of Iran, to assure gradual Soviet disengagement.

On 20 March 1946, the new Soviet ambassador, Ivan Sadchikov, informed Qavam that 'Soviets might withdraw troops from Iran if [the] Shah and Prime Minister would sign [a] letter to him assuring Russia that arrangements would be made for joint Irano-Soviet exploitation of north Iranian oil.'[40] This was the opportunity Qavam was looking for. The Soviets were signalling that keeping troops in Iran and support for the Azarbayjan autonomous movement were bargaining chips for obtaining oil concessions.

According to the 4 April 1946 Qavam-Sadchikov Agreement, the Soviet Union officially committed itself to withdrawing all its troops from Iran 'within a period of one-and-one-half months starting from March 24, 1946'. In return, Iran committed itself to the establishment of a joint Irano-Soviet oil company 'presented for ratification by the new Iranian Majlis as soon as it has been elected and . . . in any case not later than 7 months after March 24 of the current year [1946]'.[41]

The news of Soviet withdrawal of forces stunned and disquieted the Pishehvari government. Pishehvari believed that the Soviets had been duped by Qavam and that the Qavam–Sadchikov Agreement was a monumental mistake. He felt betrayed by Baqerov and his Soviet benefactors. Pishehvari was convinced that once Soviet troops left Iran, Qavam would seek revenge and all that had been gained in Azarbayjan would be lost.

Pishehvari's one-year government in Azarbayjan had a mixed record. The National Government constructed the Azarbayjan University, a national theatre, a national museum and formed a symphony orchestra. It published primary school texts in Azari, founded a women's club and promoted concerts, films, circuses, mostly Soviet ones, and began building an indoor movie theatre. The literary works of Soviet writers were widely translated and published. A radio station, provided by the Soviets, started work on 7 April 1946. Radio Tabriz aired music, news and propaganda material.

The Pishehvari government distributed government-owned and private land belonging to non-Azaris and 'enemies of the National Government' among the landless peasants. It printed letters of credit and used it as money. The Pishehvari government paved roads, introduced tarmac and brought running water and electricity to some of Azarbayjan's cities.

To alleviate hardship on consumers, the National Government established government cooperatives and stores where food and essential items were made available at controlled prices. The Pishehvari government introduced a new labour law, including an eight-hour workday, annual paid vacation and pension for workers. Finally, it credited itself for closing brothels, uprooting corruption and bribery, and decreasing theft and crime.

By mid-April, the Soviets were withdrawing their forces from Zanjan, Qazvin and Ardebil. They pressured Pishehvari to enter negotiations with Qavam, who spoke about a peaceful settlement of differences with Azarbayjan. Suddenly the tables were turned in favour of Qavam and the Soviets instructed Pishehvari to be as compliant as possible towards the demands made by his government (Figure 4.2).

On 28 April 1946, Pishevari went to Tehran for negotiations that lasted a week and bore no tangible results. Towards the end of Pishehvari's stay in Tehran, the Soviet troop withdrawal was completed. The Soviets were now convinced that they should support Qavam against the reactionary forces of Seyyed Zia and Qavam led them to believe that he was inclined towards Soviet policy in Iran. Qavam played a calculated

Figure 4.2 Ahmad Qavam. *Source: Wikimedia Commons.*

and impressive game with the Soviets and outwitted Stalin. He kept his cards so very close to his chest and played his hand so masterfully that at times the Americans, the British and the young shah suspected his motives and loyalties.

Qavam Co-opts the Tudeh Party to Appease the Soviets

On 29 June 1946, with all foreign troops out of the country, Qavam announced the creation of the 'Democrat Party of Iran' in contrast to the existing 'Azarbayjan Democrat Party'. Preparing for the full control of the 15th Majles, he threw his full weight behind a strong government-sponsored party. Qavam wished to rally all progressive, anti-reactionary, as well as middle-of-the-road forces, primarily interested in the political and economic independence of Iran, behind his party. He aimed at marginalizing the pro-British forces of Seyyed Zia and undermining the appeal of the pro-Soviet Tudeh Party. Qavam knew that by preventing pro-British Majles candidates from being elected, he would be effectively pulling the carpet from underneath the shah and his supporters. Yet, with his repressive political background, he had difficulty presenting himself and his party as anti-reactionary and progressive.

Shah Weary of Qavam

[The] Shah is afraid Parliament to be elected will be divided between outright Soviet spokesmen and Deputies loyal to Qavam . . . Real basis for Shah's concern is his fear that new Parliament, elected under control of Qavam and Muzzafar Firuz, would be hostile to him and to western democracies. (G. Allen, US ambassador to Iran).[42]

Membership in Qavam's new party ballooned. They came from all classes, with conflicting interests and the sole common objective of attaining political power. Some of its more known players were Khosrow Eqbal, Tafazoli and Hasan Arsanjani, with roots in the old Combat Party, while others such as Reza Hekmat (Sardar Fakher) and Mohammad-Taqi Bahar (Malek al-shoara) were progressive veteran politicians. Qavam's second in command was Mozaffar Firuz, an old companion of Seyyed Zia, who had tilted Left. A contingent of thirty members of the Socialist Party led by Abolhasan Haerizadeh, Zeinolabeddin Foruzesh and Abolhasan Amidi-Nuri also joined Qavam's Party. New and young bloods such as Mozaffar Baqai and Hoseyn Makki, who became key players in the Mosaddeq era, joined Qavam's bandwagon.

Within a month, July 1946, to the utter surprise of many, Qavam's Democratic Party of Iran formed a coalition in preparation for the 15th Majles, with the Tudeh Party and the technocratic and US-leaning Iran Party. Both parties had supported the Azarbayjan movement. To concretize this new alliance, Qavam's cabinet (formed on 1 August) included three members of the Tudeh Party, Iraj Eskandari, Fereydun Keshavarz and Morteza Yazdi, and one from the Iran Party, Allahyar Saleh. This move brought the Tudeh Party into the government camp and made it complicit in all its decisions which further ostracized Pishevari (Figure 4.3). Presented as a government of national reconciliation, the move was particularly aimed to put Stalin's mind at ease.

The honeymoon between Qavam and the Tudeh Party was, however, brief and officially ended on 19 October 1946, when Qavam reshuffled his cabinet and ousted the three Tudeh ministers. Qavam must have felt that he no longer needed to placate the Soviets, that the Tudeh Party was becoming too strong and that the shah was becoming ever more disgruntled with their growing power. In Tehran and the

Figure 4.3 Jafar Pishevari. *Source: Wikimedia Commons.*

provinces, the supporters of the Democrat Party of Iran and the Tudeh Party clashed on the streets. The daily *Iran Democrat*, the Democrat Party's official newspaper wrote, 'our ideology is to respond to word with words and to fist with fists'.

Celebrating its 100th-day anniversary, Qavam's party organized huge demonstrations from 24 to 26 October 1946 in Tehran and the provinces. Hundreds of trucks filled with some 6,000 demonstrators passed through the main streets of Tehran. What was most spectacular was the participation of some 1,100 to 2,000 unarmed military personnel, the 'Rescue Guards' wearing special uniforms while air force planes distributed leaflets reading, 'Long live the sole refuge of patriots, of industrial and agricultural workers of Iran, the national, freedom-loving Democrat Party of Iran.'[43]

Right after announcing his new party, Qavam had reappointed as chief of the general staff Gen. Haj Ali Razmara, the St. Cyr Academy graduate known for his honesty, and knowledge. This was against the shah's will, who viewed Razmara as 'disloyal, dishonest and little better than a Russian agent'.[44] Qavam was gradually purging pro-British and pro-court officers such as Gen. Hasan Arfa and Col. Abdolhoseyn Hejazi and replacing them with independently minded and popular officers. The shah, who had always been sceptical of Qavam, saw these changes as a further impingement on his power.

Qavam had promised the Soviets an oil concession, to be officialized and legalized by Parliament after the withdrawal of their forces. Once the Soviets left Iran, they pressured Qavam to organize elections to the 15th Majles and get the north oil concession ratified. At that point, Qavam threw a spanner in the works arguing that new elections could not be held unless the Azarbayjan crisis was resolved.

Under the pretext of providing secure elections scheduled for 7 December 1946, Qavam ordered the dispatch of government troops throughout Iran, including Azarbayjan. Pishevari reacted by threatening to attack the murderous central government and defend Azarbayjan, while Sadchikov recommended against such a move. On 4 December, the Iranian Army moved with full force against Azarbayjan. Seven days later, the Soviet authorities convinced Pishehvari to stand down and begin evacuating prominent ADP members, officers of the Azerbayjan Army and members of his government to the Soviet Union.

On 13 December 1946, the Iranian Army entered Tabriz with hardly any bloodshed. The backlash against the Pishehvari government began with the pillage and smashing of ADP headquarters and pro-ADP shop and centres. Within a few days, many were imprisoned and some 500–760 were killed and executed. The teaching of Azari was prohibited in schools, Azari textbooks were burnt and the Azari-language press was shut down. Some 2,925 members of the ADP migrated with their families to Soviet Azarbayjan.

Two days after the fall of Tabriz, the eleven-month-old Kurdish Republic of Mahabad, led by Qazi Mohammad, surrendered to the central government. The

Kurdish Republic of Mahabad, with the Soviet Union's initial blessing, had claimed its independence on 4 March 1946. Its fate was closely intertwined with that of the National Government of Azarbayjan.

> ### Havoc after the Fall of Azarbayjan
>
> For months afterward nearly every public square in Azerbaijan and northern Kurdistan sported rows of rebels swinging from crude gibbets. (R. Rossow)[45]

Seven months after the collapse of the Pishehvari government, the 15th Majles, in which Qavam's Democratic Party of Iran had a resounding majority, opened on 17 July 1947. The Tudeh Party failed to have a single deputy elected. Qavam's machinations had made sure of that. Once Pishevari's government fell, the Iran Party also parted ways with the Tudeh Party. The political landscape of Iran which had turned red between the end of June and December 1946, became paler after the fall of Azarbayjan.

The last chapter of the Qavam–Stalin drama came to a climax on 22 October 1947. Qavam went to the 15th Majles and gave a highly detailed report of his activities in relation to Azarbayjan and Soviet withdrawal of forces. He condemned the ADP and the Pishevari government as unconstitutional, traitorous and rebellious, but insisted on the importance of friendly ties with the Soviet Union.

During that same session, the Iranian Parliament voted 102 to 2 that the Qavam–Sadchikov Agreement was null and void. The Majles also passed a single bill article instructing the government to negotiate all agreements concerning natural resources and restore the nation's rights where Iran's interests had been impaired, especially in relation to southern oil. In a clearly well-rehearsed act, the Majles overturned Qavam's promise and denied the Soviets its oil concession.

What seemed especially unexpected was that the Majles, packed with Qavam's deputies would refer to the AIOC agreement as unfair and mention the need to renegotiate its terms. The British military attaché quickly picked up on the reference to British oil interests in the south and wrote: 'That a strongly nationalistic feeling about her oil resources has risen in Persia . . .'[46]

From Qavam's Fall to Mosaddeq's Rise

Once Qavam secured the withdrawal of Soviet forces, resolved the Azarbayjan crisis, and skilfully prevented the Soviets from obtaining an oil concession in the north, the shah was more than ready to get rid of him. During the almost ten-year period, from 27 August 1941 to 29 April 1951, when Mohammad Mosaddeq became prime minister, Iran had eleven different prime ministers. Three of them, Ali Soheyli, Ahmad Qavam and Mohammad Saed, had formed two governments non-successively and Ebrahim Hakimi had formed three. Governments during this period would last from less than a month to twenty-two months.

Qavam's second term in office was the longest of any prime minister. His success in dealing with the Soviets, consequent popularity and consolidation of executive and legislative power, worried the shah. Most significantly, the shah felt completely overshadowed by Qavam during the Azarbayjan crisis. While credit was poured on Qavam for 'saving' Azarbayjan, the shah, who wished to be considered as the mighty commander-in-chief of the Army, found himself overlooked and neglected. Soon pro-court newspapers began attacking Qavam as an 'unbridled dictator in domestic and foreign policy'.[47] Some requested the shah to dissolve the 15th Majles in which Qavam had a majority.

The shah succeeded in forcing eight of Qavam's ministers to resign while turning Reza Hekmat, the president of the 15th Majles, and an old ally of Qavam, against him. Qavam refused to resign and chided his ministers for going against the Constitution by handing their resignation to the shah, instead of him. Six days later, on 10 December 1947, Qavam failed to obtain a vote of confidence. He left the office with another sensational stunt. He went on radio, and this time he baited the British, declaring that talks were underway about the AIOC concession and that Bahrain, then British territory, was an inalienable part of Iranian territory.

On 21 December 1947, the Majles cast 54 votes for Ebrahim Hakimi and 53 votes for Mohammad Mosaddeq. A week later, the 77-year-old Hakimi became prime minister for the third time. Qavam left for Switzerland on 30 December. Hakimi's cabinet reflected the shah's return to the political central stage. The shah wished to regain the grounds he had lost to Qavam, during his premiership, and exert his authority.

Enter Iran's New Shii Game Changers

At 9.00 am on 11 March 1946, while Qavam was in the thick of negotiations with the Soviets, and all attention was focused on the withdrawal of foreign troops, news came that Ahmad Kasravi was assassinated in broad daylight. Kasravi, who had been charged with writing anti-Islamic books in the summer of 1945, was attending a court hearing, when his assailants entered the court chanting, 'God is Great (*Allah o akbar*)!' and escaped the scene leaving behind their victims riddled with bullets and knife wounds.

Ahmad Kasravi was born in 1890 and attended seminary school in Tabriz. He was a participant in the Constitutional Revolution and had written one of the best accounts of this event. He had also written an important work on the principles and branches of Islam and Shiism. In his everyday life, Kasravi noticed practices and beliefs which he could neither find in the Quran nor explain rationally. The inconsistencies in the religious practices of his fellow Muslims, and their inattention to improving their socio-economic conditions bothered Kasravi.

Kasravi exited the clerical order and became convinced that Shiism along with other monotheistic religions had become perverted and incapable of guiding people towards spiritual and material progress. By 1943, having breathed in Reza Shah's secular Iran, Kasravi claimed that existing Islam was an institution run by the clerics, beneficial to no one, and the source of great misfortunes. In the same year, Kasravi wrote his most disparaging works towards Shiism, Bahaism and Sufism. While in his book *The Practice of Shiism*, sometimes referred to as *Read and Judge*, he remained respectful towards imams Ali and Hoseyn, he chided Imam Jafar Sadeq, the highly revered Sixth Shii Imam and founder of Shii jurisprudence (*fiqh*). Kasravi also attacked Shii rites and rituals developed during the Safavid dynasty.

Kasravi remained a deist but revolted against all religions, including Islam, which he considered responsible for the misfortunes of Arabs, Iranians, Egyptians and Indians. In 1943, Kasravi published *Varjavand bonyad* (Divine Foundations), in which he announced his new faith, *Pakdini* or the Clean Faith, a superior religion willed by God. Kasravi labelled all other faiths as imbued with falsities, out of touch with modern times and the sciences and in need of total abandonment.

He claimed that his new faith, had the power to save monotheism, uphold virtues, assure welfare in this world, and most significantly, confront materialism, the most fearful 'misguidedness' in the world. Kasravi did not directly proclaim himself a new prophet, but in his writings, he left hardly any doubt that he was the chosen one (*barangikhteh*). He stated that he did not *claim* to be a prophet, but that he had *done the work* of prophets.

For the Shii community and their clerical leaders, Kasravi had crossed the Rubicon when he challenged the concept of imamate, or the right of Imam Ali and his lineage to the religious and temporal leadership of the Islamic community and rejected the infallibility of the Twelve Imams. Kasravi refuted the central Shii principle of the Twelfth Imam's occultation and his promised return on earth. What became particularly insulting to the Shii community was Kasravi's demeaning of imams, and Fatemeh, the daughter of the Prophet and Imam Ali's wife.

At the time, Kasravi was not the only voice criticizing actually existing Shiism for its deviations, superstitious beliefs, practices and irrationalism. Shariat Sangelaji, a man of the frock, had also begun propagating his modernist and severe criticism of certain Shii ideas in the 1930s and early 1940s. He had argued that polytheism, obscurantism and ignorance had eclipsed the Muslim world and a new age of *jaheliyyeh* (ignorance) had come to prevail. Sangelaji's rejection of Shii reports, the occultation of the Twelfth Imam, the return of the dead before Judgement Day, shrine-/grave-worshipping, superstitious practices and beliefs, and the innovations of Mohammad Baqir Majlesi, were systematic and thoroughly documented.

Taking advantage of Reza Shah's secularization drive, Sangelaji launched a Luther-like debate calling for a return to the Quran to reform the faith. Whereas Sangelaji's reformation movement was a measured and scholarly endeavour against popular Shiism and Majlesi's Shiism, Kasravi's anti-Shiism was more of a sharp-tongued zealous rhetorical campaign, almost comparable in intensity to the fanaticism of his detractors and enemies.

The organization responsible for assassinating Ahmad Kasravi and his secretary and bodyguard, Mohammad-Taqi Hadadpour, was the newly born *Fadaiyane Eslam* or Devotees of Islam, an organization somewhat similar to the Egyptian ***Ikhwan al-Muslemin*** **(Muslim Brotherhood)**. In late February 1946, Mojtaba Navab-Safavi (Mir-Lowhi), a 22-year-old cleric issued a manifesto called 'Blood and Vengeance', announcing the birth of the Devotees of Islam. Kasravi's murder came ten days after Navab-Safavi announced the creation of his organization, and ten months after his initial failed attempt to murder Kasravi.

Navab-Safavi had been radicalized during his short stay at Najaf as a seminary student, where he came across Kasravi's *The Practice of Shiism* and had been offended by it. He subsequently obtained two fatwas from Ayatollahs Hasan Tabatabai-Qomi and Abdolhoseyn Amini who had pronounced Kasravi to be an apostate whose blood was forfeited. From the moment of his return to Iran, Navab-Safavi, a passionate orator, began his anti-Kasravi campaign and gradually attracted young Moslems among 'the neighborhood thugs and ruffians who disturbed the peace' and turned them into zealous soldiers of his cause.[48]

In the name of religious uprightness and vengeance, Navab-Safavi promised to spill the blood of an unspecified number of evil doers who were to be condemned in the 'divine court of justice'. He called on Muslims of the world to revolt and regain their rights, promising that those who died in the cause of God would forever be alive and basking in the bounties and grace of God. Navab-Safavi's call to Islam was a direct reaction to Reza Shah's forced marginalization of religion and restrictions on religious practices, the diminished political clout of the clergy and the rise of modern cultural and social mores and practices, incompatible with a conservative and traditional Islamic outlook. For Navab-Safavi, the antidote to the sense of inferiority of Iranians towards Westerners, was the embracing of a jingoistic and extremist Islam.

Navab-Safavi was a non-intellectual voluntarist, disdainful towards the educated, especially the Westernized types. He wished to revive an Islamic government based on the *sharia* (Islamic law), and through the application of revolutionary terror. Navab-Safavi believed that lust and sexual promiscuity undermined the Islamic foundation of society. Therefore, he ruled that the public display of a women's body (unveiledness), novels, poetry, films, theatres, cabarets, nightclubs, prostitution and music, provoking lustfulness had to be prohibited. He longed for a society in which alcohol, opium, gambling and cigarettes were banned and their consumers were punished.

To usher in an Islamic society, Navab-Safavi recommended building a mosque in every office building and factory, where congregational prayers could be held. For Navab-Safavi, the assassinations committed by his organization were not illegal acts of terrorism, but religiously sanctioned holy wars against those who were spreading corruption on earth and stood in the way of implementing the Islamic code of conduct.

> ### Navab-Safavi's Ideal Society
> The source of all decadence and misfortune is the absence of faith and the lack of an Islamic education. Iran would become a heaven on earth if faith and an Islamic educational system came to reign in this country. (M. Navab-Safavi)[49]

The assassination of Kasravi sent three political signals to the community. First, Navab-Safavi proved that a cleric was perfectly capable of taking the law into his own hands, prosecuting, sentencing, and executing the 'enemies of Shiism'; second, that a junior ranking clergy was now in command of a powerful and obedient armed organization; third, that in pursuit of establishing his perception of an Islamic order, he was fearless, ruthless and resolute. The awe and fear that Navab-Safavi and his organization generated turned them into a coveted asset in Iran's competitive political environment where the budding modern process of political engagement could readily be supplemented by coercion, intimidation and murder if need be.

Sometime between September of 1945 and February 1946, before Kasravi's assassination, Navab-Safavi met with Seyyed Abolqasem Kashani at the latter's house and entered a covenant with him to enforce Islamic edicts. The 21-year-old Navab-Safavi accepted the 68-year-old Kashani as his source of imitation and pledged his loyalty to the Ayatollah in the hope that he would strive for the establishment of an Islamic government. From 1945 to 1951, a solid axis was formed between the two men.

Navab-Safavi looked upon Kashani as a militant politicized cleric, different from the established clergy, who were only interested in their scholarly activities at the seminary schools. But, contrary to Navab-Safavi, as Kashani's political fortune ascended, he looked upon the implementation of divine laws more as an effective promise to obtain political power rather than an attainable end. Once Navab-Safavi realized this fact, he turned against his mentor and leader.

Kashani had been a student of Molla Kazem Khorasani, the renowned constitutionalist, residing in Najaf. Kashani had been elected to the Constituent Assembly and had voted in favour of ending the Qajar dynasty and installing Reza Shah's monarchy. Shortly after Reza Shah's departure, on 8 October 1941, Kashani voiced his grievances to Mohammad-Ali Forughi, the prime minister. In a letter, he emphasized the necessity of applying the 'divine laws' and criticized the gradual replacement of old religious schools with modern schools as well as the unacceptable behaviour of the police bothering veiled women and turbaned clerics.

Kashani was a staunch anti-British activist and was arrested and imprisoned in June 1944 by the British for his collaboration with the German fifth column in Iran. He made his political return by getting elected from Tehran to the 14th Majles, which he was never able to attend due his bouts of imprisonment. After the fall of Qavam, Kashani resurfaced.

Already in 1947, in response to the UN partition of Palestine, Kashani and Navab-Safavi had begun their common political activities by campaigning for Palestinians against British policy and Zionist encroachments in the region. From January 1948, they started issuing fiery communiqués and organized a series of high-profile demonstrations and marches in Tehran. In his declarations and speeches, Kashani usually attacked the Qavam and later the Hajir governments for their corruption and mismanagement of the affairs of the nation, their propagation of immorality and impiety, the persistence of poverty, prostitution, injustice and the continual pillage of the country by the country's leaders. Navab-Safavi, in turn, focused on intimidating women who did not wear the veil by organizing demonstrations in front of Tehran's bazaar to prevent them from entering. He also went to Sari, in Mazandaran, calling on shopkeepers not to sell their goods to veilless women.

As soon as Abdolhoseyn Hajir succeeded Ebrahim Hakimi's third short-lived premiership on 13 June 1948, the Kashani and Navab-Safavi axis increased its anti-government activities (Figure 4.4). Hajir had the shah's solid support. He was known as an Anglophile and his cabinet included several ministers known for their pro-British sympathies. Hajir's political programme was based on reducing the cost of living, implementation of the economic Seven-Year Plan, increasing the power of local government and administrative reform. At his first press conference, Hajir raised the issue of negotiations with the AIOC and the question of Bahrain.

Figure 4.4 Abdolhoseyn Hajir. *Source: Wikimedia Commons.*

Kashani, however, was not willing to give him any time to implement his programmes. From the moment Hajir was appointed prime minister, daily demonstrations against him were organized by Kashani and Navab-Safavi, rocking Tehran, Qom, Mashhad and Esfahan. Demonstrators carried pictures of Kashani and chanted slogans of 'Death to the traitorous Hajir!' On 17 June 1948, Navab-Safavi led some 2,000 demonstrators carrying red and green flags from Kashani's house to the Majles. The crowd clashed with the police and were only dispersed after the police opened fire, leaving behind several people wounded. The electric week of agitation in mid-June of 1948 died out abruptly without attaining its objective of forcing Hajir to resign.

The anti-Hajir campaign was a complex one, typical of murky behind the scenes alliances. Seyyed Zia, at the time, opposed Hajir, although both were suspected of being Anglophiles. Jockeying for premiership, Seyyed Zia threw his weight behind the Kashani and Navab-Safavi axis. The majority of those who attended the five-day demonstrations led by Kashani and Navab-Safavi in Tehran were supporters of Seyyed Zia. John Le Rougetel, the British ambassador in Iran (1946–50), considered Kashani as Seyyed Zia's 'mouthpiece'.[50]

Collaboration against Hajir between Kashani, the devout anti-British cleric and the former cleric Seyyed Zia, well known for his Anglophile tendencies, was certainly an enigmatic one. Hajir was not only accused of being pro-British by his opponents but was labelled as an apostate who had converted to Christianity at the age of 18. He was also charged with being a propagator of Bahaism.

The anti-Hajir campaign became even more perplexing, when on the evening of the 17 June 1948 demonstrations, Navab-Safavi, the pious and revolutionary cleric attended the Anti-Dictatorship Press Front at the posh Tehran Ritz Hotel. The Anti-Dictatorship Press Front had been formed in response to the shah's growing appetite for power and his move to change the Constitution and obtain the right to dismiss Parliament. It was at this secular gathering, launched by Seyyed Zia and the Tudeh Party, that Navab-Safavi was introduced as Kashani's special envoy.

On 7 August 1948, Kashani kept the momentum of his political offensive and led the traditional **Eyde Fetr (Eid al-Fitr)** congregational prayers. In a spectacular show of religious power, pictures of which were printed in the press, some 40,000 people prayed behind Ayatollah Kashani in Tehran. Under the watchful eyes of the army, Shams Qanatabadi, a junior cleric and Kashani's lieutenant, led the ceremony.

In December 1948, Shams Qanatabadi, went on to found the 'Society of Muslim Mojaheds' (*Majma mosalmanan mojahed*). A few months later, on 3 February 1949, the Central Committee of this organization was elected with Qanatabadi as its leader. Its members were estimated between at 200 and 2,000. At this time, in addition to Navab-Safavi, the awe-inspiring soldier of God, Kashani needed a more mundane, pragmatic and suave diplomat-cum-muscleman. Shams Qanatabadi's multi-task organization became Kashani's reliable religious and political executive arm and mouthpiece, especially after the Devotees of Islam broke off ties with Kashani.

Attempted Regicide and Its Consequence

In the afternoon of 4 February 1949, during Mohammad Saed's second government, the shah attended the official celebration ceremony marking the anniversary of Tehran University. Naser Fakhr-Arai, a photographer and reporter, stood at about two metres from his target and shot five bullets at the shah. When his sixth bullet jammed, Fakhr-Arai was shot and killed on the spot, even though the shah had shouted out that the assailant should be arrested and not killed. Unbelievably, the shah escaped the assassination attempt with minor injuries, with three bullets ripping through his hat.

With Fakhr-Arai dead, his motives remained a mystery, generating different possible scenarios. First, Fakhr-Arai had sympathies for and was an adherent of the Tudeh Party, so he may have been prompted by the Tudeh Party, which was again gaining momentum around its criticism of the AIOC concession. Second, Fakhr-Arai had attended the ceremony as a reporter for the religiously oriented newspaper, *Parcham Eslam* (Flag of Islam), the managing director of which was Abdolkarim Faqihi-Shirazi, a close friend of Kashani. It was suggested that Kashani had personally introduced Fakhr-Arai to the newspaper, therefore Kashani may have been the mastermind. Third, Fakhr-Arai was said to have been in a romantic relation with the daughter of the gardener at the British Embassy, thus implicating the British. Fourth, Gen. Haj Ali Razmara, the popular chief of the general staff, whose star was rapidly rising at the time and who sought to become prime minister, could have been the mastermind behind the assassination attempt. Finally, there was the possibility that Fakhr-Arai was an angry and discontent lone wolf acting on his own behalf.

From the five scenarios, the shah opted for the first two which best served his political purposes. Gen. Razmara identified the chief culprits as Kashani and the Tudeh Party. British authorities believed also that 'there was little room for doubt' that the Tudeh Party was behind the assassination attempt and that it had made various preparations in Tehran and the provinces to instigate 'widespread social disorder'.[51] The Tudeh Party, however, had the most to lose and the least to gain from the shah's assassination. At the time, the Tudeh Party's appeal and power was on the rise, and it aimed to send deputies to the 16th Majles. It was also unlikely that either Kashani or Faqihi-Shirazi had any knowledge or role in the assassination attempt. Kashani had also nothing to gain from the shah's assassination. The net beneficiaries of the failed assassination were actually the shah, Gen. Razmara and the Western powers, who wished to see the demise of the Tudeh Party and the curtailment of religious zeal.

Immediately after the failed assassination attempt, martial law and a curfew were imposed in Tehran and later extended to other provinces. The Tudeh Party was outlawed and dissolved, and its members and sympathizers were rounded up in Tehran and the provinces. Newspapers unkind to the court and those with Tudeh Party sympathies were shut down and their editors arrested and sentenced to prison terms of one to five years. After seven years of open activities, all centres and clubs affiliated with the Tudeh Party and the Central United Council of Iran's Workers and Toilers (CUCIWT) were closed.

> ## The Wave of Repression
> Of the Tudeh-CUC [CUCIWT] leaders who could be found, five hundred were arrested. Among the first group were such familiar figures as Dr. Hossein Jowdat, Ebrahim Mahzari, Dr. Morteza Yazdi, Noureddin Kianouri (later to become the leader of the Tudeh Party), Ammanollah Ghoreishi, and Zia Alamouti. (H. Ladjevardi)[52]

At 1.00 am on the morning of 5 February 1949, Tehran's chief of police, Gen. Mohammad Daftari entered Kashani's house and arrested him in connection with the shah's assassination. Kashani was sent to the infamous Falak al-aflak fortress before being put on a plane and sent first to Damascus and then to Beirut.

On 8 February 1949, the Majles passed a repressive press law, effectively banning any criticism of the court, the government or Parliament. Twenty days later, the shah issued a royal edict ordering the formation of the Second Constituent Assembly. This Assembly would enable the shah to dissolve the Majles, it would legislate the creation of an upper house, the Senate, and establish procedures by which the Constitution could be amended in all matters except the regime and the religion of the country – that is to say, Iran would remain a monarchy and its religion, Shiism. All three of these measures, legislated by 10 May 1949, reduced the power of the Majles and strengthened the political power of the shah. The elections to the Constituent Assembly had been openly manipulated by the minister of interior, Manuchehr Eqbal and Gen. Razmara.

The wave of political repression against all opposition forces after the failed attempt on the shah's life created a backlash in the Majles. When the 15th Majles opened after its annual recess, Hoseyn Makki, Mozaffar Baqai and Abolhasan Haerizadeh came to form a new opposition nucleus to Saed's second government, which had succeeded Hajir's on 13 November 1948.

Makki and Haerizadeh censured the Saed government for the illegal closure and censorship of newspapers, irregularities in the elections to the Constituent Assembly, martial law, the arrest and exile of Kashani, and the government's inattention to speeding up the revision of the AIOC concession of 1933. Baqai's long and theatrical speeches focused on the political interferences of Razmara, while acquitting the shah from any wrongdoing.

The Oil Issue

From April and May 1948, the Iranian press, and the 15th Majles, focused on the Anglo-Iranian Oil Company (AIOC) concession, seriously questioning its terms. During Hajir's five months in office, opposition deputies censured his government on the AIOC concession and pressed for its revision. The government, in turn, opened negotiations with the AIOC on the 'Iranianization' article of the concession. Preliminary discussions on the 1933 oil concession opened in Tehran on 28 September 1948.

Iran claimed that the royalties it received compared unfavourably with those in Iraq, Kuwait and Venezuela in particular, where the principal of 50/50 profit sharing between the government and the oil companies had already been introduced. Other complaints involved British taxation and dividend limitations; the sterling/gold exchange rate used in calculating royalty payments; the prices charged by the company for its oil products in Iran; and the Iranianization of the company.

On 3 February 1949, one day before Fakhr-Arai's attempt on the shah's life, some 2,000 students marched to the Majles and demanded the cancellation of the AIOC concession. A new round of negotiations began on 13 February 1949 between Neville Gass, the AIOC director, and Abbasqoli Golshayan, the Iranian minister of finance, and culminated in the 17 July 1949 Supplemental Agreement. Two days later, the Supplemental Agreement, supported by the shah and the AIOC, was sent to the Majles in the form of a bill, in the hope of a quick ratification.

The Supplemental Agreement raised the royalty per ton paid to Iran from 4 to 6 shillings. The AIOC was to pay £5,090,909 ($21,890,908) to the Iranian government within thirty days of the Supplemental Agreement coming into force. In return for continued exemption from Iranian taxation, the company agreed to increase its commutation payments on production from 9 pence to 1 shilling per ton. Finally, it was agreed that the AIOC would increase its discounts on the price of products sold for consumption in Iran. Apart from the one-off payment of £5,090,909, the royalty and tax payments under the Supplemental Agreement was set at £18,667,786 ($80,271,479) for 1948 and £22,890,261 ($98,428,122) for 1949. Even though the AIOC was conceding to higher payments and more favourable terms, it was far from a 50/50 deal, nor did it agree to the payment of taxes to the Iranian government.

Deliberation on the bill was obstructed by Makki until the 15th Majles came to an end and the fate of the Supplemental Agreement remained in limbo. The Baqai, Makki and Haerizadeh trio strongly criticized the government, defended political freedoms and lobbied for the release and return of Kashani in the 15th Majles. They received the support of Mosaddeq once they began resisting the Supplemental Agreement.

On 23 July 1949, Makki read Mosaddeq's letter pleading with the deputies not to ratify the unjust and discriminatory agreement that had its roots in a dictatorial past.

Mosaddeq who was not a deputy, pursued the logic of a 'negative equilibrium' thesis. Having prevented Kavtaradze from obtaining a Soviet oil concession, Mosaddeq now pushed for ridding Iran of the unfair British agreement, thus creating an equilibrium and maximizing national interests. 'Negative equilibrium' was Mosaddeq's motto for economic democracy and liberation. To the British, however, the agreement's failure to pass through Parliament was a 'deplorable failure' and they hung all their hopes on a 'friendlier' 16th Majles.

Battle over the 16th Majles

The Baqai, Makki, Haerizadeh trio became the essential conduit between two popular politicians, both out of the centre stage. Kashani, the political cleric was in exile and Mosaddeq, the ethical politician considered himself retired. From late July 1949, Iranian nationalism, anti-British colonialism and the quest for political freedom and democratic rule, suddenly raged like wildfire throughout the country. Iranians became intransigent in the face of colonialism and rising political authoritarianism. The shah and Hajir, his new minister of court, were determined to fix the elections to increase royal political power within the 16th Majles. Gen. Razmara, on the other hand, was trying to engineer the elections for his own agenda and ambitions.

> ### Hajir on the 16th Majles Elections
> The Shah feels bound to ensure that those whom he considers 'subversive' should not be elected.[53]

At the end of September 1949, from exile, Kashani issued a directive about elections to the 16th Majles, inviting people to vote for Mosaddeq, Haerizadeh, Makki, Baqai, Abdolqadir Azad, Ali Shayegan and Mahmud Nariman. Kashani instructed Navab-Safavi's 'Devotees of Islam' and Qanatabadi's 'Association of Muslim Mojaheds' to enter into a tactical and operational alliance with Mosaddeq's supporters.

Faced with Navab-Safavi's irritation at collaboration with liberal-nationalist figures, whom he did not consider sufficiently pious, Kashani argued that at the time, religious forces did not possess religious notables skilled in the art of politics and were compelled to work with nationalist politicians. Navab-Safavi acquiesced and the Kashani, Navab-Safavi axis joined forces with what would become the National Front.

The protracted battle over the staggered elections to the 16th Majles mobilized the Iranian society and unleashed a pro-democracy movement. Elections for the 16th

Majles began in the provinces in August/September 1949. On 14 October 1949, at the invitation of Mosaddeq, a group of some 200–700 walked to the Marble Palace, protesting foul play, rigged ballots, military and government engineering of elections, stuffing ballot boxes, multiple voting and ineligible voters casting votes during the 16th Majles elections. The protestors demanded the annulment of the elections and the appointment of a trusted supervisory committee overlooking the election process.

In the old Iranian tradition of political sit-ins (*bast*), the protestors sought sanctuary in the Palace to open a parley with the shah. Mosaddeq and 19 others were allowed into the Palace where they took residence for four days and left two days after the parliamentary elections in Tehran began on 16 October 1949. While the shah claimed that there had been no complaints about irregularities during the elections, the protestors insisted that these elections had been illegal and fixed. The protestors left the palace empty-handed, but Mosaddeq's peaceful protest had jolted Iran's political scene. It placed the two juxtaposed issues of political and economic change at the centre stage. Mosaddeq was demanding free elections and democracy, while pushing for 'negative equilibrium'.

Five days after their departure from the Palace, on the evening of 23 October 1949, all those who had participated in the sit-in gathered at Mosaddeq's house. After three hours of discussion, the *Jebhehye Melli* (National Front) was born under the leadership of Mosaddeq. This was an umbrella organization, presenting a united front and composed of various nationalist parties and personalities.

Despite all efforts to keep a close watch on the polling stations, widespread government intervention and fraud led to the gradual elimination of the opposition candidates. Although the shah, Hajir and Eqbal, the minister of interior, had promised a fair process, the elections turned out to be an utter farce. There were widespread reports that during the last days of election in Tehran, the ballot boxes containing the name of Mosaddeq's coalition had been replaced with boxes filled with the name of candidates supported by the shah, the army and Hajir.

Whereas initially it was said that 8 out of the 12 seats in Tehran had gone to Mosaddeq's allies, by the last day of the election, irregularities assured that neither Mosaddeq nor Kashani were elected. Mosaddeq's speeches tying the fate of the 16th Majles to the Supplemental Agreement, made the outcome of the elections hypersensitive.

On 4 November 1949, Tehran was once again shocked by a political assassination. Twelve days after the creation of the National Front, Hajir was shot to death by the 25-year-old Hoseyn Emami. Hajir was implicated in the election irregularities favouring the shah's list of deputies ready to ratify the Supplemental Agreement. Hoseyn Emami was an old member of Navab-Safavi's Devotees of Islam, who had assassinated Kasravi in March 1946.

Back then, Qavam, the prime minister, had discussed what to do with Emami at a cabinet meeting. Allahyar Saleh, minister of justice, had opposed Emami's release, while Hajir, the minister of finance, had defended him and insisted that Kasravi was an apostate and his blood was forfeit. Emami had thus been set free in 1946.

On the heels of Hajir's assassination, a state of emergency was announced, prominent figures of the National Front were arrested and Mosaddeq was banished for a short time to his private estate at Ahmadabad. For their part, the Devotees of Islam immediately issued a declaration accepting responsibility for the assassination. They announced that, 'Hajir was condemned to death by the order of God' and that 'the elections needed to be annulled and new elections held, in which the people could vote freely, and the ballot boxes would not be switched'.[54] Emami was hanged, without any publicity, at the very early hours of 9 November 1949.

On 10 November, the Chair of the Election Supervisory Committee confirmed widespread irregularities and riggings in the elections and announced the Committee's decision to nullify the results in Tehran. Ten days later, the election results of Tabriz were also announced null and void. Consequently, new elections were ordered for Tehran and the Mosaddeq–Kashani axis reactivated their electoral campaign with regular elections meetings, which attracted more and more people.

On 11 April 1950, the results of the second round of elections for Tehran were announced and the Mosaddeq–Kashani coalition came out clearly on top. Mosaddeq obtained the highest vote from Tehran, Baqai the second, Makki the third, Haerizadeh the fourth, Kashani, who was in exile, the fifth, followed by Abdolqadir Azad, Shaygan and Nariman.

By mid-May, the British Embassy was astounded by the 'degree of moral ascendency' that Mosaddeq and the National Front had established over the prime minister and the government.[55] Mosaddeq's moral superiority, impeccable honesty, 'negative equilibrium' and democratic politics endeared him to the people and made him a formidable opponent for his ill-wishers.

Ironically, however, it was the extremist political act of the undemocratic Devotees of Islam which enabled 8 out of the 12 members of Mosaddeq's coalition from Tehran to enter the Majles. This act of terrorism perpetrated by an organization which completely disagreed with man-made laws via a parliamentary system and only believed in an Islamic government under the strict laws of the *sharia*, became the guarantor of free elections in Tehran and renewed interest in the democratic process.

Oil Nationalization

On 10 June 1950, Kashani returned home from exile and was given a hero's welcome with a crowd of some 15,000 to 100,000 greeting him on his way from the airport to his house. Four days after his return, Kashani attended a National Front meeting at Mosaddeq's house. He politely shunned membership in it, but informally accepted to take charge of its parliamentary group and participated in the National Front meetings.

Immediately after Kashani's arrival, the two leaders set their political targets; Iranian oil had to be returned to Iranians and the growing dictatorial aspirations of the monarch had to be harnessed. As Mosaddeq and Kashani grew more powerful, the shah's interest converged more with the British. Ali Mansur, the prime minister appointed by the shah on 23 March 1950, was to present the Supplemental Bill to the Majles, but he was hesitant and reluctant. When he finally presented the bill, the Majles opted to elect a Special Committee of 18 to discuss it and report back.

On 26 June 1950, Mosaddeq was elected chair and Makki the rapporteur of the Special Committee. On the same day, the shah reacted by appointing Gen. Razmara, the first military man since Reza Khan as prime minister (Figure 4.5). The shah and the British needed a strong man to stand up to the spiking nationalist and anti-dictatorial fervour. North Korea crossing the 38th parallel into the South on 25 June 1950, had raised US anxieties over Soviet designs on Iran. Razmara was the tough, Reza Khan-like man of the hour.

Both Mosaddeq and Kashani opposed Razmara whom they viewed as a military dictator intent on stifling the rule of parliamentary democracy, as well as a British stooge charged with ratifying the Supplemental Agreement. Both men appealed to the people to stand up to Razmara, whom they characterized as a threat to the country.

During Razmara's thirty-three weeks in office, the Mosaddeq–Kashani axis challenged him incessantly on several fronts and using different levers. Razmara and his bills were opposed in Parliament, he and his policies were attacked in the press, the Supplemental Agreement was rejected in the Special Commission, and he faced systematic and regular street demonstrations, which often ended in bloody clashes. At this time, brawls and altercations between the thugs of each side were a normal occurrence in the streets and even inside the Majles.

Razmara retaliated by closing opposition newspapers and throwing their editors in jail. The battle over Baqai's paper *Shahed* (Observer), probably the most popular daily, went to extremes when Razmara ordered a physical assault on its printing

Figure 4.5 Gen. Ali Razmara. *Source: Wikimedia Commons.*

press while Kashani ordered Navab-Safavi and Qanatabadi to mobilize their boys to defend it.

On 25 November 1950, the Special Commission voted unanimously that the Supplemental Agreement was insufficient to secure the interests of Iran and therefore, turned it down. On the same day National Front members of the Commission wrote a letter to the Majles, suggesting that 'in the name of the Iranian people's welfare ... the oil industry throughout Iran should be nationalized, and all activities such as exploration, extraction and production be placed in the hands of the government'.[56] No sooner was the National Front's letter published that Kashani issued a formal fatwa ordering the people to demand the nationalization of the oil industry. On Friday, 22 December 1950, a few thousand responded to Kashani's call to demonstrate in favour of oil nationalization.

V. J. Northcroft, the Resident Manager of the AIOC who met regularly with Razmara on Friday afternoons at the latter's house, and who blatantly intervened in Iranian politics, exerted systematic pressure on Razmara to get the Supplemental Agreement ratified. Sensing the strong public opinion against the Agreement, and its dim chances of ratification, Razmara withdrew the bill on 26 December 1950, hoping to take the wind out of the parliamentarian opposition and stem the call for oil nationalization.

As the deadlock between Razmara and the opposition over the oil issue dragged on, Kashani and Mosaddeq intensified their campaign to unseat Razmara. Their anti-Razmara and pro-nationalization demonstration on Friday, 29 December 1950, attracted some 40,000–60,000 people. As such demonstrations multiplied, the Devotees of Islam, regular organizers and participants of such demonstrations, became more radical and more entitled. During their 26 February 1950 demonstration, Abdolhoseyn Vahedi, the second in command of the Devotees of Islam, sniped at the National Front that their popularity was due to the activities of the Devotees of Islam and declared that the Devotees were ready for holy war.

On 7 March 1951, while Razmara attended a funeral ceremony, Khalil Tahmasebi shot and killed the prime minister. Tahmasebi was arrested and confessed to being a member of the Devotees of Islam. One day after Razmara's assassination, Kashani told foreign reporters that his murder was religiously sanctioned and that Tahmasebi was Iran's saviour.

In a huge demonstration on 8 March 1951, Makki and Baqai, two leading figures of the National Front, congratulated the Iranian people for the death of Razmara. At this same meeting, Navab-Safavi threatened the shah and the authorities that if Tahmasebi was not released immediately and the authorities failed to officially apologize to him, leading politicians would face Razmara's fate. The Devotees of Islam were openly using terror to dictate their wishes.

Amid disbelief and awe, the British Foreign Office informed the British ambassador in Iran, Francis Shepherd, that it was necessary for a strong character to become prime minister. The Foreign Office insisted that the most appropriate person was

Seyyed Zia, demonstrating that after thirty years, the British continued to have faith in him. The shah immediately invited Seyyed Zia and asked him to form his government. Seyyed Zia responded that he needed to prepare and plan and would take on the position after the New Year holidays, around 28 March 1951. Blind to the rapidly changing conditions, Seyyed Zia thought that the opposition would go to sleep for three weeks, allowing him to muster his forces and become prime minister when he was ready.

> ### CIA's View of Iran on 23 April 1951
>
> Most observers, however, believe Ala will be replaced by Seyyid Zia . . . If Seyyid Zia becomes Prime Minister, he would apparently inaugurate a strong man type of government. It is believed that the Shah would order dissolution of the Majlis after Seyyid Zia obtained a vote of confidence, call for new elections and support Seyyid Zia in governing by decree and forcefully suppressing opposition. (Kermit Roosevelt)[57]

On 15 March 1951, eight days after Razmara's assassination, despite a flurry of letters of objection by the British Embassy and the AIOC's persistent demand that their oil agreement be respected, the Iranian Majles voted unanimously in favour of nationalizing the oil industry throughout the country. National celebration ensued in Tehran and the provinces. The public mood and opinion was so much in favour of oil nationalization that the conservative Senate followed suit even though half its members were the shah's appointees. The shah signed the Oil Nationalization Law on 20 March 1951.

On the same day that the shah signed the Oil Nationalization Law, he declared martial law in Tehran. Also on the same day, the oil workers at Abadan and other oil installations in Iran began a long and bloody strike. Some 12,000 to 30,000 workers and students taking their cue from Tudeh and National Front organizers, working independently of one another, brought Abadan to standstill.

Mosaddeq's 28 Months in Office

On 20 March 1951, faced with Seyyed Zia's request for some time to prepare, the shah appointed Hoseyn Ala as prime minister. Five weeks later, Ala resigned. In a totally unexpected development, on 28 April 1951, Jamal Emami, an Anglophile deputy, nominated Mosaddeq as prime minister, to test his resolve. The 69-year-old Mosaddeq immediately accepted the nomination and obtained the votes of 79 out of the 100 deputies present. It was rather bizarre that the Majles would, without previous negotiation with the shah, choose a prime minister. As Mosaddeq reached the summit of political power, he raised Kashani, his comrade-in-arms, with him to the top. Kashani benefitted from exercising executive power without any accountability, as he had no official state position. He was a deputy, but hardly ever attended Majles sessions.

The British had closely and furiously observed how Mosaddeq, the chair of the Special Committee, had gradually steered Parliament towards not only rejecting the Supplemental Agreement but preparing the legal grounds for nationalizing Iran's oil industry. With Mosaddeq in power, the British were dealing with a politician whom they could neither impress, pressure, intimidate nor bribe into accepting their terms.

Mosaddeq had three key characteristics, the sum of which made him a formidable political opponent. First, he was a true patriot who believed in placing Iran's benefits above all else, irrespective of the risks. Second, Mosaddeq was inflexible, relentless, and stubborn. Once he was convinced of the righteousness of a cause or a principle, factors such as convenience and expedience could hardly persuade him to change his position. Finally, he was an old-style honourable statesman, who would not compromise the principle of Iran's independence and prosperity.

Back in 1944, as a member of the 14th Majles, Mosaddeq had denounced Seyyed Zia and Reza Shah for carrying out a British coup. He had accused Reza Shah of being a dictator and criticized his policy of forcefully prohibiting the veil. He had argued that neither despotic rule nor politico-economic intervention of foreigners could be justified in the name of economic progress. Mosaddeq had distinguished between honourable and dishonourable British functionaries and thanked the American government and President Woodrow Wilson, for having respected and supported the sovereignty of Iran in the face of Anglo-Russian conspiracies.

Mosaddeq was Western-educated and a Westernized member of Iranian notables. He was a man of law, familiar with Western institutions and their ways of doing politics. On 1 May 1914, Mosaddeq obtained his doctorate degree from the newly founded University of Neuchatel in Switzerland, making him the first Iranian to receive a doctorate degree in law (hence Dr Mosaddeq to Iranians). The title of his thesis was, 'Le Testament en Droit Musulman (Secte Chyite)' (Testaments in Islamic (Shii) Jurisprudence).

According to his own autobiography, after his four-year stay in Switzerland, he fell in love with that country, the cradle of modern democracy. Yet, contrary to most Western-educated politicians, he did not mistake admiration for Western political and economic achievements with veneration of Western governments and their condescending attitude towards non-Western countries. As much as he longed to modernize and democratize Iran, he opposed foreign colonialism, intervention and hegemony. Mosaddeq believed that his power was just and enforceable, only if it emanated from the people and their representatives in the Majles. Throughout his crisis-ridden premiership, he would stand up in the Majles and inform the opposition deputies to give him a vote of no confidence if they wanted him to stand down.

The British government owned 51 per cent of AIOC, which was a highly lucrative business contributing significantly to the British economy. The nationalization of the AIOC could not be taken lightly. The British investment in Abadan was 'the greatest single overseas enterprise in British commerce', making a profit of £170 million in 1950.[58] It was therefore not surprising that the British ambassador, Shepherd, deeply disliked Mosaddeq as a person and resented his ideas.

One day after Mosaddeq received his vote of confidence from Parliament, Shepherd set the tone for British policy towards the new prime minister and informed the shah that Britain did not trust Mosaddeq and that his premiership would only be a disaster. Subsequently, Shepherd referred to the Iranian prime minister as a 'lunatic' who was 'both cunning and slippery and completely unscrupulous'.[59]

On 30 April 1951, the nine-point law articulating the objectives of oil nationalization was ratified by the Majles. It aimed to establish Iran's sovereignty, ownership and control of the country's oil industry and resources, eradicate British political and economic influence and dominion in Iran, and mobilize financial resources to realize economic development plans. On 3 May 1951, Mosaddeq introduced his non-partisan cabinet to the Majles. He identified the implementation of the Oil Nationalization Law and reform of the electoral laws as the two objectives for his government. Mosaddeq's oil nationalization mandate was to throw his premiership into an interminable foreign crisis, which would become a domestic crisis and lead to his forceful removal from office.

Mosaddeq's International Saga

Britain had engaged in a vast nationalization project of its own services and industries since 1946 and was in the process of nationalizing its iron and steel industry in 1951. But what was good for colonial Britain was not desirable for colonies and unofficial colonies. Iran's oil nationalization left unpunished was seen as a formidable blow to Britain's overseas economic investments and a serious threat to the empire.

From 5 May to 27 September 1951, the British planned different military operations, from the invasion of Iran's southern oil fields under the code name 'Operation Buccaneer' in late June to the deployment of airborne troops to take over Abadan and the oil refinery in July. On 27 September 1951, Clement Attlee, the Labour prime minister, announced that the UK would completely abandon the idea of a direct military intervention in Iran because of US opposition to it.

With the military option off the table, Britain embarked on a multipronged strategy. It announced an embargo on the international sale of Iranian oil to disrupt the country's urban economic activities, with the objective of fostering discontent and hardship and bringing about the fall of Mosaddeq (Figure 4.6). To implement the embargo, the UK announced that it would pursue all parties purchasing Iranian oil

Figure 4.6 Mosaddeq with Allahyar Saleh (left of photo). *Source: Via Alamy Images.*

in the courts. On 28 September, the UK lodged a complaint against Iran at the Security Council of the UN.

Mosaddeq was drawn into a long string of oil discussions and meetings at home and abroad, continuously studying and discussing proposals and counter-proposals on the details of implementing nationalization, while warding off British harassments of all sorts, and hoping to reach an agreement with them. To this end, Mosaddeq engaged in oil discussions proposed by the Jackson Mission (11–21 June 1951), the Stokes Mission (4–21 August 1951), the International Bank for Reconstruction and Development (IBRD) or World Bank (November 1951) and the Churchill–Truman Proposal (30 August 1952 and 20 February 1953). On 16 September 1952, Mosaddeq took the first Churchill–Truman proposal to the Majles, presented his arguments against it and asked for a vote of confidence, which he obtained by a unanimous vote.[60]

The second Churchill–Truman proposal (20 February 1953) supported by the US was the best offer Iran had received. It accepted nationalization and left it to the International Court of Justice to determine the compensation due, although it stipulated that this compensation had to be settled according to English law. The proposal recognized the right of Iran to manage and control its oil industry in Iran but not its exclusive right to foreign sales. Iran was required to export its oil through an international consortium. Concerned with the ambiguity of the sum of compensation to be decided in the future, and the danger that Iran would be caught in paying long-term reparations paralyzing its economy, Mosaddeq refused to sign the second Churchill–Truman proposal.

On the international scene, Mosaddeq embarked on a series of high-profile overseas visits to defend Iran's right to nationalize her oil industry. When the British lodged a complaint against Iran at the UN Security Council, Mosaddeq flew to New York on 7 October 1951. Having heard the Iranian case, the Council ruled itself incompetent in the matter and voted to postpone discussion until the International

Figure 4.7 Premier Mosaddeq and the shah, shortly after the premier's return from the US. *Source: Via Alamy.*

Court of The Hague had ruled on its own competence to address the Iran–UK litigation. This was a diplomatic victory for Iran and a blow to the British. Iran had staved off the UK's first international legal assault (Figure 4.7).

On 7 January 1952, *Time* magazine named Mosaddeq Man of the Year for 1951 and splashed his face across its January 1952 issue. Even though the article on him was far from complimentary, it reflected the world impact of a highly popular Iranian leader, who was challenging unfair UK colonial practices since 1907. The *Time* article depicted Mosaddeq as 'a weeping, fainting leader of a helpless country' which posed a danger to the West, yet 'for all its power', the West was unable to cope with him.

On 28 May 1952, Mosaddeq went to The Hague to attend the hearing of the International Court regarding the UK complaint to the Security Council. The UK maintained that Iran had unilaterally annulled the 1933 oil agreement with AIOC and had broken International Law. It considered that nationalization had been illegal according to international law. Once again, Mosaddeq came out on top when on 22 July 1952, the International Court of Justice ruled by 9 votes to 5 that the Court had no jurisdiction to deal with or rule over the dispute.

This was a final blow to Britain's claim that according to international law, Iran had acted illegally. Since the Security Council had ruled that it would defer the decision of jurisdiction to the International Court, the non-jurisdiction rule of the International Court had rendered Britain's complaint to the Security Council null and non-pursuable.

Britain's Economic Embargo

Even though the British legal claim against Iran was turned down at both the Security Council of the UN and the International Court of Justice, initially Britain succeeded in impounding foreign oil tankers carrying Iranian oil. In July 1952 British warships intercepted the Italian oil tanker *Rose Mary* which carried 700 tons of Iranian oil and forced it into the port of Aden, a British protectorate.

The British successfully argued before their own court that *Rose Mary* was in possession of 'wrongfully detained' or 'stolen goods belonging to the British'. In the end, the oil embargo succeeded in reducing Iranian oil production from around 700,000 barrels per day in 1950 to some 28,000 barrels per day in 1952–3. The dramatic decrease in oil production reflected Iran's inability to export oil, which in turn, adversely effected the Iranian economy.

Gradually, however, Iran succeeded in concluding agreements with Supor, an Italian company. On 14 February 1953, the oil tanker *Miriella* emptied its cargo of 4,600 tons of Iranian oil in Venice. The British tried to impound the contents of the ship, but on 11 March a Venice court rejected the British 'application for judicial sequestration' of *Miriella*'s Iranian oil.[61] On 10 April, *Miriella* arrived in Venice with a second cargo of Iranian oil and two days before, another Italian tanker, the *Alba*, had unloaded 10,000 tons of Iranian oil at the Port of Leghorn in Italy.

The Japanese followed the Italian lead in running the blockade. The Japanese company Idemitsu Kosan signed an agreement with Iran and obtained a 50 per cent price discount. Paying no heed to British threats on 13 April 1953, *Nissho Maru* loaded 22,000 tons of Iranian oil at Abadan and sailed to Japan. The British filed complaints, but eventually dropped their case. The blockade, the last act of British aggression short of war against Mosaddeq, was failing.

On 19 August 1953, the day Mosaddeq was overthrown, another 18,000-ton tanker, the *Koiemaro* belonging to Idemitsu, entered Abadan to load Iranian oil for Japan. Iran's sale of her oil to small companies threatened the hold of what came to be the **Seven Sisters**, disrupting the existing oligopolistic oil market. Mosaddeq was not only a nuisance to the British, but to the established international oil producers dominated by a few Western countries.

Mosaddeq and Domestic Policies: The Mosaddeq–Kashani Alliance

The interaction between domestic political forces and Mosaddeq went through two broad phases. The first phase began with Mosaddeq's premiership in late April 1951 and lasted until 21 July 1952, when Mosaddeq was returned to power after a five-day revolt against Qavam's premiership. During this first period, Mosaddeq was confronted with the opposition of the radical Islamic Devotees of Islam, the pro-Soviet communist Tudeh Party and the royalists strongly supported by the British. Mosaddeq, however, enjoyed widespread popularity as the hero of the oil nationalization movement and was supported by the parties and organizations constituting the National Front, as well as Kashani's widespread religio-political network.

Immediately after Mosaddeq became prime minister, the Devotees of Islam parted ways with the Mosaddeq–Kashani axis. They felt used and abandoned after Razmara's assassination. Navab-Safavi saw Razmara as the major obstacle to oil nationalization and hoped that by liquidating him, the Mosaddeq–Kashani alliance would come to power and pave the way for the implementation of Islamic edicts and an Islamic government.

Mosaddeq, however, refused Navab-Safavi's requests to move society towards an Islamic state. Navab-Safavi had instructed Mosaddeq to make Friday prayers compulsory at government offices, impose the veil, fire women from government offices and ban alcoholic beverages. Kashani stood by Mosaddeq, emphasizing that the oil nationalization was the principal preoccupation of the day.

Convinced that he had been betrayed, Navab-Safavi turned against both Kashani and Mosaddeq, and threatened to assassinate them. In June 1951, Navab-Safavi was arrested and remained in prison until January 1953. In February 1952, *Nabarde Mellat* (People's Combat), the Devotees of Islam's paper which continued to be published by Amirabdollah Karbaschian, was calling Mosaddeq mad, hysterical and syphilitic.

Mosaddeq on Political Alignments in September 1951

In this country there are three outlooks. First, the supporters of British policy in Iran . . . Second, the outlook of those inclined to left ideologies . . . seeking help from others . . . Third, the outlook of patriots . . . whose supporters argue that Iran should control whatever is hers . . . (M. Mosaddeq)[62]

The Tudeh Party's reaction to Mosaddeq and the National Front was negative and hostile. As early as 25 September 1950, the Tudeh Party paper, *Besuye Ayandeh* (Towards the Future) labelled National Front representatives in the Majles as hypocrites and demagogues, who spoke about the people but knew nothing about their hardships. The paper described Mosaddeq as colonialism's last resort and considered the National Front, as 'reactionary . . . vile . . . and a false reformist organization'.[63] The Tudeh Party had a hard time digesting the fact that Mosaddeq and Kashani, hardly the typical revolutionary leaders, had replaced them in Iran's anti-colonial and anti-imperialist struggle.

The Tudeh Party's papers and political rallies aimed at destabilizing Mosaddeq's government and accused him of being an American stooge. The first of these demonstrations attracted 20,000 workers on 15 July 1951. The date conveniently coincided with the arrival of Averell Harriman, the US secretary of commerce. Harriman was delivering a message from President Truman, to mediate between the

British and the Iranian governments. The Tudeh Party demonstrators clashed with the anti-Tudeh members of Baqai's Party. The police and army had to intervene, leading to the death and injury of many. The Tudeh Party held Mosaddeq responsible for the attack on its demonstration.

On 28 July 1951, the Tudeh Party's newspaper wrote, 'the anti-patriotic government of Dr. Mosaddeq has stepped towards murdering the people, [embracing] fascism, lying, and obeying the colonial policies of the US'.[64] By July 1951, Tudeh Party supporters were chanting slogans such as 'death to Mosaddeq' at their rallies. In August, Mosaddeq was accused of resolving the oil issue to the benefit of imperialism and of treachery towards Iranians. During the elections to 17th Majles in January 1952, the Tudeh Party newspapers continued to treat Mosaddeq as a stooge of US imperialism.

The shah had wanted the 63-year-old Seyyed Zia, the British candidate, to replace Razmara, and his reaction to Mosaddeq's premiership was at best lukewarm. He could not openly oppose Mosaddeq, because of his popularity, but constantly complained about him to his advisors. The shah suspected that Mosaddeq had a republican agenda. In mid-July 1951, the shah informed Shepherd that 'he was convinced that Mussadiq must be got rid of as soon as possible'.[65]

The shah had initially hoped to oust Mosaddeq through normal parliamentary channels. For this purpose, he had mobilized his loyal deputies, such as Mohammad-Ali Shushtari, Jamal Emami and Hadi Taheri, who also happened to be well-known pro-British politicians, to attack Mosaddeq in the Majles. To further undermine Mosaddeq's government, the court and the British constantly prompted Seyyed Zia, who had a considerable political network to revive his National Will Party and intensify his anti-Mosaddeq activities on the streets.

An assortment of newspapers, such as Abolhasan Amidi-Nuri's *Daad* (Justice), Mehdi Mirashrafi's *Atash* (Fire), Ali Hashemi-Haeri's *Tolu* (Dawn) and Abbas Shahandeh's *Farman* (Edict) acted as the court's mouthpiece against Mosaddeq and Kashani, hurling abuse at them. *Atash* regularly called Mosaddeq a British agent and the enemy of freedom. It labelled Mosaddeq's government as filthy and murderous and went as far as claiming that the prime minister's blood was forfeit as he was not a Muslim. With Mosaddeq's ascension to power, the press experienced a freedom never experienced before, as Mosaddeq refused to censor or silence even the worst of his detractors.

Unable to unseat Mosaddeq and faced with his growing popularity despite the prolongation of the oil crisis and the increasing economic hardship caused by the blockade, on 26 December 1951, the shah informed Loy Henderson, the US ambassador to Iran, that 'since there was no organized effective opposition to Mosaddeq in [the] country, he did not see how any change could be effected except by [a] coup'.[66]

As long as the Mosaddeq-Kashani alliance held, the anti-Mosaddeq forces remained unsuccessful in destabilizing his government. Mosaddeq's focus on foreign and oil policy, left the management of the National Front and internal politics to

Kashani. Since becoming prime minister, Mosaddeq had announced that he no longer belonged to the National Front. He also refused to pack his government with National Front members, alienating some of his original allies who had hoped for a position in his government.

As Mosaddeq withdrew from the National Front and ceased to attend its meetings, Kashani took greater control of the National Front. Mozaffar Baqai and his political organization, *Hezbze zahmatkeshan mellat Iran* (Iranian People's Toilers Party), which he had founded on 17 May 1951, allied themselves with Kashani, intentionally driving a wedge in the Mosaddeq–Kashani alliance. As early as 21 June 1951, Baqai sought to cause jealousy between the two by referring to Kashani as 'the great religious leader', knowing that Mosaddeq was called the 'national leader'.

Kashani, however, stood firmly by Mosaddeq. Under Kashani's leadership, Qanatabadi and Baqai organized and mobilized huge street demonstrations and rallies in the name of the National Front. When opposition deputies attacked Mosaddeq on 11 December 1951, and chants of, 'Death to Mosaddeq!' in the Majles were countered with, 'Death to British lackeys!', Mosaddeq decided to resign. At that crucial moment, it was Kashani who stood firm and dissuaded him. Two days later, Kashani organized a massive demonstration in support of Mosaddeq.

The elections to the 17th Majles, which began on 27 December 1951, caused the first fissures in the Mosaddeq–Kashani alliance. In the absence of Mosaddeq on the domestic political scene, the National Front, relegated all important decisions concerning the selection of candidates, arbitration of internal disagreements and the election campaign to Kashani.

Kashani repeatedly announced that he would not intervene in the elections, yet he and his close allies Qanatabadi and Baqai, bent the rules. They exerted local pressure, and even interfered in the election to get their own candidates elected. Criticism of Kashani's cronyism and nepotism during the election, created rifts within the National Front, and exposed Mosaddeq's government to serious attacks and accusations.

Irregularities on the part of Kashani's friends reflected poorly on Mosaddeq and his claim to run fair elections. Mosaddeq's stopping or suspension of elections in 55 districts, raised questions. It is true that in some cases the elections were stopped because of the army's meddling, but in other cases, the elections were aborted simply because it seemed as if the National Front's rivals were ahead in the polls.

The elections to the 17th Majles ended up being a mixture of free elections and engineered ones and there was evidence of tampering from both sides: the court and the army, Kashani and Mosaddeq. The upshot was that Mosaddeq obtained a parliamentary faction of around 30 members out of 73 deputies. The remaining 43 deputies were either anti-Mosaddeq deputies or independents. The outcome of the Majles election had left Mosaddeq in a fragile state which was only worsened when an attempt was made on the life of his minister of foreign affairs on 15 February 1952. Mohammad-Mehdi Abdekhodai, a 15-year-old member of the Devotees of Islam, tried to assassinate Hoseyn Fatemi but failed (Figure 4.8). Abdolhoseyn Vahedi, who had taken over the Devotees of Islam while Navab-Safavi was in prison, had ordered the hit.

Twelve days later, when on 27 April 1952, the 17th Majles was inaugurated by the shah, Mosaddeq brooded and stayed home. Mosaddeq was critical of his own government for failing to prevent illegal interferences and influence-peddling. The honeymoon between Kashani and Mosaddeq came to an end as each blamed the other. Kashani became a reproachful and fault-finding partner, while Mosaddeq felt that his understanding of political democracy and free elections differed from Kashani's.

Both parties continued, however, to stand by one another temporarily ceasing outright hostility. Kashani brushed aside rumours of their differences and schisms, while he began looking for alternative alliances. By 11 March 1952, the British Embassy in Iran was reporting that Kashani had met Gen. Zahedi, who by this time had become a British favourite to replace Mosaddeq. As the oil dispute dragged on, it wore down and strained all sides to the dispute. And as the Mosaddeq camp became enfeebled by internal dissent, the opposition became more organized, focused and belligerent.

On 5 July 1952, upon his return from The Hague, as was the democratic political protocol, Mosaddeq tendered his resignation to the new Majles and on the next day, 52 out of the 65 deputies voted in favour of his renewed premiership. Ten days later, Mosaddeq met with the shah to discuss the members of his new cabinet. The shah objected to Mosaddeq nominating himself minister of war, and Mosaddeq retorted that the Ministry of War had become a government within the government, and he needed to be sure of the loyalty of his ministers. The shah and the prime minister reached a dead end on this issue, and Mosaddeq resigned on the evening of 16 July 1952.

Figure 4.8 Mosaddeq with Hoseyn Fatemi (to his right) and Hoseyn Makki (third to his left). *Source: Via Alamy.*

On Thursday 17 July 1952, while the Majles was surrounded with tanks, armoured vehicles, and soldiers and as the pro-Mosaddeq faction refused to attend the parliamentary session, the Majles voted in favour of Qavam, as prime minister. Qavam's appointment had the full support of the British and American governments which were delighted by the seemingly smooth removal of Mosaddeq from power and felt that the road was paved for a 'reasonable' government.

Qavam's government lasted five days. Throughout these five days, Qavam and Hoseyn Ala, minister of court were in close contact with George Middleton, the British chargé d'affaires in Tehran, while the shah was in contact with Henderson, the American ambassador to Iran. Henderson and Middleton, in turn were in close contact with one another. Once news of Mosaddeq's resignation and his replacement reached the provinces, shops closed in protest.

In Tehran, from early Friday morning 18 July, crowds shouting slogans in favour of Mosaddeq and against Qavam spontaneously poured out and converged on Baharestan, the seat of the Majles, which was surrounded by the military. Clashes began in Tehran, while Qavam went on radio and promised to solve the oil crisis. Qavam threatened that he would deal with the opposition by setting up revolutionary courts and punishing criminals.

On the same day, Kashani came to Mosaddeq's defence and called on the people to rise in his support. The bazaar closed completely, the bus services came to a halt, phone lines connecting government services and offices were disabled and people took over the streets, refusing to go home. The Tudeh Party, indifferent to Mosaddeq's resignation, nonetheless joined the anti-Qavam camp on 20 July at Kashani's behest. The Tudeh Party continued to blame Mosaddeq for collaborating with the court and imperialism, yet it was more fearful of Qavam's repression once he had consolidated his power.

Tehran was completely paralyzed as a rainbow opposition to Qavam took shape and the people were in outright rebellion. On Monday, 21 July 1952, Tehran was the scene of bloody clashes as the army opened fire on the people, killing some 25 to 63 and wounding approximately 280. Despite the British and American efforts to convince Qavam to hold on to power in the afternoon of 21 July, Tehran Radio announced the prime minister's resignation. On the next day, the Majles voted in favour of Mosaddeq. With Mosaddeq's triumphant return to power, his domestic enemies, Seyyed Zia, Asadollah Rashidiyan and Mehdi Mirashrafi, contacted the British and suggested a coup to get rid of him.

The British Chargé d'Affaires on Mosaddeq

It now looks as though the only thing to stop Persia falling into communist hands is a coup d'état. (G. Middleton)[67]

The 21 July uprising, known to Iranians as *Qiyame Siye Tir*, demonstrated that the soft approach to removing Mosaddeq was doomed to failure. Faced with Mosaddeq's rising popularity, the idea of a military intervention or a coup was resuscitated among his opposition. But to move ahead with this plan, Mosaddeq had to be isolated, Kashani had to be turned, Gen. Zahedi who was popular among the forces loyal to the shah had to be groomed to lead the coup and, most importantly, the US had to give the green light.

The British assessment of the shah's political role in fostering change after the 21 July uprising was bleak. Middleton wrote, 'The Shah hates taking decisions, and cannot be relied upon to stick to them; he has no moral courage and easily succumbs to fear; he is pre-occupied with his personal position on the throne and thinks to retain it by a policy of appeasement.'[68] The coup had to take place in the shah's name but without any direct help from him.

Mosaddeq and Domestic Policies: The Kashani–Zahedi Alliance

From 21 July 1952 to 19 August 1953, when Mosaddeq was ousted by a coup, his adversaries closed rank, reorganized and succeeded to co-opt Kashani and his allies. During this period, however, faced with the imminent danger of a joint British–court coup, Mosaddeq's old foe, the Tudeh Party, reluctantly supported the prime minister. Relying on information obtained by its military organization, the Tudeh Party papers warned of the anti-Mosaddeq plots in the army and pressed the prime minister to punish the traitors decisively.

Following the uncovering of a coup plot involving Zahedi, Baqai and the Rashidiyan brothers and reports that Middleton, the British chargé d'affaire, was among the plotters, Iran severed diplomatic ties with Britain on 22 October 1952. In mid-November 1952, Montague Woodhouse, the Secret Intelligent Service (SIS) station chief in Tehran before the severance of diplomatic relations, travelled to Washington and proposed 'Operation Boot' to overthrow Mosaddeq.

From February to August 1953, while the CIA and the SIS prepared for a last resort coup against Mosaddeq, their domestic accomplices fomented well-coordinated and planned crises. For six months, every effort was made by the anti-Mosaddeq forces to destabilize the Mosaddeq government and force it to fall without going to the extreme of ousting it through a coup.

On 28 February 1953, against the advice of Mosaddeq, the shah announced that he would leave the country on vacation. Kashani and his new ally, the well-known pro-British Ayatollah Mohammad Behbahani, used this opportunity to present Mosaddeq as a power-hungry villain who intended to chase the shah away from the country, change the regime and impose a dictatorship. The anti-Mosaddeq forces composed of members of Baqai's Toilers Party and three smaller parties, Ariya, SUMKA and Zolfaqar, mobilized their troops and brought the ruffians of south Tehran onto the streets.

The Ariya Party was the brainchild of the anti-communist, pro-British Gen. Hasan Arfa, with connections to Baqai's shock troopers. SUMKA, was Iran's fascist National Socialist Workers Party, led by Davud Monshizadeh. Its members wore black shirts and armbands with an insignia very similar to the fascist swastika and greeted one another with the standard Nazi salute. Supported by members of pro-Shah retired and active officers, a large right-wing crowd gathered around the shah's house pleading with him not to leave the country.

Once the shah agreed to stay, the crowd tried to break into Mosaddeq's house. For two days, Tehran was the scene of clashes between pro-Mosaddeq and anti-Mosaddeq forces. By the evening of 2 March, the first attempt of the anti-Mosaddeq front had failed. Yet, it had succeeded in driving an irreconcilable wedge between the shah and Mosaddeq and presented Mosaddeq as the shah's enemy. This tactic forced non-politicized people, who were not privy to political details, to choose between the monarch and Mosaddeq. Meanwhile, Mosaddeq continued to remain loyal to the monarchy.

After the unrest of 28 February, the press supporting the newly formed Kashani–Zahedi–Behbahani axis, representing the court, hammered at the myth that Mosaddeq and his friends were intent on changing the regime, dismembering the country, establishing a republic, banishing clerical leaders and dismantling the army. Their propaganda presented Mosaddeq in league with the communists and the Tudeh Party, and a Soviet puppet paving the way for a communist Iran. On 4 April 1953, Allen Dulles, the director of the CIA, authorized a budget of $1 million to be used 'in any way that would bring about the fall of Mosaddeq'.[69]

Sixteen days later, Lt Gen. Mahmud Afshartus, Mosaddeq's chief of police was abducted in Tehran. Afshartus, a popular officer, was one of the four founding members of the pro-Mosaddeq 'Nationalist Army Officers'. His dead body was found on 26 April 1953. The military officers involved in Afshartus' abduction and murder were members of the two overlapping pro-Zahedi, pro-Shah and anti-Mosaddeq organizations of the 'Retired Officers' Association' and the 'Devotees of the Shah'. Both organizations had played a crucial role in the unrest of 28 February and would also play a key role in the August 1953 coups. The military personnel involved constituted the operational team while the planning and commandeering team was composed of two civilians, the enigmatic Hoseyn Khatibi and Mozaffar Baqai.

The murderers of Afshartus aimed at destabilizing Mosaddeq's government, eliminating a very effective and daring pro-Mosaddeq officer, demonstrating the government's vulnerability and ineptitude, disseminating fear among the military supporters of Mosaddeq, fostering an atmosphere of insecurity, forcing Mosaddeq's resignation by arresting or liquidating other key supporters of his, and eventually abducting or murdering the prime minister.

On the Majles front, from 16 April 1953, Ala, the court minister in collusion with Henderson, the American ambassador, decided to paralyze the legislative process. To this end, pro-court deputies were ordered not to attend parliamentary sessions. Many left Tehran for the provinces. In the absence of a quorum, the Majles was unable to legislate and the affairs of the country were left in limbo. The country was again plunged into another crisis.

By mid-May, having failed to attain their objective of bringing down the Mosaddeq government, pro-court deputies were instructed to change tactics and resume attendance. Subsequently, the Majles became the arena of unusual verbal abuse and physical clashes between the deputies supporting and opposing Mosaddeq. Turning Parliament into a vulgar circus was the opposition's new tactic of bringing the legislature to a halt.

On 1 July 1953, the anti-Mosaddeq coalition was served a major blow when Kashani lost the presidency of the Majles to Abdollah Moazami, a Mosaddeqist deputy. Tired of a dysfunctional parliament, which had become a centre of agitation, commandeered by the court and foreigners and weary of the daily plots against his government, Mosaddeq announced holding a referendum on the dissolution of the 17th Majles. In a not entirely democratic process of voting, with separate booths for those who agreed and disagreed, the yes vote to dissolve the 17th Majles won by an overwhelming majority.

The Coups

On 25 June 1953, a meeting took place in Washington with eleven high-powered government, diplomatic, military and secret service officials. In the presence of Allen Dulles (director of the CIA), John Foster Dulles (secretary of the state), Charles Wilson (secretary of defence), Loy Henderson (the American ambassador to Iran) and Kermit Roosevelt (chief of the coup operation), the plan to overthrow Mosaddeq was given official approval. According to Kermit Roosevelt, the original proposal of TPAJAX had come from British intelligence. This was to be a three-way cooperative and clandestine operation involving the shah, Churchill, Eden and other British representatives, Eisenhower, John Foster Dulles and the CIA. The clearly stated objective of the operation was to overthrow Mosaddeq.

As of 19 July 1953, the CIA agents in charge of the coup entered Tehran beginning with Kermit Roosevelt and followed by George Carroll. Efforts had to be made to make the shah overcome his fear of the coup. The shah had to be prepared, prepped and cajoled. Having met with Princess Ashraf in France to obtain her cooperation, Asadollah Rashidiyan met with the shah six times to convince him that the US and the UK were fully on board, involved in and behind the coup. Kermit Roosevelt met with the shah twice, and the key Iranian military players briefed the monarch on those involved in operation.

Late at night on Saturday, 15 August, the first coup began by officers and soldiers of the Iranian army loyal to the shah. This was a military coup minutely planned by the CIA, with an important legal aspect to it. Col. Nasiri, commander of the Imperial Guards, was to serve Mosaddeq with the shah's royal edict dismissing him as prime minister. In case Mosaddeq disobeyed, he was to be arrested by Nasiri. At this time, Gen. Zahedi who had another royal edict which appointed him as prime minister, was to step in and replace Mosaddeq.

Nasiri arrived at Mosaddeq's house at around 1.40 am on Sunday, 16 August. He handed Mosaddeq his dismissal edict but was subsequently arrested by the military personnel defending Mosaddeq's house. The troops that were supposed to help in Mosaddeq's arrest if he was to refuse the royal edict, which he did, were delayed. They showed up after Nasiri's arrest, and then turned around and went back to their barracks empty-handed.

Simultaneously, the coup officers had planned to arrest Gen. Mohammad-Taqi Riyahi, the chief of staff, Hoseyn Fatemi, minister of foreign affairs, Jahangir Haqshenas, minister of roads, and Ahmad Zirakzadeh a high-profile Mosaddeqist deputy. Even though they succeeded in capturing Fatemi, Haqshenas and Zirakzadeh, their nocturnal assault to arrest Riyahi and occupy his headquarters was a complete flop. Gen. Batmanqelich, who was tasked to lead this key operation 'lost heart and went into hiding'.[70] The first radio announcement of the aborted coup went on air at 7.00 am on 16 August. At 10.15 am on the same day, having received coded news of the failed coup, the shah left for Baghdad. The monarch fled his country, heartbroken and baffled.

> ### The Shah's state of mind in Baghdad
> The Shah said that he is utterly at loss to understand why the plan failed. Trusted Palace officials were completely sure of its succeeding. The American friend was absolutely confident of its success. When he had said to the American if it should fail what should he do, the American scouted the possibility of failure adding when pressed, that the Shah should go to Baghdad. (Burton Berry, US ambassador to Iraq)[71]

While the shah was brooding in Baghdad, a second coup was hatched within the US Embassy compound. This 'council of war' was attended by Roosevelt, Carroll, the Zahedis (father and son), Gen. Hedayatollah Gilanshah, Col. Abbas Farzanegan and the three Rashidiyan brothers, and it was decided that action should be taken on Wednesday 19 August. The key feature of this second coup was that it would not be triggered by the military, which had been infiltrated by Tudeh and nationalist officers, but by the ruffians of south Tehran. Once the thugs, controlled by Rashidiyan,

Behbahani and Kashani occupied strategic and symbolic locations in Tehran, pro-shah army personnel would be sent in to fraternize with them, giving a semblance of the people and the army uniting against Mosaddeq.

The new plan neither specified a precise schedule for the completion of its various phases nor did it stipulate a deadline for the termination of activities. It was an open-ended operation until the objective of overthrowing Mosaddeq was realized. At this time, the movement of groups and crowds in Tehran was not particularly alarming as the previous two days had seen many such commotions. Therefore, until the crowds began chanting slogans, no one could tell who they supported. Whereas a movement of tanks and troops could have caused suspicion, the movement of crowds provided the best disguise until they stated their allegiance through their slogans. That is why the plan only involved tanks and soldiers in its last phase. Their arrival on the scene and fraternization with the 'patriotic' crowd, would announce the successful conclusion of the overthrow operation.

On 19 August 1953, the second coup unfolded as planned. Between 6.30 and 9.00 am, some 1,500–3,000 thugs armed with clubs and sticks, moved from four different points in the south of Tehran, and occupied the strategically significant streets and squares. Between 10.00 am and 3.00 pm, numerous trained undercover agents connected with the **TPBEDAMN** organization guided the newly injected military forces and the thugs to destroy previously designated opposition headquarters and papers. They subsequently occupied government buildings, took over the police and the military police headquarters, and most importantly Tehran's radio transmission station, which would broadcast Zahedi's victory over Mosaddeq.

From around 3.00 pm, Mosaddeq's house, where all his ministers had congregated, was attacked by the military using tanks. At around 7.00 pm, Mosaddeq ordered the military defending his house to lay down their arms and he and his close followers escaped from his house. By then, all five main army garrisons in Tehran were in the hands of pro-Zahedi officers. By nightfall, the Mosaddeq government had been overthrown by the combined effort of the CIA, SIS and their Iranian co-conspirators.

Factual and Analytical Questions

1. Why was Iran invaded by the Allies during the Second World War? What was the excuse and what were the real motives?
2. Explain and discuss the economic crises following the Allied invasion.
3. Explain the underlying causes of the clash between Qavam and the shah in the 1940s and contrast it with the clashes between Mosaddeq and the shah in the 1950s. Provide specific historical examples.
4. Evaluate the rule of the Azarbayjan Democratic Party.
5. What was the significance of the Qavam–Sadchikov Agreement?

6. Compare and contrast Qavam's Democratic Party of Iran with the Tudeh Party of Iran.
7. Who was Ahmad Kasravi? What was his message? What were his contradictions?
8. Who stood to gain from Mohammad-Reza Shah's assassination by Naser Fakhr-Arai? Make a case for Fakhr-Arai's motive to assassinate the shah.
9. Why did the Devotees of Islam assassinate Hajir and Razmara? Who stood to benefit from each assassination?
10. What is the gist of the 'Supplemental Agreement' or the 'Gass-Golshayan Agreement'? Why was it not acceptable to Iran? Speculate on whether Iran would have agreed to it had a 50/50 agreement been proposed by the British? Provide your arguments based on the prevailing realities and mood of the times.
11. Compare the political methods, objectives and principles of Kashani and Mosaddeq, what did they have in common and what distinguished them?
12. Outline the two phases in Mosaddeq's premiership. Could he have done something to assuage his enemies without compromising his principles?
13. Explain the origin and evolution of the idea of a coup against Mosaddeq.

Seminar Questions

1. 'The Azure Party, simply nationalist and not fascist.' Discuss. How many of its key figures played determining roles in the August 1953 coup against Mosaddeq?
2. 'The Tudeh Party was part nationalist and part a blind disciple of the Soviet Union.' Provide arguments with specific cases supporting one or another of these cases, or both.
3. 'The Azarbayjan Democratic Party and the autonomous movement of Azarbayjan were Stalin's bargaining chips for obtaining oil concessions in Iran.' Assess the degree of veracity of this statement.
4. Compare the political methods and principles of Qavam and Mosaddeq, what did they have in common and what distinguished them.
5. Analyse and assess the impact of Navab-Safavi and the Devotees of Islam on Iranian politics between 1946 and 1952. Did they serve or hinder democratization?
6. Why would the British Labour Party, the architect of nationalizing British industries and services, oppose nationalization of Iranian oil? Double standards? Logic of colonial and semi-colonial relations, politico-economic domination?
7. 'The oil nationalization movement would have succeeded had Mosaddeq and Kashani not separated.' Assess the above statement, with an eye to the reasons why they parted ways.

8 'The motives of the British, the Americans, the court and Kashani, with their associated co-conspirators, were different for supporting the coup against Mosaddeq.' Assess the above statement.

Discussion Questions

1 'The political consequences of the Allied invasion were both positive and negative. How did it disrupt and aid the development of democratic political institutions? To what extent did it allow for endogenous political initiative?' Discuss.
2 'The economic consequences of the allied invasion disorganized and retarded Iran's economic development for some five years.' Discuss.
3 'The Azarbayjan crisis brought the world close to a major US–Soviet confrontation.' Myth or fact, discuss.
4 'The reason why the Soviets withdrew their forces from Iran, abandoned Pishehvari and did not get an oil concession in Iran was because Qavam seduced and deceived Stalin or/and because of US diplomatic pressure and threat to use force.' Discuss. Can you think of any other possible argument?
5 'Kasravi was a product of Reza Shah's secularization campaign and Navab-Safavi was an extremist response to secularization and Kasravi's radical anti-Shiism.' Discuss and evaluate.
6 'Mosaddeq's "negative equilibrium" was a rash and zero-sum-thesis, harmful to Iran and discordant with laissez-faire economics and Cold War realities.' Assess and evaluate.
7 'During the oil crisis, Mosaddeq and the British spoke two different economic, political and cultural languages, even though Mosaddeq was Western-educated and Westernized.' Discuss the validity of this statement and if accurate, why?
8 'A coup against Mosaddeq was inevitable from the moment the oil was nationalized and Mosaddeq pursued its complete implementation.' Discuss by reviewing the chronology of events.

Glossary

Eyde Fetr (Eid al-Fitr) The feast of breaking the fasting month of Ramadan, during which Muslims fast from dawn to dusk.

***Ikhwan al-Muslemin* (Muslim Brotherhood)** A religio-political organization founded in 1928 by Hasan al-Banna to combat what he perceived as the economic, political and cultural invasion of Egypt by the West. Banna believed that the Quran provided a complete and perfect system of managing politics, society and the economy. The Muslim Brotherhood sought to impose an Islamic government. In 1940, the Brotherhood created an armed special branch to carry out political assassinations. By 1945, its membership grew to some 0.5–1 million. On 12 February 1949, Banna was gunned down by King Farouk's secret police.

Lend Lease On 11 March 1941, the US Congress passed an Act setting 'up a system that would allow the United States to lend or lease war supplies to any nation deemed "vital to the defense of the United States"'. Lend Lease enabled a neutral US to lease arms to Britain against the Axes. 'The supplies dispersed under the Lend-Lease Act ranged from tanks, aircraft, ships, weapons and road building supplies to clothing, chemicals and food.'[72]

Seven Sisters The term was coined by Enrico Mattei, the head of the Italian state oil company, and referred to the consortium that dealt with the international sale of Iranian oil after Mosaddeq's fall. It referred to the seven oil companies that controlled the world oil industry. The exclusive cartel was composed of the Anglo-Persian Oil Company (BP), Royal Dutch Shell, Standard Oil Company of California, Gulf Oil, Texaco, Standard Oil Company of New Jersey and Standard Oil Company of New York.

TPBEDAMN In the late 1940s, the CIA set up a covert organization under the code name 'Operation TPBEDAMN' in Iran to counter communism, the Tudeh Party and the Soviet threat. The TPBEDAMN's Iranian leaders were Ali Jalali and Farrokh Keyvani. According to Gasiorowski, it was the TPBEDAMN network which constituted the 'CIA's main political action network in Iran' and at the end of May 1953. 'Jalali and Keyvani had over one hundred sub-agents in their network.'[73]

Tudeh Faction/Group in the 14th Majles This faction was composed of Taqi Fadakar (Esfahan), Fereydun Keshavarz (Bandar Pahlavi), Reza Radmanesh (Lahijan), Ardashes (Ardeshir) Avanesiyan (Armenian), Abdolsamad Kambakhsh (Qazvin), Iraj Eskandari (Sari), Valiollah Shahab-Ferdows (Tabas), Mohammad Parvin-Gonabadi (Sabzevar), Zeinolabeddin Rahimzadeh-Khoi (Tabriz) and Rahmanqoli Khalatbari (Babol).

5

From Post-Coup to Post-Uprising, August 1953–June 1963

Chapter Outline

Iran after the Coup	233
Ala's Caretaker Government	243
Eqbal in Office	248
Two Elections, Sharif Emami's Brief Premiership and a Cursed 20th Majles	253
Amini's Premiership	257
Alam, the White Revolution and the Eclipse of Mosaddeqists	264
Ayatollah Khomeyni, the New Contender for Power	271
Glossary	280

Iran after the Coup

On Thursday, 20 August 1953, Iranians woke up to a new reality. The political hustle and bustle of the Mosaddeq days, typical of a society experimenting with democratic principles and modes of behaviour, albeit muddled, had given way to a deadly silence. Now, tanks watched over the comings and goings on the main streets of Tehran. Military rule followed its proper logic, and its expectations of correct conduct were different from what Iranians had been used to under Mosaddeq. The people needed to adjust quickly.

For twenty-eight months, Iranians had become accustomed to Mosaddeq's liberal and democratic style of government. Mosaddeq's tolerance of freedom of expression and criticism had raised the bar of democratic liberties in Iran. Citizens had come to take their freedoms for granted. The baby steps of political tolerance and dialogue were central in developing democratic values. The 1953 coup gagged this newly found voice of a people, practicing freedom even though not always successfully. It clipped their national pride and self-confidence.

> ## US Assessment of Mosaddeq in the Eye of Iranians Five Weeks after the Coup
>
> Some Iranians offer the unilateral explanation that the lingering favor for the former Government represents the hold on the public of Mosadeq's personality. Representatives of all shades of opinion stubbornly cling to the belief that Mosadeq was a patriot sincere in purpose. (R. M. Melbourne)[1]

The 1953 coup removed a prime minister who had remained loyal to the full implementation of the nationalization law, unyielding to British interests and unaccommodating to US recommendations for reconciliation with the British. The shah returned to Iran on Saturday 22 August indebted to his coup-making patrons for his crown. During his private meeting with Loy Henderson, the US ambassador to Iran, the shah 'expressed deep appreciation of the friendship which the US had shown him and Iran during the period'. The shah added that 'he would always feel deeply indebted for this proof of genuine friendship'.[2]

But for those who had been politically active and invested in the oil nationalization movement, proud of Iran's new status as a self-governing country and appreciative of Mosaddeq's attempt at democratization, the coup was cataclysmic. Post-coup Iranian poets and intellectuals conveyed a compelling sense of calamity in their works. They mourned the fate of Iran and Iranians.

> ## My House is on Fire
>
> My house is on fire, a life-burning fire, this fire is burning in all directions . . . I walk in all directions weeping amidst the smoke-filled flames . . . from their rooftops, my enemies watch over me while I am on fire, elated with victorious sly smiles on their lips, as I run in all directions weeping, I howl against this injustice, oh grief . . . By sunrise, they know that all my being will perish, my kind neighbours are sleeping happily in their beds, by morning only ashes will remain of me, oh grief, will my neighbours raise their heads from their sleep to help me, this unjust fire is burning me, I am howling alas, oh alas. (M. Akhavan-Sales)[3]

From 1953, the shah's regime strived to write its own history of events, while preventing the other side to express itself. Official post-coup accounts vilified the Mosaddeq era as one of chaos and destruction, saved by the 'national uprising' of

19 August 1953. The coup was presented as a spontaneous popular movement in favour of the shah.

For many Mosaddeq was a democratic and patriotic national hero overthrown by the CIA and SIS, with the collaboration of Iranian traitors, and for others, he was a power-hungry demagogue who had abused the well-founded nationalist sentiment of Iranians for his anti-constitutional, anti-monarchic and anti-democratic political ends. These two extreme positions were irreconcilable and even became more acute in time.

> ## US Assessment of CIA Influence in Iran after the Coup
>
> The change of government has resulted in greatly improved CIA contacts in government and military circles. Consequently, CIA capabilities have become greatly enhanced both in terms of short-term political action programs designed to support the existing government and in terms of long-range programs designed to promote the internal stability, general welfare, and strong western orientation of the country. (CIA)[4]

Political Consequences of the Coup

Within five days of the coup, some 200 people were arrested. Among them were Mosaddeq, his cabinet members, old pro-Mosaddeq Members of Parliament, high officials and the military personnel loyal to him. Four months after the coup, around 3,000 'suspect' government employees lost their jobs. This included around 1,000 teachers. According to the minister of education, the purge among 'deviant' teachers in September 1953 was such that the country faced a severe shortage of teachers during the 1953–4 academic year.

Born almost immediately after the coup, *Nehzate Moqavemat Melli* (National Resistance Movement) announced its existence by publishing and circulating 2,000 copies of a leaflet entitled *The Movement Continues*. The National Resistance Movement (NRM) was the first political organization opposing the coup. It had chosen a name reminiscent of the French resistance movement in Nazi-occupied France. This Mosaddeqist political group promised to pursue the goals of the national movement by opposing colonialism, as well as foreign-imposed and corrupt governments. It pursued reinstating the independence and rule of the people by following Mosaddeq's path and opposing the Zahedi government.

The coup had taken place in the heat of the Cold War and on the pretext of pre-empting a communist takeover. The new government was obsessed with purging the country of the Tudeh Party. On 23 September, 1,200 people were arrested on charges of being Tudeh Party members. The detention of ordinary citizens under the pretext of being Tudeh Party members became so pervasive that on 30 September 1953, the commander of the military police in Tehran reported that prisons under his command were swamped, and new detainees had to be interned at police stations throughout the city.

Newspapers reported that a 'Tudeh Party training centre' had been uncovered where different kinds of weapons were found along with books and pamphlets on the use of weaponry and guerrilla warfare. Zahedi's government fanned the anti-Tudeh hysteria to such an extent that the pro-government press reported on innocent individuals and even opponents of the Tudeh Party being denounced out of personal animosity and arrested. Reports spread that under orders of the military governor, who was acting as the administrator of martial law, Tudeh Party members had been mutilated in public, with noses, ears and fingers chopped off.

As the prisons swelled with inmates, opposition to the coup-government increased. On 8 October 1953, the NRM organized its first major demonstration. The triad of bazaar, high school and university students constituted the opposition's main social base. The bazaar went on strike along with Tehran University and several politicized high schools in Tehran. The tanks and armoured vehicles positioned in front of the bazaar did not deter the demonstrators, 300 of whom were later arrested. Concurrently, more than 2,000 high school students congregated in three different parts of the city chanting, 'Mosaddeq is victorious!' as they marched through the streets of Tehran.

On 7 November 1953, Mosaddeq's trial opened in Tehran. Placing Mosaddeq on trial was tantamount to putting the oil nationalization movement on trial. Yet, the regime had no alternative as it claimed that on 19 August the people had risen against a traitor. Protesting against Mosaddeq's trial, the NRM demonstration of 12 November once again brought high-school and university students, civil servants, members of the professional classes and bazaar workers to the streets.

Anticipating unrest, the government issued a decree ordering the police to shoot anyone writing anti-government slogans on walls. The police and soldiers were told to shoot after a single warning. By the day's end, many were injured, two were reported killed, and some 218 of those arrested were dispatched to the inhospitable prison on Khark island. When the Tehran bazaar closed its shutters in protest again, a targeted raid, led by troops and a special engineering unit, demolished sections of the bazaar ceiling.

What to Do with Mosaddeq

The Shah has decided that former Prime Minister Mossadeq must be tried and condemned to death, but he has not decided whether Mossadeq should then be pardoned by royal decree and immediately banished from Iran or immediately executed. (K. Roosevelt).[5]

A Hot December in Tehran

With all eyes on Mosaddeq's sensational trial, a joint communique was published simultaneously in Tehran and London on 1 December 1953, announcing the resumption of diplomatic relations between Iran and Britain. Reacting to this news and to Denis Wright's arrival as Britain's new chargé d'affaires, students at Tehran University staged a demonstration.

On 2 December, student disturbances spilt into the streets outside the university grounds. Four days later, soldiers clashed with students leading to injuries and arrests. Vice President Richard Nixon was scheduled to visit Iran the following week, on 9 December 1953. To pre-empt any further instabilities, the Zahedi government ordered troops to enter Tehran University, repress unrest and arrest dissident students and faculty.

On 7 December 1953, the atmosphere at Tehran University remained agitated as students continued to protest. At the Faculty of Engineering, a corporal entered the building with four machine-gun-toting soldiers and arrested two students. The students, who were accused of being disrespectful, were beaten up by the soldiers in front of their peers. As tensions mounted, recess bells were sounded to calm the commotion. Students poured out of their classrooms towards the main exit doors, only to find them blocked by armed soldiers. Surrounded by aggressive and nervous soldiers, the students started chanting, 'Military: hands off the university!' and 'Long live Mosaddeq!', as they moved towards the southern exit doors.

The soldiers opened fire on the students in the hallway, in the classrooms and even outside the building. The Faculty of Engineering building, splattered with blood, was shut down by the military and no one was allowed to enter or exit. At the end of the day, three students, Ahmad Qandchi-Mazandarani, Azar (Mehdi) Shariat-Razavi and Mostafa Bozorgnia, succumbed to their wounds and died. The date of 7 December or 16 Azar would come to symbolize the university's resistance against authoritarian rule and has been henceforth commemorated as 'university students' day'.

On the same day that violence broke out in Tehran University, the Intelligence Bureau of the Police informed printing houses in Tehran that only 47 out of the 432 licence-holding publications would be permitted to go to press. From the list of 47, some 20 had long been inactive, a handful were specialized professional publications and some 15 belonged to the old anti-Mosaddeq press which were now staunch Zahedi supporters.

Two days after the university events and concurrent with Richard Nixon's arrival in Tehran on 9 December 1953, student demonstrations erupted again. The students protested against the arrival of the US vice president and the presence of the military on Tehran University campus. High school students, mostly girls, took to the streets, chanting anti-Nixon slogans and distributing anti-Nixon pamphlets, both in Persian and English.

On 21 December 1953, when Denis Wright and his British diplomatic team of sixteen arrived at Tehran airport, the capital was placed under tight security. After fourteen months, the British Embassy in Tehran opened. Wright and the entire British delegation were met at the embassy door by demonstrators hurling bags of garbage and rotting kakis. Ironically, on the same evening, Mosaddeq's trial had come to an end after thirty-five court sessions. The presiding military judges had condemned Mosaddeq to three years of prison. The announcement caused another wave of student protest, mostly at Shahdokht High School for Girls.

Zahedi's Brief and Grief

The tug of war over Iranian oil, which had thrown the country into a crisis since March 1950, had to be dealt with under Zahedi's watch. What came to be called the 'oil problem' after the coup, had to be resolved to the satisfaction of international oil interests. The shah wished the problem resolved as quickly as possible. Legalizing any agreement needed the approval of the Parliament. The shah and Zahedi needed predictable and obedient parliamentarians, which could only be obtained by fixing the upcoming 18th Majles. Zahedi had assured Henderson that with a carefully concocted Majles, he could get the oil settlement passed. Even though the National Resistance Movement and the Mosaddeqists tried their luck in the Majles elections, they were completely shut out. The 136 deputies elected to the 18th Majles were carefully hand-picked and agreed upon by the shah and Zahedi. The deputies were the outcome of a selection rather than an election process.

> ### CIA Report on Its Involvement in the 18th Majles
>
> The Shah and the Prime Minister are in agreement on a joint slate of candidates to be supported for election to the Majlis. The Station believes that in most constituencies the government supported candidate will win and the Station has been very active in influencing the composition of the government slate. (J. Waller)[6]

For Zahedi, the forceful shutting-out of the Mosaddeqist opposition was easier than dealing with a new and powerful adversarial block. The shah had always been suspicious of independent minded and strong prime ministers such as Qavam, Razmara and Mosaddeq. They overshadowed him and made him feel weak. After his 'triumphant' return, the shah wanted to start on a clean slate and exert his authority, beginning with direct control over military appointments and affairs. Less than a month after the coup, Zahedi and the shah disagreed over the minister of defence and whether the chief of staff should report to the shah or the prime minister.

To undermine Zahedi, the shah prompted deputies, officers, politicians, religious leaders and newspaper editors such as Hasan Akhavi, Nader Batmanqelich, Mozaffar Baqai, Ayatollah Mohammad Behbahani and Abbas Shahandeh, all pro-British figure, to write and speak against him. Finally, Zahedi also started to lose the support of some of his key allies. Influential religious and political figures, such as Ayatollah Kashani, Hoseyn Makki and Abolhasan Haerizadeh, who had defected to Zahedi's camp against Mosaddeq before the coup, were growing restless with Zahedi's conciliatory approach to British interests. Baqai played a complicated game. He pretended to be on Kashani's side, but contrary to Kashani, Baqai was supported by the shah, the post-coup officers and the British.

On 18 February 1954, Kashani complained to journalists that conditions in Iran had never been so disturbing and pitiful. He denounced fraud and the absence of freedoms during the elections and warned that whatever agreement was ratified by the unrepresentative 18th Majles would not be acceptable to the people. Kashani, the staunch anti-British, opposed efforts by the shah and Zahedi to quietly resolve the 'oil problem'.

At the inauguration of the 18th Majles, on 18 March 1954, the shah announced his pleasure at having been 'faithful to his oath of safeguarding the constitution' despite 'unfortunate events' and promised that the 'oil problem' would be quickly resolved. Negotiations between representatives of the international oil consortium and the Iranian government began on April 14.

The Consortium negotiation team was at first headed by Orville Harden, vice president of Standard Oil Company. The Consortium oil pie was divided between Britain (40%), the US (40%), Netherlands (14%), and France (6%). Aside from Consortium–Iranian government negotiations, there were also regular meetings between the Iranian delegation and the British delegation to work out the compensation issue. Behind the scenes, there were lengthy discussions between the trio of the British and American ambassadors, plus Herbert Hoover of the Department of State and the duo of Ali Amini and Abdollah Entezam, the ministers of finance and foreign affairs. Whenever Amini and Entezam met an obstacle in their negotiations with either the Consortium or the British delegation, they turned to the two Americans, Henderson and Hoover.

Aware of the public's mistrust towards British and US designs, the sensitive negotiations with the Oil Consortium were led by Amini in a highly secretive manner. Neither the lower nor the upper chamber of the Parliament were privy to the secret discussions, and there was a complete ban on any discussion pertaining to oil negotiations. Even though the shah and Zahedi wished to see the oil issue resolved, they also needed to save face by claiming that the principle of oil nationalization was being fully respected.

While the 18th Parliament was in a prolonged summer recess, an announcement was made that on 5 August 1954 an oil agreement had been reached between Ali

Amini and the new head of the Consortium, Howard Page. The press, under close surveillance, limited its reactions to commenting that 'this was the best that could be obtained under the prevailing international circumstances' and that there was 'no other choice than to solve the oil problem'.[7]

> ### An Assessment of the Agreement by an Iranian Oil Expert
>
> The 1954 Agreement failed to achieve the main objectives of the 1951 oil nationalization which were the complete control and management of the oil industry by the National Iranian Oil Company (NIOC). (P. Mina)[8]

The Iranians in effect outsourced the operation, development and international sale of their 'nationalized' asset to the Consortium. 'In no case could the host country interfere in the running of the concession.'[9] The agreement was a 'resounding triumph for the British and the International Petroleum Cartel, and a catastrophic defeat for the national aspiration of Iran'.[10]

Some two and a half months after publicizing the oil agreement, Zahedi, dressed in full military garb, attended the special session of Parliament ratifying the Amini–Page oil agreement on 21 October 1954. Out of the 120 deputies present, 113 voted in favour and 5 voted against the oil agreement. Just as the shah and Zahedi felt beholden to the US and the UK, the carefully hand-picked members of Parliament, in turn, felt indebted to the shah and Zahedi.

In accordance with the shah's wishes, Zahedi had fixed the Majles and repressed all dissenting voices to get the oil agreement ratified. Five months earlier, the shah had wished to replace Zahedi and sought approval from Henderson. But Henderson had assured him that 'it would be preferable not to change horses in mid-stream unless really necessary'.[11]

The Demise of the Tudeh Party

On 27 December 1953, the powerful position of Tehran's military governor changed hands. Gen. Farhad Dadsetan, a Zahedi protégé, was replaced by Gen. Teymur Bakhtiyar who had the reputation of an iron-fisted and ruthless commander (Figure 5.1). With an eye to fixing the 18th Majles and assuring the smooth ratification of the oil agreement, the opposition of all shades and forms had to be tightly controlled. Even the soft opposition press and those politicians such as Baqai who had the shah's permission to act as fiery antagonists of the regime, had to tread carefully.

Figure 5.1 Gen. Teymur Bakhtiyar. *Source: Wikimedia Commons.*

On 11 September 1954, Teymur Bakhtiyar announced that the Officers' Organization of the Tudeh Party had infiltrated the army, the police and the gendarmerie and planned to overthrow the monarchy. The barrage of news on uncovering this clandestine, powerful and communist organization overshadowed all other national stories, especially the Amini–Page oil agreement. The Officers' Organization was the Tudeh Party's military and clandestine branch led by Khosrow Ruzbeh. With a twelve-year record of infiltration and covert operations, it had established a widespread network throughout the armed forces.

Between 19 October 1954 and 17 August 1955, twenty-seven were executed in connection with the Officers' Organization. All were officers except one civilian, the poet, journalist and literatus, Morteza Keyvan. Furthermore, 421 members of the Officers' Organization received sentences from life to 18 months' imprisonment. During this same period, some 3,469 members of the Tudeh Party, not to be confused with members of the Officers' Organization, were also arrested.

In Bakhtiyar's assault on the Tudeh Party and its various organizations, three members of the party's five-man Executive Committee, Mohammad Bahrami, Morteza Yazdi and Ali Owlovi, were arrested. The other two, Hoseyn Jowdat and Nureddin Kianuri, remained in Iran clandestinely and left the country by early 1956, relegating all affairs to Khosrow Ruzbeh. The rest of the Tudeh Party leaders were already abroad. The Officers' Organization had planned and executed the daring escape of ten high-profile Tudeh Party leaders from prison on 15 December 1950. Seven went overseas, while others trickled out of the country gradually, gravitating towards East Germany.

Khosrow Ruzbeh was one of the founders of the Officers' Organization of the Tudeh Party back in 1942 and had successfully escaped many arrests. Ruzbeh was a shrewd and nimble covert operator. In the absence of the Tudeh Party leaders, and the ruinous assault on Tudeh members and sympathizers and the Party's subsequent disintegration and collapse, Ruzbeh tried to salvage the remnants of the organization. He was, however, arrested on 6 July 1957 after a shoot-out with the security forces and secretly executed on 11 May 1958.

With the death of Ruzbeh, the active presence of the Tudeh Party ended in Iran and would not resurface until after the 1979 revolution. After his execution, Ruzbeh became a hero of the Tudeh Party and was praised as a symbol of selfless resistance and combat. Siyavush Kasrai, the notable Iranian modern poet and a Tudeh Party member, dedicated his now classic compilation of epic poems, *Arash the Archer*, to the memory of Khosrow Ruzbeh.

Aside from the widespread execution of Tudeh officers, two killings marked Iranians. Before sunrise on Wednesday, 10 November 1954, Hoseyn Fatemi, Mosaddeq's outspoken minister of foreign affairs and the editor of National Front's organ *Bakhtare Emrooz* (Today's East), faced the firing squad. He was 38 years old, bold and a republican at heart. Even though a few influential politicians tried to intervene and prevent Fatemi's execution, they failed. Fatemi's execution was as senseless as the murder of Amir-Mokhtar Karimpur-Shirazi on 15 March 1954. Karimpur-Shirazi was the staunch pro-Mosaddeq editor and director of the daily *Shuresh* (Insurgence). After the coup, he had been arrested, imprisoned and said to have been tortured before being set on fire. At the time of his cruel death, Karimpur-Shirazi was 33.

In both cases, the shah seemed to be taking disproportionate revenge for the fiery editorials of two journalists who had spoken against him and his court. In his fiery speech on 16 August 1953, Fatemi had referred to the Pahlavi Court as ignoble, murderous, corrupt and a thirty-year-old British base. The shah was gradually imposing his authority and displaying his power to dispense justice as he saw fit.

Exit Zahedi

After the 1953 coup, Zahedi had succeeded in repressing the nationalist opposition, crushing the Tudeh Party and its military organization, enforcing order, putting Mosaddeq on trial and behind bars, re-establishing diplomatic relations with Britain and most importantly, getting the Amini–Page oil agreement ratified by the Majles. In the process, Zahedi had strengthened his position domestically as well as internationally. The popularity of Zahedi caused the envy and suspicion of the shah and his entourage.

Zahedi's usefulness had come to an end and in January 1955, a loud chorus of deputies in the Majles and newspapers began attacking the prime minister. Zahedi was suddenly accused of failing to act according to national interests and of misusing a $75 million grant from the US as well as a $25 million aid from the Point Four Program.

On 30 January 1955, Jafar Behbahani, who had been made deputy because of the services his father had rendered during the coup, accused Zahedi's government of corruption, embezzlement, arbitrariness, repression, torture and disregard for individual freedoms. Without support from the court and Teymur Bakhtiyar, Behbahani would never have dared to make such a speech.

The shah was eager to turn the page. Zahedi would be the last of the strong-willed, hard-nosed and proud prime ministers who did not consider himself to be the shah's obedient servant. In a 1955 private conversation with E. A. Bayne, the shah confided in him that the life of a man who decides to 'rule instead of reign' was indeed a 'lonely and unhappy one'. The shah informed his interlocutor that, 'I am going to rule.'[12]

Zahedi's stature as a powerful general and prime minister was also a painful reminder of a time when the shah had been a weak monarch incapable of maintaining his reign, let alone his rule. With Zahedi out of the picture, the shah hoped to erase that memory. On 12 March 1955, the shah returned from his three-month-long trip to the US and Europe. On 6 April 1955, while Parliament was in recess, he demanded Zahedi's resignation and appointed Hoseyn Ala as prime minister. The shah wished to rule and was no longer going to ask Parliament to nominate a prime minister. Zahedi left Iran for Switzerland.

Ala's Caretaker Government

Hoseyn Ala was a seasoned politician who had served in numerous sensitive positions, both at home and abroad. He was British-educated and had already served as prime minister for a short time after Gen. Razmara's assassination. Ala was the shah's trusted choice of prime minister whenever he needed a moment of respite to think things over. Ala posed no threat to the monarch and was highly respected in the West. He had been Iran's chargé d'affaires in Washington, Paris and London, and spoke English and French fluently. He was 73 at the time of his appointment and, according to his doctor, needed to travel abroad immediately to have a prostate operation.

The shah was now in command of the army and the executive. State security was left in the hands of generals Teymur Bakhtiyar, Tehran's military governor, and Mehdiqoli Alavi-Moqaddam, the chief of police, who reported directly to the shah. In April 1955, the National Resistance Movement published and circulated a pamphlet claiming that the post-coup regime had betrayed the objectives of the oil nationalization movement, and when faced with a popular backlash, had intimidated and repressed the people. Key members of the NRM, such as Mehdi Bazargan and Yadollah Sahabi, were rounded up and banished internally. The wave of arrests continued through May and included National Front members, such as Abdollah Moazami, Baqer Kazemi and Mehdi Amir-Alai.

The most important task of Ala's government, however, was to facilitate Iran's adherence to the Baghdad Pact which included Turkey, Iraq, the UK and Pakistan. This was a security and defence protocol against possible Soviet aggression. For the US, the defence of the 'Northern Tier' of the Middle East against communist threat remained a major preoccupation. John Foster Dulles, the secretary of state, was very keen on bringing Iran into the Baghdad Pact. In return, however, he was not prepared to commit the US to the specifics of military and economic assistance to Iran which the shah eagerly expected. In the end, the shah agreed to join the Baghdad Pact only under considerable pressure from the US. On 22 October 1955, members of the Iranian Parliament unanimously voted in favour of it.

Iran's adherence to the Baghdad Pact was the shah's first significant foreign policy move. Contrary to Mosaddeq, who had believed in keeping Iran neutral in the Cold War, the shah enjoyed the security of being on the side of the West. The shah personally took charge of Iran's foreign policy, abandoned the Mosaddeqist neutralist foreign policy doctrine of 'negative equilibrium' and joined the anti-communist 'free-world' camp led by the United States.

The Devotees of Islam's Last Assassination Attempt and the Eclipse of Kashani

On 17 November 1955, one day before his departure to join the summit conference of the five member-states of the Baghdad Pact, Ala escaped an assassination attempt. The attack was in protest to Iran's membership in the Baghdad Pact. The next day, Ala left for Baghdad with minor injuries. His assailant, Mozaffarali Zolqadr, a member of *Fadaiyane Eslam* (Devotees of Islam), readily admitted that Navab-Safavi had ordered the hit.

Navab-Safavi had been in prison for twenty months during Mosaddeq's government and was released in January 1953. Upon his release, he refused to take sides between Mosaddeq and his opponents and effectively ceased his political activities. Two months before the coup against Mosaddeq, while Kashani and his followers were committed to ousting Mosaddeq from power, Navab-Safavi offered to protect Mosaddeq against all dangers only if he were to implement the 'holy edicts of Islam'. Navab-Safavi played no political role in the events that led to the coup against Mosaddeq's government and remained an unaligned observer.

Four months after the coup, Navab-Safavi left Iran for Jordan to attend an Islamic conference, where he met King Hoseyn of Jordan. During this trip, he also accepted the invitation of the Muslim Brotherhood and visited Egypt, where he gave a fiery speech at Al-Azhar and met with **Seyyed Qutb**. Navab-Safavi returned to Iran in early January 1954 and even briefly toyed with the idea of standing for elections as deputy to the 18th Majles.

Within two weeks of the attempt on Ala's life, Navab-Safavi, Abdolhoseyn Vahedi, Khalil Tahmasebi, Habibollah Zolqadr, Mohammad Vahedi and some thirty members of the Devotees were arrested. They were put on trial, and on 18 January 1956, Navab-Safavi and three of his associates were executed by firing squad. The tumultuous life of the Devotees of Islam organization ended, even though some of its members and sympathizers would later join another historically significant religio-political organization.

The attempt on Ala's life also led to an effective intimidation campaign against Kashani and his close associates, who had criticized Zahedi's government over the oil agreement. Amid Navab-Safavi's stormy trial, the Military Prosecutor rounded up 22 politicians, journalists, members of Parliament and prominent bazaar figures such as Mozaffar Baqai, Ali Zohari, Hoseyn Makki, Abdolqadir Azad and Amirabdollah Karbaschian, on the grounds of their suspected involvement in prime minister Razmara's assassination back in March 1951.

On 19 January 1956, Ayatollah Kashani was arrested and then subsequently released on 14 March 1956. After his release and until his death on 14 March 1962, Ayatollah Kashani was deserted by his friends and followers, and he kept clear from politics. The regime succeeded in marginalizing, demoralizing and depoliticizing him.

The Shah's Expanding Purview, Western Anxieties and the Birth of SAVAK

The election to the **19th Majles** which began in the winter of 1955–6 was so openly rigged that the Iranian press were predicting certain results with uncanny precision months before the results became known. The shah, with the help of his military brass, was able to engineer the outcomes to their taste. The preselected and non-representative nineteenth Parliament was inaugurated on Thursday, 31 May 1956.

> ### The British Embassy on Elections
> The elections were rigged most thoroughly and were conducted in an atmosphere of cynical apathy. (R. Stevens)[13]

By October 1956, the shah had ordered Ala's ministers to report to him directly. Ministers were obliged to provide the shah with weekly and monthly reports on their respective ministries. The shah was on the way to becoming his own prime minister and the head of the judiciary. Under pressure from the shah, the minister of justice, Abbasqoli Golshayan, was extended emergency powers by the Majles to 'decree laws'.

Golshayan presented a press law legalizing censorship and closure of newspapers by the police. Publications deemed against national security or suspected of disseminating seditious news against the government or anti-religious sentiments could be shut down. A repressive customary practice was legalized.

As long as the shah remained a loyal political, military and economic partner of the US, he received their support. The importance of Iran's oil and its geopolitical location outweighed concerns with the shah's growing appetite for absolutist power and dictatorial rule. CIA Director Allen Dulles believed that if the US were to show any sign of hesitation in its support for the shah, 'anti-regime extremist elements' would be encouraged in Iran, and 'facilitate the eventual re-emergence of another Mosaddeq-type government backed by fanatical nationalist elements and the Communists'.[14]

Yet, as early as January 1957, there were voices within the US administration arguing for the urgency of economic development 'benefitting the urban classes, and general modernization of the social and political structure'. The alarmist voices contended that, in the absence of reforms, the maintenance of 'internal stability' would become 'increasingly dependent on uninterrupted maintenance of strong controls'. They predicted that since the government had become ever more identified with the shah, and 'because of the firmness of these controls', future opposition movements 'are likely to include him [the shah] as a target and to take a more revolutionary cast than in the past'.[15] The shah's ever-greater direct involvement in all affairs of the state, compounded with the police state securing his rule, left no buffer between him and his people. The monarchy, thus, became responsible for the country's fortunes and misfortunes.

On 25 April 1955, the US chargé d'affaires, William Rountree, sent a report on Iran's security position to the Department of State and emphasized that the shah was the 'Chief bulwark of internal security.' He concluded that the shah recognized the need for 'positive [and] constructive countermeasures to communist subversion', as well as 'repressive measures' to assure 'a better standard of life' for his people in the future. Rountree emphasized that 'Iran will require continued outside assistance toward this end.'[16]

One of the most important domestic events of 1956 was the drafting of the bill concerning the State Organization for Intelligence and Security (SAVAK). The shah appointed Teymur Bakhtiyar to head the new security agency. SAVAK performed the equivalent functions of the FBI and the CIA. SAVAK's Third Bureau dealt with internal security, while the Seventh and Eighth Bureaus were respectively responsible for foreign intelligence analysis and counter-intelligence. The Third Bureau, which became feared and dreaded, was charged with discovering, pursuing, arresting and interrogating political opponents suspected of subversive activities. This department had free rein to operate across the entire society and throughout the land, and its power was unlimited. SAVAK was accountable only to the shah.

> ### SAVAK, Whence It Came
> It was established with the full assistance of the United States, which put its own intelligence forces at the Shah's disposal in SAVAK's formation. Israeli intelligence also played a major part in the creation of SAVAK. (J. Bill)[17]

Lt Gen. Hasan Alavi-Kia, one of Bakhtiyar's deputies at SAVAK, maintained that it was primarily the Americans and the British who had suggested the formation of SAVAK as a centralized intelligence-gathering organization. Gen. Haj Ali Kia, the head of the army's Second Bureau (counter-intelligence), believed that the Americans drew up SAVAK's organizational structure. He confirmed that US technical assistants, sent to Iran, played an instrumental role in drafting SAVAK's organizational and operational charts.

On Thursday, 14 March 1957, the bill concerning the creation of SAVAK passed in the Majles with a majority rising in favour. SAVAK was legally endowed with incontestable plenipotentiary and extra-judiciary powers to enforce national security through intimidation and repression. SAVAK was intended to be scary and the fact that Teymur Bakhtiyar was appointed as its director sent the clear message that this organization was to be dreaded.

> ### Bakhtiyar's Performance by October 1957
> The internal situation remained exceptionally stable thanks largely to the emergence of SAVAK, General Bakhtiyar's security and information organization as an efficient, loyal, and feared secret police. (J. W. Russell)[18]

SAVAK initially began its operations from a four-storey yellow-brick building in Tehran. Its original officers came either from the Office of the Military Governor or Military Security. Gradually, it expanded its offices in Tehran, and each Bureau moved into a separate building. Over time, SAVAK opened branches in key provinces such as Khorasan, Fars, Azarbayjan and Khuzestan. Before long, SAVAK was operating in major European countries, such as Germany, Britain, France, and Italy.

The creation of SAVAK was a crucial step in the shah's consolidation of his rule. It helped to concentrate power in the shah's hands by keeping tabs on not only dissidents, but politicians, businessmen, bureaucrats, and technocrats, rendering them servile under the threat of exposing their secrets. It quickly replaced the role of the judiciary where political issues were concerned. The shah grew to believe that by relying on the military and SAVAK, he could single-handedly rule the country.

Eqbal in Office

On 3 April 1957, Manuchehr Eqbal became prime minister and Ala slipped back into his old position of court minister (Figure 5.2). Since January 1957, the US had been critical of Ala's government for its suppression of civil liberties, indifference to popular grievances and 'the preoccupation of its leading figures with matters of personal advantage'.[19] Eqbal was a seasoned 47-year-old politicians who had the shah's full trust and confidence. He had served as governor, cabinet minister, chancellor of Tehran University, senator and minister of court. As minister of interior, he had been instrumental in fixing the elections of the 1949 Constituent Assembly and the 16th Majles in favour of the shah's candidates. He had no personal ambitions threatening to the shah and viewed his role as the implementor of His Majesty's 'royal will' and 'royal commands'.

Eqbal stated unabashedly that his government would do nothing without the permission of His Majesty. In October 1957, Eqbal was questioned by a Majles deputy about the arrest of some 60 to 70 members of the National Resistance Movement in Tehran and Mashhad, and its subsequent cover up. Having labelled those arrested as traitors and followers of Mosaddeq's thesis, Eqbal informed Parliament that his government was in power because *Shahanshah* (Shah of Shahs) had desired it. He reminded them that he would hold his position for as long as the shah willed it and would leave when the shah decided. Eqbal instructed the Members of the Parliament that 'this is the way it is, irrespective of whether everyone agrees or not.'[20]

Confident of the regime's iron grip on society, less than two weeks after he became prime minister and some five years after the coup, Eqbal lifted martial law. Having dissolved the Military Governor's Office, he introduced Teymur Bakhtiyar as his deputy and director of SAVAK. With the shah's consent, Eqbal committed himself to

Figure 5.2 Manuchehr Eqbal. *Source: Wikimedia Commons.*

some sort of political liberalization and democratization and promised to reinstate the freedom of the press, association and political parties, except for the Tudeh Party.

For nearly four years, the Iranian political system had functioned without legal parties and Majles deputies had been elected without party affiliations. Suddenly, on 23 April 1957, the shah spoke of the importance of a two-party system. The problem, however, was that since all parties had been dissolved after the coup, new ones had to be created.

Contrived Parties and Party Politics

For the shah, the two-party system was a response to 'a kind of sentimental desire on the part of the Americans and the British to have a Westminster-type of democracy in Iran'.[21] In 1957, the shah was highly sensitive to American and British perception of his rule. Satisfying their wish, however, created an untenable domestic situation. Political competition and freedom raised political expectations, which the shah did not wish to fulfil and had painstakingly stamped out. Before the 1953 coup, Iranians, however, enjoyed a multiparty system, which did not survive the subsequent repression. The shah also wished to set up the two parties to 'offset the effectiveness of the National Front'.[22] To expedite the formation and development of two pro-court parties, the shah allocated monthly funds to each party.

On 16 May 1957, Asadollah Alam announced the creation of *Hezbe Mardom* (the People's Party) which proposed a socially-progressive and even radical programme. The core of Alam's programme would later find its way into the shah's 'White Revolution'. The People's Party's programme revolved around four key issues: distribution of large landholdings among peasants working the land; equitable distribution of income by limiting large fortunes to eradicate class disparities; making workers shareholders in the profits of large factories; and allowing women to participate in elections. Starting in October 1957, the party published a daily organ.

Despite the shah's insistence on the quick formation of a governing party, it took about ten months for Eqbal to form it. On 24 May 1958, the prime minister was elected president of the new *Hezbe Melliyoun* (Nationalists' Party). The Nationalists' Party had no ideology 'that could be labelled as left or right-leaning'.[23] Its political platform was broad and contrary to that of the People's Party, it had no delineating features. The Nationalists' Party was committed to supporting Iran's material and spiritual well-being, upholding the constitutional monarchy and national unity, combining Iran's religion and culture with modern science and industry, providing individual and social freedoms, assuring public health for all, supporting a balanced budget and increasing output.

As soon as the two parties were formed, the deputies in the 19th Majles were instructed to join one or the other party. The two parties, however, failed to obtain a broad and dedicated membership. While Eqbal's party had no clearly defined platform to mobilize its members, Alam's party could not freely promote its programme, as it was supposed to remain the minority party. The two parties were attractive primarily to bureaucrats and aspiring politicians seeking self-promotion, career development, proximity to the centres of power and a political ladder to fame and fortune. Membership of lower-echelon civil servants and private sector employees in each party was determined by the allegiance of their superiors. The rank and file did not adhere by choice but were forced into membership.

Plots Destabilizing the Shah's Newly Found Confidence

From February 1958, two political events rattled the shah. On 27 February 1958, a veiled official announcement mentioned that 'a few Iranians had tried to solicit the help of foreigners to bring a new government to power' and had promised their foreign cohorts to protect their interests in Iran.[24] Most importantly, the official statement added that the foreigners in question had not agreed to help the conspirators.

The key figure implicated in this conspiracy was Gen. Mohammadvali Qarani, the chief of army intelligence, an honest, well liked and progressive officer, who was also highly trusted by the shah (Figure 5.3). Qarani, who was supposed to be the eyes and ears of the shah in the army, was said to be plotting against him. The shah had pushed Qarani up the ladder of promotion, from colonel to general in four short years, a trajectory which was usually completed in ten years. The discovery of the plot led to about 39 arrests. The army's prosecutor general announced that Qarani was arrested for 'misuse of his authority and meddling in state affairs that were not his business'.[25]

Figure 5.3 Gen. Mohammadvali Qarani. *Source: Wikimedia Commons.*

Qarani was 'arrested for attempting to overthrow the government' with the involvement of 'an unnamed foreign power'.[26]

> ## Qarani's Political Objectives
>
> Qarani's basic goal was to bring to power a new government that would curtail the power of the traditional upper class, force the Shah to act as a constitutional monarch, and carry out extensive reforms. (M. J. Gasiorowski)[27]

Qarani had gathered a group of 2,000 intellectuals, 1,200 of whom were US-educated. Members of his group were said to be pro-American and liberal in their political outlook and intent on forming a government which would force the shah to reign, but not rule. To attain their political end, Qarani and members of his group had directly met with and spoken to high-level US officials, but the US had concealed those discussions from the shah.

As the chief of army intelligence, Qarani had met with 'the CIA station chief, US military attachés, and members of the US Military Assistance Advisory Group (MAAG)' in Iran.[28] It is probable that the US wished to place an honest, anti-corruption military crusader in a position of authority. Rather than removing the shah from power, the US had been looking for someone who could stand up to the shah and harness his authoritarian drive.

The Qarani Affair convinced the shah that he had to endear himself further to the US to offset their preference for a constitutional monarch. Domestically, the shah minimized the possibility of collusion and a coup, by prohibiting his officers from establishing personal relations with one another and with foreign embassies. One year after the Qarani Affair, Hoseyn Fardust, the shah's childhood companion, was sent to MI6 for training. On his return, the shah created another intelligence organization and appointed Fardust to head the all-powerful intelligence-gathering bureau called *Daftare Vijeh Ettelaat* (the (Special Bureau of Information).

Qarani was sentenced to three years in prison, a very light sentence for a sensitively positioned general suspected of colluding with foreign powers to change the government. The shah must have been convinced that even though there had been contacts between US officials and Qarani, they were not plotting to remove him from power.

Less than five months after the Qarani Affair, the shah went to Istanbul, where he joined the leaders of Turkey and Pakistan and the US and British foreign ministers for a high-level Baghdad Pact meeting. On 14 July 1958, the heads of state awaited the arrival of King Faisal of Iraq and his prime minister, Nuri Said, when news came of a bloody coup in Baghdad. Brig. Abdolkarim Qasem and Col. Abdolsalam Aref had dissolved the monarchy and proclaimed a republic. King Faisal of Iraq, Crown Prince Amir Abdollah, Nuri Said and several prominent Iraqis had been executed.

The unexpected and violent events in neighbouring monarchical Iraq, which had close affinity to the Iranian monarchy, was the second seism ruffling the shah's peace of mind. The shah came to realize that membership in the Baghdad Pact may reduce the chances of a Soviet aggression but could not protect him from what had just happened in Iraq. The shah had survived Qarani's attempt to curb his powers. Now, he was worried that the coup in Iraq would embolden disenchanted young officers, perhaps even more radical than Qarani, to make a bid for power.

> ### Shah's Reaction to the Coup in Iraq
> The Shah suspected that the coup in Iraq would overflow into Iran and was highly anxious about his own safety. (A. Kia)[29]

The shah was 'somewhat frightened' and 'apparently depressed' after his return to Tehran. He ordered the strengthening of his palace guards by transferring more tanks to the palace grounds.[30] A month after the Baghdad coup, on 14 August 1958, the US Embassy reported that 'between four and eighteen Iranian Army and Gendarmerie officers, most of field grade, were arrested during the past two days for alleged anti-regime political activity.'[31]

After the Qarani Affair, the shah had asked the Americans to stop contacting Iranian dissidents, and they had agreed. The coup in Iraq made him insecure and forced him to reverse his decision and seek US help in keeping a close eye on Iranian dissidents. On 1 August 1958, the shah met with the American ambassador and expressed the hope that the American Embassy in Iran 'was being vigilant and keeping track of what was going on in Iran.'[32]

A month later, having heard the American ambassador's report and assessment of 'underground movements and unrest' in Iran, the shah 'was impressed with US intelligence work.'[33] The confluence of the two key events in 1958 convinced the shah that, to strengthen his insecure position at home, he was more than ever needy of US involvement and an expanded SAVAK purview.

The coup in Iraq also strengthened the view in the US Administration that unless the shah initiated 'some dramatic internal reforms, his days will be numbered.'[34] By 15 August 1958, Allen Dulles proposed that: 'It might be well if this Government considered whether we could not exert some pressure on the Shah to carry out some of the most needed reforms, especially in land tenure and taxation.'[35]

The US subsequently pushed for two types of reforms in Iran. First, a major social, economic and administrative overhaul of the country centred around 'land reform and revision of landlord-peasant relationships'. This measure, it was believed, would 'improve Iran's economic progress as well as reduce popular discontent.'[36] Second, the shah was prompted to abandon his long-term goal of ruling. The US wished to see the shah modify his 'dictatorial role to allow some scope for opposition sentiments', delegate 'specific administrative responsibilities to competent subordinates' and liberalize 'legislative and judiciary practices' to 'insure his position and syphon off the growing discontent'.[37]

Two Elections, Sharif Emami's Brief Premiership and a Cursed 20th Majles

On 7 January 1960, the shah issued a royal edict ordering elections to the 20th Majles. This was to be a historically significant election. The shah would oversee his experimentation with the two-party system while the US would test the shah's commitment to implementing political reforms. From May 1960, the election campaigns gradually picked up momentum. In the meantime, a third political organization, known as *Monfaredin* (the Independents), had appeared on the political stage. It was composed of Jafar Behbahani, Fatollah Forud, Asadollah Rashidiyan and Ali Amini, all influential politicians, closely connected to the court.

The Independents were loyal to the shah and considered themselves best suited to realize his intentions and desires. They believed that, for his own good, the shah should rule, but perhaps a little less brashly. After much ado about a two-party system, the Independents were informally allowed to participate. All three political parties were more interested in interpreting and executing the shah's desires than in representing the interests and wishes of the people. By June, both the shah and Eqbal promised and guaranteed free elections.

Amidst the general excitement over free elections, the Mosaddeqist forces acted as though they too had been invited to participate in the election and eagerly embraced this opportunity. On 26 June 1960, the National Resistance Movement announced its intention of benefitting from the legal right and freedom to participate in the election. One day later, in an open letter, Allahyar Saleh announced the National Front's entrance on the Iranian political scene after nearly eight years. Saleh stated his eagerness to work within Iran's constitutional framework and test the shah's promise of free elections and a return to democracy.

On 21 July 1960, the order to begin elections was issued. On the same day, the National Front announced its official resumption of activities. The newly revived political formation identified itself as the Second National Front, distinguishing itself from the organization which had existed up to 19 August 1953. Having sensed a political opening, and possibly having been encouraged by US officials, the National Front prepared to participate actively in the elections.

The shah's reaction was immediate. He pointed out that freedom did not imply the freedom to commit treason and argued that what constituted treason was determined both 'by law and the people's popular opinion'. In the absence of legal barriers preventing the National Resistance Movement and the National Front from participation in national elections, the shah was accusing Mosaddeqists of treason.[38] The National Front and Mosaddeqist forces were viewed as spoiling the shah's game of democracy.

The voting started on 1 August and was staggered according to localities. Elections for Tehran started on 17 August and lasted three days. As soon as they began, the press began to talk about 'the election scandals', 'cheating', 'the unnatural election process' and 'filling of the ballot boxes'.[39] In the second week of August, Ali Amini met with the shah and presented him with evidence he had gathered demonstrating misconduct, cheating and Eqbal's meddling in the elections.

One day before elections began in Tehran, the university students associated with the National Front organized a series of demonstrations against the rigged election. The tempo of mobilization against the electoral process accelerated between 19 and 25 August. Cries of foul play, rigging and government manipulation were coming in from all corners of the country. Contrary to plans, the shah and his prime minister had lost control of the situation. Once the results of Tehran's election were announced, it turned out that all those elected were candidates of Eqbal's party.

The shah held a press conference on 27 August 1960 and under pressure from the US made a complete volte-face, announcing his displeasure with the election process. He explained that since the beginning of the election, he had been privy to incessant complaints about it. The shah blasted the members of the National Front for their opposition to the election and seemed to blame them for the rigged elections. The shah was desperately looking for a way out of this election without losing face. Forty hours after the shah's press conference, Manuchehr Eqbal, the obedient executor of the shah's orders, took the fall after forty-one months in office. At the time of his replacement, he had been Mohammad-Reza Shah's longest-serving prime minister.

On 29 August 1960, the shah appointed the 50-year-old Jafar Sharif-Emami as prime minister (Figure 5.4), and on 1 September, he called on the newly elected

Figure 5.4 Jafar Sharif-Emami. *Source: Wikimedia Commons.*

members of Parliament to resign collectively, thus annulling the summer election. A few months after Sharif Emami's appointment, without consulting his prime minister, the shah issued a royal decree announcing a new round of elections for the end of the year. The announcement came 3 weeks after President Kennedy's election to the White House. Sharif-Emami believed that the shah was worried that Kennedy did not have a high opinion of him and wished to show his liberal colours by holding new elections before Kennedy took office.

While Sharif-Emami was not privy to why the shah was rushing the Majles elections, the British ambassador to Iran was in the know. Harrison reported that the shah wished to have elections earlier because he was wary of foreign criticism that his regime was 'in reality a dictatorship'. The shah was especially sensitive to Kennedy's criticism of past US administrations giving aid to military dictatorships. The shah also needed the Majles to pass the budget. Finally, the shah, was embarrassed about not having a parliament during the visit to Iran by the queen of England. The shah spoke of the 'unseemliness of not having a parliament' when the queen of England was to visit Tehran.[40]

Once the winter elections started, however, Sharif-Emami recalled that the shah intervened directly to fix them. The National Front threw itself with full force into this second round. The election of President Kennedy had been welcomed by the National Front as a factor which would strengthen the possibility of free elections in Iran. The new US president had a reputation for supporting liberalization in autocratic countries. Optimism about free elections prompted the National Front to present candidates in several constituencies. It was even rumoured that, under US pressure, the shah would allow a few National Front candidates to enter the 20th Majles.

After long negotiations, the National Front managed to open its Club and political headquarters. Soon the National Front was attracting thousands of people. Its political message highlighted reviving the rule of law, guaranteeing individual and socio-political rights and freedoms, respecting the Universal Declaration of Human Rights, upholding parliamentary democracy and ensuring Iran's independence.

The National Front rallies attracted some 12,000–20,000 people, although deprived of an official publication to publicize the events. As the numbers attending National Front meetings swelled and student demonstrations in its favour multiplied, government repression against Mosaddeqists increased. The police clashed with student demonstrators, arresting them and closing Tehran University and the Teacher Training College. In constituencies where National Front candidates were poised to win, direct orders came from Tehran to manipulate the results. The success of government-approved candidates had to be guaranteed.

> ## On the Winter Elections
> The elections were largely rigged, and diverse opposition political forces have not been able to force their cancellation, despite several minor riots in Tehran and a few disturbances in other parts of the nation . . . the Shah is now the dictator of Iran for all practical purposes . . . ruling through the security forces. (US State Department)[41]

At last, the 20th Majles convened on 21 February 1961. Only half the people who had cast their votes during the first round of elections had bothered to vote again. According to official figures only about 17 per cent of eligible voters had cast a ballot in Tehran. However, in spite of all the manipulations, the outcome was that of some 178 deputies, at least 20 truly elected candidates found their way to Parliament. Dressed in full military uniform, the shah delivered a short inaugural speech and praised the exceptional work of the 19th Majles.

The shah called on the new deputies to operationalize the laws voted in the previous Majles, such as land reform, supervision of the wealth of cabinet ministers and civil servants, and tax reform. He reminded the people and their representatives that the 'spectacular and unprecedented progress' attained so far had been because of the 'political and social stability' in the land, and emphasized the importance of preventing 'traitors, demagogues and corruptors' from meddling in the country's affairs.

The 20th Majles was very short-lived. It held twenty sessions and lasted some ten weeks (21 February–3 May 1961), three of which were spent in recess. While it lasted, Allahyar Saleh, the National Front deputy, and the sole opposition figure, made waves by criticizing the Sharif-Emami government for violently and illegally intervening in the second round of elections, trampling on constitutionally guaranteed freedoms, closing Tehran University and arresting students, political notables and members of the bazaar.

Saleh asked the rhetorical question, 'Mr. prime minister, are you aware of the dangerous road on which you have embarked? Do you know which ideology is promoted when pens are broken, and mouths shut?' Saleh pointed out that, 'if autocracy, the rule of fear, and the terror of ideas were a solution to social problems', 'despotism would not have given way to constitutionalism, dictatorship to democracy, and slavery to freedom'.[42] These were bold words in the politically sanitized atmosphere of the post-coup Majles.

While Saleh was addressing the Majles, throngs of students gathered in Baharestan Square in his support and demonstrated on the streets. A political dynamism reminiscent of the Mosaddeq era was in the air. After eight years of a tight leash on political expression and activity, Sharif-Emami needed to navigate between popular demand for liberal democracy, and the shah's reluctance to give up the absolute powers he had gained since the 1953 coup.

On 2 May 1961, while deputies in the Majles were busy discussing a bill to increase the salaries of teachers, outside Parliament, teachers and students congregated. The crowd had been mobilized by the Tehran Teachers' Association. Mohammad Derakhshesh, its leader, had called for a strike. Derakhshesh was the liberal and nationalist member of the 19th Majles. He was also the representative of Tehran's Teachers' Association and head of the Mehregan Club, where teachers had met regularly since February 1961, demanding a pay rise, and patiently waiting for the government to meet their demands.

The police tried to disperse the peaceful crowd of some 50,000 people, sitting down on the tarmac. It used at first water cannons, then Major Naser Shahrestani, the chief of the Baharestan police station, ordered his men to attack the protesting teachers, leaving behind one dead and three injured. The CIA station chief in Tehran described the shah's reaction to the strikes as 'the only thing to do was to put this down by force.'[43] The gravity of the 2 May events was such that the regime decided to put Iranian military units on alert. The death of Abolhasan Khanali, a 29-year-old high school teacher, who was shot in the back of the head on 2 May, triggered widespread student demonstrations.

After three days of continuous unrest and mounting popular discontent, Sharif-Emami, became the new scapegoat. On 5 May 1961, after eight months in office, the shah replaced Sharif Emami with the 55-year-old Ali Amini. On 9 May, four days after Amini became prime minister, the shah dissolved the three-month-old 20th Majles. The 21st Majles would not be inaugurated for another 29 months, on 6 October 1963.

Amini's Premiership

Amini presented himself as the economic saviour of an almost bankrupt economy, a political mender and healer, promising national reconciliation between the people and the regime. Amini insisted that the welfare of the people could only be assured by respecting the Constitution and the social and political rights stipulated in it. In the same breath, he threatened to stand firmly against disorder and sedition.

The Majles closed less than a week after his premiership, placing Amini in an untenable position with respect to liberal and democratic opposition forces (Figure 5.5). Amini had become the prime minister of an unconstitutional, 'parliament-less' monarchy. He and the monarch were ruling illegally, unconstitutionally and by fiat. Amini's vacillations between promoting and violating the Constitution would cripple his entire term in office.

Figure 5.5 Ali Amini. *Source: Wikimedia Commons.*

The dominant perception among the people, the press, and the political elite was that Amini had been imposed on the shah by the Kennedy administration. This common belief placed Amini in a delicate position, both of weakness and strength. Two months after Amini's premiership, the British Embassy in Iran reported that one of the serious criticisms against Amini's government was that it was 'made in the U.S.A.'[44]

To help Iran's 'cash crisis', the US extended a grant of $15 million. Yet, it established a quid pro quo. With Amini in power, the US would try to push forward with reforms while letting the shah think that the idea was his.

The Anti-Corruption Campaign

Immediately after his appointment, Amini launched his highly publicized anti-corruption campaign. On 8 May 1961, he replaced Fatollah Forud, Tehran's mayor, with Mohsen Nasr. Forud had been a fixer, broker and veritable godfather figure, very much like his best friend, Asadollah Rashidiyan. Forud's dismissal was a hostile act against the powerful and well-connected clique of the shah's devotees, clustered around Rashidiyan, who believed themselves to be politically invincible.

On the heels of Forud's dismissal, on 14 May 1961, Amini arrested four highly influential generals: Gen. Haj Ali Kia, the powerful former chief of army intelligence; Gen. Mehdiqoli Alavi-Moqadam, Sharif-Emami's minister of interior; Gen. Ali-Akbar Zargham, Sharif-Emami's minister of finance; and Gen. Ruhollah Noveysi, the former chief of fisheries. On the next day, Gen. Ahmad Ajudani, the former head of the National Electricity Company, was arrested for misappropriation of public funds. Before the end of May, the former managing director of the Ministry of Finance, Javad Tabatabai, joined the detainees.

This was the first time that the heads of such high-ranking military officers were rolling on charges of misappropriation of funds and embezzlement. Bringing to justice those who had supposedly emptied the coffers of state and lined their own pockets endeared Amini to the people. Yet, after its initial splash, Amini's anti-corruption campaign ran out of steam very quickly. Six weeks after taking office, Amini was facing complaints about delays in pursuing the corrupt. At a news conference, Amini provided a new list of thirty additional detainees, but none were big fish.

The Mosaddeqist Opposition, the Shah and the US

On 11 May 1961, less than a week after Amini assumed office, Mehdi Bazargan wrote a letter to Mosaddeq to announce the formation of *Nehzate azadiye Iran* (the Iran Freedom Movement). This was a nationalist and Islamic political force founded by Mahmud Taleqani, Mehdi Bazargan, Yadollah Sahabi, Mansur Atai, Hasan Nazih and Rahim Atai.

> ### The Iran Freedom Movement
> We are Muslim, Iranian, followers of the Iranian Constitution, and Mosaddeqists . . . we do not distinguish between faith and politics . . . and are committed to the principles of justice, equality and fraternity [as well as] Iran's independence and the maintenance of good relations with other countries. (M. Bazargan)[45]

The Iran Freedom Movement was launched on 17 May 1961. At its first meeting, Bazargan pledged the loyalty of his organization to the Constitution and vowed to defend the freedom of thought, press and assembly and respect the separation of powers. He announced that Mosaddeq had been the only head of government in Iranian history truly elected by the majority. The Iran Freedom Movement reiterated its attachment to the National Front and instructed members and sympathizers to attend the National Front rally on 18 May 1961 at the large Jalaliyeh field close to Tehran University.

On Thursday, 18 May 1961, Tehran witnessed an unprecedented National Front gathering officially permitted by the Amini government and the chief of police, Mohsen Mobasser. According to foreign news agencies, some 60,000 to 80,000 were in attendance. These numbers were particularly telling when contrasted with the 50,000 to 100,000 votes cast in Tehran's summer election and the 65,451 voters registered during the winter election. The numbers at the Jalaliyeh rally demonstrated the lasting popularity of Mosaddeq and the National Front almost eight years after the coup.

The Jalaliyeh rally unfolded while the shah was away on an official state visit to Norway. A startling feature of this gathering was the peaceful and disciplined behaviour of the crowd. University students, wearing special insignia, were responsible for the rally's safety and security. Some seventeen truckloads of soldiers, twenty-nine police jeeps, four trucks equipped with water cannons and a group of mounted police stood by observing.

During speeches by Karim Sanjabi, Gholamhoseyn Sadiqi, and Shapur Bakhtiyar, the large crowd was silent, and on three occasions when the speakers mentioned Mosaddeq's name, the people broke out into heavy and long rounds of applause lasting some ten minutes. The speakers condemned injustices committed by previous governments, violations of human and political rights, illegal imprisonment and cheating during elections. They criticized the unconstitutional closure of the Majles, called for immediate elections to the Majles and prompted the government to withdraw from the Central Treaty Organization (CENTO, what used to be the Baghdad Pact). Taking advantage of Amini's promise of freedom, the press gave substantial and positive cover to the rally. It praised the orderly conduct of the participants and expressed astonishment at the unprecedented numbers present.

On 19 May 1961, President Kennedy presided over the National Security Council (NSC) which recommended that 'the US make a major effort to back the new Government in Iran as the best instrument in sight for promoting orderly political, economic and social evolution in Iran, and for averting serious and damaging political developments'. But it maintained that while the US supported the monarchy, it should 'more actively encourage the shah to move toward a more constitutional role'.[46]

The Jalaliyeh rally, and the subsequent show of force by the Mosaddeqists, rattled the liberal Amini and Kennedy administrations. Both hoped to hem in the shah's powers and turn him into a constitutional monarch, but neither had expected to see the re-emerging power and popularity of the Mosaddeqists after eight years. The Kennedy administration, which had hoped to guide and nudge the shah to play a 'more constitutional role', came to realize that it was impossible to expect the shah to be democratic and safeguard US ideological and economic interests in the country. The Mosaddeqist emphasis on neutralism, however, irked the US. Meanwhile, Amini realized that playing the democratic and liberal card provided political space for the Mosaddeqists to grow and threaten his government.

From May 1961, the prime minister ordered SAVAK to forbid the opening of National Front offices in the provinces and restrict their activities. The Amini government took charge of the offensive against Mosaddeq's partisans by denigrating and sullying the National Front. Employing a stratagem used by anti-Mosaddeq forces before the 1953 coup, and appealing to the US, the Amini government suggested that the National Front was nothing but a naive tool of the communists.

> ## US Reaction to Mosaddeqists' Growing Power
> Principal danger [to the] independence and integrity of Iran flows from pressures [brought to bear by] Mosadeq partisans and their allies on government. (C. Bowles)[47]

The Kennedy–Amini axis moved away steadily from their liberal-democratic point of departure to join the shah's anti-democratic and authoritarian outlook. During Amini's premiership, alarmed by the Mosaddeqist upsurge, they moved from opponents to proponents of the shah's growing dictatorial powers. Having failed to generate political reforms, they contended themselves with implementing economic reform centred around land reform.

From July 1961, Amini used force to prevent the National Front from holding meetings and demonstrations. Leaders of the National Front and the Iran Freedom Movement were rounded up. Tehran University was occupied by police and the army, and tanks and armoured vehicles were deployed in Tehran to confront Mosaddeqist rallies. Anti-Amini student demonstrations were repressed, and students were beaten up and jailed. Faced with the cautious approach of the National Front leadership in confronting Amini's abuse of the Constitution and repression of the National Front, its student wing radicalized and began parting ways, arguing for action rather than strong worded declarations.

By mid-August 1961, Amini spoke in the reverential language of Eqbal. He pointed out that his government was appointed by the highest authority in the land, the shah, and had his confidence. Amini promised to carry out the shah's reformist objectives and called on the people to rally behind the shah. He warned that destabilizing the regime would imperil the country. After four months in office, Amini accused all those who thought differently from the shah of being traitors.

To protest the illegal expulsion of high school students associated with the National Front for their political activities, the National Front Youth Organization invited all students to a rally on 21 January 1962. The students announced that if 'the despotic system of government and the illegal minister of education ignores our protest and prevents the return of students to their schools', they would 'return them to their schools by force'.[48] The students were threatening the government with insubordination and insurrection if necessary. Their tone was firm, focused and belligerent.

On 21 January, Tehran University experienced an unprecedented mayhem. The University was assaulted by the military, mostly parachutists. Their bloody operation lasted for some two hours. The troops engaged in a destructive rampage. Entire classrooms, offices, chairs, tables, windows, doors, typewriters, cabinets, mirrors, lamps and even sinks were vandalized and smashed. Cars parked on campus were smashed and their windows shattered. Two motorbikes belonging to the university postal system were set on fire.

The university clinic, where some of the lightly injured students were receiving treatment, was attacked. Wounded students and the doctors treating them were given a beating. More seriously injured students who lay inside ambulances were dragged out and the drivers assaulted. Two American students at Tehran University were roughed up and robbed by soldiers who forced their way into their rooms and ransacked them. Later, the American Embassy in Iran lodged an official complaint with the Ministry of Foreign Affairs.

According to the government, 120 students and 96 government forces were injured. The National Front and Iran Freedom Movement referred to some 600 to 800 injured students, among whom 200 to 400 were seriously wounded and hospitalized. Some 56 to 300 students were arrested. The indiscriminate and ferocious student bashing, along with the senseless physical destruction of university property, was aimed at intimidating and subduing students. The shah wished to discipline the students. This was the first of many messages stating that university students had best get on with their studies and abandon political engagements.

In the days following 21 January 1962, clashes between students and government forces spread to the universities of Shiraz, Tabriz, Mashhad, Esfahan and Ahvaz. The unrest led to more arrests and closure of universities. The high school students in Tehran, Tabriz, Shiraz, Esfahan, Ahvaz, Abadan and Qazvin staged demonstrations in solidarity with the student movement in Tehran. The government shut down Tehran University and subsequently the Teacher Training College, Karaj University of Agriculture and Tehran's Polytechnic University, to prevent further disorder. Notwithstanding the closure of universities, student confrontations continued in Tehran with different degrees of intensity for at least another month. Tehran University remained padlocked for about two and a half months and was only reopened after the Iranian New Year holidays in early April 1962.

Arsanjani and Land Reform

Initially, the US Administration had supported Amini as a counterweight to the shah. As Amini lost his use and appeal and the US changed its position, Amini's future became uncertain. Accepting the inevitability of a ruling Shah also meant that the US had to recognize the failure of the Amini experiment to 'prevent a developing and hardening dictatorship' in Iran.[49] Starting in October 1961, the shah signalled to his foreign benefactors that he wished to take on more responsibilities and, in effect, rule directly and absolutely.

> ## US Objectives in Iran in October 1961
> To prevent Soviet domination of Iran must be our immediate and overriding objective. This requires the continuance in power of a pro-Western regime, for the ultimate alternative is a weak neutralist government which could not withstand Soviet pressures and maintain Iran's independence. (P. Talbot)[50]

In November 1961, the shah issued an edict giving full powers to Amini to quickly implement reforms in six specific areas, the most important of which was land reform and forming cooperatives, promoting import substitute industries and profit-sharing schemes, and expanding the scope of free education at all levels. These objectives were discussed at the **Iran Task Force** meeting of 14 October 1961 in Washington, one month before the publication of the shah's royal edict commanding reforms.

From the first days of Amini's government, Hasan Arsanjani, his flamboyant and radical minister of agriculture, was adamant on overhauling the land tenure system in Iran. On 9 January 1962, a new land reform law was in place. The law stipulated that land owned by a landowner in excess of one village or the equivalent of six parts was subject to distribution. On 2 March 1962, the much-publicized land reform initiative, which had been keenly sought by various US administrations since 1956, was finally operationalized. Three landlords signed off to state authorities the ownership of a part of their estates in Maragheh (Azarbayjan), one of the most fertile regions in Iran.

Arsanjani congratulated the Iranian people, thanked the shah for backing this important initiative, and hailed the collapse of Iran's semi-feudal system. On 8 March, Arsanjani travelled to Azarbayjan and signed the legal documents transferring the ownership of the lands obtained by the government from the landowners to the peasants. Five days later, accompanied by Arsanjani, members of the government, Iranian dignitaries and the foreign diplomatic corps, the shah attended a benchmark ceremony in the district of Varjuy in Maragheh. On this special occasion, he handed land ownership deeds to some 520 landless peasants. In the absence of Amini, this was the first act of the much promised land reform which was to revolutionize the socio-economic profile of the country. Arsanjani had become the public face of land reform as Amini was sidestepped.

Internationally, the shah was unhappy with the US, especially after his 10 April 1962 trip to Washington. There he was advised to concentrate on social and economic reforms or a 'controlled revolution' instead of building up Iran's military arsenal. In Washington, Dean Rusk, the secretary of state, had advised His Majesty to reduce his army of 200,000 to 150,000 men in return for a military assistance package of $330 million over five years. In their meeting in Washington, on 12 April 1962, when the shah had asked for continuing budget support, Kennedy had 'indicated that Iran could expect no such aid in the future'.[51]

The US position had prompted the shah to push ahead with reforms, become their uncontested leader, take all political credit for them, endear himself to his people, and bide his time. When Amini requested a reduction in the budget of the Ministry War, on par with other ministries, to narrow the country's $150 million budget deficit, the shah, who had for months tried to remove Amini from power, found the ideal moment. On 17 July 1962, the shah accepted Amini's resignation.

The land reform was a watershed moment in Iran's modern history, transforming the country socially, economically and politically. For the 431,743 to 512,975 peasant families who benefitted from land reform in the following years and up to 1966, the shah was their benefactor, the Crowned Father, and the source of their entitlement. Land reform gave peasants a sense of self-esteem, belonging and dignity, generating loyalty towards the shah. Naturally, all the political credit associated with land reform accrued to the shah, providing him with an important social base, different from his traditional pillars of support.

Land reform gave also the best excuse for the shah to further his political designs. To counter the political criticism of his opposition, he hammered at two interlinked arguments, highlighting the inappropriateness of democracy in Iran. He argued that relying on normal parliamentarian procedures had proven ineffective and that political parties in Iran were usually the handiwork of foreigners. The shah would now argue that 'political democracy is meaningless, without economic democracy'.[52]

Alam, the White Revolution and the Eclipse of Mosaddeqists

On 19 July 1962, the 42-year-old Asadollah Alam became prime minister (Figure 5.6). The most significant aspect of this change of the guard was that the shah, the veritable 'owner' of the country, was now fully and firmly in control. He felt liberated from Amini, whom he suspected of imposing US designs on him. The shah's new ticket to ensure his reign was an audacious socio-economic action plan, a White Revolution.

By 20 October 1962, the US government had overcome all previous ethical qualms about supporting a dictatorial monarch. Robert Komer of the National Security Council wrote: 'Crudely stated, our goal in Iran is enough stability to avoid violent revolution, from which we doubt we'd emerge the gainers.' Komer hoped for 'rapid enough progress to satisfy growing popular frustrations'. Speaking on behalf of the US administration, he wrote: 'we need a controlled revolution rather than an uncontrolled one in Iran'. Komer proposed that the US should, 'soft-pedal for a while

Figure 5.6 Asadollah Alam. *Source: Wikimedia Commons.*

longer on elections and a parliament'. In the name of 'realpolitik', Komer blurted, 'let's strengthen the internal security apparatus'.[53] Assuring the stability of the shah's regime now took precedence over all else for the US. The Kennedy administration now stood firmly behind a Shah with despotic designs.

Once Alam came to power, at the behest of the shah, he tried to woo the National Front. In August, the Iran Freedom Movement (IFM), led by Mehdi Bazargan, had targeted the person of the shah for the political ills in the country. The IFM's frontal attack on the shah prompted the monarch to drive a wedge between the radical IFM and the cautious members of the National Front leadership, thus splitting the Mosaddeqist front.

In late September 1962, Alam met with Allahyar Saleh and Mehdi Azar of the National Front and informed them that the shah wished to benefit from their ideas in managing the country. In return they were expected to support his socio-economic reforms and close their eyes to the monarch's wish to rule rather than reign. These negotiations lasted until 28 November, when the National Front publicly reported on their contacts with the prime minister, turned down the offer and condemned the existing dictatorial and absolutist rule. The shah mistook the cautiousness of the National Front leadership for their willingness to renounce their fundamental constitutionalist principles.

A Tale of Two Congresses

In December 1962 and January 1963, Tehran witnessed two historic events, the first post-coup Congress of the National Front, and the first Congress of Iran's Rural Cooperatives. For three consecutive weeks, with one week of respite in-between, the two major contenders for political power in Iran engaged in two very different kinds of gatherings. The Congress of Iran's Rural Cooperatives, convened by the regime, was perfectly planned, organized and executed. Its participants were happy peasants, the beneficiaries of land reform, brought to Tehran to celebrate their new status, praise the shah, and support his White Revolution initiative.

The Mosaddeqist National Front Congress, in contrast, opened with incomparably meagre resources, and under substantial political pressure. Those attending were independently minded political activists, and difficult to manage. Most of them possessed exemplary credentials in their anti-regime struggles, had their own political and organizational agendas, and were not submissive to authority. The slightest detail of the Congress of Iran's Rural Cooperatives was widely covered and commented on enthusiastically in the Iranian press. News of the National Front's Congress, on the other hand, was completely stonewalled by the press, which was instructed to ignore it. So, while the Congress of Iran's Rural Cooperatives took place under national floodlights, the National Front's Congress went unnoticed by the politically uninitiated.

Mosaddeq had embodied the essence and soul of the National Front. The process of transcending him without undermining his legacy or rupturing with his spiritual guardianship was a most challenging task. During this crucial gathering, the National Front needed to articulate Mosaddeqism, its political ideology, objectives, methods and ethics, and boldly declare: 'Mosaddeq is no longer, Long live the National Front'. The self-appointed leadership had to assert its authority while charting the course of the struggle against the regime.

The National Front Congress opened on Tuesday, 25 December 1962, with 176 members in attendance, and ended after thirteen sessions at 00.30 am on Wednesday, 2 January 1963. The pent-up tensions and gaping differences among the different groups and parties present, quickly pierced through the bubble of unity and cohesion, presaging the demise of the Second National Front. The National Front was a nationalist, constitutionalist, reformist, and moderate umbrella organization, composed of different political organizations and lacking a distinct ideology. It was bereft of a well-defined organizational structure and conducted its affairs in an informal manner. Two major topics of disagreement haunted and crippled the proceedings.

First, The Congress split over two conflicting views of how the National Front should be structured. One faction supported retaining the National Front's original umbrella organizational structure. It imagined the National Front as a collection of tendencies, a popular front, representing a diversity of parties, all united in their belief in the Mosaddeqist ideals and objectives. The second faction advocated a single disciplined and homogeneous organization. The notion of a 'big and uniform organization' required the affiliated parties and organizations to disband and morph into a new National Front Party. This faction envisioned a party with a single identity and ideology closing ranks and no longer prepared to house diverse Mosaddeqist groups.

Second, even though the Iran Freedom Movement (IFM) consistently considered itself as a part of National Front, it was never officially admitted into the Front. The question of the Iran Freedom Movement's membership in the National Front became another controversial issue. Many at the Congress supported IFM's membership. They were those who opposed a homogeneous single identity, National Front Party.

The faction blocking IFM's admission were composed of the heavyweights such as Saleh, Sanjabi, Sadiqi and Bakhtiyar. The antipathy of this faction towards the IFM was rooted in the latter's pronounced emphasis on Islam as both a belief system as well as a politically liberating force, which did not sit well with the secularism and laicity of this faction. Concurrently, IFM's radical and non-conciliatory stand towards the shah went against the National Front leadership's cautious and pragmatic politics. The popular student wing of the IFM was viewed as radical, extremist, and adventurist by the conservative leadership of the National Front.

Differences of opinion on the political acumen, foresight, management, and work of the leadership, caused deep divisions among the participants. The young political activists were irritated with the leadership's procrastination and irresolution. To them, the political stalling of the leadership was rooted in their desire not to provoke and antagonize the shah and remain on good terms with the US government. The radicals believed that pursuing an independent, nationalist, democratic and anti-despotic political agenda was incompatible with the leadership vision.

The tension between the radical, action-oriented and more blatantly anti-Shah faction and the more established, compromising and pragmatic dignitaries of the National Front that had been brewing, erupted during the Congress. For the first time, the leadership and the rank and file came face to face during the lengthy sessions, exposing their irreconcilable differences. The fact that Mosaddeq, in absentia, was more supportive of the militant faction than the pragmatists, strengthened the confrontational posture of the radicals towards the leadership.

During the entire Congress, the leadership proved incapable of entertaining or presenting new ideas on how to compete with or challenge the regime's much-touted reforms. The National Front leadership was living and thinking in the past and was at best reactive to day-to-day problems. It failed to develop a modern reform discourse looking towards the future.

The First Congress of Rural Cooperatives in Tehran, organized by Arsanjani, brought together some 4,200 to 4,800 farmer delegates from all over the country. The opening session of the Congress, on 9 January 1963, coincided with the first anniversary of the land reform law. The shah addressed the free tenants, during the opening session, and claimed that land reform had laid the foundations of a free, democratic and prosperous society. He identified the nation's enemies as 'the red forces of destruction' and the 'black reactionary elements' resisting change and progress. He warned that 'red forces' intended to hand over the country to the foreigners, while 'black forces' were defending their 'private interests'.

The climax of the shah's speech came with the presentation of his revolutionary socio-economic package. He sought its approval through the direct vote of the people, namely a referendum. This six-pointed new Northern Star constituted the framework of the shah's White Revolution with its 'six-point principles': (1) the abolition of the landowner–tenant system through land reform; (2) nationalization of forests throughout the country; (3) sale of shares in state-owned factories to finance land reform; (4) benefit/profit sharing of workers in industries; (5) reform of the electoral law; and (6) establishment of a literacy corps.

On 13 January, while the Congress was still in progress, Alam surprised the country by announcing that the 'six-point principles' would be put to a vote on Sunday 26 January 1963. The Congress, which ended on 15 January, was an unprecedented public relations feat and all-out success for the shah, who appeared as a visionary leader with socially progressive ideas. The shah was hailed as 'just' for spearheading the social reforms, and was praised for having closed Parliament, which was labelled as the 'gathering place of the landowners'. Moreover, the Congress gave legitimacy to the shah's referendum on the White Revolution.

The Congress, fruit of Arsanjani's ideas, stamina and labour, turned out to be the beginning of his downfall. Throughout the proceedings, the peasants displayed genuine appreciation and affection for the work he had done. This outpouring of affection towards Arsanjani did not sit well with the shah. During the distribution of land deeds in the provinces, the shah had witnessed the gratitude of peasants to Arsanjani (Figure 5.7). Less than two months after the end of the Congress, it was officially announced that the shah had accepted Arsanjani's resignation on 11 March 1963.

On 26 January 1963, more than 99 per cent of the Iranians who participated in the referendum approved of the White Revolution and the shah's political vision of a future Iran. The outcome of the referendum provided the shah with the legitimacy he had lost on 19 August 1953. Irrespective of the conditions under which the voting took place, the shah could announce to his people and to the world that 99.9 per cent

Figure 5.7 The shah handing out land deeds. Hasan Arsanjani (right of photo) with Amini and Alam present. *Source: Wikimedia Commons.*

of Iranians supported his egalitarian, just and progressive social policies. For the first time during his reign, the shah had a popular national project, which he could claim to be as important as Mosaddeq's oil nationalization undertaking.

Iranian dailies presented a euphoric mood on 26 January 1963, especially among women who had flocked to the voting booths for the first time. Confusion reigned over women's suffrage as their vote did not yet officially count. However, they were permitted to organize separate voting booths and subsequently announce their results. This exercise was to be the prelude to extending voting rights to women. Later the shah considered women's suffrage as the most important aspect of reforming the electoral law, the fifth principle of the White Revolution.

Opposition to the White Revolution

The White Revolution disarmed the Mosaddeqist opposition. The reform package had been devoid of political items, but the socio-economic benefits were glaring enough to temporarily shut out any and all criticisms. The opposition, including the Tudeh Party living overseas, had consistently argued that the shah was not defending the majority's interest and was responsible for Iran's backwardness. With the White Revolution, the shah could no longer be accused of acting against the majority's interest and lacking public legitimacy or representation. The opposition had not expected the shah to proclaim himself a revolutionary, robbing them of their potential peasant–worker social base.

The Central Committee of the Tudeh Party boycotted the referendum one day before it took place. It condemned the 'kingly referendum' imposed on the Iranian people in the absence of freedoms and under the watchful eyes of SAVAK and accused the shah of being 'a trickster and a swindler' whose tactics combined 'the cruelty of cowards and the chicanery of imposters'.[54] After the referendum, the Tudeh Party argued that the reforms were intended to 'reinforce and consolidate the shah's regime'. It maintained that reforms would help 'to continue the anti-nationalist policy of remaining at the beck and call of imperialism ... and expand capitalist relations in the country'.[55]

Three days before the referendum, the National Front and the Iran Freedom Movement (IFM) issued their respective communique against the referendum. The IFM considered the US and the shah as the principal beneficiaries of the White Revolution since it forestalled the rise of communism and strengthened the pillars of the shah's despotic rule. The IFM announced that the landowner–tenant system in Iran was unacceptable, that a real referendum required democratic preconditions guaranteeing freedoms of expression, press and assembly, inexistent in Iran. The IFM directly attacked the shah and announced that when 'revolution and reform' take place at the hands of 'the source of all corruption and misfortune in this country', one could not expect a better process of implementation.[56]

The National Front position echoed that of the IFM. Their declaration condemned holding the referendum in the absence of political freedom and warned that the country was on the verge of transitioning from a constitutional democracy to a reactionary and dictatorial system. The National Front concluded that it was in favour of land reform but opposed to despotism. Short of accusing the person of the shah of despotism, the NF held him responsible for all the country's problems. The National Front no longer blamed 'the system' or 'the ruling clique', but the person of the shah.

Alarmed by student unrest and demonstrations leading to the referendum, the government had taken necessary precautions and arrested some 150 members of the opposition, among them many leaders of the National Front and the Iran Freedom Movement. After the referendum, however, the immediate threat to the shah's power had shifted. It was no longer the Mosaddeqist opposition whose members and sympathizers were rounded up and packed into the prisons. The real danger to the shah's power came now from the Shii clerical establishment, which wielded immense power, yet its relationship with the monarchy had been cryptic

The influential religious leaders and Sources of Imitation enjoyed unquestioned allegiance among believers. This powerful spiritual force, usually allied with the monarchy, had occasionally challenged the monarchical power and brought kings to their knees. The shah's experience with the last absolute authority of the clerical establishment had been with the towering figure of Grand Ayatollah Borujerdi. Borujerdi had neither fallen out with the shah nor allowed the monarch to impose his will upon him. Aware of Borujerdi's status and popularity among the people, the shah had feared the consequences of alienating or contradicting him openly, and Borujerdi had seldom interfered in politics, unless he felt religiously obliged to do so.

In December 1961, after the death of Borujerdi and before the emergence of a single authoritative religious figure, Amini travelled to Qom and met the four high-ranking religious dignitaries, Kazem Shariatmadari, Shahabeddin Marashi-Najafi, Mohammad-Reza Golpaygani and Ruhollah Khomeyni. All four were contenders for the highest Shii position of the absolute Source of Imitation. This meeting was reported in the press along with a picture of the prime minister and the four clerics. This gathering was of great political significance as it expressed the non-objection or non-opposition of Borujerdi's successors to Amini, his policies and land reform.

Even though Grand Ayatollah Borujerdi had opposed the first land reform law of 12 March 1960, Khomeyni remained silent on the issue. In December 1961, he did not object to meeting with Amini. The second land reform bill was made into law on 9 January 1962, only eighteen days after Amini met with Khomeyni. The actual transfer of land began on 2 March 1962, and even then, Khomeyni had not objected to land reform.

Ayatollah Khomeyni, the New Contender for Power

Khomeyni's first verbal attack on the regime came on 3 September 1962, some one-and-a-half months after Asadollah Alam became prime minister. The targets of Khomeyni's attacks were multiple. They spanned from the shah's pro-Israel and anti-Islamic foreign policy to cultural policies which 'corrupted' the youth, and the spread of Western civilization and communist propaganda. Khomeyni bemoaned the weakening of the religious establishment in the name of modernity, and the regime's support for Israelis and Bahais.

Khomeyni opposed the 8 October 1962 law on Regional and Provincial Councils, intended to introduce some degree of democratic participation at the local level. One day after the law had gone into effect, Khomeyni sent a polite telegram to the shah, objecting that Islam had not been specified as a requirement for those standing for election. He also objected to women's right to vote. Having noted his two religio-cultural objections, Khomeyni had ended his message by praying for the shah's health. Khomeyni followed up his open letter campaign against the law on 'Regional and Provincial Councils', by writing to Alam. During his campaign against the law on 'Regional and Provincial Councils', Khomeyni's name gradually caught the people's attention.

Faced with the staunch opposition of the clergy, the government dropped the idea of Regional and Provincial Councils in December 1962. Expediently, the Alam government took a small tactical step back only to push through its reform programme with greater vigour once it had rallied the free tenants to its cause. The Congress of Iran's Rural Cooperatives signalled the clergy that rural Iran supported the shah and his reforms. The conflict between Khomeyni and the regime intensified once the shah decided to solidify his rule through the referendum on the White Revolution.

Once Khomeyni opposed the referendum, the regime set aside all subtleties and embarked on insulting, intimidating, and arresting the Ayatollah's rebellious partisans. On 24 January 1963, right before the referendum, the shah went to Qom, the home of the clergy, and delivered a frontal attack. The shah accused the opposing clergy of obstructing his efforts to improve the people's well-being. He called them a bunch of hidebound and thick-headed people with ossified and immutable minds. The shah argued that Islam was the most progressive of all religions and criticized those who justified exploitation in its name. He slammed the clerical opposition and said that he pitied the deplorable black reactionaries because they were simply incapable of understanding ideas and concepts. The shah was in a combative mood, announcing his intolerance for opposition to his reforms.

After the referendum, in which women had participated unofficially, the issue of women's suffrage came to fore. From early February 1963, there were signs that

Iranian women would obtain the right to vote. On 17 February 1963, Khomeyni and eight high-ranking clerics issued a communique against the government's decision to give women the right to vote. They argued that it would only result in 'misfortune, perversion/corruption and prostitution/vice'. They reasoned that Islam was against this kind of mingling which jeopardized women's 'chastity and virtue'.[57] On 2 March 1963, the government decreed that women were eligible to vote and stand for election to the Majles and the Senate.

Khomeyni's speeches soon took on a more political tone and targeted the person of the shah. From 26 February 1963, Khomeyni criticized the regime's harsh and repressive domestic measures and instructed the shah to desist from relying on the bayonet and imprisoning citizens. He accused the government of being in cahoots with the US and Israel to destroy the Quran and squash the clergy. Khomeyni warned the regime that if it were to continue its anti-Islamic policies, a 'revolution from below would ensue'.[58]

The shah's response to Khomeyni was twofold. First, he poured verbal abuse on him and the clergy, calling them dejected snakes, or better still, lice entangled in their own filth, and threatened to 'descend on them like thunder, irrespective of their garb, ending their filthy and ignominious lives'.[59] Second, he ordered a physical attack on the Fayziyeh Seminary School at Qom. Government forces went on a rampage, destroying property, carpets and books. In the aftermath of the attack, some seventy people were hospitalized in Qom.

The violent attack was a reminder to Khomeyni that, irrespective of his religious status, he would be dealt with in the same brutal manner as anyone challenging the shah. After the attacks, the government upped the ante by announcing that any opposition to the women's right to vote or any of the reforms would be considered 'as an act of treason vis-à-vis the nation'. Yet, Khomeyni's religio-political manoeuvres endeared him to believers, including in rural Iran. In March 1963, SAVAK reported that the most esteemed clergy in Qom had decided to follow Khomeyni on social issues and had effectively chosen him to replace Grand Ayatollah Borujerdi. This news signalled that Khomeyni had taken charge of the clerical establishment and spoke for it.

The 5 June or 15 Khordad Uprising

The political atmosphere in Iran was tense and volatile between 22 March and 5 June 1963. There were growing signs of pent-up anger and frustration with the regime's heavy-handed and sharp-tongued post-referendum theatrics. The loyalty of Iranian free tenants and workers to the shah, which had seemed cemented by land reform and the White Revolution, suddenly seemed shaky. In the eyes of the pious rural folk who were favourable to the shah, the regime's attack on the Fayziyeh Seminary School was perverse. The masterfully projected image of victimized and bloodied clergy echoed the historical suffering and martyrdom of Imam Hoseyn and his followers.

The government's arbitrary decision to arrest seminary students and send them off to military service began on 13 April 1963. This policy of humiliating the young would-be clergy came across as excessive vengefulness. It embarrassed and alienated some of the influential pro-shah clerics, who could not with good conscience support the shah, thus driving a deeper wedge between them and the regime.

Khomeyni and the regime were preparing themselves for a show of force during the Moharram and Safar months when believers mourned the martyrdom of Imam Hoseyn at Karbala. Since May 1963, Khomeyni had stood in open defiance of the shah. He had instructed preachers throughout the country to set aside their fears and speak against the 'despotic regime' which was 'closely collaborating with Israel and its lackeys'. Khomeyni had ordered religious speakers to voice their hatred for the participation of women in social activities, the equality of rights, and the anti-Islamic regime. He accused the shah of being irreligious and spoke about the necessity to 'deal with him' and 'revolt' against him.[60] The cocktail of Khomeyni's charges against the shah was lethal. In the name of religion and God, Khomeyni was dynamiting the traditional symbols of the regime's legitimacy: God, Shah, Fatherland.

Nine days before the 5 June uprising, SAVAK recognized that since the Iranian New Year (21 March 1963), the balance of power between the regime and the clergy had become increasingly complicated. It identified delays in the serious implementation of the second phase of land reform, the attack on Fayziyeh, and forced dispatching of seminary students to military training, as factors causing general dissatisfaction. The anti-government mood was exacerbated by the steep increase in the price of oil, sugar and other basic needs. The constellation of these negative factors, SAVAK maintained, was playing into the hands of the clergy.

On 3 June 1963, Tehran witnessed a huge pro-Khomeyni demonstration, which the police and army did not attempt to disperse, except when demonstrators approached the shah's palace. On the same day in Qom, Khomeyni lambasted the regime in a fiery speech. Addressing the shah as 'Mr Shah', Khomeyni told the mighty monarch that unless he wished to see the people rejoice at his fall from power, he should recant, come back to the fold, and heed the advice of the clergy. Khomeyni threatened the shah directly and openly, saying that he could declare the shah to be a disbeliever and the people would 'kick him out' and 'make his life impossible'.[61]

Before dawn on 5 June 1963, in the dark of the night, troops surrounded Mostafa Khomeyni's house in Qom, where his father was staying. They arrested the Ayatollah and dispatched him in a Volkswagen Beetle to a prison in Tehran. News of Khomeyni's arrest reached Tehran at about 5.00 am. His supporters, primarily organized around what came to be known as the Islamic Coalition of Mourning Groups, set out immediately to organize a riposte. From 8.30 am crowds began to congregate and from 10.30 am, the army received orders to shoot at will at the demonstrators.

From around 10.00 am to 1.00 pm, government troops had great difficulty neutralizing the revolt. The protesters barricaded certain areas around the bazaar. Some of the unarmed protesters wore black shirts and carried black flags along with pictures of Khomeyni. A good number of the demonstrators coming from Southern Tehran, carried pictures of Khomeyni, and were armed with sticks and iron rods, vandalizing property on their rampage. According to SAVAK reports, shots were fired in the bazaar area before 11.00 am. The angry protesters set fire to buses, army jeeps, fire engines, army trucks and booths selling bus tickets. They attacked government buildings, banks, police headquarters and targets such as Shaban Jafari's Athletic Club, the Automobile Club and several cinemas

From around 1.00 pm, tank columns began rolling into the areas where protesters were putting up considerable resistance. The protesters had been out on the streets since 8.30 am, marching, shouting, running, clashing with soldiers, and destroying property. From around 10.00 am, the central and southern parts of Tehran witnessed an unprecedented theatre of war. At about 5.00 pm, the protesters tired. The wind was knocked out of the uprising as demonstrators began to scatter and head home. As the military regained control of the streets, the demonstrators abandoned parts of the city that looked like veritable war zones.

Tehran radio announced martial law in Tehran, with Gen. Nematollah Nasiri, the chief of police, as military governor. Martial law imposed a curfew from 10.00 pm to 5.00 am, outlawed all assemblies and gatherings, and entitled the police and the military to arrest suspects and enter houses without a warrant. The announcement reminded the public that anyone acting against the constitutional government, public peace, and public security would be sentenced to death, if they were found guilty of treason.

By nightfall on 5 June, Tehranis living in the centre and southern parts of the city had experienced scenes of death and injuries, wailing and screaming faces, people ducking flying bullets and exploding grenades. The rubble, and columns of smoke rising to the sky were reminiscent of a war-torn city. The number of demonstrators on 5 June varied according to different sources from 4,000 to 49,000. The number of those arrested between 5 and 6 June were estimated between 418 and 704.

At 7.00 pm on 5 June, SAVAK claimed 42 dead in Tehran and 22 in Qom. Two days later, official sources placed the number of dead in Tehran and Qom at eighty-six. On 24 June, the American Embassy in Tehran reported that: 'The death toll is probably about 125 persons, with [the] possibility [of] a few more who were wounded and carried off by friends to places where they died later and were not reported.'[62] Alam, the prime minister, talked about 200 dead, only 85 of whom had been identified.[63] A study by Emadeddin Baqi, after the revolution, placed the number of dead at 32.

> **The US Chief of Staff's Assessment of Iran after the 5 June Uprising**
>
> In view of the mounting dissatisfaction among an increasing number of diverse and geographically dispersed elements in Iran, the current threat to internal security is believed to be greater than at any time since the Shah was forced to flee the country in August 1953. (V. H. Krulak)[64]

The shah could neither risk putting Khomeyni on trial nor execute him, lest another round of upheavals would bring his regime to its knees. Yet, someone had to pay for the uprising. The least dangerous and most well-known candidate to implicate was Tayyeb Haj-Rezai, a loyal servant of the shah, decorated by him for services rendered in toppling Mosaddeq. The extent of Tayyeb's involvement with the 5 June events was that he had in absentia consented to close the Tehran's vegetable market. However, the regime framed him for paying and arming the rioters with sticks and clubs to rebel in support of Khomeyni and against the shah. On 2 November 1963, Tayyeb Haj-Rezai and Haj Esmail Rezai were executed for what had happened on 5 June.

The Alarming Political Aftermath of the June 5 Uprising

Some ten years after the coup against Mosaddeq, during which the shah felt he had strengthened his power, he was once again challenged by a new contender with religious and political clout. Even though he felt victorious, he relapsed into his post-coup 1953 mood of mistrusting his rebellious and 'ungrateful' people. In turn, he was once again appreciative of his army and falsely insisted that the insurgents had been traitors in collusion with foreigners. He called the demonstrators mercenaries who had received 25 rials to take to the streets.

Bloodshed ushered fear and political conservatism. The aftermath of 5 June crippled traditional political parties and organizations. The leaders of the Iran Freedom Party who had been arrested before the uprising were given long prison terms of four to ten years. The state accused the defendants of disrespecting the law and the Constitution, preparing the conditions for a 'regime change' and 'establishing contacts with foreigners' to implement their plans. The leaders of the Second National Front, argued that 'the ruling clique had become very powerful, and the National Front had become very weak', and so adopted 'a policy of patience and awaiting' and eventually permanently closed shop on 9 February 1964.[65]

The people's intimidation emboldened the shah. While a majority followed where the shah led them, a small but young and committed minority dug in their heels to oppose the shah and his regime. A new political opposition was born out of the 5 June uprising. As the regime's criminalization of democratic dissent pushed political activity underground, clandestine student circles flourished and murmurs of radical and revolutionary armed struggle percolated.

Before the end of June 1963, the National Front publication in Europe, *Irane Azad* (Free Iran), published by Iranian students in France, Germany and Switzerland, reacted to the 5 June uprising. The editor of the paper, Ali Shariati, maintained that everyone in Iran 'hated those who unjustly and coercively ruled over them' and that 'everyone hoped for a revolution with deep social impacts'. In Shariati's assessment, 'the June revolution was a flash of lightning in the deadening silence and darkness of Iran'. Obviously, his feisty article did not bear his name.

Shariati wrote, 'Yes! The epoch of peaceful struggle has come to an end.' He identified 'the overthrow of Mohammad-Reza Shah' as a political objective and suggested that 'the enemy's flood of fire and steel' should be responded to 'with the expressive language of guns and the destructive force of war'.[66] The overseas students of the National Front were proposing a new path to political change.

By March 1964, *Payame Daneshju* (Message of University Students), the unofficial organ of the radical and student-driven Third National Front, echoed the revolutionary call of their overseas cohorts. They posited that the National Front was responsible for 'leading the people's discontent' to the final stage of 'smashing the diabolical forces of despotism and overthrowing colonial rule'. In the name of the National Front, the students appropriated the leadership and issued a revolutionary alert. They reminded their readers that 'rebellions without a proper plan and roadmap would fail'. Yet, the students declared war on the regime and wrote, 'We intend to obtain freedom, and it is to this end that we will be at war with dictatorship, bullying and despotism.'[67] The idea of revolutionary university intellectuals substituting themselves for a party or the working classes and leading the armed revolutionary movement started in the aftermath of the 5 June uprising.

The Shah Looks to a Bright Future

For the shah, however, Iran's political and economic future was bright. Some 29 months after the closure of the 20th Majles, the country prepared itself for elections to the 21st Majles. Eleven weeks after the 5 June uprising, on 27 August 1963, the Congress of Free Men and Women opened in Tehran to set the stage for the Majles elections. It was attended by 600 representatives of Iran's farmers, 130 representatives of Iran's workers, and 270 representatives of the country's various urban professional and guild groups. This gathering was supposed to be a 'People's Congress' representing a coalition of farmers, workers, professionals, women and intellectuals. Those gathered were supposed to discuss the White Revolution or the 'priceless/wonderful gift given to them' by the shah. The one thousand delegates swore allegiance to defend the White Revolution with their blood.

Through a seemingly democratic, inclusive and participative process, this government-selected Congress produced a list of 193 candidates for the 200 parliamentary seats available. The people subsequently voted for them during the election on 17 September 1963. On the surface, 'appropriate' deputies were identified by members of this all-encompassing People's Congress rather than the opaque engineering methods of the past. Furthermore, nominations by this Congress rendered party politics redundant. The Congress of Free Men and Women was the embryo of a single mass party, and a dress rehearsal for the future single party called *Hezbe Rastakhize Mellate Iran* (the Resurgence Party of the People of Iran), imposed in 1975.

The single-day election on 17 September 1963 displayed unusual speed and efficiency. For the first time in Iranian history, women participated in elections. Women voters surpassed male voters in numbers. Two days after the election, the results were announced in the press. The list presented by the Congress won a sweeping victory. Of its 193 candidates, 182 were elected. Abdollah Riyazi, who became the president of the 21st Majles and served in that post until 1978, received the highest vote among the fifteen deputies from Tehran. Some 29 per cent of the deputies had spent some part of their education abroad. The exceptional feature of the 21st Majles was the debuting of six female deputies, one of whom, Farrokhru Parsa, became the first female minister in August 1968.

The 21st Majles

In this, the Twenty-first Majles, the regime promoted the candidacy of new educated professional middle-class members- individuals who represented a growing salariat that was increasingly challenging the system of monarchical rule. (J. Bill)[68]

Hasan-Ali Mansur, a young, dashing and rising political star, was one of the key architects and planners of the Congress of Free Men and Women and the elections to the 21st Majles elections. Mansur, along with a few like-minded educated and Westernized liberals, such as Amir-Abbas Hoveyda, Manuchehr Kalali, Hadi Hedayati and Gholamreza Nikpay, were the founder of the *Kanune Moteraqi* (Progressive Centre) in February 1961. Mansur's plans and preparation for the 21st Majles were well known to the American Embassy in Iran. More than three months before the elections, Stuart Rockwell had informed the State Department from Tehran that: 'The study of suitable candidates is proceeding, and the elections will be carried out well, and in a manner, which can cause no complaints.'[69]

Satisfying the shah's quest for an economically and culturally modern Iran required energetic Western-educated technocrats and bureaucrats. This new Iranian elite needed to be depoliticized and loyal to the shah's vision of a modern Iran. In the Progressive Centre, the shah found the dynamic and ambitious cadres ready to carry out his modernizing dream for Iran.

Mansur's young and educated circle of friends were best situated to direct and manage the kind of economic modernization the shah yearned for. They were familiar with the latest theories of economic growth and development in the West. They understood their models and the technical jargon involved. The Progressive Centre helped the shah to successfully substitute economic growth and welfare for political reform and liberalization.

After the 21st Majles elections, Mansur, Hoveyda and Ataollah Khosravani founded *Hezbe Irane Novin* (New Iran Party). On 15 December 1963, the fifty-six members of the Central Committee were elected, and Mansur was unanimously voted as general secretary. From this date, the New Iran Party, strongly supported by the shah and the US, formed a strong majority in the Majles, threatening Alam's government.

Five days before Mansur became prime minister, the acting assistant secretary of state hailed the formation of the New Iran Party as a 'most noteworthy internal political development'. He added that this move was 'part of an attempt to marshal public support for the [shah's] reform program and prepare the groundwork for the long-planned accession of the Party's leader, Hasan-Ali Mansur, to the premiership'.[70] On 7 March 1964, Alam resigned and the shah appointed Mansur prime minister. After his dismissal, Alam became minister of court. Mansur's government was primarily composed of members of his own party. The shah charged the new government with the implementation of the White Revolution.

Factual and Analytical Questions

1 How did post-coup freedom of expression, political association and assembly differ from the Mosaddeq era?
2 What were the objectives of the National Resistance Movement?
3 What happened on 'University Students' Day'? Did it have a single cause? Explain.
4 What were the accomplishments of the Zahedi government?
5 What was the significance of the Bagdad Treaty and Iran's participation in it?
6 Why was the US interested in reforms in post-coup Iran?
7 Why did the shah opt for a two-party political system? What were the two parties? How successful was this experience? Why?

8   What was the 18 May 1961 Jalaliyeh National Front rally indicative of? Why did it rattle both the Amini and the US government?
9   What were the 'six-point principles' of the shah's White Revolution? What do you think was the purpose of the 'White Revolution'? Support your position with historical facts.
10 Outline the process by which Ayatollah Khomeyni became the leader of the opposition to the shah's regime before he was banished to Iraq.
11 In what ways are Amini and Mansur similar and in what ways are they different? Why did the shah trust Mansur and not Amini?

Seminar Questions

1   Provide historical evidence for the position that Mosaddeq was a democratic and patriotic national hero overthrown by the CIA and SIS, with the collaboration of Iranian accomplices.
2   Provide historical evidence for the position that Mosaddeq was a power-hungry demagogue who abused the well-founded nationalist sentiment of Iranians for his anti-constitutional, anti-monarchic and anti-democratic political ends.
3   Assess the importance of the Officers' Organization of the Tudeh Party, and the circumstances and consequences of its demise.
4   'Iran's abandonment of her neutralist foreign policy position during Ala's premiership guaranteed its independence.' Provide the pro and con arguments for this statement.
5   'The Mosaddeqist National Front and Iran Freedom Movement had similar political objectives and methods.' Provide historical evidence for your response.
6   'Kashani, Navab-Safavi and Khomeyni, three political Islams, with three different methods of struggle and three different political outcomes.' Assess the validity of this statement.

Discussion Questions

1   Zahedi faced different kinds of domestic opposition after the coup. Categorize and discuss each.
2   'The Amini–Page Oil Agreement did achieve the objectives of the Oil Nationalization Law.' Assess the validity of this statement.
3   Compare and contrast the governance styles of Zahedi, Eqbal and Amini.

4 'The Qarani Affair paved the way for Amini's rise to power.' Assess this statement in view of US political interests in Iran.
5 'Amini's vacillations between promoting and violating the Constitution crippled his entire term in office.' Discuss the validity of this assertion.
6 'Ayatollah Khomeyni's initial criticisms of the regime were cultural and not political.' Assess the validity of this statement.
7 'The 5 June 1963 uprising in support of Khomeyni, changed the opposition's alignment of forces and their tactics of confronting the Shah in more than one way.' Assess and explain.

Glossary

19th Majles From the 1st to the 18th Majles, the length of parliamentary terms was limited to two years. From the 19th Majles onwards, the term was extended to four years. The Islamic Republic retained the four-year term of the Majles.

Iran Task Force In May 1961, alarmed by the death of Khanali and a 'potentially dangerous situation' in Iran, President Kennedy ordered an interdepartmental 'crisis-type task force' called the Iran Task Force to monitor the political situation in Iran and provide policy proposals on how to deal with the country's problems.

Seyyed Qutb (1906–66) Qutb worked as a teacher in the Egyptian Ministry of Education and joined the Muslim Brotherhood at the age of 46 and after his two years' stay in the US, which left a most negative mark on him. Qutb was a staunch anti-Westerner and believer in forging an Islamic government based on Islamic laws in Egypt. He was imprisoned by Jamal Abdel Naser in 1958, where he wrote his most important religio-political works. In 1964, he was released from prison, re-arrested after eight months and executed on 29 August 1966.

6

The Shah's Push towards the Gates of the Great Civilization, 1964–77

Chapter Outline

The Architects of the New Iran and Their Enemies	281
Landmarks of Transitioning to Despotism	289
The Roaring Years: Economic and Cultural Transformations	303
The Queen's Soft Cultural Revolution	311
Glossary	325

The Architects of the New Iran and Their Enemies

On 8 March 1964, the 41-year-old Hasan-Ali Mansur introduced his cabinet to the shah (Figure 6.1). Of Mansur's 26-member cabinet, 14 held doctorate degrees, and only six were old members of Alam's government. Members of his government who had not yet adhered to the New Iran Party, joined now. The minister of foreign affairs and the three military cabinet members, including the ministers of war and of agriculture, and the deputy minister in charge of SAVAK, directly under the shah's control, were exempt from party affiliations. Iran was now officially governed by the New Iran Party, with a resounding majority in the legislature and dedicated to implementing the shah's modernization policies.

Within three weeks, Mansur conducted a major house cleaning campaign in Iran's ministries, central and provincial government offices, and bureaucracy. Some 300 new appointments changed the surface of Iran's political face. For the first time, two

Figure 6.1 Hasan-Ali Mansur. *Source: Wikimedia Commons.*

women occupied the positions of general directors in the Ministries of Water and Electricity and of Housing and Construction. With women deputies in the Majles and now women in the government, Mansur was following the shah's wish to speed up women's participation and involvement in Iranian socio-political life. Unveiled women gradually found their way into liberal professions, entertainment, movies, arts and especially the teaching world at all levels.

Mansur hoped to mend fences with the clergy. One month after he became prime minister, he eulogized the clerical institution and emphasized that the government had the highest regard for it. He added that the shah was the protector of the faith. On 7 April 1964, after ten months of house arrest in Tehran, Khomeyni was released and returned to Qom.

Since March 1962, the US had been pushing for the ratification of the 'Status of Forces Agreement', exempting US military personnel from being held accountable for crimes committed in Iran. This bill provided the US with sole jurisdiction over its military personnel in the country. Litigations involving US personnel would not be judged according to Iranian law but according to American law. Realizing the delicacy of this issue for a sovereign state, the governments of Amini and Alam had refused to go through with it. Stuart Rockwell of the American Embassy in Iran recalled that Mansur 'knew we wanted it and I guess it was decided that it would be useful to oblige us'.[1]

'Status of Forces Agreement', Whence it came

The Shah . . . rammed through the Iranian Parliament, at our insistence and with considerable risk to his domestic position, a highly unpopular measure extending immunities and privileges to American military personnel in Iran. (P. Talbot)[2]

The bill was put to the Majles on 13 October 1964. In a parliament where Mansur's New Iran Party enjoyed a comfortable majority, the bill was ratified by 74 votes in favour and 61 against. The tepid response to this burning foreign policy issue was far from the expected overwhelming support. Even members of the government, such as Jamshid Amuzegar, Ali-Naqi Alikhani and Ataollah Khosravani, strongly objected to the bill, calling it a 'shame which shall forever taint the party [New Iran] and the government'.[3] The regime was understandably preoccupied with the public reaction.

Less than two weeks later, on the shah's birthday (26 October 1964), Khomeyni lambasted the 'Status of Forces Agreement', referring to it as the capitulation agreement. He condemned it for rendering Iran a US colony and claimed that it had 'shamelessly reduced the Iranian people to a status lower than American dogs'. He accused the parliamentarians who had supported the bill of treason and declared that he did not accept the legitimacy of the Majles, the Senate, and the government, and prayed that God would destroy all who betrayed the faith, the Quran and the country. Khomeyni was once again calling on his supporters to overthrow the regime. Within two hours, transcribed texts of his speech were duplicated and distributed in Tehran.

Five days later, Mansur explained the necessity and importance of this agreement for the country's well-being. He pointed out that other countries, large and small, as well as Iran's neighbours had signed similar agreements. On 4 November 1964, nine days after his speech against the 'Status of Forces Agreement', Khomeyni was again arrested and rushed from Qom to Tehran, where he was placed on a plane and banished first to Turkey and then Iraq. SAVAK issued a declaration informing the public that Mr Khomeyni had been exiled from Iran because of his activities 'against the people's interest and that of national independence and self-sovereignty'.[4]

Khomeyni's first arrest had brought the country to the verge of a revolution. Now, almost seventeen months later, the news did not make much of a ripple, except in the seminary schools. The people in Tehran, Qom, and other major cities went about their lives as usual. Even among Khomeyni's staunch followers, the anger, zeal and stamina manifested during the 5 June uprising had dissipated. It was partly sublimated, partly neutralized by increasing economic prosperity and partly driven underground.

On 24 November 1964, Mansur's government suddenly doubled the price of gasoline from 5 to 10 rials per litre and introduced a 60 per cent increase in the price of kerosine. The additional income from the price hikes was to be spent on necessary infrastructural expenditures. Protesting the price rise in gasoline, some 16,000 taxi drivers went on strike. A very cold Tehran without taxis made life difficult for people to get around. Rumours circulated about a general strike involving grocers, butchers, and bakers. On 12 January 1965, the prime minister partially reversed the price hikes and informed the Majles that the shah had personally ordered the price decreases. Frustrated with the setback, Mansur saved face by claiming that his government was courageous enough to change its mind for the sake of the people.

Bullets Aimed at the Prime Minister

During the first nine months of 1965, the Iranian political scene witnessed two assassination attempts on the highest officials of the land, one state funeral and an unsuccessful armed uprising. The cycle of armed operations, arrests, trials, sentencing and the execution of sentences overlapped and lasted from January 1965 to April 1966.

On Thursday, 21 January 1965, Mansur was shot twice at very close range as he was getting out of his car in front of the Majles. His assailant Mohammad Bokharai was captured, and Mansur was rushed to hospital. By nightfall on 21 January, Bokharai's two other accomplices, Reza Saffar-Harandi and Morteza Niknejad, were arrested. The prime minister was pronounced dead at 11.00 pm on Tuesday, 26 January.

Mohammad Bokharai, Mansur's 21-year-old assassin, was a member of the armed branch of the Islamic Coalition of Mourning Groups, a religious-political organization founded around April 1963 at the behest of Ayatollah Khomeyni to propagate and implement his vision of an Islamic-Iranian state and society. The rank and file of the Coalition were non-clerical Muslim zealots. A good majority of the members were engaged in commerce and petty trade primarily in Tehran's bazaar. The Coalition members had a high school education at best and did not include women or intellectuals. To create an ideal Islamic society, they believed that Muslims needed to be obedient to the clergy not only in the religious and spiritual realm but also in social and political domains. The organization and mobilization of the 5 June uprising had been the work of the Islamic Coalition of Mourning Groups.

From the inception of the Coalition, a small faction led by Sadeq Amani and Mehdi Araqi favoured the formation of an armed branch within the organization. Both men had been active in Navab-Safavi's Devotees of Islam. About a month after Khomeyni's exile, Amani argued for a radical operation against the regime to avenge its repeated blows against the religious institution. Araqi maintained that by January 1965, the Islamic Coalition of Mourning Groups had 500 operational cells in Iran with some 5,000 members. Some 300 of these cells operated in Tehran.

Mansur's assassin, Mohammad Bokharai, was born into a humble urban family and had eight siblings. He had been involved in National Front demonstrations. In 1963, through neighbourhood friends Reza Saffar-Harandi, aged 17, and Morteza Niknejad, aged 21, he became familiar with Khomeyni's ideas and was recruited by Amani and Araqi. Within ten days of Mansur's assassination, members of the Armed Branch, including Araqi and Amani as well as all influential members of the Coalition, were arrested.

Thirteen people were implicated in Mansur's assassination. They were accused of crimes ranging from overthrowing the regime and murdering Hasan-Ali Mansur to possession and sale of illegal arms and sheltering culprits. Their trial began in a military court on 27 April 1965. Bokharai, Saffar-Harandi, Niknejad and Sadeq Amani were executed on 16 June 1965, and others received prison sentences. With the arrest, execution, and imprisonment of the founders and influential members of the Islamic Coalition of Mourning Groups, the organization went into a long hibernation period, only to resurface in 1979.

The Big Wheel Keeps on Turning

Immediately after Mansur's assassination, the shah appointed as prime minister Amir-Abbas Hoveyda, Mansur's close friend and minister of economy (Figure 6.2). The shah praised his slain prime minister for his hard work in implementing the White Revolution, musing on what the poor man had done to be assassinated. The shah quickly moved on, reminding Iranians that not a moment should be lost in implementing the reforms and concluded that they should march towards the bright future.

On 27 January 1965, twenty-four hours after the death of Mansur, Hoveyda introduced the members of his government to the shah. Hoveyda and the shah were

Figure 6.2 Amir-Abbas Hoveyda. *Source: Via Getty Images.*

the same age. Iran's new 45-year-old prime minister had spent some 40 years of his life abroad, growing up, studying and working. When he became prime minister, Hoveyda's French was better than his Persian. He was an affable, open-minded, honest, good-humoured and sociable intellectual. In love with French culture and art, he had unwittingly found himself at the centre stage of Iranian politics. He started his premiership with a walking cane and was always remembered with a pipe in a corner of his mouth and an orchid in his lapel.

His cabinet was composed of twenty-six ministers and deputy prime ministers, the majority of whom spoke English. The most significant change in line-up was the removal of Hasan Pakravan as director of SAVAK and his replacement with Nematollah Nasiri. The shah replaced the honest, well-educated, legally minded and liberal Pakravan with an obedient servant, and SAVAK took a sharp turn for the worse. Pakravan moved on to become Iran's first minister of information. Hoveyda announced that the programme of his cabinet would remain exactly the same as Mansur's.

On 28 January 1965, Mansur was given a state funeral. Hoveyda and his cabinet, members of Mansur's family, although not his wife, and the diplomatic corps in Iran were present mourning the death of the slain prime minister. Riazi, the president of Majles, praised Mansur as one of nation's greatest martyrs and a minute of silence was observed in his honour. The shah did not attend the funeral. Instead, he sent his brother, Shapur Gholamreza, as his representative along with a 3-metre-long wreath.

Bullets for the Shah

On 10 April 1965, some seventy days after Mansur's assassination, Reza Shamsabadi, a 23-year-old conscript soldier of the elite Royal Guard, opened fire on the shah. As the shah entered the Marble Palace and made his way to his office, Shamsabadi, on guard on that day, fired thirty shots at him in less than a minute. Two of the shah's bodyguards were killed, a palace gardener and a butler were wounded, and Shamsabadi was gunned down. The shah escaped the assassination attempt unscathed. This experience added weight to his conviction that he enjoyed God's special protection.

Reza Shamsabadi was born in a poor rural family on the rim of the desert, near Kashan. He was 10 when his family migrated to the city of Kashan in search of work. In 1960, at the age of 20, Shamsabadi joined the Mosaddeqist *Hezbe Mardome Iran* (People of Iran Party) in Kashan. He allegedly got into trouble for throwing acid at Prime Minister Amini's car and was said to have been expelled from the party for his 'left' tendencies.

Since the 1953 coup, the shah had been increasingly reliant on his military and security organizations, which were rewarded lavishly. The Shamsabadi case exposed the incompetence of the country's counter-intelligence services, including the army, the Royal Guard, police, gendarmerie and SAVAK. Embarrassed by its fatal shortcoming, and with Shamsabadi dead, Nasiri's SAVAK team fabricated an imaginary plot with seemingly plausible culprits.

On 8 May 1965, almost a month after the incident, SAVAK revealed a sinister plot, supposedly masterminded by Parviz Nikkhah, Ahmad Mansuri-Tehrani and Ahmad Kamrani, members of the **Confederation of Iranian Students in Europe**. These young, educated and left-wing students who had returned from Europe were identified as Shamsabadi's puppeteers and arrested. In total, seven left-wing intellectuals were accused of plotting to unleash guerrilla war in Iran. SAVAK shifted attention from Shamsabadi and focused on imaginary conspirators. The concocted scenario was so far-fetched that even the shah did not believe the trumped-up charges.

Even though it was evident that the framed culprits were not behind Shamsabadi's action, the Military Court sentenced Ahmad Mansuri-Tehrani and Ahmad Kamrani to death, and Nikkhah to life imprisonment. On 26 December 1965, the shah commuted the two death sentences, and the press praised him for his compassion and benevolence. SAVAK whitewashed its incompetence and came out as omnipotent, and the shah ended up looking like a just ruler, forgiving dangerous would-be assassins. All came out winners except those arrested and tortured by SAVAK.

What Spurred the Assassination Attempts

It was unquestionably the milieu of discontent and malaise permeating Tehran, but especially the poorer sections surrounding the bazaar, that spawned the assassins. (M. Zonis)[5]

Shamsabadi was a restless, lone wolf, who had long been thinking of assassinating the shah. Whatever his motives, Shamsabadi acted alone. He had spoken of his intention to a few friends, but no one knew the exact details of where, when and how. Neither Mohsen Mobasser, the chief of police, nor Ardeshir Tajbakhsh, the head of army counter-intelligence, believed that Shamsabadi had any connection with the Confederation of Iranian Students.

On 20 October 1965, or about ten days before the Military Court ruled on the fate of those arrested in connection with the attempt on the shah's life, shots were exchanged throughout the night in the hills of northern Tehran. Mohammad-Kazem Bojnurdi and four of his close associates had attempted to disarm the Ozgol Gendarmerie Station when they came under attack by the police and gendarmerie, which had them under surveillance for a while. The assailants were surrounded and arrested. Three months later, on 20 January 1966, the government announced that 55 members of *Hezbe Mellal Eslami* (the Party of Islamic Nations), an armed clandestine party intent on unleashing armed insurrection, had been arrested.

Bojnurdi had founded his Party of Islamic Nations in early 1962 and begun preparing for armed struggle to overthrow the regime. The Party of Islamic Nations was composed essentially of young, educated men, around age 22. Bojnurdi believed that since political activities 'in the Shah's undemocratic and police state' would be 'severely repressed', it made sense 'to respond to the bayonet with a bayonet'.[6]

Bojnurdi and members of his organization had participated actively in the events of 5 June 1963. They assessed the support for Khomeyni and the opposition to the shah as the readiness of the masses to support any religious movement against the regime. After 5 June, Bojnurdi placed armed struggle on the agenda of the party to overthrow the regime.

On 6 February 1966, members of the Party of Islamic Nations went on trial. The military prosecutor, asked for the death penalty for eight of the defendants, each accused of a different crime, from overthrowing the regime to involvement in an anti-monarchic party, insulting the monarch, illegal possession of arms and armed resistance. On 17 April 1966, the Military Appeals Court condemned Bojnurdi to death and sentenced the others from life to six months' imprisonment. About two weeks later, on the birthday of Prince Ali-Reza, the shah's second son, the shah pardoned Mohammad-Kazem Bojnurdi. His death sentence was commuted to life imprisonment.

Domestic Politics

With the New Iran Party, the shah had found the motor for realizing his dreams. The party attracted upcoming young, educated and professional technocrats who looked up to the West, especially the US. These were overwhelmingly nonideological men and women eager to enter the expanding Iranian civil service, producing the end product desired by the shah. All sorts and types could be found in the party. Some were nationalists in the sense that they wished to build an economically powerful and socio-culturally modern Iran for their children, some were corrupt, some were honest, some were ambitious, while some were good civil servants. Oppositional politics, which was a high-risk affair in Iran, was not their cup of tea. This new elite of managers and builders were pragmatists, utilitarian, interested in modernization and loyal to the shah.

With Mansur as his prime minister, the shah felt confident that an efficient, technocratic machine, closely following his vision of progress, without political liberalization, had been installed. His assassination had delayed the launching of his project. This two-year period of adjustment and fine-tuning came to an end in 1966.

From 1967 to 1970, Iran experienced a period of general tranquillity, while the shah consolidated his despotic rule, channelling his energies towards economic growth, greater oil revenue and building his military arsenal. From 1970 to 1978, Iran asserted its authority and independence internationally with the oil consortium, became an important player on the international chessboard, and side by side with Israel became the US's most reliable ally in the region. During this period, Iran made great economic and social strides towards an economy of affluence and speeded up the drive towards socio-cultural Westernization. These roaring years had the cultural and artistic climate of a *belle époch*. It began in Tehran and permeated to provincial centres.

During this period, the shah imposed a one-party system, Iran became a theatre of armed struggle, and the regime became evermore intolerant of dissent and repressive. From 1970 to 1978, the shah pursued a model of governance, well embraced by the international community. It combined a drive towards economic affluence, an open and accommodating international economy, with political repression at home. Long after the shah's death, his model of government came to be called the Chinese model of development. The shah could not maintain his iron-fisted repressive regime, once he erroneously thought that the West and especially the US was abandoning him, and from 1978, all fell down.

Landmarks of Transitioning to Despotism

On 15 September 1965, to extol the shah's outstanding and historically unprecedented services during his twenty-five years of rule, both houses of Parliament held a joint session. One speaker after the other fawned over the monarch, labelling his reign as the most glorious in Iran's twenty-five centuries of history. Sharif-Emami, the president of the Senate, read out a laudatory commendation and conferred the title 'Aryamehr' on the shah. Aryamehr could mean the love/favourite of the Aryans. The new title, however, intended to frame the shah as the Sun of Aryans (Iranians). Shojaeddin Shafa, who had coined the term, posited that the title expressed the light, which the shah exuded on all Iranians.

All kinds of urban projects and events, prestigious and not so prestigious, popped up bearing the name Aryamehr. The Aryamehr Stadium, Aryamehr Industrial University, Aryamehr Steel Complex (Esfahan), Shahyad Aryamehr Monument and even the Aryamehr Tennis Cup and Aryamehr Horse-Racing Cup, were intended as physical expressions of the shah's grandeur and omnipresence. Aryamehr presented a superhuman image of the shah, necessary for the construction of his cult of personality. The media, government officials, politicians and all Iranians quickly adopted the title. Until the end of his reign, he was called 'Shahanshah (king of kings) Aryamehr, the sublime leader of the country.' The shah, who lacked both charisma and a heroic political past, tried to present himself as being chosen and protected by

God to fulfil a mission. Therefore, more stringent efforts were required to stage him as a fearless, decisive and loved hero of the people.

Intuiting the Shah's Desires as State Policy

From October 1965, the leaders of the three branches of state government, legislative, judiciary and the executive, as well as their supposed watchdog, the press, outdid one another to emphasize that their mission was to intuit and implement the shah's intentions and desires. This new development openly acknowledged that the three branches and the press had no responsibility to the people but the person of the shah.

By November 1966, the shah had constituted his team of executive secretaries. With Alam as minister of court, Hoveyda as prime minister, Sharif-Emami as president of the Senate, Riyazi as the speaker of the Majles, Eqbal as the chairman of the National Iranian Oil Company and Nasiri as the director of SAVAK, the six pillars of the shah's rule were in place. These men retained their positions for some eleven to fifteen years. The shah was now happy with his employees.

It became common political practice for Riyazi, the Speaker of Iran's Parliament to invite the parliamentarians to 'implement Shahanshah Aryamehr's lofty wishes', or 'ensure the majestic satisfaction of Shahanshah Aryamehr'. The Speaker of the Senate, Sharif-Emami, implored that 'it is imperative that we attain the objectives determined by Shahanshah Aryamehr'. The role of the Parliament was reduced to facilitating the implementation of the shah's 'illuminous and towering ideas and plans'. For Mohammad Sururi, chief of Iran's Supreme Court for eleven years, the judiciary's job was to 'do its utmost to fully implement the Shahanshah's intentions and desires' in the domains of enforcing justice, welfare and security. Sururi acknowledged that the judiciary, like the legislative served only at the shah's pleasure.

Hoveyda, throughout his almost thirteen years as prime minister, repeatedly asserted that his government was guided and inspired by the towering ideas of Shahanshah Aryamehr and exerted all efforts to carry out the magnificent programmes and projects of the Shahanshah. For Hoveyda, the prime minister and the government were accountable only to the shah and there to serve him. The ticket to Hoveyda's longevity in office, as that of the other five pillars, was their skill at understanding or guessing the shah's intentions and desires and trying to implement them.

Hoveyda and the Shah

Prime Minister Hoveyda first accepted and then promoted the idea that policy was the Shah's, development was the Shah's, and consequently all the progress the nation made was the Shah's. The monarch, he insisted, was the boss, the final arbiter, the supreme decision maker. (G. R. Afkhami)[7]

From 1966, even the soft opposition newspaper editors, who were still allowed to publish, threw in the towel. Rahmat Mostafavi, a one-time supporter of Mosaddeq, spoke on behalf of the Iranian press at the 1966 New Year audience with the shah. Mostafavi announced that: 'the press is proud to communicate/propagate the shah's lofty ideas among the people'. Mostafavi assured the monarch that the press 'was honoured to participate in the rebirth of Iranians', which he attributed to 'the Shah's grace and his progressive ideas'.[8]

By March 1966, the press had forfeited its mild checks-and-balances role and had become the loudspeaker of a single person. From 1964 to 1978, the shah was the only captain of Ship Iran, and the three branches of government were window dressings. The press could enter politics only if it sang the praise of Shahanshah Aryamehr.

A Bonapartian Coronation

On 26 January 1967, half a million copies of the shah's second book, *Enqelabe Sefid* (The White Revolution), were published and it was made into a required text in school. It told the story of the shah's miraculous achievements and the treachery of his opponents. The book explained in detail the six-plus-three principles constituting the White Revolution and elaborated on the shah's vision of international politics. The royal text was supposed to serve as an ideological manifesto galvanizing all Iranians, just as Mao's Little Red Book had rallied the Chinese three years earlier.

On Saturday, 19 August 1967, the shah and Queen Farah went to the Senate and inaugurated the Constituent Assembly, which subsequently revised the Constitution. The deputies voted unanimously that in case of the monarch's death, while the crown prince was still underage, Empress Farah Pahlavi would act as regent until he turned 20. The revision took away the decision-making power of the two legislative houses deciding on a regent and legalized the shah's appointee as regent. The hand-picked Constituent Assembly assured the continuity of the Pahlavi dynasty the way the shah had wanted it.

All was ready for the shah to celebrate his achievements by crowning himself on the twenty-fifth year of his kingship. The designated date of 26 October 1967 was also the shah's birthday. These festivities were only the first of a two-leg ceremony. The October 1967 festivities were a domestic affair, which the shah wished to celebrate with his big family, the Iranian people. The commemoration of Iran's 2,500 years of monarchy, scheduled for 1971, was to be the second leg of the celebrations and an international bash. The shah needed to be appreciated at home and abroad.

Preparations started with Tehran getting a facelift. The squares and streets were beautified, and potholes were repaired. Luminous arches and crowns, multicoloured bulbs, and strings of light were strewn across the city. Some 200 triumphal arches were constructed in Tehran and 52,000 throughout the country. Garden parties, carnivals,

Figure 6.3 Coronation of the shah of Iran in 1967. *Source: Photo by Angelo Cozzi, Archibio Angelo Cozzi via Getty Images.*

fairs, sports activities, parades, military marches and exhibitions entertained the people, in Tehran and other cities, towns and villages. On the evening of their coronation, the royal couple inaugurated Tehran's new performing arts complex, the Rudaki Hall, with a capacity of 1,350 spectators. Consecutive nights of fireworks illuminated the skies of Tehran. Climbers even decorated the peak of the Alborz Mountains with crowns.

On Thursday, 26 October 1967, the Austrian-built gold and royal blue carriage, pulled by four pairs of Hungarian white horses, carried the royal couple to the Golestan Palace. At 11.07 am, the shah placed the Pahlavi Crown on his own head (Figure 6.3). Within minutes, Queen Farah knelt before him and the shah crowned her. Crown Prince Reza sat attentively on a little throne to the shah's left. Clothed in full military regalia, he would turn 7, five days later.

During the coronation ceremony, Hoveyda, Sharif-Emami and Riyazi outdid each other in showering the shah with praise and announcing the festivities as the people's genuine expression of gratitude towards him. On their way to and from the Golestan Palace, the streets were lined with people cheering the royal carriage, while many Iranians watched the ceremony on television.

The golden crown worn by the queen weighed 2 kilos and was studded with diamonds, pearls, and rubies. The shah's gold and silver crown with some 3,300 diamonds was slightly heavier than 2 kilos. The shah wore the same crown as his father did during his 1926 coronation. Outside the palace, planes dropped 17,705 stalked flowers on Tehran, each symbolizing a day in the shah's life.

In the spirit of Middle Eastern dreamy fantasias, the festivities lasted seven nights and seven days. The newly built (21 January 1963) luxurious Hilton Hotel hosted balls for dignitaries. Food was flown in from France and fireworks from Germany. The shah and the people visited the industrial fairs displaying Iran's advancements. The celebrations cost 25,388,780 tomans ($3,626,960). The coronation festivities were the shah's way of sharing his joy with his people.

Iran's 2,500 Years of Monarchy: Just a Celebration?

Four years after the coronation festivities, came the celebration of Iran's 2,500 years of monarchy. This was a very different event and expressed fundamental changes in the shah's outlook of his monarchy. It was a four-day (12–16 October 1971) international feast, celebrating the monarchical system, the shah and his vision of Pahlavism. The shah had become used to Iranians celebrating him and now he felt entitled to being honoured and praised by world leaders and embraced as a world-class player on the international scene.

The celebrations coincided with a phase during which the shah turned his attention from Iran to the region and the world. He had come to believe that he could now extend his experiences and services to the world. His growing self-absorption and self-admiration and his long-held spiritual fixation that he was chosen and protected by God and the Shii Imams added to his missionary sense of responsibility to Iran and the world. The shah became less interested in domestic issues, riding roughshod over whatever was in dissonance with his vision.

The combined economic and diplomatic achievements rendering the shah oblivious to internal issues were real and significant. Iran's oil revenues had increased substantially since the Tehran Conference of 14–15 February 1971. The agreement had been brokered by Amuzegar and commandeered by the shah, who had long wished to increase his oil revenues to build up his military arsenal and become the dominant regional power. For some three years, the shah had been irritated by the Consortium preventing Iran from increasing its oil revenue.

Flexing his muscles, and with the support of OPEC countries, the shah threatened the Consortium and the US with a shutdown of oil supplies. At the Tehran Conference, the posted price of Persian Gulf oil was finally raised from $1.80 to $2.18 per barrel, thereby increasing Iran's oil revenue by some $350 million. The shah came out of the Tehran Conference as a proud politician who had finally got his way with his world-class partners. The shah's ego was boosted by his success with the Consortium and the fact that he no longer needed to beg the US for armaments.

> **Iran's Arms Procurement Policy**
> Iran's request for US arms are a function of the Shah's perception of Iran's strategic requirements and the amount of revenue Iran has available to purchase arms in the US (Committee on Foreign Relations)[9]

The Arabian Nights account of the celebrations with 600 guests and a long list of world dignitaries, including one emperor, numerous kings, sheikhs, queens, princes, princesses, presidents, vice presidents and prime ministers, became the main news of the international press. Almost everything concerning the celebrations at Persepolis (Shiraz), the tents, linen, towels, hairdressers, cosmetics, chefs, bakers, waiters, food (except for Persian Caviar), wine, cutlery, plates and glasses were imported mainly from France. From Germany came 250 Mercedes-Benz cars to transport the dignitaries and celebrities to and from Persepolis. The cost of the festivities was estimated anywhere between $22 million to $200 million.

In preparation for the smooth unfolding of the celebrations, SAVAK took precautionary measures and rounded up students, and suspected opponents of the regime while some faculty members were instructed not to attend their classes or go to university until the celebrations were over.

The celebrations were criticized both at home and abroad for their ostentatious display of extravagance, while many Iranians lived in poverty and squalor. The celebrations sharpened the public's sense of injustice. The armed operations of the nascent Iranian guerrilla movement launched some eight months before the celebrations, intensified the socio-political atmosphere of polarity. The regime's execution of arrested guerrillas exasperated the student opposition to the celebrations and plunged Iranian universities into a wave of demonstrations and disturbances.

The Celebrations Council tried to connect the celebrations to the lives of Iranians. They decided to build 'twenty-five-hundred new schools in the villages to correspond to the twenty-five-hundred anniversary of the founding of the Persian Empire'.[10] Funding for these 'Commemoration Schools', showcased as a significant stride towards 'the Great Civilization', came from private contributions.

From 5 April 1971, the press reported how businessmen, captains of industry, landowners, wealthy dignitaries, civil servants and even workers were rushing to participate in this school-building race. The contributors were competing to win the shah's good graces. By the start of the celebrations, 3,200 'Commemoration Schools' were built and inaugurated by the members of the Literacy Corps. Yet, the state-engineered aspect of this effort made it seem as another show of coerced charity.

> ### Pahlavism as an Ideology
> Three elements made up *homo Pahlavicus*. The first element was primordial and eternal faith in the imperial system. Second was the concept of empire that symbolized the golden ages of the past and the future . . . Pahlavism's third emphasis was on Aryanism. (Z. Shakibi)[11]

The extravagant celebration was the shah's debutant ball coming out on the international stage as a rising star. The festivities also had a solemn message for Iranians, uninvited to the event. At Pasargad, the tomb of Cyrus the Great, the founder of the Iranian Empire, the shah addressed him as one king to another. The shah referred to 'this glorious moment in Iran's history' and assured Cyrus to, 'Rest in peace, for we are awake, and will always rest awake to safeguard your magnificent heritage.' He promised Cyrus that just as in his days, 'Iran's name is now associated with respect and admiration throughout the world.' The shah was tracing his royal lineage to Cyrus and completely ignoring Iran's Islamic heritage.

The shah told the world that as long as he remained vigilant, Iran would prosper. He had come to believe that he embodied Iran and that he was Iran. The main show of the celebrations was a grand military parade by some 4,000 soldiers and officers of the Iranian army re-enacting 2,500 years of the Persian Empire. Dynasty after dynasty, represented by their soldiers, faithfully clad in uniforms of their times, and accompanied by the music of their age, marched before the guests. For the shah, it was military might that symbolized the Empire throughout its evolution. Just as Cyrus the Great had created the vast Achaemenid Empire, the shah saw himself walking in his footsteps.

The Shah, Nixon and Kissinger: Money Brings Political Romance

Having acquired the finances he needed, the shah was eager to purchase the military hardware he had always longed for, particularly advanced US fighter planes. In January 1969, President Richard Nixon had articulated what came to be known as the 'Nixon Doctrine'. The major setbacks of direct US intervention in Vietnam had led President Nixon to look for alternative ways to guarantee US interests in sensitive regions of the world. The 'Nixon Doctrine' promised that the US would stand by its allies, help them financially and militarily, but would not enter into a conflict on their side, avoiding situations such as Vietnam. The 'Nixon Doctrine' minimized US involvement in regional conflicts by placing the responsibility of safeguarding the security of US allies on their governments.

> ### US View of the Shah's Role in the Region in April 1970
> The Shah's Iran is an island of stability in an otherwise unstable area which includes not only the broader Middle East but also the Persian Gulf from which the British will withdraw next year . . . From our viewpoint, he is a good friend . . . Given the above factors and Iran's rapid economic growth, there seems little reason not to give the Shah whatever he wants. (H. Kissinger)[12]

The 'Nixon Doctrine' liberated the shah from the cautious approach of previous US Administrations that had, to different degrees, hemmed in his desire to build up his military strength. The shah could now obtain the latest military weapons and technology and impose himself as the guardian of a politically volatile and economically crucial region.

The military withdrawal of the British from the Persian Gulf, announced in January 1968 and effectuated on 1 March 1971, created a potential power vacuum. The shah saw a golden opportunity. The US had alienated the Arab world after her support for Israel in the Six-Day War and was delighted to see the shah, an old benefactor and a reliable ally, fill that vacuum.

In April 1969, the shah had already obtained a major regional victory. He had used brinkmanship by threatening Iraq to use force and had secured the annulment of the 1937 Tehran Treaty, which gave Iraq sovereignty over the entire Shatt al-Arab waterway. By October 1970, the shah knew that he had a stern ally in Kissinger and Nixon and that the US would bend backwards to accommodate him. When it came to choosing the guardian of the Persian Gulf after the UK withdrawal from the region, the US would acknowledge that 'that Iran is in fact the preponderant power in the Gulf'.[13]

On 20 February 1971, the shah threatened that if Tonb and Abu Musa, in the Persian Gulf, were not returned to Iran, he would take them by force. On 30 November 1971, less than three weeks after the end of the celebration of Iran's 2,500 years of monarchy, the Iranian armed forces landed on the three tiny islands of Greater Tonb (some 10 square kilometres) and Lesser Tonb (some 2 square kilometres) and Abu Musa (some 12 square kilometres) in the Persian Gulf and hoisted the Iranian flag. With Britain out of the Persian Gulf, the shah, with US support, marked his territory.

President Nixon was invited to the Persepolis celebration, but dispatched Vice President Spiro Agnew and his wife to the royal bash. Less than six months later, however, Nixon, accompanied by Kissinger, arrived in Tehran on 30 May 1972. This was immediately after attending the historical Moscow Summit of 1972, where he signed the first **Strategic Arms Limitation Talks (SALT)** with Soviet leader Leonid Brezhnev. Twelve days earlier, Israeli Prime Minister Golda Meir had travelled secretly to Iran and met with the shah for two and a half hours.

Nixon's two-day visit provided the shah with what he had always wanted. This was the first official visit of an American president since Eisenhower's short stay in December 1959. During the first day, the shah told Nixon that 'Iran, like Israel, must be able to stand alone', and to do this, 'Iran also had to have the most modern weapons.'[14] On the second day of their meeting, the shah revealed his foreign policy designs. He said, 'the Persian Gulf was key. Iran had established relations with Ethiopia and South Africa to make sure there was a common policy in the Indian Ocean. Iran would deal even with Australia for this purpose.' The shah mentioned that he had told Oman that he 'would fulfill any request they had for assistance in defeating the guerrillas'.[15]

At the end of the two days, the shah received an unprecedented carte blanche to purchase any number and type of conventional weapons available in the US arsenal, without any questions asked. Iran was subsequently exempt from the sales reviews practiced by the State and Defense Departments. Nixon was operationalizing his doctrine, and the shah was finally getting the kind of alliance he always wished. The agreement between the shah and Nixon made the shah the gendarme of the Gulf region. This historical agreement triggered an unprecedented process of military, political and financial enmeshment and entanglement between the US and Iran.

Was the Shah a Client of the United States?

We must reexamine the popular myth of the shah as a pliant Third World client of the United States during the global Cold War. What this history of the origins of Iranian primacy suggests is that Mohammad Reza Pahlavi was an architect, not an instrument, of the Nixon Doctrine in the Persian Gulf. (R. Alvandi)[16]

Arms Build-Up and the Regional Gendarme

In August 1972, the shah engaged Iran in a proxy war. His neighbour, Sultan Qabus of Oman, had been fighting against the Dhofar Marxist-Leninist rebels with the secret help of the British since 1963. In 1972, Iran pledged to help Sultan Qabus in fighting the communist threat supported by China and the Soviet Union. The theatre of war in Oman was an ideal testing ground for Iran's growing military power and her newly acquired weapons, especially US fighter jets and helicopters.

The Shah on the Dhofar Rebels

Just imagine that these savages should seize the other bank of the Ormuz Straits, at the mouth of the Persian Gulf. Our life depends on that. And those people at war with the Sultan are savages. They may even be worse than communists. (C. L. Sulzberger)[17]

In August 1972, the shah began shipping arms to Qabus, and in October 1972, he dispatched 150 special forces to Oman. By 1975, there were some 3,000 Iranian soldiers of the Imperial Army fighting some 1,800 insurgents in Oman. The arrival of the Iranians, accompanied by their air superiority, shifted the fortunes of war to the advantage of Sultan Qabus in 1974–5.

Iranian forces secured the coast and Western Dhofar, assured transportation links inland, and the Imperial Iranian Navy dispatched to the Arabian Sea prevented outside support from reaching the rebels from South Yemen. On 11 December 1975, Sultan Qabus claimed victory over the rebellion. The shah, who micromanaged the operations in Oman, took credit for Iran's role as the saviour of the region, and the Iranian military remained in Oman until the revolution. The casualties of the Imperial Iranian Army's involvement in Dhofar amounted to some 500 dead.

Who Decides What Weapons to Buy

The defense decision-making process in Iran is relatively simple. The Shah decides on all major purchases; his Vice Minister of War, Air Force General Hassan Toufanian, implements these decisions. (Committee on Foreign Relations)[18]

Between 1970 and 1976, the Iranian defence budget increased from 8.2 per cent to 14.2 per cent of the GNP. US military sales agreements with Iran leapfrogged: $113 million (1970), $519 million (1972), $2.1 billion (1973), $4.3 billion (1974), $3.0 billion (1975), $1.3 (1976) and $5.7 (1977). The increase in arms purchases, helicopters, fighter jets, destroyers, submarines and missiles, was almost in tandem with the quadrupling of oil prices in 1973/74, which increased Iran's per-barrel oil revenue from $2.18 in January 1971 to $9.49 in 1974.

This sudden jump in oil prices solved Iran's foreign exchange constraints and increased Iran's domestic and foreign expenditures. For the shah, the financial resources to realize his promised 'Great Civilization' and become 'the fifth world power' were now at hand. The shah, however, remained impervious to the dangers of overheating an economy saddled with inadequate infrastructural facilities and skilled labour constraints.

In 1977, the Iranian market accounted for 50 per cent of all US arms sales. Iran's purchase of sophisticated US arms and technology made Iran into a regional superpower on paper. The shortage of trained personnel to operate such sophisticated weapons however, created a major bottleneck, pre-empting the possibility of taking full advantage of them.

> ## Arms Build-Up, Economic Deterioration and Collapse
> The Shah's military build-up directly led to the economic deterioration preceding and perhaps precipitating the overthrow of the regime. (R. E. Looney)[19]

The shah's military build-up created at least three interrelated economic, ethical-political and cultural problems. First, it placed considerable strains on the Iranian economy. From 1973, the shah acted as though he was not bound by the traditional guns versus butter dilemma. Iran's defence budget jumped by 141 per cent from 1973 to 1974 and another 72 per cent from 1974 to 1975. By the fiscal year 1977, the resources allocated to military and security expenditure constituted some 33–40 per cent of the total Iranian budget.

It may be difficult to estimate how much economic growth would have 'improved if military expenditures were held at their pre-1973 levels'. However, 'the economy would have been healthier, perhaps sufficiently so to defuse the tensions that ultimately resulted in the overthrow of the regime'.[20]

Second, on the heels of huge contracts between Iran and Western corporations, which craved Iranian business, came corruption, kickbacks, bribery and ill-gotten gains. Iranians who occupied sensitive military, governmental and professional positions, with connections to the shah, stood to gain. The traditional system of patronage, networks and nepotism benefitted some. Soon there were talks of multimillion-dollar 'bribes' and 'commissions'. Grumman, Northrop, Rockwell International and McDonnell-Douglas, giants of US arms industry were allegedly paying commissions to Iranian officials. It has been suggested that between 1972 and 1975, Iranian officials pocketed some $200 million from the contracts negotiated with US arm companies.

Third, the expansion of trade, and especially the import of arms, resulted in a growing American presence in Iran. Training Iranians on the use and maintenance of sophisticated US military technology necessitated the presence of American military technicians and personnel. By mid-1975, forty-four military-related companies operated in Iran, with 60 per cent of their personnel located in Tehran. In 1973, the Department of Defence (DOD) personnel in Iran stood at 760, not counting their dependents. In 1976, approximately 17,000 to 24,000 Americans associated with the DOD community and US contractors lived in Iran.

By 1978, the number of Americans in Iran was somewhere between 35,000 and 54,000 compared to some 15,000 in 1972. The salary of the US military personnel paid by the Iranian government was anywhere between $12,000 and $24,000 per month. The housing of this growing number of Americans, with a pronounced disproportionate purchasing power, compared to the local population, placed pressure on the price of local rentals. The increasing presence of American personnel in Iran also gave rise to a service sector tailoring to their cultural, entertainment and leisure needs.

The inflow of young, single American males, especially Bell Helicopter flight and maintenance personnel in Esfahan, created socio-cultural problems and tensions. While the mingling and dating of American personnel with Iranian women went largely unnoticed in Tehran and especially northern Tehran, such socializing gave rise to religious objections in Esfahan. The casual and lax moral comportment of American personnel in society, at their place of work and even on military bases created cultural misunderstandings and conflicts. The '**Ugly American**' was at times rowdy, arrogant and rude. The salary disparities fuelled jealousies. In Iran's growing anti-American and radical atmosphere of the 1970s, the loud presence of American military personnel caused social consternation and malaise.

The One-Party System

Between 1970 and 1973, the shah became increasingly arbitrary and consequently more intolerant of the slightest act, event or word not in compliance with his wishes. He continued to set higher economic objectives. However, Iran was besieged by weak institutions, wanting infra-structural facilities, underdeveloped work ethics, managers and technocrats fearing to take initiative and administrative red-tape. The shah, therefore, chose to manage selectively.

He required key officials to report directly to him, as he mistrusted all and worried about collusion, slacking, and conspiracies. As the economy, bureaucracy and army expanded, the breadth, width, and depth of the shah's purview for micromanagement increased, forcing him to over-spread himself. Convinced that one man could manage all, the task of dealing with everything became ever more impossible.

To obtain results and prevent failures, the shah inculcated fear in the hearts of his subjects, functionaries and even relatives, hoping to increase loyalty, efficiency and greater identification with his goals. The armed struggle conducted by the guerrillas and the growing unrest in Iranian universities was an important source of concern, preoccupying him and making him bitter.

In 1961, the shah had been proud that 'most Iranians' were 'industrious and hard-working'. By 1972, in close circles, the shah referred to Iranians as good for nothing, villains, moaners, groaners and lazy loafers.[21] He saw himself at loggerheads with his own people, whom he believed were neither wholeheartedly supporting his regime, nor invested in his ideas.

> **The Shah on His People**
>
> Usually this is the way Iranians are. If you stand up to them, you are the winner, and if you retreat before them, you are finished. (A. Alam)[22]

The shah failed to understand why the people were unhappy with his governance at home while his prestige was surging on the international scene. From 1973, the shah and his people became politically disconnected. Yet, the shah was adamant about making them understand the importance of absolute monarchy and their duty to rally behind him.

In June 1973, he had come to believe that the 'highest form of participation' was for a group of experts to share their opinions with the shah on matters of the state.[23] Searching for new forms of increasing the people's political participation in his modernization scheme, ironically, the shah opted for a single-party system.

Another ominous sign of the regime's growing political intolerance for a minimum of plurality came on 20 August 1974. Sixty-three newspapers and publications, including popular weeklies, were shut down. By 1974, newspapers were already under heavy censorship, yet the obsession to completely homogenize ideas and weed out, not actual but possible, dissent was driving the regime towards a dangerous precipice.

On 2 March 1975, the shah ended decades of his uncomfortable coexistence with a formal two-party system (at times a multi-party system) and imposed the ultimate straight jacket of a single-party system on the people. In a lengthy televised interview-cum-monologue, resembling a stream of consciousness, he recapitulated his vision of Iranian history and his role in it.

But most significantly, he divided Iranians into two groups: those who believed in the Constitution, the monarchical system and the White Revolution and those who did not. The shah instructed those who believed in the tripod of his make-shift ideology to immediately join the new *Hezbe Rastakhiz* (Resurgence Party) and announced the immediate dissolution of all existing parties. The shah appointed Hoveyda, the prime minister, as the secretary-general of the new party for at least two years.

The shah accused those who would not join the Resurgence Party of 'belonging to illegal organizations', being Tudeh Party sympathizers and 'stateless traitors'. He announced that 'their place is in prison'. Offering the opposition, a way out, he said, 'If they wish, we will willingly issue their passports, without charging them with the regular exit duties and allow them to go wherever they want . . .'

In his at times muddled speech, the shah acknowledged a third category. He said those who neither believed in this movement nor were traitors 'were free'. However, he warned this latter category that they should not expect anything, assumingly rewards or jobs, from the state. He treated those Iranians who did not aspire to his dreams as a disenfranchised community and chastised those who refused to commit to the regime in the face of the opposition, without explicitly saying so.[24] The Resurgence Party was charged with 'guarding the White Revolution'. By fiat, the shah believed, he had made the people the keen guardians of his throne and his ideas.

Everyone in Iran, pro and anti-regime and even political bystanders were taken off-guard and perplexed. No one knew or understood what was going on and why? Yet, everyone in power praised the decision as an act of genius. The Resurgence Party was to separate the devotees of the shah, whom he thought were the overwhelming majority, from the hard-core opposition and push anyone on the sidelines to join the devotees.

The shah was closing ranks to lead his people towards the 'Great Civilization'. On 10 April 1975, the statute, regulations and organizational structure of the Resurgence Party were published and three weeks later, the party's newspaper *Rastakhiz* appeared to propagate the ideas of the shah and the party. To inject some political excitement, on 9 July 1975, Hoveyda announced the creation of two wings within the Resurgence Party. Jamshid Amuzegar, the interior minister and a bright technocrat who led Iran's OPEC team would head *Jenahe Pishro va Taraqikhah* (The Progressive Wing) and Hushang Ansari, the entrepreneurial minister of economy would take charge of *Jenahe Sazandeh* (The Constructive Wing). The pro-American leaders of both wings were serious contenders for the post of prime minister.

On 28 October 1976, Amuzegar replaced Hoveyda as secretary-general of the Resurgence Party (Figure 6.4). Less than nine months later, on 7 August 1977, he would replace him as prime minister. The last secretary-general of the party was Javad Saeed, who took over this position on 27 September 1978. Four days later, Saeed resigned and the party, which boasted some 5.4 million members, disappeared after three and a half years of unsuccessful activity.

One of the main initiatives of the Resurgence Party was the dramatic change in Iran's calendar system. While Iran was celebrating the fiftieth anniversary of the Pahlavi dynasty, Iranians woke up to a curious piece of news. On 14 March 1976, four days before the Iranian New Year of 1355, a joint session of the Majles and the Senate, whose members were all candidates of the all-encompassing Resurgence Party, voted that Iran's Muslim solar calendar be changed. Iran's new calendar would base its origin on the coronation of Cyrus the Great instead of the solar Hejira date when the Prophet Mohammad's migrated from Mecca to Medina. Overnight, Iran's new imperial calendar jumped from 1355 to 2535.

This was yet another initiative indicative of the shah's growing hubris and disinterest in what his people were thinking. It was a logical follow-up to the impetuous decision to impose a single party and have his functionaries work out the details. The idea of a new calendar system had been aired during the 2,500-year celebrations but was swept aside by Hoveyda. The shah felt that his Great Civilization had to reconnect with the grandeur of Cyrus's great empire and severe ties with its Islamic origins. Iran's history no longer reflected its religious lineage but relied entirely on the history of its monarchs.

Figure 6.4 Jamshid Amuzegar. *Source: Keystone Pictures USA via Alamy.*

The Great Civilization

The Great Civilization is one in which the most insightful and scientifically minded individuals are employed to attain the highest standards of material and spiritual wellbeing for all members of society . . . The special capability of this civilization, which has always been the source of the Iranian civilization's power and dynamism is its ability to comingle with other civilizations and cultures, co-opting their best features to create a more perfect and global combination . . . This is the ideal culmination point of Iran's historical and cultural evolution throughout thousands of years. (M.-R. Pahlavi)[25]

The Roaring Years: Economic and Cultural Transformations

From 1964, Iran experienced a distinctive roaring period of economic prosperity accompanied by cultural and social transformations in Tehran and a handful of other urban centres. This period was somewhat similar to the 'Roaring Twenties' in the West. The economic boom, fuelled by oil revenues, allowed for a significant rise in economic welfare and spectacular and concomitant changes in consumption patterns.

The shah's Westernization drive, and his particular emphasis on personal and individual freedoms, to balance his refusal to allow for political rights, revolutionized the mode of urban life. That segment of society at ease with cultural liberalization was unchained from its traditional family and religious vestiges, creating an atmosphere of the *Années folles*. During these years, the youth could rebel against all symbols of authority, except the shah's despotism and the state.

The shah wished his 'Great Civilization' to replicate life in Paris, New York and London. Where political freedom was in short supply, the shah offered economic, moral and cultural liberalism and the freedom to pursue individual tastes and pleasure. The shah's selected snide remarks about corruption, decay and decline of morals in Western societies were more of an intellectual show. He wished to appear opposed to moral degeneration and **Westoxication** but never took steps to curtail the spread of Western lifestyle in Iran.

The shah privately grumbled about the increasing number of long-haired Iranian hippies and their hashish abuse. Gen. Mohsen Mobasser, the chief of Tehran's police, took the monarch's criticisms seriously. He ordered the police to round up the long-haired men in northern Tehran and cut their hair. The anti-hippie raids had spread as far as Tehran's most exclusive discotheque, the Key Club, which was said to have been inaugurated in 1965 by members of the royal family. One day after the anti-hippie operations, on 28 September 1970, Mobasser was removed from his post.

On 28 and 29 September 1970, the leading newspapers published an important Court announcement. Citizens were assured of 'freedom of lifestyle, dressing, etc.' and any interference in personal and individual liberties was condemned as 'an infringement of liberties'.[26] By the mid-1970s, the regime officialized its green light to the Iranian youth to conduct their private lives as they pleased.

Growing Prosperity and Crippling Convulsions

The story of Iran's economic success between 1964 and 1977 could be told in different ways. From a strictly economic growth point of view, Iran's performance during these thirteen years was exceptional. In 1964, Iran's Gross Domestic Product grew at a respectable 9.2 per cent. From 1965 to 1977, growth rates averaged an impressive 11.2 per cent, while the population grew at an average of 2.7 per cent, enabling the country to comfortably join the ranks of the fastest-growing nations of the world. Iran's growth rates came close to the Republic of Korea and surpassed Turkey, Venezuela and Mexico. By standard growth criteria of the times, since 1965, Iran was in its sustained economic 'take-off' stage.

Iran's rate of inflation during the Third Development Plan (1963–7) remained at a very low figure of 0.6 per cent. The increasing size of the economic pie with an almost non-existent increase in prices enhanced the purchasing power of Iranians and enabled them to have more. During the Fourth Developmental Plan (1968–72), price levels increased by 3.4 per cent. From 1973, inflation rates became double-digited and soared to 27 per cent in 1977, before dropping to an average of 11 per cent during 1978 and 1979.[27]

During Iran's Fifth Development Plan 1973–7, and after the quadrupling of oil prices, the steady-state Iranian economy was jolted and experienced a turbulent period. The economy was not ready to absorb the enormous financial inflow. The increase in government oil revenues from $2.8 billion (1972/3) to $17.8 billion (1974/5) generated a substantial demand shock. The economy could not deliver what the cash inflow expected.

The previously impressive double digit growth rates fell into single digits in 1973 and 1974 before becoming -2.3 per cent in 1975, then peaked to 18.2 per cent in 1976 and then dipped into negative single and then negative double digits until December 1979. The dramatic negative growth rates were primarily due to the 30 per cent drop in Iran's oil sales, which in turn, was the result of the recession-driven decrease in demand in the West. The increase in expenditures running faster than the increase in revenues in 1976–7 brought economic realities crashing down on the shah, making Iran a borrower.

Shah, Hoveyda and Economists

The Shah and Hoveyda showed a certain contempt for the cautious views of the economists who could not see beyond problems to the broader vision of an industrialized Iran. (R. Graham)[28]

For the shah, the post-1973 staggering jump in revenues was a blessing as it released him from budget and financial constraints, enabling him to attain his 'Great Civilization' before the end of the twentieth century. The miracle was to happen through a spending-binge that would remove bottlenecks, resolve the unavailability of skilled labour, infrastructure and organizational structures necessary to absorb the magnitude of the financial injection.

The shah's ambitious and outlandishly expensive idea of launching into a nuclear programme, for example, was a poisoned fruit of the 1973 leap in oil prices. The Atomic Energy Organization of Iran (AEOI) was born on 10 April 1974. By 1976, it employed over 1,000, and its budget stood at $1.3 billion. It had also signed letters of intent with France and Germany for four large nuclear plants.

> ### The Shah's Rush to Nuclear Energy
>
> The shah's decision to rapidly expand Iran's nuclear energy in 1974 had been made without consulting Washington and with Iranian, not American, interests in mind. (R. Alvandi)[29]

Economics is a Pain!

With the increase in oil revenues, came the opportunity to realize the social dimension of the 'Great Civilization'. From 21 July 1974, the state committed itself to forge an impressive welfare state characterized by free schooling, free school meals and free feeding of newborns until the age of 2 and finally a comprehensive social, health and retirement insurance programme. These measures became the fifteenth, sixteenth and seventeenth principles of the White Revolution.

Expenditures on this vast social programme along with ambitious economic projects and military purchases had consequences. Something had to give. The gap between aggregate demand and aggregate supply at 1972 price levels became ever-more glaring. By early 1975, the transportation system and especially the ports crumbled under the weight of imports. By mid-1975, 'over 200 ships were waiting to unload their cargoes' at Khorramshahr, the main port in southern Iran.[30]

Furthermore, Iran's spectacular growth did not improve the standard of living of all Iranians equally. All ships were not rising with the tide. As in the case of almost all developing capitalist economies, glaring disparities emerged. The rural fell way behind the urban. The rural–urban migrants created their own makeshift shanty towns in the urban centres. These urban slums inhabited by the poor were a sour sight. They lacked amenities, services and employment opportunities in comparison to the modern spaces of the lower-middle, middle, upper-middle and upper-class neighbourhoods. The income and wealth disparities further marred the overall results.

> ### Income Distribution in Tehran in 1974
>
> Inequality of income was most pronounced in Tehran where in 1974, 60 per cent of the city's total income was distributed among the top 20 per cent income group. (F. Kazemi)[31]

The stagnating and backward rural sector provided an unlimited supply of labour for the large and booming cities. These poor and traditional rural migrants felt culturally alienated and economically impoverished in the fast-moving, glittering,

Westernized and promiscuous social atmosphere of Iran's big cities. 'The 1966–76 period experienced a 22% increase in the rural-urban migration rate (a total of 3.5 million), relative to an 11% increase in this rate over the previous decade (a total of 1.6 million).'[32] The rural–urban migrants, huddled together, lived in marginal settlements in the periphery of big cities and were neglected by the government. Every once in a while, the government tried to evict them from the squatter settlements. This wronged and numerically increasing social strata found solace and security in traditional networks of mosques and religious congregations.

You Can't Tell a Market Economy What to Do

In the summer of 1975, it became clear that increasing expenditure to remove infrastructural and manpower-related bottlenecks was not reducing inflation. The shah, therefore, resorted to instituting price controls in his own authoritarian manner. He sought a scapegoat for his economic mismanagement and decreed prices to roll back. On 14 July 1975, the shah gave an ultimatum to 'profiteers and hoarders'. He threatened that inflation had to be curbed within a month, otherwise, the military courts would prosecute the culprits.

Combatting profiteering was decreed as the 14th principle of the White Revolution. Three weeks later, the shah labelled profiteers as 'the people's blood-suckers' and 'exploiters'. Through executive order, the price of 640 commodities was to be reduced by 10 per cent within days. Shopkeepers, boutique owners, retailers, wholesalers, restaurant owners, entrepreneurs, merchants and industrialists were threatened with expropriation, arrest and banishment.

> ### Iranian Economy in 1975
> By 1975 the economy was indeed out of control, and Iran as a nation was losing on two accounts. First, inflation was disrupting the socioeconomic equilibrium of years past; second, the nation was losing real resources (barrels of exported oil) as the cost of development projects soared. (H. Razavi and F. Vakil)[33]

Within a month of the shah's order, thousands of inspectors, including student shock-troopers of the Resurgence Party, were unleashed. Shops were closed and merchants were arrested. At least 16,000 were fined for profiteering. Some of the highly influential members of the business and commercial community were humiliated by the campaign. Among those arrested were Habibollah Elqaniyan, the founder of Iran's plastic industry, Hamid Kashani-Akhavan, a pioneer of department-store chains; Javad Barq-Lame, the owner of the largest towel factory in Iran;

Mohammad Vahabzadeh, a well-known merchant and sales representative of BMWs; and Saeed Khalili, the highly respected general manager of Butan Gaz, Iran's major producer and distributor of liquid gas and appliances.

Soon the wave of arrests spread to mayors, deputy-governors, government bureaucrats, guild members and leaders, contractors and even a Member of Parliament, all accused of collusion with the profiteers. In the summer and fall of 1975, the press reported on and printed the pictures of economic or political saboteurs. A flustered Shah, unable to impose his will on inflation, declared war on everyone, even the loafers in the ministries.

The unproductive, if not destructive anti-profiteering campaign, waned down after a while. By November 1976, some fifteen months after the shah's war on inflation, the Iranian press regularly reported on power outages, shortages of cement, poultry, charcoal, salt and even sumac. Forcing down inflation by edict and criminalizing business had failed to contain prices but had succeeded in alienating an important social class that had benefitted from the roaring years and supported the shah. The business community, large and small, were being penalized because blame had to be deflected from the monarch. The outcome was capital flight, reduction in investment and output, a thriving black market and increasing economic discontent.

The Tangible Results of the Economic Boom

Iran's GDP per capita (in current prices) had risen from $221 in 1964 to $2,315 in 1977. Even though the GDP per capita indicator represents the average and therefore a general level of prosperity, the tenfold increase of this measurement in thirteen years was a sign of the staggering rate at which the economic fortune of Iranians improved.

The growing demand fostered by the rise in oil export earnings fuelled an average 30 per cent increase in wages during 1974/5. During this period, unskilled construction workers could earn $5.50 a day, pipefitters around $450 per month, a good bilingual secretary approximately $1,200 per month, a foreign-educated engineer around $2,000 a month and finally, a well-educated manager could earn as much as $4,500 a month at the age of 30. These spectacular incomes, at first, gave a sense of prosperity and happiness.

Iran of 1976 had a population of over 33 million, with 48 per cent living in urban areas. Tehran, the heart of the country, had a disproportional share of everything. Some 4.4 million lived in Tehran, which housed 60 per cent of all industry and 22 per cent of the country's workers. For urban consumers, the variety and availability of goods and services had dramatically changed between the late 1950s and the late 1960s. From the late 1960s to the late 1970s, however, the change was phenomenal. The face of the big urban centres had transformed quantitatively and qualitatively.

The automobile industry

In 1951, Tehran had 8,000 privately owned cars and 50,000 in 1961. In 1977, Tehran was packed with 667,608 privately owned cars, 130,000 taxis, and 2,947 buses. In 1966, the entrepreneurial Khayami brothers had signed a contract with Talbot automobile manufacturers to assemble Hillman Hunters/Arrows. By the end of the year, their automobile company, Iran National, produced 7,000 cars called *Paykan* (Arrow). Twelve years later, in 1978, Iran National's output was 136,000 *Paykans*.

Paykan became Iran's veritable national car. Prime Minister Hoveyda drove around in one, and so did almost all taxicab owners. *Paykan* became the motor car of the emerging middle class, and its advertisement read, 'In the hope that every Iranian would one day own a *Paykan*.' In 1972, a total of some 120,000 *Paykans* roamed the cities of Iran, and in 1978, this number jumped to 432,000 units. Even though imported cars had increased sixfold from 10,000 in 1955 to 63,000 in 1977, Iran was producing twice more *Paykans* than it was importing foreign cars in 1977.

One year after *Paykan* came off the assembly line, in 1967, another Iranian entrepreneur Jafar Akhavan, who had already started assembling Wheeler Jeeps in Iran back in 1960, began rolling out American Motor's Ramblers under the names of *Arya* and *Shahin*. These models were classier sedans for the upper-middle classes. Akhavan's share of the automobile market remained modest, with an average of 8,000 vehicles per year between 1967 and 1972.

In 1974, Akhavan concluded a partnership agreement with General Motors and the Pahlavi Foundation. His company, Iran's General Motors, assembled brand vehicles such as Chevrolets, Buicks and Cadillacs. Akhavan aimed at winning the luxury car market of the upper classes. Between 1974 and 1978, Iran's General Motors sold 63,500 cars in Iran.

While the British *Paykan* won the hearts of the Iranian middle class and the American General Motors, that of the upper classes, Antoine Ayseh entered the Iranian car market with the French workman's car or the intellectual's ride, the famous Citroen Dyane. Ayseh, an Iranian-Armenian-Lebanese, formed a partnership with Citroen called SAIPAC. From 1968, *Jiyane*, the Iranian version of Diyane, entered the Iranian market at the low price of 8,000 tomans or $1,100. *Jiyane* sold some 123,000 units until 1975, when Ayseh decided to produce Renault 5, a more comfortable workman's car.

The evolution of the consumption and variety of cars was just one example of how the lifestyle of Iranians evolved. Iranian car output, even though it was more of an assembly/montage nature with some 30 per cent of the final good produced in Iran, increased by leaps and bounds. Home assembled cars took over the market and overshadowed imports.

Home appliances, food industries and department stores

The surge in homemade products and their variety occurred not only in the automobile industry but also in home appliances including, water heaters, refrigerators, water-cooled air conditioners, pressure cookers, ovens, gas cookers, kerosine cookers, televisions and radios. Iranian entrepreneurial families of great genius expanded their production and provided consumers with sturdy, fashionable and competitive home products.

Famous Iranian brands such as Arj, Azmayesh, Pars Electric-Pars Toshiba and Butan, were providing middle-income consumers with high-quality and affordable goods. These companies were founded respectively by Eskandar Arjomand, Mohsen Azmayesh, Mohammad-Taqi Barkhordar and Mohsen Khalili. Between the end of the 1960s and the beginning of the 1970s, Mohsen Azmayesh produced some 200,000 home appliances per year, while the annual output capacity of Eskandar Arjomand's company reached some 450,000 by 1975.

> ### Iran's Economy under the Pahlavis
> Despite worsening social and economic disparities, the standard of the living of the majority of the population improved substantially under the Pahlavis . . . However, oil proved to be a curse as well as a blessing. (H. Pesaran)[34]

The face of Iranian households, especially the middle and lower-middle classes living in cities was transformed by the surge in the domestic production of home appliances in these golden years. The upper classes continued to furnish their homes with imported goods. In 1962, Iran produced 600 sets of televisions and 8,580 radio sets. In 1969, production rose respectively to 66,566 television sets and 136,789 radio sets. By 1978, Barkhordar's Pars Electric alone produced 120,076 black and white televisions, 46,301 colour televisions and 24,000 radios.

The food industry in Iran underwent a similar revolution. In 1962, Iranians were familiar with two main factory produced biscuits. Reza Tehranchi and his brothers marketed Vitana, the first of its kind with its famous *Madar* (Mother) brand. Ali Gorji followed suit and produced the Gorji brand. It was not until 1965 that Ali Khosrowshahi's Minoo Industrial Company revolutionized the Iranian biscuit, wafer, chocolate, chewing gum, bubble gum, candy, toffee, and cheese puffs market. In 1965, Iranians consumed the Minoo brand of Kit Kat and Smarties produced under license from Rowntree-Mackintosh. Minoo's production, management, and marketing know-how offered Iranians homemade, high quality and internationally recognized brands. The popularity of its products quickly made Minoo a household name and a giant of Iran's food industry. In 1976, Minoo produced the Iranian version of 'Digestive'. The cylindrical-shaped, red, and gold package of the biscuit appeared even in remote rural Iran. In 1974 Minoo was producing some 2,150 tons per month of its assorted products. This figure jumped to 3,540 tons per month in 1977.

Iranian companies were churning out an impressive array of consumer goods from shoes to textiles, ice cream to soft drinks, ballpoint pens to pencils, cooking oil to salad dressing, soap to shampoo, washing powder to detergents, canned food to pickles, alcoholic beverages to cigarettes and home furniture to beauty products.

In the 1970s, Iran needed modern distribution hubs in line with the leaping growth in its consumer goods output. The bazaar, traditionally the supplier of goods and located in a specific geographical location had been losing its status since the end of the 1950s. It was less accessible and appealing to the emerging middle and upper-middle class, looking for more Westernized products.

Already in the 1940s, the first Iranian quasi-department store had been founded by Hasan Pirayesh and his German wife. In 1957, the Ferdowsi Department Store, founded by Amir Motaqi in cooperation with German interests opened its doors to the public. This was more of a modern department store. In the 1960s, Pirayesh and Ferdowsi were Tehran's leading chic department stores.

On 30 November 1967, the shah and the queen inaugurated the ten-storey Iran Department Store, owned by Hamid Kashani-Akhavan. In 1970, Akhavan opened another modern department store, Kurush (Cyrus). These American-style department stores provided mass consumption for Iran's growing middle and upper-middle classes. By 1979, Kurush had 13 other branches. Small fashionable boutiques such Keyvan Khosravani's 'Number One' and Pari Zolfaqari's 'Miss Number One' offered the elite stylish Iranian-designed and produced clothings. Towards the end of the 1970s, Iran's urban and rural population enjoyed consumption levels never experienced before.

The Queen's Soft Cultural Revolution

Queen Farah Pahlavi and her entourage of young, Western-educated, culturally and artistically avant-garde advisers played an instrumental role in introducing and supporting modern art, music, cinema, theatre, fashion, literature, poetry, painting and sculpture. The youth were encouraged to express themselves freely in these domains yet keep clear of any political insinuations. Political art in the shah's Iran was subversive and, therefore, other alternative arts, such as art for art's sake, was strongly promoted. Non-politicized arts were advanced to elevate the cultural standard of Iranians, bring them joy and amuse them.

Educated at L'École Spéciale d'Architecture in Paris, Farah Diba had a taste and sharp eye for the arts. After becoming queen, she realized that her husband's interests and political proclivities were different from hers. By October 1972, the queen would confide in Alam, the minister of court, that, 'my views differ from the Shah's in all domains'.[35] Much later, however, she would write, 'My husband and I actually had no basic differences. He believed that Iran's economic awakening was still too fragile to survive a complete liberalization of society, a Western-style liberalization.'[36]

The queen quickly carved out a sphere of culture and arts for herself and began a soft cultural revolution. The shah was happy to give her a free hand in a domain that he was not attached to and had no particular appreciation for. The shah was said to refer to intellectuals as 'shit-tellectuals' or *Ann-tellectuel*, with an emphasis on *Ann*, which in Persian means excrement.

The queen attempted to cultivate and propagate an eclectic Iranian-Western culture, familiarizing Iranians with the Western arts while emphasizing and promoting homespun and traditional arts. She became the patron of museums, lectures, seminars, conferences, art exhibits, film and music festivals, both national and international. Her cultural policy, however, found expression in two important projects.

> **The Queen's Cultural Mission**
>
> One of my growing concerns in the second half of the sixties was not to forget culture in the march of progress. (F. Pahlavi)[37]

From 1964, the queen gradually gathered different groups of young, talented and Western educated individuals. Most of them were around her own age of 26. The two projects with a transformative effect on shaping and developing Iranian art and culture were *Kanune Parvaresh Fekriye Koudakan va Nojavanan* (Organization for the Intellectual Development of Children and Young Adults) and *Jashne Honare Shiraz* (Shiraz Art Festival). While *Kanun* (for short), outlived the revolution, the Shiraz Art Festival would become a prime target of wrath for the revolutionaries.

Organization for the Intellectual Development of Children and Young Adults

Lily Jahan-Ara was a school friend of the queen at Razi, one of the francophone schools in Tehran. Later, educated in France and the US, she became a librarian. In 1964, Lily Jahan-Ara presented the queen with the idea of setting up a national network of children's libraries and producing relevant books for such a project. The idea was well received, and soon Lily Amir-Arjomand (after her marriage) stood at the apex of Iran's most important cultural institution, the Organization for the Intellectual Development of Children and Young Adults (*Kanun*).

Amir-Arjomand was assisted by Homa Zahedi and Firuz Shirvanlu. *Kanun*'s main objective was to try a new educational approach in a country with an illiteracy rate of 70 per cent. It hoped to make a mark by starting with children and working its way up. It planned to get children reading books, trigger their creativity, widen their horizons, and foster their personal and social development. The task necessitated mobilizing the experts who could contribute to and realize the various stages of this vast project.

Kanun quickly spread its activities from establishing libraries to translating and publishing children's books and operating a countrywide distribution network through mobile libraries. It later added film-making, animation, music and theatre to its activities. Soon it became a thriving centre for talented translators, writers, poets, essayists, editors, illustrators, painters, art designers, graphic designers, cameramen, sound engineers, documentarists, musicians and directors. During its fifteen-year activity, it produced hundreds of children's books, videos, audio cassettes and films.

> ## Children's Libraries in Tehran's Parks
> The libraries obviously had to be available to all free of charge, from nursery school to age sixteen, and we would need talented staff members for each age group. (F. Pahlavi)[38]

In 1966, the Organization launched its annual International Festival of Films for Children and Young Adults, which became one of the most prestigious annual festivals of its kind. Films produced by the *Kanun* soon found fame in international film festivals. In 1970, the Organization launched the Children's Film Training Center, the Music Training Center, and the Theatre Center, which housed the Children's Theater Activities and Puppet Show. It also established the Centre for Cultural and Social Surveys to provide the planners and the project managers with facts and figures on the ground. From 1974, the *Kanun* established its training centres in the provinces. The long and impressive list of those young novices who participated in the Organization and subsequently became references and celebrities in their respective fields, is a 'who's who' of Iran's leading artists of the time and even after the revolution.

In 1966, the *Kanun* had ten libraries. By the mid-1970s, it had '222 libraries serving also as cultural centres and 30 mobile libraries throughout the country'. It employed around 1,000 librarians and over 1,000 worked at art training shops and associated services.[39] The *Kanun* had become an imposing cultural pillar. Among the hundreds of high-quality books produced by the *Kanun*, one stood out as the epitome of the many contradictions that this organization embodied. In 1968, *Kanun* published Samad Behrangi's classic children book, *The Little Black Fish*. The book, masterfully illustrated by Farshid Mesqali, was about the armed guerrilla movement that was to sweep Iran between 1971 and 1976. Had it not been for the support and patronage of Queen Farah, the intellectual, liberal and progressive *Kanun* would have been shut down by SAVAK.

The Shiraz Arts Festival and the Theatre Workshop

Reza Qotbi was the queen's first cousin and almost like a brother to her. He studied engineering in Paris while Farah Diba was attending architectural school. Qotbi returned to Iran in Fall 1965 and was put in charge of establishing the government television network. The Iranian National Television officially began operations on 5 November 1966.

In March 1967, the queen launched the idea of the Shiraz Art Festival. From its inception, the queen's dynamic and modernist artistic team was at loggerheads with the conservatively minded Ministry of Art and Culture. Since December 1964, Mehrdad Pahlbod, the shah's brother-in-law, a musician, had been the minister of culture and arts, in charge of all programmes produced for the national radio.

The statute of the Shiraz Art Festival was approved by the queen on 23 May 1967 (Figure 6.5). The purpose of this organization was 'to propagate and honor genuine Iranian arts and raise the standard of the arts in the country, as well as celebrate the work of Iranian artists and introducing foreign arts and artists to them'.[40] The queen wished the Shiraz Film Festival to be a meeting place of Western and Third World art, and especially an arena for traditional, modern and avant-garde Iranian artists to expose their latest works, influence and be influenced by the rest of the world.

Figure 6.5 Shiraz Arts Festival. *Source: Wikimedia Commons.*

The main engines behind this project and the bulldozers which paved the way for its realization were Reza Qotbi, the festival director, and Farrokh Ghaffari, the deputy director, who was in effect in charge of the programme selection process. The French-educated and progressive film director, producer and intellectual, Ghaffari was Qotbi's close associate and his deputy at the Iran National Television.

The first Shiraz Art Festival was held from 11 to 21 September 1967, this was about a month before the shah's coronation. The queen called it the 'most important artistic event of recent years'. The annual ten days to a fortnight festival included, opera, Iranian folk music, religious passion plays, puppet shows, dance, film, and theatre from Iran and the world. Around the main events, there were film festivals of various renowned film producers, painting and photo exhibitions along with seminars and discussions of the main artistic events in the city of Shiraz.

The second Shiraz Arts Festival opened on 3 September 1968. This event coincided with the devastating earthquake in Khorasan that prevented the queen from attending the opening ceremonies. Instead, she assisted in the closing events of the festival, from 13 September 1968. In her absence, two very different plays rocked Iran's artistic community. The only thing they had in common was their view of a society that seemed to be going through its golden years but was deeply marked by an internal state of confusion, malaise and alienation.

A profound, colossal, and modern research into the fossils of the 25th, or 14th or 20th geological era etc., it does not really make any difference was the work of the Iranian playwright Abbas Nalbandian and directed by Arby Ovanessian. The play was as unusual as its title. Nalbandian was a 20-year-old newspaper seller, who had only an official fourth-grade education and had been unknown until this play. Ovanessian was a 26-year-old film director who had come back to Iran in 1966 from his studies at the London School of Film Technique.

The play, *A profound, colossal, and modern research* was framed in the unreal world of nine wandering spirits in a cave, very much like the Seven Sleepers of Ephesus. Each character walked around with a thick rope around their necks, searching for the individual who had done them wrong. They would tell their sordid story and start looking for their lost ones, continuing their unending odyssey.

The play had no action, no identifiable beginning or end, but words, sometimes disjointed, sometimes complete sentences. Iranians heard references to 'the old man of Ahmadabad', a familiar codename for Mosaddeq, as well as repeated references to Marx and veiled references to Lenin and Stalin. The spirit of the assassinated politician talked about his 'choice between surrender and violence', and that of the young soldier suggested that 'politicians and thieves are same'. The young soldier argued that for the 'good of the country and the people' action was necessary, and therefore, recommended making heterosexual and homosexual love. A woman on the stage swore at the soldier who asked her whether she was a prostitute. She said, 'Yes, motherfucker, I am a prostitute,' and then burst out in tears. The statements uttered were like highlights of newspaper titles, with no discernible social message.

The play caused considerable controversy among critics. Some argued that art was supposed to respond to people's tastes. Others believed that artists should be free of producing works for the general public. The allegorical and emblematic Nalbandian-Ovanessian production was labelled elitist, an 'absolute delirium', and 'a montage in the era of assembly lines'.

The Nalbandian-Ovanessian production did not resonate with most theatre critics, let alone with the people. Bijan Mofid's *Shahre Qeseh* (City of Tales), the second important play of the festival, on the other hand, was an instant hit. Mofid was a 33-year-old experienced playwright and director. His satirical and musical production weaved together old Iranian folk tales, songs and accounts of individuals transitioning in an imaginary modern city, very much resembling the Tehran of the late 1960s, with all its complexities and contradictions. *City of Tales* appealed to young and old and cut across the bubbling ideological schism in the country. The players wore animal masks, representing their duplicity and duality.

Mofid described his work as an allegorical play about people and their forsaken and bleak lives behind masks. The bear represented the superstitious geomancer and the fortune-teller. The fox personified the cleric, and the donkey, the worker. The craftsman wore a camel mask. The monkey, Mofid explained, portrayed 'today's castrated intellectual class who is cognizant of all problems, but his work remains at the level of being an audience'.[41] The elephant was the naive newcomer, whose compliance and good manners brought him pain as he went through an agonizing and confusing assimilation process. The two young lovers, mister Mouse and Aunty Beetle, characters based on an old Persian children's story, represented the pure and unsullied souls and wore no masks.

Mofid wished to show that no one could come out of this society, which he called a 'cesspool', unsullied. The play ended with a jazz song performed by the elephant who mourned his lost identity. He shouts out, 'Damn you, the public-bath owner, that I have become this!' The audience leaves the theatre wondering who the public-bath owner is.

The *City of Tales*, contrary to the Nalbandian-Ovanessian production, became a big hit and people from all walks of life and all social classes, high and low, white and blue-collar, veiled and miniskirt-clad, went to see it. Mofid succeeded in his objective of bridge-building between Iran's intellectuals and the common folk, who were having a complicated time transitioning the roaring decades.

On 4 June 1969, under the auspices of Qotbi and with the National Iranian Television's support, the experimental *Kargahe Namayesh* (Theatre Workshop) was officially born. This new cultural institution was a direct outgrowth of the two theatrical experiences of the 2nd Shiraz Art Festival. The statute of the Theatre Workshop was written by Ovanessian, Fereydun Rahnema and Khojasteh Kia. Four different work groups were organized by the avant-garde team of Bijan Saffari, Arbi Ovanessian, Iraj Anvar and Abbas Nalbandiyan. The Theatre Workshop became an influential school for training and giving voice to scriptwriters, directors, actors, actresses and musicians. It produced more than 50 plays until 1978.

After the 2nd Shiraz Art Festival, the organizers pushed the frontiers of innovative and experimental arts giving voice to another type of artist, in tune with the Western frontiers of non-politicized art. This was sometimes too avant-garde even for highly Westernized Iranians. In the realm of music, the festival succeeded in promoting Iranian traditional and provincial productions.

Right from its inception, the Shiraz Art Festival was a thorn in the side of the opposition and dissident voices in Iran. The freedom of expression and the liberating spirit of experimental and avant-garde arts in Persepolis and Shiraz clashed with the reality of political intolerance, torture and repression in the country. As opposition to the regime took more of a religious turn, and the art at Shiraz became more risqué, the festival became a veritable theatre of war over moral-correctness and promiscuity.

During the eleventh and last Shiraz Art Festival, 17–26 August 1977, the Hungarian Squat Theatre staged *Pig, Child, Fire*. Their play featured a symbolic rape scene with no nudity. A male soldier grabbed a female from the back and simulated the act of rape. The fact that ordinary passers-by, some of them veiled, could see the performance in a large store with a perfect view from Ferdowsi Street, added to the lewdness and violence of the scene, caused great commotion and resentment. The performance was in bad taste for people. The flawed judgement of the festival's organizers would have probably been forgotten had it not been for the politically charged atmosphere of the country at the time.

By February 1977, the country was going through a crisis and sensitivities had been heightened. Newspapers were already showing exceptional irritation towards the immodest and revealing clothing of women attending the festival.[42] *Pig, Child, Fire* had shocked the population in Shiraz. The Iranian press, especially *Keyhan* gave it considerable negative coverage and turned it into a national issue. The controversy surrounding the performance played into the hands of the shah's opposition, as they hammered at his regime's propagation of moral corruption and debauchery.

While primarily apolitical, cultural institutions under the queen's patronage were shielded from SAVAK's excesses, others equally talented were not. In 1968, *Anjoman Teatre Iran* (Iran's Theatre Association) was founded by two gifted Left artists, Saeed Soltanpur and Naser Rahmaninejad. Later Mohsen Yalfani joined them. The group began its performances in Rasht. Without any state support, they staged plays in Tehran, mostly at the theatre hall of the Faculty of Fine Arts at Tehran University and the Iran-American Society. One of their plays, *The Bus Station*, was even broadcast by National Iranian Television around 1969.

In 1972, they staged Bertolt Brecht's *The Visions of Simone Machard* for two weeks at their regular venue of performance, the Faculty of Fine Arts. Once they asked to extend their successful performance, they were refused the space. On 12 December 1974, SAVAK raided their rehearsal of Maxim Gorky's *The Petty Bourgeoisie*. The group had performed this play in Rasht a year before and were preparing for its Tehran performance.

Some 15 people, actors, staff and spectators were rounded up at first, and the sweep culminated in some 40 to 60 arrests in connection with the initial detainees. The majority were put on trial and given prison terms of three to six years by the military tribunal for acting against state security and propagating communist ideas.

The Swinging and Sizzling Tehran of the 1970s

The October 1966 census had revealed that Tehran's population was some 2,719,000 million, of which 62.7 per cent were literate and only half of its population were born in Tehran. The capital city had 4,234 doctors, 4,513 engineers and 197,706 civil servants. Tehran had 565,968 households, most of whom lived in single-room accommodation, packing in between one and ten individuals. The majority of Tehranis lived in rented homes. Of the 354,346 housing units in Tehran, 292,588 had electricity and 249,787 had running water.

For the academic year 1966/7, 28,000 applicants participated in Tehran University's general entrance exam, of which around 5,000 were admitted. Women constituted 48 per cent of the applicants, and 30 per cent of those who took the national entrance exam wore miniskirts. In early 1970, the press quoting experts reported that 80 per cent of Tehran's males and females were wearing Western clothing.

From the early 1960s, Tehran experienced a cultural transformation based on a Western liberalization model. The urban centres underwent a state-supported trend altering prevalent social norms by creating public recreational spaces for the youth and liberalizing intergender relations.

Intellectual cafés and popular cabarets

In the aftermath of the 1953 coup, Tehran had two spatially distinct centres. One was the old male-dominated hub of cultural, artistic and intellectual interaction, concentrated around the old heart of Tehran, namely Eslambol, Naderi and Qavam al-saltaneh Streets. These famous 1950s and 1960s hangouts of Iran's literary, artistic and intellectual luminaries, both young and old, included the cafés Naderi, Lalehzar, Ferdowsi, Fard, Nobakht, Firuz and old Riviera. They were the equivalents of the smoke-filled, politicized and talent-packed, Parisian Cafés Flore, Les Deux Magots and La Rotonde, with the exception that almost all of those in attendance were male.

Attendants of these political-cum-literary spaces were there to see each other, read out their poetry aloud, discuss arts, poetry, and politics, and figure out what they should do about the arrests of their peers. Sometimes the oversized and frustrated egos would butt heads. These cafes entertained the **giants of Iran's literary society**. Simin Daneshvar, Ale-Ahmad's wife, was a singular female figure who appeared in these male-dominated café circles.

The second, and very different male-dominated space, not far from the intellectual hubs, was a cluster of cabarets, café-cabarets and theatre houses. This space, along the famous Lalehzar Street, Tehran's Champs-Elysées at daytime and Pigalle without its ladies of the street, at night, came into vogue after the coup and was frequented by ruffians who had attained a privileged social status because of their involvement in overthrowing Mosaddeq on 19 August 1953.

In these Persianized cabarets, most famous among them, Ofoq Talai, Jamshid, Mostafa Payan, Lalehzar, Nur, Pars and Continental, women served vodka and beer. Female and male singers and local bands of Iranian popular music entertained their male customers. The most popular Iranian singer of the late 1950s and early 1960s, Masumeh Azizi-Borujerdi, better known as Mahvash, began her singing career at Café Jamshid, the favourite hangout of the most well-known Tehran ruffians.

The lyrics to her songs were simple, rap-like and concerned with everyday topics in the lives of the common folk. In one of her most popular songs, 'When I returned from India', she would engage her audience in a joyful and amusing question and answer session. She would ask her audience, 'This hand askew?' and her band members, along with the audience, would respond, 'Who would think that, I ask you?' Teasingly, she would then say, 'This ass askew?' and once again they would repeat, 'Who would think that, I ask you?'[43] Mahvash's lines were repeated by millions, young and old. Mahvash sang, jested, danced and brought joy to her very many fans, mostly from the lower classes.

By modern standards, Mahvash had neither a golden voice nor a stunning physique or appearance. She was an odd mixture of an Iranian Edith Piaf, the voice adored by the common folk, and an Iranian Marilyn Monroe, the sex symbol. Mahvash, later became an actress. To increase movie sales, producers randomly inserted one or two shots of Mahvash singing and dancing. Famous ruffians drew knives and broke bottles, fighting over her attention at Jamshid and Ofoq Talai cafés. Her fans spanned Afghanistan, Kuwait and Iraq. On 16 January 1961, she died in a car accident and some 100,000 to 500,000 people attended her funeral.

Movies and the television

Since 1958, to combat the post-coup morose and apathetic national mood and lift the morale of the people, the government had been providing financial incentives for more movie theatres to be built. In 1963, Tehran had 52 cinemas and in 1977 it had some 115. Of Tehran's 115 cinemas, 25 were built between 1960 and 1965, and 32 were constructed between 1966 and 1970. To promote the building of modern movie theatres and movie-going, the shah and Queen Farah would inaugurate them.

On 29 August 1966, the royal couple watched *The Sound of Music* at the newly inaugurated Diamond Movie Theatre.

The popular films screened were westerns, war movies, romance, thrillers and musicals. The gender interaction screened in such movies reflected the acceptable moral and sexual mores of the West. In October 1958, Brigitte Bardot's appearance in *And God Created Woman* was considered offensive to public morality and was banned after its first-night screening in Tehran. The issue of what to do with sexual promiscuity in Western imported films became a non-issue as time went by, and gradually Iranian films incorporated a large dosage of the semi-nudity and promiscuity expressed in Western-made films.

By January 1968, *The Oldest Profession*, a comedy history of prostitution showcasing Raquel Welch, Anna Karina and Elsa Martinelli, was issued an age rating of 18+, renamed *From Love to Passion* in Persian and advertised as the gathering of 'the sexiest and most seductive international actresses'. The screening of lustful movies no longer made any ripples. In ten years, the moral standards of urban Iranians had shifted.

By the late 1960s, the Iranian film industry had its own numerous sex bombs and sex symbols appearing half-naked in blockbuster movies. In 1973, Khosrow Heritash's 'Speeding naked till high noon' with two nude lovemaking scenes was screened for about a month before it was banned. The film's provocative scenes were censored and in 1976 it was allowed to be screened.

In April 1960, the government made ad-hoc attempts to prohibit the youth from attending cinemas during school hours. Soon such unrealistic measures were abandoned. In the late 1960s and the 1970s, cinemas became an ideal place for romantically involved – or to become – couples, to enjoy some privacy. High school and university students, skipping classes, found the 1.00–3.00 pm and the 3.00–5.00 pm shows most convenient. The dark and discreet interior of movies and the passionate or tender amorous content of the films made cinemas an ideal dating location. In Tehran, Radio City, Empire and Takhte Jamshid were cool movie theatres for the youth to hang out.

On 3 October 1958, the first television network in Iran, Iran Television (ITV), owned by Habibollah Sabet, began transmitting. The appearance of the magic box was an important event inaugurated by the shah. Sabet was a well-established business tycoon. He was the chairman of Firuz Trading Company, owned the Pepsi-Cola franchise in Iran and was the sole distributor of Volkswagen and Studebaker. As a part of his deal with the government, Sabet obtained a lucrative agreement according to which, he had the monopoly to import some 10,000 TVs free of custom duties.

ITV was a commercial network broadcasting in Tehran. In 1960, it began broadcasting in Abadan and Ahvaz. Sabet was responding to the entertainment needs of Oil Consortium employees in the region. In the early 1960s, Sabet's television offered news, talk shows, children's programmes, cartoons, predominantly dubbed

Western films, musical shows, rock and jazz concerts and ballet performances. ITV's most popular shows were dubbed western series such as *Flash Gordon, Danger Man, Annie Oakley, Richard Diamond: Private Eye* and *The Fugitive*. The Iranian public was receiving a taste of the West through a different medium.

About a year later and right before Christmas, 23 December 1959, the American Armed Forces Radio and Television Services (AFRTS) started broadcasting its first television programme. AFRTS's primarily audience were some 2,000 American military personnel stationed in Iran at the time. Those privileged Tehranis who were in possession of a television set and understood some English were now exposed to solely US entertainment and American culture, art, taste and way of life.

ARFTS attracted considerable attention among the upper classes. Tehranis came to watch the *Ed Sullivan Show, Jack Benny Program* and the *Glenn Miller Show* for light entertainment, *Perry Mason* and *Untouchables* for detective stories, and *Gun Smoke* and *Bonanza* for good old westerns. By 1965, Tehran had some 100,000 televisions and Abadan approximately 40,000.

On 27 March 1969, Sabet's television station, Iran Television, ceased to broadcast. The government bought it out, and its facilities were incorporated into the National Iranian Television (NIT). By law, NIT was a financially and administratively independent government organization. On 21 June 1971, the Iranian radio network, or Radio Iran, was merged with the National Iranian Television to form the National Iranian Radio and Television (NIRT). From this date, Reza Qotbi became the director-general of Iran's most influential propaganda, entertainment and broadcasting machine.

The National Iranian Radio and Television succeeded in partially moving the content of attractive television shows from Western to Iranian productions. The transition was a gradual process. In the early 1970s, Iranians viewed Western, and particularly American shows. Provincial as well as urban Iranians watched cartoons such as *The Flintstones*, action serials such as *Mission Impossible, The Six Million Dollar Man, Streets of San Francisco, Perry Mason, Columbo, The Persuaders* and *Charlie's Angels*, soap operas such as *Peyton Place, Days of Our Lives* and sitcoms-musicals such as *I Love Lucy, The Monkees, Mary Tyler Moore Show* and *That Girl*.

By the mid-1970s, however, a good share of soap operas, film series and variety shows were produced by NIRT. The NIRT entertainment channel became so popular with all social classes that on specific nights when certain Iranian shows or series were broadcast, people would cut short their parties and gatherings to watch them. The subject of these homespun series dealt with the concerns, everyday problems, habits and idiosyncrasies of Iranians and every social group found something with which they identified.

From 1969, Iranian made series gradually won over the Iranian public. Popular productions such as Manuchehr Mahjubi's *Khaneh Qamar khanum* (Mrs Qamar's House), Parviz Sayyad's *Samad va Qalicheh Hazrat Soleyman* (Samad and the Prophet

Solomon's Carpet), Behzad Eshtiyaqi's short 10–15-minute satirical skits, *Aqaye Marbouteh* (The Designated Person), Iraj Pezeshkzad and Naser Taqvaie's *Daie Jan Napoleon* (Dear Uncle Napoleon) and Ali Hatami's historical series of *Soltan-e Sahebqaran* (The Long-Lasting Sultan), were prized programmes.

Young and talented producers were promoted and given reign to innovate and attract viewers. Farshid Ramzi returned from Britain in the mid-1960s and pioneered the production of music shows in the late 1960s. These shows were an Iranian and timid adaptation of the BBC classic *Top of the Pops*. Ramzi's famous shows *Cheshmak* (Wink) and *Studio 11* presented modern pop and jazz music, dance, art deco type decorations and the latest styles of Western fashion. These shows introduced and launched many future musical stars, such as Farhad Mehrad, Gugoush, Ramesh, Aref and Aqasi.

NIRT was also successful in launching trendy Iranian showmen with their own musical shows, also featuring popular Iranian singers and bands. Parviz Qarib-Afshar and Fereydun Farrokhzad hosted popular musical variety shows peppered with situation comedies. Iranians would watch their favourite celebrities on their shows, *Jomeh sho* (The Friday Show), *Rangarang* (Rainbow) and *Mikhak Noqrehi* (Silver Carnation).

Even an Iranian Charlie Chaplin-type called *Mohandes Billy* (Engineer Billy) was created by NIRT. Hasan Khayatbashi impersonated the bow tied *Mohandes Billy*, whose comedy musical programme, *Shabakeh Sefr* (Network Zero), became an instant hit. Qotbi's NIRT put into motion a well-oiled cultural machine that discovered and supported Iranian talents in all fields of modern and traditional arts. These talents, in turn, found their way into the hearts and minds of Iranian audiences.

By 1979, NIRT was the prime source of popular entertainment for Iranians, understanding their taste, forming it and responding to it. By this time, NIRT gave radio coverage to 100 per cent of the population and television coverage to some 75 per cent. It began its operation in 1966 with a staff of 56 and by 1978, it employed some 9,000.

A new genre of hangouts

The government encouraged people to have fun, even before student discontent became endemic and the guerrilla movement broke out. From 1961, the government pursued a conscious policy of creating a modernized/Westernized leisurely and recreational atmosphere for Iranian youth, where they could be happy and amused. Around 1965, a new kind of space mushroomed in Tehran. These were the modern and female-friendly cosy cafés, restaurants, discotheques and jazz clubs designated for the youth. Yet, they were culturally appealing to and financially affordable for the middle class, upper-middle class and the upper class. These were not intellectual, political or ruffian joints. They were modern spaces for the happy go lucky to enjoy life.

New cafés, restaurants, dancehalls with afternoon dancing (*thé dansant*) and nocturnal discotheques appeared in the northern part of the city and altered the socio-cultural face of Tehran. This new generation of recreational facilities, intended for pleasurable social interaction and connection, popped up mostly along Pahlavi Street. The youth and the less young gathered to eat or drink, socialize, flirt and seduce. Chatanooga, Sorento, Riviera, The Shoppe (Hot Shop) and Casbah became the relaxed restaurants for Tehranis to meet up for pleasure and work. The more intimate and cosy discotheques like Couchinie, Borj (La Tour), Labyrinth, Cheminée, Cave d'Argent and Key Club were the sexually charged spaces for the fun-loving youth, dancing through the night and taking advantage of Iran's cultural and sexual revolution. These modern spaces soon developed their regular clientele.

From 1963 to 1965, private Western-style leisure and sports centres opened in Tehran. Initially, due to their relatively high costs, these new spaces were reserved for upper-middle-class and upper-class Iranians. The opening of bowling clubs, tennis clubs, drive-in movies, swimming clubs, amusement parks, mini-golf courses made Tehran a fun place to be in. Tehran's Ice Palace on Pahlavi Street had an indoor swimming pool with a spacious skating rink. It also housed a dance space with popular musical bands. Tehran's Ice Palace, inaugurated by the royal family, epitomized a new type of amusement centre, geared to the modern taste of a culturally evolving society. In the 1970s, many of these venues became frequented by middle-class youth seeking a space to socialize and meet.

On 25 October 1966, the shah and the queen inaugurated Tehran's *Kakhe Javanan* (Youth Palace). This government-subsidized arena was a modern space intended for those who could not afford to go to the pricy ice-skating rinks, bowling clubs, swimming clubs and discos. This mixed-gender youth complex was a cultural, artistic and entertainment hub providing amusement and diversion for university students.

The 'Youth Palace' included an amphitheatre seating 250 people for conferences, film projections, concerts and speeches, a billiard and ping pong hall, a chess room, a library, a music hall equipped with different musical instruments. It had a variety of social spaces, a restaurant, a television hall and a heated and filtered swimming pool with modern changing rooms and showers. The 'Youth Palace', which was replicated in other areas, was a peace offering, by the government, to the disgruntled university youth and intended to introduce them to fun and games instead of politics.

University students were not protected from arbitrary detention and torture by the state when they engaged in politics but were free in their personal lives to follow Western fashion and modes of interaction. Boys could wear their hair long, and girls could wear maxi- or miniskirts. Imported Western political ideas, challenging the regime, were repressed. Non-political countercultures, in vogue in the West, were, however, tolerated if not promoted.

Iranians were flooded by magazine articles, fiction, poetry, films, television shows and advertisements all propagating love stories with sexually arousing content, gender mixing and moral laxity. The flourishing of new spaces for social interaction facilitated the realization of the sexual promiscuity promoted in the media. The meeting, mingling and free association of opposite sexes in the late 1960s constituted a veritable sexual liberation movement.

The politicized intellectuals of the late-1960s and 1970s for whom the battle against political despotism was of primary importance feared that an open, permissive, and promiscuous cultural atmosphere would detract the youth from focusing on the political. They often rallied against cultural and sexual liberation, pitting the satisfaction of romantic and sexual personal experiences against social commitment and responsibility. Romantic and sexual abstinence became a distinctive aspect of the code of conduct of those who dedicated their lives to armed struggle.

Factual and Analytical Questions

1. How was Mansur's government different from previous governments? Assess the pros and cons of his policies?
2. Why was Prime Minister Mansur assassinated? Who were the assailants? Which organization did they belong to?
3. Why, when and how did Iran become militarily involved in Oman?
4. Why did the shah launch his anti-profiteering campaign in the summer of 1975? How successful was it economically and politically?
5. Compare and contrast the Organization for the Intellectual Development of Children and Young Adults with the Shiraz Arts Festival.

Seminar Questions

1. What made the New Iran Party appealing to the shah?
2. What were the shah's relations with the three branches of state government, legislative, judiciary and the executive, as well as the press from 1965? Explain.
3. 'The celebrations of the 2,500 years of monarchy were more of historical landmark in the evolution of the shah's vision of himself and his future role as a world-class leader.' Discuss the veracity of this statement by providing historical evidence.
4. What fuelled Iran's military build-up in the 1970s? How was it related to the 'Nixon Doctrine'?
5. Assess the overall impact of the rise in revenues due to the jump in oil prices on the Iranian economy from 1971 and 1977?

6 'The celebrations of the 2,500 years of monarchy, the single party Resurgence Party and the anti-profiteering campaign were different manifestations of the shah's despotism.' Discuss the validity of this statement and provide counter-arguments to it.
7 'Iran was experiencing a sexual revolution in the late 1960s and early 1970s.' Explain the factors that contributed to this revolution.

Discussion Questions

1 'Members of the Confederation of Iranian Students in Europe were behind the assassination attempt on the shah's life.' Discuss the merits of this statement.
2 'The title Aryamehr was a title bestowed by the people to praise the shah's services to the country.' Discuss the validity of this statement.
3 The celebrations of the 2,500 years of monarchy endeared the regime to the people, alienated them or antagonized them? Explain your position with historical evidence.
4 Discuss the interrelated economic, ethical-political and cultural problems triggered by Iran's arms binge in the 1970s.
5 'Iran experienced its "crazy years", "roaring years" or *Années folles* between 1964 and 1977.' Assess the validity of this statement.
6 Discuss the achievements and shortcomings of Queen Farah Pahlavi's cultural programmes.
7 What kind of a culture was permeated in Iran in the 1960s and 1970s through movies, television and meeting places? Choose one of the three spaces and make your argument.

Glossary

Confederation of Iranian Students in Europe An Iranian student organization which began its activities initially in Europe to protect the welfare and living condition of students. In the 1960s, the organization became more political and in April 1960 representatives from Germany, France and England met in Heidelberg and established the Confederation of Iranian Students in Europe. Soon, the Confederation became a highly influential anti-Shah political organization, exposing the regime's violation of human rights and mobilizing Western public opinion against the regime.

giants of Iran's literary society A few names, among this distinguished group include, Nima Yushij, Sadeq Hedayat, Bozorg Alavi, Mojtaba Minavi, Masud Farzad, Jalal Ale-Ahamd, Mehdi Akhavan Sales, Ahmad Shamlu, Nader Naderpur, Siyavush Kasraie,

Hushang Ebtehadj, Nosrat Rahmani, Manuchehr Atashi, Fereydun Moshiri, Gholamhoseyn Saedi, Esmail Khoie, Nemat Mirzazadeh, Mohammad-Reza Shafie Kadkani and Reza Baraheni.

Strategic Arms Limitation Talks (SALT) On 26 May 1972, US President Richard Nixon and Soviet leader General Secretary Leonid Brezhnev signed two historical documents aimed at limiting the production of strategic missiles capable of carrying nuclear weapons. This was a crucial step in consolidating the détente policy between the US and USSR.

Ugly American The title of a 1958 political novel by Eugene Burdick and William Lederer. The book attributes the loss of US political power and influence in South-East Asia to the failure to understand the local culture. The term encapsulates the insensitivity of Americans to cultures and behaviours other than their own. It stereotypes the boorish expat behaviour, exuding superiority towards the locals.

Westoxication The name of Jalal Al-e Ahmad's very popular book which was published in September/October 1962. The book described 'Westoxication' or being afflicted by the West as a disease which came from the West and arrested the endogenous development of underdeveloped Third World countries. The term encapsulated all that was negative about the West and blamed the fate of Iranians only on the West. Al-e Ahmad's Third Worldist critique of Westernization influenced the youth of the 1960s and 1970s and was a powerful manifesto against the Iranian roaring years.

7

The Revolutionary Transition from Monarchy to Republic, March 1977–March 1979

Chapter Outline

The Rise of Subversive Forces	328
Dismantling the Monarchy, Step by Step	343
The Regime Retaliates, Retreats and Strikes Back	348
The Shah Vacillates and Khomeyni Rams through the Revolution	359
Glossary	374

In his new year message of 21 March 1977, the shah announced that he and his people were at the gates of the Great Civilization and in the process of constructing a historical national and international masterpiece, a historical epic. He was thrilled with the advances and achievements of the country and prompted Iranians to work harder and become ever more armed with patriotism, faith, and moral values. Less than two years later, on 16 January 1979, the shah and Queen Farah left the country with tearful eyes, never to return.

As Iran celebrated the overthrow of a despot, different people looked forward to different kinds of future. All believed that any system of government replacing the shah's would be a 'better one'. The wiser among them wondered how the principal slogans of the revolutionary movement, would pan out in practice. In the spectacular marches, the multitudes chanted, 'Independence, freedom and Islamic Republic!'

What seemed like an abrupt transition from monarchy to the Islamic Republic had been long in the making and went through three chronological steps. First, since the late 1960s, 'subversive' forces and discourses radicalized and gave heart to Iranians nibbling away, like termites, at the shah's self-confidence, his authority and his decision-making powers. This had set the stage for what was to follow. Second, under pressure from the new Carter administration at the White House, the shah agreed to a liberalization policy, leading to gatherings such as the Ten Nights of Poetry Reading at the Goethe Institute in October 1977. This unprecedented cultural event, in turn, opened wide a dam of resentment and anger towards the shah, by secular and religious forces, unleashing uprisings which culminated sixteen months later with the army's surrender on 11 February 1979. The third and final step was on 1 April 1979 when the Islamic Republic was founded and Ayatollah Khomeyni could at last impose his will on the nation.

The Rise of Subversive Forces

On 8 January 1968, news came that Gholamreza Takhti had passed away. Takhti was Iran's wrestling gold medalist at the 1956 Melbourne Olympics and a two-time silver medalist at the Helsinki and Rome Olympics. Takhti was not only a revered sportsman. He also symbolized what was held as socially, politically, and ethically noble among the common folk. He was a national hero, and his membership in the Mosaddeqist National Front made him a model of political opposition to the shah. Takhti's funeral became an occasion for the opposition to show its pent-up anger toward the regime. Student activists of all shades, many of whom would later join various 'subversive' groups, were present. In retrospect, Takhti's funeral became a watershed in the revolutionary movement against the shah.

In the absence of freedom of assembly, funerals in Iran gauged the socio-political sensitivities and allegiances of Iranians. In the 1960s, the funeral ceremonies of Mahvash, Takhti and Grand Ayatollah Borujerdi attracted the most glaring numbers of people. Each one of them symbolized very distinct life-styles and values. But their general appeal disclosed something about the complex proclivity and identity of urban Iranians in the 1960s.

The People's Fadai (Self-Sacrificing) Guerrillas: A Revolutionary Marxist Movement

On 9 January 1968, one day after the death of Takhti, Bijan Jazani was arrested. Jazani was a 30-year-old Tehran University graduate who had been active in student politics since the early sixties. With the help of his uncle, Manuchehr Kalantari, and Hasan Zia-Zarifi, another Tehran University graduate, he had founded a Marxist-Leninist study group. By March 1966, the 'Jazani Group' had entered semi-clandestinity and by August formed a politico-propaganda branch and a military branch.

Barely two years later, in December 1968, Jazani and his group faced trial for 'founding a communist group and propagating communist ideas' as well as 'conducting activities against state security'. The military court handed down sentences of three to fifteen years to the '14-man group'. The original 'Jazani Group' went behind bars, with the exception of Ali-Akbar Safai-Farahani and Mohammad Saffari-Ashtiyani, who had succeeded in crossing the border into Iraq and joining the Palestinian armed resistance and Hamid Ashraf whose identity was unknown to the authorities.

Another revolutionary group, the 'Jungle Group', was founded by two militants, Ghafour Hasanpur and Hamid Ashraf. In September 1964, Hasanpur had independently begun recruiting anti-shah militants at Tehran Polytechnic University. After being put in contact with the 'Jazani Group' in June/July 1966, Hasanpur had organized a network in his hometown of Lahijan, Gilan. Hasanpur's discretion shielded his networks from being compromised after the arrest of the 'Jazani Group'. Hamid Ashraf, a Tehran University student, had been recruited by Jazani back in August 1966 and joined the mountain team of the military branch in April/May 1967. His vigilance and intentional avoidance of becoming embroiled in student politics had kept his identity a secret for some five years.

After the arrest of the 'Jazani Group', Hasanpur and Ashraf reconstructed and reactivated old networks and fostered new ones. From October/November 1968, Hasanpur and Ashraf organized their recruits into three specialized guerrilla teams: urban, mountain and weapons procurement.

In June 1970, having discovered the existence of a robust politico-military network in Iran, Safai-Farahani and Saffari-Ashtiyani returned clandestinely from Jordan with a cache of arms to begin the armed struggle. In August 1970, the 'H-A-S Group' (Hasanpur, Ashraf and Safai-Farahani) were ready to strike.

Parallel to, and unbeknown to the 'H-A-S Group', another Marxist-Leninist network of university students had taken shape in fall 1966. Three different regional Marxist political circles, in Sari, Mashhad and Tabriz had coalesced to form another revolutionary group committed to a guerrilla war against the regime. The 'P-A-M Group' (Pouyan-Ahmadzadeh-Meftahi) was founded between July and September 1967, by Amir-Parviz Pouyan, a 21-year-old National Front sympathizer with a religious background and raised in Mashhad and Abbas Meftahi, also 21, with a Marxist-Leninist background from Sari.

Pouyan and Meftahi met at Tehran University, and it was Meftahi who had converted Pouyan to Marxism. Meftahi was also 21 and had created a Marxist-Leninist circle in Sari and subsequently merged his group with Pouyan. Within a couple of months, Masud Ahmadzadeh, a close friend of Pouyan from Mashhad, turned to Marxism and joined the group.

In 1969 the 'P-A-M Group' joined forces with two revolutionary groups in Tabriz. One belonged to the circle that had been formed around the famous Left Iranian writer Samad Behrangi and his friends Behrooz Dehqani and Kazem Saadati. The other was composed of students at Tabriz University who had gathered around Asadollah Meftahi, Abbas' younger brother. The 'P-A-M Group' soon incorporated a vibrant circle of Marxist students at Mashhad University into their expanding network. The Mashhad branch was cultivated and formed by Pouyan and included Hamid Tavakoli, Bahman Ajang, Gholamreza Galavi, Shahin Tavakoli and Saeed Aryan. By 1970 the 'P-A-M Group' claimed around sixty-six adherents.

> ## The Responsibility of the Revolutionary
>
> To Pouyan, studying Marxist literature in small clandestine circles and continuing one's peaceful life without any meaningful attempt at changing the status quo, while waiting for the 'right moment' and the 'appropriate conditions' was an 'opportunistic' excuse born out of paralysing fear. (A. Rahnema)[1]

What distinguished the P-A-M group from the H-A-S group was that the former had produced two theoretical treaties, which were to become the recruitment manifesto of the revolutionary Marxist-Leninist guerrilla movement in Iran. Between March and May 1970, Pouyan wrote his influential treatise, *Zarurat Mobarezeh Mosalahaneh va Rade Teoriye Baqa* (The Necessity of Armed Struggle and the Refutation of the Theory of Survival). Two months later (July–August), Masoud Ahmadzadeh wrote the group's theoretical manifesto, *Mobarezeh Mosalahane ham strategy ham Taktik* (Armed Struggle, Both Strategy and Tactic). Both writings explained the immediate necessity for intellectuals to act as the vanguard of the masses and enter armed struggle to overthrow the regime.

These revolutionary works were written under pressure, in an environment of fear and danger. Their contents were subjective, goal-oriented, often polemical, peppered with passionate invocations and ideological postulates. They called on the revolutionaries to dispel the double myth of the regime's invincibility and their own powerlessness, which prevented the masses from joining the revolutionary movement. To survive, Pouyan and Ahmadzadeh promoted attacking first. These two writings jolted Iranian intellectuals and university students into action.

> ## Ahmadzadeh's Marxism
>
> Ahmadzadeh was rebelling against the well-articulated orthodox edifice that the Tudeh Party had constructed based on a set of timeless Marxist–Leninist laws, formulations, and generalizations. As such, Ahmadzadeh's work was not only a manual for liberation from the shah's regime, but a clarion call to free Marxist revolutionaries from the theoretical straitjacket of non-revolutionary Marxism. (A. Rahnema)[2]

Starting in mid-August 1970, each group independently attacked and robbed banks in Tehran without disclosing their identities and by February 1971, the two groups were waging war on the state. On 3 February 1971, the Tabriz branch of the 'P-A-M Group' attacked a police station in Tabriz, disarmed and killed two policemen. Five days later, on 8 February 1971, a combined guerrilla force of one P-A-M member and seven H-A-S members led by Safai-Farahani attacked and disarmed the Siyahkal Gendarmerie Station in Mazandaran. The army and gendarmerie poured troops into the area and within nineteen days, the guerrillas were routed, six captured and two killed.

After 8 February 1971, the newly renamed organization of *Cherikhaye Fadai Khalq* (the People's Fadai Guerrillas, or the People's Self-Sacrificing Guerrillas, hereafter Fadais), composed of the remaining forces of the P-A-M and H-A-S groups, conducted a protracted and bloody urban guerrilla war against the regime. In August 1971, only Ashraf, out of the six founders of the Fadais, remained alive. By October 1971, the guerrillas had lost 90 per cent of their fighters and were on the precipice of total annihilation. They nonetheless had an indelible impact on the Iranian society.

Between 21 March 1971 and 20 March 1972, the lead article of fifty-one issues of Iran's most influential Iranian dailies was dedicated to the Fadais. Typically, guerrilla-related news appeared on the top half of the front page in large fonts, sometimes in red, describing tales of shootings, bombings, explosions, street gun battles, deaths of policemen, 'innocent bystanders', 'partisans' and 'saboteurs'. The official term employed by the state-controlled mass media to describe the guerrillas had become *Kharabkar* (saboteurs).

As the guerrillas recovered from their losses, in the fall of 1973, the newly created **Anti-Sabotage Joint Committee** imposed a news blackout on all guerrilla activities. This new policy aimed to spare embarrassment to the shah, who had announced the end of guerrilla activities on 27 September 1973. From 27 September 1973 to 20 March 1974, no news of guerrilla activities appeared in the press despite a flurry of guerrilla activities in February and early March 1974. To counter the news blackout, the Fadai guerrillas published their underground publication, *Nabarde Khalq* (Combat of the Masses), which first appeared on 21 January 1974. Other than theoretical issues, it reported on the military activities of the Fadais and some of the Mojahedin, a non-Marxist Islamic guerrilla organization.

The very short life expectancy of a guerrilla, typically six months, the increasing number of executions, the widespread arrests and prison terms in Iran's university milieus, extrajudicial executions and the tales of torture in Iranian prisons, indicated the firm resolve of the state to uproot the movement. Yet, from early 1975, the Fadais succeeded in replenishing and reconstructing their ranks and cells by attracting new combatants from Iranian universities. There was also a surge in the number of released political prisoners seeking to take up arms.

The influx of recruits caused substantial absorption, organizational and security problem. On 6 January 1974, the partial media coverage of the court proceedings of

Khosrow Golesorkhi and his eleven co-defendants on trumped up charges followed by his execution and that of Keramatollah Daneshiyan deeply touched and disturbed even non-political Iranians and created an impressive wave of sympathy for the armed combatants.

Following the assassination of Brig. Gen. Reza Zandipur, the head of the Anti-Sabotage Joint Committee by the Mojahedin, the SAVAK retaliated. On 18 April 1975, seven members of the 'Jazani Group', including Jazani and Hasan Zia-Zarifi, along with two members of the Mojahedin, all serving prison terms, were executed. The regime justified the extrajudicial execution of political prisoners by falsely claiming that they were attempting to escape.

> ### US Warnings about Guerrilla Activities in May 1975
>
> There are almost daily skirmishes with terrorist elements on the streets in terms of leaflet distribution and sniping at policemen, but that only the highly organized assassination teams' infrequent successes are being reported to the Shah. (Intelligence Information Cable)[3]

From January 1976, the Fadais came under sustained and debilitating attacks by the Anti-Sabotage Joint Committee, which had changed its surveillance tactics and had even infiltrated the recruits. In May, the organization suffered huge losses. Five of their safe houses were attacked and lost in Tehran, and three in Karaj, Rasht and Qazvin. Crowds witnessed gun battles and car chases in the busy neighbourhoods.

On 29 June 1976, the leadership team of the Fadais gathered at a safe house in Tehran for a meeting to assess the organization's situation. They were attacked from land and air. The battle was conducted by the elite forces of forty teams (around 200 men) and lasted approximately four hours. The press, some of which had three reprints on that day, referred to the fighting as 'a major armed clash in Tehran' during which 'Hamid Ashraf, a member of the Siyahkal group, was killed,' and 'the main headquarters of the communist terrorists of Iran was destroyed.' With the fall of Ashraf, the last of the founders of the Fadais, after six years of struggle, the revolutionary Marxist guerrilla movement in Iran went into hibernation.

The People's Mojahedin (Holy Warriors): A Revolutionary Islamic Organization

The failed experience of the 'Iran Freedom Movement' in the early 1960s to initiate change had convinced its younger members and sympathizers that transformations in a despotic system were only possible through armed struggle. Just as the founders of the Fadais had their roots mainly in the National Front and a few in the Tudeh Party, the revolutionary Islamic movement had its roots in the Iran Freedom Movement. Both groups believed in making revolution and their leadership was composed of university-educated intellectuals. Both forces were influenced by Regis Debray's *Revolution in Revolution*, and Carlos Marighella's *Handbook of Urban Guerrilla Movement*.

Mohammad Hanifnejad, Saeed Mohsen, Ali-Asghar Badizadegan and Abdolreza Nikbin, the founders of the Mojahedin, were all four members of the Iran Freedom Movement and their ages ranged between 23 and 26. On 6 September 1965, they formed a clandestine group to launch an armed struggle. With the help of Ayatollah Mahmud Taleqani (Figure 7.1), one of the founders of the Iran Freedom movement, their ideological branch began an exegesis of the Quran and worked on Imam Ali's collection of sermons and letters. Based on Islamic sources, these young revolutionaries sought to construct a modern, progressive and revolutionary Islamic ideology.

From 1967, the group began recruiting and forming cells of three to four members. Members were practising Muslims and committed to armed struggle. By the summer 1967, the group had started studying Marxist literature to master 'the science of combat'. For the group, a true Muslim struggled against exploitation, dictatorship, and imperialism. Hanifnejad, the group's leader, believed that the Iranian political situation was incapable of reform and needed a revolution.

Figure 7.1 Mahmoud Taleqani gifts a Quran to Gholamreza Takhti. *Source: Via Alamy.*

From 1971, the ideological branch of the group circulated a series of homespun works, such as *Shenakht* (Cognizance), *Takamol* (Evolution), *Rahe Anbiya, Rahe Bashar* (Path of Prophets, Path of Humankind), *Eqtesad be Zabane Sadeh* (Economics made simple) and *Rahe Hoseyn* (Hoseyn's Path). These publications incorporated the Marxist concept of historical determinism yet propagated the idea that struggle for the oppressed, in the cause of God, was the responsibility of a Mojahed, a holy warrior. The ideological works of the group aimed at convincing the Muslim youth that it was time to act and take up arms against all the injustices of the regime. These texts intended to empower the religious revolutionaries and dispel their inferiority complex regarding the Marxist revolutionaries.

The 8 February 1971 attack on Siyahkal's gendarmerie station and the approaching 2,500th anniversary celebrations prompted the group to expedite its military activities. The group recalled their trainees from the Palestinian training camps and regrouped. In the summer of 1970, the group had contacted the 'Palestinian National Liberation Movement' and dispatched some 25 members to *Fatah* military training camps. By July 1971, the group had approximately 150 members and some twenty teams of 4 members each. Members were preparing to 'set fire to the celebrations', which were due to commence on 12 October.

But from fall 1970, SAVAK, having infiltrated the group through an old Tudeh Party member, had the members under close surveillance Once it was known that the group was looking for arms and preparing for operations during the celebrations, SAVAK moved in. On 23 August 1971, it raided various hideouts in Tehran and rounded up 30 members. After two months, some 120 members were rounded up in Tehran, Tabriz, Mashhad and Esfahan. They were imprisoned and subjected to torture. Finally, sometime between 18 and 25 October 1971, Mohammad Hanifnejad, the last of the leadership team, was arrested and subsequently their group was almost dismantled.

Ahmad Rezai, age 26, who had been recruited by his brother Reza in 1969, picked up the dismantled pieces of the organization, regrouped the members who had been cut off from one another after the raids and began a new recruitment and mobilization drive. On 24 November 1971, Reza Rezai, who had been arrested back in August 1971, escaped from prison and joined his brother. Under the auspices of the Rezai brothers, the group began its armed urban operations in January 1972. During 1972, 9 members of the 12-man leadership team of the group would be executed, including Hanifnejad, Mohsen, Badizadegan and Abdolrasoul Meshkinfam.

In spite of these setbacks, the group announced its organizational identity on 20 February 1972 under the name *Sazemane Mojahedine Khalqe Iran* (People's Mojahedin Organization).[4] The Mojahedin identified an antagonistic contradiction between the Iranian people and world imperialism led by the US and the shah's puppet regime. The only way to resolve this opposition to the benefit of the people, they claimed, was through armed struggle. They targeted high profile Iranian and US military personnel, foreign and Iranian economic and cultural companies and offices, police stations, and government buildings.

After his arrest, Mehdi Rezai, the youngest of the Rezai brothers, was put on trial. On 27 August 1972, to discredit the Organization in the eyes of believers, the prosecutor labelled him and his organization 'Islamic Marxists'. The Mojahedin categorically rejected this appellation and called it a ruse by the regime to undermine their revolutionary Islamic credentials. Mehdi Rezai was executed on 7 September 1972. Eight months earlier, on 31 January 1972, his brother Ahmad, cornered by the security forces, had put up a fight but had finally taken his own life. On 15 June 1973, Reza Rezai also committed suicide after being injured in his getaway from the security forces. The Organization nonetheless continued with its military operations forcing the regime to enforce a widespread nocturnal door-to-door search for the guerrillas in the southern parts of Tehran. The Anti-Sabotage Joint Committee started its new method of hunting guerrillas on 2 December 1974.

After the death of the Rezai brothers, Mohammad-Taqi Shahram, Bahram Aram and Majid Sharif-Vaqefi took charge of the Organization. Under the influence of Shahram, Aram, the military brain of the Organization gradually converted to Marxism-Leninism. In 1973–4, an ideological tug of war broke out between the Shahram-Aram newly Marxist-Leninist leadership and Sharif-Vaqefi, who kept fast to his original revolutionary Islam. Instead of seceding from the Organization and forming a new group, Shahram and Aram purged the group of its Muslim members. Some eighty-five members converted to Marxism-Leninism, and the ideological debate turned into the physical liquidation of Sharif-Vaqefi on 6 May 1975.

The Marxist-Leninist tendency expropriated the Organization's Islamic name and deleted the famous Quranic verse, 'Allah has graced those who wage jihad over those who sit back with a great reward,' in its logo. In September/October 1975, they issued an ideological manifesto called *Bayaniyeh elame mavaze ideologik sazeman mojahedin khalqe Iran* (The declaration stating the ideological positions of the People's Mojahedin Organization). Written by Shahram, it ripped through Islam, old and new, denounced Islamic revivalists such as Seyyed Jamaleddin Asadabadi and Ali Shariati (Figure 7.2), and blamed all the Organization's shortcomings on its previous eclectic ideology. The coup by the Shahram-Aram group sowed confusion and created an identity crisis among members and sympathizers of the Organization. It also confirmed the regime's accusation that the Organization had been Islamic Marxist and that it was now coming out and announcing its true colour.

On 28 August 1976, while the shah was in the US, the Marxist-Leninist Mojahedin attacked and executed three American military advisers in Tehran. This was one of their last operations. On 19 November 1976, Bahram Aram fought a one-hour street battle, finished his ammunition and finally blew himself up with his last grenade. After that the Organization went into hibernation and Taqi Shahram left the country

Figure 7.2 Ali Shariati. *Source: Wikimedia Commons.*

in July/August 1977. Subsequently, the Organization announced its temporary dissolution.

Ali Shariati, the Ideologue of a Revolutionary Islam

Back in June 1963, Ali Shariati, who was in Paris, wrote, 'Yes! The epoch of peaceful struggle has come to an end,' and suggested that 'the enemy's flood of fire and steel' should be responded to 'with the expressive language of guns and the destructive force of war'. Shariati was born on 24 November 1933, grew up in Mashhad, was a National Front supporter in his youth and was steeped in his father's progressive and modernist Islam taught at the Centre for Propagation of Islamic Truths.

In 1955, when Shariati was a student at Mashhad University, he translated and published a book called *Abu Zarr Qifari, the God-Worshipping Socialist*. From Abu Zarr, the famous companion of the Prophet Mohammad, Shariati chiselled out a Muslim revolutionary hero, role model and an archetype, who defied wealth, power and religious authority to save the 'authentic' Islam of the poor and the oppressed. By recreating Abu Zarr, Shariati engaged in a transformative genealogy of concepts. This exercise enabled him to retrace Western socio-political and economic ideas, which had reached Iran through Western intellectual thought, to an Islamic origin, reappropriating and rendering them native.

Upon graduation in September 1958, Shariati qualified for a newly established scholarship. The shah wanted the best university graduates sent abroad for the continuation of their education. Ali Shariati, who had studied French as a foreign language at university finished top of his class and was sent to Paris in late May 1959.

For a young man who had spent the entire 26 years of his life in provincial Khorasan, Paris of the late 1950s and early 1960s was more than a cultural shock. After complaining about the promiscuity of Paris, he soon fell in love with it.

> ### Shariati on Paris
> I wish I had never come here and never tasted the meaning of freedom. I should have stayed back there and read about it only in books. (A. Shariati)[5]

Having defended his doctoral thesis on 21 June 1963, Shariati returned home in March 1964. In his highly controversial piece, *Maboudhaye man* (My Idols), which was later widely used against him by his clerical detractors, Shariati provided a list of those Western intellectuals who had left their imprint on him and marked the development of his thoughts in Paris. Shariati wrote, 'I bowed down to Gurvitch, and considered Massignon a saint. Lefebvre, Sartre and Gurvitch filled my mind, nourished my reasoning, and taught me how to think, while Cocteau fascinated me.'[6]

Shariati was forthcoming about acknowledging his intellectual debt to Westerners. In Paris, he came to realize that a revolutionary and modern political discourse that would appeal to the Iranian youth necessitated theoretical bridge-building and the blending of various aspects of dominant Western thoughts such as existentialism and socialism with Islam. He intentionally tried to burn down all religious, national and ideological distinctions, barriers and taboos.

He irked the sensitivities of the traditional clergy when he claimed that Gurvitch, his teacher, a Jewish former communist, who had fought against fascism, Stalinist dictatorship and French colonialism in Algeria, was closer to the spirit of Shiism than Ayatollah Mohammad-Hadi Milani. Shariati added that Milani, one of Iran's principal Sources of Imitation, had never engaged himself in a just cause or struggle. Shariati's Islam was openly challenging the traditional Islam of the clergy.

> ### Shariati's Modernist Islam
> All that Pascal, Marx and Sartre contributed to Europe could be found in Shiism under the name of Ali. (A. Shariati).[7]

On 20 March 1966, almost two years after his return, Shariati was admitted to the University of Mashhad as an assistant professor of history. The appearance of a Western-trained professor, using the language and jargon of Western philosophers and social scientists couched in Islamic terminology, was a novelty. In his lectures, age-old religious concepts, considered obscure and narrow-minded by students, were imbued with socio-politically relevant contents. As time passed, Shariati's classes became more popular, and his Islamic interpretations resonated with a growing number of inquisitive university students.

By autumn 1968, one of his courses, the History of Philosophy and Art, attracted over 250 students. Aside from his novel ideas Shariati's personality and captivating oratory bewitched his students. In January 1969, his book *Eslamshenasi* (Islamology), composed of his lectures during 1966–7, and one of the few academically well-documented books among the 35 volumes of his published works, came onto the market. The first part of this 640-page book, *What is Islam?* contained the germ of Shariati's future works.

In *Islamology*, Shariati refuted the traditional charges of conservatism and close-mindedness against Islam. He argued that in Islam, reason and religion were one and the same, and that contrary to the views of the clergy, Darwin's ideas were defendable from an Islamic perspective. Shariati insisted that during Islam's early years, individual liberties and the freedom of thought and expression, even of disbelievers, had been respected and guaranteed. Shariati's Islam was a religion of tolerance. He believed that institutionalized religion would ultimately lead to reaction and dogmatism, perpetrating 'religious and clerical despotism'.[8]

Shariati engaged in another essential innovation. He transformed the classical Islamic notion of *shirk*, polytheism or belief in many gods, and accorded it a socio-political meaning. Polytheistic acts, he argued, were those arrogating God's rights and substituting oneself for Him. For Shariati, absolute rule, power, dominance and ownership were the monopoly of God alone, and those who assumed such positions became polytheists. Shariati's 'monotheistic world outlook' was an open invitation to Iranian Muslims to rebel against all false gods, which he later identified as wealth, power, and religious duplicity. One of Shariati's main themes was his notion of polytheistic Islam against monotheistic Islam. For Shariati, monotheistic Islam was a revolutionary religion which pressed upon its adherents to 'change and destroy whatever they found to be false and unacceptable'.[9]

By January 1969, from his classes at Mashhad University and the modern pulpit at Hoseyniyeh Ershad in Tehran, Shariati was relying on Islam and socialism to challenge the shah and the clerical institution, both, in his view, being the causes of the people's misery. Shariati's call to rebellion against both King and established religion came sometime before the Fadais and the Mojahedin had made their revolutionary discourse public.

Shariati had given the first of his many lectures at Hoseyniyeh Ershad, Tehran's modernist Islamic Centre, on 25 October of 1968. Neither the speakers nor the audience at Ershad were traditional religious types, they were there to discuss an Islam which addressed the socio-political problems of their times. From late May 1969, Shariati had begun to openly construct his revolutionary Islamic ideology in a language that his students and audience would understand but which would elude SAVAK.

Shariati aroused his jam-packed young audience, saying that, 'Islam was both an ideology and a social revolution which intended to construct a classless and free society based on equality and justice, where enlightened, responsible and free people could live.'[10] The more Shariati lectured at Ershad, the more he became popular. Accidently or intentionally, the 'Youth Palace', situated on the Old Shemiran Road, to supposedly depoliticize the youth, had been constructed almost in front of Hoseynieh Ershad.

Between March 1970 and 1971, the gist of Shariati's lectures at Ershad evolved. His socialist Islamic discourse, decrying gaping class distinctions and exploitation, morphed into a powerful call for a religious revolution. He accused the 'deceitful custodians of religion', who had historically justified and rationalized the unjust status quo, of being 'idolaters'. In the tradition of Abraham and his religion, which Shariati greatly admired, he had begun smashing the idols.

The repression and violence unleashed after the Fadai attack on Siyahkal further radicalized Shariati. During his lectures throughout 1971, he would call on his audience of 1,500 to 5,000 to confront the injustice of the usurpers, 'engage in a political and armed insurrection' and reinstitute the people's rights through a revolution.

In his famous speech *Shahadat* (Martyrdom), delivered on 25 February 1972, after the revolutionary suicide of Ahmad Rezai and the death sentence of the founders of the Mojahedin, Shariati upped the ante. He argued that once the *mojahed*, the combatant for the cause of God/guerrilla fighter – a direct reference to members of the Mojahedin Organization – is defeated, the time comes for the *shahid* or the martyr to enter the stage. The martyr and his movement represented the last exasperated attempt of righteous and responsible intellectuals who knew that though their act was almost suicidal, it remained the only possible course of action for the collective and social good. Shariati concluded his insurrectionary speech by saying, 'kill if you can and be killed if you cannot'.[11]

It took SAVAK some time to realize that Hoseyniyeh Ershad, under the heavy intellectual influence of Shariati, had become a sanctuary for propagating seditious and revolutionary thoughts. Hoseyniyeh Ershad was a haven for distributing anti-regime pamphlets of the Mojahedin Organization and their recruiting ground. A good number of future high-profile Mojahedin militants attended Shariati's lectures. Early in the morning of Friday, 17 November 1972, Hoseyniyeh Ershad was sealed-off by a cordon of police surrounding it. Shariati's pulpit was closed.

Shariati went into hiding until 29 September 1973, when he was arrested and interrogated. The popularity of Shariati's message and the wide distribution of his books throughout the land continued to worry the authorities. On 23 January 1973, Nematollah Nasiri (Figure 7.3), the head of SAVAK, ordered the confiscation of all Shariati's books for their seditious, pernicious and revolutionary content. Possession of his books was grounds for being arrested.

Figure 7.3 Gen. Nematollah Nasiri. *Source: Wikimedia Commons.*

Shariati spent 18 months in solitary confinement at the notorious Komiteh Prison. He was never put on trial or physically tortured before being released on 19 March 1975. Although he was prohibited from travelling abroad, he left the country on 16 May 1977 and settled in England. On 19 June 1977, his dead body was found lying on his back at the entrance of his room in Southampton. The coroner's report, issued on 21 June, identified 'cardiac failure' as the cause of his sudden death.

Shariati's revolutionary discourse continued to mobilize the Muslim youth even after the closure of Hoseyniyeh Ershad and his death. His subversive political and religious Islamic ideology gave educated modernist Muslim youth an identity and a purpose. During the 1979 revolution, his pictures adorned the demonstrations. His ideas permeated the post-revolutionary debates, marked the Iranian political scene and haunted the clerical establishment. Even Khomeyni wavered on how to deal with Shariati.

CISNU: The Student Movement Abroad

The regime was becoming impatient with Iranian students overseas, who were freely engaging in anti-government activities and exposing the regime's excesses. Gen. Siyavosh Behzadi, the military prosecutor general, threatened students overseas to end their membership in the Confederation of Iranian Students National Union (CISNU) by 21 March 1971 or else face prosecution. The activities of the Confederation were regarded as opposed to 'national interests' and 'against state security'. According to the Iranian security apparatus, the Confederation was being manipulated by communists and was a pawn in the hands of foreign powers. The government labelled its members as 'terrorists', 'agitators' and 'saboteurs'.

The outbreak of guerrilla activities in Iran provided the CISNU with a focus and direction energizing and revitalizing it. Consequently, many politicized students abroad sided with the armed struggle movement in Iran and supported it. To help the guerrilla movement, CISNU relied on different levers. It informed, petitioned, and obtained the active involvement and support of international human rights and legal organizations.

In European and US cities, they organized campaigns, hunger strikes, demonstrations, marches, press conferences and teach-ins against the Iranian regime to impact public opinion. It established close links with the Western press and informed them about the practices of the regime, and the predicament of political dissidents, activists and prisoners. CISNU also reached out to internationally known personalities, intellectuals, artists and Western parliamentarians, petitioning them to demand greater transparency and accountability from the regime.

> **Student and Guerrilla Opposition**
>
> Perhaps the group most thoroughly opposed to the shah and his regime are students, inside and outside Iran, and the terrorists for whom they provide a fertile field for recruitment. (J. Farland, US ambassador to Iran 1972–3)[12]

At its 15th Congress (2–11 January 1974), the Confederation warmly embraced the Mojahedin's message of solidarity, which emphasized that along with the Fadai guerrillas, they believed in armed struggle as the sole means of liberation. A year later, during its 16th Congress (8–15 January 1975), CISNU fully aligned its objectives with those of the guerrilla movement. It adopted a new charter, reiterating its adherence to the overthrow of the regime and pledging to employ all means available to serve the 'revolutionary movement'. They promised to spread their message, follow their guidelines and 'keep the Fadai's brave flag of struggle hoisted'.[13] From January 1974, CISNU acted as a potent auxiliary force for the guerrilla movement.

The guerrilla forces called on the Confederation to expose the regime's atrocities and sway public opinion against the shah's regime. They asked for campaigns defending the cause of Iranian political prisoners, support for their families and publicizing the heroic feats of the guerrillas. Finally, they appealed to members of CISNU to prepare and eventually join the theatre of war at home.

CISNU staged demonstrations and hunger strikes across Europe and on 8 March 1974 occupied Iran's embassies in Brussels, Stockholm and The Hague. The students denounced repression, arrests, torture, political executions and Iran's interference in the internal affairs of Oman and the press gave them ample coverage. Their operations became better coordinated, more violent and more targeted, and had an impact on public opinion in the West. CISNU succeeded over time to turn significant international organizations, with substantial moral authority and weight, against the shah. The change in perception towards the shah forced Western policy-makers to deal more cautiously with him. News of Iran's human rights abuses alerted the US Congress, jeopardizing the shah's traditionally secure and almost unlimited access to US arms.

> ## The Success Story of CISNU
>
> The students' one real success to date has been to influence international opinion in their favor, but so long as the Shah is prepared to ignore such opinion, and he is quite capable of doing so, it seems unlikely that the students or the terrorists will succeed in forcing political change on their country. (Airgram from the embassy in Iran to the Department of State)[14]

In the 1974–5 annual report of Amnesty International, Secretary-General Martin Ennals wrote that 'the Shah of Iran retains his benevolent image despite the highest rate of death penalties in the world, no valid system of civilian courts and a history of torture which is beyond belief'.[15] On 4 March 1975, US Democratic Congressman Pete Stark, relied on articles in the US media about Iran's repressive regime and Amnesty International's data on torture in Iran to warn members of the Congress. According to Roy Atherton, deputy assistant secretary of state for the Near East, the shah was worried about 'the hostile attitude of the Congress towards him'.[16]

On 3 August and 8 September 1976, the Subcommittee on International Organizations of the US House of Representatives met to discuss human rights in Iran. Donald Fraser, Chairman of the subcommittee, opened the meeting by announcing that 'the situation in Iran has been one of primary concern to a number of international nongovernmental organizations active in the field of human rights'.[17] William Butler, president of the International Commission of Jurists, reported to the subcommittee on his findings during his fact-finding mission to Iran in September and October 1975. Butler's report on human rights in Iran was alarming, if not damning. He reported on 6,000 political prisoners, three-quarters of them being held in provisional detention and subjected to torture. From 1975, criticism of the Iranian regime in the international press became recurrent and common. While in the past, this would have been bothersome to the shah, now it was an outright threat.

Between March and November 1976, two highly reputable international organizations, Amnesty International and the International Commission of Jurists, published three damaging reports on Iran's human rights abuses. The pace and intensity of criticism intensified.

The shah's reaction to these reports was twofold: on the one hand, he interpreted the negative coverage incorrectly as an implicit vote of no confidence in his regime by the US administration and his European allies. With Nixon's departure from office and the interim presidency of Gerald Ford, the shah lost his security blanket and became insecure and defensive. Reacting to the orchestrated wave of anti-regime reporting in the media, the shah became paranoid and suspected that a conspiracy against him was in the making. Richard Helm, the American ambassador to Iran, reported to Kissinger that the shah and other Iranian leaders 'were convinced that the United States was looking for some kind of confrontation with Iran'. On the other hand, even before Jimmy Carter's presidency, somewhere around the Fall of 1976, the shah started mulling over a carefully controlled 'sprinkle' notion of providing human rights and freedom of 'constructive criticism'. The shah's concession to the international community's outcry was a constrained liberalization policy.

Dismantling the Monarchy, Step by Step

Carter in the White House

After President James Carter entered the White House on 20 January 1977, the Iranian regime became defensive. The opposition in Iran welcomed Carter's presidency and was rejuvenated and emboldened by it. It hoped that a president in the White House, who emphasized human rights as a criterion for friendly international relations, would pressure the shah to begin political liberalization.

Beating a retreat before Western pressure, on 2 February 1977 the Iranian government announced that: 'Iranian prisons were open to foreign journalists.' One day later, 66 political prisoners, who had been previously condemned in military courts, were released. Key figures of the old 'Islamic Coalition of Mourning Groups' were among those freed. According to Amnesty International in February 1977, the shah 'had reportedly ordered the abolition of torture in Iran'.[18] By 19 August 1977, the government released some 650 political prisoners.

The shah wished to placate what he suspected to be Carter's reproach to his rule. In his inauguration speech, Carter had said, 'Because we are free, we can never be indifferent to the fate of freedom elsewhere. Our moral sense dictates a clear-cut preference for those societies which share with us an abiding respect for individual human rights.' These words had unsettled and destabilized the shah, adding to his paranoia.

The shah was hoping for a tightly controlled Iranian glasnost. His overtures to uphold human rights sent a warm signal to the Iranian opposition while conveying a confusing one to SAVAK's Internal Security branch. SAVAK was used to exercising arbitrary violence to obtain results. But now, it was ordered to put on a velvet glove and accommodate the opposition. The shah's modification of his style of rule destabilized SAVAK and threw a wrench in a well-oiled oppressive machine.

SAVAK's operations relied on imposing the strictest of censorship, the exercise of repressive techniques of surveillance, intimidation, arrest, interrogation, torture and imprisonment. Now, the shah expected SAVAK to do the impossible: desist from brutal methods and keep the shah in power. Meanwhile, the shah's 'drip-drop' reforms were construed as a sign of his weakness, emboldening the opposition. Faced with an ever-growing and radicalized opposition, the shah's hesitations and oscillations rendered the Ship Iran captain-less.

Open Letters and Ten Nights of Poetry Reading

On 10 January 1977, Ali-Asghar Haj-Seyyed-Javadi, a well-known and secular journalist, submitted a long letter to the shah. This new letter-writing campaign was followed by others, including by three old Mosaddeqists, Karim Sanjabi, Shapur Bakhtiyar and Darush Foruhar, on 12 June 1977. They called on the shah to respect the Constitution, honour the separation of powers, reign and not rule, observe human rights, hold free elections, end censorship, free all political prisoners, assure the safe return of all political refugees, end the single-party system and dissolve SAVAK. These were reformist demands, and their implementation meant undoing the shah's despotism. These letters did not provoke the wrath of SAVAK against its authors and were followed by more. Something had changed in the land.

> ### The Shah's Position in September 1977
> I am a combative person and will neither tire nor rest until I reach my objective . . . My objective is a first-class Iran . . . The hammer and sickle communism, the Union Jack communism, the Islamic looking communism, and the new communists, who are looking for new masters, have all failed to stop us. (The shah)[19]

The formation of professional organizations with political proclivities, constituted the second step of reformist activities. Re-organizing non-governmental guilds meant that groups could assemble in a space unrestricted by SAVAK. Freedom to congregate was yet another novelty. The most important professional and non-governmental associations were the Iranian Writers' Association (24 June 1977) and the Iranian Committee for the Defence of Freedom and Human Rights (27 November 1977), attracting familiar figures from the old Iranian opposition groups, such as the Iran Freedom Movement, the National Front, the Tudeh Party, Khalil Maleki's Socialist Society and a good number of independents.

The third step in undermining the shah's authority involved reaching out to people and organizing public events. Starting on Monday, 10 October 1977, the Goethe Institute in Tehran organized ten nights of poetry reading and speeches by the revived, politicized and dissident Iranian Writers' Association. The German Club opened its spacious garden to Iran's most influential cultural figures and their fans. The mainstream press was not only allowed to publish the Iranian Writers' Association's advertisement, inviting the people to attend the event, they were also later allowed to print a favourable coverage of the nightly events. The poetry-reading nights ended on 19 October 1977.

A few details made these nights a historical benchmark in the events leading to the 1979 revolution. Under the rain, some 15,000 to 20,000 attended the first night of this unprecedented cultural gathering. Night after night, educated youth and members of the middle class came to hear the previously censored words of their cultural icons. During this well-planned cultural festival, speakers crossed traditional red lines, broke taboos and used hitherto disallowed words. Every night, the large crowds gathered and dispersed in an orderly fashion. Security forces were present but did not interfere. On the sixth night, Baqer Parham read the Iranian Writers' Association statement reiterating that it aimed to obtain and protect 'the freedom of thought and expression' as stipulated in Iran's Constitution and the Declaration of Human Rights.[20]

The fact that a significant gathering of intellectual dissidents and attended by the people could take place unmolested for ten nights marked the successful transition from tacitly obtaining the freedom of expression to winning the freedom of assembly. Such events helped shed the fear of political objection. The secular opposition was furthering its agenda of pressing for more freedoms within Carter's human rights policies and taking full advantage of the new period of political relaxation. The traditional religious opposition, loyal to Khomeyni, seemed either aloof or asleep.

Khomeyni Prods the Sleepy Religious Forces to Wake Up

From his exile in Najaf, Ayatollah Khomeyni kept in touch with events in Iran. He was the uncontested spokesman of a conservative political Islam opposed to the shah's reign and rule. On 12 March 1975, Khomeyni ruled that the shah's Resurgence Party was opposed to Islam and the interests of Iran's Muslim people. He prohibited the believers from joining it. In concert with the general mood among Iranians abroad, Khomeyni denounced the shah's imprisoning of the youth and intellectuals and promised the destruction of the monarchy. Khomeyni called on the religious dignitaries in Iran to mobilize the people.

On 26 September 1976, Khomeyni wrote a letter to all Muslims and students both inside and outside Iran. Reacting to the sexual revolution in Iran, he lamented the propagation of 'centers of moral corruption and prostitution' aiming to destroy the Iranian youth. On the heels of the Fadais loss of their leadership on 29 June 1976 and the Marxist-Leninist Mojahedin's execution of three American military advisers in Tehran on 28 August 1976, Khomeyni ended his letter in an enigmatic manner by inviting 'the intellectual and learned youth' to 'avoid unfounded adversities, set aside the unfounded doctrines of others and turn to the progressive doctrine of Islam'.[21] He then asked them to unite and annihilate falsehood. With the demise of Marxist and Islamic revolutionaries, Khomeyni was jockeying for power.

Almost a year later, by July–August 1977, Khomeyni began to lash out at the followers of the Mojahedin and Shariati as 'traitors' without naming them. He announced that he 'hated and despised' anyone who deviated from Shiism and disrespected the Shii clerical institution and Shii scholars. Khomeyni sternly warned unnamed Left and progressive Muslim intellectuals, most probably the proponents of Shariati and perhaps Taleqani. He implored 'the honorable writers and thinkers not to engage in the interpretation and exegesis of the Quran and Islamic edicts'.[22] Khomeyni invited all to unite under his banner of Islam.

Khomeyni was putting his own Shii house in order and re-establishing his leadership of the radical Islamic movement, which had slipped under Shariati's influence and partially under the Mojahedin's. He cautioned that understanding and speaking for Islam was the work of only a few jurists, including himself. With the death of Shariati in June 1977, whom Khomeyni refused to call a martyr, a popular political contender for the leadership of the Islamic movement had disappeared leaving the path clear.

Until the end of 1977, Khomeyni's declarations and interventions did not receive the echo he hoped. On 21 October 1977, two days after the end of the poetry-reading event, and while the secular forces basked in the glory of their cultural and political feat, Khomeyni sent a glum and pessimistic message to one of his close clerical associates, Jalaleddin Taheri-Esfahani. A dispirited Khomeyni expressed his worries about the 'clerical institution' and the 'final defeat' that may be awaiting it due to its own doing. He concluded that perhaps God's grace would 'wake us up' and hoped that the clergy would survive through 'appropriate reflection' and 'action according to their responsibilities'.[23] Observing the mobilization among the opposition, Khomeyni was frustrated with the inactivity of his religious followers and the clergy.

Mostafa Khomeyni's Death

Two days after Khomeyni's depressing letter to Taheri-Esfahani, Mostafa Khomeyni, the Ayatollah's elder son who had accompanied his father to exile, passed away in Najaf at age 47. The unexpected death of Mostafa Khomeyni on 23 October 1977 provided a golden opportunity for the clerical forces to enter the political scene. The people's mistrust of the regime fed the rumour mill that Mostafa Khomeyni, like Ali Shariati, had been killed by SAVAK's operatives overseas.

From 28 October 1977, ceremonies were held in his memory in Qom and Tehran. In Tehran, some 8,000 people from different walks of life, including members of the

National Front, the Iran Freedom Movement, *Bazaaris*, members of the Coalition of Islamic Mourning Groups, students and politicized clergy, came together to mourn the death of Mostafa Khomeyni.

At Tehran's Ark Mosque, *Jameeye rowhaniyat mobarez* (Association of Combative Clergy) convened the ceremony. This significant and newly constituted clerical organization was composed of Khomeyni's old students and clerical supporters. This important gathering was summoned by Morteza Motahhari, Khomeyni's favourite and loyal student, and organized by Haj Mehdi Araqi of the Coalition of Islamic Mourning Groups, who had been released from prison some eight months before.

The keynote preacher was a 29-year-old clergy. Hasan Rowhani, who later became Iran's president called Khomeyni the Abraham of his time and bestowed the title of 'Imam' on him. Rowhani concluded that the people loved Khomeyni and his movement. While the Ark Mosque was surrounded by military vehicles, soldiers and police, those inside unanimously demanded the return of Khomeyni from exile. The death of Mostafa played a significant role in reviving Ayatollah Khomeyni's forgotten name and promoting his image among the people. The pious common folk were reminded of Khomeyni's political legacy and opposition to the shah since June 1963.

Khomeyni Regains His Voice

From Najaf, on 1 November 1977, Khomeyni delivered his first public speech since the death of his son. Khomeyni unveiled his stoicism, political acumen, view of Islam and strategy for leading the anti-shah movement. He minimized the importance of his son's death as one of God's 'hidden favours'. He said, 'if we were not so impatient, we would understand 'that there must have been a good, a favour, and a reason in this'. Khomeyni did not blink or show the slightest emotion on the death of his son.

Khomeyni refrained from labelling intellectuals and university students traitors for deviating from Shiism and disparaging the Islamic scholars. He recategorized them as unfamiliar with Islamic jurisprudence and history, and rather excessive in their analysis. Posing as the leader of the anti-shah movement, Khomeyni spoke at length about how religious scholars had historically spearheaded revolts against despotism and called for an alliance between the clergy and the university students against the shah. Poaching in Shariati's and Mojahedin's territories, Khomeyni denounced the possibility of Islam without clerics and reminded his audience that it was he who had led the 5 June 1963 revolt.

In the same speech, Khomeyni pressed on his clerical followers to follow the lead of those non-religious forces in Iran that had launched the open-letter campaign. Khomeyni said, 'Today we are faced with an opportunity [an opening] in Iran … various parties find fault and voice their criticism in signed letters. You too should write, and one hundred learned clerics (*olama*) should sign'. Khomeyni assured the conservative clergy that if they were to sign petitions, 'nothing would happen to them'.[24]

From his place of exile in Najaf, Khomeyni lashed out at the 50-year-old Pahlavi dynasty as illegal and a child of foreign powers. He referred to Reza Shah's reign as a dark period during which Iranians were murdered, pillaged and enchained. He called Mohammad-Reza Shah worse than Genghis Khan and accused him of murder and torture, alleging that he had murdered 15,000 on 5 June 1963. Khomeyni described the shah as an ally of Israel and an enemy of the Arab and Palestinian cause.

By mid-November 1977, barely two weeks after his first speech, Khomeyni started to distance himself from the secular and reformist forces that had participated in the open-letter campaign. He denounced such conciliatory approaches as a ruse to whitewash the atrocities of the Pahlavi regime and called on the people to support 'our endeared Islam and uphold its life-giving ordinances', which 'guarantee the freedom and independence' of this country.[25] Khomeyni enjoined the army and its leadership to free themselves from subjugation to foreigners and save their country from demise.

Khomeyni's instructions to his supporters would remain the same from 12 November 1977 until the shah's overthrow. Khomeyni called on Muslims to desist from collaborating with those forces that did not accept the Islamic character of the movement, and at the same time, he called for unity under his leadership.

The Regime Retaliates, Retreats and Strikes Back

The regime's quasi-liberalization policies had opened the floodgates of some twenty-four years of dammed up discontent. The sudden surge in oppositional activities of secular forces, and demonstrations at universities leading to clashes and closing of classes, worried SAVAK. The country witnessed increasing support for Khomeyni, and the widespread distribution of his 'subversive' speeches and letters.

It was not until 16 November 1977 that SAVAK resorted to dispatching its club-wielding agents in civilian clothes to beat up, scare, and abduct opposition secular intellectuals who planned to give lectures at various universities in Tehran and the provinces. On 24 November 1977, some 2,000 people attended a gathering of the National Front just outside Tehran when they were attacked by busloads of agents, under cover of workers, chanting, 'Long live the shah!' They indiscriminately battered the attendants, destroyed property and smashed some 150 vehicles.

SAVAK's hands, however, were tied behind its back, since the shah had disallowed arbitrary detention, torture, and imprisonment. The new bullying tactics of beating up the opposition did not suffice and failed to deter the opposition. On 20 December 1977, after almost fourteen years of 'patience and awaiting', the National Front announced the formation of the 'Alliance of National Front Forces'. The shah's political ghosts of the past were one by one reappearing. Parviz Sabeti, SAVAK's strongman and mastermind, believed that the shah's refusal to prohibit the religious ceremonies held for Mostafa Khomeyni, and again his objection to widespread arrests of the opposition, had led to the mass mobilization of the religious forces that brought down the monarchy.

Violent Street Demonstrations

Bringing demonstrators out on the streets, a new stage in the anti-shah movement, was ironically the work of the shah's anger and hubris. Insulted by Khomeyni's attacks on the Pahlavis, the shah fell into the trap of a mudslinging match. Miscalculating the situation and mistaking it for an echo of June 1963, the shah ordered a personal attack on Khomeyni in the press.

On 7 January 1978, *Ettelaat*, one of the country's leading newspapers published an opinion piece under the title *Estemare sorkh va siyah* (Red and Black Colonialism). It was signed by Ahmad Rashidiye-Motalaq, probably Ali Shabani's pen name, and appeared on page seven. Rashidiye-Motlaq, accused Khomeyni of being an agent of black and red reactionary and colonial powers. The article called Khomeyni an adventurist, a faithless and ambitious character who was in the pay of colonial centres and in search of political fame and glory. The piece warned against enemy plots, even among those in the holy and respectable garb of the clergy. It labelled the 5 June 1963 revolt, Khomeyni's pride, as a disastrous, shameful and unpatriotic plot against Iran which had been financed by the British.

This provocative piece was another godsend for Khomeyni as the regime insulted and vilified him on issues for which his record was transparent and almost impeccable. To call Khomeyni an agent of colonial powers and in British pay irked Iranians, secular and religious. The article compelled non-politicized key Shii Sources of Imitation such as Ayatollah Golpaygani, Marashi-Najafi and Shariatmadari, who were not fond of Khomeyni's political Islam, to rally behind him. The united voice of notable Sources of Imitation helped Khomeyni's cause and added further fuel to the recurring demonstrations, which grew in size and demands.

Two days after the anti-Khomeyni article appeared, anti-shah demonstrations and closure of shops began in Qom and spread to Tehran, Tabriz, Mashhad, Esfahan and Ahvaz. Demonstrators took to the streets, chanting 'long live Khomeyni', and clashed with the police. On 9 January 1978, the army opened fire on pro-Khomeyni demonstrators in Qom and killed 6, mostly seminary school students. Four days later, on 13 January 1978, the regime tried to turn the tide by mobilizing its supporters. The

Resurgence Party and SAVAK organized pro-Shah rallies in Qom, Tabriz, Khorramshahr, Ahvaz and Tehran. The regime claimed that 50,000 people had participated in the 17 January rally in Tabriz and some 300,000 in the 26 January rally in Tehran. Participants in these rallies chanted, 'Long live the shah!' and pledged to sacrifice their lives for the 'Shah and People Revolution.'

On 19 February 1978, a vast outburst of violence occurred in Tabriz as the people commemorated the fortieth day of 6 demonstrators killed in the Qom demonstrations on 9 January. This date marked the beginning of violent, endemic and relentless anti-shah demonstrations that embroiled the country into a permanent low-intensity civil strife.

From 10.00 in the morning to late at night, thousands of anti-shah and pro-Khomeyni protesters in Tabriz, aged between 15 and 20, caused havoc, while chanting, 'Death to the shah!' Operating in groups of around 100, rioters attacked, looted, and burnt shops, cinemas, banks, hotels, bars, restaurants, sports clubs, government buildings, Youth Palaces and the headquarters of the Resurgence Party. For two days, Tabriz was a city under siege and all daily activities came to a halt. It did not stop until the army intervened, leaving some 12 dead and at least 125 wounded. The majority of the 670 arrested were high-school students. A handful were apprehended for reproducing and distributing Khomeyni's taped speeches. Iran's cassette tape revolution had started.

In the Senate, the industrial tycoon Ali Rezai called for the punishment of Tabriz rioters and a policy of zero tolerance towards the culprits. He criticized the freedoms extended and argued that it had provided an excuse for rabble-rousers to disrupt the peace. Rezai told his fellow senators that the few demonstrators were opposed to Iran's progress and growth and were servants of foreigners who did not favour a strong Iran. The Iranian ruling class, completely cut off from the majority, seemed to live on a different planet.

Shah's Assessment of the Political Situation in February 1978

We will continue to follow the policy of maximum freedoms, since the foundations of the nation built upon the shah and People's Revolution and the people's resurgence is so solid that these symbols of the last breaths of this unholy alliance [red and black] cannot do it the slightest harm. (M.-R. Pahlavi)[26]

The campaign of open letters, peaceful cultural assemblies and the rejuvenation of professional organization and old political parties quickly gave way to heated religious rallies, demonstrations, clashes, arson, riot and tumult. From February 1978 to

February 1979, the country experienced an endless cycle of anti-government riots, engagement with the army, injuries and deaths. As time went by, mid-size and smaller Iranian cities also witnessed anti-shah riots.

Khomeyni: Natural Leader of the Anti-Shah Movement

With each bloody confrontation, the rage and sense of injustice felt by the demonstrators throughout Iran increased rendering them more justified and intent to continue their cause with a heightened level of vengeance. Khomeyni was on the offensive, insulting and shattering the shah's image in his speeches. The shah was on the defensive, desisting from attacking Khomeyni personally while repeating the old notions that he and the patriotic forces would not hand the country to foreigners and communists. On the shah's explicit orders and against the advice of Sabeti, the Iranian press was allowed to report on demonstrations and clashes. News of Iran in the grips of civil strife was publicized almost daily.

During this period, Khomeyni effectively overshadowed the secular forces and assumed the leadership of the revolution. From abroad, he masterfully united the most diverse ideologies with his powerful mantra, 'The shah must go.' The shah, however, kept on his course of liberalization. Hoveyda, now the minister of court, and Gen. Azhari, the army chief of staff, met with the top brass of the armed forces at the shah's behest and insisted that the ongoing events were calculated and there was no reason to panic and what was happening in the country was necessary.

The Shah Changes Tactics, Confusing His Supporters

On 9 May, widespread riots shook Qom, Shiraz and Tabriz and spread to ten other cities. Beyond hurling stones and setting fire to the usual targets, protestors were now attacking police stations, only to be pushed back when the army opened fire. The situation was getting out of hand. Changing tactics, the shah conceded to Sabeti's demand to tighten the reigns. The government issued a stern ultimatum that it would 'no longer tolerate lawlessness and sedition', and threatened the troublemakers and saboteurs with the harshest of punishments.

Sabeti later claimed that he had proposed to arrest 1,500. The shah, however, had only agreed to the arrest of 300 clerical supporters/students of Khomeyni, identified as the ringleader of the demonstrations. From 18 May 1978, the news of unrest subsided, and it seemed as though worried about the scale of the regime's backlash, the opposition had become cautious in its activities. Even the 5 June commemorations, which Khomeyni had insisted on observing, went by without any incidents. On 10 June 1978, alarmed by the slump in anti-shah activities, Khomeyni warned that the people 'should not allow the just struggle to falter and waver'.[27]

> ### Khomeyni on National Reconciliation in June 1978
>
> The military, parties and the clergy should be in touch with one another and plot the fall of this person [the shah]. The people of Islam and Iran will not reconcile with this person. If someone talks of reconciliation, he would be a traitor . . . This is a divine responsibility . . . we are obliged to revolt against him. (R. Khomeyni)[28]

On 6 June, the meaningful changing of the guard at SAVAK made news. Gen. Nasiri, whose management of SAVAK was associated with tales of torture and abuse of human rights, was packed off to Pakistan as ambassador. Both Nasiri and Sabeti, his second in command, were known for their hawkish position on national security. In contrast, Nasiri's replacement, Naser Moqadam, had the reputation of being a dove. The change in SAVAK's leadership was a further sign of liberalization. Less than a month after the ultimatum and arrests, the opposition and forces loyal to the shah witnessed the shah's resolve to maintain the 'maximum freedom' course.

According to Sabeti, Moqadam followed a policy of reconciliation with the opposition and gradually released the 300 arrested clerics. Subsequently, from 25 July, after two months of relative calm, the protest movement picked up speed and intensity with a vengeance. The vigour of the protests and the death of at least 38 people in Shiraz and Esfahan, forced the government to declare martial law in Esfahan on 11 August 1978. In tandem with the spectacular presence of tanks and armoured vehicles in Esfahan, the government imposed a curfew from 8.00 pm to 6.00 am and prohibited the congregation of more than three people.

On 19 August 1978, violence reached a new hysterical pitch when the Rex Movie Theatre in Abadan was set on fire by Khomeyni's supporters, and attributed to the regime, causing the death of 377. The habit of burning movies, bars, cafes and restaurants, symbols of Iran's new cultural liberation, was routine among religious protestors, but to purposefully cause the death of hundreds of innocent people was a novel phenomenon.

Change of Prime Ministers

On 27 August 1978, amidst widespread demonstrations throughout the country, and after almost a year in office, Amuzegar was replaced by Jafar Sharif-Emami. Amuzegar had been chosen by the shah to fix the economy, combat corruption and supervise the monarch's new liberalization policy. He handed to Sharif-Emami a country on the brink of collapse. The new prime minister announced that the motherland was in danger and tried to play the religious card to calm down tempers. He presented his government as that of national reconciliation.

Sharif-Emami committed his government to abolish the monarchical calendar, shut down cabarets and casinos, accept the legitimacy of a multiparty system, free political and clerical prisoners, and recognize the right of peaceful demonstrations. Such measures may have been curative back in September of 1977, but by August 1978 they fell short of what the popular mood demanded. The accommodation policy of the shah and Sharif-Emami further emboldened Khomeyni, who knew that the shah was losing his grip day by day.

> ### Khomeyni's Winning Card
> Khomeini's genius was in realizing that by criticizing the greatest defects of the Shah's regime as perceived by a large majority of the people – the absence of democracy and freedom; overt dependence on and alignment with the United States and widespread corruption- he could gain the widest base of support possible. (Rahnema and Nomani)[29]

Two Days of Massive and Peaceful Demonstrations

The next stage in the anti-shah movement unfolded on 4 and 7 September 1978. Khomeyni's partisans demonstrated their impressive numerical strength by organizing massive, peaceful and well-organized marches throughout Iran. Some 3 million people participated in the most spectacular demonstrations ever in Tehran. They walked through some 20 kilometres of the city's main arteries, chanting, 'Independence, freedom and Islamic republic!', 'Death to the shah!', 'Onwards to the destruction of the monarchy in Iran!' and 'Khomeyni is our leader and Iran is our country!'

The security and military forces stood by. These demonstrations were organized by militants associated with the Islamic Coalition of Mourning Groups, the Iran Freedom Movement, and the Association of Combative Clergy. The clerical group of Morteza Motahhari, Mohammad Beheshti, Ali-Akbar Hashemi-Rafsanjani and Mohammad-Javad Bahonar, comprising the nucleus of the Association of Combative Clergy, was gradually rising in prominence and power.

To curtail the escalation and extension of the demonstrations, which were taking control of the capital, the government imposed martial law on 12 cities, including Tehran. On Thursday, 7 September, Sharif-Emami's government imposed a curfew from 9.00 pm to 5.00 am and warned that all demonstrations were illegal, and transgressors would be punished according to the law. Gen. Gholamali Oveysi, who had the reputation of a hawk, was named military governor of Tehran.

Black Friday and Its Consequences

Despite martial law prohibiting the congregation of more than two, crowds gathered at Jaleh Square on Friday, 8 September. The troops ordered the people to disperse. Based on the army's peaceful comportment during the past few days, the crowd refused to obey orders. As more people joined, filling Jaleh Square, the officers in charge, who had received orders to shoot in the face of insubordination, instructed soldiers under their command to fire on the crowd.

> ## Khomeyni on Black Friday
>
> The world has to know that this [Black Friday] is Iran's glasnost and this is the shah's democratic regime, and this is the way the shah and his government act according to Islam and reason. (R. Khomeyni)[30]

The troops fired into the crowd as well as in the air. The opposition claimed somewhere between 400 and 3,000 deaths. After the revolution, it became known that 88 had been shot dead during the carnage that came to be known as 'Black Friday' (Figure 7.4). On

Figure 7.4 Black Friday on Jaleh Square. *Source: Wikimedia Commons.*

that day, seventy-eight cases of arson were reported throughout Tehran, targeting buses, restaurants, cinemas, banks and department stores. The shah's vacillation between liberalization and crackdown confused and infuriated people.

The events of Jaleh Square played directly into the hands of the opposition. The shah came off as a bloodthirsty despot. The bloodshed, however, scared the monarch and made him revert to his policy of prohibiting the army from shooting on people as a means of crowd control. 'Black Friday' was the gateway to the victory of the opposition over the shah. On Sunday 10 September 1978, two days after 'Black Friday' and the onset of the strikes, President Carter called on the shah to assure him of his support.

US Assessment of the Iranian Situation before September 1978

We were assured by the judgement of the ambassador, the experts in the State department, the CIA, and other agencies and foreign governments that even though he might be required to make political compromises that would dilute his power, the shah was not in serious danger. (C. Vance)[31]

Strikes

In addition to daily demonstrations and rioting, and despite martial law, the opposition resorted to another potent weapon of civil disobedience, namely strikes and work stoppage. The first of these strikes, most probably completely spontaneous, occurred at the heart of Iran's industrial complexes. On 5 September 1978, some 2,000 workers went on strike at the Tabriz Machine Factory and another 2,000 at the Arak Machine Factory. One day later, 850 stopped work at Mashhad Water Company.

The striking workers demanded higher pay, housing allowances and an increase in the duration of paid holidays. Soon the strikes spread to the Tehran and then Abadan oil refinery. In tandem with industrial work stoppages, on 6 September, 1,000 employees of the Iranian Central Bank went on strike. On 14 September, nine days after the first strikes, Khomeyni called on the 'great and victimized people of Iran to strike'. In a vocabulary different from his own, Khomeyni called the government 'fascist', and then returning to his own language, accused the shah of turning the country into a 'ruinous cemetery'.[32]

Hundreds of oil workers in Ahvaz stopped working on 23 September 1978. One by one, gas pipeline workers at Bide Boland, Esfahan Steelworkers, the Sarcheshmeh Copperworkers, Abadan Petrochemical workers, railroad workers and subsequently workers in the private sector crippled economic activities.

By 9 October, strikes spread to the banking, insurance, telephone, post, water, railway, transportation, hospital, publishing and electricity sectors. Employees of the ministries of justice, education, health, interior, economy and finance, housing and urban development, culture and arts, agriculture, information and tourism also joined in the strikes. There was hardly an economic sector, ministry or government office that was immune to strikes, which like the demonstrations and the rioting, spread like wildfire across the country.

The impact of the strike by the oil depot workers at Shahre Rey, added to that of the 5,000 striking oil workers in Abadan, crippled the distribution of kerosine and gasoline in Tehran. The outcome was long lines, causing a mixture of frustration and disorder. But it also fostered revolutionary compassion, solidarity and bonding as the youth helped the elderly carry their heavy petroleum jerries and buckets home. With teachers and students on strike, students throughout Iran were free to participate in the revolution.

The continuous string of work stoppages led to an intermittent general strike, seriously interrupting oil exports. On 26 October, Carter noted in his diary that, 'Iran is running into serious trouble because of strikes preventing the shipment of oil to foreign markets. The shah will have to take action soon'.[33] The two-months strike of Iran's Radio and Television network and the mainstream press began on 6 November 1978. They both resumed work on 6 January 1979, ten days before the shah would leave the country.

The front page of the daily *Ettelaat* on Saturday, 6 January, looked very different. For the first time, it had a big picture of Khomeyni and smaller pictures of Mosaddeq and Takhti. What was banned by the shah was now on public display. *Ettelaat*'s headline read, 'The people's revolution is at the gate of victory.' In the two months between November 1978 and January 1979, victory was at hand. The burning issue, however, was how to transfer the power.

The Saint under the Apple Tree: Khomeyni at Neauphle-le-Château

On 6 October 1978, under pressure from the Iranian government, Khomeyni was forced to leave Iraq after 13 years stay. He and his close entourage tried to enter Kuwait but were refused entry. At the behest of Ebrahim Yazdi, Khomeyni flew to Paris, demanded, and was accorded political asylum. Overnight, Khomeyni turned the quiet village of Neauphle-le-Château in the Yvelines, some 45 kilometres west of Paris, into an international hub.

Moving to France brought him closer to his objective of overthrowing the shah. With the growing international interest in Iran's complex political situation, news agencies, journalists, radio and television reporters gave extensive coverage to

Khomeyni, the enigmatic spiritual leader. Khomeyni's interviews found their echo in Iran, boosting his status and popularity. From his idyllic suburban residence, in the heart of secular France, Khomeyni and his growing circle of followers directed the Islamic anti-shah movement in Iran.

From his arrival in France, Khomeyni bombarded Iranians with his moving messages, instructing them to keep up the revolutionary momentum. In the first of his almost daily, if not more, messages recorded on cassette tapes, Khomeyni remained focused, clear, and adamant. He identified three concrete goals for his partisans in Iran: dismantling the monarchy, chasing out, and punishing all those who had collaborated with the shah, and ending foreign intervention, be it the US, USSR or Great Britain.

In France, Khomeyni had the opportunity to freely meet with the Iranian opposition and plan for the future. The representatives and leaders of the National Front, Iran Freedom Movement, the Coalition of Islamic Mourning Groups and the Association of Combative Clergy all flooded Neauphle-le-Château. When both Alexandre de Marenches, the head of the French Secret Service and Counterespionage, and French President Valéry Giscard d'Estaing approached the shah about expelling Khomeyni from France, the shah was not in favour of the idea. The shah had lost the will either to take risks or to fight.

Khomeyni's famous Paris discourse was influenced by his non-clerical Western-educated advisors, Abolhasan Bani-Sadr, Ebrahim Yazdi and Sadeq Qotbzadeh. His new locution became more all-embracing, pluralistic and inclusive, giving the impression of a politically and religiously tolerant and democratic Islam. In France, Khomeyni had a double discourse.

His primary target were the religious masses, who looked up to him as almost an infallible imam. In this discourse, he drew upon popular Shii sources and emphasized the implementation of Shii Islam in all its political, economic, religious and cultural facets. He lashed out at Iran's moral degeneration and corruption at the hands of the shah. The modality of his Islamic Republic was a work in progress and even Khomeyni did not know what it would ultimately resemble.

Khomeyni's Paris discourse was also for those Iranians who were not convinced that Islam and Shiism alone possessed solutions to all modern problems. As the leader of the Iranian Revolution, in contrast to the Islamic Revolution, Khomeyni needed to attenuate and smooth out his intolerant and harsh positions towards the 'other'. At the time, Iran was predominantly a society of Shii believer, although Iranian religiosity was widely diverse. It ranged from a hidebound inflexible Islam to a liberal, inclusive, modernist and left Islam.

The young political activists of the Islamic movement were mainly the children of Shariati, the Mojahedin and Mahmud Taleqani. The middle-aged pious professionals interested in the revolution were followers of Bazargan and Shariatmadari. The Sunni Kurdish minority followed the Left-leaning, culturally progressive Ezeddin Hoseyni.

These other Islamic leaders shared very little with Khomeyni's world outlook. Aside from the rainbow of Muslim tendencies, Iran was also the home of religious minorities, such as Orthodox Armenians, Jews, Zoroastrians and Bahais, as well as a significant, vibrant and solid secular contingency. This non-religious bloc included monarchists, constitutionalists, Mosaddeqists, liberals, modernists and Marxists of various shades.

In Paris, Khomeyni's worldly non-clerical advisers taught him how to speak to that rainbow of Iranians who did not share all his Shii beliefs. In his interviews with foreign journalists, Khomeyni began to emphasize commonalities rather than divergences. This intelligent move enabled various socio-political and even most non-religious groups in Iran to find some common ground with his ambiguous post-shah project. Minimizing potential differences in the future helped Iranians focus on the immediate anti-shah project. Khomeyni's unprecedented political feat was his ability to unite Iranians of very different persuasions under one umbrella, offering each something they could identify with.

From November 1978 until his return to Iran on 1 February 1979, Khomeyni made a long list of promises that he would later not keep. Khomeyni went on an effective campaign of charming his non-partisans, domestic and foreign by reiterating that the Islamic Republic would be a democratic government in the proper sense of the word, that it would hold free elections and provide for the equality of economic and political opportunities, that it would uphold freedoms of speech, the press and party politics, and that it would respect all religious minorities. Communists would obtain freedom of expression, men and women would be regarded as equal from a human rights point of view, and women would be allowed to choose their work and garb, even though they would have to comply by certain standards.

The Islamic Republic would rely on the people's vote and will in the political process, would allow the public to scrutinize and criticize governments, would not be xenophobic, would not be a dictatorship and would not rule by the bayonet. It would be a republic, both democratic and Islamic, maintain cordial relations with the US as long as the US remained cordial towards Iran, and cooperate with regional powers to maintain stability and peace. The Islamic Republic would provide justice and economic affluence/comfort, uproot state pillage, theft and coercion, and end inequalities between slum-dwellers and the those who lived in luxurious villas inside and outside Iran.

But most significantly, Khomeyni vowed that the clergy would not become personally involved in governing the country, even though they would act as observers and guides. He asserted that the clergy would not act as guardians (*motekafel*) of the government. Amid his flowery promises, however, Khomeyni made a statement about opposition forces in Iran that sounded disturbingly like the shah's old leitmotif. Iran's future leader said, 'all groups are free to express their beliefs, but we will not allow treachery'.[34] Freedom, Khomeyni said, was respected in Islam unless it became harmful to the country and a source of corruption.

The Shah Vacillates and Khomeyni Rams through the Revolution

The daily clashes between the military and civilians, reports of fraternization between soldiers and the protestors, the economic standstill due to strikes and Khomeyni's inflexible position, drained the shah. The monarch was unable to restore order, and even though he was getting support from the US, he had lost confidence in Carter's friendship. The shah's shift from his comfort zone of ruling as a despot and keeping a tight ship to becoming the protector of political freedoms and human rights had destabilized him. The shah was out of his element and in unchartered waters without his usual safety nets.

> ### A Hesitant Shah in November 1978
> The shah expressed deep concern about whether to set up an interim government, a military government, or perhaps even to abdicate. We encouraged him to hang firm and count on our backing. (J. Carter)[35]

The shah's indecision, aggravated by the fact that he was battling cancer, made it impossible for him to make important decisions at a moment in history when all held in the balance. His entourage, who had long learnt not to voice an opinion lest they upset the monarch, did not know what to do in a crisis of this magnitude. Alam, the shah's only true friend, who had his ears, was his quasi-therapist and had pulled him out of the June 1963 crisis, died on 14 April 1978. The monarch was compassless, scared and completely paralyzed. The shah's conflicting and half-baked decisions only strengthened the position of Khomeyni and the revolutionary forces in the country. He had become his own worst enemy, incapable of going to the logical end of any action plan.

On 6 November 1978, a month after Khomeyni arrived in France, and following seventy days of massive demonstrations, strikes, riots and the full coverage of the revolution in the press, the shah changed course again. His new course, composed of three elements, was a deadly combination of contradictory policies.

The first element was that he replaced Sharif-Emami's civilian government of 'national reconciliation' with Gen. Gholamreza Azhari's military government, while still giving strict orders that the military should avoid shooting at the people (Figure 7.5). The second element was that, on the same day, the shah addressed the people and apologized for appointing a military government.

In his historical concession speech, the shah said, 'As Iran's monarch and as an Iranian, I cannot, but endorse the Iranian people's revolution.' He lamented the riots and the strikes that had crippled the country and cautioned about the threat to the

Figure 7.5 Gen. Gholamreza Azhari. *Source: Wikimedia Commons.*

country's independence. The shah was apologetic about forming an interim military government and remorseful about his style of government in the past. In a rather pathetic statement, he said, 'I, too, have heard the message of your – Iranian people's – revolution and as guardian of the constitutional monarchy ... I will guarantee whatever you have shed your blood for'.[36]

The third and final element was that on 6 November 1978, the shah ordered the arrest of six ex-ministers, in addition to the arrests of Nasiri, the ex-head of SAVAK, and of Jafarqoli Sadri, the former chief of police. And on the following day, he ordered the arrest of Hoveyda, his loyal prime minister of 13 years. The shah's futile attempt to appease Khomeyni and the opposition by arresting his old functionaries and loyal subjects only weakened his already meagre support base. Threatened by the arrests, one by one, high officials took flight, most importantly Parviz Sabeti, Hushang Ansari and Jamshid Amuzegar.

While the shah was beating a retreat, Khomeyni began his effective psychological campaign of gradually undermining the resolve and loyalty of the Iranian armed forces. On 7 November 1979, Khomeyni called on the military to disobey the orders of their superiors and called on them to join the people and enjoy the final victory. Three weeks later, he declared the government outlaw/illegitimate and standing against the will of the people and the *sharia*. He threatened the officials in power that if they continued to work with the regime, they would be gravely dealt with after the revolution's victory and called on the soldiers to desert.

On 1 December 1978, at 9 pm, sudden chants of '*Allah o akbar!*' (God is great!) and '*La elahe ellallah!*' (There is but one God!) disrupted the deadly nocturnal silence. In Tehran, which was under curfew, these chorus-like chants were the people's new method of psychological warfare, sowing panic among soldiers and martial law authorities. On the first night, surprised by the chants, the military fired shots thinking they were under attack. Every night thereafter, Iranians went to their rooftops, balconies or their windows for about twenty minutes to demonstrate their solidarity with the revolution and voice their protest differently.

Azhari's toothless military government lasted a mere seven weeks. During this time, protests, demonstrations, and riots continued throughout Iran. Sometimes the soldiers opened fire on protestors, and sometimes, as on 10 and 11 December, they stood by and even disappeared. This massive two-day demonstration, called by Ayatollah Mahmud Taleqani, brought out 1–3 million people on the streets of Tehran. The shah allowed the marches because he feared his troops would disobey orders to shoot at the crowd.

The demonstrations were a spectacular show of disciplined force by all shades of the opposition. The portraits brandished by the throngs who filled Shahyad Square demonstrated the unity of purpose and the political plurality of the participants. Portraits included Khomeyni, Mosaddeq, Shariati, Taleqani, Hanifnejad, Badizadegan, Mohsen, Samad Behrangi, Takhti, Pouyan, Ahmadzadeh, Hamid Ashraf and Khosrow Rouzbeh.

The preponderance of Khomeyni's portrait reflected his popularity and attested to his leadership. Khomeyni called the demonstrations a veritable referendum in favour of Shah's departure and regime change. He again ordered the young army officers to turn their backs on their commanders and join the movement.

Shapur Bakhtiyar's Civilian Government

Iran was at a dysfunctional gridlock. On 26 December 1978, the shah asked William Sullivan, the American ambassador to Iran, whether the US 'would support a policy of brutal repression' in Iran.[37] Zbigniew Brzezinski, President Carter's national security advisor, supported a hardline position towards the opposition. Cyrus Vance, the secretary of state, favoured a more moderate approach, opposing the iron fist option. As of 3 January 1979, Ambassador Sullivan recommended that the US 'advise the shah to abdicate'.[38] Clearly the US government was divided on how to deal with the shah and the anti-shah uprising. The US answer to the shah was unclear. It voiced a preference for a moderate government but recommended a firm military government if the army was in danger of becoming more fragmented.

On 30 December 1978, the shah replaced Azhari's military government with Shapur Bakhtiyar's civilian government. The fact that in the span of 17 months (August 1977–January 1979) the shah had felt obliged to try out four very different types of prime ministers was a sign of his confusion, indecision, disorientation, imbalance, and finally stupor. By January 1979, neither the shah nor the US had a clear vision of what to do.

Shapur Bakhtiyar was a hard-headed, ambitious and Westernized politician who took pride in his secular French education and time in the French resistance movement. He was also proud of his National Front heritage and did not hide his deep respect and affinity for Mosaddeq. The shah had spent some 26 years belittling and insulting Mosaddeq and the National Front and accusing them of treason. Now, the shah had chosen Bakhtiyar, a Mosaddeqist, to save his crown. Belatedly, the shah was prepared to reign as a constitutional monarch.

Bakhtiyar boastfully referred to himself as a legendary 'thunderbird' and seemed under the illusion that he could fly in unimaginable storms when no one else could. On the day that Bakhtiyar was appointed prime minister, his old political family, the National Front, expelled him from their fold. Khomeyni's response to a Shah-appointed prime minister was predictable. He labelled the new government illegitimate and treacherous and those cooperating with it, as traitors.

The Guadeloupe Consensus

On 3 January 1979, four days after nominating Bakhtiyar as prime minister, the shah sent word to the US that he would leave Iran only if he was advised to do so by President Carter. By this time, there was talk of army generals planning a coup. Far away from the tumult in Iran, the leaders of the US, UK, France, and Germany were gathered for a three-day meeting at the French Caribbean Island of Guadeloupe. The three-day summit, commencing on 4 January 1979, was called by Giscard d'Estaing, and one of the main items on the agenda was the Iranian crisis. British Prime Minister James Callaghan and Jimmy Carter maintained that the shah had lost his political legitimacy and control of the country. German Chancellor Helmut Schmidt believed that 'the megalomaniac shah would be brought down'.[39] Carter informed the three European heads of state that the shah could no longer stay in power. All four powerful Western allies decided on non-support for the shah and full support for Bakhtiyar.

Guadeloupe Decision on 6 January

I then discussed Iran and found little support among the other three for the shah . . . They were unanimous in saying the shah ought to leave as soon as possible. (J. Carter)[40]

On 4 January, the US responded to the shah's inquiry about leaving the country. Ambassador Sullivan told the shah that Carter 'concurred in the shah's intention to leave Iran under a regency council and assured him that he would be welcome in the United States'.[41] This was in line with what would be decided in Guadeloupe. The Iranian generals interpreted the Guadeloupe decision as the green light by the four powers for the shah to leave the country. The generals believed that this was a departure, 'for which there was no return'.[42]

Planning the Shah's Departure

Having informed the shah that he could leave Iran, the US action plan remained muddled, haphazard, and unrealistic. The US hoped that in the absence of the shah, the Iranian army would fully support the moderate, pro-Western Bakhtiyar and that, by some miracle, Bakhtiyar would be able to restore order. In case Bakhtiyar was unsuccessful, the US proposed 'contingency plans … to restore order'.[43] Neither Carter nor his administration were in any way similar to Eisenhower and his administration in 1953. Carter's administration thought about a coup, and wanted a coup, but was too reluctant to be seen as Nixon in Chile. In terms of hesitancy and reluctance to use violence, the shah and Carter were birds of the same feather.

> ### The Huyser Mission
> His mission was murky. Subsequent conversations with White House officials suggested that his purpose was to make a military coup. This impression, however, was contradicted by other officials at the State Department. The dominant impression was of confusion and growing danger to American interest. (A. Haig)[44]

On 5 January 1979, Gen. Robert Huyser, deputy commander of the Supreme Allied Command in Europe, arrived in Iran. Huyser had travelled to Iran before and closely knew many of Iran's top brass. He was dispatched by the US administration and given an impossible task. Huyser was to assure the army's unity and cohesion in the shah's absence, prevent its collapse and a possible coup by the hardliner generals. He was to give heart to the generals by promising them that the US remained behind them. But Huyser was also in Iran to stage a coup as a last resort. The shah had forbidden the army to use an iron fist while expecting it to restore order. Now it was Huyser's task to both prevent the hawkish Iranian generals from staging a coup, while planning for a coup with them if need be.

While Ambassador Sullivan pushed for the army to enter negotiations and reconciliation with Khomeyni, Huyser continued to encourage Bakhtiyar and the generals to hold down the fort. A few days after Bakhtiyar became prime minister, he met with Mehdi Bazargan. Conflicting signals from US representatives further confused the Iranian generals.

From 16 January 1979, the US opened a channel of communication with Khomeyni in Paris through Ebrahim Yazdi, a close confidant of Khomeyni and a naturalized US citizen. In Tehran, Ayatollah Abdolkarim Musavi-Ardebili and Bazargan met with Sullivan, while negotiations were also conducted between John Stemple, US Embassy political officer, and Abbas Amir-Entezam, Bazargan's envoy. Concurrently, the generals entered talks with Mehdi Bazargan and Ayatollah Beheshti. Beheshti was Khomeyni's key political representative in Iran and both Beheshti and Musavi-Ardebili were members of the six-man Revolutionary Council, secretly established by Khomeyni in December 1978. On 12 January 1979, Khomeyni announced the formation of *Showraye enqelabe eslami* (Council of the Islamic Revolution), without revealing its members and mandated it to study and prepare the conditions for the Provisional Government.

A Monarchy without the Monarch

Seventeen days after appointing Bakhtiyar and asking his top military commanders to support his designated prime minister, the shah left Iran. On Tuesday afternoon of 16 January 1979, Tehran was windy and cold. The haughty shah of Iran and his queen were at the Mehrabad Airport prepared to leave the country. A handful of staunch followers were present, seeing them off with tearful eyes. The royal pavilion at Mehrabad Airport, which had seen many a glorious and spectacular days was morose and grey. There was neither a band to play the national anthem nor was Seyyed Hasan Emami, Tehran's Friday Prayer Leader, who always murmured the religious prayers in the shah's ears for a safe trip, present. A member of the Royal Guard threw himself on the tarmac at the monarch's feet, begging him to stay.

The shah's 38-year rule had come to a tragic end. The people, in whose name he had ruled with an iron fist, wanted him out. The jewel of the shah's eyes, the military and SAVAK, were impotent to prevent his departure. A dejected, physically ill and broken-hearted Shah, rushed to the Boeing 727 that took him and a small entourage to Cairo. Oh, how the proud and mighty fall. Within sixteen months, enraged Iranians had chased the shah out of the country (Figure 7.6).

Figure 7.6 The shah and the queen, Farah Diba, leaving Iran, with Shapur Bakhtiyar (right of photo). *Source: Wikimedia Commons.*

On the news of the shah's departure, the people throughout the country took to the streets in an ecstatic state of joy and euphoria, dancing and singing that, '*Shah raft!*' (The shah is gone). The cars in Tehran honked incessantly, brandished Khomeyni's portraits, and passengers with their bodies halfway out of the windows waved and flashed V-signs. Joyful and proud pedestrians distributed sweets and flowers. Men and women veiled and unveiled hugged and kissed. Tehran witnessed a momentary carnival of carefreeness and delight. It felt like a liberated city. Fear and anxiety had dissipated, and the people fraternized with the military, hugged them and placed flower reefs around their necks.

On that same day, there were also signs of vengefulness and wrath. Crowds threw the shah's portraits out of government buildings and angrily trampled on, broke, tore, and burnt them. Some pulled down statues of the shah and his father, others brandished 100 rial notes with the face of the shah plucked out of it. The provinces were also in an equally festive and vengeful mood. Khomeyni congratulated Iranians on the departure of the shah and called on the people to keep pressure on the government through demonstrations and strikes and urged all members of Iran's armed forces, irrespective of rank, to join the people.

Khomeyni Returns

At 9.27 am on 1 February 1979, Khomeyni's Air France plane landed at Mehrabad Airport. Some 1,000 people, his official reception team got their first glance of Iran's new leader. The 76-year-old cleric walked down the stairs leaning on the hand of an Air France personnel. Fifteen years before, when he left Iran, there had been hardly any reaction to his forced exile. On his return, there were few Tehranis who decided to stay home and not to welcome him. Among those who accompanied him on his flight from Paris and those selected new dignitaries who welcomed him, a good number would soon be chased out of Iran into exile, imprisoned, killed in street battles and executed by the new revolutionary state.

Upon his arrival, Khomeyni wanted to pay his respects to the martyrs of the revolution. Some 2,781 to 2,838 were killed between the start of the clashes in Qom on 9 January 1978 and 11 February 1979, the fall of the monarchy. From Mehrabad Airport to Tehran's main cemetery, Behesht Zahra, crowds of zealots packed the 32-kilometre trajectory, eager to welcome the Imam. At Behesht Zahra, more than 100,000 congregated to hear his first speech at home.

In his first face-to-face with Iranians after fifteen years, Khomeyni criticized the shah and his father for having destroyed Iran, its economy and having helped fill and flourish the cemeteries. These words would linger in the ears of post-revolutionary generations of Iranians. Khomeyni accused the shah of founding all sorts of whorehouses, such as the national radio and television and the cinemas. But he reminded his audience that he was not against either cinema nor radio and television, but against prostitution.

Looking into the immediate future, Khomeyni warned Bakhtiyar and said, 'I will appoint a government. I will punch this government in the mouth. With the support of the people, and since the people want me, I will appoint a government.' Khomeyni added that, 'the government that I am talking about is reliant on the people's vote and God's edict, you [Bakhtiyar] would have to either negate God's edict or the people's will'.[45]

Khomeyni's new vision of government was now based on potentially contradictory sources of power. It drew its legitimacy on the one hand from God and the Guardian Jurist (*valiye faqih*) as the Twelfth Imam's spokesperson and, on the other hand, from the people. This mixture of theocracy and democracy, designated as the Islamic Republic, was very different from Khomeyni's initial concept of Islamic government, articulated in January and February 1970 in Najaf.

Back in 1970, Khomeyni had argued that without a religious guardian to watch over and direct the people, and in the absence of an honest leader who would teach them Islamic injunctions and beliefs and enforce Islamic laws, the pursuit of private interests would lead to personal and social corruption, chaos and destruction. The necessity for a religious custodian of the people was primarily based on his posited belief that, 'the people are [mentally] deficient and in need of completion or perfection'.[46]

Nine years earlier, Khomeyni believed that people in general needed guidance in the same way that minors had to follow the instructions of their legal custodians. Leadership and rule, Khomeyni argued, belonged to the *fuqaha* or legal experts of Islamic law. The deserving and just expert on Islamic law, he believed, possessed the same rights and powers to govern as did the Prophet and the imams. In Khomeyni's original concept of an Islamic government, the people had no right or voice in the administration of the state, the legislative, judiciary and the executive. On his return to Iran, when it came to the source of legitimacy of his political rule, Khomeyni placed the weight on the people's will and his religious role as the Guardian Jurist.

Bazargan's Provisional Government

On 4 February 1979, Khomeyni introduced Mehdi Bazargan as the first provisional prime minister of the Iranian Revolution and charged him with organizing a referendum to change the regime to the Islamic Republic, convening a Constituent Assembly of the people's elected representatives to draw up and ratify a new constitution, which would then prepare for a new parliament composed of the people's representatives. Bazargan's brief reflected Khomeyni's order of priorities in expediting the formation of democratically-elected legal institutions and consolidating the revolutionary regime.

> ### What Khomeyni Did Not Include in Bazargan's Brief but Expected of Him
> Acting in a revolutionary manner ... employing violence, exclusion and destruction, promoting Islam and the implementation of the *sharia* as a government programme, exporting the revolution, combatting world arrogance, liberating the disinherited of the world, and combating disbelief. (M. Bazargan)[47]

For five days, Iran had two prime ministers, one of the Ancien Régime and the other of the revolutionary regime. In the interim, widespread demonstrations in support of Bazargan broke out throughout the country. Gen. Huyser left Tehran, and a large number of *homafaran* (non-officer technical personnel of the air force) visited Khomeyni in their military uniforms, at his residence in Refah School and pledged allegiance to him.

On Friday night, 9 February 1979, bloody clashes broke out at the Doshantapeh Air Force Garrison between the pro-Khomeyni *homafaran* and the elite Royal Guard. On 10 February, the fighting at Doshantapeh Garrison continued and around 8.30 am, protesters entered the garrison, broke into the armoury and obtained arms. They subsequently armed the rebellious military personal, went out of the garrison and began building barricades against the Royal Guards. Tehran witnessed its first revolutionary battles. In the afternoon, the people attacked and occupied several undefended police stations, expropriating arms, ammunition and wireless equipment. The police personnel were the first to desert.

At around noon of 10 February, some 50,000 supporters of the Marxist-Leninist Fadai Organization gathered at Tehran University. They were commemorating the attack on the Gendarmerie Station at Siyahkal in 1971 and were supposed to march towards Shahyad Square. Once they got news of the fighting at Doshantapeh Garrison, they marched instead to Foziyeh Square, close to the garrison. The demonstrators chanted 'we will turn the whole of Iran into Siyahkal' as they rushed towards the centre of the armed clashes. Worried about the Fadai march towards Doshantapeh, Bakhtiyar moved up the curfew to 4.30 pm.

By nightfall of Saturday, February 10, Doshantapeh Garrison was in the hands of the rebel forces. On the same night, personnel of the Gendarmerie began deserting their garrisons. At 3.00 am on Sunday, thirty tanks deployed by the Royal Guard Division were intercepted by the people, who had defied the curfew. The people destroyed most of the tanks, and the few remaining went back to their base. The ammunition factory in Tehran which had been under attack since very early hours of Sunday fell to the people at 8.00 am on 11 February. The fighting which had started on Friday 9 February at 9.00 pm was effectively over by Sunday, 11 February at 9.00 pm.

The High Council of the Armed Forces met on 11 February 1979. They began their deliberations at 10.00 am and ended at 12.30 in the afternoon, issuing a determining communique that would turn the course of Iranian history. The document signed by 27 generals asserted that, 'To prevent further bloodshed and chaos,' the army 'has decided to announce its neutrality in the political disputes and has ordered all units to return to their barracks'.[48]

The 11 February 1979 Collapse

On 11 February, the abandoned army garrisons in Tehran, after the army declared neutrality fell one by one as the people helped themselves to the armories and armed themselves. The symbols of repression, including SAVAK headquarters, the notorious Evin, Komiteh and Qasr Prisons, were occupied. Various royal palaces, the Majles, the Senate, the Prime Minister's Office, Mehrabad Airport and the national radio and television transmission centres fell to the people. In the afternoon, Khomeyni's message of victory, read by Rafsanjani, was broadcast on television, now renamed, 'the face of the revolution'. The 'voice of the revolution' began broadcasting its radio programme at 6.00 pm.

After 57 years, the Pahlavi regime had come tumbling down in two days without much resistance. The official number of dead during the final clashes of the revolution was put at 235. From 12 February, armed youth began hunting down and arresting civilian and military officials of the old regime throughout the country. Striking workers resumed work, parties mushroomed, and Fadais and Mojahedin began reorganizing, arming and attracting members.

With victory, came the widespread purges in all government ministries, organizations, universities and, most importantly, the armed forces. The private sector was not immune to such arbitrary cleansing. In the name of revolutionary fervour, Iran's technocrats, professionals, managers and experts were gradually purged and forced to the sidelines or exile. Khomeyni threw out the baby and the bathwater.

Bazargan, the tie-wearing, reformist, Islamic and Mosaddeqist prime minister, tried hard to reign in the excesses by establishing a reasonable modus vivendi with his imposing clerical partners. For Bazargan, the fall of the Pahlavi dynasty marked the end of the destructive and violent stage of the revolution and the beginning of reconstruction and wise management. He wished to retain the experts, managers and technocrats and have them serve the Islamic Republic.

However, Khomeyni continued to be in a belligerent mood. He believed that victory over the shah marked only the halfway line to the end of the revolution. He intended to thoroughly transform the old state, society and economy, and Islamize it. Khomeyni did not trust the experts, technocrats and managers, who had worked in the shah's regime and considered them corrupted. Unfamiliar with the difficulties of running an economy, he wished to replace them with Islamic zealots of his liking. On 1 March 1979, Khomeyni announced that the revolutionary movement should continue until the instalment of 'an Islamic government'. To pursue his dream, he needed more time to cleanse, change and homogenize society.

On 15 February 1979, four days after the end of the Pahlavi dynasty, heads began to roll. The first of a repeated series of summary trials behind closed doors by the Islamic Revolutionary Courts condemned Generals Nematollah Nasiri, Reza Naji, Mehdi Rahimi and Manuchehr Khosrowdad to death for 'corruption on earth'. Khomeyni approved the sentences carried out at 11.45 am. Armed guards around Khomeyni's residence rejoiced at the coming of 'the day of judgement and punishment'. The second round of executions followed on 19 February.

On 6 March 1979, Bazargan, Yadollah Sahabi, Motahhari, Beheshti and Musavi-Ardebili, all members of the Islamic Revolutionary Council and effective managers of revolutionary Iran, condemned the executions. Beheshti suggested the replacement of Mohammad-Sadeq Khalkhali, the clerical revolutionary judge appointed by Khomeyni to preside over the trial of key former regime personalities. But Khalkhali remained in his position for another year.

On 12 March 1979, the execution machine continued and began targeting civilians, whose real crime was their involvement with the old regime. Parviz Nikkhah, who had been persecuted and imprisoned by the Pahlavi regime and an employee of NIRT, Mahmud Jafariyan, deputy manager of the NIRT and Gholamhoseyn Daneshiyan, a cleric and Majles deputy, were the first of many more civilians to be executed by the Islamic Revolutionary Courts. Gory pictures of bullet-ridden corpses of the old regime's high officials became a regular feature on the first page of Iranian newspapers. The macabre face of the Islamic Revolution was showing itself.

The single voice and order of the shah had gradually faded away, and while Khomeyni's was undoubtedly the domineering one, he was incapable of imposing his power immediately. A liberated Iran had freed all kinds of voices, opinions and expectations in a country where different shades of the opposition were dreaming of their ideal post-revolutionary government and society. Everyone felt as though they were stakeholders in the revolution. It would take time for the Islamic Revolution to replace the people's revolution.

Even among the Shii clergy, there was an undeclared power struggle. Ayatollah Taleqani was very popular among the progressive, culturally and socially tolerant and economically radical segments of the population. He had lingered in prison for years and knew first-hand the old anti-shah combatants and was highly respected by most, secular and religious. He was the spiritual father of the Mojahedin and the favourite of the Fadais. Taleqani represented an enlightened, pluralistic, modern, anti-imperialist and equitable Islam.

Ayatollah Shariatmadari was one of Iran's four Sources of Imitation and a real contender for religious leadership. He was a cautious and moderate man with a solid base of support in Azarbayjan and a large following among moderate Muslims and the propertied classes. He believed in reform and a more pluralistic society. Neither Taleqani nor Shariatmadari approved of Khomeyni's style and his autocratic posture after the revolution succeeded.

A Referendum on an Islamic Republic

From the morrow of victory, Khomeyni began making his voice heard over and above others, clerical and civil. He ordered the changing of primary school, high school and university textbooks and the cleansing of 'those photographs and subjects in the interest of colonialism and despotism'. He commanded their replacement with 'revolutionary-Islamic' subjects and photos.[49]

The Fadais announced that they would march towards Khomeyni's residence on 22 February to 'support the just initiatives of Imam Khomeyni'. They invited all revolutionaries to join them. On the eve of 21 February, Khomeyni's office retorted that the march was 'by communists, and Muslim brothers and sisters should desist from participating in it'. The announcement added that Khomeyni would not accept to see the demonstrators. Humiliated by Khomeyni's open rejection, the Fadais cancelled the march and called for a gathering at Tehran University.

The Fadai's 23 February gathering at Tehran University attracted some 150,000 people. They called for unity and praised 'the progressive clerics under the leadership of Imam Khomeyni and Ayatollah Taleqani' for their anti-imperialist positions. The Fadai's held gatherings on the same day at Tabriz and Ahvaz (*Jondishapur*) University. On all three occasions, a group of some 50-100 zealot supporters of Khomeyni, interrupted and disrupted the gatherings chanting, 'The only party, Party of God (*Hezbollah*), the only leader, Ruhollah!'

Less than two weeks after the victory of the revolution, club-wielding shock troopers, who would soon become known as *Hezbollahi*s, were organized and unleashed by Khomeyni's lieutenants to impose the Imam's hegemony through intimidation and violence. The *Hezbollah* began by bullying the Fadais and Mojahedin. They then turned against smaller Marxist organizations, unveiled women, and finally attacked all those who disagreed with Khomeyni.

Sadeq Qotbzadeh was appointed head of the Iranian radio and television network. He was the non-clerical close aid of Khomeyni, who had flown to Tehran with him, after a long sojourn in Europe. In one of his first addresses, he informed his employees that Iran's radio and television belonged to 'the Muslim People of Iran'. The artists employed in this organization, he said, had to use their crafts in the service of 'the people's Islamic revolution'. He reiterated that Iran's radio and television would be 'completely in the service of the leadership of this Islamic revolution'.[50] One day after his speech, Qotbzadeh came under substantial attack in newspapers. Reza Baraheni ended his criticism of Qotbzadeh's speech and wrote, 'Iranian revolutionaries! Strangle censorship in its embryo!'

On the heels of victory, society began debating the options presented to voters on the day of the referendum, determining the name of Iran's news system of government. Suddenly, on 1 March 1979, Khomeyni bulldozed the debate, rejected all alternative options raised by Bazargan, Shariatmadari, and various other political organizations, which were different from his. He said, 'What our people want is an Islamic Republic, not a simple Republic or a Democratic Republic, and not a Democratic Islamic Republic... whoever follows Islam *must want* an Islamic Republic.' Yet, he added that the people were free to vote, but that he was going to vote for the Islamic Republic.'[51]

Before the referendum on the name of the new regime scheduled for 31 March 1979, the left political organizations of the Mojahedin, Fadais, the newly born left-wing of the old National Front, the Democratic National Front, the Democratic Party of Kurdistan, and Sheykh Ezeddin Hoseyni, the Left-leaning politico-religious Kurdish leader, boycotted the referendum. All objected to the formulation of the question in the referendum: 'The Islamic Republic, yes or no.' The Left stood up to Khomeyni's preferred and dictated formula and were joined in by a few smaller newly created political parties.

One day before the referendum, Khomeyni used his tactic of acting democratic after having categorical pronounced his dictatorial edict. He encouraged everyone to vote. He changed his tone and tried to appease the opposition by saying that all were free to vote and that people could add whatever form of government they wished in their ballots. Khomeyni urged the women to vote and for the sake of political expediency, falsely claimed that, 'Islam had established greater rights for women than men.'[52] On Friday, the day of the referendum, a female foreign journalist covering the event in Qom was asked to cover her hair. The officials informed her that it was not obligatory, but it would be advisable to look like the women of Qom. The reporter complied.

Of those who participated in the referendum, 98 per cent voted for the Islamic Republic. The handling of the referendum provided a glimpse of how Khomeyni was to conduct his 'democratic dictatorship'. He would allow options within narrowly confined constraints established by himself. On 1 April, Khomeyni announced that Iran was herewith an Islamic Republic. By this time, in Kurdistan and Gorgan armed dissidents were clashing with Khomeyni's newly formed parallel military organization, 'The Guardians of the Revolution.'

Factual and Analytical Questions

1 What role did the two books *The Necessity of Armed Struggle and the Refutation of the Theory of Survival* and *Armed Struggle, Both Strategy and Tactic*, play in

the Marxist revolutionary movement of the Fadais? What was it promoting and what was it opposing?
2 How was the Fadai Guerrilla Organization born? Provide a chronological survey.
3 Trace and explain the birth, development, and demise of the Mojahedin. What role did the Marxist-Leninist schism within the organization play in its demise?
4 Who was Ali Shariati and how did his discourse prepare the grounds for the revolution against the shah?
5 Why did the shah feel compelled to initiate political liberalization? Was the Presidency of Jimmy Carter the only factor?
6 In the run-up to the revolution, when and how did Khomeyni's messages first find an echo in Iran?
7 What were Khomeyni's charges against the Pahlavi dynasty? What was his battle strategy in Najaf? Who was he appealing to in Najaf?
8 When and why did 'Black Friday' take place?
9 What was the domestic and international significance of Khomeyni's Paris Discourse? How successful was it as a tactical stratagem to establish his leadership of the revolution?
10 When and why did the US withdraw its support from the shah? Was it a consequence of the Guadeloupe Summit? Explain and provide historical evidence for your argument.
11 What was Gen. Robert Huyser's mission in Tehran? How realistic was his brief?
12 Describe and explain the events that unhinged the monarchy between 9 and 11 February 1979.

Seminar Questions

1 Assess the success or failure of the Fadai guerrilla movement in terms of its objective to bring about change through armed struggle.
2 In what ways were the Fadais and Mojahedin different and/or similar?
3 Fadais, Mojahedin and Shariati were all targeting the educated youth as the vanguards of the revolution. In view of what happened during the revolution, were they correct in their analysis?
4 Assess the role of the Confederation of Iranian Students National Union (CISNU) in turning Western public opinion against the shah's regime.
5 What was the political significance of the ten nights of poetry reading at the Goethe Institute?
6 To what extent did the shah's hesitations, procrastinations and wavering help the revolution?

7   How would you interpret the routine burning of movies, bars, cafes, restaurants and clubs by the protestors during the latter period of the revolution?
8   The Iranian Revolution employed multiple protest tactics against the shah. Provide a chronological list of these methods of protestation. Which do you think were the most effective? Why?

Discussion Questions

1   'The guerrilla movement of the Fadais and Mojahedin succeeded in breaking the reign of fear among the people and the regime's image of invulnerability.' Discuss the strengths and weaknesses of this statement.
2   'Shariati's eclectic and iconoclastic teachings challenged, political despotism, capitalist exploitation and religious dogmatism in Iran'. Assess the veracity of this statement.
3   'The synergy between the guerrilla movement in Iran and the Confederation of Iranian Students National Union (CISNU) abroad played an important role in bringing down the shah's regime.' Discuss the validity of this statement.
4   'The initial oppositional steps in the Iranian Revolution were taken by secular forces aiming to reform the system'. To what extent is this statement true? Provide historical examples to support your arguments.
5   'The shah's political bungling and Khomeyni's good fortune helped turn the tide in favour of the revolution.' Assess this statement. Provide historical evidence for your arguments.
6   '"Black Friday" was the gateway to the victory of the opposition to the shah.' Assess the veracity of this statement. If you disagree, what in your opinion, was the gateway?
7   'Khomeyni's Paris discourse played an important role in mobilizing his non-partisans behind the anti-shah movement and the success of the revolution.' Assess the historical validity of this statement.
8   'There was a logic to the shah's change of prime ministers from Amuzegar to Bakhtiyar.' Discuss with a chronological account what each government represented and was intended to do.
9   'Shapur Bakhtiyar's government was doomed to fail.' Discuss the historical merits of this statement with historical evidence.
10 'From the immediate aftermath of victory, the autocratic and intolerant tendencies of Khomeyni and his partisans became clear.' Assess this statement with reference to historical evidence.
11 Was the revolution Iranian or Islamic? Support your argument with historical evidence.

Glossary

Anti-Sabotage Joint Committee (ASJC) Between 1971 and 1976, the Anti-Sabotage Joint Committee (ASJC) disposed of 50 teams of mobile undercover, surveillance and assault personnel. Each team was composed of 4 members in cars, armed with Uzi machine guns, colts, M-10s and grenades. There were 25 teams operating from morning till noon and another 25 teams continued the relay from noon to evening. Once the political targets were arrested, they were turned over to the interrogation branch of the ASJC for the extraction of information. It was at this stage that torture became a systematic and routine method of interrogation at Iranian security prisons. The interrogation branch of ASJC possessed 8 interrogation teams. It is essentially from 1971 that recurrent tales of horror and abomination gradually leaks out of prison.

8

Khomeyni's Islamic Republic, 1979–89

Chapter Outline

Mehdi Bazargan's Nine-Month Government: A Knife without a Blade 377
The Rise and Fall of Bani-Sadr: The Paris Discourse is Gone for Good 407
Khomeyni's Last Two Years: Haughtiness, Desperation and Anger 439
Glossary 453

Ayatollah Khomeyni's tenure was eventful, consequential, complex and full of surprises. In a matter of ten years, he created the Islamic Republic from scratch and consolidated it. He simultaneously destroyed the vestiges of the past regime, de-Pahlavized and Islamized Iran, and forcefully imposed a homogeneous life-style, demeanour and set values, in accordance with his vision of Islam. He introduced and imposed a new vocabulary which helped advance and disseminate his style of Islam.

Khomeyni crusaded against liberals, democrats, constitutionalists, Marxists, leftists, Mosaddeqists, Shariatists, freethinkers, monarchists, freemasons, Bahais and whatever creed, religion or ideology he believed was a threat to his interpretation of Islam and the clerical institution. He even ended up fighting prominent members of the clerical establishment when their brand of Islam was not in tune with his.

Since the Constitutional Revolution, Iranians had accumulated substantial non-Islamic political, ideological and cultural luggage. Erasing all that was not an easy task. Not all who participated in the anti-Shah movement believed in Khomeyni's Islamic discourse. In the beginning, Iranians followed Khomeyni as the charismatic leader of the anti-despotic movement. Quickly, however, a vocal but numerically small faction began to distance themselves from Khomeyni's vision and polity. In time the opposition grew and was joined by Khomeyni's own partisans. The multitude of parties and organizations that mushroomed demonstrated the plurality of political beliefs.

In post-revolutionary Iran, there were at least three Trotskyist groups: the Revolutionary Workers Party, the Socialist Workers Party of Iran and the Kandokav Group. Several small Maoists groups were active, the most important of which was the Toilers Party of Iran and the Organization of Combat for the Liberation of the Working Class (the offshoot of the Marxist Mojahedin). The small Marxist-Leninist-Maoist League of Iranian Communists made waves when around 100 launched a Siyahkal-type attack on Amol, occupied it on 26 January 1982 and were subsequently crushed within two days. And the Moscow-oriented pro-Khomeyni Marxist-Leninist Tudeh Party had a long-standing history in the country.

Since the revolution, the old revolutionary Marxist-Leninist Fadais had split into the Minority and Majority factions. The Majority subsequently splintered again when one section joined the Tudeh Party and the other seceded. The Organization of Communist Unity and Organization of Revolutionary Workers of Iran (The Worker's Way) represented Iran's New Left groups. To these many parties should be added the plethora of nationalist, liberal, and social-democratic organizations and associations.

Although the majority of Iranians were Muslim believers, they were not necessarily the kind of Muslims Khomeyni wished them to be. Islamizing Iranians in the image of Khomeyni was the arduous task of homogenizing a very heterogeneous society. Relying on the underclasses, the dispossessed and those politically, economically and culturally marginalized in the Pahlavi regime, as his foot soldiers, Khomeyni destroyed all manifest opposition to his rule, once again leading Iranians to sublimate their anger and discontent.

After an initial two-year battle to impose the absolute authority of the Islamic Republic by silencing and physically exterminating its opponents, Khomeyni hoped to form a uniform and pugnacious Islamic community, *ummah*, steeped in his vision of Islam and a pre-modern way of life. Over time, however, he realized that unity and uniformity even among his old students and followers was as impossible as an Islamic monolith.

The Danger of Political Plurality

These gentlemen are now once again forming groups, every day there is a new group . . . these are harmful to the country. We want these groups to return and form one group, an Islamic group useful to and serving the country. (R. Khomeyni)[1]

Mehdi Bazargan's Nine-Month Government: A Knife without a Blade

Khomeyni had appointed the 72-year-old Mehdi Bazargan as prime minister before the fall of the Pahlavi regime (Figure 8.1). On 13 February 1979, Bazargan moved into the Prime Minister's Office on Pasteur Street, and gradually formed his government composed of old members and sympathizers of the Iran Freedom Movement, the National Front, and its offshoots.

Bazargan had been Mosaddeq's deputy minister of culture and was sent to Abadan by Mosaddeq to oversee the oil nationalization process. After the 1953 coup, Bazargan had stood up to the shah's rule, been arrested several times and spent some five years in prison. He was a well-respected French educated engineer, a university teacher and a political militant. Bazargan was known for his honesty, uprightness, sense of humour and quick-wittedness.

Bazargan had been in close contact with Morteza Motahhari and Mohammad Beheshti, Khomeyni's closest post-revolution confidants since 1961. He was the only non-clerical member amidst an intellectually high-powered clerical group, including Taleqani, who discussed the pressing topic of religious leadership and the fate of the clerical institution after the death of Grand Ayatollah Borujerdi.

Bazargan had the trust and confidence of the old generation political activists, who knew him as a Mosaddeqist nationalist and a progressive and modernist Muslim. But to those in their twenties, who were the makers of the revolution, Bazargan seemed too slow, cautious and conservative.

The revolutionary mood demanded abrupt and radical action. Bazargan, on the contrary, was mild-tempered, liberal-minded and averse to radicals and their excesses.

Figure 8.1 Ayatollah Khomeyni and Mehdi Bazargan. *Source: Wikimedia Commons.*

He believed in change, but not revolutionary change. As a self-proclaimed reformist, he abhorred violence, vengefulness, rash decisions and disorder. During his tenure, Bazargan fought on four different fronts. First, the impatient young public who wanted quick revolutionary fixes. Second, Khomeyni who supported his prime minister but did whatever he wanted without consulting him. Third, Khomeyni's mushrooming revolutionary institutions and clerical nominations. Finally, even though Bazargan was a member of the Council of the Islamic Revolution, his brief as prime minister was often interfered with by this body.

> ## The 'Council of the Islamic Revolution'
> It has been repeatedly said that the Council [of the Islamic Revolution] has two responsibilities: to act as the parliament and to lead the revolution. (M. Beheshti)[2]

During its 18-month activity, the Council of the Islamic Revolution ratified some 2,000 bills. The Council of the Islamic Revolution was only accountable to Khomeyni, from whom it received its directives. It often acted as the executive, bringing it into conflict with Bazargan's Provisional Government. Until 5 November 1979, when the Bazargan government resigned and his government was incorporated into the Council of the Islamic Revolution, Iran had a government within a government, causing friction, disruption and confusion. The Council of the Islamic Revolution was finally dissolved on 20 July 1980 after the Islamic Republic elected its president and parliament.

The appointees of Khomeyni in political, economic, military and bureaucratic domains were required to perform their duties under the supervision of either the Council of the Islamic Revolution (also referred to as Revolutionary Council) or the Provisional Government. This provision created a dual structure in the chain of command and decision-making. Khomeyni's network was limited to the clergy, with no management or professional experience. They viewed expertise as synonymous with Western influence and non-religious tendencies. Hence, from the beginning, the clerical leadership was suspicious of Bazargan's expert nominees and instead emphasized Islamic doctrinarism of managers.

Bazargan's task of managing Iran's transition towards an Islamic Republic, while restoring order, was a herculean one. After eighteen months of turmoil and disorder, the state and economy had to be fixed and put back on track. Disrupted farms, businesses, banks, shops, schools, universities and ministries had to be reopened. Most significantly, the army had to be reconstituted. The old regime's experienced managers, directors, officials, factory owners and landowners were under the threat of arrest and execution. Bazargan had to salvage and protect whoever of this group he could in order to reconstruct country. The revolutionary segments of the population wanted to continue dismantling, and the clergy wanted Bazargan out. The revolution had unleashed pent-up demands, ethnic, religious and regional, putting pressure on Bazargan's meagre resources.

New Revolutionary Institutions: Outside Bazargan's Reach

As Bazargan started his term, Khomeyni was already issuing edicts and ad hoc orders, laying the foundation of new revolutionary bodies. Even though the Revolutionary Council and Bazargan's government were supposed to implement his orders, no one had the slightest idea how to operationalize them. Running these new institutions and foundations became a nightmare as the prime minister realized he had no control over them. These foundations provided job opportunities, identity and social mobility for Khomeyni's disinherited partisans.

Bazargan on the Impediments to His Government's Activities

We are impotent because of the Revolutionary Courts, the [Islamic Revolution] Committees, the Party [Islamic Republic Party] and the radio and television (M. Bazargan)[3]

The Islamic Revolution Committees

On 13 February 1979, Khomeyni announced the victory of the revolution, called for the creation of the Islamic Revolution Committees, and placed them under the supervision of the clergy. Mohammad-Reza Mahdavi-Kani was put in charge of this newly constituted security force. Tehran was divided into twelve headquarters, each under the control of a different cleric. The mandate of the Islamic Revolution Committees was to bring counter-revolutionaries and members of the old regime to justice and provide for urban and rural security. Members of these committees were neighbourhood and mosque vigils who had come together during the months before the revolution.

From 20 February, less than ten days after the victory of the revolution Bazargan began grumbling about the intrusion and interference of the Islamic Revolution Committees arresting people in government offices and ministries, threatening their wives and children, intimidating foreigners, and whipping up fear. Feeling as if they were the ultimate law in the land, these young and sometimes adolescent members of the Islamic Revolution Committees regularly interfered in the private lives of people, bullying, disrupting the peace and sowing insecurity.

On 28 February, came the first of many announcements by Bazargan that his government was fed up with the unruly Islamic Revolution Committees. His government had no control over these overzealous, untrained, gun-wielding paramilitary bands. Within a fortnight after the victory of the revolution, Bazargan and Khomeyni were at loggerheads over the reckless and hot-headed behaviour of the Islamic Revolution Committees.

The Revolutionary Islamic Courts

On 14 February 1979, Khomeyni appointed the 52-year-old Mohammad-Sadeq Givi-Khalkhali, better known as Khalkhali, to the sensitive and delicate position of religious judge of the Revolutionary Islamic Courts. Khalkhali considered himself only accountable to Khomeyni and did not consider himself bound by any established customary or secular rules, regulations, and due process of law. Khalkhali's court hearings were short, and the accused were neither allowed a defense counsel nor a jury. Once he passed his summary judgement of 'spreading corruption on earth', which covered an amalgam of almost unverifiable accusations, victims were sent to the gallows within 24 hours.

Khomeyni on Human Rights

Those who play the game of human rights wish to conspire, and their human rights is to the benefit of capitalist super-powers and to the detriment of small countries. They make a big deal of executing traitors. (R. Khomeyni)[4]

By 13 March 1979, 62 faced the firing squad, and by October 1979, the number had reached 600. Most were military and civilian supporters of the shah's old regime. The Revolutionary Courts also handed out death sentences for adultery, homosexuality and prostitution. In the meeting of the Revolutionary Council on 26 April 1979, Abolhasan Bani-Sadr reported that, in the prisons of the Islamic Republic, detainees were 'tortured, beaten up, prevented from sleeping', and wardens were 'demanding money to allow prison visits'.[5]

Revolution and Property

In the 1979 revolution, however, the legitimacy of property as 'excessive wealth', the source of economic power of the Iranian oligarchy, and in the form of foreign capital came under attack. (S. Behdad)[6]

On 28 February 1979, Khomeyni ordered the expropriation of the assets belonging to the shah, the royal family, and those associated with them. To justify his unorthodox Islamic edict, he called such assets war booty. This edict subsequently applied to industrialists, landowners, merchants, military officers, and government officials accused of being associated with the old regime. In the provinces, even small businesses were expropriated. The wave of expropriations came to include the next of kin of individuals expropriated.

Islamic Revolutionary Guard Corps

Around 28 February 1979, Khomeyni issued an edict creating the Islamic Revolutionary Guard Corps (IRGC) and placed it initially under the supervision of Bazargan's government. The IRGC was composed of various groups of devout Khomeyni followers who had armed themselves after expropriating the garrisons. None of its young, streetwise leaders had any previous military training. Their main concern was to defend the Islamic Revolution against internal threats, especially the rising power and popularity of the Mojahedin and the Fadais, who were not about to turn in their arms.

On 4 March 1979, the first head of the IRGC, Hasan Lahuti-Eshkevari, appointed by Khomeyni, gave an interview to the press. Lahuti, who had been a militant clergy, long imprisoned by the Pahlavi regime, pointed out that Iran's new military organization would only recruit Muslim youths. He announced that the communists and Fadais would not be admitted to the IRGC. Lahuti emphasized that the army's job was to defend the borders while the IRGC would be responsible for protecting the revolution in the cities and villages.

The IRGC issued its first official declaration on 15 April 1979, three days after a group within it abducted Ayatollah Taleqani's two sons and daughter-in-law. The detainees were blindfolded, insulted and refused access to restrooms. Mojtaba Taleqani, the main target of IRGC's arrest, was a member of the Mojahedin, who had later joined the Marxist branch. The incident threw the country into a near crisis as massive demonstrations broke out in support of Ayatollah Taleqani, who was dearly loved by a large public (Figure 8.2). For a few days, pro-Taleqani demonstrators chanted anti-IRGC slogans, and Tehran looked like a theatre of war between Taleqani and Khomeyni supporters.

While Ayatollah Taleqani compared IRGC's practice to SAVAK's behaviour. The IRGC denied involvement in the affair and under public pressure, the Taleqanis were released after some 72 hours. The Taleqani Affair presaged a bloody settlement of scores with all dissident groups, especially the Marxist Mojahedin. But more importantly, it was a sign of the coming battle between members of Khomeyni's revolutionary military and paramilitary groups with the growing popularity of the Muslim Mojahedin and Taleqani, their spiritual father.

Figure 8.2 Mahmud Taleqani, Sadeq Qotbzadeh and Ebrahim Yazdi. *Source: Via Alamy.*

On 22 April 1979, a new edict relieved Bazargan's government from supervising the IRGC and placed it under the control of the Revolutionary Council. In a heated debate among Council members on the qualifications for recruitment in the IRGC, the majority argued that applicants should be 'anti-communist, anti-imperialist and anti-Zionist'. Ayatollah Taleqani dissented, arguing that 'if the IRGC were to be anti-communist, then it would engage in communist-killing … dragging us towards fascism'.[7] Hashemi-Rafsanjani interjected that Khomeyni condoned bashing the communists. On 24 November 1979, Seyyed Ali Khamenei replaced Lahuti as the head of the IRGC. The new establishment clerics had always suspected Lahuti of supporting the Muslim Mojahedin (Mojahedin). The new appointment placed the IRGC under the command of Khomeyni's lieutenants.

The Foundation of the Oppressed/Disinherited

On 12 March 1979, the Council of the Islamic Revolution followed Khomeyni's instructions and announced the creation of the Foundation of the Oppressed. This Foundation received and managed the assets expropriated by the Revolutionary Courts, supposedly for the benefit of the poor. The para-governmental Foundation became a substantial economic and financial powerhouse unaccountable to the government and exempt from taxes. Whatever assets were confiscated by the

Revolutionary Courts, such as the 200 factories, agri-businesses, banks, hotels and trading companies of the Pahlavi family, were transferred to the Foundation.

Khomeyni placed Ali-Naqi Khamushi, a 39-year-old member of the Islamic Coalition of Mourning Groups, at the head of the Foundation. Khamushi was concomitantly the head of the Iran Chamber of Commerce. The two financial supervisors of the Foundation, appointed by Khomeyni, were also members of the Islamic Coalition of Mourning Groups. What was to become one of Iran's richest economic agglomerations was put in the hands of middle-ranking merchants with ties to the bazaar. In 2020, Khamushi was reputed to be the sixth wealthiest man in Iran and nicknamed the 'godfather' of the Iranian petrochemical industry because of his hold on that sector.

> ### Khomeyni on the Foundation of the Oppressed, a Year after Its Birth
> Is it true that the foundation of the oppressed has become the foundation of oppressors, if it is, then purging it is necessary and neglecting to do so is religiously forbidden. (R. Khomeyni)[8]

After a year, reports circulated about mismanagement and embezzlement in the Foundation, and Khomeyni ordered an investigation into its dealings. The probe uncovered 800 cases of embezzlement in 1980 and 4,000 instances of misappropriations in 1983, although in the end no one was held accountable. In 1982, the Foundation possessed: '203 manufacturing and mining enterprises, 472 commercial farms, 101 construction companies, 238 trade and other services enterprises, and 2,786 real-estate properties.'[9]

Imam's Assistance/Relief Committee

On 20 March 1979, another newborn revolutionary institution, the Imam's Assistance/Relief Committee, called on Iranians to help the 'injured and martyred' of the revolution and 'families left without caretakers'.[10] A year later, this charity organization morphed into another para-governmental institution. On 15 March 1980, Khomeyni appointed Mehdi Karrubi as the head of the Martyrs' Foundation of the Islamic Revolution.

The 10-item responsibility of the Martyrs' Foundation included providing free housing, furniture, insurance and health services for martyrs, the disabled and their families. Most importantly, Khomeyni ordered that the families of the martyrs and disabled be given priority in terms of employment and access to schools and universities. During and after the Iran–Iraq War, the martyrs, veterans and their families were placed under the financial care of this Foundation.

By 1990, the Foundation owned some 150 companies in various economic activities, and in 1994, it expanded its economic activities by founding the Shahid Investment Company and obtaining another 50 companies. By September 2000, the Foundation provided 'support for the families of just over 188,000 people who lost their lives during the war'.[11]

The Construction Jihad

On 16 June 1979, Khomeyni called on university students, engineers and the skilled to reconstruct the 'ruinous country' left behind by the shah. He called for a Construction Jihad in the rural and tribal areas to provide asphalt roads, dispensaries, electricity, piped water and new houses. While extending an invitation to the youth to go help the rural population, he warned the locals to reject and drive away any un-Islamic elements who may carry out 'seditious propaganda'.[12]

> ### The Construction Jihad
>
> The [Construction] Jihad would provide a means of obtaining rural support for the revolution and spreading the message of the revolution amongst the villagers . . . the Jihad was generously funded and enjoyed excellent facilities. (A. Shakoori)[13]

Among others, the goal of the Construction Jihad was to: 'assist rural economic development', 'increase literacy among peasants' and 'propagate Islamic culture and Islamic Revolution in rural areas'.[14] Within two years, the Construction Jihad claimed having built some 13,000 kilometres of roads, 1,700 schools, 1,600 public baths and 110 health centres. In the decade of 1980–90, the Construction Jihad claimed to have supplied 11,428 villages with potable water and provided 10,680 villages with electricity.

In August 1983, the responsibilities of the Construction Jihad expanded. It took over the responsibility of various ministries in the domain of rural development, such as building schools and roads, as well as the provision of agricultural implements such as fertilizers, seeds, tractors and the construction of irrigation networks.

On 26 February 1984, this organization was converted into the Ministry of Construction Jihad. During the Iran–Iraq War, members of the Construction Jihad went to the fronts and made considerable engineering contributions to the war effort by providing logistical and infrastructural support, building roads and particularly suspension bridges, canals, bunkers and trenches.

Among all the organizations created by Khomeyni, to alleviate hardship and provide useful services and welfare, this was probably the most useful and beneficial. As time went by and the initial revolutionary fervor rescinded, the duplication and overlap of responsibilities and subsequent rivalries with various ministries hampered the activities of the Construction Jihad. When in December 2000, the Ministry of Construction Jihad was merged with the Ministry of Agriculture, there was nothing left of the original enthusiasm, zest and excitement of its young, rugged pioneering volunteers.

Pushing Out the Uncommitted, Making Room for Doctrinaires

The long-term impact of Khomeyni's revolutionary institutions outside the legal control of the government was twofold. First, he created new military and financial bodies responsible to himself. Second, he filled those new institutions with the disinherited who demonstrated religious fervor and came under his patronage. Employment in revolutionary organizations meant prestige, social status and power. Khomeyni was creating a new ruling class, beholden to him.

> ### Growth in the Public Sector
> Public sector employment more than doubled after the revolution, from 1.7 million in 1976 to 3.5 million in 1986. According to one estimate, within three years of the revolution, one in six Iranians above the age of fifteen belonged to one state and revolutionary body or another. (K. Ehsani)[15]

The post-revolutionary purges in the military, private and government sectors had forced out many thousands, predominantly among the middle and upper echelon of white-collar functionaries, bureaucrats, technocrats, managers, intellectuals, journalists, artists, musicians and actors. By 26 March 1979, barely a month after the revolution, some 206 had been purged from the Ministry of Foreign Affairs. This number reached 402, including half the political personnel of the Ministry by December 1979. In late May 1981, the Ministry of Foreign Affairs recruited some 40 applicants, and gave them forty days of training before dispatching them overseas as ambassadors, chargé d'affaires and cultural and press attachés.

> ### Khomeyni on Brain Drain and Purges
> They say brains will run away, well, let these rotten minds run away ... Let these minds that corrupted the minds of our children for thirty, forty years run away and let upright minds replace them. Now that well-meaning people want to purge, you are sitting and moping about the purges and the executions ... Offices, culture and universities should be purged. (R. Khomeyni)[16]

The thorough purge of the state structure and its replacement with suitable devout Muslims, in tandem with generating employment for Muslim doctrinaires in the revolutionary institutions, changed the socio-cultural composition of Iran's civil service. The middle and upper-level management of the country underwent a radical change as it passed on to the clergy and the religiously doctrinaire low, lower-middle and middle classes, with a lower general level of education and skills.

The revolution created upward social mobility for the underclasses with claims to firm Islamic beliefs, and downward social mobility for the opposition, the educated, non-compliant with new regulations, experienced and the experts. The social, class and cultural composition of the state apparatus and society experienced a long-lasting change.

Ethnic Opposition, Self-determination and Clashes

The fall of the shah's regime took the lid off the accumulated frustrations of Iran's ethnic minorities, who had long felt culturally and politically ignored by the central government. For some three years, the authority of the new central government remained contested in the provinces as competing armed groups vied for power.

Kurdistan

Kurdistan, a predominantly Sunni province speaking Kurdish, had a history of armed struggle against the central government. After the revolution, it became a stronghold of non-clerically approved political organizations threatening the newly installed government. On the eve of 18 March 1979, Sanandaj, the capital of Kurdistan, was in turmoil. The army headquarters, the gendarmerie outpost and Sanandaj's radio and television, were overrun by anti-government forces, and the town's main garrison was under siege. In this first attack launched by the rebel forces some 120 were killed and 200 injured.

The anti-government movement was composed of different groups. The Marxist-Maoist Komaleh Organization (Kurdistan's Society of Revolutionary Toilers) organized peasants against landlords. Komaleh had a strong following among the underclasses, as well as Kurdish urban intellectuals and radicals. It called for a people's army and the transfer of power to local councils.

Sheykh Ezeddin Hoseyni, the progressive Sunni Friday Prayer Leader of Mahabad, was the veritable religious leader of Kurdistan. The Komaleh and the Marxist Fadais, seeking a provincial base, worked under Hoseyni's revolutionary Left umbrella for self-determination and self-governing councils throughout Kurdistan.

Kurdistan possessed other important contending forces. On 12 February 1979, the Kurdish Democratic Party of Iran (KDPI), after some three decades of clandestine activity, occupied the police stations and gendarmerie outposts in Mahabad and emptied out the armouries. A week later, supporters of KDPI, Komaleh and Ezeddin Hoseyni, who had laid siege to the Mahabad garrison, entered and expropriated all the light and heavy weaponry.

Abdolrahman Qasemlu, the KDPI leader, was French-educated, secular and a social-democrat. The KDPI, the most significant Kurdish opposition force was highly respected in the region. Qasemlu believed in 'autonomy for Iranian Kurdistan within the framework of a democratic Iran'. The politics of the KDPI was more conservative than Komaleh nevertheless, Qasemlu sided with the loose Left coalition around Ezeddin Hoseyni and against the central government.

A different key player in the region was the influential pro-Khomeyni Ahmad Moftizadeh, who first took sides with the government and was later sidelined and persecuted, after the defeat of the Kurdish movement. Moftizadeh was a non-cleric who had organized Quranic schools back in 1977 and gradually spread his religious influence among Islamic zealots. As hostilities broke out, Moftizadeh was the central government's only Kurdish ally in the region.

Bazargan's government intended to resolve ethnic demands through peaceful means. A series of brittle ceasefires were negotiated and failed. The political situation in Kurdistan became increasingly more volatile as cities witnessed clashes between rebel forces and the army. The dispatch and installation of IRGC and Islamic Revolution Committee members in Kurdistan further complicated the situation. The increased presence of IRGC members in Kurdistan caused consternation among the insurrectionary forces, who now called the Revolutionary Guards, SS troops.

Clashes continued in Sanandaj, Naqadeh, Jaldiyan, Marivan and Paveh. The siege of Paveh's army garrison and armed confrontations in Sanandaj brought matters to a head. On 18 August 1979, in the name of commander in chief of Iran's armed forces, Khomeyni ordered the army, gendarmerie and the IRGC to rush to Kurdistan, arrest the 'bandits', and bring them to justice immediately. Khomeyni threatened his commanders that if his orders were not followed within 24 hours, he would hold them responsible.

The Paveh confrontations gave Khomeyni the excuse to purge Kurdistan of opposition forces. On 19 August 1979, government forces attacked Paveh and the rest of Kurdistan with full force. Their land and air operation aimed at purging the province of the armed forces of the KDPI, Komaleh, Ezeddin Hoseyni and the Fadais. Throughout September, the Iranian air force carried numerous missions bombing the strongholds of the KDPI in Paveh, Mahabad, Saqez and Baneh. An F-4 Islamic Republic Airforce jet and two helicopters were shot down by the Kurdish opposition forces, killing four pilots. Clerical officials accused the KDPI of secessionism and collusion with counter-revolutionaries and foreign powers. The party was officially banned, and a warrant was issued for the arrest of Ezeddin Hoseyni. Khomeyni called the KDPI 'Satan's Party'.

Figure 8.3 Mohammad-Sadeq Givi-Khalkhali, Hoseyn-Ali Montazeri, Mohammad-Taqi Falsafi and Mostafa Chamran. *Source: Wikimedia Commons.*

The number of casualties after the assault on Kurdistan was put at approximately 400, of whom 300 were Kurds. Khalkhali was dispatched by Khomeyni to deal with Kurdish counter-revolutionaries (Figure 8.3). During his nine-day tour of Kurdistan, Khalkhali executed between 51 and 79, including soldiers and officers of the army and the gendarmerie. Among the executed was Dr Abolqasem Roshvand-Sardari, a respected physician at Paveh Hospital.

Hostilities continued in 1980, abated but lingered until December 1982. During the almost four-year conflict, some 8,000 to 10,000 were killed and approximately 200,000 displaced. The leadership of the KDPI was eventually forced to leave Iranian Kurdistan and its forces settled across the border in Iraq, at war with Iran.

Turkman Sahra

A more limited ethnic conflict broke out in Gonbad Kavus, Gorgan. In this area, too, most of the population were Sunnis and of Turkman origin. On 26 March 1979, hostilities broke out over the shooting of a 22-year-old local man. Armed clashes ensued between members of the Islamic Revolution Committee and the IRGC against the Left-leaning and radical Cultural and Political Centre of the Turkman People, supported by the Fadais. The two sides barricaded the city, while the Left militants overran the gendarmerie and police headquarters.

The Left Turkman Sahra Council, closely connected with the Cultural and Political Centre of the Turkman People and the Fadais, demanded the creation of freely elected revolutionary councils, the distribution of lands belonging to the royal family and their associates among landless peasants, the annulment of all debts incurred by workers, peasants and petty civil servants to banks and the Turkman people's right to self-government in a free and unified Iran. After six days of clashes, an armistice was signed between the two sides. The bloody confrontations left 85 dead and 250 wounded.

Almost a year later, war flared up again in Gonbad Kavus when, on 8 February 1980, four influential local members of the Fadais and the Turkman Sahra Council were abducted. Concomitantly, a Fadai meeting was attacked by members of the

IRGC. These assaults were acts of provocation to cleanse the city of the Fadais and their local allies. Gonbad Kavus became once again barricaded and the scene of bloody battles. On the same day, the Fadai meeting in Borujerd (Lorestan) was also attacked by the IRCG, leaving behind one dead.

On 12 February, the army entered the conflict in support of the IRGC, and by the next day, the combined forces of the Turkman Sahra Council and the Fadais were defeated and dispersed. The newspapers reported that Khalkhali had been sent to the area and Khomeyni's revolutionary judge promised that he was not there to create a bloodbath. The clashes left behind some 48 dead and 142 wounded.

On 18 February 1980, the executed and abandoned remains of the four abducted leaders of Turkman Sahra Council were discovered. The authorities promised to investigate the matter and bring the culprits to justice but failed to follow through. Khomeyni had reportedly said, 'it was not a big deal since they were disbelievers (*murtad*)'.[17] Later it became clear that during his visit to Gonbad Kavus, Khalkhali had executed 26 members and sympathizers of the Turkman Sahra Council, although he had previously denied having any knowledge of it.

Khuzestan

With the defeat of the old regime, Sheykh Mohammad-Taher Ale-Shobeyr-Khaqani, the most influential clerical figure of Khorramshahr, took effective control of the oil-rich Khuzestan province. He disbanded the local Islamic Revolution Committees and replaced them with members of his Political Organization of the Arab People. The appeal of his organization was an ethnic one with a strong emphasis on the Arab origins, language and heritage of the region. The Left-leaning local intellectuals founded the Cultural Centre of the Arab People. This organization operated in tandem with Shobeyr-Khaqani, and both demanded the total withdraw of the newly formed Islamic revolutionary militias.

Iran's Arab neighbours were taking a particular interest in the budding Arab identity in Khuzestan. Claims by all opposition organizations in Khuzestan to self-government worried the new regime, which interpreted it as a prelude to secession. The appointment of Admiral Ahmad Madani, a tenacious National Front member, as the governor of Khuzestan was a stern message to the possible secessionist aspirations of Shobeyr-Khaqani and his allies.

On 18 May 1979, Madani ordered the disarming of all unauthorized individuals and organizations in Khuzestan and announced that only government forces were responsible for maintaining peace and security. When the Political Organization of the Arab People refused to comply, Madani promised to crush the counter-revolutionaries, downplaying the Arab–Persian division and emphasizing the importance of a unified Iran. Concomitantly, units of the army and the IRGC entered Khorramshahr.

From 28 May 1979, the political situation in Khorramshahr deteriorated rapidly. In retaliation against the arrest and disarmament of Shobeyr-Khaqani's partisans in Abadan, his supporters disarmed a gendarmerie outpost and killed IRGC members. Subsequently, Khorramshahr, Abadan and Ahvaz became veritable war zones. The intermittent clashes lasted about a month and ended with an agreement between Madani and Shobeyr-Khaqani. The accord relegated the security and military affairs of Khuzestan to the government forces. The clashes left some 50 to 70 dead and some 169 to 400 wounded. On 19 July 1979, Shobeyr-Khaqani was exiled to Qom by Khomeyni.

The three ethnic movements in the West, North and South of Iran failed to obtain self-determination and self-control for the Kurds, Turkmans, and the Arabs. All three movements were supported by Left organizations and especially the Fadais. Shobeyr-Khaqani's movement was the only one benefitting from outright foreign support. Within five years of taking power, the central government succeeded in quelling ethnic challenges to its authority with the help of the blooming IRGC and the decisive role of the army.

Three New Islamic Parties

Khomeyni's religio-revolutionary institutions outlived him, expanded, mutated and continued to be a fixture of the Islamic Republic into the twenty-first century. Post-revolutionary Islamic parties and organizations, however, had relatively short life spans. In due course, none proved to be deep-rooted, organized and robust enough to resist closure and dissolution. The curse of custom-made, fickle parties with no history, programme or ideology, had been plaguing Iran since the Constitutional Revolution, and was to continue in post-revolutionary Iran. Khomeyni was not at ease with the notion of political parties, which implied ideological plurality, debate and theoretical rivalry. In Khomeyni's mind, the Muslim community, the *ummat*, was based on uniformity and the single voice of its leader. The popular slogan of zealots, 'Party, only Party of God, Leader, only Ruhollah,' best encapsulated this idea.

The Islamic Republic Party

On 18 February 1979, five clerics close to and trusted by Khomeyni announced the formation of *Hezbe Jomhuriye Eslami* (Islamic Republic Party). Four of them, Mohammad Beheshti, Abdolkarim Musavi-Ardebili, Ali-Akbar Hashemi-Rafsanjani and Mohammad-Javad Bahonar, were original members of the powerful Revolutionary Council. The fifth was Ali Khamenei, the future president and Supreme Leader of Iran. In their first announcement, they identified the purpose of their party as combating counter-revolutionaries and their plots, defending and sustaining the Islamic Revolution and moving towards a classless society.

The Islamic Republic Party (IRP) pledged to create a powerful and disciplined organization and opened its doors to all followers of what became known as the 'Imam's line'. It quickly became a melting pot of various Islamic shades and orientations loyal to Khomeyni. The military, however, were barred by Khomeyni from entering political parties or becoming in any way involved with politics. On 30 May 1979, IRP began publishing its own newspaper, of the same name, with Mir-Hoseyn Musavi as its editor.

> ## IRP's Dilemma
> The IRP did not have a coherent development ideology around which to organize civil corps . . . The IRP also lacked a mass base, since none of its organizers had any lasting claim to national leadership outside their association with Khomeini. (E. Ferdows)[18]

Even though Khomeyni did not favour political parties and relied on his one-man initiative style, he gave his consent to the creation of the Islamic Republic Party. Hashemi-Rafsanjani (hereafter Rafsanjani) had approached Khomeyni and convinced him that since the clergy had no experience managing the country, they needed to identify and mobilize religious and skilled cadres to run the Islamic Republic. A party would help them do that. Rafsanjani and Beheshti sought to create a tight and homogeneous organization of Islamic bureaucrats, civil servants, managers and technocrats imbibed in Khomeyni's thoughts.

Bazargan's team had the skilled manpower to manage the state and the economy. But right from the beginning, the clergy in power sensed that Bazargan's notion of Islam was different from and too liberal for them. Finding him too independent, the clergy were determined to remove the 'liberal religious-nationalist' Bazargan group as soon as possible. For that eventuality, they needed to organize a modern party, attracting perhaps a few members of Bazargan's team in the process. The clergy had no idea how to form and run a party. The whole exercise was trial and error and learning on the job.

> ## The Sole Purpose of the Islamic Republic Party
> The party is important and useful to us as long as it serves the interests of the Islamic Revolution and ensures the survival and blossoming of the Islamic Republic. (M. Beheshti)[19]

The Islamic Republic Party was committed to defending the revolution according to Khomeyni's vision and announced that it was 'subservient to the rule of the

Guardian Jurist and an unquestionable ally of the principled/true clergy'.[20] The IRP sought to purge the country of all remnants of 'despotism, exploitation and colonialism', install 'a 100% Islamic economic system', Islamize education and culture, and 'uproot all remnants of corruption, prostitution, all prohibited things and materialist tendencies'.[21]

Muslim People of Iran's Republic Party

On 24 February 1979, six days after the Islamic Republic Party came on stage, a second Islamic party supported by Ayatollah Kazem Shariatmadari, a top-ranking figure in Iran's clerical institution, announced its formation. The Muslim People of Iran's Republic Party (MPIRP) made its debut by announcing that Islamic democracy in Iran necessitated the end of a one-party system and welcomed the birth of progressive parties. MPIRP was Shariatmadari's response to IRP.

The MPIRP's statute emphasized the establishment of individual and social freedoms and the freedom of the press based on Islamic principles. It insisted on benefitting from 'the constructive and healthy experiences of the modern world', did not refer to fighting against imperialism, and called for mutual respect towards all friendly countries.

The MPIRP published its newspaper, the Muslim People, which soon became a platform for Iran's opposition voices, before being gradually silenced. The declarations of opposition groups, including the Fadais, Mojahedin, National Front, Democratic National Front and even smaller Marxist organizations, were reflected in the pages of the Muslim People. From late August 1979, MPIRP's Friday public gatherings and speech-making became the meeting place of nationalists, leftists, intellectuals and dissidents. Contrary to the IRP, the MPIRP was a pluralist and democratic Muslim party.

In the traditional Shii hierarchy, Grand Ayatollahs Kazem Shariatmadari, Shahabeddin Marashi-Najafi and Mohammad-Reza Golpaygani were on par with Khomeyni from a religious point of view. Shariatmadari was from Azarbayjan and had a solid political base in that province. Nationally, he was known for his moderate political tendencies. He believed in the primacy of the people's political choice and free vote.

The first signs of disagreement between Shariatmadari and Khomeyni and their respective parties appeared during the referendum on the name of Iran's new political system. Two different Islamic approaches to Iran's post-revolutionary political structure confronted one another. Khomeyni insisted on a ballot with only a yes or no option to the question, 'should Iran become an Islamic Republic'. Shariatmadari favoured giving people more options to choose from and opposed limiting the public's choice to only an Islamic Republic (Figure 8.4). Khomeyni did not wish to entertain any other name and hammered that people should vote on an 'Islamic Republic' nothing more or less.

Figure 8.4 Ayatollah Kazem Shariatmadari. *Source: Photo by Claude Salhani/Sygma via Getty Images.*

From its inception, the MPIRP acted as a democratic party opposed to IRP's hegemonic stream rolling and Khomeyni's imposition of a straitjacket on the country. MPIRP lasted for eleven months. The first official rebuke against MPIRP came from Khalkhali on 22 April 1979. In a newspaper article, he wrote that two Islamic parties may suggest disagreement and discord between Khomeyni and Shariatmadari and accused the MPIRP of attracting old members of SAVAK, the Resurgence Party and royalists, who wished to oppose the Islamic Republic.

In Tabriz and Tehran, large demonstrations took place in support of Shariatmadari and condemning Khalkhali's article. Meanwhile the IRP issued a proclamation denying any involvement in the article. The pro-Shariatmadari demonstrators asked for legal action against Khalkhali and called for a 'true Islamic government under the flag of which a thousand flowers of freedom would bloom'.[22]

> ### Shariatmadari on Islamic Laws
> Islamic laws do not permit any group to commit violence and despotism . . . People have to be given freedom to talk without fear. (K. Shariatmadari)[23]

Shariatmadari's political positions and those of his party gradually became intolerable for Khomeyni. By November 1979, Khomeyni categorized the MPIRP as a creation of the US. He sent word to Shariatmadari to denounce his party in the press, radio and television and disassociate himself from it. Shariatmadari's refusal and his statements against the rule of the Guardian Jurist, or the absolute rule of a cleric, heightened tension between the two. Khomeyni was now manifesting the shah's symptoms, imputing all opposition and dissent to foreign forces. The shah's nemesis was communism, Khomeyni's was the US.

Shariatmadari opposed Khomeyni on several issues, but their difference came to a head, when on 1 December 1979, Sharitmadari officially objected to the rule of the Guardian Jurist, the linchpin of the new Constitution. Shariatmadari argued that the rule of the Guardian Jurist contradicted popular sovereignty and took position against the new Constitution, which legalized Khomeyni's unrestricted powers.

On 2 December, Tabriz, and numerous cities in Azarbayjan reacted to Shariatmadari's open opposition to the Constitution, and people assembled in his support. Three days later, on 5 December, Shariatmadari's house in Qom and his supporters came under attack. An armed bodyguard on his rooftop was shot dead by unidentified assailants.

The intimidation tactics of Khomeyni's supporters sent Azarbayjan into a tantrum. Huge crowds overran and took control of Tabriz radio and television station, the governor's headquarters and the airport. The task of maintaining peace fell to Shariatmadari's supporters, who along with army personnel, gendarmerie, police and air force stationed in Azarbayjan had pledged their allegiance to him. The 'liberated' Tabriz radio publicly condemned the new Constitution for laying the grounds of a dictatorship. On 7 December 1979, Shariatmadari called for a return to calm and the cessation of demonstrations and rallies.

In Tehran, pro-Khomeyni organizations warned that US plotters, Westernized elements, and stooges of imperialism had infiltrated the MPIRP. In unison, they pleaded with Shariatmadari to dissolve the MPIRP, and called on Azarbayjanis to cleanse their ranks of MPIRP members. On 9 December, after nightfall, the IRGC attacked the Tabriz television station, as well as, the governor's headquarters. After a few hours of a gun battle, the IRGC prevailed.

On 15 December 1979, the MPIRP announced that it had ceased all activities and was closing all its offices throughout Iran. Three weeks later under pressure, Shariatmadari publicly stated that any resumption of political activities by the party would not have his support. On the next day, Tabriz experienced clashes leaving 15 dead and 100 injured. In Tehran, MPIRP's headquarters was seized.

The IRGC succeeded in putting down the second Tabriz uprising and rounding up Shariatmadari sympathizers. The Tabriz revolutionary court sent 15 to the gallows, 4 of whom were army officers. Khomeyni had at last silenced Shariatmadari's MPIRP, which challenged his vision of Islam. More importantly, Khomeyni wished to crush Shariatmadari to demonstrate his indubitable religio-political power over all other high religious authorities in the land who may have become weary of his policies.

The Mojahedin of the Islamic Revolution

On 27 March 1979, a new paramilitary political organization called the Mojahedin of the Islamic Revolution (MIR), composed of seven small militant groups, announced its activities. MIR was a semi-clandestine body committed to supporting the Islamic revolution, the leadership role of Khomeyni, and combatting all enemies of the Islamic Revolution, be they imperialists and Zionists or internal deviants such as the 'hypocrites', the pejorative term used for the Muslim Mojahedin.

The common denominator of these seven groups was their theoretical or practical interface of sympathy-then-enmity with the Mojahedin and their newfound allegiance to Khomeyni. The degree of old love and new hate in relation to the Mojahedin varied among the seven groups. MIR announced that as a last resort in their campaign against internal enemies, meaning the Left, communists and the Mojahedin, it was prepared to engage with them militarily.

MIR had strong connections with Rafsanjani. Their choice of name intended to sow confusion among people as to which organization was the authentic successor to the past legacy of the revolutionary Islamic Mojahedin. Crafting a new Mojahedin to combat the old Mojahedin was the logic of the new organization, causing the old Mojahedin to object to the organization's name. Before the revolution, it was the Marxists that had hijacked their name. Now it was a zealous pro-Khomeyni group. On 5 April 1979, MIR held its first rally at Tehran University. Abolhasan Bani-Sadr and Hani al-Hasan, the Palestinian envoy to Iran, were present at this rally. A representative of MIR condemned the divisive activities of non-Kurds and non-Turkmans in the unrests of those regions.

MIR was always at the forefront of anti-Mojahedin and anti-Left rallies and worked closely with the IRP, IRGC and the Islamic Revolution Committees to mobilize the pro-Khomeyni masses. They were instrumental in preparing placards for the participants to carry and slogans for the zealots to chant. Their motorcyclists and minibuses invited people to join the marches in advance. Their armed militia, indistinguishable from the Islamic Revolution Committees and the IRGC, provided muscle for breaking up protestors and roughing up dissidents.

The relation between MIR and IRGC was very close. Many MIR members were involved in both organizations. With Rafsanjani's support, MIR played a determining role in Kurdistan and founded the pro-Khomeyni Muslim Kurds **Pishmarga** Organization to confront the Left Kurdish forces. Mohammad Borujerdi, the 28-year-old member of MIR, and a member of Khomeyni's bodyguards after his return to Iran, became the commander of the Muslim Kurds Pishmarga Organization and later became the commander of the IRGC in Kurdistan until his death in May 1983. Mohsen Rezai, another founding member of MIR, became the commander of the IRGC during the Iran–Iraq War.

MIR and Forqan

Ayatollah Morteza Motahhari was assassinated on 1 May 1979 (Figure 8.5). The 60-year-old cleric was the Islamic revolution's ideological beacon and a beloved student and trusted advisor of Khomeyni. Even though Motahhari had initially been Shariati's mentor, he later fell out with him and came to consider Shariati as an eclectic

Figure 8.5 Ayatollah Morteza Motahhari. *Source: Wikimedia Commons.*

and deviant whose leftist ideas were dangerous for Muslims. Motahhari went on to be a steadfast opponent of Marxists, Shariati and the Mojahedin.

Six months after Shariati's death in 1977, Motahhari and Bazargan wrote a letter in response to the growing popularity of Shariati's works. Having confirmed that Shariati was a Muslim, they denounced his many errors and attributed them to his ignorance of the certitudes of the Quran, the reports (***ravayat***) and Islamic jurisprudence. Motahhari and Bazargan announced that they planned to criticize and correct Shariati's deviations. Two days after the publication of this letter, Bazargan withdrew his signature. In rebuttal to the Motahhari–Bazargan letter, a 20-year-old stoic cleric called Akbar Gudarzi, threatened Motahhari and all enemies of Shariati in the name of Islam.

Motahhari's assassins belonged to the clandestine and militant Forqan Group, which was devoted to Shariati's anti-clericalism and Imam Ali's Shiism. Their name, Forqan was a direct reference to the title of **Surah** 25 in the Quran and means that which distinguishes right from wrong. Akbar Gudarzi, a low-ranking cleric, was the leader of Forqan. Members of his group believed in destroying what Shariati identified as the three symbols of polytheistic Islam, capitalism, coercion/dictatorship and clerical duplicity. In February/March 1978, Gudarzi's Group published the first issue of their paper, also called *Forqan*.

In the name of killing polytheists and the godless, Forqan assassinated a long list of Islamic Republic's notables, including General Mohammadvali Qarani, the first post-revolution army chief of staff (23 April 1979), Taqi Tarkhani, a prominent and wealthy member of the bazaar (8 July 1979), Mehdi Araqi, one of the leaders of the

Islamic Coalition of Mourning groups, and his son Hesam (26 August 1979), Ayatollah Mohammad-Ali Qazi-Tabatabai, Khomeyni's representative and the Friday Prayer Leader of Tabriz (1 November 1979) and Dr Mohammad Mofatteh, a rising clerical star of Iran's new political elite (18 December 1979).

On 25 May 1979, Forqan attempted to assassinate Rafsanjani, but he survived the attack. While hospitalized Rafsanjani met up with three leading figures of MIR, Behzad Nabavi, Morteza Alviri and Mohammad Salamati. He provided them with cars and wireless equipment and urged them to deal with Forqan. A month later, on 27 June 1979, Ali Khamenei, the Friday Prayer leader of Tehran escaped an attempt on his life by Forqan. After a while, MIR succeeded in infiltrating Forqan and went on to play a determining role in dismantling the group.

Sometime between 8 and 12 January 1980, the Green Berets, IRGC and MIR attacked approximately 17 Forqan safe houses and arrested some 35–70 members, including Gudarzi. Members of MIR participated in the interrogations, and rumours circulated about the use of torture techniques. Some 106 members of Forqan were rounded up and some 30–40 were executed. Those who had participated in the arrests were rewarded with plots of land and loans and henceforth became homeowners.

Iran's New Constitution: A Lost Opportunity

In retrospect, no event in Iran's post-revolutionary history was as significant as writing the new Constitution. After about seven months (22 May–3 December 1979), the original draft of the new Constitution became an unrecognizable document sanctioning a theocracy. The original draft respected the division of powers, upheld popular sovereignty, and did not concentrate exceptional jurisdiction in the hands of a single person. After seven months, the Constitution legitimized the religio-political leadership of a Guardian Jurist endowed with far more legal powers than the shah, paling his despotic powers.

The original draft of the new constitution was the work of Hasan Habibi, Abdolkarim Lahiji, Fatollah Bani-Sadr, Naser Katouzian and Jafar Langerudi. This group of non-clerics, including outstanding lawyers, had consulted the Algerian, French and Soviet constitutions, as well as the Human Rights Charter. Khomeyni was pleased with the original draft, made a few alterations and sent it to the Sources of Imitation in Qom. On 15 March 1979, the draft was returned to Khomeyni with suggestions made by the high-ranking jurists and was then forwarded for final review to a committee supervised by Yadollah Sahabi, in the Provisional Government. This committee ratified the proposed constitution and sent it to the Revolutionary Council, the legislative body at the time.

The Revolutionary Council altered the composition of the Guardian Council, the religious body overlooking the Islamicness of all legislatures in favour of non-clerical members. From the 6 Islamic jurists (clerics) and the 6 legal experts stipulated in the original draft, the Revolutionary Council decreased the number of Islamic jurists to 5, deliberately diminishing the clergy's legal power. The Revolutionary Council ruled that decisions by the Guardian Council on the compatibility of the laws passed in Parliament with Islamic ordinances needed a two-thirds majority vote of the members. Furthermore, the Guardian Council was denied the right to review every law ratified by Parliament, to assure its compliance with Islam. Only those laws that the Sources of Imitation, the president or the prosecutor general, requested a closer and more critical examination of would go to the Guardian Council. These alterations made by the Revolutionary Council significantly weakened the say and authority of Islamic jurists in the legislative.

The influential clerical figures and devotees of Khomeyni who sat on the Revolutionary Council approved this initial draft of the Constitution which made no references to the rule of the Guardian Jurist. On the issue of whether women could stand for the presidency or become judges, Beheshti argued that, 'we have documents proving that women could become judges'.[24] The final draft did not specify the gender or sect (Shii or Sunni) of either the president or the prime minister.

During the final round of drafting the Constitution, however, Khomeyni inserted a few alterations, thus ensuring that the president would be male and Shii, and judges were all males. He also rejected the proposition which allowed the practice of Sunni jurisprudence in the realm of family law in the Sunni regions of the country. Finally, Khomeyni wished to see the emblem on the national flag change from the sun and lion to something else. Khomeyni's concerns were adopted, and the final form of the first draft of the new constitution was made public.

Article 3 of the draft Constitution stipulated that ,'governance is based on the popular vote', and Article 6 maintained that, 'no individual, group or person in authority is entitled to deny the freedoms of opinion, speech, expression and other legitimate freedoms for reasons of state, except during war'.[25] Article 126 assured that the judiciary would be independent, and that the president would guarantee its independence.

The question that remained was the procedure that would render this document legitimate: should it be put to a referendum immediately, or should it be ratified by an elected Constituent Assembly? Two views clashed. Pragmatically, Khomeyni insisted that the draft approved by the Provisional Government, the Revolutionary Council and the religious authorities be put to an immediate referendum, bypassing a Constituent Assembly's review process.

Khomeyni worried that a future Constituent Assembly with 350–600 representatives reviewing 151 articles carefully would take 6–18 months, delaying the process of legitimizing the foundations of the new Islamic Republic. Furthermore, without a constitution in place, presidential and legislative elections were impossible. Khomeyni was pressed for time.

> ## Khomeyni on the Draft Constitution
> Give me the draft constitution and I will personally put it to a referendum.[26]

The proponents of presenting the draft to a popularly elected Constituent Assembly believed that the people through their representatives were entitled to review and debate the articles before the people's final vote. They further argued that Khomeyni had promised the people a Constituent Assembly. During one of their debates, Rafsanjani, himself a proponent for an immediate referendum, argued that if elections were to be held for a future constituent assembly, at least 70 to 80 per cent of its members would be clerics and unlikely to approve the contents of the draft constitution. Prophetically, Rafsanjani concluded that those in favour of a Constituent Assembly would eventually regret a constitution produced by such a body. Rafsanjani cautioned the members of the Revolutionary Council that the composition of the Constituent Assembly would be a reactionary and hidebound one that would not approve the contents of the draft constitution.

Faced with a deadlock, on 22 May 1979, the two sides met with Khomeyni in Qom. The discussion lasted six hours. Faced with the strong opposition of Bazargan, Yadollah Sahabi and Bani-Sadr to a direct referendum, Khomeyni tilted towards a compromise. Beheshti, the powerful and shrewd clerical member of the Revolutionary Council, proposed a small-size assembly of 10 to 48 experts to review the draft. Khomeyni agreed, and it was decided that an elected small-size assembly would study, review and approve the Constitution in one month. On 28 and 29 of May 1979, the draft was published in the press.

The Assembly of Experts and the Rule of the Guardian Jurist

The public was informed that the Assembly of Experts would replace the Constituent Assembly, and an election date was determined. Khomeyni encouraged the candidates to rapidly review and approve the final draft. But around 20 June, or some two months before the election to the Assembly of Experts, Khomeyni had a sudden change of heart, prodding the clergy to carefully review every article of the draft and make recommendations on what would be beneficial for Islam and absent in the initial draft.

In the first post-revolution election, the people went to the voting booths on 3 August 1979. The Mojahedin, Fadais, Shariatmadari's Muslim People of Iran's Republic Party and the Tudeh Party participated in this election. There were widespread reports of foul play and election engineering by the alliance of Khomeyni supporters, the Great Islamic Coalition, led by the Islamic Republic Party. The elected representatives turned out to be of 50 clerics, 23 non-clerics, with one female representative among them, Monireh Gorji-Fard, a candidate of the Islamic Republic Party and a Shariati disciple. Of the 73 elected representatives, 58 had been on the list of the Great Islamic Coalition, 8 belonged to Bazargan's Iran Freedom Movement and 7 were candidates of Shariatmadari's the Muslim People of Iran's Republic Party.

On 19 August 1979, the Assembly of Experts convened to review the draft, and instead set aside the initial draft completely and began rewriting the new Constitution. On 12 September 1979, Article 57 of the new Constitution that established the controversial Rule of the Guardian Jurist was ratified, with 53 votes in favour, 8 against and 4 abstentions. This game-changing article stated that leadership and rule in Iran were the sole purview of a just and pious jurist, whose authority the majority had accepted.

The new Constitution put to a referendum was approved on 3 December 1979. According to Article 110 of Iran's new Constitution, the Guardian Jurist appointed all six clerical members of the Guardian Council, as well as the head of the judiciary. He was also the commander-in-chief and was entitled to dismiss the president. Less than ten months after the shah's fall, Iran abruptly shifted from a despotic monarchy to a despotic theocracy, with unprecedented legal powers in the hands of one man.

Imposing Islamic homogeneity

During the early days of the revolution, the Iranian press had experienced a revival. After years of censorship, it was liberated and reported as it saw fit. Of the pre-revolution newspapers, *Ayandegan* and *Keyhan* took their job seriously. They gave coverage to Khomeyni, the government and the Council of the Islamic Revolution, as well as the growing voices of dissent. As tensions and clashes increased between the zealot supporters of Khomeyni and various diverging and discordant social, political and ethnic groups, *Ayandegan* reflected what was going on in the country. It gave coverage to dissenting views of personalities who did not see eye to eye with Khomeyni. *Ayandegan* did not belong to any political organization unlike newspapers such as *Azadi* (The Democratic National Front of Iran), *Ommat* (Movement of Militant Muslims), *The Muslim People* (Muslim People of Iran's Republic Party), *Kar* (Fadais), *Mojahed* (The People's Mojahedin of Iran), *Mardom* (Tudeh Party of Iran) and many more.

By 10 May 1979, Khomeyni was tired of public criticism of the state affairs and weighed in against *Ayandegan* and the independent press. He declared *Ayandegan* 'deviationist' and acting 'against the welfare of Muslim people'. Khomeyni announced that 'he would no longer read this newspaper and that its contents did not meet his approval'.[27] On the same day, Khomeyni also accused *Peygham Emrooz*, an independent Left publication of deviation and deception.

Ayandegan's sin was that it had published an investigative piece on the Forqan Group and their motive behind assassinating Motahhari. While Khomeyni and

Bazargan blamed the communists and anti-Muslims for the attack, *Ayandegan* had demonstrated that the assassins were anti-communist and staunch Muslims, followers of Shariati and fervent proponents of an Islamic government without the clergy.

Khomeyni's first condemnation of *Ayandegan* and *Peygham Emrooz* prompted the **Hezbollah** to attack, occupy and firebomb their offices in Tehran and the provinces. Both papers briefly stopped publication, but resumed work after a week. During this time, *Keyhan* reported on and denounced the aggressions committed against its professional cohorts.

On 14 May 1979, the workers at *Keyhan* barred some twenty members of its editorial board from entering their offices, and announced their expulsion. They then visited Khomeyni in Qom, obtained his full support and gratitude, and carried out a most successful coup. *Keyhan* fell into the hands of 'Khomeyni's soldiers', the Muslim proletariat and its new leadership promised, 'to listen to the commands of the esteemed leader to further the objectives of the Islamic revolution'.[28]

In solidarity with the expelled journalists, 130 *Keyhan* writers, reporters, journalists and editors went on strike. Bazargan's government watched helplessly while the Islamic Republic Party and MIR congratulated the 'revolutionary' action of *Keyhan*'s workers. The first victim of 'Khomeynizing' the press was *Keyhan*, one of the two most famous flagships of the Iranian news media.

Khomeyni on the Dissident Press and the Unruly Parties

We made a mistake in not acting in a revolutionary manner . . . We would not have had such problems, had we from the beginning, having defeated the corrupt, been revolutionary: breaking pens, banning the press and all the rotten media, putting their manager on trial, banning all corrupt parties, and setting up gallows in the main squares and slaying them all . . . [Then], we would have had one party: *Hezbollah*, the party of the oppressed/disinherited. (R. Khomeyni)[29]

The election results of the Assembly of Experts on 3 August 1979 demonstrated the hegemonic position of pro-Khomeyni forces. Four days later, a new wave of censorship and repression swept the country. On 7 August 1979, armed men occupied the central office of *Ayandegan* and arrested thirteen journalists. The prosecutor of the Islamic Revolutionary Courts ordered the closure of *Ayandegan* and the transfer of its assets to the Foundation of the Oppressed. On the same day, the satirical Left paper *Ahangar* and the daily *Peygham Emrooz* were also ordered shut. The prosecutor argued that these newspapers were working against the welfare of Muslims and the Islamic Republic.

The opposition reacted by organizing a rally in defence of the freedom of the press and against *Ayandegan*'s closure. The pronounced erosion of hard-won democratic freedoms left the opposition in a bind. They did not wish to provoke the wrath of Khomeyni, the *Hezbollah* and the Revolutionary Courts, leading to their dissolution, yet silence in the face of repression meant acquiescence and gradual disappearance.

The Democratic National Front, which had the support of major Left political organizations, called for a rally against the suppression of freedom of thought at Tehran University. Khomeyni had already warned against anyone who disturbed public peace with strikes, sit-ins, demonstrating, and rallies and was particularly annoyed with the activities and statements of the Democratic National Front.

A few days before the demonstration, an unknown group, *Hezbe Towhidi* (Monotheistic Party) called on its members to stand up against all conspiracies. The new pro-Khomeyni *Keyhan* condemned political unrests and agitations as *haram* or religiously forbidden. The Mojahedin of the Islamic Revolution (MIR) warned that puppets of 'plunderers and colonialists' will object to the revolutionary act of closing *Ayandegan*, but 'faced with the people's will, they will fail'.[30] Fereydun Tonokaboni, the renowned writer and satirist, reflected the Tudeh Party's position. He condemned the 'well-off urban intellectuals' and the 'liberal bourgeoisie' for grumbling about the absence of freedoms and called for 'unity of expression under the Imam's flag'.[31]

> ## Khomeyni on Democracy
> We will allow one or a few parties that act properly to function and will ban all the rest. All these [opposition] publications were against Islam and Muslims, and we will destroy them all. (R. Khomeyni)[32]

On 12 August 1979, the peaceful meeting in support of *Ayandegan* turned into an unprecedented bloody clash leaving behind some 270 to 600 injured. The well-organized *Hezbollah* militants pelted the demonstrators with stones and bricks and assaulted them with brass knuckles. The hostile pro-Khomeyni crowds chanted, 'Party, only Party of God [*Hezbollah*]!', while their victims responded, 'Death to fascism and death to reaction!'

On the next day, 13 August 1979, the offices of the Fadais were overtaken by some 200 club-wielding members of the *Hezbollah*, who gutted them before handing them over to the Islamic Revolution Committee of Tehran's fourth district. The Mojahedin managed to temporarily stave off attacks on their headquarters guarded by some 5,000 supporters. Their offices subsequently fell to the IRGC on 22 August 1979. When members of *Hezbollah* tried attacking the headquarters of the Tudeh Party on 13 August, they were repulsed by the IRGC.

On 21 August 1979, the Office of Tehran's Prosecutor of the Islamic Revolutionary Courts and the minister of guidance ordered the closure of 41 dailies and weeklies throughout Iran. These included organizational, party and independent publications that had been critical of the excesses of the new regime. By September 1979, prominent political opposition groups and organizations were stripped of their democratic rights and privileges.

To further limit the circulation of independent information, the Islamic Republic curbed the activities of the foreign press. Journalists working for the BBC, *Financial Times*, *Express* and two West German papers were told to leave the country immediately. The closure of the offices of the Associated Press followed on 5 September 1979.

American Embassy Falls

On 22 October 1979, Khomeyni lashed out against the deviationists who were talking about dissolving the Assembly of Experts which had recently included the Rule of the Guardian Jurist in the Constitution. He accused them of being ignorant of Islam and the Rule of the Guardian Jurist. He thundered that 'the Rule of the Guardian Jurist is not a dictatorship but against it!'

Later it became known that around 19 October, Abbas Amir-Entezam, Bazargan's deputy and later Iran's ambassador to Sweden, had proposed the dissolution of the Assembly of Experts, and had obtained the approval of Bazargan and 18 cabinet members. Khomeyni categorically rejected the proposal to dissolve the Assembly of Experts, and it became clear that Bazargan, who had offered his resignation many times before, needed to go.

On the same day, 22 October, the shah flew from Mexico to the US, his jet landed at New York's La Guardia Airport, and the shah immediately entered New York Hospital to have his gall bladder removed on the next day. After much hesitation, the US Administration had admitted the shah to the US on humanitarian grounds due to his urgent cancer condition. Khomeyni's reaction to the shah's admission to the US was defiant. In a meeting with students in Qom, on 29 October, Khomeyni declared that: 'Foreigners are responsible for the problems in the East . . . The US is responsible for all our problems . . . Let us forget the West.'[33]

In Iran, officials demanded the shah's immediate extradition from the US. On 31 October 1979, as anti-US sentiments were rising, Mehdi Bazargan flew to Algiers to attend the 25th anniversary of the commencement of Algeria's war of independence. On this first-post revolution Iranian diplomatic mission, the prime minister, was accompanied by Ebrahim Yazdi, minister of foreign affairs, and Mostafa Chamran, minister of national defence. On the recommendation of Bruce Laingen, the US chargé d'affaires in Tehran, the Iranian delegation met with Zbigniew Brzezinski, Carter's national security advisor. The two sides met and had a cordial 90-minute meeting.

> **One View of Why the Hostage Crisis Happened**
>
> Brzezinski told Bazargan that the United States was open to any relationship and partnership the Islamic Republic wanted and shook his hand. The day after newspapers published photographs of the Brzezinski-Bazargan handshake, protests rocked Iran, culminating in outraged students seizing the American embassy. (M. Rubin)[34]

On the heels of Khomeyni's anti-American speech, pro-Khomeyni political organizations called for an anti-US demonstration on 1 November. Even though the march was supposed to end in front of the US Embassy, it did not. Participants in this colossal anti-imperialist demonstration chanted, 'America, America, you are our people's enemy!' On the same day, Khomeyni called on the students to 'bolster their attacks against the US and Israel with all their might and compel the US to return the murderous Shah.'[35]

The Islamic Republic Party openly challenged Bazargan and his meeting with Brzezinski. It enquired, 'When the Imam and the Islamic community (*ummat*) are vehemently condemning America's interventionist policies, is meeting with Brzezinski in accord with the movement of Iran's Muslim people?'[36] The prime minister did not think that he needed to seek the approval of the Imam for whatever he thought was in the interest of the country. But he was wrong. Everything was now in place for the clergy around Khomeyni to get rid of Bazargan.

The Den of Spies

On 4 November 1979, schools and universities closed to commemorate the bloodshed at Tehran University in 1978, and students were invited to congregate on Tehran University's campus. A group of 400 students, supposedly on their way to Tehran University, climbed the walls of the US Embassy and entered the grounds at around 11.30 am (Figure 8.6). By 1.30 pm, they fully occupied the buildings and had taken 63 embassy staff hostage. The occupiers of the US Embassy called themselves the Student Followers of the Imam's Line (SFIL).

By the end of the day, neither the IRGC nor the Revolutionary Committees had intervened to expel the occupying students, confirming that the occupation had the blessing of Khomeyni. In the first of their many declarations to come, the Student Followers of the Imam's Line began their statement with a quote from Khomeyni's speech on 1 November, which prompted students to attack the US with all their might. In the third declaration, they announced that Ayatollah Mohammad Musavi-Khoeiyniha had joined them in the embassy. Musavi-Khoeiyniha was a radical cleric close to Khomeyni and a close friend of Khomeyni's son Ahmad. He had been the spiritual father of the Student Followers of the Imam's Line and the real mastermind behind the

Figure 8.6 Iranian demonstrator burning the American flag on top of the US Embassy. *Source: Photo by Bettmann via Getty Images.*

occupation. On 5 November, Bazargan's government resigned and the Revolutionary Council, dominated by Khomeyni's clerical supporters, took over its functions.

> ## US Pressure to Assure the Release of Hostages
>
> On November 9, the cessation of all shipment of military parts and equipment to Iran was ordered. On November 13, imports of Iranian oil were banned. On November 14, a key measure, freezing Iranian assets held in American banks and their foreign branches, was put into effect. (C. Vance)[37]

Khomeyni's position on the hostage situation quickly surfaced. He referred to the American Embassy as the 'Den of Spies' the US as the 'Great Satan' and President Carter as Iran's enemy. He assured Iranians that the 'US cannot do a damn thing.' Khomeyni prohibited Iranian officials from negotiating with the US, arguing that Iran neither feared military action nor economic sanctions. Subsequently, some $14 billion of Iranian assets were frozen in US and European banks.

Khomeyni now posed as the heroic Third World anti-imperialist leader, challenging and belittling the US by violating international law (Figure 8.7). The US-led 1953 coup had poisoned Iranian perception of the US for generations. Hostage-taking reversed the gaze, and contaminated US perception of the Islamic Republic, with dire economic consequences that would last decades.

Figure 8.7 Poster with the Iranian leaders Mohammad Mosaddeq, Ayatollah Ruhollah Khomeyni, Ahmad Khomeyni and Abolhasan Bani-Sadr. *Source: Via Alamy.*

The occupation of the American Embassy was a second revolution, saving Khomeyni from his growing domestic problems. It enabled him to focus the attention of Iranians on another enemy, the US, and thus force the Islamic and the majority of the communist Left to support his momentous anti-imperialist initiative. By the time the new and controversial Constitution legitimizing Khomeyni's rule as the Guardian Jurist was published in Iranian newspapers (17 November 1979), and the referendum on it had taken place (2–3 December 1979) officializing Khomeyni's uncontested political position, Iran was fully in the grips of an anti-imperialist hysteria.

Bazargan's Resignation Closes the Democratic Window of Opportunity

The resignation confirmed the fact that Iranian domestic politics had become too inhospitable for moderate Islamic activists and secular democratic forces. Democracy's moment had passed, and with rising revolutionary fervor on the streets, the militants saw pro-democracy forces—whom the Left derided as 'bourgeois' and 'liberal,' and whom fundamentalists called 'pro-Western'- as dispensable. (A. Gheissari and V. Nasr)[38]

The occupation of the US Embassy forced Khomeyni's considerable Left opposition to support his anti-imperialist initiative. The Imam had temporarily pacified the Left and purged the nationalist, liberal and Muslim politicians of Bazargan's type, thereby tightening the circle of Iran's new ruling class. After the hostage-taking, Khomeyni's tone and attitude hardened against the West and he began hammering at the idea of exporting the Islamic Revolution. The hostage crisis strengthened the hands of the radicals and caused a cold war between the US and Iran, which would last much longer than the original Cold War.

The Rise and Fall of Bani-Sadr: The Paris Discourse is Gone for Good

Eighty days after the fall of Bazargan, and almost a year after the victory of the revolution, Abolhasan Bani-Sadr won Iran's first presidential election. On 25 January 1980, in the most unconstrained and competitive election in the history of the Islamic Republic, 96 candidates participated, and Bani-Sadr obtained 75 per cent of the votes, crushing Hasan Habibi, the Islamic Republic Party's candidate who came in third with 3 per cent of the votes.

Bani-Sadr promised to put an end to censorship, to the multiple centres of power and decision-making, and to despotic governance in Iran. From early 1980, pressure on the Mojahedin had mounted as they were constantly harassed and beaten up during their rallies or while selling their newspapers. On the eve of the presidential elections, their medical relief centre in Tehran was attacked and fired on by armed men. The state military and security organizations denied all responsibility for the attacks.

Even though Khomeyni supported Bani-Sadr at first, and named him commander-in-chief, his protégé was an outsider to the clerical clique in the Islamic Republic Party. Bani-Sadr, who had criticized Bazargan for his inability to impose his authority in the face of lawlessness, now found himself in his shoes. Bani-Sadr mistakenly believed that his special relationship with the Imam would give him greater power and leverage with the clerical clique.

Bani-Sadr had a long wish list: a quick release of the hostages, an end to purges in government organizations and ministries, stopping *Hezbollah* attacks on demonstrations, opposition headquarters and newspapers, and finally curbing the excesses of the Revolutionary Courts. To attain those objectives, he needed to curtail the growing power of the clergy who controlled the IRP.

The clerics, however, already controlled the judiciary, the Revolutionary Courts, the Revolutionary Committees, the IRGC and the national radio and television. Now, the Student Followers of the Imam's Line (SFIL), whose credo was an anti-liberal crusade at home and an anti-American policy abroad, was added to the list. The SFIL selectively published compromising information it had discovered in the American Embassy on various politicians they deemed liberal and Westernized. Based on such information, the Islamic Revolutionary Prosecutor arrested politicians, such as Naser Minachi, Bazargan's minister of information and Abbas Amir-Entezam, the Spokesman of Bazargan's government and the ambassador to Sweden.

On 8 May 1980, while Bani-Sadr was president, and on the eve of the second round of elections to the first Parliament, the Revolutionary Courts executed Farrokhru Parsa, the first female minister in Iran. The outrageous and trumped-up charges were 'plundering the public coffers, corruption and propagating prostitution at the Ministry of Education'.[39] Bani-Sadr was opposed to such excesses and in his newspaper, the Islamic Revolution, which had begun publication on 19 June 1979, referred to Farrokhru Parsa as 'lady' and expressed his criticism in the following way, 'being categorical is not the same as blind coercion and murder'.[40]

Khomeyni on Prolonging the Hostage Crisis

We will keep the hostages and once we have fulfilled our domestic tasks, we will release them. Today the hostage issue has united the people, the opposition does not dare oppose us and we will easily get the new Constitution ratified. Once we conclude the Presidential and Parliamentary elections, we will release them. (A. Bani-Sadr)[41]

The first round of elections to the first Parliament of the Islamic Republic took place on 14 March 1980. These elections demonstrated the strength of the Islamic Republic Party and its allies, the Mojahedin of the Islamic Revolution, the Coalition of Islamic Mourning Groups, and the Association of Militant Clergy (*jameeye rowhaniyat mobarez*). In spite of calls of foul play from prominent personalities such as Khomeyni's brother, Ayatollah Morteza Pasandideh, members of Bazargan's government and members of the Revolutionary Council, complaints went unheeded.

To further consolidate Khomeyni and his powerful clerical nucleus, a crisis engulfing universities was fomented. This diverted the attention of Iranians between the two election rounds. Unsurprisingly, the Islamic Republic's first Parliament came under the control of the IRP. These elections brought into the open the rivalry between Bani-Sadr and the clerical nucleus of Beheshti-Rafsanjani-Khamenei.

A Cultural Revolution

On 21 March 1980, Khomeyni lashed out against Iranian universities, inciting violence and hostility. Very much like the shah, Khomeyni had come to dread if not hate university students, who actively and vocally opposed his ideas. He announced that 'A fundamental revolution was necessary for all Iranian universities to purge professors connected to the East, or the West, and for universities to become healthy environments for the teaching of Islamic sciences.'[42]

For the new clerical establishment, universities were counter-revolutionary centres, where the student organization of the Mojahedin and the Fadais were active and in control. To impose a religio-political homogeneity, ethnic minorities had to be crushed, non-compliant politicians neutralized, opposition voices muzzled and university students needed to be subdued and silenced. Under the pretext of a Cultural Revolution, the universities were ordered to no longer provide sanctuary for demonstrations, rallies and the germination of anti-Khomeyni ideas.

Closing the Universities

The Student Followers of the Imam's Line planned to close the universities because they felt that the hostage crisis fever had fallen, and a new cause was needed to keep public opinion mobilized and involved. (A. Bani-Sadr)[43]

On 15 April 1980, the Student Followers of the Imam's Line occupied Tabriz University and called for a Cultural Revolution. The pro-Khomeyni forces in universities constituted a mere 10 per cent of the student body. The clerically manipulated Students Followers of the Imam's Line, supported by the state's official and non-official repressive machine, began storming universities.

For a week, various student political organizations put up a bitter fight, especially those who had offices inside university campuses, such as the Mojahedin's *anjoman daneshjuyan mosalman* and the Fadai's *pishgam*. Bani-Sadr, who initially opposed the occupation, joined the assailants, and argued that universities should not house offices of political organizations. The takeover of Iranian universities by Khomeyni's supporters, with the help of Bani-Sadr, was completed on 22 April. The political organizations vacated their offices. The bloody battles with stones, bricks, knives and guns left at least 2,500 wounded and approximately 28 dead. Khomeyni was conducting a successful trench war against his opponents. One by one he took out the pockets of resistance.

> ## Khomeyni on the Iranian Universities, 21 April 1980
> Our universities are [as though they were run by] colonial [powers]. Our universities educate ... Westernized types, many of our teachers are Westernized and raise our youth Westernized ... universities have to undergo fundamental changes and to be built anew ... Our youth need to have an Islamic education. (R. Khomeyni)[44]

Iranian universities resumed their activities once they had been 'Islamized'. In June 1980, Khomeyni appointed a seven-man team to the Cultural Revolution Headquarters (CRH), whose task was to homogenize and Islamize the universities. The CRH was responsible for replacing the deviant 'Westernized' or liberal and 'Easternized' or Left faculty and students with religio-politically 'correct' zealots. The CRH was also responsible for changing the curriculum, thoroughly reviewing and 'fixing' the social sciences and developing appropriate Islamic courses. Lastly, universities had to be 'sanitized'. Lax and promiscuous gender mixing and coed merrymaking had to cease.

The Cultural Revolution was a myopic attempt at forcefully chasing out 'undesirable' ideologies and practices. Just as Reza Shah, the secular despot, had been under the false assumption that he could stamp out Islamic practices and beliefs, Khomeyni, the religious despot was under the erroneous impression that he could stamp out curiosity, mental inquisitiveness, passion and fun among the youth.

Iranian universities remained closed for three academic years. They reopened their doors in September 1983, with some 35–40 per cent of the teaching staff and 35 per cent of the students purged. Those who had been purged adhered to different ideologies, ways of life, and religions, yet they had one thing in common. They had failed to convince the Islamic admission/inquisition committees that they were not a threat to a homogeneous body of the devotees of the Imam's vision of Iran. From September 1983, in addition to academic entrance exams for majors, new students were now required to take ideological and Islamic admission tests (*gozinesh*) to ascertain their religio-political eligibility. Women were now barred from engineering, agriculture, and veterinary studies.

Decades later, the objectives of the Cultural Revolution, to transform Iranian universities according to Khomeyni's values remained unattained. Iranian youth, products of 'Islamized' universities, ended up being more than ever distanced from Islam and infatuated with the West and with Western culture, morals, attitudes and mores.

The Failed US Rescue Operation

On 7 April 1980, after five months of unsuccessful diplomatic efforts to free the US hostages, the US government broke off all diplomatic ties with Iran and imposed full sanctions. Carter's decision came after Khomeyni turned down Bani-Sadr's proposal to transfer custody of the American hostages from the Student Followers of the Imam's Line to the Revolutionary Council.

> **Carter Losing Patience**
>
> In response to the abhorrent act in Iran, our Nation has never been aroused and unified so greatly in peacetime. Our position is clear. The United States will not yield to blackmail. (J. Carter)[45]

Under considerable public pressure at home and faced with Khomeyni's intransigence, Carter opted for a military operation to rescue the hostages. Public opinion in the US and Iran was that Carter would never endorse military action. On 24 April 1980, while Iranian universities were reeling from bloody clashes, and the IRGC and the army were under heavy attack by Kurdish opposition forces in Sanandaj, Operation Eagle Claw to free the hostages commenced. The operation benefitted from the element of surprise.

The complex and high-risk five-step military plan to rescue the remaining 52 embassy staff involved eight helicopters and six C-130 planes. It was to be executed by 118 soldiers from the Delta Forces and Green Berets and two former Iranian military officers, acting as advisers. The operation was supposed to be over in three days and two nights. The first step of the operation involved eight Sea Stallion helicopters and four C-130 planes, transporting fuel and soldiers to meet at 'Desert One', located 320 kilometres south-east of Tehran in South Khorasan Province, near Tabas. For the mission to proceed, at least six helicopters were necessary to carry the soldiers to 'Desert Two', near Garmsar, 80 kilometres south-east of Tehran. Of the eight helicopters, only six arrived at 'Desert One'. Once there, one of the six helicopter encountered technical problems and had to be abandoned.

Unable to complete the first step of the rescue operation, the mission was aborted. The withdrawal of US forces proved to be even more catastrophic. Refueling in the middle of a sandstorm with reduced visibility caused a helicopter pilot to crash into the C-130 fuel plane, immediately blowing up both air crafts. Members of the rescue mission had to carry five injured comrades, mount the three remaining planes and fly back to Masirah Island, Oman, leaving behind the bodies of eight burnt US servicemen, and all helicopters, one charcoaled and four intact.

The failure of this rescue operation sealed the fate of the hostages and Carter's bid for a second term in office. Khomeyni presented the failed US operation as proof of the Divine's love for the revolution and the Islamic Republic. His first response to the military operation was one of anger and enmity towards the person of Jimmy Carter, whom he called 'stupid' and a 'murderer', who wished to prolong his presidency. Khomeyni held Carter responsible for the bloody clashes in Kurdistan, the universities and Iraq's border incursions.

Khomeyni set four conditions for the release of the hostages. The US would pledge not to interfere in Iran's internal affairs, it would return all Iran's frozen assets and cancel all claims against Iran, and finally, restitute the shah's assets abroad. On 15 September, Sadeq Tabatabai, Ahmad Khomeyni's brother-in-law, met with a high-ranking American mission in the presence of the West German Foreign Minister Hans-Dietrich Genscher in Bonn. The two parties came close to mutually acceptable terms for the release of the hostages. On 20 January, after President Ronald Reagan took his oath of office, Iran released the hostages after 444 days of captivity.

> **What was Materially Gained from Hostage-Taking**
>
> In response to the four Iranian demands, we gave away nothing of value that was ours; we simply returned a relatively small part of what was theirs and the balance held back to pay off much what Iran owed to our claimants . . . Arguably, therefore, if substantial concessions were made by anyone during the negotiation process, virtually all were made by Iran. (R. Owen)[46]

Bani-Sadr's Initial Skirmishes with the IRP

Once he became president, Bani-Sadr found himself, like his predecessor Bazargan, in a war of attrition with the Islamic Republic Party and especially Beheshti, Rafsanjani and Khamenei, who enjoyed Khomeyni's support. Whereas Bani-Sadr could counter-attack and publicly denounce the IRP's efforts against himself, he could not attack Khomeyni. The Imam liked Bani-Sadr, but he liked the clergy more. More significantly, and again like Bazargan, Bani-Sadr was not partial to revolutionary coercion and violence as a means of resolving problems. As soon as he became president, the Islamic Republic Party gnawed at the powers of his office, reducing it to a purely ornamental and symbolic one.

Starting on 11 May 1980, Bani-Sadr became involved in a tug of war over the appointment of the prime minister. Bani-Sadr's newspaper warned against an approaching 'religious fascism', 'chaos' and the rise of a 'just despot' while hammering at the necessity for 'moderation' and 'order'. Concurrently, Ayatollah Khalkhali was busy destroying Reza Shah's mausoleum with Khomeyni's approval, and the Revolutionary Prosecutor was banning 40 'counter-revolutionary' publications.

In mid-June 1980, club-wielding thugs and militia chanting, 'Party, only Party of God [*Hezbollah*], Leader, only Ruhollah (Khomeyni)!', increased the intensity of their violence against the opposition in the name of Islam and the imam. Bookstores in front of Tehran University, especially those of the Left, were regularly attacked, destroyed and looted. Mojahedin's rallies in Tehran with permission from the minister of interior, were assaulted leaving 150 injured and 1 dead. The *Hezbollah* was openly provoking the opposition.

When Ahmad Khomeyni objected to the attacks on the Mojahedin, his father immediately repeated his condemnation accusing the Fadais and the Mojahedin of acting against the revolution and being US pawns. On 25 June 1980, Khomeyni chastised his son and said, 'some people connected with me are not aware that the problem is not the club-wielders, but those who foment unrest and tumult'. Khomeyni set the stage for an all-out war against the Mojahedin when he said, 'They want to destroy us with the Quran and the **Nahjolbalaqeh** and then destroy the Quran and the Nahjolballaqeh.'[47] In reaction to these attacks and in the hope of preventing further bloodshed, the Mojahedin announced the closure of their offices throughout Iran.

Imposing the Islamic Attire

A month after the revolution, on 12 March 1979, Khomeyni had attempted to impose the veil but had backed off after widespread protests by women. On 1 July 1980, Khomeyni lashed out again at the continuing un-Islamic dressing of women in the workplace. He held the Western-educated (his president) responsible. In his speech, Khomeyni said, 'Ministries are not brothels, universities are not whore houses, they ought to be centers of education.' He attacked the manner in which women were clad in public spaces and referred endlessly to 'self-purification' versus 'corruption', never mentioning the word *hejab* or veil.[48]

Khomeyni on the Islamic Attire

Now I have the power and I am obliged to implement the religion of God. (A. Bani-Sadr)[49]

Starting on the very next day, women were obliged to wear Islamic attire in all government offices. At the Congregational Friday Prayers of 4 July 1980, Hojatoleslam

Khamenei explained the importance of the Islamic *hejab* and invited women to cover their 'naked bodies' and don their *hejab* to defeat the enemies of the revolution. The following day, some 3,000 women protested the imposition of *hejab*, chanting, 'We did not make a revolution to go back in time' and 'death to reactionaries'. Bani-Sadr met with their representatives and promised that nothing would be imposed.

In the evening of 5 July, the Revolutionary Council announced that it was mandatory that women wear the veil. Bani-Sadr buckled under pressure and asked women to wear the Islamic attire in their workplace. On the next day, two women were lapidated in Kerman on charges of prostitution. This novelty in the Islamic Republic's judicial repertoire, was condemned as 'harmful' by Bani-Sadr, in his newspaper. Following the anti-*hejab* rally, 8 women were arrested, and 139 women in the army and the defence industries, who had been wearing black in sign of mourning and protest against the imposed *hejab*, were dismissed. This was the start of a long string of layoffs among women throughout Iran on charges of not observing the *hejab*. Once again, Khomeyni had won over another trench by forcing upon Iranian women his concept of chaste and virtuous fashion.

> ## Khamenei's Reference to Women Mourning the Veil by Wearing Black
>
> We do not claim that all of them were prostitutes, it is possible that some of these types were among them and some of them may not have been. But we can tell them that they are all liars and counter-revolutionaries.[50]

The Failed Nojeh Coup

On 12 July 1980, the press reported on a coup attempt to overthrow the Islamic Republic. The coup, code-named NEGAB (The Mask), the Persian acronym for Saving the Insurrection of Great Iran, had been planned by royalist officers, financed by Shapur Bakhtiyar, aided by certain members of the Iran Party and was to be carried out by army and air force personnel. They had recruited around 700 officers.

The main targets of the overthrow operation included 'Ayatollah Khomeini's home in Tehran, the Fiyziyih [Fayziyeh] seminary in Qom, the headquarters of the revolutionary court system, the prime minister's office, the Revolutionary Guard intelligence branch, two other Revolutionary Guard bases in Tehran, several Tehran *kumitih* [Islamic Revolution Committee] bases, and air-force runways in Tehran and other cities'.[51] To pound their designated targets, the conspirators needed planes which they intended to obtain by seizing the Nojeh (Shahrokhi) Air Base in Hamedan.

On 9 July, two groups were scheduled to go from Tehran to the Nojeh Air Base. Group One, composed of approximately 300 military personnel and paratroopers was designated to travel in small groups, penetrate the base and seize it, making way for the next group. Group Two, including some 40 air force pilots, were to travel to Hamedan, enter the neutralized base, join some 30 like-minded pilots, board the Phantom planes and embark on their mission.

The coup was compromised before the plotters even reached the Nojeh Air Base. The IRGC rounded up some of the pilots at their meeting point, Laleh Park in Tehran, before heading to Hamedan. Members of Group One made their way to Hamedan but were arrested near the Nojeh Air Base. By 10 July, the plot had folded, the military ring leaders, Generals Ayat Mohaqeqi and Saeed Mahdiyoun, Maj. Kurush Azartash and Lt Naser Rokni, with some 300 other participants were arrested. On 19 July, basing his ruling on the Quran, Khomeyni condemned the accomplices to death. Approximately 122 to 144 of those arrested were executed.

Of the many scenarios of how the coup attempt was compromised, the most restated one according to those directly involved with the affair is that the Tudeh Party of Iran had reported the plot to Ahmad Khomeyni and Ayatollah Khomeyni. On 18 July, the organizer and financier of the coup, Shapur Bakhtiyar, escaped an assassination attempt in Paris. His Lebanese would-be assassin, Anis Naqash, was released from his French prison in July 1990, and went on to live in Tehran and Beirut.

The failed coup further strengthened Khomeyni and his hardline clerical supporters. Rafsanjani accused members of the National Front and the Democratic Party of Kurdistan of colluding with the coup plotters. To denigrate the opposition the press charged that the Fadais had approved of the coup, and the Mojahedin knew of it. On the heels of such accusations, the offices of the National Front were attacked and occupied by 'Muslim youths' in Tehran, Rasht and Ahvaz. The attempted coup had provided the ideal excuse to accuse the opposition of treason and exert repression.

Iraq Attacks

On 22 September 1980, a week after the Iran–US meeting in Bonn aiming to resolve the hostage crisis, Iraq launched a full-scale land and air attack against Iran. Iraq invaded Iran across a 630-kilometre wide front and on four separate axes from Qasr Shirin in Kermanshah Province to the oil jugulars of Khorramshahr and Abadan in Khuzestan. The Iraqi Air Force attacked ten major Iranian air bases, including Tehran.

Both sides had been engaged in virulent propaganda attacks against one another. The Shii revolution in Iran threatened Saddam Hoseyn's rule in Iraq. The deportation of some 16,000 Shii Iraqi citizens by Saddam Hoseyn and the murder of the prominent Ayatollah Mohammad-Baqer Sadr in April 1980 had brought relations between the

Figure 8.8 Iran–Iraq War. *Source: Photo by Homer Sykes via Alamy.*

two countries to a new low. On 17 September 1980, Saddam Hoseyn unilaterally abrogated the Algiers Agreement signed by the shah. This significant international treaty recognized that the water border of Shatt al-Arab (Arvand Roud), separating the two countries, was drawn down the centre. For about a week before the all-out attack, border clashes had intensified, and each side accused the other of border violations (Figure 8.8).

Saddam Hoseyn was convinced that, faced with an Iranian army in disarray, an air force without spare parts and an inexperienced and unruly IRGC, Iraq could win a quick victory. A widespread purge of the army in September 1979 had laid off some 10,000 officers, giving Saddam Hoseyn reason to believe that the Iranian military apparatus was most vulnerable. Khomeyni called the war a blessing as it once again united the people behind him against a real foreign enemy. The nation embarked on a war footing, a siege mentality developed, nationalism and defense of the Islamic Motherland surged, and all shortcomings of the regime were attributed to the imposed war.

Khomeyni announced that a war against Iran was a war against Islam, the Quran and the Prophet of God, thus turning the battle into a holy crusade against Saddam and the US, the Great Satan. Khomeyni succeeded in enticing and engaging the pious Iranian youth emotionally, religiously and morally, turning them into the backbone of the war. To go to the front was promoted as a religious happening, where believers could emulate the ordeals of Imam Hoseyn and his followers in Karbala.

A strong sense of religious puritanism, fraternity, selflessness, valour and collective compassion for the sake of the higher ideals of faith and country were promoted. For zealot Muslims, especially the youth, going to the fronts and attaining the lofty status of martyrdom became a godly deed reserved for the blessed and the beatified. The war fronts became 'the land of light' where the scent of love and God filled the air. In this euphoric religio-mystical ambiance, zealots yearned for ascension to the hereafter and meeting the Beloved.

In the immediate aftermath of Iraq's invasion, tens of thousands of volunteers rushed to the fronts. On 13 October 1980, Khomeyni created a seven-man central command post, the Supreme Defense Council, to coordinate and manage the war under Bani-Sadr, the commander-in-chief. In addition to the professional and regular army, the revolution had mobilized its own warriors, the IRGC and a new military organization, the volunteers' corps of the Mobilization of the Oppressed (MOO), better known as *Basij*. The *Basiji*s came predominantly from the provinces. They were young, some even child soldiers, and untrained, yet highly motivated, full of faith and gumption and ready for martyrdom. MOO was initially an independent organization, but the IRP-dominated Majles promptly incorporated it into the IRGC on 3 December 1980.

On 27 September 1980, Iraqi forces laid siege to Abadan. On the next day, having shelled Khorramshahr for seven days, and hoping that the Arab population of the city would welcome them with open arms, 20,000 Iraqi troops tried to enter the city defended by 3,000. After a month, Iraqi forces occupied Khorramshahr on 24 October 1980, leaving 6,000–7,000 killed and wounded.

Starting on 28 January 1981, due to the war condition, the economic sanctions, reduction in imports and paucity of necessities, the Iranian government started issuing ration coupons. Ten necessities, such as sugar, cooking oil, rice, kerosene, soap and detergent, were rationed, and the government began familiarizing the people with the rationing system. The coupons enabled consumers to purchase these necessities at fixed and lower than market prices. This rationing system remained in place throughout the eight years of war.

The End of Bani-Sadr and All Opposition Groups

As soon as the first Parliament began to work, Khomeyni unveiled the last stage of his plan, which was to cleanse society of its past vestiges and implement an Islamic government. In a historical, 20 June 1980 speech, some two months before Iraq was to attack Iran, Khomeyni had instructed Parliament to vote for a '100% pious, Islamic, revolutionary, doctrinaire and categorical' cabinet. He had emphasized that ministers had to know how 'Islam was to be implemented in Iran' and added that 'We cannot tolerate the idea that these European-educated gentlemen, wish to fix this country.'

Khomeyni called for the application of Islamic punishments in society. He warned President Bani-Sadr that if he were to introduce non-revolutionary ministers, the

Majles would be obliged 'to refuse them'. Khomeyni informed Iranians that he would 'no longer tolerate nationalists, democrats, and anyone other than Islamic'.[52] Khomeyni's words were the perfect ammunition the IRP needed to begin destabilizing Bani-Sadr and eliminate the political opposition, especially the Mojahedin, who had lost their spiritual father, Ayatollah Taleqani, on 9 September 1979.

Bani-Sadr stands up to Khomeyni

Starting in the summer of 1980 and for the next eleven months, irreconcilable differences emerged between Bani-Sadr and Khomeyni and Iran became the scene of unprecedented political agitation and social strife. While Bani-Sadr stood up to the excesses of Khomeyni and the IRP, defended what he called 'these minimum freedoms' and warned about the imminent return to the 'age of ignorance' and 'fascism', the opposition and the Mojahedin found common grounds with the beleaguered president.

In a Majles led by Rafsanjani and dominated by the IRP, Bani-Sadr's legal battles began with the choice of a prime minister. After a lengthy tug of war, on 10 August 1980, the Majles gave the IRP candidate Mohammad-Ali Rajai a vote of confidence. Bani-Sadr considered Rajai dogmatic, and inexperienced. On 31 August 1980, Rajai presented his ministers to the Majles, and Bani-Sadr opposed most of them. The overwhelming majority of Rajai's ministers were either members of the IRP or MIR. Rajai considered himself a humble follower of Khomeyni, obedient to his 'directives'.

With all power in the hands of the IRP and its clerical leadership team, Bani-Sadr became a voice of opposition and anti-despotism. He adopted Shariati's discourse and attacked the 'concentration of power, and wealth in the hands of a few' as 'disbelief and polytheism'.[53] From 9 September 1980, hostilities between Bani-Sadr and the IRP became public. Bani-Sadr called the IRP liars, agitators, despots and polytheists, while Rafsanjani labelled him a liberal and accused him of slander against the Majles, ministers and the revolutionary institutions.

On 10 September 1980, Rajai's cabinet obtained a vote of confidence from the Majles. Twelve days later, on 22 September, Iraq launched a full-scale war against Iran, putting a temporary lid on the open feud between Bani-Sadr and the IRP. While Bani-Sadr as the commander-in-chief was fully involved with the war effort, IRP continued to stymie his efforts and discredit him. Bani-Sadr referred to his predicament as 'fighting on two fronts'.

While Bani-Sadr and the IRP fought their political battle, the judiciary under the control of Beheshti carried out its persecution of religious minorities. On 8 September 1980, seven Bahais were executed in Yazd. To dissimulate religious persecution, Bahais were accused of being 'Agents of International Zionism' and espionage. On 2 May 1981, three more Bahais were executed in Shiraz, followed by seven others on 11 June 1981 in Hamedan.

The appointment of Asadollah Lajevardi, an IRP member known for his intolerant and extremist views towards the Left and the Mojahedin, as Tehran's prosecutor general, sent a clear signal that political freedoms and the right to dissent were no longer tolerated. The arrest of Sadeq Qotbzadeh on 7 November 1980 indicated that the IRP intended to get rid of all three non-clerical and trusted advisers of Khomeyni in Paris. Bani-Sadr, Yazdi and Qotbzadeh were responsible for Khomeyni's liberal Paris discourse. On Khomeyni's orders, after a few days, Qotbzadeh was released.

One after the other, pro-Bani-Sadr rallies in major cities such as Mashhad, Esfahan, Hamedan, Rasht, and Tehran were disrupted by groups of club-wielding *Hezbollahi*s chanting slogans in favour of Rajai. For the IRP, Bani-Sadr and his allies especially the Mojahedin, were against the rule of the Guardian Jurist, Khomeyni's leadership and dangerous counter-revolutionaries.

Ironically, the communist party of Iran, the Tudeh Party, which had become a firm follower of the Imam's anti-imperialist line, remained a tolerated force and a trusted ally against liberalism. On 7 April 1981, Bazargan's newspaper, *Mizan*, was closed and its managing director arrested. One of the charges against it was that *Mizan* had referred to the Tudeh Party as one of the followers of Imam's Line. Although the statement was correct, the IRP wished to minimize this unholy alliance.

Bani-Sadr was determined to report on all the problems in the country and used his rallies to hammer at IRP's threat of taking the country down the road of despotism. This created deep-seated divisions at and behind the fronts, to which Khomeyni could not remain indifferent. Internal bickering could weaken the resolve of his soldiers. Khomeyni first invited both sides to reach an agreement, and then prohibited Bani-Sadr, Rajai, Beheshti and Rafsanjani from making public speeches until the end of the war. Khomeyni constituted a three-man committee to resolve the differences between the two sides, before finally siding with the clerics.

Bani-Sadr's alliance with the Mojahedin

On 5 March 1981, Bani-Sadr spoke at a rally in Tehran University commemorating the death of Mosaddeq. This rally escalated the tension between Bani-Sadr and the Mojahedin with the IRP and its allies. The Mojahedin's militia forces reacted forcefully to the assault of some 200 club-wielding *Hezbollahi*s. They gave them a good beating, confiscated their weapons, and arrested some 70. The identity cards found on the *Hezbollahi*s proved their membership in the IRGC, the Islamic Revolution Committees, Special forces of the Prime Minister's Office (Rajai's), and IRP affiliated foundations. The combined power of Bani-Sadr and the Mojahedin shook the IRP to its core.

For Khomeyni, any attack against the clergy was construed as an attack against the Islamic Republic and himself. Bani-Sadr and the Mojahedin's vocal criticism of the

IRP and their growing popularity made them first-class enemies of the state. On 26 April 1981, a well-coordinated attack was launched against the Mojahedin in Gorgan, Borujerd, Shahr Kord, Babol and Babolsar. Their poster and photo exhibitions were disrupted and torn down and their newspaper sellers attacked. The confrontations that ensued left hundreds injured. After a 50,000-strong demonstration by the Mojahedin in Tehran, further skirmishes with the *Hezbollah* spread to Tehran, Esfahan, Qazvin, Dorud, Yasouj, Karaj, Arak, Zanjan and Qazvin.

When the Mojahedin requested to meet with Khomeyni on 2 May 1981, to explain their side of the events, Khomeyni refused to see them. Ten days later, Khomeyni announced that the Mojahedin needed to lay down their arms, embrace the Islamic Republic, stop threatening the state with armed uprising and recant from their past positions. Khomeyni pointed out that deviant parties [the Tudeh Party], which were not even Muslims, had retained their freedom and newspapers because 'they were not intent on armed insurrection and engaged in political interaction'. Khomeyni's message to the Mojahedin was clear: either toe the Imam's Line, as did the Tudeh Party or else accept the consequences.[54]

The Mojahedin agreed to lay down their arms only if Bani-Sadr guaranteed political freedoms as stipulated in the Constitution. Bani-Sadr, in turn, claimed that since his hands were legally tied and he was unable to guarantee political freedoms, he would call for a referendum. The threat of a referendum unsettled not only the IRP but also Khomeyni, who feared that Bani-Sadr would put the Constitution and the rule of the Guardian Jurist to another public vote. Based on their growing popularity at rallies, Bani-Sadr and the Mojahedin sensed a change in the tides in their favour and felt confident that they could challenge the regime.

The long-expected civil war erupted in June 1981 between the status quo forces of Khomeyni and the IRP and its contenders Bani-Sadr, Mojahedin, the National Front and the Left, except the Tudeh Party and the Majority Faction of the Fadai. The opposition to Khomeyni who were becoming defiant and popular had to be silenced. On 7 June 1981, Bani-Sadr's paper, *Enqelabe Eslami*, was closed along with five other newspapers, including those belonging to the National Front and Bazargan. The banned newspapers were accused of propagating dissent and division.

The final blow by Khomeyni and his followers

Bani-Sadr and the Mojahedin invited the people to resist the return of tyranny, despotism, and reaction. Khomeyni lashed out at Bani-Sadr, saying, 'Dictator is the one who would not bow before the Majles, the Guardian Council, the Judiciary and the Prosecutor General.' Khomeyni told the people that it was their religious obligation to hand over the agitators to the courts.[55] The headquarters of Bani-Sadr's political organization, 'The Office Coordinating the Cooperation of the People with the President,' was seized and its personnel beaten up.

> ## Khomeyni on Bani-Sadr, Mojahedin and the National Front
>
> He [Bani-Sadr] wanted to turn me into a dictator . . . These people are ignorant and faithless. (R. Khomeyni)[56]

Starting on 8 June, pro-Bani-Sadr and pro-Mojahedin forces had daily clashes with pro-Khomeyni *Hezbollahi*s. The first group chanted 'Death to despotism, death to reaction', while Khomeyni's supporters chanted, 'Party, only Party of God, Leader, only Ruhollah [Khomeyni]!' and 'Death to the enemies of the Guardian Jurist!' Mojahedin militia and supporters constituted the backbone of the demonstrators, as they spread every day throughout the cities, disappeared and then reappeared in other parts. The significant presence of women in the pro-Mojahedin and pro-Bani-Sadr rallies was remarkable. Every day, Tehran and other major cities witnessed bloody clashes, leaving behind many wounded and dead.

On 10 June 1981, Khomeyni relieved Bani-Sadr as commander-in-chief of the army. Five days later, the National Front invited the public to demonstrate against the despotic ruling class and against a specific bill formulated by the judiciary which imposed Islamic punishments, including the law of talion (*qisas*). When the bill had been made public in April 1981, jurists, judges, non-clerical legal experts and intellectuals had strongly objected to retributions such as cutting off a limb or an ear, or else plucking out an eyeball or extracting teeth. They had argued that such punishments were inhuman and uncivilized.

On 15 June, right before the National Front rally, Khomeyni announced that since the National Front considered the law of God, the law of talion as being inhuman, it had committed apostasy. He invited the National Front and Bazargan's Iran Freedom Movement to recant. The National Front demonstration quickly petered out as its supporters, mainly of the middle and upper-middle classes, proved to be no match for the ferocity of some 500 *Hezbollahi*s, who attacked the demonstrators chanting, 'Where are the sissies, hiding in mouseholes?!' On the same day, 15 June 1981, Bani-Sadr, the president and now, the leader of the opposition, went into hiding.

Three days later, the Mojahedin declared a defensive war on the Islamic Republic by promising revolutionary retribution against all who attacked them. All Left organizations, except the Tudeh Party and the Majority Faction of the Fadais, revolted against the regime. On 20 June 1981, the opposition's show of force shook Tehran and the provinces. In Tehran, a few hundred thousand Mojahedin militia clashed with the *Hezbollah* and the IRGC, leaving eight killed and hundreds wounded and arrested. From this day on, and until February 1982, for eight months, Iran was in the throes of a civil war while the majority remained concerned bystanders.

On 21 June 1981, the Majles removed Bani-Sadr from office. Khomeyni confirmed this decision on the next day, and by the evening of 22 June, the summary executions began. At 9.00 pm, Mohammad Mohammadi-Gilani, the head of Tehran's Revolutionary Courts, and Asadollah Lajevardi, the revolutionary prosecutor, sent six to the gallows on charges of having cooperated with and supported the Mojahedin. A policy of on-the-spot execution when arrested in demonstrations was immediately put into place by special courts. Thousands of young, many of whom were minors, were shot for their political opposition and armed resistance. Three months after the Mojahedin uprising, and by 21 September 1981, Iran's revolutionary courts had 'sent 1,000 people to firing squads'.[57]

Eight months of brisk and screaming turnovers, June 1981–February 1982

As soon as Bani-Sadr was deposed, his three nemeses, Beheshti, Rafsanjani and Rajai, constituted the Provisional Council of the Presidency with Rajai as prime minister. But a week later, on 28 June 1981, at 9.00 pm, a thunderous explosion at the headquarters of the IRP killed 75, including Beheshti, 12 Majles deputies, 4 of Rajai's ministers and 12 undersecretaries. Rafsanjani had left the IRP meeting before the blast. Mohammad-Javad Bahonar, the minister of education and one of the founders of the IRP had been dissuaded from attending, and Khamenei was still in hospital after an assassination attempt on his life on the previous day. The explosion signaled the start of the Mojahedin's targeted urban military operations to overthrow the regime.

The bombing of this important meeting of IRP leaders was carried out by Mohammad-Reza Kolahi, a 22-year-old undercover member of the Mojahedin. Kolahi had infiltrated the IRP and won Beheshti's trust. One day after the blast at the IRP headquarters, Mohammad Kajoui was assassinated at his place of work. He had been the warden of the dreaded Evin Prison, where prisoners were held, tortured and executed. The Mojahedin were targeting influential and principal members of the regime.

The assassinations and the Mojahedin's show of daily force on the streets destabilized the regime. An atmosphere of fear settled among members of the ruling class. On 2 July, Khomeyni invited the people to identify the saboteurs, inform on their whereabouts and even arrest them. Conducting an armed urban uprising forced the Mojahedin to depend heavily on hideouts in the middle of the cities. These safehouses were often so crowded that they looked more like military barracks and attracted suspicion in the neighbourhood. The daily *Ettelaat* ran a lengthy and detailed article on, 'How to identify safe houses' and what constituted 'suspicious behaviour'.[58] The piece was probably a manual penned by the nascent security and intelligence agencies of the Islamic Republic.

Amid civil strife, daily armed confrontations in all major cities, group executions, and mass arrests, the Islamic Republic managed to hold its second presidential election on 24 July. Rajai won the election and presented Mohammad-Javad Bahonar, one of the founders of the IRP, as his new prime minister.

Masud Rajavi, the leader of the Mojahedin, and Bani-Sadr escaped from Iran on an Iranian Air Force plane commandeered by Mojahedin sympathizers. They arrived at Evreux Air Force base some 95 kilometres from Paris on 29 July 1981 to lead 'the resistance' against Khomeyni. In Iran, on 13 August, Mohsen Rezai, an old member of MIR, a member of IRGC's leadership council and the future commander-in-chief of the IRGC, announced that 70 per cent of the Mojahedin's organization had been annihilated.

Khomeyni on Incessant Explosions

These explosions prove Iran's stability. If the country was unstable, these things would not happen. (R. Khomeyni)[59]

Yet, less than three weeks later, on 30 August, a deadly explosion killed the newly elected president and his prime minister, and once again a Provisional Council of the Presidency was formed. On 6 September, another bomb exploded that killed Ali Qoddusi, the prosecutor general of the Islamic Revolution. The scale of the Mojahedin assassination campaign of state officials was unprecedented in Iranian history. With each new execution or bombing, the level of hatred and violence kept rising between the two sides.

The stamina, steadfastness and proactive response of Khomeyni in the face of political calamity assured continuity and stability amid havoc. Khomeyni did not flinch. The Majles approved Mohammad-Reza Mahdavi-Kani as prime minister on 2 September 1981. Mahdavi-Kani reinstated Bahonar's ministers, and the executive was back on track as though nothing had happened. In the meantime, Tehran was witnessing armed clashes, sometimes lasting eight hours.

The daily demonstrations and clashes of September and October resulted in large-scale arrests and executions. On average, some 40–50 were executed on a daily basis by the Revolutionary Courts. Exceptionally, on 20 September, 109 were executed, the great majority were Mojaheds. The Mojahedin had hoped to attract the masses, through their political assassinations and demonstrations. Having failed to do so, they now aimed to paralyze the state by assassinating as many high officials, Friday prayer leaders, clerics, members of the IRP, IRGC, Islamic Revolution Committees or any other revolutionary institutions and anyone whom they suspected of being a member of *Hezbollah*.

By the end of October 1981, the IRGC obtained the upper hand in the war with the Mojahedin and became apt at identifying and destroying their safe houses and arms depots. Concomitantly, the number of daily executions dropped. Yet, whenever the Mojahedin carried out a bombing or an attack, the Revolutionary Courts responded by executing large numbers.

> **The Prosecutor General of the Revolutionary Courts on the Executions**
>
> The number of executions is less than the number of assassinations and explosions and these executions will continue until these small groups stop their terrorist activities, explosions, destructions and the creation of fear. (H. Musavi-Tabrizi)[60]

Eight-Year Presidency of Seyyed Ali Khamenei

While the war raged in Khuzestan, Iranians went to the booths for a third time to elect a president. In the 2 October 1981 election, Ali Khamenei, who had replaced Bahonar as the secretary-general of the IRP, obtained 94 per cent of the votes and became Iran's third president. With Khamenei as president, Rafsanjani as the Speaker of the Majles and Musavi-Ardebili as the head of the judiciary, the clerical founders of the Islamic Republic Party continued to control all the three powers in Iran. Khomeyni had appointed Rafsanjani as his representative in the High Council of National Defence, thus placing the armed forces under clerical command. Some still remembered Khomeyni's promise that the clergy would not become involved in politics. Homogenization of the clerical ruling class gave the false semblance of political unity and harmony.

No sooner was Khamenei sworn in as president that he encountered the same problem as Bani-Sadr. His clerical garb could not stamp out ideological and personal differences. Khamenei introduced Ali-Akbar Velayati, a 36-year-old paediatrician and member of the IRP to the Majles as his prime minister. Even though the IRP held a majority in the Majles and Khamenei was the party's secretary-general, Parliament turned down Velayati. The Majles did not even warm up to Khamenei's other choices, neither the second (Mohammad Qarazi), nor the third (Ali-Akbar Parvaresh). So much for Iranian party politics.

Finally, on 29 October 1981, after a week of negotiation, the Majles gave the 40-year-old Mir-Hoseyn Musavi its vote of confidence. Musavi, an architect and sympathizer of Ali Shariati represented the left wing of the IRP, while Khamenei belonged to the right-wing of the Party. At this time, the economic future of the country and appropriate economic policies during the war divided the Left from the Right. The economic Left believed in minimizing the role of the market and increasing the presence of government through planning to produce and equitably distribute necessities, while the economic Right believed in providing an almost free hand to the market. Tension and rivalry between Khamenei and Musavi began right away and was to continue throughout their eight years of political cohabitation (1981–9).

> ### Iran's new Prime Minister on His Economic Programme
>
> The government's economic policies would be that of supporting the oppressed/disinherited . . . without deviating from Islamic jurisprudence, the Guardian Jurist and the constitution. (M.-H. Musavi)[61]

Members of Musavi's first cabinet were almost entirely from the IRP. They included economically Left-leaning members such as Behzad Nabavi and Mohammad Salamati of MIR, as well as right-wing conservative members such as Habibollah Asgarowladi, Ali-Akbar Parvaresh, and Ahmad Tavakoli. For the sensitive position of the minister of foreign affairs, Khamenei and Musavi did not meet eye to eye. Musavi, therefore, managed this ministry for six weeks until he finally conceded to Khamenei's candidate, Velayati. While on the surface, it had seemed as though Khomeyni's partisans were like-minded and in unison, the reality was quite different.

Crushing All Domestic Foes

The Islamic Republic was busy celebrating the third year of the fall of the Pahlavi dynasty when news came that on 8 February 1982, a Mojahedin safe house had been attacked, and its inhabitants killed after a four-hour gun battle. Among the 20 killed were Musa Khiyabani, the military commander of the Mojahedin, and his wife, along with Ashraf Rabei, Masud Rajavi's wife and a symbol of struggle and resistance among the Mojahedin.

Masud Rajavi's prediction that 'with the death of 60 per cent of the IRP's leaders, a Medieval regime cannot survive' was proven wrong. After the death of its high-ranking military commanders, and suffering enormous casualties, Mojahedin's urban guerrilla activities waned considerably in 1983, and petered out by 1986. In October 1987, the Mojahedin published a detailed list of 14,028 members executed by the Islamic Republic since June 1981.

> ### The Five-Month Bloodbath, June–November 1981
>
> The Mojahedin attempt to overthrow the regime in June 1981 set off waves of repression unprecedented in Iranian history. Between June and November 1981, the Revolutionary Tribunals executed 2,665 political prisoners . . The slain included 2,200 Mojaheds and 400 leftists. (E. Abrahamian)[62]

Even though the Mojahedin constituted the backbone of the June 1981 uprising, the smaller Marxist-Leninist-Maoist Organization *Sazeman peykar dar rahe tabaqeh karegar* (Combat for the Liberation of the Working Class) had preceded the Mojahedin in attacking the regime. They had begun their political-military operations on 10 April 1980. They viewed the Iran–Iraq War as a conflict between two reactionary regimes and hoped to see it morph into civil war in Iran. Combat for the Liberation of the Working Class opposed the Mojahedin, the Tudeh Party and the IRP. After the June uprising, more than 300 of its members and its entire leadership were arrested and 246 were executed.

The Majority Fadais

The fate of the two Marxist-Leninist organizations, the Tudeh Party and the Majority Fadais, who had both chosen to ally themselves with the IRP and the clerical regime, would in the end be lamentable. Both organizations had sided with the regime throughout the June uprising. Even though their offices were regularly attacked by the *Hezbollah*, they never wavered in supporting the Imam's anti-imperialist line.

As early as October 1979, the Fadai leadership had split into two factions, the Majority and the Minority. The division had occurred over a few issues: the assessment of the political and social nature of the Islamic regime, the manner of interacting with the regime, and the question of armed struggle which the Majority faction wished to put aside.

The rupture between the two factions was made public in June 1980, as the regime's intolerance towards the Left increased. The representatives of the Majority faction reached out to Beheshti and arranged a modus vivendi, which included accepting the political leadership of Khomeyni, and adopting a policy of cohabitation and later cooperation and collaboration with the regime. The Minority faction of the Fadais, on the other hand, identified the overthrow of the regime as their strategic objective in late June 1980.

During the summer 1981 uprising, the Majority faction of the Fadais sided with the regime and condemned the National Front, Bani-Sadr and the Mojahedin for opposing it. They labelled those who participated in these uprising as 'terrorists'. When Siyamak Asadiyan, one of the oldest members of the Fadais and one of the leaders of the Minority Fadais, was killed on 5 October 1981, fighting the regime, the Majority Fadais' newspaper referred to him as a member of SAVAK, a pawn of imperialism, leftist, misguided and a counter-revolutionary.[63]

For the Majority faction, the Mojahedin were allies of reactionary, feudal and capitalist circles who were betraying the revolution. The Mojahedin's 'armed demonstrations' were labelled 'political hysteria', and their leaders were accused of 'stupidity', 'treason', and 'murder'. The Majority faction warned that the Mojahedin exposed their organization to destruction and annihilation. By October 1981, the Majority faction viewed all opposition to the Islamic Republic as enemies. Even when the Islamic revolutionary courts were executing members of the Majority faction, the organization brushed it under the carpet as 'a mistake'.[64]

On 2 October 1981, even though the candidates of the Majority faction and the Tudeh Party had been barred from participating in the parliamentary mid-elections of 24 July 1981, the two organizations issued a joint statement announcing their support for Khamenei's candidacy in the third presidential election. Meetings between the leaders of the Majority faction and the Tudeh Party for an eventual unification had been in progress since summer 1981. By 4 November 1981, the merger between the two Marxist-Leninist-Khomeynist organizations was made official by a joint declaration. Quoting Imam Khomeyni's statement that 'We are at war with the US,' they promised to defend the revolution in unison with those who struggled 'in the line of Imam Khomeyni'.[65]

The Tudeh Party

After the revolution, taking its cue from the Soviet Union, the Tudeh Party saw Khomeyni and the Islamic Revolution as a bulwark against the US. From the beginning of its activities, with Nureddin Kianuri at the helm of the party, Imam Khomeyni was regarded as a progressive and tireless anti-imperialist militant and the sole worthy leader of the revolution.

Euphoric about the occupation of the American Embassy, the Tudeh Party called on all its members to unite with 'the active revolutionary forces under the command of Ayatollah Khomeyni and block all collaborationist attempts'.[66] In its admiration for Imam Khomeyni, the Tudeh Party went through the pain of proving that since 5 June 1963, it had been a 'supporter of Khomeyni's anti-imperialist and mass line'.[67] By May 1981, the Tudeh Party was said to have '30,000 members and sympathizers'[68]

The Tudeh Party's Attitude towards Khomeyni

To improve its tarnished image, the Tudeh deified Khomeini, rendering it difficult to distinguish its exaltations from those by the Imam's devotees. It unwaveringly claimed that its support for the Imam was strategic and sincere, not tactical and deceptive. (M. Milani)[69]

On 6 February 1983, having eliminated the Mojahedin and all Left opposition, the IRGC descended on Kianuri's house at 4.00 am and arrested him, his wife, his stepdaughter and his 11-year-old grandson. The arrest of the secretary-general of the party, who had fully supported the regime signaled the start of a massive round-up operation. The 'Amir al-Momenin' operation, led by the intelligence office of the

IRGC, arrested 300 cadres of the civilian and military leadership and some 1,000 members and sympathizers in Tehran and the provinces. Some 80 safehouses were seized, including arms depots, printing presses and secret archives of the party.

The suppression of the Tudeh Party was rumoured to be linked to the defection of Vladimir Kuzichkin, a Soviet diplomat and KGB major, stationed in Tehran. The information he had provided to the British was subsequently passed on to Iranian authorities, triggering the arrests. Members of the Tudeh Party were accused of espionage for the Soviet Union and conspiring against the Islamic Republic.

On 1 May 1983, Kianuri and Mahmud Etemadzadeh (Behazin) participated in a televised interview, which seemed more like a staged confession session under duress, much like the ones during the shah's rule. They confessed to espionage, treason, association with the Soviet Communist Party and plotting to overthrow the government. On 7 May 1983, the Tudeh Party was banned.

In late February 1984, ten military officers of the Tudeh Party were executed on charges of treason, espionage and plotting to overthrow the government. Admiral Bahram Afzali, commander of the Islamic Republic Navy, who had shown valour in the sinking of 11 Iraqi ships in November 1980, was among the executed. The military court did not present any hard evidence proving that the Tudeh Party members had been plotting to overthrow the government, nor that they posed a threat to state security.

The Tudeh Party had always been Iran's most organized and well-disciplined political formation. The confessions and recantations of its leadership, albeit forced, and the political conversion of many of its members in prison, represented a major moral and ideological defeat for the Party. The Tudeh Party collapsed without a whimper or a volley, and the Islamic Republic spared its political leadership. Kianuri was released from prison in 1996 and passed away on 6 August 1998.

The unfortunate fate of Qotbzadeh and Shariatmadari

On 7 November 1980, in a taped televised debate, Sadeq Qotbzadeh, the former member of the Revolutionary Council, former foreign minister and former head of the Islamic Republic's television, criticized the Student Followers of the Imam's Line for being pro-Russians and lefties and characterized the National Television as a den of fascists propagating lies and libel. Qotbzadeh also criticized the executions and the expropriations conducted by the revolutionary courts. Most importantly, Qotbzadeh attacked the IRP, calling it the filthiest party in Iran. On the next day, Tehran's Prosecutor, Asadollah Lajevardi, ordered his arrest for divisive and disruptive statements at a time of war. Qotbzadeh was released on bail three days after his arrest, allegedly on Khomeyni's orders.

Qotbzadeh was one of Khomeyni's three key advisers during his exile. He was always well-dressed, and contrary to Bani-Sadr and Yazdi, often wore a suit and tie.

Qotbzadeh was bold, outspoken, a lone maverick and a loose cannon. His arrest indicated that the clerical leadership would no longer tolerate his open and biting criticism of state affairs. Qotbzadeh was an active member of the ruling circle and subsequently sidelined by the clergy. He was said to be against the Iran–Iraq War, believing that it was avoidable.

On 6 April 1982, Qotbzadeh and a few others were arrested on charges of conspiring a coup plot to overthrow the Islamic Republic and attempt to exterminate Khomeyni. The accusations against Qotbzadeh were deadly, yet there was no evidence that he had colluded with the foreign powers, created a military network, or intended to blow up Khomeyni's residence with '500 kilos of TNT' and then 'bombard it'.[70] The Islamic Republic was replicating SAVAK's system of framing the opposition.

Two weeks after Qotbzadeh's arrest, Ayatollah Shariatmadari was also implicated in Qotbzadeh's coup plot. He was said to have known about it and had promised to lend his support once it had succeeded. In an unprecedented move, unheard of in Shii practice, the teachers at Qom Seminary School ruled that Shariatmadari was no longer apt to be a Source of Imitation and informed his followers to cease acting according to his religious directives. This new twist demonstrated that the regime still worried about Shariatmadari's influence in Azarbayjan and considered him a viable religious rival and alternative to Khomeyni. Also worried about Qotbzadeh being a loose cannon, the regime had decided to frame the two.

Discrediting and dishonouring Shariatmadari sent a historical signal to other discontented Sources of Imitation, such as Ayatollahs Mohammad-Sadeq Rowhani, Mohammad Hoseyni-Shirazi, and Hasan Tabatabai-Qomi. The intervention of the Qom Seminary School as a supervisory political institution judging the credibility of the Sources of Imitation indicated the end of the clerical institution's long-cherished independence. Shii religious authorities were now obliged to toe the line of a single person, not out of respect, but out of fear.

An Insider's View of the Qotbzadeh Affair

The account of pouring explosives in a well close to the Imam's house is a complete fabrication and was only for the purpose of framing Shariatmadari. (H.-A. Montazeri)[71]

On 14 August 1982, Qotbzadeh and four of his supposed accomplices were put on trial at a military tribunal headed by Hojatoleslam Mohammad Mohammadi-Reyshahri. On 15 September 1982, Qotbzadeh faced the firing squad, while others were given prison terms. It must be noted that Mohammadi-Reyshahri had a prior history with Shariatmadari and his supporters. In the January 1980 uprising in Tabriz, he had sent fifteen supporters of Shariatmadari to the gallows. After Qotbzadeh's trial,

Shariatmadari was placed under house arrest, his seminary school was confiscated and his son-in-law imprisoned.

Settling scores with Bazargan and the Hojatiyyeh Society

The Qotbzadeh Affair provided a golden opportunity for the ruling clerics to settle scores with various independent notables such as Bazargan, Yazdi, and members of the Iran Freedom Movement in the Majles. In a fiery parliamentary speech, Khalkhali referred to Qotbzadeh's plot, and added that Bazargan, Yazdi and Kazem Sami, Bazargan's former minister of health, were even worse than Qotbzadeh, and people needed to deal with them. From September 1982, Bazargan, his friends and the Iran Freedom Movement were subjected to a widespread defamation campaign. Their houses were firebombed, their friends threatened and wherever they went, there was always an organized group on hand to insult, jeer and heckle them.

The 1st Majles of the Islamic Republic, which included deputies of the Iran Freedom Movement such as Bazargan and Yadollah Sahabi ended on 28 May 1984. From that date on, Bazargan and his friends were barred from competing for office. When Bazargan tried to run for the fourth presidential election on 16 August 1985, his candidacy was rejected by the Guardian Council, which permitted only three candidates to run, Habibollah Asgarowladi, Mahmud Kashani, and Ali Khamenei. The Islamic Republic was not only purging old associates of Khomeyni such as Qotbzadeh and Bazargan or leading Sources of Imitation such as Shariatmadari, but it was tightening its grips over all possible contending Islamic forces.

Anjoman hojatiyyeh mahdaviyyeh or the Anti-Bahai Society was established in 1953 by Ayatollah Mahmud Zakerzadeh-Tavalai, better known as Sheykh Halabi. The Society focused on the importance of the Twelfth Imam, Mahdi (the Hidden Imam) and directed its activities against members of the Bahai faith. During the shah's regime, the Anti-Bahai Society was given free rein since it provided a safe outlet for religious radicalism that could otherwise become subversive. It gradually attracted numerous followers and even became popular among the youth.

The Society was anti-Communist, preferring an Islamic monarchy to atheist communist rule. Most importantly, the Society believed that establishing a just Islamic society was only possible after the reappearance of the Twelfth Imam. Until the coming of the Mahdi, it kept strictly away from politics and only prepared the conditions for the reappearance of the Hidden Imam while combatting Bahais.

The Islamic Revolution and its victory placed the Society, which had many influential members in the rising political, military and clerical elite, in an awkward position. The Society had a low opinion of Khomeyni and the rule of the Guardian Jurist, which they viewed as a usurpation of the Hidden Imam's position. Only the infallible Hidden Imam could rule in a just manner. After the revolution, the Society focused on anti-communist and anti-Left activities, without addressing its theoretical and religious differences with Khomeyni and the rule of the Guardian Jurist.

On the Iran–Iraq War, the Society took a consistent position, and Halabi argued that only an infallible individual had the authority and credentials to proclaim war against another Islamic country. On 1 November 1981, Ahmad Jannati, a member of the Guardian Council who had been appointed by Khomeyni, pressed the Society to clarify its position on the rule of the Guardian Jurist, or the absolute authority of Khomeyni. Unbeknown to the public at the time, but probably known to Jannati, Abolqasem Khazali, another clerical member of the Guardian Council, who was also an appointee of Khomeyni, was a member and an outspoken supporter of the Society. The issue of the Society's infiltration in high government offices, and their questionable allegiance to Khomeyni, was reflected in the press.

The Tudeh Party was instrumental in villainizing and attacking the Hojatiyyeh Society as a powerful mysterious, and reactionary clerical force, opposed to the 'progressive' IRP leadership. On 27 December 1981, President Khamenei came to the Society's help and accused its detractors of creating a 'false crisis'. Khamenei's favourite candidate for the post of prime minister, Ali-Akbar Velayati, was said to be a member of the Hojatiyyeh Society.

Aware of their religious proclivities and opposition to the rule of the Guardian Jurist, Khomeyni did not trust them. After Khomeyni took power, Halabi offered to put his approximately 15,000 specialist and educated professional cadres at his disposal to run the country. Khomeyni refused the offer. Yet, members of the Society succeeded in penetrating sensitive government and even military positions.

Fearful of divisions within his own clerical ranks over the Hojatiyyeh Society, and faced with its growing opposition, on 13 July 1983, Khomeyni fiercely attacked the Society. He did not mention it by name, but it was obvious who he was reproaching. Ten days after Khomeyni's rebuke, the Society issued a statement, acknowledging that Khomeyni had been referring to them. The Society announced that it would discontinue its activities. And even though the Society did cease its public activities, it actually only went under the radar. Khomeyni's clamp down on the Hojatiyyeh Society had intended to keep his ruling class out of theoretical Islamic debates and confrontations. Factionalism, however, had become endemic to the Islamic Republic.

The Islamic Republic Party Implodes

On 10 May 1983, four years after entering the political scene, the Islamic Republic Party (IRP) convened its first Congress. By this time, with Khomeyni's support, the IRP had successfully eliminated all clerical and non-clerical political rivals. Everyone in the political structure of the Islamic Republic claimed to follow the Imam's Line, his vision and interpretation of Islam.

The IRP had Khomeyni's ear and its members ran the country according to his command. Ali Khamenei, an IRP founder and the party's secretary-general, was Iran's president and Prime Minister Mir-Hoseyn Musavi was one of the IRP's initial members. Abdolkarim Musavi-Ardebili, another architect of the IRP, was Khomeyni's appointee as the head of the judiciary, and Rafsanjani, a founding member of the party, was the speaker of Iran's first Islamic Parliament. Nevertheless, on the fifth anniversary of the revolution, in February 1984, Khomeyni underlined the three critical problems facing the Islamic Republic, the war with Iraq, a deepening economic crisis and nagging factional disputes among the clerical leadership.

Khomeyni was aware of the deep schisms over economic policy pitting Khamenei against Prime Minister Musavi. On the one side stood pro-bazaar free-marketers and laissez-faire protagonists, led by Habibollah Asgarowladi, minister of commerce, Ahmad Tavakoli, minister of labour, and Ali-Akbar Nateq-Nuri, minister of interior. They enjoyed Khamenei's support and stood against the growing role of government in economic activities. They approved of a stern and invasive Islamic government in the political and cultural domains but not in the economic sphere.

On the opposing side stood the Left-leaning interventionists or statists, led by Behzad Nabavi (minister of industry), Mohammad Khatami (minister of culture) and Mohammad Salamati (minister of agriculture), who supported greater government control of the economy. The interventionists, supported by Musavi, believed that equitable distribution of basic needs during the war was best attained by rationing, controlled markets, price-fixing and a greater intervention of the government. For Khomeyni, who had always minimized the role of economics in the revolution, it must have been painful to see his lieutenants fighting over material economic policies.

The Ministry of Commerce

When Asgar-Owladi was appointed minister of commerce, the merchants virtually monopolized the ministry and related offices. The Ministry of Commerce granted the merchants a monopoly over the distribution of imported and local goods, which they often sold at high prices in the free market. (M. Moaddel)[72]

In a country fully committed to complying with Islamic jurisprudence, the choice of appropriate policies in all conceivable domains, including economics, had to be grounded in Islamic jurisprudence. The problems of the Islamic Republic proved to be unresolvable once the new political elite realized that Islamic jurisprudence was not a fixed and singular canon. Their compass could have different norths and souths. The laws of the land, including economic ones, had to be drawn from the primary sources, the Quran and the four principal Shii books of reports.

These primary ordnances in economic matters included the right to private property, prohibition of usury and the obligation to pay the two types of Islamic taxes, **zakat** and **khums**. Those jurists who believed in the use of primary ordinances in determining the direction of the state and economy were the proponents of traditional jurisprudence and supporters of a market-dominated economy. To the traditionalists, the statists, who rejected free trade and the market mechanisms as economic regulators, were communists.

But Islamic jurisprudence also allowed the possibility of relying on secondary ordinances for deriving Islamic laws. Secondary edicts could trump the primary ones to attain a higher social order of priority. Pressing needs, the satisfaction of social welfare and exigencies justified the use of secondary ordinances. The jurists allowing the application of flexible and ad hoc secondary edicts were proponents of dynamic jurisprudence. Khomeyni's revolutionary expropriation order was a case of invoking secondary edicts, to which the traditional clergy objected. The Left-leaning proponents of a statist economy argued that during exceptional conditions, be it war, the public's convenience, or reason of state, the use of secondary ordinances could be called to prevail.

The End of the Islamic Republic Party

In the beginning, the mission of the party was to combat those opposed to Islamization of the country. Gradually as the opposition faded away, so did IRP's mission. (A.-A. Hashemi-Rafsanjani)[73]

Khomeyni tried in vain to use his influence to reconcile the differences between the economic Left and Right factions of the Imam's Line. It took some three years for these fundamental differences to boil over into uncontrollable enmity leading to the closure of the Islamic Republic Party. Islamization had been successful, but the struggle over which kind of political Islam was to become the dominant paradigm, determining policy, was about to begin.

Khamenei was the unsurprising winner of the fourth presidential election on 16 August 1985. After his re-election, Khamenei informed Khomeyni that he did not consider Musavi a suitable prime minister and tried to replace him with Velayati. Khomeyni insisted on Musavi and went as far as saying that appointing anyone other than him would be 'treason to Islam'. Khamenei appeared to comply, though reluctantly. Yet, even though, formally, it was the job of the Majles to approve the prime minister proposed by the president.

The second Islamic Majles elected on 15 April 1984 was entirely composed of IRP members and their allies, the Association of Militant Clergy. Yet, the Majles debates reflected deep disagreements and resentments among deputies. On 27 September 1985, in a letter to the Majles, Khomeyni publicly supported Musavi's premiership. On 13 October 1985, in a secret ballot at the Majles, 73 deputies voted against Musavi's Premiership, 26 abstained and 162 voted in favour.

At the beginning of this sensitive Majles session, the partisans of each side insulted one another. Despite Khomeyni's clear directive, 99 deputies refused to follow him and made a valiant stand against both Khomeyni and the radicals. They were however defeated. After almost six years, Khomeyni had lost his invincible and infallible aura among his own devout followers. For a second term, Khamenei remained a powerless and bitter president. In Musavi's new cabinet, the prominent conservative figures, vocal in the previous government, were absent.

On 1 June 1987, four years after its first Congress, Rafsanjani and Khamenei requested that Khomeyni dissolve the IRP and the Imam responded positively. At first, they had suggested that since the Islamic Republic had consolidated its power, neutralized counter-revolutionary plots and belligerent foreign powers were kept at bay, the party had completed its task and was no longer necessary. Eventually, Rafsanjani and Khamenei presented the real reason for their demand. The IRP had become an arena for 'division/dissent and schism/bipartisanship', and its members were clashing with one another and wasting their energies. Khomeyni responded positively. The Imam feared that polarization among his functionaries would destabilize the regime and further diminish his religio-political authority.

During its eight years of activities, the IRP played a determining role in the political transition of post-revolutionary Iran. IRP's governing track displayed ineptitude and disarray in managing society and setting it on a long-term path. Even though the constituent parts of a political system were put in place, key decisions were made by Khomeyni's ad hoc and arbitrary will.

The Imam vacillated, sometimes clamping on dissent among his followers and sometimes promoting it. The despotic element in Khomeyni's Islamic political project prevented a clear-cut perspective of what the future of Iran should look like, other than it should be Islamic. After Khomeyni's death, irreconcilable differences between Left and Right factions spread to other domains besides economics. The two sides continued their battles over domestic, foreign, cultural and social policy.

The End of MIR

The fate of the Mojahedin of the Islamic Revolution was no different from that of the IRP. MIR and the IRP fought side by side to purify and consolidate the Imam's Line, and both ended up with irreconcilable ideological differences that brought about their demise. A month after MIR's birth, members discovered that despite being zealot believers in Khomeyni's leadership, and their combat against the shah's regime, their world views had little in common. Topics such as the appropriateness of issuing a supportive proclamation on the occasion of the First of May (the International Workers' Day) or mourning Shariat's death became divisive issues.

As long as MIR was battling external enemies such as the Mojahedin, the Left, Bazargan, or later Bani-Sadr, it maintained a tenuous unity. Under the clerical and conservative leadership of Hoseyn Rasti-Kashani, disagreements were initially glossed over. The Left faction of MIR was never happy with Rasti-Kashani's conservative leadership, while its Right faction welcomed it. Once all opposition forces were crushed and members of MIR found themselves in leadership positions, it imploded.

By January 1983, 37 members of MIR's left wing, including Behzad Nabavi, Mohsen Armin, Mohammad Salamati, Morteza Alviri and Mostafa Tajzadeh, left the organization. Many of them joined Musavi's government and formed its backbone. Amongst the remaining right-wing, members such as Mohsen Rezai, Mohammad-Baqer Zolqadr and Ali Shamkhani, joined the IRGC and attained the summits of military command.

For the next three years, the MIR existed on paper, but it had been gutted and become purposeless. On 29 September 1986, Rasti-Kashani requested and obtained Khomeyni's approval to dissolve the Organization. In his letter to Khomeyni, Rasti-Kashani mentioned that he had eliminated the threat posed by the 'deviants' in the Organization. Behzad Nabavi objected to Rasti-Kashani's implication that the left wing was a deviant force, and Khomeyni issued a declaration insisting that he had only agreed to the dissolution of the Organization and did not concur with Rasti-Kashani's insinuations.

From a Defensive to an Offensive War

After an eight-month lull in the war with Iraq, Iran launched a counteroffensive, involving some 30,000 warriors. Between March 1981 and November 1981, Iraq had occupied approximately 14,000 square kilometres of Iranian territory. Iraqi forces, however, proved incapable of expanding their territorial gains. On 29 November 1981, Iran launched a military operation, named Path to Jerusalem, and regained the town of Bostan in Khuzestan, as well as some 350 square kilometres of its territory, and most significantly opened the road to retaking Khorramshahr. In this operation, mainly involving the IRGC and the *Basij* or volunteers' corps, *Basiji* soldiers were used as human waves for the first time (Figure 8.9). In an eight-day battle, the Iranian victory came at high human costs. Approximately 6,000 Iranians were killed compared to some 2,500 Iraqis.

From November 1981, in a concerted effort, the Friday Prayer leaders and the IRGC called on Iran's youth to go to the fronts and join the volunteer forces to defeat Saddam. The notion of martyrdom as the highest honour and worthiest possible distinction in the eyes of God, was steadily and forcefully cultivated and disseminated. The defence of the motherland was put on par with defending the Quran, and

Figure 8.9 Basiji Forces. *Source: Wikimedia Commons.*

Khomeyni praised the status of going to the fronts by claiming, 'I wish, I, too, was a Revolutionary Guard.'

> ## IRGC's Call to the Fronts
>
> The Iran–Iraq War is a war of Islam and disbelief (*kofr*), and Islam and anti-Islam. Our honor and prestige are contingent on such wars . . . We invite the martyr-cultivating Iranian community (*ummat*) to help Iranian warriors by flocking to the fronts, as they had done in the past.[74]

On 24 May 1982, Khorramshahr, now dubbed Khuninshahr (the bloodied city) was retaken by the Iranian army and the IRGC. Though signs of disagreement and tension between the army and the IRGC began to emerge, this battle was in retrospect a critical turning point in the war. The Iraqis left behind some 16,000 wounded and dead and some 19,000 prisoners. Iran's heavy casualties were put at 30,000 wounded and killed.

The importance of this Iranian victory led to the intercession of Saddam's Persian Gulf allies. The Gulf Cooperation Council offered Iran $25 billion in war reparations in exchange for a peace treaty. On 20 June 1982, Saddam Hoseyn sued for peace, announcing a cease-fire and promising to withdraw within ten days all Iraqi forces from Iran to the international borders. All the conditions were at hand to end the war.

Khomeyni did not want to occupy Iraqi territory. The IRGC commander, Mohsen Rezai and the army commander Qasem-Ali Zahirnejad convinced him that entering Iraq was of strategic importance as a bargaining chip in negotiating for peace. Domestically, the war faced opposition from Bazargan's Iran Freedom Movement and even Hoseyn-Ali Montazeri, Khomeyni's heir. But the military had regained its self-confidence and claimed that they could easily defeat, punish, and even overthrow Saddam. Khomeyni conceded. Once Iran entered Iraqi territory, Khomeyni rallied for victory, the capture of Basra and the overthrow of Saddam.

On 13 July 1982, Operation Ramazan marked a new phase in the war. Just as Saddam had falsely believed that by entering Khuzestan, its Arab inhabitants would welcome his troops with open arms, Khomeyni now invited Iraqis to rise against Saddam. Some 150,000 Iranian forces, composed of 100,000 IRGC and voluntary *Basiji*s, hurriedly crossed into Iraq towards Basra.

After initial successes and having penetrated 15 kilometres into Iraqi territory, the 17-day operation turned into a disaster. The ill-conceived, and rushed operation used untrained human-wave assaults by the *Basij* forces, resulting in some 20,000 dead and wounded, while the Iraqi losses were some 8,000 dead and wounded. The net gain of the operation was of only 50 square kilometres of Iraqi territory.

On 31 December 1983, Rafsanjani said, 'in order to win this war we have to continue our mobilization effort and depend on our self-sacrificing volunteers'.[75] From 15 January to 15 February 1984, the Iranian press reported on the dispatch of thousands of fresh volunteers to the fronts. 'To conquer Karbala, onwards to the fronts' became the battle cry of the volunteers.

Saddam now wished to bring Iran to the peace negotiation table as soon as possible. In pursuit of this objective, he engaged in new military operations. On 7 February 1984, Iraq launched the 'war of the cities', using its air force and missiles to attack major Iranian cities. The attacks, causing havoc on civilians, lasted until February 1988. Initially, the bombing of cities did not demoralize Iranians, its persistence, however, weighed.

To place greater pressure on Iran, Saddam ordered the 'tanker war' in March 1984, to hinder oil export, and the importation of arms. Saddam intended to internationalize the war in the Persian Gulf, thereby forcing Iran to the peace table. In tandem with the 'war of the cities', the attack on oil tankers, merchant ships as well as war ships lasted four years. The use of French Super-Etendard combat aircrafts and Exocet anti-ship missiles facilitated Iraq's 'tanker war'.

From February 1984, Saddam began using mustard gas to stop Iranian advances during the Kheybar Operation. A month later, Iraq also used tabun, a nerve gas. From October 1987, Iraq relied on a variety of nerve gases. On 16 March 1988, Iraq dropped chemical bombs on its own village of Halabja, in Kurdistan, which was under Iranian occupation. This unprecedented four-hour massacre of civilians employed mustard and other nerve gases, slaughtering 3,500 to 5,000 and injuring between 7,000 and 10,000. Iraq's sustained chemical attacks incurred 'more than 50,000 casualties' on Iran.[76]

Chemical Weapons

During 1983, Iraq began to use chemical agents with some regularity against Iranian troops. It is generally accepted that Iraq's first major employment of chemical agents occurred in July or August 1983 during the Val Fajr II campaign near Haj Umra. (J. Ali)[77]

But Iran had its eyes on Basra and its capture became the military's Achilles heel. Operations, Al-Fajr I, V, VI, VIII (March 1983, February 1984, February 1986), Kheybar (February 1984), Badr (March 1985), and Karbala IV and V (December 1986), all failed at a considerable human cost. Karbala IV was to prepare the grounds for the capture of Basra, but it was compromised before it started and aborted two days after its launch. Karbala V became the costliest Iranian operation, both in manpower and weapons. Iran inched towards Basra but was unable to consolidate and maintain its gains.

During the March 1984 Kheybar Operation, Iran captured the strategic Majnoon Islands, 80 kilometres north of Basra. During this 20-day battle, Iraq employed widescale chemical weapons, resulting in 30,000 wounded and dead Iranians, and 15,000 Iraqis. During this Operation, IRGC lost two of its most competent field commanders, Mohammad-Ebrahim Hemmat and Hamid Bakeri. Almost a year later, in February 1985, the Al-Fajr VI offensive stopped at 24 kilometres of the Basra–Baghdad main road. A month later, during the Badr Operation, Iranian troops cut off the Basra–Baghdad Road for the first time but were pushed back by Iraqi forces.

On 17 September 1985, Khomeyni permitted the IRGC to expand its branches and constitute its own navy and air forces. The news caused considerable joy and excitement among IRGC's commanders who interpreted their new responsibilities as a sign that Khomeyni approved of their military operations. After this date, the Islamic Republic possessed two parallel armed forces, one traditional, a remnant of the Pahlavi regime, and another religio-revolutionary army, favoured by the regime.

In February 1986, Iran launched its two-pronged Al-Fajr VIII operation. This well-prepared surprise amphibious attack by the IRGC involved some 150,000 to 200,000 men. Iran's highly successful offensive led to the capture of Faw Peninsula, 20 kilometres south-east of Basra. Iraq was caught off guard and lost two principal oil terminals, seriously hampering its oil exports. In the aftermath of the Faw victory, a state of euphoria reigned among Iranian leaders. Rafsanjani announced that 'real peace was unattainable without eliminating the Baath Party'. Khomeyni declared that 'rest assured that you are the victors'.[78]

Call for Recruits

Today, filling the fronts with trained soldiers and preparing for the defense of Islam and Iran is the most important of all divine obligations for all social strata. (R. Khomeyni)[79]

During the war, Iran relied heavily on the religious and revolutionary fervor of its selfless *Basiji* volunteers, who countered Iraqi arms superiority with their human-wave assaults. By early 1987, however, Iran faced a dangerous crisis mobilizing volunteers for the fronts. Seven years of war, sanctions, inability to purchase sufficient arms and spare parts, foreign exchange crunch, and economic hardship were taking their toll.

To end its international isolation and as a sign of appeasement towards the Persian Gulf supporters of Iraq, in October 1984, the Iranian government had announced abandoning its initial claim of exporting its revolution. Between the beginning of the war and the capture of Faw by Iran (February 1986), Iraq had received some $40 billion in financial aid from the Persian Gulf states (GCC). Iraq also received sophisticated arms exports from the USSR, China, the US, and France, while Iran's primary arms suppliers were China, North Korea and the USSR. The Iraqi air force outnumbered Iranian combat aircrafts by 7 to 1 and tanks by 4 to 1.

By 1988, the Iranian military faced a dwindling number of volunteers. The targets set by the IRGC in terms of recruitment were falling seriously short. War weariness and frustration in the absence of tangible military gains were taking hold. Khomeyni's exhortations to the youth 'to fill the war fronts' were no longer falling on receptive ears. In January 1988, as draft-dodging increased, the government extended conscription from 24 to 28 months. The increase in deployment of soldiers between 12 and 16 demonstrated that recruitment was becoming a real problem.

On 15 April 1988, Rafsanjani announced that the war had reached a most critical point and called on the youth to 'rush to the fronts'. Within two days, Iraqi forces outnumbering Iranian *Basij* soldiers 6.5 to 1, used sarin nerve gas with heavy bombardments, and retook Faw. The loss of Faw, which had been Iran's most important prize since it entered Iraqi territory, marked the beginning of a series of defeats for Iran.

Khomeyni's Last Two Years: Haughtiness, Desperation and Anger

On 20 July 1987, the UN Security Council issued Resolution 598, calling for a ceasefire and negotiations between Iran and Iraq to reach a peace agreement. Iraq accepted the resolution, and Iran procrastinated. Ten days later, at Khomeyni's behest, Iranian pilgrims to the *Haj* turned the religious ritual into a political rally, calling for unity among Muslims and chanting 'Death to America, and Death to Israel'. Weeks before the incident, Saudi officials had warned against political agitation at the *Haj*.

Iranians had planned to take over the Great Mosque (*Masjed al-Haram*) at Mecca and chant 'Death to America!' over its loudspeakers. The scheme was a reactive game of desperation. The Saudi military confronted the crowd, and the Iranian demonstrators assaulted them. Saudi forces opened fire, killing 402 and injuring 629.

The Absolute Rule of the Guardian Jurist: A New Landmark in Iranian Despotism

In 1987 the war was raging with increasing casualties, cities were under intense Iraqi attacks, the religio-revolutionary fervor of fighting was ebbing, and the fall of Basra seemed less and less realistic. Meanwhile, Iran's new ruling class did not cease bickering among themselves. Musavi's government and the Majles clashed with the Guardian Council and President Khamenei over how to best manage a war economy. Eight years of incessant infighting, on top of the Iran–Iraq War, had worn out the country. Unresolved key issues had accumulated, the economy stagnated and articulating long-term national plans and policies stalled. After eight years, the revolution did not have much to show for, except forced Islamization, hardship, war and death.

In 1986 and 1987, despite rationing coupons, the price of necessities increased, and shortages of many commodities intensified. Efforts by Musavi's government to curtail speculation and hoarding and control prices were frustrated by the conservative Guardian Council's strict interpretation of religious laws. Khomeyni had to intervene on Musavi's behalf to push through laws supporting consumers and against hoarders, speculators and those charging exorbitant prices.

Clashes came to a head over a bill on labor laws presented by Musavi, approved by the Majles, and rejected as un-Islamic by the Guardian Council. The bill hoped to regulate the labor market by imposing standards on employers. It compelled employers to provide insurance for workers, observe a minimum working age and set a ceiling on maximum working hours. The Guardian Council ruled that contracts between employers and employees were a voluntary agreement between individuals, and the government had no right to impose conditions on either side.

On 28 November 1987, Abolqasem Sarhadizadeh, minister of labour, wrote a letter to Khomeyni, inquiring whether the government could impose conditions on firms and employees. Khomeyni confirmed the government's right to impose conditions, thereby overturning the Guardian Council. He abrogated the Constitution and overruled the verdict of the legal supervisors of Islamicness in the land. Musavi rejoiced at having circumvented the Guardian Council to secure certain minimum rights for employees.

On 11 December 1987, in a surprising move, Khamenei reacted to Khomeyni, undermining the authority of the Guardian Council. In his Friday Prayer sermon, he defended the Constitution, pointed out that its purpose was to 'avoid the concentration of power at one point', and prodded the Guardian Council to do its job.

On 1 January 1988, Khamenei threw himself into a religio-legal debate. He interpreted Khomeyni's ruling on the government's right to enforce labour laws and suggested that the Imam's ruling was limited to 'conditions permissible within acceptable Islamic ordinances and not beyond them'. It remains a mystery why Khamenei thought he could hem in the Imam.

On 6 January 1988, Khomeyni issued a fatwa-like statement, sharply chiding Khamenei for misunderstanding his ideas. In this historical statement, Khomeyni introduced the novel concept of the 'absolute rule of the Guardian Jurist'. He confirmed that statesmanship/government or absolute rule was a position conferred to the Prophet by God and was a primary ordinance that trumped all secondary edicts such as prayers, fasting, and pilgrimage (*Haj*). Khomeyni concluded that if the government deemed it necessary, it could suspend pilgrimage, a paramount religious obligation.

Overnight, Khomeyni had claimed that he stood above the Constitution, and most importantly, above Islamic principles specified in the Quran. He declared that he had the religio-political right to abrogate Islamic edicts for the reason of state. Khomeyni was now arrogating the powers of the Prophet and more. The absolute rule of the Guardian Jurist, as claimed by Khomeyni and immediately accepted by all, combining unlimited religious and political power in the hands of one person, was unprecedented in Iran's modern history. The country was entering a level of despotism far more advanced than that during the Pahlavis.

On the Absolute Rule of the Guardian Jurist

The claim that since government is one of the primary principles of Islam and therefore the ruler can, according to his personal judgement, dispense with religious edicts is incorrect and opposed to the Quran and the tradition of the Prophet . . . From a socio-political view the absolute rule of the Guardian Jurist is nothing but arbitrariness/tyranny or religious and governmental despotism leading to the annihilation of freedom, identity, and independence. (Iran Freedom Movement)[80]

Instead of restoring the weakened position and authority of the Guardian Council and making amends with its conservative clerical members, Khomeyni further reduced their power by adding a new institution to the complex governmental structure of the Islamic Republic. On 6 February 1988, Khomeyni issued an edict that an 'Expediency Discernment Council of the System' (*Majma tashkhis maslahate nezam*) be established to resolve the differences and conflicts between the Guardian Council and the Majles. This new mediating body would be entirely nominated by Khomeyni.

Religion against Religion: Mohammaden vs American Islam

The conflicts and divisions long tucked under the semblance of unity surfaced rapidly. On 20 March 1988, the younger and more radical members of the Association of

Militant Clergy seceded. The Association of Militant Clergy, composed of fervent followers of Khomeyni were instrumental in mobilizing the clergy before the revolution, and symbolized the unity of the clerical institution. Now, with Khomeyni's permission, a group of prominent radical clerics, led by Mehdi Karrubi and Musavi-Khoeiyniha, split from the mother organization and established the Assembly of Militant Clerics (*majma rowhaniyoun mobarez*).

This new rival organization made the already apparent splits in the IRP and MIR over economic and social policies, official. The radical/Left was establishing its own clerical organization distinct from the conservative/Right. The Assembly of Militant Clerics supported the Musavi government. It promoted anti-Americanism in foreign policy and egalitarianism and anti-capitalism in economic policies.

The split was in preparation for the third parliamentary elections in May 1988. Neither Khamenei nor Rafsanjani joined the new clerical organization. On 31 March 1988, eleven days after the Assembly of Militant Clerics was born, Khomeyni, the absolute Guardian Jurist, threw his weight behind the new organization and took sides in the ongoing factional rivalries.

In a message on the upcoming parliamentary elections, Khomeyni asked the people to elect candidates who were defenders of 'the poor' and 'the Islam of the oppressed/disinherited', whom he equated with 'the defenders of pure Mohammaden Islam'. Khomeyni warned against electing those who were supporters of 'an American Islam', namely the supporters of 'capitalist Islam', the 'Islam of the arrogant and the well-to-do' and 'the Islam of the opportunists.'[81]

The third Majles, dominated by the radical wing of the Imam's Line, began deliberating on 28 May 1988. The Assembly of Militant Clerics and their allies had a resounding majority with 170 deputies, while the conservatives, led by the Association of Militant Clergy mustered only 100 deputies. Having obtained the victory of his preferred faction, Khomeyni called on the two blocs to set aside their difference and unite, as if nothing had happened.

Between the first round of Majles elections (8 April 1988), and the second round (13 May 1988), the devastating news of the defeat at Faw on 17 April 1988, shook the regime. After six years of fighting on Iraqi soil, Iran had lost its only main gain and was left with naught for all its hardship. The hope of ever reaching and taking Basra was dissipating. After Iran's military setbacks, a general mood of frustration and gloom descended upon the leadership.

Ending the War: Khomeyni Drinks the Poisoned Chalice

On 3 July 1988, the USS *Vincennes*, cruising in Iranian waters, launched two surface-to-air missiles at Iran Air Flight 655. The commercial flight travelling from Bandar

Abbas to Dubai with 290 onboard crashed at 10:45 leaving no survivors. The US eventually claimed that the ship had mistaken the commercial Airbus A 300 for an Iranian F-14 fighter. The case appeared before the International Court of Justice, and the US expressed deep regrets and agreed to pay $61.8 million to the victims' families.

The murder of civilians by the US military came when Iran's leaders were most vulnerable due to their misfortunes in the war. Even though Iranian authorities threatened the US with revenge for its 'murderous', 'criminal' and 'terrorist' attack, their thunderous warnings remained in words only. On 4 July, Khomeyni issued a bellicose message ordering Iranians to go to the fronts and prepare for an all-out war against the US and its allies. Khomeyni wrote, 'hesitation in whatever form is an act of treason towards Islam, and negligence towards problems of the war is treason towards the Prophet of God'.[82] Events were to show that behind Khomeyni's firm assertions lurked major doubts that the shooting of the Iran Air flight might be the prologue of a massive international attack against Iran.

Two weeks after Khomeyni's threatening assertions, on 18 July 1988, Rafsanjani announced that Iran has agreed to comply with Resolution 598, calling for a ceasefire with Iraq and a withdrawal of troops to international borders. In a historical message on 20 July, Khomeyni presented a paradoxical and conflicted stance, at once belligerent and aggressive, and desperate and vanquished.

Khomeyni expressed hope that soon the slogan 'death to the US and the USSR' would be heard not only in the Muslims' Kaaba but also in Christian churches. Khomeyni called the acceptance of Resolution 598 'a truly bitter and unpleasant event' for himself, yet he asserted that it was 'to the benefit of the revolution and the system'. By emphasizing that for him, accepting the Resolution was 'more deadly than poison', he was passing on the message that he was selflessly acting for the good of the country.[83]

Eight years of war ended at last because Khomeyni willed it. The Imam was not apologetic, but rather sad and angry that he had to end the conflict without having attained any of the objectives he and his leadership team had promised. The war had cost Iran approximately $330 to $445 billion and had left between 218,000 to 750,000 dead and some 574,000 to 670,000 disabled. One to two million were displaced, jobless and homeless. Khorramshahr, Abadan, and Iran's port and oil facilities were in ruin. Cities, towns and villages in the five provinces at the centre of the conflicts were levelled, gutted and in need of reconstruction.

The Mojahedin Attack: 'Operation Eternal Light'

Less than a week after the ceasefire, on 25 July 1988, the Mojahedin's National Liberation of Iran Army entered Iran from Iraq. Since his departure from Iran in July

1981, Masud Rajavi, the leader of the Mojahedin, had resided in Paris and formed the National Council of Resistance in Iran (NCRI) with Bani-Sadr. The organization included distinguished figures from the opposition and combative political organizations such as the Kurdish Democratic Party of Iran.

The NCRI initially seemed like a viable and democratic alternative to the Islamic Republic, yet it quickly succumbed to Masud Rajavi's growing authoritarian and anti-democratic predispositions. From June 1983, the influential members of NCRI, including Bani-Sadr, left the organization. Rajavi's secret meeting with Tariq Aziz, Iraq's powerful deputy prime minister in December 1982, and the signing of an agreement with him, irked most non-Mojahed forces gathered in the NCRI.

On 10 March 1985, the Mojahedin's Central Committee announced that Mariam Azodanlou-Qajar was promoted to the leadership position and would be co-responsible and co-leader of the Organization, on par with Rajavi. This 'Ideological Revolution', which was more of a political women's liberation revolution among old Muslim revolutionaries, culminated in Azodanlou-Qajar divorcing her husband, the number two of the Organization, and asking Rajavi, the number one, to marry her.

Rajavi imposed his sexual liberation movement on all members. Women were forced to divorce their husbands, abandon their families, and devote themselves entirely to the Organization. In the name of sexual equality, battling against patriarchy, and the commodification of women, the Organization turned into a cult, forcing blind imitation and absolute obedience to the whims and decisions of its leader. Rajavi wished to create an organization that would follow him out of sheer devotion and unquestioned trust.

After five years of exile in France, Rajavi flew to Baghdad on 7 June 1986, received an official welcome, and accepted Iraq's military and financial support to mount an attack against Iran. After his arrival, Rajavi met with Saddam Hoseyn, shook hands, and made promises. Soon his followers poured into 'rebel bases' placed at Rajavi's disposal by Saddam. On 20 June 1987, Rajavi inaugurated the 'National Liberation Army of Iran' (NLAI). By aligning himself with Saddam against Iran, Rajavi, the one-time symbol of democratic and nationalist resistance to Khomeyni, lost all respect and esteem among his countrymen. Rajavi and his followers were seen as collaborators with an enemy who had been killing, maiming, and gassing Iranians in and behind the fronts.

Even though Iraq had accepted a ceasefire according to Resolution 598, Saddam Hoseyn approved Rajavi's attack on Iran, and provided his army with air and land support. In the early afternoon of 25 July 1988, the NLAI, composed of 4,500 to 7,000 soldiers, captured Qasr Shirin, Sar Pol Zahab, Karand and Eslam Gharb. The Mojahedin army swept through some 120 kilometres without much resistance and advanced towards Kermanshah.

The Iranian Army, led by Lieutenant General Ali Sayyad-Shirazi, began its counter-offensive at 6.00 am on 26 July. The Mojahedin's thrust was halted at Chahar Zebar,

40 kilometres west of Kermanshah. In three days, the NLAI was completely routed. The Mojahedin incurred 1,200–2,500 dead, some 2,000 injured and 300 prisoners. Eleven years later, in April 1999, the Mojahedin retaliated by assassinating Sayyad-Shirazi.

Prison Massacres

Already shaken, angry and shamed by the fall of Faw, the shooting of Iran Air Flight 655, and the acceptance of Resolution 598, all within four months, the surprising swift advance of the Mojahedin infuriated Khomeyni. On 24 July 1988, Khomeyni directed his anger and despair at the military and ordered Hojatoleslam Ali Razini, head of the Justice Organization of the Armed Forces, to set up a special war tribunal to investigate wartime offences and infractions. Khomeyni ruled that any activity that may have led to defeats in the war was punishable by execution.

After the defeat of Mojahedin, Khomeyni turned his frustration and wrath towards their members and sympathizers lingering in Iranian prisons since the June 1981 uprising. On 31 July 1988, he issued a vengeful edict arguing that since 'the treacherous hypocrites [Mojahedin] are by no means believers in Islam ... and since they are fighting against Islam and have waged war in the South and West of the country ... and have spied for Saddam against our Muslim people ... those in prison who remain steadfast in their hypocritical beliefs are in fact fighting against Islam and are sentenced to execution'.

Khomeyni assigned a three-man commission to carry out his edict throughout the country and wished them to 'obtain God's pleasure by exercising wrath and revolutionary vengeance against the enemies of Islam'. Khomeyni warned them against 'doubt, hesitation or wavering' in their decision making.[84] The sessions determining the religious and political position of prisoners lasted a few minutes during which, responses to three or four short questions determined the fate of prisoners. In these vengeance kangaroo courts, prisoners who had been tried and given prison sentences by the Islamic Republic's judiciary system were re-sentenced and sent to the gallows. The initial edict of dealing with Mojahedin prisoners was soon to be extended to all Left and Marxist political prisoners.

Iran's Political Prisoners were Executed in Two Waves

In the 're-trials' they faced, the first group was asked about their political affiliation – those who answered 'Mojahedin' were sent to their death. Some were asked if they were willing to clear the minefields for the army of the Islamic Republic. The second group was questioned about their religious faith – again, a wrong answer resulted in a death sentence. (Amnesty International)[85]

This unprecedented political massacre of the opposition in prisons was incomparable to the execution of seven Marxist and two Mojahedin prisoners ordered by the shah in April 1975. Amnesty International concluded that 'the massacre of political prisoners was a premeditated and coordinated policy which must have been authorized at the highest level of government'. The number of executions during July, August and September 1988 has been estimated to be between 2,800 and 12,000. Even much higher figures have been suggested.

In August and September 1988, while the death committees were liquidating the opposition and the Imam talked about the importance of post-war reconstruction, schisms at the highest levels of leadership were becoming more gaping. On 5 September, Musavi resigned from his position as prime minister, and this was not the first time he had quit. However, the fact that the news leaked out was unusual and reflected growing incoordination, disarray and disjointedness within the leadership.

In an official resignation letter to Khamenei, published in the press on 6 September, the prime minister complained about his growing disagreements with the president. Musavi informed the public that he had difficulty agreeing with Khamenei on suitable candidates for ministerial positions and that sometimes their differences could delay the process by a whole year. In a separate private letter to Khamenei, Musavi outlined other reasons for his resignation, which included being sidelined in foreign policy matters, particularly concerning Afghanistan, Iraq and Lebanon, and being kept in the dark about military operations abroad.

Musavi expressed hope that Khamenei would find someone as prime minister with whom he would be able to work. Nothing would have suited Khamenei more than Musavi's resignation, but Khomeyni ordered Musavi to continue his services 'in the bunker of the Prime Minister's Office'. Neither Khamenei nor Musavi obtained what they wanted and both were forced to continue their unhappy partnership.

The *Satanic Verses*

Far from the Iranian scene, the *Satanic Verses* by Salman Rushdie appeared in England on 26 September 1988. The book inflamed the anger of millions of Muslims as it was considered blasphemous and critical of Islam. Pakistan, India, Saudi Arabia, Egypt, Somalia, Malaysia, Qatar, Bangladesh, Sudan and South Africa banned the book. On 13 February 1989, in one of the bloodiest demonstrations against the *Satanic Verses* that had swept Pakistan, five died and some 80 were injured, as angry crowds marched on the American Cultural Centre in the middle of Islamabad. Srinagar, in India, experienced clashes of similar amplitude.

Suddenly, on 14 February 1989 Khomeyni, who had been informed of the book issued a religious pronouncement. He announced that the book was 'against Islam, the Prophet and the Quran', and the author of *Satanic Verses* and its publishers were condemned to death for blasphemy. Khomeyni gave a religious carte blanche to all

Muslims to execute the culprits 'as quickly as possible, wherever they found them' so that no one else should dare to insult the sanctities of Islam. Khomeyni added that whoever dies in this cause is a martyr.[86] An Iranian religious foundation, '15 Khordad', completed Khomeyni's fatwa by promising a $1 million reward to anyone who would assassinate Rushdie.

Khomeyni's house was in disorder. He needed to assert his spiritual and temporal authority and forge a unity that had eluded him since the revolution. The Rushdie fatwa, which intended to unite the people against an external enemy of Islam, in fact caused dissent in the leadership camp. Khamenei, exercised caution and promoted reconciliation, even accepting Rushdie's apology, but Khomeyni remained steadfast on his conflictual track, rejecting Rushdie's apology and insisting on his fatwa.

The Montazeri Affair: Rise and Fall of Khomeyni's Heir

On 16 July 1985, the Assembly of Experts met and secretly designated Hoseyn-Ali Montazeri as heir to Khomeyni. The news of his appointment as Khomeyni's deputy was not made public until 16 November 1986. In the Majles, nonchalantly, Rafsanjani thanked the Grand Ayatollah Montazeri, for his role as deputy of the eminent leader. For 16 months, Iranians did not know that Khomeyni had an heir. On 1 December 1986, the Iranian press officially addressed Montazeri as 'Deputy of the Leader.'

Montazeri and Motahhari, his classmate at the Fayziyeh Seminary School, were two of Khomeyni's favourite students. Montazeri was not only a highly knowledgeable theologian, well versed in Islamic jurisprudence, but a militant revolutionary who had been Khomeyni's plenipotentiary representative in Iran while he was in exile (Figure 8.10). Montazeri had been regularly imprisoned and exiled during the shah's regime. In June 1975, he was sentenced to ten years in prison and was released with Taleqani on 30 October 1978, a few months before the victory of the revolution.

The job of the 82 Islamic jurists, elected to the Assembly of Experts of the Leadership in December 1982, was different from the Assembly of Experts that had written the Constitution. This Assembly of Experts had the single and crucial task of choosing the Guardian Jurist and the leader of the Islamic Republic and supervising his activities. Worried about Khomeyni's heart condition and his general state of health, Rafsanjani was anxious to avoid a power vacuum in case anything happened to him. Even though the Constitution did not provide for an heir or a deputy, it was imperative to have Khomeyni's successor in place for a smooth transition of power.

Montazeri was a devout believer in the rule of the Guardian Jurist and follower of Khomeyni. Yet, he represented a force of moderation and transparency in contrast to Khomeyni and his lieutenants. Montazeri was almost a liberal Muslim in domestic

Figure 8.10 Ayatollah Hoseyn-Ali Montazeri. *Source: Photo by Michel Setboun/Gamma-Rapho via Getty Images.*

politics and an anti-imperialist in his foreign policy. He was also in favour of ending the Iran–Iraq War. Montazeri openly criticized shortcomings in the ministries, the judiciary, the IRGC and the army. He believed that transparency was for the good of the country. His criticism of the excesses of revolutionary institutions, and the Ministry of Information, SAVAK's successor, which had come into being on 18 August 1983, made him powerful enemies.

Montazeri had disagreed with the harsh and rapid court decisions, house arrests, imprisonments, expropriations and executions. In December 1984, he was instrumental in removing Asadollah Lajevardi from all positions of power. Lajevardi had been known for his notoriously violent behaviour, torture, cruelty and summary executions of the Mojahedin and the Left opposition.

Furthermore, Montazeri was involuntarily at the centre of a power struggle. He believed that Ahmad Khomeyni and Hojatoleslam Reyshahri, minister of information, were intent on discrediting him and stripping him of his deputyship position before Khomeyni's death. Ahmad Khomeyni had voiced disagreement with Montazeri as deputy, even before the Assembly of Experts appointed him to this position. Gradually, Montazeri felt sidelined about secret meetings and deals such as the US and Israeli arms exports to Iran between August 1985 and November 1986.

Through his own sources, Montazeri learnt about Robert McFarlane's secret trip and arms delivery to Iran on 25 May 1986. Khomeyni, his son, Ahmad, Rafsanjani, Khamenei, Musavi, the prime minister, and Musvai-Ardebili were all hiding crucial foreign policy decisions from Montazeri, even though he was the Imam's deputy. Khomeyni supported the initiative to obtain desperately needed Western arms for the war effort, but Montazeri could not swallow the idea of importing secretly from the US, let alone Israel.

From Montazeri the Deputy, to Khomeyni the Leader

Do you know that in the Islamic Republic's prisons there are atrocities being committed in the name of Islam that were unheard of in the shah's evil regime. (H.-A. Montazeri)[87]

In a scathing letter dated 9 October 1986, Montazeri confronted Khomeyni with a series of most embarrassing questions. He asked the Imam if he knew that many had died under torture in prisons, that girls had been raped in prisons, that people were openly cursing the leaders of the Islamic Republic, including Khomeyni, while waiting in long lines of necessities, that bribery was rampant in ministries and courts, that grand scale corruption and theft by people in the uniform of guardians of revolution and revolutionary committees had plunged the people into insecurity, that poverty and high prices had made life difficult, that in the Islamic Republic, contrary to Islam, neither life nor people's property was respected, and that finally did he know that drug addiction was raging and all the executions had done nothing to control it.[88]

Montazeri summed up Khomeyni's performance in the most brutal terms. He wrote, 'For about eight years, we have ruled with violence, lots of executions and arrests, along with unnecessary expropriations, and they have gotten us nowhere ... The only people who did not benefit from our expropriations were the oppressed/ disinherited.'[89] Montazeri was not only questioning the performance of the Islamic Republic but Khomeyni's statesmanship and religiosity.

On 12 October 1986, Mehdi Hashemi, a cleric, a five-year member of the IRGC's Command Council and the brother of Montazeri's son-in-law, Hadi, was arrested by the Ministry of Information. He was put on trial at the Special Court for the Clergy and executed on 28 September 1987 for 'spreading corruption on earth' and 'fighting against God'. The indictment against him included undermining Khomeyni and Montazeri, and sowing division among the state's leadership team. Khomeyni and his allies were making a concerted effort to villainize Montazeri's close advisors.

Mehdi Hashemi had been very close to Montazeri. It is rumored that he was arrested and executed for his role in making public McFarlane's secret visit to Iran in

May 1986, thus embarrassing Khomeyni and his associates. The pressure on Montazeri to purge his trusted advisers increased once his son-in-law Hadi Hashemi was arrested and then released on 7 July 1987 on the condition that he would desist from intervening in the political and current affairs of Montazeri's office. Khomeyni was trying to cleanse Montazeri's office in Qom from individuals he considered undesirable and bring his old student under his own control. Little did he know that Montazeri had become his own man.

After Khomeyni ordered the execution of Mojahedin prisoners who continued to stand firm on their political convictions, Montazeri wrote him a letter, questioning his decision. In his first letter dated 31 July 1988, Montazeri warned that Khomeyni's decision would be construed as vindictiveness, that violence and execution would not yield any results, and that at least women should be spared. He concluded that 'executing a few thousand in a few days would be neither free of adverse reactions nor would it be free of errors'.[90]

It was not surprising that on 26 March 1989, Montazeri, whose leadership may have changed the course of the Islamic Republic, was stripped of his title by Khomeyni. Once again, the Imam threw one of his closest and most beloved, though disobedient and dissenting, protégés to the wolves. Khomeyni wrote that he was convinced that after him, Montazeri would hand the country and the revolution to the Mojahedin and the liberals, and therefore ruled that Montazeri had lost 'the authority and legitimacy to lead the system/regime in the future'. Khomeyni prohibited Montazeri from ever engaging in political activities since he was 'a simpleton' who would become 'quickly incited'.[91]

Khomeyni's glorious pre-revolution days were coming to a dramatic end. On 4 June 1989, Iranians learnt that Khomeyni had passed away on the previous night. Millions participated in his funeral procession, shedding genuine tears, mourning, and grieving. Khomeyni had taken over an economically and culturally modern, albeit despotic, country, which had been well integrated into the international political and economic order and respected by the international community. He had turned Iran into the opposite, without ridding it of despotism.

In his ten-year leadership, Khomeyni by far outdid the Pahlavi regime in establishing an unprecedented violent religio-political despotism. The chaos of the revolutionary days subsided after ten years. The lofty promises in Paris were long forgotten, while their opposites were enforced. Even in the eyes of his fervent Islamic followers, the hyped-up escapades of occupying the American Embassy and continuing the war into Iraq, did not obtain the promised ends. For ten years, the arbitrary decisions of one man had taken the country on a downward spiraling path. At the time of his death, Iran's GDP per capita ($2,246) was less than what is was before the revolution in 1979. 'Iran's GDP per capita ended up 25 percent below that of Turkey, while it had surpassed Turkey by that measure in the early 1960s.'[92]

Khomeyni was an excellent leader of the opposition, but not a statesman whose actions assured the economic welfare and political liberties of his country. To his successors he left a country in limbo, a fractured and scheming leadership, a devastated economy in which corruption had become endemic, a legacy of hard-nosed visceral anti-Americanism and international isolation, a new and upcoming military nomenklatura intent on reclaiming its economic and political booty of the war and a population still yearning for democracy and freedom.

Factual and Analytical Questions

1. Who was the first post-revolutionary prime minister of the Islamic Republic? What were his responsibilities and the problems that he faced in his capacity as the head of the executive?
2. What was the composition, role and responsibility of the Council of the Islamic Revolution and how well did it coalesce with government?
3. What were the objectives of the three ethnic opposition movements? What did they have in common? How successful were they?
4. What was the purpose of the Islamic Republic Party? Who were its founders?
5. Which political players in Iran benefitted from the hostage crisis and who did not benefit? Explain by providing historical examples.
6. What was at the roots of Iran's Cultural Revolution? How was it attained? What were its objectives? How successful was it?
7. Assess Operation Eagle Claw. Was it doomed from the start? How did it affect Iranian and American relations?
8. What were the objectives of the Nojeh coup? Who was behind it? Why did it fail?
9. Explain the cause of the Bani-Sadr and Mojahedin revolt against the Islamic Republic. How was it conducted? What was the result?
10. Why was Ayatollah Shariatmadari placed under house arrest? Why was he stripped of his position as a Source of Imitation and what did this imply for the independence of Shii authorities and the clerical institution in the Islamic Republic?
11. What were the salient features of the eight-year Iran–Iraq War? Explain why retaking Khorramshahr and the fall of Faw were turning points in the war?
12. What was the UN Security Council Resolution 598?
13. When and under what circumstances did Khomeyni accept Resolution 598?
14. What was the content of Khomeyni's fatwa against Salman Rushdie? What was its purpose?

Seminar Questions

1. Why did Khomeyni decree the creation of revolutionary institutions? Explain your answer with reference to the Revolutionary Courts, Committees and the Revolutionary Guards.
2. Which segments of society were drawn to these revolutionary institutions and why?
3. Analyse and assess the process by which the opposition press and political organizations came under attack between May and September 1979. What role did the *Hezbollah*, the IRGC and the Revolutionary Courts play in this wave of repression?
4. 'The occupation of the American Embassy was a solution to domestic political problems with long-lasting international consequences.' Assess the validity of this statement.
5. Compare and contrast Bani-Sadr's Presidency with that of Bazargan's Premiership. In what ways did they resemble and differ?
6. How would you assess the interaction between the leadership of the Islamic Republic and the Tudeh Party of Iran? Why did it degenerate?
7. Did the Iran–Iraq War have a winner?
8. What is the religious and political significance and difference between the rule of the Guardian Jurist and the absolute rule of the Guardian Jurist?

Discussion Questions

1. What was the objective of the purges in the ministries and the private sector?
2. Compare Shariatmadari's Muslim People of Iran's Republic Party (MPIRP) with the Islamic Republic Party (IRP). What were their similarities and differences?
3. Compare Gudarzi's Forqan Group with Navab-Safavi's the Devotees of Islam Group. What were their similarities and differences?
4. 'The Islamic Republic could have avoided a despotic theocracy if Khomeyni had his way and put the draft Constitution to a referendum.' Discuss the above assertions with reference to historical facts.
5. 'Crisis generation was an aspect of Khomeyni's mode of governance.' Assess and discuss the validity of this statement. Support your argument with historical evidence.
6. Assess the role of the Islamic Republic Party in the formation of the Islamic Republic. How successful was it in consolidating Khomeyni's rule? What caused its demise?

7 'The Islamic Republic under Montazeri would have been a different country today'. Assess the above statement with an eye to the core disagreements between Montazeri and Khomeyni.
8 'Arbitrary decisions of one man characterized Khomeyni's ten-year legacy. He took the country on a downward spiraling path.' Critically assess the validity of this statement.

Glossary

Hezbollah The term means the Party of God. Before t became an Iranian surrogate force in Lebanon (1985), it referred to an aggressive pro-Khomeyni pressure group in post-revolution Iran. Ayatollah Khomeyni called it 'the party of the oppressed/disinherited' and wished it to become the only political force in the country. During the first few years of the revolution, *Hezbollah* operated as a militia of zealous shock-troopers intimidating the opposition. They attacked and broke up opposition gatherings, demonstrations and headquarters, insulting and injuring dissidents.

khums The term means 'one-fifth'. For the Shii, it is a flat 20 per cent tax on their annual income derived from ownership of natural resources, mines and profits from all permissible economic activities.

Nahjolbalaqeh The term means 'Path of Eloquence.' It refers to the collection of Imam Ali's sermons, sayings and letters. Ali ibn Abu Taleb was the cousin and son-in-law of Prophet Mohammad and the first of the Shii Imams. Nahjolbalaqeh, collected by Seyyed Razi in the tenth century ad provides a rich source of inspiration of what Shii Islam represents and stands for.

Pishmarga Kurdish combatants who are ready to face death. They are the fighters of Kurdish guerrilla groups and organizations. The term is said to have been coined by Qazi Mohammad, the founder of the Kurdish Democratic Party of Iran and president of the Republic of Mahabad, in March 1946.

ravayat The Persian term for *hadith*s. It means reports and refers to the sayings or acts of the Prophet or the Shii Imams transmitted through a Shii imam to a compiler. After the Quran, it constitutes the second primary legal source for deriving Shii jurisprudence. The Shii have four major report/hadith books, compiled by Kolayni and Ibn Babawayeh and two compilations by Sheykh Tusi.

Surah The Quran is broken down into chapters and verses. Surah is the equivalent of chapter and Ayeh is the equivalent of verse. The Quran is composed of 114 Surahs. Surahs are not chronologically compiled in the Quran, they are of unequal length, and usually divided between those revealed to the Prophet in Mecca and those revealed in Medina.

zakat The term means that which purifies. Zakat, alms or poor tax is an annual levy or tax stipulated in the Quran. Its amount for simplicity's sake is quoted as 2.5 per cent of savings and wealth above a limit (Nisab). It is not an income tax but rather a wealth tax on certain specific items. It is a religious duty by which Muslim are required to cleanse their property.

9

President Rafsanjani, the Crusader of Construction, 1989–97

Chapter Outline

Transitioning to Post-Khomeyni Iran	455
The Rafsanjani–Khamenei Duo	458
Domestic Politics, July 1989 to July 1997	459
Rafsanjani's Economic Reform: Hopes and Challenges	468
Rafsanjani's Political Conundrums	474
Glossary	489

Transitioning to Post-Khomeyni Iran

In the immediate post-Khomeyni period, two events significantly marked the future of Iran. First, some forty days before his death on 24 April 1989, Khomeyni ordered the reappraisal and revision of the Constitution. The Council for the Reappraisal and Revision of the Constitution finished its task after Khomeyni's death. On 28 July 1989, the amendments to the Constitution were ratified by 95 per cent of Iranians who participated in the referendum.

The new revisions in the Constitution eliminated the position of prime minister and empowered the president to form a government. They also incorporated the Expediency Discernment Council of the System into the Constitution. This body, constituted by Khomeyni in February 1988, was tasked with arbitrating and passing final judgement on issues where the Guardian Council and the Majles disagreed. This new body could overturn the decisions of the Guardian Council and uphold that of the Majles.

While the new constitution weakened the role of the Guardian Council in terms of its authority with Majles rulings, it strengthened it in another determining domain.

The Guardian Council was now legally empowered to supervise presidential and parliamentary elections as well as elections to the Assembly of Experts of the Leadership. The nature of this supervision, which later became a powerful vetting weapon of candidates standing for election, was not defined or determined at the time.

The most far-reaching revision of the Constitution concerned the qualifications and the purview of the Islamic Republic's future Leader. The controversial position of *Velayat Faqih* or the rule of the Guardian Jurist was omitted and replaced with that of the Leader (*rahbar*). The Leader was no longer required to be among the highest clerically ranking *maraje taqlid* (Sources of Imitation). The Islamic qualifications of the clerical leader was watered down, making any junior or middle ranking **mojtahed** eligible to take Khomeyni's place. Khomeyni had the unique position of being both a religious and political leader. After his death, no one could combine both positions and therefore, the political leader could be a cleric, whose religious status and authority would be inferior to some.

Concomitantly, the Council for the Reappraisal and Revision of the Constitution increased the powers of the Leader. In addition to his previous powers as the Guardian Jurist, the Leader was empowered to determine and supervise the macro policies of the *nezam* (system/regime), appoint the head of National Radio and Television, and coordinate the three branches of the government. The new amendments bolstered the absolute rule of the clerical leader.

The second significant event occurred on the eve of June 3rd, immediately after the death of Khomeyni. The Assembly of Experts of the Leadership was urgently convened to designate a successor and until that time, news of Khomeyni's death was not to be made public. On 4 June, in a highly secretive meeting of the Assembly of Experts of the Leadership and after some deliberation, Hojatoleslam Khamenei became Iran's new Leader. Out of 70 or 74 members present, 56 or 60 voted for Khamenei as the provisional Leader. His position was made permanent on 6 August 1989.

Reluctant to accept the leadership position, Khamenei was seemingly pushed into it by Rafsanjani. Secret discussions about designating Khamenei as successor had been going on between the two for at least two weeks before Khomeyni passed away. To secure Khamenei's nomination, Rafsanjani spoke at length during the Assembly of Experts session on 4 June, quoting Khomeyni on Khamenei as a befitting successor. During that session, Rafsanjani had even taken over the job of Ali Meshkini, the Chair of the Assembly of Experts of the Leadership, to obtain his desired outcome.

Khamenei knew that he had neither the necessary religious authority, status, nor acceptability for the position. Politically, he was not a consensus builder. While Rafsanjani had tried to keep his distance from the two warring factions for eight years, Khamenei had sided with the conservative and Right faction. Khamenei candidly told the Assembly that his leadership would be a superficial and nominal one. Rafsanjani, the shrewd, pragmatic and politically gifted powerbroker, believed that he could happily share power and even control the weak and insecure new Leader. On 6 June 1989, the public was informed that Khamenei was designated as the new Leader and to bolster his stature, Rafsanjani addressed him as Ayatollah instead of Hojatoleslam.

On 28 July 1989, Iranians voted on the amendments to the Constitution and the new president simultaneously. The system/regime was in a rush to consolidate and legitimize the leadership of Khamenei and make the transition to the post-Khomeyni period smooth. Iranians were not given much of a choice. Of the 79 presidential candidates, the Guardian Council approved the qualification of only 2, Rafsanjani and Abbas Sheybani. Even Bazargan's candidacy was rejected. This marked the beginning of a systematic and unabashed filtering of candidates to elected positions of the state by the Guardian Council, appointees of the new 'Leader of the Revolution'. Rafsanjani won 95 per cent of the votes in a very unequal battle and became president (Figure 9.1).

Khomeyni, the charismatic Leader of the revolution, adored by the zealots, had not prevented the emergence of dissent and factionalism among his followers. Given his status and authority, Khomeyni could suppress discord at will. After his death, the interpretation of the Imam's Line or his vision became open to debate. Each faction read into Khomeynism, what it wished, and there was no single powerful individual to say the last word. The confusion over the orientation, general policies and the kind

Figure 9.1 Rafsanjani with newly elected Supreme Leader Ali Khamenei, 1989.
Source: Wikimedia Commons.

of state and society the Islamic Republic wished to become remained ambiguous and unsettled.

Debates over the state's legitimizing identity (Islamic versus Republican), style of government (popular will/democracy versus rule of the Guardian Jurist), the economy (statism versus crony capitalism), foreign policy (detente and rapprochement versus anti-Western hostility and belligerence), cultural policy (openness and tolerance versus dogmatism and religious sanctimoniousness), and individual and political freedoms continued to divide society preventing it from attaining a stable equilibrium.

The Rafsanjani–Khamenei Duo

Starting in July 1989, the duo of Rafsanjani and Khamenei ruled Iran. Their partnership and power relation were not always smooth. Irrespective of their long history of friendship and common struggle against the shah, they had different temperaments, different visions of the Islamic Republic and different Islamic world views. In time, Khamenei shed his insecurities and began to spread his wings and Rafsanjani realized that he had made a huge mistake not becoming Leader. During Rafsanjani's first term in office as president, however, a tacit division of labour, and the threat of a common rival, the economic Left, united them and minimized tension.

Khomeyni's last words to Rafsanjani

If you remain united the revolution will make headway. Especially you and Mr. Khamenei. You should not let the sneaky knaves foment sedition between you.[1]

Rafsanjani's favourite Iranian statesman was the modernist Amir Kabir, the prime minister of Nasereddin Shah, about whom he had written a book at age 30. Like Amir Kabir, Rafsanjani wished to see his country prosper and therefore, as president, he plunged into post-war reconstruction. Rafsanjani did not shun technical know-how and financial capabilities, necessary for realizing his economic objectives.

Both Amir Kabir and Rafsanjani were men of action interested in tangible results. They wished to strengthen the system/regime by modernizing and developing it from the top. They were firm believers in expertise, technocracy and strong-handed economic growth. Neither Amir Kabir nor Rafsanjani were fans or enemies of democracy and political liberalism. If they felt that political liberties hindered growth objectives, they would willingly forego the former for the benefit of the latter, and even suppress such freedoms for the sake of economic progress.

Khamenei, on the other hand, was under the influence of Seyyed Qutb. At age 26, he had translated Qutb's book *Islam the Religion of the Future* and published it in 1966. Four years later he had begun translating Qutb's long and influential book, *In the Shade of the Quran*, but did not pursue it once he discovered that someone else was translating it. Qutb had spent two years in the US from 1949 to 1951, and had become radically opposed to all things Western, its way of life, culture, society and, most of all, its modernization project. To some extent, Khamenei shared Qutb's view that the West was an infested community of moral, political, and civilizational decadence, a community of ignorance and evil.

Even though the realities of running a country did not allow Khamenei to strictly adhere to Qutb's radical views, he was smitten by his discourse of a closed and introverted Islam as the antidote to the West and its way of doing things. Khamenei shared Qutb's view that Islam was constantly threatened and besieged by the repugnant Western camp of *jaheliyyeh* (ignorance). Khamenei often spoke of the clash of the two discourses and worlds.

Qutb was very different from Amir Kabir, who felt the need to learn from the West to compete with it. Khamenei, too, was equally different from Rafsanjani. The latter had an acute curiosity for the world and had visited Europe and the US several times before the revolution and had even taken a road trip through the US with his brother, visiting some 20 states.

Domestic Politics, July 1989 to July 1997

For the conservative/Right clergy who had been chastised by the Imam for their liberal economic policies and 'Capitalist Islam', the post-Khomeyni period was one of respite and optimism. Their long-time supporter, Khamenei, was now the Leader. The Left/radicals, however, clustered around Musavi and members of the Assembly of Militant Clerics (*majma rowhaniyoun mobarez*), faced a reversal. They had lost their mentor, and with the elimination of the position of the prime minister, they forfeited their power base in the executive.

On 19 August 1989, Rafsanjani presented his bi-partisan cabinet. He refused to include Ali-Akbar Mohtashamipur, Musavi's minister of interior, and a hard-nosed anti-Western follower of Khomeyni, who had been instrumental in founding the Lebanese *Hezbollah*. Despite a letter of support for Mohtashamipur signed by 136 deputies of the 3rd Majles, Rafsanjani introduced a low-ranking cleric, Abdollah Nuri, sympathetic to the Left faction. Rafsanjani also refused to yield to the Left's nominee for the minister of health or Ahmad Khomeyni's pressure to include Mohammad Musavi-Khoeiyniha in his cabinet. Musavi-Khoeiyniha had been a founder of the Assembly of Militant Clerics, the spiritual father of the Student Followers of the Imam's Line, and the mastermind of the American Embassy takeover.

Relying on its majority in the Majles, the Left faction threatened to turn down Rafsanjani's proposed cabinet. Surprisingly, however, even though the Assembly of Militant Clerics and their allies claimed 170 deputies, Rafsanjani's ministers obtained a quick vote of confidence. The highest vote (246) went to Mohammad Khatami, minister of culture and Islamic guidance and a founding member of the Assembly of Militant Clerics. Rafsanjani referred to the Majles vote as 'a disgrace for the radical faction, which despite [friendly] advice, were defeated'.[2]

Rafsanjani's victory in the Majles demonstrated his non-confrontational and smooth political style. He was respected by both factions and savvy at networking across ideological and organizational alignments. Over the years, he had created a vast patronage system. In time, however, Rafsanjani's attempt at keeping both sides happy while pursuing self-interested politics made him a target for both the Left faction and the Right.

While presenting his ministers to the Majles, Rafsanjani outlined his plans for reconstructing Iran, admitted that not much had been done since the revolution, and prayed that he would not become a despot. He insisted that Iran's independence was contingent upon reviving Iran's economy, relying on a five-year plan, revitalizing stagnant industries, drawing upon Iranian expertise and know-how, promoting exports and creating jobs. Rafsanjani held out an olive branch to the nearly 1 million educated specialists and owners of capital who had fled the country. He asked them to return and conceded that he needed help from abroad.

To reconstruct the Iranian economy, Rafsanjani needed professionals and managers. He, therefore, sought to alter the revolutionary culture of prioritizing zeal and doctrinairism in society over expertise and know-how. Rafsanjani paid lip service to the abstract ideals of the Islamic Revolution to assuage the Leader and comfort those who had sacrificed life and limb in the war such as the selfless and pious *Basijis*.

Khamenei's vision of the future Iran was a continuation of the past order. He emphasized cultivating and pampering the *Basiji* and the *Hezbollahi* ethos, as Khomeyni had done. Relying on the old backbones of the regime and maintaining the wartime social status quo was Khamenei's way of taking on Khomeyni's role. In Rafsanjani's modernist vision, on the other hand, the ascetic *Basiji* mentality had to be transformed while maintaining their deep sense of loyalty to the system. Rafsanjani needed to replace austerity as a social value with self-improvement and material gain to fuel his economic reconstruction project.

Rafsanjani began by discrediting sloppy, coarse and unpoised personal appearances, dogmatic and sectarian views and anti-materialism as the identifier of a good revolutionary Muslim. Rafsanjani swam against the current he had once been instrumental in creating. The bearded, black-shirted, angry and pugnacious zealots, who dogmatically opposed everything and anything socially, economically and culturally Western, had to be mollified and eventually assimilated.

Fostering a fundamental and sudden attitudinal shift from selflessness to materialism was not to happen overnight and without resistance. Those old veterans, *Hezbollahi*s and *Basiji*s, who did not have the drive, ability or willingness to join and benefit from Rafsanjani's new Islamic Eldorado were sidelined. Rafsanjani's economic reconstruction became the ideal incubation environment for crony capitalism. It opened the way for corruption, rent-seeking and quick illicit money for those willing to jump on Rafsanjani's bandwagon, including many with a proven record of service during the war.

Two classic Iranian films best captured the estrangement, displacement, and alienation of true *Basiji*s after the war. 'Marriage of the Blessed' by Mohsen Makhmalbaf in 1989 chronicled the insurmountable challenges faced by a war veteran to reintegrate into a rapidly shifting post-war society. Ten years later, Ebrahim Hatami-Kia, in his 1998 production, *Glass Agency*, depicted how *Basiji*s, who did not wish to benefit from patronage and favouritism, became broken and unhinged in a self-seeking and self-promoting society.

No sooner was Rafsanjani's cabinet in place that a degree of emphasis in discourse differentiated the president from the Leader. On 31 August 1989, Khamenei announced that relieving the hardships of a people who had endured an eight-year war did not mean taking distance from ideals and spiritualities. He reminded the authorities that they 'are obliged to be attentive equally to the material and spiritual concerns of the people'.[3]

At the 18 November 1989, Friday Prayers, Rafsanjani took a first step in promoting his attitudinal change and characterized 'action and work as the essence of worship'. To those who dreamt of exporting the Islamic Revolution, he proposed building Islam in one country first, and said, 'we can only export our revolution when we have a flourishing, prosperous, and developed society'.[4]

Rafsanjani's Friday Sermon was so bold and non-conformist that the daily *Ettelaat*, which supported his views, did not publish all of it. Later, Rafsanjani's detractors dubbed it 'the parade of luxury' sermon. Rafsanjani lashed out at the culture that pigeonholed Muslims as 'unbeautiful and unattractive'. He warned his zealous audience that it would be detrimental to Islam if all things beautiful were non-Muslim and all uncomely things were Muslim. He invited all those who attended the Friday Prayers to wear their best clothes and adornments, embellish themselves so that the weekly religious event would turn into a place of parading luxuries.[5]

In the controversial part of his sermon censured by *Ettelaat*, Rafsanjani criticized the disagreeable foot stench of sweaty Mosque-goers, and requested that they wear perfume, comb their hair, groom their beard, and wear clean clothes. For Rafsanjani's opponents, his slogan of 'welfare/prosperity' was a 'dangerous plot' to make the country 'economically dependent' and eventually 'destroy the revolution'.[6]

To integrate *Basiji*s into society, Rafsanjani issued a directive mandating universities to set aside a quota for the admission of those who had been at the war fronts for at least six months. To Rafsanjani, higher education was one way to change attitudes. While pushing to change mentalities, Rafsanjani tried to hem in the excesses. He ordered the Islamic Revolutionary Committees to stop inspecting and aggressively interrogating passengers in their private cars. Imposing religious codes of modesty and virtue, such as checking on alcohol consumption, gender mixing, and acceptable social conduct had become a regular activity of the Revolutionary Committees. Rafsanjani prohibited the public execution of drug dealers and sought educational rather than punitive measures for dealing with the growing social problem of 'insufficient veiling', a euphemism for women trying to minimize the covering of their head, hair and body.[7]

A silent majority welcomed Rafsanjani's call for moderation. An important article in *Ettelaat* signaled a degree of opening and tolerance in the tightly government-controlled press. Under the guise of supporting Rafsanjani's Islamic modernity project, Ali-Akbar Saeedi-Sirjani, a scholar, writer and journalist questioned Khomeyni's legacy. He criticized certain post-revolutionary practices that had become the modus vivendi of a loud segment of Iranians. Saeedi-Sirjani attacked past excesses such as hostage-taking, irrational and angry comportments, the 'Death to America' slogan, growing corruption and privileges of protected social categories, the invitation to austerity, the futility of the war and its prolongation. Saeedi-Sirjani welcomed the president's message of 'tolerance and leniency'.[8]

The Duo Purging the Left Faction of the Imam's Line

The Left controlled a number of revolutionary institutions including the Majles and student organization of the Office of Consolidating Unity. They, however, remained unrepresented in the key decision-making bodies. As of January 1990, they began undermining Khamenei and voiced their opposition to Mohammad Yazdi's appointment as the new head of the judiciary. Yazdi, a stubborn and conservative cleric, had replaced the centrist and senior clergy, Musavi-Ardebli.

With Khomeyni out of the picture, the Guardian Council, now dominated by heavyweight anti-Left conservative clerics close to Khamenei, felt entitled to intervene in the coming bi-election of the third Majles. In mid-January 1990, they, almost secretively and without any accountability, annulled the results of 80 ballot boxes in Tehran. Besides annulling ballot boxes to obtain the intended outcome, they started to exclude 'undesirable' candidates. Even though certain of the Left candidates such as Mohtashamipur and Abolqasem Sarhadizadeh, were eventually elected in the second round, the Guardian Council's outright tampering with votes was alarming. Besides annulling ballot boxes to obtain the intended outcome, another 'efficient' method was fashioned to exclude 'undesirable' candidates.

In mid-July 1990, the Assembly of Experts of the Leadership met and passed a resolution empowering the Guardian Council to ascertain the eligibility of candidates applying to the Assembly of Experts. This unconstitutional move was made in anticipation of elections to the Second Assembly of Experts of the Leadership in October 1990. Subsequently, the Guardian Council, appointed by the Leader, would vet the candidacy of those who were to supervise the activities of the leader, gathered in the Assembly of Experts of the Leadership.

The Guardian Council now imposed a qualifying exam to measure the applicant's knowledge of Islamic jurisprudence (*fiqh*) and ascertain whether they were *mojtaheds*, whenever they deemed it necessary. The higher-ranking conservative clerics, appointed by Khamenei, concocted a self-serving procedure to keep out the junior Left clerics who may criticize the activities of the Leader. The battle for hegemony between the Republican and Islamic aspects of the Islamic Republic had begun.

Of 180 candidates who registered for elections to the Second Assembly of Experts of the Leadership, 62 failed the written and oral exam, 11 were rejected and 24 retracted. On 29 September 1990, the Guardian Council announced the eligible candidates for election. Only four prominent members of the Left were among them. The credentials of renowned Left figures of the Assembly of Militant Clerics such as Mohtashamipur, Asadollah Bayat, Sadeq Khalkhali and Hadi Khamenei, the Leader's brother, were rejected. In protest at the widespread purge of the Left clerics, Khoeiyniha, Mohammad Tavasoli and Mohammad Abaie-Khorasani, whose credentials were approved, withdrew their candidacy. The Guardian Council confirmed the credentials of all members of the conservative Right for Tehran.

The Left wrote a letter to Khamenei, denouncing what seemed more like an appointment process than free elections, and both the Majles and the press condemned the machinations of the Guardian Council. On 3 and 4 October 1990, Khamenei and Rafsanjani retaliated with force. Khamenei announced that he would 'not tolerate' anyone insulting the Guardian Council and upheld their actions as legal and appropriate.[9] Having commandeered and supported the illegal and undemocratic initiative of the Guardian Council and infringed upon the rights of the opposition, the Khamenei–Rafsanjani duo called on the opposition to fall in line and observe unity, lest enemies of the state benefit from internal divisions.

On 13 January 1991, the Left deputies challenged Rafsanjani's policies and interpellated Iraj Fazel, Rafsanjani's capable US-educated minister of health, and removed him from office. This incident rattled and frustrated Rafsanjani. Faced with an almost blackout in the mainstream press and deprived of a mouthpiece, the Left began to launch its own factional publications.

In June 1990, Mohtashamipur had published the monthly *Bayan* (Expression), the unofficial organ of the Left and the Assembly of Militant Clerics. Its pages criticized Rafsanjani's economic policies, the American and Capitalist Islam of the Right and meddling by the Guardian Council. Subsequently, Hadi Khamenei published the daily *Jahane Eslam* (The World of Islam), and finally, on 9 February 1991, the daily

Salam (Greetings/Salutations) appeared on the stands. Musavi-Khoeyniha was the managing director of *Salam*.

When Rafsanjani became president, he created a think tank attached to the President's Office, called the Centre for Strategic Studies, and placed Musavi-Khoeiyniha at its helm. Both the Centre for Strategic Studies and *Salam* became the hub of young and talented university graduates of the Left student organization, Office of Consolidating Unity. Most of these young militants had been involved in the occupation of the US Embassy. Among those who ran or collaborated with *Salam*, many would later become leaders of the reformist movement, such as Saeed Hajjariyan, Abbas Abdi, Feyzollah Arab-Sorkhi, Mohsen Mirdamadi and Ebrahim Asgharzadeh.

Having successfully kept the Left out of the Assembly of Experts, the Guardian Council officially defined and extended its supervisory role. Instead of overseeing the election process, the Guardian Council arrogated the role of vetting the credentials of candidates to the Majles, rendering free elections of the legislative meaningless. On 22 May 1991, the Guardian Council dropped a bombshell. Through a letter, it institutionalized the invasive concept of 'approbatory supervision' rather than its original passive role of 'informational supervision'. The Guardian Council announced that it had the right to supervise the Majles elections, 'including the rejection and approval of applicants' credentials'.[10]

Eleven months before the elections to the 4th Majles, Khamenei and Rafsanjani, through the good office of the Guardian Council, prepared the elimination of the Left gadflies who had challenged and bothered them. Less than two months before the Majles election, Khamenei announced his full backing of all decisions made by the Guardian Council, called it 'the most dependable and incorruptible' of all state institutions, and commanded Iranians to obey its decisions.

Under the same breath, Khamenei instructed the Guardian Council to disqualify those who were 'financially, morally, or politically corrupt'. Those who 'should not enter the Majles', Khamenei mandated, were the 'seditious' who 'challenged the system/regime or obstructed its activities'. The Leader ordered the Guardian Council to bar the opposition and those who opposed the rule of the Guardian Jurist, while imploring them not to act on a 'factional' or 'political' basis.[11]

While Iranians were on their New Year vacation, the Guardian Council carried out its widespread purge of the candidates. On 1 April 1992, the axe fell, and 58 deputies of present and previous Parliaments were disqualified. Among the approximately 70 disqualified Left candidates were two of Khomeyni's prominent judicial appointees, Sadeq Khalkhali, Khomeyni's first revolutionary judge, and Hoseyn Musavi-Tabrizi, chief of revolutionary courts in Azarbayjan and later the prosecutor general of the Islamic Republic. On 3 April, the new Friday Prayer Leader of Tehran, Ahmad Jannati, the rising star of the Guardian Council, announced that those disqualified had 'financial and ethical' problems.[12]

> **Strangling of the Republic**
>
> The vetting process undertaken by the Guardian Council marked the first time that the factionalism inherent in the Islamic Republic's political fabric since the early 1980s had the effect of heavily conditioning an electoral race prior to the same taking place. (S. Randjbar-Daemi)[13]

Many of those who ended up disqualified were veterans or family members of war martyrs. The Left contemplated boycotting the elections, but Khamenei informed Karrubi, the Majles president and a leading Left figure, that his faction was compelled to participate in the elections. Karrubi obliged and cobbled a list, while a few Left candidates, such as Mohsen Armin, whose eligibility was confirmed, withdrew their nomination in protest.

The candidates of the Right/conservative coalition, led by *jameeye rowhaniyat mobarez* (the Association of Militant Clergy) campaigned under the slogan of, 'Following the Imam's Line, obedience to the Leader, support for Hashemi [Rafsanjani].' Their candidates won an overwhelming victory in the 4th Majles. All 30 candidates representing Tehran belonged to the Right, and the new Majles was composed of approximately 134 Right, 86 independent and 40 Left deputies.

The handpicked and vetted 4th Majles sent the Left into hibernation. Parliament convened on 28 May 1992 and replaced Karrubi with Ali-Akbar Nateq-Nuri, the

Figure 9.2 Ali-Akbar Nateq-Nuri. *Source: Wikimedia Commons.*

emerging Leader of the conservative-dominated Parliament (Figure 9.2). Prematurely, Rafsanjani felt confident that his days of tension with the Majles were over, and that his economic policies would glide through the new legislative, with no resistance.

Forced out of politics, the Left focused on intellectual pursuits, assessing the past and reflecting on the future. On 2 October 1991, the left-wing of the Mojahedin of the Islamic Revolution, which had seceded from its Right-leaning allies in January 1983, founded Iran's Mojahedin of the Islamic Revolution (IMIR). This new organization had a closed membership and was composed of like-minded militants and cadres interested in providing society with food for thought. Three years later, in October 1994, they published the biweekly *Asre Ma* (Our Epoch), their theoretical organ, which would later play a considerable role in promoting a democratic political discourse and paving the grounds for the reform movement.

Asre Ma promoted the idea that in Islam, it was the people's will that legitimized governance, and even the rule of the Guardian Jurist. After some fourteen years, the club-wielding anti-democratic Khomeyni zealots who had supported his Absolutist Rule of the Guardian Jurists were now questioning the fundamentals of clerical rule. The ideological transformation of their founders, among them Behzad Nabavi, Mohammad Salamati and Mohsen Armin, was genuine.

The Leader's Nightmare of a Western Cultural Onslaught

The lifestyle, and religious sensibilities of zealous *Basiji*s, represented the archetype that Khamenei yearned for in Iranian youth. The *Basiji*s became exemplars of the ideal Islamic culture; puritanical, austere, self-sacrificing, and anti-Western. *Basiji* religiosity was rooted in the notion that the position of the Guardian Jurist was 'sacred'. Their blind following of his directives made them a priceless socio-political power base. Threatened by the marginalization or metamorphosis of his devout followers, in the process of Rafsanjani's economic reconstruction, Khamenei created a new *raison d'être* for them under his command.

With no grand project to mobilize the people in a common cause and connect with them, Khamenei opted for a path already taken, a second 'cultural revolution'. This scheme was to rejuvenate the *Basiji*s and *Hezbollahi*s, by giving them a new mission and a sense of purpose. But most importantly, the second cultural revolution would provide a lever to control Rafsanjani and his reconstruction and economic modernization project. Khamenei wished to put his imprint on the construction and development projects sweeping the country, passing Rafsanjani's materialist construction project as a spiritual 'jihad' for and by the pious war veterans. But the golden age of *Basiji* spirituality had passed. Rafsanjani's initial economic successes, and the gains from the booming crony capitalism had undermined innocence and selflessness of the wartime *Basiji*s.

The Political Significance of *Basij* and *Hezbollah* for the Leader

If it was not for our pious forces, the *Basiji*s and *Hezbollahi*s ... those who since the beginning of the revolution have confronted all mishaps ... we would have been vulnerable. (A. Khamenei)[14]

In the middle of Rafsanjani's economic reconstruction, Khamenei launched his cultural war against the West and its cultural 'onslaught, pillage, and slaughter'. The Leader hammered that, 'The *Basiji*s need to be involved, to retain the virtues of the revolution.' 'The enemy,' he said 'is trying to rob our youth by propagating a wrong culture, perversion/immorality, and prostitution'. In his speech of 14 July 1992, Khamenei ordered the *Basiji*s and *Hezbollahi*s to take the initiative and impose the proper Islamic cultural and moral code by **enjoining good and forbidding wrong**. He called on the zealots to take matters into their own hands and warned that 'some have confused reconstruction with materialism'.[15]

Four days after Khamenei's heated speech on the necessity of fighting the cultural onslaught, the press reported on the anticipated change in the Ministry of Culture and Islamic Guidance. Mohammad Khatami's highly politicized resignation letter dated 24 May 1992, which Rafsanjani had resisted accepting until 18 July 1992, was published in full in *Ettelaat*.

In his letter, Khatami referred to his differences with 'eminent positions of responsibility' and concluded that it was impossible to continue his task. He identified 'reactionary, hidebound and ossified ideas' as the gravest threat to the system/regime and expressed anxiety over the 'disappointments and sense of insecurity among Iran's artists and intellectuals/thinkers'. Khatami boldly promised to continue 'defending the legal rights and freedoms of the people and society to the best of his abilities'.[16]

Khatami had come a long way. In the spring of 1983, as Musavi's minister, Khatami had supervised the prohibition of video cassettes and projectors in Iran. The widespread use of non-censored videos containing music, films and serials, were deemed culturally and morally corrupting and an affront to Islamic values. Many possessing such videos were arrested, flogged and fined, but neither supply nor demand for them had subsided. After almost ten years in office, Khatami had come to realize the absurdity of such prohibitions and had become open-minded and moderate. But a tolerant Khatami in the sensitive position of minister of Culture and Islamic Guidance made him the ideal target for Khamenei's newfound campaign against the Western cultural onslaught.

Khatami did not share Khamenei's cultural concerns about a 'Western cultural onslaught'. Rafsanjani, on the other hand paid lip service to the Leader's rantings, even repeating them while pursuing his own objectives. Khatami, the official face of the Islamic Republic's cultural policies was out of synch with the Leader and needed to be changed. Since December 1991, he had made his differences known to Rafsanjani.

After his unaccepted resignation letter, Khatami sounded more like a poised member of the opposition than a cabinet member. He publicly announced that: 'the will of the people constituted the basis of the government and that the social livelihood of the revolution depended on all people'. He criticized 'intolerance and irritability' in society and pressed that 'an environment of logic and reflection should prevail, where ideas are confronted with ideas'.[17]

To replace Khatami, Rafsanjani nominated Ali Larijani, son of the Grand Ayatollah Hashem Amoli, a conservative figure with close ties to the Islamic Coalition of Mourning Groups and the IRGC. Rafsanjani hoped that by relegating the cultural realm to the conservatives, he could obtain the full support of the Leader and the Majles for his economic policies.

Rafsanjani's Economic Reform: Hopes and Challenges

Rafsanjani inherited a war-torn economy that had been on a war footing for eight years. Most importantly, he needed to halt the decline of the Iranian economy. He began by promoting GDP growth, which registered a -5.4 to -3.5 per cent in 1988, by reactivating the manufacturing sector which operated at 40 per cent of capacity, reconstructing the war devastated-zones, the oil refineries and ports, and increasing oil and gas revenues, which had sharply dropped from approximately $29 billion in 1977 to $9.6 billion in 1988. The post-revolution economic disorder and the 8-year war had diminished national output and investment. 'Over the period 1978–88, the real output and investment fell by average annual rates of 1.8 and 6.6 % respectively.'[18]

Since the revolution and the war, Iran had undergone some fundamental changes, two of which were rapid population growth and urbanization. Population shot up from 34.8 million in 1977 to 53 million in 1988. This rapid increase in population was concomitant with a rapid rate of urbanization. In 1977, some 47 per cent of the population lived in urban areas compared to 55 per cent in 1988. The population and urbanization pressure required long-term policies in terms of education, health, job creation and housing. The cultural and political demands of a bulging teenage population needed reflection, understanding and planning.

Rafsanjani's reform project took its lead from the economic package suggested by the International Monetary Fund and the World Bank, known as Structural Adjustment Policies (SAP). The Iranian SAP (*Tadil eqtesadi*) aimed to place the economy on the track of an efficient market-oriented economy. Implementing SAP meant disengaging the economy from government involvement, unloading the heavy role and burden of the government, and moving away from a self-sufficient economy.

Putting the Iranian economy on an unfettered capitalist path implied promoting competitive markets, the appropriate consumer and producer behavior, namely maximizing utility and profit. The pursuit of the SAP capitalist path conflicted with the *Basiji* mentality championed by Khamenei and his aversion to detente with the West. Most significantly, the successful implementation of SAP meant dismantling powerful religious, political and military vested interests and terminating the opaque, monopolistic and lucrative operations of the para-state foundations and the IRGC's economic wing.

The main features of Rafsanjani's economic reform reflected in the first Five-Year Development Plan (1989–93) included trade liberalization, privatization, and deregulation. The linchpin of trade liberalization was the herculean task of unifying the existing seven different exchange rates and hopefully establishing a single floating rate. Rafsanjani was also faced with three other major problems. First, he was not the sole decision-maker on determining Iran's economic system and its path and method of development. Second, he had inherited a disjointed and uncoordinated economy, in which organizations, foundations, and ministries acted autonomously and independently of one another, making coordinated planning impossible. Finally, Rafsanjani was a staunch supporter of IRGC involvement in the economy, the growing monopolistic activities of which was irreconcilable with competitive market activities.

Years after the revolution, and particularly after the war, economic and financial decision-making centres, each with their entrenched vested interests and appropriate political clout, had multiplied. Unsupervised and arbitrary dispensations, permits, quotas, favours and licenses created and hardened networks of nepotism and cronyism, encouraging corruption. Rafsanjani needed to bring order, consistency and transparency to an opaque patronage capitalism which he had been instrumental in creating. Real reform jeopardized the handsome gains of those with political, military and religious clout and connection, namely the ruling elite.

Furthermore, Khomeyni's legacy of villainizing the West and especially the US rendered normal economic and diplomatic relations taboo. Yet, Rafsanjani could not pursue his economic reforms without a change in foreign policy and detente with the West. Khamenei feared that Rafsanjani's economic modernization would result in the normalization of relations with the West and political and cultural liberalization at home. For Khamenei, the change of course intended by Rafsanjani undermined his ideological legitimacy, authority, and raison d'etre, while eroding the support of his power base, the doctrinaire *Basijis*, *Hezbollahis* and the IRGC. The already hardened vested interests around the ruling class feared that the opening of Iran's markets to foreign investment would end their monopolistic hold on lucrative investment projects.

Rafsanjani was initially successful in attracting foreign capital and investment and bringing Iran out of its international isolation. On 3 May 1991, Roland Dumas, the French foreign minister, visited Tehran, followed by Hans-Dietrich Genscher, the West German foreign minister, on 6 May 1991. Rafsanjani's international overtures paid off and he obtained credit from European, South Korean and Japanese banks to finance Iran's imports. 'In 1991, Tehran signed preliminary agreements with Japanese and European countries for developing several oil and gas fields,' while welcoming the return of American corporations Coca-Cola and Pepsi Cola.[19]

Between 1989 and 1993, the real GDP grew by an average annual rate of 7.0 per cent. Oil exports increased 'from around 2 million barrels per day in 1989/90 to 2.8 million barrels per day in 1993/94'. Investment as a percentage of GDP 'increased from 11 percent in 1989/90 to 14 per cent in 1992/93'. The removal of trade and foreign exchange restrictions led private consumption expenditures to grow 'by the staggering rates of 19.5 and 9.5 percent over the years 1990/91 and 1991/92, respectively' as compared to '2.5 percent in 1989/90'.[20]

In 1989, exports and imports were equal. A year later, the external deficit (export–import) stood at some $7 billion, and in 1991 it jumped to $11 billion before it returned to $7 billion in 1992. Iran's successive current account deficits and its inability to repay brought the country close to crisis. By the end of 1993, the country's foreign debt stood at around $23 billion. Even though Germany and Japan stepped in to reschedule Iran's debt repayment and prevented a debt crisis, Rafsanjani was forced to reconsider his economic reforms.

After almost three years in office, Rafsanjani's economic policies faced the discontent of the have nots. Since March 1992, the dispossessed manifested socio-economic resentment. Riots broke out in Tehran, Arak, Shiraz and Mashhad, as demonstrators attacked government buildings, banks, and police stations. Since the demonstrations of the early 1980s, this wave of unrest was a novelty.

In Tehran, protestors were mainly underprivileged disabled war veterans demonstrating against 'mismanagement at the state-run Foundation of the Oppressed', and 'squatters protesting their forced eviction from their illegally built homes'. The Mashhad riots of 30 May 1992 involved squatters who were defending their illegally built homes against 'demolition squads and security forces with trucks and bulldozers'. The riots left approximately 17 dead. Some 600 rioters were arrested, and eight were executed. In Mashhad, 'when the army could not suppress the crowds, the central government dispatched *Basij* (volunteer militia) units' to take back the city.[21]

Rising prices of goods and services were pinching the pockets of the lower classes. The timid inflation rate of 9.0 per cent during 1990–1 had jumped to 20.7 per cent in 1991–2, and further up to 24.4 per cent during 1992–3. The contraction in the purchasing power of the poor reduced the already meagre consumption of their basic necessities. The regime was becoming extra sensitive to the unwanted socio-political consequences of Rafsanjani's economic reforms.

Structural adjustment, economic restructuring, and unburdening the state from financing a highly bloated government sector and a heavily subsidized standard of living necessitated an initial worsening of the livelihood of the low and middle classes. Rafsanjani faced an inevitable choice. He could spend Iran's fluctuating oil revenues on maintaining the subsidized standard of living of a continuously growing population. This choice minimized public discontent and maximized the clergy's hold on power at the cost of capital formation, growth, and building for future generations. Or, by eliminating subsidies and accepting the probable short-run consequence of socio-political unrest, Rafsanjani could allocate oil revenues to investments and infrastructural development. The political cost of no subsidies was greater than its economic benefits.

Around 1993, economic conditions worsened, and Khamenei supported the conservative opponents of Rafsanjani's economic reforms. Rafsanjani's vocal economic opponents were the old *Bazaari* followers of Khomeyni, represented by the Islamic Coalition of Mourning Groups (ICMG). This powerful anti-statist and pro-mercantile group had at first embraced Rafsanjani's privatization policies and his drive to attract foreign trade and capital, but later withdrew their support. Rafsanjani's reforms jeopardized their mercantile-cum-capitalist interests on the one hand and their politically obtained legal, economic and financial privileges on the other hand.

Bazaar, the Islamic Coalition of Mourning Groups and State Patronage

Individual *bazaaris*, or those with *bazaari* roots, who were 'correct, religious, and skilled' were to be rewarded with government portfolios and protection from property seizures. Many of these figures were part of the ... ICA [Islamic Coalition Association]. (A. Keshavarzian)[22]

After the revolution, the Islamic Coalition of Mourning Groups (ICMG), which always emphasized its unswerving fidelity and loyalty to Khomeyni and the clerical establishment, was handsomely rewarded by the Islamic Republic. Members became deeply entrenched in the Iranian private, government and para-statal sectors of the economy and were equally well represented in Iranian politics.

In January 1986, the ICMG in close collaboration with the influential and conservative Ayatollah Ahmad Azari-Qomi, had founded the daily *Resalat* (Calling), which became an important anti-Rafsanjani mouthpiece. The ICMG disliked Rafsanjani's modernist entourage, their Westernized outlook and cultural tendencies, as well as his economic policies. They feared that their privileged access to import permits, domestic credit and cheap foreign exchange, the sources of their new and ill-gotten gains, may be threatened.

Privatization, Subsidies and Exchange Rate Unification

An important aspect of Rafsanjani's economic reforms was to end price distortions that were the result of the difference between the low government-set prices and the much higher real market prices. In the Iranian economy the most glaring cases of price distortions were that of subsidized basic goods, a vestige of the war economy and the price of foreign currency, principally the dollar. Their result was the inefficient allocation of resources, the disproportionate growth of the service sector and a rise in rent-seeking activities or making money without contributing to the economy because of political connections.

The removal of government subsidies on basic necessities meant a sudden leap in price of basic necessities such as bread, sugar, cooking oil and fuel, detrimental to most vulnerable economic groups. On 6 March 1992, Rafsanjani claimed that 'the government pays for the lion's share of the people's livelihood' and gave specific and glaring examples of the scope of subsidies. The government, he said, bought a kilo of wheat from farmers at 15 tomans, turned it into flour and sold it to bakeries at one toman. Rafsanjani added that the government was effectively giving consumers 1.2 million barrels of oil a day for free. He acknowledged that such subsidies could not be terminated at once since it would wipe out the livelihood of the most vulnerable but hoped for their gradual 'adjustment'.[23]

Political considerations, social stability and the need to retain the loyalty of the most vulnerable to the system/regime, however, prevented Rafsanjani from even gradually eliminating subsidies. Unable to reduce or end the subsidies, Rafsanjani left the lingering financial problem to future administrations.

Rafsanjani's attempt at unifying the exchange rates, another gordian knot of the Iranian managed economy, proved equally unsuccessful. Even though in 1993 the economy was encountering problems, the government tried to move towards a single unified exchange rate. From the end of March 1993, other than the official government exchange rate for the import of essential goods (consumer, defence, medicine) at $1=1,268 rials, Iran had two 'floating exchange rates'. The Central Bank announced a so-called 'floating exchange rate' of $1=1,542 rials, available through the banking system and a real free-floating exchange rate of around $1=1,640 rials, determined by market forces. The free market floating exchange rate representing the 'real price' of the dollar kept increasing and the gap between the official rate and real rate widened.

By 1995, the free market rate for the dollar jumped to 4,030 rials, while the official rate of the Central Bank was at 1,750 rials. The beneficiaries of this price distortion were those with privileged access to the artificially low 'official' rate. Rent-seeking, dishonest practices, corruption, and quick enrichment were encouraged when in 1995 a windfall gain of 2,280 rial could be made by gaining access to $1 at the official rate.[24] Faced with a fall in oil prices, a rapidly depreciating rial on the free market due to international payment imbalances, a growing external debt, a 23 per cent inflation rate and the inability to attract sufficient foreign investment, Rafsanjani backtracked, leaving the price distortions in the economy as they were and their beneficiaries untouched.

Privatization and Militarization of the Economy

An important component of Rafsanjani's economic reforms was the privatization of nationalized firms, which he began in 1990. Even though the Majles blocked his initiative in 1994, privatization was resumed in 1995 and ran through 1997. But the outcome fell short of its objectives. From 770 to 3,000 state-owned enterprises, only 391 to 400 were 'privatized'. Government enterprises were sold through direct negotiations with buyers and not through auctions or tenders, which raised the issue of cronyism, favouritism, nepotism and corruption. In the 1995 round of 'privatization', under the guise of sales to war veterans and martyred families, shares were sold to the foundations, enhancing the economic power of parastatal mega-holdings.

> ### State Owned Enterprises in Iran
> Since 1980 the Iranian economy has been characterized by prevalence of highly subsidized, inefficient, and overstaffed state-owned enterprises [SOEs] that account for a major share of the economy's output. SOEs in the industrial sector alone account for 70 per cent of the sector's value added, which is equivalent to 15 per cent of GDP . . . Available data suggests that a large number of SOEs are loss making and highly dependent on substantial government subsidies. (P. Alizadeh)[25]

Privatization failed to sell state-owned enterprises to the private sector. Instead, nationalized firms were transferred to unsupervised and unaccountable parastatal holdings. The most important of these holdings, the Foundation of the Oppressed, was directed by Mohsen Rafiqdust, a member of the Islamic Coalition of Mourning Groups and the former minister of the Islamic Revolutionary Guard Corps. Later, Mohsen Rafiqdust's brother, Morteza, became implicated in one of the most spectacular embezzlement cases in the history of Iranian banking. Morteza Rafiqdust's co-defendant, Fazel Khodadad was sentenced to death and executed. Morteza was initially sentenced to life imprisonment but was pardoned and released after eight years.

On 19 August 1989, Mohsen Rezai, the commander of the Islamic Revolution Guardian Corps, asked Rafsanjani for a 10 per cent hike in IRGC's budget. Instead of agreeing to a budget increase, Rafsanjani recommended that the IRGC place its engineering capabilities developed during the war at the service of the reconstruction effort. He directed the IRGC to become involved in national economic projects to secure a lucrative source of income. Rafsanjani referred to the Tehran–Tabriz highway and the Ilam tunnel as potential projects for the IRGC and quipped that with IRGC's involvement in reconstruction, civilians would be kept out of the process.

In 1989, at Rafsanjani's behest, *Qarargah sazandegie khatam al-anbia* (Construction Base of the Seal of the Prophets) entered the economic scene. This new military entity, a holding of the IRGC, became Iran's biggest post-war recipient and contractor of governmental projects. Rafsanjani hoped to attain three objectives by involving the IRGC in economic projects. He intended to create an independent source of income for them, draw upon their highly skilled engineering corps, and finally, coopt the demobilized *Basiji*s and the aimless young commanders and cadres of the IRGC in his economic reconstruction projects. Rafsanjani hoped to rally the war veterans to his own cause by giving them a taste of power and material well-being.

During Rafsanjani's tenure, *Khatam al-anbia* benefitted from preferential contracts in all economic domains, including oil, gas, electricity, minerals, pipeline, highway, railway, tunnel, dam and hospital projects throughout the country. Iran's economic isolation and the international sanctions against it eliminated all competition for *Khatam al-anbia*, providing the military with unprecedented colossal financial gains.

Rafsanjani's Political Conundrums

The years 1992 and 1993 were difficult ones for Rafsanjani. On 11 June 1993, in the sixth presidential election, he ran against three candidates and won. But his major contender, Ahmad Tavakoli, supported by the Islamic Coalition of Mourning Groups, obtained an unexpected 24 per cent of the vote. Tavakoli hammered at Rafsanjani's failure to properly implement privatization, reduce the size of government expenditures and bureaucracy. He reproached the management style of Rafsanjani's ministers and officials, which he believed were not sufficiently Islamic. Tavakoli objected to Rafsanjani's disregard for vulnerable social groups, inattention to social justice and the rise of self-indulgence and extravagance among his team.

Toeing Khamenei's line, Tavakoli criticized Rafsanjani's infatuation with the capitalist economic models proposed by the World Bank and the International Monetary Fund and intuited that the president and his team were not convinced that Islam could manage all aspects of society. In matters of foreign policy, Tavakoli followed the Leader's line and insisted that Iran's foreign policy be based on the understanding that the Islamic government faced 'an essential and serious enemy'.[26]

The conservative coalition wished to reduce Rafsanjani's power and authority and boost Khamenei's. The sixth presidential elections brought to the surface new cleavages among the conservatives and sharply expressed the morose mood of Iranians. Fifteen years after a cataclysmic outburst of political zeal, Iranians had become almost indifferent to politics as only 50.6 per cent of eligible voters participated in the presidential elections.

In 1992 Khamenei's snide comments to thwart Rafsanjani's reform efforts, and impose his authority over the president, made Rafsanjani's political life cumbersome. In the middle of Rafsanjani's all-out effort to attract foreign investment, on 2 July 1992, Khamenei announced that, 'This country ought to be constructed by Iranians as non-Iranians are untrustworthy. Officials must rely on the people's talents.'[27] Again, on 22 October 1992, Khamenei declared that Europeans and the superpowers 'were liars, with a dagger hidden behind them [in one hand] and another hand [ready] for pillage'.[28]

Khamenei Challenges Rafsanjani

At this time, Azari-Qomi, the outspoken clerical founder of the daily *Resalat* (Calling), Nateq-Nuri, the Majles president, Ahmad Jannati, the head of the Guardian Council, and Mohammad Yazdi, the head of the judiciary, formed a powerful pro-Khamenei clerical coalition. In their sycophant statements, they systematically presented Khamenei as the defender of the pious and Islamically conscious destitute and disinherited and bolstered his status by emphasizing his unassailable position as the Ruling Guardian Jurist. Their exaltations of Khamenei were also warnings to Rafsanjani to obediently follow the Leader. It was natural for this significant power bloc to rally behind Khamenei, from whom it derived its politico-economic interests.

Rafsanjani chose his new cabinet with Khamenei's consent. On 15 August 1993, Rafsanjani went to the Majles to introduce his ministers. He told the deputies that he had already dropped those candidates that the Leader might have opposed. The conservative deputies, however, insisted on cabinet ministers with strong 'Islamic' credentials who were in tune with Khamenei's line, now called the Guardian Jurist's Line (*khate velayat*). The conservative Majles turned down Mohsen Nurbakhsh, one of the key architects of economic reform, as minister of economy and finance.

On 9 November 1993, Khamenei wrote a letter to Rafsanjani on the general directions of the Second Five-Year Plan. He called on the president to ensure the strictest compliance of all aspects of the plan, economic, financial, social and cultural, with Islamic jurisprudence (*sharia*). Khamenei directed Rafsanjani to guarantee the attainment of social justice and support the disinherited, prioritize the allocation of resources to those possessing Islamic values and support and consolidate the revolution and the Islamic system.

Khamenei instructed the president to promote religious beliefs and revolutionary values, prevent profligacy and consumerism, move towards a self-sufficient economy, be very cautious with privatization, expand interest-free credit centres (*sandoqhaye qarz al-hasaneh*) within the national banking system and avoid external indebtedness. Khamenei's letter did not demonstrate a coherent national plan or programme, but it succeeded in throwing various wrenches in Rafsanjani's plans. Khamenei was announcing that his vision of an ideal Islamic Republic was a hermetic one, tightly protected from all non-Islamic and Western influences, economic, cultural, social, and political.

On 13 February 1994, Khamenei demonstrated his displeasure with Rafsanjani's cultural policies by appointing Ali Larijani to the sensitive post of director of the Islamic Republic of Iran Broadcasting (IRIB). The national radio and television organization was a most potent propaganda tool. Khamenei wanted it run by someone who shared his sense of urgency to confront the Western cultural threat. Larijani believed that the Western cultural onslaught was permeating Iranian society with its 'decadent music, art, and clothes' and one would have to be blind not to see it.[29]

Ali Larijani had first replaced Mohammad Khatami as minister of culture and Islamic guidance. The Leader was now firing Mohammad Hashemi-Rafsanjani, the president's brother, and putting Larijani in his place. Since July 1990, Mohammad Hashemi-Rafsanjani had been under pressure and attack by members of the Islamic Revolutionary Committees and *Hezbollahi*s for his unacceptable cultural policies. From September 1993, the conservative Majles deputies attacked the IRIB for its un-Islamic television programmes, spreading Western culture and corrupting the minds of the youth through its Western films and decadent music.

Khamenei was gradually marking his territory and curtailing Rafsanjani's power. Mohammad-Mostafa Mir-Salim, a French-educated engineer and a member of the Islamic Coalition of Mourning Groups, replaced Larijani as minister of culture and Islamic guidance. Mir-Salim believed that culture was an ideological affair, and his responsibility was to propagate Islamic values endorsed by the high clergy and Khamenei.

Mir-Salim pursued Larijani's promotion of Islamic cultural activities in mosques. While Mir-Salim was minister, the use of satellite dishes was prohibited (17 April 1994). Rafsanjani's minister of interior, Mohammad-Ali Besharati informed the public that Law Enforcement Forces would enter people's homes, inspect their roofs, and confiscate the illegal dishes.[30] Thus began a long and futile cultural war against satellite dishes ending in the capitulation of the system to the people's will for a different kind of entertainment.

The press was closely controlled during Mir-Salim's tenure. Maverick publications such as *Jahane Eslam*, *Gardun*, *Bahman* and *Payame Daneshju*, and at least three others were closed. The system was intolerant towards those publications that represented opposition organizations or crossed the red lines set by the Leader.

Hadi Khamenei, the Leader's brother, was *Jahane Eslam*'s editor and one of the founders of the Left Assembly of Militant Clerics (*majma rowhaniyoun mobarez*). Abbas Maroufi, *Gardun*'s editor, was an active member of the Iranian Writers'

Association, critical of the government's violations of the freedom of expression. Ataollah Mohajerani, the editor of *Bahman*, was close to Rafsanjani and Karbaschi. In April 1990, Mohajerani had proposed improving relations and direct negotiations with the US. Heshmatollah Tabarzadi, the editor of *Payame Daneshju*, was one of the founders of the Left, Office of Consolidating Unity, a vocal and popular student organization.

The power struggle reigned, as long as the Khamenei–Rafsanjani duo did not feel that the system/regime was in danger. Rafsanjani acquiesced to Khamenei's inroads and placed a brake on his economic reforms with its cultural consequences. Instead, he turned to building dams, roads and electricity and nuclear plants, and developing heavy industries and bolstering infrastructural capacities. His attempt to clamp down on profiteering failed to prevent the rising inflation, which reached a peak of 49.5 per cent in 1995–6.

Karbaschi, the Modernist and Entrepreneurial Mayor of Tehran

Facing resistance to economic reforms, Rafsanjani took an indirect route to effectuate part of his socio-economic and cultural change. On 4 January 1990, Abdollah Nuri, the minister of interior, introduced Gholamhoseyn Karbaschi as the mayor of Tehran. Karbaschi had attended Tehran University after three years of theological studies at Qom, and epitomized the market-oriented, go-getting, innovative managers and technocrats that Rafsanjani took pride in surrounding himself. Karbaschi's years in office from January 1990 to April 1998 transformed Tehran and the life of Tehranis.

> ### The Mayor Who Lifted Morales
>
> In the spring of 1990, shortly after assuming office, Karbaschi asked Tehranis to put flowerpots at their doorsteps, at home and at work. Outside homes and shops, offices and hotels, the city's residents obliged the new mayor with displays of color and greenery. (L. Secor)[3]

Karbaschi's multi-faceted urban policies left an undeniable physical mark on the city and the morale of Tehranis. What happened in Tehran under Karbaschi's auspices soon permeated throughout other major cities in Iran. The to-be cleric-turned-modernist revamped Tehran's municipality into a robust financial entity through wheeling and dealing with the private sector. He twisted arms and ignored the terms of Tehran's Comprehensive Plan to raise money for Tehran's municipality and make it financially viable and independent.

By selling permits to developers to construct high-rises in Tehran, he destroyed Tehran's beautiful and virgin skyline. Yet, between '1990 and 1998, he raised $6 billion, three quarters of it from the sale of density'.[32] Karbaschi invested 'three fourths of it in the city's infrastructure and urban fabric'.[33] Thanks to his cavalier management approach, the construction industry in Tehran picked up and flourished and many went from rags to riches due to patronage, while skyscraping super-luxury apartments came into vogue.

Karbaschi's flagship project to enliven the morose life of middle and lower class Tehranis was his Bahman Cultural Centre. This 5,000-square metres complex was composed of sports facilities and grounds, a concert hall, indoor swimming pool, sauna, library, movie theatre, arts and computer classes, children's playgrounds, cafés, science fairs and auditoriums. Bahman Cultural Centre, the first of approximately 130 Cultural Centres, was built where Tehran's ugly and stinking slaughterhouse used to stand. While Khamenei's choice for the Ministry of Culture attempted to revitalize the mosques, Karbaschi was paving another path (Figure 9.3).

Karbaschi built some 600 parks, freeways, fast-lane bus services, clean streets and well-maintained greens and squares with colourful flowers, adorned with sculptures and water fountains. Karbaschi, like Rafsanjani, appreciated beauty, cleanliness and a colourful city that smelled nice. At the time, the hidebound conservatives opposed planting flowers in public spaces and even argued against planting grass in city squares and instead argued for growing lucerne, alfalfa and even eggplants.[34]

On 15 December 1992, Karbaschi launched a full-coloured professional daily called *Hamshahri* (Fellow Citizen/Townsman), addressing the problems and concerns of citizens, from traffic to city sanitation, crime, housing problems, and current issues. Karbaschi's *Hamshahri* looked and sounded different from all other newspapers. Almost apolitical, it promoted Rafsanjani's modernist cultural, social and economic ideas against the weighing conservatism of Khamenei.

Figure 9.3 Gholamhoseyn Karbaschi. *Source: Wikimedia Commons.*

About two months after its publication, Khamenei warned the mayor about the nonconformist cultural content of *Hamshahri* and its promotion of non-Islamic values. Karbaschi fired the editor and found a replacement who had Khamenei's approval to assure the continuation of the paper. The paper became in vogue as it appealed to a wide spectrum of the population. Its circulation reached 400,000 after three years and laid the grounds for Iran's reformist movement.

On 2 March 1995, Rafsanjani, flanked by his ministers and Karbaschi inaugurated the first *Refah* (Welfare) supermarket in Tehran's upper-middle-class neighbourhood of Yusefabad. This brainchild of Karbaschi was the first of a chain of super and hypermarkets which soon spread throughout Tehran and Iran. The *Refah* stores were public joint-stock companies raising some 65 per cent of their capital from the sale of bonds at a fixed 20 per cent rate of return. Tehran's municipality remained the manager of these stores.

The *Refah* stores were Karbaschi's market-oriented response to price rises, profiteering and overpricing of goods in retail outlets. By cutting out the mark-up of middlemen, *Refah* provided some 11,700 products at prices 20 to 30 per cent lower than the market. *Refah* was also Karbaschi's way of promoting a modernist market mentality and getting middle-class Iranians to invest their capital in the stock market and participate in the economy. The chief opponents of *Refah* stores were the bazaar and the Islamic Coalition of Mourning Groups, which considered the supermarkets and hypermarkets as threats to their monopoly of the economy's distribution and retail network.

The 5th Majles: The Right Splits into Traditional and Modern

The ongoing divide between Rafsanjani's modernist technocrats and the traditional clerical guardians of the status quo deepened before the elections to the 5th Majles (8 March 1996). Those born during the revolution had come of age and were seriously challenging the merits of a theocracy. In November 1995, the conservative beneficiaries of the system/regime closed rank behind the Leader and lambasted the public's growing mistrusts and uncertainties as seditious and the handmake of the foreign enemy and the domestic liberals and technocrats.

The Youth's Growing Estrangement

If one day the youth become indifferent towards Islamic and revolutionary values, the country will become vulnerable. (A.-A. Nateq-Nuri)[35]

Carried away by a false sense of popularity, aware of the growing rift between Khamenei and Rafsanjani, and encouraged by the decrease in Rafsanjani's votes in the previous presidential election, the traditional Right moved to marginalize Rafsanjani. The Association of Militant Clergy (*jameeye rowhaniyat mobarez*) and the Islamic Coalition of Mourning Groups set out to win the 5th Majles, without Rafsanjani's cooperation.

During internal discussions of the Association of Militant Clergy, Rafsanjani tried to convince his more doctrinaire colleagues to break their sectarian mould and include different Islamic political tendencies in their list of candidates. Once negotiations over the inclusion of 5 names proposed by Rafsanjani in the list of 30 Tehran candidates supported by the Association of Militant Clergy fell through, the Right split and Rafsanjani's followers went their own way.

On 18 January 1996, the press published a declaration signed by 16 members of Rafsanjani's team, including ten ministers, four undersecretaries, the head of the Central Bank and the mayor of Tehran. The announcement praised the contributions of Rafsanjani, labelled him the 'commander of construction and development', and announced their participation in the elections to the Fifth Majles. The signatories called themselves 'the executives of construction and development' and 'the people's servants'.

This new political formation announced that the revolution was no longer threatened by external dangers but by underdevelopment. They proposed to overcome it by 'efficiency and expertise' in the economic and social domains. Rafsanjani's technocratic and professional team announced that they would compete in the elections to pursue economic and social reforms and boost the people's faith in their own ability to 'manage the Islamic government'.[36] The 'liberals' and 'technocrats' dreaded by the conservative clergy were already propagating their ideas through the weekly *Bahman*, whose editor Ataollah Mohajerani was one of the 16 signatories.

To extend an olive branch, *Kargozarane sazandegie Iran* (Iran's Executives of Construction) included nine candidates of the Association of Militant Clergy (*jameeye rowhaniyat mobarez*) in their list of 30 candidates for Tehran. Some of these candidates such as Iran's future president, Hasan Rowhani, and Mahmud Doai, the wise and moderate editor of *Ettelaat*, were ideologically closer to the modern rather than the traditional Right.

The presence of Faezeh Rafsanjani, the president's nonconformist daughter, on the list of Iran's Executives of Construction sent a meaningful and disparaging message to the traditional and conservative clergy. Faezeh was an outspoken modern character, a staunch supporter of women bicycling, and a nemesis of the conservative clerics.

The Guardian Council excluded some 2,130 candidates for a variety of reasons. Under the veneer of unity and alliance, a fierce ideological rivalry was underway among the old conservative followers of the Imam's Line. Convinced that the candidates of Iran's Executives of Construction posed no threat, Khamenei made the tactical mistake of giving them his blessing.

But as soon as Iran's Executives of Construction entered the political scene, they generated an unexpected favourable momentum. The conservative and traditional political competitors reacted by warning the people against electing 'liberals' who would 'jeopardize Islamic thoughts in the country in the name of freedom', dilute the 'religious and revolutionary values of the people', initiate 'the separation of politics and religion', and 'seek to negotiate and establish relations with the Great Satan (the US)'.[37] Little did they know that their objections would serve the popularity of Iran's Executives of Construction.

Another surprising element in the elections was the return of the Left political formations, Iran's Mojahedin of the Islamic Revolution, and the Assembly of Militant Clerics (*majma rowhaniyoun mobarez*). While Rafsanjani and his colleagues had moved away from the ideas of the traditional Right, the Left had also evolved. The old Left had become more nuanced: politically democratic, economically social-democratic, culturally more liberal and religiously more tolerant and inclusive.

Despite manipulations to keep all political forces deviating from Khamenei's Line out of the Majles, candidates of the new social-democratic Left and the technocratic and modern Right entered the Majles. In Tehran seven exclusive candidates of Iran's Executives of Construction, headed by Faezeh Rafsanjani and another 8 joint candidates with the conservative Association of Militant Clergy (*jameeye rowhaniyat mobarez*) entered the Majles.

The Fifth Majles was convened on 1 June 1996, and on 2 June, the new balance of power in the Majles became evident. Nateq-Nuri, the influential conservative incumbent president of the Majles, secured his leadership position by obtaining only 27 votes more than Abdollah Nuri, the joint candidate of the Left and the Executives of Constructions. The big loser of the 5th Majles was the Islamic Coalition of Mourning Groups. Habibollah Asgarowladi and Asadollah Badamchiyan, the Coalition's pillars and stalwarts, failed to get elected. The outcome of elections to the 5th Majles was a warning to the conservative leadership that Iranians sought a different life than the one they currently had.

Less than a year after the opening of the 5th Majles, the Islamic Republic was scheduled to hold its Seventh presidential election on 23 May 1997. The conservatives had a natural candidate in Nateq-Nuri, whom they hoped would follow Rafsanjani's path of becoming president after having presided over the Majles. From the end of August 1996, Rafsanjani's followers openly campaigned for reforming the Constitution to allow Rafsanjani to run for a third term. Nateq-Nuri and his political base opposed the prolongation of Rafsanjani's office and the greater entrenchment of his ideas. Nateq-Nuri argued that Khamenei was also opposed to 'entertaining such a discussion'.[38]

When on 14 October 1996, Rafsanjani officially opposed the idea of a third term, the traditional Right breathed a sigh of relief. On the next day, Karrubi announced that the Assembly of Militant Clerics was resuming its activities after a six-year hiatus.

The new Left wanted Mir-Hoseyn Musavi to enter the race and worked hard to obtain his candidacy. But on 28 October 1996, Musavi thanked his supporters and officially declined his candidacy for the presidency. Musavi's bow-out seemed to pave the way for Nateq-Nuri. The new political trio, composed of Iran's Executives of Construction, the Assembly of Militant Clerics and Iran's Mojahedin of the Islamic Revolution, were now in a desperate search for a suitable candidate.

Assassinating the Opposition Abroad and Its Consequences

On 13 July 1989, Abdolrahman Qasemlu, the leader of the Kurdish Democratic Party of Iran, was assassinated in Vienna during a meeting with the representatives of the Islamic Republic. Rafsanjani referred to the killing as the death of 'a few counter-revolutionary Kurds'. Less than two years later, on 18 April 1991, Abdolrahman Borumand, a political opponent of the regime and a close associate of Shapur Bakhtiyar, was stabbed to death in the lobby of his apartment in Paris. On 6 August 1991, Shapur Bakhtiyar, the shah's last prime minister and the leader of the National Movement for the Iranian Resistance, a pro-democracy and anti-Islamic Republic Organization, was stabbed to death at his Paris apartment, along with his secretary. All three assassinations were believed to be the work of the Islamic Republic's death squads liquidating the opposition.

On 6 August 1992, the German police discovered the mutilated body of Fereydun Farrokhzad, with ten stab wounds in his body, at his apartment in Bonn. Farrokhzad was a famous showman, TV host, singer and poet who had left the country after the revolution. In exile, he had become a staunch enemy of Khomeyni, the clergy and the Islamic Republic, and was associated with royalist organizations opposed to the Islamic Republic. The German authorities did not implicate the Islamic Republic, although the style of murder bore their trademark.

> ### Iran's War against Its Own Opposition Abroad
> Iran's involvement in international terror is extensive and has long been the cause of persistent problems between Tehran and the West. (Scotsman)[39]

Less than six weeks after the assassination of Farrokhzad and three years after the assassination of Qasemlu, on 17 September 1992, Sadeq Sharafkandi, who had succeeded Qasemlu as leader of the Kurdish Democratic Party of Iran, was assassinated along with two of his associates, at Mykonos, a restaurant in Berlin. The three were in Berlin attending the XIX Congress of the Socialist International. The spokesman for Iran's Foreign Ministry rejected any implication by the Iranian government in the murders and attributed it to internal Kurdish disputes.

The Mykonos Affair became a real headache for the Islamic Republic. In May 1993, five were indicted and put on trial on 28 October 1993. Three and a half years later, on 11 April 1997, the German judiciary ruled that the Iranian political leadership had ordered this crime. A 'Committee of Special Operations' was identified as the body that had carried out the operation. Germany's prosecutor general named Khamenei, Rafsanjani, Velayati, the minister of foreign affairs, and Ali Fallahiyan, the minister of intelligence, as members of the 'Committee of Special Operations' and directly implicated them in 'state terrorism'. The German prosecutor general named Khamenei as the 'mastermind/commander of the initial murder orders' and upheld the warrant issued for Fallahiyan's arrest on 14 March 1994.[40]

The Consequences of the Mykonos Executions

The verdict delivered by the Berlin court, was the most serious blow to Iran-Germany relations and subsequently to Iran-Europe relations. (H. Musaviyan)[41]

After the court verdict, the European Union (all except for Greece) withdrew its ambassadors from Iran, expelled Iran's intelligence personnel, ceased ministerial-level meetings and ended its 'critical dialogue' (1992–7). Europe, and in particular Germany, Iran's chief trade partner that had made great efforts to accommodate Rafsanjani's economic reforms, abandoned Iran.

It is difficult to understand the rationale behind alienating friendly European countries by conducting assassinations on their lands. Economically, the overseas assassinations were suicidal and politically, of dubious merit, except to intimidate the Iranian opposition. If there was a will to torpedo Rafsanjani's economic and foreign policy reforms, the overseas assassinations were the best means to go about it. The Islamic Republic's rash adventurism in Europe isolated the country and forged an alliance between the European Union and the US against Iran.

One year into Iran's honeymoon with the European Union (May 1993), Martin Indyk, the US presidential advisor and national security advisor on Arab–Israeli issues, Iraq, Iran and South Asia, had articulated US President Bill Clinton's 'dual containment' policy to detain and deter Iran and Iraq. At the time, 'Dual containment' did not share Europe's favourable view of Iran. It considered Iran a rogue state and called for its 'active containment'. Clinton referred to Iran's nuclear and missile programme as one of his reasons for sanctions. He labelled Iran's role in the Middle East 'as an inspiration and paymaster to terrorists'.[42] Between March and May 1995, all US firms, and their subsidiaries, were prohibited from trade, financial and commercial transactions with Iran.

The US sanctions sent the rial to dollar exchange rate into a tailspin. In January 1995, the dollar was worth 2,500 rials on the free market (black market), and by May 1995, one dollar exchanged for 6,500 rials. On 5 August 1996, Clinton signed the Iran–Libya Sanctions Act (ILSA), threatening 'penalties on third countries that invested more than $20 Million in Iran's energy sector'.[43] Even though Europe tried to stand up to the ILSA, the verdict on the Mykonos Affair pushed it into US arms.

Repression at Home

In May 1990, some nine months after Rafsanjani became president, Bazargan's political organization, the Association for Defence of Freedom and the Sovereignty of the Iranian Nation, wrote him a lengthy letter. The letter argued that after ten years of absolutist rule, mismanagement and repression, Iran stood at the edge of a dangerous precipice. Many of the 90 signatories had been involved in the provisional government and the Revolutionary Council. The old revolutionaries reminded Rafsanjani of the grave economic, political and social problems. They requested him to prevent the wrongdoings, restore the rights stipulated in the Constitution, and allow the activity of law-abiding organizations and the press. They asked the president to permit the press to publish their letter and thereby take the first step toward ending censorship.

About a month after the letter, Rafsanjani responded with increased repression and intimidation. The Ministry of Intelligence arrested 23 of the 90 signatories, including Ezatollah Sahabi, Abolfazl Bazargan and Hashem Sabbaqiyan. A few signatories withdrew their names under coercion. The detainees were interrogated for three to five months, kept in isolation, tortured, and some recanted under pressure. Later, the Iranian National Television aired their forced statements as proof of their guilt. They were sentenced to between six months and three years' imprisonment but were released after some twelve months.

On 14 March 1994, Saeedi-Sirjani, Rafsanjani's once outspoken supporter, was arrested by the Ministry of Intelligence. He had written several bold letters to Khamenei, criticizing the repressive cultural atmosphere in the country, the censorship of his books and inviting the Leader to reflect. Sirjani was accused of numerous 'crimes', including possession of drugs, homosexuality, and espionage. Secular and not necessarily politicized intellectuals and writers pressing for artistic and cultural freedoms were labelled domestic foot soldiers of the Western cultural onslaught. On 25 November 1994, Sirjani was killed in prison. Ali Fallahiyan's repressive programme at home and abroad ushered a bloody war on intellectuals and activists thinking differently from the clerical regime.

Silencing Iranian Writers' Association

Iranian intellectuals who were in the process of reviving the old Iranian Writers' Association and who had written a text denouncing the murder of Sirjani were summoned to the Ministry of Intelligence and warned not to make waves, lest they be treated as criminals against national security. Their response was a bold text, 'We Are Writers,' signed by 134 of Iran's eminent writers, poets, critics, translators and researchers.

On 15 October 1994, the in-embryo Iranian Writers' Association claimed that it was their 'natural, social and civil right' to publish their work 'freely and without interference'. The Iranian intellectual community reminded Rafsanjani, Mir-Salim and Fallahiyan that they were well and alive. Defiantly, they stressed that even if threatened, they would maintain that 'No individual or institution has the right to obstruct the publishing process for whatever excuse.'[44] They demanded recognition as writers and their organization as a professional body. The text of 'We Are Writers' was sent to the press, and to the Ministry of Culture and Islamic Guidance. The latter ruled that the press was forbidden to print it. But Mansur Kushan's publication *Takapou* braved the wrath of the intelligence community and published it.

The insubordination of the intellectual community infuriated Fallahiyan and the Ministry of Intelligence. In a vengeful act of ideological retaliation, it launched a daunting intimidation campaign of surveillance, interrogations, arrests, frame-ups, kidnappings, torture and finally murders. Writers, especially those implicated in reviving Iranian Writers' Association, were regularly summoned by the Ministry of Intelligence, and warned to desist from 'political and organizational activities'.[45]

On 26 July 1996, Fallahiyan's intelligence apparatus tried to intimidate both the German authorities before the verdict of the Mykonos trial and the Iranian intellectual community. Iranian security agents raided the residence of Jens Gust, the German Cultural Attaché, who had invited six members of the revived Iranian Writers' Association for dinner. The six writers, three men and three women, had been signatories of the letter, 'We Are Writers'. The security forces interrogated, filmed, arrested, and then released them, warning them that they could be arrested for espionage.

On 6 August 1996, the plot to murder 21 members of Iranian Writers' Association failed. The Ministry of Intelligence had apparently planned to send the bus transporting Iranian writers to Armenia for a series of conferences to the bottom of a cliff. About a month later, on 8 September 1996, 14 influential writers who had finalized the charter of Iranian Writers' Association and were to sign it, were arrested and warned that they should end their meetings and activities.

In the subsequent months, the Ministry of Intelligence notched up its arrests, kidnappings, and beatings of writers. Those arrested were explicitly told that unless they ceased their activities, they would be murdered. The chief intelligence operator in charge of the campaign against writers, intellectuals, and Iranian Writers' Association, was Fallahiyan's US-educated undersecretary, Saeed Emami. The sombre Saeed Emami believed that liberals, intellectuals and seculars were the Trojan Horse of the Western onslaught. As opponents of the clerical state, they deserved to die.

In tandem with the physical harassment and persecution of intellectuals, in the summer of 1996, Channel One of the Islamic Republic's National Television launched a weekly programme on Thursday nights called *Hoviyat* (identity). The masterminds of this programme, Saeed Emami and Hoseyn Shariatmadari, formed a team of harrowing cultural hardliners obsessed with pursuing Khamenei's directive of countering the Western cultural onslaught. They aimed at breaking, exposing, and silencing the so-called Western domestic foot-soldiers. To obtain conformity, they exercised character assassination. Hoseyn Shariatmadari had been an IRGC commander during the war and an old employee and interrogator of the Ministry of Intelligence. On 22 December 1993, Khamenei appointed him to the highly prestigious position of director of the daily *Keyhan*.

Every Thursday night, the Islamic Republic's National Television, engaged in spreading a mixture of vile lies and a few facts, about Iran's cultural luminaries, including Abdolhoseyn Zarinkoub, Iraj Afshar, Ahmad Shamlu and Hushang Golshiri. Sometimes, the crude confessions obtained from detainees under torture, such as Ezatollah Sahabi's, were released during the *Hoviyat* (identity) series. Those slandered during this programme were accused of a premeditated and deliberate plot to subvert the youth in collusion with foreign powers.

The Challenge of Islamic Intellectuals

The real problem facing the Islamic Republic was that after seventeen years of revolution, the youth showed less and less interest in the Islamic discourse and was more and more attracted to Western culture, mores and its way of life. Even the early day zealous stalwarts were gravitating towards non-clerical Islamic discourses, questioning the Rule of the Guardian Jurist or the necessity of the unity of state and religion.

Abdolkarim Sorush (Hoseyn Haj Faraj-Dabbagh) had been the star theoretician of the Islamic Republic in the early days of the revolution and had impeccable religio-revolutionary credentials. The monthly *Keyhan Farhangi* (Cultural Keyhan) had first appeared in the summer of 1984 and gathered a group of bright, progressive religious intellectuals. This publication was the cultural and scholarly monthly of the daily *Keyhan*, which was headed by Khatami. In April 1988, *Keyhan Farhangi* published Sorush's path-breaking 'Theoretical contraction and expansion of the *sharia*' in a series of articles.

Sorush's central concepts of the indeterminateness and incompletion of man's understanding of the Quran and Islam frazzled the clerical leadership. Sorush posited that as time changed and the human mind evolved, the understanding of the eternal Quran and religion also evolved. Sorush denied the clergy their primordial claim to an absolute and time-frozen knowledge and grasp of religion.

On the relation between religion and state, Sorush was equally revolutionary. He rejected 'any government that claims legitimacy based on the implementation of some notion of Islamic methods of governance'. A democratic government was 'the only one compatible with his notion of Islam'.[46] Sorush rejected Islam as an ideology, arguing that it was richer than a one-dimensional ideology. He also refuted the cleric's interpretation of religion to legitimize a religious political system. Modern methods of government, he argued, could neither be derived from nor based on Islamic law. Sorush's modernist religious ideas shook the pillars of political Islam.

In November 1991, the influential monthly *Kiyan* appeared on the newsstands. Its contributors were principally composed of the *Keyhan Farhangi* group, and its editor was Mashallah Shamsolvaezin. Sorush and his iconoclastic critique of the hegemonic post-revolutionary view of religion and religious rule constituted the soul of *Kiyan*. Sorush's ideas, their extensions, spillovers, associations, cross-germinations and even criticisms in *Kiyan* created a veritable democratic, pluralistic and agnostic incubation space. *Kiyan* became an innovative intellectual platform as well as the conveyor of intellectual dialogue, tolerance, and reasoning.

The articles in *Kiyan* were written by an ideologically heterogeneous group of Islamic modernists, leftists, liberals and seculars with intellectual, journalistic, academic, administrative and activist backgrounds. Once Khatami came to power, the intellectual and technical producers of *Kiyan* fanned out into various reformist newspapers, ministries and universities. They became the messengers, practitioners and ideologues of the reformist movement and the nemesis of the conservative traditionalists and their rule.

Factual and Analytical Questions

1 Explain the process by which Hojatoleslam Khamenei became the Leader. In what specific ways were his credentials for leadership different from Khomeyni's?
2 What was the purpose of Rafsanjani's policy of changing attitudes? How did he intend to implement it?
3 What were the levers used by the Guardian Council between 1990 and 1992 to eliminate the Left opposition? Provide specific cases.
4 What is the difference between 'approbatory supervision' and 'informational supervision'?
5 What were the main features of Rafsanjani's economic reforms? How successful was he in implementing them?

6. How did Khamenei's Islamic world outlook differ from Rafsanjani's?
7. Explain the European Union's 'Critical Dialogue' with Iran and how it differed from Clinton's 'Dual Containment Policy' between 1992 and 1997?

Seminar Questions

1. 'Rafsanjani's Structural Adjustment Policies (SAP) were incompatible with the economic and cultural interests of the ruling oligarchy and were doomed to failure from the beginning'. Discuss. Why did Rafsanjani embark on them?
2. 'Khamenei's Western cultural onslaught theory and his campaign against it was a politically and religiously motivated move to control Rafsanjani, subvert his economic reforms, establish his political authority and keep the country on a conservatively defined religious path.' Discuss each of these possibilities and provide historical evidence.
3. 'What Rafsanjani could not do for the country during his presidency, Karbaschi did for Tehran.' Assess the validity of this statement by providing specific examples for and against.
4. Provide a rationale for the Islamic Republic's state terrorism in Europe between 1989 and 1992. What were its international consequences?

Discussion Questions

1. 'The Islamic Republic could be divided between pre- and post-Reappraisal and Revision of the Constitution.' Explain why and provide specific evidence.
2. If leaders could be distinguished and analysed through their role models and their political projects, how did Rafsanjani and Khamenei compare?
3. To what extent were Rafsanjani's economic reforms victim of a power struggle between him and Khamenei? What were Khamenei's religious and ideological arguments justifying his stance against Rafsanjani?
4. 'From 1990 to the end of his term in office, Rafsanjani and his minister of intelligence, Fallahiyan, embarked on a systematic campaign of silencing political and cultural figures who thought differently from regime.' Discuss and provide specific evidence.

Glossary

enjoining good and forbidding wrong Sometimes referred to as commanding what is just and forbidding evil (*Amre be marouf va nahye az monker*) is an Islamic duty incumbent upon Muslims. The notion has its roots in the Quran and is considered a social obligation by the Shii. The question of how to apply this principle has long been debated. The means available to enforce it have been argued to be, the heart, the tongue, the hand and the sword. The Quran does not specify how.

mojtahed A clergy who has passed all stages of theological studies, introduction, basics/surface, advanced/beyond and has obtained permission from an established Islamic jurist to derive edicts or ordinances from the body of Islamic jurisprudence, the Quran, the Tradition of the Prophet, analogy and reason. The Mujtahid has mastered the science of *fiqh* (Islamic jurisprudence) and *usul* (principles of the faith).

10

Khatami's Presidency

A Democratic Opportunity Deflected and Foregone, 1997–2005

Chapter Outline

Khatami's Sweeping Victory	493
Stifling Reform	498
State-Sponsored Terror	503
The Rise of Iran's New Civil Society Press	507
Laying Siege to the Reform Movement	512
The Revolt of the Maverick 6th Majles	516
Khatami's Re-election	520
Khatami's Foreign Policy	526
Khatami's Economic Legacy	529

On 30 January 1997, having obtained Khamenei's non-opposition to his candidacy, Mohammad Khatami, announced his readiness to run in the presidential election. In his quest, he had the support of Iran's Executives of Construction, the Assembly of Militant Clerics, and Iran's Mojahedin of the Islamic Revolution. Khatami, the 54-year-old cleric, had served as minister of culture and Islamic guidance in both Musavi and Rafsanjani's governments and had the support of both. From 1992 to 1997, he headed the National Library, and had been away from politics for five years. He spent this time reflecting, engaging in intellectual speculation and dialogue with Iranian social scientists and thinkers. In Khatami's election campaign, political and cultural development occupied the centre stage.

Khatami had his ears to the ground and realized that perceptions, values and expectations were shifting rapidly. He was aware that Iranian society did not adhere to a rigid interpretation of Islam promoted by the conservative traditionalists. Khatami knew that hammering at blind obedience to the ruler and forcing a cultural and political straitjacket was far from what the majority wanted and expected. Yet, Khatami was conscious that he could jeopardize the confirmation of his candidacy by the Guardian Council unless he paid his official respects to Khamenei's line.

Khatami's discourse, however, was a breath of fresh air in Iran's politically and culturally stale environment. He invoked ideas such as 'assuring the people's rights and freedoms', 'a reason-revered religion', 'making religion more attractive as a way to counter the cultural onslaught', 'the constitution as the regulating mechanism of society', 'institutionalizing plurality of ideas, tolerance and competition within the system/regime', 'honour and respect for different ideas', 'civil rights of citizens', an open society in which no single group or tendency can consider itself 'as the epitome of Islam', 'equal opportunity for all', 'preventing violations against legal freedoms and rights', 'familiarizing the people with their rights and enabling them to attain the legal freedoms of expression, pen, and association', 'combatting lawlessness and violence', 'assuring the active participation of the youth and women', the Islamic ruler's obligation to 'listen to criticism' and the Guardian Jurist being also 'the leader of the minority, the leader of atheists'.[1] His ideas clashed with the monotonous discourse of the clerical leadership and excited Iranian society.

By late April 1997, Khatami's campaign picked up, and he was neck to neck with Nateq-Nuri in the unpublished surveys and polls. Khatami was attracting the youth, who usually abstained and the silent majority who desperately wanted change. From mid-May, the youth mobilized massively and spontaneously in his favour. They voluntarily joined his election campaign headquarters throughout the country and filled the streets, handing out his pamphlets and canvassing passersby. The public enthusiasm for Khatami snowballed. The conservatives who believed in Nateq-Nuri's easy victory panicked. Khatami's campaign speech in Mashhad was disrupted. His opposition launched an elaborate vilification and demonization operation against him.

Mir-Salim, minister of culture and Islamic guidance, informed Iran's cultural community and sportspeople to desist from supporting candidates. His strange comment was in response to the overwhelming support of intellectuals, academics, artists, musicians, actors, directors and sports celebrities for Khatami's candidacy. Right before the elections, during the night of Ashura, a night of sorrow and mourning for the Shii, the ruling conservatives organized a festive carnival. They attributed this religious transgression to Khatami's supporters, conveying their insensitivity to the faith.

Two days before the election, Ayatollah Mohammad-Reza Mahdavi-Kani, the influential leader of the traditionalist Association of Militant Clergy (*jameeye rowhaniyat mobarez*), made a desperate and most unconventional move. The newspaper *Abrar* quoted Mahdavi-Kani in large fonts at the top of its front page that, 'I guess the esteemed leader favours Nateq-Nuri.'

Khatami's Sweeping Victory

From the 238 who presented their candidacy for the presidential election, the Guardian Council had approved only four, including Nateq-Nuri and Khatami. On 23 May 1997, Iranians went to the polls, and on 24 May, the press reported on Khatami's landslide victory. The Khatami phenomenon had attracted 80 per cent of the eligible voters. Only 51.8 per cent had participated in the previous presidential election. Khatami obtained 20 million votes against Nateq-Nuri's 7.2 million. The Second Khordad (23 May) Movement was a veritable second revolution The vote against Nateq-Nuri was also a vote against Khamenei. The Leader was far from happy with his new president and thus began another four years of turbulence between the highest powers of the state.

The 23 May tsunami expressed an overwhelming demand for change, giving Khatami and his followers a solid mandate to implement his projects. It was a victory of the 'People's will' against the 'Leader's will,' and a resounding vote of confidence in the Republican aspect of the system/regime and a categorical no to its clerically defined Islamic facet. Like Rafsanjani, Khatami had a national project.

On 23 May 1997, a long tug of war began between two perceptions of the Islamic Republic. One defended a theocracy and arbitrary rule, the other a civil society and the rule of law. Most significantly, Khatami and his supporters sought to minimize the role of the Guardian Jurist to that of a symbol of national unity. In this attempt, they resembled the monarchical reformists, the National Front, who had tried to make the shah reign but not rule. Once above the law, neither the shah nor Khamenei were willing to accept constraints.

> ## Khatami's Presidency
>
> The presidential tenure of Mohammad Khatami also represented a period during which the uneasy balance between popularly mandated state institutions and clerically supervised ones reached levels of perilous instability. (S. Randjbar-Daemi)[2]

Khatami believed in gradual political and cultural liberalization to allow dissenting voices to express themselves. For him, recognizing plurality, entering a national dialogue and tolerating different outlooks, were ways to reduce social resentment, relieve tension and normalize life, thereby assuring the maintenance of the system/regime. Khatami was not a revolutionary but a reformist who sought solutions within the system. Khatami's respect for the system implied that he was committed to the role of the Guardian Jurist. Nevertheless, he intended to modify Khamenei's function from ruling and intervention to supervision and guidance.

Khatami's democratic discourse and liberalization project constituted an existential threat to Khamenei and the oligarchs appointed by him. The Pahlavi dynasty had taught the ruling clergy a compelling lesson: when despots open wide the floodgates holding back public resentment and opposition, it will wash them away. The Khamenei camp quickly grasped the reality that if unchecked, the 23 May Movement would loosen its grip on power. More alarming was Khatami's sociopolitical base running ahead of him, with more radical demands. Controlling the Khatami fervor required severing the bond and trust fostered between the new president and his 20 million voters. His supporters had to see that Khatami's promises were undeliverable. As Khatami prepared to implement his reforms, the coalition around Khamenei was poised to stunt them.

> **President Clinton's First Public Reaction to Khatami's Election**
>
> Now, as to Iran, obviously it's a very interesting development . . . it's at least a reaffirmation of the democratic process there. And it's interesting, and it's hopeful. (B. Clinton)[3]

During Khatami's first presidential term (May 1997–May 2001), Khamenei relied on the judiciary, the Special Clerical Courts, the Law Enforcement Force of the Islamic Republic, the IRCG, and the old thugs and *Hezbollahis*, now called 'pressure groups', to hem in the 23 May Movement and its objectives. The Leader experimented with containment and repression through trial and error. He tested the degree of obedience of his subjects, hoping that they would comply with his wishes without him having to resort to force. Khamenei examined the limits and possibilities of a constrained democracy, just as the shah had done.

Khatami, His Cabinet and Initial Waves

On 20 August 1997, Khatami presented his cabinet to the Majles and obtained a vote of confidence for each of them. His ministers were composed of Iran's Executives of Construction, his own religious and political formation, the Assembly of Militant Clerics, and a few independents. He faced his first challenge in choosing an appropriate minister of intelligence acceptable to Khamenei and eventually settled on Qorbanali Dorri-Najafabadi, who was not high on his list of candidates for this post. Khatami got his way with his ministers of foreign affairs, interior and of culture and Islamic guidance, demonstrating that the leader was giving him latitude and the benefit of the doubt.

Figure 10.1 Abdollah Nuri. *Source: Photo by Atta Kenare/AFP via Getty Images.*

For almost sixteen years, Ali-Akbar Velayati, the Leader's protégé, had occupied the influential position of the minister of foreign affairs and had seemed untouchable. Replacing him with Kamal Kharrazi, the US-educated Iranian representative to the United Nations (1989–97), must not have been easy. Khatami's minister of interior, Abdollah Nuri, had already occupied the same position under Rafsanjani but had been dropped in 1993, under suspicion that Khamenei disapproved of him (Figure 10.1).

The new minister of culture, Ataollah Mohajerani, was a controversial figure who had called for direct negotiation and relations with the US and was a staunch proponent of 'indulgence and tolerance'. Mohajerani was an Islamic liberal and different from his illiberal predecessor, Mir-Salim. Mohajerani told the deputies before their vote that if he were to become minister of culture, he would oppose 'almost all of the methods and policies that existed in that ministry'.[4] Mohajerani did not believe in dictating to writers, artists, and people of reflection, what to do. Khatami's economic, financial, commercial, oil and planning ministries and portfolios were filled with specialists and technocrats from Iran's Executives of Construction, indicating that economically he was pursuing Rafsanjani's plans.

Khatami thought of himself as a peacemaker reconciling his alienated fellow citizens with an open, indulgent, liberal and democratic Islam. He told the Majles that he did not believe in resolving problems by 'arresting, imprisoning, beating up, and assaulting'. All prohibitions he announced needed to be 'within the law', and individuals could not take the law into their hands.[5] Khatami saw his mission as harnessing arbitrariness, unaccountability and subjectivity by lawfulness, accountability and objectivity.

Khamenei, however, would not stand for change. Meeting with the top brass of the IRGC, he promised to hold a steady course as had been set by Khomeyni. Angrily he lashed out that 'to the despair of the enemies (*kuriye chesm doshman*), we will not budge an inch backwards or forward'. Khamenei reiterated that 'the line and path of the revolution' was the same as 'that articulated from the first day of the revolution'.[6]

Khamenei's first reaction to the new situation was guarded. He failed to see the need for change and refused to acknowledge the demands and discourses different from his ideals. Denying the obvious realities in the country, he repeated that differences among the regime's high authorities, the desire on the part of some in the system/regime to open up to the West and the US and the diminution in the people's belief in the system/regime, and Islam, were myths and enemy propaganda.[7]

On 14 November 1997, Khamenei was subjected to a scathing challenge by no less than Ayatollah Montazeri. Khomeyni's first designated successor, and a cleric of the highest religious stature, reinterpreted the position of the Guardian Jurist as a supervisory role without plenipotentiary powers and the right to intervene in all affairs. Montazeri advised Khatami to inform the Leader that the people had spoken and voted for him massively, giving him the legitimacy to manage their choice. Montazeri also warned against the seminary schools and the religious institutions losing their independence and becoming dependent on the government. One day after his speech, Montazeri's residence in Qom was assaulted by a group of pro-Khamenei zealots, looted, wrecked and occupied. Montazeri was placed under house arrest until January 2003.

Three days later, Ayatollah Meshkini, the Chair of the Assembly of Experts of the Leadership, claimed that the Guardian Jurist was a 'perfect human being and unassailable'.[8] The conservative Association of Militant Clergy, the self-proclaimed guardian of the system's Islamicness, responded to Montazeri's bombshell by insinuating that he was an enemy who had chosen this moment to question the authority of the Guardian Jurist because he had figured that, 'the recent presidential elections illustrated a dilution in the people's belief in Islam, the revolution and the Rule of the Guardian Jurist'. The Association of Militant Clergy were equally in denial as their Leader. They asserted that Khatami's success at the elections merely demonstrated the people's support of the 'revolution, the system/regime and the Leader'.[9]

Khatami was caught between a rock and a hard place, a position that defined his eight years of presidency. He must have appreciated Montazeri's interjection and his interpretation of the supervisory role of the Guardian Jurist. But he was the president and Khamenei was the Leader. Khatami's reaction had to be nuanced. The reformist president announced that 'according to the constitution, the rule of the Guardian

Jurist was one of the principles of the system, and therefore defense of the law meant defending the Guardian Jurist'.[10]

Khatami's Islam is Different from Khamenei's

Khatami, however, also pursued reforms that Khamenei did not appreciate. On 7 January 1998, Khatami told Christiane Amanpour, CNN's famous Iranian-British correspondent, that his Islam sought 'dialogue, understanding and peace with all nations'. Khatami raised the issue of two Islams, one 'progressive' and the other 'reactionary'. He chided the American government for attacking the 'Islam which seeks democracy, progress and development; an Islam which calls for benefitting from the achievements of human civilization including that of the West'.

In this crucial interview, Khatami conceded that he faced opposition and contrary to the Leader accepted the existence of 'internal differences' in terms of 'opinions' and 'tendencies'. He referred to a 'tall wall of mistrust' between Iran and the US and optimistically added that through a 'dialogue between civilizations', 'relations between Iran and the American people would open up'.[11] The American and Iranian media welcomed Khatami's statements, and negotiations with the US became a hot topic. A survey in Iran indicated that 82 per cent of Iranians believed that Khatami's comments on establishing relations with the US were 'good' and 'very good'.[12]

Khamenei's response to Khatami's overtures was dismissive, muddled, and passive aggressive. He thanked Khatami for his principled statements, although adding that 'relations and negotiations with the US were useless for the Iranian people' and even 'detrimental for the Iranian people and the world Islamic movement'.

Khamenei escalated his attack, targeted his president, and announced that breaking the taboo of negotiating with, and establishing relations with America, was 'a US propaganda objective'. Khamenei believed that belligerence towards the US united the people behind him. The enemy he claimed was trying to shatter this unity, and reconciliation with the US was a rejection of the revolution's ideals and an act of surrender. Khamenei deplored the Iranian press which was welcoming negotiations with the US.[13]

On 5 February 1998, Khamenei articulated his concept of Islamic democracy, by emphasizing that believing in, and wholeheartedly obeying the 'rule of the Guardian Jurist' was the lynchpin of the Islamic Republic's representative system. He announced that 'the rule of the Guardian Jurist and the negation of foreign hegemony constituted the two main pillars of Islam's governance system'. Allegiance to the rule of the Guardian Jurist, Khamenei claimed, was on par with all other Islamic jurisprudential ordinances.[14] The national project of the Leader was now to convince Iranians that the US was their eternal enemy and that they needed him to protect them from the US.

Seven months after Khatami's election, Khamenei slammed on the brakes of his president's political, cultural and foreign policy reforms and moved against the reformer. The seeds of doubt about the role of religion in government, sown by eminent religious intellectuals such as Sorush and Mohammad-Mojtahed Shabestari, the renowned Iranian theologian, philosopher and hermeneutist, added to Montazeri's criticisms, were dangerous and seditious for the traditional clerical oligarchy.

The Khamenei camp knew that Khatami and his reformist theoreticians were employing Islamic arguments to weaken and redefine the rule of the Guardian Jurist, separate religion from politics and empower the people's vote at the expense of religious leadership. To vilify the reformists in the eyes of the faithful the traditionalist Right presented them as anti-Islamic, inspired and financed by foreigners, conspiratorial and treacherous, the veritable Trojan Horse of the enemy.

Stifling Reform

To push back against Khatami's reforms, Khamenei's supporters used three main levers. The judiciary played a determining role in arresting reformist *persona non grata*, putting them on trial and sending them to prison on trumped-up charges. Extremist groups within the Ministry of Intelligence played a more sinister role. They indulged in assassinations which came to be known as state 'serial/chain killings' of 'non-desirable deviants'. Finally, the *Hezbollah* thugs resurfaced, very much like the 1980s. They attacked legal assemblies and assaulted reformist speakers, including ministers such as Mohajerani and Nuri. The *Hezbollah* thugs would attack the offices of leading reformist newspapers, such as *Jameeh* (Society) and break up peaceful student conferences and demonstrations in favour of the reform movement. Their battle cries were, 'Death to the enemies of the rule of the Guardian Jurist!' and 'Death to the liberals!'

The anti-Khatami forces relied on four channels to shape public opinion and whip up emotion and rage among the zealous against reform. First, the conservative members of the Majles led by Nateq-Nuri, the Majles president and his deputy Mohammad-Ali Movahedi-Kermani made speeches, gave interviews and wrote articles in *Resalat* deploring the state of the country after Khatami's election. The conservative minority faction in the Majles also wrote open letters firmly condemning the government's political and cultural deviations, the excesses of the press and the weakening of Islamic values.

Second, Friday Prayer leaders, the most extreme among them Mohammad-Taqi Mesbah-Yazdi, used their sermons throughout the country to attack political and cultural reforms. Third, rallies in various cities such as Tehran, Qom, Mashhad, and Esfahan were organized by institutions under the Leader's control. The participants demanded the resignation of Khatami's key ministers, such as Nuri and Mohajerani. Lastly, IRGC's leading military brass, including its commander, Yahya Rahim-Safavi, appointed by Khamenei, openly threatened and intimidated Khatami, his supporters and the nascent reformist press with outright violence.

Attack on Karbaschi

On 4 April 1998, the judiciary arrested Gholamhoseyn Karbaschi, Tehran's mayor, and charged him with embezzlement and bribery. All political forces who had supported Khatami's election condemned Karbaschi's arrest as a 'political maneuver' to destabilize Khatami and his government. Faezeh Rafsanjani, a Majles deputy, called it an act of vengeance by those who lost the election to Khatami, and an attack on democracy. The head of the judiciary, Mohammad Yazdi, an appointee of Khamenei, defended the arrest in the name of the anti-corruption campaign underway. In the judiciary's ambush against Karbschi's Tehran Municipality some 100 employees were rounded up and interrogated. The detainees were even questioned about the mayor's private and personal life, such as what he ate, whether he did his prayers or whether he had extramarital relations.

Karbaschi had become the hero of many Tehranis for his efforts to bring colour, scent, cleanliness, greens, highways, cultural centres and chain stores. His real guilt was his unequivocal support for Khatami's presidential bid. Khatami requested that the Leader order Karbaschi's release until his case received a thorough review. Khamenei conceded, and Karbaschi was free after eleven days. On 7 June 1998, Karbaschi was put on trial and was accused of embezzlement, participation in briberies and misappropriation of public funds. In his trial, the prosecutor, Gholamhoseyn Mohseni-Ejehi, was also the judge.

Karbaschi denied all charges and insisted that his trial was political and not juridical. He provided details of his mistreatment and of the threats against others to obtain false testimony against him. Karbaschi's trial was fully reported in the press and on television. The six hearings quickly became a national hit and opinions polarized around the mayor's guilt or innocence. A survey suggested that 69 per cent believed that there had been 'payments which were unaccounted for in the Tehran Municipality', 68 per cent thought that Karbaschi should be acquitted, and 58 per cent considered the trial to be 'a political affair'. Only 8 per cent believed that Karbaschi had 'pillaged public funds and deserved execution'.[15]

On 23 July 1998, Karbaschi was sentenced to 5 years in prison and 20 years' suspension from all government services and given a hefty fine. Faezeh Rafsanjani's newly published newspaper *Zan* (Woman) dedicated its first issue to the Karbaschi trial. Its headline read a statement by Karbaschi, 'Had the court been unbiased, I would have been acquitted.'[16]

Karbaschi's sentence was subsequently reduced to 2 years' imprisonment and 10 years suspension from government services. On the Leader's recommendation and after Rafsanjani's interventions, Karbaschi was pardoned on 25 January 2000, having spent some 18 months in prison. Upon his release and on the eve of the elections to the 6th Majles, Karbaschi founded the daily *Hammihan* (Compatriot), with the talented young journalist Mohammad Quchani as its editor. Karbaschi subsequently engaged in politics through his publications and his leadership role in the Executives of Construction Party.

Gagging Nuri and Kadivar

Khatami's minister of interior, Abdollah Nuri, was bold and firmly committed to political liberalization and advancing people's participation in the political process. Nuri issued permits for meetings of alternative voices, which were suppressed in the past and hoped to turn Park Laleh into Tehran's Hyde Park Corner. Nuri did not, however, have the power to guarantee the security of such meetings. Unable to prevent Nuri from issuing permits, the conservative Right unleashed the *Hezbollah* to attack the participants with stones, sticks and chains. They destroyed the loudspeakers and broke up peaceful rallies by throwing tear gas at the participants.[17]

Nuri's statements and activities were anathema to the anti-Khatami coalition. He insisted that Islam was a 'defender of freedoms' and that presenting Islam as 'repressive and despotic' was 'the biggest blow to Islam'.[18] Arguing that Islam was not only compatible with but equal to democracy and freedom went against the current discourse of the pro-Khamenei conservative camp. From Friday, 6 February 1998, Mesbah-Yazdi, the chief anti-Khatami theoretician, spoke every other Friday at Tehran's Friday Prayers. He expounded an anti-democratic, repressive, hidebound and violent Islamic discourse.

On 10 June 1998, after Karbaschi's first day of trial, 28 conservative deputies wrote a letter to the Majles president demanding Nuri's impeachment, and accusing him of fomenting tension in society, issuing permits for political meetings leading to violence and making provocative speeches. Nuri's 'misdeeds' included widespread new appointments in the Ministry of Interior, defending Karbaschi and rendering the country insecure.

Eleven days later, on 21 June 1998, Nuri went to Parliament, faced his opponents and informed them that illegal pressure groups [*Hezbollah*] and not the legally assembled citizens were the cause of insecurity. He reminded them that contrary to 'despotic systems/regimes', where only the security of government officials is guaranteed, 'in popular/democratic systems', the security of all citizens needs to be assured.[19]

The conservative revolt of the traditionalist deputies paid off. On the morrow of the Iranian football team's 2–1 victory over the US during the World Cup and the outburst of public jubilation and dancing in the streets, 137 deputies voted in favour of Nuri's impeachment and 117 opposed it. Khatami appointed Nuri as his deputy for 'Development and Social Affairs' and replaced him with Abdolvahed Musavi-Lari. Khamenei did not think that the new minister of interior was appropriate for the task.

> ## Why Nuri was Impeached
> The Right faction has impeached Nuri, to obtain its own ends in the elections to the Assembly of Expert, the [City and Rural] Councils, and the Sixth Majles. (Qodratollah Nazarinia, Majles Deputy)[20]

On 5 December 1998, Nuri launched his newspaper, *Khordad*, which became a veritable Islamic pro-democracy and anti-despotic juggernaut. It attacked the traditional Right for its insatiable appetite to monopolize all power, intimidate reformists and intellectuals and impose a dogmatic and hidebound Islam on society. The readership of *Khordad* skyrocketed as it exposed the machinations and involvements of the extremist conservatives in the political serial/chain killings that swept the country. Nuri resigned his position as Khatami's deputy to have a free hand in defending the people's constitutional rights.

In February 1999, Nuri and another progressive cleric, Mohsen Kadivar, were summoned to the Special Court for Clerics for the subversive contents of *Khordad*. Concurrently, Nuri entered the elections to the first Rural and City Councils held on 26 February 1999. He headed the pro-Khatami list of the Islamic Iran Participation Front, a new political party born on 5 December 1998 and the pro-Rafsarjani list of Iran's Executives of Construction Party.

Mohsen Kadivar was arrested one day after the elections to the Rural and City Councils, which proved to be a sweeping success for the reformists. The Special Court for Clerics charged him with 'propaganda against the Islamic Republic system', 'inciting public opinion' and 'propagating lies'. The anti-Khatami coalition was rooting out alternative political and religious expressions as heresy. Kadivar's arrest caused a widespread backlash among prominent clerical figures such as Grand Ayatollahs Musavi-Ardebili and Yusef Sanei, Qom clerics, journalists, political activists, students and the reformists at large.

> ## Is the Leader Appointed by God?
> The perception of some, that the Leader is appointed by God, or the Divine Lawgiver, and does not require supervision, is religiously reprobate and legally highly questionable. (M. Kadivar)[21]

Mohsen Kadivar was put on trial primarily for an interview published in *Khordad* on 14 and 15 February 1999 which insinuated that the Islamic Republic was a 'monarchical Islamic system' and that the 'relations and norms' of the monarchy had persisted in the form of 'a system in which one ruler has unlimited and absolute powers'. Kadivar opined that 'the people revolted to decide for themselves, not so that decisions be made for them, even if the decision-maker was a righteous person'.

Kadivar, questioned the Islamic Republic's record of providing freedoms and suggested that had it not been for the Khatami years, 'its performance would have obtained a failing grade'.[22] His criticisms were too radical for the pro-Khamenei coalition to hear. After a single court hearing, he was sentenced to eighteen months' imprisonment and sent to Evin Prison. He served his full term and was released on 16 July 2000.

The Rural and City Council elections again demonstrated the widespread popularity of reformists. In Tehran, Nuri came in first followed by Saeed Hajjariyan (Kashani) and Jamileh Kadivar, Mohsen Kadivar's sister. From the 15 seats on Tehran's City Council, the pro-Khatami reformists won 13 seats. Nuri was voted in as president of Tehran's City Council.

The Rural and City Council elections were the only true free elections since the Guardian Council had no say in sifting candidates and tilting the scales in favour of candidates. Ayatollah Jannati, the head of the Guardian Council, lamented that Council elections were a major catastrophe as the candidates' credentials were not vetted.

On 30 October 1999, Nuri was put on trial and charged with 'libeling and insulting the system's authorities and institutions', 'propagating lies to incite public opinion', 'propaganda against the system', 'opposing the views of the Imam [Khomeyni] and insulting him' and, finally, 'propagating ideas against religious principles/standards and insulting religious sanctities'. The prosecutor of the Special Court for Clerics based his accusations on articles in *Khordad*.

Nuri turned his six court hearings into a veritable indictment of the conservative Right and their assault on freedoms and democracy in the name of Islam. Nuri's iconoclastic defence of a modern and liberal Shiism and political democracy against religious and political despotism was reminiscent of Emile Zola's *J'accuse* and Martin Luther's *Ninety-Five Thesis*.

He thundered, 'the leadership is not above the law ... and cannot deprive the clergy or members of any other profession or group of their legal freedoms stipulated in articles 36, 37 and 168 of the constitution!' Nuri lambasted the conservative coalition's belief that 'diplomats were spies, intellectuals were bought, the Left were anarchists and coup-makers, the youth were corrupt deviants, thugs and hoodlums were revolutionaries, women were potential satanic symbols and all tie-wearing middle-aged men were royalists'.[23]

On 23 November 1999, Nuri was condemned to five years of prison, five years of deprivation from press activities and the payment of fines. The judge revoked

Khordad's permit and forced its closure. One day after Nuri's sentence was made public, Khamenei threw his weight behind the Special Courts for the Clergy and supported their decisions as 'seemingly just'. Khamenei also defended the Guardian Council's sifting of candidates for elections to the Majles, the Assembly of Experts and the presidency as legal and for the protection of the people. He rejected allegations that the Guardian Council was politically biased and motivated.

State-Sponsored Terror

Under Khatami, the blossoming of the free press, the rejuvenation of civil society and the increasing mobilization of pro-reform student actions had rapidly changed the Iranian political scene. Khatami's insistence on following through with his reforms and supporting the newly founded liberties confronted the anti-Khatami coalition with a glaring dilemma. Putting Karbaschi, Kadivar and Nuri behind bars did not suffice to dampen the dammed-up socio-political and cultural enthusiasm and expectations unleashed by Khatami's presidency. The system/regime, therefore, resorted to violence and intimidation.

On 4 September 1998, Mohajerani and Nuri participated in the funeral of war martyrs whose corpses had been returned to Iran. They were suddenly attacked by *Hezbollahi*s and given a good beating in broad daylight. The assailants were zealous supporters of Khamenei, who chanted 'death to liberals' and 'death to the opponents of the Rule of the Guardian Jurist'. Violence against reformists, irrespective of their position, was placed on the agenda of the pro-Khamenei coalition.

About a month after beating up Khatami's ministers, the *Hezbollahi*s carried out another provocative and illegal operation. This time, they attacked American tourists and businessmen visiting Iran. Khamenei had been displeased with Khatami's overtures to the US since the January 1998 CNN interview. A significant aspect of Khatami's opening to the world had been attracting foreign tourists. His adversaries equated his reach-out policy with the spread of 'degenerate' Western culture. Khamenei's followers wished Iranians and foreigners to understand that political and cultural opening was not to be.

On 21 November 1998, a new group of thugs called 'The Devotees of Mohammad Mostafa Navab's Pure Islam' went to Esteqlal [Hilton] Hotel.[24] They attacked a bus carrying 13 American tourists with stones and iron rods, breaking windows, and terrorizing its passengers. The Americans tourists were called spies, and threatened that next time, the assailants would put into practice the slogan of, 'Death to America.' In a statement, they announced that their operation served also as a warning to the those who had invited the Americans. Soon the conservative clerical leadership discovered that even attacking and beating up ministers was not enough to curb the ardor and energy of the people for change. To push back reforms, more extremist tactics were employed.

> **The Price of Political Reform**
>
> If civil society's project of political development leads to the removal of the right-wing faction from power, they are prepared to carry a coup and turn Iran into Lebanon. (A. Ganji)[25]

The Execution of Darush Foruhar and Parvaneh Eskandari

At 10.50 pm on 22 November 1998, eight plainclothesmen who were later identified as members of the Ministry of Intelligence, entered the house of Darush Foruhar and Parvaneh Eskandari. The assassins stabbed Darush 12 times, and Parvaneh, his wife, 25 times. Darush was 70 and Parvaneh was 59. The mission completed, Mehrdad Alikhani, the team leader, informed his superior Mostafa Kazemi, the vice deputy of intelligence of the Ministry of Intelligence, that the 'work was done'. When Mostafa Kazemi sought reassurance and asked, 'both', Alikhani confirmed. Kazemi asked again, 'definitely finished?' and Alikhani ascertained, 'yes'.[26]

The Foruhar couple were Mosaddeqists, nationalists and secular social democrats who had a long, upstanding, and honorable political track opposing the shah's despotic regime. Darush Foruhar had spent many years lingering in the shah's prisons and some five months in Khomeyni's. Parvaneh Eskandari was one of the two women present at the National Front Congress of December 1962. Darush Foruhar was the founder of *Hezbe Mellat Iran* (Nation of Iran Party), minister of labour in Bazargan's post-revolution government and a member of the Islamic Revolutionary Council. Both were known for their frankness and courage (Figure 10.2).

In the 1990s, the Foruhars had reached the conclusion that political change was only possible with the separation of religion from the state and the reinstatement of people's rule or democracy. The Foruhars objected to the violation of political and individual rights. They believed that change was possible by relying on the mobilization of domestic forces in the form of syndicates, unions, professional, student and political organizations. The couple were peaceful, yet radical opponents of the regime and religious despotism. After Khatami's election, their political discourse gained more attraction. The Foruhars flaunted the idea that Khatami had his hands tied, faced with Khamenei's powers. The Foruhar murders shocked society. Political and student organizations called for bringing the culprits to justice. Khatami called the murders 'abominable' and ordered immediate identification and pursuit of the 'law-breaking murderers'.

Figure 10.2 Darush Foruhar and Parvaneh Eskandari. *Source: Wikimedia Commons.*

Hunting Writers and Intellectuals

Within a fortnight, news came of four other political murders. Majid Sharif, a writer and translator, a follower of Shariati, a member of the National-Religious Forces of Iran, and a writer for the reformist press, had gone missing on 19 November 1998. His body was found abandoned on 25 November. Mehrdad Alikhani, a member of the Ministry of Intelligence's assassination squad, recounted that Sharif was abducted, made unconscious and then given a lethal injection.

Mohammad Mokhtari, a poet, writer and translator, signatory of 'We Are Writers', and an active member of the inner circle of Iranian Writers' Association, was the next victim. He had gone out to buy milk on 3 December 1998 and never returned home. He was found strangled far away from his house on 9 December 1998. On the same day that Mokhtari's body was found, his friend and colleague, Mohammad-Jafar Puyandeh, another well-known writer and translator, also a signatory of 'We Are Writers', and an active member of Iranian Writers' Association went missing. Puyandeh's body was discovered strangled and abandoned on 19 December 1998. The orders to carry out the political and cultural executions again came from Mostafa Kazemi, the vice deputy of intelligence of the Ministry of Intelligence.

With the revelation of these assassinations, gradually previous ones were disclosed. Piruz Davani, a Left writer and journalist, had gone missing on 25 August 1998. His body was never recovered. Davani had Tudeh Party sympathies and was the president and spokesman of a group called 'Unity for Democracy in Iran'. He had spent some three and half years in the prisons of the Islamic Republic, and upon release in 1994, he had tried to forge unity among the Left opposition of all shades. It was Darush Foruhar who had divulged his abduction.

Once the unofficial list of some 25 to 80 state executions emerged as 'serial killings', 'chain killings' or 'suspect killings', Davani's name was among them. The names of the murdered included two Protestant Armenian priests, a priest who had converted from Islam to Christianity at the age of 14, writers, translators, journalists, scholars, a car dealer, an interpreter of the Quran and a stewardess. The list also included Kazem Sami, Bazargan's minister of health, and Ahmad Khomeyni, Ayatollah Khomeyni's son.

Khatami's insistence to get results, and the investigative journalism of Nuri's *Khordad* and Saeed Hajjariyan's *Sobhe Emrooz* (This Morning), yielded unprecedented results. *Sobhe Emrooz* had come on the newspaper stands on 15 December 1998. The two papers committed themselves to getting to the bottom of the political and cultural serial killings. Khamenei and his coalition forces reacted to the murders by calling them the work of Zionists and foreigners. The reformist press countered that only those who wished to destabilize Khatami's government had a motive to carry out such butcheries.

On 5 January 1999, 'The Devotees of Mohammad Mostafa Navab's Pure Islam', issued a statement accepting responsibility for the murders. This was only a subterfuge to distract the public from identifying the real masterminds. It was thanks to the popular pressure from below, the press from the middle, and Khatami's pressure from above, that on 6 January 1999, the Ministry of Intelligence issued an unprecedented historical statement.

For the first time in Iranian history, the secretive and much feared security and intelligence apparatus acknowledged guilt. The Ministry of Intelligence officially announced that it had identified and arrested the network responsible for the 'recent despicable murders in Tehran'. It added that, 'Most regrettably, a few irresponsible, deviant, and rogue colleagues of this Ministry . . . were among those who perpetrated these murderous acts.'[27]

Five days later, Khamenei spoke at Tehran's Friday Prayers. He condemned the killings, defended the Ministry of Intelligence and its hard-working personnel, and expressed his 'surprise' at the 'infantile and foolish' behaviour of some of Iran's newspapers, which he insinuated may be 'spiteful and connected [to foreigners]'. Khamenei posited, 'I cannot believe and accept that these murders were not part of a foreign scenario.'[28] The minister of intelligence, Qorbanali Dori-Najafabadi, and his predecessor, Ali Fallahiyan, were said to have been implicated in the murders. On 10 February 1999, Dori-Najafabadi was replaced by Ali Yunesi. According to an unwritten rule, all ministers of information need to be *mojtahed*s, and therefore clerics.

Almost two years later, on 19 January 2001, a closed military court passed judgement on 18 suspects implicated in the murders of the Foruhars, Mokhtari and Puyandeh. All but one of the accused were members of the Ministry of Intelligence. Three were acquitted, and the remainder received sentences from 30 months in prison to the death penalty. The two death sentences were never carried out. The mysterious mastermind of the murders, Saeed Emami, died under very suspicious circumstances. The press reported that Emami had committed suicide in prison on 20 June 1999. Rumour had it that the highest authority in the land had sanctioned the hits.

The Rise of Iran's New Civil Society Press

One of the chief beneficiaries of Khatami's liberalization effort was the press which produced critical, analytical and investigative journalism. The people yearned for uncensored and independent news and analysis. The public's fascination with the reformist press was dangerous as both raced to break religious and political taboos one after the another. Once the growing bond between the reformist press and civil society snowballed, the anti-Khatami coalition had no other option but to gag the press and harness the public's enthusiasm.

On 5 February 1998, a different-looking, different-speaking and an intellectually seductive newspaper called *Jameeh* (Society) appeared on the newsstands and sold like hotcakes. The title on the first page of the paper read '*Salam bar jameeh*' or 'greetings to society'. Right below the title was the picture of a handsome woman, covered in a yellow headscarf and coquettishly revealing an eye, an eyebrow and some forehead.

Jameeh had come to loosen tongues, break taboos, promote pluralism and serve the blossoming civil society, but jar and rattle the conservative ruling class. Giving license to such a newspaper and the others that followed was by the grace of Khatami's cultural team, Ataollah Mohajerani and especially his broadminded deputy, Ahmad Burqani. *Jameeh* had come to provide non-governmental news, politicize society differently, foster informed political participation, and build a bridge between non-governmental theoreticians, political activists, modernist clerics, journalists, artists and writers. It became a seminal newspaper and a school of journalism.

The pages of *Jameeh* covered controversial cultural and political topics gave voice to dissident thinkers, and debated religion, democracy and despotism, roughening many conservative and extreme Right feathers. On 27 April 1998, two and a half months after the appearance of *Jameeh*, Yahya Rahim-Safavi, the new commander-in-chief of the IRGC appointed by Khamenei, made an outlandish speech in Qom. He said, 'These days, newspapers and journals threaten our national security,' and added, 'We will have to behead some and cut out the tongue of some. Our language is our sword.'[29]

It was clear that Rahim-Safavi had the Leader's blessing. On 2 June 1998, Rahim-Safavi identified the strategy of the Islamic Revolution Guardian Corps (IRGC) towards the reformists and said, 'We threw a stone in the den of vipers injured by the revolution and allowed them to come out.' He then added, 'When the proper time comes, we will remove the masks of this group and will demonstrate the foreign hands behind these "pens", and "masks"'. In plain language, Rahim-Safavi warned that, 'When the time comes, we will pick the ... ripened fruit with the hands of you Basijis.'[30] Within a month and a half, this was the third time the IRGC was threatening the reformists.

On 24 July 1998, *Jameeh* (Society) published its last issue. *Jameeh*, the first pathbreaking post-Khatami independent newspaper which revived the significance and power of the fourth pillar of democracy, a free press, was ordered shut by the judiciary. *Jameeh*'s plaintiffs were the IRGC, the Organization of Prisons and the head of Tehran's Department of Justice.

One day after the closure of *Jameeh*, on 25 July, Mashallah Shamsolvaezin, the editor of *Jameeh*, published a new paper called *Tus*, with the headline 'After the ban on *Jameeh*, starting today *Tus* will be in service of *Jameeh* (Society)'.[31] *Tus* lasted less than two months and was also closed by the judiciary, but this time, a number of its editorial board were arrested and imprisoned in Evin Prison.

The daily *Neshat* (Joy) picked up the relay of the reformist press. On 18 February 1998, it appeared on the newsstands with the headline, 'Joy in Society'.[32] The investigative journalism of *Neshat* continued to provide a platform for all reform-minded voices in society, breaking down the political 'them' and 'us' categorization employed by the conservatives and extremists. On 4 September 1999, *Neshat*, too, was banned.

As the conservative-dominated 5th Majles came to the end of its four-year term, it sought to assure that once a reformist 'subversive' newspaper was closed, no new ones would take its place. On 6 July 1999, the Press Law was on the agenda of the Majles. On the same day, the Left cleric's influential newspaper *Salam* published a sensational piece of news. It revealed a letter dated 8 October 1998, in which Saeed Emami, the mastermind of the serial murders had recommended the policies advocated by the revised Press Law.

In this letter, Saeed Emami had informed Dori-Najafabadi, the minister of intelligence at the time, that the existing Press Law was insufficient to prevent 'conspiracies' and 'the only way to withstand this [cultural] assault, was to deal with individual cases legally and ban them from writing and publishing'.[33] On 7 July 1999, the Majles ratified the revised Press Law, and on the eve of the same day, the Special Court for Clergy banned *Salam* on the charge of having published a confidential letter.

Assaulting Universities for Defending the Free Press

On Thursday night, 8 July 1999, after the news of *Salam*'s closure became public, Tehran University students began peacefully demonstrating both inside and outside

Figure 10.3 NOPO Special Forces. *Source: Wikimedia Commons.*

of their dorms. First, the paramilitary *Hezbollah* ruffians (*Ansare Hezbollah*) attacked the students with sticks and stones. At 4.30 am, the paramilitary forces, accompanied by the newly constituted anti-riot NOPO Special Forces (*niruhaye vijeh pasdaran velayat*), entered the student dorms without permission from the Ministry of Interior (Figure 10.3). The students were beaten up, insulted, arrested, injured and shot to death (two to seven, depending on accounts).

The invading assailants gutted dorm rooms, broke down doors, set a few rooms on fire, devastated others and destroyed the students' personal belongings. By resorting to wanton violence and taking bloody revenge on university students who were defending the freedom of the press, the conservative leadership hoped to intimidate the defiant and re-establish its waning authority. The students, however, were becoming more radical and responding to violence with violence.

From 10 July, student unrest and strikes snowballed, and tensions rose in Tehran, Tabriz, Rasht, Shiraz, Mashhad, Hamedan and Esfahan. Students condemned the violence against their cohorts and the dorms and demanded the immediate identification and arrest of the perpetrators. Their slogans quickly turned political, with, 'Long live Khatami, death to the dictator' and, 'Law enforcement forces are a reminder of SAVAK.'[34]

As student anger and frustration grew, non-students joined the crowds, armed with sticks and stones. They marched through the streets, insulting the Leader, clashing with law enforcement forces, attacking their vehicles, destroying government property, banks and buses, and finally marching on police headquarters. The protesters chanted, 'Independence, freedom and Iranian Republic!' Political liberalization was paving the way for replacing the Islamic Republic with a Republic. Tehran and major cities were experiencing their first significant riot since the early 1980s.

On 12 July 1999, Khamenei announced, 'The bitter event of the university dorms has injured my heart.' Failing to take responsibility, the Leader attributed the planning of the occurrences to 'espionage services', the Americans, and 'the enemy who wishes to infiltrate the students and cause corruption and doom in their name'. The Leader advised the political factions and their leaders to establish and observe 'red lines' for political activities.³⁵ Once again, Khamenei deflected attention from the domestic masterminds and perpetrators of violence very close to him by blaming his usual bogeyman, the foreign enemies, spies and US conspirators.

Two days after the Leader's statement (14 July), the president distanced himself from the violence on the streets. Khatami warned about a 'deviationist tendency' among the students and preached 'fighting violence with non-violence'. On the same day, Khamenei issued an aggressive message contradicting Khatami's Gandhian call. The Leader promised, 'severe repression' of the 'bandits' supported by 'foreign enemies', who wish to 'pave the road for the hegemony of murderous America over our dear country'.³⁶

The University of Tehran was padlocked, and riot police surrounded it. Student activists, journalists and non-compliant clerics were arrested and interrogated. With demonstrations banned, *Basiji*s and *Hezbollahi*s occupying the main streets and helicopters circling overhead, calm was restored at a high cost. For two years, Khatami had preached peaceful reform and the conservative ruling clique had exercised repression, violence and terrorism to thwart it. A segment of Khatami's young supporters was becoming impatient and ready to renounce peaceful means of seeking change. The radical youth were distancing themselves from Khatami, while the pro-Khamenei camp became more virulently opposed to the president and his policies.

Khamenei was conducting a proxy war against his popularly elected president through all the means available to him, be they the judiciary, the Council of Friday Prayer speakers, the Guardian Council, the Assembly of Experts, IRGC, *Basij*, or the law enforcement forces and influential conservative political and religious groups such as the Islamic Coalition Mourning Group and the Association of Militant Clergy (*jameeye rowhaniyat mobarez*).

An unusual and surprising letter signed by 24 high-ranking commanders of the IRGC to Khatami was published on 20 July 1999. The military leadership were openly disregarding Khomeyni's strict orders that they should keep out of politics. The IRGC commanders referred to the aftermath of the assault on the students and held the president responsible for emboldening the enemies of the revolution and the disillusionment and frustration of its supporters.

The IRGC commanders denounced the insulting slogans of the students and the public against the Leader and called them enemies of the state. They enquired how long they would have to wait with tears in their eyes and watch the anarchy and the insults while 'practicing democracy and exercising revolutionary patience at the cost of surrendering the system/regime'. The IRGC commanders warned Khatami that their patience was at an end, and if he did not reconsider, they would no longer wait.³⁷

On 1 September 1999, the Leader reacted to an article published in *Neshat* referring to *qisas* and told his IRGC and *Basiji* audience that 'If some deny the necessities of religion, one of which is the *qisas* (the law of talion), they renounce the faith (*mortad*), the punishment for which is clear in Islam'.³⁸ Two days later, Mesbah-Yazdi, the system's anti-democratic theoretician, used the Friday Prayer tribune to officially encourage Muslims to kill whomever they thought were insulting Islamic values and principles. He announced that, 'Islam allows all Muslims to kill a person who insults the sanctities of Islam.' This position, he said, was an Islamic edict and 'did not need a court' to approve or pronounce it.³⁹

On 4 September, in a speech to *Basiji*s gathered at their educational camp, Khamenei extolled Mesbah-Yazdi. Khamenei added a personal touch to his comments and referred to nearly 40 years of friendship with Mesbah-Yazdi, for whom he said he had 'a heartfelt regard' as 'an Islamic jurist (*faqih*), philosopher, thinker and expert on fundamental Islamic issues'.⁴⁰

On the same day, Mahdavi-Kani, the secretary-general of the conservative Association of Militant Clergy (*jameeye rowhaniyat mobarez*), told his audience that he felt threatened by 'those who acted under the guise of supporting Khatami and weakened the people's religious zeal'. He warned that once religious sentiments were insulted, believers may 'God forbid, do things that are not desirable in the Islamic Republic.'⁴¹ Mahdavi-Kani was threatening the opposition with violence (Figure 10.4).

The Assembly of Experts of the Leadership called for a special session in Mashhad on 6 September 1999. The urgent meeting was to tighten the pincer movement against Khatami. The senior clerics called on Khatami to stop 'the attacks on the

Figure 10.4 Mohammad-Reza Mahdavi-Kani at Friday Prayer, with nuclear negotiator, Ali Larijani, former foreign minister, Kamal Kharrazi, and commander of the IRGC, Yahya Rahim-Safavi. *Source: UPI Photo/Mohammad Kheirkhah via Alamy*

Islamic government in the recent years' and the 'weakening of religious pillars'. Ayatollah Meshkini attacked the reformist press without naming them and said, 'Today what some are writing does not represent the freedom of the pen, but the freedom to conspire.'[42]

On its front-page issue of 27 September 1999, Saeed Hajjariyan's reformist newspaper, *Sobhe Emrooz* (This Morning), published a colour picture of Gen. Mohammad-Reza Naqdi in his military uniform. Naqdi, the head of the intelligence and security division of the Law Enforcement Forces told the Law Enforcement personnel that if the authorities were to remain silent in the face of insults, he would personally 'carry out God's edict against the insulters' in public without any concern for its outcome. The general said, even if they 'execute me', I will do what I must. Mesbah-Yazdi had provided the religious justification for lawless acts of terrorism, Khamenei supported his discourse, and Naqdi pledging to execute it in the name of God, was setting himself as a model for the zealots.

The Devotees of Khamenei

This is the way we are supporters of the Rule of the Guardian Jurist (*velayati*), if agha [Khamenei] says yogurt is black, I swear to the Quran that we see yogurt as black. (R. Borji, a *Basiji* artist)[43]

Laying Siege to the Reform Movement

Between the anti-Khatami camp flaunting the idea of killing peaceful but 'deviant' dissidents in the name of religion and its execution, the turn of events further empowered the reformist camp. The elections to the 6th Majles on 18 February 2000, ended in a crushing victory for Khatami's reforms and his discourse, especially in Tehran. Of the eligible voters, 67 per cent participated in the parliamentary elections, registering the highest rate of participation in any parliamentary election. The people had spoken, and Khamenei and his coalition were in disarray. The absolute parliamentary majority of the Islamic Iran Participation Front and its allies, the Executives of Construction, and the Assembly of Militant Clerics (*majma rowhaniyoun mobarez*) emboldened the reformists and created deep-seated anxiety for Khamenei and his coalition. The republican pillar of the system was pointing in one direction, and the custodians of its conservative Islamic column another.

The reformists' trench by trench advance, despite threats and assaults, left the conservatives with few options. The Guardian Council, in consultation with the Leader, spent three months deciding on what to do with the sixth parliamentary elections. They could either approve the outcome of the elections, another victory for the reformists, or else, annul all results or that of Tehran. Worried about the backlash of dissolving the elections in Tehran and the whole country, the Guardian Council opted for partial engineering.

On 26 February 2000, the Guardian Council suddenly dropped a bombshell. It announced that due to complaints, it had to recount the votes and eventually invalidated numerous ballot boxes in the provinces, which had reported reformists as winners. In Tehran, the fate of 30 candidates was held up as the Guardian Council dragged its feet for three months. In the meantime, it invalidated 726,266 votes to make sure that Gholamali Haddad-Adel, Khamenei's in-law, would enter the Majles, and Ali-Reza Rajai, a reformist journalist and a Nationalist-Religious activist, would be barred from entry. The conservative clergy distrusted the Nationalist-Religious Activists, who were a modernist, Islamic social-democratic group under the leadership of Ezatollah Sahabi. They traced their intellectual lineage to Bazargan, Taleqani and Shariati. The people voted Rajai to go the Majles, and the Guardian Council replaced him with Haddad-Adel.

The Hajjariyan Affair

Ten weeks before the opening of the new Majles, on 27 May 2000, Iran went through another crisis. The conservative and extremist pro-Khamenei coalition upped the ante with terror. At 8.30 am on 12 March 2000, as Saeed Hajjariyan was about to enter Tehran's City Council, two motorcyclists stopped in front of him. One of them called him by name and then pointed his Makarov pistol at his temple and shot him twice before escaping from the scene. Hajjariyan survived the assassination attempt, and his shooting galvanized a new wave of sympathy for him and the reformists.

Hajjariyan had symbolized the transformative personal journey of Iran's revolutionary youth that the conservative clerics dreaded. A pro-Shariati revolutionary at the outset of the revolution, Hajjariyan had joined the Islamic Revolutionary Committees, proven his zeal, entered various counterespionage and intelligence organization of the Islamic Republic, before becoming the architect of the Ministry of Information. Over time Hajjariyan had gravitated toward political reform, popular participation, a free press and the importance of supporting elected institutions against unrepresentative transgressions. The zealous follower of clerical leadership had turned into the reformist theoretician of democratizing clerical despotism.

Why Shoot Hajjariyan?

Hajjariyan contributed much to the reformist' basic rethinking of the Islamic Republic's political theology, but apart from his penchant for ideas, he stands out as perhaps the grand strategist of the reform movement in the second half of the 1990s. (E. Sadeghi-Boroujerdi)[44]

Hajjariyan had evolved and moved away far from the dogmas of the conservative Right. He was now considered a pernicious danger. Twenty days before the assassination attempt, Hajjariyan received a tape. In it, Reza Ahmadi, a self-proclaimed member of the *Ansare Hezbollah* and founding member of the Young Devotees of the Guardian Jurist, had contended that Hajjariyan's crime was 'being against the rule of the Guardian Jurist and an apostate'. A reason for sentencing Hajjariyan to death was that he had 'refused to sign the form of allegiance to the absolute rule of the Guardian Jurist' when filing his candidacy application for Tehran's City Council.[45]

The anti-reform strategies of the conservative coalition around Khamenei were backfiring as even the non-reformist press reported on: 'National loathing in reaction to terrorizing a religious reformist.' Condemnations of violence came from most quarters, and Khatami announced that the only result obtained by the murderers was 'the growing hatred of the people towards them'.[46]

On 15 March, Khamenei issued a message condemning the attempt on Hajjariyan's life as 'part of a dangerous conspiracy against national security, the people and the Islamic system'. Yet, he also warned those who would take advantage of this incident to create an atmosphere of suspicion against 'the personnel of public security'. Khamenei attacked those who accused individuals and factions at home for the assassination attempt as 'conscious or ignorant helpers of the enemy'.[47] Sentiments against the paramilitary, plainclothesmen, *Basiji*s, and *Hezbollahi*s had reached such a pitch that Khamenei needed to intervene and calm down the public clamour against his allies by deflecting attention from the perpetrators at home and once again accusing foreigners.

On 25 March 2000, the Ministry of Intelligence named those involved in the assassination attempt. Eight were arrested and put on trial. Saeed Asgar had shot Hajjariyan, and his accomplice, who commanded the operation, was Mohsen (Morteza) Majidi, a member of the IRGC. The culprits were members of a group founded after the attack on Tehran University dorms. They were fanatical lovers of Islam and the Leader and had participated in two other assassination plots and a case of arson.

Even though Khamenei condemned the assassination attempt, the scare and intimidation effect of terrorism had to be maintained and intensified to keep dissidents in check. On 15 April 2000, the IRGC issued a lengthy declaration criticizing 'American and Western-style reforms, intended to obliterate revolutionary Islam.' In a most belligerent tone, the IRGC threatened that when the time comes, 'the enemies, small and big, will feel the blast of the revolution's hammer in the space of their skulls, in such a way that they would be forever, impeded from conspiring and committing treason'.

The statement vindicated IRGC and *Basij* members as warriors in the path of God, who 'had and would overnight disrupt the calculations of many'. These 'God's warriors' were credited for executing 'the law of revolutionary violence' and 'descending like thunder upon murderers on orders from the leader and guide'.⁴⁸ Khatami's reaction was a call for national peace and tranquility.

Silencing the Independent Press

Within a week of IRGC's ominous announcement came Khamenei's menacing discourse. On 20 April 2000, Khamenei spoke of internal enemies, lackeys of the enemy, two-faced saboteurs and those in authority who were negligent. These enemies, he said, wanted to dethrone the religious and Islamic government. Khamenei extolled the president as a pious cleric who wished to propagate the faith but reproached some of his mid-level managers.

Khamenei announced that some '10 to 15 newspapers, seemingly directed from the same centre' had become the enemy's base, weakening the people's trust in the officials and 'insulting the main institutions in the country'. Khamenei called these newspapers 'charlatans' that accused the IRGC, the *Basij* and the clergy of foul play when 'someone was assassinated'. Khamenei ruled these newspapers 'to be harmful to the youth, the future, the revolution and the people'.⁴⁹

Three days after Khamenei's speech, on 23 April 2000, twelve flagship reformist newspapers and weeklies, among them Hajjariyan's *Sobhe Emrooz* (This Morning) and the Islamic Iran Participation Front organ *Mosharekat* (Participation), were ordered shut down by the judiciary. On 23 April, Karbaschi's moderate reformist paper, *Hammihan* (Compatriot), was also closed. One month later, the judiciary, blocked the publication of three new reformist newspapers. The judiciary informed the minister of culture and Islamic guidance that the newly registered press was forbidden to print before obtaining its permission.

Following Khamenei's directive, the judiciary revoked the authority of the Ministry of Culture and Islamic Guidance over the press and took full charge of it. New permits for reformist publications were denied, and the reformist press shut down. Consequently, newsstands in Iran displayed homogeneous news and ideas reflecting Khamenei's views. In May 2000, the Ministry of Culture and Islamic Guidance conducted a survey in Tehran among newspaper readers of age 16 and above. Their reaction to the blanket closure of the reformist press reflected the gap between Khamenei's state of mind and that of the public. Of those polled, 70 per cent opposed the closures, 20 per cent favoured them and 6 per cent had no opinion.⁵⁰

The reformists lost their means of communication with the people. From April 2000, under different pretexts, influential journalists were arrested. They were put on show trials and sent to prison. Mashallah Shamsolvaezin, Akbar Ganji, Emadeddin Baqi, Latif Safari, Ezatollah Sahabi and Ahmad Zeydabadi were among the victims. Reformists viewed the closure of their press as vengeance against their success in winning the 6th Majles.

Figure 10.5 Saeed Hajjariyan. *Source: Photo by UPI/Fars News Agency via Alamy.*

Having silenced the reformist press, the Islamic Revolutionary Court put Hajjariyan's assailants on trial. After three open court hearings, the Revolutionary Court announced its verdicts on 18 May 2000. Saeed Asgar, who had shot him, was sentenced to 15 years in prison, and Majidi, his accomplice, to 10 years. Both had openly acknowledged their role and had stated that Hajjariyan (Figure 10.5) was a corrupt element, undermining the faith. Asgar left prison after a year. Hajjariyan believed that Saeed Asgar was just a trigger and others had pulled 'it'. The masterminds who had ordered his assassination never became known.

The Revolt of the Maverick 6th Majles

The new reformist-dominated Majles had several items on its legislative agenda, which threatened the conservatives' hold on power. The reformist deputies proudly spoke about removing impediments to a free press, reversing the restrictive Press Law of the 5th Majles, introducing legislature to review the management of the National Television, legalizing the use of satellite dishes, legislating against the entry of law enforcement and military personnel to university campuses and dorms, and finally legalizing the establishment of private radio and television stations. They even spoke of introducing legislature amending Election Laws that would end the Guardian Council's approbatory and subjective role of vetting candidates standing for elective offices.

Frustrated with the arbitrary repression of reformists and the judiciary's whitewashing of crimes committed by extremist conservatives, the 6th Majles challenged Ayatollah Mahmud Hashemi-Shahrudi (hereafter Shahrudi), the new head of the judiciary. In an open letter on 19 June 2000, 151 reformist deputies deplored the unconstitutional closure of the press and the unnecessary arrest of individuals. The deputies demanded clarity on the condition and legal situation of those imprisoned and announced that they were obliged 'to safeguard the people's rights'.[51] By 16 August 2000, the number of reformist newspapers closed by the judiciary had reached 20, including *Bayan* (Locution), one of the few remaining reformist publications.

Shahrudi responded that his responsibility was to 'safeguard the people's religion and doctrine' and that the judiciary in the Islamic Republic 'had its own specific structure, which could not be criticized employing any criteria or standard'.[52] Two days later, Khamenei supported the head of the judiciary and asked him to stand firm against those factions weakening and intimidating the judiciary with their 'fussing and criticisms'.[53]

The judiciary further curtailed the executive's real power. In the case of the serial murders, attacks on the universities and attempt on Hajjariyan's life, it prohibited the Ministry of Intelligence to 'summon, interrogate and arrest' suspects. The Ministry of Intelligence which had unlimited powers in the past, now needed a warrant from the judiciary to investigate national security issues. The Ministry of Intelligence under Khatami's control was no longer trustworthy. The judiciary had taken over the job of the Ministry of Intelligence, leaving it in the dark on arrests and interrogations. In turn, Khamenei relied on the intelligence bureau of the IRGC as his reliable base, an institution which later became the all-powerful intelligence hub in the land.

On 9 July 2000, Ayatollah Khamenei had presented the nation with his domestic policy doctrine. Faced with the rising enthusiasm for reforms in the country, he paid lipservice to their necessity but spoke at length about dangerous and distorted kinds of reform. For Khamenei the US, UK, and world support for reforms in Iran proved that a conspiracy was being hatched by the enemies of the Islamic Republic. The reforms were a complex conspiracy 'a detailed and multi-faceted US project' that aimed 'to repeat the collapse of the Soviet Union in Iran'.

Khamenei warned the people not to be duped, as the Soviets had been duped, by 'so-called iconoclastic slogans, support for a plurality of the press, Western-style freedom of expression and the propagation of Western cultural symbols and images'. He prohibited the press from promoting 'misguiding, empoisoning, and deviating reforms'. Khamenei indirectly referred to the new reformist majority in the Majles and their upcoming Press Bill, guaranteeing the freedom of the press. He cautioned the reformist deputies not to 'enter a confrontational phase'.[54]

The reformist Majles, however, failed to demonstrate the blind respect and submission Khamenei expected. Mohammad-Reza Khatami, the president's brother, had obtained the highest number of votes in Tehran during the Parliamentary elections and was both the Deputy president of the 6th Majles and the secretary-general of the Islamic Iran Participation Front. As an embodiment of the reformist movement, Mohammad-Reza Khatami minimized Khamenei's rule as the Guardian Jurist by saying that it was 'the people's will which defined reforms'.[55]

On 16 August 2000, all eyes were on the Majles. Despite Khamenei's strict orders, the reformist deputies had decided to present and discuss their revised Press Bill. Even before discussions began, in a closed session, contrary to the internal by-laws and procedures of Parliament, Mehdi Karrubi, the president of the Majles, tabled the Bill and refused to consider it.

Faced with the frustration of the deputies, Karrubi announced that the Leader had sent a letter, a State Edict (*hokm hokumati*) demanding that the Bill be taken off the Parliament's agenda. Khamenei had returned to his old theme that 'if the enemies of Islam, the revolution and the Islamic system were to take control or infiltrate the press, a major danger would threaten security, unity and the belief of the people'. Karrubi's response to the objections of the deputies was that 'the Constitution strongly emphasizes the absolute rule of the Guardian Jurist, and this is what absolutist Guardianship is'.[56]

Karrubi upheld Khamenei's State Edict and validated his absolute power to trump the will of the people's representatives. On 16 August 2000, with considerable help from Karrubi, Khamenei demonstrated who was the country's real decision-maker. Again, on 17 July 2001, Karrubi refused to allow the deputies to consider the bill, 'Investigating and Inspecting the National Radio and Television'. He argued that the institution in question was under the direct authority of the Leader and out of Majles' jurisdiction. The most reformist and progressive Majles in the Islamic Republic's twenty-year history learnt a bitter lesson in the limitations of reform faced with the absolute rule of the Guardian Jurist.

Reformist Majles and the Guardian Council

The Deputy Speaker, Behzad Nabavi, noted with indignation that within the first six months of the new parliament, 17 of the 44 bills ratified by the Majlis had been rejected by the Guardian Council, while the Speaker, Mehdi Karroubi, protested at infringements on parliamentary privilege and the barely disguised comments emanating from the Guardian Council about possible prosecution of wayward deputies. (A. Ansari)[57]

The Judiciary Muzzles the Executive and the Legislative

Even though the reformists could no longer disseminate their ideas through a free press, the reformist Majles deputies continued conveying their message through their defiant speeches. In the repressive political atmosphere imposed by the conservative coalition, the reformist could only talk. But soon, the judiciary made the immunity of deputies from prosecution conditional and subject to revocation.

On 11 March 2001, 21 Nationalist-Religious activists were rounded up. Four days later, 10 were released. But, less than a month later, on 7 April, 42 members of this group were rounded up in Tehran and the provinces. The detainees were accused of plotting to overthrow the system. The reformist Members of Parliament challenged the arbitrary arrests by the judiciary and spoke against them. Mohsen Armin, a reformist deputy, polemically asked, 'Do we respect the right of existence of the opposition?' He criticized the judiciary for its intolerance toward peaceful criticism. The arrest of the Nationalist-Religious activists became more unjustifiable when Yunesi, the minister of intelligence, told the Majles that those arrested were not seeking to 'overthrow the system'.[58]

Hoseyn Loqmaniyan, the young deputy from Hamedan, criticized the arrests and accused the judiciary of injustice, propagating fear and disenchantment. He had previously criticized Shahrudi, the head of the judiciary. Despite his parliamentary immunity, Loqmaniyan was imprisoned for twenty days. When Fatemeh Haqiqatju, another 'insubordinate' deputy, questioned Ayatollah Khamenei about the serial murders, the commanders of the attack on the university dorms and Hajjariyan's assailants, she, too, was put behind bars.

Khatami entered the fray on the side of the persecuted deputies. On 11 October 2001, he sent a soft legal warning to Ayatollah Shahrudi (Figure 10.6), referring to the imprisonment sentences and fines handed to Loqmaniayan and Haqiqatju. He pointed to Articles 84 and 86 of the Constitution, stipulating that a deputy was free to express his or her opinion in Parliament and could not be legally pursued or arrested for such expression. Khatami evoked his rights and duties according to Article 113 of the Constitution and clause 15 of the president's responsibilities to notify and caution the head of the judiciary to 'correctly apply the constitution and refrain from its violation'.[59] In his mild-mannered style, Khatami was standing up to Khamenei's appointee.

Within a week, Shahrudi refuted Khatami's arguments and suggestions. He informed the president, that judges ruled on their independent deductions, and even the head of the judiciary could not tell them what to do. Shahrudi rejected the notion that Article 113 gave the president the prerogative to supervise the judiciary and reminded Khatami tersely that he should avoid giving the impression that there was disunity among the system's leaders.[60]

The president's skirmish with the Judiciary entered a heightened phase as the head of Tehran's Justice Department wrote a letter to Khatami. He informed the president that the Supreme Court was monitoring his infractions, and 'if the Leader were to see fit, his removal from office would be prepared'.[61] The judiciary and the Leader were now threatening the president with removal from office if he were to exercise his minimum legal powers. As the endemic tension between the opposite visions of the Leader and the president flared up sporadically, the high authorities of the Islamic Republic invited all to unity, calm and cooperation.

Figure 10.6 Judiciary Chief Sadeq Larijani sits next to former Judiciary Chief Ayatollah Hashemi-Shahrudi. *Source: Photo by UPI/ILNA Hoshang Hadi via Alamy.*

> ### Khatami on Cemeterial Security
>
> In a society inflicted by despotism, and hinging on fear, insecurity and hopelessness, security means inertia and silence, which is today known as 'cemeterial security'. This security is certainly not [a desirable] national security. (M. Khatami)[62]

Over the issue of arbitrary political arrests and closure of the reformist press, relations between the Majles and the judiciary deteriorated considerably and became contentious. The deputies sought transparency and accountability, but like the Guardian Council, the judiciary hid behind their security blanket of being Leader-appointed bodies and indulged in opaqueness. The deputies made speeches against the illegal actions of the guardians of the law, but nothing made a dent in the judiciary's armour. During the tumultuous 6th Majles, some 60 deputies were summoned and interrogated for their speeches.

Khatami's Re-election

Somehow, Khatami weathered all adversities, and resiliently hammered at his own liberal and democratic ideals. In his speeches and interviews, he encouraged Iranians to exert their rights against all odds and promoted his pluralistic and inclusive vision of an Islamic Republic. He launched the slogan 'Iran for all Iranians', breaking religious, ideological, factional, gender and ethnic boundaries and divisions between 'them' and 'us'. Abhorred by the idea, his foe, Mesbah-Yazdi called it 'a sign of the collapse of religious culture'.[63]

Khatami emphasized the role of the people and buttressed the Republican aspect of the state by saying, 'whatever we have is by the people's grace'. He rebutted Khamenei's fear of the free press and said, 'freedom of the press and criticism of the government is the people's right'. Khatami targeted the youth and implored them to 'take their destiny into their own hands'. He condemned attempts at 'pitting religion against freedom' and would tell his adversaries that 'we have no other option than democracy'. As the conservative coalition tightened the grip of repression, Khatami harkened that 'in a despotic atmosphere, both religion and ideas will be harmed'.[64]

> ## Polls on Khatami's Popularity before the 2001 Elections
>
> 83.9% of those polled [Tehranis of 16 and above] wanted Khatami to stand for a second time . . . 78% approved 'the people's rule and respect for the majority's vote', while 9.9% disapproved.[65]

On 8 June 2001, Iranians went to the polls to elect their president. Khatami ran his campaign, arguing that reform had become a historical demand of the people and a dominant discourse even among his opponents. He announced that the election would be a referendum on his reform policies and promises, warned against excesses and emphasized that reform would result from 'moderation' and 'patience'. Khatami reminded Iranians that the freedom he proposed would be within Islamic law and that the absence of liberties would lead to despotism.

Khatami won a second landslide and obtained 77 per cent of the votes cast, while his main rival, Ahmad Tavakoli, received only 16 per cent. Khatami's number of votes was even higher than in the 1997 election. The conservative coalition seemed resigned to Khatami's re-election. They had no distinctive candidate and did not put up any serious resistance, preparing themselves for the 2005 elections.

Khatami's inaugural ceremony on 2 August 2001 set the pace for the four agitated coming years. Seyyed Ali Khamenei validated Khatami's presidency and added that his confirmation was conditional upon the president continuing the path of 'Islam, and its shining ordinances . . . and resisting arrogant and unjust enemies.' Khamenei suggested that the president should 'prioritize responding to the needs of the oppressed/dispossessed and promoting the lofty ideals of the faith and the revolution at the world level'.

Khatami responded politely, diplomatically, and firmly. He emphasized that his position made him responsible to the Leader and the Majles, but most importantly to the people who had elected him and had expectations of him. He reminded the Leader that all were responsible before the people who had the right to criticize, supervise, protest and demand their rights from 'the highest of the powers'. Khatami informed the Leader that 'people's rule prevailed and that all officials, especially the highest ones, had to be constantly under scrutiny and supervision to avoid despotism and arbitrariness'.[66] The two highest officials in the land were at loggerheads, speaking two different languages.

The Sad Fate of Reform: Acquiescence and Confrontation

Khatami was a reformist who believed in the rule of law, nonviolence, and the Islamic Republic's Constitution. He was neither a radical nor a revolutionary. Faced with the reality of impotence before the legal and extra-legal powers of the Leader, Khatami returned to the Constitution and sought to unearth and realize its untapped potentials to counterbalance the absolute rule of the Leader. He tried to find clauses and articles which would enhance his legal prerogatives, make the position of a popularly elected president more meaningful and effective than just a figurehead.

Deputies of the 6th Majles were becoming restless with the obstructionist methods of the judiciary and the Guardian Council, halting reforms and rolling back achievements since the election of Khatami. They were the radical voice of reform, prodding Khatami to take a firm position against the conservative coalition. On 21 May 2002, the Majles deputies wrote an unprecedented letter to Khamenei. Instead of beating around the bush, they addressed the Leader as the person obstructing change.

In an audacious letter, 135 deputies lamented the efforts by the conservative coalition at proving 'that the people's will, for a change in perceptions and behaviors, was ineffectual'. They told Khamenei that the country was at a fork in the road, either 'dictatorship and despotism' or 'a return to the principles of the constitution and an honest submission to democratic rules'. They emphasized that the direction the country was to take depended on Khamenei.

The deputies proposed that the Leader take the bitter pill of making fundamental changes in the appointed institutions and force them to 'act fairly and objectively'.[67] They called on him to keep the judiciary, Guardian Council, the national television and the IRGC out of the struggle between the two factions. The deputies accused the Guardian Council of obstructing change and acting as though all religious and constitutional laws were a function of the one principle of the Rule of the Guardian Jurist. They lambasted the judiciary for systematically restricting freedoms in social, cultural and political domains.

The deputies suggested that the fate of the 'Twin Bills' under discussion in the Majles would test the conservative coalition's real intentions. Their historical letter expressed their irritation at their inability to legislate. Two days later, Khamenei responded to the radical deputies indirectly, accusing them of being 'cowards (*na javanmard*), 'traitors and eternally damned', 'weak' and 'attracted to the US'.[68]

On 28 August 2002, frustrated by his own inability to obtain results through behind the scenes negotiations, Khatami relaunched his attempts to effectuate real change. At a press conference with domestic and foreign reporters, Khatami contended that one aspect of his responsibility was to ensure the proper implementation of the Constitution. To this end, he announced presenting a bill to the Majles which would enhance his powers within the purview of the Constitution. Khatami lashed out at those who wished to impose a single voice in society and were intolerant of dissent. He criticized the judiciary and announced that political trials without a jury were against the Constitution.

> ### A Religious People's Sovereignty
> Because of the revolution, an auspicious unity has occurred between religion and people's sovereignty . . . so that people could change their government without bloodshed and rebellion and replace it with another. (M. Khatami)[69]

What became known as Khatami's 'Twin Bills' was the litmus test of the president's reformist and republican push against the absolutist rule of the Guardian Jurist. The first bill, 'Reform of the Election Law of the Islamic Majles', was sent to Karrubi, the president of the Majles, on 26 August 2002. It listed 15 specific cases according to which the Guardian Council could reject the credentials of a candidate. This bill intended to limit the arbitrary elimination of reformist candidates to the Seventh Majles. Among other articles, it specified that candidates would have representatives present at the voting booths and that annulling ballot boxes by the Guardian Council would have to be supported by hard evidence and proof.[70]

On 23 September 2002, Khatami sent to Karrubi his second bill, 'Determining the powers and responsibilities of the President.' This two-article bill sought to reconfirm the president's power to enforce the proper implementation of the Constitution, warn against the violations of the Constitution and expect a detailed report from transgressing institutions within two months. The bill enabled the president to prevent ad hoc actions and rulings by the judiciary until the time when proper legal procedures had led to a conviction. On 8 April 2003, the bill was approved by the Majles and sent to the Guardian Council.

Six months after the Parliament approved the 'Reform of the Election Law of the Islamic Majles', the Guardian Council rejected it on 31 March 2003. The Majles amended the bill, addressing the issues raised by the Guardian Council, and returned it to the Council. On 11 August 2003, the Guardian Council rejected the bill for a second time. On 7 May 2003, the Guardian Council turned down the president's second bill, 'Determining the Powers and Responsibilities of the President'. Through his appointed institutions, the Leader successfully obstructed all attempts by Khatami to implement change.

On 23 February 2003, elections were held for City and Rural Councils for the second time. The results reflected the disarray and disillusion among the once determined and united reformist forces. Without any interference from the Guardian Council, a new conservative political group, the *Usulgarayan* (Principlists), in alliance with the Islamic Coalition of Mourning Groups, routed the reformist candidates. Mahmud Ahmadinejad, the dynamic leader of the Coalition of Islamic Iran's Developers (*Eetelaf abadgarane Iran eslami*), the leading Principlist force in the elections, was catapulted to the centre of the political stage. On 3 May 2003, Mahmud Ahmadinejad became Tehran's mayor.

Nationwide participation in the first City and Rural Council elections had been 62 per cent and 40 per cent in Tehran. In the second elections, only 40.5 per cent of all eligible voters participated and in Tehran, only 13 per cent went to the voting booths. In Tehran, reformist voters sulked, and all fifteen seats went to conservative candidates. Tehran's City Council changed hands from the reformists to a new breed of Islamic conservatives. The outcome showed people's disillusionment with the possibility of reform, resulting in their withdrawal from politics.

Khatami spoke about his disappointments and frustrations on 22 May 2003. He announced that without the powers that he had sought and was denied, he had 'hardly any functions' and in certain respects, 'his powers were less than an ordinary citizen'.[71] Khatami was being pushed by the reformists in the Majles to consider a radical stand, call for a referendum or resign. The reformist deputies believed that the reform programme conducted from within the governance system had been completely blocked by the conservatives and that they had no option but to resign and find another solution outside the governance structure.

The reformist deputies knew that Khatami's movement and their presence in Parliament had given to the Islamic Republic domestic and international legitimacy and a semblance of democratic practice. Incapable of operationalizing their promises, they felt politically and morally obliged to withdraw from power. But Khatami was not a man of confrontation. When dialogue and behind the scenes negotiations failed, Khatami chose the 'legal' solution and complied with the decision of the Guardian Council. On 2 June 2003, Khatami announced that he would obey the Constitution. Even though indignant, he threw in the towel but continued with his attempts to seek the release of political prisoners, verbal promptings, preaching democracy and consciousness-raising.

The Leader's Representative to the IRGC on Elections to the 7th Majles

You [*Basijis*] should be on your guard against God forbid another Majles like the Sixth Majles, which opposed the Leader and made his life miserable (*khoon be del rahbar kard*). (M. A. Movahedi-Kermani)[72]

From January 2004, it became clear that the Guardian Council was intent on the widespread rejection of reformists candidates, especially those who had been 'bothersome' during the 6th Majles. Of 8,157 nationwide candidates for the election to the 7th Majles, 3,650 were excluded. In Tehran Province, 52 per cent of the applicants were rejected, as compared to 9.2 per cent in elections to the 6th Majles. Some 80 deputies of the 6th Majles who wished to stand for re-election were barred. To avoid another unruly Majles, the Guardian Council 'legally' paved the way for the victory of Khamenei's conservative coalition.

On 11 January 2004, the 6th Majles took another unprecedented step. In a dramatic act of last resort, some 140 deputies took sanctuary inside the Majles. Concurrently, many governors and deputy governors decided to resign in protest against the purge of reformist candidates. The minister of interior intervened to stop them from resigning. Even though Khatami asked the deputies to end their sit-in, they continued their action. Khamenei had at last succeeded in splitting the reformist movement.

The radical reformists, mostly but not entirely non-clerics, composed of the Islamic Iran Participation Front and Iran's Mojahedin of the Islamic Revolution (IMIR), parted ways, exiting the system. Khatami and his religious and political organization, the Assembly of Militant Clerics (*majma rowhaniyoun mobarez*), acquiesced to the Leader and accused their old allies of being 'radicals', 'disruptive' and 'unlawful'.[73]

Despite Khatami and Karrubi's best efforts, 109 deputies resigned on 1 February 2004. That number swelled to 125 within a couple of days. The deputies announced that they would boycott the upcoming election as 'the people have been denied their right to elect and be elected'.[74] Khamenei responded that resignation 'was against the law and religiously forbidden (*haram*)'.[75] Impervious to threats by the Leader, the rebellious deputies ended their sanctuary on 6 February and disbanded.

On 20 February 2004, ornamental elections to the 7th Majles took place. National participation rates dropped. Only 28 per cent of eligible voters in Tehran went to the booths. The myth of people's participation in the Islamic Republic dissipated. In a perfectly engineered election, the candidates of Khamenei's conservative coalition won a sweeping victory. The Principlist Coalition of Islamic Iran's Developers obtained 67 per cent of the Majles seats. Haddad-Adel, who had entered the 6th

Majles through manipulations of the Guardian Council, received the highest vote in Tehran.

Khamenei praised the elections for being conducted in 'a completely healthy and legal manner, and in a completely free environment'. He added that, 'irrespective of its results, which will be of utmost credibility, the people and the officials would not give a hoot about the judgement of the arrogant and blabbering Americans'.[76]

The reformist 6th Majles, a unique experience in the history of the Islamic Republic, had failed to get its progressive bills approved by the Guardian Council. A glance at the numerous bills promulgated by the Majles and rejected by the Guardian Council indicates how the Islamic Republic would have evolved politically, socially and economically had the reformists succeeded. These legislatures included, defining political crimes, mode of operation of student organizations, banning human trafficking, the annual budget for the year March 2004–5, modality of government procurements, preventing the parcelization of agricultural lands, joining the UN Convention against Torture and Other Cruel, Inhuman or Degrading Treatment or Punishment, prohibition of torture, joining the UN Convention on the Elimination of All Forms of Discrimination against Women, modality of the use of satellite dishes, reform of the Press Laws and joining the Convention concerning International Carriage by Rail (COTIF).

Khatami's Foreign Policy

On 22 September 1998, Khatami addressed the General Assembly in New York and impressed his audience with an erudite speech promoting dialogue as the means to understanding and cooperation among nations. He proposed that the UN declare 2001 as the 'year of dialogue among civilizations', to obtain 'universal justice and liberty'.[77] Bill Clinton, the US president, stayed behind to hear his speech. There was talk that the two were supposed to meet 'accidentally', but this did not happen as it was against the Leader's wish.

After almost twenty years of harsh words for the West and especially the US, Khatami held an olive branch. Very much a corollary of his domestic approach, Khatami believed that tolerance and openness to 'the other', could secure world stability and prosperity. Consequently, he did not view the West or the US as a permanent threat, constantly conspiring to undermine Iran's national security through political, social and cultural means.

A near Muslim replica of Desmond Tutu, Khatami was a bridge-builder and disdained castigation, exclusion and segregation. He opposed Samuel Huntington's polemical and intolerant civilizational dichotomy of 'them' and 'us' and feared its international and domestic ramifications. Khatami's rebuttal of Samuel Huntington's clash of civilizations was also a camouflaged refutation of Khamenei's world outlook and methodology. Khatami based his foreign policy on mutual respect for sovereignty, non-interference in the affairs of other countries, peaceful coexistence with friendly countries and detente towards countries at odds with the Islamic Republic.

Following in the footsteps of Rafsanjani, Khatami placed primary emphasis on the pursuit of national interests in foreign policy rather than ideological or religious commitments and allegiances. Khatami did succeed in wooing hostile countries, normalizing relations with Iran's estranged Persian Gulf neighbours and European countries. He did succeed in attracting foreign capital and investment and drove hard to end Iran's international isolation.

Within six months of Khatami's election, EU ambassadors, who had left Iran over the Islamic Republic's involvement in the assassination of Iran's Kurdish Democratic Party leaders in 1992 returned to Tehran. Concurrently Khatami and his like-minded minister of foreign affairs, Kamal Kharrazi were invited abroad. The Italians were the trailblazers. On 28 February 1998, Lamberto Dini, the Italian foreign minister, visited Tehran on behalf of his own country and the EU, and Kharrazi spoke of going beyond 'critical dialogue'. Thomas Klestil of Austria followed suit in September 1999. He was the first EU president to visit Tehran since Iran's Islamic Revolution in 1979.

On 9 March 1999, Khatami's first state visit was to Italy, where he was warmly received by the Italian prime minister and president, Parliament and the pope. The international community lauded his comforting and friendly words as a sign of Iran's new policy of detente. Khatami continued his goodwill-globetrotting by state visits to Saudi Arabia, Syria and Qatar (May 1999), France (October 1999), the United Nations (September 2000), Japan (November 2000), Russia (March 2001), Austria and Greece (March 2002), Turkmenistan and Uzbekistan (April 2002), Turkey and Spain (October 2002), Pakistan (December 2002), India (January 2003), Lebanon (2003), Malaysia (October 2003), Switzerland (January 2004), Tajikistan (September 2004), Algeria, Sudan and Oman (October 2004), Austria, France and Italy (April 2005) Croatia, Bosnia and Venezuela (March 2005).

After 1998, relationship between Iran and the EU improved and entered a phase of 'comprehensive dialogue', leading to a Trade and Cooperation Agreement in 2000, linked to a Political Dialogue Agreement. 'Within the scope of this agreement were four main areas: human rights, non-proliferation, terrorism, and the Middle East peace process.'[78] Iran–US relations, however, remained unfriendly. As much as Khatami tried, he was unable to soften Khamenei's obsessive anti-Americanism and end a quarter of a century of distrust and resentment. A few weeks after his CNN interview, Khatami's 'wrestling diplomacy', raised hopes and expectations of a thaw in US–Iran relations. On 17 February 1998, the US wrestling team received a warm welcome in Tehran. The American flag, among eleven others, was hung from the ceiling of the Azadi stadium and the Americans were cheered by the crowd during the opening ceremony.

> ## US Wrestlers in Tehran
>
> The visit to the bazaar was terrific. People were very friendly. They said hello to us and asked for our pictures to be taken. It was really nice. (Larry Sciacchetano, President of USA Wrestling)[79]

In August 1998, Clinton sent a secret letter to Khatami, attempting to establish contact with him through the Swiss ambassador in Tehran. In March 1999, the US removed its sanction against sales of spare airline parts, food, and medicine to Iran. In another sign of appeasement, in March 2000 Madeleine Albright apologized to Iran for US involvement in the 1953 coup and her support for Saddam Hussein during the Iran–Iraq War. As a gesture of goodwill, the US allowed the import of carpets, pistachio and caviar from Iran. However, Iran's active support of *Hezbollah*, Hamas and the Palestine Islamic Jihad, as well as its nuclear programme, prevented reconciliation with the US. An opinion poll published on 31 July 2000, revealed that 91 per cent of Tehranis were satisfied with Khatami's foreign policy initiatives, 90 per cent approved of his 'Dialogue among Civilizations' and 86 per cent supported his policy of détente with European countries.[80]

The 11 September 2001 attack on the US, and American President George W. Bush's reference to Iran as a member of the 'axis of evil' on 29 January 2002, strengthened Khamenei's hands and weakened Khatami's (Figure 10.7). The invasion

Figure 10.7 President Mohammad Khatami. *Source: Photo by Patrick Kovarik/AFP via Getty Images.*

of Afghanistan (October 2001) and Iraq (March 2003) added to the rhetoric of regime change, strengthened xenophobia and reinvigorated the anti-US stance of Khamenei's conservative coalition.

Khatami, however, continued to work hard to neutralize threats to Iran under the pretext that the country was moving towards producing weapons of mass destruction. He signed the Additional Protocol to the Nuclear Non-Proliferation Treaty (NPT) in December 2003. Before leaving office, and in the middle of US accusations that Iran was 'actively working' on methods to deliver a nuclear warhead, Khatami temporarily suspended 'the manufacture and importation of gas centrifuges and related components, as well as the assembly, installation, testing, or operation of such centrifuges', and promised to refrain from 'all tests or production at any uranium-conversion installation.'[81]

Khatami's Economic Legacy

Khatami believed in a sequential process of political development first and then economic development. He was interested in economic development but believed that democracy and transparency would assure participation, and people's enthusiasm and mobilization would fuel economic growth. He belonged to the generation for whom unbridled capitalism was neither philosophically desirable nor morally acceptable. He was a proponent of growth with equity. Khatami's eight-year economic record was quite acceptable for someone always said to be less interested in economics.

Iran had been saddled with numerous economic problems when Khatami came to power in June 1997. To top it all, between October 1997 and March 1998, oil prices dropped by some 40 per cent. In a televised interview on 14 March 1998, Khatami discussed his economic preoccupations. He referred to the country's 'sick economic structure' in production, distribution, business laws and regulations. He lamented the slowdown in industrial output and rates of growth, the decrease in oil prices, Iran's dependence on oil, the high inflation rates and unemployment, the unequal distribution of income, the tendency of capital to move towards speculative and unproductive activities, insecurity for investment and the inability of the government to cover its expenditures from taxes.[82] In July 1998, the unprecedented tanking of oil prices to a 25-year low of $11.90 complicated managing Iran's oil-dependent economy. But from 2000, oil prices picked up, attaining $27.39 and reaching $50.04 in 2005. With the rise in oil prices, the Iranian economy picked up.

Iran's general economic indicators during Khatami's eight-year presidency were respectable. The economy grew by about 5 per cent per year, and the per capita income increased from $1,823 to $3,226. Inflation averaged around 16 per cent, a sharp drop from the average annual 35 per cent rates of Rafsanjani's second term in office. Some 5 million jobs were created, and household welfare improved, but the overall unemployment rate remained at 12.8 per cent. The Iranian currency (rial) depreciated during Khatami's Presidency. The exchange rate for a dollar went from around 6,400 in 1997 to about 9,000 rials in 2005. By 2013, before the end of the second term of Khatami's successor, the Iranian currency stood at 35,000 rials for $1.

> ## Unemployment among Urban Youth
> [Khatami] did not do enough to help the young people, especially young women . . . Urban women's unemployment rate was 60 percent in 2004 . . . This is an astronomically high figure. For men 20–24 years of age, it's also very high – 25 percent. (D. Salehi-Isfahani)[83]

Khatami was not successful in decreasing the economy's dependence on oil exports. On the contrary, the government's budget reliance on oil income increased. He did, however, succeed in creating an Oil Stabilization Fund to protect the government from sudden oil price falls. When he left office, the Oil Stabilization Fund had some $10.6 billion.

The Khatami Presidency was also characterized by a last-ditch effort to curtail and even push back the greed of IRGC's economic wing. Khatami tried to keep the economic ambitions of the IRGC and its Construction Base of the Seal of the Prophets (*Qarargah sazandeggiye khatam al-anbia*) at bay, hemming in their economic hegemony, monopoly and corrupt practices. Nine months after Mahmud Ahmadinejad was elected mayor of Tehran and eighteen months before Khatami left his office, Ahmadinejad announced that the Construction Base of the Seal of the Prophets would be involved in Tehran's construction projects. He added that because of their 'superior quality and low prices', he had bypassed 'the high-cost superfluous bureaucratic procedures'.[84] The IRGC-supported mayor of Tehran was repaying his political debt with economic favours.

On 8 May 2004, the IRGC physically occupied the newly constructed Imam Khomeyni International Airport on the opening day of the international flights. Unable to win in a 31-company bid to manage operations and provide services for the airport, the IRGC conducted a military operation and closed the airport. The IRGC claimed that it would keep the airport shut until the 'security conditions' were met and 'foreign personnel' ceased to operate the airport.

With Khatami's support, Ahmad Khorram, minister of roads and transportation and a member of the IRGC in his youth, had refused to concede to IRGC's aggressive and extra-economic strategy of gobbling a lucrative government project. On 3 October 2004, four months after Khorram put up a futile fight against IRGC's illegal demands, the new conservative-dominated 7th Majles impeached him. He was charged with mismanagement, disregarding legal procedures in concluding contracts and encouraging embezzlement in his Ministry. Khorram was also accused of being 'dismissive of domestic technical know-how and management capabilities, with an unnecessary penchant for foreign companies'.[85]

When Khatami left the Presidential Palace on 3 August 2005, the Leader and the conservative coalition around him breathed a deep sigh of relief. A popular movement for change, liberalization and democratization was finally vanquished. Constitutionalists had once again been defeated by despotic absolutists. The pro-Khamenei forces alienated reformists of all colours, rendering politics more polarized than ever. Moderate politicians like Khatami and Karrubi and the younger radicals were thrown together into the pool of potential 'foreign collaborators' and 'enemies of the revolution'. A large disenfranchised and dejected majority stood face to face with an oligarchical group around the despot. The ruling class monopolized political, military and financial power.

At the apex of the ruling class stood Khamenei, guarded by the self-appointed all-power institutions of the judiciary, Guardian Council, Expediency Discernment Council, IRGC and National Radio and Television. Khatami and the maverick 6th Majles taught the Leader that freeing himself from unpredictable elected offices, where non-compliant individuals could take office, needed 'managed elected offices'. These so-called elected offices were 'legally' converted into appointed offices by the Leader. From 3 August 2005, Iran had a theocratic-despotic system of governance.

Factual and Analytical Questions

1. What was the contribution of Abdolkarim Sorush and his monthly *Kiyan* in laying the intellectual groundwork for the rise of Khatami's reformist movement?
2. How did Khatami's CNN interview of 7 January 1998 and Khamenei's response to it encapsulate the difference of world outlook between the two? Provide specific examples.
3. How did the ani-Khatami forces shape public opinion and whip up fervour against reform? Provide specific examples.
4. In what way did Khatami's election help the emergence of an independent and free press? How did the conservative clergy muzzle it? Provide specific examples of threats against the press.
5. Explain the process by which the judiciary took over the tasks of Khatami's Ministries of Culture and Islamic Guidance and Intelligence. Why were these two ministries targeted and neutralized? Provide evidence for your response.

6. Explain and discuss the relation between the judiciary, on the one hand, and Khatami and the 6th Majles, on the other hand. Provide evidence for or against the independence of the judiciary.
7. What were the 'Twin Bills'? Why were they considered to be the litmus test for Khatami's success? What was its fate?
8. Analyse the elections to the 7th Majles. What lessons did the Guardian Council learn from the 5th and 6th Majles elections?
9. What were Khatami's economic and foreign policy legacies?

Seminar Questions

1. How did Khatami's discourse differ from Khamenei's? What were the changes that Khatami was promoting which Khamenei did not wish to see changed? Provide specifics to support your arguments.
2. What were the three levers used by Khamenei's supporters to push back against Khatami's reforms. Use specific cases to support your answer.
3. 'The history of the Islamic Republic vindicates Shariati's dictum of "Islam versus Islam" or does it vindicate the notion that religions and ideologies are means of political struggle for personal power and glory.' Discuss by reference to two of the following: (a) Khomeyni vs Shariatmadari; (b) Khomeyni vs Montazeri; (c) Khamenei vs Rafsanjani; (d) Khamenei vs Khatami.
4. What was the relation between the victory of the reformists in the 6th Majles, the criticism of the free press by conservative religious and military leaders of the Islamic Republic and the attempt on Hajjariyan's life. Explain your answer by tracing through the events.
5. 'Had Khatami resigned as the 125 Majles deputies did in February 2004, barriers to reform would have been reduced or removed, and Khamenei's rule would have been fragilized and even threatened.' Assess the validity of this statement. What kind of conclusions could be drawn from your analysis?
6. 'From 3 August 2005, Iran had a theocratic-despotic system of governance.' Assess the validity of this statement. Provide historical evidence to support your arguments.

Discussion Questions

1. 'The trials of Karbaschi and Nuri were intended to weaken the resolve of Khatami's reformist strategy, raise the cost of open criticism and discourage political change.' Discuss and provide specific evidence.

2. 'The chain killing of opposition politicians and discontented intellectuals was an act of desperation to intimidate rather than random acts of terrorism.' Assess the above statement. What was the common denominator between those assassinated?
3. 'The religious justification for violence and terror during Khatami's presidency against religiously, culturally and politically "undesirable elements", was provided by Khamenei, Mebah-Yazdi and Mahdavi-Kani and its affirmation and execution was left to the IRGC, *Basij* and *Hezbollah*.' Assess the validity of this remark by tracing the events and statements that would support or refute it.
4. 'Khamenei's State Edict (*hokm hokumati*) demanding that the Press Bill be taken off Parliament's agenda and the president of the Majles' acceptance of it as an authoritative decision that could trump the voice of the people's representatives, proved that the Islamic Republic was an Islamic government ruled by a despot.' Assess the validity of this statement, while addressing the distinction between an Islamic Republic and an Islamic government?
5. 'Had the 6th Majles been allowed to legislate its progressive bills, the Islamic Republic would have been a totally different system than it is today.' Assess the validity of the above statement. Prove or disprove it with specific examples.

11

The Ahmadinejad Presidency, 2005-13

Chapter Outline

Khamenei's Search for an Appropriate President	535
Ahmadinejad's Atypical and Folksy Politics	546
Society Pushes Back against Ahmadinejad	559
The June 2009 Presidential Elections: The People Confront the Leader	564
Ahmadinejad's Turn to Fall Out with Khamenei	575

Khamenei's Search for an Appropriate President

For the past sixteen years, Khamenei had found himself at loggerheads with his clerical presidents. Contrary to Khomeyni, who merely nodded and intimated and policies followed, Khamenei felt badgered and threatened by Rafsanjani's economic initiatives or with Khatami's political and cultural reform movement. Rafsanjani was a worthy rival who had Khomeyni's blessings and the support of the ruling elite. Khatami had overwhelming public support. Both men proved to be vibrant proponents of their own novel ideas, not easily discarded and dispensed.

Khamenei was not interested in modernization and reform and saw change as a threat. He was tired of his second in commands innovating and pushing society in directions he did not appreciate. Khamenei wished to slow down, stop, and turn back the political, cultural and social outcomes of the last sixteen years of change brought about by Rafsanjani and Khatami. The Leader yearned for a society that followed its Guardian Jurist and helped him protect the realm from the dangers of Westernization, Americanization, globalization and all non-Islamic '-isms'.

Khamenei's first two presidents had close ties with Khomeyni. They had their primary allegiance to the Imam and felt equally able to interpret Khomeyni's thoughts and the path he wished to take the country. Rafsanjani more, and Khatami to a lesser extent, were members of the same prestigious revolutionary club as Khamenei. The credentials, supporting organizations and networks of both Rafsanjani and Khatami carried weight and made harnessing their efforts difficult. Khamenei needed a new face, without long-standing administrative experience, with no links to Khomeyni, who would defy the old guards and their networks of the Right and Left and form new networks under instructions from the Leader. Khamenei longed for an obedient president who would implement his ideology and wishes with no fuss.

From the end of January 2005, Khamenei's speeches rotated around three main topics. First, without directly naming the reformists, the Leader criticized them for sowing despair and almost handing the country to its enemies. Second, he invited the people to elect an 'efficient, pious and revolutionary' president. One who would be 'a capable and strong manager and administrator', 'combat poverty, discrimination, and corruption', and make plentiful the 'people's food table/tablecloth (*sofreh*)'. Third, Khamenei attacked the US and its contention that Iran was 'building a nuclear bomb', calling it 'a myth and an untruth' and ascertained Iran's right to benefit from nuclear energy and technology and lambasted the US for its accusation that Iran violated human rights and supported terrorism.[1]

Khamenei's Advice to the Youth before the 2005 Elections

The youth should avoid getting involved in certain futile issues. You should study, be pious, engage in healthy pastimes and be happy. (A. Khamenei)[2]

In view of the coming presidential election, Rafsanjani and Karrubi's names appeared as potential candidates. Both had been Khomeyni's close disciples, companions, and appointees. Karrubi represented the cautious reformist and Rafsanjani the conservative pragmatist.

The non-clerical candidates had varied service records. Ali Larijani was Khatami's minister of culture and Islamic guidance and Khamenei's head of National Radio and Television. He came from a clerical family and was well connected to Qom. Mohammad-Baqer Qalibaf had been commander of the IRGC's economic branch, *Qarargah sazandegie khatam al-anbia* (Construction Base of the Seal of the Prophets) in 1994, the commander of the IRGC's Air Force in 1997 and the commander of the Law Enforcement Forces in 2000. Both Larijani and Qalibaf owed their careers to Khamenei. Mohsen Rezai, on the other hand, had been appointed commander of the Islamic Revolution Guardian Corps by Khomeyni, and had served in this position throughout the war until 1997. All three were conservative and loyal followers of Khamenei.

On the reformist side, Mostafa Moin had been a Member of Parliament and minister of science in Rafsanjani and Khatami's governments. Moin was supported by the radical reformists. A third and less well-known reformist candidate was Mohsen Mehralizadeh, a one-time governor general of Khorasan and a deputy of Khatami.

The reformist votes were divided between Karrubi, Moin and Mehralizadeh, while the traditional conservative votes were split between Larijani, Qalibaf, Rezai and the newcomer Mahmud Ahmadinejad. The conservatives now referred to themselves as *usulgarayan* (Principlists). Rafsanjani, however, stood all by himself somewhere in the middle, part *eslahtalab* (reformist) and part *usulgara* (Principlist).

Ahmadinejad, the Populist Miracle-Maker

Among the Principlist candidates, Mahmud Ahmadinejad was the least known (Figure 11.1). The 49-year-old mayor of Tehran was previously governor general in the province of Ardebil between 1993 and 1997. He represented a new breed of non-clerical Islamic neo-conservatives. His discourse, mannerism, public relations and style were distinct from the stale apparatchiks. Ahmadinejad was not the conservative mainstream's candidate. While mainstream candidates spoke about the same old themes in the same old monotonous and drab language, Ahmadinejad criss-crossed Iran, mixed with the common people and delivered a sparky, vivacious and different discourse.

Figure 11.1 Mahmud Ahmadinejad's election poster with Mohammad-Ali Rajai (to the right). *Source: Photo by Jaber Yazdankhah Kenary via Alamy.*

Ahmadinejad claimed that Islam provided 'answers for all current problems and questions', economic, cultural, scientific and social. Countering Khatami-era's minimization of Islamic values and criteria, Ahmadinejad argued that revolutionary managers, functionaries and administrators needed 'to believe in the ability of Islam to provide for all human needs', and 'rely on God'. Very much like Khamenei, he believed that the country's problems were rooted in 'enemy plots', 'infiltrators', 'party politics' and most significantly Western-style management. Ahmadinejad revived the idea that the Islamic Revolution in Iran had 'the historical mission of preparing for a world government'.[3]

Ahmadinejad passionately hammered at inequalities, poverty and corruption in the language of the masses, and gradually made his way into the hearts of the pious. To denigrate and contrast Khatami's style of so-called Western style of government, with his proposed revolutionary Islamic style, Ahmadinejad used unverifiable alarmist tactics. To show how the common people's rights was being abused he would refer to an unnamed minister who received 'a 12 million toman [around $1,500] allowance in addition to his salary and served eight or nine different kinds of food at a dinner reception', imposing unjustifiable costs on the people.[4]

Ahmadinejad flaunted his empathy for the dispossessed and the underdogs. As the mayor of Tehran, he joined the street sweepers late at night, wore their orange uniform and cleaned the city. He then had his high-placed supporters recount the 'event' to journalists and the people, eulogizing the mayor's humility, simplicity, and sense of service. Ahmadinejad distinguished himself from his main competition by playing the honesty, simplicity and equalitarian card. While Rafsanjani and Karrubi were embroiled in rumors about financial misconduct, Ahmadinejad emphasized that he did not belong to the well-off rent-seekers.

Ahmadinejad criticized the existing social, economic and cultural polarities, blamed Khatami for them and presented himself as the defender of the poor, the voiceless pious and the *Basiji* and *Hezbollahi* ideals. To drive his message home, he recreated the duality of the arrogant (*mostakbarin*) and the oppressed/dispossessed (*mostazafin*), the haves and have nots, the revolutionaries and counter-revolutionaries much in vogue during the revolution. He lashed at the new 'palace-dwellers' and the profligate consumerists, who had separated themselves from the people and could not understand their pains and problems. He promised that by establishing an Islamic government, upholding social justice and propagating the *Basiji* culture, he would put the country back on its revolutionary and religious track.

Politically, Ahmadinejad presented himself as an independent outsider, detached from existing political parties and organizations. The new anti-establishment man of the people criticized and admonished the past sixteen years of Iran's history. He blasted Rafsanjani and Khatami's economic record, arguing that they had ignored social justice, allowed for the concentration of wealth and power in the hands of a few and the geographical centralization of investments, services, and facilities in Tehran.

His criticism of poverty and underdevelopment of the provinces fell on many receptive ears.

As with all populists, blanket criticisms came with the promise of quick solutions. Ahmadinejad promised to solve 'the country's major problems in five years'. He told his supporters that 'eradicating poverty and unemployment can be solved with resolve and dedication'.[5] Despite his growing popularity, twenty days before the elections, a government poll indicated that Rafsanjani had the highest intention of votes with 33 per cent, followed by Ali Larijani, 17.26 per cent and Qalibaf with 15.86 per cent.[6] A week before the elections, polls conducted by the conservatives indicated that Rafsanjani was ahead of Larijani and Qalibaf.[7] Ahmadinejad did not seem to pose a real threat.

The Making of a President

By the time the 2005 presidential elections came around, it became clear that Ahmadinejad had been groomed by Mesbah-Yazdi. Mesbah-Yazdi, a member of the Assembly of Experts of the Leadership since 1999, was a clerical figure whom Khomeyni had never really trusted. He was associated with the quietist anti-Bahai Hojatiyyeh Society, which always remained on the good side of the Pahlavi regime, rather than siding with Khomeyni's revolutionary anti-Shah stance.

After the revolution, Mesbah-Yazdi was never offered an administrative, executive or judicial position, yet he had obtained some national recognition because of his televised debates with various Left and communist leaders in the spring of 1981. He had a strict and traditional Shii view, with an exaggerated emphasis on the presence and intervention of the Twelfth Shii Imam in everyday affairs. Even though the Twelfth Imam had been in occultation since the ninth century, Mesbah-Yazdi spoke as if the Hidden Imam interacted with the material world, and Mesbah-Yazdi was privy to his intentions, wishes and thoughts.

Acting as the implicit medium between the infallible Hidden Imam and believers, Mesbah-Yazdi had presented himself as a religious authority whose political positions derived from Islam could not be challenged. It was most convenient that this new spokesperson of the Hidden Imam was now wholeheartedly loyal to the Leader, enhancing the latter's position. Mesbah-Yazdi claimed that enmity towards Khamenei was a kind of polytheism and on par with opposition to God and the Shii imams.

Shortly following Khatami's presidency, in January 1998, Mesbah-Yazdi began propagating his ideas at Tehran's Friday Prayers. Concurrently, he and his followers launched their publication *Partove Sokhan* (Beam of the Word), defending religious values, the Islamic system and the Rule of the Guardian Jurist against 'anti-religious and deviationist thoughts'. In January 2005, Mesbah-Yazdi claimed that 'Islam was in danger' and a 'supporter of Islam' who 'pained for the faith and wished to implement the real Islam' had to be elected president to save the country.[8]

Ahmadinejad benefitted from the full support of conservatives connected with Khamenei's son, Mojtaba Khamenei, and Mesbah-Yazdi in the *Basiji* and *Hezbollahi* organizations, the IRGC, the Guardian Council and the instrumental network of *maddahan* (preachers-performers). The preachers-performers who regularly addressed the devout and zealous believers, in all religious gatherings wielded considerable influence among the pious through their emotionally charged religious sermons.

The influential clerical organization of the Association of Militant Clergy (*jameeye rowhaniyat mobarez*), headed by Mahdavi-Kani, threw its weight behind Rafsanjani's candidacy, but Mesbah-Yazdi, who did not belong to this organization of Khomeyni's old followers, went his own way. On 9 June 2005, twenty-two junior clerics unknown to the public but associated with Mesbah-Yazdi, issued a statement of support in favour of Ahmadinejad. The signatories included the employees of 'Imam Khomeyni Educational and Research Institute', an organization founded in 1995 by Mesbah-Yazdi and fully supported by Khamenei.[9]

Iranians went to the voting booths on Friday, 17 June 2005. By Saturday noon, from the 22,459,714 votes counted, Rafsanjani gained 4,825,863 votes, followed by Karrubi with 4,527,355 votes. Ahmadinejad with 3,940,419 votes and Qalibaf with 3,501,444 votes came in third and fourth. None of the candidates had obtained more than 50 per cent of the votes, so the first two candidates, Rafsanjani and Karrubi, were poised to compete in the second round.

On Sunday morning, 19 June 2005, however, the tables turned. After counting 6,941,146 more votes, the Guardian Council announced that out of 29,400,860 votes cast, Rafsanjani had 6,190,132 votes and Ahmadinejad 5,718,129 votes, and these two candidates would go to the second round, while Karrubi with 5,073,800 votes was eliminated.[10]

On the same day, Karrubi wrote a bold letter to Khamenei contesting the results and accusing the *Basij*, the IRGC and the preachers-performers (*maddahan*) of meddling in the provinces. Karrubi spoke of the Guardian Council's coup-like move and accused Mojtaba Khamenei, the Leader's eldest son, of interfering in the election in support of Ahmadinejad. In defiance of the Leader, Karrubi resigned his posts in the Expediency Discernment Council of the System and informed the Leader that he would subsequently form a political party.

The political atmosphere after the first round of elections was tense, and accusations reached a new pitch as the run-off elections approached. Ahmadinejad's camp accused Rafsanjani, his family and associates of corruption and ill-gotten wealth. The reformist supporters of Karrubi and Moin had no other option but to support Rafsanjani. Many brooded and abstained from participating in a game they thought was already rigged in favour of Ahmadinejad.

Mohammad Quchani, editor of the reformist daily *Sharq* (East) underlined the need to form an anti-fascist front in defence of the Republic and called on Iranians to rally behind Rafsanjani. To defend the Republic, Iranians were called to rally behind Rafsanjani. The anti-Ahmadinejad coalition warned against a reactionary backlash and the establishment of Talibanism, the Red Khmers, dictatorship, despotism, fascism and insecurity, if Ahmadinejad were elected.

On Friday, 24 June, Iranians voted and on Sunday came the second great upset. Mahmud Ahmadinejad was announced as the sixth president of the Islamic Republic. Out of 27,959,253 votes cast, he obtained 17,428,782 as compared to Rafsanjani's 10,046,701. In the second round, 1,441,607 fewer Iranians had voted. Within the week between the first and second rounds of elections, Ahmadinejad tripled his votes and Rafsanjani's votes increased by 1.6 times.

Rumours about electoral fraud in favour of Ahmadinejad were widespread after the election. Ali Mirbaqeri, managing director of the Ministry of Interior and Jafar Habibzadeh, the legal director of the Ministry of Interior, gave details of cheating and accused the Guardian Council and the armed forces of having intervened in the elections. Rafsanjani spoke of organized interferences directing the votes towards a particular candidate.

In Mesbah-Yazdi's first official meeting with Ahmadinejad, he told the victorious president that 'the future generations will conclude that this election was replete with miracles and *keramat* (thaumaturgic gifts)'. Mesbah-Yazdi described the election as a miracle and hailed its results as the proof of the Hidden Imam's favour towards Iranians and hoped for the eventual reappearance of the Twelfth Imam.

Mesbah-Yazdi's Role in Ahmadinejad's Victory

Ayatollah Mesbah-Yazdi's support was instrumental in Doctor Ahmadinejad reaching the run-off elections and his ultimate victory over Rafsanjani. (R. Sanati)[11]

Mesbah-Yazdi compared Ahmadinejad's mission to that of the Prophet, to establish an 'Islamic government', aided by miracles and the blessing of the Hidden Imam. Ahmadinejad candidly thanked Mesbah-Yazdi for 'intelligently and graciously entering into this scene [the election] and managing it'.[12]

Ahmadinejad's Islamic Government: The Leader's Dream Come True

Khamenei's reaction to the election results exuded satisfaction and relief. The Leader thanked the people for 'demonstrating their will, orientation and resistance to the

Figure 11.2 The Bushehr Nuclear Power Plant. *Source: Wikimedia Commons.*

world'. Khamenei hoped for a 'pious, motivated forceful and efficient government' that would fulfil the election promises in cooperation with other state institutions. The Leader spoke of the Islamic government creating an Islamic state, giving birth to an Islamic civilization, a culture that would prevail over humanity.[13] The two conservative presidential candidates close to Khamenei, who had lost to Ahmadinejad, were also rewarded with prominent positions. Larijani replaced Hasan Rowhani as the secretary of Iran's Supreme National Security Council, instrumental in the nuclear discussions and Qalibaf became Tehran's new mayor (Figure 11.2).

On 21 August 2005, Ahmadinejad went to the Majles and presented his cabinet, who shared his world outlook and highlighted the four axes of his government: justice, kindness, service to God's subjects, and ensuring spiritual and material progress. He criticized the Western cultural onslaught, liberalism and the disregard for religion and religious culture in politics and economics. The new president promised to support religious teachings in schools, universities, mosques and seminary schools.

Three days later and to everyone's surprise, the conservative Majles dominated by the Principlists turned down four of Ahmadinejad's proposed ministers, three of whom had been his colleagues at the Tehran City Council. The vote demonstrated how concerned and anxious the traditional conservatives had become as they faced the Ahmadinejad coalition. Ahmadinejad had blown apart the fragile unity that existed among the Principlists. Khamenei sat back and watched his loyal forces compete.

In his initial statements and interviews, Ahmadinejad reiterated that the pronouncements by *maqam moazame rahbari* (Supreme Leader) on society, governance, justice and other issues, constituted the theoretical charter, which he intended to operationalize. The Leader, in turn, warned against undermining the new government, prompted all to support it, and announced that 'realizing the promises of the government was to everyone's benefit'.[14]

> ### Khamenei's Praise for Ahmadinejad
>
> The present situation of the government, the favourable position of the president, and the verbal and practical interaction that now exists with the people has created a most conducive atmosphere. The people have become earnestly hopeful. If you visit governmental offices today – and I know – people are complaining less . . . because they feel progress in all areas. (A. Khamenei)[15]

With domestic politics under his control, Khamenei, focused on a new interest. Iran's nuclear programme was to become his anti-Western project, a means of presenting himself as the commander of resistance forces, standing up to US arrogance and intimidation. Khamenei believed that unjustifiably, the US wished to prevent the Islamic Republic from developing its own nuclear fuel and to keep Iran dependent on the West's provision of processed uranium. To the Leader, the Bush Administration was 'a warmonger in search of world domination and an empire'.[16] Even though Khamenei insisted on Iran mastering the technology of nuclear fuel production, he had since early August 2005, issued a fatwa forbidding the production and use of nuclear weapons.

> ### US view of Iran's Nuclear Program
>
> On Iran's nuclear program, Bush administration strategy was to rally the international community to confront the Iranian regime with a strategic choice. Tehran could transparently and verifiably give up its pursuit of a nuclear weapons capability, especially its enrichment facility at Natanz. If it did, the international community would respond with substantial diplomatic, economic and security benefits. These would include the relaxation of existing economic sanctions and active international support for a truly peaceful civilian nuclear program, including the supply of nuclear fuel so Iran would not need an enrichment facility. If it rejected this choice, the regime would only be further isolated diplomatically, incur increased economic sanctions, and run the risk of military action. (S. J. Hadley, national security advisor to President George W. Bush)[17]

A Bombastic and Sanctimonious President

On 17 September 2005, Ahmadinejad travelled to New York to address the UN General Assembly. He asserted Iran's right to develop peaceful nuclear energy and enrich its own uranium fuel for that purpose. He argued that Iran was a 'victim of terrorism and chemical weapons', referred to Iran as 'a symbol of true democracy', and concluded his political speech with a prayer for the return of the Twelfth Shii Imam, who would lead the world to justice and absolute peace.

To Ahmadinejad and his ardent supporters back home, the speech at the UN, and the reference to the promised Hidden Imam reawakened, and reinvigorated the pride, honour and authority of Shiism in the world. Later, Ahmadinejad presented a highly controversial supernatural account of his General Assembly speech. He intimated the presence of the Twelfth Imam in the form of a 'column of light' or 'halo of light' and spoke of a paranormal hand holding the delegates motionless gazing at Ahmadinejad's face during his speech. The president's dramatic depiction of his so-called supernatural experience was recorded on film and seen by millions.[18]

The spread of superstition around the presence of the Hidden Imam became a hallmark of the forces around Mesbah-Yazdi and Ahmadinejad. Gholamhoseyn Elham, the spokesperson of the Guardian Council, whom Ahmadinejad had appointed as the government's spokesperson, told reporters that, 'it was undeniable that an interested hand extended from the world of angels was focused on [concerned with the lot of] our people'.[19] The new leadership played on the innocent beliefs of pious believers to pass the new president as an appointee of the Twelfth Imam and therefore irreproachable. They also propagated the idea that with the coming of Ahmadinejad, a novel spiritual and paranormal era reigned over the country, during which believers could visit the Twelfth Imam and forget their mundane and worldly considerations.

In 2007, two years into Ahmadinejad's presidency, Hojatoleslam Morteza Aqa-Tehrani, a student and protégé of Mesbah-Yazdi, published a book on the Twelfth Imam, with the subtitle, *The Practical Ways of Meeting the Twelfth Imam*. It tells how such encounters were made possible and enumerated them. Aqa-Tehrani's book encouraged the devout Shii to strive toward meeting with the Hidden Imam as their prime objective in life. It prodded believers to forget their pressing material needs until they had met the Hidden Imam in this world.[20]

On 9 November 2005, some eleven weeks after Parliament rejected four proposed ministers, Ahmadinejad sent another four nominees to the Majles. Ahmadinejad's newly proposed minister of oil, Sadeq Mahsuli, caused an uproar in the Principlist Majles. The commotion should be understood in light of an ethical and political covenant, which Ahmadinejad had obliged his ministers to sign on 15 August 2005. His ministers committed themselves to 12 principles. The second, fourth and tenth items stressed that ministers should have a frugal lifestyle, be honest, appoint colleagues based on merit, desist from cronyism, patronage and factionalism and combat forcefully extravagant and luxurious lifestyles.

Mahsuli came from a humble background. He had joined the IRGC, fought in the Iran–Iraq War and became an IRGC commander in Azarbayjan. He went to the same university as Ahmadinejad, the University of Science and Industry. Ahmadinejad and Mahsuli, along with Parviz Fatah and Mojtaba Samareh-Hashemi, formed the 'Orumiyeh circle', known for their role in repressing supporters of Bazargan, Bani-Sadr and Shariati in 1979. Ahmadinejad and Mahsuli became closer in 1980, when Ahmadinejad was governor of Maku and Mashsuli served as governor of Orumiyeh, both in Azarbayjan Province. Once Ahmadinejad became president, Parviz Fatah became his minister of energy and Mojtaba Samareh-Hashemi, a senior aide to the president.

After the war, when Ahmadinejad became governor general of Ardebil in 1993, he was said to have been instrumental in helping Mahsuli win a bid involving oil swaps with Nakhjavan in the Republic of Azarbayjan through IRGC-connected companies. The lucrative profits from the oil contracts became the seed money for Mahsuli's future financial and real estate empire. In 2005, when he was Ahmadinejad's presidential campaign manager, his wealth was said to be around 160 billion tomans ($160 million).

During the hearings on Mahsuli's credentials, a Majles deputy called him the 'billionaire general', a nickname that stuck. The majority of deputies were not satisfied with his explanations of how he had obtained his wealth. Some deputies argued that he had obtained it through 'special relations', an embarrassment for a government which claimed to be bent on justice, combatting corruption and the frugal life-style of its members. Mahsuli, in turn, argued that his wealth was only in his trust, while in truth, it belonged to the Hidden Twelfth Imam. Learning that the Majles would turn him down, Mahsuli withdrew his nomination. Ahmadinejad accepted the setback, appointed him as his second senior aide and praised him as an honest and anti-corruption commander.

From mid-2007, Ahmadinejad's relationship with the conservative dominated 7th Majles gradually soured. The president did not possess a solid faction in the Majles, and after two years, some of his earlier staunch supporters became vocal opponents of his policies. The loyalties of Principlist deputies were now divided between Rafsanjani, Ali Larijani and Mohsen Rezai. Ahmadinejad's haughty attitude towards the Majles alienated his supporters and pushed them into opposition. Unhappy with bills passed by the Majles, Ahmadinejad ignored their implementation, partially implemented them and sometimes delayed acting on them.

At the end of December 2007, Ahmadinejad wrote a severe letter to Haddad-Adel, the president of the Majles. He complained that the deputies were intervening too much in the affairs of the government and crippling its activities. Ahmadinejad was not happy with the deputies criticizing his policies and opposing his withdrawals from the Reserve Fund to finance his current expenditures. The Majles feared higher inflation rates while the president wanted to have his way.

Ahmadinejad's Atypical and Folksy Politics

During his first term in office (2005–9) Ahmadinejad benefited from the unqualified endorsement of Khamenei. The Leader dismissed the complaints of his detractors as unfair and repeated that the president 'lived a simple life', and was 'tireless', 'a people's person', 'brave' and with a lot of 'self-confidence'. At this time, Ahmadinejad followed Khamenei's wishes and took initiatives approved by him and, in return, the Leader gave him free rein, unprecedented in his dealing with past presidents. The two men were convinced that national interest was a function of ideological correctness, a blend of Islamicness and anti-Westernism, pushing Iran into a camp of populist, authoritarian and anti-American countries such as Syria, Russia, North Korea, Cuba, Bolivia and Venezuela.

Iran's Nuclear Policy

Khatami had suspended Iranian uranium enrichment during talks with France, Germany, and United Kingdom. Five days after Ahmadinejad took office, the Natanz facility in Isfahan began producing uranium hexafluoride, used in enriching uranium. The decision to move again towards uranium enrichment and embark on a costly nuclear programme was made by Khamenei, who expected Ahmadinejad to take Iran's nuclear programme to the people and transform it into a national mission. The move's immediate consequence, however, was that France, Germany, and the United Kingdom stopped all further negotiations with Tehran.

On 24 September 2005, the International Atomic Energy Agency (IAEA) passed a resolution that 'the nature of Iran's nuclear activities and the lack of assurance in their peaceful nature fall under the purview of the UN Security Council'.[21] By April 2006, Iran announced having enriched uranium for the first time. Foreign Minister Manuchehr Mottaki announced the end of Iran's voluntary cooperation with the IAEA.

The IAEA reported Iran to the UN Security Council for noncompliance with the NPT Safeguards Agreement. Despite Iran's repeated denials, the world community suspected Iran of pursuing military nuclear objectives. Meanwhile, throughout 2006, initiatives by the European Union and Russia to provide Iran with civilian nuclear technology and enriched uranium for peaceful purposes were rejected by Iran.

Ahmadinejad's boastful statements about Iran's nuclear capabilities that were meant for boosting domestic morale proved counterproductive in the West, as they strengthened suspicions about Iran's military nuclear ambitions. On 11 April 2006,

Ahmadinejad announced that Iran had completed the nuclear fuel cycle and bragged that this achievement placed Iran among the 'nuclear countries of the world'.²² Four months later, Ahmadinejad inaugurated the heavy-water-production plant at Arak. Critics feared that heavy water reactors could eventually produce nuclear weapons.

Iran and the West were on a collision course. Ahmadinejad promised to operationalize 60,000 nuclear centrifuges, 3,000 of which would be ready by March 2007. The president pledged to 'fully nuclearize' Iran by 2007.²³ He argued that sanctions would have no effect and that the nuclear programme was unstoppable. Khamenei escalated the hype by making the nuclear programme into a national anti-Western project, reminiscent of Mosaddeq's anti-colonial oil-nationalization project.

Khamenei claimed that the people 'adamantly demanded this [nuclear programme] right'. He announced that 'nuclear energy is the future and destiny of Iran' and brushed off those criticizing the high cost of the energy programme and those who deemed it 'unnecessary for the country'. He called them 'shallow-minded and short-sighted'.²⁴ In the name of resisting Western hegemony, he pushed right ahead with uranium enrichment at home, and testing rocket launches into space.

Holocaust Denying and Wiping Out the Zionist State

The Khamenei-Ahmadinejad synergy created a new level of rhetoric against the Zionist state which, added to the fast-paced nuclear programme posed as a threat to Israel. Iran's nuclear programme rattled Israeli officials. On 11 December 2006, Khamenei met with Ismail Haniyeh, the prime minister of the Palestinian National Authority, who was also a member of Hamas, the Islamic Resistance Movement. Khamenei assured Haniyeh of Iran's full support, hoping that Palestine (Israel) would eventually be managed by Palestinians. Haniyeh, in return, announced that Palestine was an Islamic state and that Hamas would never recognize the Zionist regime. He insisted on 'resistance' as the sole mean of liberating Palestine.

On the same day, Mottaki, the minister of foreign affairs, inaugurated an international conference in Tehran called *Reviewing the Holocaust: Global Vision*. Sixty-seven representatives from thirty countries were in attendance. Mottaki claimed that the seminar was neither to negate or ascertain the Holocaust but to allow intellectuals to freely discuss this issue and share their scientific findings. Mottaki himself condemned antisemitism and insisted that it was a Western phenomenon. David Duke, an American white supremacist, anti-Semitic conspiracy theorist and former Grand Wizard of the Knights of the Ku Klux Klan, was, however amongst the attendees, as were members of the zealous anti-Zionist Orthodox Jewish community of Neturei Karta.

On 12 December, Ahmadinejad addressed the conference. He said that, 'thanks to God's will, the life expectancy curve of the Zionist regime has taken a downward turn and is falling. This is God's promise and the wish of the world's people ... Just as the Soviet Union was wiped out (*mahv*), and there is nothing left of it today, so will the Zionist regime and humanity [will be] freed.'[25]

A year before, President Ahmadinejad had referred to the Holocaust as a myth, drawing strong condemnations from Israel and the European Commission. Now, he and his counselor, Mohammad-Ali Ramin, were introducing the Iranian public to the term Holocaust. At the time, curious Iranians scrambled to find what Holocaust meant. Morris Motamed, a Jewish-Iranian deputy in the Majles, criticized the seminar and called the Holocaust one of the most, if not the most significant of human catastrophes. Motamed wrote to Ahmadinejad that negating the Holocaust was an affront to the Iranian Jewish community.

Throughout his presidency, Ahmadinejad continued a campaign of virulent anti-Zionist attacks with anti-Semitic overtones. He consistently attacked and provoked Israel by referring to it as 'a source of corruption', a bunch of 'criminals', 'thieves and murderers', 'a group of hypocrite racists' and 'a minuscule minority ... dominating ... the financial, monetary, and political decision-making centres of some European countries and the US in a deceitful, complex, and furtive manner'. Ahmadinejad incessantly called for the dismantlement of Israel and referred to the Holocaust as 'a lie'.

Israel retaliated by taking macabre measures. A string of assassination attempts in the heart of the capital, targeted Iranian nuclear scientists. Masoud Alimohammadi was assassinated in January 2010, followed by Majid Shahriyari on 29 November 2010. Fereydun Abbasi survived an attempt on his life on the same day as Shahriyari was murdered. Darush Rezainejad was assassinated in July 2011, followed by Mostafa Ahmadi-Roshan in January 2012. All assassination attempts were linked to the Israeli intelligence service Mossad. In an interview with the German weekly, *Der Spiegel* in August 2015, Israel's defence minister hinted that Israel had been behind the killings of Iranian nuclear scientists. Moshe Yaalon said, 'Ultimately it is very clear, one way or another, Iran's military nuclear program must be stopped.' He added that 'We will act in any way [necessary] and are not willing to tolerate a nuclear-armed Iran. We prefer that this be done by means of sanctions, but in the end, Israel should be able to defend itself.'[26]

International Sanctions

As Khamenei insisted on leading the resistance against 'world arrogance', the international community pushed ahead with further isolating the Islamic Republic. From July 2006, the Security Council adopted resolutions 1696 (July 2006), 1737 (December 2006), 1747 (March 2007), 1803 (March 2008), 1835 (September 2008) and 1929 (June 2010) against Iran's nuclear activities.

In October 2007, the US began a spiraling series of sanctions on Iranian banks, government, and para-state companies, including oil, gas, petrochemical and shipping. It blacklisted the IRGC and its affiliated organizations and institutions, government officials, military commanders, nuclear scientists and politicians. By June 2010, the US imposed unilateral sanctions on Iran, tightening restrictions on Iran's banking and energy sector, and penalizing countries doing business with Iran. Foreign banks conducting transactions with Iranian banks or the IRGC were sanctioned and deprived of access to the US financial system. In June 2011, the number of blacklisted Iranian banks reached 21, and further sanctions were imposed on the Islamic Revolutionary Guard Corps, the *Basij* Resistance Force, and Iran's Law Enforcement Forces.

In November 2011, President Obama issued Executive Order 13590, imposing new sanctions targeting Iran's petrochemical sector and comprehensive energy sanctions. The US and EU restrictive measures forced almost all Iran's oil buyers to either reduce or halt their purchases. Washington warned countries importing Iranian oil that their banks would be cut off from the US financial system if they did not comply with oil sanctions.

In May 2012, talks between Iran and the P5+1 reached another dead end. The six world powers insisted that Iran stop enriching uranium at 20 per cent purity, a grade just below the level to allow for nuclear weapons production. Tehran demanded the easing of economic sanctions and insisted on the P5+1 recognizing its 'right to enrich'.

The sanctions gradually took their toll. Iranian oil exports dropped from 2.2 million barrels per day at the end of 2011 to approximately 1 million barrels per day in September 2012. Iran's monthly revenues from crude oil exports dropped from around $8 billion in 2011 to $6.3 billion in the first half of 2012 and $3.4 billion in the first half of 2013. When Ahmadinejad had come to power in 2005, international oil prices had been $105. He was fortunate that by May 2008, they had reached an all-time high of $169 per barrel, partially compensating for the drop in exports.

The Effect of Sanctions

The sanctions rippled across the Iranian economy. As parts became difficult or more costly to import and longstanding relationships with foreign firms were ruptured, much of Iran's indigenous capacity was devastated. (S. Maloney)[27]

Ahmadinejad's Economic Policies

Ahmadinejad had come to power promising to improve the living standard of the poor, the lower classes and the dispossessed. He had vouched for uprooting inequalities and ending corruption, favouritism and nepotism. His performance, however, proved to be mixed.

Ahmadinejad took strides to improve the lot of those he and the Leader considered the socio-economic backbone and defenders of the system, namely the *Basij* and the IRGC. His method of supporting them, however, further divided and polarized their members along economic lines. At the time of their creation, members of *Basij* and IRGC were economically homogeneous and quite modest. Ahmadinejad's policies empowered the new elite at the apex of *Basij* and IRGC, enjoying exceptional military, financial and political powers. Yet, the rank and file of those organizations remained lower-middle-income personnel, subject to the vagaries of a market under sanctions. The genie of enriching IRGC members let out of the bottle by Rafsanjani and contained by Khatami was fattened by Ahmadinejad.

The collapse of oil prices after the 2008 international economic crisis and its cumulative economic consequences had an inevitable effect on the Iranian economy, but the country's disastrous mismanagement was primarily caused by the Khamenei–Ahmadinejad duo. The crippling sanctions, disregard for basic economic theory and sound fiscal and monetary policy, support for opaque and unaccountable para-state economic units, favouritism in allocation of loans and foreign exchange, repression of labour unions, indulgence towards the financial misappropriation of those connected to the centres of power and a policy of financially rewarding/bribing the IRGC, were all outcomes of conscious executive decisions.

Khamenei's call for economic jihad and resistance in 2011 were mercantilist and protectionist responses to a continuously deteriorating welfare situation. Self-sufficiency and self-reliance could make sense for an economy with a robust industrial and agricultural base. Iran's economy, which was driven by oil exports, imports of all kinds and sorts and the real-estate market, was a far cry from what was required to become self-sufficient. When the full force of the sanctions impacted the Iranian economy, Ahmadinejad was ill-equipped and unprepared to cope.

Ahmadinejad staked the success of his tenure on four specific projects, which he believed would quickly achieve socio-economic progress, justice and equity. They were the Quick Impact and Return Projects (QIRP), the Mehr Housing Project (MHP), the Justice Shares Scheme (JSS) and the (Cash Payments Scheme) (CPS).[28]

On 10 November 2005, the government ratified the by-laws of 'Quick Impact and Return Projects'. Ahmadinejad believed that identifying and providing low-interest capital to small-scale local firms of less than 50 employees, would quickly solve Iran's unemployment problem, assist development in the provinces, and increase output. From 2006 to 2010, the government was to invest 47,000 billion tomans (some $47 billion) in QIRPs and generate 3.1 million jobs. In the end, however, only 20,000 billion tomans (some $20 billion) was allocated, generating 1 million jobs. By 2011, the Majles Research Centre concluded that, '30% of the capital paid out to the QIRPs were diverted to other purposes or to units which demonstrated no economic activities'.[29]

The small scale of the units, the absence of economies of scale, and the lack of managerial and marketing skills of the loan recipients made the output of these firms costly and uncompetitive. A large proportion of these projects were purely fictional, and the funds received were spent elsewhere or diverted to other purposes, such as purchasing real estate and investing in the more lucrative housing sector.[30] Although, Ahmadinejad labelled the QIRPs as one of the most successful projects of his government, many Iranian economists and politicians differed, arguing that the QIRPs failed to attain their objectives and became a major inflationary factor.

The Mehr (affection) Housing Project (MHP) was a social housing initiative included in the 2007–8 annual budget and intended to provide cheap and affordable housing for low-income families. Since 2006, real estate prices had skyrocketed by some 50 per cent in less than a year. To make everyone a 'homeowner', the government announced the construction of 4 million residential units, with at least half of them in the provinces and rural areas. Applicants were extended loans ranging from $7,000–$10,000. In 2011, Ahmadinejad announced that the MHP had been a success story and that by the end of his presidency, Iran would be free of its housing problem.

At the end of Ahmadinejad's presidency, approximately a million residential units were completed. These low-income housing projects were built on the periphery of cities and towns, and at first lacked the basic infrastructure (tarmac roads, public transportation), amenities (electricity, piped water, gas), and social services (schools, shops, medical and leisure facilities, parks, sanitation services, mosques). The quality of construction material used in these units was questionable and proved non-resistant during earthquakes.

As of January 2011, the Iranian banking system had paid out $10.2 billion in loans. The money came from the government borrowing from the Central Bank and fueling inflation. Hasan Rowhani, Ahmadinejad's successor, labelled MHP 'one of the largest hurdles to Iran's economic recovery' and 'the main culprit behind the country's still-rampant inflation'.[31] Yet, despite all its shortcomings, the MHP enabled millions of low-income people, never properly sheltered, to benefit from what gradually became respectable suburbs and communities.

The distribution of Justice Shares or the JSS was a corollary to Ahmadinejad's attempt at privatization, an ongoing affair since Rafsanjani's presidency. In July 2006, the Leader charged the government to implement Article 44 of Iran's Constitution which defines the three sectors of ownership in the Islamic Republic, the state, the cooperative and the private and enlarge the private sector by selling 80 per cent of all state-owned enterprises. The outcome of this 'privatization' was the eventual transfer of significant petrochemical, power and telecommunication companies to IRGC-controlled consortiums and holding companies of the Social Security Investment Company, known by its Persian acronym Shasta.

As a part of Ahmadinejad's promises of equitable distribution of income, poverty reduction and income generation for low-income families, on 29 January 2006 the government ratified the executive bylaw of Justice Shares Scheme (JSS). Unbeknown to shareholders, a large number of shares in particular state-owned companies were bought by the government and sold to low-income categories (initially the bottom 20 per cent of income owners). The circle of those eligible expanded gradually and included war veterans, families of martyrs, villagers, tribespeople, mosque employees, seminary school students, journalists, retired government employees, carpet weavers, single-mother households and patients with rare diseases. Shares were sold at different discounts based on family incomes. The purchase, management and distribution of the profits of these shares were entirely in the hands of the government. The new shareowners became joint beneficiaries of a government-controlled investment fund in the so-called 'privatized enterprises' but held no title as proof of this ownership. The companies had become formally privatized as their shares were held by government designated individuals.

On 18 April 2009, right before the presidential elections, Ahmadinejad distributed the 'profits' of the JSS to some 9 million shareholders, raising eyebrows among his presidential rivals. This 'one-time' profit distribution was the equivalent of some $80 per shareholder. After this initial payment, profits were no longer paid out but accrued to the government treasury. In November 2009, the distribution of Justice Shares came under much criticism from independent economists and Majles deputies. Critics believed that it had been an unsuccessful initiative.

By 2019, some 49 million people were the nominal joint shareholders of some 60 firms worth some $18.7 billion. Stockholders did not know the enterprises in which they held their shares, had never participated in a stockholders' meeting, never voted and had no knowledge of the profit or returns to their titles.

Logic of Cash Payments

This is an important initiative to achieve social justice. The people's rights should be returned to them and the government intends to place those rights in their individual pockets for them to manage. (M. Ahmadinejad)[32]

Like all his two predecessors, Ahmadinejad concluded that the heavy load of subsidies paid out to Iranians, was untenable, especially under the pressure of sanctions. He, therefore, began a two-pronged approach, explaining why it was imperative to gradually decrease subsidies on gasoline, gas, electricity, bread and water, all essential items in the budget of low-income earners. To cushion price shocks, attenuate hardship on the low-income categories and avoid social unrest, Ahmadinejad introduced a Cash Payments Scheme.

On 11 November 2010, the government announced that it would deposit a monthly payment of approximately $45 in the accounts of 67,482,000 Iranians. The government hoped that recipients would save the cash payments, and not rush to consume it, feeding inflation. On 19 December 2010, the great price adjustment or 'surgery' went into effect, raising the price of petroleum by 1.75 times, gas for home cooking by 7 times, electricity by 2.7 times, and water by 3.5 times. In 2012, Iran remained the highest subsidy-paying country in the world.

Once Hasan Rowhani became president, the Ministry of Economy published a report in June 2014 suggesting that the cash payments had reduced the purchasing power of Iranians by 25 per cent, dipping 31 per cent of the population below the poverty line. In 2015, the minister of oil complained about the crushing burden of cash payments as a 'great disaster' and claimed that about 80–90 per cent of the sales of Iran's Gas company and 80 per cent of Iran's revenues from refining and distribution of processed goods were going towards the payment of Cash Subsidies.

The Politics of Voluntaristic Economic Decisions

Ahmadinejad was not an economist, nor was he interested in what they said. He did not appreciate experts, as they often disagreed on the soundness of his policies and methods. Gradually the circle of professionals and technocrats in his entourage dwindled. Ahmadinejad's stubbornness and can-do attitude enabled him to impose his political and personal voluntarism on the economy during his first four years in office when he enjoyed Khamenei's support. His cavalier approach, however, caused his undoing during his second term in office. Rushed and lightening decisions to do first and deal with the grave consequences later typified Ahmadinejad's economic policies during his tenure.

The minister of economy, Davud Danesh-Jafari, and the director of the Central Bank, Ebrahim Sheybani had consistently assured depositors that interest rates would remain stable, and they would not have to worry about a reduction in the return on their savings. In late June 2007, Ahmadinejad suddenly issued two directives. Interest rates on savings was lowered to 12 per cent in state banks and 13 per cent in private banks. Interest rates on loans to investors in the industrial, agricultural, and mining sectors was ordered at 10 per cent. With inflation hovering around 20 to 23 per cent, depositors had no longer any incentive to place their money in saving accounts. Well-connected and privileged elites with access to lowered interest loans found unprecedented opportunities to make lucrative windfall gains from the administratively low price of capital in a capital-scarce country.

When it came to running the affairs of the state, the list of Ahmadinejad's arbitrary and rash decisions abounded. Faced with the rising financial burden of importing petroleum and the wish to remove subsidies, Ahmadinejad's government suddenly announced rationing petroleum. Iranians, who had been used to unlimited access to very cheap gas, were caught by surprise. The government introduced a dual price system. Car owners were suddenly limited to 100 liters per month at subsidized prices of 1,000 rials ($0.11/litre). Those consuming more than the 100 liters ration per month had to pay four times as much per litre. On 16 June 2007, cars lined up for six hours in front of gas stations, as angry consumers went on a rampage, vandalizing between 12 to 24 gas stations across Tehran, and setting them on fire. The police arrested at least 80 in Tehran.

Ahmadinejad's reaction to the criticism of the experts to his economically unsound and impulsive initiatives were a series of vindictive actions, effectively gagging criticism of his policies. For 60 years, Iran possessed one of Asia's most experienced indicative planning institutions. With disciplined oversight and an effective system of checks and balances, the five-year plans had been assiduously carried out by the Management and Plan Organization (MPO), the successor to the Plan and Budget Organization. On 9 July 2007, Ahmadinejad ended the independence of MPO. He issued a directive, dissolving the original body and incorporating it into the President's Office. MPO was the government's accountant, and one of its jobs was to supervise and monitor the government's revenues and expenditure. Ahmadinejad did not like autonomous institutions overlooking the economic activities of his government.

A month later, the president did away with another independent financial and economic supervisory body. On 14 August 2007, Ahmadinejad dissolved the Money and Credit Council (MCC), the professional watch-dog organization of the Central Bank articulating and supervising monetary policy. The MCC had disagreed with the reduction of interest rates and the creation of interest-free (*qarz al-hasaneh*) banks.

In March 2008, an increasing number of well-connected borrowers who had obtained substantial low-interest loans had defaulted on payment. Danesh-Jafari, the minister of economy and finance who had been at loggerheads with Ahmadinejad over the lowering of interest rates, gave the president a list of 200 mega-debtors strongly attached to the centres of power. Among them was Mahsuli, Ahmadinejad's close friend. On 21 April 2008, he openly criticized Ahmadinejad's economic policies and mocked his economic advisers. He was dismissed the following day. Ahmadinejad's erratic and unstudied decisions and his hostile reactions to criticisms were inimical to putting the Iranian economy on a steady and calculated path.

Economic Performance during Ahmadinejad's Presidency

Ahmadinejad's economic policies were mostly based on his populistic view that generous government spending to please and help the dispossessed masses would solve Iran's socio-economic and political problems. During Ahmadinejad's presidency, some fifty Iranian economists wrote four different letters (2006, 2007, 2008, 2013), warning him about the disastrous consequences of his 'rushed policies lacking any scientific base and expertise'. They cautioned against rising inflation and recession, capital flight, slowing growth rates, decreasing inflow of foreign direct investment and increase in oil-revenue driven government expenditures and imports. They warned against the windfall gains of those privileged few who benefitted from obtaining lowered interest rates from the banking system.[33] He did not heed their warnings and continued to do his own thing.

In 2005, the economy had been growing (real GDP growth) at approximately 3.2 per cent. During 2012 and 2013, it was registering negative growth rates. Inflation rates, which were about 15 per cent in 2005, reached 40 per cent in 2013. During Ahmadinejad's presidency, the free market price of the dollar increased from 9,000 rials to every dollar in 2005 to almost 35,000 rials by 2013. The steep depreciation of the rial caused the chicken shortage of July 2012. In Tehran, the free market price of chicken tripled to about 7,500 rials per kilo due to the rise in price of imported chicken feed. Consumers would wait in line for up to six hours to buy frozen chicken from Turkey, which was subsidized at 4,000 rials per kilo.

In 2013, the price of a standard staple of Iranians, bread and feta cheese skyrocketed. The price of *Barbari* bread, one of the four main kinds of Iranian bread, soared from about 1,000 to 5,000 rials per unit, while the price of Iran's feta cheese tripled. Beef prices jumped by five times and rice prices soared by about ten times. Towards the end of Ahmadinejad's presidency, the traditional food items in the consumption basket of the low and even middle classes had shrunk.

On the sensitive issue of poverty reduction and lowering income inequalities, Ahmadinejad's social assistance, in the form of cash payments, proved to be successful at first until economic realities caught up with it and inversed the results. 'The main reason why poverty did not rise was the huge cash transfer program instituted by the populist President Mahmoud Ahmadinejad.'[34] But high inflation ate into the real value of cash transfers, causing poverty and inequalities to increase. Despite 'a sharp fall in poverty and inequality during 2009–2012', both gradually increased after 2012.[35]

Finally, during Ahmadinejad's presidency, corruption worsened. Based on the Corruption Perception Index, with a score of 100 representing no corruption, Iran's score was 29 in 2005, ranking 92 among 152 countries. It dipped to 25 in 2013, and Iran ranked 145 among 175 countries.

The IRGC: Beneficiary of Ahmadinejad's Presidency

After the Iran–Iraq War, demobilizing, reorientating, and reintegrating those who had served in the IRGC and the *Basij* forces became a pressing problem. Having shown their loyalty to the system by risking their lives, the war veterans had to be rewarded and incorporated into society. Those veterans with technical, engineering, economic, financial, and managerial skills soon constituted a trusted and entitled new bourgeois-military class. This loyal, young and upcoming bourgeoisie, soon pushed out the Islamic Republic's traditional commercial bourgeoisie represented by the old Islamic Coalition of Mourning Groups and the new Islamic Coalition Party.

As the post-war star of the old commercial bourgeoisie descended, that of the new one ascended and Ahmadinejad's presidency embodied this transition in an exemplar fashion. Both the new and old bourgeoisie had obtained their privileged financial positions as a reward for their political loyalty to the clerical and political power in place and not because of their entrepreneurship, know-how and merit. The ruling clerical-political leadership added the military-bourgeoisie to its crony capitalist partners.

The Supreme Leader was the commander-in-chief of Iran's Armed Forces. His most powerful and reliable power base was the approximately 120,000-strong Islamic Revolutionary Guards Corps (IRGC) and its auxiliary *Basij* Resistance Forces of about 1 million. Khamenei nominated commanders, fostered personal relations with the top brass of the IRGC and had clerical representatives in IRGC's army, navy and air force. The IRGC was a most potent military organization on which Khamenei relied to secure his rule and through which he exerted political, cultural and ideological pressure on non-compliant social and political actors whenever needed.

Khamenei and the IRGC

The relationship is increasingly symbiotic, politically expedient for the Leader and economically expedient for the guards. He is their commander-in-chief and appoints their senior commanders, who, in turn, are publicly deferential to him and increasingly reap benefits by playing a more active role in political decision making and economic activity. (K. Sadjadpour)[36]

At its inception, the IRGC was mandated to stay out of politics, protect the revolution, and defend the country against foreign threats. But, even during Khomeyni's leadership, the Imam got the IRGC involved in domestic politics. Under Khamenei, occasions on which his authority was challenged increased and with it grew his reliance on the IRGC's military might. The IRGC entered politics regularly at home to support the faction favoured by the Leader, and consolidate his power, in the face of domestic unrest. Overseas, the IRGC's Qods Force pursued Khamenei's dream of expanding and strengthening the anti-American resistance front. Under the command of Qasem Soleymani, the Qods Force became a veritable regional power broker with interests in Iraq, and in Lebanon, Syria and Yemen.

The economic and financial influence of the IRGC expanded significantly during Ahmadinejad's presidency, as did its political clout. Between 2009–13 Ahmadinejad's cabinet included 19 former IRGC members. The 290-seat Ninth Majles had about 40 former members of the IRGC in it. The IRGC's presence in the executive and the legislative, was clearly a trend approved by Khamenei. In 2007, Ahmadinejad 'convinced' the Central Bank of Iran to allow the *Basij* to open its own bank, *Mehr*, and in 2009, the IRGC founded its bank, *Ansar*. Never before in the history of the Islamic Republic, were the IRGC and its affiliates given such financial latitude.

The IRGC engineering affiliate, *Khatam al-anbia*, had obtained handsome contracts during Rafsanjani's period, but its unbridled stranglehold over the Iranian economy received a determining boost during Ahmadinejad's presidency. The Ahmadinejad era contracts given to *Khatam al-anbia* in construction, highways, dams, infrastructure, oil and gas projects were mostly no-bid handouts.

The $1.3 billion contract to build a 900-km natural gas pipeline from Asaluyeh to Iranshahr in 2006, and the contract to complete phases 15 and 16 of the Pars Jonubi oil fields and refinery construction, were handouts to *Khatam al-anbia*. The IRGC was not accountable to anyone but Khamenei. No one questioned why the Pars Jonubi project, which was to be completed in about four years and cost $3 billion, was finished after nine years (2006–15) at twice the cost ($6 billion).

The lucrative no-bid contracts allotted to *khatam al-anbia* left those private companies previously benefitting from government contracts hanging out to dry. As the Oil Ministry chose *Khatam al-anbia* over the Iran Industrial Sea Company (SADRA), the now blacklisted old giant contractor in the oil and gas field, nosedived after 2005 and was purchased by *Khatam al-anbia* in 2009. In 2003, SADRA shares were worth 2,000 tomans each, and in 2009, *Khatam al-anbia* bought its shares for 100 tomans.

In 2011, the commander of the IRGC ordered *Khatam al-anbia* not to get involved in small projects of less than $80 million. IRGC's economic activities were free of oversight, lacked transparency and were exempt from taxation. Khamenei's support for the IRGC provided it with leverage to appropriate what it wanted and shielded it from legal accountability and supervision. The IRGC, as Khamenei's personal domain, had a solid legal shield and became an unsupervised economic juggernaut.

The IRGC's Economic Reach

From laser eye surgery and construction to automobile manufacturing and real estate, the IRGC has extended its influence into virtually every sector of the Iranian market. (F. Wehrey, J. D. Green, B. Nichiporuk et al.)[37]

The greater involvement of the IRGC in the Iranian economy diluted its ideological, selfless, and ethical values. The IRGC became a vehicle for social mobility, with its more fortunate members abandoning their origins and humble lifestyles. Religious standards and zeal waned among its members, while worldly pursuits and quick money-making became virtues, especially among its upper echelons. The IRGC's special and preferential economic and political privileges spawned cronyism and corruption. When soldiers turned into merchants, traders, and sellers, they relied on brute force to maximize gains. The IRGC became a major armed economic stakeholder in the system. Since the dawn of the twentieth century, the Iranian military had never been in such a privileged and lucrative position.

> ## The Role of IRGC in the Iranian Economy
>
> In the profit-making sector, the role of Sepah [IRGC] has been primarily that of a contractor. In other words, it has some 5,000 private sub-contractors, among which it distributes its contracts. The primary role of the Sepah is not in controlling the Iranian economy, but one of profit-making for individual members of the Sepah . . . In this sense, the Sepah is a broker. (M. Vahabi)[38]

The sanctions strengthened the hands of the IRGC. In March 2012, the European Union decided to intensify financial sanctions by disconnecting Iran from the global SWIFT system and preventing it from cross-border financial transactions. Iran could no longer legally pay for its imports or receive money for its exports. Iran's oil exports of 2.5 million barrels per day in 2011 dropped to 1 million by 2014. As it became impossible to conduct international transactions, the IRGC stepped in. It employed its military and under-the-radar networks to circumvent the sanctions. The IRGC's experience and savviness in the 'shadow economy' helped it become the singular power to put holes in the sanction shield around Iran.

In August 2012, Iran's revenue from the export of oil and gas to Turkey was converted to gold and returned to Iran straight from Turkey or via Dubai. Turkey's 'gold export to Iran rose to $6.5 billion in 2012, more than 10 times the level of 2011, while its exports to the United Arab Emirates – much of it for onward shipment to Iran or conversion to hard currency – rose to $4.6 billion from $280 million'.[39]

The IRGC played a determining role in helping sustain Khamenei's 'resistance economy'. The IRGC took the lead in all resistance schemes elaborated by the Supreme Leader against the Western enemy and stood at the forefront of combatting the economic, cultural and political onslaught while continuing to pay lip service to an ever more abstract notion of Islam. Obsessed with the US threat of regime change, Khamenei's Islamic Republic fortress had now one multi-purpose defender, the IRGC.

While Ahmadinejad's dissonance with Khamenei increased, the president continued to hammer at his direct relations with the Hidden Imam, rendering the role of the clerical intermediary superfluous. Consequently, the Leader and the clergy panicked about his political intentions even more. The IRGC leadership rebuked the president and ruptured ties with him. In May 2011, Gen. Aziz Jafari, the commander of the IRGC, accused Ahmadinejad of deviation, forgetting the values of the revolution and disrupting the essence of Islam. On 4 July 2011, Ahmadinejad retaliated by criticizing 'our own smuggling [IRGC] brothers', the illegal ports and jetties they operated, and their involvement in the approximately $1.4 billion contraband cigarette market in the country. Directly attacking the IRGC, Ahmadinejad jabbed that corruption rears its head wherever there are extra-legal rights.

Society Pushes Back against Ahmadinejad

After Ahmadinejad's rise to power, international human rights organizations warned that his Ministry of Intelligence had 'substantially increased its surveillance of dissidents, civil society activists, and journalists'. Ahmadinejad's presidency differed from its predecessors in 'the great expansion in scope and number of individuals and activities persecuted by the government'.[40]

Women activists, independent journalists, students, teachers, bus drivers, labour union activists, civil society activists, bloggers, scholars and dissident clerics were arrested, interrogated and imprisoned throughout Ahmadinejad's tenure. Behind the tough and popular veneer of his government lurked a politically insecure system that suspected the mildest of dissent as a threat to its national security. To make matters worse, the peaceful political transformations of power in Georgia, Ukraine and Kyrgyzstan under the rubric of the Rose Revolution (2003), Orange Revolution (2004) and Tulip Revolution (2005), respectively, began to haunt to Khamenei. Crowds, protests, assemblies and organizations were now suspected of acting against state security and preparing a soft, colour revolution.

Workers' Movement

On 22 December 2005, the Bus Workers' Syndicate announced a strike protesting work conditions. The regime feared economic demands becoming political and arrested Mansur Osanlu, their leader. In January 2006, the workers retaliated by scheduling another strike, demanding Osanlu's release. The government responded by detaining hundreds of bus drivers and labor organizers in late January 2006. Osanlu was released in August 2006 but was subsequently in and out of prison, repeatedly kidnapped and beaten. The regime became highly sensitive to Osanlu's connections with the International Transport Workers Federation and the

International Trade Union Confederation. He was arrested again in 2007 and sentenced to five years in prison. When he was temporarily released, Osanlu fled the country in February 2013.

Teachers' Movement

On 14 March 2007, when teachers gathered peacefully in front of the Majles to protest their wages and benefits, the police attacked them, arresting tens. Yet, the teachers insisted on their rights, desisted from attending their classes, and called for another demonstration in May 2007. By mid-April, some sixty per cent of schools in Tehran were experiencing work stoppages. Between March and May 2007, more than 300 teachers were arrested. Most of them were released in June on exorbitant bails, but pressure was maintained on their leaders by handing out suspended prison terms. The government tried different kinds of intimidation tactics, ranging from suspensions and reprimands, to wage reductions, and forced early retirements. The cycle of protests, arrests, and imprisonment continued. The initiative spread from Tehran to regional Teachers' Guild Centers, and the movement itself became more active and militant.

The protesting teachers arrested were accused of 'acting against national security', 'instigating strike action', 'assembling', and 'refusing to comply with police'. Depending on the intensity of the protest, the regime adjusted its repression. Farzad Kamangar, a teacher and a member of the Teachers' Guild Center of Kurdistan, had been arrested in July 2006, tortured, and kept in solitary confinement. He was executed by hanging on 29 April 2010, along with four others on trumped-up charges. Kamangar became a symbol for the teachers' movement.

Women's Movement

During a peaceful rally by women's rights activists on 12 June 2006, 42 women and 28 men, among them a deputy of the 6th Majles, were arrested on charges of participation in an illegal assembly and acting against national security. Iranian women's rights activists launched a campaign called the 'One Million Signatures for the Repeal of Discriminatory Laws' in August 2006. The campaign pushed for equal rights in marriage settlements, divorce, child custody, inheritance and criminal law. Women who tried to collect signatures were arbitrarily arrested, and anyone associated with the campaign was harassed, arrested and/or imprisoned. The campaign lasted five years but eventually died out, when its leaders, the journalists, Nushin Ahmadi-Khorasani and Parvin Ardalan were sentenced to three years in prison.

In late January 2008, Ahmadinejad's minister of culture closed the monthly publication *Zanan* (Women) for endangering the spiritual, mental and psychological health of its readership. The articles in *Zanan*, had originally addressed women's issues from a progressive and intellectual Islamic perspective, questioning discriminatory practices through fresh interpretations of Islamic jurisprudence. *Zanan* gradually addressed more current affair problems, such as daily discriminatory and criminal activities against women. Iran's only Islamic feminist publication, which had weathered the country's prevailing patriarchal and macho political and cultural environment for sixteen years was at last silenced.

On 14 November 2012, the conservative dominated Majles approved a bill proposed by Ahamdinejad's cabinet, restricting travel for single women under the age of 40 by requiring them to obtain the written permission of either a husband or a male guardian. The bill met with immediate resistance from women's organizations, lawyers and former Majles deputies. Some 2,500 artists, actors, filmmakers and directors wrote an open letter, protesting the discriminatory law. Three months later, faced with the opposition of the women's faction of the Majles and the Majles Women and Family Committee, the law was rescinded.

Scare Tactics against Intellectuals

The system's obsession with imminent soft revolutions caused it to target Iranian journalists, intellectuals, and scholars who travelled abroad to participate in conferences and seminars as well as Iranian scholars and professionals living abroad with double nationalities, who traveled to Iran. This worldly group of idea-influencers, 'peddling Western ideas', was now regarded by the system as enemy collaborators and spies.

On 27 April 2006, Ramin Jahanbeglu, a prominent young academic, was detained at the airport on his way to a conference in Hungary. Jahanbeglu had published articles and interviews in the Iranian and foreign press but had no prior political activities or affiliations. He was, however, an intellectual who had criticized Ahmadinejad's revisionist stand on the Holocaust.

On 1 July 2006, Mohseni-Ejehie, the minister of intelligence, announced that 'the arrest was in relation with US attempts to foster a velvet and soft revolution in Iran … and he was on a mission to provide information'.[41] On 18 July 2006, Ramin Jahanbeglu, Haleh Esfandiyari and Yahya Kiyan-Tajbaksh, appeared on a televised programme, *Be name demokrasi* (In the name of democracy), airing their coerced 'confessions'. Haleh Esfandiyari was the director of the Middle East programme at the Woodrow Wilson Center, and Yahya Kian-Tajbakhsh was a consultant for George Soros's Open Society Institute. Esfandiyari had been arrested on 8 May 2007 and Tajbakhsh on 11 May 2007.[42]

The political show *In the Name of Democracy* hoped to convince Iranians that overseas academic conferences were a recruiting ground for spies and a hub for passing sensitive information to the enemy. Furthermore, the show intended to prove that non-government organizations (NGOs), both in Iran and abroad, were potential dens of espionage. The Ministry of Intelligence sent the clear message that Iranians involved in overseas academic or civil society conferences or receiving grants from foreign universities or foundations were now suspect of being spies and subject to persecution.

During Ahmadinejad's presidency, free-thinking journalists and academics continued to be the target of the wrath of the system/regime. In September and October 2006, four reformist publications, including *Sharq* (East) were shut down and throughout 2006 dozens of journalists were summoned and interrogated by the Ministry of Intelligence. Academics suspected of liberal and secular tendencies were either forced into early retirement or else were fired. 'Around this time, an estimated 150,000 to 180,000 educated Iranians were leaving Iran each year.'[43] Distinguished public figures such as Akbar Ganji (2006), Mohsen Kadivar and Hoseyn Bashiriyeh (2007), Hasan Yusefi-Eshkevari and Shirin Ebadi (2009), left the country to escape persecution and were forced to live abroad.

Elections to the 8th Majles: The Ruling Elite Squabble as the People Abstain

In preparation for elections to the 8th Majles, the Guardian Council rejected the credentials of 82 reformist applicants, including ten members of the Seventh Majles and three deputies of the Sixth Majles. Mohammad-Reza Aref, one of the few prominent reformists allowed to stand for election, withdrew his candidacy in protest. To assure the victory of the conservatives, Gen. Mohammad-Ali Jafari, the commander of the IRGC, emphasized the absolute and indispensable necessity and 'divine duty' of the country's revolutionary forces to support the Principlists. As if openly telling his troops to interfere in the elections, Jafari said that the *Basij* should know how to proceed with the upcoming election.

On 14 March 2008, Iranians went to the voting booths to elect their Guardian Council-sifted parliamentary representatives. The turnout was far from enthusiastic. Only 51 per cent of the eligible voters in the country and 30 per cent of Tehranis voted. Predictably, the Principlists won 74.8 per cent of all seats in Parliament and Ali Larijani became the new president of the Majles.

Yet, in spite of this apparent homogeneity, there were deep cleavages among the Principlists. From 27 May 2008, tension simmered within the ruling class. Ahmadinejad turned against Mostafa Purmohammadi, his minister of interior, and fired him on 17 May 2008. The president had been outraged that Purmohammadi had made an independent report to Khamenei on election malpractice and fraud during the first round of elections without consulting him. Ahmadinejad replaced Purmohmmadi, who was Khamenei's man, with Ali Kordan.

From August 2008, an ethical and political crisis brewed around Ahmadinejad's new minister of interior. Ali Kordan claimed to have a BA and an MA from the Free Islamic University and an honorary DPhil from Oxford University. From the day after his appointment, it became evident that he had faked all his higher education certificates and had only an Associate of Arts degree. Ahmadinejad supported his dishonest appointee, who was known for his hardline position against dissident social and political activities. For the new minister of interior, cyberspace, internauts, deviant intellectuals, secularists, democracy activists, environmentalists, feminists, modernists, syndicalists, human rights and student activists, all fell into the same dangerous bag, and posed a threat to the system.

The Majles pressured Kordan to resign and avoid the humiliation of a vote of no confidence. Ahmadinejad, however, prompted him to stay and resist the pressure. Ahmadinejad defended him by saying, 'to serve the people, there is no need for such useless pieces of paper'.[44] On 4 November 2008, Kordan went to the Majles, and after three months in office, the deputies gave him a vote of no-confidence and impeached him for faking his degrees. The 'Kordan Affair' once again shook the people's confidence in Ahmadinejad's claim to upholding honesty.

On the next day, Khamenei strongly reprimanded those who had spoken against the government, shown enmity towards it and undermined the system. In full support of Ahmadinejad's government, and seemingly upset at Kordan's treatment by the Majles, Khamenei warned that people 'should mind what they say and what they do'.[45] Khamenei's support gave heart to Ahmadinejad to re-introduce another questionable candidate as minister of interior.

Less than two weeks after Khamenei chided the Majles for upsetting Ahmadinejad, the president made a bold move. On 18 November 2008, he introduced as Kordan's replacement, Sadeq Mahsuli, his old and wealthy friend, who in 2005 had failed to obtain the consent of the Majles. With presidential elections less than seven months away, Ahmadinejad needed a trusted figure to run his elections. Mahsuli, the billionaire general, became Ahmadinejad's minister of interior.

During his eight years of presidency, Iranians never got used to Ahmadinejad's brash and erratic method of governance. Contrary to the Rafsanjani and Khatami administrations, Ahmadinejad's ministers never had much autonomy and independence. When Ahmadinejad was about to form his first government, Mohammad-Reza Bahonar, a heavyweight pragmatist conservative deputy and one of his early supporters, suggested that he should choose his ministers from established and experienced conservative figures. Ahmadinejad is said to have responded, 'I need soldiers, not generals.'[46]

During his tenure, Ahmadinejad fired 14 ministers, including his first secretary, almost a prime minister position, without explanation or justification. Discharged ministers were usually informed by a third party not to attend cabinet meetings. In one of the most controversial cases, the president fired his minister of foreign affairs of five years, Manuchehr Mottaki, a career diplomat, while he was on an official mission to Senegal (13 December 2010). Ahmadinejad did treat his ministers as foot soldiers.

Ahmadinejad's unpredictable positions and U-turns were sometimes contradictory to what he seemed to stand for. On 24 May 2006, to everyone's surprise, Ahmadinejad issued a directive to the head of Iran's Sports Organization *Sazemane tarbiyat badani* (Physical Training Organization), ordering him to provide Iranian women and families with a specific seating area in football stadiums. The Islamic Republic had, however, barred women from attending sports arenas.

Ahmadinejad's nonconformist directive did meet with opposition from his mentor Mesbah-Yazdi and a number of high positioned clerics. Mesbah-Yazdi argued that in Islam men were prohibited from looking at women's bodies, be they young, old, single or married. Neglecting this principle, he posited, would lead to decadence and moral corruption. Faced with the clergy's staunch opposition, women's attendance at football games, was once again banned.

The June 2009 Presidential Elections: The People Confront the Leader

Nine months before Iran's tenth presidential election of June 2009, Khamenei launched a not so veiled campaign in favour of Ahmadinejad. On 24 August 2008, he heaped unprecedented praise on Ahmadinejad as president, and on his government for their enduring 'energy, vigour, stamina, joyfulness at work and persistence to serve the people'. He eulogized Ahmadinejad for his courageous decisions, revival of national honour and independence, and his stand against corruption and world arrogance, the code word for US imperialism. The Leader rejoiced that the Ahmadinejad government had 'blocked the very dangerous penetration of Westernized and secular ideas into Iran's managerial body politics'. Khamenei predicted that Ahmadinejad's government would become even more popular among the people.[47]

On 10 March 2009, to everyone's surprise, Mir-Hoseyn Musavi announced his candidacy for the presidency. After Khamenei's leadership and Rafsanjani's presidency in 1989, Musavi, who had never seen eye to eye with Khamenei, had withdrawn from political life. Six days after he announced his candidacy, Khatami officially pulled out of the race in favour of Musavi. Khatami promised to remain involved in the election campaign and work for unity in the reformist camp. The popular former president said, 'I believe that at present, Musavi has the competence and ability to foster change . . . and has the potential for being elected.'[48]

The reformists failed to unite and entered the election with two candidates, Musavi and Karrubi (Figure 11.3), while Principlists had a leading candidate,

Figure 11.3 Mehdi Karrubi. *Source: Photo by Jaber Yazdankah Kenary via Alamy.*

Ahmadinejad, with Mohsen Rezai tagging along. To reformists, who had lost faith in the Islamic Republic's democratic process and withdrawn from political participation, the Guardian Council's approval of Musavi's credential was an encouraging sign. Musavi's rocky relation with Khamenei in the past was not a secret. His return to politics was reassuring and a sign that these dire times required extraordinary measures.

Musavi's track was transparent. He had belonged to the Left and radical faction of Iranian politics, deeply committed to and strongly supported by Khomeyni. His discourse on social justice, anti-corruption and equality had long preceded Ahmadinejad's. Like his Left colleagues, he too had embraced political, religious, economic, cultural and social reformism. He no longer held his inflexible anti-Western stance in foreign policy and was a known and trusted politician admired for his honesty, integrity and resolve. To those who remembered him during the Iran-Iraq war, his administration was a reminder of wartime economic hardships but also low inflation and availability of basic needs for all.

Musavi was coming back to politics after twenty years and was almost unknown to the young voters in the country, whereas Khatami was still popular, especially after four years of Ahmadinejad's administration. Musavi's close ties with Khomeyni did not excite the youth, but Khatami's genuine support and his active campaigning throughout the country in favour of Musavi convinced the young generation that the soft-spoken, gentle, bespectacled and grey-haired candidate, a painter and a Shariati fan, was worth fighting for. Musavi's campaign colour was green, he wore a green scarf which Khatami had symbolically put around his neck, and his movement came to be known as the Green Movement.

The Televised Debates, the Youth and Musavi's Green Wave

Musavi was not a charismatic leader but a well-poised, seasoned, combative and sturdy politician. In the famous 3 June 2009 presidential debates, a novelty in Iranian politics, millions of Iranians saw two politicians with distinctly different ethics, behaviors and outlooks on the country. Musavi spoke of two methods of managing Iran. One relied on 'adventurism, instability, flashy conduct, pretentious heroism, daydreaming, superstition, deception, dissimulation, self-centeredness, lawlessness, superficiality, routineness, and extremism'. The intimations were clear, and he did not need to say whom this system belonged to but added that the present management was dangerous for the country.

The second system of managing the country, Musavi proposed, would be 'based on realism, anti-superstitiousness, transparency, honesty and reliant on collective wisdom and moderation' (Figure 11.4). He labelled Ahmadinejad's foreign policy statements such as 'the fall of such and such civilization or taking over world management as reverie'. He criticized Ahmadinejad's Holocaust statements and argued that it had ended up to Israel's benefit. Musavi criticized Ahmadinejad's policies towards universities, the youth, teachers, writers, and artists. He concluded that 'the country has been dishonored' during his presidency.[49]

Figure 11.4 Supporters of Mir-Hoseyn Musavi. *Source: Photo by UPI Photo/Mohammad Kheirkhah via Alamy.*

During the televised presidential debates, Ahmadinejad's attempt at presenting himself as the anti-establishment and anti-elite candidate, fighting against the conspiratorial trio of Musavi, Khatami and Rafsanjani, was a futile long-shot attempt. After four years in office, and Khamenei's unwavering support for him, Ahmadinejad was the veritable candidate of the establishment and the ruling elite.

In an unbecoming fashion, Ahmadinejad engaged in mudslinging to divert attention from his four years in office. In an aggressive style, he engaged in sensationalism, suggesting that Rafsanjani was paying for Musavi's campaign, that Rafsanjani and Nateq-Nuri and their sons had become wealthy through ill-gotten gains and that he was the victim of the political conspiracy of the corrupt. In a last-ditch attempt to discredit Musavi, he accused Zahra Rahnavard, Musavi's wife, of faking her diplomas and becoming president of a university through nepotism.

Musavi responded levelheadedly that Ahmadinejad was accusing people who were absent to defend themselves. Musavi walked away from the debate as a rational, seasoned and solid leader, and Ahmadinejad as a bombastic, theatrical and jittery politician. After the TV duel, the wave of support for Musavi picked up at an increasing rate.

Khatami on the Debate

Artists oppose lies, intimidating people and turning values into anti-values...What I witnessed during the debate between Ahmadinejad and Musavi was the confrontation between artlessness and artfulness. (M. Khatami)[50]

The engine behind Musavi's nationwide and successful campaign was the National Headquarters of Khatami's Young Supporters (Setad 88). This political formation had come to existence in the Fall of 2008, at the initiative of 88 young reformist civil-rights activists and journalists. To convince Khatami to enter the presidential race, they had organized headquarters in 30 provinces. Once Musavi entered the race, there were 233 centres in various counties and cities, and 22 in Tehran alone. With Musavi as their new candidate, they organized rallies throughout the country, inviting high profile reformist speakers, and carrying out incessant grassroot canvassing in cities and the rural areas. Their work galvanized the people and restored hope in the democratic process.[51]

As the campaign wounded up, thousands of joyful, ardent, and peaceful young supporters occupied the streets and squares of Tehran and the big cities advocating for their respective candidates. Iran was experiencing a democratic revival. Artists, intellectuals, journalists, film stars, academics, Islamic modernists, athletes, children and families of martyrs, and clerics signed petitions in Musavi's support, and his rallies attracted up to 100,000 supporters.

On the last days of campaigning, the Musavi camp insisted on 'people's sovereignty, freedom of speech, press, thought and expression'. Musavi reminded the people that they had all gathered to rid Iran of 'lies', 'close-mindedness', and those who 'opposed the law and pinched public funds'. Ahmadinejad's camp told the people that 'the US wants anyone but Ahmadinejad to be President'. It hammered that the election of anyone, but Ahmadinejad would mean that 'Iranians are rejecting their faith and Islam.'[52]

As the election approached, the campaign headquarters of Musavi and Karrubi warned against ongoing wrongdoings. They cautioned that a secret meeting had taken place between the minister of interior, Mahsuli and all governors general. The reformist candidates claimed that the Ministry of Interior had published 2.6 million more ballots than it had announced.[53]

Two days before the election, Rafsanjani wrote an open letter to Khamenei, lamenting the accusations made by Ahamdinejad in his televised debate. Rafsanjani told the Leader that he did not believe that the continuation of the present situation, namely Ahmadinejad's presidency, was beneficial for the country. One day before the election, surveys by Ahmadinejad's Ministries of Intelligence and Interior suggested that neither candidate, Ahmadinejad nor Musavi, had a fifty plus one majority in the first round, and elections would go to a run-off.[54]

Unexpected Election Results

In 2009, Iran had 30.2 million mobile phone users. Mobile phones and SMS messages became the opposition's primary means of communication. Before the election, Iranians were probably exchanging millions of SMS messages per day. During the election campaign, Twitter, Facebook and SMS played a pivotal role in providing information. From 11.00 pm on Thursday June 11th, the eve of the election day, SMS messaging was shut down and remained unstable for the next 40 days. Consequently, news of the attacks on Musavi's HQ at Qeytariyeh, and the eviction of his representatives from the election centres could not be relayed. At 5.00 pm on Friday, the Law Enforcement Forces put on a show of force throughout Tehran to 'provide security' during the election.

On Friday evening, after the polls had closed, officials from the Ministry of Interior informed Musavi that he had won the elections. Simultaneously, Ali Larijani, president of the Parliament, Nateq-Nuri, the director of the Leadership's Inspection Office, and Mostafa Purmohammadi, the director of the National Inspectorate Organization, called on Musavi to congratulate him on his victory. At around 11 pm, Musavi announced that he had won the elections. But half an hour later, IRNA (Islamic Republic News Agency) pronounced Ahmadinejad the winner.

On Saturday morning, 13 June, at 8.00 am, the press reported that Ahmadinejad had received over 19.7 million votes (64.7 per cent) as compared to Musavi's 9.8 million votes (32.2 per cent), followed by Rezai with 2.7 per cent and Karrubi with 0.88 per cent of the votes. The results were a crushing defeat for Musavi and a humiliating one for Karrubi. Contrary to government polls right before voting, the fate of the election was sealed in the first round. On the same day (Saturday, 13 June), the Leader called the elections an 'unprecedented and captivating epic' and asked Ahmadinejad's rivals to 'unanimously support and help him'. Rushing to formalize the presidency of Ahmadinejad, Khamenei issued his announcement even before the Guardian Council had confirmed the election results. With the danger of a new reformist president removed, Khamenei wished to get back to business as usual.

Where is My Vote: The Green Movement is Born

The June 12 election and its outcome plunged the country into an unprecedented political crisis that lasted for almost seven months. Iran was thrown into a near revolution as the Green Movement challenged the authority of the Leader and the coalition supporting him. The shock, deception and frustration which overwhelmed Musavi's partisans on Saturday morning quickly turned into anger, insubordination, and resistance against those that had stolen their vote (Figure 11.5). Saturday morning

Figure 11.5 Where is my vote? *Source: Photo by WENN Rights Ltd via Alamy.*

began with protests, clashes and arrests. Images and footings of anti-riot troops beating up protesters circulated on Facebook and YouTube. The regime reacted by blocking them.

On the same Saturday, while Khamenei was confirming Ahmadinejad's presidential victory, Musavi issued his first statement at noon. He called the election outcome a 'charade' and contested the results. He warned that he would 'not surrender to this dangerous staging' and spoke about 'lies and despotism'. Musavi's thinly veiled recommendation to the Supreme Leader was to 'safeguard the people's vote before it was too late'. On Saturday afternoon, Khamenei sent an envoy to Musavi warning him to back off. Instead, Musavi insisted on the annulment of the election. Karrubi joined him, refused to accept the election results, and called them 'astonishing and comical'.

From Saturday night, independent and reformist newspapers were prohibited from printing Musavi's announcements, headquarters of reformist organizations and parties were attacked, their offices ransacked and sealed, and their newspapers closed. The system/regime moved with great urgency to nip the opposition in the bud. It rounded up journalists, prominent reformist politicians and theoreticians, campaign activists and aides to Musavi and Karrubi *en masse*. By nightfall, the government also reported having arrested 100 protesters. The Musavi camp called the wave of repression a 'soft coup against the people's sovereignty'.

Election Results: Foul or Fair

All the available evidence (forensic analysis of the voting figures, along with socio-historical analysis) suggests that fraud was perpetrated by the governing elite on order to give Ahmadinejad a landslide election victory surpassing that of Khatami in 1997. (A. Ansari)[55]

On Sunday, 14 June 2009, Tehran witnessed four defining and very different moments. First, Mohsen Rezai, the second conservative candidate, filed a complaint about the election process to the Guardian Council. Rezai's reaction, given his loyalty and devotion to Khamenei, was a clear indictment of the level of fraud at play. Without openly joining in the call by Musavi and Karrubi for new elections, he came as close to it as he could.

Second, Musavi met the Supreme Leader. Khamenei encouraged him to accept the election results and pursue his grievances through the Guardian Council. He referred to the clashes as the work of Iran's enemies and invited all parties to peace and calm. Undeterred, Musavi announced that he would lead a peaceful protest march on Monday, 15 June at 4.00 pm from Enqelab Square to Azadi Square. The authorities announced Musavi's march illegal and vowed to stop it.

Third, in the afternoon, Ahmadinejad addressed some 50,000 supporters at Vali Asr Square. He denied tampering with the election results and announced that the elections were perfectly free, proper and unblemished. The re-elected president called those protesting the vote count a few 'impotent dregs and dead plants incapable of glowing before the pure river of the Iranian people'.

Fourth, late on Sunday night and in the early morning hours of Monday, riot police and plainclothesmen attacked university dorms in Tehran and Esfahan, where students had been protesting the election results. The assault and battery lasted around four hours leaving behind injured students, ransacked rooms and destroyed property. The extent of brutality was such that Larijani, the Majles president, another loyal subject of Khamenei, asked for an investigation into the 'rash and incorrect' treatment of the students (Figure 11.6).

On Monday, 15 June, according to different sources, 1–3 million people participated in a spectacular peaceful and mostly silent show of force. Tehran had not witnessed anything like this since the pre-revolution pro-Khomeyni rallies. The sea of green demanded that their vote be counted, and their rights respected. 'Where is my vote?' had become the pacifist slogan of Iran's Green Movement. From the roof of a car encircled and hidden by the people, Musavi spoke of his resolve to oppose the 'widespread electoral fraud' and passively 'resist' the incursions against 'the people's rights'. He proposed 'annulling the irregular election' and promised to 'pay whatever price for realizing the people's ideals'. The grand demonstration attended by Khatami and Karrubi unfolded peacefully throughout the day.

Figure 11.6 Iranians run from the riot police, 2009. *Source: Photo by UPI Photo via Alamy.*

> **The Green Movement**
>
> Begun and continued as a civil rights movement...this uprising has seen phases of civil disobedience and shades of civil unrest-but its skeletal vertebrae is a nonviolent drive toward democratic institutions that the current republic will either accommodate and survive, or else resist and be washed aside. (H. Dabashi)[56]

Towards the end of the march protesters attacked a *Basij* base, hurling Molotov cocktail at it. The *Basij* forces opened fire from the rooftop of their headquarter. In Esfahan, Shiraz, Mashhad, Rasht, Ahvaz, Babol and Kerman, riot police attacked protesters chanting, 'Death to the dictator!', leaving many injured. Eight people were killed during the Monday clashes. Widespread and intense protests and repression continued, while a total blackout was imposed on reporting the protests.

On Friday, 19 June, Khamenei spoke at the Tehran Friday Prayers. Ever since he had become the Supreme Leader, at every election, Khamenei had tried to present himself as a neutral and fair umpire, not taking sides. Now, he was faced with an open challenge to his authority by the powerful trio of Musavi, Khatami and Karrubi, with the implicit support of Rafsanjani. Khamenei, therefore, threw off all appearances and spoke of the enemy's scheme of undermining trust in the system/regime by spreading rumours about rigged elections. Rejecting the annulling of elections, Khamenei stood his ground and asserted that he was not conceding to 'illegal innovations', jeopardizing the people's trust in future elections. He ordered the people not to come out on the streets and warned that they would be responsible for any 'bloodletting, violence and chaos'.[57]

On Saturday, 20 June, Iranians ignored the Supreme Leader's warnings and occupied the streets of Tehran. Neda Aqa-Soltani, a 26-year-old university student, was shot dead by what eyewitnesses described as two *Basiji*s on a motorcycle. She became the innocent, young and bloodied face of the Green Movement's quest for freedom and democracy.

Repression Works

After six months of resistance by the people and systematic repression by the system, the Green Movement folded. All state instruments of power and coercion were employed to clamp down protest and terrorize those defying the untrustworthy vote-snatching system. Law enforcement, riot police and *Basij* forces arrested, shot at, injured and killed protestors. Prison authorities overlooked the beating, torture, rape and murder of detainees. The Ministry of Intelligence, and the Intelligence Branch of the Islamic Revolutionary Guard Corps, interrogated and prepared the dossier of those arrested and passed them on to the judiciary.

The judiciary, under close supervision of the intelligence organizations, passed judgement on the ordinary people, politicians, former deputies, journalists, students, academics, lawyers, human rights and women activists, filmmakers and clerics arrested. The collective trial of around 100 reformist political prisoners accused of plotting against national security, disturbing public order, and attempting a velvet revolution began on 1 August 2009.

> ## Ayatollah Khamenei on Court Confessions
> I need to say that when in courts - aired on television - something is attributed by an accused to another person, this statement does not constitute a religious proof. Yes, whatever the accused says about himself in court is credible proof. Those who say that if someone confesses against himself in court is not valid, are talking nonsense and their talk is baseless. No, all confessions of an accused in a court, before cameras and millions of viewers is customarily and religiously valid, acceptable, and binding among rational people. (A. Khamenei)[58]

The system accused the Green Movement of sedition against a just ruler, a *fetneh*. Most of the culprits on trial accepted blame before the TV cameras and praised Khamenei as the honest and wise leader. The show-like hearings of the old political elite and fervent Khomeynists accused of treason closely resembled Stalinist trials. The recent events were said to have been a foreign plot hatched against the Islamic Republic, and the protestors had been its foot soldiers. In the end, approximately 4,000 to 7,000 individuals had been arrested, and 72 to 107 killed. Over 100 journalists had been arrested, some 20 publications banned, and the remaining press was to bear heavy censorship.

The shah crushed the pro-Khomeyni 5 June 1963 uprising, won the day but lost his political legitimacy among the politicized. Khamenei defeated the Green Movement in six months and lost the trust and confidence of those who believed the system/regime was salvageable. On both occasions, demonstrators shouted, 'Death to the dictator!' But most significantly, whereas the shah's actions rekindled interest and faith in political Islam, Khamenei, the protagonist of political Islam, did the exact opposite. He undermined the faith of ordinary non-politicized Iranian Muslims in Islam and turned them against political Islam.

On 27 and 28 December 2009, the Green Movement rattled the regime for the last time. The Ashura protests in Tehran, Shiraz, Esfahan, Mashhad, Tabriz, Ardebil, Qom,

Kerman, Babol and Arak became violent. The outpour of popular rage mixed with passive civil disobedience embroiled the country in a spiral of violence. Government forces, overwhelmed as never before, were ordered to open fire on the protesters. Intent on preventing the people from joining each other and forming human waves, troops and plainclothesmen scurried from one point in the city to another, assaulting what came their way.

Angry protesters attacked, beat up, and wounded security forces, plainclothesmen, and riot police, whenever they could corner them, setting their cars and motorcycles ablaze. Tehran became a war zone covered in tear gas as protesters battled government forces in spontaneous, hit and run operations. The protesters pouring out on the streets were in a combative mood, chanting, 'Death to Khamenei!' and 'Khamenei is a murderer, his rule as the Guardian Jurist is illegitimate!' The Green Movement offensive, almost on the cusp of victory, recoiled before the government's firepower which left behind 11 dead in Tehran. In Tehran alone, some 300 people were arrested.

On 30 December 2009, a state-organized demonstration in Tehran brought people from all over Iran by bus for a show of solidarity with Khamenei. The government claimed the gathering to be millions, while foreign sources reported hundreds of thousands. Ahmad Alam al-hoda, a rising clerical star, Mashhad's Friday Prayer Leader, a member of the Assembly of Experts and a sycophant, addressed the crowd. He announced that whoever does not recognize the Rule of the Guardian Jurist and refuses to acknowledge that 'Imam Khamenei' is heir to the Twelfth Imam is opposed to the Quran and a member of Satan's Party.

Alam al-hoda's function was to reestablish the lost authority of the Supreme Leader among believers. He labelled the throngs protesting on 27 December as 'warriors against God' and warned that if the leaders of the sedition (*fetneh*) do not recant, they, too, will be dealt with as 'warriors against God'. His message to the Green Movement and its leaders was clear, accept the leadership of Khamenei or prepare for death.

Musavi, Karrubi and Khatami did not oblige. On 14 February 2011, after eight months of protest, constant verbal assault on Khamenei's person and the rapid erosion of his legitimacy, the system incarcerated the two main contestants of the elections and the vocal leaders of the Green Movement. Musavi, his wife Zahra Rahnavard, and Karrubi with his wife, Fatemeh Haji-Sharifi, were put under strict house arrest and completely cut off from the outside world. The house arrest of Musavi, Rahnavard and Karrubi has lasted more than eleven years. Khatami was not placed under house arrest but faced restrictions in his movements and meetings. A ban was placed on his public appearance and speaking, and neither his picture nor any news relating to him was allowed to appear in the press or broadcast on television.

Ahmadinejad's Turn to Fall Out with Khamenei

While Khamenei was trying to impose his authority on the rebellious Green Movement contesting Ahmadinejad's election, his own protégé for whom he had compromised his reputation began defying him. In his obstinate manner of conducting politics, during his visit to Mashhad, on 17 July 2009, about a month after the outbreak of the protest movement, Ahmadinejad furtively announced the appointment of six new government deputies and senior advisers. All but one of his appointees were his old friends, and the most controversial among them was Esfandiyar Rahim-Mashai.

The Rahim-Mashai Affair and Its Consequences

Esfandiyar Rahim-Mashai had an especially tight spiritual bond with Ahmadinejad since their days in Kurdistan in 1984. At the time, Rahim-Mashai had been busy setting up the IRGC's intelligence bureau, while Ahmadinejad was governor of Khoy. Since then, Rahim-Mashai, exerted considerable influence on Ahmadinejad. Rahim-Mashai was a most complicated character, who was said to have been in contact with the Twelfth Imam, while holding Iran-centric, anti-clerical and liberal positions.

In 2008, as Ahmadinejad's deputy and director of Cultural heritage, Handicrafts and Tourism, Rahim-Mashai, had half cryptically and half plainly made statements contrary to established Islamic and Revolutionary values and positions. With Ahmadinejad's full support, he nonchalantly challenged certain fundaments of the system. He sniggered at the conservative clergy's fear of tourists and their cultural impact on Iranians. Referring to their apprehensions, he said 'They still think that if head scarves were to budge or loosen a little, the world would fall apart.' He then jabbed at an old religious belief concerning Satanic temptations of looking at women. 'Beauty,' he said, 'is not an instrument of Satan ... but darkness, poverty, evil and wrongdoing are.' Rahim-Mashai made fun of the clergy and some of their deep-felt beliefs and got away with it. He made light of women's headscarves slipping off their heads, a social reality, that the establishment denied.

On two occasions, he challenged Iran's official foreign policy position since the revolution. Rahim-Mashai opined that 'no people in the world is our enemy'. He also spoke about the 'friendship between the people of Iran and Israel' and announced that 'we consider the American people as one of the most superior people of the world'.[59] An Iranian statesman referring to Israel by name was a novelty, let alone claiming friendship with it. By doing so, Rahim-Mashai, the gadfly, was rejecting

Khamenei's axial theory that Iran was constantly faced with and besieged by enemies. Iran's political establishment jumped on Rahim-Mashai's statements, and he retreated.

On 19 September 2008, Khamenei reacted to Rahim-Mashai's statements while staunchly defending Ahmadinejad's record and criticizing his detractors. The Supreme Leader admonished Rahim-Mashai's comments and the uproar they had caused. Khamenei spoke of, 'misplaced and unnecessary comments by the political elite, creating futile problems which needed to end quickly'. He added that, 'the statement about our friendship with the people of Israel, like all other people of the world, is wrong'. Rahim-Mashai immediately wrote a letter to the Guardian Jurist declaring his allegiance to him. He assured Khamenei that he was 'convinced of world Zionism's destruction'.[60] Having caused an intentional fuss, Rahim-Mashai retracted, but Khamenei did not forget his propositions.

As if nothing had happened between Khamenei and Rahim-Mashai, on 17 July 2009, Ahmadinejad appointed Rahim-Mashai as his First Deputy. Ahmadinejad must have believed that confronting Khamenei with a *fait accompli* would force him to accept his appointment rather than create another crisis. What becomes most confusing is understanding why Ahmadinejad, who spoke of wiping the Zionist state off the map of the world, would want to insist on supporting his bosom friend, who had upset the Supreme Leader by speaking of friendship with Israel. Under the illusion of his resounding victory at the elections, Ahmadinejad was testing Khamenei's resolve, who was already under considerable pressure.

The next day, 18 July, Khamenei issued a decree commanding Ahmadinejad to revoke Rahim-Mashai's appointment. The implementation of the Supreme Leader's direct order took a long week, causing significant infighting among the Principlists. Faced with Ahmadinejad's insubordination, deputies in the Majles condemned any deviation from the Leader's path and position and invited the president to obey Khamenei. Irritated by Ahmadinejad's insolence, his ministers of intelligence, culture and Islamic guidance, labour and health objected to Ahmadinejad's defiance in a cabinet meeting. But Ahmadinejad told his ministers that 'Mashai was Ahmadinejad and Ahmadinejad was Mashai'.[61] Ahmadinejad refused to personally fire his first deputy, so the announcement that Rahim-Mashai had relinquished his position was made public by Mojtaba Samareh-Hashemi, the president's senior aide.

Two days later, in a defiant mood, Ahmadinejad appointed Rahim-Mashai, whom Khamenei had identified as a bad choice and 'against the President's interest and a source of division', as his aide and chief of staff. In cabinet meetings, Rahim-Mashai usually sat to the left of the president, while Ahmadinejad's new first deputy, Mohammad-Reza Rahimi, sat on his right. On 27 July 2009, a day after Mashai's appointment was made public, Mohseni-Ejehei, the powerful minister of intelligence, was fired and Saffar-Harandi, the minister of culture and Islamic guidance, resigned. Both ministers had fallen out with Ahmadinejad over Rahim-Mashai.

On 3 August 2009, as Iranians continued to refuse Ahmadinejad's election and he brooded over the 'Rahim-Mashai Affair', Khamenei officiated his endorsement ceremony. The heavy presence of law enforcement forces and sporadic clashes with protesters signaled the unusual circumstances of Ahmadinejad's second term in office.

Ahmadinejad: Sudden Defender of Pre-Islamic Persia

Ahmadinejad's second term in office proved complicated and agitated. The ruling elite, busy fighting the Green Movement, had little time for his idiosyncrasies. His popularity among his electoral base had subsided, as promises were not delivered. And a significant number of Iranians believed that he had robbed them of their vote. His old tactic of dismissing all criticism of his administration as a conspiracy against his person, had lost its appeal.

Ahmadinejad needed a new angle and a new pitch to regain his lustre. The mastermind behind his new action plan was said to be Rahim-Mashai. As of May 2010, Ahmadinejad engaged in a new discourse shifting from Islamo-centricism to Irano-centricism. He suddenly began eulogizing the pre-Islamic civilization, identity and culture. He delved into Ferdowsi's Book of Kings, celebrated pre-Islamic heroes such as Rostam and Arash as liberators, and claimed that it was Iran that had kept the unjust and plunderers in check. On the face of it, Ahmadinejad's emphasis on Iranian chauvinism and jingoism was compatible with Iran's nuclear and foreign policy positions.

But reviving the old sense of pride of Iranians in their pre-Islamic civilization, as the Pahlavi's had done, meant bypassing, and neglecting Islam, and Islamic Iran. The president was shifting his target audience and hoping to attract the attention of the middle class and the youth who contested his presidency. But he was also snubbing Khamenei and the clerical elite's insistence on identifying Iranians with Islam only.

In August 2010, Rahim-Mashai developed Ahmadinejad's new paradigm and argued that Iran had been historically synonymous with 'science, culture, civilization, humanity and God'. He asserted that 'Iran had been the founder of human civilization.' In an audacious and confused statement, Rahim-Mashai argued that Arabs were indebted to Iranians for their language. And that 'had it not been for Iran, Islam would have undoubtedly been buried under the illusion of Arab nationalism'.[62]

Two days after his first speech, Rahim-Mashai gave glad tidings that 'a new age has started for Iranians ... one in which Iran will bloom and grow again ... and the dark nights that had covered this country for hundreds of years was about to disappear'. He launched his idea of the Iranian School of Thought and rebuked those who 'chided him for talking about Iran's rather than Islam's school of thought'. He concluded that, 'from now on, we should present the Iranian School of Thought to the world'.[63]

Rahim-Mashai's comments reflected Ahmadinejad's earlier statement situating Iran's cultural and civilizational superiority, not in its Islamic but pre-Islamic history. This paradigm shift questioned the thirty-year religious management of the country, Khamenei's twenty-year rule in the name of Islam and even the Islamic Revolution. Ahmadinejad and Rahim-Mashai's Irano-centric discourse was certainly threatening to the clergy and was construed as an attempt to 'delete Islam' and replace it with Iran. The clergy reminded the public of Khomeyni's famous quote that 'our movement is Islamic, before being Iranian'.

One after the other, the coalition around Khamenei condemned the new Irano-centric discourse of the Iranian School of Thought as 'apostasy' and 'unacceptable to our Muslim community'. Haddad-Adel, the Supreme Leader's adviser, spoke on his behalf and said, 'the only school of thought acceptable to the Leader is that of Islam'. He attributed talk of separating Iran from Islam and emphasizing a school of thought different from Islam to the 'enemies'.[64] Ahmadinejad, in turn, kept on course and on 7 August 2010, reiterated that 'today Iran is a . . . path and a School of Thought'.

Frost Sets in between the Leader and His President

In August 2009, a conservative website, Alef, offered a nuanced message that both justified Khamenei's absolute and despotic rule over the people and all branches of government and undermined the president's legitimacy. 'Let's assume . . . that there had been fraud and irregularities and that Musavi should have been president, not Ahmadinejad. Now, once the highest legal authority in the land, the Guardian Jurist, confirms the election results, wouldn't protests be meaningless?'[65] This was the kind of message the Leader wished the people and the high officials of the country to understand and internalize.

On 30 August 2009, the Majles began debating Ahmadinejad's new cabinet. It rejected three of his proposed ministers and approved 18. For the first time in the history of the Islamic Republic, a woman, Marziyeh Vahid-Dastejerdi, entered the cabinet as minister of health. During his second term in office, Ahmadinejad's relationship with Parliament, the Guardian Council and the Leader became tenuous and contentious. Khamenei's words of praise for his president dried up. The Majles pushed the president to abide by the law, follow the Fourth Developmental Plan, and be more transparent about his current expenditures and unending provincial financial commitment. And Ahmadinejad pushed back, ignoring Majles directives.

Even the government press began questioning the president's unfulfilled promises and his ready-made prescriptions for the rest of the world while he failed to deliver them at home. Unappreciated in Tehran, Ahmadinejad spent a considerable part of his second term travelling. He spent 320 days travelling to about fifty-two provinces, often accompanied by his whole cabinet. Constantly repeating far-fetched ideas such as Iran's 'wise and firm participation in world management' and administering 'the new world order', Ahmadinejad spent at least 110 days travelling abroad and visiting thirty-eight different countries.

The shortcomings of Ahmadinejad's management and policies were becoming manifest, and he felt under pressure from quarters that had unreservedly supported him in the past. In May 2010, the Supreme Audit Court reported on the plethora of financial offences and wrongdoings in institutions and ministries under the president's control. In October 2012, the Majles Audit Office announced that $12.2 billion from the sale of crude oil had not been deposited in the Foreign Exchange Reserve Fund. Reports of outright corruption and embezzlement blemished Ahmadinejad's claim to honesty. An $87-million oil rig bought by the Ministry of Oil went missing and ended up in Mexico. Three high-tonnage oil tankers with cargos worth about $100 million went missing. The government commissioned an intermediary to purchase airplane parts worth $400 million, but the order never arrived.

The Leader continued to cohabit with his erratic president but without the previous sense of complicity, harmony, and even affection. Post-election events had affected and separated the two. Ahmadinejad's haughtiness and stubbornness over the Rahim-Mashai affair had embittered the Leader who had staked his legitimacy over Ahmadinejad's election. Khamenei's response to Ahmadinejad's insubordination was to limit his powers. But Ahmadinejad still had his own staunch followers, and his defiance found its ripple effect in the Majles, where his partisans clashed with pro-Larijani deputies. Disputes and collisions among the Principlists trickled down into society. Ahmadinejad's confrontations with Khamenei during the last two years of his presidency became a nightmare for the Leader.

The Moslehi Affair

On 17 April 2011, Heydar Moslehi, the minister of intelligence resigned, and Ahmadinejad readily accepted his resignation and appointed him to the ceremonial post of his Intelligence Adviser. This was the tip of the iceberg. Behind the scenes, there were two rumors about his sudden dismissal. First, Moslehi was said to have wiretapped Rahim-Mashai's phone. Second, it was said that Moslehi had insisted on firing one or two deputies, close to Rahim-Mashai, and Ahmadinejad had opposed the decision.

A day after Moslehi's resignation, the Leader, in a letter addressed to the president, ordered him back. In his letter Khamenei reminded his president that 'the Islamic Republic is a mighty system, and the Leader is sternly standing on his correct positions'.[66]

The dispute between the Leader and his president was now open and public. Ahmadinejad showed his discontent with the Leader's decision to meddle in his affairs by staying home and refusing to attend government functions. Ahmadinejad met with Khamenei and set three conditions for his return to work. He demanded the reinstatement of Rahim-Mashai as his First Deputy, the dismissal of Moslehi and the removal of Saeed Jalili, Khamenei's representative at the High Council of National Security.

Khamenei refused to budge, and Ahmadinejad provoked an unprecedented national crisis by refusing to carry out his state responsibilities. He brooded and stayed at home for eleven days. He finally returned to work on 1 May 2010, claiming his subservience to the Supreme Leader and announcing that his government was 'totally committed to and obedient towards the rule of the Guardian Jurist'. One day after the president resumed his activities, the security forces arrested his Cultural Adviser and the Prayer Leader of the President's Office, Abbas Amirfar, along with several individuals associated with Rahim-Mashai's circle. The humiliated president was reprimanded for his misconduct. His close circle of friends had now lost their shield of immunity.

Ahmadinejad Besieged

The election to the upcoming Ninth Majles in 2012 was essentially an inhouse competition among the Principlist forces. All pretenses to political plurality and people's sovereignty were dropped, and the prominent reformist political forces boycotted the election. Thirty-nine notable imprisoned reformists wrote a letter lamenting the 'complete political blockage' in the country and the instauration of 'an undeclared martial law'. They concluded that participating in the Majles elections would be 'helping despotism'. The quasi-reformists allowed to stand eventually obtained 6.9 per cent of the seats.

Amongst the Principlists, the escalating animosity between the supporters of Khamenei and Ahmadinejad cast a shadow on the elections. Ahmadinejad's opponents called him and his associates deviant, corrupt, dictatorial, seditious, and opposed to the rule of the Guardian Jurist. The split between the Principlists deepened as each camp accused the other of plotting to overthrow the system. The vocal spokesperson of the Ahmadinejad camp was Ali-Akbar Javanfekr, the president's press adviser and the director of the official Iranian News Agency, IRNA. For the ruling elite, the threat of the 'deviant group', the new name for Ahmadinehad and Rahim-Mashai, overshadowed the danger of the Green Movement. Khamenei now feared Ahmadinejad winning the Ninth Majles and even getting his friend Rahim-Mashai elected as the next president.

The Principlists demonstrated their deep divisions and four different formations entered into competition. The run-off elections on 4 May 2012 witnessed the rise of a new Principlist force. This was Mesbah-Yazdi's well-financed *Jebheye paydariye enqelabe eslami* (Islamic Revolution Perseverance Front), composed of his ardent clerical followers of the Eighth Majles, and influential figures of Ahmadinejad's first cabinet, such as Mahsuli. Even though Mesbah-Yazdi was highly suspicious of Rahim-Mashai's deviationist tendencies and had distanced himself from Ahmadinejad, he did not break off relations.

On 27 May 2012, the Ninth Majles was inaugurated. A divided Principlists bloc composed of a majority of anti-Ahmadinejad political formations and a minority of pro-Ahmadinejad groups, obtained a majority. The government announced that 63.8 per cent of eligible voters had participated in the election, while other sources put the participation rate at a maximum of 54 per cent. Khamenei praised the victory of the national will and invited the three governing branches to cooperate and avoid tensions.

On 24 September 2012, Ahmadinejad arrived in New York on his last official trip to attend the UN General Assembly. He was accompanied by an entourage of 140. Two days later, the president addressed the Security Council. At the same time, back in Tehran, Ali-Akbar Javanfekr, Ahmadinejad's close ally and the director of the Iranian News Agency, was arrested. Javanfekr was sent to Evin Prison on charges of insulting the Leader and publishing articles contrary to Islamic standards and public morality.

Returning from New York, Ahmadinejad did his best to secure the freedom of his aide but failed to do so. On 2 October 2012, he requested to visit Evin Prison and meet with Javanfekr. Sadeq Larijani, head of judiciary, refused and informed him that it was not an appropriate time. Ahmadinejad was no longer the darling of either Khamenei or the ruling elite, and doors would no longer swing wide open on his command.

Ahmadinejad was a lame duck during his last year in office. He was neither appreciated nor liked by the conservative circles, the majority of Principlists, clerics, and institutions that had supported him unconditionally at the beginning of his first term in office. The prodigious protégé of Khamenei, Mesbah-Yazdi, IRGC, *Basij* and *Hezbollah*, whose presidency was celebrated as a divine gift and was to save the system/regime from the menace of reformists, had fallen from grace. When 3 August 2013 came around and Ahmadinejad left the Presidential Palace, again Khamenei was relieved. His relationship with his three presidents had been troubled. Yet, Ahmadinejad continued to have his supporters among the people. It would be difficult to guess his popularity, but it was not negligible.

Factual and Analytical Questions

1. What distinguished Ahmadinejad from other conservative presidential candidates in 2005? Why did he appeal to the pious masses? What did he promise? Provide examples for your answer.

2   What was the 'Mahsuli Affair' of 2005? How did Mahsuli's appointment comply with the charter Ahmadinejad had his ministers sign? What did it say about Ahmadinejad?
3   What was the 'Kordan Affair' of 2008? How did Ahmadinejad and the Supreme leaders react to this affair? What do their reactions say about their values?
4   What were the four major economic initiatives of Ahmadinejad? Assess their success and shortcomings.
5   How successful was Ahmadinejad in improving the welfare of Iranians, reducing poverty and stamping out corruption? Provide examples.
6   'Was fraud perpetrated during the June 2009 presidential elections?' Discuss and provide circumstantial evidence.
7   What was the 'Moslehi Affair' of 2011? How did Ahmadinejad and the Supreme leaders react to this affair? What do you think was at stake?
8   How did sanctions strengthen the role and position of the IRGC in Iran's economy? Provide evidence for you answer.

Seminar Questions

1   What were the determining factors in Ahmadinejad's victory in the 2005 presidential elections? Provide examples for your argument.
2   How can Ahmadinejad's claim to a supernatural experience at the UN National Assembly be explained? What did he wish to achieve politically?
3   Explain how the Supreme Leader's fear of 'colour revolutions' or 'velvet revolutions' shaped domestic policies during Ahmadinejad's presidency.
4   What were the short- and long-term causes of the Green Movement? Why did it peter out?
5   What was the objective of Esfandiyar Rahim-Mashai's non-conformist statements and policy positions? Pick one of his themes and explain how and why it was offensive to the ruling elite.

Discussion Questions

1   Present Iran's case for uranium enrichment and the West's case against it. Present arguments for and against both sides.
2   Discuss the state of the Iranian economy during Ahmadinejad's presidency. Provide arguments and examples for your position.
3   'During Ahmadinejad's presidency, repression of dissidents, civil society activists, intellectuals, women's right activists, trade union organizers and

journalists substantially increased.' Discuss and assess the validity of this statement by providing examples.

4 'During the 2009 presidential elections, Musavi and Ahmadinejad presented two very different visions of how Iran should be governed.' Discuss and explain their fundamental differences in character, style, world outlook, programmes and ethical values.

5 'The Green Movement was reformist and not revolutionary.' Discuss the validity of this statement. Provide evidence for your arguments.

6 How would you assess the disputes between the Leader with Mir-Hoseyn Musavi and Ahmadinejad? Were they ideological or character clashes? What did they signify in terms of the Islamic Republic's governance system?

7 Distinguish between Ahmadinejad's first and second term in office. What are the main distinctive features of each term? Why did Khamenei fear him and how did he control him?

12

Rowhani Smiles, Hope and Moderation Dashed, 2013–21

Chapter Outline

Rowhani, the Surprise Victor of the 2013 Presidential Elections	586
Rowhani's First Term 2013–17: Somewhat Euphoric	590
Rowhani's Very Bumpy Second Term in Office	605
The Second Social Calamity	611
In Closing	618

The Iranian society of 2013 had shifted dramatically from what it had been in 1989. Social attitudes and behaviours, especially among the youth and women, displayed a marked tendency away from religious and traditional values and towards modern values. The Westernization of Iranians and their estrangement from Islamic and conventional practices had multiple manifestations. Embracing all things Western by a growing majority was also a constant reminder of the failure of the system to impose its alternative culture.

Iranians had to different degrees, turned away from doing their prayers, frequenting mosques and observing Ramadan. A good majority believed in separating religion from the law of the land. A growing number of women opposed compulsory veiling and openly violated the dress code to the extent possible. The flourishing cafés, restaurants, cultural centres, art galleries, athletic clubs, underground cinemas, theatres and music clubs, private parties, malls and parks in cities across Iran lent themselves to gender mixing and the breakdown of sexual segregation and repression. As many as about a third of adults even broke the prohibition laws and indulged in the consumption of alcoholic beverages.

By 2013 when Iranians were once again called to the ballot box to choose a new president, some 33 per cent of the population (25 million) were internauts, and a growing number of households obtained their news and home entertainment from Persian language networks abroad. All these programmes had one thing in common, they propagated Western culture, mores, way of thought and life. Mohammad-Reza Shah's compulsive Westernization had Islamized the Iranian youth. His revolutionary Islamic successors who had imposed compulsive Islamization had Westernized their young. Neither, however, delivered political freedom, rule of the law or democracy.

Rowhani, the Surprise Victor of the 2013 Presidential Elections

On 22 May 2013, the Guardian Council announced that it had approved the credentials of eight out of 686 candidates. From the list of eight, two desisted, leaving Iranians to choose between Saeed Jalili, Mohamad Qalibaf, Ali-Akbar Velayati, Mohsen Rezai, Hasan Rowhani and Mohammad Qarazi. The six represented a perfect rainbow of conservatives, from the extreme-traditionalist Jalili to the almost reformist Rowhani (Figure 12.1). Rezai and Qalibaf were defeated veterans of past presidential elections.

Figure 12.1 Supporters of Iranian President Hasan Rowhani. *Source: Photo by Majid Saeedi via Getty Images.*

Amongst those whose credentials were rejected was one of the principal architects of the Islamic Republic, Ali-Akbar Hashemi-Rafsanjani. The behind-the-scenes story of this political scandal was that Moslehi, the minister of intelligence, had attended a meeting of the Guardian Council and informed them that according to pre-election polls, Rafsanjani was poised to obtain over 70 per cent of the votes in the first round and win the elections. At that meeting, Moslehi, a devout supporter of Khamenei, had suggested that Rafsanjani's presidency was against the interests of the system/regime. The Leader was indeed averse to a Rafsanjani presidency because he had been favourable to the Green Movement and unsupportive of Khamenei in 2009. Furthermore, Rafsanjani was almost his equal with whom Khamenei did not wish to share power again.

In reaction to this, Zahra Mostafavi, Khomeyni's daughter, addressed an open letter to Khamenei, requesting him to oppose 'dictatorship' and order the approval of Rafsanjani's credentials. In her support for Rafsanjani, she revealed an important secret. She informed Khamenei that she had been present in the room when her father spoke about the eligibility of Khamenei as the future Leader. Mostafavi reminded the Leader that on that day, Khomeyni had suggested two possible names for leadership, Khamenei and Rafsanjani.[1] Ironically, by rejecting Rafsanjani's credentials, the Guardian Council and Khamenei made him a national hero.

The other not-so-surprising disqualification was Eskandar Rahim-Mashai. During the last months of his presidency, Ahmadinejad had campaigned hard to present Rahim-Mashai as his true heir and trusted successor. His candidacy went clearly against the wishes of the Leader. Aside from the person of Rahim-Mashai, any collaborator of Ahmadinejad was *persona non grata* for Khamenei. The roster of candidates had been cleaned of all 'undesirables' by the Guardian Council.

Among the six that were permitted to run, all but Velayati had some degree of affiliation with the war fronts. Qalibaf and Rezai were generals and commanders in the IRGC. Qarazi was one of the founders of the IRGC. Jalili had participated in the war as a volunteer *Basiji* and had lost his right leg. Between 1985 and 1997 Rowhani had directed the general headquarters of *Khatam al-anbia* (not to be confused with the engineering branch of the IRGC), the highest body planning, coordinating, and supervising the military activities of the armed forces during the Iran–Iraq War.

Hasan Rowhani (Fereydun) was neither an unknown figure nor a newcomer to the Iranian political scene. He was a cleric with a law degree from Tehran University, who had been a zealous supporter of Khomeyni before the revolution. Rowhani had joined the Association of Militant Clergy (*jameeye rowhaniyat mobarez*) before the revolution and was close to Motahhari and Beheshti. In a sermon in October 1977, the 28-year-old Rowhani addressed Khomeyni as Imam, and the title had stuck. Before the revolution, Rowhani had gone to the UK to study law. His studies were interrupted in October 1978 when Khomeyni arrived in Paris. It was not until eleven years later that he obtained his PhD from Glasgow Caledonian University in 1999.

After the revolution, Rowhani occupied sensitive state functions. He was a five-time Majles deputy, member of the High Council for National Defence and secretary of the Supreme National Security Council for sixteen years. He had Khamenei's trust. Right after the revolution, at Khamenei's behest, he began his responsibility at *Setade moshtarek artesh* (the Army Combined Centre). Ten years later, in November 1989, Khamenei as the newly chosen Supreme Leader, appointed him as his representative to the Supreme National Security Council. Rowhani had never wavered in his loyalty to Khamenei when political lines needed to be drawn. To cite an example, on 14 February 2011, when protesters demonstrated against the house arrest of the Green Movement leaders, Rowhani sided with Khamenei and accused the protesters of sedition.

Unlike Khamenei, however, Rowhani was a modernist committed to the system/regime and the two differed on how Iran should proceed to overcome its problems. To compensate for his ideological dissonance with Khamenei's static outlook, in his campaign speeches, Rowhani insisted on his 45-year devotion to Khamenei. Rowhani signalled the Leader that whatever he may believe, in the last analysis, he would remain obedient to the Guardian Jurist. By the end of the election campaign, however, the Principlists were calling for a re-evaluation of Rowhani's credentials with the hope that the Guardian Council would eliminate him from the list of presidential candidates.

Rowhani's solution to the crippling standoff in the country was threefold. He proposed getting the sanctions lifted by resolving the nuclear issue, securing the release of Musavi and Karrubi from house arrest, and generating trust in the system's ability to foster change through protecting constitutional and political rights and freedoms. In his electrifying election campaigns, adorned by the slogan 'Government of wisdom and hope,' a key symbolized his intention to resolve problems through moderation, reason and dialogue. He called for an end to the heavy security environment that weighed upon the country and announced that the people had the right to exercise their freedoms and criticize. Rowhani emphasized that the government needed to alter its view of the youth and begin trusting them.

Rowhani's language and discourse were very different from Ahmadinejad's. His campaign speeches were well prepared, poised and polite, combining Khatami's political development ideas with Rafsanjani's economic development, peppered with sarcasm. Rowhani called the youth the 'heroes and saviours of the country' and promised freedom, respect for civil rights and the Constitution, clean air, pursuit of national interests, befriending the world community and change. At his rallies, the youth chanted, 'Free political prisoners!' and Rowhani retorted, 'Why only political prisoners and not all prisoners?' On the economic front, the presidential candidate insisted that he would work towards alleviating the sanctions to improve the livelihood of Iranians. Rowhani seldom referred to Islam, the Guardian Jurist or the revolution.

Rowhani had the full support of Rafsanjani and his moderate and pragmatic conservative supporters. In the absence of any reformist candidates, he also became the proxy candidate of that segment of the Green Movement, which still felt as though the system was salvageable. Rowhani chose purple as the colour of his campaign and created an unexpected political momentum out of the general political despair and apathy that reigned since 2009. His election posters included a picture of him in the middle, flanked by Khatami to the right and Rafsanjani to his left. The Green Movement, with the precise political objective of, 'Where is my vote?', had passed on the baton to the Purple Movement, the ambiguous motto of which was moderation.

On Friday, 14 June 2013, the people went to the polling booths, and in the afternoon of Saturday, 15 June, to everyone's surprise, Rowhani was declared the winner in the first round with 50.7 per cent of the votes cast. His Principlist runners-up Qalibaf and Jalili received 16.5 per cent and 11.3 per cent of the votes. The minister of interior reported that 72.7 per cent of eligible voters and approximately 50 per cent of Tehranis had voted. Khamenei had, it seems, decided to bring back some trust and confidence to the election process, which had become ever more arbitrary and meaningless in the eyes of the people.

The national and international reactions to Rowhani's unexpected victory were warm and encouraging. For true-blooded Iranian reformists, the election results proved that the system could allow change from within. Swept away by optimism and hope, they quickly forgot that the same system had most arbitrarily excluded Rafsanjani from running in the elections. From the international standpoint, Rowhani was known to Western statesmen and politicians as Iran's capable chief negotiator with the International Atomic Energy Agency and the international community between 2003 and 2005.

On 3 and 4 August 2013, Rowhani was sworn in. The Majles rejected three of his eighteen proposed ministers, two of whom were rebuffed for their association with Karrubi, Musavi, and the Green Movement. Rowhani's choice of cross-party ministers represented his concern for a well-experienced and specialized team with managerial and technical skills in their related fields. His economic team were cautious, pragmatic and moderate free marketers interested in economic stabilization, liberalization and privatization.

Rowhani's cabinet included three clerics, including himself and a considerably higher number of ministers and deputies educated in the US and the UK than the previous governments. Rowhani was the first Iranian president who obtained his final degree (PhD) from a Western country. Out of 21 members of Rowhani's team, including his chief of staff, 10 were Western trained, some at the best US and UK universities. Rowhani's ministers of intelligence and interior were doves with no previous security, intelligence or IRGC employment. His minister of culture and Islamic guidance, suspected of being a conservative at first, turned out to be a full-blown reformist.

Rowhani's First Term 2013–17: Somewhat Euphoric

Rowhani's first four years were rather smooth and though his actions were in line with his promises, he was less successful with his goal of forging national unity around moderation and reconciliation at home and abroad. In time, Rowhani became jammed between the Leader who pressed him to tone down his reformist discourse, which was becoming as dangerous to the system as Khatami's, and the popular will which had surpassed Rowhani's moderate liberalization and demanded more, transgressing the Islamic Republic's red lines. In his nuclear policy, Rowhani, had painstakingly finessed a compromise acceptable to the Leader, but then had the misfortune of having to deal with Donald Trump, the new US president whose political grandstanding resembled Ahmadinejad's.

The Zarif–Soleymani Duo

Rowhani's first term in office was marked by nuclear negotiations and semi-clandestine military exploits overseas. By April 2015, the Iranian media flaunted two smiling faces, one bustling and the other timid, as national heroes and two sides of the Islamic Republic's winning coin. One was the diplomatic grand master, Mohammad-Javad Zarif, and the other was the shy-looking, insignia-less victorious military mastermind, Qasem Soleymani. The two had little in common, except that they were about the same age and had become legends in Iran for defending national interests and rekindling patriotism, glory and pride.

Zarif came from an urban well-off religious family. He had completed his last year of high school in San Francisco, obtained his BA and MA in International Relations from San Francisco State University and received his PhD in International Law and Policy from the University of Denver. Soleymani, on the other hand, came from a humble provincial family and had to leave school at the age of 13 to work (Figure 12.2).

Zarif was presented as a Mosaddeq-like symbol, defending the country's economic interest against foreigners. Soleymani was paraded as the chivalrous and unassuming knight, fending off the barbarian hoards of the Islamic State of Iraq and Syria (ISIS). The two had become icons of a gushing sense of Iranian nationalism, one speaking the language of international law and diplomacy and the other, the language of the gun.

In 1997, Khamenei had appointed Soleymani to command the IRGC's Qods Force. Through Qasem Soleymani and the Qods Force, Khamenei hoped to realize his international project of expanding the Axis of Resistance. At home, Khamenei had

Figure 12.2 Gen. Qasem Soleymani. *Source: Wikimedia Commons.*

been unsuccessful in keeping Iranians revolutionary, pious and anti-Western. His legitimacy at home was waning. With the Qods Force, he hoped to expand his influence and power overseas in the name of defending oppressed Muslims of the Axes of Resistance against the Great Satan. Unappreciated at home, Khamenei looked abroad for recognition.

The brutalities of the ISIS (Daesh) and the Qods Force's war against them in Syria and Iraq helped the benevolent image of the Islamic Republic. Iranians felt chuffed that as countries in the region fell into chaos and became subjected to ISIS atrocities, Soleymani kept them safe and secure in their country. The Qods Force's presence in Syria, Iraq, Lebanon and Yemen was highlighted as the Islamic Republic's selfless protection of friendly states against ISIS and the guarantor of domestic security.

The threat of the Taliban, Al-Qaida and especially ISIS temporarily muddied the clear lines of demarcation between the Axes of Resistance and World Arrogance, as the West and the US were referred to by the Iranian regime. The ISIS victories in Iraq and Syria posed a common threat to the old enemies and created a space for Iran, with its Qods Forces on the ground, to cooperate with US forces in the region.

> ### The British Prime Minister's Olive Branch to Soleymani, 2014
>
> Iran should also be given the chance to show it can be part of the solution, not part of the problem. Earlier today I met with President Rouhani. We have severe disagreements. Iran's support for terrorist organisations, its nuclear programme, its treatment of its people. All these need to change. But Iran's leaders could help in defeating the threat from ISIL[ISIS]. They could help secure a more stable, inclusive Iraq; and a more stable and inclusive Syria. And if they are prepared to do this, then we should welcome their engagement. (D. Cameron)[2]

In the US, too, serious voices opined that Iran was a natural US ally and at least they could coordinate their efforts and collaborate in Iraq and Syria against the Islamic State. In September 2014, reports indicated that Ayatollah Khamenei had 'sanctioned' Soleymani 'to work with forces fighting IS, including the US'.[3] On 15 September 2014, however, the Supreme Leader announced that the Islamic Republic had rejected Washington's invitation for cooperation in Iraq. Once the tides turned against ISIS after their defeat first at Palmyra (Syria) in March 2016 and at Mosul (Iraq) in October 2016, there remained no reason for cooperation.

Rowhani's Illusions

On 8 January 2014, Rowhani delivered an upbeat and enthusiastic speech, like some of Khatami's early speeches. Rowhani had fallen under the euphoric spell that he could push his moderate reform agenda and foster change without much resistance from the Leader. Addressing the artistic and cultural community, Rowhani held out a rose without thorns. He insisted that 'true art could not be created, in the absence of freedom' and that his government did not intend to 'intervene in the domain of arts and culture'. Rowhani said, 'We should remember, and all should know that art is not dangerous, and artists do not endanger national security'. Rowhani seemed to be apologizing for the macabre days when the Ministry of Intelligence exterminated 'troublemaking' writers, poets, and artists to thwart the cultural onslaught.

The president admitted that the system had 'red lines' (censorship) to be observed but promised that they would become 'transparent, specific and legal'. He suggested that 'supervision of films, books and music' be left to artists in their respective fields and the professional and guild organizations involved. Rowhani proposed that artists accept a part of the responsibilities in the Ministry of Culture and Guidance.

The highlight of his speech was a passing reference to his vision of his responsibilities as president. 'The inherent responsibility of the government,' he said, 'is to deal with significant national issues such as security, foreign policy and diplomacy'. He identified these domains as 'the sole purviews of the government' and insisted that 'no other institution has the right to intervene in them'. Rowhani realized that he had gone too far and added, 'of course, according to the constitution, the broad foreign policy issues are determined by the Supreme Leader'.

Rowhani insisted on 'minimizing the control and oversight of the government in the economic and cultural realms'. He signalled to the ruling class that his laissez-faire approach and opposition to government command and management in economics, equally applied to the political realm. This approach, he believed, would lead to 'national reconciliation and unity'. Rowhani warned the 'extremists' and the 'violent' in the regime that if 'mouths are shut, and pens are broken, the public's trust will disappear'.[4]

The zealous protectors of the Leader and Islamicness soon jolted Rowhani out of his cultural, artistic, and intellectual Islamic-liberal dreams. On 15 February 2014, a pro-Rowhani tabloid, *Aseman* (Sky), appeared on the newsstands. *Aseman* was the first newspaper to obtain a publishing license in Rowhnai's presidency and was an intellectual and independent paper in favour of moderation. After an official complaint by the prosecutor of the Revolutionary Courts, *Aseman* was closed on 20 February 2014, five days after it appeared. The paper was shut for referring to the law of talion (*qisas*) as inhuman. The executive's hands-off policy in the cultural realm was corrected by the hawk-eyed judiciary. When elected bodies reflected the public will and 'faltered', appointed institutions did their job and put them in their place.

In April 2014, Pharrell William's catchy song 'Happy' brought joy to the people worldwide. Videos of young and old singing and dancing in the streets, cafes, train stations, hospitals, offices, schools, and universities filled YouTube and cyberspace. People in 153 countries joined the 'Happy' fever and let off steam. Iranian youth followed suit and joined their global counterparts. They posted dance videos in parks, in streets and private compounds. Others avoided public places and danced on rooftops, balconies and inside their homes. The girls dancing wore loose head scarves, and some took them off.

On 20 May, the system clamped on the 'Happy' videos and arrested seven youngsters. They were quickly released, but the message was clear. The security apparatus was watching and could clamp down whenever it wanted. The custodians of correct morality disapproved of how the youth dressed, mingled, moved their bodies, laughed, and were carefree. While the system found what 'Happy' symbolized as offensive, a rapidly growing segment, if not most of the Iranian youth, identified with it as their fully adopted culture and identity.

Those who chanted and danced to 'Happy' were not Iran's typically politicized youth. They were happy-go-lucky, *carpe diem*-types who wished to live the life of their global counterparts and be left alone. Contrary to Khamenei and the conservatives, Rowhani and the reformists understood this growing and irremediable cultural cleavage. Rowhani tweeted, 'Happiness is our people's right. We shouldn't be too hard on behaviors caused by joy.'[5]

With all means of repression at its disposal, the conservative coalition oscillated between a reluctant tolerance of cyberspace and substantially raising the risk of employing it. The appointed institutions loyal to the Leader, however, continued their crusade against the 'cultural onslaught'. In May 2014, eight were condemned to a total of 127 years in prison for using Facebook, and in June, another eleven were convicted and sentenced to up to 11 years for 'designing sites, websites, and creating content for media hostile to the regime'.[6]

The clampdown on cyberspace activists continued in April 2016, with the courts condemning six social media users to terms between five and seven years in prison for their Facebook posts on charges of 'assembly and collusion against the national security' and 'insulting the sanctities.' In June 2016, Atena Farqadani was condemned to 'a total of 12 years and 9 months imprisonment in connection with a critical cartoon she drew and posted on her Facebook page ... that depicted members of Iran's parliament as animals'. Her sentencing was followed by 'a wave of arrests of social media users and activists'.[7] In 2016, 'hundreds of social media users, in particular on the Telegram messaging application and Instagram, have been summoned or arrested by the IRGC for commenting on controversial issues, including fashion'.[8]

The conservative coalition also put pressure on Rowhani to cleanse his government of controversial figures. Ali Jannati, minister of culture and Islamic guidance was the political opposite of his father, Ayatollah Ahmad Jannati. Ali Jannati was close to Rafsanjani and Rowhani's line of thought. His liberal views to ease the stifling cultural atmosphere and inject some spontaneity and joy bothered the hardliners and the traditional conservatives like his father.

Already in 2014 Khamenei (Figure 12.3) had shown his dissatisfaction with Jannati's liberal cultural policies by not attending Tehran's Book Fair, organized by the Ministry of Culture and Islamic Guidance. Traditionally, the Leader took an interest in Book Fairs and attended them regularly. When Ali Jannati became minister, his predecessor in Ahmadinejad's government had ordered the closure of the 'House of Cinema'. Jannati rescinded his order and reopened Iran's most important film industry organization. He gave license to rap music performers and supported music concerts throughout the country, even in the holy cities of Qom and Mashhad. Ali Jannati believed in minimizing filtering access to Facebook and other social media. He resisted pressure from all conservative quarters to ban 'politically inconvenient' films, permitted them to be screened and opposed censuring books.

After an open run-in with the hardline conservative cleric Ahmad Alam al-hoda over musical concerts in Mashhad, Ali Jannati resigned on 19 October 2016. Alam al-hoda, the Leader's representative in Khorasan Province, had become Mashhad's

Figure 12.3 Supreme Leader Ayatollah Ali Khamenei, Secretary of Drug Control and Police Chief Esmail Ahmadi Moqqaddam, Army Commander Ataollah Salehi, Armed Forces Joint Chief of Staff Hasan Firuzabadi, Head of Revolutionary Guards Mohammad-Ali Jafari and Defence Minister Mostafa Mohammad Najjar. *Source: Photo by UPI Photo via Alamy.*

strongman after his firm support for Khamenei in the summer of 2009 uprisings. He was the Friday Prayer Leader of Mashhad, but unlike some 800 other Friday Prayer Leaders throughout the country, he had the political power to oppose concerts in his city.

The Pashai Affair: Widening and Deepening Cultural Cleavages

On 14 November 2014, the 30-year-old songwriter and pop singer Morteza Pashai died of cancer. Less than a month earlier, on 24 October, the 83-year-old Ayatollah Mahdavi-Kani, a major religious and political player in post-revolution Iran, had died in the same hospital (Bahman). For Pashai, streets and parks in Tehran as well as 26 other cities filled spontaneously with mourners, men and women wearing black, singing his songs. Mahdavi-Kani was given a state funeral, attended by the heads of the three branches of government. The two very different personalities represented two distinct values and symbols in the historical evolution of the Islamic Republic.

Pashai had reached fame by first posting his songs on the internet. His gentle, bespectacled face, almost perfectly chiselled, long hair, tender voice, and melancholic love songs resonated with Iranian youth. He sang about love, its joys and longings, broken hearts, amorous deceptions and painful separations. Pashai and his fans longed for social and cultural normalcy, where experiences of softness, warmth, and affection were not considered seditious threats to national security and punished. Mahdavi-Kani had been a pillar of Iran's conservative religious institution and a staunch supporter of the Supreme Leader's world outlook. He had been provisional prime minister and president of the Assembly of Experts of the Leadership. Thousands attended Pashai's funeral. Tehran was shocked by the numbers in attendance who peacefully grieved their deceased musical icon. Social observers sarcastically compared the throngs displaying their affection for Pashai and his music with the typical types who had attended the state-initiated funeral for Ayatollah Mohammad-Reza Mahdavi-Kani.

Conscious of the youth's cultural transition to a different way of life the regime selectively made an example of un-Islamic and unrevolutionary behaviour. In June 2014, Parliament discussed the increasingly un-Islamic clothing of women. To demonstrate the threat of a new 'perverse' fad, large monitors inside the Majles displayed women wearing leggings clasping their legs and thighs. The Majles deputies questioned Rowhani's minister of interior about his negligence towards women wearing leggings.

In April 2016, the system announced the creation of a 7,000 mixed men and women special undercover morality police force in Tehran. The unit was tasked to monitor and report on improper veiling in public, un-Islamic dressing and conduct, and the increasing incidence of women removing their headscarves inside cars. This was not the first time morality police were instructed to monitor un-Islamic clothing. This attempt, like all previous ones, failed to reverse the trends.

On the Role of Police in Society

The Police is not responsible for imposing Islam, but to implement the law. (H. Rowhani)[9]

Incapable of imposing its values on the youth or even curtailing the spread of Western morality and identity in Tehran and the big cities, the system gave up on systematic and continuous harassment. The morality police (*gashte ershad*) imposed its authority randomly and irregularly, showing teeth mainly in the provinces and at times of crisis. In 2016, a couple in Golpayegan, was sentenced to 100 lashes for 'having an illegitimate relationship'. In Qazvin, 35 young men and women were charged with 'engaging in acts incompatible with chastity which disturbed the public opinion' and sentenced to 99 lashes each for partying. The morality police became a scarecrow badgering people for comportment non-compliant with Islam. It targeted women relentlessly resisting and pushing back against the forced dress code.

Social Movements and Demands

Unfulfilled promises by Rowhani caused resentment and protest. According to a report attributed to the Interior Ministry, 'there were around 43,000 protest demonstrations in Iran between 2013 and January 2018, or 30 protests per day'. In the World Happiness Report Survey conducted between 2013 and 2018, Iran ranked between 115th and 106th among 152 countries. Different social categories found themselves persecuted by the state. If imprisonment and repression were once reserved for political activists, dissident intellectuals and journalists, from 2013, worried about the people's growing expectations in response to Rowhani's promises, the conservatives tightened the noose.

The accumulated demands of the working-class movement came to a head in January 2014. Some 3,000 workers at the Chadormalu mine in Yazd, the biggest iron mine of its kind in Iran, protested and downed tools demanding pay increases in line with inflation, the reinstatement of fired labor leaders, and payment of unpaid overtime wages. The authorities retaliated by arresting 25 workers, among them labour union leaders. The system's fear of widespread political instability made it suspicious of assemblies, demonstrations and protests.

On 1 May 2014, Rowhani celebrated May Day by attending a large government-organized workers' meeting. He praised the working class, spoke about more workers' rights and promised that his government would 'pave the way for independent trade unions'. On the same day, worker activists demanding non-government-controlled independent unions, higher wages and better work conditions congregated in Tehran. Their assembly was attacked, 25 were arrested and, as a preventive measure, 2 union activists were also been arrested the previous night.

Throughout Rowhani's first term, tension between workers and the state increased. In 2015, Iran registered some 410 cases of labour protests. The state responded by imprisoning members and leaders of trade unions. The arrested labor activists received hefty prison terms. From 2013 to 2021, protests, strikes and labour actions grew across sectors, in incidence and numbers involved. The provinces registered a greater number of incidences than Tehran.

The Iranian Teachers Association became vocal and active in mobilizing and representing teachers. Between 2014 and 2020, nine peaceful teachers' actions per year spanned some 40 to 60 cities. The protesting teachers demanded higher pay, better social security coverage, job security, freedom of imprisoned teachers and the right to establish independent unions. Repression against the members and leaders of the Teachers' Association began in July 2015 with the arrest of some 130 teachers. In November 2016, Esmail Abdi, secretary-general of the Teachers' Trade Association, was condemned to ten years in prison for his guild activities.

Women, human, civil, children and environmental rights activists became targets of repression. In May 2015, Narges Mohammadi, a human rights activist and journalist, and Atena Daemi, a child and civil rights activist, were sentenced, respectively, to 6 and 14 years in prison for 'assembly, collusion and propaganda against the state' and 'insulting the Supreme Leader and religious sanctities'. In May 2016, Narges Mohammadi's sentence was increased to 16 years in prison. One of the charges against her was membership in a banned campaign to stop the death penalty.

As a means to counter these moves, on 19 December 2016, Rowhani signed a 120-article 'Charter on Citizen's Rights', reiterating his government's commitment to upholding the rights and freedoms of individuals, women, and minorities. Most of the articles stipulated in the Charter were already in the Constitution. Those rights and freedoms remained, however, unattainable because the judiciary and the law enforcement agencies chose to ignore and violate them. The executive's Charter never went to the Majles to become law.

The Domestic Balance of Forces

In the summer of 2014, the radical conservatives of Mesbah-Yazdi's parliamentary faction, the 'Islamic Revolution Perseverance Front', began agitating among the Principlists in the Majles to undermine Rowhani's authority. Their first successful action was to impeach the minister of science and higher education on 24 June 2015. Reza Faraji-Dana was an academic and former president of Tehran University, educated in Iran and Canada and respected among academics at Tehran University. The deputies opposed to Faraji-Dana, accused his appointees at Tehran University of having participated in the 2009 'sedition' and allowing the return of dissident students banned from their studies and dismissed faculty to universities.

In December 2014, under fire from Mesbah Yazdi's 'Islamic Revolution Perseverance Front', Rowhani opened a new front against the radical conservative pillars of the system. He challenged the mighty and sacrosanct IRGC at a seminar on combatting corruption. In a scathing attack, he shared his predicament with the people and said, 'If information, guns, money, newspapers, news agencies, and other sources of power become concentrated in one institution . . . it would become corrupt.'[10] Rowhani was telling the people that the IRGC juggernaut, the pride of Khamenei, had become corrupt.

On June 2015, members of the 'Islamic Revolution Perseverance Front', who were by now nicknamed the 'anxious bunch', tried to impeach Rowhani's minister of education, Ali-Asghar Fani but failed. However, the pressure on Rowhani did not abate. His success with the nuclear negotiations was taking the country down a path unwanted by the hardliners, the traditional conservatives and the IRGC. They were obsessed with keeping Iran isolated, beleaguered, protected from Western influences and conducive for rent and ill-gotten gain.

Rowhani's Foreign and Nuclear Policy, 2013–17

Rowhani was committed to resolving Iran's economic problems through detente, rapprochement, and negotiation with the West. In his interactions with Western politicians and diplomats, he had learned that they pursued their national interests and were not necessarily bent on regime change in Iran. He believed in putting an end to sanctions without Iran losing face. As Javad Zarif, his foreign minister would often say, the Rowhani team looked for a win-win solution, a concept alien to the Supreme Leader.

On 24 September 2013, Rowhani was in New York attending the UN General Assembly and speaking to US President Barack Obama on the phone. The conversation was the first direct and open contact between an Iranian leader and a US president since the revolution. Rowhani broke the sacrosanct precedence of Iranian leaders not speaking to their US counterparts. From that point, events unfolded rapidly, with consequential ups and downs.

On 14 July 2015, Iran and the P5+1, the five permanent members of the Security Council plus Germany, reached a comprehensive nuclear deal, the Joint Comprehensive Plan of Action (JCPOA). After 21 months of complex, delicate and exhausting negotiations, a historical accord was signed. The deal had the consent and support of Khamenei. The Iranian diplomats and experts, led by Javad Zarif, reversed the shortcomings and incompetence of the previous team, led by Saeed Jalili.

They proved that Iran had to be taken seriously, as a worthy negotiation partner knowledgeable of the dossier at hand and with skills and capabilities on par with its Western interlocutors. Diplomatic negotiation over such a delicate matter was a game of brainpower and intelligent maneuverings, not empty threats, conspiracy theories and cussing. JCPOA 'laid the groundwork for the Security Council to lift nuclear-related sanctions on Iran when Tehran completed key steps under the deal that restricted its nuclear activities'.[11] Security Council Resolution 2231 endorsed the deal ending a ten-year embargo on Iran.

As the historical wall of distrust towards the West was demolished by Rowhani's team, the supporters and opponents of his diplomatic feat lined up at home. For Rowhani, the agreement was a substantial victory. He had delivered on one of his central campaign promises, the key to lifting sanctions and improving the economic condition of the people. Before the agreement took effect on 16 January 2016, the opponents of Rowhani's peaceful coexistence foreign policy went to work neutralizing and undermining his diplomatic efforts.

On the eve of Saturday, 2 January 2016, two weeks before JCPOA went into effect, a 'spontaneous' crowd of some 700 zealots chanting, 'Death to Saud Family!' attacked, ransacked and fire-bombed the Saudi Embassy in Tehran. After the initial damage, the police appeared, evicted the protesters from the embassy grounds and extinguished the fire. A similar attack was conducted in Mashhad on the very same day, where protestors tore down the Saudi flag.

The violence was in response to the execution of Sheykh Nimr Baqer al-Nimr, a Saudi Shii cleric, announced on 2 January 2016. Al-Nimr was an outspoken critic of the Saudi monarchy and the spiritual leader of the 2011 anti-government protests in the Shii dominated Eastern Province of Qatif. He was arrested in July 2013 and decapitated along with 46 others by the Saudi government on charges of anti-state activities and sedition.

On Sunday, 3 January, Saudi Arabia broke off diplomatic relations with Iran and gave Iranian diplomats 48 hours to leave the country. The diplomatic rupture between Iran and Saudi Arabia was a setback for Rowhani's rapprochement policy. Saudi Arabia was a major regional player and was already engaged in a proxy war with Iran in Yemen. The diplomatic crisis complicated Rowhani's plans to mend fences with the Saudis, the Gulf States and the Arab world. The attack on its embassy gave Saudi Arabia a golden opportunity to harden its position against Iran, further isolate it in the region, and accuse it of being a terrorist rogue state, in breach of international law and a security threat in the region.

Rowhani condemned the execution of al-Nimr as a violation of Islamic and Human Rights but called the attack on the Saudi Embassy 'totally unjustifiable' and 'an insult to the system and an affront to Iran's reputation'. He called the perpetrators 'rogue elements' and asked the responsible authorities to identify and bring them to justice.

The man behind the attack was Hasan Kordmihan. He managed several *Basij* headquarters in Tehran and Karaj and had been Mohammad Qalibaf's campaign manager in Karaj during the 2013 presidential elections. Kordmihan publicly announced that his actions were in tandem with Khamenei's intentions.

On 20 January 2016, 18 days after the attack on the Saudi Embassy, Khamenei first said a few words condemning the attack as 'a very bad operation' and that 'whoever did it was wrong' and praised the hard work of the JCPOA negotiating team. He then embarked on the main thrust of his speech. Khamenei warned against the US's 'ruse and deception' and reminded the public that 'the enemy remained the enemy', and that the Obama Administration was not different from the Bush Administration in its animosity towards Islam and the Islamic Republic. Both administrations, he believed, were intent on regime change. Khamenei then went on to eulogize the revolutionary and pious youth, whom he believed were devotees of Islam and the revolution and understood issues and analysed them even better than some senior authorities. Khamenei warned against undermining and accusing this zealous youth of attacking the Saudi Embassy.[12] Khamenei was not willing to abandon his conspiracy theory and hate speech.

The signing of the JCPOA caused a new alignment of forces on the Iranian political scene. The zealot members of the 'Islamic Revolution Perseverance Front' continued to vociferously oppose it as an agreement that could result in economic, military, and cultural hegemony of foreigners. Since Khamenei had ruled that the Majles should vote on JCPOA, the 'anxious bunch' hoped to rally the deputies to vote against it. However, the influential president of the Ninth Majles, Ali Larijani, and his faction rallied in support of JCPOA and joined forces with Rowhani's supporters in the Majles.

On 11 October 2015, the Majles approved JCPOA with 139 deputies voting for 100 against and ten abstaining. Larijani's management of the Majles secured the quick approval of JCPOA in twenty minutes. Larijani's helping hand could not have been without the consent of Khamenei, who wished to avoid taking sides and responsibility for the possible adverse consequences of the agreement. On the day the Majles voted, hysterical members of the 'Islamic Revolution Perseverance Front', sensing defeat, threatened that if JCPOA was ratified, they would kill the soft-spoken chief of Iran's Nuclear Organization, Ali-Akbar Salehi and execute Javad Zarif.

Rowhani's agenda was to break Iran out of its isolation and re-integrate it into the international economy by removing sanctions. Iran was an oil-exporting economy, and the welfare of its people was highly dependent on its single crop. In February 2014, Khamenei had relaunched his notion of an insular economy, which he had called 'a resistance economy' back in 2010. The idea implied an autarkic, self-sufficient economy with almost no trade, suitable for a country domestically capable of providing for all it needed, not one like Iran.

The Leader and Rowhani promoted two different paths of dealing with sanctions and relieving economic hardship. Khamenei viewed the Western world – the US in particular – and everything that had to do with it as an eternal source of evil to avoid. To Rowhani, economic collaboration, necessitating political understanding and cordial relations with the West and the US was desirable as it alleviated hardships and improved the livelihood of Iranians.

Khamenei's position was more complicated, as he lived in two parallel realities. For his power base at home, he needed to minimize the crippling impact of the sanctions, turn it into a blessing and harp on the importance of the self-reliance and increased diversification at home, resulting from it. Yet, he was also aware of the desperate state of the economy. Iran had $100 billion in frozen overseas assets, and its oil exports had halved, constituting a loss of $160 billion in revenue between 2012 and 2015. The Iranian currency, the rial, lost 56 per cent of its value within two years after the 2012 sanctions, and inflation reached 40 per cent.[13] The oil price plunge of 2014–16 further aggravated the sanction shock on the economy.

Khamenei knew that dire economic conditions could quickly take a political turn and pose serious security threats. The Leader appreciated the fact that an improved standard of living resulting from JCPOA would reduce the threat of public unrest. This explains his green light for signing the deal and its adoption in the Majles. He nonetheless felt obliged to hold on to his anti-Western discourse, which identified him and had legitimated his rule for some 35 years.

The implementation of the JCPOA did improve Iran's economic situation. In 2012, the Iranian Gross Domestic Product (GDP) shrunk by 3.7 per cent, indicating a net diminution in the national pie of goods and services produced. In contrast, Iran's GDP increased by 8.8 per cent in 2016. The high inflation rate of 36.6 per cent in 2013 dropped to 7.2 per cent in 2016, a low not experienced since 1985. The economy picked up in 2016 improving living standards, particularly in the urban areas.

The unemployment problem, however, persisted despite the overall positive economic climate. In 2013, 34 per cent of the youth aged between 15 and 24 were neither employed, studying, nor in training. By 2017, overall youth unemployment did not improve. This increasingly educated and unemployed youth with rising expectations and dismal employment opportunities, became increasingly frustrated and prone to social unrest.

The Surprise Elections to the 10th Majles and the Fifth Assembly of Experts

From January 2016, the political forces in Iran began preparing for the 10th Majles elections. Khamenei adopted a new approach and openly invited those 'who did not accept the system/regime to participate in the elections'. He insisted that those who did not accept the system should vote, but those candidates unfavourable to the system be barred from standing for election. In an irrational and inconsistent approach, the Leader wanted the opposition to participate in the election process but not be able to vote for the candidates of their choice.

Khamenei also slammed the brakes on the 'moderation craze' promoted by Rowhani and his supporters. If moderation was a virtue, then excessiveness was a vice. Khamenei rejected the association between the young revolutionary and pious *Hezbollahi*s and the hardliners and fanatics. He credited his zealot powerbase, which Rowhani's supporters were labelling as excessive hardliners, and said the revolutionary *Hezbollahi*s had always been ready to 'enter the battlefield' and defend 'the frontiers' and the 'national identity'.[14]

On 24 February 2016, two days before the first round of elections, in a speech at Najafabad (Esfahan), Khamenei warned against 'the fake polarity' between 'moderates and hardliners/fanatics', concocted by 'the enemy' for election purposes. He went out of his way to deny the glaring political cleavage in the country and called it 'a lie'. For him, Iranians stood united behind the revolution, the thoughts of Imam Khomeyni, and his rule as the Guardian Jurist and leader. Khamenei warned against 'infiltrators' and called for a new Majles composed of 'pious, politically and religiously committed' deputies who would 'defend the revolution', 'stand up to the excesses of the Westerners', and 'not be intimidated by the US'.[15]

Figure 12.4 John Kerry and Javad Zarif. *Source: Photo via Alamy.*

Targeting Rowhani and Zarif, who during the JCPOA talks had exchanged smiles and handshakes with personalities such as John Kerry, the US secretary of state (Figure 12.4), Khamenei said, 'if the enemy praises you, pause and question your behaviour and your doings'. At home, Rowhani and Zarif were modifying the old negative and deceitful image of Western and particularly American politicians, rendering them human and indulgent.

On 26 February 2016, Iranians voted in the tenth parliamentary election since the Revolution and the fifth election for the Assembly of Experts of the Leadership. The run-off elections were held on 29 April 2016, and the results proved most disappointing for the Principlists. The coalition formed by the reformists and moderates called *Omid* (hope), obtained 42 per cent of the Majles seats. The Grand Coalition of Principlists, composed of Mesbah-Yazdi's hardline 'Islamic Revolution Perseverance Front' and the traditional conservatives under the leadership of Haddad-Adel, father to Khamenei's daughter-in-law, obtained only 28 per cent of the Majles seats. The other seats went to various shades of reformists and conservatives, giving a general outcome of some 47 per cent reformist/moderate deputies, 41 per cent conservative/hardliner and 10 per cent pro-Khamenei independent deputies.

All 30 seats representing Tehran went to the reformist and moderate coalition. The heavyweight conservative and hardline Tehran deputies in the Ninth Majles, such as Haddad-Adel, Ahmad Tavakoli and Morteza Aqa-Tehrani, were dealt a humiliating blow. Tehran's blanket rejection of conservative and hardline candidates was most telling. The hardline cleric, Jafar Shojooni said, 'This was not an unexpected event. Tehran is the bastion of those who oppose the revolution, and the Rule of the Guardian Jurist.' To the defeated hardliners, Tehran was the city of fallen angels composed of a new middle-class with a quasi-modern lifestyle and quasi-intellectual demands. The system deemed Tehranis as being 'impious, unreligious, and Westernized'.[16]

On the same day Iranians also voted for the Fifth Assembly of Experts of the Leadership. The results were equally disappointing for Principlist clerics and much more alarming for Khamenei. This crucial clerical body, elected every eight years, had three responsibilities. It supervised the Leader's activities, could remove him from office if he was no longer fit to rule, and when the time came chose his successor. The elected members of the Assembly of Experts had the country's political future in their hands and, subsequently, its composition and political outlook were of extreme sensitivity to the Leader (Figure 12.5).

Prior to the elections, the Guardian Council, the gatekeeper of all key elected institutions, had, as always, done its job of 'weeding out' the undesirable candidates. It, nevertheless, shocked Iranians when it rejected the credentials of prominent moderate and reformist clerical figures such as Hasan Khomeyni, the Imam's grandson, Mohammad Musavi-Bojnurdi, Ali-Mohammad Dastgheyb, Mahmud Amjad and Majid Ansari. The Guardian Council had by now perfected the art of doctoring candidates. In six provinces, their vetting was so extreme that the number of approved candidates equalled the seats that needed to be filled, leaving the electorate with no formal choice. Rafsanjani reacted uncharacteristically harshly to the non-approval of Hasan Khomeyni and questioned the authority and legitimacy of the Guardian Council.

Figure 12.5 Assembly of Experts of the Leadership. *Source: Photo by Maryam Rahmanian via Alamy.*

Despite the Guardian Council's manipulations, the Fifth Assembly of Experts was not composed of homogeneous hardline conservatives. While the Principlists obtained 38 per cent of the seats, the moderates took 32 per cent and the conservative independents 28 per cent of the seats. The hardcore hardliners were irate at the success of Rafsanjani's list, the 'People's Experts'. This list, composed of moderate and conservative clerics close to Rafsanjani, won 15 of the 16 seats in Tehran, even though it included seven members on the list of the conservative and hardline coalition.

It was embarrassing for Khamenei that two of his star allies and ardent anti-Rafsanjani protégés failed to enter the Assembly of Experts. Rafsanjani, on the other hand, received the highest vote in Tehran. Mohammad Yazdi, head of the Society of Seminary Teachers and the chairman of the Fourth Assembly of Experts, and Mohammad-Taqi Mesbah-Yazdi, the real power behind the 'Islamic Revolution Perseverance Front', failed to get elected from Tehran.

The election challenged Khamenei's design to keep the Assembly of Experts packed with members fully committed to him and his vision. Rafsanjani's emerging popularity disturbed and worried the Leader. During the elections, Khamenei had thrown his full weight behind the trio of Jannati, Yazdi and Mesbah-Yazdi and asked Iranians to vote for them, while Rafsanjani had opposed the three. The spectre of Rafsanjani's rise to power haunted Khamenei.

Rowhani's Very Bumpy Second Term in Office

For Rowhani, 2017 began with the ominous news of Rafsanjani's unexpected death. On 8 January 2017, the 82-year-old healthy and fit Ayatollah Rafsanjani was announced dead following a cardiac arrest. His body was found in the indoor swimming pool of the Kushk Building, in Shemiran, where he had his office. He frequented the private pool for his regular weekly swimming exercises. On the day of his death, he swam alone, without his bodyguards present and the surveillance cameras were out of order. Rafsanjani's family believed that his death was not natural and that he was murdered. Later, the level of radioactivity in Rafsanjani's body was determined at '10 times what is considered permissible'.[17]

Rafsanjani was an unmistakable clerical alternative to Khamenei. Aside from his role in the revolution, friendship with Khomeyni, and eight years of presidency, he was of the same religious stature as Khamenei and had been reborn as a symbol of reason and reform after the 2009 elections. Rafsanjani had sway throughout all state institutions, including the IRGC. His death was a blow to Rowhani, who was preparing for legislative elections, as well as the moderates, reformists, and conservative pragmatists. The only strong candidate who could have replaced Khamenei, and perhaps altered the course of the Islamic Republic, from within the system was dead. Khamenei and his hardline conservatives remained the big winners.

In the presidential election of 19 May 2017, Rowhani was the most well-known ticket among the candidates. He carried Rafsanjani's mantle and was riding on the wave of his successful closing of the nuclear deal, efforts to liberalize the political and cultural atmosphere and the prospect of more prosperous economic times ahead. The Iran nuclear deal had opened the clogged-up oil exports to Europe, resulting in a 30 per cent increase in Iran–EU trade between 2016 and 2017. Although the direct effect of these developments on the standard of living of Iranians was not immediate, the expectation for substantial improvements resulted in a resounding vote of confidence for Rowhani.

In this election, two clerics were the leading contenders, with two non-clerics, Mostafa Mir-Salim and Mostafa Hashemi-Taba, tagging along. The Guardian Council had barred Ahmadinejad from running for president again. The 68-year-old Rowhani, representing a coalition of reformists, moderates, and pragmatic conservatives, obtained 57 per cent of the votes. The runner-up, Ebrahim Raisi, age 56, representing the Principlists and Khamenei's implicit candidate, received 38 per cent of the votes. The election results seemed to indicate that the 73 per cent participating in the elections were either content with the status quo or believed in the system's ability to change peacefully. But, seven months later, the buoyant mood of Iranians turned sour and hostile. Iran faced an intense period of violent turmoil, protest, and rejection of the system.

The Enqelab Street Girl

Irrespective of inner-system rivalries, in the winter of 2017, signs of discontent and frustration were everywhere. On 27 December 2017, an unassuming 31-year-old woman stood on an elevated electricity box in Tehran's very busy Enqelab Street. Passers-by saw her defiantly standing almost like a statue, exposing her uncovered long black hair, holding a white headscarf on a stick and waving it like a flag. She was arrested for not complying with the Islamic Republic's headscarf code.

At first unidentified, the picture of the brave 'Enqelab Street Girl', Vida Movahed, went viral on social media and immediately became a new symbol of the women's long and hard-fought battle against forced veiling. Overnight, the cause of the 'Enqelab Street Girl' turned into a spontaneous movement as protesting women bared their hair. In February 2018, the unveiling protesters were attacked and 29 were arrested. Even though President Rowhani's Special Assistant on Citizen's Rights objected to the physical use of force against the protesters, the judicial authorities threatened the civil disobedience movement with 'inciting moral corruption', carrying a maximum of ten years in prison.

The Curse of Endemic Corruption

One day after the 'Enqelab Street Girl' challenged the Islamic Republic's 'legalized' discrimination against women's fundamental right to choose their attire, Iranians protested another structural defect of the Islamic Republic. For years Iranians had heard of officials and individuals at or well connected to centres of power misappropriating funds and enriching themselves. These centres of power included members of government, Majles deputies, high officials in the judiciary, mayors, prominent clerics, the IRGC and its financial holdings, the security apparatus, provincial governors, directors of banks and insurance companies and close confidants of the Leader. Politically linked economic and financial corruption and cronyism had become an endemic curse.

Over ten years, unprecedented numbers of corruption, bribery, embezzlement, and scam cases became public. They all involved the pillage of funds in the public sector and state institutions. Between 2011 and 2021, and based on 11 court cases, some $91 billion of primarily government funds went fraudulently missing. The most famous scandals involved scams and misappropriation of public funds in the banking sector, oil deals through private individuals, the Martyrs Foundation, the petrochemical, tourist and car industries, and fraud in the foreign exchange, sugar and gold coins markets. The sanctions added to the unaccountability of politically protected individuals and institutions, facilitating corruption.

The list of presumed corrupt personalities went right to the top of the ladder. In June 2008, Abbas Palizdar, an aide to the Economic Commission of the Seventh Majles and a supporter of Ahmadinejad, unleashed a national scandal. In a few public speeches, he named 50 high-profile state and religious officials and accused them of 'economic corruption', 'rent-seeking' and having connections with the country's 'economic mafia'.[18] Every once in a while, a few had been put on trial and given sentences, even death sentences. But to the public, the real perpetrators were systematically protected by centres of power, enabling them to act with total impunity and immunity to scrutiny and legal pursuits.

Revolting Against Corruption

On 28 December 2017, a few thousand people, men, women, children, and elderly, gathered at Mashhad's Shohada Square to denounce rising prices and the high cost of living. Among them were those who protested their loss of investment and fortune in three famous fraud cases. The three Mashhad-based entities, the *Caspian* and *Samen al-Hojjaj* Credit Institutions and the *Padideh Shandiz* Tourist and Urban Development Scheme, had embezzled money from hundreds of thousands of middle-income families, ruining their savings and livelihood. The three institutions had attracted depositors and investors with promises of exorbitant returns and then refused withdrawals or repayments. The religious, political and military ruling class were suspected of involvement in the three scam cases.

The crowd chanting anti-Rowhani slogans were summoned by SMS messages from circles close to Ahmad Alam al-hoda, the Friday Prayer Leader and Khamenei's representative in Mashhad. Hardline Principlists wished to weaken Rowhani and his government. Within hours, the crowd snowballed and metamorphosed. Slogans of 'Death to Rowhani' and 'Death to the high cost of living' were quickly replaced by angry cries of 'Death to the dictator!' and 'Death to Khamenei!' The Mashhad protests triggered a vast and spontaneous uprising against the system/regime in every province in the country. The government's first response was to deploy the anti-riot police and shut down access to social media.

For ten days, protests rocked 80 to 150 cities throughout the country. In some 40 cities, the crowds turned violent. Protesters communicated through social media when available and gathered at various city locations. The number of participants during the ten-day upheaval is unknown, but it may have been in the hundreds of thousands. Protesters were overwhelmingly under thirty years of age and with a high school education. They were from the lower middle classes, with access to cell phones, social media, the internet, Telegram, Instagram and overseas anti-regime platforms, sites and television programmes.

They were the new dispossessed and oppressed. Thirty-eight years earlier, the revolution had claimed to be speaking in their name. Pent-up political and economic dissatisfaction against the leadership and a complete loss of trust had brought about this unprecedented outpour of rage and loathing. The protesters demanded the removal of Khamenei from office and a different system of governance. Their demands were encapsulated in their chants, 'Death to Khamenei!', 'Death to the dictator!' and 'Principlists, reformists, the adventure is over!' The latter slogan ruled out solutions and change from within the system.

The leaderless and unorganized angry youth attacked and set fire to the Islamic Republic's political, financial, religious and military symbols. Government offices, provincial headquarters, banks, *Basij* headquarters, police stations and the office of some 60 Friday Prayer Leaders and 20 seminary schools were attacked and set on fire. The young rioters attacked the special anti-riot forces, law enforcement forces, the IRGC and *Basij* forces with stones and bare hands, and the government responded with water cannons, tear gas and gunshots. The clashes that lasted ten days left some 25 to 50 dead and 150 to 340 injured. Anywhere between 3,800 and 5,000 were arrested.

For Khamenei, the ten days of protests were 'a battle between the people and the anti-people, Iran with anti-Iran and Islam with anti-Islam'. He announced that the revolts were 'planned by the US and the Zionists', financed by 'one of the filthy rich states around the Persian Gulf [Saudi Arabia] and implemented by the 'Monafeqin

[Mojahedin] Organization'. In Khamenei's mind, the hardships and desperation of the people had nothing to do with the unrest. After ten days, the uprisings were repressed, yet society remained feverish and the Leader in denial.

Repressing Workers, Teachers, Environmentalists and Sufis

On 7 January 2017, workers of the Haft Tapeh sugar-cane factory in Khuzestan went on strike. Within a week other units of this major agribusiness joined. A wave of labor unrest followed as workers at Arak's Heavy Equipment Production Company (Hepko) went on strike, followed by the transportation workers at Esfahan oil refinery, workers at Tabriz Tractor Manufacturing Company and Mahshahr Petrochemical plant. The striking workers protested delayed wages of up to ten months. Between May 2017 and October 2019, Iran experienced some 8,200 labour actions, including strikes, sit-ins and marches.

> **Teachers' Actions**
>
> On four separate occasions over the 2018–2019 period—in May 2018, November 2018, March 2019, and May 2019—the Coordinating Council of Teachers Syndicates in Iran encouraged protests, which resulted in sweeping teachers' demonstrations across the country. These protests occurred in at least 55 cities and 16 provinces, as teachers decried low salaries, poor health insurance, and a lack of job security. Some also demanded the right to unionize and insisted that the Iranian regime release teachers detained in previous strike. (S. Jones)[19]

On 24 and 25 January 2018, the Intelligence Organization of the Islamic Revolutionary Guard Corps (IOIRGC) arrested nine members of an environmental group called the Persian Wildlife Heritage Foundation. The IOIRGC was a parallel intelligence unit under the command of a hardline cleric, Hoseyn Taeb, accountable to Khamenei alone. Fifteen days after the arrest of Kavous Seyyed-Emami, a prominent Iranian-Canadian academic and the founder of the Foundation, it was announced that Seyyed-Emami had committed suicide in prison. With the probable exception of the ruling class, no one believed the official suicide scenario.

A year later, on 30 January 2019, the surviving eight environmentalists appeared in court. Eight months later, on 24 October 2019, the Tehran prosecutor general announced that four of those arrested were charged with 'spreading corruption on earth', a sentence usually carrying the death penalty. The other four, were charged with 'espionage' and 'assembly and collusion against national security'. The Foundation was accused of 'infiltrating' the Iranian scientific community and acting as a front for the CIA and Mossad to channel sensitive military information.

Rowhani; his minister of intelligence, Mahmud Alavi; and Issa Kalantari, the head of Iran's Environmental Protection Organization rebutted the trumped-up charge of espionage against the environmentalists. Government officials testified to the absence of evidence indicating espionage. The IRGC Intelligence Organization, in harmony with the judiciary, insisted on their guilt, and they were given sentences of four to ten years in prison.

On 3 February 2018, followers of the spiritual pole of the Gonabadi Sufi order, Nourali Tabandeh, poured into the Golestan Street of northern Tehran from all over Iran. The devout Sufis feared the arrest of 90-year-old Tabandeh. The presence of large numbers of Tabandeh's partisans irritated the authorities and minor clashes broke out around his house. Tension rose until on 19 February, police and plainclothesmen attacked the Sufis protecting Tabandeh's house and violence flared up. The continued clashes led to the death of five law enforcement personnel and the arrest and beating up of some 300 to 500 Sufi protesters. A 50-year-old bus driver, trying to fight off the attack against Tabandeh's partisans, ran over three law enforcement personnel. Mohammad Salas, was arrested, put on trial, and executed on 18 June 2018. Another 40 or more Sufi protesters were given sentences of two to seven years in prison, 74 lashes and banishment for disrupting public order and national security.

Trump Pulls the Plug

President Donald Trump entered the White House on 20 January 2017. Trump had repeatedly referred to the Iran nuclear agreement as 'a disastrous deal' and had promised that one of his priorities would be 'to dismantle it'. Trump's threat to withdraw from JCPOA and force Europeans to abandon their deals and investments with Iran eroded Rowhani's position and significantly strengthened the Principlists. High officials in the IRGC welcomed Trump's threat of withdrawing from JCPOA, claiming that it would give them a freer hand to operate.

On 8 May 2018, against the counsel of his European partners, President Trump withdrew the US from the Joint Comprehensive Plan of Action (JCPOA), reimposing sanctions. By doing so, Trump vindicated Khamenei's conspiracy theories about the unreliability and eternal enmity of the US towards Iran. The US president's move also sealed the political fate of the moderates and reformers, who had relied on improving domestic economic conditions by reintegrating Iran into the international economy and subsequently rallying the people behind Rowhani's political and cultural reforms. The labours of Rowhani and his team came to naught.

> ### Beneficiaries of Sanctions
>
> Sanctions have also resulted in significant advances in the areas of missiles and other military-related technologies. It is estimated that IRGC control between 10–30 per cent of the economy, with large stakes in the oil and gas sectors, construction, telecom, banking, and tourism. One could argue that IRGC has been a major beneficiary of U.S. sanctions. (D. Laudati and M. Hashem Pesaran)[20]

By September 2018, foreign firms that had entered the Iranian market after the nuclear deal began pulling out under the threat of US retaliation. 'Thirty-one European and Asian firms in the Global 500 announced they would be leaving the Iranian market or hinted their exit was imminent'. The list included: France's Total, Airbus and PSA/Peugeot; Denmark's Maersk; Germany's Allianz and Siemens; Italy's Eni; Japan's Mazda and Mitsubishi UFJ Financial Group; and the UK's BP.[21]

By 2020, oil exports dropped to about 400,000 barrels from over 2 million barrels a day in 2017. In 2020, Iran's GDP registered a -6 per cent growth rate and inflation surged to about 36 per cent. The income per capita dropped lower than in 2005. High inflation rates and significant contractions in the size of the economic pie between 2018 and 2020 reduced purchasing power. The impact of lower purchasing power was higher on the middle and the lower classes.

> ### Consequences of Re-imposing Sanctions on Poverty
>
> The deepening economic crisis following the Trump administration's 'maximum pressure' campaign is evident in the sharply rising poverty rates across the country, from 8.1 percent in 2017 to 12.1 percent in 2019. The increase of four percentage points means that 3.2 million Iranians fell into poverty in two years. (D. Salehi-Isfahani)[22]

The Second Social Calamity

The return of sanctions turned the summer of 2018 into another intense period of social strife in Iran. Grievances and anger were waiting to erupt, all they needed was another piece of bad economic news. On 25 June, the Tehran Bazaar, for long a pillar of the Islamic Revolution, pulled down its shutters, protesting the economic depression, the high prices and the spiraling exchange rate of the dollar. The dollar on the free market more than quadrupled in price from 3,000 tomans in 2016 to 13,500 tomans in 2018.

The black or khaki-clad Robocop-style special riot police lined up in and around the heart of Tehran's traditional commercial district, subsequently charging the longtime supporters of the system with teargas and riot batons. Within ten days, similar protests by the commercial classes and ordinary people broke out against the rapid depreciation of the national currency in Karaj, Mashhad, Shiraz, Esfahan, Rasht, Qazvin and Bandar Abbas, among other cities. The incidents left behind two dead in Karaj and many arrested throughout the country.

On 1 July 2018, disturbances erupted in Ahvaz, Khorramshahr and Mahshahr as riot police attacked and tried to disperse crowds protesting the shortage of potable water and the saltiness of available water resources. Khorramshahr's pipe water project, contracted to IRGC's *Khatam al-anbia*, was delayed, and people were pushed to violence, demanding water. At the end of July, violent protests against the high cost of living and economic hardships erupted for about a week in Karaj and Esfahan, leading to attacks on public buildings, injuries and arrests.

Environmental protests, mainly related to water and pollution, were added to the people's long list of outrage, with some 260 cases between January 2018 and October 2019. The Leader and the ruling class insisted that unrests were the work of foreigners, spies and enemies. In June and August 2019, two open letters, one by 14 men and women political activists, and the other by 14 women activists, called on Khamenei to resign and for the Constitution to change. Out of 28 individuals, 13 were arrested and 1 was sentenced to 13 years in prison.

On Friday, 15 November 2019, the government announced the tripling of the price of non-rationed gasoline from 1,000 to 3,000 tomans per liter. The marked decrease in oil exports, and the reduction in government revenues forced it to tighten its belts. To compensate for the price rise of subsidized goods Rowhani had continued with Ahmadinejad's across-the-board Cash Payment Scheme, on which the needy had become highly dependent. The main problem with the Cash Payment Scheme under Rowhani was that the public continued to receive the same 45,000 tomans per person per month, that they received in 2010. By 2018, inflation had eaten into the real value of the 45,000 tomans cash payment and made it less than half of what it was in 2010, a mere pittance.

The response to the November 2019 price hikes was immediate, spontaneous, leaderless, and violent. Protests spread across the country, engulfing 29 out of 31 provinces. In Esfahan, which ranked third among the provinces with most incidents of clashes, confrontations erupted in 110 different locations. More than 200 cities, small and large, were embroiled in protests that invariably led to violent clashes. According to Yadollah Javani, political deputy of the IRGC, 'This event, with such a stretch and extent, was unique in the forty-year life of the revolution.'[23]

The November 2019 unrests were even more violent and radical than the December 2017 movement. Official figures put the number of participants in the almost two-week unrests at some 130,000 to 200,000. The first five days of the protests were the bloodiest, and the protesters' main target of rage was Khamenei. The protesters chanted slogans against Khamenei and set his pictures on fire. The system/regime responded by deploying riot police to disperse the angry crowds and shut down the internet throughout the country for almost a week. Internet access was gradually restored from 21 November 2019 after an almost complete blackout.

On the second day of unrest, the Leader backed the government's decision to raise prices and blocked attempts by the Majles to rescind the decision. He called the protesters thugs and hooligans. On the same day, 17 November 2019, a distraught Khamenei met with a handful of top political, security and military officials and said, 'The Islamic Republic is in danger. Do whatever it takes to end it. You have my order.'[24]

By the third day of upheavals, riot police and IRGC were shooting indiscriminately at angry crowds. The smell of gunfire, burning debris and teargas filled the air. The number of dead was estimated at between 304 and 1,500, and the number of wounded was between 2,000 and 8,500. According to Amnesty International, 'The majority of the deaths ... occurred as a result of gunshots to the head, heart, neck, and other vital organs indicating that the security forces were shooting to kill.'[25]

The participants in the uprising were more sociologically diverse than during the December 2017 outbursts although they remained predominantly of the lower and disenfranchised classes, the traditional bastion of the system. The protesters used stones, knives, and Molotov Cocktails. The riot police, *Basij* and the army, on the other hand, employed riot batons, tear gas, rubber bullets and live ammunition. The protesters attacked and destroyed 3,000 ATMs (automated teller machines), some 1,200 banks, 183 military vehicles, 140 government buildings, some 50 police and *Basij* outposts, 75 department stores, numerous religious centres, gas stations and buses. Protesters even attempted to occupy the Radio and Television Station in Tehran.

The gruesome events in Mahshahr, with a population of some 280,000, epitomized the ruthlessness of the system under siege. Mahshahr is an industrial and petrochemical county located in the south-western province of Khuzestan and composed of a mixed Arab and Fars population. Protests in five areas, mostly suburban poor, began on 15 November 2019. On the second day, demonstrators began closing the roads leading out of the city when they were shot at from the rooftop of a *Basij* headquarter, killing one protester. On Monday, 18 November, the protesters blocked all the exit roads. Contrary to other angry cities, government buildings, property or banks were not assaulted by the people of Mahshahr.

The protesters kept the sensitive energy roads closed for a few days, took control of five poor suburbs, and continued demonstrating. Heavily armed IRGC special forces accompanied by tanks, armored vehicles, and heavy machine guns entered the suburbs to end the protests and break their hold. Shots were exchanged between a few armed townspeople and the soldiers. A group of unarmed protesters took shelter in the marshes close by and were gunned down. The massacre of the urban poor by the IRGC left some 47 to 100 dead.

On 25 November, the government staged a pro-Khamenei counter-demonstration. The participants, numbering thousands, condemned the Leader's enemies and chanted, 'Death to America!' and 'Death to Israel!' The main speaker at the rally was the commander-in-chief of the IRGC, Hoseyn Salami. He announced the end of a war that had begun in the streets of Iran, which he attributed to a worldwide conspiracy against the country. The IRGC commander praised Khamenei as a 'divine man' who defeated the US in Lebanon, defended the Syrian people and freed the Iraqi people from the threat of disintegration, forging a Muslim community.

Two days later, Khamenei referred to the protest movement and announced that 'a deep, expansive, and most dangerous conspiracy, had been obliterated'.[26] But the protests had shaken the regime's confidence to the bone and turned a significant page in the history of the Islamic Republic. It made plain that the regime's social base was disappearing, and for Khamenei to hold on to power, he needed to rely on repression. Even lower and lower-middle-class *Hezbollahi*s were becoming counter-revolutionaries.

Rowhani's Nightmarish Final Months

In the twenty-one months between the bloody uprising of mid-November 2019, and Rowhani's departure from office on 3 August 2021, neither the people nor the president had a moment of respite. Mismanagement, poor governance, ineptitude and international adventurism produced catastrophe after catastrophe. The wedge between the people and the ruling class and within the ruling class deepened.

On 3 January 2020, President Donald Trump ordered a drone attack in Baghdad, Iraq. It killed seven people, including Gen. Qasem Soleymani, the head of Iran's Qods Force, and Abu Mahdi al-Muhandis, the leader of Iraq's *Hezbollah*, a militia founded by Iran's Qods Force in 2003. Soleymani was the strategist and tactician par excellence of Iran's regional expansion. He was an able and honest soldier to most Iranians, credited for keeping them safe from the Islamic State (ISIS). For Khamenei, he was an irreplaceable commander who had realized his dream of humiliating the US and its allies by exerting military control over Lebanon, Iraq, Syria and Yemen.

With Soleymani's death, Khamenei's only 'successful' project, that of uniting overseas anti-Western Muslims around the Axis of Resistance, was seriously threatened, if not thwarted. Having lost credibility, authority and legitimacy at home, Khamenei was dealt a severe blow with the death of his respected and liked military contact person abroad. Soleymani was more than a general. On 25 February 2019,

Bashar Al-Assad came to Tehran almost secretly to meet with and pay his respect to his saviour, Ayatollah Khamenei. Aside from members of Khamenei's Special Office, Soleymani was present, while foreign minister Zarif was absent.

Soleymani was the veritable foreign minister and military commander in relation to Lebanon, Iraq, Syria and Yemen. The Leader had vested him with plenipotentiary powers. In April 2021, when Zarif explained the delicate relationship between the military designs of the system in the region and his diplomatic efforts, he pointed out that Soleymani's priorities trumped all diplomatic considerations and determined all final decisions. Zarif believed that the system sacrificed diplomacy for military objectives in the region.

One day after the extrajudicial assassination of Soleymani, President Trump threatened to hit 52 Iranian sites, including cultural sites. Four days after Trump's bellicose comments, Iran retaliated. Under the code name, 'Operation Martyr Soleymani', the IRGC launched 12 missiles at American forces stationed at Ayn al-assad Airbase in Iraq. The attack at 1.30 am on 8 January 2020 lasted three hours and caused extensive damage to the military base. No one was killed as the US military had received prior warning of the attack.

After the attack on the US airbase, Iranian authorities were nervous about US retaliation and anxious about Trump's reaction. At 6.12 am, or about 102 minutes after the end of the Iranian missile attack, a Ukrainian International Airlines Boeing 737-800 took off from Tehran's Imam Khomeyni International Airport. The plane was heading to Kyiv with 176 people on board. Its passengers were predominantly Iranian-Canadians and Iranian students and academics travelling back to Canadian universities via Ukraine. Six minutes after takeoff, the airliner crashed, killing all on board.

The Iranian government's first reaction was that the plane crash was due to technical malfunctions. On the following day, Canadian authorities spoke about a missile having downed the plane. Iranian authorities categorically denied this theory. Three days later, on 11 January, Amirali Hajizadeh, commander of IRGC's Aerospace Force, admitted that the Ukrainian plane had been mistaken for an entering cruise missile and shot down accidentally by the IRGC. He explained that Iran had been at the highest levels of alert and had received information about incoming cruise missiles. Iranian high officials apologized and regretted the human error.

Less than two months after the bloody repression of the November protests, the ineptitude of the IRGC and the death of innocent people, including 83 Iranians, and 55 Iranian Canadians, caused another public outrage. On Saturday, 11 January 2020, right after the IRGC's admission of responsibility, university students demonstrated in Tehran, accusing the regime/system of 'lying' and 'deception' and called for the resignation of Khamenei as the Chief of the Armed Forces.

Similar demonstrations broke out in some two dozen large cities, with ordinary people joining in. The anti-riot police responded by firing tear gas at the crowds, assaulting and arresting protesters. Unrest swelled on Sunday and Monday as thousands took to the streets and the slogans became more violently targeted at Khamenei. After about six days, the protests abated. Tens were arrested and sentenced to prison terms and lashes. The judiciary, however, failed to put on trial or sentence those responsible for the shooting of the passenger plane.

As Iran was busy protesting the downing of the Ukrainian plane, the Guardian Council disqualified thousands of applicants to the 11th Majles. With the angry anti-system wave of protests, the Guardian Council, probably in concert with the Leader, decided to put aside all pretenses to the fake claim of free elections and eliminate all voices of dissent within the system. Dealing with both the people's opposition and dissenting voices from within had become unbearable for the ruling class.

The Guardian Council rejected the credentials of 6,800 candidates, among them 90 incumbent deputies, predominantly moderates, reformists and pragmatic conservatives. The moderates and reformists had no real candidates to run in the elections. Mostafa Tajzadeh, the prominent and vocal reformist figure who had spent seven years in prison after the 2009 election fraud, held Khamenei responsible for turning the elections into an appointment process. Tajzadeh tweeted, 'I will vote in an election, not an appointment.' Political activists, reformists and the public were in no mood for playing politics and boycotted the elections.

The Majles election outcome was predictable. Nationally, only 42 per cent of eligible voters participated, the lowest turnout in the history of the Islamic Republic. In Tehran Province, only 26 per cent of the eligible voters cast their ballots. The mild and watered-down reformists represented only 13 per cent of the deputies, with the pre-selected hardline Principlists obtaining a resounding victory. The president of the new Majles was the ex-IRGC commander and mayor of Tehran (2005–17) Mohammad-Baqir Qalibaf. In the new Parliament, the IRGC and the *Basij* were well represented with some 24 deputies, most of them holding high military ranks.

Iran was struck by the global COVID-19 pandemic between the first and second rounds of elections. On 18 February 2020, Iran announced its first cases, shutdown partially for about two months, and pushed back the run-off legislative elections from 17 April to 21 September. Amid a health crisis, Iran received another economic blow. In April 2020, Iran's price of heavy crude plummeted to $12 per barrel from $44 in February, with exports at an unprecedented low of 70,000 barrels per day.

Iran was experiencing cataclysmic days. As the pandemic peaked again in June, an explosion rocked the Natanz nuclear enrichment site on 2 July. The substantial damages, setting back the country's nuclear plans by several months, proved that despite Iran's claim of airtight security, the Israelis could strike at the heart of Iran's nuclear programme. The Iranian authorities admitted that 'advanced equipment and precision measurement devices' were damaged and destroyed.

In November 2020, Israel carried out another surgical operation near Tehran. In plain daylight, Mohsen Fakhrizadeh, a most discreet personality and always under very tight security, was assassinated by a satellite-controlled machine gun with artificial intelligence. Fakhrizadeh, an ex-IRGC member, was believed to have been the Executive Officer of Iran's covert nuclear weapons programme. The impunity of Israeli security forces highlighted the vulnerability of the IRGC and the security apparatus against their sworn enemy.

After the third coronavirus peak in September 2020, the health authorities announced that one person was dying of the disease every four minutes, and hospitals were running out of beds to treat new patients. By January 2021, Iranian officials reported 55,540 deaths due to the pandemic. Zero per cent of the population had been vaccinated, and it was generally believed that the actual number of deceased was twice the government reports.

On 8 January 2021, the Supreme Leader prohibited the import of vaccines from Britain and the US, arguing that they were untrustworthy, and that Iran would obtain its vaccines elsewhere. The Supreme Leader was hoping for the development of home vaccines and wanted to avoid the cost of importing Western vaccines. As the death toll soared and protests against the mishandling of the health crisis led to arrests, the ruling class became worried about another wave of social unrest. Six months after Khamenei's insistence on his resistance policy against all things Western, Iran approved the use of Western vaccines (Figure 12.6). By January 2022, the official death toll reached 131,620 and 71 per cent of the population had received at least one dose of the vaccine.

Figure 12.6 Supreme Leader Ayatollah Ali Khamenei (on screen) speaking during an online meeting with members of the Iranian Parliament in Tehran, 27 May 2021.
Source: Photo by ZUMA Press Inc. via Alamy.

In May 2021, the Guardian Council conducted a thorough cleansing operation of potential candidates for Iran's presidential elections on 18 June. The Guardian Council criminalized any record of political dissent and included it as a cause for barring candidates. The rejection of Ahmadinejad's credentials or that of Tajzadeh did not come as a surprise. But the system/regime continued to surprise its own supporters when news came that the former president of the Majles, Ali Larijani, a stalwart supporter of Khamenei, who had abandoned the Principlist camp and joined the pragmatic conservatives, was barred from standing for election.

After being besieged by the people, challenged, and contravened by his four presidents, each in his own way, the Supreme Leader longed for a loyal and obedient president and an equally devoted head of the legislative. He believed that a homogeneous ruling group, reflecting his visions, would solve the problems. Khamenei was tired of tolerating and paying lip service to the quasi-diversity of Islamic opinions and outlooks within the ruling class, an 'unfortunate' vestige of the Khomeyni era. He wanted a homogeneous group of individuals in power who would remain committed to his doctrine of an all-encompassing resistance at all costs. On 18 June 2021, only 48.8 per dent of Iranians went to the polls and elected Ebrahim Raisi, a cleric, as president. Rowhani handed over the executive to his successor on 3 August 2021.

In Closing

For over a century, from the Constitutional Revolution to the Presidency of Raisi, the Iranian people have demonstrated an enduring, and irrepressible desire for freedom, democracy, and the rule of law. In time this thirst has entered the Iranian DNA and broadened its reach. What used to be the dream of a few intellectuals familiar with Western ideas at the turn of the twentieth century has now become the popular demand of even teenage high schoolers in the Islamic Republic.

Iran's search for the holy grail of freedom has led this nation down a spiraling and at times convoluted path of trial and error, at immense social and human costs. Throughout their century-old struggle, Iranians have sought new answers to release them of their state of political and economic underdevelopment. Sometimes they looked forward and sometimes backward. Disappointed with the dysfunctionality, insecurity and fragility of their initial parliamentary experience, Iranians opted for an iron-fisted authoritarian system that would at least provide security and order. Even though Reza Shah ushered physical modernization and progress, Iranians found themselves stifled by political repression. Their reaction to years of foreign intervention and colonial manipulations was the oil nationalization movement and Mosaddeq's short-lived experiment with a democratic constitutional monarchy.

In the latter half of the twentieth century, Mohammad-Reza Shah's economically and culturally modernizing, and politically repressive rule gave birth to contradicting socio-political reactions. The flourishing middle class, the supposed new anchor of society, gradually came to adopt a love and hate relation towards Westernization. Some embraced and emulated it, while some rejected it and searched for answers in Islam. The politicized Iranian youth condemned 'Westoxification' and gravitated towards revolutionary Marxism and Islam, while those who had bought into Mohammad-Reza Shah's vision of a modern but repressive Iran enjoyed the cultural and social fruits of modernization, without the least loyalty to his absolutist monarchy. A large segment of the Iranian population, those left out of the modernization process, alienated, disaffected and discontented remained on the sidelines.

The 1979 revolution was another moment of national unity against oppression. Its major achievement was in ridding Iran of despotism. But once again the holy grail of freedom eluded the people. The political system of the Islamic Republic backpaddled, ignored its republican promises and replaced elective offices with appointed offices. It, too, like its preceding dynasties, one by one, stifled all attempts at reform, and started devouring its own children. The Islamic and revolutionary system re-acquired all those undesirable, arbitrary, arrogant, and undemocratic traits that it had so despised in the Pahlavi regime. Soon, Iranians turned against their own doing and returned to the streets to demand justice.

For more than a century, Iranian leaders who believed that they could forcefully impose their will on the people failed at cloning Iranians in their own image. From Mohammad-Ali Shah Qajar to Khamenei, unpopular and unrepresentative leaders succeeded at appointing loyal commanders and spending lavishly on the forces of repression in the hope of sustaining their rule. Concerned with a semblance of democracy, a sham democracy, they sought an executive, legislative and judiciary, dancing to their tune, forgetting that the people could see through their threadbare ruse.

Having gradually become obsessed with their sense of self-grandeur, these leaders distanced themselves from their people. Their paranoia with the incessant opposition of the people to their arbitrary and unjust rule has made them almost loathe their people for 'misunderstanding them'. From Mohammad-Ali Shah Qajar to Khamenei, Iran's rulers have come to live in a dream-like bubble, pretending that all is rosy. The Pahlavis believed Iranians had become modernized and Westernized and had abandoned their religion and traditions. Khamenei believes that Iranians are all in love with his Islam, the Islamic Republic and their Supreme Leader. He seems to think that the country enjoys freedom and democracy and is jubilant and flourishing. While Iranians did not like being pushed either towards Mohamad-Reza Shah's gate of the 'Great Civilization' or the Guardian Jurist's gate of 'Heaven', their presumptuous leaders blindly thought that they have their best interests and heart.

Each system, traditional, secular, or religious, became unresponsive to the people's basic demands and closed its eyes to the corruption, injustice and abuses committed by their appointees and functionaries. Each whitewashed its own transgressions and blamed the socio-political outcomes of its evildoings on foreigners and their domestic foot soldiers and mercenaries. One day it was the Soviet communists and the Black and Red conspiracy and the other, the American-Zionist atheists, liberals, and monarchists. The unrepresentative Shahs and Absolute Guardian Jurists neither accepted responsibility for the damage they incurred nor accepted that they were unwanted.

The Islamic Republic is sitting on an active volcano of amassed discontent. The unity of word and action created around Islam by Khomeyni to forge the 1979 revolution has long been lost and gone. The system has remained in power by ever-more ruthlessly repressing the recurring cycles of violent uprisings. The leadership is ruling over a fractured, dysfunctional, gridlocked and failed state. Ethical, cultural, social, political, religious and economic decay, deceit and corruption have permeated society, posing a monumental problem for future politicians concerned with Iran's welfare.

Despotic regimes are incapable of hearing and recognizing mass discontent, owning up to it, and analysing its root cause and are seldom amenable to reform. Their myopic narcissism leads them to believe that reform is a confession to mismanagement and the slightest admission of weakness and easing of the reign of terror would commence the domino effect of their departure. Iranian society, however, has always shown vital signs of life, zest, and vivacity. It has taken to the streets, downed tools, demonstrated, picked up arms, shouted and kicked whenever its fundamental demands for human rights fell on deaf ears. Iranians of all social categories and classes have not always reacted in unison, but when they did, they turned the tables and sent their unwanted leaders packing and running. In unison, they rid their country of the unwanted despots, but often found themselves bound once again and the vicious cycle of protest, repression and increasing violence followed.

But after more than a century of trial and error, the overwhelming majority of Iranians now know what they do not want and what they do want. Other than a constitution in accord with every little detail of the charter of human rights and approved by the majority, they will not stand for any dos and don'ts. They will celebrate the May 1968 slogan of Parisian students *Il est interdit d'interdire!* 'it is forbidden to forbid'. Only time would tell when the next uprising would change the tides and having tried a plethora of political systems, what type of government would they put into place this time.

Factual and Analytical Questions

1 Why did the Guardian Council reject Rafsanjani's credentials to stand for the presidential election of 2013?

2. How would you qualify Hasan Rowhani's 2013 electoral promises? Who was his target audience? How did his campaign discourse differ from Ahmadinejad's?
3. Was there a surge in organized labour, women and human rights activities between 2013 and 2021? Why did it increase, spread and intensify during Rowhani's terms in office?
4. Why were the 2016 elections to the Majles and the Assembly of Experts alarming for Khamenei? Explain what happened in each election and what the results indicated?
5. What were the roots of the 28 December 2017 uprising? How was it different from the June 2009 uprising?
6. What triggered the 15 November 2019 uprisings? How was it different from the December 2017 uprising?

Seminar Questions

1. Does the Supreme Leader control the IRGC or vice versa? Provide evidence for your argument.
2. 'Rowhani fell under the euphoric spell that he could push his moderate reform agenda and foster change without much resistance from the Leader.' Assess the veracity of this statement and provide evidence to support your position.
3. How can Khamenei's hot-and-cold attitude towards the JCPOA be explained? Provide examples of his support and his reservations towards it. If he believed in the deceitfulness and unreliability of the West, why did he give the green light for the signature of the JCPOA? To what extent did the hardships caused by the sanctions play a role in his decisions?
4. Who in Iran were the beneficiaries and losers of Donald Trump's decision to withdraw from JCPOA? Provide evidence for your arguments.
5. 'Israel's surgical operations against Iran on her proper soil, reveal real fault lines in Iran's security and intelligence system.' Discuss the veracity of this statement and provide evidence for your arguments.

Discussion Questions

1. 'Mohammad-Javad Zarif and Qasem Soleymani were symbols of Iran's nationalism and pride.' Discuss the veracity of this statement. In what ways were the two similar and different?
2. 'The cultural cleavage between the Leader and the youth becomes more blatant in 2014.' Discuss the veracity of this statement by providing historical evidence.

3 'The Leader and Rowhani promoted two different paths of dealing with sanctions and relieving economic hardship.' Assess the veracity of this statement. Support your arguments with historical evidence.
4 'With the death of Qasem Soleymani, the Supreme Leader's regional vision of the Islamic Republic at the head of the "Axis of Resistance" combatting the US is seriously compromised if not ended.' Discuss the merits of this statement.
5 What can be concluded about the Islamic Republic's state of mind and decision-making process from the shooting-down of the Ukrainian International Airlines Boeing 737-800?

Notes

Introduction

1. E. H. Carr, *What is History* (London: Pelican Books, 1987), 11.
2. W. Rybczynski, 'Waiting for the Weekend', *The Atlantic* (August 1991).
3. G. G. Gilbar, 'The Persian Economy in the Mid-19th Century', *Die Welt Des Islams*, 19, no. 1/4 (1979): 177–211, available at JSTOR online: www.jstor.org/stable/1569923 (accessed 23 February 2021). Statistics in this section are based on this article unless otherwise indicated.
4. E. Abrahamian, *A History of Modern Iran* (Cambridge: Cambridge University Press, 2008), 2; J. Bharier, 'A Note on the Population of Iran, 1900–1966', *Population Studies*, 22, no. 2 (1968): 273–9, available at JSTOR online: www.jstor.org/stable/2173024 (accessed 27 February 2021).
5. J. Bharier, 'The Growth of Towns and Villages in Iran, 1900–66', *Middle Eastern Studies*, 8, no. 1 (1972): 51–61, available at JSTOR online: www.jstor.org/stable/4282398 (accessed 27 February 2021).
6. E. Fakhrai, *Gilan dar jonbesh mashrutiyat* (Tehran: Jibi, 1352), 48.
7. Gilbar, 'The Persian Economy'.
8. For sources with an estimate of as much as 50 per cent of the population nomadic and only 30 per cent rural, see: A. Amanat, *Iran: A Modern History* (New Haven, CT: Yale University Press, 2017), 260.
9. Gilbar, 'The Persian Economy'.
10. A. Seyf, 'Commercialization of Agriculture: Production and Trade of Opium in Persia, 1850–1906', *International Journal of Middle East Studies*, 16, no. 2 (1984): 233–50, available at JSTOR online: www.jstor.org/stable/163101 (accessed 26 February 2021).
11. R. A. McDaniel, 'Economic Change and Economic Resiliency in 19th Century Persia', *Iranian Studies*, 4, no. 1 (1971): 36–49, available at JSTOR online: www.jstor.org/stable/4310077 (accessed 26 February 2021).
12. H. Katouzian, *The Persians: Ancient, Medieval and Modern Iran* (New Haven, CT: Yale University Press, 2010), 168.
13. S. Mahdavi, 'Irano-Russian Trade and Travel: Haj Muhammad Hassan Amin Al-Zarb and Others', *Iranian Studies*, 46, no. 2 (2013): 207–26, available at JSTOR online: www.jstor.org/stable/24482833 (accessed 26 February 2021).
14. A. Seyf, 'Iran and Cholera in the Nineteenth Century', *Middle Eastern Studies*, 38, no. 1 (2002), 169–78, available at JSTOR online: www.jstor.org/stable/4284215 (accessed 24 February 2021).

15. C. Elgood, *A Medical History of Persia and the Eastern Caliphate* (Cambridge: Cambridge University Press, 2010), p. 497; Seyf, 'Iran and Cholera'.
16. Elgood, *A Medical History*, p. 515.
17. Seyf, 'Iran and Cholera'.
18. S. Okazaki, 'The Great Persian Famine of 1870–71', *Bulletin of the School of Oriental and African Studies*, 49, no. 1 (1986), 183–92, available at JSTOR online: www.jstor.org/stable/617680 (accessed 25 February 2021).
19. Ibid.
20. Elgood, 517.
21. Ibid.
22. Okazaki, 'The Great Persian Famine'.
23. S. Yazdani, *Ejtemaiyun Amiyun* (Tehran: Nashre Ney, 1391), 97, 100–1.
24. Okazaki, 'The Great Persian Famine'.

Chapter 1

1. E. Browne, *The Persian Revolution of 1905–1909* (Cambridge: Cambridge University Press, 1910), 32.
2. G. Curzon, *Persia and the Persian Question*, vol. 1 (London: Longmans, Greene & Co., 1892), 480.
3. G. Jones, 'The Imperial Bank of Iran and Iranian Economic Development, 1850–1952', *Business and Economic History*, 16 (1987): 69–80.
4. Browne, *The Persian Revolution*, 50.
5. Y. Mostasharodolleh Mirza Yusuf Khan, *Resaleh-e yek kalameh*, 1287, 3, available online: https://static.wpb.tam.us.siteprotect.com/var/m_5/50/503/56100/631574-One_Word.pdf (accessed 20 July 2020); F. Akhoundzadeh, *Maktobat, namehhay-e kamalodolleh be shahzadeh jamalodolleh*, Entesharat-e mard azad, 1985, 11, 22–3, available online: http://cdn.zandiq.com/books/Maktoobat_Name_haye_kamal_odddole_be_shahzade_jamal_oddole.pdf (12 July 2020).
6. Akhondzadeh, *Maktobat*, 8.
7. Ibid.,15, 22, 76.
8. J. Jafarof, *Mirza Fathali Akhondoff* (Baku: Nashriyat-e Dowlati-ye Azarbayjan, 1962), 24.
9. Mostasharodolleh, *Resaleh-e*, 56, 61.
10. Ibid., 3–4, 6, 28, 37, 47.
11. A. Talebof, *Ketabe Ahmad ya safineh talebi*,(ba moqadameh va havashiye Baqer Momeni) (Tehran: Shabgir, 2536), 6–7.
12. Ibid., 125–7.
13. Ibid., 128.
14. Ibid., 195.
15. Ibid., 128.
16. Ibid., 202.

17. Z. Maraghehi, *Siyahatnameh Ebrahim beyg* (be kousheshe M.A Sepanlou) (Tehran: Entesharate agah, 1397), 124.
18. Ibid., 409.
19. Ibid., 520.
20. Ibid., 493.
21. Ibid., 121, 380. Maraghehi uses the Persianized term *parlement* (Parliament).
22. Seyf, 'Iran and Cholera', 169–79.
23. G. G. Gilber, 'The Opening Up of Qajar Iran: Some Economic and Social Aspects', *Bulletin of the School of Oriental and African Studies*, 49, no. 1 (1986): 76–89.
24. *Habl al-Matin*, 2–23 March 1905, cited by Ervand Abrahamian, 'The Causes of the Constitutional Revolution in Iran', *International Journal of Middle East Studies*, 10, no. 3 (1979): 381–414.
25. N. al-Eslam Kermani, *Tarikh Bidari-e Iranian*, vol. 1 (Tehran: Nashr-e peykan, 1377), 243–6, 256–60.
26. Ibid., 322.
27. Ibid., 364.
28. Ibid., 405.
29. Browne, *The Persian Revolution*, 115–16.
30. Ibid., 123.
31. *Habl al-Matin*, 28 December 1903, no. 17.
32. M. Etehadiyeh, *Maramnamehha va nezamnamehhaye ahzabe siyasie Iran, dar dorehye doovome majles showraye melli* (Tehran: Nashr tarilk Iran, 1361), p. davazdah.
33. M. Bayat, *Iran's Experiment with Parliamentary Governance: The Second Majles, 1909–1911* (Syracuse, NY: Syracuse University Press, 2020), 36.
34. *Habl al-Matin*, no. 114, cited in Browne, *The Persian Revolution*, 187.
35. Browne, *The Persian Revolution*, 159.
36. Ibid., 166.
37. A. Kasravi, *Tarikh-e Mashruteh-ye Iran*, vol. 1 (Tehran: Amir Kabir, 1363), 528.
38. Browne, *The Persian Revolution*, 200–1.
39. Ibid., 221.
40. V. I. Lenin, 'Inflammable Material in World Politics', *Collected Works*, 15 (Moscow: Progress Publishers, 1973), 182.
41. Lenin, 'Events in the Balkans and Persia', *Collected Works*, 15, 221.
42. M. Bayat, *Iran's First Revolution* (Oxford: Oxford University Press, 1991), 241.
43. Browne, *The Persian Revolution*, 248–9.
44. Bayat, *Iran's First Revolution*, 237.
45. Ibid., 241.
46. Lenin, 'Events in the Balkans and Persia', 230.
47. Kasravi, *Tarikh-e Mashruteh-ye Iran*, vol. 1, 891.
48. Bayat, *Iran's First Revolution*, 251–2.
49. Yazdani, *Ejtemaiyun Amiyun*, 79–84; S. Yazdani, *Mojahedine-e Mashruteh* (Tehran: Nashre Ney, 1388), 172–4.
50. Browne, *The Persian Revolution*, 316.

51. R. Farmanfarmaian, *War and Peace in Qajar Persia: Implications Past and Present* (Abingdon: Routledge, 2008), 220.
52. Bayat, *Iran's Experiment*, 114.
53. M. M. Sharif-Kashani, *Vaqeat etefaqiyeh dar ruzegar*, Be koushesh Mansureh etehadiyeh va Syrus Sadvandiyan, vol. 2 (Tehran: Nashr-e tarikh-e Iran, 1362), 376.
54. Yazdani, *Mojahedin-e Mashruteh*, 190.
55. Bayat, *Iran's Experiment*, 117.
56. Sharif-Kashani, *Vaqeat etefaqiyeh dar ruzegar*, vol. 2, 421.
57. Browne, *The Persian Revolution*, 345.
58. Ibid., 346.
59. Etehadiyeh, *Maramnamehha*, 6–8.
60. Ibid., 99–100, 107–8, 112, 116, 119.
61. M. Shuster, *Strangling of Persia* (New York: The Century Co., 1912), 236.
62. Bayat, *Iran's Experiment*, 217.
63. Yazdani, *Mojahedin-e Mashruteh*, 232.
64. M. Mojtahedi, *Taqizadeh va rowshangariha dar mashrutiyat-e Iran* (Tehran: Moasesseh Entesharat va chape daneshgahe Tehran, 1357), 162; B. Aqeli, *Ruzshomare tarikh Iran*, vol. 1 (Tehran: Nashr-e Goftar, 1369), 50 puts the date of this letter on 28 July 1910. See Sharif-Kashani, *Vaqeat etefaqiyeh dar ruzegar*, vol. 3, 869–70.
65. Yazdani, *Mojahedin-e Mashruteh*, p. 241
66. Ibid., 253.
67. Bayat, *Iran's Experiment*, 290.
68. *Majles showraye melli*, Mashruhe mozakerate dorehye dovvom, Shanbeh, 9 Rabi al-aval 1329.
69. Bayat, *Iran's Experiment*, 301.
70. Yazdani, *Mojahedin-e Mashruteh*, 264.
71. E. Browne, *The Persian Crisis of December 1911* (Cambridge: University Press, n.d.), 13.
72. Shuster, *Strangling of Persia*, 37.
73. Ibid., 69.
74. Ibid., 75.
75. *Majles showraye melli*, Mashruhe mozakerate dowreh dovvom, doshanbeh, 26 zihajjeh 1329
76. Shuster, *Strangling of Persia*, 242.
77. Ibid., 242.
78. Ibid., 183.
79. Browne, *The Persian Crisis*, 15.
80. Yazdani, *Mojahedin-e Mashruteh*, 277.

Chapter 2

1. M. Etehadiyeh (Nezam-mafi), *Ahzabe siyasi dar majle-e sevom* (Tehran: Nashr-e tarikh Iran, 1371), 60–1.

2. According to Naser al-molk he was 18. Mansureh Ettehadiyeh maintains that the shah was 18. See Ettehadiyeh, *Ahzabe siyasi dar majlese sevom*, 11.
3. M. al-saltaneh Hedayat, *Khaterat va khatarat* (Tehran: Zavvar, 1334), 270.
4. P. Sykes, *A History of Persia*, vol. 2 (London: Macmillan, 1921), 443.
5. M. al-dowleh Sepehr, *Iran dar jang bozorg (1914–1918)* (Tehran: Chapkhaneh bank melli, 1336), 163.
6. Wm. J. Olson, *Anglo-Iranian Relations during World War I* (London: Routledge, 2016), 81.
7. Sepehr, *Iran*, 175.
8. Ibid., 60.
9. S. McMeekin, *The Berlin–Baghdad Express: The Ottoman Empire and Germany's Bid for World Power* (Cambridge, MA: Belknap Press, 2010), 283.
10. O. Bast in *Didgah: New Perspectives on UK-Iran Cultural Relations* (London: British Council, 2015), 92.
11. *Majles showraye melli*, Mashruhe mozakerate dowreh sevvom, Jaleseh 52, Shanbeh 23 Shaban 1333.
12. Sepehr, *Iran*, 188.
13. Ibid. 229, 337.
14. A.-H. Sheybani (Vahid al-molk), *Khaterat-e mohajerat*, (be kousheh-e Iraj Afshar va Kaveh Bayat) (Tehran: Shirazeh, 1396), 22.
15. F. Kaveh, *Iran at War: 1500–1988* (Oxford: Osprey Publishing, 2011), 237.
16. Etehadiyeh, *Ahzabe siyasi dar majlese sevom*, 171.
17. Sepehr, *Iran*, 382.
18. J. Tabrizi, *Asrar-e tarikhi-ye komiteh mojazat* (Tegran: Majaleh vahid, 1352), 15.
19. Sepehr, *Iran*, 421.
20. Tabrizi, *Asrar-e tarikhi-ye komiteh mojazat*, 73.
21. Sepehr, *Iran*, 430.
22. Sykes, *A History of Persia*, vol. 2, 433–4.
23. Sepehr, *Iran*, 410.
24. Sykes, *A History of Persia*, vol. 2, 480.
25. Ibid., 486.
26. F. Safiri, 'The South Persian Rifles', PhD thesis, University of Edinburgh, 1976, 211–12, available online: https://era.ed.ac.uk/handle/1842/6926 (accessed 27 January 2023).
27. Ibid., 216.
28. Olson, *Anglo-Iranian Relations*, 202.
29. Safiri, 'The South Persian Rifles', 301.
30. Sykes, *A History of Persia*, vol. 2, 468.
31. Safiri, 'The South Persian Rifles', 252.
32. Ibid., 277.
33. Ibid., 265.
34. L. C. Dunsterville, *The Adventures of Dunsterforce* (London: Edward Arnold, 1920), 27.
35. Ibid. 78.
36. C. Chaqueri, *The Soviet Socialist Republic of Iran, 1920–1921: Birth of Trauma* (Pittsburgh, PA: Pittsburgh University Press, 1995), 73.

37. Ibid., 49.
38. Dunsterville, *The Adventures of Dunsterforce*, 28.
39. E. Mirfakhrai, *Sardar-e jangal* (Tehran: Entesharat-e Javidan, 1357), 75.
40. *Jangal*, yekshanbeh 19 shahr shaaban al-moazaam, 1335.
41. *Jangal*, jomeh 24 zihajeh al-haram, 1335.
42. Sykes, *A History of Persia*, vol. 2, 491.
43. *Jangal*, yekshanbeh 23 safar 1336.
44. Those directly named by *Jangal*, among others, were (Abdolhoseyn) Farmanfarma, Zel al-soltan, Naser al-molk, Amin al-molk, Nosrat al-dowleh, Sarem al-dowleh, Sheykh Khazal, Sepah Salar (Mohammad vali) Tonokaboni, (Hasan) Vosuq al-dowleh, Qavam al-saltaneh.
45. *Jangal*, panjshanbeh 10 rabialsani 1336.
46. Dunsterville, *The Adventures of Dunsterforce*, 59.
47. Mirfakhrai, *Sardar-e jangal*, 219.
48. The only dissenting voice is Mohammad Gholi Majd, who puts the number of dead at 8–10 million. See M. G. Majd, *The Great Famine & Genocide in Iran* (Lanham, MD: University Press of America, 2013).
49. T. Atabaki, 'Persia/Iran', in *1914-1918-Online. International Encyclopedia of the First World War*, available online: https://encyclopedia.1914-1918-online.net/article/persiairan (accessed 2 April 2021).
50. M. H. Donohoe, *With the Persian Expedition* (London: Edward Arnold, 1919), 92.
51. Sykes, *A History of Persia*, vol. 2, 519.
52. Dunsterville, *The Adventures of Dunsterforce*, 103.
53. Ibid., 123–4.
54. Ibid., 103.
55. Donohoe, *With the Persian Expedition*, p.117
56. Ibid., 118.
57. Sykes, *A History of Persia*, vol. 2, 515.
58. A. Afkhami, 'Compromised Constitutions: The Iranian Experience with the 1918 Influenza Pandemic', *Bulletin of the History of Medicine*, 77, no. 2 (2003): 367–92, available at JSTOR online: www.jstor.org/stable/44447742 (accessed 3 April 2021).
59. Ibid.
60. Ibid.
61. Olson, *Anglo-Iranian Relations*, 214.
62. Papers Relating to the Foreign Relations of the United States (FRUS), *The Paris Peace Conference, 1919*, vol. I (Washington, DC: Government Printing Office), document 285.
63. Olson, *Anglo-Iranian Relations*, 220–1.
64. FRUS, *The Paris Peace Conference, 1919*, vol. I, documents 284, 285.
65. Olson, *Anglo-Iranian Relations*, 218–19.
66. FRUS, *1919*, vol. II, document 677. At the time, Arthur Balfour was the British secretary of state for foreign affairs.
67. Olson, *Anglo-Iranian Relations*, 233.

68. Ibid., 228.
69. A. S. Hershey, 'The New Anglo-Persian Agreement', *American Journal of International Law*, 13, no. 4 (1919): 749–54, available at JSTOR online: www.jstor.org/stable/2187556 (accessed 10 April 2021).
70. Hershey, 'New Anglo-Persian Agreement.'
71. Ibid. Hershey was Professor of Political Science at Indiana University and a staff member of the American Commission to Negotiate Peace, 1918–19.
72. M. Habibi, *Interface France–Iran 1907–1938: Une diplomatie voilée* (Paris: L'Harmattan 2004), 181.
73. FRUS, *1919*, vol. II, document 677.
74. H. Katouzian, 'The Campaign against the Anglo-Iranian Agreement of 1919', *British Journal of Middle Eastern Studies*, 25, no. 1 (1998): 5–46, available at JSTOR online: www.jstor.org/stable/195846 (accessed 12 April 2021).
75. Mirfakhrai, *Sardare jangal*, 192–3.
76. Olson, *Anglo-Iranian Relations*, 244–5.
77. A. Nahidi-Azar, *Jonbesh azadistan, sheykh Mohammad Khiyabani* (Tehran: Nashr-e akhtar, 1379), 41.
78. A. Azari, *Qiyam-e sheykh Mohammad Khiyabani dar Tabriz* (Tehran: Safialishah, 1354), 182.
79. Ibid. 267, 269.
80. Ibid. 295.
81. Ibid. 460.
82. Hedayat, *Khaterat va khatarat*, 312, 317.
83. Ibid., 355.
84. Azari, *Qiyam-e sheykh*, 309.
85. Not to be confused with Nasereddin Shah's prime minister Mirza Hoseyn Qazvini Sepahsalar (Moshir al-dowleh).
86. Mirfakhrai, *Sardar-e jangal*, 249.
87. Twenty-five years later, Pishehvari founded the Soviet-supported Autonomous Government of Azarbayjan.
88. Mirfakhrai, *Sardar-e jangal*, 301.
89. Lord Ironside (ed.), *High Road to Command, The Diaries of Major-General Sir Edmund Ironside 1920–1922* (London: Leo Cooper, 1972), 157.
90. Ibid.
91. Amanat, *Iran*, 417.
92. S. Elahi, *Seyyed Zia: Marde avval ya marde dovvome kudeta* (Los Angeles, CA: Ketab Corp., 2011), 56.
93. Ibid. 60, 72.
94. Ironside, *High Road*, 117.
95. S. Blair Brysac, 'A Very British Coup: How Reza Shah Won and Lost His Throne', *World Policy Journal*, 24, no. 2 (2007): 90–103, available at JSTOR online: www.jstor.org/stable/40210096 (accessed 27 April 2021).
96. Ironside, *High Road*, 161.
97. Elahi, *Marde avval ya marde dovvome kudeta*, 79.

98. M. P. Zirinsky, 'Imperial Power and Dictatorship: Britain and the Rise of Reza Shah, 1921–1926', *International Journal of Middle East Studies*, 24 (1992): 639–63.
99. Elahi, *Marde avval ya marde dovvome kudeta*, 59–60. In his 7 March 1944 speech in the Iranian Parliament, Seyyed Zia refers to 200,000 tomans as the monthly allowance.
100. Zirinsky, 'Imperial Power'.
101. R. M. Burrell, *Iran Political Diaries 1881–1965*, vol. 6 (1921–1923) (Wiltshire: Archive Editions, 1997), 8.
102. Ibid., 136.

Chapter 3

1. *Kaveh*, 22 January 1920.
2. Ibid., 6 August 1921.
3. Ibid., December 1921.
4. *Nameh Farangestan*, Shomareh yek, May 1924.
5. Ibid.
6. *Marde Azad*, shomareh 12, 14 February 1923, shomareh 80, 20 June 1923.
7. Ibid., shomareh 11, 12 February 1923.
8. Ibid., shomareh 95, 23 July 1923.
9. Ibid., shomareh 88, 4 July 1923, 45, 22 April 1923.
10. Ibid., shomareh 104, 28 July 1923.
11. Ibid., shomareh 101, 22 July 1923.
12. Ibid., shomareh 88, 4 July 1923, 101, 22 July 1923.
13. Ibid., shomareh 120, 28 August 1923, 122, 30 August 1923.
14. Ibid., shomareh, 157, 31 October 1923.
15. H. E. Chehabi, *Culture Wars and Dual Society in Iran* (Amsterdam: Farman-Farmaian Family, International Institute of Social History, 2018), 27.
16. M. T. Bahar, *Tarikh-e mokhtasare ahzabe siyasi*, vol. 1 (Tehran: Jibi, 1357), 95.
17. Burrell, *Iran Political Diaries*, vol. 6, 136.
18. S. Cronin, *The Army and the Creation of the Pahlavi State in Iran 1910–1926* (London: I.B.Tauris,1997), 96.
19. Ibid., 98.
20. Ibid., 99.
21. Bahar, *Tarikh-e mokhtasare ahzabe siyasi*, vol.1, 152.
22. Burrell, *Iran Political Diaries*, vol. 6, 145.
23. K. Bayat, *Kudetay-e Lahuti* (Tehran: Shirazeh, 1376), 45.
24. Burrell, *Iran Political Diaries*, vol. 6, 153.
25. Bayat, *Kudetay-e Lahuti*, p. 107.
26. Ibid., p.77.
27. Burrell, *Iran Political Diaries*, vol. 6, 66.
28. Ibid., 122.

29. Ibid.
30. A. C. Millspaugh, *The American Task in Persia* (London: T. Werner Laurie, 1924), 45.
31. Burrell, *Iran Political Diaries*, vol. 6, 65–166.
32. Ibid., 210.
33. R. Rais-Nia, *Akharin sangar azadi* (Tehran: Shirazeh, 1377), 6.
34. G. E. Baldwin, *Planning and Development in Iran* (Baltimore, MD: Johns Hopkins University Press, 1967), 9–10.
35. *Majles showraye melli*, Mashruhe mozakerate dowreh chaharom, 20 Dey (Jaddy) 1301, Neshast 206, available online: https://mashruteh.org/wiki/index.php?title (accessed 25 August 2021).
36. Burrell, *Iran Political Diaries*, vol. 6, 145.
37. *Marde Azad*, shomareh 120, 28 August 1923.
38. Millspaugh, *American Task*, 200.
39. B. Aqeli, *Ruzshomare tarikhe Iran*, vol. 1 (Tehran: Nashre Goftar, 1369), 127–8; Burrell, *Iran Political Diaries*, vol. 6, 625.
40. *Setareh Iran*, shomareh 12, 9 Dalv (Bahman) 1302.
41. Burrell, *Iran Political Diaries*, vol. 7 (1924–1926), 19.
42. Ibid., 27.
43. N. S. Fatemi, *Aineh ebrat* (London: Nashre Ketab, n.d.), 355.
44. Mokhber al-saltaneh Hedayat, *Khaterat va khatarat*, 364.
45. Ibid., 366.
46. Fatemi, *Aineh ebrat*, 354.
47. *Majles showraye melli*, Jaleseh haft, Surate mashruhe majles, yome panjshanbeh 30 Hute 1302.
48. Mokhber al-saltaneh Hedayat, *Khaterat va khatarat*, 367.
49. Burrell, *Iran Political Diaries*, vol. 7, 53.
50. Ibid., 81. Every Indian crore was the equivalent of some 5.3 kilos.
51. M. Bahar, *Tarikhe mokhtasare ahzabe siyasi*, vol. 2 (Tehran: Amir Kabir, 1363), 110.
52. Some sources refer to 18 July rather than 20 July.
53. C. Ghani, *Iran and the Rise of Reza Shah* (London: I.B. Tauris, 1998), 259.
54. Ibid., 259.
55. Ibid., 337.
56. M. Purshalchi, *Qazaq, Asr Reza Shah Pahlavi* (Tehran: Entesharat morvarid, 1384), 189.
57. Baldwin, *Planning and Development*, 10.
58. M. Bonakdarian, 'U.S.–Iranian Relations, 1911–1951', in *The United States and the Middle East: Diplomatic and Economic Relations in Historical Perspective*, ed. A. Amanat (New Haven, CT: Yale Center for International and Area Studies, 2000), 9–25.
59. Baldwin, *Planning and Development*, 12.
60. E. Ehlers and Willem Floor. 'Urban Change in Iran, 1920–1941', *Iranian Studies*, 26, no. 3/4 (1993): 251–75, available at JSTOR online: www.jstor.org/stable/4310857 (accessed 31 June 2021).
61. Ibid.

62. J. Bharier, *Economic Development in Iran 1900–1970* (London: Oxford University Press, 1971), 176.
63. K. Mohaddes and H. Pesaran, *One Hundred Years of Oil Income and the Iranian Economy: A Curse or a Blessing?* (December 2012), 4, available online: https://www.econ.cam.ac.uk/people-files/emeritus/mhp1/wp12/100-Iranian-Oil-27-December-2012.pdf (accessed 15 June 2021).
64. P. J. Beck, 'The Anglo-Persian Oil Dispute 1932–33', *Journal of Contemporary History*, 9, no. 4 (1974): 123–51, availabe at JSTOR online: www.jstor.org/stable/260294. (accessed 15 June 2021).
65. Ibid.
66. Ibid.
67. M. Elm, *Oil, Power, and Principle: Iran's Oil Nationalization and Its Aftermath* (Syracuse, NY: Syracuse University Press, 1992), 38.
68. J. Bharier, *Economic Development in Iran 1900–1970* (London: Oxford University Press, 1971), 94.
69. Ibid., 195, 197.
70. D. N. Wilber, 'Architecture vii. Pahlavi, before World War II', *Encyclopædia Iranica*, II/4, 11 August 2011, 349–51, available online: https://iranicaonline.org/articles/architecture-vii (accessed 30 June 2021).
71. Ehlers and Floor, 'Urban Change in Iran'.
72. Ibid.
73. Ibid.
74. Bharier, , *Economic Development in Iran* 203.
75. P. Elwell-Sutton, *Modern Iran* (London: Routledge, 1941), 97.
76. Ibid., 133.
77. C. Schayegh, 'Sport, Health, and the Iranian Middle Class in the 1920s and 1930s', *Iranian Studies*, 35, no. 4 (2002): 341–69, available at JSTOR online: www.jstor.org/stable/4311478 (accessed 30 June 2021).
78. H. E. Chehabi, 'Staging the Emperor's New Clothes: Dress Codes and Nation-Building under Reza Shah', *Iranian Studies*, 26, no. 3/4 (1993): 209–29, available at JSTOR online: www.jstor.org/stable/4310854 (accessed 16 June 2021).
79. N. Nabavi, *Modern Iran* (Princeton, NJ: Markus Weiner, 2016), 86.
80. Hedayat, *Khaterat va khatarat*, 407.
81. Burrell, vol. 8 (1927–1930), 59.
82. Elwell-Sutton, *Modern Iran*, 126.
83. I. Sadiq, *Yadegare Omr*, vol. 2 (Tehran: Ketabforoushye Dehkhoda, 1354), 315.
84. Nevile Butler was counsellor at the British Legation in Tehran. Burrell, vol. 10 (1935–1938), 300.
85. Issa Sadiq maintains that the prohibition of veiling in schools was for the academic year 1313 (1934–5). Sadiq, vol. 2, p.306. This date does not seem correct given the chronology of events.
86. Sadiq, *Yadegare Omr*, vol. 2, 306, 314.
87. Ibid., 310.
88. Hedayat, *Khaterat va khatarat*, 373.

89. Burrell, *Iran Political Diaries*, vol. 9 (1931–1934), 436.
90. Hedayat, *Khaterat va khatarat*, 371.
91. Burrell, *Iran Political Diaries*, vol. 8, 39, 47.
92. Purshalchi, *Qazaq*, p. 347; Burrell, *Iran Political Diaries*, vol. 8, 53.
93. Hedayat, *Khaterat va khatarat*, 386.
94. Burrell, *Iran Political Diaries*, vol. 8, 281.
95. Ibid., vol. 9, p.436.
96. A. Matin-Asgari, *Both Eastern and Western* (Cambridge: Cambridge University Press, 2018), 95.
97. Horace Seymour was the British minister in Iran, 1936–9. Burrell, *Iran Political Diaries*, vol. 10, 300.
98. Ibid., vol. 11, 299. R. Bullard served as British minister and later ambassador in Iran (1939–46).
99. Burrell, *Iran Political Diaries*, vol. 9, 498.
100. Ibid., 654–5.
101. H. Katouzian, *State and Society in Iran* (London: I.B. Tauris, 2000), 319.
102. S. Cronin, 'Popular Politics, the New State and the Birth of the Iranian Working Class: The 1929 Abadan Oil Refinery Strike', *Middle Eastern Studies*, 46, no. 5 (2010): 699–732, available online: www.jstor.org/stable/20775071 (accessed 2 July 2021).
103. Ibid.
104. M. Reza Ghods, 'The Iranian Communist Movement under Reza Shah', *Middle Eastern Studies*, 26, no. 4 (1990): 506–13, available at JSTOR online: www.jstor.org/stable/4283395 (accessed 2 August 2021).
105. A. Mirsepassi, *The Discovery of Iran: Taghi Arani, a Radical Cosmopolitan* (Stanford, CA: Stanford University Press, 2021), 31, 57.
106. Burrell, *Iran Political Diaries*, vol. 11 (1939–1942), 298, 385.
107. Elwell-Sutton, p.166.
108. Burrell, *Iran Political Diaries*, vol. 11, 122.
109. Ibid., 376.
110. A. L. P. Burdett, *Iran, Political Developments, 1941–1946*, vol.1, 1941, pt 1 (Wiltshire: Archive Editions, 2008), 374.
111. Ibid., pts 2 and 3, 54.
112. Burrell, *Iran Political Diaries*, vol. 11, 434.
113. Ibid., 385.

Chapter 4

1. Burdett, *Iran*, vol. 1, pt 1, 392.
2. Ibid., 424.
3. Burrell, *Iran Political Diaries*, vol. 11, 618.
4. Burdett, *Iran*, vol. 1, pt 1, 648–50.

5. T. H. Vail Motter, *The Persian Corridor and Aid to Russia*, United States Army in World War II: The Middle East Theater Series (Washington, DC: Center of Military History, United States Army, [1952] 2000), available online: https://history.army.mil/books/wwii/persian/chapter02.htm (accessed 13 July 2021), 444.
6. A. Millspaugh, *Americans in Persia* (Washington, DC: The Brookings Institution, 1946), 5–60.
7. Burrell, *Iran Political Diaries*, vol. 11, 648.
8. FRUS, *1942*, vol. IV, document 232.
9. Vail Motter, *The Persian Corridor*, 34.
10. Ibid., 241.
11. M.-H. Khosrowpanah, *Sazeman afsarane hezbe Tudeh Iran* (Tehran: Shirazeh, 1377), 14.
12. Ibid., 14.
13. FRUS, *Diplomatic Papers, 1943, The Near East and Africa*, vol. IV, document 399.
14. Burrell, vol. 11, 631.
15. FRUS, *1942*, vol. IV, document 235.
16. Burrell, vol. 11, 623.
17. B. Tayarani, *Ahzabe siyasie Iran*, vol. 2 (Tehra: Entesharate sazemane asnade melli, 1376), 303.
18. Trott and Seyyed Zia met at Gaza on 24 September 1942.
19. I. Eskandari, *Khaterat Siyasi* (be ehtemam Babak Khosravi va Fereydun Azarnur) (Bakhshe Dovvom, France: Jonbesh Tudehihaye mobareze enfesali, 1366), 44.
20. Central Intelligence Agency, 'The Tudeh Party: Vehicle of Communism in Iran', 18 July 1949, 16, 19, available online: https://www.cia.gov/readingroom/docs/DOC_0000258385.pdf (accessed 5 August 2021).
21. Khosrowpanah, *Sazeman afsarane hezbe Tudeh Iran*, 20.
22. Burrell, *Iran Political Diaries*, vol. 12 (1943–1945), 56.
23. The number of candidates varies according to different sources.
24. Burrell, *Iran Political Diaries*, vol. 12, 82.
25. A. Milani, *The Shah* (New York: Palgrave Macmillan, 2011), 97.
26. FRUS, *Diplomatic Papers, 1942, The Near East and Africa*, vol. IV, document 222.
27. Ibid., *Diplomatic Papers, 1944, The Near East, South Asia and Africa, the Far East*, vol. V, document 487 (hereafter, FRUS, *1944*, vol. V).
28. Ibid., document 490.
29. The number of demonstrators varies between 4,000 and 35,000 based on different sources.
30. Khosrowpanah, *Sazeman afsarane hezbe Tudeh Iran*, 29–30.
31. Wilson Center, Digital Archive, Secret Soviet Instructions, 'Measures to carry out special assignments throughout Southern Azerbaijan and the Northern provinces of Iran', 14 July 1945, available online: https://digitalarchive.wilsoncenter.org/document/112018 (accessed 5 August 2021).
32. E. M. Mark. 'Allied Relations in Iran, 1941–1947: The Origins of a Cold War Crisis', *Wisconsin Magazine of History*, 59, no. 1 (1975): 51–63, available at JSTOR online: www.jstor.org/stable/4635007 (accessed 13 July 2021).

33. 'Memo Concerning the Azerbaijani Democratic Party and the Situation of Political Immigrants from Iran Living in the Azerbaijan SSR', 3 July 1956, History and Public Policy Program Digital Archive, GAPPOD, f.1, op.89, d.203. Obtained for CWIHP by Jamil Hasanli and translated for CWIHP by Gary Goldberg, available online: http://digitalarchive.wilsoncenter.org/document/120512 (accessed 12 August 2021).
34. 'Message from Bagirov and Maslennikov to Beria on Arming the Autonomous Movement in Iranian Azerbaijan', 21 October 1945, History and Public Policy Program Digital Archive, GAPPOD, f.1, op.89, d.[95]. Obtained for CWIHP by Jamil Hasanli and translated for CWIHP by Gary Goldberg, available online: https://digitalarchive.wilsoncenter.org/document/120542 (accessed 5 August 2021).
35. FRUS, *1945, The Near East and Africa*, vol. VIII, document 409.
36. Ibid., document 419.
37. J. Hasanli, *Faraz o forud ferqehe democratic Azarbayjan*, trans. M. Homami (Tehran: Nashr Ney, 1386), 110.
38. FRUS, *1945, The Near East and Africa*, vol. VIII, document 503.
39. Hasanli, *Faraz o forud ferqehe democratic Azarbayjan*, 123.
40. FRUS, *1946, The Near East and Africa*, vol. VII, document 274.
41. Ibid., document 306.
42. Ibid., document 395.
43. R. M. Burrell and R. L. Jarman, *Iran Political Diaries, 1941–1946*, vol. 13 (1946–1951) (Wiltshire: Archive Editions, 1997), 175.
44. Ibid., 101.
45. R. Rossow, 'The Battle of Azerbaijan, 1946', *Middle East Journal*, 10, no. 1 (1956): 17–32, available at JSTOR online: www.jstor.org/stable/4322770 (accessed 11 August 2021).
46. Burrell and Jarman, *Iran Political Diaries*, vol. 13, 380.
47. *Khandaniha*, 4 Mehr 1326.
48. M. Araqi, *Nagoftehha* (Tehran: Rasa, 1370), 26.
49. M. Navab-Safavi, *Barnameh enqelabi Fadaiyane Eslam* (Tehran: n.p., n.d.),.71.
50. The National Archives (TNA), Kew, FO 371/68705, 13 March 1948.
51. Burrell and Jarman, *Iran Political Diaries*, vol. 13, 512.
52. H. Ladjevardi, *Labor Unions and Autocracy in Iran* (Syracuse, NY: Syracuse University Press, 1985), 92.
53. Burrell and Jarman, *Iran Political Diaries*, vol. 13, 557.
54. D. Amini, *Jamiyat Fadaiyane Eslam* (Tehran: Markaze asnad enqelabe eslami, 1381), 175.
55. Burrell and Jarman, *Iran Political Diaries*, vol. 13, 615.
56. H. Makki, *Ketab Siyah*, vol. 1 (Tehran: Amir Kabir, 1363), 307.
57. FRUS, *1952–1954, Iran, 1952–1954*, vol. X, document 17.
58. Wm. R. Louis, *The British Empire in the Middle East* (Oxford: Clarendon Press, 1984), 682, 689.
59. Ibid., 651–2.
60. For details of the arguments and counter-arguments, see Keesing's Record of World Events (formerly Keesing's Contemporary Archives), Vols VIII–IX, September, 1952

Persia, Persia Page 12457, available online: http://web.stanford.edu/group/tomzgroup/pmwiki/uploads/3195-1952-09-Keesings-a-OEP.pdf (accessed 25 August 2021).
61. R. M. Burrell and R. L. Jarman, *Iran Political Diaries, 1941–1946*, vol. 14 (1952–1965) (Chippenham: Archive Editions, 1997), 223.
62. *Majles showraye melli*, Mashruhe mozakerate dowreh shanzdahom, 17 Shahrivar 1330.
63. *Besuye ayandeh*, 8 Azar 1329, as cited in Jami, *Gozashteh cheragh rahe ayandeh ast* (Tehran: Qoqnus, 1362), 585–6.
64. *Shojaat* (*Besuye ayandeh*), 26 Tir 1330, as cited in Jami, *Gozashteh cheragh rahe ayandeh ast*, p. 610.
65. TNA/FO 248/1514, 12 July 1951.
66. FRUS, *1952–1954, Iran, 1952–1954*, Vol. X, p. 299.
67. TNA/FO 248/1531, 28 July 1952, original underlining.
68. TNA/FO 416/105, 6 August 1952.
69. D. Wilber, 'Clandestine Service History: Overthrow of Premier Mossadeq of Iran', on 16 June 2000, the *New York Times* published PDF files of this secret CIA report on its website, available online: http://cryptome.org/cia-iran.htm (accessed 30 August 2021), 3.
70. Ibid., 42.
71. FRUS, *1952–1954, Iran, 1952–1954*, vol. X, document 271.
72. *Lend-Lease Act*, History.com, 4 November 2019, available online: https://www.history.com/topics/world-war-ii/lend-lease-act-1 (accessed 12 July 2021).
73. M. Gasiorowski, 'The 1953 Coup d'État against Mosaddeq', in *Mohammad Mosaddeq and the 1953 Coup in Iran*, ed. M. J. Gasiorowski and M. Byrne (Syracuse, NY: Syracuse University Press, 2004), 236.

Chapter 5

1. FRUS, *1952–1954, Iran, 1951–1954*, vol. X, document 325.
2. A. Rahnema, *Behind the 1953 Coup in Iran* (Cambridge: Cambridge University Press, 2015), 3–5.
3. Mehdi Akhavan-Sales, an icon of modern Iranian poetry, was 25 when the coup happened. In this famous poem, he immortalized the post-Mosaddeq mood of polarization and gloom. For a selection of Akhavan-Sales' poems, including 'My House is on Fire', see online: https://files.tarikhema.org/pdf/sher/Akhavan_salas.pdf (accessed 13 December 2020).
4. FRUS, *1952–1954, Iran, 1951–1954*, vol. X, document 326.
5. Ibid., document 327.
6. J. Waller, Chief, Iran Branch, Directorate of Plans, Central Intelligence Agency, 1953, FRUS, *1952–1954, Iran, 1951–1954*, vol. X, document 354.
7. *Khandaniha*, 19 Mordad 1333.
8. P. Mina, 'Oil Agreements in Iran', *Encyclopædia Iranica*, online edition, 2004, available at: http://www.iranicaonline.org/articles/oil-agreements-in-iran (accessed 10 November 2019).

9. J. Bill, *The Eagle and the Lion* (New Haven, CT: Yale University Press, 1988), p. 109, quoted from F. Fesharaki, *Development of the Iranian Oil Industry: International and Domestic Aspects* (New York: Praeger, 1976), 50.
10. Bill, *The Eagle and the Lion*, 109, quoted from J. Walden, 'The International Petroleum Cartel in Iran: Private Power and Public Interest', *Journal of Public Law*, 11 (Spring 1962): 51–2.
11. FRUS, *1952–1954, Iran, 1951–1954*, vol. X, document 466.
12. E. A. Bayne, *Persian Kingship in Transition* (New York: American Universities Field Staff, 1968), 66.
13. Burrell and Jarman, *Iran Political Diaries*, vol. 14, 507; TNA/FO 371/120712, 4 July 1956.
14. FRUS, *1955–1957, Near East Region*, vol. XII, document 315.
15. 'The Outlook for Iran', Digital National Security Archive, 20 January 1957, available online: http://search.proquest.com/docview/1679097286 (accessed 17 February 2017).
16. FRUS, *1955–1957, Near East Region*, vol. XII, document 308.
17. Bill, *The Eagle and the Lion*, 98.
18. Burrell and Jarman, *Iran Political Diaries*, vol. 14, 569. Russell was Her Majesty's chargé d'affaires in Iran.
19. 'The Outlook for Iran'.
20. *Majles showraye melli*, Mashruhe mozakerate doreh nuzdahom, 7 Aban 1336.
21. Bayne, *Persian Kingship*, 108.
22. Ibid., 107.
23. A. Ansari, *The Shah's Iran* (London: I.B. Tauris, 2017), 82.
24. *Khandaniha*, 13 Esfand 1336
25. Ibid.
26. FRUS, *1958–1960, Near East Region*, vol. XII, document 229, p. 542.
27. M. J. Gasiorowski, 'The Qarani Affair and Iranian Politics', *International Journal of Middle East Studies*, 25, no. 4 (1993): 625–44, available at JSTOR online: www.jstor.org/stable/164538 (accessed 9 September 2021).
28. Ibid.
29. Haj 'Ali Kia, Iranian Oral History Collection, Harvard University, Transcript 2, pp. 16–19. Kia was Iran's chief of army intelligence.
30. 'Iran One Month after the Iraqi Coup', Digital National Security Archive, 15 August 1958, available online: http://search.proquest.com/docview/1679098138 (accessed 7 March 2017).
31. FRUS, *1958–1960, Near East Region*, vol. XII, document 247.
32. Ibid., document 246.
33. Ibid., document 250.
34. Ibid., document 248.
35. Ibid., document 248.
36. Ibid., document 257
37. Ibid., document 257.
38. *Khandaniha*, 4 Mordad 1339; A. Shoja va A. Tayarani, *Asnad, bayaniyehha va sourate jalasate jebhehye mellie dovom*, vol. 1 (Tehran: Chapakhsh, 1394), 58.

39. *Khandaniha*, 25 Mordad, 1 Shahrivar 1339.
40. TNA/FO 371/157599 EP1015/6, 31 December 1960, classified under 1961.
41. 'The Current Internal Political Situation in Iran', Digital National Security Archive, 27 March 1961, available online: http://search.proquest.com/docview/1679123998 (accessed 14 June 2017).
42. *Majles showraye melli*, Mashruh mozakerate doreh bistom, 23 Esfand 1339.
43. 'The Reminiscences of Gratian Yatsevitch in an Interview with William Burr', 12 January 1989, Oral History of Iran Collection of the Foundation of Iranian Studies, 62.
44. NTS/FO 371/157609 EP1015/203, 6 July 1961.
45. Mizan Khabar, *Gharaz az tasise nehzate azadie Iran*, speech by Mehdi Bazargan, Mizan Khabar, 1961, available online: https://nehzateazadi.org/%D9%85%D8%AA%D9%86-%D8%B3%D8%AE%D9%86%D8%B1%D8%A7%D9%86%DB%8C-%D8%A2%D9%82%D8%A7%DB%8C-%D9%85%D9%87%D9%86%D8%AF%D8%B3-%D9%85%D9%87%D8%AF%DB%8C-%D8%A8%D8%A7%D8%B2%D8%B1%DA%AF%D8%A7%D9%86%D8%8C-%D8%A7 (accessed 18 January 2023).
46. FRUS, *1961–1963*, vol. XVII, *Near East Region, 1961–1962*, document 51.
47. Ibid., document 61.
48. Shoja' va Tayarani, *Asnad*, vol. 1, 544, 549–550.
49. 'The Reminiscences of Gratian Yatsevitch', 155.
50. FRUS, *1961–1963*, vol. XVII, *Near East Region, 1961–1962*, document 127.
51. Ibid., document 243.
52. M.-R. Pahlavi, *Enqelab-e Sefi* (Tehran: Chapkhanehye banke melli, 1345), 198–9.
53. FRUS, *1961–1963*, vol. XVIII, *Near East Region, 1962–1963*, document 85.
54. *Mardom*, 15 Bahman 1341.
55. Ibid., 1 Esfand 1341.
56. Mizan Khabar, *Iran dar astanehe yek enqelabe bozorg*, declaration by the Iran Freedom Movement, 3 Bahman 1341, available online: https://nehzateazadi.org/%D9%85%D8%AA%D9%86-%D8%B3%D8%AE%D9%86%D8%B1%D8%A7%D9%86%DB%8C-%D8%A2%D9%82%D8%A7%DB%8C-%D9%85%D9%87%D9%86%D8%AF%D8%B3-%D9%85%D9%87%D8%AF%DB%8C-%D8%A8%D8%A7%D8%B2%D8%B1%DA%AF%D8%A7%D9%86%D8%8C-%D8%A7 (accessed 18 January 2023).
57. R. Khomeyni, *Sahifehye emam*, vol. 1 (Tehran: Moasessehye tanzim va nashre asare emam Khomeyni, 1382), 145–50.
58. Khomeyni, *Sahifehye emam*, vol. 1, 153–4.
59. *Ettelaat*, 25 Esfand 1341.
60. Khomeyni, *Sahifehye emam*, vol. 1, 229–30, 238–9.
61. Ibid., 243–8.
62. FRUS, *1961–1963*, vol. XVIII, *Near East Region, 1962–1963*, documents 263, 279.
63. A. Alam, *Yaddashthaye Alam*, ed. A. N. Alikhani, vol. 4 (1353) (Bethesda, MD: Ibex, n.d.), 159.
64. FRUS, *1961–1963*, vol. XVIII, *Near East Region, 1962–1963*, document 271.
65. *Khabarha-ye hafteh*, Hezb-e mellat-e Iran, 9 Bahman 1342, va 21 Bahman 1342, available online: http://www.forouharha.net/ (accessed 8 October 2017).

66. *Iran-e Azad*, shomareh-ye 10, Tir mahe 1342 barabar ba juane 1963.
67. *Payam-e Daneshju*, Farvardin 1343.
68. Bill, *The Eagle and the Lion*, 163.
69. FRUS, *1961–1963*, vol. XVIII, *Near East Region, 1962–1963*, document 279.
70. FRUS, *1964–1968*, vol. XXII, *Iran*, document 6.

Chapter 6

1. Stuart Rockwell, Iranian Oral History Collection, Harvard University, Transcript 2, p. 12.
2. FRUS, *1964–1968*, vol. XXII, Iran, document 62. Phillips Talbot was the US assistant secretary of state.
3. Be ravayate asnade savak, *Rejale asre Pahlavi, Ataollah Khosravani* (Tehran: Markaze barrasie asnade tarikhi, 1396), 39.
4. *Ettela'at*, 13 Aban 1343; *Khandaniha*, 16 Aban 1343.
5. M. Zonis, *The Political Elite of Iran* (Princeton, NJ: Princeton University Press, 1971), 98.
6. K. Bojnurdi, *Khaterat* (Tehran: Sazemane tabliqate eslami, 1378), 16.
7. G.-R. Afkhami, *The Life and Times of the Shah* (Berkeley, CA: University of California Press, 2009), 427.
8. *Ettelaat*, 6 Farvardin 1345.
9. Committee on Foreign Relations, U.S. Military Sales to Iran, 94th Congress, second session, July 1976, p. 3, available online: https://ufdc.ufl.edu/AA00022204/00001/1x (accessed 26 September 2021).
10. Afkhami, *The Life and Times of the Shah*, 409.
11. Z. Shakibi, *Pahlavi Iran and the Politics of Occidentalism: The Shah and the Rastakhiz Party* (London: I.B. Tauris, 2020), 140.
12. FRUS, *1969–1976*, vol. E-4, *Documents on Iran and Iraq, 1969–1972*, document 62.
13. ibid., document 91.
14. Ibid., document 200.
15. Ibid., document 201.
16. R. Alvandi, 'Nixon, Kissinger, and the Shah: The Origins of Iranian Primacy in the Persian Gulf', *Diplomatic History*, 36, no. 2 (2012): 337–72, available at JSTOR online: http://www.jstor.org/stable/44376155 (accessed 3 October 2021).
17. 'Interview with the Shah by C. L. Sulzberger', *International Herald Tribune*, 19 March 1975.
18. Committee on Foreign Relations, U.S. Military Sales to Iran, 94th Congress, second session, July 1976, p .7.
19. R. E. Looney, 'The Role of Military Expenditures in Pre-Revolutionary Iran's Economic Decline', *Iranian Studies*, 21, no. 3/4 (1988): 52–83, available at JSTOR online: http://www.jstor.org/stable/4310605 (accessed 17 October 2021).
20. Ibid.

21. Alam, *Yaddashthaye Alam*, vol. 2 (1349 va 1351) (Bethesda, MD: Iranbooks, 1993), 152, 294; ibid., vol. 3 (1352) (Bethesda, MD: Iranbooks, 1995), 165.
22. Ibid., vol. 2, 21.
23. Ibid., vol. 4, 99.
24. *Ettelaat*, 12 Esfand 1353.
25. M.-R. Pahlavi, *Be suye tamadon bozorg* (Tehran: Markaze pajuhesh va nashre farhang siyasiye doran Pahlavi, n.d.), 250–2.
26. *Ettelaat*, 6, 8 Mehr 1349.
27. World Bank, 'Inflation, Consumer Prices (Annual %) – Iran, Islamic Rep.', available online: https://data.worldbank.org/indicator/FP.CPI.TOTL.ZG?locations=IR and 'GDP Growth (Annual %) – Iran, Islamic Rep.', available online: https://data.worldbank.org/indicator/NY.GDP.MKTP.KD.ZG?end=2020&locations=IR&start=1961 (accessed 2 October 2021).
28. R. Graham, *Iran: The Illusion of Power* (London: Croom Helm, 1979), 79.
29. R. Alvandi, *Nixon, Kissinger and the Shah* (New York: Oxford University Press, 2014), 171.
30. Graham, *Iran*, 87.
31. F. Kazemi, 'Urban Migrants and the Revolution', *Iranian Studies*, 13, no. 1/4 (1980): 257–77.
32. H. Mohtadi, 'Rural Inequality and Rural-Push versus Urban-Pull Migration: The Case of Iran, 1956–1976', *World Development*, 18, no. 6 (June 1990), 837–44.
33. H. Razavi and F. Vakil, *The Political Environment of Economic Planning in Iran, 1971–1983: From Monarchy to Islamic Republic* (London: Routledge, 2019), 83.
34. H. Pesaran, 'Economy ix. in the Pahlavi Period', *Encyclopædia Iranica*, vol. VIII, fasc. 2, pp. 143–56, available online: www.iranicaonline.org/articles/economy-ix (accessed 8 October 2021).
35. Alam, *Yaddashthaye Alam*, vol. 2, 313.
36. F. Pahlavi, *An Enduring Love* (New York: Mirmax Books, 2004), 234.
37. Ibid., 227.
38. Ibid., 146.
39. F. Moezi Moghadam, 'Kānunš-e Parvare-e Fekri-e Kudakān va Nowjavānān ii. Libraries', *Encyclopædia Iranica*, XV/5, pp. 504–5, available online: http://www.iranicaonline.org/articles/kanun-e-parvares-e-fekri-e-kudakan-va-nowjavanan-libraries (accessed 11 October 2021). Information on the organization in this section is primarily based on Moezi Moghadam's excellent series of article in *Encyclopædia Iranica*.
40. Be ravayate asnade savak, *Jashne Honar Shiraz* (Tehran: Markaze barrasaie asnade tarikhie vezarate ettelaat, 1381), 4.
41. Negin, Azar 1347.
42. *Ettelaat*, 31 Mordad 1356.
43. I am grateful for this neat translation of the Persian to Mina Ebtehadj-Marquis.

Chapter 7

1. A. Rahnema, *Call to Arm: Iran's Marxist Revolutionaries* (London: Oneworld Academic, 2021), 37.
2. Ibid., 44.
3. FRUS, *1969–1976*, vol. XXVII, *Iran; Iraq, 1973–1976*, p. 346, available online: http://goodtimesweb.org/frus/frus1969-76v27.pdf (accessed 29 October 2021).
4. *Bakhtare Emrooz*, Esfand 1350.
5. A. Shariati, Collected Works 34 (no publisher, n.p., n.d.), 66.
6. Ibid., Collected Works 13 (Tehran: Chapakhsh, 1365), 320–1, 327.
7. Ibid., Collected Works 2 (no place of publication, n.p., n.d.), 51.
8. Ibid., Collected Works 30 (Tehran: Chapakhsh, 1363), 24–5.
9. Ibid., Collected Works 22 (Tehran: Sabz, 1361), 25.
10. Ibid., Collected Works 26 (Tehran: Nilufar, 1362), 630.
11. Ibid., Collected Works 19 (Tehran: Qalam, 1361), 195.
12. FURS, *1969–1976*, volume XXVII, *Iran; Iraq, 1973–1976*, p. 5.
13. H. Showkat, *Tarikh bist saleh*, vol. 2 (Saarbruecken: Nashr-e baztab, 1372) 579–81.
14. FURS, *1969–1976*, vol. XXVII, *Iran; Iraq, 1973–1976*, p. 5.
15. *Amnesty International Annual Report 1974/75* (London: Amnesty International Publications, 1975), 8.
16. FRUS, *1969–1976*, vol. XXVII, *Iran; Iraq, 1973–1976*, document 118.
17. Human Rights in Iran: Hearings before the Subcommittee on International Organizations of the Committee on International Relations, House of Representatives, Ninety-Fourth Congress, second session, August 3, and September 8, 1976.
18. *Amnesty International Report 1977* (London: Amnesty International Publications, 1977), 291–2, 297.
19. *Khandaniha*, 26 Shahrivar 2536.
20. M.-H. Khosropanah, *Shabhaye nevisandegan va shaerane Iran* (Tehran: Nashre payam emruz, 1396), 154.
21. R. Khomeyni, *Sahifeh emam Khomeyni*, vol. 3, 170–2.
22. Ibid., 203–5.
23. Khomeyni, *Sahifeh emam Khomeyni*, vol. 3, 232.
24. Ibid., 234–2.
25. Ibid., 260–2.
26. *Ettelaat*, 9 Esfand 2536.
27. Khomeyni, *Sahifeh emam Khomeyni*, vol. 3, p421–3.
28. Ibid., 404–18.
29. A. Rahnema and F. Nomani, *The Secular Miracle* (London: Zed Books, 1990), 167.
30. Khomeyni, *Sahifeh emam Khomeyni*, vol. 3, 459–61.
31. C. Vance, *Hard Choices* (New York: Simon and Shuster, 1983), 325–6.
32. Khomeyni, *Sahifeh emam Khomeyni*, vol. 3, 464–5.
33. J. Carter, *White House Diary* (New York: Farrar, Straus and Giroux, 2010), 255.
34. Khomeyni, *Sahifeh emam Khomeyni*, vol. 4, 159–60.

35. Carter, *White House Diary*, 257.
36. *Khandaniha*, 20 Aban 1357.
37. Vance, *Hard Choices*, 332.
38. Ibid., 272.
39. Ibid., 274.
40. Ibid., 275.
41. Vance, *Hard Choices*, 335.
42. A. Qarabaghi, *Haqayeq dar bareh bohran Iran* (Paris: Soheyl, n.d.), 280.
43. Vance, *Hard Choices*, 335.
44. R. E. Huyser, *Mission to Tehran* (New York: Harper and Row, 1986), vii.
45. Khomeyni, *Sahifeh emam Khomeyni*, vol. 6, 10–19.
46. R. Khomeyni, *Hokumat Eslami* (no place of publication, n.p., n.d.), 4.
47. M. Bazargan, *Enqelab Iran dar do harekat* (Tehran: nehzat azadi-ye Iran, 1363), 78.
48. Qarabaghi, *Haqayeq dar bareh bohran Iran*, 464, 467.
49. *Ettelaat*, 1 Esfand 1357.
50. Ibid.
51. *Ayandegan*, 12 Esfand 1357.
52. Ibid., 11 Farvardin 1358.

Chapter 8

1. *Bamdad*, 5 Tir 1358.
2. Tarikh Irani, *Sourat jalesat showraye enqelab*, 19 Farvardin 58, 15/25.
3. Ibid., 10 Tir58, 24/62.
4. *Ettelaat*, 26 Ordibehesht 1358.
5. Tarikh Irani, *Sourat jalesat showraye enqelab*, 6 Ordibehesht 58, 7/40.
6. S. Behdad, 'The Post-Revolutionary Economic Crisis', in S. Rahnema and S. Behdad (eds), *Iran after the Revolution* (London: I.B. Tauris, 1991), 101.
7. Tarikh Irani, *Sourat jalesat showraye enqelab*, 9 Ordibehesht, 58, 14/40.
8. Khomeyni, *Sahifeh emam Khomeyni*, vol. 12, 202–10.
9. Behdad, 'The Post-Revolutionary Economic Crisis', 101.
10. *Ettelaat*, 29 Esfand 1357.
11. A. A. Saeidi, 'The Accountability of Para-Governmental Organizations (Bonyads): The Case of Iranian Foundations', *Iranian Studies*, 37, no. 3 (2004): 479–98, available at JSTOR online: http://www.jstor.org/stable/4311651 (accessed 27 November 2021).
12. *Ettelaat*, 27 Khordad 1358.
13. A. Shakoori, *State and Rural Development in Post-Revolutionary Iran* (London: Palgrave Macmillan, 2001), 83.
14. E. Ferdows, 'The Reconstruction Crusade and Class Conflict in Iran', *Middle East Research and Information Project* (*MERIP*), 113 (March/April 1983).
15. K. Ehsani, 'Survival through Dispossession: Privatization of Public Goods in the Islamic Republic', *MERIP*, 250 (Spring 2009).

16. Khomeyni, *Sahifeh emam Khomeyni*, vol. 10, 398–404.
17. A. Bani-Sadr, *Khiyanat be omid* (no place of publication, n.p., n.d.), 100.
18. Ferdows, 'The Reconstruction Crusade'.
19. *Keyhan*, 27 Bahman 1358.
20. K. Esmaili, *Hezbe Jomhuriye Eslami* (Tehran: Markaze Nashre Enqelabe Eslami, 1386), 54.
21. Ibid., 52–4.
22. *Ettelaat*, 4 Ordibehesht 1358.
23. *Bamdad*, 3 Ordibehesht 1358.
24. *Yadavar* (Azar va Zemestan 1388).
25. *Ettelaat*, 26 Khordad 1358, available online: https://www.bbc.com/persian/world-50269721 (accessed 5 December 2021).
26. Tarikh Irani, *Sourat jalesat showraye enqelab*, 1 Khordad 1358, 2/36.
27. *Ettelaat*, 20 Ordibehesht 1358.
28. *Keyhan*, 25 Ordibehesht 1358.
29. Khomeyni, *Sahifeh emam Khomeyni*, vol. 9, 280–4.
30. *Ettelaat*, 20 Mordad 1358.
31. Ibid.
32. Khomeyni, *Sahifeh emam Khomeyni*, vol. 9, 296–305.
33. IIbid., vol. 10, 388–94.
34. M. Rubin, 'Relearning the Iran Crisis' Lessons', *Commentary*, 4 November 2016, available online: https://www.commentary.org/michael-rubin/relearning-iran-crisis-lessons/ (accessed 19 January 2023).
35. *Keyhan*, 12 Aban 1358.
36. Ibid., 13 Aban 1358.
37. Vance, *Hard Choices*, 377.
38. A. Gheissari and V. Nasr, *Democracy in Iran and the Quest for Liberty* (Oxford: Oxford University Press, 2006), 95.
39. *Ettelaat*, 18 Ordibehesht 1359.
40. *Enqelabe Eslami*, 18 Ordibehesht 1359.
41. Bani-Sadr, *Khiyanat be omid*, 169.
42. Khomeyni, *Sahifeh emam Khomeyni*, vol. 12, 202–10.
43. Bani-Sadr, *Khiyanat be omid*, 127.
44. Khomeyni, *Sahifeh emam Khomeyni*, vol. 12, 248–52.
45. President Jimmy Carter, State of the Union, Jimmy Carter Presidential Library and Museum, 23 January 1980, available online: https://www.jimmycarterlibrary.gov/assets/documents/speeches/su80jec.phtml (accessed 23 January 2023).
46. W. Christopher et al. (eds), *American Hostages in Iran* (New Haven, CT: Yale University Press, 1985), 324.
47. Khomeyni, *Sahifeh emam Khomeyni*, vol. 12, 456–72.
48. Ibid., 490–501.
49. Bani-Sadr, *Khiyanat be omid*, 414.
50. *Ettelaat*, 21 Tir 1359.
51. M. Gasiorowski, 'The Nujeh Plot and Iranian Politics', *International Journal of Middle East Studies*, 34, no. 4 (2002), 645–66.

52. *Ettelaat*, 30 Tir 1359.
53. *Enqelabe Eslami*, 18, 19 Shahrivar 1359.
54. *Ettelaat*, 22 Ordibehesht 1360.
55. Ibid., 19 Khordad 1360.
56. Ibid., 3 Tir 1360.
57. Reuters, 'Execution of 149 Reported in Iran', *The New York Times*, 21 September 1981.
58. *Ettelaat*, 14 Mordad 1360.
59. Ibid., 17 Shahrivar 1360.
60. Ibid., 29 Mehr 1360.
61. *Jomhuriye Eslami*, 9 Aban 1360.
62. E. Abrahamian, *Tortured Confessions*, Berkely: University of California Press, 1999, p. 129
63. *Kar*, Aksariyat, 29 Mehr 1360.
64. Ibid., 22 Mehr 1360.
65. Ibid., 13 Aban 1360.
66. *Mardom*, 16 Aban 1358.
67. Ibid., 14 Khordad 1360.
68. 'Information about the Activity of Leftist Organizations in Iran', 4 May 1981, History and Public Policy Program Digital Archive, BStU, MfS, HVA, Nr. 6. Obtained by Roham Alvandi, available online: https://digitalarchive.wilsoncenter.org/document/134851 (accessed 5 December 2021).
69. M. M. Milani, 'Harvest of Shame: Tudeh and the Bazargan Government', *Middle Eastern Studies*, 29, no. 2 (1993): 307–20, available at JSTOR online: http://www.jstor.org/stable/4283563 (accessed 12 December 2021.
70. S. Khalkhali, *Khaterate Ayatollah Khalkhali* (Tehran: Nashre Sayeh, 1379), 405.
71. H.-A. Montazeri, *Matn kamel khaterate Ayatollah Hoseyn-Ali Montazeri*, Etehad nasheran Irani dar Euroupa, 1379 (2001,) 268.
72. M. Moaddel, 'Class Struggle in Post-Revolutionary Iran', *International Journal of Middle East Studies*, 23, no. 3 (1991): 317–43, available at JSTOR online: http://www.jstor.org/stable/164485 (accessed 17 December 2021).
73. *Keyhan Chape Landan*, 25 June 1987.
74. *Ettelaat*, 1 Bahman 1360.
75. Ibid., 11 Bahman 1362.
76. R. Wright, 'Iran Still Haunted and Influenced by Chemical Weapons Attacks', *Time*, 20 January 2014.
77. J. Ali, 'The Nonproliferation Review', Spring 2001, available online: https://www.nonproliferation.org/wp-content/uploads/npr/81ali.pdf (accessed 30 December 2021).
78. *Ettelaat*, 13 Ordibehesht, 29 Tir 1365.
79. Ibid., 16 Farvardin 1365.
80. Nehzate Azadi Iran, *Velayate motlaqeh faqih* (no place of publication, n.p., 1367), 97, 150.
81. Khomeyni, *Sahifeh emam Khomeyni*, vol. 21, 9–12.

82. *Ettelaat*, 14 Tir 1367.
83. Ibid., 29 Tir 1367/
84. M. Niyazi, 'Bazkhanie hokme tarikhe emame rahel pas az amaliyate mersad', Shabestan News Agency, 8 Mordad 1399, available online: http://shabestan.ir/detail/News/954591 (accessed 3 January 2022).
85. 'Iran Still Seeks to Erase the "1988 Prison Massacre" from Memories, Twenty-Five Years On', Amnesty International, available online: https://www.amnesty.org/en/latest/news/2013/08/iran-still-seeks-erase-prison-massacre-memories-years/ (accessed 3 January 2022).
86. Khomeyni, *Sahifeh emam Khomeyni*, vol. 21, 263.
87. Montazeri, *Matn kamel khaterate Ayatollah Hoseyn-Ali Montazeri*, 511.
88. Ibid., 511–12.
89. Ibid., 512.
90. Ibid., 520.
91. Khomeyni, *Sahifeh emam Khomeyni*, vol. 21, 330–2.
92. H. S. Esfahani and M. H. Pesaran, 'Iranian Economy in the Twentieth Century: A Global Perspective', Cambridge Working Papers in Economics, Faculty of Economics, University of Cambridge, 2008, p. 8, available online: https://www.econ.cam.ac.uk/research-files/repec/cam/pdf/cwpe0815.pdf (accessed 2 February 2022).

Chapter 9

1. A.-A. Hashemi-Rafsanjani, *Karnameh va khaterat sale 1368* (Tehran: Nashr maaref enqelab, 1391), 143.
2. Ibid., 292.
3. *Ettelaat*, 9 Shahrivar 1368.
4. Ibid., 27 Aban 1368.
5. Ibid., 9 Azar 1368.
6. Ibid., 8, 10 Bahman 1368.
7. Hashemi-Rafsanjani, *Karnameh va khaterat sale 1368*, 305, 314.
8. *Ettelaat*, 30 Mordad 1368.
9. Ibid., 12 Mehr 1368.
10. J. Etaat, *Entekhabat va nezarate showraye negahban*, Nashriyeh hoquq assasi, sale dovvom, shomareh dovvom, Tabestan 1383.
11. *Ettelaat*, 4 Esfand 1370.
12. Ibid., 16 Farvardin 1371.
13. S. Randjbar-Daemi, *The Quest for Authority in Iran* (London: I.B. Tauris, 2018), 90–1.
14. *Ettelaat*, 23 Tir 1371.
15. Ibid.
16. Ibid., 27 Tir 1371.
17. Ibid., 4 Tir 1371.

18. M.-H. Pesaran, 'Economic Trends and Macroeconomic Policies in Post-Revolutionary Iran', 2000, 2, available online: https://www.econ.cam.ac.uk/people-files/emeritus/mhp1/iran98_0.pdf (accessed 8 February 2022).
19. S. Maloney, *Iran's Political Economy since the Revolution* (Cambridge: Cambridge University Press, 2015), 213.
20. All quotes in this paragraph are based on M. Karshenas and M. H. Pesaran. 'Economic Reform and the Reconstruction of the Iranian Economy', *Middle East Journal*, 49, no. 1 (1995): 89–111, available at JSTOR online: http://www.jstor.org/stable/4328773 (accessed 7 September 2022).
21. All quotes in this paragraph are from A. Bayat, 'Squatters and the State', *MERIP*, 191 (November–December 1994).
22. A. Keshavarzian, *Bazaar and State in Iran* (Cambridge: Cambridge University Press, 2007), 155. Keshavarzian's Islamic Coalition Association (ICA) is the same as the Islamic Coalition of Mourning Groups (ICMG).
23. Markaz asnad ayatollah Hashemi-Rafsanjani, Namaz jomeh Tehran be emamate ayatollah Hashemi-Rafsanjani, jomeh 16 Esfand 1370.
24. A well-placed person could obtain a dollar for 1750 rials and sell it on the free market at the market rate of 4030 rials and make 2280 rials by the grace of political connections.
25. P. Alizadeh, 'Iran's Quandary: Economic Reforms and the "Structural Trap"', *Brown Journal of World Affairs*, 9, no. 2 (2003): 267–81, available online: http://www.jstor.org/stable/24590483 (20 December 2021).
26. *Ettelaat*, 18 Khordad 1372.
27. Ibid., 11 Tir 1371.
28. Ibid., 30 Mehr 1371.
29. M. Moslem, *Factional Politics in Post-Khomeini Iran* (Syracuse, NY: Syracuse University Press, 2002), 214; *Ettelaat*, 21 Mordad 1371.
30. *Resalat*, 29 Farvardin 1374.
31. L. Secor, *Children of Paradise: The Struggle for the Soul of Iran* (New York: Allen Lane, 2016), 219.
32. Ibid., 221.
33. K. Ehsani, 'Municipal Matters', *MERIP*, 212 (Fall 1999).
34. Tarikh Irani, Marashi: hashemi porsid nazar Karbaschi dar mored gol chist?, available online: http://tarikhirani.ir/fa/news/3523/ (accessed 18 February 2022).
35. *Ettelaat*, 9 Esfand 1374.
36. Ibid., 28 Dey 1374.
37. Ibid., 22 Farvardin 1375.
38. Ibid., 12 Shahrivar 1375.
39. 'West Powerless to Back Suspicion with Firm Action', *Scotsman*, 11 April 1997.
40. Alan Cowell, 'The Berlin Court Says Top Iran Leaders Ordered Killings', *New York Times*, 11 April 1997; H. Musaviyan, *Chaleshhaye ravabet Iran va gharb, barrasiye ravabet Iran va Alman* (Tehran: Markaze tahqiqat estretejik, 1385), 131, 213, 225. Musaviyan was the Iranian ambassador to Germany (1990–7).
41. Musaviyan, 224.

42. Maloney, *Iran's Political Economy*, 452.
43. Ibid., 453.
44. *Avaetabid*, Zemestan 1398, Shomareh 13.
45. F. Sarkoohi, *Yas va Das* (Sweden: Baran, 2002), 148.
46. V. Vakili, *Debating Religion and Politics in Iran: The Political Thought of Abdolkarim Soroush* (New York: Council on Foreign Relations, 1996).

Chapter 10

1. *Ettelaat*, 15 Bahman 1375, 1, 4, 8, 9, 16, 28 Esfand 1375.
2. Randjbar-Daemi, *The Quest for Authority in Iran*, 120.
3. President Clinton's speech, 'Press Conference by the President and Prime Minister Blair', Whhite House, 29 May 1997, available online: https://clintonwhitehouse5.archives.gov/WH/New/Europe/19970530-3336.html (accessed 21 January 2022).
4. *Ettelaat*, 30 Mordad 1376.
5. Ibid., 30 Mordad 1376.
6. Ibid., 27 Shahrivar 1376, 1 Mehr 1376.
7. Ibid., 13 Dey 1376.
8. Ibid., 26 Aban 1376.
9. Ibid., 28 Aban 1376.
10. Ibid., 27 Aban 1376.
11. Ibid., 18 Dey 1376, http://edition.cnn.com/WORLD/9801/07/iran/interview.html (accessed 2 March 2022).
12. *Ettelaat*, 27 Bahman 1376.
13. Ibid., 27 Dey 1376.
14. Ibid., 16 Bahman 1376.
15. *Tus*, 5 Mordad 1377.
16. *Ettelaat*, 3 Mordad 1377.
17. *Jameeh*, 5 Khordad 1377.
18. *Ettelaat*, 10 Tir, 1377.
19. Ibid., 1 Tir 1377.
20. *Hamshahri*, 1 Tir 1377.
21. *Mobin*, 31 Mordad 1377.
22. M. Kadivar, 'Negahi be karnameh bist saleh jomhuriye Eslami', *Khordad*, 25, 26, 27 Bahman 1377, available online: https://kadivar.com/780/#_ftn1 (accessed 8 March 2022).
23. A. Nuri, *Shokaran Eslah* (Tehran: Tarhe No, 1379), 23, 25, 59–66.
24. The name remains a mystery. If by Navab, this new extremist group was alluding to Mojtaba Navab Safavi, the leader of the old *Fadaiyane Eslam*, then their error of calling him Mohammad Mostafa goes to show their ignorance of Iran's religio-political history.
25. *Rahe No*, 10 Mordad 1377.

26. Interrogation reports of Mehrdad Alikhani, MelliunIran, n.d., available online: https://melliun.org/simayenezam/s09/01/31marzp.htm (accessed 9 March 2022).
27. *Ettelaat*, 16 Dey 1377.
28. Ibid., 20 Dey 1377.
29. *Jameeh*, 10 Ordibehesht 1377.
30. Ibid., 13 Khordad 1377.
31. *Tus*, 3 Mordad 1377.
32. *Neshat*, 1 Esfand 1377.
33. *Asre Ma*, 16 Tir 1378.
34. *Neshat*, 21 Tir 1378.
35. *Ettelaat*, 22 Tir 1378.
36. Ibid., 23 Tir 1378.
37. *Asre ma*, 30 Tir 1378, for the full text see online: https://web.archive.org/web/20090611044911/http://www.aftabnews.ir/vdcftjydw6de.html (accessed 13 March 2022).
38. *Ettelaat*, 11 Shahrivar 1378.
39. *Neshat*, 12 Shahrivar 1378.
40. *Ettelaat*, 14 Shahrivar 1378.
41. Ibid., 13 Shahrivar 1378.
42. Ibid., 15 Shahrivar 1378.
43. *Shalamcheh*, 8 Azar 1377.
44. E. Sadeghi-Boroujerdi, *Revolution and Its Discontent* (Cambridge: Cambridge University Press, 2020), 340.
45. *Ettelaat*, 23 Farvardin 1378.
46. Ibid.
47. Ibid., 26 Farvardin 1378.
48. Ibid., 29 Farvardin 1379.
49. Ibid., 3 Ordibehesht 1379.
50. *Bahar*, 7 Tir 1379.
51. Ibid., 30 Khordad 1379.
52. *Ettelaat*, 8 Tir 1379.
53. Ibid.
54. Ibid., 20 Tir 1379.
55. *Bahar*, 29 Tir 1379.
56. Ibid., 17 Mordad 1379; *Ettelaat*, 16 Mordad 1379.
57. A. Ansari, *Iran, Islam and Democracy: The Politics of Managing Change* (London: Gingko Library, 2019), 233.
58. *Ettelaat*, 22 Farvardin 1380.
59. Ibid., 19 Mehr 1380.
60. Ibid., 24 Mehr 1380.
61. Ibid., 26 Mehr 1380.
62. Ibid., 30 Mehr 1380.
63. *Bahar*, 26 Ordibehesht 1379.
64. Ibid., 23 Bahman 1378, 10 Esfand 1378, 17 Farvardin 1379, 14 Ordibehesht 1379, 2, 16 Khordad 1379, 7 Tir 1379.

65. *Ettelaat*, 21 Farvardin 1380.
66. Ibid., 11 Mordad 1380.
67. Open letter to Khamenei by 135 MPs of the 6th Majles (explanations are in the text), Mashregh News, 31 Ordibehesht 1381, available online: https://cdn.mashreghnews.ir/d/2019/07/09/0/2552193.pdf (accessed 23 March 2022).
68. *Ettelaat*, 2 Khordad 1381.
69. Ibid., 6 Shahrivar 1381.
70. Showraye Negahban, 'Layeheh eslah qanun entekhabat entejhabat majles showraye eslami' (The Bill to Reform Elections to the Islamic Parliament, presented by the Government to the Parliament [Majles]), 20 Mordad 1381, available online: http://nazarat.shora-rc.ir/Forms/FileLoad.aspx?id=8ncV7rDqhXQ=&TN=l7tLyhyOobj0SooAFUE3m9d5XYGi044i6e4f+1NCQCI=&NF=bHiIRfspeW0= (accessed 22 March 2022).
71. *Ettelaat*, 1 Khordad 1382.
72. 'Majles sheshom nabayad tekrar shaved', speech by Ayatollah M. A. Movahedi-Kermani, 30 Mordad 1394, available online: https://www.jahannews.com/analysis/ (22 March 2022).
73. *Ettelaat*, 27 Dey 1382.
74. Ibid., 12 Bahman 1382.
75. Ibid., 16 Bahman 1382.
76. Ibid., 3 Esfand 1382.
77. Statement by H. E. Mohammad Khatami, President of the Islamic Republic of Iran before the 53rd Session of the United Nations General Assembly, New York, 21 September 1998, *Pars Times*, available online: http://www.parstimes.com/history/khatami_speech_un.html (accessed 4 April 2022).
78. R. Fiedler, 'Iran and the European Union after the Nuclear Deal', *CES Working Papers*, ISSN 2067-7693, Alexandru Ioan Cuza University of Iasi, Centre for European Studies, Iasi, Vol. 10, no. 3 (2018): 291–305.
79. 'U.S. Wrestlers Venture into Tehran's Streets and Receive Warm Welcome, *Chicago Tribune*, 19 February 1998.
80. *Bahar*, 10 Mordad 1379.
81. 'Iran Agrees to Temporarily Suspend Uranium-Enrichment Program', available online: https://www.armscontrol.org/act/2004-12/iran-nuclear-briefs/iran-agrees-temporarily-suspend-uranium-e.nrichment-program (accessed 25 March 2022).
82. *Ettelaat*, 24 Esfand 1376.
83. Bill Samii, Fatemeh Aman and Maryam Ahmadi, 'Iran: Khatami Receives Mixed Marks for His Economic and Political Legacies', RadioFreeEurope and RadioLiberty, 4 August 2005, available online: https://www.rferl.org/a/1060400.html (accessed 28 March 2022).
84. 'Taqdime projehhaye Tehran be Khatam', Eqtesad News, 18 Mehr 1400, available online: https://www.eghtesadnews.com/.
85. *Ettelaat*, 13 Mehr 1383; 'Majles Iran ray be barkenariye vazir rah dad', Persian BBC, 3 October 2004, available online: https://www.bbc.com/persian/iran/story/2004/10/041003_he-censure (accessed 27 March 2022).

Chapter 11

1. *Hamshahri*, 11 Bahman 1383, 25 Esfand 1383, 14 Farvardin 1384.
2. Ibid., 25 Esfand 1383.
3. Ibid., 14, 26, 27 Bahman 1383, 22 Esfand 1383, 4 Khordad 1384. *Ya Lesarat*, 30 Dey 1383, 19 Esfand 1383.
4. *Ya Lesarat*, 30 Dey 1383.
5. *Hamshahri*, 17, 18 Khordad 1384.
6. Ibid., 7 Khordad 1384.
7. Ibid., 21 Khordad 1384.
8. *Partove Sokhan*, 7 Bahman 1383.
9. R. Sanati, *Goftoman Mesbah* (Tehran: Markaz asnade enqelabe eslami, 1387), 191.
10. *Ettelaat*, 28, 29 Khordad 1384.
11. Sanati, *Goftoman Mesbah*, 893.
12. *Partov Sokhan*, 7 Bahman 1383, 8, 15 Tir 1384. Sanati, *Goftoman Mesbah*, 862.
13. *Ettelaat*, 29 Mordad 1384.
14. Ibid., 10, 19 Shahrivar 1384.
15. Khamenei, IR (Islamic Republic), Speech to the Minister of Interior and Governors General, 27 February 2006, available online: https://farsi.khamenei.ir/speech-content?id=3331 (accessed 23 April 2022).
16. *Ettelaat*, 30 Mehr 1384.
17. S. J. Hadley, 'Iran Primer: The George W. Bush Administration', Frontline Tehran Bureau, 3 November 2010, available online: https://www.pbs.org/wgbh/pages/frontline/tehranbureau/2010/11/iran-primer-the-george-w-bush-administration.html (accessed 18 April 2022).
18. A. Rahnema, *Superstition as Ideology in Iranian Politics* (Cambridge: Cambridge University Press, 2011), 37–42.
19. *Sharq*, 23 Azar 1384.
20. Rahnema, *Superstition as Ideology*, 54–6.
21. 'Timeline of Nuclear Diplomacye with Iran', Arms Control Association, last reviewed January 2023, available online: https://www.armscontrol.org/factsheets/Timeline-of-Nuclear-Diplomacy-With-Iran (accessed 21 April 2022).
22. *Ettelaat*, 22 Farvardin 1385.
23. Ibid., 24 Aban 1385.
24. Ibid., 29 Bahman 1385.
25. Paygahe ettelaat resaniye riyasat jomhuri, 'Sokhanrani dar didar ba andishmandane sherkatkonandeh dar hamayeshe holocaust', speaker Mahmud Ahmadinejad, Official Website of the President, Islamic Republic of Iran, 21 Azar 1385, available online: available online: https://dolat9-10.president.ir/fa/Archive?t=1&y=1385&m=9&c=120 (accessed 22 April 2022).
26. 'Israel behind Assassinations of Iran Nuclear Scientists, Ya'alon Hints', *Jerusalem Post*, 7 August 2015, available online: https://www.jpost.com/Middle-East/Iran/Israel-behind-assassinations-of-Iran-nuclear-scientists-Yaalon-hints-411473#article

=10373NUNGNTA2NjIyRjVDMTdGMTk0RDQ1MkQ5RjY1ODRGRjE= (accessed 21 April 2022).
27. Maloney, *Iran's Political Economy*, 358.
28. *Bongahhaye zood bazdeh* (Quick Impact and Return Projects), *Tarhe Maskane mehr* (Mehr Housing Project), *Tarhe sahame edalat* (Justice Shares Scheme) and *Tarhe yaraneh* (Cash Payments Scheme).
29. *Donyaye eqtesad*, 9 Azar 1391.
30. *Shahrvand Emrooz*, 7 Mehr 1387.
31. M. Hulpachova, 'Iran's Economy Struggles to Suport Ahmadinejad's Ill-Conceived Housing Vision', *The Guardian*, 30 January 2014, available online: https://www.theguardian.com/world/iran-blog/2014/jan/30/irans-economy-struggles-to-support-ahmadinejads-ill-conceived-housing-vision (accessed 6 June 2022).
32. *Ettelaat*, 26 Mehr 1389.
33. Nameh avval 50 eqtesaddan be rais jomhur Ahmadinejad, available online: https://www.daraian.com/fa/paper/9472 (accessed 23 April 2022); *Sharq*, 22 Khordad 1386.
34. D. Salehi-Isfahani, 'Poverty and Income Inequality in the Islamic Republic of Iran', *Revue internationale des études du développement*, 229, no. 1 (2017): 113–36.
35. F. Hayati, M. Kazemi Najaf Abadi, M. Reinholdt Andersen, A. Atamanov, M. G. Wai-Poi, M. Mostafavi Dehzooei, D. Salehi Isfahani, *Iran Economic Monitor: Weathering Economic Challenges* (English) (Washington, DC: World Bank Group, Fall 2008).
36. K. Sadjadpour, *Reading Khamenei: The World View of Iran's Most Powerful Leader* (Washington, DC: Carnegie Endowment, 2009), 8.
37. F. Wehrey, J. D. Green, B. Nichiporuk, A. Nader, L. Hansell, R.Nafisi and S. R. Bohandy, *The Rise of the Pasdaran* (Santa Monica, CA: RAND Corporation, 2009), xv.
38. M. Vahabi, *Jaygahe Sepah dar eqtesade Iran*, text of a speech at Anjoman goftego va democraci, available online: http://asre-nou.net/php/view.php?objnr=36960 (accessed 12 May 2022).
39. Reuters, 29 March 2013, available online: https://www.reuters.com/article/turkey-iran-sanctions-idINL5N0CL0UK20130329 (accessed 14 May 2022).
40. Human Rights Watch: World Report 2007, Iran. Events of 2006, '"You Can Detain Anyone for Anything", Iran's Broadening Clampdown on Independent Activism', *Human Rights Watch*, 20, 1 (January 2008).
41. *Ettelaat*, 12 Tir 1385.
42. Jahanbeglu was freed on 30 August 2006, and Esfandiyari was released on 21 August 2007. Tajbakhsh was released on 19 September 2007, only to be arrested again in July 2009.
43. Migration Policy Institute, 'Iran Loses Highly Educated and Skilled Citizens during Long-Running "Brain Drain"', 22 April 2021, available online: https://www.migrationpolicy.org/article/iran-brain-drain-emigration (accessed 30 April 2022).
44. *Shahrvand Emrooz*, 5 Aban 1387.
45. *Ettelaat*, 16 Aban 1387.

46. Mashregh, https://www.mashreghnews.ir/news/215539/%DB%B1%DB%B4- (accessed 26 April 2022).
47. *Ettelaat*, 3 Shahrivar 1387.
48. Ibid., 27 Esfand 1378
49. Monazereh bi sabegeh entekhabati miyan Ahmadinejad va Musavi, BBC Farsi, available online: https://www.bbc.com/persian/iran/2009/06/090603_op_ir88_mousavi_ahmadinejad_debate (accessed 1 May 2022).
50. *Ettelaat*, 17 Khordad 1378.
51. M. Michaelsen (ed.), *Election Fallout*, 41–7 https://library.fes.de/pdf-files/iez/08664.pdf (accessed 1 May 2022).
52. *Ettelaat*, 12, 13 Khordad 1388.
53. Ibid., 18 Khordad 1388.
54. Ibid., 17 Khordad; H. Bastani, Mahramanehhaye Entekhabat 1388, BBC Farsi, available online: https://www.bbc.com/persian/48596921 (accessed 1 May 2022); and H. Bastani, Nagoftehhaye Entekhabat 1388,BBC Farsi, available online: https://www.bbc.com/persian/46110885 (accessed 1 May 2022).
55. Ansari, *Iran, Islam and Democracy*, 438.
56. H. Dabashi, *The Green Movement in Iran* (London: Routledge, 2017), 69.
57. *Ettelaat*, 30 Khordad 1388.
58. Ayatollah Khamenei, 'Paygahe ettelaat resaniye daftar maqame moazam rahbari', 29 Shahrivar 1388, available online: https://www.leader.ir/fa/speech/5898/ (accessed 4 May 2022).
59. *Shahrvand Emrooz*, 3 Shahrivar 1387. The quote in the previous paragraph also belongs to this source. *Ettelaat*, 31 Tir 1387. Rahim-Mashai maintained that he had not spoken about friendship with Israel, but the absence of animosity.
60. *Ettelaat*, 30 Sharivar 1387.
61. Iranian Students News Agency, 15 Mordad 1392, available online: https://www.isna.ir/news/92051508916/ (accessed 6 May 2022).
62. *Ettelaat*, 12 Mordad 1389.
63. *Keyhan*, 14 Mordad 1389.
64. *Ettelaat*, 16, 20 Mordad 1389.
65. Peyk Iran, 20 Mordad 1388, available online: https://www.peykeiran.com/Content.aspx?ID=5102 and Flickr, https://www.flickr.com/photos/36514175@N0 (accessed 5 May 2022).
66. *Ettelaat*, 1, 4 Ordibehest 1390.

Chapter 12

1. *Ettelaat*, 2 Khordad 1392.
2. PM speech at the UN General Assembly, 25 September 2014, available online: https://www.gov.uk/government/speeches/pm-speech-at-the-un-general-assembly-2014 (accessed 19 May 2022).

3. BBC, 'Iran "Backs US Military Contacts" to Fight Islamic State', 5 September 2014, available online: https://www.bbc.com/news/world-middle-east-29079052 (accessed 20 May 2022).
4. *Mehr Nameh*, Dey 1392; *Ettelaat*, 19 Dey 1392. The quotes are from *Mehr Nameh*.
5. The United States Institute of Peace, 'More "Happy" Videos Go Viral in Tehran', 5 June 2014, available online: https://iranprimer.usip.org/ (accessed 20 May 2022).
6. Human Rights Watch, *World Report 2015: Iran*, available online: https://www.hrw.org/world-report/2015/country-chapters/iran (accessed 20 May 2022).
7. Ibid., *World Report 2016: Iran*, available online: https://www.hrw.org/world-report/2016/country-chapters/iran (accessed 22 May 2022).
8. Ibid., *World Report 2017: Iran*, available online: https://www.hrw.org/world-report/2017/country-chapters/iran (accessed 22 May 2022).
9. H. Rowhani, 5 Ordibehesht 1394, available online: https://news.gooya.com/politics/archives/2015/04/196197print.php (accessed 23 May 2022).
10. BBC News Farsi, available online: https://www.bbc.com/persian/iran/2014/12/141208_l57_iran_corruption (accessed 12 May 2022).
11. 'UN Security Council Resolutions on Iran', Arms Control Association, last reviewed January 2022, available online: https://www.armscontrol.org/factsheets/Security-Council-Resolutions-on-Iran (accessed 20 April 22).
12. A. Khamenei, 30 Dey 1394, available online: https://farsi.khamenei.ir/speech-content?id=32040 (accessed 19 May 2022).
13. Council on Foreign Relations, International Sanctions on Iran, 15 July 2015, available online: https://www.cfr.org/backgrounder/international-sanctions-iran (accessed 26 May 2022). The quote and all the information in this paragraph are based on this source.
14. Khamenei, 30 Dey 1394.
15. A. Khamenei, 5 Esfand 1394, available online: https://farsi.khamenei.ir/news-content?id=32395 (accessed 24 May 2022).
16. Khabaronline 12 Esfand 1394, available online: https://www.khabaronline.ir/news/515477/ (accessed 24 May 2022).
17. S. K. Dehghan, 'Iran Reopens Investigation into Rafsanjani Death', *The Guardian*, 9 January 2018, available online: https://www.theguardian.com/world/2018/jan/09/iran-reopens-investigation-into-rafsanjani-death (accessed 2 June 2022).
18. Radio Farda, *Do sokhanraniye janjali*, 19 Khordad 1387, available online: https://www.radiofarda.com/a/f4_Palizdar_corruption_clerics_Iran/451145.html (accessed 30 May 2022).
19. S. G. Jones, 'Iran's Protests and the Threat to Domestic Stability', Center for Strategic and International Studies (CSIS), Washington, DC, 8 November 2019, available online: https://www.csis.org/analysis/irans-protests-and-threat-domestic-stability (accessed 1 June 2022).
20. D. Laudati and M. Hashem Pesaran, 'Identifying the Effects of Sanctions on the Iranian Economy Using Newspaper Coverage', available online: https://www.econ.cam.ac.uk/people-files/emeritus/mhp1/wp21/LP_Iran_Sanctions_July_27_2021 (paper_&_supplement).pdf (accessed 28 May 2022).

21. D. Adesnik and S. Ghasseminejad, 'Foreign Investment in Iran: Multinational Firms' Compliance with U.S. Sanctions', Foundation for Defense of Democracies, 10 September 2018, available online: https://www.fdd.org/wp-content/uploads/2018/09/MEMO_CompaniesinIran.pdf (accessed 27 May 2022).
22. D. Salehi-Isfahani, 'Impact of Sanctions on Household Welfare and Employment', available online: https://www.rethinkingiran.com/iranundersanctions/salehiisfahani (accessed 26 May 2022).
23. Sardar Javani, 'Abaade eghteshshate akhir az fetneh 88 gostardehtar bood', speech, Khabargozariye Tasnim, 8 Azar 1398.
24. Reuters, 'Special Report: Iran's Leader Ordered Crackdown on Unrest – "Do Whatever It Takes to End It"', available online: https://www.reuters.com/article/us-iran-protests-specialreport-idUSKBN1YR0QR (accessed 1 June 2021).
25. Amnesty International, 'Iran: Thousands Arbitrarily Detained and at Risk of Torture in Chilling Post-Protest Crackdown', 16 December 2019, available online: https://www.amnesty.org/en/latest/news/2019/12/iran-thousands-arbitrarily-detained-and-at-risk-of-torture-in-chilling-post-protest-crackdown/ (accessed 1 June 2022).
26. 'Bayanat dar didare basijiyan', speech, Ayatollah Khamenei's Official Site, Khamenei.IR, 6 Azar 1398.

Bibliography

Books in English

Abrahamian, E. *Tortured Confessions*. Berkeley, CA: University of California Press, 1999.
Abrahamian, E. *A History of Modern Iran*. Cambridge: Cambridge University Press, 2008.
Afkhami, G.-R. *The Life and Times of the Shah*. Berkeley, CA: University of California Press, 2009.
Alvandi, R. *Nixon, Kissinger and the Shah*. New York: Oxford University Press, 2014.
Amanat, A. *Iran: A Modern History*. New Haven, CT: Yale University Press, 2017.
Ansari, A. *The Shah's Iran*. London: I.B. Tauris, 2017.
Ansari, A. *Iran, Islam and Democracy: The Politics of Managing Change*. London: Gingko Library, 2019.
Baldwin, G. E. *Planning and Development in Iran*. Baltimore, MD: Johns Hopkins Press, 1967.
Bayat, M. *Iran's First Revolution*. Oxford: Oxford University Press, 1991.
Bayat, M. *Iran's Experiment with Parliamentary Governance: The Second Majles, 1909–1911*. Syracuse, NY: Syracuse University Press, 2020.
Bayne, E. A. *Persian Kingship in Transition*. New York: American Universities Field Staff, 1968.
Bharier, J. *Economic Development in Iran 1900–1970*. London: Oxford University Press, 1971.
Bill, J. *The Eagle and the Lion*. New Haven, CT: Yale University Press, 1988.
Browne, E. *The Persian Revolution of 1905–1909*. Cambridge: Cambridge University Press, 1910.
Browne, E. *The Persian Crisis of December 1911*. Cambridge: University Press, n.d.
Burdett, A. L. P. *Iran, Political Developments, 1941–1946*, vol. 1, *1941*, part 1 and vol. 2, *1941*, parts 2 and 3. Wiltshire: Archive Editions, 2008.
Burrell, R. M. *Iran Political Diaries 1881–1965*, vol. 6 (1921–1923), 7 (1924–1926), 8 (1927–1930), 9 (1931–1934), 10 (1935–1938), 11 (1939–1942), 12 (1943–1945). Wiltshire: Archive Editions, 1997; and vol. 14 (1952–1965), Chippenham: Archive Editions, 1997.
Burrell, R. M. and R. L. Jarman. *Iran Political Diaries, 1941–1946*, vol. 13 (1946–1951), 14 (1952–1965). Wiltshire: Archive Editions, 1997.
Carr, E. H. *What is History*. London: Pelican Books, 1987.
Carter, J. *White House Diary*. New York: Farrar, Straus and Giroux, 2010.

Chaqueri, C. *The Soviet Socialist Republic of Iran, 1920–1921: Birth of Trauma.* Pittsburgh, PA: Pittsburgh University Press, 1995.
Chehabi, H. E. *Culture Wars and Dual Society in Iran*, Amsterdam: Farman-Farmaian Family, International Institute of Social History, 2018.
Cronin, S. *The Army and the Creation of the Pahlavi State in Iran 1910–1926.* London: I.B. Tauris, 1997.
Curzon, G. *Persia and the Persian Question*, vol. 1. London: Longmans, Greene & Co., 1892.
Dabashi, H. *The Green Movement in Iran.* London: Routledge, 2017.
Donohoe, M. H. *With the Persian Expedition.* London: Edward Arnold, 1919.
Dunsterville, L. C. *The Adventures of Dunsterforce.* London: Edward Arnold, 1920.
Elgood, C. *A Medical History of Persia and the Eastern Caliphate.* Cambridge: Cambridge University Press, 2010.
Elm, M. *Oil, Power, and Principle: Iran's Oil Nationalization and Its Aftermath.* Syracuse, NY: Syracuse University Press, 1992.
Elwell-Sutton, L. P. *Modern Iran.* London: Routledge, 1941.
Farmanfarmaian, R., ed. *War and Peace in Qajar Persia: Implications Past and Present.* Abingdon: Routledge, 2008.
Fesharaki, F. *Development of the Iranian Oil Industry: International and Domestic Aspects.* New York: Praeger, 1976.
Ghani, C. *Iran and the Rise of Reza Shah.* London: I.B. Tauris, 1998.
Gheissari, A. and V. Nasr *Democracy in Iran and the Quest for Liberty.* Oxford: Oxford University Press, 2006.
Graham, R. *Iran: The Illusion of Power.* London: Croom Helm, 1979.
Habibi, M. *Interface France-Iran 1907–1938: Une diplomatie voilée.* Paris: L'Harmattan, 2004.
Huyser, R. E. *Mission to Tehran.* New York: Harper and Row, 1986.
Katouzian, H. *State and Society in Iran.* London: I.B. Tauris, 2000.
Katouzian, H. *The Persians, Ancient, Medieval and Modern Iran.* New Haven, CT: Yale University Press, 2010.
Kaveh, F. *Iran at War: 1500–1988.* Oxford: Osprey Publishing, 2011.
Keshavarzian, A. *Bazaar and State in Iran.* Cambridge: Cambridge University Press, 2007.
Ladjevardi, H. *Labor Unions and Autocracy in Iran.* Syracuse, NY: Syracuse University Press, 1985.
Lenin, V. I. *Collected Works*, 15. Moscow: Progress Publishers, 1973.
Lord Ironside, ed. *High Road to Command: The Diaries of Major-General Sir Edmund Ironside 1920–1922.* London: Leo Cooper, 1972.
Louis, W. R. *The British Empire in the Middle East.* Oxford: Clarendon Press, 1984.
Majd, M.-G. *The Great Famine & Genocide in Iran, 1917–1919.* Lanham MD: University Press of America, 2013.
Maloney, S. *Iran's Political Economy Since the Revolution.* Cambridge: Cambridge University Press, 2015.
Matin-Asgari, A. *Both Eastern and Western.* Cambridge: Cambridge University Press, 2018.

McMeekin, S. *The Berlin–Baghdad Express: The Ottoman Empire and Germany's Bid for World Power*. Cambridge: Belknap Press, 2010.

Milani, A. *The Shah*. New York: Palgrave Macmillan, 2010.

Millspaugh, A. C. *The American Task in Persia*. London: T. Werner Laurie, 1925.

Millspaugh, A. *Americans in Persia*. Washington, DC: Brookings Institution, 1946.

Mirsepassi, A. *The Discovery of Iran, Taghi Arani, A Radical Cosmopolitan*. Stanford, CA: Stanford University Press, 2021.

Moslem, M. *Factional Politics in Post-Khomeini Iran*. Syracuse, NY: Syracuse University Press, 2002.

Nabavi, N. *Modern Iran*, Princeton, NJ: Markus Weiner, 2016.

Nomani, F. and S. Behdad. *Class and Labour in Iran*. Syracuse, NY: Syracuse University Press, 2006.

Olson, Wm. J. *Anglo-Iranian Relations during World War I*. London: Routledge, 2016.

Pahlavi, F. *An Enduring Love*. New York: Mirmax Books, 2014.

Rahnema, A. *Superstition as Ideology in Iranian Politics*. Cambridge: Cambridge University Press, 2011.

Rahnema, A. *Behind the 1953 Coup in Iran*. Cambridge: Cambridge University Press, 2015.

Rahnema, A. *Call to Arms: Iran's Marxist Revolutionaries*. London: Oneworld Academic, 2021.

Rahnema, S. and S. Behdad. *Iran after the Revolution*. London: I.B. Tauris, 1991.

Rahnema, A. and F. Nomani. *The Secular Miracle*. London: Zed Books, 1990.

Randjbar-Daemi, S. *The Quest for Authority in Iran*. London: I.B. Tauris, 2018

Razavi, H. and F. Vakil. *The Political Environment of Economic Planning in Iran, 1971–1983: From Monarchy to Islamic Republic*. London: Routledge, 2019.

Sadeghi-Boroujerdi, E. *Revolution and Its Discontent*. Cambridge: Cambridge University Press, 2020.

Sadjadpour, K. *Reading Khamenei: The World View of Iran's Most Powerful Leader*. Washington, DC: Carnegie Endowment, 2009.

Secor, L. *Children of Paradise: The Struggle for the Soul of Iran*. New York: Allen Lane, 2016.

Shakibi, Z. *Pahlavi Iran and the Politics of Occidentalism: The Shah and the Rastakhiz Party*. London: I.B. Tauris, 2020.

Shakoori, A. *State and Rural Development in Post-Revolutionary Iran*. London: Palgrave Macmillan, 2001.

Shuster, M. *Strangling of Persia*. New York: The Century Co., 1912.

Sykes, P. *A History of Persia*, vol. 2. London: Macmillan, 1921.

Vakili, V. *Debating Religion and Politics in Iran: The Political Thought of Abdolkarim Soroush*. New York: Council on Foreign Relations, 1996.

Vance, C. *Hard Choices*. New York: Simon and Shuster, 1983.

Wehrey, F., J. D. Green, B. Nichiporuk, A. Nader, L. Hansell, R. Nafisi and S. R. Bohandy. *The Rise of the Pasdaran*. Santa Monica, CA: RAND Corporation, 2009.

Zonis, M. *The Political Elite of Iran*. Princeton, NJ: Princeton University Press, 1971.

Books in Persian

Akhoundzadeh, F. *Maktobat, namehhaye kamalodolleh be shahzadeh jamalodolleh*. Entesharate mard azad, 1985.
Alam, A. *Yaddashthaye Alam*, ed. A. N. Alikhani, vol. 2 (1349 va 1351). Bethesda, MD: Iranbooks, 1993.
Alam, A. *Yaddashthaye Alam*, ed. A. N. Alikhani, vol. 3 (1352). Bethesda, MD: Iranbooks 1995.
Alam, A. *Yaddashthaye Alam*, ed. A. N. Alikhani, vol. 4 (1353). Bethesda, MD: Ibex, n.d.
Amini, D. *Jamiyat Fadaiyane Eslam*. Tehran: Markaze asnad enqelabe eslami, 1381.
Aqeli, B. *Ruzshomare tarikh Iran*, vol. 1. Tehran: Nashre Goftar, 1369.
Araqi, M. *Nagoftehha*. Tehran: Rasa, 1370.
Azari, A. *Qiyame sheykh Mohammad Khiyabani dar Tabriz*. Tehran: Safialishah, 1354.
Bahar, M. T. *Tarikhe mokhtasare ahzabe siyasi*, vol. 1. Tehran: Jibi, 1357.
Bahar, M. T. *Tarikhe mokhtasare ahzabe siyasi*, vol. 2. Tehran: Amir Kabir, 1363.
Bani-Sadr, A. *Khiyanat be omid*. n.p., n.d.
Bayat, K. *Kudetaye Lahuti*. Tehran: Shirazeh, 1376.
Bazargan, M. *Enqelab Iran dar do harekat*. Tehran: nehzat azadi-ye Iran, 1363.
Be ravayate asnade savak. *Jashne Honar Shiraz*. Tehran: Markaze barrasaie asnade tarikhie vezarate ettelaat, 1381.
Be ravayate asnade savak. *Rejale asre Pahlavi, Ataollah Khosravani*. Tehran: Markaze barrasie asnade tarikhi, 1396.
Bojnurdi, K. *Khaterat*. Tehran: Sazemane tabliqate eslami, 1378.
Elahi, S. *Seyyed Zia, Marde avval ya marde dovvome kudeta*. Los Angele, CA: Ketab Corp., 2011.
Eskandari, I. *Khaterat Siyasi (be ehtemam Babak Khosravi va Fereydun Azarnur), Bakhshe Dovvom*. France: Jonbesh Tudehihaye mobareze enfesali, 1366.
Esmaili, K. *Hezbe Jomhuriye Eslami*. Tehran: Markaze Nashre Enqelabe Eslami, 1386.
Etehadiyeh, M. *Maramnamehha va nezamnamehhaye ahzabe siyasie Iran, dar dorehye dovvome majlese showraye melli*. Tehran: Nashr tarilk Iran, 1361.
Etehadiyeh (Nezam-mafi), M. *Ahzabe siyasi dar majlese sevom*. Tehran: Nashr-e tarikh Iran, 1371.
Fakhrai, E. *Gilan dar jonbesh mashrutiyat*. Tehran: Jibi, 1352.
Fatemi, N. S. *Aineh ebrat*. London: Nashre Ketab, n.d.
Hasanli, J. *Faraz o forud ferqehe democratic Azarbayjan*, trans. M. Homami. Tehran: Nashr Ney, 1386.
Hashemi- Rafsanjani, A.-A. *Karnameh va khaterat sale 1368*. Tehran: Nashr maaref enqelab, 1391.
Hedayat, M. S. *Khaterat va khatarat*. Tehran: Zavvar, 1334.
Jafarof, J. *Mirza Fathali Akhondoff*. Baku: Nashriyat-e Dowlati-ye Azarbayjan, 1962.
Jami, *Gozashteh cheragh rahe ayandeh ast*. Tehran: Qoqnus, 1362.
Kasravi, A. *Tarikhe Mashrutehye Iran*. vols 1 and 3. Tehran: Amir Kabir, 1363.
Kermani, N. A. *Tarikh Bidari-e Iranian*, vol. 1. Tehran: Nashr-e peykan, 1377.

Khalkhali, S. *Khaterate Ayatollah Khalkhali*. Tehran: Nashre Sayeh, 1379.
Khomeyni, R. *Hokumat Eslami*. n.p., n.d.
Khomeyni, R. *Sahifehye emam*, vols 1, 3, 4, 6, 9, 10, 12, 21. Tehran: Moasessehye tanzim va nashre asare emam Khomeyni, 1382.
Khosrowpanah, M.-H. *Sazeman afsarane hezbe Tudeh Iran*. Tehran: Shirazeh, 1377.
Khosropanah, M.-H. *Shabhaye nevisandegan va shaerane Iran*. Tehran: Nashre payam emruz, 1396.
Makki, H. *Ketab Siyah*, vol. 1. Tehran: Amir Kabir, 1363.
Maraghehi, Z. *Siyahatnameh Ebrahim beyg (be kousheshe M.Ayn Sepanlou)*. Tehran: Entesharate agah, 1397.
Mirfakhrai, E. *Sardare jangal*. Tehran: Entesharate Javidan, 1357.
Mojtahedi, M. *Taqizadeh va rowshangariha dar mashrutiyate Iran*. Tehran: Moasesseh Entesharat va chape daneshgahe Tehran, 1357.
Montazeri, H.-A. *Matn kamel khaterate Ayatollah Hoseyn-Ali Montazeri*. Etemad nasheran Irani dar Euroupa, 1379 (2001).
Musaviyan, H. *Chaleshhaye ravabet Iran va gharb, barrasiye ravabet Iran va Alman*. Tehran: Markaze tahqiqat estretejik, 1385.
Nahidi-Azar, A. *Jonbesh azadistan, sheykh Mohammad Khiyabani*. Tehran: Nashr-e akhtar, 1379.
Navab-Safavi, M. *Barnameh enqelabi Fadaiyane Eslam*. Tehran: n.p., n.d.
Nehzate Azadi Iran, *Velayate motlaqeh faqih*. N.p., n.d.
Nuri, A. *Shokaran Eslah*. Tehran: Tarhe No, 1379.
Pahlavi, M.-R. *Enqelab-e Sefid*. Tehran: Chapkhaneheye bank melli, 1345.
Pahlavi, M.-R. *Be suye tamadon bozorg*. Tehran: Markaze pajuhesh va nashre farhang siyasiye doran Pahlavi, n.d.
Purshalchi, M. *Qazaq, Asr Reza Shah Pahlavi*. Tehran: Entesharat morvarid, 1384.
Qarabaghi, A. *Haqayeq dar bareh bohran Iran*. Paris: Soheyl, n.d.
Rais-Nia, R. *Akharin sangar azadi*. Tehran: Shirazeh, 1377.
Sadiq, I. *Yadegare Omr*. Tehran: Sherkate sahamiye tabe ketab, 1340.
Sanati, R. *Goftoman Mesbah*. Tehran: Markaz asnade enqelabe eslami, 1387.
Sarkoohi, F. *Yas va Das*. Sweden: Baran, 2002.
Sepehr, M. D. *Iran dar jang bozorg (1914–1918)*. Tehran: Chapkhaneh bank melli, 1336.
Shariati, A. *Collected Works*, vols 2 (no place of publication, n.p., n.d.), 13 (Tehran: Chapakhsh, 1365), 19 (Tehran: Qalam, 1361), 22 (Tehran: Sabz, 1361), 26 (Tehran: Nilufar, 1362), 30 (Tehran: Chapakhsh, 1363), 34 (no place of publication, n.p., n.d.).
Sharif-Kashani, M. M. *Vaqeat etefaqiyeh dar ruzegar, Be koushesh Mansureh etehadiyeh va Syrus Sadvandiyan*, vol. 2. Tehran: Nashr-e tarikh-e Iran, 1362.
Sheybani A. H. (Vahid al-molk), *Khaterat-e mohajerat, (be koushesh-e Iraj Afshar va Kaveh Bayat)*. Tehran: Shirazeh, 1396.
Shoja, A. and A. Tayarani. *Asnad, bayaniyehha va sourate jalasate jebhehye mellie dovvom*, vol. 1. Tehran: Chapakhsh, 1394.
Showkat, H. *Tarikh bist saleh*, vol. 2. Saarbruecken Nashr-e baztab, 1372.
Tabrizi, J. *Asrar-e tarikhi-ye komiteh mojazat*, Tegran: Majaleh vahid, 1362.

Talebof, A. *Ketabe Ahmad ya safineh talebi (ba moqadameh va havashiye Baqer Momeni)*. Tehran: Shabgir, 2536.
Tayarani, B. *Ahzabe siyasie Iran*, vol. 2. Tehran: Entesharate sazemane asnade melli, 1376.
Yazdani, S. *Mojahedine Mashruteh*. Tehran: Nashre Ney, 1388.
Yazdani, S. *Ejtemaiyun Amiyun*. Tehran: Nashre Ney, 1391.

Recommended Further Reading

Constitutional Revolution

Afary, J. *The Iranian Constitutional Revolution, 1906–1911: Grassroots Democracy, Social Democracy, and the Origins of Feminism*. New York: Columbia University Press, 1996.
Ansari, A. *Iran's Constitutional Revolution of 1906 and Narratives of the Enlightenment*. London: Gingko Library, 2017.
Berberian, H. *Roving Revolutionaries: Armenians and the Connected Revolutions in the Russian, Iranian, and Ottoman Worlds*. Berkeley, CA: University of Californian University Press, 2019.
Bonakdarian, M. *Britain and the Iranian Constitutional Revolution of 1906–1911: Foreign Policy, Imperialism and Dissent*. Syracuse, NY: Syracuse University Press, 2006.
Chehabi, H. and V. Martin. *Iran's Constitutional Revolution: Popular Politics, Cultural Transformations and Transnational Connections*. London. I.B. Tauris, 2010.
Farzaneh, M. M. *The Iranian Constitutional Revolution and the Clerical Leadership of Khurasani*. Syracuse, NY: Syracuse University Press, 2015.
Martin, V.*Islam and Modernism: The Iranian Revolution of 1906*. London: I.B. Tauris, 1989.
Martin, V. *Iran Between Islamic Nationalism and Secularism: The Constitutional Revolution of 1906*. London: I.B. Tauris, 2013.
Sohrabi, N. *Revolution and Constitutionalism in the Ottoman Empire and Iran, 1902–1910*. Cambridge: Cambridge university Press, 2011.

First World War, Its Aftermath and the Qajars under Siege

Atabaki, T. *Iran and the First World War: Battleground of Great Power*. London: I.B. Tauris, 2006.
Cronin, S. *Iranian-Russian Encounter: Empires and Revolutions since 1800*. New York: Routledge, 2013.
Moberly, F. J. *Operations in Persia, 1914-19*, History of the Great War Based on Official Documents. London: Stationery Office Books, 1987.
Sabahi, H. *British Policy in Persia, 1918–1925*. London: Frank Cass, 1990.

Wynn, A. *Persia in the Great Game: Sir Percy Sykes, Explorer, Consul, Soldier, Spy*. London: John Murray, 2003.

Reza Shah

Atabaki, T. and E. Zurcher. *Men of Order: Authoritarian Modernization under Attaturk and Reza Shah*. London: I.B. Tauris, 2004.
Bakhash, S. *The Fall of Reza Shah*. London: I.B. Tauris, 2022.
Cronin, S. *Soldiers, Shahs and Subalterns in Iran: Opposition, Protest and Revolt, 1921–1941*. New York: Palgrave, 2010.
Cronin, S. *The Making of Modern Iran: State and Society under Riza Shah*. London: Routledge, 2017.
Devos, B. and C. Werner. *Culture and Cultural Politics under Reza Shah: The Pahlavi State, New Bourgeoisie and the Creation of a Modern Society in Iran*. London: Routledge, 2013.
Enayat, H. *Law, State, and Society in Modern Iran: Constitutionalism, Autocracy, and Legal Reform, 1906–1941*. New York: Palgrave Macmillan, 2013.
Majd, M. G. *Great Britain and Reza Shah: The Plunder of Iran, 1921–1941*. Gainesville, FL: University Press of Florida, 2001.
Rezun, M. *The Soviet Union and Iran: Soviet Policy in Iran from the Beginning of the Pahlavi Dynasty until the Soviet Invasion in 1941*. London: Routledge, 1988.
Stewart, R. *Sunrise at Abadan: The British and Soviet Invasion of Iran*. New York: Praeger, 1988.

Mohammad-Reza Shah, Oil Nationalization, Mosaddeq and the Coup

Abrahamian, E. *The Coup: 1953, the CIA, and the Roots of Modern U.S.-Iranian Relations*. New York: New Press, 2013.
Abrahamian, E. *Oil Crisis in Iran: From Nationalism to Coup d'Etat*. Cambridge: Cambridge University Press, 2021.
Atabaki, T. *Azerbaijan: Ethnicity and the Struggle for Power in Iran*. London: I.B. Tauris, 2000.
Azimi, F. *Iran: The Crisis of Democracy*. New York: St. Martin's Press, 1989.
Bill, J. A. and W. R. Louis. *Musaddiq, Iranian Nationalism, and Oil*. Austin, TX: University of Texas Press, 1988.
de Bellaigue, C. *Patriot of Persia: Muhammad Mossadegh and a Tragic Anglo-American Coup*. New York: Harper Perennial, 2013.
Diba, F. *Mohammad Mossadegh: A Political Biography*. London: Routledge, 1986.
Elwell-Sutton, L. P. *Persian Oil: A Study in Power Politics*. London: Lawrence and Wishart, 1995.
Gasiorowski, M. and M. Byrne. *Mohammad Mosaddeq and the 1953 Coup in Iran*. Syracuse, NY: Syracuse University Press, 2004.

Hasanali, J. *At the Dawn of the Cold War: The Soviet-American Crisis over Iranian Azerbaijan, 1941–1946*. Lanham, MD: Rowan and Littlefield, 2006.
Katouzian, H. *Musaddiq and the Struggle for Power in Iran*. London: I.B. Tauris, 1990.
Katouzian, H. *Khalil Maleki*. London: Oneworld, 2018.
Kinzer, S. *All the Shah's Men: An American Coup and the Roots of Middle East Terror*. Hoboken, NJ: John Wiley and Sons, 2003.
Koohi-Kamali, F. *The Political Development of the Kurds in Iran*. New York: Palgrave Macmillan, 2003.
Siavoshi, S. *Liberal Nationalism in Iran: The Failure of a Movement*. Boulder, CO: Westview, 1988.
Zabih, S. *The Communist Movement in Iran*. Berkeley, CA: University of California University Press, 1966.

Mohammad-Reza Shah, 1953–79

Alam, A. *The Shah and I: The Confidential Diaries of Iran's Royal Court, 1969–1977*. London: I.B. Tauris, 1991.
Amuzegar, J. *Dynamics of the Iranian Revolution: The Pahlavis' Triumph and Tragedy*. New York: State University of New York Press, 1991.
Behrooz, M. *Rebels with a Cause: The Failure of the Left in Iran*. London: I.B. Tauris, 1999.
Boroujerdi, M. *Iranian Intellectuals and the West: The Tormented Triumph of Nativism*. Syracuse, NY: Syracuse University Press, 1996.
Gheissari, A. *Iranian Intellectuals in the Twentieth Century*. Austin, TX: University of Texas Press, 1998.
Katouzian, H. *The Political Economy of Modern Iran: Despotism and Pseudo-Modernism, 1926–1979*. New York: New York University Press, 1981.
Milani, A. *The Persian Sphinx: Amir Abbas Hoveyda and the Riddle of the Iranian Revolution: A Biography*. Washington, DC: Mage Publishers, 2004.
Mirsepassi, A. *Intellectual Discourse and the Politics of Modernization: Negotiating Modernity in Iran*. Cambridge: Cambridge University Press, 2000.
Naficy, H. *A Social History of Iranian Cinema*, vols 1 and 2. Durham, NC: Duke University Press, 2011.
Naficy, H. *A Social History of Iranian Cinema*, vols 3 and 4. Durham, NC: Duke University Press, 2012.
Rahnema, A. *The Rise of Modern Despotism in Iran: The Shah, the Opposition, and the US, 1953–1968*, London: Oneworld, 2021.
Ramazani, R. *Iran's Foreign Policy, 1941–1973: A Study of Foreign Policy in Modernizing Nations*. Charlottesville, VA: University Press of Virginia, 1975.
Shawcross, W. *The Shah's Last Ride: A Cautionary Tale*. London: Chatto and Windus, 1988.
Takeyh, R. *The Last Shah: America, Iran, and the Fall of the Pahlavi Dynasty*. New Haven, CT: Yale University Press, 2021.

Vahabzadeh, P. *A Guerrilla Odyssey: Modernization, Secularism, Democracy, and Fadai Period of National Liberation in Iran, 1971–1979*. Syracuse, NY: Syracuse University Press, 2010.

Vahabzadeh, P. *A Rebel's Journey: Mostafa Sho'aiyan and Revolutionary Theory in Iran*. London: Oneworld, 2019.

Zabih, S. *The Left in Contemporary Iran: Ideology, Organization, and the Soviet Connection*. London: Croom Helm, 1986.

Zonis, M. *Majestic Failure: The Fall of the Shah*. Chicago, IL: University of Chicago Press, 1991.

The 1979 Revolution

Adib-Moghaddam, A. *A Critical Introduction to Khomeini*. Cambridge: Cambridge University Press, 2014.

Afary J. and K. B. Anderson. *Foucault and the Iranian Revolution: Gender and the Seductions of Islamism*. Chicago, IL: University of Chicago Press, 2005.

Afshar, H., ed. *Iran: A Revolution in Turmoil*. Albany, NY: State University of New York Press, 1985.

Arjomand, S. A. *The Turban for the Crown: The Islamic Revolution in Iran*. New York: Oxford University Press, 1988.

Bakhash, S. *The Reign of Ayatollahs: Iran and the Islamic Revolution*. London: I.B. Tauris, 1985.

Dabashi, H. *Theology of Discontent: The Ideological Foundations of the Islamic Revolution in Iran*. New York: Oxford University Press, 2013.

Fischer, M. *Iran: From Religious Dispute to Revolution*. Cambridge, MA: Harvard University Press, 1980.

Ghamari-Tabrizi, B. *Remembering Akbar: Inside the Iranian Revolution*. New York: OR Books, 2016.

Kazemi, F. *Poverty and Revolution in Iran: The Migrant Poor, Urban Marginality and Politics*. New York: New York University Press, 1980.

Keddie, N. R. *Modern Iran: Roots and Results of Revolution*. New Haven, CT: Yale University Press, 2006.

Kurzman, C. *The Unthinkable Revolution in Iran*. Cambridge: Cambridge University Press, 1980.

Martin, V. *Creating an Islamic State: Khomeini and the Making of a New Iran*. London: I.B. Tauris, 2000.

Milani, M. M. *The Making of Iran's Islamic Revolution: From Monarchy to Islamic Republic*. Boulder, CO: Westview Press, 1988.

Moaddel, M. *Class, Politics, and Ideology in the Iranian Revolution*. New York: Columbia University Press, 1992.

Moin, B. *Khomeini: Life of the Ayatollah*. London: I.B. Tauris, 2009.

Mottahedeh, R. P. *The Mantle of the Prophet: Religion and Politics in Iran*. New York: Simon and Shuster, 1985.

Parsa, M. *Social Origins of the Iranian Revolution*. New Brunswick, NJ: Rutgers University Press, 1992.
Sachedina, A. A. *The Just Ruler in Shi'ite Islam: The Comprehensive Authority of the Jurist in Imamite Jurisprudence*. Oxford: Oxford University Press, 1988.
Satrapi, M. *The Complete Persepolis: Volumes 1 and 2*. New York: Random House, 2007.
Sick, G. *All Fall Down: America's Tragic Encounter with Iran*. New York: Random House, 1985.

The Islamic Republic of Iran

Abrahamian, E. *Khomeinism: Essays on the Islamic Republic*, London: I.B. Tauris, 1993.
Adelkhah, F. *Being Modern in Iran*. New York: Columbia University Press, 2000.
Afary, J. *Sexual Politics in Modern Iran*. Cambridge: Cambridge University Press, 2009.
Afshari, R. *Human Rights in Iran: The Abuse of Cultural Relativism*. Philadelphia, PA: University of Pennsylvania Press, 2011.
Alimagham, P. *Contesting the Iranian Revolution: The Green Uprisings*. Cambridge: Cambridge University Press, 2020.
Alizadeh, P. and H. Hakimian. *Iran and the Global Economy: Petro Populism, Islam and Economic Sanctions*. New York: Routledge, 2014.
Amir Arjomand, S. *After Khomeini: Iran under His Successors*. Oxford: Oxford University Press, 2009.
Ansari, A. *Iran under Ahmadinejad: The Politics of Confrontation*. London: Routledge, 2007.
Axworthy, M. *Revolutionary Iran: A History of the Islamic Republic*. London: Penguin, 2019.
Bakhtiari, B. *Parliamentary Politics in Revolutionary Iran: The Institutionalization of Factional Politics*. Gainesville, FL: University Press of Florida, 1996.
Barlow R. and S. Akbarzadeh. *Human Rights and Agents of Change in Iran: Towards a Theory of Change*. London: Palgrave Macmillan, 2018.
Bayat, A. *Street Politics: Poor People's Movements in Iran*. New York: Columbia University Press, 1997.
Christopher, W., H. H. Saunders, G. Sick, R. Carswell, R. J. Davis, J. E. Hoffman, Jr., R. B. Owen, O. Schachter and A. A. Ribicoff, eds. *American Hostages in Iran*. New Haven, CT: Yale University Press, 1985.
Chubin, S. and C. Tripp. *Iran and Iraq at War*. Boulder, CO: Westview, 1991.
Dabashi, H. *Iran: A people Interrupted*. New York: New Press, 2007.
Ehteshami, A. and M. Zweiri. *Iran's Foreign Policy: From Khatami to Ahmadinejad*. London: Ithaca Press, 2012.
Farzaneh, M. M. *Iranian Women and Gender in the Iran–Iraq War*. Syracuse, NY: Syracuse University Press, 2021.
Fathollah-Nejad, A. *Iran in an Emerging New World Order: From Ahmadinejad to Rouhani*. London: Palgrave Macmillan, 2021.
Ghamari-Tabrizi, B. *Islam and Dissent in Postrevolutionary Iran: Abdolkarim Soroush, Religious Politics and Democratic Reform*. London: I.B. Tauris, 2008.

Juneau, T. *Squandered Opportunity: Neoclassical Realism and Iran's Foreign Policy.* Stanford, CA: Stanford University Press, 2015.

Kamrava, M. *Iran's Intellectual Revolution.* Cambridge: Cambridge University Press, 2008.

Kamrava, M. *Triumph and Despair: In Search of Iran's Islamic Republic.* London: Hurst Publishers, 2022.

Kazemzadeh, M. *Islamic Fundamentalism, Feminism, and Gender Inequality in Iran under Khomeini.* Lanham, MD: University Press of America, 2002.

Kazemzadeh, M. *Iran's Foreign Policy: Elite Factionalism, Ideology, the Nuclear Weapons Program, and the United States.* London: Routledge, 2020.

Keshavarzian, A. and A. Mirsepassi. *Global 1979: Geographies and Histories of the Iranian Revolution.* Cambridge: Cambridge University Press, 2021.

Mahdavi, P. *Passionate Uprisings: Iran's Sexual Revolution.* Stanford, CA: Stanford University Press, 2008.

Maloney, S. *The Iranian Revolution at Forty.* Washington, DC: Brookings Institution Press, 2020.

Menashri, D. *Post-Revolutionary Politics in Iran: Religion, Society, and Power.* New York: Routledge, 2001.

Mirsepassi, A. *Democracy in Modern Iran: Islam, Culture, and Political Change.* New York: New York University Press, 2011.

Murray, W. *The Iran–Iraq War: A Military and Strategic History.* Cambridge: Cambridge University Press, 2014.

Ramazani, R. *Revolutionary Iran: Challenge and Response in the Middle East.* Baltimore, MD: Johns Hopkins University Press, 1986.

Razoux, P. and N. Elliot. *The Iran–Iraq War.* Cambridge, MA: Harvard University Press, 2015.

Saffari, S. *Beyond Shariati: Modernity, Cosmopolitanism, and Islam in Iranian Political Thought.* Cambridge: Cambridge University Press, 2017.

Samuel, A. T. *The Unfinished History of the Iran–Iraq War: Faith, Firepower, and Iran's Revolutionary Guards.* Cambridge: Cambridge University Press, 2021.

Sansarian, E. (2006), *Religious Minorities in Iran.* Cambridge: Cambridge University Press, 2006.

Schirazi, A. *The Constitution of Iran: Politics and the State in the Islamic Republic.* London: I. B. Tauris, 1998.

Siamdoust, N. *Soundtrack of the Revolution: The Politics of Music in Iran.* Stanford, CA: Stanford University Press, 2017.

Tazmini, G. *Khatami's Iran: The Islamic Republic and the Turbulent Path to Reform.* London: I.B. Tauris, 2009.

Overarching Books

Abrahamian, E. *Iran between Two Revolutions.* Princeton, NJ: Princeton University Press, 1982.

Aghaie, K. S. and A. Marashi. *Rethinking Iranian Nationalism and Modernity*. Austin, TX: University of Texas Press, 2014.

Ansari, A. *The Politics of Nationalism in Modern Iran*. Cambridge: Cambridge University Press, 2012.

Ansari, A. *Modern Iran since 1797: Reform and Revolution*. London: Routledge, 2019.

Arjomand, S. A. *Authority and Political Culture in Shi'ism*. Albany, NY: State University of New York Press, 1988.

Axworthy, M. *A History of Iran: Empire of the Mind*. New York: Basic Books, 2016.

Azimi, F. *The Quest for Democracy in Iran: A Century of Struggle Against Authoritarian Rule*. Cambridge, MA: Harvard University Press, 2008.

Cronin, S. *Social Histories of Iran: Modernism and Marginality in the Middle East*. Cambridge: Cambridge University Press, 2021.

Ghazvinian, J. *America and Iran: A History, 1720 to the Present*. New York: Knopf, 2021.

Kashani-Sabet, F. *Frontier Fictions; Shaping the Iranian Nation, 1804–1946*. Princeton, NJ: Princeton University Press, 1999.

Richard, Y. *Iran: A Social and Political History since the Qajars*. Cambridge: Cambridge University Press, 2019.

Shannon, M. K. *American-Iranian Dialogues: From Constitution to White Revolution, c. 1890s–1960s*. London: Bloomsbury, 2021.

Index

1908 coup xxii, 43–45
1921 coup 110–112
    and Britain 112, 129
    and *Haqiqat* (Truth) (newspaper) 129
    and the Iron Committee 108–109
    and plotting of 109–110
    and Russia 112
1953 coup 218, 226–228
    and Britain 224, 226
    and the CIA xxix, 178, 224, 225, 226–227
    and plotting of 224, 226
    and SIS 224

Abaie-Khorasani, Mohammad 463
Abbasi, Fereydun 548
Abdekhodai, Mohammad-Mehdi 221
Abdi, Abbas 464
Abdi, Esmail 597
Abu Zarr 336
Achaemenids 8–9
Adl, Mansur al-saltaneh 109, 525
Afghanistan 16, 19, 25, 72, 319, 446, 529
Afshar, Iraj 486
Afzali, Bahram 428
Agnew, Spiro 296
Ahmad Shah xxii, xxiii, xxv
    and the Anglo-Persian Agreement (1919) 98
    and Britain and Russia 75–76, 78–79, 106
    and the clergy 134
    and constitutional monarchy 74
    and dethronement of 142–143
    and the First World War 69–70, 81–82
    and flight from Iran 132
    and the Jangalis 90–91, 105–106
    and Reza Khan's campaign against him 134, 136, 141–142
    see also 1921 coup

Ahmadi, Reza 514
Ahmadi-Khorasani, Nushin 560
Ahmadi-Roshan, Mostafa 548
Ahmadinejad, Mahmud
    and anti-Semitism 548
    and campaign for re-election as president 567–568
    and Cash Payments Scheme 550, 552, 612
    and corruption 579
    and economic policies of 550–555
    and election as president 540–541
    and Holocaust denial 548
    and international sanctions 549–550
    and the IRGC 530, 556–557, 559
    and Justice Shares Scheme 550, 552
    and Khamenei xli, 541–542, 546, 550, 558–559, 564–565, 575–580
    and Mesbah-Yazdi 539–540, 541
    and monetary policy of 554
    and network of *maddahan* (preachers-performers) 540
    and nuclear programme 543–544, 546–547
    and opposition to 559–561, 571–572
    and pre-Islamic Persia 577–578
    and presidency of xl–xlii, 563–564, 581
    and presidential candidacy of 537–539
    and Quick Impact and Return Projects (QIRP) 550
    and re-election as president 568–571
Ahmadzadeh, Masud 329, 330, 361
Ahrami-Tangestani, Morteza 50
Ajarg, Bahman 330
Ajudani, Ahmad 258
Akbar, Fatollah (Sepahdar Rashti) 107, 112
Akhavan, Jafar 309
Akhavi, Hasan 239

Akhundzadeh, Fathali 23–24
Al-Assad, Bashar xliv, 615
al-Muhandis, Abu Mahdi xliv, 614
al-Nimr, Nimr Baqer 600
Ala al-dowleh, Ahmad Khan 30–31
Ala al-saltaneh, Mohammad-Ali 69, 74, 84, 85–86
Ala, Hoseyn xxx, 213, 223, 226, 243–244, 248
   and assassination attempt on 244–245
Alam al-hoda, Ahmad 574, 594, 608
Alam, Amir Shokat al-molk 124
Alam, Asadollah
   and creation of the People's Party 249
   and premiership of xxxi, 264–265, 271, 278
   and the Shah 267–268, 359
Alam, Jamshid 178
Alamuti, Ziaeddin 162
Alavi, Bozorg 162, 181
Alavi, Mahmud 610
Alavi-Kia, Hasan 247
Alavi-Moqaddam, Mehdiqoli 243
Albright, Madeleine xxxix, 528
Ale-Ahmad, Jalal 319
Ale-Shobeyr-Khaqani, Sheykh Mohammad-Taher 389–390
Aliabadi, Abdolhoseyn 179
Alikhani, Ali-Naqi 283
Alikhani, Mehrdad 504, 505
Alimohammadi, Masoud 548
Alviri, Morteza 397, 435
Amani, Sadeq 284–285
Amanpour, Christiane 497
America, *see* United States of America
Amidi-Nuri, Abolhasan 196, 220
Amin al-molk, Hasan Khan 55
Amin al-zarb, Haj Mohammad-Hoseyn 11, 38, 55
Amin-Soltan (Atabak Azam and Atabak), Ali-Asghar 26, 34, 38, 40, 57, 63
Amini, Abdolhoseyn 201
Amini, Ali
   and the Amini–Page oil agreement xxx, 239–240
   and anti-corruption campaign 258
   and Khomeyni 270
   and opposition to 259–260, 261–262
   and premiership of xxxi, 257–258, 264
   and the US 260, 262–263
Amir Bahador, Hoseyn Pasha Khan 41–42
Amir Kabir (Mirza Taqi Khan Farahani) xxi, 18–19, 458
Amir-Ahmadi, Ahmad 111, 184
Amir-Alai, Mehdi 243
Amir-Arjomand, Lily 312
Amir-Entezam, Abbas 363, 403, 408
Amjad, Mahmud 604
Amnesty International xxxii, 342, 445, 446, 613
Amoli, Hashem 468
Amuoghlu, Heydar 43, 56, 57, 58, 105, 123
Amuzegar, Jamshid xxxiii, 283, 293, 302, 352, 360
Anglo-Iranian Oil Company (AIOC) 147
   and Iran's oil nationalization 215, 217
   and the Supplemental Agreement (1949) 207–208, 212
   see also Anglo-Persian Oil Company
Anglo-Persian Agreement (1919) 96–99, 121
Anglo-Persian Oil Company (APOC) xxii, 147–148
   and the 'Abadan Agreement' (1909) 50, 71
   see also Anglo-Iranian Oil Company
Anglo-Persian War (1856–7) xxi, 19
Ansari, Hushang 302, 360
Anglo-Russian Convention xxii, xxiv, 40, 88, 95
Ansari, Majid 604
Anti-Bahai Society, *see* Hojatiyyeh Society
Anti-Foreigners Party (*Hezbe Zedde Ajnabi*) 158
Anti-Sabotage Joint Committee 331, 332, 335, 374
Anvar, Iraj 317
Aqa Mohammad Khan Qajar 15
Aqa-Soltani, Neda 572
Aqa-Tehrani, Morteza 544
Aqasi, Nematollah 322
Aqevli, Farajollah 176
Arab-Sorkhi, Feyzollah 464
Aram, Bahram 335
Arani, Taqi 162–163
   and the Arani Group 162, 180

Araqi, Mehdi 284, 347, 396–397
Ardalan, Amanollah (Ezz al-mamalek) 74, 131
Ardalan, Parvin 560
Aref, Mohammad-Reza 562
Arfa, Hasan 197
   and the Ariya Party 225
Ariyana, Bahram 177Arjomand, Eskandar 310
Armin, Mohsen 435, 465, 466, 519
Armitage-Smith, Sydney 104
Arsanjani, Hasan xxxi, 196, 262–263, 267–268
Aryan, Saeed 330
Aryanism 289, 295
Asadabadi (Afghani), Jamaleddin xxi, 22, 64, 335
Asadi, Mohammadvali 156
Asadiyan, Siyamak 426
Asgar, Saeed 432, 514, 516
Asgarowladi, Habibollah 425, 430, 432, 481
Asgharzadeh, Ebrahim 464
Ashraf, Hamid 329, 332
Ashura 33, 492
Assembly of Experts (of the leadership)
   and 2016 elections 603–605
   and the Constitution xxxv, 399–400
   and designation of Khamenei as Leader xxxvii, 456
   and the Guardian Council xxxvii, 455–456, 462–463, 464, 604–605
   and Khatami 496–497, 511–512
   and proposed dissolution of 403
   and the rule of the Guardian Jurist 496–497, 574
   and secret designation of Hoseyn-Ali as Khomeyni's successor xxxvi, 447–448
Assembly of Militant Clerics
   and establishment under Khomeyni 441–442
   and Khamenei's reign 459–460, 463
   and political resurgence of 481–482
Association of Militant Clergy
   and the Assembly of Militant Clerics 442, 465
   and Khomeyni's reign 408, 433, 442
   and Khamenei's reign 481, 496, 540

Association of Combative Clergy 347, 353, 357
Atai, Mansur 259
Atai, Rahim 259
Ataturk, Kemal xxvi, 144, 155, 158–159
Atherton, Roy 342
Atomic Energy Organization of Iran (AEOI) 305
Attlee, Clement 215
automobile industry 309
Avanesiyan, Ardashes 183, 192
'axis of evil' xxxix, 528
Ayandegan (Future Generations) (newspaper) 400–402
Ayn al-dowleh, Abdolmajid 28, 30–32, 36–37, 76, 78, 86
Ayrom, Mohammad-Hoseyn 160, 161
Ayseh, Antoine 309
Azad, Abdolqadir 178, 208, 210, 245
Azali Babis 34, 63
Azar, Abdolreza 182, 187, 188
Azar, Mehdi 179, 265
Azarakhshi, Reza 178
Azarbayjan Democratic Party (*Ferqehe democratic Azarbayjan*) xxiv, xxviii, 100, 101–102, 190
Azari, Abbas 162
Azari-Qomi, Ahmad 475
   and *Resalat* (Calling) (newspaper) 471
Azartash, Kurush 415
Azhari, Golamreza xxxiii, 351, 359, 361
Azmayesh, Mohsen 310
Azod al-molk, Ali-Reza 51, 57
Azodanlou-Qajar, Mariam 444
Azure Party (*Hezbe Kabud*) (of Nobakht) 176–177

Bab 17–18, 63
Babi movement 17–18; *see also* Azali Babis, Bab, Bahaism, Bahaollah
Badamchiyan, Asadollah 481
Badizadegan, Ali-Asghar 333, 334
Bafqi, Mohammad-Taqi 154
Baghdad Pact (1955) xxx, 244, 251–252, 260
Bahais
   and oppression of 138, 418

and origins of their faith 18, 63, 64
see also Bab, Babi movement, Bahaollah, Hojatiyyeh Society
Bahaollah 63
Bahar, Mohammad-Taqi (Malek al-Shoara) 98, 143, 161, 196
Bahman Cultural Centre 478
Bahonar, Mohammad-Javad 353, 390, 422–424
Bahonar, Mohammad-Reza 563
Bahrami, Farajollah 130, 160, 185
Bahrami, Hoseyn Khan 135
Bahrami, Mohammad 162, 241
Bakeri, Hamid 438
Bakhtiyar, Shapur
    and his civilian government xxxiii, 361–362
    and the failed Nojeh coup 414–415
    and Khomeyni 366
    and killing of 482
    and Western support for 362, 363
Bakhtiyar, Teymur 240–241, 243
    and SAVAK 246–247, 248
Bakhtiyari, Najafqoli (Samsam al-saltaneh) 49, 58
Bakhtiyari, Sardar Asad (Aliqoli Khan) 50, 52, 160
Balfour, Arthur 95, 114
Bani-Sadr, Abolhasan
    and alliance with the Mojahedin 419–420
    and *Enqelabe Eslami* (Islamic Revolution) (newspaper) 420
    and escape from Iran 423
    and growing rift with Khomeyni 417–419, 420–421
    and Islamic attire 413–414
    and occupation of the universities 409
    and presidency of xxxv, 407–408, 412–413
    and removal from office 422
    and the US hostage crisis 411
Bani-Sadr, Fatollah 397
Baqai, Mozaffar 196, 206–208, 210–212, 220–221, 224–225, 239–240, 245
Baqer Khan xxii, 47–48, 53, 55, 57
Baqerov, Mir Jafar xxvii, 189–192, 194
Baqi, Emadeddin 274, 515

Baraheni, Reza 326, 370
Barkhordar, Mohammad-Taqi 310
Barq-Lame, Javad 307
Bashiriyeh, Hoseyn 562
Basij (volunteers' corps of the Organization for Mobilization of the Oppressed)
    and 2018 anti-corruption protests 608, 613
    and Ahmadinejad 538, 540, 550, 555–556, 557
    and the Green Movement protests 572
    and the Iran–Iraq War 435, 437, 438–439
    and the Islamic Revolution 417
    and Khamenei 460, 466–467, 511, 514–515
    and role after the Iran–Iraq War 461–462
Baskerville, Howard 49, 67, 103
bast (sanctuary) 30, 32, 39, 63, 77, 209
Bateman-Champain, H. F. 89
Batmanqelich, Nader 176, 227, 239
Bayandor, Gholamali 165
Bayandor, Yadollah 165
Bayat, Asadollah 463
Bayat, Mortezaqoli 170, 179, 186
Bayne, E. A. 243
Bazaar (*Bazaari*)
    and opposition to the 1953 coup government 236
    and the Constitutional Revolution 32, 42, 56, 57
    and opposition to Rafsanjani 471
    and role in society 11, 63, 311, 383
    and US sanctions 611–612
Bazargan, Mehdi
    and 1979 revolution 363–364
    and barring from political office 430
    and the Iran Freedom Movement 259, 265
    and *Mizan* (Measure) (newspaper) 419
    at odds with Khomeyni 368–369, 371, 379–380, 382, 391
    and premiership of xxxiv, 366–367, 377–379, 403–405
    and Shariati 396
Behbahani, Jafar 243, 253
Behbahani, Mohammad (Ayatollah) 224–225, 228, 239
Behbahani, Seyyed Abdollah 29–32, 34, 37–38, 42, 45, 54–56

Behesht Zahra 365
Beheshti, Mohammad xxxv, 353, 364, 369, 377–378, 390–391, 398–399, 408, 412, 418–419, 422, 426, 587
Behrangi, Samad 313, 329, 361
Behzadi, Siyavosh 340
Besharati, Mohammad-Ali 476
Besuye Ayandeh (Towards the Future) (newspaper) 219
Bey, Ali-Ihsan 81
Bicherakov, Lazar 89
Biriya, Mohammad 189
Black Friday xxxiii, 354–355
Blumkin, Yakov 105, 115
Bohlul, Mohammad-Taqi 155
Bojnurdi, Mohammad-Kazem 287–288, 604
Bokharai, Mohammad 284–285
Bolsheviks 49, 89, 95, 104, 107, 111; *see also* Russia
Bonakdar, Mohammad-Taqi 38
Borujerdi, Hoseyn (Grand Ayatollah) 270, 272, 328, 377
Borujerdi, Mohammad 395
Borumand, Abdolrahman 482
Bozorgnia, Mostafa 237
Britain
    and the 1921 coup 110–111, 129
    and the 1953 coup 226
    and Ahmad Shah 78
    and the British Empire 8, 16, 106
    and control over Iranian economy xxi, 19–20, 21, 69, 99
    and Embassy in Iran 238
    and end to presence in the Persian Gulf xxxii, 296
    and fight against ISIS 592
    and Imperial Bank of Persia 21–22, 26
    in Iran during WWI xxiii, 50–51, 58, 71, 74–76, 78–79, 80–81, 82, 86–90
    in Iran during WWII xxvi, xxvii, 164–165, 169–171, 174–177, 182, 184–185
    and Iranian oil xxiii, xxix, 26, 50, 71, 112, 139–140, 147–148, 185, 207–208, 213, 215, 217–218, 239–240
    and Khazal's control of Arabestan (Khuzestan) 140–141
    and Mohammad-Reza Shah 249
    and Mohammad Shah's siege of Herat 16
    and Mosaddeq xxix, 207–208, 210, 214, 215–216, 223–224
    and Mozaffareddin Shah 26
    and Nasereddin Shah xxi, 19–20, 21
    and occupation of Mohammareh in the nineteenth century 19
    and 'Operation Buccaneer' xxix, 215
    and post-WWI designs on Iran 94–97
    and post-WWI military presence in Iran 106, 107
    and Reza Shah 110, 157, 159, 162, 163, 164–165
    and SAVAK 247
    and Seyyed Zia 108, 110, 111, 212–213
    and Tehran Conference xxvi
    see also Anglo-Iranian Oil Company; Anglo-Persian Agreement; Anglo-Persian Oil Company; Anglo-Persian War; Anglo-Russian Convention; Churchill, Winston
Brzezinski, Zbigniew 361, 403–404
Bullard, Reader 161, 163, 165, 177, 180, 183
Burqani, Ahmad 507
Bush, George W. xxxix, 522, 528, 543
Butler, William 156, 286, 342
Buzarjomehri, Karim 149
Byrnes, James 192

Caldwell, John 95
Callaghan, James 362
Capitalist Islam 442, 459, 463
Carter, Jimmy xxxii, 328, 343, 345, 355–356, 359, 361–363, 403, 405
    and failed hostage rescue operation xxxv, 411–412
CENTO (Central Treaty Organisation) 260
Central Bank of Iran 355, 472–473, 551, 553, 554, 557
Central United Council of Iran's Workers and Toilers (CUCIWT) 182, 206
Chamran, Mostafa 388, 403
cholera 8–9, 12–13, 27, 67, 92
Churchill, Winston xxvii, 71, 83, 86, 170, 172–173, 216, 226

CIA
    and the 1953 coup xxix, 178, 224, 225,
        226–228
    and TPBEDAMN Organization 228, 231
    and US influence in Iran after the 1953
        coup 235, 238
Clemenceau, George 119, 167
Clinton, Bill xxxvii, xxxviii, 494, 526, 528
    and 'dual containment' policy 483–484
    and the Iran–Libya Sanctions Act (1996)
        xxxvii, 484
Coalition of Islamic Iran's Developers (*Eetelaf
    abadgarane Iran eslami*) 525
colonialism 2, 99, 180–181, 208, 214, 219, 235,
    337, 349, 370, 392
Combat Party (*Hezbe Peykar*) (of Khosrow
    Eqbal) 178, 196
Confederation of Iranian Students National
    Union (CISNU) 287, 325, 340–341
Congress of Free Men and Women xxxi,
    276–277
Congress of Iran's Rural Cooperatives
    265–266, 271
Consortium
    and the Amini–Page oil agreement xxx,
        239–240
    and Mohammad-Reza Shah 289, 293
    and Mosaddeq 216
    and the Seven Sisters 218, 231
Constitution
    and arguments of Europeanized
        intellectuals against 117–119
    and Council for the Reappraisal and
        Revision of 455–456
    and endorsement by Mozaffareddin Shah
        xxii, 32
    and the Islamic Republic 397–399, 400,
        403, 496–497, 519, 522–524, 612
    and Khamenei xxxix, 551
    and Khomeyni xxxv, 366, 375, 394,
        398–399, 403, 455–456
    and Mohammad-Reza Shah 183, 204, 206,
        360, 362
    and the Pahlavi dynasty xxvi, 143, 291
    and the Supplement to the Constitution
        39–40, 41
    and the suspension of 45
    and threats to 257, 261, 270
    see also Constitutional Revolution,
        constitutionalists
Constitutional Revolution
    and anti-constitutionalists 36–37, 39–40
    and the assassination of Prime Minister
        Atabak 40–41
    and assaults on Parliament 42, 43–44
    and assessment as a failure 119–120
    and the attempted assassination of the
        shah 43
    and background to 13–14, 23–25, 27–28
    and Britain 58, 69, 71–73
    and civil war in Tabriz (1908–9) 47–50
    and the clergy 29–30, 31–32, 37, 42–43,
        46–47, 51–52
    and the constitutional law of 1906 33
    and demonstrations 30, 31, 42, 44
    and the dissolution of Parliament 45
    and the first Constituent Assembly 32
    and Lenin 45
    and the liberation of Tehran 49–50
    and *mashruteh* vs. *mashrueh* system of
        governance 37, 46, 64
    and Mohammad-Ali Shah xxii, 33–34,
        41–42, 43–44, 45, 46, 51, 58
    and political assassinations 56
    and Russia 37, 45, 52–53, 58, 59–62, 69,
        71–73
    and transition to a constitutional
        monarchy 73–74
    see also constitutionalists, Short/Lesser
        Despotism
constitutionalists (*mashruteh khahan*)
    and the British Legation 32, 44
    and demand for a house of justice
        (*edalatkhaneh*) xxi, 30–31
    and disintegration of the movement 52, 57
    and the first Majles 38
    and the High Commission 51
    and make-up of the movement 28–30, 34
    and the Punishment Committee 83–85
    and the removal of Mohammad-Ali Shah 51
    and secret societies 28–30, 35
    and Sepahsalar Mosque 44

Construction Base of the Seal of the Prophets, see *Qarargah sazandeggiye khatam al-anbia*
Construction Jihad 384–385
consumer goods 310–311
Cossacks xxv, 31, 37, 43–45, 60–61, 90, 105–111, 122, 125–126
Council of the Islamic Revolution (Revolutionary Council) (*Showraye enqelabe eslami*) xxxiv–xxxv, 364, 369, 378–380, 382, 390, 397–400, 405, 408, 411, 414, 428, 484, 504
Cox, Percy 50, 95, 99, 104
Curzon, George xxv, 20, 96, 99, 103–104, 106, 108, 110
Cyrus the Great 295, 302

D'Arcy, William Knox xxi, 26, 50
D'Arcy Concession 26, 147
Dadgar, Adl al-molk 109, 160
Dadsetan, Farhad 240
Daemi, Atena 598
Daftari, Mohammad 157, 176, 206
Danesh-Jafari, Davud 553–554
Daneshiyan, Gholamhoseyn 369
Daneshiyan, Keramatollah 332
Daneshvar, Simin 319
Dar al-fonun (Abode of Skills) (polytechnic) 12
Dargahi, Mohammad 137, 158
Darwin, Charles 7, 338
Dashti, Ali 112, 133, 160, 178
Dastgheyb, Ali-Mohammad 604
Davani, Piruz 505
Davar, Ali-Akbar 118–120, 131, 146, 152, 158
Davatgar, Karim 83–84
Debray, Regis 333
Dehkhoda, Ali-Akbar 44, 54
Dehqan, Mohammad 129
Dehqani, Behrooz 329
Democratic National Front of Iran (of Hedayatollah Matin-Daftari) 371, 392, 400, 402
Derakhshesh, Mohammad 257
despotism
  and intellectuals' arguments against 22–25, 100–102
  and the Islamic Republic 400, 418–419, 420–421, 441, 531
  and Khamenei 522, 578
  and Khomeyni 375–376, 410, 441
  and Mohammad-Reza Shah 300–302, 344, 355, 359
  and the National Front's opposition to 270, 276, 421
  and weaknesses of despotic regimes 620
  see also Guardian Jurist, Short/Lesser Despotism
Devotees of Islam (*Fadaiyane Eslam*) (of Navab-Safavi) xxviii–xxix, 201, 204, 208–210, 212, 218–219, 221–222, 244–245, 284
  and *Nabarde Mellat* (People's Combat) (newspaper) 219
Devotees of the Shah 225, 302
Diba, Farah 311, 314, 364
Dickson, Harold 104
Dini, Lamberto 527
discotheques 322–323
Doai, Mahmud 480
Donya (World) (periodical) 162
Doostdar, Ehsanollah Khan 84, 92, 105
Dorri-Najafabadi, Qorbanali 494, 506, 508
Doshantapeh Garrison 367
Dowlatabadi, Yahya 143
Dreyfus, Louis 177
Dulles, Allen xxix, 225–226, 246, 252
Dulles, John Foster 226, 244
Dunsterforce 88–89, 94
Dunsterville, L. C. xxiv, 88–90, 93

Ebadi, Shirin 562
Eden, Anthony 226
Edmonds, Cecil John 102, 110
Eftekhari, Yusuf 162
Eisenhower, Dwight D. 226, 297, 363
Elham, Gholamhoseyn 544
Elqaniyan, Habibollah 307
Emam Jomeh, Seyyed Abolqasem 30, 36, 46, 51
Emami, Jamal 178, 213, 220
Emami, Saeed xxxviii, 486, 506, 508
Emami, Seyyed Hasan 364

Ennals, Martin 342
Entezam, Abdollah 239, 363, 403, 408
Eprem Khan (Eprem Davidian) xxii, 49–51, 56–58, 61, 69
Eqbal, Khosrow 178, 196
Eqbal, Manuchehr xxx, 206, 209, 248–249, 253–254, 261, 290
Esfahani, Jamaleddin (Vaez-Esfahani) 29–31, 42, 44–45, 346, 530
Esfandiyari, Haleh 561
Eskandani, Ali-Akbar 182, 187–188
Eskandari, Iraj 162, 180–181, 183, 192, 196, 231
Eskandari, Parvaneh xxxviii, 504–505
Eskandari, Soleyman Mirza 53–54, 76, 130
Etemad al-saltaneh, Mohammad-Hasan Khan 22
Etemadzadeh, Mahmud 428
Ettelaat (Information) (newspaper) xxxiii, 178, 349, 356, 422, 461–462, 467, 480
Evin Prison 422, 502, 508, 581
Expediency Discernment Council of the System (*Majma tashkhis maslahate nezam*) 441, 455, 540

Fadais, *see* People's Fadai Guerrillas
Fakhr-Arai, Naser 205, 207
Fakhrizadeh, Mohsen 616–617
Falak al-aflak fortress 206
Fallahiyan, Ali 483–486, 506
famine xxvii, 12–13, 27, 67, 92–94, 174–175
Fani, Ali-Asghar 598
Faqihi-Shirazi, Abdolkarim 205
Faraji-Dana, Reza 598
Fardust, Hoseyn 251
Farivar, Gholamali 179
Farmanfarma, Abdolhoseyn 75–79, 82, 84, 87–88, 96, 112
Farrokhi-Yazdi, Mohammad 112, 133, 160
Farrokhzad, Fereydun 322, 482
Farzanegan, Abbas 227
Fatah, Parviz 334, 545
Fateh, Mostafa 54, 179–181
Fatemi, Hoseyn 222, 227, 242
Fathali Shah Qajar 16
fatwas xxxvi, 22, 47, 51, 63, 72, 212, 441, 447, 543

Fazel, Iraj 463, 473
Fellow Travellers/Confederates Party (*Hamrahan*) (of Mostafa Fateh) 179–189
Feuvrier, Jean-Baptiste 19, 22
fiqh (Islamic jurisprudence) 63–64, 200, 463, 489
First World War
    and the Allied Powers 70–74, 76, 79, 82–83, 85–86, 94
    and the Berlin Circle 72
    and British forces in Iran 75, 87–89
    and calls to wage jihad against the Allied Powers 72, 87–88
    and famine in Iran 92–94
    and Iran's National Forces 80–81, 90
    and Iran's policy of 'strict neutrality' 67, 70, 74–75, 77
    and Iran's pro-German National Defence Committee xxiii, 80–82, 90
    and the Jangalis' guerrilla war against Russian forces 90–92
    and Ottoman forces in Iran 70–71, 77–78
    and Provisional National Government xxiii–xxiv, 81
    and Spanish flu in Iran 94
    see also 'Sepahsalar Agreement'
Firuz, Mozaffar 180, 196
Firuz, Nosrat al-dowleh 96, 160
Flaubert, Gustave 7
food industry 310–311
Ford, Gerald 88, 342
Forqan Group (of Gudarzi) xxxiv, 395–397, 400
Forud, Fatollah 253, 258
Forughi, Mohammad-Ali 155–158, 171, 203
Foruhar, Darush xxxviii, 344, 504–505
Foruhar, Sadeq 176–177
Foruzesh, Zeinolabeddin 196
Foundation of the Oppressed 382–383, 401, 470, 473
Fraser, Donald 342
freemasons 35, 51, 375
Friday Prayer Leader 30, 364, 386, 397, 464, 574, 595, 608
Fuad, Fowziyeh 163

Galavi, Gholamreza 330
Ganji, Akbar 504, 515, 562
Gass, Neville xxviii, 207
gendarmerie xxxii, xxxiv, 59, 75–76, 79, 87, 98, 108, 122, 184, 187, 190, 241, 252, 287, 331, 334, 367, 386–388, 390, 394
Genghis Khan 348
Genscher, Hans-Dietrich xxxvii, 412, 470
Ghaffari, Farrokh 315
Ghaffari, Gholamhoseyn 43
Gilanshah, Hedayatollah 227
Giscard D'Estaing, Valery 357, 362
Goethe Institute (Tehran) xxxiii, 328, 344
Golesorkhi, Khosrow 332
Golestan Palace 32, 292
Golpaygani, Mohammad-Reza (Ayatollah) 270, 349, 392
Golshayan, Abbasqoli xxviii, 207, 245–246
Golshiri, Hushang 486
Gorji, Ali 310
Gorji-Fard, Monireh 400
Gowharshad Uprising 156
Green Movement xli, 566, 569, 571–575, 577, 580, 587–589
  and the Ashura protests 573–574
Grey, Sir Edward 110, 364, 565
Group of Fifty-Three 162; *see also* Arani, Taqi
Guadeloupe Conference (1979) xxxiv, 362
Guardian Council
  and 'approbatory supervision' vs. 'informational supervision' 464
  and the Assembly of Experts xxxvii, 462–463, 464
  and elections xxxvii, xxxix, xlii, xliv, 430, 462, 464–465, 480, 493, 512–513, 525–526, 540–541, 562, 586–587, 604–605, 606, 616, 618
  and Khatami's attempts to reform 523–524
  and powers of 397–398, 440–441, 455–456, 464
  and Rural and City Councils elections 502
Guardian Jurist
  and the absolute rule of 441
  and the Assembly of Experts 447–448
  and the *Basiji* 466

  and the Constitution 397, 398, 400, 456, 518
  and the Hojatiyyeh Society 430–431
  and legitimacy of political rule 366
  and political opposition to the rule of 419–421, 493, 496–498, 517–518, 522–523
  and Shariatmadari's opposition to the rule of 392–394
  and the Young Devotees of 514
Gudarzi, Akbar 396–397
Gust, Jens 485

Habibi, Hasan 397, 407
Habl al-matin (Strong Cord) (newspaper) 34, 52, 63, 153
Habl al-matin, Seyyed Hasan 52
Hadadpour, Mohammad-Taqi 201
Haddad-Adel, Gholamali 513, 545, 578, 603
Haerizadeh, Abolhasan 196, 206–208, 210, 239
Haj-Rezai, Tayeb 275
Haj-Seyyed-Javadi, Ali-Asghar 344
Haji-Sharifi, Fatemeh 574
Hajir, Abdolhoseyn xxviii, 203–204, 206–210
Hajizadeh, Amirali 615
Hajjariyan (Kashani), Saeed xxxix, 513–516; see also *Sobhe Emrooz*
Hakimi, Ebrahim xxviii, 170, 187, 191–193, 199, 203
Halcane, Almeyr 107
Hanifnejad, Mohammad 333–334, 361
Haniyeh, Ismail 547
Haqiqatju, Fatemeh 519
Haqshenas, Jahangir 179, 227
Harriman, Averell 219
Hartwig, H. G. 37, 43–44
Hasanov, Hasan 189
Hasanpur, Ghafour 329
Hashemi, Mehdi 449
Hashemi, Mir-Hoseyn 102
Hashemi-Haeri, Ali 220
Hashemi-Rafsanjani, Ali-Akbar
  and the 1979 revolution 368
  and the 2005 presidential election 536–539, 540–541

and the 2013 presidential election 587
and assassination attempt on 397
and the Association of Militant Clergy 480
and Bani-Sadr 418
and the Centre for Strategic Studies 464
and the Constitution of the Islamic
    Republic 399
and corruption 461
and death of xliii, 605
and economic policies of 468–474,
    477–478
and the Fifth Assembly of Experts
    604–605
and the Iran–Iraq War 437, 438, 439, 443
and the Islamic Republic Party xxxvi, 391,
    422, 433, 434
and the Islamic Revolution Guardian
    Corps 473–474
and Khamenei 458–459, 463, 464–465,
    466–467, 474–477, 535–536, 568, 605
and the Mojahedin of the Islamic
    Revolution 395, 397
and the Mykonos Affair 483
and presidency of xxxvii, 458–462
and repression of political opponents
    484–486
and selection of Khomeyni's successor
    447, 456–457
and Structural Adjustment Policies
    468–469
Hashemi-Rafsanjani, Mohammad 476
Hashemi-Shahrudi, Mahmud 517, 520
Hashemi-Taba, Mostafa 606
Hasibi, Kazem 179
Hatami, Ali 322, 461
Hatami-Kia, Ebrahim 461
Haussmann, Georges-Eugène 7
Hayyim, Shmuel 160
healthcare
    and the American Mission Hospital 12
    and the COVID-19 pandemic 616–617
    and the Martyrs' Foundation of the
        Islamic Revolution 383
    and the National Hospital 12
    in the nineteenth century 12–13
    in the twentieth century 151

and the White Revolution 306
see also cholera, famine, influenza
Hedayat, Mehdiqoli (Mokhber al-saltaneh)
    75, 102–103, 125, 156–159, 162
Hedayati, Hadi 277
hejab, see veil
Hejazi, Abdolhoseyn 197
Hekmat, Reza (Sardar Fakher) 155, 196, 199
Helm, Richard 343
Hemmat Organization 49
Hemmat, Mohammad-Ebrahim 49, 438
Henderson, Loy 220, 223, 226, 234, 238–240
Herat (Afghanistan) 16, 19
Heritash, Khosrow 320
Hesam-Vaziri, Mohammad-Hoseyn 176
Heshmat, Ebrahim 92
Hezbollah xliv, 370, 401–402, 407, 413,
    420–421, 423, 426, 453, 459, 467, 498,
    500, 509, 514, 528, 533, 581, 614
High Council of National Defence 424, 588
Hojatiyyeh Society (*Anjoman hojatiyyeh
    mahdaviyyeh*) 430–431
Holman, Adrian 170
holy war, *see* jihad
Hoover, Herbert 239
Hoseyni, Ezeddin 357, 371, 386–387
Hoseyni-Shirazi, Mohammad 429
Hoseyniyeh Ershad xxxii, 338–340
Hoveyda, Amir-Abbas xxxi–xxxiii, 277–278,
    285–286, 290, 292, 301–302, 305, 309,
    351, 360
Hoviyat (Identity) (Islamic Republic TV
    show) 486
Huyser, Robert xxxiv, 363, 367

Imam Ali 200, 333, 396, 453
Imam Hoseyn 46, 273, 416
Imam Khomeyni International Airport xliv,
    530, 615
Imbrie, Robert xxv, 138
Independence Party (*Hezbe Esteqlal*) (of
    Abdolqadir Azad) 178
Indyk, Martin 483
inflation
    during Ahmadinejad's presidency 551,
        553, 554–555

during Khatami's presidency 529–530
during the Mohammad-Reza Shah's reign 305, 307–308
during Rafsanjani's presidency 470, 477
during Rowhani's presidency 601–602, 611
during the Second World War 173–174
influenza 67, 92, 94
Intelligence Organization of the Islamic Revolutionary Guard Corps (IOIRGC) xliii, 517, 575, 609–610
International Atomic Energy Agency (IAEA) xl, 546
International Court of Justice at The Hague xxix, 216–217, 443
International Monetary Fund 468, 474
international oil consortium, see Consortium
Iran Freedom Movement (*Nehzate Azadiye Iran*) (of Bazargan) 259, 261–262, 265–266, 269–270, 332–333, 344, 347, 353, 357, 377, 400, 421, 430, 436, 441
Iran Party (*Hezbe Iran*) (of Farivar, Saleh, Zirakzadeh, Hasibi, *et al.*) 179, 196, 198
Iran Television (ITV) xxx, 320
Iran's Executives of Construction (*Kargozarane sazandegie Iran*) (of Rafsanjani) 480–482, 491, 494–495, 501
Iran's Mojahedin of the Islamic Revolution (IMIR) 466, 525
  and *Asre Ma* (Our Epoch) (newspaper) 466
Iran's Red Revolution Group 104
Iran's Theatre Association (*Anjoman Teatre Iran*) 317
Iran–Iraq War (1980–8) xxxix, 415–417, 435–439
  and Al-Fajr operations 437, 438
  and ceasefire 439, 443
  and chemical bombing of Halabja by Iraq 437
  and the Faw Peninsula xxxvi, 438–439, 442, 445
  and Kheybar Operation 437–438
  and Operation Ramazan 437
  and the Supreme Defence Council 417
  and the 'tanker war' 437
  and the 'war of the cities' 437

Iranian People's Toilers Party (*Hezbe Zahmatkeshan Mellat Iran*) (of Baqai) 221
Iranian Writers' Association xxxiii, xxxvii, 344–345, 485–486, 505
Iron Committee 108–109
Ironside, Edmund 104, 106–110, 120
Islamic Coalition of Mourning Groups (*Heyathaye motalefeh eslami*) xxxix, 273, 284–285, 343, 347, 353, 357, 383, 397, 468, 471, 473–476, 479–481, 524, 556
Islamic Coalition Party (*Hezbe motalefeh eslami*) 556
Islamic Iran Participation Front (of Mohammad-Reza Khatami) 501, 512, 515, 518, 525
Islamic jurisprudence, see *fiqh*
Islamic law, see *sharia*
Islamic Republic News Agency (IRNA) 568, 580
Islamic Republic of Iran Broadcasting (IRIB) 476
Islamic Republic Party (*Hezbe Jomhuriye Eslami*) (of Beheshti, Rafsanjani, Musavi-Ardebili, *et al.*) xxxiv, xxxvi, 379, 390–392, 399–401, 404, 407–408, 412, 424, 431, 433
Islamic Revolution Committees 379–380, 389, 395, 419, 423
Islamic Revolution Perseverance Front (*Jebheye paydariye enqelabe eslami*) (of Mesbah-Yazdi and Mahsuli) 581, 598, 600–601, 603
Islamic Revolutionary Courts xxxv, 369, 379–380, 382–383, 401–403, 407–408, 422–424, 427–428, 464, 593
Islamic Revolutionary Guard Corps (IRGC)
  and 2018 arrests of environmentalists xliii, 609–610
  and 2019 protests 613–614
  and abduction of Ayatollah Taleqani's sons and daughter-in-law 381
  and Ahmadinejad 550, 555–559
  and the assassination attempt on Hajjariyan xxxix, 514

and conflict in Khuzestan 390
and conflict in Kurdistan 387
and conflict with the Mojahedin 423–424, 427–428
and creation of xxxiv, 381
and economic power of 557–558
and ethnic conflict in Gonbad Kavus 388–389
and involvement in politics 510, 514–515
and the Iran–Iraq War xxxvi, 435–437, 438–439
and Khamenei 556
and the Mojahedin of the Islamic Revolution 395
and the Nojeh coup 415
and 'Operation Martyr Soleymani' xliv, 615
and post-war reconstruction xxxviii, 473–474
and the Revolutionary Council 382
and Rowhani 598
and shooting down of Ukrainian International Airlines flight xliv, 615
and the Tabriz uprisings of 1979 394
and US sanctions 549, 610–611
see also Jafari, Mohammad-Ali; *Qarargah sazandeggiye khatam al-anbia* (Construction Base of the Seal of the Prophets); Qods Force; Rahim-Safavi, Yahya; Soleymani, Qasem
Israel xliv, 271–273, 289, 296–297, 348, 404, 439, 449, 547–548, 566, 575–576, 614, 616
ISIS (Islamic State of Iraq and Syria) 590–592, 614

Jafari, Mohammad-Ali (Aziz) 559, 562, 595
Jafariyan, Mahmud 369
Jahanbeglu, Ramin 561
Jahansuz, Mohsen 163
jaheliyyeh (age of ignorance) 200, 459
Jalali, Ali 178, 231
Jalaliyeh rally 259–260
Jaleh Square massacre, *see* Black Friday xxxiii, 354–355
Jalili, Saeed 580, 586–587, 589, 599
Jam, Mahmud 156–157, 339

Jamalzadeh, Mohammad-Ali 72
Jameeh (Society) (newspaper) xxxviii, 498, 507–508
Jangalis (Men of the Woods) 90–91, 92, 104–105
and *Jangal* (Forest) (newspaper) 90–91
Jannati, Ahmad 431, 464, 475, 502, 605
Jannati, Ali 594
Javanfekr, Ali-Akbar 580–581
Jazani, Bijan xxxii, 328–329, 332
jihad 47, 87–88, 117, 212, 335
Joint Comprehensive Plan of Action (JCPOA) xlii, 599, 600–601, 610–611
Jowdat, Hoseyn 206, 241
Justice Party (*Hezbe Edalat*) (Baku-based communist party) 105, 122, 125
Justice Party (*Hezbe Edalat*) (of Ali Dashti) 178

Kadivar, Jamileh 502
Kadivar, Mohsen 500–503, 562
Kajoui, Mohammad 422
Kakhe Javanan (Youth Palace) 323
Kalali, Manuchehr 277
Kalantari, Issa 610
Kalantari, Manuchehr 328
Kamangar, Farzad 560
Kambakhsh, Abdolsamad xxviii, 183, 189, 192, 231
Kamrani, Ahmad 287
Kanitz, George 77
Karbala 17, 32, 142, 273, 416, 437
Karbaschi, Gholamhoseyn xxxvii–xxxviii, 477–479, 499–500, 503, 515
and *Hamshahri* (Fellow Citizen/Townsman) (newspaper) 478
and *Hammihan* (Compatriot) (newspaper) 500, 515
Karbaschian, Amirabdollah 219, 245
Karimpur-Shirazi, Amir-Mokhtar 242
Karrubi, Mehdi xli, 383, 442, 465, 481, 518, 523, 525, 531, 536–538, 540, 564–565, 568–572, 574, 588–589
Kashani, Jalaleddin 35, 63
Kashani, Seyyed Abolqasem xxviii–xxix, 176, 202–212, 214, 218–224, 226, 228, 239, 244–245, 307, 311, 430, 435, 502

Kashi, Nayeb Hoseyn 69
Kasmai, Ahmad 92
Kasrai, Siyavush 242
Kasravi, Ahmad 102, 199–202, 209–210
Katouzian, Naser 397
Kaveh (newspaper) 72, 117–118, 123
Kavtaradze, Sergei xxvii, 185–186, 188, 208
Kazemi, Baqer 243
Kazemi, Mostafa 504–505
Kazemzadeh (Iranshahr), Hoseyn 72
Kennedy, John F. 255, 258, 260–261, 264–265
Kermani, Mirza Reza xxi, 22
Kermani, Nazem al-eslam 29
Kermanshahi, Yar-Mohammad 58
Kerry, John 603
Keshavarz, Fereydun 183, 188, 196, 231
Ketabchi, Antoine 26
Keyhan Farhangi (Cultural Keyhan) 486–487
Keyhan, Masud Khan 109, 111
Keyhan (newspaper) 317, 400–402, 486
Keykhosrow, Arbab 160
Keynes, John Maynard 96, 115
Keyvan, Morteza 241
Khajehnouri, Ebrahim 178
Khalatbari, Rahmanqoli 183, 231
Khalesizadeh, Mohammad 158
Khalili, Mohsen 310
Khalili, Saeed 308
Khalili-Tehrani, Mirza Hoseyn 34, 42, 46
Khalkhali, Mohammad-Sadeq 369, 380, 388–389, 393, 413, 430, 463–464
Khalou Qorban 92, 105
Khamenei, Ali
  and the 2016 attack on the Saudi Embassy 600
  and Ahmadinejad xli, 541–542, 550, 558–559, 564–565, 575–580
  and anti-West rhetoric of 467, 486, 503, 517, 536, 600, 603
  and the assassination attempt on Hajjariyan 514
  and the Axis of Resistance 590–591
  and *Basiji*s 466–467, 510–511, 514–515, 556, 572
  and clashes with the 6th Majles 522–523, 525
  and COVID-19 617
  and economic jihad 550
  and elections 462, 463, 464–465, 525–526, 562–563, 572, 604–605, 616, 618
  and the Fifth Assembly of Experts 605
  and Forqan's assassination attempt on 397, 422
  and the Guardian Council 460, 462–463
  and the Guardian Jurist's Line (*khate velayat*) 475
  and Hashemi-Rafsanjani 458–459, 463, 464–465, 466–467, 474–477, 535–536, 568, 605
  and the *hejab* 413–414
  and *Hezbollahi*s 466–467, 498, 500, 503, 510, 514, 602
  and the Hojatiyyeh Society 431
  and the Intelligence Organization of the Islamic Revolutionary Guard Corps 609
  and the Islamic Revolutionary Guard Corps 382, 497, 556–557
  and Khatami 467–468, 494, 495–497, 510, 517–518, 521–522
  and Khomeyni 433, 440–441, 535–536
  and Mesbah-Yazdi 511
  and Montazeri 496
  and the Mykonos Affair 483
  and nomination as Khomeyni's successor xxxvii, 456–457
  and nuclear programme 543, 546–547
  and Palestine 547
  and press censorship 515
  and presidency of xxxv–xxxvi, 424–425, 433, 434, 446
  and protests against xliii, 509–510, 571–572, 573–574, 608–609, 612–614, 615–616
  and Rowhani 588, 601, 602–603
  and the rule of the Guardian Jurist 497, 518
  and Seyyed Qutb 459
  and Shariatmadari 486
  and Soleymani and the Qods Force 590–591
  and Soleymani's death 614–615

and Trump 610
and US invasions of Afghanistan and Iraq 528–529
and violence against opponents 498–499, 503, 505–506
and war against ISIS 592
and Western sanctions 550, 601
and 'world arrogance' 367, 548, 564, 591
and Zahra Mostafavi (Khomeyni's daughter) 587
Khamenei, Hadi 463, 476
Khamushi, Ali-Naqi 383
Khanali, Abolhasan 257
Kharrazi, Kamal 495, 511, 527
Khatam al-anbia, see *Qarargah sazandeggiye khatam al-anbia*
Khatami, Mohammad
  and Abdollah Nuri 500–501
  and Additional Protocol to the Nuclear Non-Proliferation Treaty 529
  and attack on Karbaschi 499
  and attacks on his ministers 503
  and conservative opposition to 510–512, 514, 518–520, 523–524
  and 'dialogue among civilizations' 526, 528
  and economic legacy of 529–530
  and foreign policy of 527–528
  and the Foruhar murders 504
  and Khamenei 467–468, 494, 495–497, 510, 517–518, 521–522
  and liberalization 492, 493–494, 500, 503, 520–521
  and Oil Stabilization Fund 530
  and Paris discourse 357
  and presidential campaign of 491–492
  and presidency of xxxviii–xl, 494–496, 522, 529–531
  and President Clinton 526, 528
  and re-election as president 521–522
  and reformist faction in the Sixth Majles xxxix, 512, 518–519, 522–523, 524–526
  and reformist press 506, 507–508
  and resignation as minister of culture and Islamic guidance xxxvii, 467–468
  and the role of the Guardian Jurist 493, 496
  and suspension of uranium enrichment xl, 529
  and the 'Twin Bills' 523–524
  and the US 497, 527–528
Khatami, Mohammad-Reza 517–518
Khatibi, Hoseyn 225
Khayami brothers 309
Khayatbashi, Hasan 322
Khazal bin Jabir al-Kabi (Sheykh Khazal) xxv, 50, 69, 71, 139–141, 160
Khazali, Abolqasem 431
Khiyabani, Musa 425
Khiyabani, Sheykh Mohammad xxiv, 61, 99–103, 126
Khomeyni, Seyyed Ahmad 404, 406, 412–413, 415, 448, 459, 506
Khomeyni, Seyyed Mostafa xxxiii, 346–347, 349
Khomeyni, Seyyed Ruhollah Musavi
  and 1963 arrest of 273–274, 282
  and the 1979 revolution 366–370
  and the 1988 prison massacres 445–446
  and absolute rule of the Guardian Jurist 440–441
  and 'Mohammaden' vs 'American' Islam 442
  and anti-shah rhetoric of 271–272, 273, 283, 345–346, 347–348, 351, 360–361
  and attacks on the press 400–403
  and banishment from Iran in 1964 xxxi, 283
  and Bani-Sadr 417–419, 420–422
  and Bazargan 377–379
  and the Constitution xxxv, xxxvi, 366, 375, 394, 398–399, 403, 455–456
  and death of 456
  and the death of his son Mostafa 346–347
  and demonstrations in support of xxxiii, 273–274, 349–351, 353–355, 361
  and establishment of the Islamic Republic 371, 375–376
  and exile in Paris 356–358
  and Fadais 370, 413, 427
  and fatwa against Salman Rushdie xxxvi, 446–447
  and *Hezbollahi*s 370
  and the Hojatiyyeh Society 430–431
  and Imam's Assistance/Relief Committee 383–384

and the Imam's Line 391, 431, 433, 434, 442, 457, 457
and the Iran–Iraq War 416–417, 443
and Islamic government 417–418
and the Islamic Revolution Committees 379–380
and the Islamic Revolutionary Guards Corp xxxiv, xxxvi, 381
and Islamization of Iranians 376
and Islamization of the universities 409–410
and Islamic attire 413–414
and Khamenei 433, 440–441, 535–536
and Kurdistan 386–389
and the Mojahedin of the Islamic Revolution 394–395, 434–435
and Montazeri xxxvi, 447–450
and the National Front 421
and the Nojeh coup 414–415
and the People's Mojahedin xxxv, xxxvi, 413, 419–421–422
and post-revolutionary purges 385–386
and Qotbzadeh 428–430
and return to Iran xxxiv, 365–366
and Revolutionary Islamic Courts 380
and Shariatmadari 392–394, 429
and Sources of Imitation 349, 397, 429, 456
and state executions 380, 415, 445
and the Tudeh Party 427
and the US 363, 403–404, 442–443
and the US Embassy hostage crisis 404–407, 412
and violence of supporters xxxiii, 352, 402, 413
and women's suffrage 271–272
see also Assembly of Militant Clerics, Association of Militant Clergy, Construction Jihad, Council of the Islamic Revolution, Foundation of the Oppressed, Islamic Coalition of Mourning Groups, Islamic Republic Party, Islamic Revolutionary Guards Corp, Student Followers of the Imam's Line
Khorasani, Akhund Molla Mohammad-Kazem 34, 42, 46, 52, 56
Khorram, Ahmad 530–531

Khosravani, Ataollah xxxi, 278, 283
Khosravani, Keyvan 311
Khosrowdad, Manuchehr xxxiv, 369
Khosrowshahi, Ali 310
Kia, Khojasteh 316
Kianuri, Nureddin 241, 427–428
Kissinger, Henry xxxii, 295–296, 343
Kiyan (monthly periodical) xxxvii, 487
Kiyan-Tajbaksh, Yahya 561
Klestil, Thomas 527
Kolahi, Mohammad-Reza 422
Komaleh Organization (Kurdistan's Society of Revolutionary Toilers) 386
Komer, Robert 264–265
Komiteh Prison 340, 368
Kordan, Ali 562–563
Kordestani, Asadollah Khan 54
Kordmihan, Hasan 600
Kupal, Mohammad-Sadeq 176
Kurdish Democratic Party of Iran (KDPI) xxxiv, xxxvii, 386, 444, 453, 482
Kurdish Republic of Mahabad xxviii, 197–198
Kushan, Mansur 485
Kuzichkin, Vladimir 428

Lahiji, Abdolkarim 397
Lahuti, Abolqasem xxv, 125–127, 381–382
Lahuti-Eshkevari, Hasan 381
Lajevardi, Asadollah 419, 422, 428, 448
Lambton, Anne 180–181
Land reform xxxi, 54, 252, 256, 261–265, 267–268, 270, 272–273
Langerudi, Jafar 397
Larijani, Ali xliv, 468, 476, 511, 536–537, 539, 542, 545, 562, 568, 571, 579, 601, 618
Larijani, Sadeq 520, 581
Law of Talion (*qisas*) 421, 593
Le Rosey xxvi, 163
Le Rougetel, John 204
Liyakhov, Vladimir Platonovich 37, 43–44, 50
Loqmaniyan, Hoseyn 519

MacNeil, John 16
Madani, Ahmad 389–390
Mafakher al-molk, Ali-Naqi 51

Mahdavi-Kani, Mohammad-Reza 379, 423, 492, 511, 533, 540, 595–596
Mahdiyoun, Saeed 415
Mahjubi, Manuchehr 321
Mahsuli, Sadeq 544–545, 554, 563, 568, 581
Mahvash (Masumeh Azizi-Borujerdi) 319, 328
Majd al-molk, Mohammad-Khan 22
Majidi, Mohsen (Morteza) 514, 516
Majles
    and fifteenth session 177, 195–199, 206–207
    and fifth session 120, 133, 135, 160
    and first session 36, 38–39, 54
    and fourteenth session 177–180, 182–183, 186, 190, 203, 214, 231
    and fourth session xxv, 90, 98, 100–101, 122, 126, 128, 131–132
    and nineteenth session 245, 249, 256–257, 280
    and second session 51, 68, 73
    and sixteen session 205, 208–209, 246
    and third session xxiii, 73–74
    see also Majles of the Islamic Republic
Majles of the Islamic Republic
    and eleventh session xxvi, 159, 616
    and fifth session 479–481, 508, 516
    and first session 430
    and fourth session 464–465
    and seventh session 523, 562, 607
    and sixth session xxxix, 500, 512, 515–517, 520, 522, 525–526, 531–533, 560
    and third session 459
Majlesi, Mohammad-Baqer 10, 200–201
Makhmalbaf, Mohsen 461
Makki, Hoseyn 196, 206–208, 210–212, 222, 239, 245
Makui, Mortezaqoli Eqbal al-saltaneh 137
Malek al-motekalemin, Nasrollah 29
Maleki, Khalil 344
Malkam Khan 20–22
    and *Qanun* (The Law) (newspaper) 21
Mansur, Ali 157, 165, 211
Mansur, Hasan-Ali xxxi, xxxii, 277–278, 281–286, 288, 485, 559
Mansuri-Tehrani, Ahmad 287
Manuchehri, Hoseyn 177

Maraghehi, Zeinolabeddin 22–23, 25, 29
Marashi-Najafi, Shahabeddin 270, 349, 392
Marble Palace xxxii, 150, 172, 209, 286
Mardom (People) (newspaper) 180–181
Marenches, Alexandre de 357
Marighella, Carlos 333
Marling, Charles 75–76, 82, 86
Maroufi, Abbas 476
Marriage of the Blessed (film) 461
martial law 44, 98, 111, 121, 124, 126, 129–130, 138, 142, 171, 177, 187–188, 205–206, 213, 236, 248, 274, 352–355, 360, 580
Martyrs' Foundation of the Islamic Revolution 383–384
Marx, Karl 7, 315, 337
Marxism 162, 329–330, 335, 619
Marxist-Leninist xxxii, 297, 328–330, 335, 345, 367, 376, 426–427
Mashrueh (sharia-based or religiously grounded system), *see* Constitution 37, 46, 64
Mashruteh (constitutional system), *see* Constitution
Masudi, Abbas 178
Matbui, Iraj 155
Matin al-saltaneh 84
Matin-Daftari, Ahmad 157, 176
Mayer, Franz 176
Mazandarani, Sheykh Abdollah 34, 42, 46, 52, 56
McFarlane, Robert 449
Mecca 17, 115, 302, 439, 453
Meftahi, Abbas 329–330
Meftahi, Asadollah 330
Mehrabad Airport 364–365, 368
Mehralizadeh, Mohsen 537
Mehregan Club 257
Meir, Golda 296
Melli Bank 145, 146
    and Agricultural and Industrial Bank 146
Mesbah-Yazdi, Mohammad-Taqi 498, 500, 511–512, 521, 539–541, 544, 564, 580–581, 598, 603, 605
    and *Partove Sokhan* (Beam of the Word) (newspaper) 539

Meshkat al-mamalek, Mohammadnazar Khan 83
Meshkinfam, Abdolrasoul 334
Meshkini, Ali 456, 496, 512
Mesqali, Farshid 313
Middleton, George 223–224
Migrants (*mohajerin*) 79, 80, 80–81
Milani, Mohammad-Hadi Milani 183, 337, 427
Mill, John Stuart 7, 346
Millspaugh, Arthur xxv, 127, 130, 132, 145, 173–174, 184
Minachi, Naser 408
Ministry of Culture and Islamic Guidance xxxvii, 460, 467, 476, 485, 491–492, 494, 515, 531, 536, 576, 589, 594
Ministry of Information 448–449, 513
Mir-Salim, Mohammad-Mostafa 476, 485, 492, 495, 606
Mirashrafi, Mehdi 220, 223
Mirbaqeri, Ali 541
Mirdamadi, Mohsen 464
Mirza Baqir 101
Mirza Ebrahim Khan 83–84
Mirza Ebrahimov 189
Mirza Kuchek Khan (Jangali) xxiii–xxiv, 49, 67, 84, 88–92, 99–100, 103–105, 122–124, 127, 190
Mirzadeh Eshqi (Mohammad-Reza Kordestani) 138
Mobasser, Mohsen 259, 287, 304
Modarres, Seyyed Hasan 74, 80, 112, 128–131, 135, 143, 159–160
Moez al-saltaneh, Abdolhoseyn 54
Moez al-soltan, Abdolkarim 49
Mofatteh, Mohammad 397
Mofid, Bijan 316
Moftizadeh, Ahmad 387
Mohajerani, Ataollah 477, 480, 495, 498–499, 503, 507
Mohammad-Ali Shah
    and assassination attempt on 43
    and attacks on the Majles 41–42, 44–45
    and attempt to return to power 58
    and the Constitution 33–34, 39
    and the constitutionalists 34–35, 38–39, 43–45
    and corruption 33–34
    and the despotic front 36, 41–42, 45–46
    and the First Majles 38–40
    and rescinding of the Constitution 45
    and removal from power 51
    and Russian support for 37, 49–50, 58
    and Sheykh Fazlollah Nuri 36–37, 39–40
    and Short/Lesser Despotism 45–48
    and siege of Tabriz 49–50
    and the Supplement to the Constitution 39–40, 41
Mohammad-Reza Shah Pahlavi
    and the 1953 coup attempt 226–227
    and the 20th Majles 256–257
    and Ala 243
    and Amini 261, 263–264
    and the armed forces 184, 185
    and assassination attempts on 205–206, 286–287
    and 'Aryamehr' (title) xxxii, 289–290
    and attack on Fayziyeh Seminary School 272–273
    and authoritarianism 204, 206, 248, 300–302
    and the Baghdad Pact 244
    and Borujerdi 270
    and Britain 163, 165, 183, 224
    and cancer treatment in New York 403
    and Carter 343–344, 362
    and the celebration of 2,500 years of monarchy 293, 295
    and the clergy 271, 272–273
    and the Confederation of Iranian Students National Union 340–342
    and coronation of 291–293
    and departure from Iran 364–365
    and economic policies of 304–305, 306–308, 308–311
    and election rigging 208–209, 238, 245, 253–256
    and Eqbal 248–249
    and his Great Civilization 294, 298, 302, 303, 305, 327
    and growing opposition to 344–345, 348–349, 350–351 353–356, 361
    and the June 1963 uprising 272–275

and Khomeyni 271–272, 273–275, 347–348, 349–350, 351–352, 356–357, 359–360, 381, 403
and land reform 264, 267–268
and Mosaddeq 220, 222, 224–225
and the National Front 242, 253–254, 265, 270
and Nixon 295–297
and nuclear programme 305
and oil 213, 293
and Pahlavism 293, 295
and popular discontent 257
and press censorship 206, 291, 301, 331
and proxy war with the Dhofar Rebels in Oman 297–298
and the Qarani affair 250–251
and Qavam 184–185, 197, 198–199
and regional expansionism 296
and referendum on the White Revolution 267–269
and reign of xxvii–xxxiii, 288–289, 327–328
and repression of opposition 205–206, 240–242, 250, 261–262, 270, 275–276, 307–308
and return to Iran aged sixteen xxvi, 163
and SAVAK 246, 348–349
and the Second Constituent Assembly 206
and Shapur Bakhtiyar 361
and Special Bureau of Information (*Daftare Vijeh Ettelaat*) 251
and sprinkling reforms 334, 344
and the Tehran Conference 172
and the Tudeh Party 269
and two-party system 249–250, 253
and the US 234, 246, 251–253, 258, 260, 263–265, 293, 296–297, 298–300, 342–343, 362–364
and women's participation in socio-political life 277, 282
and Zahedi 238–239, 242–243
see also Resurgence Party, SAVAK, White Revolution
Mohammaden Islam 442
Mohammadi, Narges 597–598
Mohammadi-Gilani, Mohammad 422

Mohammadi-Reyshahri, Mohammad 429
Mohaqeqi, Ayat 415
Mohsen, Saeed 333
Mohseni-Ejehi, Gholamhoseyn 499
Mohtashamipur, Ali-Akbar 459, 462
and *Bayan* (Expression) (monthly periodical) 463
Moin, Mostafa 537, 540
Mojahedin of the Islamic Revolution (MIR) 394–395, 397, 401–403, 418, 423, 425, 434–435, 442
Mokhtari, Mohammad 162, 505–506
Molotov, Vyacheslav 192, 572, 613
Money and Credit Council 554
Monshizadeh, Davud 225
Monshizadeh, Ebrahim Khan 83–84
Montazeri, Hoseyn-Ali xxxvi, 388, 429, 436, 447–450, 453, 496, 498
Moqadam, Naser 258, 352
Morality police (*Gashte ershad*) 596
Mosaddeq, Mohammad xxviii–xxx, 143, 159, 169, 178–179, 186–187, 196, 198–199, 207–231, 233–239, 242, 244, 246, 248, 256, 259–260, 266–267, 269, 275, 278, 291, 315, 319, 356, 361–362, 377, 406, 419, 547, 590, 618
Mosaddeqists xxxiii, 226–227, 235, 238, 244, 253–254, 259–261, 265–266, 269–270, 286, 328, 362, 368, 377
Mosavat-Shirazi, Mohammad-Reza 29, 35
Moshir al-dowleh, Hasan (Hasan Pirnia) 20–21, 32, 75–76, 102–104, 107, 125, 128
Moslehi, Heydar xlii, 579–580, 587
Mostafavi, Rahmat 291
Mostafavi, Zahra 587
Mostashar al-dowleh, Mirza Sadeq Khan 54
Mostashar al-dowleh, Yusef Khan 22, 24–25, 54
Mostowfi al-mamalek, Hasan (Mostowfi) 74–76, 78, 80, 82, 86–87, 128, 131, 135–136
Motahhari, Morteza xxxiv, 347, 353, 369, 377, 395–396, 400, 447, 587
Motamed, Morris 548
Motamen al-molk, Hoseyn Pirnia 136

Motherland Party (*Hezbe Mihan*) (of Sanjabi, Shaygan and Azar) 179
Mottaki, Manuchehr 546–547, 564
Movahed, Vida 606
Movahedi-Kermani, Mohammad-Ali 498, 525
Mozaffareddin Shah Qajar xxi–xxii, 16, 26, 28, 31–32, 35–36
Musavi, Mir-Hoseyn xli, 363, 390–391, 404, 424–425, 431–435, 440, 442, 446, 449, 459, 462, 464, 467, 482, 491, 501, 564–572, 574, 578, 588–589, 604
Musavi-Ardebili, Abdolkarim 363, 390, 424, 432, 501
Musavi-Bojnurdi, Mohammad 604
Musavi-Khoeiyniha, Mohammad 404, 442, 459, 463–464
Musavi-Lari, Abdolvahed 501
Musavi-Tabrizi, Hoseyn 424, 464
Muslim Brotherhood (*Ikhwan al-Muslemin*) 201, 231
Muslim People of Iran's Republic Party (MPIRP) 392–394, 399–400
Mussolini, Benito Amilcare Andrea 110, 118

Nabavi, Behzad 397, 425, 432, 435, 466, 518
Naini, Mohammad-Hoseyn (Allameh) 52
Najaf xxxiii, 32, 34, 42–43, 46–47, 51, 55–56, 142, 201–202, 345–348, 366
Najaf Sources of Imitation, *see* Sources of Imitation
Naji, Reza xxxiv, 369
Nalbandian, Abbas 315–316
Nameye Farangestan (Letter of Europe) (newspaper) 118–119
Naqash, Anis 415
Naqdi, Mohammad-Reza 512
Nariman, Mahmud 179, 208, 210
Naser al-molk, Abolqasem Khan Qaragozlu 42, 57–58, 61–62, 68
Nasereddin Shah Qajar xxi, 16, 18–19, 21–24, 138, 458
Nasiri, Nematollah xxxiv, 227, 274, 286–287, 290, 339–340, 352, 360, 369
Nasr, Mohsen 258
Natanz (nuclear facility) 543, 546, 616

Nateq-Nuri, Ali-Akbar 432, 465, 475, 479, 481–482, 492–493, 498, 567–568
National Bank of Iran, *see* Melli Bank
National Front (*Jebhehye Melli*) (of Mosaddeq) xxviii, xxxi, xxxiii, xxxviii, 179, 208–210, 212–213, 218–221, 242–243, 249, 253–256, 259–262, 265–267, 269–270, 275–276, 284, 328–329, 333, 336, 344, 347–349, 357, 362, 371, 377, 389, 392, 415, 420–421, 426, 493, 504
National Iranian Television 316–317, 321
National Resistance Movement xxx, 235, 238, 243, 248, 253–254, 278
National Will Party (*Hezbe Eradeh Melli*) (of Seyyed Zia Tabatabai) 178–180, 220 and *Raad Emruz* (Today's Thunder) (newspaper) 180
Nationalist-Religious Activists 513, 519
Nationalists' Party (*Hezbe Meliyoun*) (of Eqbal) 249
Naus, Joseph 28, 30–31
Navab, Hoseynqoli Khan 53
Navab-Safavi, Mojtaba (Mir-Lowhi) xxviii–xxix, 201–204, 208–209, 212, 219, 222, 244–245, 284
Nazih, Hasan 259
Neauphle-le-Château xxxiii, 356–357
Neshat (Joy) (newspaper) 508
New Iran Party (*Hezbe Irane No*) (of Teymurtash) 158
New Iran Party (*Hezbe Irane Novin*) (of Hasan-Ali Mansur, Khosravani and Hoveyda) 278, 281, 283, 288
New York Hospital xxxv, 403
nezam (system/regime) of the Islamic Republic 450, 456–458, 464, 467, 472, 477, 479, 492–493, 496, 503, 510, 562, 570, 572–573, 581, 587–588, 602, 608, 613, 618
Nezam al-saltaneh, Rezaqoli khan 81
Nikbin, Abdolreza 333
Nikkhah, Parviz 287, 369
Niknejad, Morteza 284–285
Nikpay, Gholamreza 277
Nixon, Richard M.

and 'Nixon Doctrine' 295–297
and Strategic Arms Limitation Talks 326
and visits to Tehran xxxii, 237, 296–297
Nobakht, Habibollah 176, 318
Nojeh Coup xxxv, 414–415
Norman, Herman xxv, 104, 106–108, 110–111, 129
North Persia Force (*Norpeforce*) 89, 104
Northcroft, V. J. 212
Noveysi, Ruhollah 258
Nuclear Non-Proliferation Treaty xxxix, 529; *see also* Joint Comprehensive Plan of Action
Nurbakhsh, Mohsen 475
Nuri, Abdollah xxxviii–xxxix, 459, 477, 481, 495, 498–503, 506
Nuri, Sheykh Fazlollah 30, 32, 36–37, 39–43, 46, 51–52, 64, 84, 153

Obama, Barack xlii, 549, 599–600
Office of Consolidating Unity 462, 464, 477
Officers' Organization of the Tudeh Party
and infiltration of the armed forces 241
and the uprising of Khorasan officers 187–188
oil
and Britain xxiii, xxix, 26, 50, 71, 112, 139–140, 147–148, 185, 207–208, 213, 215, 217–218, 239–240
and disconnection from SWIFT 558
and Iron Committee 108–109
and nationalization xxvii, xxix, 169, 210, 212–213, 215, 218–219, 234, 236, 239–240, 243, 269, 377, 618
and north oil concession 197
and Oil Stabilization Fund 530
and OPEC (Organization of the Petroleum Exporting Countries) 293, 302
and Russia 193–194
and the US 216
see also Anglo-Iranian Oil Company, Anglo-Persian Oil Company, Consortium, D'Arcy concession 26
Operation Countenance xxvi, 165
opium 11, 27, 127, 129, 201

Organization for the Intellectual Development of Children and Young Adults (*Kanune Parvaresh Fekriye Koudakan va Nojavanan*) 312
Osanlu, Mansur 559–560
Ottoman Empire xxiii–xxiv, 18, 23, 44, 65, 70–73, 75–78, 81–82, 88, 127
Ovanessian, Arby 315–317
Ovey, Esmond 103
Oveysi, Gholamali 354
Owlovi, Ali 241

Page, Howard xxx, 240
Pahlavi, Ashraf 156, 163, 226
Pahlavi, Gholamreza 286
Pahlavi, Shams 155–156
Pahlbod, Mehrdad 314
Pakdini (Clean Faith) (Kasravi's new religion) 200
Pakravan, Hasan 286
Palizdar, Abbas 607
Parham, Baqer 345
Paris Peace Conference xxiv, 95–96
Parsa, Farrokru 277, 408
Party of Islamic Nations (*Hezbe Mellal Eslami*) (of Bojnurdi) 287–288
Party of the Patriots (*Hezbe Mihan Parastan*) (of Ali Jalali) 178
Parvaresh, Ali-Akbar 424–425
Pasandideh, Morteza 408
Pashai, Morteza 595–596
Payame Daneshju (Message of University Students) (periodical) 276
People's Fadai Guerrillas (*Cherikhaye Fadai Khalq*)
and the Anti-Sabotage Joint Committee 332
and attack on the Siyahkal Gendarmerie Station xxxii, 331–332, 334, 367
and establishment of 328–329
and the 'H-A-S Group' 329, 330, 331
and the *Hezbollah* 402
and the IRGC 381, 388–389
and the 'Jazani Group' xxxii, 328–329, 332
and Khomeyni 370
and Kurdistan 386–388

and Minority–Majority split 376, 426–427
and *Nabarde Khalq* (Combat of the
    Masses) (newspaper) 331
and the 'P-A-M Group' 329–331
and Tehran University demonstrations
    367, 370
and Turkman Sahra 388–389
and universities 331–332, 409
People of Iran Party (*Hezbe Mardome Iran*)
    (of Mohammad Nakhshab and Hoseyn
    Razi) 286
People's Mojahedin Organization (*Sazemane
    Mojahedine Khalqe Iran*) xxxii,
    xxxv–xxxvi, 331–335, 338–339, 346,
    357, 368–371, 381–382, 392, 395–396,
    399–400, 402, 407–409, 413, 415,
    418–427, 435, 444–446, 448, 609
People's Party (*Hezbe Mardom*) (of Alam) 249
Persepolis xxxii, 294, 296, 317
Persian Corridor 171–173, 175
Persian Empire 8, 294–295
Persian Gulf xxxii, 87, 147, 151, 172, 293,
    296–297, 436–437, 439, 527, 608
Persian Wildlife Heritage Foundation xliii,
    609
Pesyan, Mohammad-Taqi xxv, 123–125, 127
Peygham Emrooz (Today's Message)
    (newspaper) 400–401
Pezeshkzad, Iraj 322
Pishehvari, (Jafar Javadzadeh Badkubehi)
    xxviii, 105, 182, 189–190, 192–194,
    197–198
    and *Ajir* (Siren) (newspaper) 190
Pishmarga (Those who face death) (Kurdish
    military personnel) 395, 453
Pouyan, Amir-Parviz 329–330, 361
Principlists (*usulgarayan*) 524, 537, 542,
    562–563, 564–565, 576, 580–581, 603,
    605, 606, 608, 610
Progress Party (*Hezbe Taraqi*) (of
    Teymurtash) 159
Progressive Centre (*Kanune Moteraqi*) (of
    Hasan-Ali Mansur) 277–278
prostitution 201, 203, 272, 320, 345, 366, 380,
    392, 408, 414, 467
Provincial Association of Azarbayjan 47

Puladin, Mahmud Khan 125
Punishment Committee 83–85
Purdavud, Ebrahim 72
Purmohammadi, Mostafa 562, 568
Pursartip, Mohammad 178
Purzand, Abolhasan 176
Puyandeh, Mohammad-Jafar 505–506

Qalibaf, Mohammad-Baqer 536–537,
    539–540, 542, 586–587, 589, 600, 616
Qanatabadi, Shams 204, 208, 212, 221
Qandchi-Mazandarani, Ahmad 237
Qarargah sazandeggiye khatam al-anbia
    (Construction Base of the Seal of the
    Prophets) 474, 530–531, 536, 557–558,
    612
Qarani, Mohammadvali xxx, 250–252, 396
Qarazi, Mohammad 424, 586–587
Qarib-Afshar, Parviz 322
Qasem, Abdolkarim 251
Qasemlu, Abdolrahman 387, 482
Qavam, Ahmad xxviii–xxix, 112, 122–125,
    127–131, 169–170, 174, 177, 183–185,
    193–199, 203, 209, 218, 223, 228, 238,
    318
Qavam al-Molk, Ebrahim 87–88
Qavam–Sadchikov Agreement (1946) xxviii,
    193–195, 198
Qazi Mohammad xxviii, 197, 453
Qazi-Tabatabai, Mohammad-Ali 397
Qiyame Siye Tir (21 July 1952 uprising) 224
Qoddusi, Ali 423
Qods Force 556, 590–591, 614
Qom Seminary School 429
Qotbi, Reza 314–316, 321–322
Qotbzadeh, Sadeq 357, 370–371, 382, 419,
    428–430
Quchani, Mohammad 500, 540
Quran 10, 17, 42, 51, 64, 111, 135, 200–201,
    231, 272, 283, 333, 346, 396, 413,
    415–416, 432, 435, 441, 446, 453–454,
    459, 486–487, 489, 506, 512, 574

Rabei, Ashraf 425
Radmanesh, Reza 183, 231
Rafiqdust, Mohsen 473

Rafsanjani, Faezeh 480–481, 499
Rahim-Mashai, Esfandiyar 575–581, 587
Rahim-Safavi, Yahya 499, 507–508, 511
Rahimi, Mehdi xxxiv, 369, 576
Rahmaninejad, Naser 317
Rahnavard, Zahra 567, 574
Rahnema, Fereydun 316
Rahnema, Zeinolabeddin 120, 160
Raisi, Ebrahim xliv, 606, 618
Rajai, Ali-Reza 513
Rajai, Mohammad-Ali 418–419, 422–423, 537
Rajavi, Masud xxxv, 423, 425, 444
    and National Council of Resistance in Iran 444
    and 'National Liberation Army of Iran' 443–445
Ramin, Mohammad-Ali 548
Ramzi, Farshid 322
Rashidiyan, Asadollah 223–224, 226–227, 253, 258
Rashidiye-Motalaq, Ahmad 349
Rashti, Sheykh Kazem 17, 64
Rasti-Kashani, Hoseyn 435
Rasulzadeh, Mohammad-Ali 53, 58
Rauf Bey (Orbey) xxiii, 77–78
Razini, Ali 445
Razmara, Haj Ali xxix, 197, 205–206, 208, 211–213, 219–220, 238, 243, 245
Reagan, Ronald 412
Red Army xxiv, 104, 122, 186, 189
Reform Movement (Islamic Republic) 466, 498, 512–513, 579
Renewal/Modernity Party (*Hezbe Tajaddod*) (of Davar, Teymurtash, *et al.*) 120
restaurants 322–323, 350, 352, 355, 585
Resurgence Party (*Hezbe Rastakhize Mellate Iran*) (of Mohammad-Reza Shah) xxxii, 277, 301–302, 307, 345, 350, 393
    and Constructive and Progressive Wings of 302
Reuter, Baron Julius de xxi, 20–21, 98
Revolutionary Islamic Courts xxxv, 223, 369, 379–380, 382–383, 401–403, 407–408, 422–424, 427–428, 464, 593
Rex Movie Theatre xxxiii, 352

Reza Shah Pahlavi (Reza Khan)
    and the 1921 coup xxv, 103, 109–111, 120–121
    and abdication 165
    and Ahmad Shah 110, 111, 126, 131, 133–135, 142–143
    and Ali-Akbar Davar 119
    and ascent to the throne 142–143
    and attempt to establish a republic 133–136
    and Britain 110, 112, 164–165
    as commander of the army 121, 122
    and conflicts with semi-autonomous tribes 139–141
    and control over the Majles 158–159
    and corruption 137
    and the Cossack Brigade 108, 111
    and the D'Arcy Concession 147–148
    and decline in rural living standards 148
    and economic development 145–147
    and education 152, 157
    and Germany 163–164
    and the Gilan insurrection 122–123
    and *Haqiqat* (Truth) (newspaper) 129
    and Hitler 164
    and infrastructure 149–151
    and Iranians as Aryans 164
    and judicial reform 152
    and Lahuti's coup in Tabriz 125–126
    and leisure sector 153
    and *Marde Azad* (Free Man) (newspaper) 119, 131
    as minister of war 126–131
    and modernization 151
    and the New Iran Party 158–159
    and oil 147–148
    and Pesyan's Khorasan rebellion 123–125
    and political killings 137, 138
    as prime minister 131–133
    and reign of xxv–xxvi, 143–144, 157–158
    and repression of opponents 138–139, 142, 155–156, 159–161
    and Seyyed Zia 109–110, 121–122
    and 'uniform dress code' xxvi, 154
    and urban development 149–151
    and the veil 155–156
    and women's rights 153–154

Rezai, Ahmad 334, 339
Rezai, Ali 350
Rezai, Mehdi 335
Rezai, Mohsen 395, 423, 436, 473, 536, 545, 565, 570, 586
Rezai, Reza 334–335
Rezainejad, Darush 548
riots xxvii, xliii, 12, 22, 27, 142, 174–175, 256, 351, 359, 361, 470
Riyahi, Mohammad-Taqi 227
Riyazi, Abdollah 277, 290, 292
Rokni, Naser 415
Roosevelt, Franklin D. xxvii, 172
Roosevelt, Kermit 213, 226–227, 236
Rose Mary (Italian oil tanker) 218
Roshdiyeh (Mirza Hasan Tabrizi) 9
Roshvand-Sardari, Abolqasem 388
Rountree, William 246
Rowhani, Hasan xlii–xliv, 347, 429, 480, 542, 551, 553, 585–603, 605–615, 617–619
 and *Aseman* (Sky) (newspaper) 593
Rowhani, Mohammad-Sadeq 429
Royal Dutch Shell Company 185
Rule of the Guardian Jurist, *see* Guardian Jurist
Rushdie, Salman xxxvi, 446–447
Rusk, Dean 263
Russia
 and 1909 occupation of Tabriz 49, 52–53, 61
 and 1917 revolutions in 85, 86, 91
 and 1917 withdrawal from Iran 85, 86
 and attack on the Majles 44
 and Cheka 105, 114–115
 and clashes with Ottoman forces in Iran in WWI xxiii, 70–71
 and famine in Iran during WWI 92–93
 and food crisis in Iran during WWII 174–175
 and Iranian constitutionalists 37, 45, 52–53, 58, 59–62, 69, 71–73
 and Iranian oil xxvii, 185–186, 193–194, 197, 198
 and Iranian-Russian Cossack Brigade 21
 and Jangalis 90–91, 104–106
 and Kurdish Republic of Mahabad xxviii, 197–198
 and loans to Iran 26
 and Mohammad-Ali Shah 33, 45, 51, 58
 and Mozaffareddin Shah 26
 and Nasereddin Shah 21
 and nineteenth-century migration of Iranians to 13
 and occupation of Iran 60–62, 69–70, 74–77, 78–79, 80–83
 and occupation of Iran during WWII xxvi, 164–165, 169–172, 174, 175, 186
 and Russian Social Democratic Party 49
 and Russo-Japanese War (1904–5) 28
 and Russo-Persian Treaty of Friendship (1921) xxv, 112, 122
 and Russo-Persian wars 16
 and secessionist movement in Azarbayjan xxviii, 188–193, 194–195, 197
 and the Tudeh Party 180, 181, 186, 188, 428
 and White Russians 89, 104, 106, 115
 and 'zone of influence' in northern Iran 26, 36, 59–60
 see also Anglo-Russian Convention; Cossacks; Qavam–Sadchikov Agreement; Red Army; Stalin, Joseph; Tripartite Anglo-Soviet-Persian Treaty of Alliance; Trotsky, Leon
Rusta, Reza 182
Ruzbeh, Khosrow 182, 241–242

Saad al-dowleh, Javad 36, 75–76, 112
Saadati, Kazem 329
Sabbaqiyan, Hashem 484
Sabet, Habibollah, xxx, 320–321
Sabeti, Parviz, 349, 351–352, 360
Sadchikov, Ivan, xxviii, 193–194, 197, 228
Saddam Hoseyn, 415–416, 436, 444
Sadiq, Issa, 105, 119
Sadiqi, Gholamhoseyn, 260, 267
Sadr al-ashraaf, Mohsen, 105
Sadr, Mohammad-Baqer 415
Sadri, Jafarqoli 360
Saed, Mohammad xxvii, 170, 179, 185–186, 190, 199, 206
Saeed, Javad 302
Saeedi-Sirjani, Ali-Akbar 462, 484–485

Safai-Farahani, Ali-Akbar 329, 331
Safari, Latif 515
Safavid dynasty 200
Saffar-Harandi, Reza 284–285, 576
Saffari, Bijan 317, 329
Saffari-Ashtiyani, Mohammad 329
Sahabi, Ezatollah 484, 486, 513, 515
Sahabi, Yadollah 243, 259, 369, 397, 399, 430
Sajadi, Mohammad 176
Salam (Greetings) (newspaper) xxxviii, 464, 508
Salamati, Mohammad 397, 425, 432, 435, 466
Salami, Hoseyn 614
Salar al-dowleh (Abolfath Mirza) xxii, 58, 60
Saleh, Allahyar 179, 196, 209, 216, 253, 256, 265, 267
Salehi, Ali-Akbar 601
Samareh-Hashemi, Mojtaba 545, 576
Sami, Kazem 430, 506
Samsam al-mamalek, Shir-Mohammad Khan 77
Sanei, Yusef 501
Sangelaji, Shariat 200–201
Sani-Hazrat, Mohammad Khan 42, 51
Sanjabi, Karim 78, 179, 260, 267, 344
Sardar Moazez, Azizollah 125
Sardar-Afkham, Mohammad-Ali (Vakilodowleh) 22
Sardar-Etemad, Khosrow Khan (Moqtader-nezam) 42
Sarem al-dowleh, Akbar-Mirza 96, 99, 112
Sarhadizadeh, Abolqasem 440, 462
Satanic Verses, *see* Rushdie, Salman
Sattar Khan xxii, 47–48, 53, 57
Saudi Arabia xlii, 439, 608 527
    and attack on their embassy in Tehran 599–600
Saunders, M. 126–127, 130, 134
SAVAK (State Organization for Intelligence and Security) xxx, xxxiii, 245–248, 252, 260, 269, 272–274, 281, 283, 286–287, 290, 294, 313, 317–318, 332, 334, 338–339, 343–344, 346, 348–350, 352, 360, 364, 368, 381, 393, 426, 429, 509
Sayyad, Parviz 321
Sayyad-Shirazi, Ali 444–445

Sayyah, Kazem Khan 108–109, 111
Schacht, Hjalmar 163
Schmidt, Helmut 362
Schuenenmann, Max Otto 80
Second Khordad Movement of 23 May 1997 493
Second World War
    and Allied Powers 171, 174
    and American forces in the Persian corridor 172
    and the anti-fascist front 180–181
    and food crisis in Iran 174–175, 184–185
    and inflation in Iran 173–174
    and invasion of Iran by Britain and Russia xxvi, 165, 174, 175, 186
    and Iran under foreign occupation 169–170
    and pro-Axis Iranians 176–177
    and the Red Army's occupation of Azarbayjan 188–189
    and the Tehran Conference 172
    and the Trans-Iranian Railway 164–165, 172, 175, 176
    see also Tripartite Anglo-Soviet-Persian Treaty of Alliance
sedition (*fetneh*) 103, 257, 351, 458, 573–574, 588, 598, 600
Sepahdar Rashti (Fatollah Akbar) 107
'Sepahsalar Agreement' (1916) 82–83, 87
serial/chain killings 498, 501
servitors (*khadem*) or traitors (*khaen*) 68
Seven Sisters, *see* Consortium
Seyyed Qutb 244, 280, 459
Seyyed-Emami, Kavous 609
Shabani, Ali 349
Shabestari, Mohammad-Mojtahed 498
Shadman, Jalal 178
Shafa, Shojaeddin 178, 289
Shahandeh, Abbas 220, 239
Shahram, Mohammad-Taqi 335
Shahre Qeseh (City of Tales) (play) 316
Shahrestani, Naser 257
Shahriyari, Majid 548
Shahyad Square 361, 367
Shamkhani, Ali 435
Shamlu, Ahmad 486
Shamsabadi, Reza 286–287

Shamsolvaezin, Mashallah 487, 508, 515
Shapshal, Serguy Markovitch 33, 37, 42–43
Sharafkandi, Sadeq xxxvii, 482
sharia 17, 37, 39–40, 46, 56, 64, 201, 210, 360, 367, 475, 486
Shariat-Razavi, Azar (Mehdi) 237
Shariati, Ali xxxii–xxxiii, 276, 335–340, 346–347, 357, 361, 395–396, 400–401, 418, 424, 505, 513, 545, 565
Shariatmadari, Kazem 270, 349, 357, 369–371, 392–394, 399–400, 428–430, 486
Sharif, Majid 335, 505
Sharif-Emami, Jafar xxx, xxxiii, 176, 254–256, 258, 289–290, 292, 352–353, 359
Sharif-Vaqefi, Majid 335
Sharvin, Mahmud 176
Shaygan, Ali 179, 210
Shepherd, Francis 212, 215, 220
Sheriden, J. K. 174
Sheybani, Abbas 457
Sheybani, Ebrahim 553
Sheybani, Habibollah Khan 126
Shiism 35, 45–46, 99, 199–202, 206, 337, 346–347, 357, 396, 502, 544
Shikak (Simitqu), Esmail Aqa 127
Shiraz Art Festival, xxxii, 312, 314–317
Shirazi, Jahangir Khan 35, 45
Shirazi, Mirza Hasan 22
Shirazi, Seyyed Mohammad-Ali, *see* Bab
Shirvanlu, Firuz 312
Shobeyr-Khaqani, Mohammad-Taher Ale 389–390
Shojooni, Jafar 603
Short/Lesser Despotism (*Estebdad Saqir*) 45
    and Azarbayjan's Military Response to 47–48
    and religious response to 46–47
Shushtari, Mohammad-Ali 220
Shuster, Morgan 15, 55, 59–61, 63, 68, 100
Six-Day War 296
Smyth, Henry 107–110
Sobhe Emrooz (This Morning) (newspaper) 506, 512, 515
Social Democrats (*Ejtemaiyoun amiyoun*) 30, 34, 37–38, 40, 47, 53–54, 504
    and Victorious Guard (*garde fateh*) 54

Social Moderate Party (*ejtemaiyoun etedaliyoun*) 54
Society of Muslim Mojaheds (*majma mosalmanan mojahed*) (of Qanatabadi) 204
Soheyli, Ali 170, 179, 184–185, 199
Soleymani, Qasem xliv, 556, 590–592, 614–615
Soltan al-Motekalemin, Sheykh Mohammad 31
Soltan Hasan Qajar 165
Soltanpur, Saeed 317
Sorush, Abdolkarim (Hoseyn Haj Faraj Dabbagh) 486–487, 498, 531
Sources of Imitation (*maraje taqlid*) 65
    and the Constitution of the Islamic Republic 397
    and despotism of Mohammad-Ali Shah 46–47
    and the Islamic Republic 429, 456
    and Khomeyni 349
    and land reform of Mohammad-Reza Shah 270
    and Qom Seminary School 429
    and Sheykh Fazlollah Nuri 42–43
    and Taqizadeh 55–56
    see also Golpaygani, Mohammad-Reza; Khalili-Tehrani, Mirza Hoseyn; Khorasani, Akhund Molla Mohammad-Kazem; Marashi-Najafi, Shahabeddin; Shariatmadari, Kazem
South Persian Rifles xxiii–xxiv, 86–89, 91, 106
Sowlat al-dowleh, Esmail Khan 87
Spanish flu 94
Special Court for the Clergy 449
Stalin, Joseph xxvii, 172, 189, 192–193, 195–196, 198, 315
Standard Oil Company 127, 231, 239
Stark, Pete 342
Staroselski, Vsevolod 106–107
State Edict (*hokm hokumati*) (of the Islamic Republic) 518, 533
Stokes, C. B. 59, 216
Strategic Arms Limitation Talks (SALT) 296, 326

strikes
  and the 1953 coup 236
  at Abadan oil refinery 162, 213
  by the Bus Workers' Syndicate xl, 559
  by the Confederation of Iranian Students National Union 341–342
  and *Keyhan* 401
  and Mohammad-Reza Shah 355–356, 359–360
  by oil workers xxxiii, 162, 187, 213
  and petrol prices 283
  and Rowhani 598–599, 609
  by Tehran's Teachers' Association xxxi, 257
  at Tehran University Medical School 163
Student Followers of the Imam's Line xxxv, 404, 407, 409, 411, 428, 459
Sufism 200
Sullivan, William 321, 361–363
Sultan Qabus xxxii, 297–298
SUMKA Party (of Davud Monshizadeh) 225
Supplement to the Constitution, *see* Constitution
Suresrafil, Qasem 132
Sururi, Mohammad 290

Tabandeh, Nourali 610
Tabari, Ehsan 181
Tabarzadi, Heshmatollah 477
Tabatabai, Javad 258
Tabatabai, Mohammad-Sadeq 74, 179
Tabatabai, Seyyed Mohammad 29–32, 34, 37–38, 42, 45, 54, 179
Tabatabai, Seyyed Ziaeddin (Seyyed Zia) xxv, 84, 88, 98, 103, 108–112, 118, 121–122, 124, 179–180, 190, 194–196, 204, 213–214, 220, 223
Tabatabai-Qomi, Hasan 201, 429
Tabriz University xxxv, 330, 409
Tabrizi, Abbas Aqa 40
Tadayyon, Mohammad 120, 128, 130, 135, 158
Taeb, Hoseyn 609
Tafazoli, Jahangir 176, 178, 196
Taheri, Hadi 220
Tahmasebi, Khalil xxix, 212, 245

Tajaddod, Reza 120, 160
Tajbakhsh, Ardeshir 287
Tajzadeh, Mostafa 435, 616, 618
Takhti, Gholamreza 328, 333, 356, 361
Talbot, Jerald xxi, 22, 263, 282, 309
Talebof, Aboldrahim 22–23, 25, 100
  and *Ketabe Ahmad* (Ahmad's Book) 25, 100
Taleqani, Mahmud 259, 333, 346, 357, 361, 369–370, 377, 381–382, 418, 447, 513
Taqizadeh, Hasan 38, 42, 44, 48, 53–56, 72, 117–118, 123, 143, 147, 161, 189
Tarbiyat, Ali-Mohammad Khan 53, 56
Tarkhani, Taqi 396
Tavakoli, Ahmad 425, 432, 474, 521, 603
Tavakoli, Hamid 330
Tavakoli, Shahin 330
Tavasoli, Mohammad 463
Tehran Club 153, 163
Tehran University xxviii, xxx–xxxi, 150, 152, 163, 205, 236–237, 248, 255–256, 259, 261–262, 317–318, 328–329, 367, 370, 395, 402, 404, 413, 419, 477, 508, 514, 587, 598
Tehranchi, Reza 310
Ten Nights of Poetry Reading 328, 344
Teymurtash, Abdolhoseyn (Sardar Moazam Khorasani) xxvi, 92, 108, 120, 147, 153, 157–160
Theatre Workshop (*Kargahe Namayesh*) 316–317
tobacco xxi, 22, 27
Tonokaboni, Amir-Asad 122
Tonokaboni, Fereydun 402
Trans-Iranian Railway 151, 164–165, 172, 175–176
Tripartite Anglo-Soviet-Persian Treaty of Alliance xxvii, 171
Trotsky, Leon xxiv, 88
Truman, Harry S. 193, 216, 219
Trump, Donald J. xliii–xliv, 590, 610–611, 614–615
Tudeh Party of Iran (*Hezbe Tudeh Iran*) xxviii, 178–183, 185–190, 192–193, 195–198, 204–206, 213, 218–220, 223–225, 227,

231, 235–236, 240–242, 249, 269, 301, 330, 333–334, 376, 399–400, 402, 415, 419–421, 426–428, 431, 505; *see also* Officers' Organization of the Tudeh Party
Turkman Sahra Council 388–389
Twelfth Imam, Mahdi (the Hidden Imam) 17, 64, 200, 366, 430, 539, 541, 544–545, 574–575

UN Security Council xxix, xl, 216, 439, 546
United States of America
  and the 1953 coup 226–228
  and allegations of corruption in sales of arms to Iran 299
  and Americans in Iran 299–300
  and Armed Forces Radio and Television Services xxx, 321
  and assassination of Soleymani xliv, 614–615
  and the Baghdad Pact 244
  and the Consortium 239
  and Embassy hostage crisis xxxv, 404–407, 411–412, 415
  and fight against ISIS 591–592
  and human rights in Iran 342
  and Iranian oil 216
  and the Islamic Republic's nuclear programme 543, 599
  and Lend Lease xxvii, 171–172, 175, 230–231
  and Military Assistance Advisory Group 251
  and Mohammad-Reza Shah 234, 246, 251–253, 258, 260, 263–265, 293, 296–297, 298–300, 342–343, 362–364
  and the National Security Council 260, 264–265, 542, 588
  and the rebellion in Azarbayjan 191–193
  and sanctions on Iran xxxv, xxxviii, xliii, 411, 483–484, 528, 549, 610–611
  and SAVAK 247
  and the shooting down of Iran Air Flight 655 442–443
  and the 'Status of Forces Agreement' (1964) xxxi, 282–283
  see also Bush, George W.; CIA; Eisenhower, Dwight D.; Joint Comprehensive Plan of Action; Kennedy, John F.; Nixon, Richard M.; Obama, Barack; Reagan, Ronald; Roosevelt, Franklin D.; Roosevelt, Kermit; Truman, Harry S.; Trump, Donald J.; Wilson, Woodrow

Vaez-Esfahani, Seyyed Jamaleddin 30–31
Vahabzadeh, Mohammad 308
Vahedi, Abdolhoseyn 212, 222, 245
Vahid-Dastejerdi, Marziyeh 578
Vali, Qasem Khan (Sardar Homayun) 108
Vance, Cyrus 355, 361, 405
veil xxxv, 153, 155–156, 203, 214, 219, 413–414
Velayati, Ali-Akbar 424–425, 431, 433, 483, 495, 512, 586–587
von Hentig, Werner Otto 72
von Kardorff, Radolf 72
von Niedermayer, Oskar 72, 77
von Schirach, Baldur 164
Vosuq al-dowleh, Hasan 83–86, 91–92, 95–104, 108

Wassmuss, Wilhelm 72, 77, 80
White Revolution (*Enqelabe Sefid*) xxxi, 249, 264–265, 268–269, 271–272, 277–278, 285, 291, 301–302, 306–307
Wilhelm, Kaiser 72, 77
Wilson, Charles 226
Wilson, Woodrow 95, 214
women's suffrage 155, 269, 271, 277
Woodhouse, Montague 224
Wright, Denis 237–238

Xerxes 9

Yalfani, Mohsen 317
Yazdi, Ebrahim 356–357, 363, 382, 403
Yazdi, Mohammad 462, 475, 499, 605
Yazdi, Morteza 196, 206, 241
Yektai, Majid 178
Young Iran Society (of Taqizadeh) 117
Yunesi, Ali 506, 519
Yusefi-Eshkevari, Hasan 562

Zafar al-saltaneh, Azizollah 43
Zahedi, Fazlollah xxx, 176, 222, 224–225, 227–228, 235–240, 242–243, 245, 278, 312
Zahir al-eslam, Javad 46
Zahirnejad, Qasem-Ali 436
Zakerzadeh-Tavalai, Mahmud (Sheykh Halabi) 430
Zanan (Women) (weekly periodical) 560–561
Zand, Lotfali Khan 15
Zandipur, Reza 332
Zanjani, Sheykh Ebrahim 51
Zargham, Ali-Akbar 258
Zarif, Mohammad-Javad 590, 599, 601, 603, 615
Zarinkoub, Abdolhoseyn 486
Zel al-soltan (Masud Mirza) 84
Zeydabadi, Ahmad 515
Zia-Zarifi, Hasan 328, 332
Zionists xl, 203, 382, 547–548, 576, 620
Zirakzadeh, Ahmad 179, 227
Zohari, Ali 245
Zolfaqar Party (of Malekeh Etezadi) 225
Zolfaqari, Pari 311
Zolqadr, Habibollah 244–245, 435
Zoroastrians 43, 160

www.ingramcontent.com/pod-product-compliance
Lightning Source LLC
Chambersburg PA
CBHW080718230426
43665CB00020B/2556